# TEST CRITIQUES: VOLUME IX

**Daniel J. Keyser, Ph.D.**
**Richard C. Sweetland, Ph.D.**

*General Editors*

---

# TEST CRITIQUES

## Volume IX

pro·ed
8700 Shoal Creek Boulevard
Austin, Texas 78758
(512) 451-3246

Printed in the United States of America

LC 84-26895

ISBN 0-89079-521-5

pro·ed
8700 Shoal Creek Boulevard
Austin, Texas 78758

10 9 8 7 6 5 4 3 2 1    92 93 94 95 96

# CONTENTS

# ACKNOWLEDGEMENTS

The editors wish to acknowledge the special contributions of our test reviewers. They have done an outstanding job. Our thanks extend from our deep pleasure and gratitude over their participation and the quality of their work. We know many of the contributing reviewers were as "caught up" in this project as we and are now writing additional reviews for subsequent volumes. Thanks also must go to the test publishers, whose ongoing release of information and materials to the participating reviewers ensures the continuation of this series.

We thank the staff members at Westport Publishers who assisted in the compilation of this volume and Jane Doyle Guthrie, editor and typesetting coordinator. Eugene Strauss and Leonard Strauss of Westport Publishers, Inc. have continued to give us their steady support, for which we are most appreciative.

We also wish to thank the staff members at PRO-ED, Inc., now our publisher for this series. We look forward to our ongoing association.

Finally, we want to express our warmest thanks to our readers. It is their use of *Test Critiques* that gives a final validity to this project. It is our sincere desire that *Test Critiques* will consistently have a true application for them.

# INTRODUCTION

*Test Critiques* is a fulfillment of a goal of the editors and a continuation of a task begun with the publication of *Tests: A Comprehensive Reference for Assessments in Psychology, Education and Business* (1983), its *Supplement* (1984), and *Tests: Second Edition* (1986). With the *Test Critiques* series, we believe that we have moved into the final phase of this project—to include those vital parts that were not appropriate for our directory. With succeeding editions of *Tests* and the ongoing *Test Critiques* series, the reader will have a full spectrum of current test information.

When *Tests* was published, a decision was made to leave out important psychometric information relating to reliability, validity, and normative development. Normative data and questions of reliability and validity were considered simply too complex to be reduced to the "quick scanning" desk reference desired. It was also apparent to the editors that a fair treatment of these topics would unnecessarily burden less sophisticated readers. More learned readers were familiar with other source books where such information could be obtained. The editors were aware, however, that a fuller treatment of each test was needed. These complex issues, along with other equally important aspects of tests, deserved scholarly treatment compatible with our full range of readers.

The selections for each volume were in no way arbitrarily made by the editors. The editorial staff researched what were considered to be the most frequently used psychological, educational, and business tests. In addition, questionnaires were sent to members of various professional organizations and their views were solicited as to which tests should be critiqued. After careful study of the survey results, the staff selected what was felt to be a good balance for each of the several volumes of critiques and selection lists were prepared for invited reviewers. Each reviewer chose the area and test to be critiqued, and as can be noted in each volume's table of contents, some reviewers suggested new tests that had not been treated to extensive reviews. As test specialists, some reviewers chose to review tests that they had researched extensively or were familiar with as users; some chose to review instruments that they were interested in but had never had the opportunity to explore. Needless to say, the availability of writers, their timetables, and the matching of tests and writers were significant variables.

Though the reviewers were on their own in making their judgments, we felt that their work should be straightforward and readable as well as comprehensive. Each test critique would follow a simple plan or outline. Technical terms when used would be explained, so that each critique would be meaningful to all readers—professors, clinicians, and students alike. Furthermore, not only would the questions of reliability and validity along with other aspects of test construction be handled in depth, but each critique would be written to provide practical, helpful information not contained in other reference works. *Test Critiques* would be useful both as a library reference tool containing the best of scholarship but also as practical, field-oriented books, valued as a reference for the desks of all professionals involved in human assessments.

It might be helpful to review for the reader the outline for each critique contained in this series. However, it must be stressed that we communicated with each critique writer and urged that scholarship and professional creativity not be sacrificed through total compliance to the proposed structure. To each reviewer we wrote: "The test(s) which you are reviewing may in fact require small to major modifications of the outline. The important point for you to bear in mind is that your critique will appear in what may well become a standard reference book on human assessment; therefore, your judgment regarding the quality of your critique always supersedes the outline. Be mindful of the spirit of the project, which is to make the critique practical, straightforward, and of value to all users—graduate students, undergraduates, teachers, attorneys, professional psychologists, educators, and others."

The editors' outline for the critiques consisted of three major divisions and numerous subdivisions. The major divisions were Introduction, Practical Applications/Uses, and Technical Aspects, followed by the Critique section. In the Introduction the test is described in detail with relevant developmental background, to place the instrument in a historical context as well as to provide student users the opportunity to absorb the patterns and standards of test development. Practical Applications/Uses gives the reader information from a "user" standpoint—setting(s) in which the test is used, appropriate as well as inappropriate subjects, and administration, scoring, and interpretation guidelines. The section on Technical Aspects cites validity and reliability studies, test and retest situations, as well as what other experts have said about the test. Each review closes with an overall critique.

The reader may note in studying the various critiques in each volume that some authors departed from the suggested outline rather freely. In so doing they complied with their need for congruence and creativity—as was the editors' desire. Some tests, particularly brief and/or highly specialized instruments, simply did not lend themselves easily to our outline.

Instituted in Volume III, an updated cumulative subject index has been included in this volume. Each test has been given a primary classification within the focused assessment area under the main sections of psychology, education, and business. The subject index is keyed either to correspond directly to or be compatible with the classification system used in *Tests*.

It is the editors' hope that this series will prove to be a vital component within the available array of test review resources—the *Mental Measurements Yearbooks,* the online computer services for the Buros Institute database, *Psychological Abstracts,* professional measurement journals, *A Consumer's Guide to Tests in Print* by Hammill, Brown, and Bryant, and so forth. To summarize the goals of the current volume, the editors had in mind the production of a comprehensive, scholarly reference volume that would have varied but practical uses. *Test Critiques* in content and scholarship represents the best efforts of the reviewers, the editors, and the other individuals involved in its production.

# TEST CRITIQUES

**Abigail Marion Harris, Ph.D.**
*Assistant Professor, Graduate School of Education, Fordham University at Lincoln Center, New York, New York.*

# THE ABC INVENTORY-EXTENDED

*Normand Adair and George Blesch. Muskegon, Michigan: Educational Studies and Development.*

## Introduction

The ABC Inventory was developed as a preschool screening instrument for identifying children who are immature or not ready for a standard school program. The 1990 ABC Inventory-Extended is a revised and extended version of the original form. Aims in developing both the ABC Inventory and the subsequent revision were to (a) devise a screening technique that was reliable and valid; (b) construct a format that inexperienced examiners could manage easily; (c) outline administration, scoring, and interpretation procedures that were direct and uncomplicated; (d) maintain economy by minimizing equipment needs and time-consuming procedures; and (e) address children in the preschool age range (Adair & Blesch, 1985, 1990).

Both of the authors have backgrounds and experience in school psychology. Normand Adair received a master's degree in clinical and school psychology from Wayne State University. He has worked for many years as a school psychologist and is currently the director of the Alfred Binet Center of Applied Psychology and Learning Principles. George Blesch received a master's degree in school and educational psychology from Michigan State University. He has been a school psychologist as well as director of the Pupil Personnel Department of Saginaw Township Public Schools.

Construction of the ABC Inventory began in 1960. Item analysis, weighting, and refinement continued until 1962. The instrument was first copyrighted in 1965 and reprinted in 1978 and 1985. The 1990 revision of the instrument retains all of the questions from the original instrument and adds several new items. The protocol format and weighting of items were altered and a restandardization was completed. The authors did not reevaluate the test-retest reliability coefficient and their data supporting test validity, however, for the 1990 version.

The ABC Inventory-Extended is a brief screening device designed to be individually administered to children between the ages of 4 years and 6 years, 11 months. The 33 items plus draw-a-man task are arranged on an 8½″ × 14″ protocol form and typically take from 10 to 15 minutes to complete. A supply of plain white paper, a few large pencils like the ones used in the early elementary grades, the ABC Inventory form (which includes two 6″ squares of paper), and the Administration and Scoring Guide make up the necessary materials.

Items or tasks fall into four subtests or sections: Draw-Man, Verbal Understanding, Language Comprehension, and Visual-Motor. For each subtest, the examiner can use the total raw score and the child's current age in months to determine a test age. The test form provides charts for making these conversions.

The first subtest requires the examinee to draw a man on the test form. This task is similar to the Goodenough Draw-A-Man task (Harris, 1963), though directions for scoring are substantially simplified.

Sections 2 and 3 of the inventory rely on language development. The second section consists of 16 questions that draw on a child's prior experiences and learning. Like the information subtests on popular ability measures (e.g., Wechsler Preschool and Primary Scales of Intelligence; Wechsler Intelligence Scale for Children), the questions tap general knowledge and require responses that are simply stated facts. Comprehension and the application of knowledge make up the focus of the third section. According to the authors, the seven questions in this section require the child to think in "because terms" in responding to the questions.

The fourth and final section intends to measure integration of visual and motor skills. For 7 of the 10 items, examinees fold paper and count or copy simple geometric figures. The remaining three items draw on attention and auditory memory by asking children to repeat digits.

## Practical Applications/Uses

The ABC Inventory–Extended was designed to reduce, via prekindergarten screening, the risk of early school failures by identifying children of questionable maturity for the demands of school. Identifying these children in advance of school entry allows appropriate educational decisions to be made. The authors remind users that a preschool child should not be denied entrance or admission on the basis of a test score alone. Instead, children with low scores require careful study. Deferred school entrance or alternative programs might be considered in order to avoid early academic difficulties and the associated threat to self-esteem.

The manual includes several examples of how data obtained from the screening can be interpreted and used. For example, the authors propose using test scores to project end-of-year school achievement. To do this, they suggest adding 9 months to the child's September entry age and applying a formula provided in the manual. Also, the authors have developed adjustment profiles for children with different scoring patterns on the test. The following evaluation summary is provided for children who score high on Section 1 and low on Section 3:

> Teachers usually describe these youngsters as being well liked by classmates, active group contributors and high in interpersonal behavior. Achievement patterns will usually reveal higher number skill than letter ability with a tendency to be easily distracted.
>
> Suggestion: Might have difficulty with organization and classification skills. Emphasize activities that require judgement or foster independence. (Adair & Blesch, 1990, p. 16)

Profiles such as this appear for each possible subtest pair. Finally, by combining test results, achievement projections, and adjustment profiles, the authors illustrate how individual-child screening reports can be prepared based solely on the screening test data.

Although no mention is made of the types of children for whom this test would be appropriate or inappropriate, this screen appears designed for monolingual U.S. children. Questions regarding U.S. holidays, snow, sailboats, and so on limit its appropriateness with some culturally different or language-minority children.

Administration of the ABC Inventory–Extended is not very complicated. No elaborate materials are required, and the directions for administering the test are relatively straightforward. The examiner's most difficult task may be helping the child feel at ease and willing to cooperate. Often preschool children (and their parents) become apprehensive about testing, and the examiner must develop strategies for easing this tension. Although ideally one should meet with the child individually, some preschoolers become fretful and insecure when separated from their parent(s). In such cases, the manual suggests that "having an accompanying parent or other adult known to the child present does not seem to affect the results seriously" (Adair & Blesch, 1990, p. 3). However, the examiner must situate the adult in an unobtrusive location and remind him or her not to provide cues or otherwise interfere with the child's responses.

Testing should occur in a comfortable, relaxed working environment. A classroom or nursery-room setting with low work tables and small chairs is recommended. Several examiner-preschooler pairs can work simultaneously in one classroom if space allows each pair to talk quietly without disrupting one another.

The format provides considerable flexibility in the order in which the examiner can present test items. While the authors state that item arrangement reflects difficulty, they also indicate that sequential progression through the four sections of the test is not essential. The examiner need only determine whether the child can demonstrate success in any given item, regardless of its placement or sequence in the screening form. Typically a session would start with Section 1, drawing a man. In most instances, this exercise can help the examiner establish rapport. However, some children find this task threatening and will respond more securely to verbal items or to copying a simple figure such as a circle or square. The examiner must stay sensitive to the child's reactions and prepared to exercise flexibility in helping the child to meet the demands of the test.

Unless a reason arises to do otherwise, once the examinee is comfortable and ready to begin, the examiner provides a pencil and the screening form and asks the child to draw a man in a specified location on the form. Aside from mentioning specific body parts or clothing, the examiner can offer any encouragement that may be helpful in getting the child to respond or feel more secure. If the child stops after drawing a head, the manual suggests that the examiner encourage additional effort by saying "That's nice—draw the whole man" (Adair & Blesch, 1990, p. 4). When the child shows no further attempt or seems satisfied with his or her effort, the examiner collects the form and, according to the manual, continues with the screening. However, scoring this task will require that the examiner identify body parts and clothing; presumably, if the examiner cannot identify something that the child has drawn, this is the time to ask the child to describe the picture.

Sections 2 and 3 are administered orally. The examiner reads a question and the child responds with a brief statement of fact. For the most part, administering and scoring these sections is fairly uncomplicated. In the second section, possible correct answers are obvious. However, on rare occasions, a child may offer an ambiguous answer. For example, one question asks which is larger, a cat or a dog. A child might respond that his cat is bigger than his dog. Although the manual doesn't address this kind of ambiguity, the alert examiner could then ask which animal is usually bigger. If the child answers correctly, he or she apparently understands the concept of "bigger" and has the desired knowledge. Similar ambiguity could occur with questions regarding when do we swim, when does it snow, what color is grass, and so on.

For the third section, only the answers provided in parentheses can receive credit. According to the manual, "other answers which may seem logical are not scored since only those provided were standardized" (Adair & Blesch, 1990, p. 12). In all but rare instances, this shouldn't present a problem; most children will include the "correct" answer in their responses even if their explanations are more elaborate than what is required. However, what if the child responds to "What is ice when it melts?" with "liquid" instead of "water," or to "What makes a sailboat move?" with "air" instead of "wind"? One assumes the examiner can ask the child to expand on his or her answer.

The fourth section requires more attention to administer and score than those preceding. For example, the examiner must model folding a piece of paper into a triangle for the child and then place the folded paper on the table in front of him or her. According to the manual, while the child attempts the task, the examiner should "not allow [the folded triangle] to become unfolded" (Adair & Blesch, 1990, p. 5). What should the examiner do if the child tries to unfold the examiner's sample? Also, another task requires the child to repeat numbers that the examiner presents aloud at 1-second intervals. Although a familiar task for a psychologist, a less experienced examiner may need practice to master the appropriate spacing of the numbers.

A major part of the fourth section entails copying simple geometric designs. In each case, the examinee is allowed two trials if necessary to attain one successful drawing. If the first attempt fails according to the scoring procedures described in the manual, the examiner must ask the child to make another one. To make this kind of judgment, the examiner must be familiar with all of the scoring criteria and facile in applying them. Presumably, no harm stems from asking the child to make a second attempt after a questionable first, but the examiner should be able to identify successful drawings quickly and accurately.

Scoring is meant to be direct and uncomplicated. Much of it can be accomplished during administration, and very few qualitative judgments are required. In cases where children must draw or reproduce geometric designs, the manual provides examples of scoring along with the written directions. Frequently, guidelines for scoring questionable responses also are provided.

A child's score for a section is the total number of correct responses. Thus, for Section 1, the examiner counts the number of body parts or pieces of clothing the child draws. Although the manual provides specific directions (e.g., not counting arms twice, counting any facial hair as 1 point, etc.), raw scores for Section 1 can range from 1 to 20, depending on the number of allowable parts. Similarly, in

Sections 2 through 4, the examiner totals the number of correct answers. To obtain the total overall score, the examiner sums the four subtest scores, with the maximum possible total score equal to 53 (i.e., Section 1 = 20; Section 2 = 16; Section 3 = 7; and Section 4 = 10). As is evident, subtests are not weighted equally in the total score.

For the total test score and for each subtest score, the examiner can obtain a test age via tables provided on the test form. Using the child's raw score total and his or her age, the examiner locates the child's test age. It is important to note that a particular raw score does not translate directly to a specific test age. Thus, a raw score of 30 equals a test age of 4 years, 9 months, if the child is 4 years old versus 5 years, 2 months, if the child is 5 years old. This stems from the fact that the authors developed the test-age tables with data from the standardization group, which was divided into three age categories (roughly equivalent to ages 4, 5, and 6).

The manual provides a variety of possible ways in which to interpret and use test age scores. The primary purpose is to determine a Readiness Age and Readiness Quotient (RQ). The Readiness Age (simply the test age converted into years and months) is described as "the age at which this child should comfortably manage socially and achieve" (Adair & Blesch, 1990, p. 12). The Readiness Quotient takes into account the child's chronological age and compares his or her performance with that of children in the standardization group. The examiner can compute the Readiness Quotient by dividing the child's test age by his or her chronological or calendar age and multiplying by 100. The authors suggest that "readiness is doubtful" if a child achieves a Readiness Quotient of less than 90 (25.8 percentile). The manual provides a conversion table for translating Readiness Quotients to percentiles.

The authors extend interpretation beyond readiness. Their manual includes procedures for predicting future achievement and adjustment; for example, to determine end-of-year achievement, examiners need only apply a formula. Support for this procedure comes from a study involving 24 children who were first tested with the ABC Inventory and then tested 11 months later with the Wide Range Achievement Test (Jastak & Jastak, 1965) to measure achievement in spelling, arithmetic, and reading. According to the manual, "grade level achievement data for the three areas were averaged and compared with the achievement projections proposed by the ABC Inventory" (Adair & Blesch, 1990, p. 14). From the description provided in the manual, it is unclear how the grade level data were averaged, as grade equivalents are not interval scales and cannot, from a technical standpoint, be averaged. Comparing the two values for each of the children, nearly 71% were identified as approximately within .3 (or 3 months) of the projected grade level 11 months following the ABC Inventory testing.

School adjustment is another domain that, according to the authors, the test user can predict based on ABC Inventory test performance. This use derives from the assertion that, "For the most part children are fairly equal in their individual skill development. When this is not so, behavior is often affected" (Adair & Blesch, 1990, p. 15). To investigate the relationship of score patterns to adjustment, the authors conducted a follow-up study with 82 children. Presumably, although not stated in the manual, profiles of children were obtained from their teachers in the year following the administration of the ABC Inventory. The manual provides descriptors of children who score high on Sections 1 and 4 of the test, as well as of those who score high on one section and low on another. These profiles have been summarized and are included in a chart that examiners can use to predict school adjustment and obtain suggestions to facilitate school adjustment. Unclear from the chart or the manual, however, is what constitutes a "high" or a "low" score. How discrepant must two scores be for appropriate use of the chart? The manual does not include profiles for other score combinations, such as children with a fairly even performance on three of the subtests and a "low" performance on the fourth.

The authors illustrate the uses of the ABC Inventory scores by providing three sample child screening reports. Each case includes a copy of the completed test form. Data from these forms are used to create the screening reports, which resemble psychological reports. Test data, strengths and weaknesses as measured by the test, achievement and adjustment predictions, and suggestions for educational programming are presented. The reports derive entirely from test scores; no mention is made of the child's behavior during testing, the quality of his or her drawings, or the presence of emotional indicators. As such, someone other than the examiner could generate the reports, perhaps even a computer program.

**Technical Aspects**

Technical support is limited for the ABC Inventory–Extended and its proposed uses. The standardization sample consisted of 1,092 children: 270 aged 48–59 months, 654 aged 60–71 months, and 168 aged 72–83 months. No indication appears of the children's gender or ethnic or socioeconomic backgrounds. Also, no mention is made of how, where, or when the data were collected. The authors state that "because the number in the standardization sample is large and the age range small, biases in selection are believed to be diluted" (Adair & Blesch, 1990, p. 18). Although large sample size is important, there is no substitute for ensuring that the norm group accurately represents the target population.

Reliability of the ABC Inventory–Extended is also suspect. The authors use a method called rational equivalence to determine reliability (Garrett, 1948, 1959). This computation requires no item data, only the number of items, the mean, and the standard deviation. Although the resulting coefficients are reasonably high for a short measure used with young children (.64 for the 4-year-old group, .64 for the 5-year-old group, and .72 for the 6-year-old group), these figures can mislead the user because they fail to accurately reflect internal consistency. Test-retest reliability appears reasonably good: In a study using a sample of 82 children, the authors report a correlation of .74 when comparing test-retest scores collected 9 months apart.

Evidence of validity for the inventory comes from a 1962 study using the earlier version of the test. Scores for the 166 children in the original standardization sample fell into two groups: those scoring above the median ($n$ = 83) and those scoring below the median ($n$ = 83). Forty-three of the 166 children failed their first year of school (it is unclear from the manual whether this was kindergarten or first grade). Of those failing, the inventory had identified 37 or 86% accurately. Six children who failed had scored above the median, and 46 who passed had scores falling below the median (potentially at risk?). Seventy-seven or 63% who passed their first year of school had scored above the median. The manual reports a pass-fail tetrachoric correlation of .70.

## Critique

From a technical standpoint, the data supporting the use of the ABC Inventory–Extended are less than adequate. Too few studies have been done, and those that have seem methodologically questionable. In particular, the method used to establish validity (i.e., identifying all children scoring below the median as "at risk") is not the use of results proposed in the manual. What school district wants to use a screening tool that identifies half of its population as "at risk," particularly when no evidence exists that a large proportion of these children can be expected to experience difficulties?

From a practical standpoint, this inventory is fairly uncomplicated to use and has some face validity. Many of the items are identical or similar to items on other tests that have been validated. It is useful to note, though, that this inventory may measure ability rather than readiness. In a very small study using the earlier version ($N = 14$), a .78 correlation with the Stanford-Binet Intelligence Scale resulted. Researchers and examiners have long used the draw-a-man task as a measure of intellectual maturity (Harris, 1963), and popular intelligence scales often include the tasks of repeating digits and copying geometric figures. Thus children who obtain a low score may be at risk, but this risk may come from low ability rather than lack of readiness. This becomes even more apparent when one finds that a 4-year-old with a total test raw score of 35 has a Readiness Quotient of 125 (well above the desired 90), whereas a child of 6 years, 11 months, with the same raw score earns a Readiness Quotient of 89.

Furthermore, while the ABC Inventory–Extended is potentially useful as a rough screening tool, the test is inappropriate as a diagnostic measure. A low score may reflect maturation, low ability, language difficulties, poor small-motor skills, timidity, or lack of exposure to the mainstream Anglo culture; the subtests are too superficial to pinpoint the nature of the problem. Curriculum implications are at best only suggestive. Educators should consider this quick screening device primarily useful as a preliminary step toward identifying children potentially at risk for later school failure.

## References

Adair, N., & Blesch, G. (1985). *The ABC Inventory to determine kindergarten and school readiness: Administration and scoring procedures for examiners and teachers.* Muskegon, MI: Educational Studies and Development.

Adair, N., & Blesch, G. (1990). *The ABC Inventory to determine kindergarten and school readiness: Administration and scoring guide.* Muskegon, MI: Educational Studies and Development.

Harris, D.B. (1963). *Children's drawings as measures of intellectual maturity: A revision of the Goodenough Draw-A-Man Test.* New York: Harcourt, Brace, & World.

Jastak, J.F., & Jastak, S.R. (1965). *The Wide Range Achievement Test—Manual of instruction.* Wilmington, DE: Guidance Assoc.

**Gene Schwarting, Ph.D.**
*Project Director, Preschool Handicapped Program, Omaha Public Schools, Omaha, Nebraska.*

# ANTON BRENNER DEVELOPMENTAL GESTALT TEST OF SCHOOL READINESS

*Anton Brenner. Los Angeles, California: Western Psychological Services.*

## Introduction

The Anton Brenner Developmental Gestalt Test of School Readiness (Brenner Gestalt Test; BGT) was developed to predict school readiness and success of 5- and 6-year-olds in either kindergarten or the first grade (Brenner, 1964).

The instrument is based upon a long-term study (since fall, 1953) of school readiness conducted by the Merrill-Palmer Institute of Detroit, Michigan. Participants in this study have included the Pediatric Division of Henry Ford Hospital in Detroit and the Edison Institute of Dearborn, Michigan. The author, who was affiliated with the Merrill-Palmer Institute as well as with Eastern Michigan University, indicates (Brenner, 1964) that the BGT is based upon the principles of Gestalt developmental psychology and was developed to answer a perceived need for a standardized instrument to assess school readiness. The manual reports that the BGT, still published in its original form, has been in use since 1954 with over 3,000 examinees to date.

The BGT consists of five sections: Number Producing (receptive counting), Number Recognition (expressive counting), Ten-Dot Gestalt (written reproduction of patterns of dots), Sentence Gestalt (written reproduction of a printed sentence), and Draw-A-Man. Materials needed for administration include 15–20 $^1/_2$-inch cubes, a sheet of heavy paper with arrangements of varying numbers of black dots, a black or blue crayon, and a primary pencil—all of which are provided as part of the test kit. Administration takes place on an individual basis, so the examiner is an active participant in the evaluation process.

Brenner presents the instrument as appropriate for children 5 to 6 years of age, with a ceiling being reached with average 7- to 8-year-olds. The various sections of the BGT are not considered subtests, as only a total score is obtained. The test form itself consists of four pages: scores are recorded and interpreted on page 1; page 2 consists of a Likert-type social-emotional behavior scale to be completed by the examiner; a blank page 3 provides space for the draw-a-man task; and page 4 contains the ten-dot gestalt as well as the sentence gestalt items.

## Practical Applications/Uses

The BGT purports to assess school readiness, to identify early-maturing and gifted children, and to identify young emotionally disturbed children. Appropriate users would appear to be teachers in public and private preschool programs, kindergarten and first-grade teachers, elementary school counselors, school psychologists, and those responsible for screening children for school.

As Brenner indicates, this instrument is most appropriate with 5- to 6-year-old children entering kindergarten or first grade, but it may also be used with older, lower functioning children. Due to the visual nature of the items, the BGT would not be appropriate for visually impaired children, and those with physical handicaps would be penalized by its fine-motor skill requirements. The manual indicates the test would be appropriate for non–English speakers; however, the need to provide oral directions would necessitate an interpreter for this group as well as for acoustically handicapped children.

The BGT could be administered in any reasonably quiet setting, and there are no particular qualifications for the examiner. Although designed for use by teachers, with minimal instruction and practice the test could be administered by most adults. Directions for administration and scoring are limited, and for the most part fairly understandable. The manual estimates administration time at 3 to 8 minutes.

Responses are hand scored as +, –, or 0. The manual provides scoring directions as well as examples. Scoring appears overly precise on the ten-dot and number gestalt sections, considering the age of examinees and fine-motor skills at this stage of development. The raw scores for the various sections have a maximum sum of 40; then 40 is added to the result, creating a maximum total of 80. Scoring takes about 10 minutes.

The manual provides a norms table for comparison of the child's score. The table is divided into sections based upon the date of administration (October, January, or May only), with quartile score ranges. Test results are intended to provide a quantitative and qualitative evaluation of a child's perceptual-conceptual development and to identify three special groups: slowly maturing and/or retarded; early maturing and/or gifted; and emotionally disturbed.

## Technical Aspects

The BGT was normed during the 1959–60 and 1960–61 school years on the entire kindergarten classes ($N$ = 748) of the L'Anse Creuse, Michigan, school system. Data do not appear on the SES, race, sex, or other demographics of the norm group. Reliability coefficients, established through test-retest with varying time intervals, range from .55 to .74. Split-half reliability varies from .83 to .92, while the internal consistency of three sections with the total score ranges from .61 to .96.

One validity study was based on an $N$ of 351, with a correlation of .61 between BGT total scores and kindergarten teacher ratings. Another study involved an $N$ of 353, with correlations of .71 and .68 emerging between BGT scores and first-grade teacher judgments. Correlations between BGT scores and Metropolitan Readiness Tests were .66 and .75.

## Critique

The Brenner Gestalt Test does possess face validity, in that the skills sampled include some of those important for success in lower grades. However, there is a high reliance on a few specific abilities and a dependence on a precise scoring system. The norm group involves one school district in Michigan, so the development of local norms would be necessary for most users. Reliability is inconsistent, and the validity studies involve undefined "teacher ratings."

The age of the instrument, as well as the absence of recent research involving it, also raise concerns regarding its use by a school district. In addition, one would question the reason for evaluating the readiness of children already enrolled in school. Today's emphasis on developmentally appropriate kindergarten programs would appear to offer a strong argument against the need for "readiness" tests. However, if a district should have such a need, a number of instruments on the market would be much more effective.

### References

This list includes a text citation and suggested additional reading.

Brenner, A. (1964). *Anton Brenner Developmental Gestalt Test of School Readiness.* Los Angeles: Western Psychological Services.

Falik, L. (1969). The effects of special perceptual-motor training in kindergarten on reading readiness and on second reading in grade performance. *Journal of Learning Disabilities, 8,* 395–402.

**Robert A. Bischoff, Ph.D.**
*Clinical Psychologist, Meyer Rehabilitation Institute, University of Nebraska Medical Center, Omaha, Nebraska.*

**Julian J. Fabry, Ph.D.**
*Counseling Psychologist, Immanuel Medical Center Rehabilitation Center, Omaha, Nebraska.*

---

# ASSESSMENT OF CHEMICAL HEALTH INVENTORY

*Daniel Krotz. Minneapolis, Minnesota: Renovex.*

### Introduction

The Assessment of Chemical Health Inventory (ACHI), developed for use with adolescents and adults, is a 128-item computer-based instrument designed to evaluate the extent and nature of chemical/substance abuse and associated problems. The test provides a validity check, a chemical use score, and scores on nine separate factors: Family Estrangement, Use Involvement, Personal Consequences, Alienation, Depression, Family Support, Social Impact, Family Chemical Use, and Self-Regard/Abuse. In addition, the ACHI lists endorsed critical items in the areas of physical and sexual abuse, suicidal ideation, legal problems, family secrets, and eating concerns.

The manual credits Daniel Krotz, M.A., C.C.D.P., as the author of the ACHI. A practicing chemical dependency professional in Minnesota for several years, Mr. Krotz has worked for St. Joseph's Hospital, the Hazelden Foundation, and the Bridgeway Center. Currently he practices as a clinician at Divine Redeemer Hospital and is the president of Sandia Research, Inc., a company specializing in program design and quality assurance consultation. Richard Kominowski, B.S., a graduate of the U.S. Air Force Academy, is credited with developing the computer programs used in the administration and scoring of the ACHI. Mr. Kominowski has over 15 years of experience with management information systems and serves as an automation consultant for Sandia Research. Barbara Berntson, M.S.W., C.C.D.P., was the principle researcher for the ACHI and also developed its social desirability scale. She is currently the clinical supervisor for the Hazelden Fellowship Club in St. Paul, Minnesota.

The ACHI was developed to meet the assessment needs of professionals in the chemical dependency field. Despite increasing program enrollment and national attention paid to the problem, few objective instruments exist that accurately measure the nature and extent of a client's substance abuse problem. The authors also list other reasons for the need for the ACHI: the chemical dependency treatment area is maturing, medical technology is getting more sophisticated, insurance companies are requiring more documentation, and there is an ever-growing need for assessment and treatment to be accountable, high quality, and cost-effective.

Chemical dependency professionals at a well-known Minnesota adolescent treatment facility compiled the ACHI items. The initial item pool contained 508 items; items were selected if considered useful in distinguishing among chemical use, abuse, and dependency. Over an unspecified 2-year period this form was administered to 300 adolescents admitted to a Minnesota treatment center and to 116 receiving services from an outpatient facility. These adolescents were described as primarily white, from all regions of the United States, and ranging in age from 14 to 20 years. Research on these administrations determined that 255 of the initial 508 items had sufficient construct validity to be retained.

Subsequent research on the instrument's discriminant abilities has led to the current 128-item form. The ACHI has norms for adolescents and adults; the majority of the normative sample is Caucasian, with equivalent numbers of males and females. The ACHI was designed to be totally computer driven, and both the administration and scoring are computerized. The manual states that the authors decided on the computer format for a variety of reasons, including comparable reliability and validity when compared to traditional administration, positive client attitudes toward computerized testing, data that suggest increased honesty for a computerized format, and consistency of administration.

The ACHI package consists of the administration and scoring disks and a manual for administration and interpretation. Users also may purchase ACHI response forms, which allow clients to take the test without a computer. These forms either can be scored on-line with immediate reports or sent to Renovex for scoring and interpretation. The program contains client identification, a practice survey, and the 128-item ACHI.

The 10-item practice survey (which contains no actual ACHI items) familiarizes the client with the computer and the test administration while also allowing the examiner to evaluate his or her reading level and grasp of the procedure. The examiner codes in the client identification information and guides the client through the practice test, after which the ACHI is self-administered. The client responds to the ACHI questions through function keys on the computer keyboard.

There are adolescent and adult versions of the ACHI, and it can be used for clients aged 13 and up. The test is written at a fourth-grade reading level. Items are based on a 5-point Likert-type scale, offering response options of strongly disagree, disagree, no opinion, agree, and strongly agree. The ACHI does not contain subtests per se, but rather provides nine factor scores (labeled "Problem Severity Factors"): Chemical Involvement, Alienation, Family Estrangement, Personal Consequences, Depression, Family Support, Social Impact, Self-Regard, and Family Chemical Use.

The ACHI format provides for almost instantaneous scoring, and the examiner can print a profile immediately, which also includes basic demographic and client identification information. The ACHI score is reported as a three-digit number (with two decimal places) on a scale from 0.00 to 9.00. The means of chemically dependent adolescents ($M$ = 6.08) and adults ($M$ = 6.52) also appear for comparison. In addition, the profile reports the client's ACHI score graphically (in the middle column of the profile), comparing his or her results to the means of chemically dependent and non–chemically dependent respondents. The graph presents scores at 1 and 2 standard deviations above and below the mean for both the clinical and non-clinical groups. The ACHI profile also provides a "Yes-No" report on the possibility of random responding, an honesty measure, and a measure of social desirability, the Berntson Social Desirability Scale. The client's score on the latter is compared to the mean of a non-clinical reference group, with 1 standard deviation above or below this mean considered acceptable.

The nine factor scores are reported by non-clinical reference group mean, client score, and percentage of variance that each factor contributes to the total ACHI score. Below these nine factors the profile lists the non-clinical reference group's means and standard deviations for the four factors that contribute most to the examinee's total score. Client scores on these four factors are graphed to provide a quick comparison to the non-clinical reference group. The profile also provides a printout of "critical life items," which alert the clinician to endorsed items in 10 different areas that may require immediate focus or further assessment, including suicidal ideation, depression complaints, and reports of physical abuse. Additionally this report yields endorsed items that may be of use to the clinician in treatment planning.

**Practical Applications/Uses**

Although the ACHI seems to have been developed specifically with chemical dependency treatment units and professionals in mind, the survey would appear to have some usefulness in other settings. Any qualified mental health professional may find this a quick and useful screening instrument for chemical dependency that also provides other valuable information. Use of the ACHI should only be considered as part of a battery, and its results should not be the only indicator on which a diagnosis is made. Therefore, the manual recommends that only facilities with appropriately trained assessment professionals should consider this instrument. Given its nature, one could easily place too much importance on the results of this test alone. Psychologists, physicians, social workers, and chemical dependency counselors may find the ACHI useful as part of an intake or screening.

The test authors designed the ACHI to provide an easily administered, objective, cost-effective instrument that could be presented, scored, and analyzed in a short period of time. Specifically constructed to indicate a client's chemical dependency status as compared to clinical and non-clinical groups, this survey does provide limited information on other variables, including depression and suicidal intent. The ACHI would be useful to any qualified chemical dependency treatment center with the appropriate staff to interpret it as part of a battery. In addition, other professionals who have occasion to see clients with chemical dependency concerns may want to use this instrument.

This test is appropriate for anyone over the age of 13 for whom a screening for chemical dependency is desired. However, given the normative sample, the user must apply caution when interpreting the ACHI for any minority clients (e.g., Hispanics, blacks, Native Americans, etc.). In addition, forms developed to date require adequate vision and motor dexterity.

Any person familiar with the instructions may administer the ACHI, especially if the computer version is being used. The instructions are quite clear and the test is easy to administer; the entire procedure takes approximately 15–20 minutes.

As noted previously, the ACHI is computer scored—on-site, on-line, or sent to Renovex.

Although no specific requirements are necessary to administer the test, the interpreter should have the necessary depth of background in assessment battery procedures. ACHI interpretation is based on objective standards derived from norms for clinical and non-clinical samples. Clinical judgment augments the objective total and factor scores via consideration of the listed critical life items and the four-factor cluster. Interpretation of the ACHI is straightforward as far as the chemical dependency score, but analysis of the factor cluster and critical items requires clinical training.

**Technical Aspects**

The authors report several reliability and validity studies using over 2,000 participants from Detroit, Minneapolis, and Salt Lake City. The Cronbach alphas and standardized item alphas reported for the ACHI range from .74 to .94 across items within factors. The manual presents no information on test-retest reliability. Validity studies were based on the ability of the ACHI to correctly classify chemically dependent individuals versus non-clinical individuals. In these studies, various forms of the ACHI were reported to correctly classify from 94% to 99% of the participants. The ACHI reportedly has good discriminating power in identifying non-clinical (98% correctly classified) as well as chemically dependent individuals (74% to 84% correctly classified).

More data on the psychometric properties of the ACHI would be useful as well as appropriate. For instance, further research is needed on its relationship to other chemical dependency instruments, its subscale validity, and its sensitivity to age, gender, and race.

**Critique**

The ACHI appears to be an objective screening instrument for assessing chemical abuse. It offers an effective presentation format, presents a lot of information in a clear profile, and appears to have a good normative base for both clinical and non-clinical populations. The main fault lies in an inherent problem in assessing chemical abuse: that of the client's willingness to tell the truth.

The ACHI is transparent and thus conducive to faking good. The social desirability scale may pick up some faking good as defensiveness, but a sophisticated chemically dependent respondent conceivably could appear as a non-abuser. The honesty measure consists of an item that asks whether the subject has been honest in answering the questions, apparently presupposing that clients will be honest. It would be interesting to see data on the abilities of individuals with various characteristics to fake good on the ACHI. One cannot be sure how successfully this instrument would identify abusers who are deliberately being dishonest, or those who are minimizing their chemical abuse problems. Although a high ACHI score most likely would indicate chemical abuse, a low ACHI score would not necessarily rule out a problem. The issue of honesty, however, pervades the chemical abuse field.

All things considered, for clients seeking treatment the ACHI would still seem a valuable instrument in determining the severity level of a chemical abuse problem. In addition, this assessment may give an idea, through the factor scores, of concurrent or predisposing emotional or environmental concerns. Its ease of administration, immediate scoring, and clear profile and report make the ACHI at least deserving of consideration for professionals interested in screening clients for chemical abuse and associated problems.

### References

Krotz, D. (1988). *Assessment of Chemical Health Inventory.* Minneapolis, MN: Renovex.

**Mary Anne Taylor, Ph.D.**
*Assistant Professor of Psychology, Clemson University, Clemson, South Carolina.*

# ATTITUDE SURVEY PROGRAM FOR BUSINESS AND INDUSTRY

*Staff of the University of Chicago Human Resources Center. Park Ridge, Illinois: London House, Inc.*

## Introduction

The Attitude Survey Program for Business and Industry provides an assessment of attitudes toward organizational and work-related factors. The program consists of four separate surveys (Organization Survey, Managerial Survey, Professional Survey, and Sales Survey), each tailored for use with a different set of employees. Employees covered include those up to and including first-line supervisors, those above first-line supervision, professionals in staff positions, and sales personnel.

The surveys were developed by a team of researchers at the University of Chicago's Human Resources Center. In an initial form, 10 general categories covering job demands, working conditions, pay, company benefits, changes on the job, friendliness of fellow employees, supervisory effectiveness, communication, and personal satisfaction on the job were measured (Baehr, 1953). This form of the inventory contained 64 items. In an early analysis of the items, the adequacy of 3- versus 5-point response alternatives was examined; 3-point alternatives were found as effective as 5-point.

A second study conducted an extension of prior factor analytic studies to see if a selected subset of survey items defined the dimensions they were designed to measure (Baehr & Renck, 1958). Also, the relationship between different factors of attitudes was assessed. Scale revisions derived from the results of this analysis. Five factors, including organization and management, immediate supervision, material rewards, fellow employees, and satisfaction with the job, emerged from this study. A later factor analytic study derived the same five dimensions (Baehr, 1963).

Current descriptions of the survey program suggest that two basic categories are measured on all of the forms (London House, 1985): (a) motivation and morale, which encompasses the factors of organization identification (OI), job satisfaction (JS), satisfaction with pay (SWP), satisfaction with benefits (SWB), and supervisory leadership practices (SLP), and (b) organization and work effectiveness, which takes in general administrative effectiveness (GAE), supervisory administrative practices (SAP), performance and personal development (PPD), and communication effectiveness (CE).

Organization identification (OI) contains general measures of the employee's involvement with the organization. This subscale includes items that capture the perceived fairness and openness of the organization as well as the employee's feelings of organizational commitment. Job satisfaction (JS) taps reactions to the work itself. This dimension includes measures of the extent to which employees believe they can use their abilities at work and whether they think their work is important.

Attitudes toward material rewards are captured by the satisfaction with pay and benefits subscales (SWP and SWB). These dimensions contain items to assess perceived adequacy of pay and benefits, and the extent to which these material rewards are comparable to those offered by external sources. The effectiveness of pay as a motivator also is measured.

Attitudes toward administrative and supervisory personnel are assessed through subscales tapping reactions to supervisory leadership practices (SLP), general administrative effectiveness (GAE), and supervisory administrative practices (SAP). These subscales capture such diverse attitudes as beliefs regarding the fairness and decisiveness of supervisory and administrative decisions, flow of information through the organization, and relationships with supervisory personnel.

The performance and personal development (PPD) dimension includes an assessment of satisfaction with feedback, employee development, and perceived fairness and clarity of performance appraisals. In addition, attitudes toward the available support for career development and the rewards for good work are evaluated. Communication effectiveness (CE) focuses on formal and informal patterns of communications within the firm.

A final dimension (RS) assesses reactions to the survey itself. This includes a measure of the usefulness of the survey as a means to communicate with management and the extent to which results of the survey will be used. All survey forms also contain a blank sheet after the computer answer sheet that allows employees to list any information they would like to bring to the attention of management. Respondents are informed that these comments will be typed before they are returned to the organization.

An optional category for inclusion in the survey, attitudes toward equipment, safety, and health, taps employee reactions to the company's safety and health rules and regulations as well as accessibility of equipment. A second optional category, reactions to human resource management, focuses primarily on attitudes toward available career opportunities and guidance. A third optional category, attitudes toward security operations, addresses beliefs about organizational measures designed to maintain security. This dimension includes a measure of the perceived adequacy of protection against theft.

Other attitudinal measures are incorporated into selected subsets of the four surveys. Attitudes toward work associates (WA) and reactions to work organization (WO) and efficiency (WE) are included in the Organization, Managerial, and Professional surveys. The work associates dimension measures different aspects of interpersonal relationships between co-workers (e.g., cooperation within work groups). Reactions to work organization deals with the perceived efficiency of the way the work is arranged and administered. Efficiency is defined by the effectiveness of the way the work is carried out and the quality of the work itself. Relations with top management (CTM) is covered in the Managerial and Professional surveys, capturing attitudes toward communication, support, and the controlling aspects of top management. The Sales Survey includes several unique dimensions (attitudes toward sales training, company products, pricing and credit, customer service, and advertising), which allows the company to obtain feedback tailored specifically to sales concerns.

All four surveys contain 93 items and generally take less than an hour to complete. Each survey contains the questions and the answer sheet stapled within a booklet. The first page of the booklet provides a general description of the survey and clear instructions on how to use the computer-scorable answer sheet. Each item presents three response alternatives—"agree," "disagree," and "?". The testing packet also includes a booklet that describes the four attitude surveys and contains sample items drawn from each. An accompanying general explanation of how the surveys may be used provides a good overview of the instruments.

The publisher offers three standard reporting services for the Attitude Survey Program, and additional services also are available. The standard services include an executive summary profile, organization-wide comparisons, and demographic comparisons of results. The company receives these reports 2 to 3 weeks after sending the completed surveys to London House.

The Executive Summary Profile compares the scores obtained on each item within each attitudinal dimension to a national employee norm, comprised of the results of all of the organizations that have taken the survey. The profile lists the difference between the company's score and the normative score in percentage points and also provides a graphic representation of the differences (positive or negative) as a visual aid to interpretation. The statistical significance of the difference is noted as well.

The next report is the organization-wide category and item profile, which provides a summary of results by categories and by items. The scores earned by the organization are compared to either the national norm or another predesignated group. The first part of the report contains the category scores (e.g., satisfaction with pay) of both the organization and the norm group as well as the differences between the two in numerical and graphic format. The second part of the report, the organization-wide item profile, simply extends the second report by providing item-by-item results.

The third standard reporting service presents information on category and item scores as a function of demographic variables that are of interest to the organization. For instance, a company may request that results be compiled on the basis of departmental affiliation, sex, or education level of the respondents. Differences are examined as a function of the demographic variables and reported in numerical and graphic format.

The interpretation manual included in the test packet (London House, 1987b) begins with simple definitions of the basic terms. Each term or symbol that appears in the printouts is defined, including a description of the statistical significance of differences between normative and organizational scores. The manual progresses from these basics to the interpretation of the difference scores contained within the results. When more than two groups are compared within the demographic analyses, the company has the option to request contrasts in the results of predesignated groups.

A section on analysis and feedback of results allows for a more global interpretation and guides the interpreter through an analysis of potential patterns in results. Guidelines for identifying particular trends in the data also are included. The feedback section offers suggestions for the type of feedback to supply to different organizational groups. The last section supplies several examples of results and their interpretations.

The Administrator's Guide (London House, 1987a) contains information on how each stage of the administration progresses, from the initial planning phases to providing feedback on the survey results. A step-by-step guide for administration and coordination of the survey process is included. This guide is quite complete and provides the administrator with details ranging from a list of materials to an administration script. Information for both on-site and mail-out survey administrations is included, as are planning checklists for both options.

The level of detail provided in this manual minimizes demands on the administrator. The publisher's instructions are very clear and easy to follow. The administrator simply gives respondents general directions, emphasizes the point that the surveys are anonymous, and defines terms such as *supervisor* for the group. After the respondent fills out the survey, it is placed in a box that is mailed directly to the publisher for processing.

**Practical Applications/Uses**

The Attitude Survey Program was designed to assess employee satisfaction across a variety of organizational levels. The publisher notes that the surveys can be used to pinpoint sources of dissatisfaction as well as organizational strengths. These data then may be used for planning and development. Further, the program may enhance communication between different levels of the organization, provide development opportunities for managers, and track employee attitudes.

**Technical Aspects**

Although the manuals that accompany the Attitude Survey Program provide clear instructions on the surveys' use and interpretation, technical information is largely absent. For example, though the materials present feedback on comparing an organization's standing on the survey with national norms, no specific information is offered concerning the development, composition, and dates of the norms. In a brief unpublished technical report (London House, n.d.-a), the publisher notes that development of norms for different industries and occupational groups is in progress.

Information on survey structure and development is available in three early articles (Baehr, 1953, 1963; Baehr & Renck, 1958). However, the changes that have led to the present versions are not included in the manuals. Data on the factor structure of the current version of the survey and on its evolution from past to present format are needed. No information appears in the manual regarding the correlations between subscores, although the parts of the survey are treated separately in discussions throughout the manual. The high internal consistency of the survey program as a whole (.97 for both the Organization Survey and the Managerial Survey) brings into question the independence of each subscale. However, reporting scores by subscales may aid interpretation of results.

Internal consistency information on each subscale is provided by the publisher (London House, n.d.-a) and is satisfactory for most dimensions. Cronbach's alpha for the Organization Survey was computed for 304 nonmanagerial retail employees, while figures for the Managerial Survey are based on responses of 221 managers in a retail setting. The publisher reports the following reliabilities for the Organization Survey: OI (.84), JS (.75), SWP (.83), SWB (.68), SLP (.84), GAE (.80), SAP (.86), WO (.71), WE (.77), PPD (.79), CE (.79), and RE (.50). For the Managerial Survey, the following reliabilities are reported: OI (.81), JS (.49), SWP (.80), SWB (.74), SLP (.84), WA (.56), GAE (.71), SAP (.85), WO (.66), WE (.75), PPD (.79), CE (.79), CTP (.83), and RS (.48). The low internal consistency of the work associates (WA) and job satisfaction (JS) subscales are troubling. The low reliability of the reactions to the survey subscale in both samples may be due to the fact that the scale consists of only two items.

Useful information on the readability level of the surveys is available from the publisher (London House, n.d.-b). The reading grade levels as computed by the SMOG index are as follows: Organization Survey, 10.3; Sales Survey, 11.6; Managerial Survey, 10.4; Professional Survey, 10.5.

## Critique

The strengths of the Attitude Survey Program include its clearly worded manuals. These resources provide specific information that should aid each step of the survey process, from initial planning to interpretation of results. They are well written and easy to understand.

Ironically, the limitations of the program also stem from the manuals, in their lack of basic technical information (i.e., on scale structure, norms, validity, reliability). As noted, although some information on the internal consistency of the subscales and the initial factor analyses is available from past research, more information on the norms used as a standard for comparison of results is needed. So is data on the way the surveys evolved into their present form. Information on the relationship of scale scores to other satisfaction measures would also be helpful in supporting the surveys' validity. Any data on the relationship of scale scores to dependent variables of interest to organizations (e.g., absenteeism) would be welcome, as would data on the interrelationship of the subscales. This seems an important issue, as these dimensions are treated as separate measures in scale reporting.

Overall, while the manuals provide very clear and helpful instructions and scale descriptions, the statistical aspects of the instruments and the nature of the normative data need to be discussed at some point. Adding this information would greatly strengthen the technical value of the manuals.

## References

Baehr, M.E. (1953). A simplified procedure for the measurement of employee attitudes. *Journal of Applied Psychology, 37*(3), 163–167.

Baehr, M.E. (1963). A comparison of graphic and analytic solutions for both oblique and orthogonal simple structures for factors of employee morale. *Psychometrika, 28*(2), 199–209.

Baehr, M.E., & Renck, R. (1958). The definition and measurement of employee morale. *Administrative Science Quarterly, 3*(2), 157–184.

London House. (1985). *Attitude Survey Program for Business and Industry.* Park Ridge, IL: Author.

London House. (1987a). *Attitude Survey Program: Administrator's guide.* Park Ridge, IL: Author.

London House. (1987b). *Attitude Survey Program: Interpretation manual.* Park Ridge, IL: Author.

London House. (n.d.-a). *The development of the London House surveys for business and industry.* Unpublished technical document.

London House. (n.d.-b). *Readability level of the University Series surveys.* Unpublished technical document.

**Angela Carrasquillo, Ph.D.**
*Professor of Education, Graduate School of Education, Fordham University, New York, New York.*

# BASIC INVENTORY OF NATURAL LANGUAGE

*Charles H. Herbert. San Bernardino, California: CHECpoint Systems, Inc.*

## Introduction

The Basic Inventory of Natural Language (BINL; Herbert, 1979) is a criterion-referenced test designed to assess the language dominance, proficiency, and growth of students in Grades K–12. Versions are available for 32 languages, including Spanish, Chinese, Japanese, Portuguese, and Vietnamese. The BINL focuses on the measurement of oral language, specifically natural speech production in one or more languages.

Charles H. Herbert, author of the BINL, has credentials in the area of language development and language proficiency. Dr. Herbert conducted research at the doctoral level in linguistic variations and has written and lectured in the areas of language diagnosis, assessment, and individualized language learning. In developing the BINL he chose a model of language proficiency that involves two major aspects of language ability: language competence (the language the child has to express his or her thoughts) and language production (the language the child uses in communicating with others) (Herbert, 1979).

The BINL may be given in Spanish and again in English, and then the two scores may be compared to show the language in which the student is most fluent, thereby establishing the degree of command of either or both languages. The test provides a measure of language abilities in terms of the complexity of the language used by the student based on fluency (the total number of words used in the language sample), the level of complexity (command of structures), and the average sentence length. Fluency is an indicator of ability to use the vocabulary, structures, and forms of a language. The level of complexity indicates the command of the structures of the language, including the use of modifiers, phrases, and clauses. Average sentence growth is derived for the fluency count and the number of phrases or sentences used by the student.

Language samples are analyzed at three levels: word class (determiner, noun, verb, adjective, pronoun, preposition, etc.); type of phrases employed (noun phrase, verb phrase, prepositional phrase, etc.); and sentence type (simple, compound, compound complex, etc.). BINL levels of language complexity range from 1 to 5 and increase in increments of 25 (raw score) points. Raw scores are based on syntactical analysis of the student's natural speech and range from 0 to 200. The test leads to the following language classifications: (a) non-English speaking (NES), (b) limited English speaking (LES), (c) fluent English speaking (FES), and (d) proficient English speaking (PES).

The publisher attempts to justify the format of the BINL using theories from contrastive analysis to developmental studies. However, the test's theoretical basis is never clearly stated (Hargett, 1987). Each BINL test item consists of a color picture that is used to elicit language samples from examinees. The student selects between 3 and 5 out of 40 pictures and makes up a short story about each. A sample of a minimum of 10 sentences of natural language from the stories is tape-recorded by the examiner to be transcribed later for scoring. This process is repeated for each language tested.

**Practical Applications/Uses**

The BINL has been found suitable for bilingual, English as a second language, language development, and language remediation programs. In such programs, the BINL helps to determine which of the two (or more) languages the student uses is the dominant language and, to some degree, the level of proficiency in that language. The most practical uses of the BINL follow:

1. Once the individual assessment has been finished, the data may be used to place students according to language level and to prescribe classroom instruction that will provide them the opportunity to practice and develop their dominant and second language.

2. Similar BINL procedures may be used to determine the language complexity of reading material. The student's average language score can be compared with the scores of the reading material, and teachers can prescribe reading instructional materials appropriate to the student's language development.

3. BINL posters may be used for language-production activities or language-experience stories. Teachers can use these unbiased and colorful pictures to generate language experiences in the classroom.

The BINL technical manual describes test administration, scoring, and interpretation, and it provides specific instructions for administering each test item. The BINL consists of four kits. Forms A and B are elementary kits for use with Grades K–6. Forms C and D kits are used with Grades 7–12. The kits include an instruction manual, 20 full-color pictures on heavy poster board, scoring sheets, class profile cards and sorting envelopes to prepare the test for machine scoring (if desired), and materials for teaching the prescription activities included in the instruction manual.

The BINL is individually administered, and administration time varies according to the fluency of the student (10–15 minutes on average). The BINL might be time-consuming if a large number of students must be tested. Extensive experience in test administration is not necessary, but training is required for hand scoring. Language samples may be entered and holistically scored by up to three individuals. The examiner must be proficient in the language that is being tested.

Although individual administration is recommended, a small group of up to six students is permissible. Group practice sessions are required prior to testing to familiarize students with the testing materials and to allow them to become accustomed to (and uninhibited by) the recording procedure. Teachers should incorporate the practice sessions into language-development center activities for 1 to 5 days prior to testing, depending on the readiness and maturity level of the students to be tested.

**Technical Aspects**

The BINL manual provides information related to the development of the test, its validity, and reliability. According to the manual, BINL norms were established for English and Spanish. Norming participants ranged in age from 4 to 18, were from urban and rural populations, and comprised a representative sampling of males and females and ethnic groups of the areas from which they were drawn (California, New Jersey, and New York).

The test manual states that three validity studies were conducted on the BINL, one on the BINL scoring system, one on applying the BINL for determining dominance and proficiency, and the third on BINL oral language complexity. Validity of the BINL scoring system was studied in English-dominant and Spanish-dominant students from Southern California. The purpose of the study was to correlate the average sentence length attained in the test to the level of complexity scores on the BINL. The level of significance of the correlation coefficients ranged from .001 to .002. BINL language classifications (NES, LES, FES, PES) were based on the "level" of language complexity (raw) scores.

The validity of the BINL for determining dominance and proficiency was examined in Fresno, California, in 1975. The conclusion of the study included the statement that the BINL "appears to discriminate between the languages in identifying dominance and to provide a valid measure of growth in language development" (CHECpoint Systems, 1979, p. 61).

The validity of BINL oral language complexity was examined by comparing BINL scores of language complexity to that of the Gilmore Oral Reading Test, which consists of 10 graded paragraphs of increasing difficulty. According to the manual, the results suggest that the BINL average steadily rises as the levels of the Gilmore Oral Reading Test paragraphs get more difficult.

Two studies conducted in Southern California on test-retest reliability are presented in the test manual. Both studies focused on comparing the consistency of the levels of oral language complexity across the 10 sentence samples taken for each student tested. These studies employed the Spearman-Brown split-half correlation coefficient to correlate the two halves of student oral-language samples selected. These studies concluded that students dominant in English or Spanish do generate highly consistent levels in oral language complexity, with a correlation of .93 for each sample (CHECpoint Systems, 1983). Although the test manual indicates that results show a high correlation between the first 5 sentences and the second 5 sentences in the 10-sentence sample, there was no attempt to compare these sentences with a larger group of sentences. While the coefficients are acceptable, high interrater reliability would have provided more reliable statistical data (Hargett, 1987).

**Critique**

The central feature of the BINL is its focus on natural language use. In bilingual programs, the test is mostly used as a pre- and post-measure to determine native and second-language proficiency and growth. Bilingual educators like the BINL because it measures speaking proficiency and discriminates among students of greater or lesser language proficiency. Practitioners like the test because it focuses on natural language in a communicative setting and not on test-taking skills to provide a measure of language proficiency. Criticisms are directed mainly to the technical aspects of the test, especially those related to its validity and reliability. This reviewer found the following criticisms:

1. The test requires a sample only 10 utterances long, which Guyette (1985) sees as a limitation. He states "a 10-utterance sample would not appear to be large enough to meet the requirement of a 'representative sample'" (p. 139).

2. Another criticism of the BINL regards the scoring of implied meaning (Hargett, 1987). The BINL materials do not give explicit instructions on how to reconstruct these implied meanings. Also, no data are presented to suggest that this can be done reliably between two observers. This reviewer agrees with Guyette (1985) in recommending that this procedure be clarified in subsequent revisions of the test.

3. Cutoff scores are provided in four categories across the Grades K–12 (NES, LES, FLS, and PES), but there is not sufficient data indicating how the cutoff scores for the language proficiency classifications were determined (Hargett, 1987). There is essentially no difference between the cutoff points of children in first, third, fifth, sixth, seventh, or eighth grades.

4. The test manual presents information on the average complexity levels of various grades. The BINL scores increased steadily from students in kindergarten through sixth grades. However, the scores of 7th-, 8th-, 9th-, and 10th-graders are below that of the 5th- and 6th-graders. The score of the 11th grade is similar to that of the 6th, although no information or explanation is given for many of these results.

5. The test manual provides extensive information on administration and scoring procedures and on instructional teaching recommendations before and after the administration of the test, but little information is available in terms of linguistic interpretations of the test, especially as it relates to language dominance and language proficiency. On those issues the manual is too vague, especially for practitioners.

6. The normative data are not clear enough, and arguments for validity and reliability are unconventionally presented (Hargett, 1987).

In spite of these criticisms, this reviewer feels that the BINL presents an accurate measure of language proficiency and growth and recommends its continued use in bilingual and ESL programs. However, because the test is extensively used as a testing device in United States, the author should plan to address some of the unanswered questions related to the technical and linguistic aspects of the test.

## References

This list includes text citations and suggested additional reading.

CHECpoint Systems, Inc. (1983). *Basic Inventory of Natural Language: Technical report.* San Bernardino, CA: CHECpoint.

Guyette, T.W. (1985). Review of Basic Inventory of Natural Language. In J.V. Mitchell, Jr. (Ed.), *The ninth mental measurements yearbook* (pp. 139–140). Lincoln, NE: Buros Institute of Mental Measurements.

Hargett, G. (1987). Basic Inventory of Natural Language. In J.C. Alderson, K.J. Krahnke, & C.W. Stansfield (Eds.), *Reviews of English language proficiency tests* (pp. 10–12). Washington, DC: Teachers of English to Speakers of Other Languages.

Herbert, C.H. (1970). *Social role and linguistic variation.* Unpublished doctoral dissertation, Claremont Graduate School of Education, Claremont, CA.

Herbert, C.H. (1979). *Basic Inventory of Natural Language: Instructions manual.* San Bernardino, CA: CHECpoint.

O'Malley, J.M. (n.d.). *Summaries for achievement tests/Summaries for language proficiency tests.* Washington, DC: Georgetown University Evaluation Assessment Center.

Weaver, C. (1980). *Psycholinguistics and reading.* Cambridge, MA: Winthrop.

**Phyllis Anne Teeter, Ed.D.**
*Associate Professor of Educational Psychology, University of Wisconsin-Milwaukee, Milwaukee, Wisconsin.*

# BEHAVIORAL OBSERVATION SCALE FOR AUTISM

*Betty Jo Freeman and Edward Ritvo. Los Angeles, California: Neuropsychiatric Institute.*

### Introduction

The Behavioral Observation Scale (BOS) for Autism was developed as an "objective behavioral observation system (BOS) which will: 1) differentiate autistic from normal and mentally retarded children, 2) identify subgroups of autistic children, and 3) develop an objective means of describing subjects in behavioral and biological research" (Freeman, Ritvo, & Schroth, 1984, p. 588). Not commercially available, the scale can be obtained from the author at the Neuropsychiatric Institute in Los Angeles, California.

B.J. Freeman is an associate professor at the UCLA Medical School and Neuropsychiatric Institute, Division of Mental Retardation and Child Psychiatry. The BOS appears to be the result of research from several funded projects, including awards to Dr. Freeman and others from the National Institute of Mental Health, the Clinical Research Center for the Study of Childhood Psychosis (MH), the Maternal and Child Health Project, the Computing Resources Group at UCLA, the Max and Lottie Dresher Fund, the Bennin Fund, the A.H. Robbins Company, and the Food and Drug Administration.

The development of the BOS tapped well-defined groups of autistic patients that were diagnosed on the basis of the *Diagnostic and Statistical Manual of Mental Disorders* (DSM-III; American Psychiatric Association, 1980). The original version of the scale (Freeman & Schroth, 1984) measured 67 behaviors. The behaviors included in this first version were selected after "a careful review of the clinical literature on autism" and because "various clinicians . . . reported that they were important in diagnosing the syndrome of autism" (Freeman & Schroth, 1984, p. 178). The revised BOS was comprised of 24 behaviors divided into four major categories: Solitary, Relation to Objects, Relation to People, and Language (Freeman et al., 1984). Subsequent modifications defined the final scale of 47 behaviors grouped into five scales: Sensory Motor, Social Relationship to People, Affectual Responses, Sensory Responses, and Language.

### Practical Applications/Uses

The BOS evolved from a clinical research instrument at UCLA into a scale that is apparently in wider use now at other medical centers as well. Although the original scale was developed to identify behaviors that were important in the diagnosis of autism (Freeman & Schroth, 1984), later versions have examined its utility for measuring change in behaviors following treatment (Freeman, Ritvo, Yokota, & Ritvo, 1986). Because there is no manual for the BOS, it is sometimes difficult to differentiate methods used in research studies from the methods and procedures the authors suggest for other clinicians. However, it appears that the final BOS constitutes an observational system whereby patients can be observed in their natural surroundings. It is unclear how many observational sessions are needed, but the observer rates the patient over a 30-minute period and codes the occurrence of 47 target behaviors as "never" (0), "rarely" (1), "frequently" (2), and "almost always" (3).

Freeman et al. (1986, pp. 133–136) provide a description and definition of the scale items. The Sensory Motor scale includes behaviors like whirling, flapping, pacing, banging/hitting self, rocking, and toe walking. The Social Relationship scale identifies whether the child shows an appropriate response to interaction attempts, initiates appropriate physical interaction with others, ignores or withdraws from interaction attempts, and so forth. The Affectual scale covers behaviors such as abrupt affectual changes, grimaces, and temper outbursts or explosive and unpredictable behavior. The Sensory Response scale examines behaviors such as appropriate use of objects and toys, agitation after loud or sudden noises, visual detail scrutiny, and repetitive vocalizations. The last scale measures Language behaviors, including initiation or response to communication, echolalia, delusions, auditory and visual hallucinations, and noncommunicative vocalizations.

Procedures for rating the 47 behaviors are straightforward, and the scoring instructions are easy to follow. Freeman et al. (1986) include instructions for using the Ritvo-Freeman Real Life Rating Scale, which outline the steps for rating each item and scoring the BOS. The scoring is completed after each child is observed and rated (0, 1, 2 or 3) on each of the target behaviors. The user totals his or her ratings for each item and then obtains a mean score for each scale separately. Minor mathematical corrections are necessary for some scales (i.e., Social Relationship, Sensory, and Language) to control for normal behavior. For example, items 1, 2, and 3 are subtracted from the other behavioral items before the mean is calculated for the Social Relationship scale.

Once the scale means have been calculated, they are summed and divided for a total scale mean. Though scoring is not complex, Freeman et al. (1986) are not clear in how to interpret the scale scores, nor the total BOS score, after their calculation. The authors do refer the reader to a figure (p. 135) that graphically depicts scores, but it is not readily discernible what exactly these scores mean. For example, scores are plotted on a frequency axis from 0, .1, .2, .3, .4, .5 to 1.5, but the text of the article does not explain significance of these differences.

Although the authors do provide detailed validity and reliability data on the final version of the BOS, they do not provide mean scores for the scales for the different clinical samples investigated. That is, in this final version of the BOS, mean scores for each scale are not available for the autistic, the mentally retarded, or the normal groups. These scores seem essential for clinicians who want to make diagnostic use of the BOS. In summary, once scores have been obtained, their meaning and significance are unclear.

**Technical Aspects**

The original version of the BOS was developed by observing subjects in a clinic observation room arranged as a playroom, with a uniform set of toys, a child's table and chair, two toy boxes, and an adult chair (Freeman & Schroth, 1984). Participants were selected for a developmental stage if they had met criteria established by the National Association for Autistic Children and DSM-III. Subjects were 24 to 72 months of age; 46 were classified as autistic, 32 were mentally retarded, and 40 were considered normal. Two independent board-certified child psychiatrists verified diagnoses.

Children were rated on three separate occasions, 1 week apart, by two separate observers. Each child was observed through a one-way mirror and 67 behaviors were rated for frequency of occurrence. During nine 3-minute periods, the observer assigned the behavior a score of 3 if it occurred continuously during the 3 minutes, a 2 if it occurred moderately but not continuously, a 1 if it occurred rarely, or a 0 if it did not occur at all (Freeman & Schroth, 1984).

Based on the results of this study, Freeman, Ritvo, and Schroth (1984) revised the original version by identifying 24 of the original 67 behaviors that had the best reliability, validity, and discriminatory power. Over the next 2 years Freeman, Ritvo, Yokota, and Ritvo (1986, p. 130) modified the revised BOS by "abandoning the laboratory and observing patients in their real life settings."

Freeman and Schroth (1984) conducted the validity trials with the original 67-item BOS, using the aforementioned group of 46 autistic, 32 mentally retarded, and 40 normal subjects. In this study children were observed over three sessions by two different observers. Each of the original items were analyzed for frequency of occurrence, consistency of the behavior over the three sessions, discriminatory power across groups, and observer agreement. The authors found that the exact rater agreement was 75% or higher on all but 10 behaviors. Freeman and Schroth (1984, p. 186) concluded that

> for some behaviors quantification may be possible but for others, which occur infrequently, a simple categorization as to occurrence or nonoccurrence may be appropriate. Clinically, some low frequency qualitatively clinical behaviors may be more diagnostically important than quantitatively clinical behaviors with higher frequency.

Freeman, Ritvo, and Schroth (1984) conducted a validity study with the revised, shortened version of the BOS on a total of 63 autistic children, 34 mentally retarded children, and 40 normal children. The autistic group was further divided into groups based on IQ scores: high autistic children had IQs above 70 ($n = 21$), low autistic children had IQ scores below 70 ($n = 42$). All subjects were videotaped on 3 separate days, 1 week apart, and were rated by two trained observers. Formal observations were made after the two raters reached at least an 80% agreement rate on each behavior. Scoring was done on a computer, and behaviors were scored if they occurred during specified 10-second intervals. The computer program reduced errors between observers because time intervals were uniform and the number of behavioral segments were monitored.

The results of this study indicated that only four behaviors consistently differentiated the autistic groups (high and low) from their respective control groups (i.e., high autistic group with normal group; low autistic group with mentally retarded group). The autistic children differed from their controls on Purposeful Use of Objects, Nonpurposeful Use of Objects, Talks to Examiner, and Repetitive Vocalizations. In addition, the low autistic group differed from the mentally retarded group (i.e., obtained higher ratings) on three other items: Locomotion, Looks at Examiner, and Nonstimulus-related Talking. The high autistic group received higher ratings than the normal group on Hand Flapping, Finger-Wiggling, Mouthing Objects, Sniffing Objects, Stereotypic Manipulation of Objects, Vocalizations, Echolalia, and Stimulus-related Talking.

A discriminant analysis further showed that ratings on the BOS have considerable overlap for all four groups. A 75% overall accuracy rate emerged for discriminating the low autistic from the mentally retarded group. Within this comparison the accuracy rate was higher for correctly identifying the mentally retarded (82%) than for the low autistic (69%). In this analysis, 13 out of 42 low autistic children were misclassified as mentally retarded using the BOS ratings. The authors indicated that only two behaviors (Repetitive Vocalizations and Talking) were used to discriminate the groups in this analysis. Because a step-wise discriminant analysis technique was used, it is apparent that only two behaviors out of 24 were found to have discriminatory power for differentiating low autistic and mentally retarded children.

In the comparisons between the high autistic and the normal group, the overall accuracy rate reached 88%. In this analysis, five behaviors (Manipulation of Body, Purposeful Toy Play, Communicative Speech, Nonstimulus-related Talking, and Talking and Vocalizations) were found to have high discriminatory power. However, the accuracy rate was again higher for the controls (96%) than for the high autistic group (71%). Six out of 21 high autistic children were identified as normal based on BOS ratings.

This study on the revised BOS provided empirical evidence that, although these behaviors occurred infrequently, the presence of certain ones is diagnostically significant. Further, this study showed that the two autistic groups differed on some behavioral categories. For example, although both groups showed higher ratings than their control groups on the Repetitive Solitary Behavior category, it was of more significance for the high autistic group. Also, some behaviors were observed in all the children in the study but were seen less often in the autistic groups (e.g., purposeful/nonpurposeful use of objects and examiner/child interactions).

The reported interrater reliability correlation coefficients are also quite high on all behaviors but Whirling, Finger-Wiggling, Visual Detail Scrutiny, Leads Adult by Hand, Stimulus-related Talking, Nonstimulus-related Talking, Stereotypic Object Use, and Repetitive Vocalizations. The authors explained that the observers were not in high agreement on the first six behaviors because the latter occurred so infrequently, and Stereotypic Object Use and Repetitive Vocalizations were judged to be poorly defined. When these eight behaviors were excluded, reliability coefficients ranged from .72 to 1.00 on the remaining 16 items.

In reflecting on the technical adequacy of the BOS, one must consider that the methodology used to collect data for the validity studies with the final BOS is somewhat unclear. Although the number of observations are clearly stated, the age of the subjects, the number of subjects observed, and the number of observers are not. Apparently novice observers were compared to trained observers to determine correlation coefficients. Novice raters received three training sessions with the BOS, while trained observers were "familiar with autism and previously trained to score BOS videotapes" (Freeman et al., 1986, p. 131). Though novice observers made 44 pairs of observations, it is unclear how many subjects they rated. The experienced raters made 50 observations, but the reader is not told how many different children were observed. The authors do not fully describe the children observed or the conditions under which the observations were made.

The results of the correlational study indicate that novice raters show a moderate to low degree of agreement when scoring the BOS. Pearson *r* correlation coefficients for the novice group ranged from a low of .20 on the Sensory scale (items ranged from -.05 on Toe Walks to .60 on Bangs/Hits Self) to a high of .68 on Affectual Responses (items ranged from .36 on Temper Outbursts to .70 on Cries). This group yielded Pearson *r* correlation coefficients of .52 for Social Relationship to People, .45 for Sensory Responses, .55 for Language, and .48 for the Overall scale.

Correlation coefficients were higher for the experienced raters group, ranging from a low of .59 on the Language scale (items ranging from .48 on No/Brief Response to Communication to .86 on Noncommunicative Use of Delayed Echolalia) to a high of .85 on the Sensory (items ranging from .76 on Rocks and 1.00 on Toe Walks) and Social Relation (items ranging from .37 on Disturbs Others to .93 on Changes Activities) scales.

These correlational data suggest that observers need more than three training sessions to reach high rater agreement when using the BOS. Even though the authors reported that the differences between the correlation coefficients for the novice and the experienced observers did not reach statistical significance, there do appear to be some differences that may be clinically relevant.

When individual scales are correlated, the BOS scales show considerable overlap. For example, the Motor scale was moderately related to the Sensory (.479) and Overall (.608) scales; the Social scale was moderately to highly related to the Affect (.545), Language (.433), Sensory (.591), and Overall (.812) scales; the Affect scale was moderately to highly related to the Language (.381), Sensory (.548), and Overall (.746) scales; the Language scale was moderately related to the Sensory (.442) and Overall (.639) scales; and the Sensory scale was highly related to the Overall scale (.820). These data suggest that the BOS scales are highly intercorrelated and that the behaviors described in the 47 items are not independent of each other.

Finally, the relationship between the Alpern-Boll scale and the BOS was investigated. The Alpern-Boll, a developmental profile, measures behaviors in five areas including Physical, Self-Help, Social, Academic, and Communication. Moderate negative correlations with the Alpern-Boll subscales were found, ranging from -.501 on Physical, -.497 on Self-Help, -.565 on Social, -.539 on Academic, and -.564 on Communication with the Overall scale of the BOS. Generally all the BOS scales except Motor were moderately related to those on the Alpern-Boll. The relationship between these tests indicates that high scores on the BOS are related to low scores on a developmental profile. Further, these data suggest that autistic children with high pathological behaviors have lower mental ages.

In summary, studies with the final version of the BOS suggest that the observational scale has some utility for assessing the behavior of autistic children. Though the scales are highly interrelated, the abnormal behaviors measured by the BOS most likely accompany other developmental delays in children. Also, observers seem to reach a moderate degree of agreement when scoring the BOS after only three training sessions, while experienced observers have considerably higher levels of rater agreement.

## Critique

The authors of the original, the revised, and the final versions of the BOS have conducted a series of in general methodologically strong studies with this instrument (Freeman et al., 1984; Freeman et al., 1986; Freeman & Schroth, 1984). Though the development of the BOS has followed sound experimental and psychometric practices, the final version of the BOS is at present less well researched than the experimental versions of the instrument.

Generally the revised observational method seems to have relatively high reliability across raters, and it also seems to differentiate autistic from other nonautistic groups at an adequate level. However, overlap between the control groups (normal and mentally retarded) and autistic groups (high autistic and low autistic) suggest that quantitative observations on the BOS alone are not sufficient for clinical differentiation. Although these findings might lead one to conclude limited predictive validity for the BOS, it may be that autism is such a complex syndrome that the quality of performance on some behaviors is as important as the presence or absence of specific behaviors.

Initial research with the final version of the BOS is promising although not complete at this time. Adequate interrater reliability has been shown with trained observers, and there is an inverse relationship between scores on the BOS and overall development. However, studies have not investigated the predictive validity of the final version, and specifically little is known about the utility of the scales to differentiate autistic from nonautistic groups of children. Although the scoring methods are easy, the authors have not sufficiently described how scores are to be used or interpreted.

Perhaps the most serious shortcoming of the final version of the BOS is the lack of a technical manual. The reader thus cannot go to one source for a clear description of the scale's purposes and methods, or to answer questions such as how do scores vary based on the age of the child? Which age ranges are appropriate for obtaining observations? How should the BOS be incorporated into a comprehensive evaluation for identifying autism? What range of scale scores are considered to be normal?

In summary, the BOS appears to have potential for use with autistic children. However, further research is needed before this instrument can be used for clinical, diagnostic purposes.

**References**

American Psychiatric Association. (1980). *Diagnostic and statistical manual of mental disorders* (3rd ed.). Washington, DC: Author.

Freeman, B.J., Ritvo, E.R., & Schroth, M.A. (1984). Behavior observation of the syndrome of autism: Behavior observation system. *Journal of the American Academy of Child Psychiatry, 23*(5), 588–594.

Freeman, B.J., Ritvo, E.R., Yokota, A., & Ritvo, A. (1986). A scale for rating symptoms of patients with the syndrome of autism in real life settings. *Journal of the American Academy of Child Psychiatry, 25*(1), 130–136.

Freeman, B.J., & Schroth, P.C. (1984). The development of the behavioral observation system (BOS) for autism. *Behavioral Assessment, 6,* 177–187.

**Kenneth W. Wegner, Ed.D.**
*Professor of Education, Counseling Psychology, Boston College, Chestnut Hill, Massachusetts.*

# CAREER ASSESSMENT INVENTORY–THE ENHANCED VERSION

*Charles B. Johansson. Minnetonka, Minnesota: National Computer Systems/PAS Division.*

## Introduction

The Career Assessment Inventory–The Enhanced Version (CAI-EV) is a revised edition of a vocational interest inventory originally designed for a subject population oriented toward either immediate career entry or business, technical, or other limited post–high school training. The major changes from the previous editions are the expansion of items to measure more professional interests and the inclusion of 22 new scales measuring professional-level occupations. Thus an inventory that was designed originally to measure subprofessional interests has been revised to overlap with the purposes of the Strong-Campbell Interest Inventory (SCII).

The preface to the second edition of the CAI manual (Johansson, 1982) provides background on the author and the development of the inventory. Charles B. Johansson currently works at National Computer Systems (NCS), which publishes and provides computer-scoring services for a variety of tests. Between 1961 and 1970, Johansson was a student of David Campbell, a coauthor and developer of the SCII. Johansson's early work focused on revisions of the Minnesota Vocational Interest Inventory (MVII), one of the pioneering efforts to measure the occupational interests of subprofessional-level workers. The MVII contained occupational scales similar to those on the CAI-EV. Johansson also assisted in the development of the male and female versions of the Strong Vocational Interest Blank (SVIB) as the current SCII, which combines those into a single sex inventory. This research on sex differences in vocational interests provided a background for the development and rationale for a single-sex CAI.

When Johansson joined NCS in 1972, one of his first projects was the computer-generated narrative report form for the SCII. His next major project was the development of an interest inventory for subprofessional-level occupations. The first edition of the CAI was published in 1975 with content and format very similar to the SCII. There were six General Theme scales, 22 Basic Interest scales, and 42 Occupational scales. In 1976 seven more occupational scales were added. The major changes for the 1978 edition were 40 more Occupational scales and 4 new Non-Occupational scales: a Fine Arts–Mechanical scale, which appears to measure the masculinity-femininity of occupational interests; an Occupational Extroversion-Introversion scale, measuring a preference for working with people versus things; an Educational Orientation scale, measuring interest in further education;

and a Variability of Interests scale, measuring the diversity of interests. For the 1982 edition, two more Occupational scales were added. The major change was the development of combined male-female, as opposed to the previous separate sex, Occupational scales. That edition of the CAI also was translated for French- and Spanish-speaking individuals in North America.

The current edition of the CAI-EV (Johansson, 1986) was a major effort to make the inventory more universally applicable to a wider population. Revisions included (a) increasing the Occupational scales to a total of 111 via the addition of 22 professionally oriented scales and the revision or elimination of 5 previous scales; (b) adding 5 new Basic Interest Area scales and deleting 2 previous ones for a total of 25; (c) increasing the number of items in the General Theme scales by 25%; and (d) adding a validity check index to the Administrative Indices section. Johansson also emphasized that his philosophy of constructing all scales to be applicable to both genders constitutes a major difference between the CAI-EV and the Strong-Campbell and Kuder inventories.

The four-page booklet for the CAI-EV combines both the items and response format. The respondent uses a No. 2 or softer lead pencil to mark his or her reactions directly opposite the items. The first page contains general directions and space to fill in name, age, sex, and an identification number. The other three pages contain specific instructions for each of three sections and the 370 items. This increase of 65 items over previous editions of the CAI was necessary to broaden the range of interests measured. The three parts measure preferences for Activities, School Subjects, and Occupations. The response format for all items is the same, a 5-point Likert-type scale. The five possibilities range from "like very much" to "dislike very much." Johansson (1986, p. 17) states that the reading level has been upgraded to eighth grade with the new professional-type items, but he suggests use at the upper ninth grade or higher. Adults and college students should complete the inventory in 35 to 40 minutes, but high school students may take more time. There is no time limit. The inventory can be administered individually or in groups.

The guiding principles in item development were to provide items that were relevant and comprehensible to the intended subjects and to sample from a wide range of interests. Previous editions were oriented toward non-college-attending subjects and the occupations of about 80% of the work force. The enhanced version widens the orientation to a higher level of educational and occupational expectations. Two of the main purposes in additional item development were to expand the pool of professional career-type items and provide for the development of more basic interest scales. The author also placed a great emphasis on reducing the gender differences in items and claims improvement even in the Occupations section, where job titles traditionally have been susceptible to sexual stereotypes. Part I, Activities, contains 200 items, or 54% of the inventory. Part II, School Subjects, consists of 43 items (12%), and Part III, Occupations, has 127, or 34% of the total. Overall, the length of the inventory has been increased by 20%, but it remains within the acceptable limits that permit valid and reliable results without disrupting motivation and attention span.

The manual does not specify an age range for appropriate subjects, but the suggested grade levels imply that subjects should be 16 years or older. The item content does not appear to be objectionable to older adults. Because the purpose of the CAI-EV is to identify possible occupations, the recommendation for use for career exploration in the final grades of high school is appropriate. It should also be appropriate for use in post-secondary colleges and technical schools and in assisting adults making career changes.

**Practical Applications/Uses**

This revision has significantly expanded the range of the CAI's potential usefulness. As noted, previous editions focused on assessing the vocational interests of individuals who were oriented toward the subprofessional occupations that represent about 80% of the labor market. With the increased range of items and Occupational scales, the CAI-EV may be more useful to subjects aspiring to such professional occupations as biologist, dentist, economist, physician, or psychologist. As such, it now overlaps with the content and scales of the SCII, which focuses more on professional occupations. The disadvantage to this revision is that the overall increase in comprehensibility makes the inventory less applicable to younger and/or less educated individuals. The CAI-EV is probably most useful to high school or vocational counselors who are interested in providing an instrument to stimulate career exploration. In addition, because a number of occupations requiring community college or technical training are included, the counselor at these levels also would find this inventory valuable. There is not enough research on the CAI-EV in the area of personnel selection to support its use there at this time. Four-year college counselors probably should try out the CAI to determine its effectiveness with their students, even though their preference has been instruments such as the SCII.

The CAI-EV is designed to present a comprehensive view of an individual's interests. The General Theme scales provide a picture of the subject's overall interest typology and a structure for organizing the Basic Interest Area and Occupational scales. Thus the General Theme scales provide a general focus for interests, the Basic Interest Area scales an indication of job activities that may be of interest, and the Occupational scales a specific occupation to explore. The Administrative Indices and Non-Occupational scales provide validity checks and additional information about the individual's responses. The CAI-EV is most appropriate for those who desire to do career exploration and/or plan future education, as well as those who must make a change in their careers.

The blind or physically handicapped can complete the inventory by having someone else read the items and mark the responses. Although the author does not recommend it, the inventory might be used with younger subjects of high ability levels. If so, care should be taken to make sure that respondents feel free to ask questions about items they may not understand. Based on the particular attention the author has paid to sex-bias in both items and scale construction, the CAI-EV should be one of the most appropriate interest inventories to use with females.

The CAI-EV does not require special training for its administration. It is essentially self-administering, and the administrator's role primarily involves ensuring that respondents understand the instructions, answer all items, and feel free to ask questions about items they do not understand. This inventory can be completed in 40 minutes or less, with the subject's age and ability level determining whether administration will take more or less time. The user can administer the CAI-EV in large groups or classrooms without difficulty.

Due to its large number of scales and scoring complexity, the CAI-EV must be computer scored. One method entails mailing the answer sheet to NCS for processing either a profile or narrative report. The profile is printed on two-color paper and lists the Administrative Indices plus all the other scales organized by the six General Theme categories. A standard score is printed for each scale along with an asterisk indicating where that score would fall within a particular norm group. The narrative report contains a similar graphic presentation, with scale scores printed in order from highest to lowest. The narrative provides an explanation of the score on each scale and refers to more information in the *Occupational Outlook Handbook* and the *Dictionary of Occupational Titles.* Administrators also may use a teleprocessing system for immediate scoring at NCS headquarters or a table-top scanner-scorer that provides printout profiles and/or narratives on-site. The mail-in service is the least expensive option, and one can generally expect responses within a week's time.

With so many scales and scores the interpretation of the CAI-EV profile and narrative are quite complex. The profile report has general information on each scale printed on the back. The computer-generated narrative report makes an attempt to relate the individual scores to reference groups. The major problem for the client is both understanding the meaning of scores on various scales and being possibly overwhelmed by the large amount of information provided. Ordinarily the intent of an instrument such as this is to help narrow the individual's career exploration to those occupations that best suit his or her interests. It is difficult to do this here without the assistance of an interpreter with extensive background and experience in both vocational interest theory and measurement as well as its role in career exploration and choice. For example, the CAI-EV manual (Johansson, 1986) provides adequate information on the development of the General Theme scales but very little on Holland's (1985) theoretical rationale for his six types. Without this background the interpreter could bring very little richness to the individualized interpretation of the CAI-EV (or SCII) results.

**Technical Aspects**

The technical quality of the CAI-EV and manual are of the highest level, which one would expect of an author who has spent the last 30 years working on this and other similar inventories. These technical efforts appear to have emphasized such features as scale construction, clarity and comprehensibility of items, reduction of gender-bias, internal consistency, and concurrent validity. The manual does present correlations of CAI scales with similar instruments, but the reader may be disappointed both in the lack of data on the validation of the CAI Occupational scales on other than the criterion key samples and in the dearth of specific predictive validity studies reported. A discussion of the technical qualities of each class of scales follows.

*Administrative Indices.* The Administrative Indices provide information on the distribution of an individual's responses to the CAI-EV. Total Responses is a simple count of marks on the answer sheet. Omission of more than 15% of items will tend to lower scores on all scales and invalidate the results. Response Percentages provides a distribution of responses over the like to dislike continuum of items for the Activities, School Subjects, and Occupational scales. A "high" score is more than 85% of either like, indifferent, or dislike responses (the five response categories are collapsed into three on this index). Extremely high like response percentages produce very high scores on Basic Interest Area and General Theme scales, reducing their capacity to differentiate from each other. High indifferent response percentages produce average profiles on these scales, with the same differentiation problems. Very high dislike response percentages produce low scores on these scales. Response Consistency scores are based on how frequently the respondent marks both items the same in a group of 20 highly correlated pairs. A score of +5 or less suggests an inconsistent response pattern. As can be seen from the above, all of the Administrative Indices are designed to check profile validity.

There are also four Non-Occupational scales listed under the Administrative Indices. The Fine Arts–Mechanical scale was developed by contrasting response percentage on items for a group of males and females who were in the same 12 occupations. It was designed to detect gender orientation in individuals, with fine arts, creative, and culturally oriented interests on one end and mechanical, skilled trades, and outdoor-oriented interests on the other end. Standard scores of 58 or higher represent the mechanical end, and scores of 42 or lower the fine arts end. The Occupational Extroversion-Introversion scale was developed by correlating items on the CAI-EV with items on three other established extroversion-introversion scales. Scores of 58 or higher indicate a preference for working alone or in small groups. Scores of 42 or lower indicate a strong preference for working with others or helping others. The Educational Orientation scale was developed by contrasting responses to items of college-educated groups versus non-college-educated groups. A score of 50 or above is associated with having 4 years or more of college, while a score of 30 or lower represents individuals with no post-secondary education. An alternative interpretation is that a high scorer likes aesthetic and scientific activities and courses. The low scorer tends to dislike school course work or engage in it as a means to an end rather than for its intrinsic interest. The Variability of Interest scale was developed by selecting items that showed *low* intercorrelations with each other. The items were then weighted positively for a like response and negatively for a dislike response. Scores of 60 or above indicate a wide variety of interests, and scores of 40 or lower indicate very narrow interests. In general all of the above-mentioned Administrative Indices have adequate reliability and, where appropriate, internal consistency for their purposes. Their intent is to assist the counselor in interpreting overall response style and response patterning.

*General Theme scales.* Johansson describes the approach used in developing the General Theme scale items as empirical-rational. Items were selected on the basis of their relationship to working definitions of Holland's (1985) six vocational typology themes (Realistic, Investigative, Artistic, Social, Enterprising, and Conventional). The empirical validation of the scales included (a) correlating them with equivalent scales of Holland's Vocational Preference Inventory (VPI), (b) selecting items that correlate highly with their own scales but not with the others, and (c) choosing, when possible, items with small male-female differences. Although correlations with the VPI scales are not reported in the manual, correlations with equivalent SCII General Occupational Theme scales range from .70 to .86. The item-scale correlations range from .43 to .77 and appear acceptable. The internal consistencies range from .93 to .95, indicating good internal validity.

With the expansion of items from 20 to 25 per scale in this edition, it was necessary to develop new reference groups of 450 males and 450 females to norm the scales. In order to reflect a more balanced diversity of interests, individuals in each group were chosen on the basis of their highest score on one of the six themes. The criterion used was that the difference between their highest and second highest theme score had to be more than 3 points. The 75 females and 75 males for each of the six theme groups constitute a composite reference sample of 900 employed adults and students. (This group of 900 males and females also was used for item response comparisons with occupational criterion samples when Johansson developed the Basic Interest Area and Occupational scales discussed later.) The raw scores of the two gender groups were combined for conversion to a standard scored system, with a mean of 50 and standard deviation of 10. When scored by gender, differences of about a half standard deviation were found on the Realistic (males higher) and Artistic (females higher) scales. Although other differences were not as large on other scales, the decision was made to provide gender-specific norm information on the profile. The standard score demarcations on the General Themes profile represent the previously mentioned combined group of 900 males and females, and bars representing the middle 50% of scores for each gender are superimposed on that graph. This permits the use of combined or gender-specific norms in the interpretation process.

As previously discussed, high content validity was built into these scales in the item selection process. In addition, construct validity was demonstrated by intercorrelating the scales both with each other and with comparable SCII General Occupational Theme scales. The intercorrelations among the scales do not support the Holland (1985) hexagonal model (particularly for opposite types), so the author suggests the use of a linear model instead. The correlations with comparable SCII General Occupational Theme scales range from .70 to .86. The results of these analyses indicate a parallel with Holland's vocational typology but not the hexagonal model. Of course, these differences may be due to differences in the content between the various inventories. The author's argument for concurrent validity is that if the scales were operating properly, the mean of the 111 Occupational scale samples would be distributed over a wide range of scores and appear in a logical and meaningful order. In general this holds true, as there is approximately a 20-standard-score range of Occupational scale sample means for each of them, and the occupational groups that logically "fit" Holland's themes tend to score high on those themes.

Test-retest reliabilities for these scales have medians in the .90s for up to 1-month intervals, which reduce to .82 for 2- to 3-month intervals between testings. These reliability figures seem adequate for scales of this length.

*Basic Interest Area scales.* The 25 Basic Interest Area (BIA) scales are intended to measure relatively pure domains of interests. Johansson suggests that these scales are more useful for career exploration than the Occupational scales (too specific) for high school and entering college students. He also indicates that they can be useful in identifying avocational interests when respondents produce a high score on a BIA scale but not on related Occupational scales. Conversely, research on previous editions of the CAI indicates that better predictive validity has been found for high Occupational scale scores that are supported by BIA scores.

Earlier editions of the CAI contained 22 BIA scales. Expansion of the items from 305 to 370 permitted the revision of item content in old scales and the development of new ones. The old Child Care scale was deleted and the Agriculture scale was incorporated into a new Nature/Outdoors scale. Five new scales were added: Protective Service, Athletic/Sports, Medical Science, Public Speaking, and Law/Politics. Only items that intercorrelated higher than +.30 were included in a scale. In cases where an item met this criterion for more than one scale, it was assigned to a scale based on "psychological meaningfulness" (face validity). Although the manual does not present the item intercorrelations, there is an implication that some item overlap exists between scales. Selected items next were correlated with their total scale scores, resulting in values ranging from .45 (College Professor with the Educating scale) to .89 (Woodworking with the Carpentry scale). The overall internal consistency values for each scale were .86 to .95, which appear strong for scales that range from 6 items (Animal Service) to 16 items (Manual/Skilled Trades).

The 25 BIA scales were then assigned to relevant Basic Theme categories based on scale intercorrelations and intercorrelations with each of the six theme scales. In order to validate this classification system, the author subjected the General Themes and BIA scales to factor analyses. When the General Themes scales were included in the analyses, six factors emerged for both males and females, in which appropriate scales tended to load most heavily on factors similar to those six themes. Analyses of the BIA scales alone produced a seventh factor for females. The scale loadings on this factor were highest for the Athletic/Sports, Nature/Outdoors, Animal Service, Medical Science, and Medical Service scales, suggesting a separate health care/medical factor theme for females. Overall these data support the classification system by General Theme developed for the profile, with the exceptions of males showing higher factor loadings for other themes on the Athletic/Sports, Protective Service, Animal Service, and Food Service scales.

The profile for the BIA scales uses the same reference groups as the General Theme scales. Gender norms also are superimposed on the profile for each scale because male versus female scale means differ by as much as 5 standard score points in relation to the combined gender reference group. In general females tend to score higher on BIA scales related to the Artistic, Social, and Conventional themes, and males score higher on those related to the Realistic, Investigative, and Enterprising themes. These findings are similar to those yielded in other research related to gender differences on Holland typology themes.

As indicated previously, content validity (internal consistency) was established by the item selection process and subsequent factor analyses of the BIA scales. The author examined construct validity by correlating the BIA scales with similar scales on the SCII, Kuder Occupational Interest Survey–Form DD (KOIS-DD), and the Jackson Vocational Interest Survey (JVIS). Correlations with similar SCII scales range from the low .60s to the high .80s, which one would expect due to the similar content and development process for the two inventories. Lower correlations (in the .60s and below) emerged in comparisons with scales on the other two inventories. Concurrent validity was established in the same way as that for the General Theme scales—by calculating the means of the Occupational groups on the BIA scales. These data indicate that generally Occupational groups do tend to score above the mean on their closely related BIA scales and below the mean on less closely related scales. Again, these results are in the expected direction and probably represent degrees of overlap between items of the Occupational and BIA scales. For example, Veterinarians scored the highest mean (62) on the Animal Service BIA scale, possibly due to the fact that most of the six items on this scale are also weighted similarly on the Veterinarian scale. No evidence is presented for discriminant validity of the BIA scales, although this may not have been the author's purpose for the scales. For example, the Aircraft Mechanic and Machinist occupational groups both have mean scores of 59 or higher on the Mechanical/Fixing, Electronics, Carpentry, and Manual/Skilled Trades BIA scales. One interpretation of this is that high scores on all four BIA scales would support exploration of both occupations. On the other hand, it also indicates that the BIA scales may have limited usefulness in differentiating between related occupational groups.

Reliability for the BIA scales was established in the same way as for the General Theme scales. Test-retest reliabilities are in the .90s for intervals of up to 30 days, dropping to the .70s and .80s over 2- to 3-month intervals. These reliabilities appear acceptable for scales with so few items (6 to 16 each).

*Occupational scales.* The 111 Occupational scales on the CAI-EV were empirically derived in the tradition of those on the SCII. Johansson designed these scales to provide information on the similarity or dissimilarity of an individual's likes and dislikes to adults working in specific occupations. Prospective occupational criterion-group participants were solicited primarily through appropriate mailing and membership lists and professional directories. After completing the CAI, they were screened for inclusion using five criteria. The individual had to (a) be in the appropriate job, (b) have worked in it for at least 2 years, (c) indicate that he or she was satisfied in the work, (d) be less than 70 years old, and (e) have appropriate accreditation or degrees for the occupation. The size of the final groups ranged from 73 to 453, with a median of 170.

The item responses for each of these groups next were compared to those of the same reference sample of 900 males and females used in developing the General Theme and BIA scales. Although the item weighting process is too complex and lengthy to explain here, all met the two criteria of showing a significant chi-square difference between groups for both genders. Differences in response percentages across the five options for each item were also calculated to determine a weight for each option, which could range from +3 through 0 to –3. Differences of 10–19% were weighted 1, 20–29% weighted 2, and 30% or larger weighted 3 on the scale keys. Thus, in contrast to the procedures for developing the General Theme and BIA scales, both positive and negative weights contribute to high standard scores on the Occupational scales. As a result of this process, the number of weighted items for each scale range from 19 (Waiter/Waitress) to 60 (Conservation Officer).

To develop norms for these scales, the answer sheets for the Occupational criterion groups were scored on their own combined-gender scale keys. Where there were large (over 50) discrepancies between genders in sample sizes, the means and standard deviations were weighted to determine a combined standard score mean and standard deviation. Generally these differences between genders were less than 3 standard score points. In sum, these scales included only items that differentiated significantly for both genders, and the scoring of the criterion groups on their own scales suggests that the items do measure the core interests of both genders in the same occupation.

For purposes of grouping Occupational scales on the profile, the author used two criteria of correlating each scale with the General Theme scales and with mean score of a criterion group on the General Theme scales. For example, the Aircraft Mechanic scale correlated highest with the Realistic theme, and that criterion group also had its highest mean score on that theme scale. Johansson also used this process to assign a Holland theme typology code of one to three letters to each Occupational scale. For example, in addition to a primary category of Realistic, the Aircraft Mechanic also met the criteria for a secondary category of Investigative, resulting in a Holland theme code of RI for the scale. In this way approximately 35% of the Occupational scales were assigned one code letter, 38% two letters, and 27% three letters.

The manual supplies two types of validity data for the Occupational scales. Concurrent validity is expressed as the degree to which the scales separate scores of occupational criterion samples from those of the reference group. The data here show evidence for this type of validity in that the means of the general reference group range from 7.2 (on the Forest Ranger scale) to 36.4 (on the Librarian scale), some 13 to 42 points below the means of the criterion groups on their own Occupational scales. The author indicates that these differences would all be statistically significant at the .001 level, thus supporting good concurrent validity. Construct validity was demonstrated by correlating the CAI-EV Occupational scales with similarly named scales on the SCII and KOIS-DD. The results were conditioned by several issues. Both of the other inventories utilize separate gender scales, and the sample sizes were both small (61 females and 48 males for SCII comparisons and 79 males for the KOIS-DD comparisons). Also, the inventories were not administered concurrently. For 67 separate-gender comparisons between the CAI-EV and SCII scales, the median correlation was about .60; for the KOIS-DD comparisons it was about .40. Although the author claims this "fairly good" concurrent validity, it is also true (as he admits) that a wider variety of people from a wider range of occupations would be preferred to establish good construct validity.

Test-retest reliabilities for intervals of up to 3 months range from a median in the .90s for shorter intervals to the .80s for the longer intervals. The estimated test-retest reliabilities for intervals of up to 6 or 7 years are assumed to be in the .80s for the Occupational scales, based on data from previous editions of the CAI. In general these reliabilities compare favorably with those for similar inventories.

## Critique

Reviewers of the previous and current versions of the CAI-EV have generally been positive toward Johansson's approach to interest measurement. The number of research articles (and reviews), though, are limited, perhaps due to the fact that the inventory must be computer scored, and data are not available for research except through the NCS test archives. Bodden (1978) reviewed the 1976 edition, which he described as a "blue collar" edition of the SCII. His favorable review concludes with a statement calling the CAI an excellent instrument that should be valuable to counselors whose clients typically do not attend college. His only criticism was that there were too few (32) Occupational scales on that version. The current 111 Occupational scales should satisfy this objection.

Lohnes (1978) had more negative comments on the same edition. He criticized the expense of having the CAI scored and interpreted, which is probably still valid today. His major reaction (based on his own Project Talent research) was directed to the use of the Holland typology for the General Theme scales and in organizing the other scales. Lohnes suggested that the structure might be reduced to three categories, such as technical-manual, social-structural, and business. A fourth category, science, was not applicable to the 1976 version but would fit the current enhanced version, which contains professionally oriented items and scales. Despite his criticisms Lohnes admitted he would probably use the CAI for the type of client it was designed for.

McCabe (1983) reviewed the 1982 version of the CAI and criticized the lack of predictive and construct validity studies as well as the cost of administration and scoring. On the other hand, he praised the usefulness of the manual and profile and narrative reports, the references to outside sources of information, and the combined-sex applicability of the inventory. He felt that the CAI filled a significant need and accomplished its purposes quite effectively.

Bauernfeind (1989) and associates recently reviewed the 1986 version and expressed some concern about the clarity of item response options and the small samples used for some of the occupational criterion groups. Other criticisms addressed the need to thoroughly understand Holland's typology and questioned the ability of less sophisticated respondents to relate to occupational titles such as "statistician" and "psychologist." Overall, Bauernfeind's panelists rated the CAI-EV a high positive average of 8.25 on a scale of 1 to 10, particularly citing its careful development, amount of information on interests, and applicability to clients for which the SCII is not appropriate.

Rounds (1989) also reviewed the 1986 version and was much more negative, warning that counselors who use the CAI-EV should not assume the General Theme scales accurately measure Holland's typology. He also criticized the lack of evidence for the suggested use of the BIA scales to represent avocational interests. Rounds agreed with other reviewers that the strategy for constructing combined-sex Occupational scales is weak, particularly with the small samples and inadequate representation of one gender. For 33 of the scales, item selection and weighting was based on one sex, and the smaller opposite-sex group was used only to exclude items that were not common to both. For scales with mean score differences of a half of a standard deviation between genders, interpretation should be made with caution. More importantly, the relatively small size of the occupational criterion groups raises questions about the generalizability of the item weights due to the greater possibility of chance differences. Finally, Rounds stated that the manual concentrates on detailing information on scale construction and severely lacks evidence that the CAI is useful in helping clients choose satisfying careers. As a result of this, he suggested that the SCII and Holland's own Self-Directed Search may be more useful for this purpose.

The developmental technology of the CAI-EV is definitely "state of the art," following the traditional theory and psychometric approach of the SCII. Indeed, at first glance the CAI-EV looks like a clone of the SCII for a different population. It has the same types of Administrative Indices and General Theme, Basic Interest, and Occupational scales. Although these scales have internal consistency, the evidence to support construct and predictive validity are weak. One would hope that the future will bring more evidence of relationships with actual job performance, satisfaction, and persistence. The focus on combined gender scales is laudable but seems carried to the extreme and can be misleading. The Janitor-Janitress criterion group included only 3 females, and, according to the manual, 33 scales were developed from single-sex criterion groups.

With the increase in number of items and added professional occupational scales, the CAI-EV has widened its applicability to different populations. The advantage to this is greater potential for use with college-bound students. However, the addition of new occupations raises the question as to the representativeness of the Occupational scales to the actual world of work. The manual offers no rationale for the selection of these 22 new scales to represent the professional arena. As SCII covers these occupations more adequately, why bother to incorporate them on the CAI-EV?

All in all, the CAI-EV appears to remain one of the most useful and better developed inventories for measuring the interests of nonprofessionally oriented clients and will probably continue as such. Its potential for use with professionally oriented clients remains in question until more validating information becomes available. The user of the CAI-EV is again cautioned that an extensive knowledge of vocational interest theory is necessary for adequate interpretation. Users also should study the technical information in the manual to avoid misconceptions about what the scales actually measure. Most clients cannot interpret the CAI-EV adequately by themselves, despite the descriptive information provided on the back of the profile and in the narrative report.

## References

Bauernfeind, R.H. (Ed.). (1989). Review of the Career Assessment Inventory–Enhanced Version. *AMECD Newsnotes, 25,* 1.

Bodden, J.L. (1978). Review of Career Assessment Inventory. In O.K. Buros (Ed.), *The eighth mental measurements yearbook* (pp. 1548–1549). Highland Park, NJ: Gryphon Press.

Holland, J.L. (1985). *Making vocational choices* (2nd ed.). Englewood Cliffs, NJ: Prentice-Hall.

Johansson, C.R. (1982). *Manual for Career Assessment Inventory* (2nd ed.). Minneapolis, MN: NCS.

Johansson, C.R. (1986). *Manual for Career Assessment Inventory–Enhanced Version.* Minneapolis, MN: NCS.

Lohnes, P.R. (1978). Review of Career Assessment Inventory. In O.K. Buros (Ed.), *The eighth mental measurements yearbook* (pp. 1549–1550). Highland Park, NJ: Gryphon Press.

McCabe, S.P. (1983). Review of Career Assessment Inventory. In D.J. Keyser & R.C. Sweetland (Eds.), *Test critiques* (Vol. II, pp. 128–137). Austin, TX: PRO-ED.

Rounds, J.B. (1989). Review of Career Assessment Inventory–The Enhanced Version. In J.C. Conoley & J.J. Kramer (Eds.), *The tenth mental measurements yearbook* (pp. 138–141). Lincoln, NE: Buros Institute of Mental Measurements.

**Daryl Sander, Ph.D.**
*Professor Emeritus, School of Education, University of Colorado, Boulder, Colorado.*

# CAREER QUEST

*Chronicle Guidance Development Staff. Moravia, New York: Chronicle Guidance Publications, Inc.*

## Introduction

Career Quest is a recently developed interest inventory based on the U.S. Department of Labor's 1979 *Guide for Occupational Exploration* (GOE). This inventory is intended to meet the need for a career assessment tool that is (a) self-administered, (b) easily scored, (c) usable with both junior and senior high students, (d) capable of being integrated efficiently with other occupational data, and (e) a key part of a broad program of career development and planning.

Career Quest was developed by Chronicle Guidance Publications, a well-known and well-established provider of occupational information, with the aid of a group of distinguished educators who comprised a national advisory board and a panel of research and statistical consultants. Quest is published in two forms: Form L, designed for use with students in Grades 10 through 12, and Form S, for students in Grades 7 through 10. Both forms are self-contained, self-scoring, and appropriate for either individuals or groups. Form S consists of 108 items and Form L of 144. Both provide for scores on 12 scales, which correspond to the 12 interest areas used in the GOE: Artistic, Scientific, Plants and Animals, Protective, Mechanical, Industrial, Business Detail, Selling, Accommodating, Humanitarian, Leading-Influencing, and Physical Performing.

The Career Quest packet contains the following materials: Interest Inventory, Form S; Interest Inventory, Form L; interpretation guides for Form S and for Form L; *Career Paths* booklets for Form L and for Form S; a preliminary technical manual; *Career Crosswalk;* and an administrator's guide. The reading level for both forms is purported to be sixth grade. Other materials available in connection with Career Quest are occupational profile sheets, career path summary sheets, and career path charts. The Career Quest inventory is considered one component of an integrated system of career exploration and decision-making, and potential users are invited to call the publisher (1-800-622-7284) for further information about the use of related materials.

## Practical Applications/Uses

Career Quest is an untimed interest inventory; the publisher reports the average time required for Form L as 9 minutes, and for Form S, 12 minutes. Users should allow for a substantial range of time to be made available because students may vary widely in speed and efficiency of task completion. Inventory items are straightforward statements of activities. Form S requires a "Like" or "Dislike" response; on Form L, students respond by marking "VI" (very interesting), "I" (interesting), or "U" (uninteresting). Typical items would be "Paint or draw pictures" or "Wait on customers in a store." Directions for the inventory are printed on the first page of both forms, but the Administrator's Guide suggests that when administering the inventory to groups or classes, directions should be read aloud.

Upon completion of Career Quest, students are directed to tally their scores for each of the 12 scales and to record the raw scores on the "World of Work Chart." This chart is conveniently positioned as the first page of the Interpretation Guide and appears as the customary profile sheet. In the case of Form L, students count the number of checkmarks in the VI category, multiply that number by 2, and enter that product in the space under each of the 12 scales. The number of I marks is tallied next and entered under each scale. Then the VI and I numbers are totaled for each scale and plotted by circling the corresponding number on that scale. Students then connect the circles on each scale with a straight line, thereby creating a graph.

Having completed the plotting of scores, students next are directed to select the three highest interest area scores for further study. The text reminds users that there are no right or wrong profiles and encourages them to seek out counselors for further interpretation of highs and lows. Once the three highest interest areas have been clearly identified, directions follow in the use of score data for finding appropriate job titles to consider. In addition to considering these job titles, students are directed to the Appendix of the Interpretation Guide to find other occupations of potential interest and to think in terms of broader career options. Next the *Crosswalk* is introduced, and students are shown how to obtain additional occupational information corresponding to Career Quest interest scores. The *Crosswalk* is an occupational dictionary listing over 1,100 occupations and the corresponding numbers for the *Dictionary of Occupational Titles,* the *Standard Occupational Classifications,* and the *Chronicle Occupational Briefs.* This resource also provides information on which occupations have counterparts in the armed forces and which are designated "jobs for the future" (Cetron & Appel, 1984). Using this information, students may then turn to the Career Paths Summary Sheet, which is filled in workbook-style and provides a means of synthesizing data thus far obtained.

**Technical Aspects**

Career Quest has been developed in four stages leading to its present form. Form S was pilot tested with 42 male and 42 female eighth-graders, and Form S with 48 males and 42 females, in May 1987. Certain refinements were made as the result of this pilot testing.

Both construct and content validity are discussed in the Preliminary Technical Manual, as are the publisher's intentions concerning validation, but no validity correlation coefficients with customary criteria appear. The materials make no reference to predictive validity, which is the criterion-related validity of most interest to counselors. Similarly, the publisher's plans to obtain reliability data are generally described, but the manual reports no reliability data. Norms are not yet available, but the plan to acquire national normative data is mentioned.

## Critique

Career Quest makes up part of an attractive program of occupational exploration materials. Inventory items are logically arranged under each of the 12 occupational areas used in the GOE and other government publications. Further, they are written in clear, unambiguous language at a sixth-grade reading level, which should pose no problem for students in the middle or upper range of verbal skills. The newness of Career Quest certainly provides an adequate explanation for the absence of technical data and national norms; however, this lack of data may be troubling to those who seek an instrument with better known psychometric characteristics. Counselors may wish to employ considerable caution for usage other than research purposes until validity and reliability data are known.

Despite this caveat, Career Quest appears to have much promise, both for counseling practice and for research. Among the more favorable aspects are its ease of administration and scoring, and the logical and direct connection of inventory scores to occupational information sources. Further, the relatively low costs of the materials and the favorable reputation of the publisher give Career Quest added appeal.

## References

American Educational Research Association, American Psychological Association, & National Council on Measurement in Education. (1985). *Standards for educational and psychological testing*. Washington, DC: American Psychological Association.

Cetron, M.J., & Appel, M. (1984). *Jobs of the future*. New York: McGraw-Hill.

Chronicle Guidance Publications, Inc. (1989). *Chronicle Career Quest administrator's guide*. Moravia, NY: Author.

Chronicle Guidance Publications, Inc. (1989). *Chronicle Career Quest preliminary technical manual*. Moravia, NY: Author.

Kjos, D.L. (1987). Work experience and the results of an occupational search questionnaire among unemployed adults. *Career Development Quarterly, 35*, 326–331.

U.S. Department of Labor. (1979). *Guide for occupational exploration*. Washington, DC: U.S. Government Printing Office.

**Pattey L. Fong, Ph.D.**
*Assistant Professor of Psychology, California State University–Fresno, Fresno, California.*

# CHILDHOOD AUTISM RATING SCALE

*Eric Schopler, Robert J. Reichler, and Barbara Rochen Renner. Los Angeles, California: Western Psychological Services.*

### Introduction

The Childhood Autism Rating Scale (CARS) consists of 15 behaviorally rated items designed for the identification and assessment of autistic children. The CARS produces a single, overall score that is used to distinguish autistic from nonautistic, developmentally disabled children; furthermore, for individuals in the autistic range, the score reflects the degree of severity. The CARS was designed to replace subjective clinical judgments with objective criteria based on empirical research. The developers emphasize that it is a useful screening tool and should be used in conjunction with other, more extensive assessment procedures for a conclusive diagnosis of autism.

The CARS's primary developer is Eric Schopler, a professor of psychology and director of Division TEACCH (Treatment and Education of Autistic and related Communications-handicapped CHildren) at the University of North Carolina School of Medicine at Chapel Hill. Dr. Schopler has been a major force in the study and treatment of autistic individuals for the past 25 years. He has published numerous books and articles, including the highly regarded *Current Issues in Autism* series, which have been instrumental in establishing the field's current knowledge base on the diagnosis, assessment, etiology, and treatment of autistic children and adults. He is currently the editor of the *Journal of Autism and Developmental Disorders.*

An early version of the CARS—the Childhood Psychosis Rating Scale (CPRS; Reichler & Schopler, 1971)—was developed 20 years ago in response to the inadequacy of the autism classification instruments available at the time. The 1971 CPRS was based on Kanner's (1943) definition of "classic" autism and the more broadly defined criteria of the British Working Party (Creak, 1961). The term *childhood psychosis* was used in the original scale to prevent confusion with Kanner's definition of autism, as the CPRS was intended for use with a broader range of children. However, as the generally accepted definition of autism became broader over the years, the instrument was renamed the Childhood Autism Rating Scale (Schopler et al., 1980). The content of the current version (Schopler, Reichler, & Renner, 1988) remains fundamentally identical to the 1980 version with one scoring change.

Reliability and validity for the CARS were established on a group of 537 children seen at Division TEACCH over a 10-year period (Schopler et al., 1980). Fifty-five percent of the population was under 6 years of age and 11% was over the age of 10. The ratio of boys to girls was 3:1, a proportion typical of developmentally disabled populations. About 70% of the children had IQs below 70 as measured by various standardized tests of intellectual assessment (e.g., WISC, Merrill-Palmer, Bayley). The children's families were of predominantly low socioeconomic status, and the population was approximately 70% white, 30% black. These demographics are reported as being representative of the population of North Carolina at large. By 1988, the CARS had been used in the evaluation of 1,606 cases, all with demographics similar to those reported in 1980.

The 15 CARS items cover relating to people; imitation; emotional response; body use; object use; adaptation to change; visual response; listening response; taste, smell, and touch response and use; fear or nervousness; verbal communication; nonverbal communication; activity level; level and consistency of intellectual response; and general impressions. These items are based on five diagnostic classification systems of historical and/or current significance, including Kanner's (1943) original definition of autism, the British Working Party's diagnostic points (Creak, 1961), Rutter's (1978) definition, the National Society for Autistic Children (NSAC, 1978) criteria, and the DSM-IIIR (American Psychiatric Association, 1987). Although all of the diagnostic systems include Kanner's criteria for autism, each system emphasizes additional features of autism to a different degree. For the 15 CARS items, the manual indicates whether the item is primary or secondary to the diagnosis of autism according to each of the five diagnostic systems. The CARS manual describes each of the items in detail and provides instructions for rating each. Ratings are based on behavioral observation and are marked on a separate CARS rating sheet. Each item is rated from 1 to 4 depending on the degree of deviation from "normal" the child exhibits on the particular item.

Because scoring involves comparing the client to nonhandicapped peers, the scale conceivably could be used for children from toddlerhood through adolescence. However, the sample used by the authors for establishing the scale's reliability and validity consisted primarily of young children—approximately 90% were age 10 or younger. A few studies examining the use of the CARS with adolescents and young adults (Garfin, McCallon, & Cox, 1988; Mesibov, 1988) do indicate, though, that it may be of service for assessing older individuals. However, such uses may necessitate changes in scoring, and further validity studies are needed for this population (see below).

**Practical Applications/Uses**

The CARS was designed to allow for an objective and behaviorally based assessment of autism. Although the scale should not be the sole determinant in diagnosing autism, it is appropriate for screening young clients, for identifying their behavioral symptoms, and for classifying cases in which autism is suspected. The CARS is also useful in providing a quantitative assessment of degree of autism for research purposes.

This scale was designed originally for use in conjunction with a comprehensive behavioral assessment such as the Psychoeducational Profile (PEP; Schopler & Reichler, 1979); however, the manual indicates that valid scores on the CARS can be obtained through other methods, such as a parent interview, a classroom observation, or a case history chart review. The manual states that "any of these sources can be used *as long as they include the information required for rating all the scales"*

(Schopler et al., 1988, p. 6). Furthermore, the manual indicates that valid CARS ratings can be obtained from a wide range of professionals—physicians, psychologists, special educators, school psychologists, speech pathologists, and audiologists, as well as medical students and medical residents and interns. The rater's experience with autism need not be extensive, and valid ratings can be obtained after a brief (1-hour) training session on the use of the CARS. A 30-minute training videotape is available from the Health Sciences Consortium of the University of North Carolina School of Medicine at Chapel Hill.

The rater must be familiar with the descriptions and scoring criteria for all 15 scale items before making any observations. This familiarization process includes reading the CARS manual and viewing training tapes if they are available. Once the rater becomes familiar with all the scale items, he or she can proceed with the behavioral observations or acquire the information through other sources such as parent interviews or chart reviews. The CARS manual notes that "actual ratings should *not* be made until the data collection has been completed (Schopler et al., 1988, p. 6). During the observation period, notes can be recorded on a worksheet (not included with CARS materials) and later used to make the actual ratings on the CARS rating sheet. The manual is not specific about the length of time needed for adequate observation. The only specification is that enough information be available for rating all 15 items. Ratings should be made soon after the observation period.

The manual clearly presents the instructions for scoring, and, as stated previously, inexperienced raters can be trained to score the CARS in about an hour. The user gives each item a score of 1 to 4 depending on the degree of deviation from normal exhibited by the child. The manual notes that ratings should take into consideration the child's chronological age as well as the peculiarity, frequency, intensity, and duration of his or her behavior. A score of 1 indicates that the child's behavior falls within normal limits for his or her age. A score of 2 suggests mild abnormality; 3, moderate abnormality; and 4, severe abnormality. One also can establish ratings midway between the anchor points (i.e., 1.5, 2.5, and 3.5). Thus, the CARS's rating system allows for a 7-point variation from "within normal limits for that age" to "severely abnormal for that age." The manual provides examples of the different levels of severity for each scale item.

After each item has been rated, the user sums the ratings for a single CARS score. Based on clinical observations of the original sample of 537 children, the developers determined that children with CARS scores below 30 are not autistic. For those with scores of 30 or more, further distinctions in severity of autism can be made. That is, children with scores of 30 to 36 are considered to have mild to moderate autism, whereas those scoring 37 or more are considered moderately to severely affected.

The 1980 version of the CARS (Schopler et al., 1980) included an additional scoring procedure for establishing moderate to severe autism that does not appear in the 1988 version. This procedure involved determining that at least five items were rated 3 or higher in addition to obtaining a total CARS score of 37 or more. Personal communication with Dr. Schopler (October 28, 1991) indicates that the additional scoring procedure was dropped because it was redundant. That is, a review of the first 1,500 or so cases indicated that most children scoring 37 or more also were rated 3 or higher on at least five items; therefore, the additional scoring procedure did not add any new information to the basic scoring procedure. The 1988 manual does not provide an explanation for this change in the scoring procedure, and to date no published empirical reports have appeared supporting the change.

The manual does not provide differential scoring instructions for adolescent clients. Because autism is considered a lifelong disorder (Rutter, 1970), autistic children are thought to remain autistic throughout adolescence and adulthood. However, as numerous studies (e.g., Rutter, 1970; DeMyer et al., 1973) have documented mild overall improvements with age in a number of adaptive domains, the applicability of the CARS for adolescent populations, especially in its ability to distinguish autistic from nonautistic adolescents, remains unclear.

Mesibov (1988) reported that 59 children in the TEACCH program were administered the CARS before age 10 and after age 13. The mean difference between the CARS scores over time was 2, with the children exhibiting fewer autistic characteristics after age 13. Mesibov reported that, for adolescent populations, an adjusted CARS cutoff of 28 rather than 30 resulted in 92% of the sample retaining the diagnosis of autism. In another study (Garfin et al., 1988) comparing 22 autistic children (ages 6–10) and 22 autistic adolescents (ages 13–22) matched for IQ, ethnicity, and sex, CARS scores were also almost 2 points lower for the adolescents (mean CARS scores: children = 38.3, adolescents = 36.6); however, this difference was not statistically significant, and recommendations for cutoff adjustments for adolescents are not mentioned. Thus, at present the CARS appears to be sufficient as a rough screening device for detecting autism in adolescents; however, for adolescents whose CARS scores fall between the mid-20s and 30s, a valid classification of autistic versus nonautistic cannot be determined.

Interpreting CARS scores is a straightforward task except with adolescents. It is important to note that not only do the CARS developers not sanction the use of this scale as a sole instrument for diagnosing autism, they emphasize that the CARS does not provide enough information for educational/treatment placement or planning and should not be used for these purposes.

### Technical Aspects

The CARS manual describes both the scale's reliability and its criterion-related validity. Reports by other authors (Garfin et al., 1988; Teal & Wiebe, 1986) have supported certain findings described in the manual and examined discriminant validity for both children and adolescents.

Coefficient alpha as reported in the manual was .94, indicating a high degree of internal consistency. Garfin et al. (1988) reported alpha coefficients of .79 for the group of children ($n$ = 22) and .73 for the adolescents ($n$ = 22). In the same report, Garfin et al. reported alpha coefficients of .75 and .82 for groups of autistic adolescents ($n$ = 20) and handicapped, nonautistic adolescents ($n$ = 20), respectively. The Garfin et al. studies yielded reliability coefficients that are slightly lower than recommended levels; nonetheless, the internal consistency of the CARS is adequate, especially given the developers' recommendations that the instrument be used primarily as a screening device.

On a different note, both studies described in Garfin et al. (1988) showed that the item "Level and consistency of intellectual response" correlated negatively with the total CARS score; thus, eliminating this item increased the reliability coefficient (to .83 for the group of children and to .77 for the adolescent group in the first study; to .79 for the autistic group and .84 for the nonautistic group in the second study). The CARS manual also shows this item to have the lowest interrater reliability ($r$ = .55).

Interrater reliability as reported in the manual ranges from .55 to .93 for the 15 items, with an average of .71. These reliability ratings were obtained from the item scores of two independent trained raters for 280 cases. Garfin et al. (1988) reported interrater reliability of .80 or better on the total CARS scores.

Test-retest reliability as described in the manual was determined by an examination of 91 cases. Total CARS scores obtained during second- and third-year evaluations were used to avoid the effects of improvements that often occur during the first year of treatment. The means, 31.5 and 31.9, respectively, for the second- and third-year evaluations, were not significantly different. The correlation was $r$ = .88, $p < .01$. Test-retest agreement of diagnostic categorization (autistic vs. nonautistic) from the second- to third-year evaluations was 82%, which corrected for chance results in a coefficient kappa of .64.

Test-retest agreement is less clear for older autistic children. Mesibov (1988) reported a 2-point drop in total CARS scores for 59 children evaluated before age 10 and after age 13. Although he does not report whether this difference is significantly significant, Mesibov does recommend adjusting the autistic cutoff score in order to improve test-retest diagnostic categorization agreement to 92%. Mesibov (1988) reported neither the categorization agreement using an unadjusted cutoff score nor kappa coefficients to correct percent agreements for chance.

The CARS manual indicates good criterion-related validity when the total CARS scores are correlated with clinical ratings made during the same diagnostic sessions ($r$ = .84, $p < .001$). The total CARS scores also were correlated with independent clinical assessments made by a child psychologist and child psychiatrist, who based their assessments on information derived from referral records, parent interviews, and nonstructured interviews with the child ($r$ = .80, $p < .001$). The cutoff score of 30 was determined by comparing CARS scores with expert clinical classifications in 1,520 cases. This cutoff score resulted in an overall agreement rate of 87%, with a false negative rate of 14.6% and false positive rate of 10.7%. The manual does not provide specific details concerning how these clinical ratings were determined.

The manual reports good validity when the CARS is administered under different conditions, such as a parent interview, classroom observation, and chart review. Total CARS scores obtained during administration of the Psychoeducational Profile (PEP; Schopler & Reichler, 1979) were compared with CARS scores obtained from each of the previously noted conditions. CARS scores based on parent interviews (of about 1 hour) were examined in 41 cases. The resulting correlation with PEP-derived CARS scores was $r$ = .82, $p < .01$, and categorization (autistic vs. nonautistic) agreement was 90%, which corrected for chance results in a coefficient kappa of .75. For CARS scores based on classroom observations (about 1–2 hours, 20 cases), correlation with PEP-derived CARS scores was $r$ = .73, $p < .01$.

Categorization agreement was 86%, with coefficient kappa equaling .86. For CARS scores based on case history chart reviews (61 cases), correlation with PEP-derived CARS scores was $r = .82, p < .01$. Categorization agreement was 82%, with a coefficient kappa of .63. The CARS developers thus concluded that valid CARS ratings and diagnostic ratings can be made from information obtained from these various methods.

The manual also reports on the validity of CARS ratings made by 18 professionals who had minimal experience with autism and only a brief training session. These raters were visitors to the TEACCH center and included medical students, pediatric residents and interns, special educators, school psychologists, speech pathologists, and audiologists. The visitors read the CARS manual and viewed a 30-minute training tape (if time permitted) about 1 hour prior to a diagnostic session. Their ratings were compared to those made by the clinical directors observing the same sessions and resulted in good correlations ($r = .83, p < .01$). Categorization agreement was 92%, with coefficient kappa of .81.

The CARS manual reports no discriminant validity data. However, recent studies by other authors have shown that the CARS has very good discriminant validity. Teal and Wiebe (1986) found that the CARS effectively discriminated 20 autistic from 20 trainable mentally retarded children when total CARS scores were used in conjunction with the number of scales rated 3 or higher. Using this scoring procedure, discriminant analysis of the CARS resulted in no overlapping membership, producing 100% predictive accuracy. In a study by Garfin et al. (1988), the CARS also discriminated 20 autistic adolescents from 20 nonautistic, handicapped peers, with only one adolescent mislabeled on the basis of the CARS. Unfortunately, the raters in this study were not blind to the nonautistic status of the subjects, which may have affected ratings.

## Critique

Although a number of autism assessment instruments exist, the CARS has demonstrated reliability and validity as good as or better than many of its counterparts (see Parks, 1988; Teal & Wiebe, 1986). Furthermore, valid CARS scores can be obtained from a variety of assessment sources, and relatively inexperienced raters from a range of professions can be trained to make reliable ratings after a brief training period. Thus, the CARS allows for a high level of flexibility for data collection and is cost-effective in terms of training time.

The user finds other important advantages of the CARS in its reliance on behaviorally based classification systems for development of scale items and in its empirically derived scoring criteria. The scale was developed and refined with over 1,500 children and shows good interrater and test-retest reliability (for preadolescent children). Criterion-related validity and discriminant validity appear adequate, although further validity evaluations would strengthen the scale. Eliminating the item, "Level and consistency of intellectual response" from future versions of the CARS (it has a negative item-total correlation and poor interrater reliability) may improve the internal consistency of the scale.

Valid use of the CARS with adolescent and young adult populations has not yet been firmly established; in particular, questions remain concerning the appropriate cutoff score for differentiating autistic from nonautistic adolescents. Another question about scoring concerns the decision to eliminate the number of items rated 3 or higher criterion from the most recent version of the CARS. As one of the studies on the CARS's discriminant validity (Teal & Wiebe, 1986) included this procedure, users should consider retaining this additional step until data supporting its elimination have been published.

Finally, users of the CARS should keep in mind that the scale developers did not intend its use as a sole diagnostic instrument or as a determinant for placement or treatment-planning purposes. Rather, Schopler et al. view the CARS as a first step in the diagnostic process, which also should involve the comprehensive assessment of areas such as language, adaptive behavior, and biological functioning.

## References

American Psychiatric Association. (1987). *Diagnostic and statistical manual of mental disorders* (3rd. ed. rev.). Washington, DC: Author.

Creak, M. (1961). Schizophrenic syndrome in childhood: Progress report (April, 1961) of a working party. *British Medical Journal, 5,* 889–890.

DeMyer, M.K., Barton, S., DeMyer, W.E., Norton, J.A., Allen, J., & Steele, R. (1973). Prognosis in autism: A follow-up study. *Journal of Autism and Childhood Schizophrenia, 3,* 199–246.

Garfin, D.G., McCallon, D., & Cox, R. (1988). Validity and reliability of the Childhood Autism Rating Scale with autistic adolescents. *Journal of Autism and Developmental Disorders, 18,* 367–378.

Kanner, L. (1943). Autistic disturbances of affective contact. *Nervous Child, 2,* 217–250.

Mesibov, G.B. (1988). Diagnosis and assessment of autistic adolescents and adults. In E. Schopler & G.B. Mesibov (Eds.), *Diagnosis and assessment in autism* (pp. 227–238). New York: Plenum.

National Society for Autistic Children. (1978). National Society for Autistic Children definition of the syndrome of autism. *Journal of Autism and Developmental Disorders, 8,* 162–167.

Parks, S.L. (1988). Psychometric instruments available for the assessment of autistic children. In E. Schopler & G.B. Mesibov (Eds.), *Diagnosis and assessment in autism* (pp. 123–134). New York: Plenum.

Reichler, R.J., & Schopler, E. (1971). Observations on the nature of human relatedness. *Journal of Autism and Childhood Schizophrenia, 1,* 283–296.

Rutter, M. (1970). Autistic children: Infancy to adulthood. *Seminars in Psychiatry, 2,* 435–450.

Rutter, M. (1978). Diagnosis and definition of childhood autism. *Journal of Autism and Developmental Disorders, 8,* 139–161.

Schopler, E., & Reichler, R.J. (1979). *Individualized assessment and treatment for autistic and developmentally disabled children: Psychoeducational Profile* (Vol. 1). Austin, TX: PRO-ED.

Schopler, E., Reichler, R.J., DeVellis, R.F., & Daly, K. (1980). Toward objective classification of childhood autism: Childhood Autism Rating Scale (CARS). *Journal of Autism and Developmental Disorders, 10,* 91–103.

Schopler, E., Reichler, R.J., & Renner, B.R. (1988). *The Childhood Autism Rating Scale (CARS).* Los Angeles: Western Psychological Services.

Teal, M.B., & Wiebe, M.J. (1986). A validity analysis of selected instruments used to assess autism. *Journal of Autism and Developmental Disorders, 16,* 485–494.

**Harvey N. Switzky, Ph.D.**
*Professor of Educational Psychology, Northern Illinois University, DeKalb, Illinois.*

# CHILDREN'S ACADEMIC INTRINSIC MOTIVATION INVENTORY

*Adele Eskeles Gottfried. Odessa, Florida: Psychological Assessment Resources, Inc.*

**Introduction**

The Children's Academic Intrinsic Motivation Inventory (CAIMI) is a measure specifically designed to assess academic intrinsic motivation in upper elementary through junior high school students (Grades 4–8). Academic intrinsic motivation (Gottfried, 1985) is defined as enjoyment of school learning characterized by an orientation toward mastery; curiosity; persistence, task-endogeny; and learning challenging, difficult, and novel tasks. The CAIMI assesses children's academic intrinsic motivation both as a general disposition toward learning for its own sake (Haywood & Burke, 1977; Switzky & Heal, 1990) and as specific components related to different areas of the curriculum in reading, math, social studies, and science (Deci & Ryan, 1985; Harter, 1981), reflecting the principle that academic intrinsic motivation has both specific and general aspects (Brophy, 1983).

Many current learning theorists (Borkowski & Kurtz, 1987; Haywood & Switzky, 1986; Sternberg, 1985) view the efficient operation of the cognitive processes and ability systems in children as vitally linked to their internal personality and motivational processes. Inefficient motive systems can impair children's basic abilities to develop *specific strategy knowledge,* especially if they have doubts about their learning abilities. Further, such self-doubts may cause an impoverished *general strategy knowledge* base, which may limit the acquisition of new learning strategies and the higher level processes that guide the implementation of lower level strategies.

Children may have all the necessary procedural and declarative knowledge necessary to solve a problem but still be unable to bring this knowledge to bear in specific learning or problem-solving situations because of motivational deficits and the expectations of failure. On the other hand, expectations of success and possessing a high level of academic intrinsic motivation can energize the cognitive processes of children, leading them to display enhanced problem-solving performance, higher school achievement and grades, more favorable perceptions of their academic competence, lower school anxiety, and lower extrinsic orientations to school learning (i.e., less desire to do schoolwork for external incentives) (Gottfried, 1985; Haywood & Switzky, in press; Schultz & Switzky, 1990; Switzky & Schultz, 1988).

The CAIMI was carefully designed to measure children's academic intrinsic motivation as a general orientation toward school learning and across specific curricular areas to assess the motivational underpinnings of school learning (Gottfried, 1985), a most important yet neglected area of individual differences in students. To summarize from the manual (Gottfried, 1986), the CAIMI is a 44-question self-report inventory comprising 122 items and five scales, four of which measure academic intrinsic motivation in the curricular areas of math, reading, science, and social studies. The fifth measures academic intrinsic motivation as a general orientation toward school learning. Each of the scales in the curricular areas contain the same 26 items, and the General scale contains 18 items.

Items were selected to measure components of academic intrinsic motivation such as enjoyment of learning, an orientation that stresses task mastery, curiosity, persistence, and tackling challenging, difficult, and novel tasks. High scores correspond to high academic intrinsic motivation as defined. Low scores correspond to low academic intrinsic motivation, characterized by low enjoyment of learning, an orientation toward learning that stresses low interest in task mastery, low curiosity for school learning, low persistence, and easy rather than difficult or challenging tasks.

Of the 26 items in each of the curricular area scales, 24 are scored on a 5-point Likert-type scale ranging from strongly agree (1) to strongly disagree (5). The other two items are scored using a forced-choice format between an intrinsic and nonintrinsic alternative. All the 18 items composing the General scale also are scored on a 5-point scale that ranges from strongly agree (1) to strongly disagree (5). To minimize response bias, the items were balanced so that for approximately half of them, high intrinsic motivation is indicated by agreement, and for the other half, high intrinsic motivation is indicated by disagreement. For scoring purposes, items are appropriately reversed so that high CAIMI scores correspond to high academic intrinsic motivation.

The CAIMI items are contained in a 12-page booklet, which also provides directions for using the CAIMI. Students write their responses directly in the booklet. The profile sheet provided allows the examiner to plot student responses in each of the curricular areas as well as the General scale in terms of T-scores and percentiles. The latter are derived from the normative population of over 400 lower middle to upper middle class fourth- through eighth-graders on whom the CAIMI was standardized over a 6-year period in three major studies.

**Practical Applications/Uses**

The CAIMI is designed to provide a general measure of academic intrinsic motivation toward school learning as well as curricular-specific measures of such in the domains of math, reading, science, and social studies in children from Grades 4–8. One must exercise extreme caution if the CAIMI is used with children from lower socioeconomic status groups or ethnic groups not included in the standardization sample. The CAIMI should not be used with children who are not fluent in English.

The CAIMI should only be used by trained professionals who have a sophisticated knowledge of the theory and use of tests and measures. School psychologists, guidance counselors, teachers, and other members of pupil personnel team may find the CAIMI clinically useful as part of a psychoeducational battery attempting to elucidate those factors operating to cause academic failure and school learning problems. The CAIMI provides a way of separating the operation of nonintellective (i.e., motivational) from intellective factors, and for developing an intervention plan to raise school achievement and learning if academic failure is primarily due to low academic intrinsic motivation to school learning in general or just within specific academic domains.

The CAIMI may provide information useful in counseling the general population of students regarding individual program planning and their academic interests and course selection, as well as in instructional planning to stimulate academic intrinsic motivation in weak areas and in facilitating such motivation in strong areas. The CAIMI also may be of interest to school districts in evaluating areas of their programs of instruction regarding academic intrinsic motivation. Finally, this inventory may prove very useful to psychologists and other research professionals as an operational measure of academic intrinsic motivation in pure and applied programs of research.

For children of average ability the CAIMI may be administered in small groups or individually. The examiner reads aloud the instructions and practice items, and the children complete the CAIMI on their own. For older children as well as those of higher ability, unmonitored administration (i.e., both instruction and questions are self-administered) may be attempted only if the examiner is confident that the children can read and understand all the items and instructions; however, the examiner should remain available to answer the children's questions. Unmonitored administration is not recommended with groups. For children who are known to have learning, reading, or perceptual problems, the CAIMI should be administered individually and all directions and items read aloud by the examiner. Administering the CAIMI takes approximately 20–30 minutes for individual administrations and 60 minutes for groups.

The instructions and scoring procedures in the CAIMI manual are very clear. The examiner can hand score the inventory in 10–15 minutes. Ratings are entered for each item in the scoring box on the left side of the CAIMI student booklet. Each column of ratings (e.g., marked by R [Reading], M [Math], SS [Social Studies], Sc [Science], and G [General]) are totaled at the bottom of the page. Total raw scores for each scale are summed across pages and entered on the profile report in the row marked "Raw Scores." Percentiles and T-scores can be determined from the tables of elementary school (Grades 4–6) and junior high (Grades 7–8) norms and then plotted to determine a child's level of academic intrinsic motivation relative to the appropriate normative group. Percentiles and T-scores are presented on the left side of the profile report form, and T-scores plus means and standard deviations are presented on the right. The confidence intervals for each of the five CAIMI scores can be determined easily to aid in interpreting the profile. In addition to determining motivation relative to the normative group, the examiner also can compare the relative levels of a child's academic intrinsic motivational strength across the scales in order to determine nonchance differences among scale scores.

## Technical Aspects

As noted previously, development of the CAIMI occurred within three studies over a 6-year period. These trials drew from a population of more than 450 fourth-through eighth-graders who came from lower middle to upper middle SES groups. The first study, using 141 white middle-class fourth- and seventh-graders in a suburban public school district, developed the initial 38-item CAIMI. Based on this study's results, the CAIMI was expanded to the current 122 items, which were used in studies 2 and 3. Subjects in Study 2 were 260 black and white middle-class children in Grades 4–7 from an integrated public school system. The 166 subjects in Study 3 were white middle-class private school students in Grades 5–8.

Extreme care was taken in developing the CAIMI to eliminate the effects of social desirability and response bias and acquiescence. Items presented both positive and negative instances, reversals of items, and clear and unambiguous wording and directions, and administrative procedures emphasized examiner and subject rapport in order to maximize truthful responding. The wording of the CAIMI items was reviewed by a panel of elementary and junior high school teachers to ensure the appropriateness of the vocabulary and syntactic constructions for those populations. Response acquiescence tendencies were tested in Studies 1 and 2 by correlating pairs of items that were reversals of each other. In both studies, these correlations were consistently negative and significant, ranging from –.69 to –.21 ($p < .01$ to $p < .05$), indicating that children responded to the items on the basis of content; that is, they responded appropriately on the opposite sides of the scale for items worded as reversals of each other (Gottfried, 1985, 1986). There was no indication of response acquiescence and negative item bias in the CAIMI. In all the studies, a total social desirability score was obtained and correlated with each of the CAIMI scales. All correlations were not significantly different from zero, indicating that the effects of social desirability were eliminated from the CAIMI.

The internal consistency and test-retest reliability of the CAIMI scales are very high (Gottfried, 1985, 1986). To assess internal consistency, coefficient alpha was computed for each of the subscales. For the Reading, Math, Social Studies, Science, and General scales respectively, coefficient alphas were .90, .89, .91, .90, and .89 in Study 2, and .92, .93, .93, .91, and .83 in Study 3, indicating high internal consistency reliability and substantial item homogeneity within the scales. Test-retest reliability over a 2-month interval was established on a random sample of subjects in Study 2. Coefficients ranged from .69 to .75 ($df = 136$, $p < .01$), indicating moderately high stability. For both internal consistency and test-retest reliability, coefficients were consistent across grade, sex, and race.

All three studies showed the scales of the CAIMI to be intercorrelated (Gottfried, 1985, 1986). The correlations indicate that the CAIMI scales measured variance unique to each separate area, although there was some common variance between them. The proportion of shared variance between the scales ranged from .00 to .42. The average correlation was .39, indicating that the average proportion of variance shared between the scales was .15. Principal components analyses with varimax rotation conducted in Studies 2 and 3 supported the distinctions among the CAIMI scales.

Overall, the CAIMI possesses quite impressive construct validity as a measure of academic intrinsic motivation (i.e., the extent to which a measure has both content and empirical validity). To demonstrate that a measure has construct validity, evidence is usually assembled through a series of steps, as follows (Crocker & Algina, 1986):

1. Formulate hypotheses about how those who differ on the construct are expected to differ on demographic characteristics, performance criteria, or measures of other constructs whose relationship to the performance criteria has already been validated. These hypotheses should be based on an explicitly stated theory that underlies the construct and provides its definitional elaboration.

2. Select (or develop) a measurement instrument whose items assess behaviors that are specific, concrete manifestations of the construct.

3. Gather empirical data that will permit the hypothesized relationships to be tested.

4. Determine if the data are consistent with the hypotheses and consider the extent to which the observed findings could be explained by rival theories or alternative explanations (and eliminate these if possible).

On the basis of theoretical expectations, the following hypotheses were formulated and supported (Gottfried, 1985, 1986):

1. *Academic intrinsic motivation is positively and significantly related to children's school achievement as measured by both standardized achievement tests and teacher grades.* Bivariate correlations between the CAIMI scales and the national percentiles for the standardized achievement test scores were obtained from Studies 1, 2, and 3. In addition, bivariate correlations between the CAIMI scales and teachers' grades were obtained from Studies 2 and 3. The multiple correlations (with all CAIMI scales) showed that achievement (national percentiles for the standardized achievement test scores) in every curriculum domain for the most part was significantly correlated with the CAIMI, with correlations ranging from .24 to .44 ($p < .05$), showing that academic achievement motivation accounted for up to approximately 20% of the variance in school achievement. Almost identical effects were obtained when multiple correlations (with all CAIMI scales) and teacher grades were used as indices of school achievement. Most importantly, CAIMI Reading and Math scales correlated with language and math achievement, respectively, independent of the effects of psychometric intelligence, demonstrating that academic intrinsic motivation is related to achievement performance when the effects of ability are removed (Study 1; Gottfried, 1985).

2. *Academic intrinsic motivation is negatively and significantly related to academic anxiety as measured by the Children's Academic Anxiety Inventory (CAAI), an instrument to assess academic anxiety and worry about classroom learning, tests, and peer comparison with regard to school performance in the curricular areas of reading, math, social studies, and science (Gottfried, 1982).* Academic intrinsic motivation and anxiety involve opposing learning orientations. Academic intrinsic motivation involves approaching learning and mastery and challenging tasks; academic anxiety involves withdrawing from learning and mastery and challenging tasks because of the threat to the self of failure and negative self-worth. In all three studies bivariate correlations were obtained between each of the CAIMI and CAAI scales. Within each study, correlations between corresponding academic intrinsic motivation and academic anxiety curricular areas were moderately high, ranging from –.38 to –.52 ($p < .001$), compared with correlations between noncorresponding curricular area scales and the general academic intrinsic motivation scale and the academic anxiety subscales. Children with higher academic intrinsic motivation in a specific curricular area had lower academic anxiety in that curricular area than did those

with lower academic intrinsic motivation, showing that children differentiated both their academic intrinsic motivation and academic anxiety by curricular areas. Also, children with higher academic intrinsic motivation had lower academic anxiety within each specific curricular area.

3. *Academic intrinsic motivation is positively and significantly related to children's perceptions of their academic competence.* In Studies 2 and 3, children were asked to rate their perceptions of their academic competence by responding to four items (Gottfried, 1985): "I do well in reading," "I do well in math," "I do well in social studies," and "I do well in science." Each item was rated on a 5-point Likert-type scale (strongly agree to strongly disagree) so that higher scores corresponded to higher perceptions of competence. Children with higher levels of academic intrinsic motivation should experience task mastery and should perceive that they are more competent in school learning than those with lower levels of academic intrinsic motivation (Deci & Ryan, 1985; Haywood & Switzky, in press; Schultz & Switzky, 1990; Switzky & Schultz, 1988). Bivariate correlations were obtained between each of the CAIMI scales and the perception of competence items. A strong pattern emerged in which positive correlations between corresponding curricular areas were of higher magnitudes than correlations between noncorresponding curricular areas and between the general academic intrinsic motivation scale and the perception of competence items. Significant positive correlations within corresponding curricular areas ranged from .49 to .62 ($p < .001$), indicating that children with higher academic intrinsic motivation in a specific curricular domain perceived themselves as more competent in that curricular domain compared with children with lower academic intrinsic motivation.

4. *Students' academic intrinsic motivation is positively and significantly related to teachers' perceptions of students' academic intrinsic motivation.* Children with higher academic intrinsic motivation may show behaviors (e.g., investigation, concentration, persistence, etc.) that teachers would detect, resulting in a positive correlation between student ratings of academic intrinsic motivation and teachers' perceptions of this motivation. In Study 3 (Gottfried, 1985), teachers were asked to rate the degree of academic intrinsic motivation they perceived each of their students had in reading, math, social studies, science, and in general. The teachers were presented with the definition of academic intrinsic motivation and were asked to rate each student on a 5-point scale in each curricular domain and in general.

Correlations between the CAIMI scales and teachers' perceptions of students' intrinsic motivation showed the following: (a) a low yet significant pattern of correlations among teachers' ratings of students' general intrinsic motivation with the CAIMI Reading, Math, and General scales, $r(df = 146 \text{ to } 153) = .27, .22$, and .25 ($p < .01$), respectively; (b) a low to moderate yet significant pattern of correlations between teachers' ratings of students' intrinsic motivation in each of the curricular domains and students' CAIMI scores on the Math and General scales, with $r$'s ranging from .20 to .40 ($p < .05$); (c) a moderate and significant correlation between teachers' ratings of students' math motivation and the CAIMI Math scale ($r = .40$, $p < .001$). These patterns of correlations indicated that teachers' perceptions of students' academic intrinsic motivation were related to students' reports of their own academic intrinsic motivation, with the CAIMI Math and General scales showing the most consistent pattern of correlations with the teacher ratings.

5. *Academic intrinsic motivation as measured on the CAIMI is related to other measures of intrinsic versus extrinsic motivation.* In Study 3, the CAIMI was concurrently administered and correlated with three subscales from Harter's (1981) Scale of Intrinsic versus Extrinsic Motivation in the Classroom (i.e., Preference for Challenge versus Preference for Easy Work Assigned; Curiosity/Interest versus Pleasing the Teacher/Getting Good Grades; and Independent Mastery versus Dependence on the Teacher). Lower scores on Harter's scale are related to higher extrinsic motivation, and higher scores on Harter's scale are related to higher intrinsic motivation. Higher CAIMI scores are related to higher orientation toward challenge, curiosity, and mastery, and lower extrinsic orientation toward easy work, grades, and teacher dependence. Low to high significant patterns of correlations were shown, with *r*'s ranging from .17 to .64 ($p < .05$ to $p < .001$). The CAIMI showed the strongest correlations with Harter's challenge (intrinsic) vs. easy work (extrinsic) subscale, with *r*'s ranging from .32 to .64 ($p < .001$). The CAIMI Math and General scales showed the strongest correlations across the three Harter subscales, with *r*'s ranging from .35 to .64 ($p < .001$). These results showed that the CAIMI scales were positively correlated with, and showed convergent validity with, another measure of intrinsic motivation.

## Critique

The CAIMI is one of the best tests currently available to measure academic intrinsic motivation in children. It is well constructed psychometrically and has excellent internal consistency and test-retest reliability as well as construct validity. It is easy to administer and to use. The manual is easy to understand, and the student booklet and profile report form are "user friendly." As noted, practitioners in school settings will find the CAIMI a valuable clinical tool as part of a psychoeducational battery, and researchers may find the inventory an interesting operational measure of academic intrinsic motivation.

However, the CAIMI must be considered as an extremely promising but still experimental measure of academic intrinsic motivation. The CAIMI was developed on a very small heterogeneous sample of children. Research with the CAIMI needs to be expanded to samples at least 10 times the size of the original populations studied; this will ensure the internal, external, and measurement validity of this very interesting inventory.

## References

Borkowski, J.G., & Kurtz, B.E. (1987). Metacognition and executive control. In J.G. Borkowski & J.D. Day (Eds.), *Cognition in special children* (pp. 123–152). Norwood, NJ: Ablex.

Brophy, J. (1983). Conceptualizing student motivation. *Educational Psychologist, 18,* 200–215.

Crocker, L., & Algina, J. (1986). *Introduction to classical & modern test theory.* New York: Holt, Rinehart & Winston.

Deci, E.L., & Ryan, R.M. (1985). *Intrinsic motivation and self-determination in human behavior.* New York: Plenum.

Gottfried, A.E. (1982). Relationships between academic intrinsic motivation and anxiety in children and young adolescents. *Journal of School Psychology, 20,* 205–215.

Gottfried, A.E. (1985). Academic intrinsic motivation in elementary and junior high school students. *Journal of Educational Psychology, 77,* 631–645.

Gottfried, A.E. (1986). *Manual for the CAIMI.* Odessa, FL: Psychological Assessment Resources.

Harter, S. (1981). A new self-report scale of intrinsic versus extrinsic orientation in the classroom: Motivational and informational components. *Developmental Psychology, 17,* 300–312.

Haywood, H.C., & Burke, W.P. (1977). Development of individual differences in intrinsic motivation. In I.C. Uzgiris & F. Weizman (Eds.), *The structuring of experience* (pp. 235–263). New York: Plenum.

Haywood, H.C., & Switzky, H.N. (1986). The malleability of intelligence: Cognitive processes as a function of polygenic-experiential interaction. *School Psychology Review, 15,* 245–255.

Haywood, H.C., & Switzky, H.N. (in press). In E. Zuniga (Ed)., *The development of intellective processes in the child: School context.* Washington, DC: Department of Educational Studies, Organization of American States.

Schultz, G.F., & Switzky, H.N. (1990). The development of intrinsic motivation in students with learning problems: Suggestions for more effective instructional practice. *Preventing School Failure, 34*(2), 14–20.

Sternberg, R.J. (1985). *Beyond IQ: A triarchic theory of human intelligence.* Cambridge: Cambridge University Press.

Switzky, H.N., & Heal, L. (1990). Research methods in special education. In R. Gaylord-Ross (Ed.), *Issues and research in special education* (Vol. 1, pp. 1–81). New York: Teachers College Press.

Switzky, H.N., & Schultz, G.F. (1988). Intrinsic motivation and learning performance: Implications for individual educational programming for learners with mild handicaps. *Remedial and Special Education, 9*(4), 7–14.

**Ron D. Cambias, Jr., Psy.D.**
*Psychology Staff, Children's Hospital, New Orleans, Louisiana.*

**Grant Aram Killian, Ph.D.**
*Associate Professor of Psychology, Nova University, Ft. Lauderdale, Florida.*

**Jan Faust, Ph.D.**
*Assistant Professor of Psychology, Nova University, Ft. Lauderdale, Florida.*

# CHILDREN'S APPERCEPTIVE STORY-TELLING TEST

*Mary F. Schneider. Austin, Texas: PRO-ED, Inc.*

## Introduction

The Children's Apperceptive Story-Telling Test (CAST; Schneider, 1989) was developed from a conceptual foundation that encompasses Adler's Individual Psychology. This test attempts to redress the previous psychometric shortcomings of apperception tests by offering an objective scoring system and a national standardization sample. The CAST follows in a long succession of apperception tests, most notably the Thematic Apperception Test (TAT; Murray, 1971) and the Children's Apperception Test (CAT; Bellak & Bellak, 1980).

Central to apperception tests, as well as projective tests in general, is the concept of apperceptive distortion, which refers to the individual's subjective interpretation of a stimulus. Beginning in the latter part of the 19th century and continuing into the early 20th, professionals began to recognize that clients' unconscious drives and conflicts could be manifested through verbalizations made in response to an otherwise ambiguous stimulus. Through the ambiguity of the stimulus, the client "projects" his or her personality traits, drives, defenses, and unconscious conflicts. Thus, the subject's unique history of accumulated past experiences results in a distortion of current perceptions. In other words, an individual subjectively perceives more than what is objectively extant in the stimulus (Bellak, 1975). The individual's personality colors how he or she perceives the world. As a result, projective techniques like the CAST allow access to an individual's internal world.

The test author, Mary Schneider, Ph.D., is a faculty member at the National College of Education in Evanston, Illinois. As an undergraduate, she worked under Manford Sonstegard, Ph.D., an Adlerian psychologist. She continued to pursue her Adlerian studies while earning her doctorate in educational and counseling psychology at Loyola University of Chicago. Schneider's interests have lain in the area of childhood adjustment disorders and the role of school personnel in the assessment and intervention process. She first began using story-telling pictures as a school psychologist in the late 1970s, and it was at that time she decided to devise a children's apperception test that would include an Adlerian scoring system, a standardization sample, and a large clinical sample of behavior-disordered subjects (M.F. Schneider, personal communication, August 1, 1989). The CAST was developed over a 5-year span, from 1984 until the test's publication in 1989.

The CAST is developed along the lines of an Adlerian model that contains the major components of Adlerian psychology (Sweeney, 1975). The social component involves the individual's need to belong to a social group (i.e., social interest), which is played out in the context of the various life tasks the individual faces, including work, love, and friendship. The teleological component addresses the individual's movement toward goals in order to meet the demands of the social environment. Goals are the primary motivators, while emotions fuel the movement towards the attainment of goals. The degree to which the individual's goals are in accord with social interest determines the adaptiveness or nonadaptiveness of this movement. Finally, the analytic component relates to the individual's ability to redirect or to change behavior through problem solving. Problem solving, like teleological movement, can either be adaptive or nonadaptive. In addition, problem solving can entail either the presence of cognitive operations (operational) or the lack of cognitive operations (preoperational).

It is important to note that the terms *operational* and *preoperational* used here bear no relation to their Piagetian counterparts. In this context, cognitive operations refer to the mental skills required to solve day-to-day problems. Furthermore, operational problem solving entails rule-bound, concrete, means-to-end thinking, while preoperational problem solving entails more simplistic, "magical"-type solutions. For example, the ability to consider hypothetical possibilities in the resolution of conflict is an example of adaptive operational problem solving. Conversely, resolving a conflict with a simple "and they lived happily ever after" is an example of preoperational problem solving.

The CAST originated in 1984 with a study in which 119 Adlerian psychologists and 55 child and family therapists selected a number of constructs they considered reflective of the mentally healthy child. For example, some of the constructs selected were empathy, problem-solving skills, affiliation, and family harmony (Schneider, 1989, p. 69). These constructs were used in scoring the early versions of the CAST. The pilot study was conducted with a sample of 88 children from ages 6 to 16 who were matched according to age, sex, race, and socioeconomic status. Initially 25 stimulus pictures were designed to reflect the life tasks of family, peer, and school functioning as experienced by children from intact as well as from single-parent families. As a result of the pilot study, 16 stimulus pictures were chosen because of their elicitation of diverse thematic content, lack of stereotyped responses, few response delays or refusals, and self-validated or personal responses (Schneider, 1989, p. 70).

Following the pilot study, several other studies were conducted to refine further the stimulus cards, scales, and scoring system. The first study involved the readministration of the 16 stimulus cards to a group of 133 students in 1985 (Schneider, 1989). This study resulted in modifying the stimulus cards to elicit fewer negative themes, decreasing the number of scales and making them more general in content, and making the scoring system easier to understand and apply (Schneider, 1989, p. 70). The second series of studies involved the use of the experimental version of the CAST with well-adjusted and behavior-disordered subjects (Friedrich, 1987; Musgrove, 1987; Shaw, 1987; Zemel, 1986). These studies concerned the validity and reliability of the experimental version and resulted in further improvement of the CAST scoring system. Finally, the third study involved 15 child therapists rating the 16 stimulus cards on the elicitation of themes for each card, the particular life task portrayed, the affective pull of the card, and the socioeconomic status of the characters portrayed (Schneider, 1989, p. 70). The most notable changes involved increasing the elicitation of more positive affect-laden responses and addition of a stimulus card reflective of extended family support (thereby increasing the total number of stimulus cards from 16 to 17 for use with each subject). The final result was the present version of the CAST.

The CAST was standardized on a nationally representative sample of children ages 6 to 13. The standardization sample included 876 children, and an additional 322 children were in the behavior-disordered group. Schoolchildren were selected for the standardization sample who would reflect the demographic characteristics of the U.S. population according to the 1980 census reports. Socioeconomic status was measured using parental education level. Data indicate a close match between the standardization sample and the U.S. population in terms of the various parental education levels: less than high school (20.5% for the CAST sample vs. 22.5% for the U.S. population), high school graduate (38.6% vs. 39.3%), 1 to 3 years of college (21.7% vs. 21.0%), and college graduate (19.2% vs. 17.5%).

In order to ensure that these students were well adjusted, subjects were screened via behavior checklist and school personnel report. Those identified as having an adjustment problem were replaced by an alternate subject. For the behavior-disordered sample, subjects were selected in much the same manner as the standardization group except that they attended full-time special education classes and functioned within the average range of intelligence. Although the intellectual level of the standardization subjects was not measured, presumably they functioned in the average range or higher because students evidencing academic difficulties were excluded. The overrepresentation of boys to girls in the behavior-disordered sample (a 4:1 ratio) was orchestrated purposely to reflect the greater number of boys in the general behavior-disordered population.

As noted, the CAST is designed for school and clinical use with children from 6 to 13 years of age. The test user is warned against using the CAST with children outside this age range because of the lack of normative data. The CAST is sold as a small kit containing the 31 stimulus cards, the manual, and 50 scoring forms. Each of the 8½" × 11" stimulus picture cards is rendered in color. The scenes depicted in the drawings represent a child's various life tasks, including family, peers, and school. There are 14 pairs of cards for use with either males or females, and three cards that are administered to both sexes (for a total of 17 cards for use with each subject). The cards were developed with sensitivity to various ethnic groups, and blacks, Hispanics, and Asians are all represented.

The manual presents an overview of the test as well as information on administration and scoring, interpretation of test results, and the test's development and standardization. Numerous examples illustrate scoring and interpretation, including two in-depth case studies. The scoring form consists of a section for recording demographic information, an observations section, and a section to list questions derived from test results, which are asked during the confirmation process. In addition, there are also sections for scoring each of the responses, for developing the Life Task Sociogram, and for plotting the CAST Profile. The Life Task Sociogram provides information on the concentration of stories' life-task content in terms of significant story figures and four factor scores. This method allows the examiner to visualize areas of concern that could be addressed further during the confirmation process. Finally, a section is included for computing the four CAST Factor Scores.

The CAST Profile is broken down into three sections: the Thematic Profile, which is designed to measure significant themes; the Problem-Solving Profile, which is designed to measure the quality of problem-solving ability; and the Factor Profile, which reflects the general constructs that the test measures. The Thematic Profile consists of four Adaptive Thematic Scales and five Nonadaptive Thematic Scales. The four Adaptive Thematic Scales are described as follows:

1. *Instrumentality:* mastery or achievement (e.g., a boy cleans up his room).

2. *Interpersonal Cooperation:* cooperation with others toward a common goal (e.g., a group of children collect money for a charity).

3. *Affiliation:* association with other people (e.g., getting together with friends, parents adopting a child).

4. *Positive Affect:* positive feelings (e.g., a character saying she feels "happy").

As noted, there are five Nonadaptive Thematic Scales, which are as follows:

1. *Inadequacy:* accidental wrongdoing, procrastination, inability to perform or willful evasion of a responsibility, or destructive behavior (e.g., accidentally breaking a glass, waiting to do chores, refusing to do homework, purposefully breaking a toy).

2. *Alienation:* estrangement from others (e.g., character feels left out, parents get divorced).

3. *Interpersonal Conflict:* conflictual relationship with one or more characters (e.g., two characters fight over which television channel to watch).

4. *Limits:* limits or consequences applied to one's behavior in either a rational and democratic manner or an irrational and autocratic manner (e.g., mother telling her children to pick up their dirty clothes, father hitting his son for not doing what he was told, character getting killed for not listening to his mother).

5. *Negative Affect:* negative feelings (e.g., character saying he feels "horrible").

The Problem-Solving Profile includes two Adaptive Problem-Solving Scales:

1. *Positive Preoperational:* positive resolution of a story but without a concrete solution; unreflective of rule-bound thinking (e.g., Examiner: "How will the story end?" Subject: "Okay").

2. *Positive Operational:* positive resolution of a story with a concrete solution; reflective of rule-bound thinking (e.g., Examiner: "How will the story end?" Subject: "He will apologize and do as he is told").

The Problem-Solving Profile also consists of four Nonadaptive Problem-Solving Scales:

1. *Refusal:* subject refuses or claims to be unable to tell a story to the stimulus picture.

2. *Unresolved:* a problem is left unresolved (e.g., "a boy fights with his sister"; Examiner: "How will the story end?" Subject: "I don't know").

3. *Negative Preoperational:* negative resolution of a story without a concrete solution; unreflective of rule-bound thinking (e.g., Examiner: "How will the story end?" Subject: "Not good").

4. *Negative Operational:* negative resolution of a story but with a concrete solution; reflective of rule-bound thinking (e.g., Examiner: "How will the story end?" Subject: "He will steal the money and go to jail").

Finally, the Factor Profile consists of the following four factors (identified through factor analysis during the establishment of the construct validity of the CAST):

1. *Adaptive:* includes the Adaptive Thematic Scales and Positive Operational Problem-Solving Scale and reflects the adaptive dimension of the Adlerian model on which the CAST is based.

2. *Nonadaptive:* includes the Nonadaptive Thematic Scales and Negative Operational Problem-Solving Scale and reflects the nonadaptive dimension of the Adlerian model.

3. *Immature:* includes the Positive and Negative Preoperational Problem-Solving Scales and represents a simplistic problem-solving approach.

4. *Uninvested:* includes the Refusal and Unresolved scales and measures the subject's degree of uninvestment in approaching the stimulus situations.

**Practical Applications/Uses**

The CAST is most appropriate for school and clinical psychologists to use in the evaluation of children and young adolescents with emotional/adjustment problems. The CAST manual presents four major uses for the test: assessment, treatment planning, treatment progress evaluation, and research (Schneider, 1989, p. 2). One example of its use would be a school psychologist employing the CAST in an evaluation of a student who has been disruptive in class. The test results could be employed in both a confirmation interview with the student and with his or her parents and teachers as well as in the development of an appropriate treatment plan that seeks to enhance strengths and correct weaknesses. The CAST then could be readministered, perhaps 6 months later, in order to evaluate treatment progress. However, the manual presents no research supporting the effectiveness of the CAST in such an application.

An example of the CAST's use in research might be a study examining the developmental trends in children's problem-solving capacities. The utilization of relatively large samples of children for each age level in the standardization sample (i.e., approximately 100 children for each 1-year age group from ages 6 to 13) aids the researcher in distinguishing between age-appropriate abilities and developmental differences. The availability of age-graded normative data enhances the CAST's appeal as a measuring instrument in such developmental research.

The CAST is intended to be used as part of a dynamic assessment process that aims to examine the interaction between assessor and subject and thereby determine the subject's potential for learning rather than to simply apply a label (Lidz, 1987). This approach examines the process between assessment and intervention by confirming test data through close corroboration with the subject and the subject's significant others—parents, teachers, and so forth (Schneider & Perney, 1989). This method, accomplished through questioning the subject and others about test data in an interview format, helps differentiate test responses that are pure fantasy from those that more likely reflect the subject's objective life.

In the case of the CAST, the confirmation process involves presenting each stimulus card and stating the following: "The last time we met, you looked at this picture and told a story about . . . (short paraphrase of client's story). Has anything like that ever happened to you?" (Schneider, 1989, p. 60). The examiner then continues to question the subject as part of an interview process, which often includes the subject's significant others (i.e., parents and teachers). Thus, the dynamic assessment approach requires a broader role for the test examiner, involving him or her in more of a participant role rather than in the more traditional role of observer. The confirmation process interfaces assessment and intervention by revealing problematic areas to be corrected (e.g., parents with substance abuse problems, the presence of physical abuse, truancy, etc.). Thus, the method also bears directly on the development of a treatment plan aimed at addressing the specific needs of the case.

Although not explicitly discussed in the manual, the CAST presumably also may be used in the more traditional manner, that is, as one part of a full-battery assessment. Used in such a manner, the CAST may provide the same kind of personality data that projective tests in general have traditionally provided. For example, the data may be interpreted both quantitatively and qualitatively in much the same way as the Rorschach, using the Exner scoring system (Exner, 1986). In the Exner system, the structural summary provides the standardized, "objective" data. Likewise, the CAST provides profile scores that also have been objectified through standardization. Although thematic apperception tests have been shown to reduce the diagnostic validity of more psychometrically robust measures (e.g., the MMPI or the Personality Inventory for Children [Wildman & Wildman, 1975; Butkus, 1984]), a more reliable and valid instrument like the CAST may indeed complement the other personality tests within an assessment arsenal. However, until such research is established, it is questionable whether the CAST would be a robust measure as part of a test battery or, like the TAT and other projective instruments, would serve to reduce the validity of other psychometrically robust measures within the battery.

The CAST is suitable for all verbal English-speaking children from 6 to 13 years of age. Although the test author states that children whose primary language is other than English should be tested in their native language, it is not clear whether these results could be compared reliably to the standardization data. For example, the test manual does not indicate whether bilingual children were tested in their primary language and included in the normative sample. However, the test is suitable for use with black, Hispanic, and Asian children, as these ethnic groups were included in the development of the stimulus cards and the standardization sample. In order to test the ethnic representativeness of the stimulus situations, equal numbers of children from all three of the above ethnic groups and an equal number of white children rated the stimulus pictures as to each group's perception of the race of the stimulus characters (Schneider, 1989). Results generally indicated that each group could perceive its own race as well as other races in the stimulus pictures. The test requires that subjects have the basic comprehension skills to understand directions and are free of acute sensory deficits. Schneider also warns that test results from children with severe sensory deficits or neuropsychological impairments would be of questionable validity.

The CAST is administered individually in any quiet, well-lighted room that is free from distractions. Schneider (1989) claims that test examiners should have basic knowledge of test measurement, construction, and interpretation; however, it would seem that the test conceivably could be administered by anyone familiar with the procedures. Because instructions are standardized and responses are audiotaped, no special skills are necessary to administer the CAST. According to the manual, administration requires 20 to 40 minutes.

The manual strongly recommends audiotaping each administration in order to ensure accurate recording of responses. Also, this method allows the examiner to focus on building rapport with the examinee. As the CAST was standardized using audiotaping as part of the administration procedure, this method is preferred over transcribing responses by hand. This method is also consistent with TAT research demonstrating the greater efficiency of machine recording over recording by hand (Baty & Dreger, 1975).

The examiner presents the subject with each of the 17 stimulus cards in order. Testing begins with a specific set of instructions, which are similar in nature to those given with the TAT. For each picture, the child is told to describe what is happening and what the characters are feeling and saying. Each story must have a beginning, a middle, and an end. An abbreviated set of instructions may be given, if necessary, for the first three cards. The examiner offers the following five prompt questions for each card:

1. What is happening in this picture?
2. How are they feeling? or How is s/he feeling?
3. What happened before this?
4. What are they saying? or What is s/he saying?
5. How will the story end? What will happen at the end? (Schneider, 1989, p. 14)

These questions are given, regardless of whether the subject has answered them in his or her responses, in order to maintain standardized administration procedure. There is no time limit for responses; furthermore, neither latency time nor length of time for responses is measured.

Scoring involves the Adaptive and Nonadaptive Thematic Scales and Adaptive and Nonadaptive Problem-Solving Scales. Each of the individual scales is scored using a Likert-type system in which varying point values are assigned for the various scales (e.g., Instrumentality is scored along a 2-point scale, Interpersonal Conflict is scored along a 4-point scale). For example, the Interpersonal Conflict scale (one of the Nonadaptive Thematic Scales) is scored along a continuum from 1 to 4 points in terms of general, nonspecific "fighting" (scored 1 point) to physical destruction such as the death of a character (scored 4 points). Each discrete act is thus scored for each of the Thematic Scales, and the endings of the stories are reviewed and rated according to level of problem solving. The objective scoring system provides tables for converting raw scores into T-scores, which then comprise the Thematic Profile, Problem-Solving Profile, and Factor Profile. The conversion of raw scores to T-scores allows the examiner to compare the subject to others of his or her own age. The Thematic Indicators (concerning sexual abuse, substance abuse, divorce, hypothetical thought, emotionality, and self-validation) and Life Tasks (peer, school, and family) also are tallied during the scoring process. Finally, the number of themes per card (Thematic Verbosity) are summed, and the Life Task Sociogram (optional) is completed.

The Life Task Sociogram provides information about the concentration of the stories' life-task content in terms of significant story figures and the four factor scores. The completion and interpretation of the Life Task Sociogram is difficult to grasp and complex to interpret. Specifically, the examiner must synthesize numerous components: rows of life tasks (family, peer, school, and other), columns of factors (adaptive, nonadaptive, immature, and uninvested), and spaces for marking the card numbers and appropriate thematic content. The amount of concentration and energy necessary to integrate the numerous aspects of the sociogram into a meaningful whole may discourage the use of this part of the CAST. However, this method, once learned, allows the examiner to visualize areas of concern that could be addressed further during the confirmation process.

Overall, the nuances of scoring are difficult to learn, as they sometimes entail subjective discretion. For example, the Likert-type scoring invites slight scoring difficulties due to subtleties of responses. A response in which a character has not performed a responsibility (e.g., a girl does not walk the dog) is scored either as Inadequacy 1 (accidental wrongdoing) or Inadequacy 2 (procrastination). However, in this instance it is unclear which should be scored due to the uncertain intentionality of the action (e.g., did the girl forget, or did she simply put off walking the dog?). Furthermore, some responses might lead to confusion as to which scale should be scored. For instance, the Limits thematic category may not be distinguishable from the Interpersonal Conflict category in some cases. Or, in another example, a response in which the father swears at his son to get the boy to do his homework would be scored as a verbally abusive limit (scored 2 points) but not under Interpersonal Conflict as verbal abuse (also scored 2 points). Such subtleties invite some degree of scoring confusion.

Finally, despite its thoroughness in presenting scoring criteria and examples, the manual contains many confusing mistakes in the examples given (i.e., some of the scores for responses in the case studies in Appendix C are not recorded on the sample Record Forms, while others are marked incorrectly). Thus, the CAST scoring system, though specific in its conception and presentation, can be quite cumbersome and does not completely eliminate subjective judgment from the process.

The manual states that scoring each CAST protocol typically takes about 30 minutes. However, due to the number of items to be scored, an examiner would require practice on a number of protocols (perhaps 15 or more) before attaining any reasonable degree of proficiency, especially in scoring the Thematic and Problem-Solving Scales.

Interpretation involves both quantitative and qualitative analysis of test data. Quantitative analysis, referring to the examination of the CAST Profile scores, entails the following sequence of steps: (a) inspection of Factor Profiles for significant factor scores; (b) inspection of the scale scores within the significant factor for the scales that are major contributors to the factor's significance; and (c) inspection of the Thematic Indicators for significant cutoff levels (Schneider, 1989, p. 43). The CAST Profile scores are based on a T-distribution (a method for expressing a subject's relative position within a group) with a mean T-score of 50 and a standard deviation of 10. Therefore, significant scale scores are those that fall 1 standard deviation above or below the mean (outside the T-score range of 40 to 60). Any scale scores falling outside this range are considered appropriate for interpretation.

Qualitative analysis, referring to a more subjective approach to interpretation, involves consideration of behavioral observations (e.g., length of response, quality of verbal expressiveness, etc.), content analysis of stories (e.g., examination for popular thematic content, content related to thematic indicators, etc.), and review of the Life Task Sociogram data. Interpretive hypotheses, resulting from both quantitative and qualitative analyses, are tested through the confirmatory process of subject interview, in which clinical hypotheses are either confirmed or disconfirmed through interviews with both the subject and the subject's significant others. The chapter in the CAST manual describing interpretation provides numerous examples to illustrate the process.

Interpretation of the CAST is both straightforward and comprehensive. The approach allows flexibility through recourse to qualitative analysis while anchoring much of the interpretive process to empirically derived data. Bellak (1975) states that for any projective technique to be considered valid and useful, it must provide a means both for comparing the subject to the general population as well as for revealing the individual's unique personality characteristics. The CAST's interpretive process allows the examiner to walk this fine line.

The manual reports about 20 to 30 minutes for general interpretation. It also states that the examiner should have training in one of the major branches of mental health (e.g., psychology, counseling, etc.). Interpretation is moderately difficult and would require an examiner to have knowledge of child development and psychopathology on at least a master's degree level.

**Technical Aspects**

As noted before, the CAST is one of the few apperception tests developed with any amount of psychometric rigor. Several types of validity have been addressed, including content (Schneider, 1989), construct (Schneider, 1989), and criterion-related (Beckman, 1989). Likewise, several aspects of reliability have been examined: interrater (scorer) (Schneider, 1989), test-retest (Stolorow, 1989), split-half (Schneider, 1989), and coefficient alpha (Schneider, 1989).

The CAST's content validity was verified by having 22 psychologists rate the stimulus cards according to what each card "pulls for" in terms of thematic content, life task, affect, and socioeconomic status (Schneider, 1989). Ratings for thematic content generally supported claims for those themes the cards were purported to measure and indicated that each card often pulled for more than one theme. Life-task ratings suggested a preponderance of cards with a family life-task pull, with a few cards for either peer or school life tasks. In an attempt to ensure that the stimulus cards elicited positive as well as negative affect, the raters also were asked to rate the cards according to affective pull. Results indicated balanced pull in terms of negative, positive, and neutral affect. Concerning the socioeconomic status of the people depicted, most cards were rated as neutral. Finally, the ratings concerning thematic content pull were compared to the data obtained during the standardization of the CAST. Considerable agreement emerged between the psychologist raters and the students for a few of the Thematic Scales, with somewhat lesser agreement for the other scales.

In order to establish the construct validity of the CAST, three different approaches were employed: factor analysis, intercorrelations among the scales and factors, and comparison between groups of behavior-disordered children with groups of well-adjusted peers (Schneider, 1989). The relationship among the 15 CAST scales for the standardization group was analyzed by applying a principal-components factor analysis with orthogonal varimax rotation and Kaiser normalization. Results showed the four factors mentioned earlier: Adaptive, Nonadaptive, Immature, and Uninvested. Interrcorrelation matrices were created for the 15 CAST scales and four factors using data from the standardization sample, behavior-disordered sample, and total combined sample. Results indicate support for the test's factor structure; for example, the scales that make up the Adaptive Factor (Instrumentality, Interpersonal Cooperation, etc.) correlate moderately well with each other and with the factor itself.

Finally, comparisons were made between various groups of behavior-disordered children and samples of children from the standardization pool. In the first analysis, the behavior-disordered sample and a random sample of the same number of well-adjusted children from the standardization group were compared to see if the CAST could discriminate between the two groups. Both *t*-tests and discriminant function analyses were utilized in the study. Independent *t*-tests yielded significant differences between both groups for all scales and factors except Alienation and Negative Affect. A discriminant analysis was performed to see which scales would discriminate best between the two groups. The three most discriminating scales were Positive Operation Problem-Solving, Instrumentality, and Interpersonal Cooperation. The one significant discriminant function yielded an overall classification rate of 78%.

Next, a smaller sample of behavior-disordered children was matched with a sample of standardization subjects in terms of age, sex, ethnic background, and parental education level. This time independent *t*-tests resulted in far fewer significant differences, with no differences found for Positive Affect, the Nonadaptive Factor, and almost all the Nonadaptive Scales. The author attributes the lack of significant differences to an overrepresentation of children with an attention deficit disorder (ADD) in the sample. However, this interpretation is questionable, given that a separate analysis of ADD students and well-adjusted students yielded significant differences for many of the same scales that were nonsignificant in this comparison.

The last analysis involved breaking down the behavior-disordered sample into diagnostic categories and comparing each with a matched sample of well-adjusted children. Analyses were thus performed for the following diagnostic categories of students: attention deficit disorder, conduct disorder, anxiety disorder, oppositional disorder, depression, overanxious, schizoid, and pervasive developmental disorder.

Beckman's (1989) study established the criterion-related validity of the CAST by correlating the scale with the Roberts Apperception Test for Children (RATC; McArthur & Roberts, 1982). The RATC was chosen because it yields scale scores similar to those of the CAST, which then can be utilized in a correlational analysis. The study included two groups: a well-adjusted sample of 25 students, ranging in age from 6 to 13 years, and a behavior-disordered sample of 19 students, also ranging from 6 to 13. Pearson product-moment correlation coefficients were calculated using the CAST Thematic scales and factors and the RATC profile scales. Results indicate moderate correlation between many of the scales on the CAST with those of the RATC. However, the sample size in this study falls quite short of the recommended minimum of 200 subjects to ensure statistically reliable results (Kline, 1986).

Interrater reliability has to do with the consistency of results achieved by different examiners. The interrater reliability of the CAST was established using two different approaches (Schneider, 1989). In the first, six raters scored six protocols reflecting three different levels of difficulty, from easy to difficult. Pearson product-moment correlations were calculated for the 14 CAST scales (one scale did not yield sufficient data for calculation). Of the median reliability coefficients calculated, 11 were above .90, with the other 3 falling in the .80 range. In the second approach, each of the original two raters from the above study rescored the six protocols after a 7-week period. Pearson product-moment correlations were generally above .90, thus lending support for the CAST's interrater reliability.

Test-retest reliability refers to the consistency of results from one testing to another. Stolorow (1989) conducted a study in which 43 students were administered the CAST on two occasions, 8 days apart. The study involved 26 well-adjusted students and 17 behavior-disordered students. Pearson product-moment coefficients were computed for both groups separately and for the total group. Results were generally higher for the four factor scales than for the 15 individual scales. Reliability coefficients ranged from .49 to .98 (median value of .77) across both groups for the individual scales. For the factor scales, reliability coefficients ranged from .77 to .96 (median value of .90) for the combined sample. Although Schneider (1989) prudently advises the clinician to consider the factor scores as more stable measures, the sample size in this study also falls short of Kline's (1986) recommended 200 subjects.

Split-half reliability is a way of measuring the internal consistency of a test by correlating the scores from the test's two halves. Split-half reliability poses a problem in projective testing due to the possible influence of stimulus pictures on subsequent responses. However, Schneider (1989) attempted to circumvent this difficulty by separating the 17 CAST stimulus pictures into two groups based on picture content. The Pearson product-moment correlation method, with Spearman-Brown correction, was applied to the data for both standardization and behavior-disordered samples. Correlation coefficients were computed for each, with the standardization data yielding a median value of .74 and the behavior-disordered sample a value of .79. These results would seem respectable for a projective instrument.

Schneider (1989) also computed coefficient alpha, using the standardization sample data for three age ranges: ages 6 to 8, 9 to 11, and 12 to 13. The process produced median coefficients for each age level as follows: .78 (ages 6 to 8), .78

(ages 9 to 11), and .76 (age 12 to 13.). Results generally were higher for the factors and the Problem-Solving Scales, and lower for the Thematic Scales.

## Critique

When clinicians rely on clinical experience or "intuition" to interpret projective test results, they become vulnerable to misinterpretation of the data and may even project as much as the subject (Killian, 1984). By referring to established norms, the CAST makes great strides in obviating this potential pitfall. The CAST appears to be one of a new breed of apperceptive instruments for children (along with the Michigan Picture Test–Revised [MPT-R; Hutt, 1980], the Roberts Apperception Test for Children [RATC; McArthur & Roberts, 1982], and the Tell-Me-A-Story test [TEMAS; Costantino, Malgady, & Rogler, 1988]) that attempts to reconcile the psychometric shortcomings of past apperceptive tests (see Cambias, Killian, & Faust, 1992a, 1992b, for reviews of the Roberts Supplementary Test Pictures for Black Children and the TEMAS). The CAST provides stimulus pictures developed according to a sound empirical approach, with a solid theoretical background and an objective scoring system based on a national standardization sample. The choice of stimulus pictures appears to show sensitivity to both family and cultural diversity. One strong suit of the CAST is its attempt to identify and test behavior-disordered children (e.g., attention deficit disorder, conduct disorder, etc.). Indeed, the CAST is one of the few available apperceptive instruments that approximates the standards set forth in the *Standards for Educational and Psychological Testing* (American Educational Research Association, American Psychological Association, & National Council on Measurement in Education, 1985).

One standard with which the CAST may not be in compliance is the following: "When a test is translated from one language to another, its reliability and validity for the uses intended in the linguistic groups to be tested should be established" (AERA, APA, & NCME, 1985, p. 75). Although the manual warns the user against testing subjects who lack proficiency in English, the text is not clear as to whether the CAST could be used if translated into a subject's native language. If the answer is yes, then the appropriate reliability and validity studies need to be conducted and included in the manual for those specific linguistic groups.

If the CAST has one drawback, it is its newness in the field, as further independent research on its psychometric properties and use in clinical practice has not yet been conducted. At the present time, all research appears to have taken place at the National College of Education in Evanston, Illinois, where the measure was originally conceived. At this point, according to Schneider (1989), further work should focus on developing norms for children with a primary language other than English; establishing profiles for other nosological categories; forming criterion-related validation using other personality and/or behavior instruments; designing group pre- and post-test studies of treatment-effected change; conducting studies using the CAST to predict therapeutic outcome; and performing reliability and validity studies with larger populations and populations with specific characteristics (p. 125). In addition, a study on the relative effectiveness of the CAST and other apperception tests in discriminating clinical from well-adjusted samples is recommended. Such a study would demonstrate the relative effectiveness of the CAST with regard to other available instruments. However, a briefer form of the CAST (perhaps using 10 to 12 stimulus picture cards instead of the present 17 cards) with the appropriate standardization, reliability, and validity studies could increase the marketability of this promising new technique.

The CAST should be applauded for its focus on redressing some of the typical shortcomings of past thematic apperception techniques (e.g., lack of objective scoring systems, intuitive approaches to interpretation, etc.). However, the lengthy manual (274 pages, of which over 120 pages are text) and somewhat cumbersome scoring system may discourage the use of this otherwise carefully developed and promising new instrument.

## References

This list includes text citations and suggested additional reading.

American Educational Research Association, American Psychological Association, & National Council on Measurement in Education. (1985). *Standards for educational and psychological testing*. Washington, DC: American Psychological Association.

Baty, M.A., & Dreger, R.M. (1975). A comparison of three methods to record TAT protocols. *Journal of Clinical Psychology, 31*(2), 348.

Beckman, G.A. (1989). *A concurrent validity study of the Children's Apperceptive Story-Telling Test (CAST) as compared to the Roberts Apperception Test for Children (RATC).* Unpublished master's thesis, National College of Education, Evanston, IL.

Bellak, L. (1975). *The T.A.T., C.A.T., and S.A.T. in clinical use* (3rd ed.). New York: Grune & Stratton.

Bellak, L., & Bellak, S. (1980). *A manual for the Children's Apperception Test* (7th ed.). Larchmont, NY: C.P.S.

Butkus, M. (1984). Comparison of the predictive/descriptive accuracy and improvements to the incremental validity of a projective and two objective personality tests for children and adolescents. *Dissertation Abstracts International, 45,* 3930B. (University Microfilms No. 8502508)

Cambias, R.D., Jr., Killian, G.A., & Faust, J. (1992a). Roberts Apperception Test for Children: Supplementary Test Pictures for Black Children. In D.J. Keyser & R.C. Sweetland (Eds.), *Test critiques* (Vol. IX, pp. 431–437). Austin, TX: PRO-ED.

Cambias, R.D., Jr., Killian, G.A., & Faust, J. (1992b). TEMAS (Tell-Me-A-Story) Test. In D.J. Keyser & R.C. Sweetland (Eds.), *Test critiques* (Vol. IX, pp. 545–560). Austin, TX: PRO-ED.

Costantino, G., Malgady, R., & Rogler, L.H. (1988). *TEMAS (Tell-Me-A-Story) manual.* Los Angeles: Western Psychological Services.

Exner, J.E. (1986). *The Rorschach: A comprehensive system: Vol. 1. Basic foundations* (2nd ed.). New York: Wiley.

Friedrich, G.J. (1987). *A construct validity study of the experimental version of the Schneider Apperception Test for Children in a public and private school population.* Unpublished master's thesis, National College of Education, Evanston, IL.

Henry, W.E. (1956). *The analysis of fantasy.* New York: Wiley.

Hutt, M.L. (1980). *The Michigan Picture Test–Revised.* New York: Grune & Stratton.

Killian, G.A. (1984). House-Tree-Person Technique. In D.J. Keyser & R.C. Sweetland (Eds.), *Test critiques* (Vol. I, pp. 338–353). Austin, TX: PRO-ED.

Kline, P. (1986). *A handbook of test construction: Introduction to psychometric design.* New York: Methuen.

Lidz, C.S. (Ed.). (1987). *Dynamic assessment.* New York: Guilford.

McArthur, D.S., & Roberts, G.E. (1982). *Roberts Apperception Test for Children manual.* Los Angeles: Western Psychological Services.

Murray, H.A. (1971). *Thematic Apperception Test manual.* Cambridge: Harvard University Press.

Musgrove, R.A. (1987). *A construct validity study of the experimental version of the Schneider Apperception Test for Children (SAT-C).* Unpublished master's thesis, National College of Education, Evanston, IL.

Obrzut, J.E., & Cummings, J.A. (1983). The projective approach to personality assessment: An analysis of thematic picture techniques. *School Psychology Review, 12*(4), 414–420.

Schneider, M.F. (1989). *CAST: Children's Apperceptive Story-Telling Test manual.* Austin, TX: PRO-ED.

Schneider, M.F., & Perney, J. (1989, August). Utility of apperceptive assessment in the schools. In M.F. Schneider (Chair), *Utilizing personality assessment within the school context: Assessment to intervention.* Symposium conducted at the 97th Annual Convention of the American Psychological Association, New Orleans.

Shaw, C.S. (1987). *Assessing test-retest and interrater reliability of the Schneider Apperception Test for Children (SAT-C).* Unpublished master's thesis, National College of Education, Evanston, IL.

Stolorow, G. (1989). *Test-retest reliability of the Children's Apperceptive Story-Telling Test (CAST).* Unpublished master's thesis, National College of Education, Evanston, IL.

Sweeney, T.J. (1975). *Adlerian counseling.* Muncie, IN: Accelerated Development.

Wildman, R.W., & Wildman, R.W., II. (1975). An investigation into the comparative validity of several diagnostic tests and test batteries. *Journal of Clinical Psychology, 31,* 455–458.

Zemel, B. (1986). *Validity of the Schneider Apperception Test as compared to the Roberts Apperception Test with children from intact families.* Unpublished master's thesis, National College of Education, Evanston, IL.

**Jennifer Ryan Hsu, Ph.D.**
*Associate Professor of Communication Disorders, William Paterson College, Wayne, New Jersey.*

# CLARK-MADISON TEST OF ORAL LANGUAGE

*John B. Clark and Charles L. Madison. Ph.D. Austin, Texas: PRO-ED, Inc.*

## Introduction

The Clark-Madison Test of Oral Language (CMTOL) is intended to assess a child's ability to produce various syntactic and grammatical forms. The test, which is organized in five sections, includes items assessing the expression of syntactic structure, verb forms, pronouns, inflectional morphological endings, modifiers, determiners, and prepositions. The CMTOL uses a "nonimitative elicitation technique" that elicits target items in the context of a verbal prompt and a picture stimulus. Unlike standard imitation tasks, which require a verbatim repetition of the examiner's production, the CMTOL task requires the production of a sentence similar to the one modeled by the examiner but different with respect to vocabulary and critical target forms. The picture stimulus and the verbal prompt provide the auditory and visual context for the response. Thus, the task is believed to assess production of the target forms within the context of a communicative event. The test was designed for two purposes: (a) diagnosing whether a child needs a remedial language program and (b) selecting goals for those already enrolled in such programs.

The CMTOL was developed by John Clark, M.S., and Charles Madison, Ph.D. Mr. Clark, a speech-language pathologist, is currently employed as a communication disorders specialist in the Boise public school system. He was program director for Easter Seals in the state of Idaho and also worked as project clinician on a Title III program in the Boise public schools. In 1987 Mr. Clark received the DiCarlo award for outstanding clinicians from the American Speech-Language-Hearing Association. Dr. Madison, a professor of communication disorders at Washington State University, has produced numerous presentations and articles on issues related to the use of the CMTOL.

Development of the CMTOL began in 1979. The test items were administered in several studies conducted over the next 2 years, and revisions of the items, picture stimuli, and administration procedures were made on the basis of the results. In general, items retained in the final version must have elicited the desired target 85% of the time in linguistically mature respondents. However, some items that failed to achieve this criterion were retained based on the belief that they were developmentally sensitive or discriminating. A third revision of the test was administered to first- and third-grade children. Revisions followed and a fourth version was field tested. Additional studies ensued investigating the test's reliability and validity, and data from these studies were combined with data from the field studies to develop the CMTOL norms.

The manual reports the means, standard deviations, and standard errors of the mean for 144 children who are unequally distributed in 1-year groups between the ages of 4.0 to 8.11. These children are described as having no history of language disorders or delay. According to the authors, "the standardization sample is recognized to be minimal" (Clark & Madison, 1986, p. 23). However, additional studies are in progress.

Madison and Heitman (1989) report revised norms and age equivalent scores for the test. They tested an additional 100 children ranging from 4.6 to 8.11 years of age and combined the results with file data on the CMTOL. Means, standard deviations, and standard errors of the mean are reported for 392 children unequally distributed in 6-month groups between the ages of 4.0 and 8.11. The number of children in each age category ranges from 31 to 46. Madison and Heitman (1989) report that the same criteria were used to select the subjects participating in their study as those participating in the previous studies that comprise the file data on the CMTOL. The criteria involved passing hearing, vision, and language screening tests. Teacher judgments and other information also were used to ensure the selection of linguistically normal children.

The children in the 6.0 to 8.11 age groups participating in the Madison and Heitman study were randomly selected from elementary schools in the Clarkston School District in Clarkston, Washington. No geographical information is given for the remaining age groups or for the children from previous studies. In addition, neither the manual nor Madison and Heitman (1989) report information on the socioeconomic status of the standardization sample. Furthermore, there is no description of the dialects represented in the sample, the prevalence of bilingualism, or the percentage of children representing minority groups.

The CMTOL test package consists of a booklet containing the manual and the stimulus materials, a four-page Response Form, and a single-page Analysis Form. The manual provides the background information on the test as well as the procedures for its administration, scoring, and interpretation. The stimulus materials consist of 102 test pictures and 3 practice items. The stimulus pictures are organized into Demonstration plates and Response plates. With the exception of items related to color words, all the pictures are black-and-white line drawings on 8″ × 11″ pages. The back of each picture contains written instructions for the presentation of the plate while facing the child. The target response is also printed on the page in large uppercase letters.

Each page of the Response Form contains four columns of information related to the Response items in the test. The first column contains the plate numbers for the item; the second contains the target response with sufficient space for recording the child's actual utterance; the third identifies the forms and constructions assessed by the target response; and the fourth provides space for recording whether the forms or constructions contained in the target response were produced correctly. One target sentence may permit evaluation of several structures. For example, the sentence "The girl is carrying two books" is similar to the target responses used in the test. Such an item could be used to assess production of the sentence structure $N_1 + V + N_2$, the plural morpheme /s/, and the verb form "is + auxiliary." Thus, the target response would be associated with three target items and a score for each item would be entered in the fourth column. Each target item is keyed with a number indicating its location on the Analysis Form. These numbers also are listed with the directions on the back of the picture stimuli. The test includes 66 target responses and 97 target items.

The Analysis Form lists the 97 target items within five categories: Syntax (16 items); Modifiers, Determiners, and Prepositions (MDP; 21 items); Verbs (21 items); Inflections (18 items); and Pronouns (21 items). As indicated in Table 1, the 16 syntactic items include 8 types of simple active declarative sentences, 5 question forms, 1 command, 1 passive sentence, and 1 negative sentence. The 21 items in the MDP section include 4 modifiers, 8 determiners, 8 prepositions, and 1 adverb of place. Among the 21 verb forms are 5 forms of the auxiliary *be* and 8 forms of the copula *be* (both present and past tense). The section also lists 8 additional verb forms, which assess the correct use of an inflectional ending or the modal *will* independent of the specific verb used. Included in the 18 items under Inflections are 1 adjective marker, 2 adverbial markers, 5 plural markers, 1 derivational morphological ending, and 9 verb markers. In the final section of the Analysis Form, Pronouns, the 21 items include 14 personal pronouns (7 subjective and 7 objective forms) and 7 possessive pronouns.

Both the Response and Analysis forms provide a section at the top of the first page for recording subject identifying information. In addition, the Response Form provides two boxes on the back page for recording the number of structurally correct and semantically accurate responses on the 66 target sentences. The Analysis Form provides a space at the top of the page for recording the total number of correct items out of the 97 items included in the test. Five additional spaces are provided for recording the total number of correct items within each of the five subsections (Syntax, MDP, Verbs, Inflections, and Pronouns). No other profiles are provided.

The CMTOL scores only one item for each grammatical form. However, many of the forms are represented in several sentences of the test. For example, although only one item is scored for production of the article *the,* the article actually occurs 32 times in the test. Thus, there are 32 opportunities to assess a child's production of *the.* Page 25 of the manual lists additional items representing some of the categories assessed by the CMTOL. These may be used to probe production of a particular form beyond the one item formally scored in the test. However, no protocols are provided for recording and scoring responses to these additional items. Thus, the examiner must develop his or her own method for recording, scoring, and summarizing the results of probing the production of specific constructions.

In general, the stimuli used in the CMTOL are cleverly designed and likely to elicit the target structures. The quality of the pictures is very good. With the exception of only a few items, the drawings are simple, uncluttered, and appropriate for the target response. Items 44, 50, and 84 may not elicit the target items due to drawings that do not adequately represent the target response. In particular, item 44 may be more likely to elicit *was sleeping* than *slept;* item 50 does not adequately depict the adverb *slowly,* and the dog's eyes in this picture may look open to some children. Items 9, 10, 27, 48, and 86 may cause some difficulty for children who have figure-ground perceptual problems, and item 20, which is

**Table 1**

**Syntactic Structures Assessed by the CMTOL**

| *Type of Main Verb* | *Sentence Structure* | *Example of Sentence* |
|---|---|---|
| 1. Copula *be* | 1. $N_1$ + *be* + $N_1$ | The woman is a teacher. This is a truck. |
| | 2. $N_1$ + *be* + adj | The dress is pretty. |
| | 3. $N_1$ + *be* + where | The book is on the shelf. |
| 2. Intransitive verbs | 4. $N_1$ + V | The baby is crying. |
| | 5. $N_1$ + V + when | His is practicing at night. |
| 3. Transitive | 6. $N_1$ + V + $N_2$ | The boy grabbed the ball. |
| | 7. $N_1$ + V + $N_2$ + where | The girl is holding the baby in her arms. |
| | 8. $N_1$ + V + $N_3$ + $N_2$ (dative or indirect object construction) | The man is giving the boy some money. |
| 4. Copula *be* | 9. Yes/no question | Is the book on the shelf? |
| 5. Intransitive verb + *did* | 10. Yes/no question | Did it roll under the shelf? |
| 6. Copula *be* | 11. *Wh* question—*Where* | Where is the book? |
| | 12. *Wh* question—*Whose* | Whose book is this? |
| 7. Transitive verb | 13. *Wh* question—*Who* | Who can see my book? |
| | 14. Command | Get the book. |
| | 15. Passive | The book was found by the girl. |
| 8. Copula *be* | 16. Negation | That isn't my book. |

*Note.* N = noun or noun phrase; subscript 1 = subject or predicate nominative, subscript 2 = direct object, subscript 3 = indirect object.

intended to elicit the adjective *red,* may cause difficulty for children who are color blind (inability to distinguish red from green is a common form of color blindness; Roediger, Rushton, Capaldi, & Paris, 1987). Virtually all of the vocabulary is appropriate for the age range of the test, but the words *pop* (for soda) and *buggy* (for baby carriage) may not be familiar to some children who speak regional dialects. Finally, items 65, 66, and 67 may cause some initial confusion.

## Practical Applications/Uses

The CMTOL was designed to survey a child's ability to produce specific syntactic, grammatical, and inflectional forms in the context of a verbal prompt and picture stimulus. The testing procedure was developed "to circumvent some of the problems associated with spontaneous language sampling and elicited imitation" (Clark & Madison, 1986, p. 7). Unlike verbatim imitation, the CMTOL is intended to provide an assessment of the syntactic components of standard English when production is constrained by auditory, visual, and structural information. It is also believed to approximate an interactive, communicative event while eliciting specific structural forms.

According to Clark and Madison (1986), the CMTOL may be used to determine whether a child is a candidate for remedial intervention. However, limitations in the normative data (see Technical Aspects and Critique sections of this review) suggest that additional instruments should be used to confirm the diagnostic results of the CMTOL. The CMTOL also may be used to provide information relevant to the selection of goals for children already enrolled in a remedial language program. The Analysis Form provides a convenient summary of the child's performance in the areas of Syntax, MDP, Verbs, Inflections, and Pronouns. These data combined with the results of probing and information from other procedures such as language samples should assist practitioners in identifying appropriate goals for therapy. Once the goals have been identified, the CMTOL could be readministered periodically to monitor progress. The Analysis Form would be particularly useful for this purpose.

Madison (1987) reports that a system for scoring semantic relations produced in the CMTOL target responses is currently under development. He also reports preliminary data that suggest the semantic analysis system will distinguish between normal and language-impaired children. However, development of the analysis system seems to be just in the preliminary stages.

The CMTOL may be used in a variety of clinical settings. The time required for administration and scoring makes it appropriate for public school settings and private practice, as well as speech and hearing clinics. It may also be used in preschool communication-handicapped classes or private programs servicing special populations.

The manual does not discuss examiner qualifications. Both diagnostic decisions and the selection of goals involve clinical judgment. Thus, appropriate use of the CMTOL requires professionals who are knowledgeable about language disorders, language assessment, and factors relevant to planning appropriate goals. Individuals having these qualifications are likely to be speech-language pathologists, teachers of the hearing impaired, and learning disabilities teachers.

The CMTOL is intended to be used with children ranging from 4.0 to 8.11 years of age who are producing at least three-element sentences and other grammatical forms characteristic of normally developing 3-year-olds. In general, the CMTOL appears appropriate for children who are producing sentences with subjects and predicates and are in the process of acquiring the word endings and function words that elaborate these basic structures. The test is not appropriate for children at the one- and two-word stages of language acquisition.

With the exception of two infinitival sentences, the CMTOL does not include complex constructions. Thus, it is not appropriate for assessing children who have mastered basic sentence structure and the associated grammatical morphology but are experiencing difficulties in producing complex constructions; the CMTOL will not detect delays of this type. In addition, the manual states that the CMTOL is not appropriate for children with limited attention abilities or memory deficits. These are problems that may be characteristic of mentally retarded or learning disabled children. However, the manual does state that the test can be used with children who have marginal memory or attention deficits, provided they can correctly generate four of the eight sentence structures listed in Table 1 (see sentence structures 1–8).

The CMTOL was developed for use with children who have normal vision and hearing. However, the test may have some applications for assessing the language of hearing-impaired children. Although a similar test, the Grammatical Analysis of Elicited Language (Moog & Geers, 1979), has been developed for this population, it does not provide an analysis of the production of basic sentence patterns.

The CMTOL task requires an ability to understand the relationship between the Demonstration and Response items as well as the connection between the verbal prompt, the picture stimulus, and the target response. Most children who have developed the minimum level of linguistic functioning required for the test are capable of understanding the task requirements; however, those with cognitive deficits may have some difficulty. Children who have severe echolalia or jargon speech are not appropriate candidates for this test, which may limit its use with autistic or emotionally disturbed children. Finally, the CMTOL is not suitable for children who produce unintelligible speech.

The CMTOL is administered on an individual basis with the subject seated opposite the examiner. Administration requires a quiet location with adequate lighting for viewing the picture stimuli. The booklet containing the picture stimuli is placed between the subject and the examiner. Administration proceeds by presenting the pictures in consecutive order and following the directions on the page opposite each picture. The presentation consists of two parts. First, the examiner presents the Demonstration picture and models a sentence, which is preceded by the command "Listen." Next he or she presents the Response picture in conjunction with the command "Tell me" and a verbal prompt that provides a structural context for the child's reply. The task elicits a response that is constrained in several ways. The Demonstration plate establishes a relationship between the structure modeled by the examiner and a visual stimulus. The child's response is expected to incorporate the modeled structure. However, the response also is expected to modify the structure as dictated by the Response picture as well as the structural and semantic constraints contained in the verbal prompt. All target items are underlined.

The directions for administering each item must be followed carefully. In particular, gestural or pointing cues, which are indicated in parentheses following the auditory stimuli, have been found to be critical (Clark & Madison, 1986). The manual states that all directions "must be followed to insure valid testing" (p. 18). These include the directions for each test plate as well as general guidelines outlined in the manual. The examiner cannot alter the sequence of presentation of test items; however, once the test is completed, items can be readministered a second time, either as a retrial or as a probe for another grammatical form. There is no prescribed sequence for retesting other than a reminder that a demonstration item generally precedes a response item.

The instructions for each item are clearly written and extremely easy to read due to the large print. The use of upper- and lowercase letters helps the examiner distinguish between the verbal stimuli and the target responses. The CMTOL is convenient and easy to administer when given in its entirety in the prescribed order. Administration time should take from 45 minutes to 1 hour.

The manual suggests that examiners should probe those items eliciting errors after administering the test in its entirety. A list of test plates that contain additional examples of some of the forms (articles, plurals, prepositions, and verb forms) is provided. Although no directions are given, probing appears to mean that a test plate may be readministered and additional target items may be scored. If items are selected for probing, then the examiner will need to locate and mark them for administration. The time required for probing will depend on the number of items readministered.

The list of probes on page 25 of the manual contains several printing errors. For example, item 34 (under plurals) should be 33; item 32 (under the copula) should indicate that there are three examples of the target form; item 16 was omitted from the list of present progressive items; and items 84 and 66 were omitted from the list of past tense items. Additional problems with the list of probes are discussed in the Critique section of this review.

Scoring procedures are outlined for all items given during initial administration of the test. Although the procedures are likely to be the same for the probes, no explicit instructions are given. Responses are recorded by editing the target sentences listed in the second column of the Response Form. As noted previously, the fourth column of the Response Form lists numbers and spaces for each target item contained in the target sentence. This information is printed directly opposite the target items that are listed in the third column. Although no explicit directions are given, it seems that correct responses should be indicated in the appropriate spaces located in the fourth column.

According to the manual, "target structures are credited as correct whenever they occur within the subject's response, regardless of whether or not the target sentence is produced as anticipated" (Clark & Madison, 1986, p. 18). Thus, the scoring system permits identification of the ability to produce specific structures when other aspects of the child's grammatical system are still developing. This is a positive feature of the CMTOL.

There are two types of target items: those in which specific morphemes are required, and those in which an example of the structure is needed but a specific word or ending is not required. Underlining identifies the specific words and morphemes that are required. Failure to use these forms even if the response includes a semantically equivalent form would be scored as an error. The manual identifies acceptable and unacceptable responses for all of the specific morphemes included in the test. The rules are clear and easy to interpret. The manual notes that dialect variations should be considered when scoring particular morphemes, and it advises that a distinction should be made between "deviant" and "functional" productions. The latter are presumably dialect variations that are present in the child's environment, but no information is given on these possible variations.

For target items that require an example of structure, an acceptable response must satisfy the item's description, its analysis category, and the semantic constraints imposed by the picture. As illustrated in the manual, the target for Plate #8 is $N_1$ + V, and the picture stimulus depicts a boy who is running. The manual considers "Him ran" an acceptable response because it has the basic noun + verb structure and is semantically correct with respect to the gender of the subject and the event of running. The manual considers the response "She is running" incorrect because it violates the "semantic intent." Thus, a gender mismatch results in an error score, whereas a temporal mismatch resulting from an incorrect inflectional ending on the verb does not. With the structural items, the content words must be present and semantically correct, but the morphological endings may be incorrect. Word order must also be preserved. The manual identifies acceptable responses for each structural item, and most of the rules are easy to interpret. However, there appear to be some printing errors in the section labeled "Transformations," where several acceptable responses are repeated twice (e.g., "my ball"—"my ball" for the *Who* question). These errors are confusing and should be eliminated.

Learning to score the Response Form should take approximately 2 hours. The process would be facilitated by inclusion of sample protocols for clinicians to score and compare to an answer key. Once the rules are learned, scoring should take between 30 and 45 minutes.

The information recorded in the Response Form's fourth column is transferred to the Analysis Form. Although no explicit directions appear, it is evident that the total number of correct items should be determined and recorded at the top of the form. The space for the number correct is set up in such a way to suggest that the percentage of correct items should be calculated. Again, no explicit directions are given. It also appears that the total number of correct items should be tabulated for each of the five categories and recorded in the space provided on the form. The authors state that percentages should be calculated for the subtest scores. The Analysis Form contains one printing error. Item 57 should be listed as present perfect instead of past perfect. In general, completing the Analysis Form is an easy procedure.

As noted previously, no forms are provided for recording responses to probed items. Although the authors state that probe scores should be converted to percentages, they provide no directions for this calculation. Presumably the number of correct responses for a particular category would be divided by the total number of items administered from that category. The lack of explicit information is likely to discourage clinicians from using the probing option.

Interpreting the results of the CMTOL involves decisions regarding the need for a remedial program and the selection of appropriate goals for therapy. Decisions with regard to therapy are based on the total test score. Clark and Madison (1986) state that the means and standard deviations for the norms reported in the manual's Table 10 can be used to evaluate a child's total test score. A score falling within 1 standard deviation from the mean represents average performance. A score falling between 1 to 2 standard deviations below the mean may indicate a possible problem. The authors recommend that children who score in this range become candidates for language remediation if other evaluation results corroborate the finding. Thus, for children manifesting scores within this range, decisions regarding the need for remediation involve clinical judgment. Clark and Madison

(1986) also state that scores falling at least 2 standard deviations below the mean should be considered "a clear basis for remedial intervention" (p. 23). The manual does not provide any charts that summarize the critical cut scores; thus, clinicians must perform their own calculations.

Jones (1989) states that a strong possibility for the misinterpretation of test scores exists due to ambiguity in the normative data. He notes that the authors do not explicitly state whether the mean scores for the normative sample were based on raw scores or percentage scores. Furthermore, the Analysis Form seems to suggest that percentage scores should be calculated. However, the manual does not indicate whether the raw scores or the percentage scores should be compared to the information provided in Table 10. Jones (1989) concludes that the absence of this information and other problems with the normative sample should lead test users to interpret the results on their own examinees with caution (p. 169).

The manual notes that norms have not been established for CMTOL subtest scores or probes. It is recommended, however, that these scores be used to determine which of the five categories assessed in the test should be the targets of intervention. It is further suggested that clinicians convert subtest or probe scores to percentages and use these as a basis for establishing goals for children enrolled in therapy. Again users must perform their own calculations. Additionally, no guidance is offered on critical values for decisions regarding mastery.

In summary, the only explicit criterion for interpreting the results of the CMTOL relate to total test scores that fall within the range of normal performance or those that fall at least 2 standard deviations below the mean. Otherwise, clinical judgment is required for interpreting (a) test scores that fall between 1 and 2 standard deviations below the mean and (b) subtest scores and results obtained from probing. This reliance on clinical judgment makes interpretation the most difficult part of the CMTOL.

**Technical Aspects**

Clark and Madison (1986) report test-retest, internal consistency, and interrater statistics. Clark (cited in Clark & Madison, 1986) retested 16 normal children from Grades K to 3. He reported a 4- to 9-day test-retest reliability coefficient of .99 for the total test score, and reliability coefficients ranging from .88 to .98 for the five subtest scores. Kew (cited in Clark & Madison, 1986) administered the test on two occasions to 24 normal and 20 language-disordered children in preschool and kindergarten/first grade. Although the time interval between testings is not indicated, the results (reported by age group for the normal and language-disordered children) indicate that the reliability coefficients for the total test scores ranged from .89 to .95. The language-delayed K–1 group obtained the lowest coefficient. Combining the children from each grade level, the entire group of normal children obtained a reliability coefficient of .94, and the entire group of language-delayed children obtained a coefficient of .87. A combined analysis for all children yielded a coefficient of .95. The reliability coefficients reported in the Clark and Kew studies are significant at a $p < .001$ level. Furthermore, they compare favorably to the criteria for adequate test-retest reliability suggested by McCauley and Swisher (1984). With respect to internal consistency, Kew (cited in Clark & Madison, 1986) used the Kuder-Richardson procedure and reported an internal reliability coefficient of .95. This indicates that the test items are homogeneous.

Kippenhan (cited in Clark & Madison, 1986) examined interrater agreement for two examiners who scored test protocols obtained from six children. Kippenhan obtained a reliability coefficient of .99 ($p < .001$), which is an exceptionally high correlation. However, the manual does not indicate the extent to which the two examiners were trained in the use of the CMTOL, the extent of their experience in administering the test, or the heterogeneity of the sample of six children. This information is relevant to the interpretation of this coefficient. No interrater reliability statistics are reported for subtest scores. More importantly, the manual does not report any statistics indicating interrater agreement on either diagnostic decisions or the selection of goals based on CMTOL results.

Clark and Madison (1986) and several additional sources report information relevant to establishing the CMTOL's content, construct, and concurrent validity. With respect to content validity, the manual clearly specifies the domain sampled by the test. In general, the items were selected from the domain of syntactic, grammatical, and inflectional items, which appear at approximately 3 years of age or when a child has reached the stage of development characterized by the production of three-element sentences containing a subject and a predicate. Most of the items in the CMTOL were selected from structures that occur at Levels III and IV of Crystal, Fletcher, and Garman's (1976) description of language development. However, one sentence structure was included from Crystal et al.'s Level II, and some inflections were included from Level VI. Levels III and IV span the ages of 2.0–2.6 and 2.6–3.0, respectively. Crystal et al. (1976) list several structures in Levels III and IV that do not appear in the CMTOL. As noted in the manual, these include combined auxiliary elements, several negative words, and several types of *wh* and yes/no questions. In addition, the manual points out the exclusion of the possessive marker, verb phrases, and the SVCA sentence type (i.e., sentences containing a subject, verb, complement, and adverbial).

Several CMTOL items seem to represent aspects of language that develop after 3 years of age. The pronouns selected for the CMTOL span Levels I–V of Brown's (1973) description of language development. In contrast to those of Crystal et al., Brown's levels are defined in terms of mean length of utterance (MLU): Level I = 1.75–2.25 MLU; Level II = 2.26–2.75 MLU; Level III = 2.76–3.50 MLU; Level IV = 3.51–4.00 MLU; and Level V = 4.01–5.25 MLU. Owens (1988) reports that the age range for Brown's five stages stretches between 1.0 and 4.0+ years of age. Thus, it appears that some of the pronouns may develop after 3 years of age. The CMTOL also includes the full passive, which develops between 5 and 8 years of age (Owens, 1988).

In general, the items included in the CMTOL constitute a fairly representative sampling of Crystal et al.'s Level III and IV. However, the limited sampling of negative forms, question forms, and auxiliary elements other than *be* represents an omission of structures that are generally considered important aspects of development during this period. The development of these categories is emphasized by Owens (1988) in his description of language acquisition during the preschool years. Furthermore, language sampling procedures that assess the same period of development (Lee, 1974; Miller, 1981; Stickler, 1987; Tyack & Gottsleben,

1977) also identify a greater number of negative words, question forms, and auxiliary elements such as the modals *can, will,* and *may.*

A more important issue is whether the restriction of content to the simple sentence structures and grammatical forms that appear around age 3 is an appropriate limitation for a test evaluating children between the ages of 4.0 and 8.11. A variety of syntactic and grammatical forms develop during this period, and a particularly crucial aspect of this development is the appearance of complex constructions. Furthermore, several constructions, such as coordinate sentences involving the conjunction *and* and infinitival constructions following main verbs such as *want, go,* and *have,* appear around age 3. Although two infinitives are included in the CMTOL, neither represents these early developing forms. According to Owens (1988), object noun phrase complements also appear around age 3. The inclusion of the full passive, which is produced by only 80% of normal 8-year-old children (Owens, 1988), is surprising when other constructions expected in the productions of 3-year-olds are excluded.

Clark and Madison (1986) believe that the content validity of the test is also demonstrated by the fact that the items selected for inclusion elicited the target structure in 85% of linguistically mature respondents. As noted by Jones (1989), the authors did retain an unspecified number of items that did not meet this criterion. The manual states that the items were retained because they were considered to be developmentally sensitive or discriminating. Unfortunately, no data, statistics, or graphs are reported to support this claim.

Several studies report results related to the concurrent validity of the CMTOL. Sullivan (cited in Clark & Madison, 1986) administered a preliminary version of the CMTOL (Revision 3) and the Test of Language Development (TOLD; Newcomer & Hammill, 1977) to 50 normal first- and third-grade children. The manual states that the third-graders were excluded from an analysis of the relationship between the scores on the two tests. Although the manual mentions that the group manifested a skewed distribution of scores on both tests, the reasons for their exclusion is unclear. For the first-graders, the correlation of the total scores on the CMTOL and the TOLD was .73 ($p < .05$). Correlations between total test scores on the CMTOL and scores on the five subtests of the TOLD yielded two significant coefficients ($p < .05$) of .58 for Picture Vocabulary and .83 for Sentence Imitation. The TOLD Oral Vocabulary, Grammatic Understanding, and Grammatic Closure subtests yielded nonsignificant correlations of .25, .09, and .32, respectively. The low correlations for the latter two tests are surprising, as they measure similar aspects of language as the CMTOL.

Kippenhan (cited in Clark & Madison, 1986) administered the CMTOL and the Carrow Elicited Language Inventory (CELI; Carrow, 1974) to 20 normal 5-, 6-, and 7-year-old children. The correlation of the total test scores on the CMTOL and the CELI was –.64 ($p < .05$). The negative relationship is due to the fact that the total test score for the CMTOL is based on number correct; the total test score for the CELI is based on the number of errors. The correlation between the CMTOL and the CELI appears to be numerically lower than the correlation between the CMTOL and the Sentence Imitation subtest of the TOLD. This is surprising, as both the CELI and the TOLD subtests are imitation tasks that measure aspects of language similar to those measured by the CMTOL.

Becker (cited in Clark & Madison, 1986) administered the CMTOL and the Kindergarten Language Screening Test (KLST; Gauthier & Madison, 1978) to 12 language-normal and 12 language-delayed 4- and 5-year-olds. The correlation of total test scores on the two instruments was .89 ($p < .001$). The rationale for selecting the KLST, a screening instrument, as a criterion measure is unclear. (See *Standards for Educational and Psychological Testing* [American Educational Research Association, American Psychological Association, & National Council on Measurement in Education, 1985], Standard 1.11.)

The children in Becker's study were classified as normal or delayed on the basis of the KLST and the clinical judgments of speech-language pathologists. Among the 12 children classified as normal, the CMTOL identified 11 as normal and 1 as delayed (i.e., 1 false positive). Among the 12 children classified as delayed, the CMTOL identified 9 as disordered and 3 as normal (3 false negatives). It is not clear whether these findings are representative of the CMTOL's classification accuracy, as the manual does not specify how the classification rule was selected. If the rule was selected to maximize classification accuracy for the observed data rather than a priori, then these findings probably provide an overly optimistic description of the classification accuracy of the test. Furthermore, false negative decisions, which occurred more frequently than false positives, may represent a more serious type of error than the false positive decisions. Although a false positive decision may result in enrollment of the child in therapy, the error is likely to be detected during the course of therapy or with the administration of additional tests. However, a false negative decision means that the child would be considered normal. As children with this classification would not be enrolled in therapy, this type of error would be more difficult to detect.

Language samples were also obtained from the 24 children in Becker's study. Although the scoring procedures are not described, Clark and Madison (1986) report that scores were obtained that permitted classifying the children as normal or delayed. The spontaneous language samples resulted in 3 false positive decisions and 1 false negative decision (i.e., among the 12 normal children, 9 were identified as normal and 3 as delayed; among the 12 delayed children, 11 were identified as delayed and 1 as normal). Again the manual does not specify the nature of the classification rule used to discriminate between the two groups. As noted by Clark and Madison (1986), the CMTOL resulted in fewer false positive decisions than the language sampling procedures. However, the CMTOL also produced more false negatives. Among the two types of classification errors, this seems to have more serious consequences because a misclassified child is not likely to receive needed clinical services.

The language samples collected in Becker's study were analyzed to determine the number of CMTOL target items that were present in children's spontaneous productions. The percentage of items that were correctly produced on the CMTOL and the percentage of targets appearing in the language sample were calculated for each child. The correlation between the two percentages for the 24 children in Becker's study was .65 ($p < .05$). Based on these findings, Clark and Madison (1986) conclude that the CMTOL appears to be "satisfactorily predictive of spontaneous language performance" (p. 14). (This issue will be discussed further in the Critique section of this review.)

Three studies have been conducted to determine whether the CMTOL discriminates between normal and language-delayed children. Becker's study (cited in Clark and Madison, 1986) reports that the 12 normal and 12 language-delayed children manifested significant differences in their total test scores and their subtest scores ($p$ values ranged from .0001 to .0009 for 6 $t$-tests). The mean scores for each group are not reported. Clark and Madison (1986) report that the results of a step-wise discriminant analysis suggest that the Inflections category is the best discriminator between the two groups. However, specific statistics (F ratios, discriminant function weights, etc.) are not reported.

In a second study, Madison (1987) compared data from 150 normal children classified in five age groups ranging from 4.0 to 8.11 to data from 103 language-disordered children classified in three groups. Due to differences in examiners, selection procedures, and other aspects of testing, all results from the three language-disordered groups were analyzed separately. This resulted in three groups with unequal numbers and mean ages ranging from 6.5 to 7.2. Madison (1987) reports that the language-disordered children had generally lower means and larger standard deviations than all five groups of normal children. He also reports that "the language disordered children performed no better than the youngest normal language group in one comparison . . . though they were 2 years older. In all other comparisons the differences were significant" (Madison, 1987, p. 6). Unfortunately, Madison does not report the statistical tests that were used nor the obtained $p$ levels. Clark and Madison (1986) and Madison (1983) report the means, standard deviations, and standard errors of the mean for three language-impaired groups, two of which are also described by Madison (1987). (Madison, 1987, reports slightly different means and standard deviations for the two groups than those reported by Clark & Madison, 1986, and Madison, 1983.) The mean scores for the three groups fall between 1 to 3 standard deviations below the mean scores for the comparable normal age groups reported in the manual.

In a third study, McDonough (1986) administered the CMTOL to 13 aphasic, 12 learning disabled, and 15 normal children. The means for the five subtest scores and for the total test scores were consistently ordered such that the aphasic children manifested the lowest scores and the normal children the highest. Scores for the learning disabled children consistently fell between the scores for these two groups. A one-way analysis of variance yielded a significant omnibus F ratio (ANOVA $F[2,37] = 53.23$, $p < .01$). It is assumed that the analysis was performed on the total test scores, although McDonough does not explicitly state which scores were used. McDonough reports that post hoc Scheffe tests indicated statistically significant differences between all three pairs of mean scores ($p < .05$).

In summary, the comparisons between the CMTOL and established diagnostic instruments involve two tests, the TOLD and the CELI. Furthermore, although performance on the CMTOL was compared to scores from language sampling procedures, no information was given on the specific procedures (e.g., MLU, DSS scoring, etc.) used to obtain the language sample scores. Thus, the comparisons of performance of the normal and language-impaired children provide the strongest evidence of the concurrent validity of the test. Unfortunately, no information is provided on the CMTOL's predictive validity.

The manual contains limited information on the construct validity of the test.

Results indicating that the CMTOL distinguishes between normal and language-impaired children provide evidence of the test's construct validity. The differences in performance of third- and first-grade children as reported by Sullivan (cited in Clark & Madison, 1986) suggest that performance varies as a function of age. Such a relation would also relate to construct validity. Inspection of the mean performance reported by Madison and Heitman (1989) reveals a consistent increase in scores as a function of age with the exception of one age group. Additional analyses of Madison's (1987) and Madison and Heitman's (1989) data may help to clarify the nature of the relationship between scores on the CMTOL and age.

Clark and Madison (1986) analyzed Sullivan's data on 25 normal first-graders to determine the correlations between scores on the five subtests and the total test score. The correlations ranged from .42 ($p < .05$) for Syntax to .78 ($p < .001$) for Pronouns and Verbs. MDP and Inflections yielded correlations of .76 and .72 ($p < .001$), respectively. The low correlation between Syntax and total test scores is surprising. Intercorrelations between the five subtests also were determined, and 4 out of 10 were significant at the .05 level. The significant correlations ranged from .40 to .60, and the insignificant results from .08 to .36. The manual does not discuss the meaning of these results. No a priori hypotheses were formulated that predicted which tests should have significant intercorrelations and which should not. Jones (1989) notes that three of the four significant correlations involved the MDP subtest. He suggests that the authors should conduct further investigations to determine whether this subtest represents a distinct structural category.

Correlations between age, the five subtests, and total test scores are reported for three groups of language-delayed children (Madison, 1983; Madison & Clark, 1986). The correlations between total test scores and scores on the five subtests were significant at the .001 level. With two exceptions, the correlations ranged from .80 to .94. For one group, the correlation between Inflections and total test score was .66, and for the second the correlation was .76. The language-impaired children seem to manifest higher correlations between subtest scores and total test score than observed for normal children. This is particularly true for the correlation between Syntax and total test score. As language-impaired children manifest larger standard deviations than normal children, it seems likely that the lower correlations observed in the normal group reflect restricted ranges in the scores.

## Critique

There are several positive features of the CMTOL that distinguish it from other standardized language evaluation instruments. One feature is the inclusion of a section assessing basic sentences structure. Although some language sampling procedures (e.g., Tyack & Gottsleben, 1977; Crystal et al., 1976) include this type of analysis, most standardized tests do not. This aspect of language is central to a child's early linguistic development and should be included in tests used to diagnose delays as well as those used to determine goals. Thus, the inclusion of an analysis of basic sentence structure is an important feature distinguishing the CMTOL from other standardized instruments.

A second positive feature is the careful description of the domain and the identification of both syntactic structures and grammatical forms that were included as well as excluded. This feature of the test satisfies Lieberman and Michael's (1986) requirements for a definition of the domain assessed by a test. It also enables practitioners to judge whether the test is appropriate for the evaluation of a particular child.

Several aspects of the CMTOL design render the test creative and useful. With only a few exceptions, the elicitation procedures seem to be effective in eliciting the target responses. In addition, the task is likely to be enjoyable for most children. Furthermore, it succeeds in combining efficiency with an approximation of a naturalistic context for sentence production. The Analysis Form provides a convenient summary of performance by organizing responses according to the five subtests of the CMTOL. Numbers included next to each target item on the Response Form guide the examiner to the location of the item on the Analysis Form. Thus, the transfer of information is extremely easy and the child's responses are automatically classified according to the five syntactic and grammatical categories. This provides a profile of the child's performance that will facilitate the identification of potential targets for remediation and the selection of items for probing.

The active research program and expanding database related to the CMTOL provide another positive feature of this test. However, deficiencies in several areas limit its usefulness in identifying children who need remediation. As noted by Jones (1989), there is not enough information on the characteristics of the normative sample and on the manner in which this sample was selected. In particular, information is needed on the standardization sample's geographic characteristics, socioeconomic status, and predominant dialect (see McCauley & Swisher, 1984, and Standards 4.3 and 4.4 of the *Standards for Educational and Psychological Testing*). Inclusion of this information would permit informed decisions regarding the appropriateness of comparing the individual child's performance to that of the normative sample. The procedures for comparing performance to the normative statistics reported in Table 10 of the manual must be clarified. In particular, the manual should clearly specify whether these statistics were calculated on raw scores or on percentages.

Additional information is needed on (a) interrater agreement with respect to diagnostic decisions, (b) criterion-related validity with well-established criterion measures, and (c) correct as well as incorrect classification rates for large cross-validation samples. Jones (1989) comments that larger samples are needed in the research on the reliability and validity of the CMTOL. As no research on the predictive validity has been done, studies in this area would establish the importance of the test in identifying children who are likely to have significant academic difficulties at a later time in their development.

As noted previously, Madison and Heitman (1989) report age equivalent scores for the CMTOL, but there are several problems in using these scores (see Anastasi, 1982, for a review of problems associated with this type of score). One problem relates to the fact that the standard deviations vary across age groups. In particular, they are larger for younger children than for the older ones. This makes the age equivalent scores difficult to interpret because a score that is a fixed distance below a child's chronological age will have different implications for a younger child than for an older one. For example, a 5-year-old who obtains an age equivalent score 2 years below his or her chronological age would be within 1 standard deviation from the mean of 5-year-olds and would therefore be considered normal. However, an 8-year-old child who obtains an equally deviant age equivalent score (i.e., 2 years below his or her chronological age) would be 2 standard deviations below the mean of the 8-year-olds and would therefore be considered delayed. Thus, a given unit (2 years in this example) clearly does not have the same meaning in all portions of the range of age equivalent scores. Madison and Heitman (1989) recognize that there are problems in interpreting age equivalent scores and state that future research will focus on establishing additional normative information and reporting this information in terms of standard scores and percentiles for the various subtests (p. 4). Such information would "enable the test to be more widely accepted and used in language diagnostics" (Madison & Heitman, 1989 p. 4).

Another limitation in the use of the CMTOL as a diagnostic instrument relates to its content, which, with a few exceptions, is restricted to structures that appear around 3 years of age. As noted previously in the Technical Aspects section, complex constructions (a crucial aspect of development between ages 4.0 and 8.0) are excluded from this test, which limits its sensitivity in detecting delays related to the development of complex language. Furthermore, a child enrolled in therapy may manifest adequate performance on the CMTOL while continuing to experience difficulties in this area. Thus, the CMTOL should be supplemented with instruments that include complex constructions before children between 5 and 8 are classified as normal or dismissed from therapy.

The CMTOL has the positive feature of providing information related to both the diagnosis of an impairment as well as the selection of goals. A test that accomplishes both objectives could improve the efficiency of the assessment process by reducing the number of tests administered during an evaluation. However, there are some limitations to using the CMTOL in goal selection.

The CMTOL formally assesses one item for each form that is included in the test. As noted by Clark and Madison (1986), "subjects with emerging competence cannot be sufficiently evaluated on a specific item with only a one-trial assessment" (p. 17). Thus, they recommend that "the total score of a category be used to suggest language competence, and that individual items be used only to initiate probing" (p. 17). The five categories do not represent separate sets of homogeneous items. For example, the MDP category includes modifiers, determiners, and prepositions. A low score for this category is ambiguous with respect to the source of the problem. It is possible that the low score could be related to difficulties with only one of the three subcategories. Similar ambiguities exist in the remaining four categories. Inspection of the items within each category is needed to identify the nature of the problem and potential targets for therapy. Inclusion of some additional labels on the Analysis Form would facilitate such an analysis.

The items included within each category have developmental hierarchies. For example, there are developmental sequences for each of the following: the eight basic sentence patterns, yes/no and *wh* questions, past tense versus present tense markers, aspect markers, plural markers, prepositions, and pronouns (see Hsu, 1983; Ingram, 1989; Lee, 1974; Owens, 1988; Miller, 1981; Stickler, 1987; Tyack & Gottsleben, 1977). Furthermore, the five subtest categories are not equivalent from a developmental perspective. Difficulties with structures in the syntax category would be addressed before difficulties with many of the items in the pronoun category (see Hsu, 1983; Tyack & Gottsleben, 1977); therefore, individual items or categories with equal error rates may not be equally important with respect to remediation. The CMTOL does not provide developmental or any other type of information to guide one in selecting among potential targets for remediation.

Although the authors recommend probing items that elicit errors, the manual provides a list of probes for only a limited number of the forms included in the test. There are no probe lists for syntactic structure, determiners, modifiers, or pronouns. In addition, some of the categories for the existing probe lists are misleading. For example, the list entitled "past tense" includes simple past tense markers, past progressive forms, the past perfect, and the passive verb form. These forms are not equivalent in terms of complexity nor do they develop at the same time (see Lee, 1974; Owens, 1988). Accurate interpretation of performance on the list of probes in this category requires identification of the type of verb form associated with each error. Because the subcategories are not indicated on the probe lists, item classifications must be identified from the Response Form. This will be a tedious and time-consuming task.

In summary, several modifications in the manual would increase the likelihood of appropriate decisions regarding potential targets for remediation. These include expanding the probe list, identifying subcategories of items, and clarifying the procedures for scoring and interpreting the results. In addition, interrater agreement in goal selection must be established.

As noted previously, Clark and Madison (1986) suggest that problems associated with language sampling procedures and verbatim imitation tasks are circumvented by the CMTOL. Practitioners may infer from this statement and related discussion that the CMTOL can be used in place of either a verbatim imitation task or language sampling procedures. With respect to verbatim imitation tasks, the authors suggest that (a) the CMTOL task places greater emphasis on long-term memory and retrieval processes and (b) it creates structural and semantic environments that are similar to those operating in spontaneous language production. The arguments have intuitive appeal. The CMTOL does seem to share the advantages of verbatim imitation tasks, which include sampling a wide range of specific structures while incorporating structural and semantic constraints on sentence production. Roach (cited in Clark & Madison, 1986) reports that the performance of children on the CMTOL task was "significantly different" from the performance of children on a verbatim imitation task and on a verbatim imitation task with a visual cue. Unfortunately, the nature of the difference is not discussed. Other studies (see Madison, Roach, Santema, Akmal, & Guenzel, 1989, for a review) have investigated the effect of including visual stimuli on an imitation task. However, none of these studies address the crucial issue of whether the CMTOL will result in better classification rates or more appropriate goals than verbatim imitation tasks. Further research is needed to answer these questions.

With respect to language sampling procedures, Clark and Madison (1986) state that the CMTOL yields a greater variety of language structures than spontaneous language samples. This statement is based the fact that 52% of the structures that do not appear in language samples were produced on the CMTOL. Clearly the

CMTOL, like verbatim imitation tasks, is useful in assessing structures that do not appear in a language sample. Such a finding suggests that the CMTOL should be used to supplement the results of a language sample. As noted previously, Clark and Madison (1986) report a correlation of .65 between the percentage of items correctly produced on the CMTOL and the percentage of targets appearing in language samples. This finding suggests that items correctly produced on the CMTOL would be predictive of items produced in spontaneous performance. However, Clark and Madison also report that 30% of the items missed on the CMTOL were produced correctly in children's spontaneous language. This finding, which parallels results obtained for verbatim imitation tasks (e.g., Connell & Myles-Zitzer, 1982; Lahey, Launer, & Schiff-Myers, 1983; Prutting, Gallagher, & Mulac, 1975; Weber-Olsen, Putnam-Sims, & Gannon, 1983), reveals a problem that exists when the CMTOL is used in place of a language sample. Because errors on the CMTOL are used to determine goals, it appears that approximately 30% of the goals would not address actual deficiencies. Thus, it seems that errors on the CMTOL should be verified by results of a spontaneous language sample.

In conclusion, the CMTOL is a promising instrument with several features that distinguish it from other language tests. As suggested by Jones (1989), it may eventually be a viable alternative to some of the existing standardized instruments designed to evaluate production of the structural components of language. However, studies comparing correct and incorrect classification rates are needed before such a recommendation can be made. Although correct performance on the CMTOL is predictive of spontaneous production, error information requires confirmation by a language sample. Given the present need for further research and development, the most appropriate use of the CMTOL appears to be as a supplement to existing standardized and nonstandardized procedures.

## References


American Educational Research Association, American Psychological Association, & National Council on Measurement in Education. (1985). *Standards for educational and psychological testing*. Washington, DC: American Psychological Association.

Anastasi, A. (1982). *Psychological testing* (5th ed.). New York: Macmillan.

Brown, R. (1973). *A first language: The early stages.* Cambridge, MA: Harvard University Press.

Carrow, E. (1974). *Carrow Elicited Language Inventory.* Allen, TX: DLM Teaching Resources.

Clark, J.B., & Madison, C.L. (1986). *The Clark-Madison Test of Oral Language.* Austin, TX: PRO-ED.

Connell, P.J., & Myles-Zitzer, C. (1982). An analysis of elicited imitation as a language evaluation procedure. *Journal of Speech and Hearing Disorders, 47*, 390–396.

Crystal, D., Fletcher, P., & Garman, M. (1976). *The grammatical analysis of language disability: A procedure for assessment and remediation.* New York: Elsevier.

Gauthier, S.F., & Madison, C.L. (1978). *Kindergarten Language Screening Test.* Tigard, OR: C.C. Publications.

Hsu, J.R. (1983). *A developmental guide to English syntax: An aid for teachers in facilitating the acquisition of linguistic competence by hearing-impaired children.* Washington DC: Gallaudet College Press, Curriculum Bank.

Ingram, D. (1989). *First language acquisition: Method, description, and explanation.* New York: Cambridge University Press.

Jones, B.W. (1989). Clark-Madison Test of Oral Language. In J.C. Conoley & J.J. Kramer (Eds.), *The tenth mental measurements yearbook* (pp. 168–170). Lincoln, NE: Buros Institute of Mental Measurements.

Lahey, M., Launer, P.B., & Schiff-Myers, N. (1983). Prediction of production: Elicited imitation and spontaneous speech productions of language disordered children. *Applied Psycholinguistics, 4,* 317–343.

Lee, L. (1974). *Developmental sentence analysis.* Evanston, IL: Northwestern University Press.

Lieberman, R.J., & Michael, A. (1986). Content relevance and content coverage in tests of grammatical ability. *Journal of Speech and Hearing Disorders, 51,* 71–81.

Madison, C.L. (1983). *Clark-Madison Test of Oral Language: A technical update.* Unpublished manuscript, University of Washington, Pullman, WA.

Madison, C.L. (1987, November). *Simultaneous content and structural assessment of normal and disordered language.* Paper presented at the annual convention of the American Speech-Language-Hearing Association, New Orleans.

Madison, C.L., & Heitman, M.F. (1989). *Revised norms and age equivalents for the Clark-Madison Test of Oral Language.* Unpublished manuscript, University of Washington, Pullman, WA.

Madison, C.L., Roach, M.E., Santema, S.J., Akmal, E.S., & Guenzel, C.A. (1989). The effect of pictured visual cues on elicited sentence imitation. *Journal of Communication Disorders, 22,* 81–91.

McCauley, R.J., & Swisher, L. (1984). Psychometric review of language and articulation tests for preschool children. *Journal of Speech and Hearing Disorders, 49,* 34–42.

McDonough, D.D. (1986). *A comparison of spoken language abilities in children with aphasia, autism, learning disabilities and normal language abilities.* Unpublished doctoral dissertation, University of New Orleans, LA.

Miller, J.F. (1981). *Assessing language production in children: Experimental procedures.* Baltimore: University Park Press.

Moog, J.S., & Geers, A.E. (1979). *CID Grammatical Analysis of Elicited Language: Simple sentence level.* St. Louis, MO: Central Institute for the Deaf.

Newcomer, P.L., & Hammill, D.D. (1977). *Test of Language Development: Primary.* Austin, TX: PRO-ED.

Owens, R.E. (1988). *Language development: An introduction.* Columbus, OH: Chas. E. Merrill.

Roediger, H.L., III, Rushton, J.P., Capaldi, E.D., & Paris, S.G. (1987). *Psychology* (2nd ed.). Boston: Little, Brown.

Prutting, C.A., Gallagher, T.M., & Mulac, A. (1975). The expressive portion of the NSST compared to a spontaneous language sample. *Journal of Speech and Hearing Disorders, 40,* 40–47.

Stickler, K.R. (1987). *Guide to analysis of language transcripts.* Eau Claire, WI: Thinking Publications.

Tyack, D., & Gottsleben, R. (1977). *Language sampling, analysis and training: A handbook for teachers and clinicians.* Palo Alto, CA: Consulting Psychologists Press.

Weber-Olsen, M., Putnam-Sims, P., & Gannon, J.D. (1983). Elicited imitation and the Oral Language Sentence Imitation Screening Test (OLSIST): Content or context? *Journal of Speech and Hearing Disorders, 48,* 368–378.

**Stan Scarpati, Ed.D.**
*Associate Professor of Special Education, School of Education, University of Massachusetts at Amherst, Amherst, Massachusetts.*

# COGNITIVE CONTROL BATTERY

*Sebastiano Santostefano. Los Angeles, California: Western Psychological Services.*

## Introduction

The Cognitive Control Battery (CCB; Santostefano, 1988) was developed to assess the relationship between cognitive activity and learning and coping behavior in young children and adolescents. Although the author recognizes that no general consensus exists about the nature of cognition, the CCB is structured on the assumption that cognitive strategies are anchored within emotions and personality development that engender a developmental-adaptive model of cognition. In addition, the test battery utilizes direct observation of cognitive behavior in action (i.e., nonverbal responses) rather than the self-report measures typically associated with cognitive strategy assessment devices. The test is intended for use by clinical psychologists, school psychologists, special educators, counseling psychologists, psychiatrists, psychiatric nurses, and rehabilitation counselors working with children and adolescents ages 4 to 12.

The Cognitive Control Battery evolved over the past 30 years from clinical practice and research that focused on children's cognitive processes and how these processes mediated behavior (Santostefano, 1964a, 1964b; Santostefano & Paley, 1964). After receiving his Ph.D in clinical psychology from Pennsylvania State University in 1957, Sebastiano Santostefano began his work as a postdoctoral fellow in clinical child psychology at the University of Colorado Medical School. From these initial experiences with children and others in subsequent years at the McLean Hospital and Harvard Medical School, Santostefano conceptualized cognitive control as comprised of discrete subsets of cognitive strategies. The unavailability or lack of these strategies apparently interfered with children's ability to adapt successfully to their environment. The CCB's construct and structure was influenced by Klien's (1958) cognitive control model for adults and by Stroop's (1935) work that led later to his Word Interference Test. The present form of the CCB is the first published.

The construct of this battery considers that young children's cognitive behavior is global and undifferentiated, tending to become more articulated as they mature (Santostefano, 1978). The developmental changes in children that advance their cognitive control were differentiated during one cross-sectional study comprised of a series of longitudinal studies, and the manual provides details of these reports. The normative sample consisted of 1,103 well-adjusted 4- to 12-year-olds. No formal stratification process was used, but the author reports that efforts were made to use children from various racial groups (white—84%; black—15.1%;

other—.8%), socioeconomic levels (middle—54.4%; lower—45.6%), and geographic areas (East—74.3%; Rocky Mountain—13.6%; West—12.1%). Approximately equal numbers of males (55%) and females (45%) were used. The samples were of adequate size except for the "other" category (*n* = 8) for the racial groups, which the manual refers to as ethnicity. All raw score distributions were transformed into standard scores for each age level on 15 rating variables. The manual provides norm tables that convert raw scores into T-scores and percentile equivalents.

Cognitive controls are conceptualized as intervening variables between perception, memory, and motor behavior and an organism's attempt to adapt to the environment. Santostefano (1988) identifies five separate dimensions of cognitive control:

1. *Body ego-tempo regulation.* Controls are related to the manner in which individuals use images and symbols to regulate body movements and tempos.
2. *Focal attention.* This control guides the way an individual scans and surveys a field of information and, with increasing age, begins to scan more actively and in larger segments.
3. *Field articulation.* This control defines the selective attention of individuals when separating relevant from irrelevant information.
4. *Leveling-sharpening.* This control identifies the way in which an individual constructs memory images and compares them to present perceptions.
5. *Equivalence range.* This control refers to the range of categories an individual uses to sort and arrange nonequivalent information. With age, more diverse and abstract categorization occurs.

Of these five domains, the Cognitive Control Battery uses three discrete, nonverbal measures: scanning, selective attention, and images of previous information with present perceptions. This hierarchy of cognitive control represents advancing child development across the five dimensions as well as levels of increasing differentiation within each dimension. A portion of the model (field articulation) has been adapted from Witkin's (1959, 1969) cognitive style notion of field dependence and independence. Field-dependent individuals passively interact with the environment and experience difficulty separating items from their surroundings. Conversely, field independents actively take control of their surroundings.

The manual describes the three components of the CCB as follows (Santostefano, 1988 pp. 34–35):

*Scattered Scanning Test (SST).* Four forms—Motor Tempo Test (MTT), SST Training Form, and test Forms 1 and 2—are necessary to administer this test. Additionally, a line measure to calculate cumulative distances between shapes is advised. The MTT serves as a preliminary procedure to determine fine-motor speed in young children.

The practice form trains children to recognize and mark only circles and squares while scanning an array of geometric shapes (triangles, horizontal parallel lines, and crosses). Form 1, intended for 3- to 9-year-olds, contains 50 randomly arrayed shapes with 10 crosses and 10 circles. Examinees are asked to mark with a pencil as rapidly as possible only circles and squares within a 30-second time period. This simple form (printed on a single 8″ × 10″ sheet of paper) may also be used with children who have difficulty marking the circles and squares and those with developmental disabilities or severely impaired focal attention. With these groups, the child is asked to mark as rapidly as possible only the squares. Form 2 is a larger version of Form 1, printed on a large fold-out sheet of paper. This version contains 200 randomly arrayed geometric shapes with 40 circles and 40 squares and is to be used with children 9 years of age and older. The directions remain the same as for Form 1.

*Fruit Distraction Test (FDT).* This measure is comprised of four test cards and three practice strips, administered in numerical order (i.e., Card 1, Card 2, Card 3, then Card 4). Card 1 consists of 50 rectangular bars, each colored red, green, yellow, or blue, randomly arrayed in 5 rows with 10 bars in each. Card 2 contains 50 line drawings of apples, bananas, grapes, and heads of lettuce each colored naturally (i.e, red, yellow, blue, and green, respectively). The colors are arranged to match the color arrangement of columns and rows in Card 1.

Card 3 contains the same fruit and colors as Card 2 with the addition of one achromatic line drawing next to each fruit. These line drawings are of food-related objects (cake, ice cream cone, bottle of milk, spoon, glass, loaf of bread) or non-food-related objects (chair, car, airplane, shoe, telephone, clock). All fruit and objects are arranged randomly. Each object appears four times on the card, once with each of the colored fruits.

Card 4 presents the same fruit arrangements as Cards 2 and 3, but the fruit and colors are combined incorrectly. Each fruit appears in the color of each other fruit but not the correct color. For example, the apple is colored blue, yellow, and green but never red, and so on. This occurs four times for each color.

*Leveling-Sharpening House Test (LSHT).* This test uses a single, spiral-bound flip-page booklet of 60 test cards, each containing a house scene simply drawn in black and white. The examiner exposes each card for 5 seconds. The main elements of each scene depict a front door, two rectangular windows, one round window, a chimney, a weather vane, smoke rising from the chimney, ground lines, a sidewalk, a fence, a tree, a cloud, and the sun. Beginning with Card 4, and then with every third card thereafter, details are omitted from the scene cumulatively. Six training cards using Christmas tree scenes are provided at the beginning of the booklet.

**Practical Applications/Uses**

The CCB is intended for clinicians working with clients from the following groups (Santostefano, 1988, pp. 84): (a) children with atypical development attending special schools; (b) children who fail to meet the academic and social demands of a regular school program because of their distractibility, hyperactivity, and aggressive behaviors; (c) children who fail to meet the academic demands of a regular school program because they are socially withdrawn and overly anxious; and (d) children who continue to be nonreaders in spite of extensive tutoring or who raise the question whether they should repeat a grade. Additionally, the battery may be used for reevaluating children after they have received cognitive or nondirective play therapy.

The manual is well designed and written so that any practitioner with previous testing experience can become versed in administering the CCB. The author does advise that users have some prior experience working with emotionally disturbed and learning disabled students so that rapport and a working alliance can be established. The manual also states that with practice, the entire battery can be administered in about 30 minutes, and scored and interpreted in an additional 30 minutes.

This reviewer tested a typical 8-year-old child and recommends that a user spend enough time with the Fruit Distraction Test to become more than adequately proficient. This subtest is more difficult to give than the manual would indicate, in that handling the large cards and scoring protocols at the same time can be cumbersome and potentially distracting to examinees. Scoring the Scattered Scanning Test requires the user to record on the protocol the exact sequence in which a child marks each shape, numbering each response accordingly. The protocol presents a smaller version of the examinee's form, and the sequence of responses must be recorded in a mirror-image fashion. It is easy to lose track of the sequence, and the process requires an adept and flexible scanning ability on the part of the examiner.

The manual contains a series of clinical case studies of children with various and contrasting behavioral and neurological problems. These descriptions are comprehensive to a degree, include a CCB protocol, and refer to other related assessment data. They also provide some suggested remedial strategies.

**Technical Aspects**

Reliability and validity data, particularly construct and criterion-related validity, are reported along with measures that predict learning disabilities on the basis of the CCB scores.

The manual provides indirect evidence for alternate forms reliability for all three components of the CCB. With the Scattered Scanning Test, 60 hospitalized children were administered three forms that varied in emotional content and 50 object drawings. The resulting correlations ranged from .30 to .50.

In examining the Fruit Distraction Test, Cards 3 and 4 were considered as a "baseline" measure because they require the same sequence of colors to be named as rapidly as possible while confronted with distractions. In two studies with kindergartners, the correlations between Cards 3 and 4 were .58 and .46 for typical children; .71 and .54 for at risk learners; and .63 and .50 for the total sample. In two other studies with third- and fourth-graders, Card 3 and Card 4 correlations were .44 and .51, respectively. One additional study using hospitalized children reported a .40 coefficient.

With the Leveling-Sharpening House Test, two studies correlated the house pictures with scenes of a parachutist and a doctor standing in a hospital room. The resulting coefficients ranged from .08 to .75.

The stability of the battery was analyzed using a test-retest procedure that occurred at 1-week, 4-week, 4-year, and 5-year intervals with different groups of kindergarten and fourth-grade boys and girls. A fair to moderate degree of stability was reported, with larger coefficients reported in the test-retests done in adjacent years.

Evidence regarding the construct validity is provided by a series of principal component factor analyses with various intelligence measures, motor tests, personality measures, and teacher ratings. Samples of typical and atypical children at different age levels were used to generate the intercorrelation matrices. The results in general support the cognitive control construct rather than cognitive style and affirm that these factors will maintain their stability both over time and with normal and atypical children.

As for the CCB's use in predicting learning disabilities based on the assessment of cognitive controls, an entire population of kindergarten children was followed for 2 successive years. Teachers rated behaviors after 4 months of school and identified those children who were and were not adequately meeting classroom demands. The children identified as "at risk" were considered most likely to become learning disabled as they progressed in school. These children comprised the sample for three independent studies. From these studies a series of discriminative analyses scored each child in terms of their teacher ratings and scores on the CCB and how they differed on group membership. The results were moderately predictive of school difficulties in reading, mathematics, and language, but showed lower correlations with attention and perceptual-motor functioning.

**Critique**

The Cognitive Control Battery is unique as a test that purports to identify learning disabilities in children. The notion that the learning disabled are "cognitive strategy deficient" is popular in the literature (e.g., Swanson, 1987; Torgeson & Licht, 1983), and the CCB approaches the position from a cognitive-behavioral viewpoint. Most notably, cognitive control in this test relies on direct observation of children engaged in a task and not on subject self-reports or mid-task verbalizations. The battery appears better able to detect these differences in younger children than for examinees at the upper age ranges suggested.

Many researchers and practitioners do not agree on what constitutes a learning disability. Study of the construct suffers from inconclusive theories that guide research to investigate specific underlying neurological or cognitive causes to behavioristic explanations and treatments. Some would argue that social consensus alone dictates which children get identified, treated, and placed in special programs for the learning disabled. History has seen results from process-oriented assessment play an unwarranted role in the day-to-day education that LD children receive. The sense of caution one derives from the foregoing should be applied to the CCB.

The materials associated with this test battery are well constructed, and the manual is singularly the most impressive part. It is clearly written with a substantive discussion of the theory and research that supports the test construct. The directions for each subtest are easy to understand and are written in a fashion that integrates the test procedures into the test construct.

The normative sample should be questioned, however, in that it is described as ethnically diverse (Santostefano, 1988, p. 31). White and black children in the sample (98.1%) should not be classified as ethnic groups but as racial groups. The small number of "others" in the sample (.8%) may have been ethnically diverse, but a description of these subjects is not given. Cognitive activity, particularly problem-solving strategy development and use, is a culturally loaded process and should be addressed more thoroughly from this perspective in future editions of the CCB.

The CCB appears to provide valuable information about children with learning problems that could assist teachers, psychologists, and other practitioners developing educational treatment plans for these children.

## References

Klien, G.S. (1958). Cognitive control and motivation. In G. Lindzey (Ed.), *Assessment of human motives* (Vol. 2, pp. 87-118). New York: Holt, Rinehart, & Winston.

Santostefano, S. (1964a). Cognitive controls and exceptional states in children. *Journal of Clinical Psychology, 20,* 213-218.

Santostefano, S. (1964b). A developmental study of the cognitive control leveling-sharpening. *Merrill-Palmer Quarterly, 10,* 343-360.

Santostefano, S. (1978). *A biodevelopmental approach to clinical child psychology: Cognitive controls and cognitive control therapy.* New York: Wiley.

Santostefano, S. (1988). *Cognitive Control Battery manual.* Los Angeles, CA: Western Psychological Services.

Santostefano, S., & Paley, E. (1964). Development of cognitive controls in children. *Child Development, 35,* 939-949.

Swanson, H.L. (1987). Information processing theory and learning disabilities: Commentary and future prospectives. *Journal of Disabilities, 20,* 100-140.

Stroop, H.R. (1935). Studies in interference in serial verbal reaction. *Journal of Experimental Psychology, 18,* 643-661.

Torgeson, J.K., & Licht, B.G. (1983). The learning disabled as an inactive learner: Retrospectives and prospects. In J.D. McKinney & L. Feagans (Eds.), *Current topics in learning disabilities* (Vol. 1, pp. 3-31). Norwood, NJ: Ablex.

Witkin, H.A. (1959). The perception of the upright. *Scientific American, 200,* 50-56.

Witkin, H.A. (1969). Social influences in the development of cognitive style. In D.A. Goslin (Ed.), *Handbook of socialization theory and research* (pp. 687-706). Chicago: Rand McNally.

**Chester I. Palmer, Ed.D.**
*Professor of Mathematics, Auburn University at Montgomery, Montgomery, Alabama.*

# COLLEGE BASIC ACADEMIC SUBJECTS EXAMINATION

*Steven J. Osterlind and Center for Educational Assessment Staff, University of Missouri. Chicago, Illinois: The Riverside Publishing Company.*

### Introduction

The College Basic Academic Subjects Examination (College BASE) was developed to cover the general education component of a college education, normally the first 2 years. It is intended both to serve institutions interested in measuring the attainment of their students and to serve individual students by providing information regarding specific academic strengths and weaknesses. The long form of College BASE contains 180 multiple-choice items distributed across four subtests: English, Mathematics, Science, and Social Studies. The English subtest also contains an optional 40-minute writing exercise. Administration of the long form takes about 4 hours with the writing exercise, 3 hours without.

Each of the four College BASE subtests consists of two or three "clusters." The English subtest consists of two, one on Writing and one on Reading and Literature; the Mathematics subtest has clusters on General Mathematics, Algebra, and Geometry; the Science subtest has one cluster on Laboratory and Field Work and one on Fundamental Concepts; the Social Science subtest has clusters on History and on Other Social Sciences. Within each cluster are grouped two or three skills; for example, under Other Social Sciences, the skills are knowledge of geography, knowledge of political and economic structures, and knowledge of investigative and interpretive procedures. The long form provides scaled scores overall, for each of the four subtests, and for each of the clusters. It also provides a categorical score (High, Medium, or Low) on each of the skills as well as for three cross-disciplinary competencies, called interpretive reasoning, strategic reasoning, and adaptive reasoning. The categorical scores are norm-referenced, with "High" indicating more than 1 standard deviation above the mean of the reference population, "Low" indicating more than 1 standard deviation below the mean of the reference population, and "Medium" encompassing the remaining range.

College BASE was developed using a two-parameter model from item response theory (IRT), and scaled scores are obtained by standard IRT methods. As a result, the test cannot be scored locally, but must be sent to the publisher for scoring; the publisher indicates that the user should allow 20 working days for report preparation.

In addition to the long form just described, there is also a short-form College BASE, which consists of only the English and Mathematics subtests. The short form can also be administered either with the writing exercise (total time about 2 hours) or without it (total time about 80 minutes). The items on the short form are identical to those on the English and Mathematics subtests of the long form and provide the same kinds of scores. A third form, the Institution Matrix Form, is designed to provide institutional but not individual information. This form divides the items on the examination among students and requires only about 50 minutes to administer.

College BASE comes with many aids for users. In addition to the technical manual, there is an introductory manual for potential users ("Presenting College BASE"), a substantial "Guide to Test Content," several manuals for examiners and test coordinators, and an introductory leaflet for students. With the exception of the technical manual, discussed in more detail below, all these publications, like the test itself, are professional in both appearance and content. In general, these aids are a strong feature of the test. There are no special provisions for testing handicapped students; instead, administrators are asked to decide what accommodations are appropriate and to document them to the publisher.

According to the developers, the current version of the College BASE technical manual, dated August 1990, should be regarded as a draft because a newer edition is in preparation. (The copy sent to this reviewer, presumably identical to that being sent to current users, never itself suggests draft status.) The developers clearly have put a considerable amount of work into the manual. It includes an exceptional amount of information, especially regarding individual items; it also presents a number of studies relating to the reliability and validity of the various scales and scores. Unfortunately, the manual is not always easy to understand, even for the technically knowledgeable; for example, some of the writing is obscure, and terms used in the column headings of item tables are never defined, even though not all are standard. There are also some editorial problems that are annoying, although not serious; for example, occasional words and phrases are apparently left from previous drafts, and in some tables, some of the columns have been transposed. The manual itself often interprets the results of statistical studies very optimistically, to the point that some users might be misled; however, it usually provides enough information for technically knowledgeable readers to make their own interpretations. Unfortunately, the manual is incomplete in some areas, the most important of which will be addressed later in this review.

College BASE comes in alternate forms, and additional forms are still being developed. In general, new forms are produced by replacing approximately 20% of the items on an existing form, and using standard IRT methods to calibrate the new items. At this time, however, there are no two forms available that have completely different items.

Beginning in September 1988, Missouri students have been required to attain specific scores on each of the four College BASE subtests, and on the writing cluster within the English subtest, in order to be admitted to professional education. Such students typically take the test at the end of their sophomore year or the beginning of their junior year. This review does not consider the appropriateness of College BASE for this legally required use; instead, it considers the test from the point of view of users who have free choice whether to use the test. The legally mandated use may have affected some of the decisions the developers made when constructing the test.

The test specifications for College BASE were developed starting from the report *Academic Preparation for College: What Examinees Need to Know and Be Able to Do* (The College Board, 1983). The test developers worked with a large panel of experts (over 100) selected nationwide based on expertise in particular curriculum areas. This panel helped to refine the list of areas to be tested through meetings, mail review, and telephone review. The process was intended to reach consensus. No formal votes were taken. Although there is no theoretical objection to this process, it is disconcerting not to be able to hear the individual voices of the curriculum experts; it seems impossible that such a group should reach complete agreement. With the consensus procedure, the panel cannot be considered responsible for the choice of material; instead that responsibility falls on the developer, informed by the panel. A formal vote would have been more desirable, to ensure that users would be aware of any deviations from the combined judgment of the panel. In addition, there were several changes in content between the initial form of the test and all subsequent forms: apparently a cluster of items on "Writing Usage" was dropped, and some of the skills on the Science and Social Studies subtests were rearranged. The text in the technical manual describes only the newer content specifications, and only these newer specifications are discussed in this review. The technical manual does not mention the changes in content, which the reviewer discovered by comparing tables of item information. It would be desirable for the forthcoming, revised technical manual to explain these changes in content.

The number of items assigned to each subject and cluster was largely determined by a rule that there should be at least eight (in fact, either eight or nine) items per skill. Panels of experts judged the items for congruence with specific skills. The items themselves were pretested on at least 600 examinees. Only items meeting stringent selection criteria (based on both traditional item statistics and the two-parameter IRT model) were included on the test; in addition, for inclusion, items were required to pass both a subjective screen for bias and a statistical screen for bias against black candidates (which, however, because of small sample size, had quite low power for detecting aberrant items).

**Practical Applications/Uses**

A potential user considering any measure of educational achievement must consider two primary issues: the content coverage of the instrument and the quality of the items. For some possible uses, there are other important considerations, such as the availability of adequate norms or comparative data and various technical issues regarding the scores.

It is convenient to deal with item quality first, because it is the easiest of these considerations to summarize. This reviewer examined all the College BASE items and also asked colleagues who teach English, social sciences, and science to review the relevant parts of the test. There were a few isolated problems with items, especially on the Science subtest, but in general the quality is quite good, certainly far superior to that likely to be attained on a locally developed test. All of the College BASE items appear appropriate for the skills that they are intended to measure. The items on some subtests may be too easy for assessment at highly selective colleges and too difficult for assessment at colleges where the average skill level is well below the national norm; otherwise, it is unlikely that any user who is comfortable with the content specifications would have serious concern about item quality.

The appropriateness of the content coverage is much more problematic. In general, such appropriateness is determined largely by the purpose for which the instrument will be used. As mentioned earlier, College BASE is intended to serve institutions by providing measures of general education attainment of their students, but also to serve individuals by providing diagnostic information on specific strengths and weaknesses. Unfortunately, this reviewer believes that it may be simply impossible to provide much useful diagnostic information, at least at the level of detail attempted by College BASE, on a test of general educational attainment. An ideal test of general education should have *breadth*—it should contain items on an extremely wide variety of topics. In social sciences, for example, such a test might sample information from psychology, economics, political science, sociology, and education; in sciences, from physics, chemistry, biology, geology, and astronomy. Such a broad test, however, if of reasonable length, is unlikely to have enough questions on any one topic to provide reliable measurement of specific skills; after all, even an ordinary achievement test could easily devote several hours of testing to each topic area just mentioned.

Although the coverage of each College BASE subtest will be considered in more detail later, consider some examples. The Social Studies subtest contains eight items on world history. The expectation of obtaining reliable information regarding such a specific skill (defined as "Recognize the chronology and significance of major events and movements in world history") from eight multiple-choice items is at best extremely optimistic. A similar expectation with regard to the eight items in the English subtest on "Writing as a Process" (the skill is "Understand the various elements of the writing process, including collecting information and formulating ideas, determining relationships, arranging sentences and paragraphs, establishing transitions, and revising what has been written") seems ludicrous. In general, the four subject scores are adequately reliable for individuals to look for a pattern of achievement by subtest. But the reliabilities of the cluster scores are generally marginal, and only on a few of the skills are the determinations of level sufficiently reliable to be used in judging comparative achievement. (The reliability of the various measures will be discussed in more detail under "Technical Aspects" below.) Notice, however, that while these considerations suggest serious doubt regarding the utility of many of the measurements at the skills level, and even at the cluster level, coverage of many varied competencies at relatively low depth actually strengthens the value of the instrument as a measure of general education.

The coverage of College BASE is so important to potential users that it seems desirable to review it subtest by subtest. Because of space considerations, many of the skills will be presented in abbreviated form here; more detailed descriptions may be obtained from *College BASE: Guide to Test Content,* available from the publisher.

The English subtest has two clusters, Reading and Literature (reading critically, reading analytically, and understanding literature) and Writing (writing as a process, conventions of written English, and the optional essay, if included). In general, the content of this subtest drew praise from this reviewer's English consultants, who thought its breadth and balance excellent and its questions reasonable. The subtest is quite suitable for use in assessing general education skills in English, except perhaps at institutions with an average skill level well above or below the norm for U.S. colleges.

The Social Studies subtest contains two clusters, History (U.S. events and world events) and Social Sciences (geography, political/economic structures, and procedures of social sciences). Notice that, except for a few items on the skill of social science procedures, the subtest does not cover psychology or sociology at all; these omissions seems peculiar, especially because psychology is one of the social sciences that students are most likely to study during their general education in college. This reviewer's consultants in social sciences gave a generally favorable opinion of both the coverage and the items on this subtest. Once again, however, the questions are best suited for use at institutions where the average skill level is not far from the norm for U.S. colleges.

Any consideration of the content of the Mathematics and Science subtests must begin by addressing another serious issue. In the first 2 years of college, most students, regardless of major, take roughly similar courses in English composition, world history, and some social sciences. In mathematics and science, however, the normal academic program differs strongly according to major. What kind of test of "general education" in mathematics can be appropriate both for liberal arts majors, who may take a single general mathematics course that does not even require as a prerequisite the completion of 1 year of high school algebra, and also for engineering majors, who must normally complete at least five quarters of mathematics beginning with Calculus I? The mathematics curriculum for students in business normally follows a still different pattern, as most programs require a special business-oriented calculus class. In fact, there is really no agreement as to what constitutes "general education" in mathematics, and devising a single test of reasonable length seems a nearly impossible task. The situation in science is only slightly better than in mathematics. It is not clear whether "general education" in science mean Physics for Poets or Physics for Science Majors. At least there are only two, not three, sets of requirements (business can now be included with liberal arts and education). The developers of College BASE have taken definite positions on these issues, reflected in the topic selection for these subtests.

Three clusters form the Mathematics subtest: General Mathematics (practical applications, properties and notations, and using statistics), Algebra (expressions, and equations and inequalities, almost all linear), and Geometry (two- and three-dimensional figures, and geometrical calculations). The subtest primarily tests mathematical reasoning, not computing skills; in fact, students are allowed to use calculators. The Algebra skills are so elementary that they might well be covered in a pre-algebra course in seventh or eighth grade. The Geometry skills are so elementary that it is likely that eighth-graders with some experience in informal geometry could answer many of them; certainly an average student finishing a high school geometry course would find them easy. The General Mathematics cluster is more diverse. The practical applications items are grade school skills that would surely be reviewed in a seventh-grade general mathematics course (e.g., percentage, ratio and proportion, units of time). The items on using statistics would be accessible to students from some elementary and high school programs but cannot yet be regarded as standard for all students. The properties and notations items are quite diverse; some cover topics that would be covered in elementary grades, but others might not be covered until Algebra I. Thus, an average 10th-grade student who has completed 1 year of algebra and 1 of geometry in high school should do extremely well on at least six of the seven skills. Overall, the subtest is substantially less advanced than the Mathematics section of the ACT Assessment (either original or revised), which is intended for high school students. Students whose majors require college algebra or any higher course (at the reviewer's institution, this group contains over 80% of all students) will never see most of this material in college unless they take remedial courses; at most institutions, almost no students except majors in elementary education will see the geometry at all. The subtest is arguably appropriate for measuring the mathematical attainment of students majoring in liberal arts or education, provided the user has suitably low expectations. It is clearly inappropriate for students majoring in the sciences, in engineering, or in business. The developers have chosen to write to the least common denominator, even though such students represent a distinct minority of the students at 4-year colleges.

The Science subtest has two clusters, Laboratory and Field Work (observation/experimental design, laboratory/field techniques, and interpreting results) and Fundamental Concepts (concepts of life sciences and concepts of physical sciences). The cluster on Laboratory and Field Work largely tests reading skills, scientific reasoning, and the scientific method. The reviewer's science consultant, a chemist, praised the emphasis on these topics but criticized many of the test items because the experiments they presented for analysis were poorly designed, making some of the questions unrealistic. He also considered the subtest inappropriate for majors in sciences and engineering because it does not adequately test the factual information that students majoring in those areas should acquire during the first 2 years of their college education.

Overall, how suitable is College BASE for measuring the general educational level of students who have completed the general education phase of their college program, normally the first 2 years? All four subtests are reasonably suitable for this purpose for students majoring in education and in liberal arts. Three of the four subtests (all but Mathematics) are reasonably suitable for students majoring in business areas. Only two of the subtests (English and Social Studies) are suitable for students majoring in sciences or engineering, and the Mathematics subtest is very unsuitable for such students.

The availability of normative or comparative data will be important to some, but not all, potential users of College BASE. Such information is obviously vital to users wishing to compare the achievement of their students with students at other campuses, for example, but may not be very important to users doing pre- and post-testing. Item calibration (and thus also, because the test was developed by IRT methods, score calibration) was initially done on a sample of about 2,000 students from a variety of institutions. This initial sample was not very representative of those likely later to take College BASE; for example, the group was 84% female, only 4% black, and contained 24% freshman and 12% seniors or graduate students. The items were later recalibrated on a sample of about 4,000 students, the original 2,000 plus another 2,000 for whom no demographics are given in the technical manual. It is clearly imprudent, however, to believe that the mean of 300 and the standard deviation of 65 in the reference population are of much value in judging performance by other populations. College BASE has now been used at about 100 institutions, including about 70 outside Missouri. Users for whom comparative data are important should consult the test developer about the availability of data from similar schools; the developer has indicated a willingness to prepare comparison groups for particular institutions.

**Technical Aspects**

The developers of College BASE have done extensive studies of the reliability of the various scores and classifications, using three different methods for calculating reliability. For subtests scores, cluster scores, and skill classifications, they present two general reliability estimates, KR-20 as a measure of internal consistency and a reliability calculated by IRT methods using the average standard error. For the reported skill results (High, Medium, or Low), they also supply two decision consistency measures, Huynh and Subkoviak, which attempt to estimate the probability that an individual would be classified the same on another attempt using a parallel form of the test. (For a more detailed discussion of these measures and for additional references, see Feldt & Brennan, 1989, pp. 142–143.) Note that, with the dividing points set at about plus/minus 1 standard deviation from the mean, the expected frequencies of classification in the reference population are about 16% low, 68% medium, and 16% high; of course, the fact that scores are discrete means that the division is only approximate. With the expected frequencies of classification, however, it is easy to compute that the probability of agreement by chance (i.e., the "decision consistency" of random assignment) is about .51. Because the two decision consistency measures are as usual very similar, only the Huynh values will be discussed here.

Reliability measurements are generally lowest for the skills on the English subtest. The reviewer considers these values, presented below, clearly unacceptable; none of them approaches any reasonable standard for individual interpretation, and four of the decision consistency measures are negligibly above the chance level:

| *Skill* | *IRT* | *KR-20* | *Huynh* |
|---|---|---|---|
| Reading critically | .55 | .52 | .54 |
| Reading analytically | .51 | .51 | .55 |
| Understanding literature | .38 | .30 | .52 |
| Writing as a process | .33 | .32 | .53 |
| Conventions of written English | .59 | .56 | .63 |

Although the reliabilities of the skill data on the other subtests are somewhat higher than for English, they cannot be considered satisfactory. Overall, not including the optional essay, there are 22 skills assessed. The range of their KR-20 values is 9 below .50, 8 from .50 to .59, 4 from .60 to .69, and 1 from .70 to .79; of the 5 values of at least .60, 4 occur on the Mathematics subtest. The range of Huynh values for the 22 skills is 8 from .50 to .59, 12 from .60 to .69, and 2 (both on the Mathematics subtest) from .70 to .79. These values are so low that the reviewer recommends that the publisher stop providing skill data to individuals; the great majority of students, who have no training in measurement principles, will surely give far greater credence to the skill data than justified.

The KR-20 values for the nine clusters, each containing two or three skills, are .69 and .59 on the English subtest; Mathematics, .76, .82, and .72; Science, .71 and .61; and Social Studies, .75 and .70. The KR-20 values for the subtests are .77 for English, .89 for Mathematics, .78 for Science, and .83 for Social Studies. Even at these levels of analysis, some of the values are clearly lower than desirable, especially given that scores are reported to three significant digits, giving an appearance of great precision.

Perhaps as disturbing as the reliability values themselves are the interpretations made in the technical manual. Discussing the KR-20 values, it states "These coefficients, given that there are eight to nine items per skill and about 27 items per cluster, reflect adequate magnitude to demonstrate reliability in generalizing to performance in a specific content domain" (Osterlind & Merz, 1990, p. 98). Regarding the decision consistency measures, "These decision reliabilities are of sufficient magnitude that they demonstrate more than adequate decision consistency. That is, decisions made from these item generalizes [*sic*] would be consistent over the same group" (Osterlind & Merz, 1990, p. 101). These overly optimistic assessments illustrate this reviewer's belief that users must be prepared to make their own technical judgments regarding this test, relying on the data in the manual, not the interpretations.

Although the technical manual presents in detail the scoring rubric for the optional essay, it does not discuss at all the procedures for grading, nor does it provide any information on the reliability of the grading or the relationship of the score on the essay to other scores. Given the well-known difficulty of scoring essays, the absence of this information is a serious matter, which should be addressed in the forthcoming manual revision.

As usual, it is more difficult to judge College BASE's validity than its reliability. For an educational achievement test, this reviewer believes that the most important issues are the content specifications and the quality of the questions, both issues that have already been discussed. The technical manual offers several additional kinds of studies. The factor analyses of the test are generally satisfactory, although again somewhat optimistically interpreted. Studies of correlations with ACT scores, SAT scores, and grade point averages are generally less convincing because of various technical problems; for example, ACT scores, SAT scores, and grade point averages were self-reported using five categories, the time lapse between the ACT or SAT and College BASE varies widely among students, many of the analyses concentrate on statistical significance rather than estimation, and some of the samples are small (e.g., the multiple regression of the four College BASE subject scores with SAT Verbal scores has only 347 individuals while that with SAT Quantitative has 295; no explanation is provided for the different numbers of subjects.)

### Critique

College BASE is a young test; the first true operational use occurred in September 1988. In many ways, the present form of the test is a good beginning. Test development was done carefully and professionally; the work at the item level shows an especially high standard. The subtests on English and Social Studies are well conceived and executed. The developers have shown their concern for users by preparing many aids to administration and interpretation.

At present, however, there are enough problems with the test that it is difficult to recommend it except under rather special circumstances. College BASE is reasonably well suited to measuring the general educational attainment of college students majoring in liberal arts or education; three of its four subtests are suitable for business students. It is not very suitable for students in science or engineering curricula. It is also not very useful from a diagnostic point of view, at least below the level of the scores on the four subtests. With the present manual, users should be prepared to form their own judgments on technical issues.

In several ways, the developers may have been too ambitious in planning this test. It may simply be impossible to produce a test of reasonable length that has both enough breadth to measure general educational level and enough depth to provide useful diagnostic information, at least at the level of detail attempted by College BASE. It may also be impossible to provide a single test of reasonable length to measure general educational level in mathematics and science because different curricula have such different expectations in these subjects.

In conversations with this reviewer, the developers of College BASE have shown a willingness to attack some of the problems. In particular, the forthcoming revision of the technical manual may address a number of the specific criticisms made in this review. The more general problems, especially those related to the content in mathematics and science, seem more difficult. Perhaps the solution lies in the preparation of multiple versions of those subtests. Notice, for example, that the College Board finds it necessary to have two levels of its Mathematics Achievement Test for high school students.

There is no doubt that there is a trend in higher education toward the measurement of outcomes. College BASE already provides information of value in this arena. If the developers are able to solve the problem of the content in mathematics and science, College BASE may become an important measuring device in an area where there is now no satisfactory instrument.

## References

The College Board. (1983). *Academic preparation for college: What examinees need to know and be able to do.* New York: Author.

Feldt, L.S., & Brennan, R.L. (1989). Reliability. In R.L. Linn (Ed.), *Educational measurement* (3rd ed., pp. 105–146). Washington, DC: American Council on Education.

Osterlind, S.J., & Merz, W.R. (1990). *College BASE technical manual.* Columbia, MO: University of Missouri Center for Educational Assessment.

**Karyn Bobkoff Katz, Ph.D.**
*Associate Professor, School of Communicative Disorders, The University of Akron, Akron, Ohio.*
**Carol W. Lawrence, Ph.D.**
*Associate Professor, School of Communicative Disorders, The University of Akron, Akron, Ohio.*

# COMPTON SPEECH AND LANGUAGE SCREENING EVALUATION

*Arthur J. Compton. San Francisco, California: Carousel House.*

## Introduction

The Compton Speech and Language Screening Evaluation (CSLSE) was "designed to provide a quick estimate of the speech and language development of preschool, kindergarten, and first-grade children" (Compton, 1978, p. 1). The purpose of the screening procedure is to select those children who display possible speech and language problems and are therefore in need of further testing.

The author notes that this speech and language screen resulted from 6 years of research on the language development of children who were learning normally and those who were not. The initial form of the test was designed in 1975 at the Institute of Child Language and Phonology in San Francisco. Compton reports that the final version of the test followed several revisions, these based on the administration of the procedure to approximately 500 children. Comments from speech pathologists working with the instrument were also incorporated into the final revision of the test.

The CSLSE materials include the manual (describing administration and scoring procedures), response forms, and stimulus objects, all contained in a compact plastic carrying case. An array of manipulable objects provide the content for the test items; for example, socks, blocks, and plastic spoons are provided for use during testing. Two black-and-white drawings of events are also included in the manual for facilitating a spontaneous language sample. The only additional item required for test administration is an actual chair within the testing room.

This screening test is designed for a specific age range of children, 3 years to 6 years; that is, preschool, kindergarten, and first-grade children. The range is clearly stated in the manual, and age-appropriate guidelines are also included beside items on the response form.

The use of actual objects "adds a concrete dimension to the evaluation, helps stimulate interest and, generally, helps in getting young children more quickly involved in the tasks" (Compton, 1978, p. 1). The test items make use of the objects in both comprehension and production tasks, allowing the child to focus on topics presented by objects. The author further notes that the use of objects, rather than pictures, is advantageous because of the increased familiarity of the materials for children.

The CSLSE is designed in an adult-centered format. The examiner begins the session by presenting the plastic case of test materials to the child, while encouraging the child to discover what is inside. As the testing proceeds, the examiner asks the child specific questions or requests that he or she follow specific instructions. In addition, the examiner records or spontaneously analyzes responses, scoring each test item as indicated on the response form.

The test's construction allows for the screening evaluation of several areas of speech and language development. Both production and comprehension (or recognition) tasks are used. The initial consideration is of articulation and vocabulary, followed by knowledge of colors and shapes. Test administration also includes an auditory-visual memory task. The language appraisal provides an assessment of plurals, opposites, progressive and past tense verbs, prepositions, multiple commands (comprehension only), and possessive pronouns. If considered necessary, the examiner elicits a spontaneous language sample, which also allows for the observation of problems in fluency and voice. Although no specific instructions are given, the author suggests the examiner complete a "brief inspection of the oral mechanism" (Compton, 1978, p. 9) should hypernasality or other articulatory difficulties be of concern.

The examiner guides the child's performance in each of the tasks. Several are based on the assumption that if a child performs the production items successfully, he or she would be successful on the comprehension of the same items. For example, in the evaluation of color names, the examiner gives colored blocks to the child while asking for the name of each. For any colors named incorrectly, the examiner asks the child to point to the block of that particular color. The language portion of the evaluation uses a traditional cloze technique (e.g., "Here is one spoon and here are two [*spoons*])." This method serves for plurals, opposites, progressive and past tense verbs, and possessive pronouns. The preposition subtest is the only portion of the test in which comprehension is tested first, while multiple commands ("Give the fish to the man and the spoon to the woman") is only evaluated through comprehension.

The CSLSE response form (copyright 1985) allows the examiner a clear, concise method for recording the results of the assessment. The six-page form is divided into several sections, each designed for specific data. For example, the first page allows for presentation of basic information concerning the child as well as summary data of test results. Ample space is also provided for examiner comments and observations. The author specifically recommends that childrens' responses and general behaviors be observed and noted during testing.

The user can easily record the results of each subtest on the response form with information for scoring (and age expectancies) also included. The analysis of spontaneous language, fluency, voice, and the oral mechanism also can be recorded on this response form. Although not a specified component of the Compton Speech and Language Screening Evaluation, an audiogram for an optional hearing screening allows additional and pertinent audiometric data to be recorded on the same test form. Finally, the child's results can be presented on a screening profile display that includes guidelines for passing and failing the instrument. The design of this profile (which also appears on the response form) is well organized, allowing the examiner to quickly transfer the scoring information, analyze the test results, and determine the need for further assessment.

**Practical Applications/Uses**

The CSLSE was designed for use in a clinical setting along with other health screening procedures. The original goal for this procedure was to screen speech and language skills within a maximum time limit of 6 minutes. As with other screening instruments, the CSLSE is described as a measure to identify potential speech and language problems, "thereby alerting the tester and parents that a more extensive evaluation is warranted" (Compton, 1978, p. 1).

As described, this measure is designed to provide information in nine areas of speech and language. These areas of assessment encompass preschool and early school-age abilities in articulation, vocabulary, grammatical constructs, memory, knowledge of shapes and colors, and spontaneous production of language. It is worthy of note that Compton (1978) emphasizes the potential role played by the spontaneous language sample by concluding that it "is a valuable supplement to the various specific tasks and, for some children, . . . may be even more informative, constituting the ultimate basis for deciding if a child has passed or failed the screening procedure" (p. 3).

The author appears to have carefully constructed the individual components of the CSLSE with consideration for the need to obtain information within a limited timeframe. The specific items (or objects) within a task (e.g., Articulation and Vocabulary) were selected for their potential to evaluate more than one area of language at a time. For instance, the particular vocabulary items were chosen because of their familiarity for children aged 3 to 6 years and because the specific initial and final consonants of each word provide information on articulation skills. The accomplishment of this "multipurpose" approach is also noted in the use of similar items for both comprehension and expressive testing, in the use of early identified items in later tasks, and in the suggestions for focusing on several areas of speech and language while observing the child's conversational participation.

The settings appropriate for test administration would reflect the designated age range. Preschool as well as elementary school environments (through first grade) would be the most typical sites for administering the CSLSE. The information so derived would be most useful to speech-language pathologists working within these settings to provide direction for the need for further testing. In addition, CSLSE results may be useful for consultation with the teachers whose daily interactions with targeted children provide supplemental information from classroom participation. Compton includes a suggestion that for children whose performance is not clearly in the pass or fail range, teachers may play a role in providing information for clinical decisions.

This screening tool "is intended to be used as a means of selecting out those children with 'potential' speech and language handicaps" (Compton, 1978, p. 1). Therefore, the use of this measure with children already identified as "at risk" for these problems is not considered appropriate. For children with a known potential for speech and language problems, such as the hearing impaired, assessment time would be used more efficiently by administering a procedure that allows for more descriptive linguistic information.

Although appropriate for use with children typically found in groups or classrooms, the CSLSE must be administered individually and in a test environment free from distractions. The content of the manual and the response form suggest that it was designed for use by communicative disorders specialists, such as speech-language pathologists and audiologists. Instructions assume the knowledge of language development, as well as the terminology and symbol systems characteristic of the training of these professionals. For example, directions include statements such as "A brief check of the speech mechanism may prove revealing for certain problems such as . . . hyper-nasality stemming from palatal insufficiencies" (Compton, 1978, p. 4) and "Designate sound substitutions and distortions with appropriate phonetic symbols" (Compton, 1978, p. 6). In addition, both the manual and response forms utilize the International Phonetic Alphabet symbols. It is possible that under certain circumstances, the test might be administered by a "speech aide" trained to work under the close supervision of a communication disorders specialist. In such a position, the aide should have specific training in speech and language development, as well as the systems, terminology, and symbols used in the speech and hearing profession.

The instructions for administering the CSLSE are detailed and complete. It appears that a thorough reading of the manual (pp. 1–9), with response form in hand, prepares the examiner for rapid, efficient use of the screening instrument. One disadvantage is that the actual task descriptions and instructions are not listed in the manual, requiring the evaluator to go back and forth from the manual to the response form in preparation for test administration.

The procedure is best given in the order described, in that successful performance on one task may imply omission of a subsequent one (e.g., production tasks precede comprehension tasks). In addition, the Auditory-Visual Memory Span has an optional item for screening auditory and visual memories individually should the examiner choose. The directions also state that encouraging spontaneous language during the screening may allow the examiner to omit a separate section for the spontaneous language sample. It is recommended that all tasks be administered as described in the manual, in that each is designed to assess different aspects of speech and/or language.

Specific directions are provided for scoring Tasks I through IV (Articulation and Vocabulary, Colors, Shapes, Auditory-Visual Memory Span) as well as suggestions for dealing with expected variations in responses. Thus, the methods of recording responses can be swiftly learned and these task items rapidly scored. Task I, for example, involves description and transcription (using the IPA) of articulatory performance. Tasks II through IV deal with concepts, memory, and aspects of language and are easily scored on a correct/incorrect basis. Although some directions are furnished for scoring the Spontaneous Language Sample (Task VI), successful scoring depends on the examiner's ability to make rapid decisions concerning (a) the number of words produced in the longest utterance, (b) the usual number of words per utterance, (c) the general impression of child's use of language, and (d) speech intelligibility during conversation. Rapid judgments of the four parameters requires specific training and background in the clinical realm of speech and language.

The "Screening Profile and Pass/Fail Guidelines" do not appear difficult to complete, yet the manual does not include precise directions for these summaries. Because of this, initial efforts in completing the scoring may be slow and tentative. The author does not give an estimate of the time necessary to score the test, but the reviewers consider that once the scoring technique has been mastered, the Screening Profile and Pass/Fail Guidelines could be completed quickly. Tasks VII (Fluency), VIII (Voice), and IX (Oral Mechanism) are not included in the pass/fail decision, but sufficient space is provided for descriptive comments on the response form. The manual does not suggest how the examiner should use positive results noted on these screening items. The CSLSE is scored manually, with no mechanical or computer scoring available.

Screening decisions are based on task item scores and the child's chronological age (given in 1-year increments) from 3 through 6 years. Specific errors at each age are used to determine the final results of the screening. Neither the manual nor the response forms suggest any adaptation for children at the younger or older ends of the 1-year increments, and no smaller increments of age are used in this measure. The results of the test are readily useful, in that the score is interpreted as "pass," "rescreen," or "speech and language evaluation suggested." Conclusions stated in these terms are easily understood by parents, teachers, and administrators.

## Technical Aspects

In the Foreword of the test manual, Compton described this measurement as an outgrowth of 6 years of research on children's normal and abnormal linguistic development. Once constructed, the test then underwent "several revisions during the course of administering it to a population of approximately 500 children from a wide range of socio-economic and ethnic backgrounds" (Compton, 1978, Foreword). The author further notes that the revisions were based on information obtained from speech pathologists in California using the instrument. No technical data on validity or reliability are provided in the manual.

Dr. Compton has stated (personal communication, April 1990) that the developmental and norming data were in informal raw form only and thus were not available for scrutiny by outside agents. He further elaborated on the test construction by describing the individual items as based on research concerned with speech and language development. Specific researchers noted were Roger Brown, Paula Menyuk, Daniel Slobin, Mildred Templin, and Jean Berko Gleason, but specific research citations were not provided. Compton indicated that the auditory memory tasks were adapted from similar tasks on the Wechsler Intelligence Scale for Children–Revised (WISC-R; Wechsler, 1974).

After the initial form of the test was devised, 3 years were spent informally field-testing the instrument at a number of sites, including Head Start, preschool, daycare, and private school settings served by the Institute of Child Language. Seven or eight stages of revision occurred during this testing period. In all, approximately 500 children representing wide range of backgrounds were tested. According to Dr. Compton (personal communication, April 1990), the cutoff scores derived for the English-speaking subjects were confirmed later by similar results found in testing a Spanish adaptation of the instrument (administered to approximately 200 Spanish-speaking children).

**Critique**

By focusing on the role of the screening test for the speech and language professional, we can more appropriately critique the Compton Speech and Language Screening Evaluation. Emerick and Haynes (1986) have suggested that in the screening process,

> The examiner must be able to detect individuals with impaired speech while rapidly passing over the normal individuals. Although brief, the detection process should provide a sufficient sample of each person's oral communication to permit critical judgment of articulation, voice, fluency, and language abilities. (p. 61)

The procedure should allow a clinician to identify children displaying speech and language within normal limits as well as those whose skills warrant more thorough diagnostic assessment. Although the CSLSE has many very strong and positive qualities, the absence of descriptive data on reliability and validity of the measure suggests some professional caution.

Our review addresses the issue of validity in speech and language assessment from two important perspectives. The first validity concern relates to the general purpose of a screening tool and the success of the CSLSE in completing this aim. The second validity concern reflects the relationship between current notions of validity in language assessment and the methodology selected by Compton for his screening procedure.

As suggested by Emerick and Haynes (1986), the screening process should yield rapid results while also accurately identifying the particular child for which additional testing is required. Clinicians need a tool that will accomplish this goal with a minimum of overreferrals for further testing; therefore, they should approach a procedure with questions on its "hit rate" (proportion of accurate positive decision) for screening (Salvia & Ysseldyke, 1988, p. 7). It is specifically this information that is not available for the CSLSE. Although Compton has designed his test with apparent consideration of children's speech and language skills, the lack of validity measurements (i.e., predictive validity) must influence a clinician's decision to adopt the CSLSE. With minimal data reported on the precise establishment of normative comparisons, a clinician must question the appropriateness of the test for the population being served. Schetz (1985), as an example, studied the Compton Speech and Language Screening Evaluation and questioned the measurement's high overidentification of children with possible vocabulary problems. One potential solution to this concern, of course, is for clinicians who find this screening instrument practical and easy to administer to develop local norms and design and implement their own validation measures.

In addressing the second issue of validity, much concern has been raised in recent years regarding the use of norm-referenced tests in the assessment of language skills in children (e.g., Muma, 1983). The question of improving validity in language assessment is often answered by using descriptive procedures (or language sampling) in the evaluation process (Damico, 1988; Klee, 1985; Muma, 1983). The descriptive procedures have been characterized as "more valid than psychometric tests and developmental profiles because they provide 'evidence' " (Muma, 1983, p. 202) and, therefore, give a clinician a more accurate picture of the language/communication ability of a child. Although much of the CSLSE presents constrained linguistic tasks, the role of the spontaneous language sample in evaluating a child is clearly stated and emphasized. The clinician is guided by task materials, instructions, and analysis procedures in the elicitation of the sample. In his manual, for example, Compton (1978) has noted that

> Some children's performance on the various tasks may appear to be adequate, yet their speech or language will break down in conversational speech. In these cases, especially, the child's conversational speech may be more revealing than the specific tasks, thus constituting the primary indicator of a potential handicap. (p. 11)

Clinical skill and training is required to complete the manual's analysis suggestions. Yet, there is some support for clinicians with specific training successfully using clinical judgment in observing and identifying language impairment in conjunction with the results from formal testing (Allen, Bliss, & Timmons, 1981).

It is apparent that the 1978 Compton Speech and Language Screening Evaluation has been designed and constructed to optimize the efficiency of information obtained during testing, and items have been carefully selected to increase their interest and familiarity to children (e.g., toy objects). This method is consistent with some recent suggestions from Lahey (1988, p. 292) and Lund and Duchan (1988, p. 25) for conducting successful low structure and naturalistic observation of the language skills of young children.

Although certain data have not revealed a difference between phonological elicitation tasks that compare object, picture naming, and imitation (Landry & Hess, 1985), Hodson (1986) recommends the use of objects in sound system assessment. She states, "When children become involved in manipulating the objects, they tend to forget to concentrate on producing a particular sound that they are more likely to remember when naming two-dimensional pictures" (Hodson, 1986, p. xi).

In further analysis of the CSLSE, items have been chosen for their potential to elicit speech and language information that spans more than one linguistic area at a time. For instance, articulation and vocabulary are tested simultaneously by selecting words that both are familiar to children at the targeted ages and also include sounds critical for assessing children at these stages of development. For example, by asking the child to produce the name *spoon,* the test directs the clinician to evaluate vocabulary knowledge as well as the cluster /sp-/ and the final consonant /n/. In addition, Compton uses the same vocabulary items from the subtest of Articulation and Vocabulary in seven subsequent subtests (e.g, *spoon* appears in Auditory-Visual Memory Span, Plurals, Prepositions, Multiple Commands, and Possessive Pronouns). It should be noted that certain vocabulary items may not serve their intended purpose, however. The use of the word *thimble* in the Articulation and Vocabulary subtest provides one such instance. Many children are, perhaps, unacquainted with thimbles, which could affect the vocabulary score and possibly the articulation score.

The goal of swift screening has also been addressed in the CSLSE through the evaluation of production skills before comprehension is tested. Several subtests assume that if success is achieved in the production of targeted linguistic elements, then comprehension does not require additional testing time. This assumption, although not accepted by all practitioners, has been supported in a great deal of clinical literature, particularly in regard to the importance of production in intervention (Lahey, 1988).

Clinical caution must be acknowledged in selecting this evaluation procedure. The screening test does not consider the fact that Black English (BE) speakers may use different language rules and thus may not produce Compton's target responses. In Articulation and Vocabulary, some children who speak Black English may apply BE pronunciation rules, resulting in different productions than the target Standard American English pronunciation. Several studies have reported that patterns of final consonant deletion are higher for Black English–speaking children than for children who use Standard American English. Haynes and Moran (1989) reported that Black English–speaking children in preschool, kindergarten, and first grade showed final consonant deletion percentages (on single word productions) ranging from 7% to 42% on four of the final consonants tested within the CSLSE, with higher percentages demonstrated by preschoolers and kindergartners. Seymour and Seymour (1981) found that on a single word articulation test, 5-year-olds who spoke Black English showed 15% omission of final consonants, compared with a 4% omission rate for white children. These patterns might cause the child who spoke Black English to fail to produce the target response on four words, which in turn means failure of the articulation portion of the CSLSE.

In production of the Plurals subtest, a Black English speaker might apply the rule of absence of plural suffix, particularly in the presence of a modifying numeral (Wolfram & Fasold, 1974). Thus, the response to "Here is one spoon and here are two (*spoons*)" might be the correct BE *spoon*. This rule could affect all three plural production items. Finally, past tense may be unmarked in the target word *hopped* (in the Progressive and Past Tense subtest) in that Black English allows a nonobligatory plural marker (Wolfram & Fasold, 1974). Although this screening test has been used with "a wide range of socio-economic and ethnic backgrounds" (Compton, 1978, Foreword), it is important that any speech-language pathologist using it is aware of its limitations for children who speak Black English.

It must be noted that although these reviewers have not utilized the CSLSE in clinical practice, we find that many of its properties are comparable to other tests that we have used with positive results. The ease with which the procedures can be understood and learned, the simplicity of scoring, the clarity and completeness of the response all hold promise for a clinician working with young language-learning children. In fact, Pooser (1979), in her general review of the Compton Speech and Language Screening Evaluation, noted that "students in a college practicum were able to use the test simply by studying the manual" (p. 244). The inclusion of the language sampling portion of the measure also increases the value of the test for clinicians familiar with these procedures. Yet, the limited technical data regarding reliability and validity do influence the immediate strength of the CSLSE for adoption in many clinical settings.

## References


Allen, D.V., Bliss, L.S., & Timmons, J. (1981). Language evaluation: Science or art? *Journal of Speech and Hearing Disorders, 46,* 66–68.

Compton, A.J. (1978). *Compton Speech and Language Screening Evaluation.* San Francisco: Carousel House.

Damico, J.S. (1988). The lack of efficacy in language therapy: A case study. *Language, Speech and Hearing Services in Schools, 19,* 51–66.

Emerick, L.L., & Haynes, W.O. (1986). *Diagnosis and evaluation in speech pathology* (3rd ed.). Englewood Cliffs, NJ: Prentice-Hall.

Haynes, W.O., & Moran, M.J. (1989). A cross-sectional developmental study of final consonant production in southern black children from preschool through third grade. *Language, Speech and Hearing Services in Schools, 20,* 400–406.

Hodson, B. (1986). *The assessment of phonological processes—revised.* Danville, IL: Interstate Printers and Publishers.

Klee, T. (1985). Clinical language sampling: Analyzing the analyses. *Child Language Teaching and Therapy, 1,* 182–198.

Lahey, M. (1988). *Language disorders and language development.* New York: Macmillan.

Landry, R.G., & Hess, C.W. (1985). Phonological performance elicited by object naming, picture naming, and imitation. *Perceptual and Motor Skills, 61,* 406.

Lund, N.J., & Duchan, J.F. (1988). *Assessing children's language in naturalistic contexts* (2nd ed.). Englewood Cliffs, NJ: Prentice-Hall.

Muma, J.R. (1983). Speech-language pathology: Emerging clinical expertise in language. In T.M. Gallagher & C.A. Prutting (Eds.), *Pragmatic assessment and intervention issues in language* (pp. 195–214). Austin, TX: PRO-ED.

Pooser, P.B. (1979). Compton Speech and Language Screening Evaluation. *Asha, 21,* 244.

Salvia, J., & Ysseldyke, J.E. (1988). *Assessment in special and remedial education* (4th ed.). Boston: Houghton Mifflin.

Schetz, K.F. (1985). Comparison of the Compton Speech and Language Screen Evaluation and the Fluharty Preschool Speech and Language Screening Test. *Language, Speech and Hearing Services in Schools, 16,* 16–24.

Seymour, H.N., & Seymour, C.N. (1981). Black English and Standard American English contrasts in consonantal development of four- and five-year-old children. *Journal of Speech and Hearing Disorders, 46,* 274–280.

Wechsler, D. (1974). *Wechsler Intelligence Scale for Children–Revised (WISC-R).* San Antonio, TX: Psychological Corporation.

Wolfram, W., & Fasold, R.W. (1974). *The study of social dialects in American English.* Englewood Cliffs, NJ: Prentice-Hall.

**Frances Lawrenz, Ph.D.**
*Associate Professor, Department of Curriculum and Instruction, College of Education, University of Minnesota, Minneapolis, Minnesota.*

**Robert E. Orton, Ph.D.**
*Associate Professor, Department of Curriculum and Instruction, College of Education, University of Minnesota, Minneapolis, Minnesota.*

# CORNELL CRITICAL THINKING TESTS—LEVEL X AND LEVEL Z

*Robert H. Ennis, Jason Millman, and T.N. Tomko. Pacific Grove, California: Midwest Publications Critical Thinking Press.*

## Introduction

The Cornell Critical Thinking Tests, Level X and Level Z, are designed to assess general critical thinking skills. Such skills include several specific aspects of critical thinking, such as the ability to assess deductive inferences or the ability to judge the credibility of a report. The definition of critical thinking that guided the development of the tests is succinct: "Critical thinking is the process of reasonably deciding what to believe and do" (Ennis, Millman, & Tomko, 1985, p. 1). Both levels of the test contain multiple-choice questions about hypothetical situations and should take approximately 50 minutes to complete. Level X is a 71-item instrument for students in Grades 4–14, with items covering the skills of induction, deduction, judgments of observation and credibility, and identification of assumptions. Level Z is a 52-item instrument for advanced and gifted high school students, college students, and other adults, with items covering the skills of induction, deduction, judgments of observation and credibility, identification of assumptions, and determination of meaning.

Work on the Cornell Critical Thinking Tests began in the late fifties with Ennis's doctoral dissertation, and more was done in conjunction with the Cornell Critical Thinking Project in the sixties (Ennis & Paulus, 1965). The concept of critical thinking behind this work comes from an idea advanced by B. Othanel Smith (1953, p. 130, cited in Ennis et al., 1985): "Now if we set about to find out what . . . [a] statement means and to determine whether to accept it or reject it, we would be engaged in thinking which for lack of a better term, we shall call critical thinking." This concept of critical thinking was further developed by Ennis (e.g., 1962) and applied in the development of these tests. Since initial development, the tests have been administered to many groups, from fourth-graders through graduate students, as part of various investigations.

Robert Ennis is a University of Illinois Professor of Education and is regarded as one of the leading researchers in the field of critical thinking (cf. McPeck, 1981). Jason Millman is a Cornell statistician who specializes in test design and construction. The development of the Cornell Critical Thinking Tests involved extensive discussion, revision, and more discussion of each item by a team of experts in the project.

There are many ways to categorize critical thinking, and the specific categorization directly influences the development of assessment instruments. The categorization used in the design of these tests is based on three types of inferences to beliefs: induction, deduction, and evaluation. These in turn derive from four types of bases: the results of other inferences, observations, statements made by others, and assumptions. The authors point out that a general critical thinking test would also cover attitudes such as open-mindedness, caution, and valuing being well informed, but because of the difficulty and unfairness in testing for attitudes and values, the tests do not assess these attitudes. The aspects of critical thinking covered by these tests are induction, deduction, judgments of observation and credibility, identification of assumptions, and determination of meaning.

The emphasis given to each particular aspect of critical thinking in Level Z and Level X varies in accordance with the level of sophistication of the intended audience. For example, determination of meaning, which is a relatively sophisticated skill, is included in the Level Z test but not in Level X. Similarly, judgments of observation and credibility are difficult to assess in more sophisticated students (at least in a multiple-choice format), and thus this aspect of critical thinking is given more weight in Level X than in Level Z.

There has been no specific attempt to obtain national normative data for the two levels of the test, but the manual (Ennis, Millman, & Tomko, 1985) provides information on the results obtained from various groups. The manual provides the mean scores, standard deviations, and percentile information for 29 groups tested with the Level X test and 15 groups tested with the Level Z test, as well as a description of the population samples to facilitate comparisons. The population descriptions include size of the sample, approximate date of testing, age or grade level information, geographic location, other test scores, and other demographic information as available.

The only revision of the tests took place on Level X in 1982. Based on interview results with test administrators and subjects, the directions were revised to facilitate use of the test as far down as the fourth-grade level. This version of the test is labeled "Third Edition." No other versions of these specific tests have been developed, but the Ennis-Weir Critical Thinking Essay Test (1985) is another commercially available measure based on a similar definition of general critical thinking.

The 16-page Level X test and the 14-page Level Z are printed front and back on plain white 17″ × 12″ sheets, which are folded and stapled in the center. Section titles, certain descriptive terms (e.g., supports, goes against, neither) and specific directions (e.g., go on to next page) are printed in bold. All of the type is 1/8″ or larger. The example items in Level X (Level Z has no example items) are printed inside boxes.

The questions for Level X are based on a fictitious exploration of the planet Nicoma by a second group of explorers from Earth. Printed instructions continually caution examinees not to go back to change a given answer. The test is divided into four sections. In the first, students are presented with various facts and asked whether the facts support, go against, or do neither to a presented idea. Section II simultaneously presents students with sets of two reports from various exploration team members and asks them to decide which report is more believable or if both are equally believable. In section III students read a statement they are to assume is true and then must choose which of three additional statements would also have to be true. In the fourth and last section, students are given excerpts from a report and asked to identify from three statements which one represents an idea that the person making the report is taking for granted. The last paragraph of the test resolves all of the problems faced by the explorers.

The Level Z Test has seven sections, with the first divided into two parts. Section I presents respondents with sets of statements in which a conclusion is underlined and they must decide whether the conclusion follows necessarily from the statements, contradicts the statements, or if neither is true. The second section presents a set of statements containing faulty thinking and asks respondents to identify from three choices the best reason why the thinking is faulty. Sections III, IV, and V all refer to a hypothetical experiment about the effects of eating cabbage worms on ducklings. Data from the experiment appear in a table. Section III offers respondents two statements and asks them to decide whether the first or the second is more believable, or whether neither is more believable. In section IV, given a conclusion and then additional pieces of information, respondents are asked to decide if the additional information supports the conclusion, goes against it, or does neither. The format of section V presents an "if, then" statement and a set of possible predictions related to the statement; respondents are asked to pick the best prediction. In section VI, after respondents read a quoted description of something, they are then given three definitions of the "thing" and asked to pick the definition that best characterizes the original description. The seventh and final section offers respondents a statement and asks them to pick from a set of three the most probable unstated assumption inherent in that statement.

Although both levels of the test are essentially self-explanatory, the manual provides instructions that could be verbalized by a test administrator. More extensive use of verbal instructions is recommended and described in the manual for when Level X is to be used with elementary school students. It is also recommended (and printed in the Level X test booklet) that younger students stop after each section and wait for the instructions for the next section.

Though divided into sections, the tests are not divided into subtests. However, the authors suggest in the manual that the scores for the items associated with the different aspects of critical thinking (induction, deduction, judgments of observation and credibility, identification of assumptions, and, for Level Z, determination of meaning) might be combined into subtest scores for rough diagnostic purposes. The authors caution the user, however, that because of the small number of items associated with each aspect, the subtest scores should not be used to make individual comparisons. There have been four factor analytic studies of Level X (Follman, Hernandez, & Miller, 1969; Follman, Miller, & Hernandez, 1969; Landis & Michael, 1981; Michael, Devaney, & Michael, 1980) and one of Level Z (Follman, Brown, & Burg, 1970). Although these analyses were not specifically designed to ascertain the factor structure of the test as a means of supporting a possible subtest structure, the studies as a whole do seem to support the notion of the heterogeneity of the aspects of critical thinking.

The tests are designed to be answered on any standard machine-scorable answer sheet or students can mark their answers directly in the test booklet. If the examiner decides to use answer sheets, these must be purchased separately from the test booklets. The answer sheet available from Midwest Publications has name, ID, and section grids in addition to the portion for student answers. It provides circles for sex, test level, and grade (4–12) or college (freshman–grad) level as well as a section where respondents can write in the date, course, school, and instructor. In addition, marking instructions for the student with samples of correctly and incorrectly filled-in circles are given. The item half of the single-sided answer sheet has 80 items in four columns down one half of the long side of the 8½″ × 11″ answer sheet. Each item has three fill-in circles, with A, B, or C inside the circle.

**Practical Applications/Uses**

The Cornell Critical Thinking Tests are designed to measure general critical thinking ability by asking questions related to five (Level X) or six (Level Z) different aspects of this general ability. The resulting test scores would be useful in a variety of contexts. For example, these tests could be used to detect differences in critical thinking ability among groups, which would be particularly effective in determining the effect of certain factors or procedures on critical thinking ability, or to assess changes in critical thinking ability. They also could have value in a diagnostic sense if the user compared the results obtained by one group with a norm group. Furthermore, constructed subtest scores might suggest particular areas of deficiencies. One could easily expand this diagnostic function into use for program or curriculum evaluation. These tests also could serve as a basis for instruction. They provide several examples of critical thinking skills that students could discuss in cooperative groups or as a whole class. Instructors then could follow these exploration activities with explicit instruction in the skill or in the reasons for the correct answers and then apply the skill with more examples. Scores could also be used as a criterion or selection variable for participation in other activities. Finally, these tests might be useful in validity studies of other instruments.

It seems likely that with the recent upsurge of interest in thinking or problem-solving skills both levels of the Cornell tests might be used much more frequently. The most likely users would be educational researchers, researchers in cognition or thinking skills, school districts, and classroom teachers.

Both levels of the test could be used in a variety of situations. Certainly classroom testing is a possibility as well as smaller group or individual assessments. In addition the tests could be administered to very large groups at one time. The only real constraint seems to be the respondents' ability to read the items, and even this could be remedied by reading the items aloud (as is suggested for elementary school students). Naturally, as in all testing situations, it is important to keep stress levels as low as possible. The administrator should encourage respondents to think carefully but not overly long about responses before marking their answers and remind them not to go back and change any answers they have marked.

As noted previously, the two levels of this test address different levels of sophistication in critical thinking skills. Level X is constructed for subjects in Grades 5–14, with Level X Third Edition especially designed for elementary students

(Grades 4–6 or others with limited reading or test-taking skills). Approximately a third of the items on Level X focus on judgments of observation and credibility, skills that are easier to test with a multiple-choice format in less sophisticated audiences. Level X also uses as simple a language structure as possible. The authors designed Level Z for advanced secondary school students, college students, and other adults. This level focuses less on judgments of observation and credibility and more on the sophisticated skill of determination of meaning. Also, Level Z uses more complex language and syntactical structures and does not provide example items.

As the authors of the test note, the user should base his or her selection of the appropriate level on knowledge of the sample being tested. Although no adapted forms (e.g., braille) are available, one could easily adapt these tests for deaf, blind, or physically handicapped persons through the use of individual or small group administration. The examiner could provide any necessary special service, such as marking the answer sheet. As implied by the grade ranges, it would not be appropriate to administer these tests to very young children.

As mentioned previously, both forms of the test are essentially self-explanatory, and almost any type of setting could be appropriate. Although designed to be administered in a 50-minute period, both levels also could be given in sections if a 50-minute time block is not available. The manual provides approximate testing times for the various sections. Timed section administration would be necessary in the case of group administration to an unsophisticated audience where the examiner wanted to give oral instructions at the beginning of each section. These tests could be administered by anyone able to read the very brief verbal directions and clarify words within the individual items.

The scoring for both test levels is quite straightforward. The authors present a simple formula for obtaining one total score: the number of right answers minus one half the number of wrong answers. They feel this method is consistent with the test's instructions not to make wild guesses and with attempts to cultivate careful thinking habits. Despite this recommendation of a correction for guessing, the user also can simply add up the total number of correct responses. The manual provides information on norm groups using both types of score calculations. One caution: in Level X, the sample problems are imbedded directly in the numbering system and answer sheet, so the scorer must be careful not to include the answers to these items in the total score. As discussed previously, it could be possible to obtain subscores by adding up the number of correct responses (then optionally subtracting half the wrongs) for the items assigned to the various aspects of critical thinking. To help in interpreting the scores, the manual contains a detailed discussion of reasons for choosing each correct response.

Although Midwest Publications sells the scannable answer sheets, they do not provide scoring services, so machine scoring must be done elsewhere. Hand scoring the booklets or answer sheets or constructing a template also would be possible. No training in how to score is necessary, other than providing a key for the correct answers. If the total score approach is used, a scorer (or scoring program) simply adds up the number of correct responses. If the correction for guessing formula is applied, the scorer (or scoring program) must subtract one half the number of incorrect responses from the number of correct responses.

The actual interpretation of the scores is imbedded in the users' definition of critical thinking. On a simple level, a higher score on the test should mean "better" critical thinking skills. This does not necessarily mean, however, that a person who obtained a higher score would be a better problem-solver in real situations. Because of the multiple-choice format, no information on the actual thought process the respondent goes through to obtain the answer is available. Furthermore, although some norm group information is provided, absolute levels of expertise have not been determined. The detailed explanation of the keyed answers in the manuals greatly facilitates interpretation, but it probably also would be useful for the interpreter to have some background in critical thinking skills or the philosophy of argumentation or logic.

**Technical Aspects**

Both forms of the Cornell tests are technically sound. The manual provides detailed information from several studies that demonstrate the tests' reliability and validity. Two different procedures for estimating reliability have been used: Spearman-Brown (correlate odd-numbered items with even-numbered items and correct for test length) and Kuder-Richardson (internal consistency). As the authors point out, the Kuder-Richardson is not really a measure of how much the test can be depended on to give the same results repeatedly, and this is further complicated by the extent to which critical thinking skills are heterogeneous. Therefore, the estimates will be biased in the direction of underestimation. The Spearman-Brown is a somewhat less biased indicator but would still be low. Reliability data for Level X are provided from 14 different studies and range from .67 to .90. Reliability data for Level Z were obtained from 15 different studies and range from .50 to .77. Certainly these are respectable levels. An even stronger case for the acceptability of the reliability levels can be made because of the diversity of the populations used to obtain the data. Samples ranged from fourth-grade students to college freshmen for Level X and from high school students to college seniors for Level Z.

The manual also provides item analyses. Mean discrimination and difficulty scores appear for six samples for Level X and four samples for Level Z. Discrimination indices show the correlation of an item with the total score, and difficulty indices indicate the proportion of the sample getting an item correct. The range of mean difficulty ranges from .40 to .64 for Level X and from .55 to .61 for Level Z. These are right in the ideal range of about .50. The discrimination indices are low, ranging from a .15 to .36 for Level X and from .20 to .24 for Level Z. These low levels might be explained by the heterogeneity of critical thinking skills.

The manual gives the validity of the tests extensive discussion. Content validity, or the extent to which the tests cover the general skill of critical thinking, is discussed in several ways. The text stresses the careful development of the test items, including detailed discussions of each item's applicability to the aspect it was purported to measure and to the correctness of the keyed answers. The expertise of the test developers is established and the limitations of the test are carefully noted. The authors point out that critical thinking tests cannot use the "sample from a universe of test situations" approach or the table of specifications approach to support content validity. They offer instead arguments that address the significance of the coverage and the defensibility of the answers.

The construct validity of a test is a measure of the degree to which the test seems to measure what it is purported to measure or the extent to which the information about the test makes sense. The manual presents different evidence and arguments to support the construct validity of the Cornell tests. Insofar as this issue has been assessed, these tests do indeed appear to "make sense." Many studies have been conducted with a variety of samples that examine the correlation of the Cornell Critical Thinking Tests with other tests or characteristics, and the manual presents detailed information on this. The studies involved appear to be of good quality and therefore to provide credible information. Correlations of both levels of the test with other critical thinking tests cluster around .50, with the range for Level Z greater than for Level X. Although one might initially expect higher correlations among tests supposedly designed to measure the same thing, it is important to remember that these different tests have been designed with different conceptions of critical thinking and that this might account for the lower correlations. Correlations with scholastic aptitude tests range around .50 for both Level X and Level Z. Correlations with subject matter average about .50 for Level X and .35 for Level Z. In Level X, correlations with gender are about zero, and correlations with SES are low positive. These coefficients may indicate that Level Z is somewhat less biased than other paper-and-pencil tests that correlate more highly with SES. As would be expected, scores for both Level X and Z correlate with grade level.

The manual also reports on a variety of other studies conducted with these tests. In general, the results indicate that the Cornell tests operate in a manner that would be expected if they measure what they purport to measure.

## Critique

There is continuing debate over how to assess critical thinking skills. An excellent article by Norris (1989) discusses the issues involved in detail. Much of the argument centers around the definition of critical thinking and whether or not critical thinking is generalizable. The corresponding issue of whether or not cognitive skills are domain specific is discussed in another article, this by Perkins and Salomon (1989). The present reviewers believe that the middle view is the better one: that critical thinking has some general features and others that are subject specific. This point of view supports the possible development of a general test of critical thinking skills and subsequently the belief that the Cornell Critical Thinking Tests could actually accomplish what they claim.

Believing that a general test of critical thinking skills is possible, however, does not address the question of the adequacy of the Cornell tests in accomplishing that task. Many of the tests' limitations are pointed out in the manual as well as in Norris and Ennis's (1989) *Evaluating Critical Thinking*. These limitations include the division of critical skills into separate aspects, the selection of specific aspects for testing, the interrelationships among these aspects, the lack of attitude or dispositional assessment, and the multiple-choice format.

In the Cornell Critical Thinking Tests, the specific definition of critical thinking used implies seven aspects: induction; deduction; judgments of value, observation, and credibility; identification of assumptions; and determination of meaning. A different definition of critical thinking might imply different aspects, although Ennis is a leading researcher in this field and his definition of critical thinking is certainly a popular one. Not all of these aspects were selected for inclusion on these tests. Items on value judgment were not included in the interest of fairness (one value position could not be scored correct while another was scored incorrect), and items on meaning were only included in Level Z because of the sophistication necessary for dealing with this aspect. The aspects themselves are not independent. For example, arguments could be made that deduction is involved in induction or that deduction is a part of meaning or that observations are subject to credibility criteria. The authors of the Cornell Critical Thinking Tests acknowledge these problems and point out that subscores therefore are difficult to create or interpret. The manual's listing of test items associated with each aspect of critical thinking shows overlap, with several items related to more than one aspect.

The authors point out that a disposition toward critical thinking is a key issue; however, they concede that testing for this is extremely difficult in almost any format, particularly multiple choice. The multiple-choice format has many inherent difficulties for assessing any skill, but especially for assessing the complex construct of critical thinking. Multiple-choice tests are good because they are easy to score, respondents can complete many different items in a short time, and the tests can be designed to be quite reliable. On the other hand, such tests do not allow for diverse or creative answers to items, nor do they indicate why students choose the responses they do. In assessing critical thinking, these two limitations are especially important. They raise the issue of how valid a multiple-choice test of critical thinking skills could be.

It seems to these reviewers that the Cornell Critical Thinking Tests indeed do what they say they will, but users must be cognizant of the limited scope of the claim the authors make. These tests do seem able to provide information on whether students know and can use (in a limited sense) certain principles associated with critical thinking skills. They do not, however, provide information on students' dispositions to think critically, their value judgments, or their ability to combine the various principles. If users are interested in a comprehensive assessment of critical thinking skills in a particular population, they should use a variety of assessment instruments and techniques, in which the Cornell Critical Thinking Tests would be an important part.

## References

Ennis, R.H. (1962). A concept of critical thinking. *Harvard Educational Review, 32*(1), 81–111.

Ennis, R.H., Millman, J., & Tomko, T.N. (1985). *Cornell Critical Thinking Tests Level X & Level Z manual.* Pacific Grove, CA: Midwest Publications Critical Thinking Press.

Ennis, R.H., & Paulus, D. (1965). *Critical thinking readiness in grades 1–12. Phase I: Deductive logic in adolescence* (Cooperative Research Project No. 1680). Ithaca, NY: The Cornell Critical Thinking Project. (ERIC Document Reproduction Service No. ED 003 818)

Ennis, R.H., & Weir, E. (1985). *Ennis-Weir Critical Thinking Test.* Pacific Grove, CA: Midwest Publications Critical Thinking Press.

Follman, J., Brown, L., & Burg, E. (1970). Factor analysis of critical thinking, logical reasoning, and English subtests. *The Journal of Experimental Education, 38*(4), 11–16.

Follman, J., Hernandez, D., & Miller, W. (1969). Canonical correlation of scholastic aptitude and critical thinking. *Psychology, 6*(3), 3–5.

Follman, J., Miller, W., & Hernandez, D. (1969). Factor analysis of achievement, scholastic aptitude and critical thinking subtests. *The Journal of Experimental Education, 38*(1), 49–53.

Landis, R.E., & Michael, W.B. (1981). The factorial validity of three measures of critical thinking within the context of Guilford's structure-of-intellect model for a sample of ninth-grade students. *Educational and Psychological Measurement, 41*(4), 1147–1166.

Michael, J.J., Devaney, R.L., & Michael, W.B. (1980). The factorial validity of the Cornell Critical Thinking Test for a junior high school sample. *Educational and Psychological Measurement, 40*, 437–450.

McPeck, J.E. (1981). *Critical thinking and education*. New York: St. Martin's Press.

Norris, S.P. (1989). Can we test validly for critical thinking? *Educational Researcher, 18*(9), 21–26.

Norris, S.P., & Ennis, R.H. (1989). *Evaluating critical thinking*. Pacific Grove, CA: Midwest Publications Critical Thinking Press.

Perkins, D.N., & Salomon, G. (1989). Are cognitive skills context bound? *Educational Researcher, 18*(1), 16–25.

Smith, B.O. (1953). The improvement of critical thinking. *Progressive Education, 30*(5), 129–134.

**Leaetta M. Hough, Ph.D.**
*Executive Vice President, Personnel Decisions Research Institutes, Inc., Minneapolis, Minnesota.*

---

# CORRECTIONAL OFFICERS' INTEREST BLANK

*Harrison Gough and F. Lewis Aumack. Palo Alto, California: Consulting Psychologists Press, Inc.*

## Introduction

The Correctional Officers' Interest Blank (COIB) is a nonthreatening 40-item questionnaire designed to assess dependability, reliability, and responsibility. High scores on the COIB are associated with internalization of values, acceptance of societal norms, and ability to perform well in settings where rules must be respected. High-scoring individuals have strong internal values and can be counted on to behave in a dependable and rule-observing way. They are likely to be upright, honest, have a firm sense of right and wrong, and adhere strictly to principles of right and wrong.

High scorers also tend to be taciturn, diffident to shy when interviewed, better at doing things than talking about them, more interested in activities such as hunting and fishing than reading books or keeping up on current events, conventional in their role behaviors and role expectations (particularly in regard to gender), and not academically motivated. In an interview, they do not tend to make a favorable impression, do not have showy credentials, and, because of their conservative views and conventional behavior, may irritate interviewers. These are the kind of people the usual correctional officer selection programs tend, inappropriately, to overlook (personal communication, H.G. Gough, May 1990).

Dr. Harrison Gough, senior author of the COIB, is one of the most respected personality theorists and researchers in the country. A recipient of the Society for Personality Assessment's prestigious Bruno Klopfer Distinguished Contribution Award, Gough has been associated with the Institute of Personality Assessment and Research (IPAR) and the Department of Psychology at the University of California at Berkeley for approximately 40 years. He was director of IPAR and Professor Emeritus of U.C. Berkeley. His distinguished career includes over 200 publications in the area of personality assessment, and he is the author of the California Psychological Inventory.

Dr. F. Lewis Aumack received his Ph.D. from the University of California at Berkeley in 1953. For several years he was chief of psychological services at a variety of state and federal psychiatric hospitals, where he developed both diagnostic and selection tools to improve services to patients. More recently, Aumack has been involved in research and evaluation of the effectiveness of health care delivery programs.

Richard McGee, director of the California Department of Corrections, contacted Harrison Gough in the early 1950s to ask if IPAR would develop a selection tool to predict correctional officer job performance. Donald MacKinnon, head of IPAR at the time, and Gough decided IPAR would pursue the research. Funds came from a "young scholar's" grant that Ford Foundation had awarded to Gough (personal communication, H.G. Gough, May 1990). Lewis Aumack, a graduate student at the time, was involved in the very early stages of the work, contributing to the initial development and administration of the forms. By 1953, however, Aumack was no longer involved in the project. By that time, Victor B. Cline had joined the research, and he helped administer the inventory in three California institutions.

A battery of two questionnaires was prepared. One questionnaire, entitled "Correctional Officers' Preferences Inventory" (COPI), consisted of 100 forced-choice triads. Each triad consisted of three activities, beliefs, or practices, one of which respondents would choose as the best liked and one as least liked. An example (which appears as a sample in the directions in the test booklet) follows:

| *Like Most* | *Like Least* | |
|---|---|---|
| ____ | ____ | Travel by car. |
| ____ | ____ | Travel by train. |
| ____ | ____ | Travel by air. |

The triads were written to be relatively fake proof and to measure characteristics hypothesized as related to correctional officer effectiveness. These hypotheses were gleaned from consultation with experts in the field of corrections, correctional officer materials, review of correctional officer personnel issues, published papers, and Gough's own personal experience as a correctional officer at the state reformatory in St. Cloud, Minnesota (Gough, 1982; personal communication, H.G. Gough, May 1990). The second questionnaire consisted of true-false personality items, most of which came from the California Psychological Inventory. This section eventually became Part II of the inventory; the triads eventually became Part I.

These two questionnaires, along with some other materials, were administered in the spring of 1952 to 375 correctional officers in five California correctional institutions: San Quentin, Soledad, Chino, Terminal Island, and Folsom. Later that year supervisors provided confidential performance appraisal ratings on seven categories of performance for many of the officers. The performance appraisal ratings were factor analyzed. A large general factor emerged on which all seven categories of performance had significant loadings, and it was used as the overall criterion. The usefulness of each item was evaluated according to its relationship to the overall criterion. First, officers were classified into three groups based on their score on the overall criterion: high-rated officers, medium-rated officers, and low-rated officers. Then item analyses were conducted, and those items that differentiated higher rated from lower rated officers were retained. "Like most" responses were analyzed separately from "like least."

A shortened booklet was prepared that consisted of 75 triads (Part I) and 75 true-false items (Part II), and the result was entitled Correctional Officers' Interest

Inventory (COII). This measure was administered to 218 officers in 1953 at three California institutions. Supervisory ratings on job performance also were obtained, and usable predictor and criterion information was available for 194 men. Factor analysis of the supervisory ratings again revealed a general factor. From then on, Gough had supervisors evaluate correctional officers on an overall criterion.

Again, the usefulness of each item was evaluated according to its relationship to the overall criterion. As before, officers were classified into three groups—high-rated, medium-rated, and low-rated—based on their score on the overall criterion. Those items that differentiated higher rated from lower rated officers were retained. Also, as before, "like most" and "like least" choices were analyzed separately, resulting in retention of 24 triad items and 26 true-false items. These 50 items were printed in a test booklet entitled the "Correctional Officers' Interest Blank" (COIB).

The correlation between scores on the 50-item COIB and overall performance for the 194 officers in the 1953 sample for whom complete data were available was .44. The correlation between scores on the 50-item COIB and overall performance for the 285 officers in the 1952 sample for whom complete data were available was .37 (Gough, 1982).

The 50-item COIB was administered to several additional groups. In 1954, it was administered at three California institutions to 105 male applicants, of which 75 were hired. Later, supervisors rated the job performance of the officers. COIB scores correlated .47 with the performance appraisal ratings. The 50-item COIB also was administered to 694 correctional officers in four federal prisons in 1955. COIB scores correlated .35 with supervisory ratings of overall job performance (Gough, 1982).

The COIB remained the same for about 10 years. Then, in 1965 the 50-item COIB was administered to 309 correctional officers in Florida. COIB scores correlated .28 with supervisory ratings of overall performance. Item analyses revealed that 10 items (6 triads and 4 true-false items) did not adequately differentiate higher from lower rated officers. As a result, Gough dropped these 10 items, and the 40-item COIB has remained the same since 1965.

**Practical Applications/Uses**

Correctional officers need to be dependable and rule abiding. The COIB measures these characteristics and thus contributes important, often unique, information about applicants' qualifications and the probability of their success in correctional officer work. The COIB has demonstrated useful validity, often the highest validity in a battery of tests, for predicting performance in correctional work. However, as Gough (1982) points out, the COIB scores should be used in combination with a variety of other information to make decisions about applicants.

The 40-item COIB consists of 18 triads and 22 true-false items. Hand scoring is very easy. Scores on the triads can range from 0 to 24. The scoring key was empirically developed and constructed separately for "like most" and "like least" responses; thus, there is no consistent scoring pattern for the items. The only consistency is that the options are keyed either 0 or +1. Similarly, the 22 true-false items, also empirically keyed, are either 0 or +1; scores thus range from 0 to 22. Total COIB scores can range from 0 to 46. The scoring key is stringently controlled.

It is available only to qualified persons representing state, federal, or other bona fide law enforcement or judicial agencies. Gough, however, has made the key available to professionals conducting research with the COIB in appropriate work settings.

The manual, available to qualified persons, provides good information about the psychological meaning of test scores, normative score information, the development of the inventory, faking research, construct- and criterion-related validity of the COIB, and test administration instructions. The COIB is untimed and takes approximately 10 minutes to complete. It can be administered in either individual or group settings. The reading level of the instructions included in the test booklet is just below the sixth grade; the reading level of the items is fourth grade.

**Technical Aspects**

The 40-item COIB was used in a small study ($N$ = 37) in an Eastern state correctional institution in the early 1970s. Scores on this version correlated .31 with supervisory ratings of job performance (Gough, 1982). Two additional studies have analyzed the relationship of the 40-item COIB to correctional officer job performance. Peterson and Houston (1980) conducted a predictive validity study involving over 300 correctional officers in the Ohio Department of Rehabilitation and Correction. Both COIB and performance appraisal data were available for 252 correctional officers. The COIB was one of several predictor measures administered, and it correlated .22 with an overall supervisory rating of job performance, the highest of any of the measures. Sevy (1988) used the 40-item COIB in a concurrent validity study of 210 California correctional officers. The correlation between COIB scores and overall job performance was .13, the lowest value obtained in any study using the COIB.

Gough recomputed the COIB scores for the 1952, 1953, 1954, and 1955 samples using the 40-item COIB. He recalculated the validities of the COIB as well. The validity coefficients dropped on the average .04 points. The average validity coefficient (weighted by sample size) for the 40-item COIB for all the samples that are not subject to shrinkage is .27. This validity coefficient, however, is an underestimate of the true relationship between the COIB and job performance because of unreliability in supervisory ratings (Schmidt & Hunter, 1977). If one assumes interrater reliability of .75 (both Gough [1982] and Peterson & Houston [1980] report interrater reliabilities in the mid-70s), the corrected validity of the COIB is .31. Table 1 provides the validity information, sample sizes, means, and standard deviations for both the 50-item COIB (when possible) and for all samples of the 40-item version.

Relatively little information is available about possible differences in COIB mean scores for protected classes such as minorities and women. Peterson and Houston (1980) did not separately report means and standard deviations by protected class for the COIB. They included the COIB as one element in a composite and reported such information only at the composite level. Though the composite was shown to be nondiscriminatory for blacks and women, specific information about the COIB was not reported. Sevy (1988), however, analyzed the COIB scores separately by race and gender. He found no statistically significant differences in slopes or

**Table 1**

**Criterion-Related Validities of COIB with Overall Job Performance**

| *Sample* | | | *50-item COIB* | *40-item COIB* | | | |
|---|---|---|---|---|---|---|---|
| *Location* | *Year* | *Gender* | *r* | *r* | *N* | *Mean* | *SD* |
| California | 1952 | male | .37[a] | .38 | 285 | 30.38 | 4.26[a] |
| California | 1953 | male | .44[a] | .41 | 194 | 29.65 | 4.29[a] |
| California | 1954 | male | .47[a,b,c] | .37 | 75 | 31.45 | 3.39[a,b,c] |
| Federal | 1955 | male | .35[a,b] | .31 | 694 | 31.02 | 3.89[a,b] |
| Florida | 1965 | male | .28[a,b] | .42 | 309 | 31.04 | 4.35[a] |
| Eastern State | early 1970s | male | — | .31 | 37 | 30.59 | 4.14[a,b] |
| Ohio | 1980 | mixed | — | .22 | 252 | 29.48[d] | 4.30[a,b,c,d] |
| California | 1988 | mixed | — | .13 | 210 | 29.95[e] | 3.95[a,b,e] |

[a]Not corrected for restriction in range or criterion unreliability.
[b]Not subject to shrinkage (i.e., sample not used to develop key).
[c]Predictive validity study.
[d]Based on entire sample of 394, of which approximately 40 were female.
[e]Based on entire sample of 325, of which 46 were female.

intercepts when comparing blacks to whites and males to females. He concluded that according to the Cleary (1968) model, the COIB is a fair predictor of correctional officer job performance.

Test-retest reliability information is available only for the 50-item COIB. Seventy-five men who had completed the 50-item COIB as applicants did so again approximately 6 months later. Scores at Time 1 correlated .69 with scores at Time 2. An internal consistency estimate for the 50-item COIB also was computed for the entire sample of 105 applicants. The odd-even reliability was .71 after applying the Spearman-Brown correction (Gough, 1982). Odd-even reliability also was calculated for the 40-item COIB using the scores for 75 men who completed the COIB in 1954. The coefficient derived was .70 after applying the Spearman-Brown correction (Gough, 1982).

The COIB appears to be relatively unfakeable, even under directions to distort responses to appear as an ideal correctional officer candidate. In one study of 20 police officers, the mean score in the faking condition (i.e., describe oneself as an ideal correctional officer candidate) was actually lower than in the honest condition. The mean score in the honest condition was 28.45 (standard deviation of 2.58), whereas the mean score in the faking condition was 27.0 with a standard deviation of 4.84 (Gough, 1982). The effect size of the difference between the mean sores was −.39; that is, the mean score in the faking condition was approximately one third of a standard deviation lower than in the honest condition.

In another study reported by Gough (1982), 163 college students involved in an introductory psychology class took the COIB under two conditions: (a) describe oneself honestly and (b) describe oneself as an ideal correctional officer candidate. The results differed for men and women. For men ($n$ = 79), the effect size of the difference between the mean score in the honest and faking conditions was +.08. Though the mean in the faking condition was higher than in the honest condition, it was less than a tenth of a standard deviation higher. For women ($n$ = 84), the effect size of the difference between mean scores in the honest and faking conditions was +.43. The mean in the faking condition was almost half a standard deviation higher than in the honest condition. The mean score in the faking condition was 24.99, still significantly lower (approximately 1.33 standard deviations lower) than the mean scores reported in Table 1 for correctional officers.

## Critique

The Correctional Officers' Interest Blank appears to be an excellent predictor, perhaps the best single predictor, of correctional officer job performance. Additional research about possible gender and race differences in COIB scores, however, would be valuable.

The reading level of the COIB seems appropriate for correctional officer applicants. Moreover, the items appear to be nonthreatening and relatively resistant to intentional distortion.

The COIB is an excellent inventory and should be included as a part of the information gathered in the selection process for correctional officers.

**References**

Cleary, T.A. (1968). Test bias: Prediction of grades of Negro and white students in integrated colleges. *Journal of Educational Measurement, 5,* 115–124.

Gough, H.G. (1957). *Manual for the California Psychological Inventory.* Palo Alto, CA: Consulting Psychologists Press.

Gough, H.G. (1982). *Manual for the Correctional Officers' Interest Blank.* Palo Alto, CA: Consulting Psychologists Press.

Peterson, N.G., & Houston, J.S. (1980). *The prediction of correctional officer job performance: Construct validation in an employment setting.* Minneapolis, MN: Personnel Decisions Research Institute.

Schmidt, F.L., & Hunter, J.E. (1977). Development of a general solution to the problem of validity generalization. *Journal of Applied Psychology, 62,* 529–540.

Sevy, B.A. (1988). The concurrent validity of the Correctional Officers' Interest Blank. *Public Personnel Management, 17,* 135–144.

**Terry G. Roberson, Ed.D.**
*Associate Professor of Secondary Education, University of Montevallo, Montevallo, Alabama.*

**Leland K. Doebler, Ph.D.**
*Associate Professor of Counseling and Educational Psychology, University of Montevallo, Montevallo, Alabama.*

# THE CULTURAL LITERACY TEST

*The Cultural Literacy Foundation. Chicago, Illinois: The Riverside Publishing Company.*

### Introduction

The Cultural Literacy Test (CLT) is an instrument designed to assess high school students' general content knowledge in three major areas: the humanities, the sciences, and the social sciences. While some refer to this knowledge as "world knowledge" or "functional literacy," E.D. Hirsch, the originator of this notion and the author of *Cultural Literacy: What Every American Needs to Know,* refers to it as "cultural literacy." In his book, Hirsch (1987, p. 2) defines the construct as "the network of information that all competent readers possess." According to Hirsch, this broad knowledge represents stored background information that, when combined with the message of written text, enables readers to comprehend unstated, inferred meanings. To Hirsch, the role of cultural literacy is equally important to the speaking and writing processes, both of which require the context and/or content of shared cultural information in order to communicate successfully.

The CLT was developed by The Cultural Literacy Foundation with the support of the National Endowment for the Humanities. The Foundation, a non-profit group committed to the importance of cultural literacy in education, is governed by a six-member board of trustees, which at present includes Ernest Boyer, president of the Carnegie Foundation for the Advancement of Teaching; James Cooper, dean of the University of Virginia's Curry School of Education; Bernard Gifford, former dean of the University of California–Berkeley School of Education; Harold Kolb, director of the Institute for Liberal Arts, University of Virginia; Robert Payton, former president of the Exxon Educational Foundation; and E.D. Hirsch, Jr., who serves as president of the Foundation.

For those school officials who agree that cultural literacy is an essential aspect of the curriculum and perhaps that American students "lack sufficient literate information to become fluent readers" (Cultural Literacy Foundation, 1989, p. 3), the CLT is designed to assist in the assessment of student achievement of a designated, predefined body of literate knowledge. In addition, test results should help to facilitate curriculum revision aimed at enhancing students' storage and use of shared literate knowledge. The authors stress the use of CLT results as impetus for the close examination of instructional programs and priorities, not for the labeling of culturally literate and illiterate students.

The 1989 publication of the CLT culminates nearly 3 years of test development activity, beginning with the establishment of an initial and comprehensive list of items representative of cultural literacy. The list was begun by Hirsch and two of his colleagues at the University of Virginia, Joseph Kett (professor of history) and James Trefil (professor of physics). After consulting a variety of sources in the compilation of humanities, social sciences, and sciences items, and after critiquing each others' lists, the items were submitted to more than 100 experts in the various academic fields, including some consultants outside of academe (Hirsch, 1987). The resulting list was included as an appendix to *Cultural Literacy: What Every American Needs to Know* (Hirsch, 1987), and later expanded to include definitions and/or explanations in *The Dictionary of Cultural Literacy* (Hirsch, Kett, & Trefil, 1988).

Guiding the item selection process throughout was a set of three criteria: (a) whether or not the item would require explanation if published for general consumption; (b) whether or not the item was confined to a specialized field or exclusive group; and (c) whether or not the item had a recognition life of less than 15 years. An affirmative judgment on any one of these three criteria resulted in exclusion of the item from the original list.

CLT items, then, were based on these lists. Items initially were field-tested with a sample of approximately 600 high school students in California and later with a sample of high school students in both California and Virginia, with the assistance of the state education agencies in both states. Two parallel forms of the CLT were developed on the basis of these field-test results. Further field testing included concurrent validity studies with 1,035 11th- and 12th-graders in 13 school districts in Virginia and construct validity studies with 857 first-year medical students in seven medical schools. The Association for Supervision and Curriculum Development (1987, p. 3) described these field tests as important for testing Hirsch's overall rationale as well as the test items themselves.

The Riverside Publishing Company conducted national standardization efforts on the basis of a stratified random sample of 5,283 11th- and 12th-grade students from public and parochial schools across the country. Subjects for the study were systematically selected on the basis of three variables: geographic region, school district enrollment size, and community socioeconomic status. Forms A and B of the CLT were administered randomly during this study. The ethnic distribution of the normative sample was fairly representative of the general population. No revisions of the final standardized version of the CLT have appeared, but because of the somewhat tentative nature of and agreement on the content of cultural literacy, consumers are invited to provide input into the test's continuing definition and clarification.

The CLT, Forms A and B, consists of a 16-page machine-scorable test booklet, the last page of which requires the completion of demographic information about the student, teacher, school, and district. Also on that page appear test directions and a sample test item. The test itself consists of 115 five-option multiple-choice items.

## Practical Applications/Uses

The purpose of the CLT is to enable educators to improve instruction. This purpose is accomplished by providing the teacher with information regarding the range of knowledge of his or her students. This information allows the teacher to identify possible gaps in the students' knowledge base and provide experiences to fill in those gaps. Again, the authors stress that the purpose is not to label students as culturally literate or illiterate, knowledgeable or unknowledgeable, but simply to improve instruction.

The CLT was designed for use with high school juniors and seniors. The test was standardized at this level and appropriate norms are provided. These norms make it possible for a teacher to compare the performance of his or her class with that of a national sample of students. In so doing, the teacher could identify gaps in the knowledge base of his or her students and attempt to remediate those gaps. It would seem also that some benefit could be gained by administering the test to students earlier in their schooling. The test might, for example, be administered to freshmen. Although comparison to the norms would not be appropriate in this case, such an administration would allow a formative assessment of students' strengths and weaknesses and would allow more time for the remediation of the weaknesses.

The CLT normally would be administered by a classroom teacher. The test examiner's responsibilities include (a) maintaining test security, (b) becoming familiar with the test manual, (c) explaining the test's purpose to students, (d) observing test protocol with verbatim instructions, and (e) monitoring students during the entire testing period. If large groups are to be tested, the manual recommends one proctor for each 30–40 students. Standard procedures for the administration of group tests are applicable to the CLT. Specific directions for administering are provided, and the authors clearly explain why these directions must be followed word-for-word. The administrator is also cautioned to cover all maps or other materials in the classroom that might provide the student with assistance in responding to the questions. The testing time is 50 minutes, although the examiner should allow an additional 15–20 minutes to complete the identifying information on the back of the test booklet.

The test booklets may be machine scored by the Riverside Scoring Service. A raw score for each of the topic areas is provided, and in addition, national percentile ranks and local percentile ranks are reported for the Composite score and for each of the major subareas (Humanities, Social Sciences, Sciences). The manual clearly explains interpretation of the percentile ranks. Interpretation of the raw scores in the topic areas is accomplished by comparing the scores to the national average correct for each area. This information appears in Table 7 of the manual. This comparison allows the teacher to identify student strengths and weaknesses and plan instruction accordingly.

## Technical Aspects

In terms of validity, the authors note that the CLT must be judged with regard to the purpose for which it is to be used. They provide adequate information to enable the reader to assess both the content validity and the concurrent validity of the test.

The three primary content areas—humanities, social sciences, and sciences—are in turn broken into 23 topic areas. Although the latter are referred to as "test objectives" by the authors (Cultural Literacy Foundation, 1989, p. 6), they are, in actuality, topic areas and not objectives. The 23 topics fall within the content areas as follows:

A. Humanities
   1. The Bible
   2. Mythology and folklore
   3. Proverbs
   4. Idioms
   5. World literature, philosophy, and religion
   6. Literature in English
   7. World geography
   8. Fine arts

B. Social Sciences
   1. World history to 1550
   2. World history since 1550
   3. American history to 1865
   4. American history since 1865
   5. World politics
   6. American politics
   7. World geography
   8. American geography
   9. Anthropology, psychology, and sociology
   10. Business and economics

C. Sciences
   1. Physical sciences and mathematics
   2. Earth sciences
   3. Life sciences
   4. Medicine and health
   5. Technology

These 23 topics correspond to the sections of *The Dictionary of Cultural Literacy* (Hirsch et al., 1988). Each form of the test has five questions on each of these 23 topics for a total of 115 items. Although the authors acknowledge that five questions represent a small sample from each of the 23 domains, they state that if a student correctly answers most of the questions in a given area, one can assume that he or she is probably well informed in that area. They emphasize, however, that the validity of the score hinges on the fact that the student has not been coached.

Concurrent validity data are presented based on studies done in 13 Virginia school districts prior to the publication of the CLT. Correlations of the CLT with the Scholastic Aptitude Test (SAT), the Preliminary Scholastic Aptitude Test (PSAT), the SRA Achievement Series, and the SRA Educational Ability Series are reported. These correlations are consistently strong and positive, averaging about .62. As one would expect, correlations between the CLT and the verbal components of these tests are consistently higher than those with the quantitative elements. The correlations range from a high of .82 between the CLT Form A and the SAT Verbal score to a low of .41 between the CLT Form B and the SAT Quantitative score. The authors note that although the correlations are consistently high, they are low enough to indicate that the CLT is measuring a trait that is different from those measured by the other tests. The number of students included in each of the reported validity studies varies, with the minimum number being 263.

An additional study conducted with 857 first-year medical students in seven medical colleges supports the construct validity of the test. Scores of these medical students were considerably higher than those of the high school students. Mean scores of the medical students exceeded those of the high school students by 50% or more in each of the three content areas. This suggests that increased education and the resulting broadening of one's horizons leads to increased cultural literacy.

Reliability coefficients were computed using data from the entire national standardization sample. The internal consistency of the test is quite good, with KR-20 coefficients ranging from .82 in the Science area of Form A to .90 on the Social Sciences area of Form B. The KR-20 coefficients for the Composite are .95 for Form A and .94 for Form B. The standard error of measurement is 4.41 for Form A and 4.59 for Form B. No alternate-forms coefficients are reported, nor is any measure of the CLT's temporal stability.

## Critique

The CLT materials present ample evidence of the validity of both the instrument and the construct. In addition, the Kuder-Richardson reliability coefficients indicate good internal consistency. However, as stated earlier, no measures of temporal stability or equivalence are presented. Presentation of evidence of these types of reliability would greatly enhance the confidence of the user in this instrument.

Overall, the CLT seems to be a well-constructed instrument with good potential for use in American schools. The strength of the test lies in looking globally at the performance of students in order to assess curriculum in terms of its literate content. A potential danger of the test is that scores will be used to label students as culturally literate or illiterate in spite of the authors' cautions against this.

An early concern about this test stemmed from the fact that it was available only in nonreusable machine-scored booklets. The cost of $135.00 per package of 35 at the time of this writing and an additional $1.50 per pupil for the scoring service probably inhibited the use of this instrument by many schools. The publication, in 1990, of a hand-scorable edition with consumable answer sheets was a significant step in making the test accessible to more schools and thus widening the usage of the CLT.

## References

Association for Supervision and Curriculum Development. (1987). On cultural literacy: What every ASCD member needs to know. *ASCD Update, 29*(6), 1, 3.

Hirsch, E.D., Jr. (1987). *Cultural literacy: What every American needs to know.* Boston: Houghton Mifflin.
Hirsch, E.D., Jr., Kett, J.F., & Trefil, J. (1988). *The dictionary of cultural literacy.* Boston: Houghton Mifflin.
The Cultural Literacy Foundation. (1989). *Cultural Literacy Test: Manual for administration and interpretation.* Chicago: Riverside.

**Julian J. Fabry, Ph.D.**
*Counseling Psychologist, Immanuel Medical Center Rehabilitation Center, Omaha, Nebraska.*

**Robert A. Bischoff, Ph.D.**
*Clinical Psychologist, Meyer Rehabilitation Institute, University of Nebraska Medical Center, Omaha, Nebraska.*

# THE CUSTODY QUOTIENT

*Robert Gordon and Leon A. Peek. Dallas, Texas: The Wilmington Press.*

### Introduction

The Custody Quotient (CQ), currently a psychological research instrument, was developed and designed to yield a single standardized score based on ratings obtained from a variety of sources about the parenting skills of persons being assessed. The results are intended to assist courts, juries, and attorneys, as well as impartial third parties, in making custody decisions in a child's best interest. The information utilized in making ratings can come from a family history, interviews, observations, or psychological evaluations. The Custody Quotient derives from the weighted scores of the following scales: (a) Emotional Needs, (b) Physical Needs, (c) No Dangers, (d) Good Parenting, (e) Parent Assistance, (f) Planning, (g) Home Stability, (h) Prior Caring, (i) Acts and Omissions, (j) Values, (k) Joint Custody, and (l) Frankness. The Custody Quotient is the summation of weighted ratings on 10 of the aforementioned scales.

Robert Gordon, J.D., Ph.D., past chair of the Texas Board of Examiners of Psychologists and past president of the Texas Psychological Association, is a practicing psychologist and attorney. Leon A. Peek, Ph.D., is a licensed psychologist in Texas who has taught psychometrics research courses. Both psychologists have been involved in policy issues related to state legislation and in ethical issues regarding psychological practice. Both men are parents.

The authors began working on the development of the Custody Quotient in May 1987. They had been dissatisfied with the custody assessment procedures at that time. A brainstorming session helped to identify the factors relevant to obtaining information for making custody decisions. Nine scales were composed from the psychological, psychiatric, and legal literature. Pilot studies were conducted with children ranging in age from 3 to 16 to determine their definition of a good parent. These subjects came from the Dallas/Ft. Worth areas. Subsequent items developed were reviewed by parents and judges as well as lawyers, and revisions then were made according to the results of these reviews.

From the practices that lead a child toward independent living and fulfilling their biological, psychological, and social potential, good parenting for child custody was established on a continuum ranging from having no access to joint custody. A normative study was then conducted. Further research on the Custody Quotient suggested that several categories were more important in making custody decisions. Fulfilling the emotional needs of the child, ensuring that no dangers existed by living with a particular parent, and the stability of the parent's life-style were identified as paramount for a child's well-being.

The current Custody Quotient (Research Edition) consists of an $8\frac{1}{2}'' \times 11''$ loose-leaf binder manual and an eight-page protocol. The manual includes the authors' development rationale and research foundations, standardization data, ethical considerations, administration and scoring directions, tables, and remediation information. The eight-page protocol for recording responses and ratings on the various scales also contains selected relevant information about when the assessment took place as well as identifying demographic information about the parents and children. A summary of the ratings is contained in a graph on the first page, which allows for recording the scores obtained during the assessment. The remaining pages present each of the Conceptual Quotient factors and their respective items, along with the basis on which the rating was determined (i.e., standard interview, observation, etc.). The format provides ample room for notes under each factor. Information regarding the child's preference for a particular living arrangement, if known, is recorded along with any possible changes of circumstances.

Item ratings within each of the 10 factors are made on the basis of whether the parent is highly competent (2), adequate (1), or weak (0). The scores for each of the items on a particular factor are then added together. The user converts the sum score to a stanine via the table of preliminary score conversion norms. The stanines next are multiplied by weights, resulting in weighted ratings. A weighted average stanine is calculated and then converted to a Custody Quotient from Table 2 in the manual. The quotient itself is based on a mean of 100 and a standard deviation of 15.

A Joint Cooperation scale is available to help determine a Joint Custody Quotient, which is derived in the same manner as the Custody Quotient. Further, the authors have included a Frankness scale to discover if the parent under study has distorted his or her responses during the interview phase of the evaluation.

**Practical Applications/Uses**

The purpose of the Custody Quotient is to assist in making custody evaluations and changes in decrees, and to increase the possibility of coming to a fair resolution in custody disputes. However, the authors are quite clear that this is at present a research instrument and is not intended to take the place of the expert clinician's judgment. This measure seems to be constructed for social workers, psychologists, family therapists, counselors, psychiatrists, and physicians, applied primarily in outpatient settings, such as a clinician's office, but appropriate for use in hospitals or free-standing clinics and mental health centers.

The parents of the children under study are the most likely candidates for evaluation. However, stepparents, aunts, uncles, and grandparents also could be evaluated if they were being considered as part of the custody question. Social and economic status may have an effect on particular scales within the CQ, and some of these issues have been addressed by the authors in the manual.

The examiner can obtain the clinical interview in any setting with ample space and no distractions. This component usually is administered to each parent individually. In addition to an understanding of interview procedures, the examiner should have some knowledge of child development and some appreciation of the strengths, weaknesses, and limitations of rating scales. The authors suggest following the guidelines set forth by the American Psychological Association regarding the qualifications of properly trained persons and other recognized personnel. They further suggest in the manual that the examiner possess knowledge of psychometrics and an appreciation of the fair treatment of individuals. They note that if specific training is needed in addition to studying the CQ manual, they can provide it.

In addition to the interview, the evaluator can utilize conversations with the child's teachers, relatives, neighbors, and peers as well as more formal documentation by child-protective service workers, social workers, and therapists to compile rating information. Police reports, financial statements, and attorney's reports also can be used in rating a particular parent's behavior as it relates to the Conceptual Quotient.

Administration of the clinical interview appears to take approximately 2 hours. The authors suggest videotaping the interview so that it might be impartially rated by one or several professionals. The criteria used to evaluate the clinical interview and rate the individual on each of the items leave some latitude for the examiner's judgment. The total time required to arrive at the Custody Quotient after reviewing all the necessary information will vary according to the amount of information and the intensity of each case. Currently the assessment is hand scored, although the entire rating system could be computerized.

Gordon and Peek (1989) indicate that their "guiding principle" in constructing the Conceptual Quotient was so that it could be interpreted in the best interest of the child. They contend that the CQ best describes a parent at a particular point in time, and they recognize that changes can occur that would definitely affect the score. They even go so far as to include a recommendation or remediation section in the manual to accommodate for weaknesses that a parent may exhibit as a result of their evaluation. Specifically, the authors have noted from case records and clinical observations that usually no parent receives custody of a child with a Custody Quotient of less than 100. They have also discovered that family law attorneys tend to avoid taking parents into a trial with a CQ less than 115, attempting instead to resolve the custody issues before trial in such cases.

**Technical Aspects**

The CQ authors maintain that they have systematically identified the particular attributes, attitudes, and behaviors of effective parents, thereby establishing content validity for the CQ scales. They have subjected their conceptualizations to scrutinization by judges, attorneys, parents, and even children in an effort to operationalize good parenting. They recognize, however, that the Dallas/Ft. Worth area norming group is not indicative of the general U.S. population. They suggest that users may employ local norms to supplement their own endeavors to obtain a more representive general sample of the U.S. population.

Gordon and Peek used a principle components analysis of their data to establish construct validity, and three factors emerged: a general good parenting factor, a parent's life-style factor, and a joint custody factor. No criterion-related validity has been established because the authors do not believe that winning a custody suit is an acceptable criterion on which to validate their instrument.

Internal consistency reliability coefficients for the items to the total scale scores ranged from .30 for the Planning subscale to .94 for Acts and Omissions. However, most of the Cronbach alpha coefficients appear substantial. The authors did not find significant gender or rater bias in a study they report in the manual. What seemed to be interrater reliability for the two authors suggested that their degree of agreement ranged from 50% for the Good Parent factor to 100% on No Dangers.

## Critique

The Custody Quotient offers evaluators a potentially useful assessment procedure that is based on a somewhat systematic review of relevant literature and the subsequent development of criteria and ratings. The CQ fills a gap in the measurement area that addresses the issue of adequate parenting skills, which are necessary to maintain and promote the well-being of children. The authors have made a concerted effort to objectify what previously has been an area of controversy, wherein decisions were based only on opinion. The Custody Quotient helps the evaluator organize information obtained from a variety of sources so that it can be systematically reviewed, thereby aiding the formulation of custody decisions driven by the best interest of the child. Essentially, after such an evaluation, and given the abilities and skills of both parents, decision-makers can select the most functional environment in which the child could grow and develop, free from the constraints of the conflicts that brought about the dissolution of the marriage relationship. What still remains a key issue, however, is the child's choice of which parent he or she wants to live with. Depending on the child's age, a number of methods for assessing such preferences have been postulated (Skafte, 1985). The child's preference, interacting with the parent's skills, must form the foundation of what lies in the child's best interest.

The full impact of this assessment remains to be realized. However, the potential user must bear in mind that no external or criterion-related validity has been established. Ideally, individuals with good and poor parenting skills could be identified by public school officials or caseworkers in social agencies so that a study could be undertaken to determine if the Custody Quotient can differentiate between these two groups. Further research is needed to establish concurrent and construct validity as well as interrater reliability on the various CQ scales. Eventually it would be best to computerize the CQ ratings in order to minimize scoring errors.

## References

Gordon, R., & Peek, L. (1989). *The Custody Quotient: Research manual.* Dallas, TX: Wilmington Institute.

Skafte, D. (1985). *Child custody evaluations.* Beverly Hills, CA: Sage.

**Susan M. Raza, Ph.D.**
*President, The People Planner, Tulsa, Oklahoma.*

# DIABETES OPINION SURVEY AND PARENT DIABETES OPINION SURVEY

*Suzanne Bennett Johnson, Janet Silverstein, Walter Cunningham, and Randy Carter. Gainesville, Florida: University of Florida, Departments of Psychiatry, Pediatrics, Psychology, and Statistics (Division of Biostatistics).*

## Introduction

The Diabetes Opinion Survey (DOS) and its parent version, the Parent Diabetes Opinion Survey (PDOS), are self-administered, paper-and-pencil, Likert-type assessments of respondents' attitudes toward diabetes and its treatment. The DOS, designed for young people age 6 to 19, measures attitudes toward diabetes along five dimensions, and the PDOS assesses parental attitudes along eight dimensions. Both instruments contain a lie scale and measure attitudes on a 5-point scale ranging from strongly agree to strongly disagree. Lower scores indicate a stronger endorsement of the measured attitudes and, theoretically, a less favorable adjustment to diabetes.

At present the instruments are in research rather than commercial form, and there are no published normative data available. Both surveys are available for research purposes, provided the researcher agrees to share obtained data with Suzanne Bennett Johnson, the senior author. Copies of the surveys and the scoring key for the current revision can be requested by contacting her.

Dr. Johnson received her Ph.D. in clinical psychology from the State University of New York at Stony Brook in 1974. She then joined the University of Florida and is currently a professor in the department of psychiatry, with joint appointments in the departments of pediatrics and clinical health psychology. For 5 years Dr. Johnson was the director of an inpatient program for young diabetics who were experiencing adjustment problems. She is a well-known researcher in the field of diabetes, and her research has been funded by the National Institute of Health since 1980.

The DOS and the PDOS were developed by Dr. Johnson and her colleagues to measure the attitudes of young people with diabetes and their parents toward diabetes and its treatment. The fourth revision of each instrument is currently in use, and Dr. Johnson states that the instruments will be revised continually to reflect the findings from a growing database of responses.

In the early 1980s, funded by a grant from the National Institute of Child Health and Human Development, Dr. Johnson and her colleagues began a rational and statistical process that has resulted in conceptually and mathematically sound instruments. Based on a thorough review of the clinical literature and extensive interviews of clinicians and patients regarding patient and parent attitudes toward diabetes, 10 concepts were selected for inclusion in the DOS and 11 were selected for the PDOS. The initial DOS consisted of 152 items; the parent version had 130 items. Both instruments asked respondents to react to items on a 5-point Likert-type scale ranging from strongly agree to strongly disagree. The initial instruments were administered to 157 young people and 262 parents, then revised by dropping poor items and adding new ones.

The second versions were administered to a new sample of 155 young people and 275 parents, and revisions were based on those data. The third version of the DOS measured patient attitudes along seven dimensions and consisted of 78 items. The third version of the PDOS measured parental attitudes along nine dimensions and consisted of 68 items.

The fourth and current version of the scales was developed through the technique of factor analysis. Using a sample of 281 young people, factor analysis of the DOS yielded five factors. A similar analysis of the PDOS using a sample of 228 mothers yielded eight factors, which closely matched the originally conceived attitude dimensions. Including the lie scales, the current DOS and PDOS consist of 73 and 105 items, respectively.

The DOS is a completely self-administered survey typed on both sides of three pages of standard letter-size paper. The PDOS is somewhat longer and is presented on five pages. For both surveys the respondent is asked to indicate the degree of agreement or disagreement with each item by circling a number from 1 to 5 representing the range of attitudes: strongly agree, mildly agree, neutral, mildly disagree, and strongly disagree. The responses are made directly on the test.

The directions for self-administration are very clear, and the response format is convenient and easy to use. The examiner need only pass out and collect the surveys, provided the respondent can read the items. Although the DOS was designed for young people age 6 to 19, the reading level is approximately Grade 6 as estimated using the Fog Index (Gunning, 1968). This suggests that only excellent readers under the age of 11 could respond to the survey on their own. The author does not state whether the surveys in the validation studies were read to younger subjects. The PDOS also has an approximately sixth-grade readability.

The DOS assesses patient attitudes along the following dimensions or scales:

1. *Stigma* (perception that the person is treated differently because of diabetes);
2. *Rule Orientation* (rigid adherence to rules about diabetes and its treatment);
3. *Sick Role* (playing the role of a victim);
4. *Family Interruption* (perception that the disease is a source of family conflict or inconvenience); and
5. *Divine Intervention* (perception that the causes and outcomes of diabetes are controlled by supernatural forces).

The PDOS assesses parental attitudes along the following eight dimensions:

1. *Manipulativeness* (the child uses diabetes for personal gain);
2. *Rule Orientation* (rigid parental adherence to rules about diabetes and its treatment);
3. *Stigma* (perception that the child and family are treated differently because of diabetes);

4. *Divine Intervention* (perception that the causes and outcomes of diabetes are controlled by supernatural forces);

5. *Attitudes Toward Medical Staff* (negative parental ratings of the health-care professionals who treat the child);

6. *Reactions: Observations/Detections* (parental sensitivity toward fluctuations in the child's blood glucose concentration as a critical determinant of the child's behavior or well-being);

7. *Sweet Consumption* (parental concern about the child's intake of concentrated sweets); and

8. *Family Interruption* (perception that the disease is a source of family conflict or inconvenience).

**Practical Applications/Uses**

The DOS and PDOS are intended to assess attitudes about diabetes and its treatment. To the extent that attitudes are indicative of adjustment and predictive of behavior and outcomes, one might expect that "good" attitudes are positively associated with "good" adjustment, adherence to the medical regime, and metabolic control.

These instruments should be very useful to the researcher exploring the interrelationships between attitudes towards diabetes, emotional adjustment, adherence, and metabolic control, and could be of some use to the clinician or counselor working independently or as a member of a team with young diabetics and their families. Additionally, the instruments could be used by researchers interested in attitudes toward chronic diseases or in the general relationship between attitudes and behavior. The surveys are in use by at least two research teams: Dr. Johnson's group at the University of Florida and a group from the department of pediatrics at Ohio State University. These teams have found the DOS and PDOS useful for better understanding the interrelationships between attitude, adherence, and metabolic control, and one study used the instruments to explore the relationship between parental attitudes and children's disease-specific behavior problems. Unfortunately, no published normative data have appeared; therefore, the practicing clinician or counselor could only use the surveys (with permission of the author) to discuss clients' relative standing on the various dimensions measured. Such discussions could, however, open up important new avenues to explore in working with clients to improve adjustment to diabetes.

There is no manual that describes administration procedures, although the instructions on the front of the surveys and the format suggests a standard administration in which the respondent independently reads the directions and completes the survey, returning it to a designated place or individual.

**Technical Aspects**

The DOS and the PDOS are well-constructed instruments, and the technical information, an unpublished manuscript (Johnson, 1985), is presented in a logical and readable fashion. The five DOS and eight PDOS dimensions (scales) appear to be reliable measures of a person's attitudes about diabetes and its treatment.

Four of the dimensions of the DOS are similar to four dimensions of the PDOS. A study investigating these eight dimensions generally indicates acceptable convergent and discriminate validity. To date the number of research studies is quite modest. The results, however, suggest that the instruments are valid for research and counseling purposes.

The dimensions of the current DOS and PDOS have resulted from principal component factor analyses rotated to simple structure using the varimax procedure. The selected factor solutions reflect both goodness of fit and conceptual clarity, and thus present a good combination of statistical procedures and rational analyses. Items were retained for each factor if the item/factor absolute correlation was >.40 and the item had an absolute correlation of <.30 with any other factor. These methods ensure that (a) an appropriate number of factors are retained to explain the variation in the responses to the test items, and (b) the resultant factors are independent.

The reliability of a factor may be given by its consistency, the degree to which the items are well explained by the factors and are all measuring the same concept. The reliabilities of the final dimensions for both instruments were acceptably high. The reliabilities were estimated by coefficient alpha; for the DOS, coefficient alpha ranged from .69 to .77, and for the PDOS it ranged from .70 to .84. Further, for the PDOS the authors provide the results of a study using fathers' responses that replicated the reliability estimates calculated from the original validation sample (mothers' responses). This offers support of the validity of those scales.

The validity of the dimensions measured by the surveys was investigated in three ways. First, for the PDOS only, the data from the mothers' responses and from the fathers' responses were compared. The pattern and the magnitude of the intercorrelations between the factors and the calculated coefficient alpha were very similar, suggesting validity. Providing additional evidence of validity, correlations between the mothers' and fathers' factors were all statistically significant, with six of the eight scales showing moderate to high agreement ($r > .50$). Second, correlational studies investigated the relationships between the four dimensions on the DOS and PDOS that measure similar attitudes and share the same dimension name: Stigma, Rule Orientation, Divine Intervention, and Family Interruption. The correlations were statistically significant. This offers support for the validity of the instruments because they are measuring similar attitudes in different respondents using different items. Third, using the four shared dimensions and the multitrait-multimethod matrix approach, the authors provide evidence of convergent and discriminant validity. The highest correlations emerged between the same trait measured by different methods, and the lowest were between different traits measured by different methods.

The fact that the Family Interruption dimension is the least pure of all the dimensions is clearly spelled out in the technical report. The author has made it clear that the instruments are not in their final form; they are being revised regularly to further strengthen their psychometric soundness. The DOS lie scale is taken from the Children's Manifest Anxiety Scale (Castaneda, McCandless, & Palermo, 1956), and that on the PDOS was taken from the Personality Inventory for Children (Wirt, Lachar, Klinedinst, & Seat, 1977). Correlations between the lie scales and the respective attitude dimensions are reported as similar to those obtained using the original instruments from which the lie scales were taken. This suggests that the lie scales are operating in the expected manner.

## Critique

The DOS and the PDOS are well-constructed surveys that reliably measure meaningful dimensions summarizing the attitudes of young people with diabetes (DOS) and their parents (PDOS) towards diabetes and its treatment. However, the lack of an administration manual with a scoring key and normative data and the non-commercial format of the surveys limit their usefulness to researchers willing to share their research data with the senior author. The surveys provide potentially very useful information to the interested researcher and to the clinician or counselor engaged in working with young people with diabetes and their families. They can add to our body of knowledge regarding attitudes toward chronic diseases in general and to our understanding of the general relationship between attitudes and behavior. The surveys have a potential clinical and counseling use for professionals helping diabetics and their families make a more positive adjustment to diabetes. At this stage of development, the results of DOS and PDOS administration may suggest avenues that can be fruitfully explored in counseling. If the authors continue to build their database and are able to provide meaningful normative data, these surveys may eventually be useful in early identification of "at risk" individuals and parents.

## References

This list includes text citations and suggested additional reading.

Castaneda, A., McCandless, B.R., & Palermo, D.S. (1956). The children's form of the Manifest Anxiety Scale. *Child Development, 27*(3), 317–326.

Gunning, R. (1968). *The techniques of clear writing*. New York: McGraw-Hill.

Johnson, S.B., Silverstein, J., Cunningham, W., & Carter, R. (1985). *The development and current status of the Diabetes Opinion Survey (DOS) and the Parent Diabetes Opinion Survey (PDOS).* Unpublished manuscript, University of Florida, Gainesville.

Wirt, R., Lachar, D., Klinedinst, J., & Seat, P. (1977). *Personality Inventory for Children*. Los Angeles: Western Psychological Services.

Wysocki, T., Green, L., & Huxtable, K. (1989). Blood glucose monitoring by diabetic adolescents: Compliance and metabolic control. *Health Psychology, 8*(3), 267–284.

Wysocki, T., Huxtable, K., Linscheid, T.R., & Wayne, W. (1989). Adjustment to diabetes mellitus in preschoolers and their mothers. *Diabetes Care, 12*(8), 524–529.

**Lorraine Diston, Psy.D.**
*Graduate Student in Psychology, Nova University, Ft. Lauderdale, Florida.*

**Jan Faust, Ph.D.**
*Assistant Professor of Psychology, Nova University, Ft. Lauderdale, Florida.*

**Grant Aram Killian, Ph.D.**
*Associate Professor of Psychology, Nova University, Ft. Lauderdale, Florida.*

---

# DIAGNOSTIC SCREENING BATTERIES: ADOLESCENT, ADULT, AND CHILD

*James J. Smith and Joseph M. Eisenberg. Towson, Maryland: Reason House.*

### Introduction

The Diagnostic Screening Batteries (Smith & Eisenberg, 1986/1989) are computer-assisted questionnaires designed to help clinicians collect patient evaluation information consistently and then determine appropriate diagnoses of mental or emotional disorders. The overall system comprises three sets of age-appropriate questionnaires: Adolescent (ages 13 to 17), Adult (ages 18 and older), and Child (ages 2 to 17). Although these packages are sold individually to users working with the discrete target populations, each shares much in common with the other two (manuals, developmental history, format, reports, etc.); thus, this review will primarily address the system as a whole, directing specific information or remarks to the individual batteries when appropriate.

The batteries screen a range of clinical areas, identifying diagnostic criteria for the disorders listed in the *Diagnostic and Statistical Manual of Mental Disorders* (DSM-III; DSM-IIIR). The original software was developed in 1986 and drew on the diagnostic criteria of the DSM-III (American Psychiatric Association, 1980); later, when the program was revised in 1989, the developers used the newer diagnostic criteria of the DSM-IIIR (American Psychiatric Association, 1987).

The batteries have two separate and different questionnaires, one that is administered to the patient or parent and the other for the clinician to complete. Both questionnaires can be administered by one of two methods, either on the computer or as a paper-and-pencil procedure. If the latter method is used, the responses must be entered subsequently into the computer for scoring. The computer program then compares the reported symptoms, derived from the patient's answers to the questionnaires, to either the DSM-III or DSM-IIIR taxonomy, depending on whether one uses the 1986 or 1989 version of the battery. The system then generates a list of all the diagnostic possibilities that match the client-generated symptoms. It is the clinician's responsibility to decide which diagnosis is the most accurate, given the rest of the information he or she has gathered from other sources.

Educated at the University of Alberta in Canada, Joseph Eisenberg is currently in private practice in Maryland. James Smith was educated at the University of Maryland and also maintains a private practice. As practitioners themselves, the authors report that their goals in creating these three packages were to help clinicians collect and organize assessment data as well as formulate accurate diagnoses.

Computer-assisted programs designed to aid in the determination of DSM diagnoses have been available for more than 20 years. The two most widely used programs, and those that scientists have researched extensively, are the DIAGNO series (DIAGNO, DIAGNO II, DIAGNO III) developed by Spitzer and Endicott (1968) and the National Institute of Mental Health–Diagnostic Interview Schedule (NIMH-DIS) constructed by Robins, Helzer, Croughan, and Ratcliff (1981). Because computers were originally expensive and cumbersome, early such diagnostic programs were not widely used. However, the debut of the affordable personal computer, teamed with the variety of currently available software, has caused the potential for computer-assisted diagnostic programs to be examined with more interest.

The Diagnostic Screening Batteries, as well as the DIAGNO series and NIMH-DIS, use a logical decision tree model of program analysis. Older programs utilized statistical methods. Briefly, the logical decision tree method is similar to the differential diagnostic approach. A series of questions is presented, and to each the respondent replies negatively or affirmatively. This response then rules out one or more diagnoses and determines which question is presented next. The logical decision tree model operates basically as a flowchart and is an a priori method, identifying diagnoses from a descriptive rather than an etiological perspective. It has been found to be the most accurate computer method for predicting clinical diagnoses (Fleiss, Spitzer, Cohen, & Endicott, 1972).

By comparison, the statistical model employs either Bayesian classification or discriminant function analyses to identify clinical diagnoses. A developmental sample is drawn from a large number of previously diagnosed subjects. With these data in place, the computer matches new patient information to the developmental sample to determine an appropriate diagnosis. For more information about the statistical model and the logical decision tree approach, the reader is directed to Erdman, Greist, Klein, and Jefferson (1987); Robins et al. (1981); Fleiss et al. (1972); and Spitzer and Endicott (1968).

The concept of using computer programs for diagnostic evaluation began when scientists realized the advantages of the computer's reliability, accessibility, and efficiency. Researchers have identified specific computer functions as having significant value to the clinician. Barron, Daniels, and O'Toole (1987) state that the accuracy of the computer gives it perfect memory for both questions and answers. Additionally, the computer's methodical consistency with presenting questions to the patient is an important feature of this approach to diagnosing disorders (Mathisen, Evans, & Meyers, 1987; Barron et al., 1987). Others praise the computer's inexhaustible thoroughness of covering a topic (Erdman, Klein, & Greist, 1985; Mathisen et al., 1987). Erdman et al. (1985) also cite the dependability and availability of computer time as an advantage. Greist, Klein, Erdman, and Jefferson (1983), Mathisen et al. (1987), and Erdman et al. (1985) all consider the decreased cost of using a computer as compared to human hours as another important feature of the computer approach.

The computer-assisted Diagnostic Screening Batteries differ from other diagnostic programs in that the components do not identify one primary diagnosis. Rather, each will generate a list of diagnostic possibilities for as many disorders as meet the criteria of identified symptoms. The software was specifically designed to be overinclusive; therefore, the clinician has the responsibility of eliminating all diagnoses that do not apply and making the final decision.

This software is available for use with either Apple/Apple-compatible computers (with at least 64K memory and an 80-column card in slot 3) or IBM/IBM-compatible computers (with at least 128K memory and 2 floppy drives or a hard drive) (Eisenberg & Smith, 1986, 1989). Separate instructions for both systems are provided in the 1989 manual (used with the DSM-IIIR version), whereas separate manuals were produced for Apple and IBM systems for the older DSM-III version (1986). Although each of the three Diagnostic Screening Batteries is sold as a separate package, the format is essentially the same and therefore separate manuals are not needed; the instructions for running each Diagnostic Screening Battery program do not vary from the other two.

The program for each Diagnostic Screening Battery generates a Main Menu and a Utilities Menu. The Main Menu provides the following on-screen choices:

1. Run patient questionnaire
2. Run clinician questionnaire
3. Run diagnostic determination/retrieve data
4. Run patient "quick entry"
5. Run utilities
6. End program; exit to DOS

The Utilities Menu also offers several choices:

1. Print out for patient questionnaire
2. Print out for clinician questionnaire
3. Print out answer sheet for patient
4. Print out answer sheet for clinician
5. Erase old patient data
6. Create new patient file
7. Return to main menu

Depending on the package one is using, the patient questionnaire is designed to be answered by the patient or a parent/guardian. If it is more appropriate for a parent or guardian to respond, the Child Diagnostic Screening Battery becomes the preferred form as it is written in the third person. (The 1989 version has added a line for respondent's name, which is not provided for the 1986 version.) The clinical questions cover a wide range of areas, such as current and chronic medical concerns, work/school-related activities, friendships, self-attitudes and perceptions, family relationships, thought processes, mood and affect, psychosocial stressors, sexual activity/experience/attitudes, and drug use. The frequency and duration of these problems may also be noted on some questions.

The authors report that items on the Adolescent Diagnostic Screening Battery are written at about the seventh-grade reading level. However, some of the same questions also appear on the Adult Diagnostic Screening Battery, which is reportedly written at the 10th-grade level. Prout and Chizik (1988) have found that because many teenage patients also present with other problems (e.g., academic difficulties sometimes due to reading problems), assessment instruments for this group should be written at a fifth-grade level for valid readability and completion. They warn that an individual test item might be invalidated if it contains even a single word at a higher level (Prout & Chizik, 1988).

Both the patient questionnaire and the clinician questionnaire use a yes/no and multiple-choice format. Some of the questions allow multiple answers, some include "does not apply"/"none of the above," and some offer a multiple-choice option of "other," which permits the respondent to type an original answer using up to 55 characters. The DSM-III and DSM-IIIR versions of the questionnaires are identical. The Adolescent patient questionnaire has 50 primary questions and 14 subquestions; the Adult, 37 primary questions and 14 subquestions; the Child, 44 primary questions and 13 subquestions. Subquestions are additional items presented to the respondent only if primary questions need to be clarified with additional information (e.g., frequency, duration, and severity of a symptom). On the printouts these questionnaires are titled "Adolescent Questionnaire," "Adult Questionnaire," and "Child Questionnaire" rather than "Patient Questionnaire" as designated on the program menus.

The "Clinician Questionnaire," as it is identified on the Main Menu, is entitled "The Clinician's Response Form" on the printouts. Written for professionals familiar with psychological terminology, its questions cover ground pertaining to intellectual functioning, organicity, dissociative disorders, and factitious disorders. This component also provides minimal information relating to psychosis, substance abuse, and personality features. The clinician questionnaire for the Adolescent Diagnostic Screening Battery (both DSM versions) contains 13 primary questions and 15 subquestions; for the Adult battery (both versions), 13 primary questions and 12 subquestions; and for the Child battery (both versions), 9 primary questions and 6 subquestions. All serve to provide information needed for DSM Axes III, IV, and V. The two DSM versions in each battery are identical save for the wording of questions pertaining to Axes IV and V, reflecting only the differences in the reporting on these axes. The clinician questionnaire alone is not sufficient to supply a diagnosis; it presents merely an adjunct process for recording supplementary patient data.

The diagnostic determinations for each of the three batteries can be printed in two formats, the "Standard Report" and the "Short Form," both of which report information for all five DSM axes. The printout of the "Standard Report" begins with one page of patient responses and one page of clinician responses; both lists are printed by question number and letter answer. Next follows a list of critical questions and answers printed in sentence form, obtained from information gathered on both the patient and clinician questionnaires. The user next sees a page of diagnostic possibilities, which lists all five DSM axes (including all possible Axis I and II diagnoses that apply). If no information exists for any of the axes, the printout states this fact.

The "Short Form" differs from the "Standard Report" only by omitting the list of critical questions and answers in sentence form. Both options also add a page of "Refined Diagnoses," which is a list of fewer diagnostic possibilities (less under Axes I and II) and reportedly only those that relate more closely to specific pathology. The revised (1989) program printouts also include diagnostic code numbers next to each of the listed diagnoses.

If a printer is not available, or should one wish to review the results quickly, the data can be viewed on screen at the terminal. However, when output is directed thus to the screen, it runs continuously with no way to pause or stop the information flow.

Currently there is no way to hand score the questionnaires as no templates or answer keys are available. Also, this program has not been adapted for any special populations. Respondents who are blind, manually handicapped, not literate in English, or who cannot read at the required grade level would need help in answering the questionnaires.

**Practical Applications/Uses**

The Diagnostic Screening Batteries have been designed for use by psychiatrists, psychologists, and licensed clinical social workers in any clinical setting where DSM-III or DSM-IIIR diagnoses are applied. This type of program can be utilized not only in private practice, community mental health centers, and hospitals but also in university settings. With respect to the latter, this software can serve as a learning aid and/or in research, as with other computer-assisted diagnostic programs (Barron et al., 1987; Greist et al., 1987; Greist et al., 1983; Mathisen et al., 1987; Swartz & Pfohl, 1981; Spitzer, Endicott, Cohen, & Fleiss, 1974; Spitzer & Endicott, 1968).

The questionnaires are administered on an individual basis, and no real computer knowledge is necessary for respondents to answer the questions on-line. Also, neither an examiner nor a clinician is needed for the administration of the client questionnaire. However, the authors suggest that an assistant be present to instruct the respondent in using the keyboard and cursor key and to address potential problems. Studies conducted with other programs have identified patient populations that experience difficulties using computer-assisted self-report questionnaires, including those with special needs as noted above and those with acute psychotic disorders (Klein, Greist, & VanCura, 1975). Patients with mania, organic dysfunctions, and antisocial personality disorder may also show problems with this type of task (Greist et al., 1983). Even though these studies included adult populations, similar problems conceivably may arise with respect to particular adolescent populations. Hence, this should be addressed in future research.

The program begins as individual questions and possible answers appear on the screen sequentially. The respondent may choose as many answers as apply. Also, throughout the program, instructions appear on the screen that explain how to select an answer, change it, forward the program to the next question, or return to a previous question. The time estimated to complete the questionnaire is about 15 minutes; however, with all the subquestions a respondent may need to answer, a more realistic estimate might be 20–30 minutes, especially if the respondent experiences reading problems.

The authors estimate 10 minutes to complete the clinician questionnaire, which seems accurate once the clinician has become familiar with this form. Although the patient need not be present when the examiner completes the clinician questionnaire, patient background information is required. This component may be obtained from school records, medical/psychiatric records, psychological test data, and family history and background, as well as from personal contact with the patient.

During on-line questionnaire administration, the program utilizes a forced-choice response format. The system will not advance to the next question unless the respondent enters an answer from among those provided. With a few exceptions, there is generally no opportunity for the respondent or clinician to make comments or elaborate on answers. He or she may do so only with the questions that offer "other" as a choice. Conversely, the paper-and-pencil format does allow for variation, as the respondent can produce a new answer, modify an existing one, or omit a question altogether. When the examiner chooses the paper-and-pencil format, he or she must then enter the responses onto the data disk before the program can generate any diagnoses.

A better description of the manuals that accompany both the 1986 and 1989 versions of the program would be a "user's guide." The *Standards for Educational and Psychological Testing* (American Educational Research Association, American Psychological Association, & National Council on Measurement in Education, 1985, p. 94) define a "user's guide" as often a subset of the test manual, containing no information on validity or reliability (which would apply to the manuals Eisenberg and Smith provide). The manuals never clearly explain the program process as a logical decision tree method, disappointing because the gap raises endless questions about the program's efficacy (rather than simply eliminating any possible concern on the part of the authors that the manuals appear too technical).

The manuals are divided into two major parts: "Introduction" and "How to Use the IBM (Apple) System." The introductory section in both manuals contains a few simple statements about the authors' purpose, goals, and philosophy. Basically Smith and Eisenberg believe that their program offers a systematic means of providing direction and consistency within an initial evaluation as the questions represent a broad range of concerns for the clinician and respondent to consider. The manuals' sections on how to use the system contain instructions that are useful and understandable, especially to the novice. However, certain typographical errors in the 1986 IBM-version manual make for an unsuccessful installation of the program. The revised edition corrects some, but not all, of these mistakes.

## Technical Aspects

Smith and Eisenberg fail to report any technical information on this battery, either in the manuals or elsewhere. Apparently no formal reliability or validity studies have been conducted, and no normative data are provided. In a personal communication with Eisenberg (April 14, 1989), he did describe research that was attempted with the Adult Diagnostic Screening Battery at Walter Reed Hospital. The study entailed entering data on previously diagnosed adult inpatients into the program, and the results showed the patients' actual diagnoses listed among the possibilities that this software program identified on its printout. However, these findings were never published, and when Eisenberg inquired at the hospital, the data could not be found.

Eisenberg, as others (Erdman et al., 1987; Erdman et al., 1985; Fleiss et al., 1972), contends that computer-generated diagnostic programs have perfect reliability, in that the same answers given to the same questions will always produce the same diagnoses. There is a problem with this contention, though. Program errors can occur that could affect the scoring and/or the results. Software developers need to experiment with their own programs and report their findings, thus assuring themselves and their users of accurate program consistency. Even then, program consistency can be assumed only if a program is not tampered with or changed. Erdman et al. (1985) are concerned additionally that reliability studies conducted on computer-based instruments should not focus exclusively on the program. Rather, they suggest that studies of computer interviewing be geared also to include other variables, such as nonverbal language and clinician acceptance.

As described previously, this program has two administration alternatives, online or paper-and-pencil formats. These two different forms need to be examined closely and carefully, as the paper-and-pencil self-report provides more room for variability with responding than the computer questionnaire. Therefore, as recommended by the American Psychological Association (AERA, APA, & NCME, 1985), Anastasi (1982), and Ferguson (1981), separate studies need to be conducted and reported to assure parallelism. Moreland (1985, p. 222) warns, "computer-linked factors may change the nature of a task so dramatically that one cannot say the computer-administered and the conventional versions of a test are measuring the same construct"; further, statistical properties "cannot be generalized" from one form to the other. Erdman et al. (1985) compared computer and paper-and-pencil questionnaires, finding the two methods comparable. However, their study used only an adult population and limited the subjects to substance abusers. Furthermore, Erdman et al. advocate the small-scale interview, using questions pertaining to a single topic (e.g., alcohol, drugs, sex). They report the programs are more likely to be successful because, at this time, the computer's strength lies in the narrower task.

Validity studies using the DIAGNO and NIMH-DIS programs primarily have compared clinician diagnoses with program diagnoses. Greist, Klein, and Erdman (1976) have found on-line psychiatric diagnoses by computer as good as those patients obtain from admitting clinicians in a hospital setting. However, Spitzer et al. (1974) report that expert clinicians show low agreement among each other, and note that as long as there is a variance among clinicians, any software program designed by an expert will naturally reflect the same variance. These studies have identified inherent problems with computer-assisted diagnostic programs; however, further research with each Diagnostic Screening Battery needs to be conducted to identify specific areas of concern.

Eisenberg (personal communication, April 14, 1989) acknowledges this program has face validity. Although this may be helpful to define particular behaviors, empirical measures of this program's validity are never formally addressed; consequently, its validity cannot be presumed at this time.

**Critique**

This system of evaluation software is devoid of all psychometric data, which is the most important factor to consider when deciding on its purchase. When comparing the batteries to the *Standards for Educational and Psychological Testing* (AERA, APA, & NCME, 1985), these reviewers found many instances of violations and incomplete compliance.

By using a logical decision tree based on the DSM-III or DSM-IIIR, which assumes normative population, validity, and reliability criteria sufficient for computer use, Smith and Eisenberg apparently concluded they did not need to report statistical information. The decision tree process, as it functions within this system, must be assessed independently. Swartz and Pfohl (1981, p. 359) identify some problems with the DSM-III decision trees from the learning aid program used in their study, stating, "[they] are not inherently sufficient as a diagnostic schema and might lead to a dead end if blindly followed by a computerized system." This may explain why some errors occurred within the list of diagnostic possibilities when these reviewers examined each Diagnostic Screening Battery (Diston, 1989; discussion to follow).

The decision tree, as programmed for the Diagnostic Screening Batteries, was designed specifically to remain overinclusive. The rationale, as stated by the battery authors, was to assure that data not be minimized during the diagnostic decision-making process. Smith and Eisenberg define the purpose of their program as intending to assure diagnostic thoroughness and account for information that might otherwise be overlooked, not to fine-tune a diagnostic impression. This philosophy is echoed by both Erdman et al. (1987) and Greist et al. (1983), who indicate that especially at this stage of the development of diagnostic software, users must evaluate *all* criteria for a given diagnosis and thereby decide on its appropriateness.

The Adolescent, Adult, and Child Diagnostic Screening Batteries were examined by the present reviewers (Diston, 1989) to determine how well or poorly the software was able to match symptoms to diagnoses. To test, trial runs using hypothetical patients were performed on both DSM versions of each battery, and numerous errors emerged in the choices of diagnostic possibilities. Descriptions of these trials follow, grouped within the three individual batteries.

*Adolescent Diagnostic Screening Battery.* On one trial, a 13-year-old male responded to this questionnaire with suicidal ideation and behaviors as well as fears about the future. Neither version of the program chose "Depression" as an Axis I diagnostic possibility, nor any diagnosis reflecting suicidal symptoms. In addition, both versions' printouts included Axis II diagnoses of "Histrionic Personality Disorder," "Dependent Personality Disorder," and "Passive-Aggressive Personality Disorder."

In another example, a 15-year-old female selected auditory and visual hallucinations as symptoms. The printouts for both versions listed "R/O Schizophrenia" on Axis I, but both also printed a "Refined Diagnoses" list that eliminated the diagnosis of "R/O Schizophrenia." Therefore, using this function, the clinician is not alerted to this patient's psychotic symptoms.

On a third trial, both program versions assigned a 13-year-old female patient a possible Axis I diagnosis of "Identity Disorder" along with an Axis II diagnosis of "Borderline Personality Disorder." According to the DSM-III this should not happen, because the criteria for "Borderline Personality Disorder" clearly state that this diagnosis may be given if the patient is under 18 years old but does not meet the criteria for "Identity Disorder" (American Psychiatric Association, 1980, p. 323). However, the DSM-IIIR criteria for assigning these diagnoses have changed enough to allow for both these diagnostic possibilities (American Psychiatric Association, 1987, p. 336).

With a fourth trial, a 13-year-old male patient denied the use of alcohol and cannabis. However, when completing the clinician questionnaire for this patient, Diston (1989) chose to add both alcohol and cannabis abuse in an attempt to discover what diagnostic changes would occur. When utilizing both programs, the printout of "Diagnostic Possibilities" stated "No condition on Axis I" but went on to list 12 diagnostic choices. Further, "Alcohol Personality Disorder" and "Cannabis Personality Disorder" were listed among the Axis I diagnostic choices. Obviously, neither the DSM-III nor the DSM-IIIR has either of these diagnoses in its text; in addition, personality disorders are listed on Axis II, not on Axis I. Further, personality disorders generally are not assigned to patients under the age of 18. Perhaps, in a revision of the software, it might be better to list these symptoms as personality "traits" or "characteristics."

*Adult Diagnostic Screening Battery.* On one trial, a 32-year-old male had selected suicidal attempts as a symptom. With both DSM versions, the list of diagnostic possibilities did not select "Depression" as a choice. Furthermore, both versions' lists of diagnoses printed "No condition on Axis I." In addition, when the short form was generated (i.e., a list of only letter answers), the clinician then had no way of knowing that this patient admitted to being suicidal.

In a second trial, a 30-year-old male patient answered affirmatively to auditory and visual hallucinations. The DSM-III version listed an Axis I diagnosis of "R/O Schizophrenia" but eliminated it on the "Refined Diagnoses" printout. The revised program was changed, however, inasmuch as both diagnostic lists included "Psychotic Disorder NOS."

For another patient, the DSM-III version's printout of "Diagnostic Possibilities" listed an Axis I diagnosis of "Adjustment Disorder with Academic Inhibition." This, however, was a 47-year-old male who did not identify academics as an activity, much less a problem. The revised software simply listed "Adjustment Disorder NOS." In addition, this same patient was assigned a DSM-III diagnosis of "Atypical Paranoid Disorder" and a DSM-IIIR diagnosis of "Psychotic Disorder NOS," yet neither paranoid nor psychotic symptoms were selected.

*Child Diagnostic Screening Battery.* On one trial, for a 9-year-old male patient who was identified as having suicidal behavior, self-destructive behavior, and overreacting to many things, the list of "Diagnostic Possibilities" did not include "Depression" as a consideration with either DSM version. Another patient with suicidal behaviors, this time a 5-year-old male, also did not produce "Depression" on the list of Axis I "Diagnostic Possibilities." However, he was offered Axis II diagnoses of "Histrionic Personality Disorder" and "Atypical, Mixed or Other Personality Disorder" when the DSM-III version was used, and "Histrionic Personality Disorder" and "Personality Disorder NOS" when the DSM-IIIR version was tested.

Furthermore, both programs generated these same personality disorders for a hypothetical 2-year-old patient. Questions arise then regarding the appropriateness of these diagnoses, given the theories about the development of personality. Perhaps in a revision of this program, as was suggested previously for the Adolescent Diagnostic Screening Battery, a better way to identify these symptoms would be to list them as personality "traits" or "characteristics."

The "Refined Diagnoses" list generated for each battery is unnecessary and serves no practical purpose, as previously illustrated: This function eliminates some diagnoses, yet the authors state that the elimination of diagnoses is the responsibility of the clinician. The procedure of completing the clinician questionnaire also is unnecessary in the diagnostic process. The information that can be used to add to the determination of diagnoses does not have to be entered into the computer for the clinician to make his or her decisions. However, benefits of completing the clinician questionnaire on-line include convenient record keeping and the provision of information that may be necessary to complete Axes III, IV, and V.

The manuals erroneously refer to the printout as both a "report" and a "profile." The printout does not fit the definition of "profile" as presented in the glossary of the *Standards for Educational and Psychological Testing* (AERA, APA, & NCME, 1985, p. 93) as it does not utilize several tests to produce a graphic representation of test scores. This final function of the program simply generates a list of diagnostic possibilities. The program does not print out any explanations, reports, profiles, or interpretations, and none are offered from the authors or elsewhere. These must be provided by the clinician. It is important to note that the authors do include a statement on the actual printout reminding the reader to consider the diagnoses presented as only tentative; they must be either ruled out or substantiated further through additional clinical information or assessments.

This software program does not deal adequately with questions answered either "none of the above" or "does not apply." Moreland (1985) and Klein et al. (1975) report concern about important clinical information that may be lost by not knowing the reasoning behind the N/A (not applicable) answer. They consider several possibilities: a patient may misunderstand the question, a patient's answer choice may not be among those offered, or a patient may experience resistance. A partial solution to the problem of lost information due to N/A responses might be to include the opportunity for more "other" fill-in answers. Other solutions may be apparent in other programs. For instance, Erdman et al. (1987) noted that the program they used in 1980 provided a list of all the "don't know"-answered questions. The program used by Swartz and Pfohl (1981, p. 360) also provided "a list of the questions which had been answered 'undetermined information.'" The Diagnostic Screening Batteries do not provide comparable lists. Additionally, the program used by Erdman in 1980 (Erdman et al., 1987, p. 7) also indicated "which diagnoses could not be made because of missing information" or unknown criteria (e.g., frequency or duration requirements). Some researchers report this loss of clinical data as a concern of the clinicians but not especially of the patients (Barron et al., 1987; Erdman et al., 1985).

The user's guides contain problems with the presentation of information and instructions. The "Introduction" presents information in a poorly organized manner. For example, the authors begin stating their purpose for designing the program on the first page of the guide. However, it is not until pages later, hidden among other information, that they conclude their statement of purpose with the sentence, "It is up to the qualified clinician to determine which diagnoses are most valid and appropriate for each patient" (Eisenberg & Smith, 1986, p. 5; 1989, p. 3). (The role of the clinician is not as clearly worded in the printed materials as it was during a conversation with the author. Eisenberg [personal communication, April 14, 1989] succinctly stated, "The program is to *work* like a clinician *not* to *think* like one, offering a broad list of diagnostic possibilities, allowing the clinician and his/her expertise to make the final diagnosis.") Located at the end of the "Introduction" section, and before the operating instructions, one finds a small paragraph that defines the hardware requirements. This includes one sentence that suggests a printer is optional, but it does not elaborate on any benefits or limitations. The manuals do not provide information here or elsewhere regarding how to access diagnostic possibilities without a printer. (This can be accomplished only if the printer is switched off and the user gives the command to "Run Diagnostic Determinations.")

In the manuals' sections referring to use of the system, there are instructions for entering patient demographics. The user is directed to identify the patient's gender by typing only the first letter: " 'm' equals male, 'f' equals female." However, the instructions continue with " 'e' equals elephant, 'a' equals apples" (Eisenberg & Smith, 1986, p. 9; 1989, pp. 6, 15). This leads a novice program user to question the intention of the authors with respect to instruction clarity.

There are also a few typographical errors throughout the manuals and in the software program. One important typo in both versions of the Adolescent Diagnostic Screening Battery is found in the patient questionnaire. One question contains an incomplete word; the word and the question are therefore unknown. This mistake invalidates the question, along with its assumed relevance. In the Child Diagnostic Screening Battery, a typo appeared in a printed list of diagnostic code numbers. For one young patient (Diston, 1989) the list of diagnostic possibilities printed "312.00 Conduct Disorder, Group Type, Moderate"; however, 312.00 is actually Conduct Disorder, Solitary Aggressive. There are also typos that appear in the directions in the 1986 IBM version of the manual for loading the system on to a hard drive. As a result, the program cannot be installed without a telephone call to the authors for corrections. In the revised program some but not all typos were corrected, and a telephone call to the authors may still be warranted.

In conclusion, when considering a computer-assisted diagnostic program, the buyer must remember the following: this program has problems with its diagnostic decision-making process that leads to errors, and it has major typographical errors in both manuals that preclude hard-drive installation without assistance from Smith and Eisenberg. More importantly, there are serious compliance problems with regard to the *Standards for Educational and Psychological Testing*. The absence of empirical studies and psychometric information on these batteries indicates the need for extensive research. At this stage of development, these reviewers cannot recommend the Diagnostic Screening Batteries for clinical use.

## References


American Educational Research Association, American Psychological Association, & National Council on Measurement in Education. (1985). *Standards for educational and psychological testing*. Washington, DC: American Psychological Association.

American Psychiatric Association. (1980). *Diagnostic and statistical manual of mental disorders* (3rd ed.). Washington, DC: Author.

American Psychiatric Association. (1987). *Diagnostic and statistical manual of mental disorders* (3rd ed. rev.). Washington, DC: Author.

Anastasi, A. (1982). *Psychological testing* (5th ed.). New York: Macmillan.

Barron, M.R., Daniels, J.L., & O'Toole, W.M. (1987). The effect of computer-conducted versus counselor-conducted initial intake interviews on client expectancy. *Computers in Human Behavior, 3*, 21–28.

Diston, L. (1989). *Diagnostic screening batteries: A review and critique*. Unpublished manuscript, Nova University, Ft. Lauderdale, FL.

Eisenberg, J.M., & Smith, J.J. (1986). *The Diagnostic Screening Batteries manual: IBM version*. Towson, MD: Reason House.

Eisenberg, J.M., & Smith, J.J. (1989). *The Diagnostic Screening Batteries manual*. Towson, MD: Reason House.

Erdman, H.P., Greist, J.H., Klein, M.H., & Jefferson, J.W. (1987). A review of computer diagnosis in psychiatry with special emphasis on DSM-III. *Computers in Human Services, 2*, 1–11.

Erdman, H.P., Klein, M.H., & Greist, J.H. (1985). Direct patient computer interviewing. *Journal of Counseling and Clinical Psychology, 53*, 760–773.

Ferguson, G.A. (1981). *Statistical analysis in psychology and education* (5th ed.). New York: McGraw-Hill.

Fleiss, J.L., Spitzer, R.L., Cohen, J., & Endicott, J. (1972). Three computer diagnosis methods compared. *Archives of General Psychiatry, 27*, 643–649.

Greist, J.H., Klein, M.H., & Erdman, H.P. (1976). Routine on-line psychiatric diagnosis by computer. *American Journal of Psychiatry, 133*(12), 1405–1408.

Greist, J.H., Klein, M.H., Erdman, H.P., Bires, J.K., Bass, S.M., Machtinger, P.E., & Kresge, D.G. (1987). Comparison of computer- and interviewer-administered versions of the Diagnostic Interview Schedule. *Hospital and Community Psychiatry, 38*(12), 1304–1311.

Greist, J.H., Klein, M.H., Erdman, H.P., & Jefferson, J.W. (1983). Computers and psychiatric diagnosis. *Psychiatric Annals, 13*, 789–792.

Klein, M.H., Greist, J.H., & VanCura, L.J. (1975). Computers and psychiatry, promises to keep. *Archives of General Psychiatry, 32*, 837–843.

Mathisen, K.S., Evans, F.J., & Meyers, K. (1987). Evaluation of a computerized version of the Diagnostic Interview Schedule. *Hospital and Community Psychiatry, 38*(12), 1304–1311.

Moreland, K.L. (1985). Computer-assisted psychological assessment in 1986: A practical guide. *Computers in Human Behavior, 1*, 221–233.

Prout, H.T., & Chizik, R. (1988). Readability of child and adolescent self-report measures. *Journal of Consulting and Clinical Psychology, 56*, 152–154.

Robins, L.N., Helzer, J.E., Croughan, J., & Ratcliff, K.S. (1981). National Institute of Mental Health Diagnostic Interview Schedule: Its history, characteristics, and validity. *Archives of General Psychiatry, 38*, 381–389.

Smith, J.J., & Eisenberg, J.M. (1986/1989). *The Diagnostic Screening Battery: IBM version*. Towson, MD: Reason House.

Spitzer, R.L., & Endicott, J. (1968). DIAGNO: A computer program for psychiatric diagnosis utilizing the differential diagnosis procedure. *Archives of General Psychiatry, 18,* 746–756.

Spitzer, R.L., Endicott, J., Cohen, J., & Fleiss, J.L. (1974). Constraints on the validity of computer diagnosis. *Archives of General Psychiatry, 31,* 197–203.

Swartz, C.M., & Pfohl, B. (1981). A learning aid for DSM-III: Computerized prompting of diagnostic criteria. *Journal of Clinical Psychiatry, 42*(9), 359–361.

**Betty E. Gridley, Ph.D.**
*Associate Professor of Psychology–Educational Psychology, Ball State University, Muncie, Indiana.*

**David E. McIntosh, Ph.D.**
*Assistant Professor and Director of Training in School Psychology, Department of Applied Behavioral Studies in Education, Oklahoma State University, Stillwater, Oklahoma.*

---

# DIFFERENTIAL ABILITY SCALES

*Colin Elliott. San Antonio, Texas: The Psychological Corporation.*

### Introduction

Differential Ability Scales (DAS; Elliott, 1990a) is an individually administered, standardized test of intelligence, achievement, and information processing designed to measure the cognitive abilities of children and adolescents 2½ to 17 years of age. The 17 cognitive and 3 achievement measures were developed and normed together, resulting in a comprehensive and efficient instrument. Designed for psychologists and other trained professionals, the DAS may be used in school and clinical settings as well as in research. General classification of a child's ability is possible, along with a profile of his or her strengths and weaknesses across a wide range of abilities.

Colin Elliott, the author of the DAS, is currently a senior lecturer and tutor in the Centre for Educational Guidance and Special Needs at the School of Education, University of Manchester. He was born in England and obtained his bachelor's degree in psychology from Hull University, followed by a Master of Science and doctoral degree in educational psychology from the University of Manchester. He was a school teacher and school psychologist for 7 years before becoming a trainer of school psychologists. Dr. Elliott has been involved in development of the Differential Ability Scales and the British Ability Scales for over 17 years. In connection with the development of the DAS, he spent over a year in the United States. In addition to the DAS, Dr. Elliott has published widely on behavior problems in children, the relationship of temperament and personality to learning, profiles of children with learning disabilities, and the measurement of developmental stages in children. He is a Fellow of the British Psychological Society.

Development of the DAS was begun in 1984. The instrument is an adaptation of the British Ability Scales (BAS; Elliott, Murray, & Pearson, 1979) and as such shares its history with that instrument. Interest in developing a British intelligence scale arose from concerns about using American intelligence scales for English children. Specifically, the American content of some questions and the lack of British norms were criticized. At the time, psychologists also were examining available instruments for ethnic and social class bias in test scores, questioning the use of a single summary score, and developing an interest in tapping aspects of development such as those suggested by theorists such as Jean Piaget that were not measured by extant batteries.

The final version of the British Ability Scales came about after a long period (1965–82) in which the original idea for a "British Intelligence Scale" evolved into the form of the BAS that became the forerunner of the DAS. The result of this long developmental period was a cognitive assessment battery designed to provide not only a general ability score but meaningful, distinct subtest scores as well. The test's hierarchical structure was not based on a single theory of intelligence, but instead its sample of abilities derived from a variety of theoretical points of view and empirical results such as factor analyses. In order to develop homogeneous subscales, the test's authors drew on the psychometric sophistication provided by item response theory. In addition, a set of unique subtests was designed to tap cognitive abilities relevant to common learning difficulties but seldom reflected in other tests. The first edition of the BAS was released in 1979 with a revised version becoming available in 1982. This revised version was the immediate predecessor of the DAS and consisted of 21 subtests representing the process areas of speed, reasoning, spatial imagery, perceptual matching, short-term memory, and retrieval and application of knowledge.

Colin Elliott began developing an American version of the BAS in 1984. His goal was to develop a battery of homogenous subtests with good reliability and specificity from which reliable interpretable profiles of strengths and weaknesses could be obtained. The result was the Differential Ability Scales. The DAS was designed to reflect the internal structure and content of the BAS, excluding or revising those items with a distinctly British flavor. The American test also reflected a number of suggestions and criticisms of the DAS that had been voiced by educational and clinical psychologists in England, Scotland, and the United States. For example, some subtests were deleted and others added. Some subtests were made more efficient and reliable with the addition of items, particularly at the lower and upper difficulty levels. In the final version of the DAS, six BAS subtests were omitted while four new subtests were developed and incorporated.

The new test materials were administered to samples in the United States during 1985 and 1986. These tryouts were designed to provide information about administration procedures and the statistical properties of individual items that were new to the DAS. Some of the DAS subtests were not included because they were little changed from the BAS versions and the BAS standardization data were judged sufficient to guide the design of the standardization edition of the DAS. Specifically, 1985–86 tryouts were designed to test new items that replaced existing items, to evaluate suggested changes in administration procedures, and to develop new subtests. More details and a listing of those subtests are provided in the *Differential Ability Scales: Introductory and Technical Handbook* (Elliott, 1990b). In addition to tryout testing, a bias review panel met in early 1986 in order to examine questions for possible bias toward minority or ethnic groups. Revisions were made based on the tryouts and recommendations of the panel.

The DAS standardization edition was distributed during early fall 1986. The primary goals of the standardization process were to (a) obtain a norm sample that accurately represented the target population of children aged 2:6 to 17:11 along major demographic variables, (b) analyze various technical aspects including item difficulty and discrimination, subtest reliability, unidimensionality, and factor structure, and (c) evaluate each item for possible bias due to ethnicity/race, sex, and geographic region. Approximately 600 additional cases of black and Hispanic children were included to supplement the norm sample.

Standardization data were collected by trained examiners from locations throughout the United States. The standardization sample consisted of 3,475 children: 175 for each age group from 2:6 through 4:11, and 200 cases per year from ages 5:0 through 17:11. Each group was approximately equally distributed by month and by sex. Other factors monitored included race/ethnicity, parent education, geographic location, and (for preschoolers) whether subjects were attending school. The standardization sample was drawn from both public and private schools and included children who were receiving various special education services in roughly the same proportions as those found in the U.S. population. Data are presented in the manual as to specific characteristics of the sample. However, generally the sample characteristics closely matched those for the general population based on U.S. Census Bureau data for 1988. The only exception was in the previously mentioned oversampling of black and Hispanic children collected for the purpose of determining item bias. The standardization version of the DAS was normed during 1987–89, and the present version was released for general use in 1990.

The testing package consists of the *DAS: Administration and Scoring Manual* (Elliott, 1990a), the *Differential Ability Scales Introductory and Technical Handbook* (Elliott, 1990b), two different record forms (Preschool and School-Age), stimulus and consumable booklets, and manipulable materials. The materials come in a briefcase, which has partitions for the various manipulative materials. Examiners furnish a stopwatch, pencils, and blank paper.

The manual provides very detailed administration and scoring instructions. Sections on the organization of the instrument, including brief descriptions of the abilities measured by each of the subtests, and tables both for converting raw scores to a variety of standard scores and determining the significance of the differences between various scores also are included. The manual has a self-standing binder that can serve as a screen between the Record Form and the child.

The handbook gives a detailed description of the test, its structure, the rationale behind its development, and its history. Complete descriptions of the subtests are given as well as suggestions for the systematic interpretation of the test scores. Complete information on the standardization process and the technical development of the test is provided. Two chapters are devoted to describing the reliability and validity studies that took place during the development of the battery. The final chapter presents information on bias and fairness and reviews the safeguards taken during development of the DAS. An appendix that explains the Rasch model also is included. There is some overlap of information with that provided in the manual; however, the author notes that this is by design because many readers may not have the manual. In addition, the handbook can be used as a general reference because it does not contain test items or scoring rules, thereby presenting no danger to test security.

The DAS cognitive battery includes 17 subtests divided into two overlapping levels, Preschool and School-Age. The Preschool Level is actually composed of two sublevels. Children aged 2:6 to 3:5 take four core subtests, Block Building,

Verbal Comprehension, Picture Similarities, and Naming Vocabulary, which comprise a general conceptual ability score (GCA composite). Two additional diagnostic subtests, Recall of Digits and Recognition of Pictures, are also available for this age group. Children in the upper Preschool Level (ages 3:6 to 5:11) take six subtests to produce the GCA. Five of these subtests also form two ability cluster scores: Verbal Comprehension and Naming Vocabulary form the Verbal cluster, and Picture Similarities, Pattern Construction, and Copying form the Nonverbal cluster. Early Number Concepts is the sixth core subtest. Five additional diagnostic subtests are also available: Block Building, given only to children ages 3:6–4:11; Matching Letter-Like Forms and Recall of Objects, given only to children ages 4:0–5:11; and Recall of Digits and Recognition of Pictures. Estimated administration time for the preschool battery ranges from 25 to 65 minutes.

The School-Age Level is designed for children 6:0 to 17:11. Examinees are administered six core subtests, which in turn form three ability cluster scores: (a) Verbal, with Word Definitions and Similarities; (b) Nonverbal Reasoning, with Matrices and Sequential and Quantitative Reasoning; and (c) Spatial, with Recall of Designs and Pattern Construction. Three diagnostic subtests, Recall of Digits, Recall of Objects, and Speed of Information Processing, are also available. Estimated administration time is 40 to 60 minutes.

The DAS School Achievement Tests comprise three measures of basic skills: Basic Number Skills, Spelling, and Word Reading. These, too, are designed for children ages 6:0 to 17:11, with an estimated administration time of 15 to 25 minutes.

The battery includes record forms for the two age levels and four "consumable" booklets. The record booklets are very detailed. Preschool and School-Age versions are similar, the main difference lying in the subtests administered at the different levels. Similar to other test booklets, these have space for responses for each subtest, behavioral information, and the like. However, a great deal more information appears than is customary, such as the inclusion of many of the administration instructions and/or sample diagrams and scoring instructions. Helps for error analysis are provided for all three achievement subtests; for example, phonetic spellings allow for quickly recording specific errors rather than just indicating whether the word was right or wrong, the items for the Basic Number Skills subtest have been categorized, and there is room to indicate types of spelling errors (e.g., basic phonetic, order error, etc.). Tables for converting raw scores to ability scores appear for the core subtests. A chart of ages at which the subtests are normed enables the examiner to determine quickly whether a particular subtest is appropriate for a given age. The summary page includes identifying information and is perforated so that it can be removed from the actual test answers if desired. The summary page provides spaces for a number of different types of scores as well as for score comparisons. There is also room for a graphic presentation of a child's profile for core, diagnostic, cluster, and (in the case of the School-Age form) achievement tests. The number of points needed to obtain significant differences between certain scores is printed above the graphic profile.

Consumable booklets are needed for the Quantitative Reasoning (ages 6:0–10:11) and Speed of Information Processing (one booklet per age level) subtests. These booklets are of high quality paper and are used only once.

**Practical Applications/Uses**

The Differential Ability Scales were designed to identify children's strengths and weaknesses across a wide range of ability domains. Though intended primarily as a profile test, a wide variety of reliable scores makes interpretation at a number of levels possible. For example, a general conceptual ability score is available for classification purposes, the composites of which are derived from the best measures of conceptual and reasoning abilities. At the same time the DAS subtests have greater reliable specificity than many other batteries. In addition to measures of conceptual and reasoning abilities, the diagnostic subtests provide information on varied dimensions of ability such as memory, perception, and speed of information processing not found in other batteries. Achievement tests are also available, and these along with the diagnostic tests have been normed together with the other battery components.

Tables 1, 2, and 3 present summaries of the various DAS subtests, appropriate ages for each, descriptions of the tasks, and possible abilities measured. As the reader will notice very quickly, the DAS covers a wide span of ability and age ranges. Use of tailored testing allows examiners to select items appropriate for a specific child. The battery was created from developmental and educational perspectives, rather than being merely a downward extension of an adult battery. This design allows for administration to be child centered and age appropriate.

The DAS may be used by psychologists and other appropriately trained individuals in the schools, clinics, and in research. The subtests were developed to be suitable for exceptional as well as "normal" children, and include a large number of both easy and difficult items to ensure adequate "ceiling" and "floor" for a wide variety of children. Profiles for gifted, retarded, and learning disabled children are given in the handbook, and special attention was paid to investigating item bias and oversampling black and Hispanic students in the standardization sample.

The DAS is designed to be individually administered by an examiner who has had formal training in individual administration and interpretation of cognitive test batteries for children and adolescents. The test's author suggests that, before administering the battery, new examiners read over the manual and the handbook, go over the test materials thoroughly, observe an administration of the DAS, and practice administering and scoring all of the subtests two or three times prior to testing an actual child. Dr. Elliott also suggests that potential administrators complete the scoring exercises provided in the manual for the drawing subtests prior to scoring those from the practice administration. Finally, it is suggested that a colleague be asked to observe and review one's work. The procedures as outlined in the manual may suffice for those who have had specific training and extensive experience in administering other standardized ability tests, but, in the opinion of this reviewer, specific instruction and guided practice in administering and interpreting the DAS would be preferable. This training should include fundamentals such as establishing and maintaining rapport, eliciting optimum performance, following standardized administration procedures, probing responses, and maintaining test security. In addition, administration of the scales to special populations requires familiarity with the problems and concerns often encountered in testing such groups.

**Table 1**

**DAS Preschool Battery**

| *Ability Cluster/Subtest* | *Age Range*[1] | *Task* | *Abilities Measured*[2] |
|---|---|---|---|
| Block Building | 2:6–3:5<br>(3:6–4:11) | Copies two- or three-dimensional diagram with blocks | Visual perceptual matching, spatial orientation, perceptual motor |
| Early Number Concepts | 3:6–5:11<br>(6:0–6:5)<br>[2:6–3:5]<br>[6:6–7:11] | Using colored chips or pictures answers questions about number, size, or other numerical concepts | Knowledge of numerical and prenumerical concepts, nonverbal and verbal knowledge, quantitative |
| *Verbal* | | | |
| Verbal Comprehension | 2:6–5:11<br>3:6–5:11<br>(6:00–6:11) | Points to pictures, manipulates objects after examiner gives oral directions | Receptive language, understanding oral directions, using basic language concepts, memory |
| Naming Vocabulary | 2:6–5:11<br>(6:00–7:11)<br>[8:00–8:11] | Names objects and pictures | Expressive language, knowledge of picture names, language development, memory |
| *Nonverbal* | | | |
| Picture Similarities | 2:6–5:11<br>3:6–5:11<br>[6:00–7:11] | After seeing a row of four pictures, places fifth card under the picture with which the card shares an element or concept | Non verbal reasoning, visual attention to detail, level of general knowledge base |
| Pattern Construction | 3:6–7:11<br>[3:00–3:5] | Constructs design from flat squares or blocks with black and yellow patterns | Nonverbal reasoning, spatial visualization/reasoning, part-whole relationships, analysis and synthesis |

**Table 1** (cont.)

| *Ability Cluster/Subtest* | *Age Range*[1] | *Task* | *Abilities Measured*[2] |
|---|---|---|---|
| Copying | 3:6–5:11 | Reproduces (copies) a series of line drawings of progressively more complex geometric designs presented in a booklet | Ability to match visual shapes by shapes by a paper-and-pencil response, fine-motor coordination, visual perceptual organization |

[1]Extended age ranges are given in parentheses ( ), out-of-level testing is shown by brackets [ ].
[2]Representative abilities determined by factor analyses or clinical interpretation.

Both general instructions for administration and those specific to each subtest are provided. The goal of the procedure used to administer the DAS is to have a majority of the testing time devoted to items appropriate for the child's ability level. Therefore, a form of tailored testing is used, wherein subtest basals and ceilings such as one finds in other instruments are not necessary. The use of item response theory in the test's development results in a format in which fewer items are administered than in more traditional procedures. Subtests are to be administered in the specified order, with core subtests first and diagnostic subtests later. Most children take the core and diagnostic subtests prescribed for their age bands. Age ranges for several categories are given on the first page of the instructions for each subtest, for each subtest on the record form, and graphically in the manual and on the Preschool Record Form. The usual subtest selection is illustrated by the "Usual Age Range" shading on the record form or in the manual (see p. 16). As many subtests also were normed outside of these age ranges, examiners may choose those labeled "Extended Age Range" to obtain additional diagnostic information. "Out-of-level" norms also are given.

Ordinarily each subtest is started at the items indicated for a child's age. Administration then continues to the normal stopping point or what the author terms a "decision point." There the examiner must determine whether to continue or stop. The decision is made based on the total number of items the child has missed. If the child has failed at least three test items, the subtest is discontinued; if he or she has failed fewer than three items, the examiner continues testing until the next decision point. If the child passes less than three items, the examiner is expected to return to an earlier starting point and administer an easier set of items. The examiner also may choose to discontinue administering a set of items when a child fails a number of items in a row before reaching the stopping point. In this case one is instructed to use an *alternative stopping point rule.* For example, the alternative stopping point in the Naming Vocabulary subtest occurs after five consecutive failures. Except when this alternative stopping point rule is used, all children take a continuous set of items from the starting to stopping points. Conversion of raw test scores to standard scores is based on this assumption.

It is suggested that examiners follow the test procedures used in standardizing

**Table 2**

**DAS School-Age Battery**

| *Ability Cluster/Subtest* | *Age Range*[1] | *Task* | *Abilities Measured*[2] |
|---|---|---|---|
| *Verbal* | | | |
| Word Definitions | 6:0–17:11 [5:0–5:11] | Orally gives the meaning of individual words | Knowledge of vocabulary, verbal conceptualization, long-term information retrieval |
| Similarities | 5:0–17:11 [5:0–5:11] | States how three things are similar or go together | Verbal inductive reasoning, vocabulary and general verbal development, logical and abstract thinking |
| *Nonverbal Reasoning* | | | |
| Matrices | 6:0–17:11 [5:0–5:11] | Shown an incomplete matrix of abstract figures, selects one that correctly completes the matrix from among four or six choices | Nonverbal inductive reasoning, use of verbal mediation strategies in labeling diagrams, perception of visual detail, simultaneous processing, fluid intelligence |
| Sequential and Quantitative Reasoning | 6:0–17:11 [5:0–5:11] | Completes a series of abstract figures by supplying the missing figure, or finds a relationship within two pairs of numbers and supplies the missing number in another pair by applying that concept | Perception of sequential patterns or relationships in figures or numbers, analytical reasoning, ability to formulate and test hypotheses, fluid intelligence |
| *Spatial* | | | |
| Recall of Designs | 6:0–17:11 [5:0–5:11] | Produces abstract line drawing from memory | Short-term visual recall, visual memory, nonverbal reasoning |

**Table 2** (cont.)

| *Ability Cluster/Subtest* | *Age Range*[1] | *Task* | *Abilities Measured*[2] |
|---|---|---|---|
| Pattern Construction | 3:6–17:11 [3:0–3:5] | Constructs designs from flat squares or blocks with black and yellow patterns | Nonverbal reasoning, spatial visualization/reasoning, analysis and synthesis, part-whole relationships |
| *Achievement* | | | |
| Basic Number Skills | 6:0–17:11 | Solves computational problems presented on a work sheet | School knowledge, numerical computation, skill in applying a range of arithmetic operations |
| Spelling | 6:0–17:11 | Writes words dictated by examiner | School knowledge, knowledge of spelling rules, retention of facts |
| Word Reading | 6:0–17:11 [5:0–5:11] | Reads aloud a series of words presented on a card | Recognition of printed words, vocabulary knowledge, school knowledge |

[1]Extended age ranges are given in parentheses ( ), out-of-level testing is shown by brackets [ ].
[2]Representative abilities determined by factor analyses or clinical interpretation.

the DAS. These include some important differences from those customarily employed in cognitive assessments (e.g., computation of the child's chronological age, beginning and stopping points, rapid presentation rate on recall of digits, the manner in which pattern construction is timed, multiple trials across time for recall of objects), which may prove somewhat problematic for seasoned examiners. Though the examiner is expected to adhere to standardized instructions, some flexibility in adapting to the needs of each child and to the testing situation is allowed. For example, the examiner may repeat and rephrase directions if a child does not understand. He or she also may demonstrate through teaching after failure on designated items. Questioning or encouraging more elaborate responses is also allowable.

Most examiners choose to administer subtests that form the usual level for a child's age. Because the battery's School-Age and Preschool Levels actually were normed for overlapping age ranges for children 5:0 through 6:11, other options are possible. For example, complete normative information is available for some subtests, and these extended age range measures (see Tables 1–3) may be given to any child who falls within their scope. Even though norms are available, some of

**Table 3**

**DAS Diagnostic Subtests**

| *Ability Cluster/Subtest* | *Age Range*[1] | *Task* | *Abilities Measured*[2] |
|---|---|---|---|
| Block Building | 3:6–4:11 | Copies two- or three-dimensional diagram with blocks | Visual perception matching, spatial orientation, perceptial motor |
| Copying | 6:00–7:11 | Reproduces (copies) a series of line drawings of progressively more complex geometric designs presented in a booklet | Ability to match visual shapes by a paper-and-pencil response, fine-motor coordination, visual perceptual organization |
| Matching Letter-Like Forms | 4:6–5:11 [4:0–4:5] [6:0–7:11] | Must find identical match to and abstract figure from six choices | Visual discrimination, ability to follow verbal instructions and verbal cues, visual-perceptual matching |
| Recall of Digits | 3:0–17:11 [2:6–2:11] | Repeats a sequence of digits presented orally at the rate of two digits per second | Short-term auditory memory, attention, concentration, oral recall of sequences of numbers |
| Recall of Objects | 4:0–17:11 | Immediate and delayed verbal recall of the names of 20 common objects pictured on a card | Short- and intermediate-term auditory recall, concentration and attention, verbal mediation strategies |
| Recognition of Pictures | 3:0–7:11 [2:6–2:11] [8:0–17:11] | After viewing a picture of one or more objects for 5 or 10 seconds, points to same objects on a second picture | Recognition memory for pictures, short-term visual memory, verbal reasoning/ mediation |

**Table 3** (cont.)

| *Subtest* | *Age Range*[1] | *Task* | *Abilities Measured*[2] |
|---|---|---|---|
| Speed of Information Processing | 6:0–17:11 [5:0–5:11] | Marks the highest number or most boxes in a row (score for each page based on time taken to respond) | Speed in performing simple mental operations, short-term numerical memory, ability to make quantitative comparisons rapidly |

[1]Extended age ranges are given in parentheses ( ), out-of-level testing is shown by brackets [ ].
[2]Representative abilities determined by factor analyses or clinical interpretation.

these subtests are too easy for children of high ability or too difficult for those of low ability. Such applications are called "out-of-level" testing, which is most appropriate for bright younger children and less able older ones. These modifications result in subtests suitable for children of varying abilities. An examiner may choose to change to one level even after a different level has been given. If, based on a child's performance, the examiner determines that the level is too difficult or too easy, he or she can administer the more appropriate subtests. Examiners are cautioned, however, not to discontinue during a subtest, but rather to wait until a stopping point has been reached.

The manual does not provide specific instructions for administering the DAS to special populations. General considerations in testing and guidelines that include allowance for individual differences are given instead. A GCA score for very low functioning individuals may be obtained through out-of-level testing. As all types of scores are not given for all subtests, the author suggests that age equivalents be used as indicators of general developmental level. Although several of the subtests have verbal content and/or require verbal responses, a special nonverbal composite is available from a battery of nonverbal tasks. Examiners may determine that this nonverbal composite is a more appropriate measure of ability for subjects such as shy preschoolers, elective mutes, children from home environments where English is not the primary language, children suspected of having severe hearing loss, and those simply reluctant to answer verbally. Nonverbal diagnostic subtests are available at every age. The directions can be given through gestures if necessary and the child responds nonverbally by pointing, drawing, or manipulating objects. Translation of verbal subtests into another language is not recommended. For children ages 2:6–3:5, the special nonverbal composite consists of Block Building and Picture Similarities. For ages 3:6–5:11, Picture Similarities, Pattern Construction, and Copying are used. For school-age children, one can administer Matrices, Sequential and Quantitative Reasoning, Recall of Designs, and Pattern Construction.

The manual provides general scoring rules as well as specific scoring instructions for each subtest, and many are repeated on the Record Booklet. Item scoring rules were developed based on cases collected during standardization. Scoring rules also were influenced by item and subtest scaling through Rasch model analysis. As noted previously, the handbook offers a description of the procedure and an appendix explaining the Rasch model. Specific rules and a number of correct and incorrect examples are given for those subtests where judgment is involved. Most of these examples appear in the manual along with the instructions for administration.

Two appendixes in the manual detail more complete guidelines for scoring Early Number Concepts, item 1, and the drawing subtests. The author stresses that the nature and purpose of the two drawing tests makes the emphasis in their scoring different. Principles and instructions for the use of the scoring templates also are given for the Copying subtest, but the task seems no more difficult than that on many other cognitive batteries. Some differences might arise because of subjectivity in scoring certain items. Four subtests, Copying, Recall of Designs, Similarities, and Word Definitions, require a significant amount of judgment. For comparison, results of interrater reliability studies for these subtests are reported in the handbook. The authors (Shrout & Feiss, 1979) calculated a form of intraclass correlation that accounts for the differences in the scorers' leniency (i.e., level of the scores) as well as ranking. This formula appears in the handbook. The results were based on information from approximately 50 subjects at each of four age levels for Word Definitions, Similarities, and Copying, and from approximately 100 at three age levels for Recall of Designs. These correlations ranged from .74 to .98, averaging about .90 for all subtests. However, it is recommended that new examiners have their scoring checked by someone experienced before using the results for decision making.

Most items are scored correct (1 point) or incorrect (0 points). However, scores may range from 0 to 6 points on a single item. Raw scores for each subtest are calculated by adding the total number of points for all items comprising that subtest. Because the concept of basal and ceiling is not used, the raw score is not an estimate of the score a child would have obtained had all the items been given. Conversions to normed scores also depend on this assumption. Subtest raw scores are converted to ability scores based on the number of correct responses and the difficulty level of the items administered. This ability score gives the examinee's raw level of performance. The Rasch model allows for comparisons of these ability scores among subtests and for the examiner to make predictions about performance of examinees of known ability. Standard errors of measurement are reported and allow for ranges or bands of ability to be established.

Raw scores can be converted to a variety of normative scores for subtests and composites, leading to a number of possible comparisons. For example, the ability score for a subtest can be converted to an age-based standard T-score, percentile, or age equivalent. By summing the core subtest T-scores, the examiner can convert this total to a standard score ($M$ = 100, $SD$ = 15) for the cluster and the composite it represents. Achievement subtest ability scores can be directly converted to the same standard score scale, allowing the examiner to make direct comparisons between achievement and ability.

The manual gives instructions for prorating for the GCA when one subtest either is not given or is judged invalid for some reason. Cluster scores should not be prorated.

Both the manual and the handbook describe procedures for systematic interpretation of test scores. A number of tables are provided to help in making comparisons. In addition, qualitative labels such as *average, above average,* and so on for particular score ranges appear in both publications. An entire chapter of the handbook describes in detail the abilities measured by each subtest along with a number of factors that may either enhance or detract from subtest performance. Descriptions of the clusters also are given along with some possible interpretive statements.

In a second chapter of the handbook on interpretation, the author outlines a two-stage procedure. In the first, the examiner decides whether certain composites or subtests are more appropriate for describing a particular child's performance. Elliott suggests a hierarchical strategy for interpretation similar to that suggested by Kaufman (1979) for the WISC-R. Working from most general to specific, the composite score is interpreted first, the clusters next, and finally the subtest scores. For example, the cluster ability scores may be compared to the GCA to determine whether an overall score is the best measure of the child's abilities or whether a better explanation may be found in differing abilities. Cluster standard scores can be compared with each other or subtest scores with the mean score of the core subtests, and comparisons can be made between ability and achievement scores. Elliott (1990b), like Kaufman (1979), suggests an ipsative approach to interpretation; that is, that the strengths and weaknesses attributed to a particular profile will be judged most appropriately in comparison with the average overall performance for that particular individual rather than with absolute normative standards. Unlike in many other batteries, the DAS diagnostic subtests are not included in the composite score and, as such, were designed to be interpreted individually. Although they are correlated with the cognitive subtests, they have a high level of reliable specific variance that allows for this separation.

Many clinicians may wish to make ability/achievement comparisons such as those used for determining eligibility for programs for the learning disabilities. The author suggests that using the GCA score as the ability score is the most defensible in that it is the best measure of general and conceptual reasoning abilities. However, for some children the special nonverbal composite may be a more accurate measure. Two approaches to evaluating ability-achievement discrepancies are available: the simple difference and the regression equation approach. Tables with significant differences at particular levels (uncorrected for multiple comparisons) are provided for both approaches. In the simple difference approach, the clinician seeks to answer the question, "Does the child's level of achievement differ reliably from the child's ability?" The regression approach is predicated on the question, "Does the child's level of achievement differ reliably from the average of what might be expected from children of this ability level?"

Frequencies of various difference scores in the standardization sample as well information about the statistical significance of differences of various magnitudes are given in the handbook and the manual. For example, what would our conclusions be if we tested a 10-year-old child who scored 95 on the GCA and 85 on Basic Number Skills? Using the simple difference score approach, we could turn to

Table B.10 in the handbook and determine that at a significance level of .05, we would need a difference of 11.8 points to be statistically significant. Therefore, our conclusion would be that this child's achievement was not reliably different from her ability. On the other hand, if we turn to Table B.11, we would find that the predicted level of achievement in Basic Number Skills for this child's GCA would be 98. Turning to Table B.12, we would find that the difference between predicted and actual scores for this child would need to be 10.6 less (at $p < .05$) than the predicted score of 98, or 87.4 or less. Therefore, we would conclude that this child's achievement is reliably less than would be predicted based on the obtained ability level. We could also determine from Table B.13 that the obtained difference of 13 points was found for less than 15% of the students in the standardization sample.

In the second stage, the examiner interprets the profile and develops hypotheses about the underlying processes that best explain the nature of the obtained profile of scores. Such interpretations are primarily clinical rather than statistical, suggestive rather than definitive, and primarily for hypothesis generation. The author provides charts of shared underlying processes for both levels of the battery to assist this stage of interpretation. Guidelines for the process and example profiles also are given.

**Technical Aspects**

There are two chapters in the DAS handbook dedicated to reliability and validity studies as well as other technical aspects of the test's development. The first addresses not only reliability but also the topics of item development, accuracy, and specificity. The DAS was developed using the Rasch model as its psychometric basis. The Rasch model, based on the item response model of George Rasch (1966), assumes that there are one or more underlying characteristics (traits or abilities) that determine an individual's responses to test items. The model specifies an expected relationship between observed responses and the unobservable trait(s) or ability(ies). In theory the ability is a continuum on which both the individual and test items can be placed. The person's ability or position on the dimension is independent from the items taken. Each item will have the same difficulty regardless of examinee characteristics. Item response theory (IRT) provides estimates of item difficulty and person ability independent of the population on which they are determined. Therefore, the probability of a person's passing an item depends solely on the ability of that person and the difficulty of the item. Ability and difficulty level estimates were done using the MSTEPS computer program, the result of which allows for adaptive testing. The examiner can match item difficulty to the child's ability by selecting items based on his or her performance on previous items. Results of computer analyses using item response theory and through traditional item-total correlations, the developers were able to eliminate items to create a homogeneous set for the final version of the test.

For the standardization sample, examiners scored only enough to make final item selection. All responses were recorded verbatim, and the items were scored by central project staff members using both content and statistical considerations. Therefore, final scoring rules are based on results of the standardization process. Complete details of the procedures used are given in the handbook.

Because no basals or ceilings are established, the staff was unable to calculate traditional internal consistency reliability estimates. Instead, an alternate method using the item response theory results was developed. Internal consistency estimates based on traditional test theory and item response theory are given. These estimates spanned from .66 to .95 for subtests and composites for in-age or extended age range testing. Reliabilities were lower for out-of-level testings. Test-retest reliabilities give an indication of a test's stability across time. Test-retest reliabilities for a 3- to 7-week time interval ($M$ = 30 days) were obtained for 100 randomly selected students at each of three age levels. The correlations ranged from .79 to .92, with the highest stability for the CGA. Interrater reliabilities were mentioned earlier for those subtests requiring subjective scoring judgments.

The handbook also reports a number of validity studies. Correlations among the various subtests are reported, as is evidence of criterion-related validity. A variety of researchers collected data on a number of other ability batteries and measures of achievement from both the standardization sample and a number of independent samples. Construct validity, which is an indication of how well a particular test measures hypothesized underlying constructs, was supported by both confirmatory and exploratory factor analyses. Keith (1990) conducted separate, independent confirmatory and hierarchical confirmatory factor analyses. The factor structure of the DAS as proposed by its author (and therefore its construct validity) was supported by all of the reported studies. Keith also concluded that in spite of the fact that different subtests are given at various ages, the battery measures essentially the same constructs across age levels.

## Critique

With the recent proliferation of new or revised intelligence and/or ability tests, many psychologists are beginning to ask, "How necessary and useful is another one?" Interestingly, the Differential Ability Scales may become as universally used and respected as the Wechsler scales. It seems to be a well-constructed and standardized instrument. Its format has much to offer, and the information so gathered appears to have great utility in the diagnostic/evaluation process. Many features set this instrument apart from the crowd. First, use of the most advanced psychometric techniques in its development and standardization have ensured a measure in which confidence can be placed. Tailored testing allows for much information to be obtained in as expedient a fashion as possible. Unlike those for many other new instruments (e.g., K-ABC, Stanford-Binet IV), early validity studies have supported the constructs as conceptualized by the test's author. Diagnostic subtests, which are not included in the general conceptual ability battery, allow for a more "pure" measure of ability apart from processing. This is a real plus in trying to identify students who are learning disabled. Discrepancies between ability and achievement are often difficult or impossible to document when comparisons are made with other instruments, as their general ability scores often are highly influenced by those same factors one is trying to identify. In addition, co-norming of ability, diagnostic, and achievement subtests make comparisons among these scores much more meaningful than those made among tests that have been normed on separate populations. The format of the DAS and the interest levels of its items have much to offer, especially for the assessment of young children. Personally, when administering the DAS to young children, I found myself thinking of the Stanford-Binet LM and the wonderful clinical and diagnostic richness of that instrument.

My major criticism of the test is due primarily to a number of features having to do with the physical aspects of the test itself. For example, I had some difficulty in making sense of so much new information. Although the material is well presented in both the manual and the handbook, the lack of indexes is problematic. This oversight might be excused in the manual, but I would urge the author and publisher to include an index to the handbook in future editions. Another criticism is that the record booklets and consumables are fairly expensive at this time. Though they are well done, perhaps some economy could have been made without sacrificing quality. The quantity of such items included in the original test kit seemed less than that provided with a number of other tests.

I find myself in disagreement with the critique of the DAS provided by S. Elliott (1990) in the *Journal of Psychoeducational Assessment*. The majority of his criticisms were answered straightforwardly by Colin Elliott in the same volume (Elliott, 1990c) pointing out that many of the latter's criticisms stemmed from a lack of complete information. At a more basic level than criticism of the test per se, S. Elliott expressed his concern over use of intelligence or cognitive ability tests at all. Indeed, the author of the DAS prefers the use of the term *psychometric g* or *general conceptual ability* over the term *intelligence*. Regardless of what we decide to call this construct, nearly a century of scientific evidence supports the existence of some underlying general ability. Moreover, tests such as the DAS remain some of the best predictors we have of academic success. In addition, they provide clinicians a wealth of information that can be used to tailor educational interventions.

The question, "Is this just another IQ test?" remains to be answered. More empirical data need to be collected in order to verify the DAS's interpretive and predictive utility. However, the usefulness of the battery seems promising. For example, McIntosh and Gridley (1990) found reliable subgroup profiles for groups of learning disabled students from the standardization sample. Based on such initial studies and personal use, the battery seems to be a valuable addition to the psychologist's testing repertoire.

## References

Elliott, C.D. (1990a). *DAS: Administration and scoring manual.* San Antonio, TX: Psychological Corporation.

Elliott, C.D. (1990b). *Differential Ability Scales: Introductory and technical handbook.* San Antonio, TX: Psychological Corporation.

Elliott, C.D. (1990c). The nature and structure of children's abilities: Evidence from the Differential Ability Scales. *Journal of Psychoeducational Assessment, 8,* 376–390.

Elliott, C.D., Murray, D.J., & Pearson, L.S. (1979). *British Ability Scales.* Windsor, England: National Foundation for Educational Research.

Elliott, S.N. (1990). The nature and structure of the DAS: Questioning the test's organization model and use. *Journal of Psychoeducational Assessment, 8,* 406–411.

Kaufman, A. (1979). *Intelligent testing with the WISC-R.* New York: Wiley.

Keith, T.Z. (1990). Confirmatory and hierarchical confirmatory analysis of the Differential Ability Scales. *Journal of Psychoeducational Assessment, 8,* 391–405.

McIntosh, D., & Gridley, B.E. (1990). *The Differential Ability Scales: Profiles for learning disabled students.* Manuscript submitted for publication.

Rasch, G. (1966). An item analysis which takes individual differences into account. *British Journal of Mathematical and Statistical Psychology, 19,* 49–57.

Shrout, P., & Fleiss, J. (1979). Intraclass correlations: Uses in assessing rater reliability. *Psychological Bulletin, 86,* 420–428.

**Brian Bolton, Ph.D.**
*Professor, Arkansas Research and Training Center in Vocational Rehabilitation, University of Arkansas, Fayetteville, Arkansas.*

# DISABILITY FACTOR SCALES–GENERAL

*Jerome Siller. New York, New York: New York University, Department of Educational Psychology.*

## Introduction

The Disability Factor Scales–General (DFS-G; Siller, 1969a, 1970) is a multiscale self-report instrument that measures seven replicated components of attitudes toward people with physical disabilities. The DFS-G was developed in conjunction with a research program undertaken by Jerome Siller and his colleagues and students for the purpose of investigating the implications of psychoanalytic theory for understanding the nature and origins of attitudinal reactions to people with disabling conditions.

Jerome Siller is Professor Emeritus of Educational Psychology at New York University, the institution from which he received his Ph.D. in experimental psychology in 1956. He is a diplomate in clinical psychology and maintains a private practice in psychotherapy and psychoanalysis. He is a past president of the Division of Rehabilitation Psychology of the American Psychological Association. Dr. Siller has published extensively in the area of psychological adjustment to disability, but he is known best for his critically important research on the structure and psychodynamic determinants of attitudinal reactions to disability.

The historical roots of the DFS-G are located in research on reactions to physical disability that was carried out by Siller, Chipman, Ferguson, and Vann (1967) in the mid-1960s. Using data derived from objective questionnaires, projective tests, and in-depth interviews, Siller and his co-workers delineated 13 negative and 4 positive components of attitudes that transcended specific disability conditions. Several of these categories (e.g., strain in social interaction, attribution of negative qualities, loss of empathic potential, fear it could happen to self, and benevolent attitude) were operationalized in subsequent factor analytic investigations.

The distinguishing feature of Siller's research program was the explicit reliance on a psychoanalytic theoretical framework. The psychoanalytic approach to this area of inquiry is premised on the understanding that self-feelings originate in elemental body sensations and awareness, and that unconscious cues stemming from early developmental experiences influence the formation and structure of attitudes toward physical disability. Siller and his students conducted a number of studies relating attitudes toward disability to fundamental psychodynamic concepts and intrapsychic processes, such as castration anxiety, object representation, and ego defense style preferences. An integrated survey of the results of these investigations, as well as more thorough reviews of the literature concerned with personality correlates of attitudes toward disability, can be found in several book chapters by Siller (1984a, 1984b, 1988).

Rather than attempting to develop a multidimensional conception of attitudes using the ambiguous term *disability,* Siller, Ferguson, Vann, and Holland (1967) initiated their instrument construction research by focusing on three representative disabilities: amputation, blindness, and cosmetic conditions. It was only after common attitude dimensions emerged from factor analyses of these disabilities that Siller concluded it might be feasible to construct an instrument to measure general attitudes toward disability without employing the generic stimulus "disabled people" as the attitude referent. Details concerning the development of the DFS-G are contained in the Technical Aspects section of this review.

The DFS-G consists of 69 statements that express reactions, describe assumed attributes, or advocate policies toward nine types of disabling conditions: amputation, blindness, deafness, facial scars, epilepsy, cancer, paralysis, hunchback, and heart trouble. Respondents indicate their opinions about each statement using a 6-point Likert format ranging from "Strongly Agree" to "Strongly Disagree." The 69 statements require sixth-grade reading ability and can be completed in about 15 minutes. The DFS-G can be appropriately administered in small groups to most adolescents and adults. The instrument is scored objectively by summing the scores for the items comprising each attitude component.

Brief descriptions of the seven DFS-G scales, along with an illustrative item, follow:

1. *Interaction Strain* (IS; 9 items). Uneasiness in the presence of persons with disabilities and uncertainty as to how to deal with them (e.g., "I would feel nervous with a blind person because a lot of the time I wouldn't know the right thing to do").
2. *Rejection of Intimacy* (RI; 11 items). Rejection of close, particularly familial, relationships with individuals with disabilities (e.g. "I would be upset if a child of mine dated a person with bad facial scars").
3. *Generalized Rejection* (GR; 12 items). A pervasive negative and derogatory approach to persons with disabilities with consequent advocacy of segregation (e.g., "Deaf people are best off staying among themselves").
4. *Authoritarian Virtuousness* (AV; 10 items). Ostensibly a "prodisabled" orientation, though really rooted in an authoritarian context; manifests in a call for special treatment that is less benevolent and more harmful than it seems (e.g., "A person who is paralyzed can understand people better than someone who isn't").
5. *Inferred Emotional Consequences* (IEC; 8 items). Intense hostile references to the character and emotions of the person with a disability (e.g., "People with heart trouble feel sorry for themselves").
6. *Distressed Identification* (DI; 12 items). Personalized hypersensitivity to people with disabilities, who serve as activators of anxiety about one's own vulnerability to disability (e.g., "I get nervous about my own health when I hear about someone who has cancer").
7. *Imputed Functional Limitations* (IFL; 7 items). Devaluation of the capacities of people with disabilities in coping with their environments (e.g., "People with epilepsy can do things as well as anyone else").

The DFS-G was published in the sourcebook by Antonak and Livneh (1988, pp. 148–152), and the scoring key appears in Figure 1 in this review.

**Fig. 1.** Disability Factor Scales-General (DFS-G) scoring key

1. *Interaction Strain* (*N* =9; range 9–54)
   1, 7*, 14, 21, 26, 34, 41*, 48, 55*
2. *Rejection of Intimacy* (*N* =11; range 11–66)
   2, 9, 16, 23, 30, 38, 45, 51, 58*, 62, 66
3. *Generalized Rejection* (*N* =12; range 12–72)
   3, 10, 17, 20, 24, 31, 35, 39, 46, 52, 59, 64
4. *Authoritarian Virtuousness* (*N* =10; range 10–60)
   4, 11, 22, 28, 37, 44, 49, 53, 60, 67
5. *Inferred Emotional Consequences* (*N* =8; range 8–48)
   5, 12, 19, 29, 32, 40, 63, 69
6. *Distressed Identification* (*N* =12; range 12–72)
   6, 13, 18, 25, 33, 42, 47, 50, 54, 57, 61, 68
7. *Imputed Functional Limitations* (*N* =7; range 7–42)
   8*, 15*, 27*, 36*, 43*, 56*, 65*

*Reverse scoring for starred items (i.e., 1 = 6; 2 = 5; 3 = 4; 4 = 3; 5 = 2; 6 = 1).

**Practical Applications/Uses**

The Disability Factor Scales–General (DFS-G) has been applied primarily in research projects designed to investigate the nature and causes of prejudicial attitudes toward people with physical disabilities. One finds examples of such research in studies by Anderson, Asher, Clark, Orrick, and Quiason (1979), Florian, Weisel, Kravetz, and Shurka-Zernitsky (1989), Kang and Masoodi (1977), and Weisel (1988). The dissertation projects carried out by Siller's students under his direction provide additional such material (Siller, 1988).

Additionally, the DFS-G and other instruments in the series have been used in psychoanalytically oriented counseling with clients for whom physical disablement is a threatening issue and in training as a sensitization device for rehabilitation personnel. Beyond assessing prejudicial attitudes held by people without disabilities, the DFS-G can be used in counseling and research applications with persons who have disabilities, serving as a measure of self-esteem or disability acceptance for this population. However, all clinical applications must rely substantially on the analysis of item content, because the DFS-G normative data are of questionable value.

The original norms for the DFS-G consisted of means and standard deviations for more than a dozen occupational and student groups, such as teachers, nurses, physical therapists, and dental students. Milestone events in the disability rights movement, including the Rehabilitation Act of 1973 and subsequent reauthorizations culminating in the Americans with Disabilities Act of 1990, as well as renewed activity by disability rights organizations have most certainly produced significant changes in attitudes toward people with disabilities. After 20 years, new DFS-G norms should be developed for pertinent populations.

In addition to the DFS-G, the Disability Factor Scales series includes instruments designed to measure attitudes toward six specific disabilities: amputation, blindness, cosmetic conditions, deafness, obesity, and cancer. For three of these conditions (cosmesis, obesity, and cancer), disability-specific attitude components have been discovered; hence, for applications involving these disabilities, the disability-specific instruments might be more appropriately used (copies available from Jerome Siller, 808 Park Ave., Manhasset, NY 11030).

The above proviso notwithstanding, it would appear feasible to construct new instruments for other disabling conditions, employing the existing DFS-G item stems and substituting the specific disability. This strategy would be most easily justified for the seven replicated DFS-G dimensions, recognizing that it is possible for other disability-specific attitude components to emerge in factor analytic studies, as was the case for cosmesis, obesity, and cancer.

### Technical Aspects

The Disability Factor Scales–General (DFS-G) has its origins in earlier research by Siller and his colleagues and students that produced multidimensional scales to measure attitudes toward amputation, blindness, cosmetic conditions, deafness, and obesity (Siller, Ferguson, Vann, & Holland, 1967; Siller, Ferguson, Vann, & Holland, 1968; Ferguson, 1970; Vann, 1970). Because the factor analyses of the separate disability groups produced a consistent set of replicable, attitudinal dimensions, Siller reasoned that it might be feasible to construct a general measure of attitudes toward persons with physical disabilities. The strategy was to combine information on the dimensional structure of specific disability conditions with a wider variety of disabilities.

A 120-item preliminary questionnaire was assembled, with 15 items for each of the eight dimensions of attitudes previously found in work with specific disability conditions (the seven dimensions listed earlier plus Denial of Severity, which emerged in the deafness study). Item content and style paralleled earlier Disability Factor Scales questionnaires, and a number of new disability conditions were added to those for which the factorial structure had already been established.

The highest loading items for each dimension were used without change for the conditions of amputation, blindness, deafness, and facial scars. The same and other high-loading item stems also were used for the new conditions of epilepsy, cancer, paralysis, hunchback, and heart trouble. Siller et al. chose the disabilities to represent a wide variety of conditions varying in visibility and seriousness.

The research sample consisting of 772 respondents was heterogeneous with respect to sex, age, and educational attainment. A principal factors analysis with orthogonal procrustes rotation to the eight hypothesized attitude dimensions was carried out. Several varimax rotations also were performed to provide additional perspectives on the dimensional structure of the data set.

Examination of the procrustes factor loading matrix revealed good support for six of the target factors. Imputed Functional Limitations was only weakly supported, however, while Denial of Severity was not sustained. Further inspection of the factor loadings indicated that 36 items could be deleted from the DFS-G pool, either because they missed their targeted factors, were factorially complex, or represented the Denial of Severity factor.

The remaining 84 items were then rotated by the procrustes procedure to a seven-factor target solution, which established the basis for the final version of the DFS-G. By examining target and nontarget loadings, as well as the content of the items, the researchers identified a final set of the best 69 items. The seven DFS-G scales, composed of between 7 and 12 items, corresponded closely to the hypothesized attitude structure, with goodness of fit indices ranging from .72 to .87 (Siller, 1969a, 1970).

Three independent factor analyses of the DFS-G have been reported during the past decade. Ezrachi (1980) analyzed the DFS-G for a sample of 251 high school and college students and compared the results to those from a parallel reanalysis of Siller's original construction sample of 772 respondents. The two intercorrelation matrices were reduced by principal factors analysis, followed by varimax rotation of seven factors. Congruence coefficients for the seven matched factors ranged from .86 to .94, indicating that Siller's original factor structure was almost perfectly replicated.

Livneh (1985b) factor analyzed the DFS-G for a sample of 200 college students using two different condensation procedures (principal factors analysis and maximum likelihood factor analysis), each followed by orthogonal and oblique rotations. The results of the orthogonal (varimax) rotations essentially replicated the seven DFS-G factors identified by Siller, although support for Interaction Strain, Rejection of Intimacy, and Imputed Functional Limitations was weaker than for the other four factors.

The strongest evidence for the replicability of the DFS-G factors came from an analysis of a Hebrew translation of the instrument administered to 658 Jewish Israeli high school students (Weisel et al., 1988). Principal components factor analysis of the 69 DFS-G items was followed by varimax rotation of eight factors. Item loadings indicated that five of Siller's seven factors were almost completely replicated, with Generalized Rejection and Interaction Strain only partially replicated. Congruence coefficients calculated for corresponding factors from the Israeli sample and Siller's original factor loading pattern ranged from .73 to .94.

All three factor analytic investigations provided additional support for the DFS-G scale structure, with the transcultural replicability of the Israeli sample being especially impressive. Taken together, the results of these studies confirm the validity of Siller's original analyses and strengthen arguments for the psychometric integrity of the seven attitudinal constructs measured by the DFS-G.

Two other studies provide further support for the theoretical rationale and construct validity of the DFS-G. In conjunction with the development of the DFS-G, Siller (1969b) demonstrated convincingly that attitudes toward people with physical disabilities are organized primarily by attitudinal dimension, rather than by type of disabling condition. A procrustes rotation that was targeted to the nine disabilities represented in the initial 120-item set was compared to the rotation targeted to the eight attitude dimensions. Comparisons between the internal consistency coefficients and the goodness of fit indices for the two resulting factor solutions definitively supported the partition based on attitude dimensions. In other words, attitudinal reactions to people with physical disabilities are determined more by broad categories of affective response than by particular disability conditions.

An experimental investigation by Marinelli and Kelz (1973) found that high and low scoring groups on the Disability Factor Scales–Cosmetic (DFS-C) were significantly different on measures of state anxiety (heart rate) and trait anxiety (Manifest Anxiety Scale) obtained in conjunction with a standardized interaction with a person with severe facial scarring. In contrast, no significant differences occurred between high and low scoring groups on a unidimensional measure of global attitude toward people with disabilities. Because five of the six DFS-C component scales relate directly to anxiety in interpersonal interactions with persons with cosmetic handicaps, the sensitivity of the instrument to the experimental anxiety measures is fully understandable. The Marinelli and Kelz research constitutes a construct validation study of the DFS-C, and by extension supports the more general approach to measurement of attitudes toward people with disabilities followed by Siller and his colleagues.

Although orthogonally rotated factors are by definition statistically independent, unweighted scales based on orthogonal factor solutions typically evidence moderate correlations among themselves. The DFS-G scale intercorrelations calculated for two large heterogeneous samples (*N*s = 722 and 569) ranged from .04 to .60, with a median of .33, and from .03 to .52, with a median of .33, respectively. The highest correlations are reflective of the common elements measured by the scales: Interaction Strain and Rejection of Intimacy (.60/.47), Inferred Emotional Consequences and Generalized Rejection (.57/.52), Inferred Emotional Consequences and Rejection of Intimacy (.50/.40), Inferred Emotional Consequences and Interaction Strain (.47/.41), Imputed Functional Limitations and Generalized Rejection (.46/.44), and Rejection of Intimacy and Generalized Rejection (.46/.41).

These scale correlations justify two conclusions about the DFS-G. First, when the variance overlap (correlations squared) among the scales is compared to the scale reliabilities summarized below, it is apparent that the scales contain mostly variance specific to each attitude component measured. In other words, the DFS-G measures seven relatively independent facets of attitudes toward disability. Second, the pattern of scale correlations is consistent with the emergence of a broad second-order construct labeled Net Affect in three factor analyses of Disability Factor Scales instruments (Livneh, 1985a; Kohler & Graves, 1973; Siller, Ferguson, Vann, & Holland, 1967). The DFS-G scales are organized correlationally in a meaningful and replicable manner.

Internal consistency reliability coefficients for the seven scales calculated for the two research samples are Interaction Strain (.83/.76), Rejection of Intimacy (.87/.83), Generalized Rejection (.85/.89), Authoritarian Virtuousness (.83/.84), Inferred Emotional Consequences (.84/.78), Distressed Identification (.86/.86), and Imputed Functional Limitations (.76/.69). Although there are no published experimental reliability data for the DFS-G, reasonable inferences can be made from the test-retest reliabilities for the disability-specific instruments (amputation, blindness, and cosmetic condition) from which the DFS-G evolved. Test-retest coefficients for scales composed of 10 to 12 items with a 2-week retest interval ranged from .76 to .89, with a median of .84; with a 3-month interval, coefficients ranged from .68

to .87, with a median of .78 (Siller, Ferguson, Vann, & Holland, 1967, p. 31). Thus one can conclude that the DFS-G scales reliably measure seven components of attitudes toward disability.

A final issue concerns the extent to which DFS-G scales may be contaminated by social desirability influences. Two studies have correlated the Edwards Social Desirability Scale and the Marlowe-Crowne Social Approval Scale with the seven DFS-G scales (Dolak, 1979; Weisel et al., 1988). Though several significant relationships were observed in each analysis, there was only one finding common to both investigations. This limited evidence suggests that social desirability responding is not a serious problem with the DFS-G.

## Critique

The Disability Factor Scales-General (DFS-G) is the product of a psychometrically sophisticated program of research on the nature and determinants of attitudes toward persons with physical disabilities carried out by Jerome Siller and his colleagues and students. Unlike many instruments, the development of the DFS-G is embedded in a consistent theoretical framework, in this case a traditional psychoanalytic perspective.

Three major research conclusions were reached in conjunction with the construction of the DFS-G: (a) attitudes are best measured using specific disabilities (e.g., blindness, amputation, epilepsy) as stimulus referents rather than the vague term *disabled persons;* (b) attitudes toward people with physical disabilities are multidimensional in their expression rather than reducible to a single continuum of favorableness of opinion; and (c) attitudes are organized by psychosocial constructs rather than by specific disabling conditions.

The major results of the research program have been an empirical taxonomy of components of attitudinal reactions to people with physical disabilities, and a series of instruments for reliably and validly measuring attitudes toward physical disability, including a general purpose instrument, the DFS-G. The only legitimate criticisms of the DFS-G concern the absence of norms, which could be remediated by the systematic collection and publication of new normative data, and that the terminology and phrasing of some items is inappropriate by current standards and should be revised or replaced.

For an instrument that was developed almost a quarter of a century ago, the DFS-G is remarkably free of handicapist language. Fewer than one third of the items contain terminology or expressions that tend to stigmatize or devalue people with disabilities. Examples of handicapist and nonhandicapist expressions, all taken from the DFS-G, are "an amputee"/"a person who is missing a limb"; "a blind person"/"a child who is blind"; and "paralyzed person"/"a person who is paralyzed" (the latter expression in each pair is preferable). With minor rephrasing, most of the unacceptable terminology could be removed from the DFS-G.

The term *hunchback* and the phrase "person who is a hunchback" present special problems, however, because the word is clearly unacceptable by contemporary standards. *Hunchback* (or *humpback* ) refers to a person with kyphosis, an angular curvature of the upper spine caused by tuberculosis, osteoarthritis, and other diseases. Because *hunchback* occurs just five times in the DFS-G, and only two items are scored on the same scale (Rejection of Intimacy), substitution of the phrase "person with severe spinal deformity" is recommended.

In conclusion, the Disability Factor Scales–General (DFS-G) resulted from a carefully designed program of research that advanced psychological understanding about the way nondisabled people react to disability. It is the best instrument available for measuring attitudes toward people with physical disabilities.

## References

Anderson, F.J., Asher, M.A., Clark, G.M., Orrick, J.M., & Quiason, E.P. (1979). Adjustment of adolescents to chronic disability. *Rehabilitation Psychology, 26*, 177–185.

Antonak, R.F., & Livneh, H. (1988). *The measurement of attitudes toward people with disabilities: Methods, psychometrics, and scales.* Springfield, IL: Charles C Thomas.

Dolak, E.D. (1979). *Social desirability correlates of the Disability Factor Scales–General.* New York: Department of Educational Psychology, New York University.

Ezrachi, O. (1980, March). *Opinions about the disabled: Congruent dimensions in a replication.* Paper presented at the Third Annual Meeting of the Eastern Educational Research Association, Norfolk, VA.

Ferguson, L.T. (1970). Components of attitudes toward the deaf. *Proceedings of the 78th Annual Convention of the American Psychological Association, 5*, 693–694.

Florian, V., Weisel, A., Kravetz, S., & Shurka-Zernitsky, E. (1989). Attitudes in the kibbutz and city toward persons with disabilities: A multifactor comparison. *Rehabilitation Counseling Bulletin, 32*, 210–218.

Kang, Y.W., & Masoodi, B.A. (1977). Attitudes toward blind people among theological and education students. *Journal of Visual Impairment and Blindness, 71*, 394–400.

Kohler, E.T., & Graves, W.H. (1973). Factor analysis of the Disability Factor Scales with the Little Jiffy, Mark III. *Rehabilitation Psychology, 20*, 102–107.

Livneh, H. (1985a). The Disability Factor Scales–General: Second-order factor structure. *Journal of General Psychology, 112*, 279–283.

Livneh, H. (1985b). Factor structure of attitudes toward individuals with disabilities—a replication. *Rehabilitation Counseling Bulletin, 29*, 53–58.

Marinelli, R.P., & Kelz, J.W. (1973). Anxiety and attitudes toward disabled persons. *Rehabilitation Counseling Bulletin, 16*, 198–205.

Siller, J. (1969a). *The general form of the Disability Factor Scales series (DFS-G).* New York: Department of Educational Psychology, New York University.

Siller, J. (1969b). *The generality of attitudes toward the physically disabled.* New York: Department of Educational Psychology, New York University.

Siller, J. (1970). Generality of attitudes toward the physically disabled. *Proceedings of the 78th Annual Convention of the American Psychological Association, 5*, 697–698.

Siller, J. (1984a). Attitudes toward the physically disabled. In R.L. Jones (Ed.), *Attitudes and attitude change in special education: Theory and practice* (pp. 184–205). Reston, VA: Council for Exceptional Children.

Siller, J. (1984b). The role of personality in attitudes toward those with physical disabilities. In C.J. Golden (Ed.), *Current topics in rehabilitation psychology* (pp. 201–227). New York: Grune & Stratton.

Siller, J. (1988). Intrapsychic aspects of attitudes toward persons with disabilities. In H.E. Yuker (Ed.), *Attitudes toward persons with disabilities* (pp. 58–67). New York: Springer.

Siller, J., Chipman, A., Ferguson, L.T., & Vann, D.H. (1967). *Attitudes of the non-disabled toward the physically disabled* (Studies in Reactions to Disability: XI). New York: Department of Educational Psychology, New York University.

Siller, J., Ferguson, L.T., Vann, D.H., & Holland, B. (1967). *Structure of attitudes toward the physically disabled: The Disability Factor Scales—Amputation, Blindness, and Cosmetic Conditions* (Studies in Reactions to Disability: XII). New York: Department of Educational Psychology, New York University.

Siller, J., Ferguson, L.T., Vann, D.H. & Holland, B. (1968). Structure of attitudes toward the physically disabled: The Disability Factor Scales—Amputation, Blindness, Cosmetic Conditions. *Proceedings of the 76th Annual Convention of the American Psychological Association, 3,* 651–652.

Vann, D.H. (1970). Components of attitudes toward the obese including presumed responsibility for the condition. *Proceedings of the 78th Annual Convention of the American Psychological Association, 5,* 695–696.

Weisel, A. (1988). Contact with mainstreamed disabled children and attitudes towards disability: A multidimensional analysis. *Educational Psychology, 8,* 161–168.

Weisel, A., Kravetz, S., Florian, V., & Shurka-Zernitsky, E. (1988). The structure of attitudes towards persons with disabilities: An Israeli validation of Siller's Disability Factor Scales–General (DFS-G). *Rehabilitation Psychology, 33,* 227–238.

**Alan C. Bugbee, Jr., Ph.D.**
*Director of Educational Systems, The American College, Bryn Mawr, Pennsylvania.*

# DOLE VOCATIONAL SENTENCE COMPLETION BLANK

*Arthur A. Dole. Wood Dale, Illinois: Stoelting Company.*

## Introduction

The Dole Vocational Sentence Completion Blank (VSCB) is a 21-item, semiprojective, paper-and-pencil sentence completion instrument intended primarily to assist guidance counselors and school psychologists in helping junior high and high school students plan and facilitate educational and vocational goals. It is called "semiprojective" because it combines elements of both projective and objective testing. It is a projective instrument in that it requires responses to open-ended stems; it is an objective instrument in that it is scored following a fairly well-defined set of rules. According to the test manual, the VSCB is not intended to be used independently, but "to supplement and perhaps amplify in the client's own words the results of the standardized inventories such as the Kuder or Strong" (Dole, 1982, p. 1).

So used, this test seeks to bridge the differences between stated or perceived occupational and educational goals or interests revealed by interest inventories and latent aspects of personality. The latent aspects usually would not be examined in career planning, although they assuredly will have strong direct and indirect influences on these decisions and their consequences. As is pointed out in the manual, "unlike projectives such as Rorschach or TAT, VSCB is not designed to tap repressed or unconscious material or to reveal complex personality dynamics" (Dole, 1982, p. 1). It is intended to reveal more about a person than the matching of personal interests with occupations found in the interest inventories; instead, the VCSB means to provide the depth of the individual to the breadth of career goals indicated by the interest inventories.

The test's author, Dr. Arthur A. Dole, is Professor Emeritus, Psychology in Education, at the University of Pennsylvania's Graduate School of Education. During his graduate studies (M.A. and Ph.D.) at Ohio State University, while taking courses taught by Julian Rotter (author of the Rotter Incomplete Sentences Blank), Dole became interested in developing a test like the VSCB. His doctoral dissertation (Dole, 1957) was the apparent precursor to the VSCB, although an earlier version (1952) is listed in the manual. The final version of these studies is the Dole VSCB, revised in 1979. Although it is not clearly stated, it appears that the VSCB reviewed here is the fourth version. This is based on the listing of two other revised manuals (Dole, 1959, 1977) in the references of the present manual (Dole, 1982). The original manual does not appear in the references, though it may be a part of the doctoral dissertation.

**Practical Applications/Uses**

This instrument is designed principally for vocational/career counseling in junior high and high school settings. It also can be used for rehabilitation counseling. The manual also mentions (p. 1) diagnosis and therapy as a use, but does not seem to pursue that course of action. The only detailed description of use found in the manual (Dole, 1982, pp. 12–13) has to do with counseling.

As the manual makes clear from the outset, the Dole Vocational Sentence Completion Blank is intended to supplement and enhance the results of vocational interest inventories like the Strong Vocational Interest Blank and/or the Kuder Interest Inventory. It is *not* intended to stand alone in assisting students in selecting careers or life goals.

The manual says that the VSCB can be used with anyone who is literate and recommends that its completion should be voluntary. It does not, however, provide for any particular uses or groups or individuals for whom this instrument should be used. It would seem that the VSCB would best serve to assist high school students who have many possible career goals or who have several equally interesting, but diverse, goals and want assistance in career selection. As Dr. Dole points out, "The VSCB is a personal inventory whose usefulness is diminished if the respondent is resistant" (Dole, 1982, p. 13).

The Dole VSCB can be administered in almost any setting by almost anyone who can read and write. Its only real requirement is that the test takers describe their real feelings in completing each sentence. There is no time limit, but the manual mentions (Dole, 1982, p. 6) that in group-testing situations, most subjects finish in about 20 minutes. No mention is made of how long individually administered tests tend to take.

The manual provides succinct instructions for administration of this instrument, including a six-sentence statement to read aloud in group administrations. In addition, suggestions of possible answers to commonly asked questions about the Dole VSCB are provided.

Group administration instructions also suggest that the administrator should "tactfully" prevent collaboration among subjects in completing sentences and/or leaving stems blank. The instructions do not, however, provide any suggestions about how the examiner for a group administration might accomplish this, especially in light of this manual's instruction for only casual inspection of returned forms.

The VSCB consists of two separate sheets of paper, the Record Form and the Individual Score Profile. The Record Form provides brief instructions and the sentence stems for the test taker to complete. The Individual Score Profile provides a form for the scorer to classify responses within categories. The front side of the Record Form asks the subject's name, sex, age, present occupational goal, and school or college, as well as the date the form is filled out. This sheet then provides eight brief lines of instruction explaining the VSCB and how the respondent should answer it. One sentence, "Simply express your real feelings" (Dole, 1974), is italicized to urge subjects to respond as they believe best describes their true feelings. This is done to dissuade respondents from "parroting" answers or responding with what they believe a counselor wants to hear. This is further stressed by the statements that there are no correct answers and that "different people write different things" (Dole, 1974).

Twenty-one sentence stems are presented next. The taker is asked to complete each sentence within an underlined space following the stem. These spaces vary from about 4½ to 6½ inches wide. The manual mentions (Dole, 1982, p. 6) that subjects may write on the back of the sheet if they wish to elaborate on a sentence, but this is not part of the instructions on the form (it's mentioned only as a suggested answer to possible questions). Presumably, short completions are expected, though this is not specified until the subject reaches the last statement (#5) on the reverse side of the form.

The other side of the Record Form seeks Supplementary Information through five questions. The first asks the respondent to list any of the sentence stems that he or she feels did not bring out any important information. The second asks which stem(s) he or she found especially difficult to complete, and the third asks which stems brought out important information. These three questions each have one line on which to respond. The fourth question asks for any other information not covered on the 21 stems that respondents believe is important in planning their lives. The form provides about three lines for this response. As previously mentioned, the fifth statement provides space for takers to expand on their sentence completions.

The second sheet, the Individual Score Profile, is used to classify a subject's responses within a defined group of categories. This form is laid length-wise and includes the respondent's (listed as "client") name, age, sex, date (presumably of the scoring), major, and school, as well as the name of the scorer. The profile lists 29 categories from four general groupings: Concern, General Emphases, Specific Preference Areas, and Miscellaneous. The form provides eight spaces for the number of mentions in sentence completions for each category, followed by a space for counselor notes and then a section called Other Categories.

The Other Categories section of this form lists five areas—Peace of Mind, Security, Value, Obligation, and Health—within the Concerns grouping and three areas—Religion, Social Studies, and Negative Academic—within the Specific Preference Areas grouping. The Miscellaneous grouping contains a category labeled Unclassifiable. Following these areas are three spaces for recording which responses fit into these other categories.

Although the VSCB may be administered by almost anyone, scoring requires knowledge of the scoring keys and procedures. The manual indicates that "any reasonably intelligent person, irregardless of psychological experience, can learn to score VSCB in a few hours" (Dole, 1982, p. 6). The manual also suggests that a potential scorer should first complete a VSCB. After that he or she should become familiar with the instrument's general principles and definitions for scoring, collectively (about 13 pages in the manual). The scorer should then score his or her own profile. Professor Dole mentions that this method was used to educate two student clerks. He says it took about 3 hours to "attain a satisfactory comprehension of the materials" (Dole, 1974, p. 7).

According to the manual, the scoring categories used in the VSCB were selected by how well they met the following six criteria: (a) the category was more frequently correctly selected than incorrectly selected on a stem-by-stem basis;

(b) the category was independent of other categories; (c) the category was consistent with an accepted theory of career development; (d) the category had a mean of no less than .5 and no more than 3.0, with a range for each 100 subjects of at least 0 to 5; (e) at least five different sentence stems generated responses for that category; and (f) the category is a commonly recognized one, like those used on a Strong or Kuder instrument. The application of these criteria to responses (Dole, 1977) yielded 27 categories. Two additional categories, Omit and Other, were provided to allow for "unfinished, unscorable, and/or ambiguous responses and for completions assigned to categories other than the 27" (Dole, 1982, p. 3).

The assumptions section of the manual states that the VSCB is scored in terms of the frequency with which responses fit into categories. This is done because Dole assumes that "frequency of response is a sensible index of importance and that it is useful in counseling to compare categories by their frequencies" (Dole, 1982, pp. 1–2). This seems consistent with the career development interest inventories on which this instrument is attempting to expand. They, too, use ipsative scores.

Ipsative scores are those in which a person's performance (or, in this case, vocational or career interest) in a subtest or category is contrasted with that person's average performance across all subtests or categories on the instrument. This is quite different from the usual norm-referenced scoring-comparison to a normative group—or criterion-referenced scoring, "the degree to which [a test taker's] achievement resembles desired performance at any specified level" (Glaser, 1963, p. 519). Although there is controversy about this type of scoring (e.g., Anastasi, 1976, pp. 539–540; Mehrens & Lehmann, 1984, p. 461), Dole states clearly that he believes in "empirical and inductive methods applied to a single individual (idiographic, ipsative)" (Dole, 1982, p. 2). In this, Professor Dole agrees with the scoring methods of many interest inventories, especially that of the Kuder Vocational Preference Record.

This use of ipsative scoring is consistent with the VSCB's intended use as a supplement to interest inventories for counseling. This instrument seeks to provide more and deeper information about the client's career and vocational interests, as a supplement to his or her match(es) with broad areas of interest (Kuder Vocational Preference Record) or with specific occupations (Strong-Campbell Interest Inventory). Because of this, the user would not be particularly interested in the test taker's relationship with a normative group on the VSCB.

The interpretation of results is based on the objective scores of the VSCB, the result(s) of standardized interest inventories, and the judgment of the user. The objective scoring aspect of interpretation comes from the well-documented "Definitions of VSCB Categories With Examples" section of the manual. As Dr. Dole points out in the apparently unused *What Your Score Means* handout, "We assume on good evidence that the more times a person says something about himself the more important it is to him" (Dole, 1971, p. 2.32–2.34). This ties the responses on the VSCB with the scores a person received on the Strong-Campbell and/or Kuder. The judgment of the user comes into play somewhat in scoring but mostly in conducting counseling interviews, where he or she both extracts information and explains the measuring of the VSCB to the client. As Professor Dole puts it, "VSCB serves its purpose if it accelerates client movement in counseling, samples very widely, but only approximately, many current attitudes and interests, and objectifies individualities" (Dole, 1982, p. 13).

This quotation notes an important point about the interpretation of the VSCB: the attitudes and interests expressed are considered to be transient (i.e., "current") in nature, at least with the adolescents this instrument seems to be principally intended for (Dole, 1982, p. 4; Dole, 1974, pp. 1.29–1.33). As Dole states in the manual, "By choice I have accentuated impermanence, diversity, individuality, uniqueness, and open-endedness within an economical format" (Dole, 1982, p. 2).

**Technical Aspects**

The "Psychometric Properties" section of the Dole VSCB manual is short (2½ pages), but it provides much information. Unfortunately, much of the latter comes from another work (Dole, 1977). That work, the apparent preliminary manual for the VSCB, is mentioned frequently in the instruction manual. This is particularly problematic because that work is a mimeographed report that is not available from the publisher. This reviewer's inquiry to the author provided a 1974 draft of what apparently became the 1977 report. This is especially unfortunate because the VSCB's instruction manual gives the impression that the manual containing this vital information is available (i.e., "A technical manual designed for research specialists [Dole, 1977] summarizes in further detail more than 25 years of published and unpublished work on VSCB" [Dole, 1982, p. 3]), although the reference to that work (p. 29) notes that it is a mimeographed report.

It seems that the instructional manual would have the user view this 1977 report as a technical manual, but does not provide it. This lack of availability of psychometric information does not fulfill the accepted standards for tests (American Educational Research Association, American Psychological Association, & National Council on Measurement in Education, 1985). This is especially interesting in light of Dr. Dole's assertion that he tried to follow such standards and his statement "I realize that in some instances there are gaps between ideal, essential, or very desirable published standard and current information about VSCB. The closing of such gaps, as time and funds permit, is an unfinished, long-term project" (Dole, 1982, p. 2). This implies that any failure to fulfill these standards will be corrected in the future. However, there is no evidence that any new versions are in production, so it can be assumed that these "gaps" will be closed by others.

Interscorer and test-retest reliabilities are presented in the manual. Interscorer reliability is a reflection of the degree of agreement between how two or more raters score responses (see Fleiss, 1981, pp. 212–236). According to Professor Dole, experienced VSCB scorers range from 80% to 95% agreement with one another. No information, though, is presented about the scorers, how many tests they scored, what indicated agreement, what indicated disagreement, and so forth. No interrater agreement statistics (such as Cohen's kappa) are presented.

The manual mentions a blind scoring study where "differences between the means of two independent scorers on each category in samples ranging from 20 to 50 did not attain significance; when categories were ranked in the order of frequency correlations between scorers exceeded .80" (Dole, 1982, p. 3). Like the previously mentioned interscorer reliability, no information is presented about these scorers. In addition, and perhaps more importantly, no information is provided about how these means and frequencies were computed. For example, was the order of frequency based on agreement of assigning the same item to a category or only the number of assignments within a category? It is interesting to note that this important information does not appear in the draft for the 1977 manual either. This lack of information also fails to fulfill the recommended standards for psychological tests and is clearly more than a "gap" between research and standards.

The manual mentions a study of the stability of interest, concerns, and emphases (and, consequently, of the VSCB) over a 2-year period. The adolescent subjects (134 boys and 169 girls) took the VSCB and the Milwaukee Interest Inventory in the 8th grade and again in the 10th grade. This study yielded Pearson *r*'s from –.01 to .56 for the boys and .06 to .51 for the girls. Dr. Dole explains this relative lack of stability by saying that the interests of adolescents change over time. Although this extensive instability could be due to the vicissitudes of adolescent interests (e.g., see Mehrens & Lehmann, 1984, pp. 447–472), it may be due to the instability of the VSCB over time.

The Dole VSCB manual mentions six concurrent and predictive studies. As with reliability, the information is quite sparse. Considering the age of this instrument and its commercial availability, it is quite surprising that so little is available on the VSCB's validity and that what is available is presented to such a very limited extent in the manual. This conflicts with the test standards' general principle that a test developer should provide as much validity information as possible so the user can evaluate the test of the research for his own purposes (AERA, APA, & NCME, 1985).

One thing that seems peculiar about this test is that the author explains the low reliability by saying that subjects' interests change over time but then utilizes predictive studies to validate the instrument. The axiom that a test can be reliable without being valid, but not the reverse, comes to mind. However, because this instrument is intended to supplement more reliable instruments (Kuder and Strong), perhaps this is not as important.

In addition to reliability and validity, Professor Dole also covers the VSCB's relation to other variables in the "Psychometric Properties" section of the manual. He begins by stating that sex is related to a number of the VSCB's 29 categories, race is associated with some of them, but that socioeconomic status and "measured ability" are independent of a subject's vocational and career goals. He cites four studies and mentions another without citation, but fails to provide statistical information to back up his assertions. Although not of critical importance, such coverage would provide helpful information for researchers who wish to pursue this.

It is worth noting that the 1974 draft copy of the original manual for the VSCB contains considerably more psychometric information than the current manual. It is unfortunate that the manual was shortened; its present paucity of psychometric information does little to encourage its use.

The Dole VSCB is normed for urban and suburban students in 7th to 12th grades. These norms came from studies conducted between 1960 and 1969. The normative samples derive from eight schools, one in Hawaii, one in suburban Pennsylvania, and six in Philadelphia. The Hawaiian sample constitutes the 7th-grade normative male and female groups, the suburban Pennsylvania sample constitutes the 12th-grade normative groups, and the 8th-, 9th-, and 11th-grade norms were created from the Philadelphia school samples. It is noteworthy that no information appears about 10th-grade students and that some of the normative samples are very small (i.e., $N = 19$ for one group). The materials present no information about students in rural schools.

While the manual suggests that the VSCB be used with adults and college students (the scoring example is a college student), there are no norms available for such subjects. The manual's cover illustration suggests that the VSCB can be used with different age and ethnic groups, yet the manual does not provide such normative information or background. Perhaps this, too, was intended for future "gap"-filling research.

## Critique

The Dole Vocational Sentence Completion Blank is based on Dr. Arthur Dole's innovative idea to apply the concepts of the Rotter Incomplete Sentences Blank to assist in helping a subject plan vocational, educational, and life goals. It utilizes "free responses" to 21 sentence stems in order "to supplement and perhaps amplify in the client's own words the results of standardized (interest) inventories such as the Kuder or Strong" (Dole, 1982, p. 1). The VSCB has apparently existed since 1952 and has been examined in no less than 15 studies. The present form of this instrument was revised in 1979 and seems to have been printed in 1982, although the test form (Record Blank) is listed as being revised in 1974.

This instrument suffers from its stated attempt to cover many age and racial groups in many decisions. As has been pointed out elsewhere, "in attempting to be too many things, this test succeeds in validly and reliably measuring too few" (Lowman, 1985, p. 515). It appears that Professor Dole believed that his instrument could be of assistance in many things but limited his studies to helping high school students decide on vocational and/or educational choices. This tends to undercut the publisher's catalog's avowed large number of uses and may work against this test's usefulness as an aid in vocational counseling. This instrument would be better served if the author and the publisher were satisfied to refer to it as it is, an aid for high school vocational counseling, not as it may be, an omnitest for many facets of professional counseling and therapy.

As has been mentioned throughout this review, the VSCB manual provides too little information. This is especially true in the areas of validity and reliability but is also applicable to the test's norms and how they should be used. Probably the current manual's greatest flaw lies in its use of the 1977 manual as a principal source of information and research. This 1977 manual is not available from the publisher, and because it is a mimeographed report it does not appear to be available through any source other than the author. Even the author provided only a 1974 draft of the 1977 manual, which does not inspire confidence.

The foregoing criticism is not meant to say that the Dole VSCB serves no use. As indicated previously, it may be quite helpful in assisting high school students and, perhaps, college students and adults in expanding on interests revealed by tests such as the Strong Vocational Interest Blank or the Kuder Vocational Preference Record. The categories and the examples for scoring are well defined and may provide insightful and useful information. Nonetheless, the Dole Vocational Sentence Completion Blank needs more research and substantiation before it is used as any more than a discussion supplement to standardized interest inventories.

### References

American Educational Research Association, American Psychological Association, & National Council on Measurement in Education. (1985). *Standards for educational and psychological testing.* Washington, DC: American Psychological Association.

Anastasi, A. (1976). *Psychological testing* (4th ed.). New York: Macmillan.

Dole, A.A. (1957). An investigation of sentence completions as a method of measuring certain dimensions of the normal personality and as applied to prospective teachers. *Dissertation Abstracts International, 67,* 205A–209A.

Dole, A.A. (1959). *Dole Vocational Sentence Completion Blank revised manual.* Honolulu: University of Hawaii Bookstore.

Dole, A.A. (1971). *What your score on the Vocational Sentence Completion Blank means.* Unpublished report, University of Pennsylvania, Philadelphia.

Dole, A.A. (1974a). *Manual for Vocational Sentence Completion Blank draft.* Philadelphia: Author.

Dole, A.A. (1974b). *Record Form Dole Vocational Sentence Completion Blank.* Chicago: Stoelting.

Dole, A.A. (1977). *Manual for Vocational Sentence Completion Blank (revised).* Unpublished report, University of Pennsylvania, Philadelphia.

Dole, A.A. (1982). *Dole Vocational Sentence Completion Blank: Instruction manual.* Chicago: Stoelting.

Fleiss, J.L. (1981). *Statistical methods for rates and proportions* (2nd ed.). New York: Wiley.

Glaser, R. (1963). Instructional technology and the measurement of learning outcomes. *American Psychologist, 18,* 519–521.

Lowman, R.L. (1985). Review of Dole Vocational Sentence Completion Blank. In J.V. Mitchell, Jr. (Ed.), *The ninth mental measurements yearbook* (pp. 514–515). Lincoln, NE: Buros Institute of Mental Measurements.

Mehrens, W.A., & Lehmann, I.J. (1984). *Measurement and evaluation in education and psychology.* New York: Holt, Rinehart & Winston.

**David J. Mealor, Ph.D.**

*Associate Professor of School Psychology and Chair of Educational Services, University of Central Florida, Orlando, Florida.*

# EARLY CHILD DEVELOPMENT INVENTORY

*Harold Ireton. Minneapolis, Minnesota: Behavior Science Systems, Inc.*

## Introduction

The Early Child Development Inventory (ECDI) was developed as a brief screening inventory for use with children ages 15 months to 3 years. Designed to help identify children with developmental and other problems that may interfere with the ability to learn, the ECDI is based on the parent's (usually the mother's) report of the child's *present* functioning. The instrument was created to provide a brief, systematic, inexpensive method for screening children within the given age range. Although best used in conjunction with a developmental screening test, it can be used as a pretesting questionnaire.

An understanding of the ECDI derives from Harold Ireton's 21-year research experience with using mothers' reports to measure the development of young children. The foundation for the ECDI is based on the author's earlier work, the Minnesota Child Development Inventory (MCDI; Ireton & Thwing, 1968/1972). The ECDI is composed of components of the MCDI and is the fourth measure developed from that original inventory. The others are the Minnesota Infant Development Inventory (for infants in the first 15 months; 1977), the Minnesota Prekindergarten Inventory (a kindergarten readiness evaluation; 1979), and the Preschool Development Inventory (a briefer screening measure for 3- to 6-year-olds; 1984). The author notes that the ECDI is the least researched of the lot; to fully understand the ECDI, one must review the MCDI.

All ECDI items are taken from the original MCDI. The MCDI contained 320 statements describing behaviors of children from shortly after birth to 6½ years. The original norm group for the MCDI was comprised of white, middle-class children. "The scale areas and their items were derived from the child development literature, psychological tests, and mother's perspectives" (Rysberg, 1985, p. 992).

The ECDI consists of a questionnaire for the parent and a brief manual for the professional. The one-page questionnaire (front and back of a sheet) is divided into six sections: General Development (60 items), Possible Problems (24 items), Child Description (parent's brief description of the child), Special Problems or Disabilities (parent's report of problems that may be major handicaps or obstacles to learning), Questions or Concerns, and Parent's Functioning. The 60 items on Part 1 are an abbreviated form of the General Development Scale from the MCDI. The author notes that the "items are the most age-discriminating of the MCDI" (Ireton, 1988, p. 5) and cover seven developmental areas: Language Comprehension, Expressive Language, Gross Motor, Fine Motor, Self-Help, Situation Comprehension, and Personal-Social.

The first two sections of the ECDI are completed by answering "yes" or "no" to a series of behavioral statements. The remaining four sections serve as a basis for a structured interview with the parent. The instrument can be completed at home and brought to the screening or completed at the time of testing. The ECDI is easily and quickly scored, designed to alert the professional immediately to possible problem areas. The manual provides a developmental sequence (by months) for the 60 items in Part 1. Part 2, Possible Problems, items were adopted from previous child development inventory research.

### Practical Applications/Uses

The brief, inexpensive, easy to use ECDI provides professionals with a parental report of a child's development as well as of any special problems, handicaps, or concerns. Although it can serve as a pretesting database, the inventory's primary utility may be in serving as a basis for discussion with the parent(s). Although parents may view their child as doing well and having no problems, this may not be the case. A more detailed evaluation can yield a different picture. Any areas of disagreement can be discussed and possibly lead to better understanding of the child's "actual" performance. The focus of the discussion should be on the parent's perceptions.

Scoring the inventory presents a relatively simple procedure. The examiner/reviewer counts the numbers of "yes" responses for items 1–60 and records that score in a box labeled "Total." The examiner then refers to Table 1 in the manual, finds the child's age, and then reads across to the cutoff score. The cutoff scores are broken down by sex and a combined cutoff score. The user records the appropriate cutoff score in the box under the total score. If the total score is lower than the cutoff score, there may be a problem indicating the possible need for further evaluation. As the cutoff score for each age group is based on the performance of children who are 20% younger, a child's score would be below age expectations if it fell below the cutoff. All calculations are completed on the one-page answer sheet.

### Technical Aspects

As mentioned previously, any review of the ECDI must center around an understanding of the MCDI. Fortunately when one contacts the publisher about the ECDI, the author presents this information. However, when one views the manual of the ECDI, a number of technical inadequacies appear. There is little or no discussion about the inventory's reliability and validity, and the author presents no reliability or validity studies, although readers are referred to earlier work with the MCDI. Interestingly, the table used for determining cutoff scores for males and females is based on the performance of 138 males and 137 females; no other demographic information is presented. Overall, the technical aspects of the ECDI seem woefully inadequate.

Earlier reviews of the MCDI point out problems with the standardization group and recommend that other groups be included in the standardization process. Based on the information presented within the manual, at this time the ECDI should be considered as a supplement to an overall evaluation procedure. A great deal of work needs to be done with the technical aspects of this instrument. Specific reliability and validity studies should be conducted and the results included in the manual.

## Critique

Although the intent of the ECDI is admirable and the format easy to use, one cannot overlook the obvious technical shortcomings. At a time when a great deal of attention is being devoted to the age group served by the ECDI, there is a need for an instrument of this type. Unfortunately, the manual does not deal with the concerns raised about the MCDI and the other instruments derived from that original work. Earlier reviews questioned the interpretive format utilized by the ECDI, and the present manual fails to address those issues. The standardization group for the ECDI is inadequate at best, and more attention should be devoted to providing a sample representative of groups with a predisposition to developmental problems that may later interfere with ability to learn. More research is needed to determine how mothers of specific groups respond to the ECDI.

Until significant changes are incorporated and better technical information provided to the consumer, the determination of a child's need for further testing should not be based on ECDI results. The instrument can provide useful background information about the child to supplement the evaluation process, and if supported by reliability and validity studies, the ECDI should become a valuable addition to the assessment of very young children.

## References

This list includes text citations and suggested additional reading.

Guerin, D., & Gottfried, A.W. (1987). Minnesota Child Development Inventories: Prediction of intelligence, achievement, and adaptability. *Journal of Pediatric Psychology, 12,* 595–608.

Ireton, H. (1988). *Manual for the Early Child Development Inventory.* Minneapolis, MN: Behavioral Science Systems.

Ireton, H., & Thwing, E. (1968/1972). *Manual for the Minnesota Child Development Inventory.* Minneapolis, MN: Behavioral Science Systems.

Rysberg, J.A. (1985). Review of the Minnesota Child Development Inventory. In J.V. Mitchell, Jr. (Ed.), *The ninth mental measurements yearbook* (pp. 991–992). Lincoln, NE: Buros Institute of Mental Measurements.

Ullman, D.C., & Kausch, D.F. (1979). Early identification of developmental strengths and weaknesses in preschool children. *Exceptional Children, 45,* 8–13.

**Carol N. Dixon, Ph.D.**
*Senior Lecturer and Director, Education Reading Clinic, Graduate School of Education, University of California-Santa Barbara, Santa Barbara, California.*

**Priscilla A. Drum, Ph.D.**
*Professor of Educational Psychology, Graduate School of Education, University of California-Santa Barbara, Santa Barbara, California.*

---

# EDINBURGH READING TESTS, STAGES 2 AND 3 (SECOND EDITIONS)

*The Godfrey Thomson Unit, University of Edinburgh, and Morey House College of Education, in association with The Scottish Education Department and The Educational Institute of Scotland. London, England: Hodder & Stoughton Educational.*

## Introduction

The Edinburgh Reading Tests series are presented to assess students' progress in reading and to help teachers identify the particular strengths and weaknesses of individual children as well as whole classes. "There are four tests in the series: Stage 1 for ages 7:0 to 9:0, Stage 2 for ages 8:6 to 10:6, Stage 3 for ages 10:0 to 12:6, and Stage 4 for ages 12:0 upwards. Stages 1, 2 and 4 were constructed by the Godfrey Thomson Unit. . . . Stage 3 was constructed by Morey House College of Education" (Morey House College of Education, 1989, p. 5). Only Stages 2 and 3 were received for this review.

According to the manuals, there is one form of the test available for Stage 2 and two equivalent forms available for Stage 3. All stages were designed for administration to groups, although it is also possible to administer the test to individuals. No forms of the test have been developed to meet the needs of special populations (e.g., ESL students). However, a screening version of the test, called The Shortened Edinburgh Reading Test (reviewed in Keyser & Sweetland, 1990), is available.

The materials provide no biographical information on the test developers. However, the manuals indicate that test development was guided by a committee of representatives from Morey House College of Education, The Godfrey Thomson Unit at the University of Edinburgh, The Scottish Education Department, and The Educational Institute of Scotland. The committee included practicing teachers from

---

The reviewers would like to acknowledge Janet Brown for her assistance in preparing this review.

the Educational Institute and educational psychologists from Edinburgh and Strathclyde Universities.

The manual for Stage 2 indicates that test was first published in 1972, and that the second version for Stage 3 was completed in 1982. However, the manuals contain no information on the history of the test development process. Although these reviewers received second editions of both Stage 2 and 3 to review, the manuals contain no information either about the reasons for revision or their kind and extent.

The Edinburgh Reading Tests, Stages 2 and 3, are norm referenced to a population of state school children from Scotland, England, and Wales, ages 8:6 to 12:6. The populations represent two large educational districts; *authorities* is the term used for the educational divisions in the Manual of Instructions. The 100 schools in Scotland and 98 schools in England and Wales were randomly selected so that they were proportional to the population they represented. Single classes were then selected within schools, with average enrollments of 30 and an equal balance between sexes and across age ranges. The samples tested at Stage 2 (ages 8:6 to 10:6) included 5,509 children, 2,764 in Scotland and 2,745 in England and Wales. The samples tested at Stage 3 (ages 10:0 to 12:6) included 5,446 children, 3,000 in Scotland and 2,446 in England and Wales.

Both Stage 2 and 3 tests consist of a practice test and the test proper. The test proper for Stage 2 has two parts, each of which consists of three independent timed subtests of 20 items each. Part I has subtests of Vocabulary, Comprehension of Sequences, and Retention of Significant Details. Part II consists of Use of Context, Reading Rate, and Comprehension of Essential Ideas. The practice test consists of one item for each of the subtest types.

The Stage 3 test is similar in format. In addition to the practice test, the test proper consists of two parts. Part I has three independent timed subtests: Reading for Facts, Comprehension of Sequences, and Retention of Main Ideas. Part II has two subtests: Comprehension of Points of View and Vocabulary.

The Stage 2 Vocabulary subtest consists of items that ask the student to match a word with a definition, select the correct word to complete a sentence, or choose a word that means most nearly the same as an underlined word in a sentence. Comprehension of Sequences requires students to order a series of short sentences presented in a mixed up order, while Retention of Significant Details requires him or her to read a brief selection and then immediately answer short factual questions about the selection from memory. In Part II, the Use of Context items consist of pairs of unrelated sentences, each using the same word but with a different meaning. Three meaning choices are provided for the target word, and the student is to match the correct meaning for the word with the sentence. Reading Rate consists of a series of sentences presented in a modified cloze-type activity; here the student must select the appropriate choice from three possibilities for each blank in the story. The final subtest, Comprehension of Essential Ideas, asks the reader to select the correct answer to questions about a short story paragraph. The answer choices are not worded in exactly the same way they appear in the story paragraph, requiring the reader to select the correct restatement of the information provided by the paragraph.

The test tasks for Stage 3 are somewhat different. Reading for Facts requires the reader to respond "true," "false," or "don't know" to each of a series of restatements of information from a previously read paragraph. This activity is very similar to the kind of decision making required by the Comprehension of Essential Details subtest from Stage 2. Comprehension of Sequences is similar to its counterpart in Stage 2. Retention of Main Ideas is like Retention of Significant Details except that the reader is provided with four choices for each required response. Comprehension of Points of View contains two different types of tasks: In one the reader is asked to select the answer that best completes a sentence, and the other consists of a short paragraph followed by a series of statements. Here the reader must decide which of the characters described in the paragraph would have been most likely to have made each of the statements. The Vocabulary subtest asks the student to select the word that best completes the sentence. The reader must understand the meaning of each of the four choice words and then be able to select the proper consequence of the action or idea expressed in the first portion of the sentence.

Answers to test items for both stages are recorded directly in the test booklets. The tests are intended to be administered by classroom teachers and should require no special psychological expertise in administration or in interpretation as long as manual directions are followed carefully. The profile of test results is intended to allow a comparison within a child's performance rather than comparisons between children.

**Practical Applications/Uses**

A major purpose of the Edinburgh Reading Tests is to provide teachers with a tool for accessing their students' progress in reading. As such, the series is designed primarily for group administration by classroom teachers, although it can also be used as a preliminary individual diagnostic or screening measure for those who may need special help. The user obtains an overall score for each student, which can be compared to norms based on age (taken from the British Isles, Scotland, or England/Wales). This measure also presents a useful tool for comparing within-class and school averages. In addition, subtest scores can give some indications about a student's particular strengths and weaknesses. The test designers caution teachers to use subtest scores only to make comparisons within the student's own performance, or between classes of students, rather than comparing a single student with another student. Instructions are given for identifying strengths and weaknesses of whole classes. In addition to classroom teachers, these tests can be used by any educator, including resource teachers, reading specialists, and tutors.

These tests were designed for students in England, Wales, and Scotland, ages 8:6 to 12:6. The standardization samples do not include children in special schools that provide assistance for those with very low reading ability nor children in private schools, which might include those of very high reading ability. One assumes that the samples represent ethnic minorities and children whose native language is not English in numbers proportional to the characteristics of the general population, though such information is not provided in the manual. American children taking these tests might find themselves at some disadvantage because of colloquial language (e.g., one passage refers to "Groves The Stationers"), but these reviewers think these tests offer an excellent model for other test constructors to examine. An American version might be useful.

The Edinburgh tests are very straightforward and easy to administer to groups as well as individuals. Students are given a practice test first, which takes under 35 minutes and should be separated from the actual test-taking time by at least 15 minutes (but not more than 24 hours). During the practice test students are introduced to several examples of each type of item they will encounter. The class, with the teacher's help, answers each question together. A script is provided for the teacher to use in administering the test. In addition, misunderstandings can be dealt with by the teacher in a relaxed atmosphere.

The total time allotted for Part I is 40 minutes. Again, an interval of at least 1 hour (but no more than 24) should elapse before Part II is given. Part II requires a total of 35 minutes. Total testing time and recommendations for intervals between tests remain the same for both stages.

Because students mark answers directly in the test booklets, scoring is done by hand. To aid in speed and efficiency, teachers are advised to score one page at a time for the whole class, finding that soon they have memorized the answers. In this way, pages are scored relatively quickly.

The manual presents scoring procedures clearly. The user simply adds raw scores (number right for each subtest) together and converts the result into a "quotient" score, which takes into account the student's age. Conversion tables are given in a simple-to-follow manner. The last page in each student's test booklet provides a place to record subtest raw scores and quotients, and to determine confidence intervals for comparing scores. A chart is included to determine a student's "reading age," based on the raw scores and compared with norms from Scotland or England/Wales norms. The first time teachers administer this test they will need to read and follow the scoring instructions carefully. However, they should find the directions clearly written.

Interpretation is based on objective scores. As with any testing instrument, teachers are cautioned about the need to use good sense in interpreting the scores. Students who obtain exceedingly low quotients could have done so for reasons unrelated to their competency in reading. Scores need to be validated by actual performance in the classroom. However, with these cautions in mind, a teacher can use the class's average reading quotient to indicate where the group stands in relation to others, and the spread of the quotients to give a measure of the range of ability within the class.

## Technical Aspects

Where the standardization procedures differ for the two stages, they will be discussed separately. The standardization of scores for both stages is based on the total samples as normally distributed with a mean of 100 and a standard deviation of 15. The manual's conversion tables provide deviation quotients for each district by age in monthly intervals for raw scores between 3 and 95 out of a total score of 120 for Stage 2, 8:6 age students, and between 19 and 139 out of a total score of 154 for Stage 3, 10:0 age students. Extreme scores are not provided with quotient values as their accuracy is suspect.

Subtest scores are standardized across ages for both stages in order to compare a child's or a class's performance on the subtests for instructional purposes. Separate comparison lines for the two districts are provided in the tables for quotient levels and for subtest scores by sex and by age. The proportion of children scoring either very high or very low on the subtests in Stage 2 is also tabulated, with no proportion larger than .037 for any subtest except the speeded subtest for reading rate (.085 for high scorers and .097 for low scorers). These high and low scorer proportions were not provided for Stage 3.

The internal consistency of the total Stage 2 test, minus the speeded reading rate subtest, was substantial, yielding a Kuder-Richardson reliability of .97. No alternate form for the Stage 2 test is mentioned, so these reviewers assumed one was not available. Also, the manual provided no test-retest reliabilities, so again we assumed such procedures were not implemented. The internal consistency reliabilities were high for the five 20-item subtests, ranging from .814 to .913. Intercorrelations among the five subtests also were fairly high, ranging from .656 to .795 for Vocabulary, Comprehension of Sequence, Retention of Details, Use of Context, and Comprehension of Essential Ideas, but somewhat lower with reading rate, where the correlations ranged from .433 to .494. The manual warns users that these skills are interdependent, that "reading can be thought of as a unified ability" (Godfrey Thomson Unit, 1989, p. 29) and that only rather severe discrepancies should be noted and further tested. However, the correlations are not perfect, and class weaknesses might be used to judge curricular adequacy.

The same high reliability of .97 was obtained for the internal consistency of the Stage 3 total test. Again no alternate-forms reliability coefficient was provided, even though there are two forms for Stage 3. Also, test-retest procedures are not mentioned. The subtest scores for all five components (Reading for Facts, Comprehension of Sequence, Retention of Main Ideas, Comprehension of Points of View, and Vocabulary) were even higher than for Stage 2 components, ranging from .81 to .95. The intercorrelations among the components ranged from .709 to .838, even higher than those for the Stage 2 components, indicating perhaps that reading abilities become even more of a unified ability with increasing age and practice reading.

Perhaps because validity is a rather difficult standard to define, the manuals provide little attention or commentary on this phase of test construction. These reviewers believe these Edinburgh tests do represent valid measures of reading ability. The total tests and their subtest components do cover important aspects of developing reading ability. The statement that test construction was accomplished in association with the steering committee of teachers and reading experts has resulted in one of the most valid general reading tests we have examined. However, the lack of any concurrent or predictive validity measures is a weakness that must be acknowledged. One hopes that the needed experimental studies will confirm, when done, our belief in the validity of these tests.

## Critique

The Edinburgh Reading Tests are useful to examine developing reading abilities at various ages. The identification and retention of details, the sequencing of information, and the multifaceted approach to vocabulary knowledge all relate rather directly to both understanding and learning from text. In order to better evaluate the tests, these reviewers gave Stage 2 to an 8:6-year-old average reader and Stage 3 to an 11:6-year-old average reader. The children we tested liked these tests; they said that they were fun to take. The variety of item formats and the puzzle-solving nature of many of them seemed to contribute to these children's enjoyment.

The practice test appears to be a necessity because of the diverse formats within these tests. The California Achievement Tests (CAT) also provide and recommend the use of a practice test; however, it is not always administered because of time constraints. These reviewers wonder whether the practice tests for the Edinburgh are generally administered before the actual test or not. Basically, with some modification in vocabulary and typical events discussed, we feel that this series would be useful for examining reading development in the United States.

## References

American Educational Research Association, American Psychological Association, & National Council on Measurement in Education. (1985). *Standards for educational and psychological testing*. Washington, DC: American Psychological Association.

Calfee, R.C., & Drum, P.A. (1986). Research on teaching reading. In M.C. Wittrock (Ed.), *Handbook of research on teaching* (pp. 804–849). New York: Macmillan.

Drum, P.A., & Dixon, C.N. (1991). Review of The Shortened Edinburgh Reading Test. In D.J. Keyser & R.C. Sweetland (Eds.), *Test critiques* (Vol. VIII, pp. 647–651). Austin, TX: PRO-ED.

Godfrey Thomson Unit. (1989). *Edinburgh Reading Tests, Stage 2, manual of instructions*. London, England: Hodder & Stoughton.

Morey House College of Education. (1989). *Edinburgh Reading Tests, Stage 3, combined manual of instructions for test booklets A and B*. London, England: Hodder & Stoughton.

Tierney, R.J., & Cunningham, J.W. (1984). Research on teaching reading comprehension. In P.D. Pearson & R. Barr (Eds.), *Handbook of reading research* (pp. 609–655). New York: Longman.

**Loy O. Bascue, Ph.D.**
*Counseling Psychologist, Devon, Pennsylvania, and Adjunct Clinical Associate Professor, Institute for Graduate Clinical Psychology, Widener University, Chester, Pennsylvania.*

**Jed A. Yalof, Psy.D.**
*Associate Professor and Chair, Graduate Program in Counseling Psychology, and Director, Counseling and Diagnostic Testing Services, Immaculata College, Immaculata, Pennsylvania.*

---

# EGO FUNCTION ASSESSMENT

*Leopold Bellak. Larchmont, New York: C.P.S., Inc.*

### Introduction

The Ego Function Assessment (EFA) is a semistructured interview technique derived from psychoanalytic ego psychology and designed to assess psychopathology through the analysis and numerical rating of 12 ego functions: Reality Testing; Judgment; Sense of Reality and the Self; Regulation and Control of Drives, Affects, and Impulses; Object Relations; Thought Processes; Adaptive Regression in Service of the Ego; Defensive Functioning; Stimulus Barrier; Autonomous Functioning; Synthetic-Integrative Functioning; and Mastery-Competence. Interview assessments of these 12 ego functions are rated on either a 7- or 13-point ordinal scale, with lower scores indicating more serious disturbances of ego functions. The ratings are recorded on the EFA Blank (Bellak, 1989), which is a six-page report form that includes a brief definition of each ego function, sample questions to guide the interviewer in evaluating each function, a page for recording interview responses, and a graph for plotting the numerical ratings of each function.

The EFA was authored by Leopold Bellak with the support of a 5-year grant from the National Institute of Mental Health (NIMH; Bellak, Hurvich, & Gediman, 1973). Bellak has enjoyed a distinguished career as a physician and psychoanalyst and has authorship credit on more than 200 articles and 30 books. His first article examining ego functions appeared in 1949 (Bellak, 1949). He then proposed an operational definition of ego functions in 1952 (Bellak, 1952) and published the Global Ego Strength Scale for the measurement of ego functions in 1966 (Bellak & Rosenberg, 1966).

The development of the EFA interview method is detailed in *Ego Functions in Schizophrenics, Neurotics, and Normals* (Bellak, Hurvich, & Gediman, 1973), which reports the results of the NIMH research project for the study of ego functions. The book includes both an examination of the relationship of ego functions to psychoanalytic structural theory and also a description of the actual research project, including several case studies illustrating the application of the EFA interview method. The appendices provide an interview guide for EFA (Appendix A), a detailed manual for rating interviews (Appendix B), and a form for the numerical recording of interview results (Appendix C).

In addition to the EFA materials available in the project report, Bellak also has published an EFA manual (Bellak, 1988), a brief booklet that includes an initial section written by Bellak describing the development of EFA and defining the 12 ego functions and also two sections authored by Gruber (Gruber, 1989a, 1989b), which describe, respectively, an alternative interview and scoring method. For information about the validity and reliability of EFA, Bellak refers readers of the manual to his project report (Bellak, Hurvich, & Gediman, 1973) and to an additional collection of research reports (Bellak & Goldsmith, 1984).

**Practical Applications/Uses**

The EFA is an individually administered, hand-scored interview method that "is not easily learned and somewhat cumbersome" (Bellak, 1988, p. 2). The examiner's role is to conduct a brief history of an individual and then present, and modify if necessary, a series of questions in order to assess 12 ego functions that derive from the psychoanalytic structural theory of mental functioning and disturbance. Administration of the history and interview materials can take about 2 hours but is likely to vary considerably, depending on both the experience of the examiner and the personality characteristics of the patient.

The EFA interview method is likely to be of particular value in research projects that require an assessment of current personality functioning. It can be used with a wide range of personality conditions, ranging from the assessment of those without dysfunction to those with extreme pathological conditions. Although the EFA can be administered to children and adults, its use is probably restricted to individuals with some verbal ability because it is essentially an interview technique.

The strength of the EFA method appears to reside in the operational definition of each ego function, which permits the description of personality in precise terms. Such precision allows quantification of functions and consequently the application of the method to research.

Though Bellak proposes that the EFA can be used for clinical assessment as well as research (Bellak, 1988), the educational utility of the method is not stressed. Yet EFA is likely to have special appeal to educators and supervisors who want to train others in an ego-psychological framework, including the ability to describe personality in terms of explicit ego functions.

For numerical scoring, Bellak (1988) states that the 7- or 13-point rating scales can be used interchangeably. However, on the EFA Blank the graph for plotting the numerical scores is organized for the 13-point scale. Each ego function also is designated within an overlapping numerical range of adjustment on the graph: Normal (8–13), Neurotic (6–10), Borderline (4–8), and Psychotic (1–6).

The user also can rate libidinal and aggressive drive strength on a 7-point scale that ranges from +3 to -3, with higher scores reflecting higher drive strength, and superego neutralization-sublimation on a 4-point scale, with higher scores indicating higher levels of neutralization.

A limitation is that the interview method reflects theoretically a psychoanalytic structural point of view. Empirical investigations (Bellak & Goldsmith, 1984) suggest that training for the interview method can be achieved by a wide range of professionals, even those without psychoanalytic background. Nevertheless, it strains credibility to presume that users without beliefs compatible to ego psychology and some psychoanalytic training could understand and infer from an interview the accurate assessment of such concepts as, for example, *regulation of drives, affects, and impulses* or *adaptive regression in service of the ego.*

## Technical Aspects

Data concerning the reliability and validity of the EFA are presented in the book by Bellak, Hurvich, and Gediman (1973). The interview method originally was applied to a sample of 50 hospitalized schizophrenic patients, 25 neurotic outpatients, and 25 normal hospital employees. All the subjects participated voluntarily, and diagnostic groups were matched on education (1 year of college) and socioeconomic status (middle class). The schizophrenic group was somewhat older (30 years) than the neurotic (27 years) and normal (26 years) groups, and the neurotic group scored higher on an intelligence test (IQ = 118) than did the normal (IQ = 114) and the schizophrenic (IQ = 108) groups. Following training, six doctoral-level interviewers evaluated the 100 subjects. The audiotaped interviews were then evaluated by four other trained raters. Each interview was evaluated independently by two raters.

Results of the comparison between diagnostic groups by analysis of variance, based on a comparison of average scores of the two raters for each subject, showed all mean differences between pairs of groups were significant beyond the .001 level and all differences were in the predicted directions. Interrater reliability was computed between pairs of raters for 11 of the functions (data were not available for Mastery-Competence), and the derived Pearson product-moment correlations ranged from .88 for Autonomous Functioning to .61 for Stimulus Barrier, with the average mean reliability coefficient of .77 for all 11 functions. Further, on no single ego function was the average disagreement between raters as much as 2 scale points on the 13-point rating system, and the disagreement was less than 1.5 scale points for two thirds of the ratings for each of the three groups.

The initial project also examined the relationship between mean ratings and subject's social class, education, intelligence test scores, and age. Although there was a tendency for the ratings to be associated with these factors, Bellak and his associates (1973) concluded that the rating differences among groups were not attributable to any background factors.

Other than the original project report, the edited publication by Bellak and Goldsmith (1984) appears to be the most comprehensive collection of research reports concerning the EFA. In particular, the reports provide empirical evidence to suggest that the interview method can be used to differentiate among psychiatric diagnostic groups, to identify personality changes in the same individuals following treatments such as psychotherapy, medication, and substance abuse treatment, and to identify individuals experiencing psychopathology within groups of high-functioning people.

## Critique

The EFA interview method applies a psychoanalytic ego-psychological framework to the assessment of psychopathology. For researchers who want an operationally defined, quantifiable interview system of personality description based on psychanalytic theory, the EFA offers a method that has shown itself valid for the evaluation of a variety of diagnostic categories and the assessment of an array of treatment conditions. Although raters require training in the application of the EFA, research has demonstrated that the technique can be taught to a variety of professionals and that those trained can achieve good interrater reliability.

Educators and supervisors who want to promote the ability of mental health professionals to describe personality functioning in ego-psychological terms will find the EFA especially useful, as the 12 functions are both precisely defined in operation and explicitly described in quality.

A weakness of the method lies in the brevity of the manual. To become proficient in the EFA one must become familiar with the material (especially the appendices) in Bellak, Hurvich, and Gediman (1973), and it is helpful to review the reports collected by Bellak and Goldsmith (1984). The author would certainly enhance the overall process if he were to produce a revised manual that reviewed the EFA's validity and reliability, outlined a training method for raters, and provided a complete description of each function, including experiences and behaviors associated with different qualities of various functions. Even without such a manual, the EFA remains an important addition both to psychoanalytic research methodology and to the clinical practice of ego psychology. The EFA stands as another of the original contributions in the outstanding career of Leopold Bellak.

## References

Bellak, L. (1949). A multiple-factor psychosomatic theory of schizophrenia. *Psychiatric Quarterly, 23,* 738–755.

Bellak, L. (1952). *Manic-depressive psychosis and allied disorders.* New York: Grune & Stratton.

Bellak, L. (1988). *Ego Function Assessment (EFA): A manual.* Larchmont, NY: C.P.S.

Bellak, L. (1989). *Ego Function Assessment blank.* Larchmont, NY: C.P.S.

Bellak, L., & Goldsmith, L. (1984). *The broad scope of ego function assessment.* New York: John Wiley.

Bellak, L., Hurvich, M., & Gediman, H. (1973). *Ego functions in schizophrenics, neurotics, and normals.* New York: John Wiley.

Bellak, L., & Rosenberg, S. (1966). Effects of two antidepressant drugs on depression. *Psychosomatics, 7,* 106–114.

Gruber, L. (1989a). Alternate interview guide for ego function assessment. In L. Bellak (Ed.), *Ego Function Assessment (EFA): A manual* (pp. 23–28). New York: John Wiley.

Gruber, L. (1989b). Modified rating manual for ego functions. In L. Bellak (Ed.), *Ego Function Assessment (EFA): A manual* (pp. 29–43). New York: John Wiley.

**Lucille B. Strain, Ph.D.**
*Professor of Education and Coordinator, Graduate Reading Education Program, Bowie State University, Bowie, Maryland.*

# ENGLISH LANGUAGE INSTITUTE LISTENING COMPREHENSION TEST

*John Upshur, H. Koba, Mary Spaan, and Laura Strowe. Ann Arbor, Michigan: English Language Institute.*

## Introduction

The English Language Institute Listening Comprehension Test (LCT) is a 45-item, 15-minute, tape-recorded listening test. Now retired from its original use as a component in the Michigan English Proficiency Battery, the LCT is used to assess the proficiency of nonnative speakers of English who are studying in institutions of higher education where English is the language of instruction.

From 1973 to 1983, the LCT was one of three components of the Michigan English Proficiency Battery, accounting for one third of an individual's score on the total battery. Other components of the battery included a holistically scored composition and the 100-item Michigan Test of English Language Proficiency (MTELP). The LCT was used, mainly, during administration of the battery in the United States and Canada. In 1984, the proficiency battery was renamed the Michigan English Language Assessment Battery (MELAB). The LCT is now used as a single test and, according to its publisher, is not to be confused with the "Michigan Test" or the "Michigan Battery."

Specifically, the purpose of the LCT is to assess a student's ability to comprehend basic English structures presented orally. The LCT is based on the assumption that phonemic discrimination precedes comprehension of natural utterances. Therefore, the LCT does not focus on an individual's ability to make correct discriminations of the English sound system. The LCT integrates grammar and aural comprehension testing in short, isolated sentences. It does not utilize questions or statements that require processing of longer forms of discourse. Nor does it provide the test-taker with redundancies and contextual information as would occur in expanded discourse.

The LCT is presented as an aural-grammar test. All of the aural stimuli (cues) and printed responses are grammar based. The examinee hears a short question or statement and then is required to choose the printed response that either answers the question or is similar in meaning to the statement. Test sentences are not repeated nor are they slowed during the test; they are delivered at a normal speaking pace. A standard time of 12 seconds is allowed between test items. Printed answer choices are brief, and high-frequency vocabulary is used in all items.

The LCT is available in three forms—4, 5, and 6—and the same test booklet, containing identical printed answer choices, is used for all three. The audio stimuli, however, vary from form to form. Each form of the LCT consists of 45 items organized into 15 sets of structures. Each structure has three variations of the structural patterns. For example:

Item 1, Form 4, is parallel to Item 16, Form 6, and Item 31, Form 5.
Item 1, Form 5, is parallel to Item 16, Form 4, and Item 31, Form 6.
Item 1, Form 6, is parallel to Item 16, Form 5, and Item 31, Form 4.

Grammar classifications of the test include tense, parts of speech, subject, causal, connective, correlative, questions, object, and so forth.

Requirements for administering the LCT tend to be simple and easily understood. The recommended time for administration is 20 minutes, with 5 minutes for instructions and 15 minutes for actual test completion. Users must exercise care regarding the maintenance of proper security to assure continuing usefulness of the test. Examinees are not to have had an opportunity to study the test prior to taking it. The examination room should be large enough to provide alternate seating for examinees. Up to 20 examinees can be proctored adequately by one examiner. Beyond that number, additional proctors are required in proportion to the size of the group. The examiner is responsible for making sure that examinees understand the directions and the examples pertaining to the test, although these are presented by the tape.

Examiners are advised that test scores from two different oral administrations of the LCT should not be treated as scores of the same test. Other instructions include reminders that a good-quality sound system should be used for all testing sessions and there should be good amplification if the group is large.

Scoring the LCT is facilitated by use of the punched scoring stencils that the publisher provides. An additional answer key is given in Table 7 of the test manual. Raw scores, the total number of correct answers achieved by examinees, can be adjusted by use of the manual's equation table.

Although a printed script is available for providing information to examinees, it is imperative to present the test itself by means of the tape included in the test materials. This recommendation is based on several factors: The tape ensures standardization of presentation of the audio stimuli and timing, it facilitates proctoring during group administrations of the test, and the publisher stresses that reliability is better maintained if the tape is used.

A complete set of materials for the LCT includes the manual, 20 test booklets, 100 answer sheets, 3 scoring stencils, and the cassette tape. The test is available to purchasers approved by the University of Michigan English Language Institute, that is, valid institutions and researchers.

**Practical Applications/Uses**

The LCT is a means for assessing an individual's ability to comprehend spoken English. It was developed for use with college and university students whose background language was other than English. The nature of the content and the format of the LCT, however, suggest that it might serve broader uses. It seems apparent that the LCT might be used effectively with students in English as a second language (ESL) classes at any level of secondary schools. There could also be uses for it with students in ESL classes at upper elementary school level. The LCT conceivably could provide useful information regarding the ability of adult immigrants to understand spoken English for reasons other than educational. For example, businesses and industries might use the LCT as a screening aid in determining qualifications of individuals for employment. For persons whose native language is English but who, for various reasons, are accustomed to structures that differ from the standard English dialect might benefit from assessment by the LCT. No technical data exist at present, however, to support these alternative applications.

The increasing diversity of American society as reflected in the classrooms of schools and higher education institutions suggests a need for quick and effective ways to assess individuals' abilities to understand oral English. In many such situations there are no ESL classes to assume responsibility for developing the communication abilities of students with foreign-language backgrounds. The LCT might be used to indicate areas of strengths and weaknesses in ability to understand spoken English. Although the norms presently available for the LCT may not be appropriate for all individuals and groups assessed, important information might thus be acquired.

**Technical Aspects**

The LCT manual includes a large amount of information on the test's development. Test items were written by H. Koba, Mary Spaan, and Laura Strowe under the direction of John Upshur in 1972. The items were pretested on 271 subjects, and a high-low item analysis was performed on tests of 146 of these subjects. (The item responses of the top-scoring 27% were compared to those of the lowest scoring 27%.) Items that gave maximal valid discrimination were retained (i.e., those that were easy for the top scorers and difficult for the low scorers). Tables included in the manual present the results of this initial pretesting. The average discrimination indices ranged from .38 to .40, indicating that for these items about 40% more of the high scorers answered each item correctly than did the low scorers. The manual points out that as the tests were not in their final form during the pretesting stage, one cannot assume that the mean difficulties are the same.

The tests were put together into their present form after the initial pretesting. They were then administered along with the earlier standardized Michigan Test of Aural Comprehension (MTAC) in 1972 and 1973 to 269 intensive-course students at the English Language Institute of the University of Michigan (ELI-UM). In 1972, it is reported, 132 students were administered the LCT as practice followed by the MTAC as part of their final examination. The order was reversed in 1973 for 137 students. By comparing students' LCT raw scores (total number correct) to the MTAC raw and equated scores, an equation table was derived for the LCT. The equated LCT scores are not the percentage correct, but rather are scores adjusted to the scale used on the other components of the Michigan proficiency battery.

Conversion of raw scores to equated scores resulted in their equivalence to scaled scores on other components of the old Michigan battery. The norms provided in the manual (Table 9) were based on 1,486 official Michigan battery tests administered during 1983. The manual provides details for use of these norms for interpreting results of the LCT. Several important factors for users to consider in interpreting students' scores also are pointed out.

Additionally the LCT manual reports reliability and validity procedures and data. Reliability was computed by use of the Kuder-Richardson Formula 21, which yielded a coefficient of .796. Descriptive statistics appear in tables to show the comparability of the three forms of the test.

Content validity of the LCT was determined by examining the behaviors required in the test in terms of their representation of behaviors exhibited in the desired performance domain. In the case of the LCT, the desired performance domain was that part of the English language related to aural comprehension and grammatical structures. The test authors used as references the core texts in use at the ELI-UM at the time of creation of the test, and these references are given in the test manual.

In order to determine the concurrent validity of the LCT, the developers made correlations with other standardized English proficiency tests. The domain of the LCT is aural comprehension of grammar structures, the same as that of the Michigan Test of Aural Comprehension (MTAC). Correlation of the LCT with the MTAC produced the highest correlation coefficient among the comparisons made. According to information reported in the manual, however, the LCT correlated satisfactorily with other tests whose domains were in other areas of English. All correlation data appear in Table 6 of the LCT manual.

## Critique

The purpose for which the LCT was created to serve several years ago still remains viable. That purpose, which is to assess comprehension of oral English structures of college students with foreign-language backgrounds, assumes even greater importance in face of increased numbers of persons with these characteristics. The advent of students with foreign-language backgrounds into learning situations in which English is the language of instruction is becoming increasingly common at all levels of schooling and higher education. In addition to instructional situations where such an assessment might yield useful information, increased numbers of persons inexperienced in oral English comprehension seek employment in American industries and businesses. A means of assessing their comprehension of oral English efficiently in terms of both time and effort is desirable, and the LCT seems to have such potential.

Both the format and content of the LCT are appropriate in terms of its purpose. The format assures easy and uncomplicated delivery and response. The content focuses on the basic structures of English that are essential to clear communication.

Several features of the LCT are advantageous for aural testing. Presentation of the test items by tape counteracts some of the weaknesses identified in other listening tests. Use of the tape tends to ascertain that administration and timing of the test follow standardized procedures. Variations in delivery, such as have been described when different persons orally deliver test items, are prevented (Richards, 1983). That administration of the test requires only a small amount of time makes its use expedient in a variety of situations.

The manual accompanying the LCT provides exceptionally complete information regarding test development, administration and scoring, and interpretation.

The reported reliability and validity procedures and data appear adequate in terms of the LCT's purpose. In addition, all of the manual's many tables are useful to those interested in assessing the test's probable value in their particular situations.

**References**

This list includes text citations and suggested additional reading.

Epstein, N. (1978). *Language, ethnicity and the schools.* Washington, DC: Institute for Educational Leadership, George Washington University.

Garcia, R.L. (1982). *Teaching in a pluralistic society.* New York: Harper & Row.

Mehrens, W.A. (1985). Review of Listening Group Tests. In J.V. Mitchell, Jr. (Ed.), *The ninth mental measurements yearbook* (p. 864). Lincoln, NE: Buros Institute of Mental Measurements.

Richards, R.A. (1985). Review of Listening Group Tests. In J.V. Mitchell, Jr. (Ed.), *The ninth mental measurements yearbook* (p. 865). Lincoln, NE: Buros Institute of Mental Measurements.

Upshur, J., Koba, H., Spaan, M., & Strowe, L. (1976). *English Language Institute Listening Comprehension Test manual.* Ann Arbor, MI: University of Michigan, English Language Institute.

**Jan Hankins, Ph.D.**

*Senior Research Associate, University of Tennessee, Knoxville, Tennessee.*

# ETSA TESTS

*George A.W. Stouffer, Jr. and S. Trevor Hadley. Chambersburg, Pennsylvania: Educators/Employers' Tests & Services Associates.*

## Introduction

The Educators/Employers' Tests & Services Associates (ETSA) Tests form a battery of eight norm-referenced instruments that may be administered separately or in combination. The battery includes measures of general mental ability, office arithmetic, general clerical skills, stenographic skills, mechanical familiarity, mechanical knowledge, sales aptitude, and personal adjustment. The tests are to be used as an aid in personnel selection, training, and promotion decisions.

The original ETSA tests were developed by Drs. S. Trevor Hadley and George A.W. Stouffer, Jr. Dr. Hadley has taught at the University of Illinois and the Indiana State College. He also has been a high school guidance counselor and director of a college psychological clinic. During World War II, Dr. Hadley served as a research psychologist in the U.S. Air Force, developing psychomotor aptitude tests for air crew classification.

Dr. Stouffer has taught at Purdue University and the University of Pittsburgh. He has been employed over the course of his career as a clinical psychologist for the Indiana State Division of Corrections, as chief clinical psychologist for a neuropsychiatric hospital, and as a school psychologist. He also served as a clinical psychologist for the U.S. Navy during World War II and the Korean conflict. Dr. Stouffer has authored or coauthored several psychological tests.

The ETSA tests first appeared in 1957 and have been revised and updated several times. No information is available on when these updates were carried out, however. Many of the current items were included in the original tests. Others have been modified or eliminated in subsequent editions as the publishers felt they had become ambiguous, obsolete, or differentially unfair to particular groups of individuals. New items have been added to increase the tests' reliability without making them unduly long (ETSA, 1990).

There are no special forms of these tests available for either hearing or visually impaired or otherwise handicapped persons. The current ETSA manager, Charles K. Stouffer, indicated that testing for such individuals is handled on an individual basis (C.K. Stouffer, personal communication, August 16, 1990). There also are no foreign language editions available.

The ETSA tests are designed to be administered, scored, and interpreted within a business or organization by individuals who have no special training in testing or measurement (ETSA, 1985). Minimal skill is required of the administrator. In seven of the eight subtests, he or she is asked to be sure that the examinees understand the directions but is not required to read them aloud. Other than handing out pencils and test booklets and timing the tests, little is required of the administrator.

Descriptions of the individual components of the ETSA battery follow:

*General Mental Ability.* Test 1-A, General Mental Ability, is designed as a short measure of general intelligence or ability to comprehend and learn new material. It addresses abilities important in almost all types of learning. The test's verbal, computational, and nonverbal items require reasoning, the ability to comprehend, and drawing conclusions. The computational and nonverbal items are purported to provide consideration to examinees with good reasoning ability but who lack skill in reading or have poor verbal development. Approximately 200 items were selected for possible inclusion on this test. The measure was administered to a sample of approximately 200 men and women, and 125 items were eliminated as being too difficult, too easy, or ambiguous. Test 1-A is purely a power test, but a time limit of 45 minutes is suggested. No scratch paper is provided, and directions are not read aloud to the examinees. In addition, the administrator should not answer questions about the directions—reading and understanding the directions is considered part of the test. The latest revision of Test 1-A occurred in 1985.

*Office Arithmetic.* Test 2-A, Office Arithmetic, is designed to measure an individual's ability to use mathematics to solve the numerical problems encountered in most offices or other situations. It covers skills in addition, subtraction, multiplication, division, fractions, and percentages. In addition, there are a few word problems and several others that require the ability to read, understand, and use information from tables and graphs. Test 2-A contains six types of problems: whole number computation, mixed number computation, written problems, reading tables, reading graphs, and advanced office computation. ETSA surveyed "several standard textbooks in business arithmetic and in office practice" (1990, p. 9) to determine the types of mathematical operations common to many office jobs. The six problem types were chosen "because they appear to provide a fair sampling of the various number operations which met this criterion" (ETSA, 1990, p. 9). Over 100 items were selected and grouped by heading for field testing. Fifty items were selected for inclusion in the final test. Scratch paper is allowed, as are hand held calculators. Test 2-A is a power test, but the publisher suggests a time limit of 60 minutes.

*General Clerical Ability.* Test 3-A, General Clerical Ability, is administered to measure the general skills required by clerical personnel in routine office work. The developers constructed approximately 200 items using "several standard text books in general office practice as a primary source of material" (ETSA, 1990, p. 11) and grouped them as follows: alphabetization, matching of numbers, checking names, spelling, using office vocabulary, and knowledge of mailing procedures. About 69% of these items were eliminated as being too difficult, too easy, or ambiguous after initial administration. No scratch paper is necessary. Speed is considered an important component in this 131-item test, so a time limit of 30 minutes is set.

*Stenographic Skills.* Test 4-A, Stenographic Skills, is designed to measure typing, shorthand, and the general skills needed by secretaries and stenographers. The items were "specifically selected to parallel the contents of a number of standard texts in the field" (ETSA, 1990, p. 12). The technical manual states that the original test, containing approximately 180 items, was administered to a sample of 200 people employed in stenographic occupations. Approximately 80 items were eliminated as being too difficult, too easy, or ambiguous, and 120 remain on the current test (there are no details on where the additional 20 items came from). No scratch paper is necessary. The test is divided into four parts: spelling, filing, grammar, and general information relevant to the work of secretaries and stenographers. Test 4-A is considered a power test rather than one of speed, but a time limit of 45 minutes is suggested.

This component also includes supplementary evaluations of typing and/or shorthand. The typing test presents a prepared letter, complete with correct spelling, punctuation, and so forth, for the examinee to type. The supplementary shorthand test uses the same letter, which in this case is dictated to and then typed by the examinee. These supplementary measures may be administered at the discretion of the user, adding either 5 (typing) or 18 (typing/shorthand) minutes to the administration of Test 4-A.

*Mechanical Familiarity.* Test 5-A, Mechanical Familiarity, purports to measure the ability to recognize common tools and mechanical instruments. This test is essentially nonverbal and can be used with examinees of limited reading ability. The examinee's task is to match the name of a tool or instrument with a picture of that tool or instrument. If the examinee cannot read or write, the examiner may read the directions as well as the words/terms aloud and ask the examinee to mark the appropriate picture. Fifty commonly used tools, parts, and implements were selected from suggestions obtained from persons working in mechanical, electrical, or related occupations. In addition, standard handbooks, "parts" books, and so forth were used to draw the items. Test 5-A is considered a power test, but the administrator's manual suggests a time limit of 60 minutes.

*Mechanical Knowledge.* Test 6-A, Mechanical Knowledge, is included to measure mechanical understanding. It samples basic information in six areas of mechanical knowledge, covering items such as hand and bench tools, materials, measuring devices, electrical information, shop arithmetic, shop terminology and symbols, lathe tools, interpretation of schematic drawings, welding information, and so forth. The administrator's manual notes that "the test is also felt to be indicative of the examinee's understanding of mechanical movements and functions" (ETSA, 1985, p. 3). No information is provided on the test itself or in either manual that identifies all six parts. Part 3 is related to electrical symbols and Part 4 the lathe, but the others are not identifiable to someone who lacks knowledge of the mechanical field. The content is based on information from courses of study, "handbooks" of mechanical knowledge, and personal contacts with employers. Approximately 200 items were divided into several forms and administered to persons employed in mechanical, electrical, and related areas and to high school students in vocational education courses. The 50 tests with the highest scores and the 50 tests with the lowest scores were selected. Based on the count of the correct responses on these 100 tests, 121 items were chosen for the final version. Test 6-A is considered a power test, but a time limit of 90 minutes is suggested. As this measure taps mechanical knowledge that may be acquired through working, a young person is not necessarily expected to score as high as an older examinee with more experience.

*Sales Aptitude.* Test 7-A, Sales Aptitude, focuses on the abilities and skills required for effective selling. It does not primarily attempt to measure sales skill or ability but rather the individual's knowledge of basic selling principles and capacity to be a successful salesperson. The test's scope includes selling to wholesalers, retailers, and consumers, covering a variety of products from heavy capital goods sold to industry to small items sold door to door. Seven individual factors deemed important in sales are addressed: sales judgment, interest in selling, personality factors involved in selling, identification with the sales occupation, level of aspiration, insight into human nature, and awareness of sales approach. Unlike Tests 1-A–6-A, in which the individual receives only a total score, the Sales Aptitude test yields a score on each of the seven subsections of the test as well. Items were derived from a list of questions compiled from interviewing salespersons in education and vocational counseling services. Some of the original items were obtained from a list dealing with the sales field, others by talking with employers of salespersons and follow-up studies of successful and unsuccessful salespersons. Approximately 250 items were administered to 175 salespersons and 325 nonsalespersons. The 100 items that best differentiated the two groups were used in the present form. Although Test 7-A is considered a power test, the administrator's guidelines suggest a time limit of 60 minutes.

*Personal Adjustment.* Test 8-A, Personal Adjustment Index, was developed in 1956 to measure "certain" aspects of the individual's adjustment to the environment in which he or she functions. It is not a measure of personality.

This test is divided into seven areas: community spirit, attitude toward cooperation with employers, attitude toward health, attitude toward authority, lack of nervous tendencies, leadership, and job stability. As on Sales Aptitude, the examinee obtains subtest scores as well as a total score (or rating of "possible vocational adjustment"; ETSA, 1985, p. 4). The original form contained 105 items, drawn from the authors' experience and the literature on adjustment problems and constructed to minimize the influences of social desirability. The original inventory was administered to a "large number of people" at "various times" (ETSA, 1990, p. 21); after each administration an item analysis was done and changes were made as needed. The current inventory has been modified over the years only as necessary to make it more relevant to "today's milieu" (ETSA, 1990, p. 21). As with most of the other tests in the battery, this is a power test, but a time limit of 45 minutes is suggested.

The administrator's manual recommends that all examinees be given Test 1-A (General Mental Ability) and then whatever is appropriate from among 2-A to 7-A, depending on the job in question. Tests may be administered one at a time, with the test administrator determining the sequence. If the personal adjustment index (Test 8-A) is administered, the examiner should do so last. It should be given only "when the person's characteristic mode of life adjustment is felt to be a factor of importance in the job under consideration, e.g., dealing with the public or interacting with other employees" (ETSA, 1985, p. 4). The user establishes the policy on retesting, and no specific time interval between retestings is suggested.

As noted, all the tests except General Clerical Ability are power tests. The administrator's manual asserts (ETSA, 1985, p. 4) that all established time limits allow all but the slowest of persons to complete the tests. Items are ordered by approximate level of difficulty, so the hardest items are the last ones that examinees reach. No separate answer forms are required for any of the ETSA tests; all answers may be recorded directly in the test booklets.

**Practical Applications/Uses**

According to the administrator's manual, the ETSA tests were developed to be used either separately or in combination to provide for more satisfactory hiring, better employee selection and placement, better assessment of training needs and progress, and more effective promotion with an objective database. In addition, the ETSA tests have been used in secondary schools for counseling students and placing them in trade and vocational programs. Vocational-technical schools and community colleges have administered these tests to help guide students into programs and curricula appropriate for their interests and aptitudes (ETSA, 1990). The technical manual goes on to state that the results of the ETSA tests can provide career development assistance, to help individuals entering or re-entering the work force and those considering a career change.

These tests were designed to supplement the other factors on which hiring, training, and promotion decisions are based. As stated in the administrator's manual, "Tests, like any other measure, should be used as only one gauge of competence. . . . Test results are only one source of information about the examinee to be considered with all other available relevant data" (ETSA, 1985, p. 21). The tests included in this battery are appropriate for adults in business and industry as well as students in high school, vocational-technical schools, and community colleges. Qualified users include officials in charge of employment and placement, personnel managers, counselors, psychologists, and educators.

The ETSA tests are easy to score. A "Rapid Scoring Key" facilitates checking the answers recorded in the test booklet. (No scoring guide is supplied for the supplemental typing and shorthand tests, however.) All scores derive simply from number correct and are interpreted in terms of bands rather than individual scores. These bands take errors of measurement into account and cover five categories: poor, questionable, average, good, and excellent. Each test except for the supplemental typing and shorthand measures has its own score breakdown; it is up to the user to establish performance scoring bands for the latter. In addition, score bands are provided for the subscales as well as total scale scores for the Sales Aptitude test and the Personal Adjustment Index. The technical manual (ETSA, 1990) calls for great care in interpreting such "part scores," however. Despite the score breakdown categories suggested, it is the user's responsibility to determine the level of proficiency required for a particular job.

Percentile rank tables are available for the ETSA tests, but their use is not encouraged for persons without an extensive background in measurement.

**Technical Aspects**

*Norms.* As the ETSA tests are norm referenced, a discussion of norms is appropriate. The technical manual states:

> Norms for the several tests and the Personal Adjustment Index Inventory are based, where feasible, on numbers of males and females from urban and rural areas. The samples included, as the needs of the specific test dictated, a randomized population of examinees from specially selected populations. Among the populations sampled were minorities, high school seniors, trade, technical, vocational, and college students, out of school job applicants, employed workers including those with special skills, adults in occupational training programs, etc. on a regional/national basis. (ETSA, 1990, p. 5)

At present a handbook of norms is available for a small fee. According to the technical manual, this handbook contains information on construction, reliability, validity, norms, scoring rationale, and other data.

The norms for Test 1-A (General Mental Ability) derive from the performance of approximately 4,500 subjects, ranging in age from 16 to 62 years. The test was administered on a voluntary basis to a group of college applicants, clients at a college psychological clinic, and other randomly selected adults. Test 2-A (Office Arithmetic) norms were based on a "completely" random sample of 3,000 persons aged 16 to 54 years. The test was administered on a voluntary basis to an employment service's clients and a sample of randomly selected adults.

The developers based norms for Test 3-A (General Clerical) on approximately 4,000 persons, these ranging in age from 15 to 57 years. The test was administered on a voluntary basis to clients at an employment service over a 2-year period and to "other randomly selected individuals" (ETSA, 1990, p. 12). Norms for Test 4-A (Stenographic Skills) were developed from a slightly smaller group (approximately 3,900 persons) that spanned ages 18 to 55. The test also was administered on a voluntary basis to clients at an employment service over a 2-year period as well as a sample of other randomly selected adults.

A diverse group of approximately 4,000 subjects produced the norms for Test 5-A (Mechanical Familiarity). Ranging in age from 14 to 63, the participants included senior high school students in vocational education courses, college students enrolled in engineering courses, and several categories of adults: unemployed persons with previous "mechanical" experience, unskilled workers, skilled workers, and a few semiprofessional and professional workers. The persons included in the sample ranged in age from 14 to 63 years of age. The test was administered on a voluntary basis. Several special samples of women also were gathered and their results compared to these norms. Little difference was evident in the performance of two samples of women from the norming population performance.

Approximately 2,500 persons engaged in mechanical, electrical, or related work made up the norming sample for Test 6-A (Mechanical Knowledge). A small sample of high school students enrolled in vocational education courses ($n$ = 20) and college students enrolled in engineering courses ($n$ = 17) were included. Other subjects were employed mainly in skilled jobs, with some in semiskilled jobs. Ages ranged from 15 to 59 years. The norms for Test 7-A (Sales Aptitude) were gathered from 2,300 employed salespersons who represented many aspects of the field, including real estate, insurance, retail, and door-to-door. This sample ranged in age from 16 to 71 years.

The technical manual is somewhat confusing when describing the norms for

Test 8-A (Personal Adjustment Index). The first paragraph indicates that the norms were based on 860 persons from the eastern United States with a slightly higher educational level than for the country as a whole. Then the text states that the inventory was administered to 3,000 men and 3,500 women who "were secured with the help of other professional workers" (ETSA, 1990, p. 23). These individuals took the Personal Adjustment Index voluntarily. It is unclear whether these were two separate samples drawn at different times and who, exactly, were the 6,500 men and women who "were secured with the help of other professional workers." A written inquiry to the current ETSA manager resulted in some clarification: The 3,000 men and 3,500 women were an additional norming sample, which served to confirm the results of the original norming study (C.K. Stouffer, personal communication, August 16, 1990).

*Bias.* Several attempts have been made to ensure that the ETSA tests are in no way biased. Beginning in the 1960s, the developers collected data on black, Oriental, American Indian, and Spanish-surnamed Americans. Analyses revealed no significant differences from the scores obtained by a total heterogeneous population. Further, additional research has indicated no difference in performance between males and females on the ETSA tests. However, the specific statistical tests used to draw these conclusions are neither described nor discussed in the test manuals.

*Reliability.* Reliability evidence is presented for each test in the ETSA battery. Test 1-A (General Mental Ability) was administered to 238 individuals (characteristics unknown), yielding a KR-20 reliability coefficient of .91. Although the sample size for this reliability study is the same as that for the first validity study, it is not clear whether this is simply a coincidence or if the same sample (college applicants) participated in both studies. The technical manual (ETSA, 1990) states "reliability coefficients of internal consistency, test-retest reliabilities are high" (p. 7); no further information is available.

The KR-20 reliability coefficient for Test 2-A (Office Arithmetic), based on a sample of 249 individuals (characteristics unknown), was .90. The technical manual (ETSA, 1990) states that "since the criterion which the test is trying to predict is relatively homogeneous, the test itself is composed of relatively homogeneous items, thus ensuring a fair level of test reliability" (p. 9).

General Clerical Ability (Test 3-A) is a speed test, so determining a KR-20 is not appropriate. Test-retest reliability, however, based on 300 scores, was .94. The interval between the two administrations is identified only as "several months" (ETSA, 1990, p. 11), and no information is provided about the sample on which this reliability coefficient was based.

The next three tests also produced high reliability figures. Test 4-A (Stenographic Skills) showed a KR-20 reliability of .90. The sample of 300 individuals that produced this coefficient is not described in the manual, however. Test 5-A (Mechanical Familiarity) produced a test-retest reliability coefficient of .94 on a sample of 140 randomly selected persons (no further information provided) retested after 3 months. The mean gain upon retesting was less than 1 point. Test 6-A (Mechanical Knowledge) had a KR-21 reliability of .93, based on 300 persons "in mechanical, electrical, and related areas" (ETSA, 1990, p. 17). Apparently these subjects were *employed* in mechanical, electrical, and related areas.

The split-half method was applied to the seventh and eighth components in the battery. Test 7-A (Sales Aptitude) yielded a split-half reliability estimate of .77 based on 168 salespeople. The coefficient was corrected for length using the Spearman-Brown prophecy formula. The Personal Adjustment Index (Test 8-A) produced a split-half reliability estimate of .90, based on 100 men and women and corrected for length using the Spearman-Brown formula. Subjects were chosen "from the standard or normative group" (ETSA, 1990, p. 22). In addition, the developers also examined test-retest reliability on this measure, with a 6-week interval between administrations. The resulting coefficient of .94 was based on a group of 38 graduate students, "all of whom might be expected to be typical or well adjusted" (ETSA, 1990, p. 22).

*Validity.* More information is presented about the validity of the various ETSA tests than there is about their reliability. Test 1-A (General Mental Ability) was administered to 238 college applicants along with the verbal and mathematics components of the College Entrance Examination Board (CEEB-SAT), resulting in a correlation between scores of .681. Based on a sample of 67 examinees, the correlation between Test 1-A and WAIS-R scores was .593; no information, however, is provided about the examinees used in that study. One hundred sixty randomly selected individuals were administered Test 1-A and the Otis Employment Test, Test 2, Form A (Otis Self-Administering Test of Mental Ability, high school level). The resulting correlation between scores was .742. Finally, measures of criterion-related predictive validity were obtained by comparing Test 1-A scores earned by 90 students in a professional school program prior to entering school with their cumulative GPAs at the end of the program. The correlation was .505, statistically significant at the .01 level.

The technical manual (ETSA, 1990) states of Test 2-A (Office Arithmetic), "since the aptitude it measures is very specific, the test items themselves have considerable content validity" (p. 2). No information is available, however, on who reviewed the items to establish the content validity. In the first of two formal validity studies, two classes of college freshmen enrolled in a first-year business mathematics course were given Test 2-A. The instructor was asked to group students in one of two categories: satisfactory or unsatisfactory performance in the course. The course covered "essentially the same types of skills as measured by the test, so it was presumed that there would be a correlation between scores on the ETSA Test 2-A and performance in a business mathematics course" (ETSA, 1990, pp. 9–10). The resulting point-biserial correlation was .49. The technical manual goes on to say that the "ETSA tests are not intended for college students and the distributions of scores obtained from a relatively homogeneous group of college freshmen will probably yield lower coefficients than might be obtained with more heterogeneous samplings" (ETSA, 1990, p. 10). The second study involved correlating Test 2-A scores with those obtained on the School and College Ability Test (mathematics). A sample of 210 college freshmen were administered the SCAT in October and Test 2-A in February. The correlation between scores on the two tests was .61.

For Test 3-A (General Clerical Ability), the technical manual states "a good case could be made for content and/or curricular validity since the items in this test were patterned directly from material usually emphasized in books written about general office procedures" (ETSA, 1990, p. 11). In addition, Test 3-A was administered to 75 college freshmen in the business education department of a state college. At the same time instructors were asked to identify those doing satisfactory and unsatisfactory work. The point-biserial correlation between the Test 3-A scores and the instructor rating was .81. The technical manual indicates that this sample of 75 students had a mean score of 122, while a random sample of clients in an employment service had a mean score of 100. Although not clear to the present reviewer what this has to do with validity, these comparative mean scores nonetheless are presented as evidence of validity in the technical manual.

Of Test 4-A (Stenographic Skills), the technical manual states that "content validity is assumed good since the items in the test were specifically selected to parallel the material presented in several standard text books widely used to train secretaries and stenographers" (ETSA, 1990, p. 13). In addition, Test 4-A was administered to 280 college freshmen in the business education department of a state college. These subjects' instructor also had grouped them into those doing satisfactory work and those whose efforts were unsatisfactory. The point-biserial correlation between the scores earned on Test 4-A and the instructor's rating was .74.

The correlation between ETSA Tests 3-A and 4-A was .84, based on a sample of 280 students. The sample of college freshmen produced a mean score of 82 on Test 4-A, while a random sample of clients in an employment service showed a mean of 68. Again, this reviewer cannot tell what this difference in means has to do with validity, but it is presented as evidence of such in the technical manual. The validities reported are based only on the actual test; the figures do not include the typing and shorthand supplement tests. No information on the validity of these latter two instruments is reported.

To establish the validity for Mechanical Ability (Test 5-A), the distribution of scores obtained from 140 trained, work-experienced individuals and a second group of 150 untrained and inexperienced subjects was compared using a chi square statistic to determine if the difference in distributions was statistically significant. The developers also looked at differences between means of the distributions using the critical ratio technique. A chi square of 71 and critical ratio of 14.4 were both significant at the .01 level, indicating statistically significant differences in the two distributions of scores. No reference was provided for the critical ratio technique, and the author of this review was able to find only one statistical text with this term referenced (i.e., Horowitz, 1974).

The technical manual states that "the establishment of concurrent validity does not always guarantee predictive validity" (ETSA, 1990, p. 15); thus, one should be cautious in interpreting this evidence. The correlation between Test 5-A and the Otis Employment Test, Test 2, Form A (Otis Self-Administering Test of Mental Ability, high school level) for 225 individuals was −.016. This sample was composed of vocational and educational guidance clients, trade school trainees, adults employed in a variety of settings, and college students. In another study, the Otis Employment Test, Test 1, Form A (Otis Self-Administering Test, grammar school, fourth–ninth grade level) was administered to 500 job applicants with primarily unskilled work experience, who also took ETSA Test 5-A. The correlation between the scores on the Otis and ETSA tests was .82. As the technical manual states: "The Mechanical Familiarity Test would appear to measure something other than intelligence, but seems to discriminate better with average or above average level of mental functioning as measured by the Otis test" (ETSA, 1990, p. 15).

To establish criterion-related concurrent validity for Test 6-A (Mechanical Knowledge), the scores of 290 persons engaged in activities (occupations?) where mechanical knowledge is essential were compared to those of 380 individuals in other occupations. A chi square and critical ratio technique were used to compare the distributions, resulting in a chi square value of 50 and a critical ratio of 8.27 (statistically significant at the .01 level). Further evidence of concurrent validity was provided by asking supervisors of 42 mechanical, process, and electrical engineers, designers, mechanics, production supervisors, lathe operators, and draftsmen employed in an industrial plant to rate their employees' mechanical knowledge on a 5-point scale (1 = excellent, 5 = poor). The rank order correlation (Siegel, 1956) between the scores on Test 6-A and the supervisors' ratings was .67, statistically significant at the .01 level. In addition, for a sample of 150 persons (40 in occupations related to the mechanical field and 110 in other occupations), the correlation between Test 6-A and Mechanical Preference as measured by the Kuder Preference Record, Form CH, was .93.

The ETSA developers used rank order correlations, Pearson product moment correlations, and biserial correlations to determine the relationship between scores on Test 7-A (Sales Aptitude) and certain "success" groups of salespersons representing different types of selling (insurance, real estate, and door-to-door). Table 1 provides these correlations as described in the technical manual.

Concurrent validity of the Personal Adjustment Index (Test 8-A) was established by using the California Psychological Inventory (CPI) as the criterion. The CPI was chosen "because the description of what it purports to measure seems compatible with the content and expected outcomes of ETSA Test 8-A Personal Adjustment Index" (ETSA, 1990, p. 22). The correlation between scores on the two tests was .72 (no information was provided on the sample's size or characteristics). Construct validity was demonstrated by examining the test's ability to discriminate people with significant adjustment problems that hindered their productivity and ability to get along with others. Scores on Test 8-A for 50 clients with significant adjustment problems at a mental health clinic were compared to scores of 50 individuals identified by peers and/or supervisors as being "normal" or "typical." The groups were matched on age, education, gender, marital status, and other relevant factors. The mean of the typical group was 84.5, with a standard deviation of 13.1; the mean for the clinical group was 72.4, with a standard deviation of 8.2. Although the technical manual states "the inventory scores distinctly separate the two groups" (ETSA, 1990, p. 22), no statistical analysis was reported. The correlation between Test 8-A and final GPA for a 2-year technical program (information on the type of program not provided) was .316, significant at the .01 level. In addition, the prediction of performance on a state board exam (practical/vocational nursing) was significant at the .01 level, with a correlation of .342. It is unclear why Test 8-A should be highly correlated with either of these criteria. Is this provided to show divergent validity? Although the technical manual states that "careful research over a period of 10 years indicates a positive correlation between the Personal Adjustment Index and the successful hospital employee as measured by employer ratings while in training and

**Table 1**

**Correlations Between Test 7-A and Other Variables for Various Salespersons**

| | *Type of Sales* | | | |
|---|---|---|---|---|
| *Variable* | *Real Estate* (*N* = *144*) | *Insurance* (*N* = *128*) | *Door-to-Door* (*N* = *160*) | *Retail* (*N* = *112*) |
| Test 7-A and employer's rank | .71 | — | — | .82 |
| Test 7-A and salaries | — | .72 | .61 | — |
| Test 7-A and years of service | .20 | .10 | –.32 | –.03 |
| Test 7-A and education | .56 | .73 | .40 | .21 |
| Test 7-A and years of service or employer's rank | .64 | .47 | .09 | .06 |

*Note.* Date taken from ETSA *Technical Manual*, p. 20.

on the job performance" (ETSA, 1990, p. 26), an exact correlation figure is not provided.

The technical manual notes that because scores for all tests are reported in bands and because the tests make no effort to distinguish between fine differences in performance, "extremely high validity coefficients would not be necessary" (ETSA, 1990, p. 9). The user is encouraged to establish the predictive validity of the ETSA tests for her- or himself.

## Critique

There are a number of problems with the ETSA tests. First, for all but Test 8-A, only one type of reliability evidence is presented. Nunnally (1978) states that "at least two types of reliability coefficients should be computed and reported for any test that is employed widely" (p. 236). This is also implied in the *Standards for Educational and Psychological Testing* (American Educational Research Association, American Psychological Association, & National Council on Measurement in Education, 1985) in Standard 2.6.

For tests 3-A, 5-A, and 8-A, the technical manual presents evidence of test-retest reliability. Although certainly desirable, when this is the only type of evidence presented, the problems inherent in test-retest reliability may make the reliability estimates unrealistic (Allen & Yen, 1979; Anastasi, 1976; Ebel, 1965, 1972; Guion, 1965; Mehrens & Lehmann, 1984; Nunnally, 1978; Stanley, 1971).

For example, there is the potential for carryover effects between testings. The first test may influence the second, as when an examinee remembers answers given to the first test (which will lead to an overestimate of reliability) or when practice effects occur (which will lead to an underestimate of reliability). One cannot determine whether reliability has been under- or overestimated. Nunnally (1978) states, "Except in certain special instances, there are serious defects in employing the retest method. The major defect is that experience in the first testing usually will influence responses in the second testing" (p. 233). Further, in Stanley's (1971) opinion,

> In most measures of intellect, temperament, or achievement, however, repetition of the same test form and correlation of the two sets of scores is at present less defensible as an operation for determining reliability than it is for physical measurement. (pp. 406–407)

The length of time between the two testings will influence the reliability coefficient when test-retest reliability estimates are employed. Short periods make carryover effects due to memory a potential problem; a long interval makes changes in examinees more likely. As Allen and Yen (1979) summarize, "Different lengths of time may affect the reliability estimate in different ways, sometimes overestimating and sometimes underestimating the real reliability" (p. 77). Test-retest reliability is most appropriate if there is no significant change in examinee characteristic expected within the period of measurement and if memory of the items does not influence subsequent administrations. Feldt and Brennan (1989) state that "with paper-and-pencil instruments, however, the second condition will almost certainly not be met" (p. 110). They go on to say that "test-retest reliabilities are often viewed with skepticism" (p. 110).

The split-half method was used to estimate the reliability of Test 7-A and (partially) Test 8-A. The technical manual does not indicate, however, which method of splitting the tests was used, and there are a number of different options available. (Though it is beyond the scope of this review to discuss these various methods, interested readers may consult Allen & Yen [1979], Guion [1965], Gulliksen [1950], and Rulon [1939].) Halves formed by order are usually less desirable than odd/even splits because some examinees may improve with practice and others may not finish the test (Allen & Yen, 1979). Guion (1965) states that "the split-half methods are not, strictly speaking, estimates of internal consistency; rather, they provide spuriously high estimates based on equivalence" (p. 42). Nunnally (1978) indicates that the problem with the split-half method is that the correlation between the halves (and thus the reliability estimate) will vary to a degree depending on how the items are divided.

Use of the Spearman-Brown prophecy formula to correct for the lengths of split halves may also result in unreasonable reliability estimates. Technically speaking, to use the Spearman-Brown formula the two halves must be parallel (Allen & Yen, 1979). If the component tests are not parallel, the Spearman-Brown formula can under- or overestimate the reliability of a longer test (Allen & Yen, 1979), and it is impossible to know if the reliability is an over- or underestimate. If the two halves are essentially tau equivalent, coefficient alpha should be used. The latter should also be used if the scores for the halves have unequal variances or some other indication that they are not parallel. If the two halves are not essentially tau equivalent, alpha produces a lower bound estimate of reliability. If the variances of the observed scores for the two halves are equal but they are not essentially tau equivalent, the Spearman-Brown formula will produce an underestimate of reliability (Allen & Yen, 1979). Reliabilities produced by coefficient alpha and those corrected using the Spearman-Brown formula will be high if the two halves of the test are highly correlated and low if they are not. No evidence is presented that the parts formed here in the split halves were either parallel or essentially tau equivalent.

Tests 1-A, 2-A, 4-A, and 6-A have KR-20 or KR-21 reliabilities reported. Internal consistency reliability is not appropriate when the test cannot be divided into parallel or essentially tau equivalent parts or when items are not independent (Allen & Yen, 1979). Internal consistency reliability methods will be accurate only if the two components are essentially tau equivalent and only when the test measures one trait. Allen and Yen (1979) state that "a typical intelligence test, which measures a collection of verbal, spatial, and quantitative skills, would be heterogeneous. . . . Internal consistency measures of reliability are not suited for use of heterogeneous tests" (p. 83). Cureton (1958) has shown that the Kuder-Richardson formulas can be used properly only when the assumption of homogeneity is satisfied. An important question concerns the use of KR-21 instead of KR-20 for estimating the reliability of Test 6-A. Allen and Yen (1979) point out that KR-20 and KR-21 will be equal only if all the item difficulties are equal. If the item difficulties are unequal, KR-21 will be less than KR-20 and will underestimate the reliability of the test. Are item difficulties all equal for Test 6-A? No data are provided one way or the other. Ebel (1965) indicates that the more widely items differ in difficulty, the more seriously the Kuder-Richardson formulas, particularly KR-21, may underestimate reliability.

The technical manual does state for Test 2-A that "since the criterion which the test is trying to predict is relatively homogeneous, the test itself is composed of relatively homogeneous items, thus ensuring a fair level of test reliability" (ETSA, 1990, p. 9). This may be true for internal consistency reliability estimates but not necessarily for other types such as test-retest or alternate forms reliability.

No reliabilities are provided for the two tests that report subscores as well as total scores (i.e., 7-A and 8-A). In addition, no standard errors of measurement are reported for any of the tests. It is often assumed that there is "one" standard error of measurement, but this may not be the case. Such an assumption does seem to be operating, though, for the ETSA tests. Many authors (e.g., Blixt & Shama, 1986; Feldt, Steffen, & Gupta, 1985; Lord, 1984; Jarjoura, 1986; Livingston, 1982; Woodruff, 1989) have indicated that the standard error of measurement may not be the same for all score levels, and several have provided methods for estimating the standard error of measurement at different score levels. No attempt to report standard errors of measurement at the cutoff scores for the score bands has been made (see AERA, APA, & NCME, 1985, Standards 2.1 and 2.10, and Feldt & Brennan, 1989).

Although the *Standards for Educational and Psychological Testing* state that the procedures used to obtain samples for estimating reliabilities and standard errors of measurement should be described (p. 20), one finds no such descriptions in the

ETSA technical manual. Descriptions of samples are very sketchy, including phrases such as "a sample of 238 scores" (ETSA, 1990, p. 7), "a recent sample of 300 scores" (p. 11), and "140 randomly selected individuals" (p. 15). Even the latter "randomly selected individuals" gives no real indication because it fails to describe the population sampled.

Despite conventionally accepted standards (e.g., Standards 4.3 and 4.4, AERA, APA & NCME, 1985) and other published guidelines (e.g., Peterson, Kolen, & Hoover, 1989; Angoff, 1971) for test norming, the ETSA technical manual reveals shortcomings in this regard. For instance, it does not clearly describe the groups on which the normative data are based, providing instead information such as the approximate number of individuals included in the sample, their age range, and a very brief descriptors (e.g., "college applicants," "clients . . . at a college psychological clinic," "other randomly selected adults"; ETSA, 1990, p. 8). In addition, the technical manual provides only the mean and standard deviation of the normative group (and even that is not placed under the section on norming). No other information is available. The year in which the norming studies were done is not stated, and the participation rates are not included.

In the process of developing norms, it is important that the population of interest be clearly specified (Angoff, 1971; Peterson et al., 1989). How a particular person performs depends to a great extent on the norm group used, and norms based on different groups can be quite different. Angoff (1971), Ebel (1972), Ghiselli, Campbell, and Zedeck (1981), Mehrens and Lehmann (1984), Nunnally (1978), and Peterson et al. (1989) stress the importance of norms being recent and representative of the group to which users will apply them. The ETSA tests fail to meet these criteria also. For example, the technical manual says that the ETSA tests "are not intended for college students" (ETSA, 1990, p. 10). Yet, in many of the norming samples, college students compose at least part of the group(s). Why use college students in the sample if the test is inappropriate for college students? Mehrens and Lehmann (1984) state the following:

> A sampling procedure too often employed is to sample by convenience rather than by a particular technical sampling procedure. . . . Such a chosen sample *may* not be biased, particularly if the data in the sample are appropriately weighted. Nevertheless, the likelihood that such a sampling procedure will produce biased results is great enough for us to be wary of norms built in such a fashion. (p. 314)

Angoff (1971) claims that "samples of convenience will almost certainly be biased" (p. 549), and Peterson et al. (1989) agree that "convenience norms" (p. 238) have a limited usefulness. They further indicate that it is the responsibility of the test publisher to point this out to potential test users. Although the publishers of the ETSA tests do encourage employers to develop their own local norms, they do not, however, indicate that their own scoring band breakdown and norms may be of limited usefulness.

In addition to being representative, the norming sample must be sufficiently large to provide stable values (Angoff, 1971; Ebel, 1972; Ghiselli et al., 1981; Mehrens & Lehmann, 1984; Peterson et al., 1989). This appears to be less a problem for the ETSA tests than the other standards for norms. The norming samples here range from 2,500 to 6,500 for the various tests.

The *Standards for Educational and Psychological Testing* (AERA, APA, & NCME, 1985) state that "validity is the most important consideration in test evaluation" (p. 9). Mehrens and Lehmann (1984) agree. Unfortunately, there is no rule of thumb regarding exactly how high a validity coefficient should be (Cronbach, 1971). Validity coefficients for the ETSA tests ranged from -.016 to .93. As validity is the most important consideration for the test, this reviewer would like to see high validity coefficients, certainly higher than those reported for several of the ETSA tests.

As might be expected, a large number of standards cover validity. Only a few will be discussed here. Standard 1.14 indicates that when rater judgments are used as criteria in concurrent validity studies, the training and experience of the raters should be described if possible. In several cases, raters were used to establish concurrent validity of several of the ETSA tests, but there is no indication that raters were trained. Mehrens and Lehmann (1984) believe that supervisor ratings have many inadequacies as a criterion. For example, if the test score does not correlate highly with the ratings, it is not possible to determine if the test did not predict job success or whether the supervisor could not rate the individual accurately, or both. In addition, the reliability of the criterion measure will affect validity (Thorndike, 1982). An unreliable criterion measure will produce a low validity coefficient.

Standard 1.21 indicates that when studies of differential prediction are conducted, regression equations should be computed for each group in which the group is a moderator. Although Tests 5-A, 6-A, and 8-A contain such studies of differential prediction, no regression equations are presented.

Standard 10.3 calls for the rationale for criterion relevance to be made explicit. The criterion should contain important aspects *of the job*. Messick (1988, 1989) also stresses the importance of the relevance of the criteria. It is doubtful that performance in a single business class contains the important aspects of the jobs for which the General Clerical Ability and Stenographic Skills tests might be employed. It also seems doubtful that the Otis Employment Test, high school level, contains the important aspects of the jobs for which the Mechanical Familiarity test may be useful.

Standard 10.4 indicates that content validity should be based on job analysis, and Messick (1988) concurs. Looking at the "big picture," Madaus (1983) discusses several important court cases that deal with this issue. The publishers of the ETSA tests, however, do not present evidence of content validity based on a job analysis. On the contrary, they claim content validity based on the contents of "standard" and "widely used" textbooks.

Mehrens and Lehmann (1984) indicate that face validity is important from an acceptance viewpoint. If a test appears relevant, examinees may take it more seriously. Within the ETSA tests, some subscales of tests such as Sales Aptitude, Office Arithmetic, Mechanical Familiarity, and Personal Adjustment seem to lack face validity.

Guion (1965) indicates that a chi square can be used appropriately to establish evidence of validity, as the developers did for Tests 5-A and 6-A. Guion contends, however, that one should not stop with the use of the chi square (because it does not indicate the strength of the relationship), but go on to include expectancy tables. Thorndike (1982) suggests the use of *taxonomic validity,* which indicates whether persons in different occupations produce different means on the test. He also advocates the application of analysis of variance procedures and a point-biserial correlation to differentiate the two groups; this will provide evidence of the strength of the relationship.

Guion (1965) identifies predictive validity as the most relevant to personnel practice. The common practice of relying on concurrent validity is an inadequate substitute. Yet, a predictive validity study has been conducted only for ETSA Test 1-A.

This reviewer noticed some problems with the validity studies carried out for some of the ETSA tests. For example, the second validity study cited for Test 2-A involved correlating its scores with scores on the SCAT. The SCAT was administered in October, and Test 2-A followed in February. First, it is assumed that these two tests measure the same thing, which seems doubtful to this reviewer. Second, it is assumed that the trait being measured remains stable across several months for the individuals being measured (college freshmen). No evidence is provided that would support this assumption, however, and in fact it seems somewhat doubtful that tests measuring achievement would remain stable as one continues one's education.

For Tests 3-A and 4-A, instructors identified students performing satisfactorily and those who were not, and their ratings then were correlated with scores on the tests. It would be interesting to know how many students were included in each group (satisfactory and unsatisfactory). If a large number of students were rated as doing satisfactory work and only a very few as unsatisfactory, the point-biserial correlation may still be quite large. However, the very small number of persons in the unsatisfactory group would raise serious questions about the usefulness of the point-biserial correlation as an indication of validity.

The correlation between scores on Test 5-A and the Otis Employment Test was −.016 for one sample, yet using another form of the Otis and Test 5-A produced a correlation of .82 for a second group. This is a very large and interesting discrepancy. Could this be interpreted as a failure to replicate the findings between the two studies? Is this possibly an error in the technical manual? It is difficult to interpret both this discrepancy and the validity coefficients from these two studies.

For Test 6-A, supervisors ranked their employees from 1 to 5, with 1 indicating "excellent" and 5 indicating "poor." A rank order correlation then was computed between these rankings and scores produced on Test 6-A. The technical manual reports the resulting correlation as .67. This *must* be an error. If this value is reported correctly, then the correlation would indicate an *invalid* test. Where a ranking of 1 represents "excellent" and a ranking of 5 represents "poor," a low ranking should be associated with a high test score and a high ranking should be associated with a low test score. Assuming a valid test, the expected correlation would be *negative,* yet a moderately large *positive* correlation is reported. Is this simply an error in the technical manual, or is this test invalid?

Construct validity is asserted for Test 8-A by comparing scores earned by subjects "with significant adjustment problems" in a counseling setting with those of "normal" persons. The latter were identified by peers or supervisors as "normal," but the technical manual does not stipulate how the developers determined that those persons in the counseling setting actually had "significant adjustment problems." The difference between means was relatively small (84.5 vs. 72.4), particularly in view of the standard deviations (13.1 vs. 8.2). There is a good bit of overlap in the distributions of the two groups. Apparently no statistical test was carried out to determine if the difference in means was statistically significant (though even if it were, it probably would not be practically significant).

Several general comments and questions deserve mention. The administrator's manual asserts that the "ETSA tests are level A instruments, as defined by a joint committee of the American Psychological Association, American Educational Research Association, and the National Council on Measurements Used in Education" (ETSA, 1985, p. 2) but does not provide a reference. This reviewer found what appeared to be the appropriate reference (AERA & NCME, 1955) but failed to locate any definition of a "level A instrument" within. The apparent reference is the original form of the *Standards for Educational and Psychological Testing*. The committee that created these standards was composed only of the American Educational Research Association and the National Council on Measurements Used in Education. The APA was not part of the committee, as indicated by the ETSA authors. A written request for clarification produced no clear reference, but a page number was provided; however, this reviewer still could not find any such definition and apparently did not have the correct reference.

The publisher's written response to the above did indicate, however, that the most current version of the *Standards* (AERA, APA, & NCME, 1985) provides no detailed information regarding the necessary skills for administering and interpreting tests. For this reason, the ETSA publishers "have continued to use the 'old' standards" (C.K. Stouffer, personal communication, August 16, 1990). It would certainly seem prudent for test publishers to follow the criteria set forth in the most recent version of the *Standards* (1985); 30+ years have seen some significant changes in the field of psychometrics!

For Test 6-A, approximately 200 items were divided into several forms and administered to persons employed in mechanical, electrical, and related areas and to high school students in vocational education courses. The developers chose the 50 tests with the highest scores and the 50 with the lowest scores; then, based on the count of the correct responses on these 100 tests, they selected 121 items for the final test. This reviewer wonders why an item analysis was not done, as with other tests in the battery.

For the Sales Aptitude test, approximately 250 items were administered to 175 salespersons and 325 non-salespersons. The 100 items that best differentiated the two groups were used in the present form. How did the developers determine which items best discriminated—what statistics were used?

For Test 1-A, General Mental Ability, the manual indicates that no scratch paper is necessary. However, may examinees use scratch paper if they request it? Take the following problem (similar to a problem in ETSA Test 1-A):

> A store clerk receives a commission of 20% of every sale under $10 and 50% on every sale of $20 or over. In the first hour he made sales of $10.50, $20, and $22.50. What was his commission for the first hour?

Though this problem itself is not exceptionally difficult, it could be become so without scratch paper as one begins to multiply and add in one's head. Memory also plays a significant role (i.e., being able to remember the commission for each item) in order to add the appropriate amounts. Another question not addressed by the administrator's manual is whether hand calculators are allowed when taking Test 1-A.

The computational and nonverbal items on Test 1-A are purported to help the individual who lacks reading skills or who has poor verbal development. Given the problem stated above, one can easily see that this computational problem (and most of the others in the test) requires reading ability; further, the administrator's manual indicates that the ability to read, understand, and follow the directions are part of Test 1-A. This not only constitutes an "unscored" part of the test (as it is not counted in the score), it seems to contradict the purpose of the nonverbal items—to aid those with limited verbal ability.

Test 7-A (Sales Aptitude) seems to be misnamed. Parts 2 (Interest in Selling), 3 (Personality Factors), 4 (Identification of Self with Selling Occupation), and 5 (Level of Aspiration) seem more like components of an interest inventory, as illustrated by the following paraphrased items:

Part 2 (Interest in Selling): You would rather work indoors at a desk.

Part 3 (Personality Factors): You have been the officer of several clubs.

Part 4 (Identification of Self with Selling Occupation): You would rather be a psychologist than a research scientist in biology.

Part 5 (Level of Aspiration): You would rather be a politician than work in orology.

Part 7 of the Sales Aptitude test asks the examinee to match a sales slogan with the appropriate product. There is a psychometric problem with this section: as there is an exact match between the product and slogan, the process of elimination can play a role in the examinee's score. Another concern is that this section seems to measure (a) how much television one watches, (b) how closely one pays attention to commercials, (c) one's memory, or (d) a combination of a, b, and c.

No reliability or validity evidence is provided for Test 7-A and 8-A subscores. Even though the technical manual notes that Test 8-A was designed to remove social desirability effects, this reviewer found that some of the items still contained such a component. For example, asked to respond to "Schools are a neighborhood nuisance," I believe most *job applicants* would answer that they disagree, whether they actually do or not. In addition, some items on Test 8-A are of questionable relevance (e.g., the paraphrased item, "A good laxative is a poor man's doctor").

This reviewer also questions some of the "correct answers" provided by the test publisher. For example, the person who agrees with the paraphrased statement "A person who works alone is happier" would be scored as "incorrect," an indicator of adjustment problems. People who prefer to work alone are not necessarily maladjusted—perhaps they would be unsuited to occupations where they had to interact continually with others, but they quite possibly could perform well in occupations where they could work alone.

Finally, the technical manual indicates that the original Test 8-A was administered to a "large number of people" at "various times" (ETSA, 1990, p. 21), and changes were made based on an item analysis of the data. How many people are a large number? When were the various times? This reviewer attempted to obtain answers to these and other questions by telephone; however, all calls were answered by a recording machine, and none were returned to my knowledge despite messages left.

In summary, the prospective user should be aware that there are a number of problems with the ETSA tests that the publisher should address (and remedy) in future editions.

## References


Angoff, W.H. (1971). Scales, norms, and equivalent scores. In R.L. Thorndike (Ed.), *Educational measurement* (2nd ed., pp. 508-600). Washington, DC: American Council on Education.

Allen, M.J., & Yen, W.M. (1979). *Introduction to measurement theory.* Monterey, CA: Brooks/Cole.

American Educational Research Association, American Psychological Association, & National Council on Measurement in Education. (1985). *Standards for educational and psychological testing.* Washington, DC: American Psychological Association.

American Educational Research Association & National Council on Measurements Used in Education. (1955). *Technical recommendations for achievement tests.* Washington, DC: National Education Association.

Anastasi, A. (1976). *Psychological testing* (4th ed). New York: Macmillan.

Blixt, S.L., & Shama, D.D. (1986). An empirical investigation of the standard error of measurement at different ability levels. *Educational and Psychological Measurement, 46,* 545–550.

Cronbach, L.J. (1971). Test validation. In R.L. Thorndike (Ed.), *Educational measurement* (2nd ed., pp. 443–507). Washington, DC: American Council on Education.

Cureton, E.E. (1958). The definition and estimation of test reliability. *Educational and Psychological Measurement, 18,* 715–738.

Ebel, R.L. (1965). *Measuring educational achievement.* Englewood Cliffs, NJ: Prentice-Hall.

Ebel, R.L. (1972). *Essentials of educational measurement.* Englewood Cliffs, NJ: Prentice-Hall.

Educators/Employers' Tests & Services Associates. (1985). *Administrator's manual for the ETSA Tests and for the ETSA Personal Adjustment Index.* Chambersburg, PA: Author.

Educators/Employers' Tests & Services Associates. (1990). *Technical manual (a report) for the ETSA Tests and the ETSA Personal Adjustment Index.* Chambersburg, PA: Author.

Feldt, L.S., & Brennan, R.L. (1989). Reliability. In R.L. Linn (Ed.), *Educational measurement* (3rd ed., pp. 105–146). New York: American Council on Education.

Feldt, L.S., Steffen, M., & Gupta, N.C. (1985). A comparison of five methods for estimating the standard error of measurement at specific score levels. *Applied Psychological Measurement, 9* (4), 351–361.

Ghiselli, E.E., Campbell, J.P., & Zedeck, S. (1981). *Measurement theory for the behavioral sciences.* San Francisco: W.H. Freeman.

Guion, R.M. (1965). *Personnel testing.* New York: McGraw-Hill.

Gulliksen, H. (1950). *Theory of mental tests.* New York: Wiley.

Jarjoura, D. (1986). An estimator of examinee-level measurement error variance that considers test form difficulty adjustments. *Applied Psychological Measurement, 10* (2), 175–186.

Livingston, S.A. (1982). Estimation of the conditional standard error of measurement *Journal of Educational Measurement, 19*(2), 135–138.

Lord, F.M. (1984). Standard errors of measurement at different ability levels. *Journal of Educational Measurement, 21*(3), 239–244.

Madaus, G.F. (1983). Minimum competency testing for certification: The evolution and evaluation of test validity. In G.F. Madaus (Ed.), *The courts, validity, and minimum competency testing* (pp. 21–62). Boston: Kluwer-Nijhoff.

Mehrens, W.A., & Lehmann, I.J. (1984). *Measurement and evaluation in education and psychology* (3rd ed). New York: Holt, Rinehart & Winston.

Messick, S. (1988). The once and future issues of validity: Assessing the meaning and consequences of measurement. In H. Wainer & H.I. Braun (Eds.), *Test validity* (pp. 33–45). Hillsdale, NJ: Lawrence Erlbaum.

Messick, S. (1989). Validity. In R.L. Linn (Ed.), *Educational measurement* (3rd ed., pp. 13–104). New York: American Council on Education.

Nunnally, J.C. (1978). *Psychometric theory* (2nd ed.). New York: McGraw-Hill.

Peterson, N.S., Kolen, M.J., & Hoover, H.D. (1989). Scaling, norming, and equating. In R.L. Linn (Ed.), *Educational measurement* (3rd ed., pp. 221–262). New York: American Council on Education.

Rulon, P.J. (1939). A simplified procedure for determining the reliability of a test by split halves. *Harvard Educational Review, 9*, 99–103.

Siegel, S. (1956). *Nonparametric statistics for the behavioral sciences*. New York: McGraw-Hill.

Stanley, J.C. (1971). Reliability. In R.L. Thorndike (Ed.), *Educational measurement* (2nd ed., pp. 356–442). Washington, DC: American Council on Education.

Thorndike, R.L. (1982). *Applied psychometrics*. Boston: Houghton Mifflin.

Woodruff, D. (1989, March). *Derivation and application of the conditional standard error of measurement in prediction*. Paper presented at the annual meeting of the American Educational Research Association, San Francisco.

**Alice G. Friedman, Ph.D.**
*Assistant Professor of Psychology, State University of New York at Binghamton, Binghamton, New York.*

# FEAR SURVEY SCHEDULE FOR CHILDREN–REVISED

*Thomas H. Ollendick. Blacksburg, Virginia: Thomas H. Ollendick, Ph.D.*

## Introduction

The Fear Survey Schedule for Children–Revised (FSSC-R) is a self-report inventory designed to assess fear in children. The inventory consists of 80 items representing a wide range of common objects and events that children may find frightening. The directions instruct the child to respond to each item according to the word or phrase ("None," "Some," or "A lot") that best describes his or her level of fear. Each item is then assigned a score of 1, 2, or 3, corresponding to the child's reported level of fear, and summed over the items to yield a Total Fear Score and scores in each of the five factor scales: Fear of Failure and Criticism (18 items), Fear of the Unknown (19 items), Fear of Injury and Small Animals (22 items), Fear of Danger and Death (14 items), and Medical Fears (7 items). The child's score for each of the five factors may be derived by summing the responses to each of the items that comprise the factors. Higher scores indicate greater levels of fears related to that domain.

The FSSC-R was designed to be administered to children ages 7 through 16 either individually or in a group setting. The instrument was developed for use with normal children as well as those who are physically handicapped, mentally retarded, or psychiatrically impaired. Items may be read aloud to examinees who have difficulty reading or who are visually impaired. According to the author, the FSSC-R is most useful as an ipsative instrument to identify the specific objects of fear among fearful children, as a screening instrument to identify fearful children, and as an outcome measure to evaluate the efficacy of therapeutic intervention (Ollendick, 1988).

The scale is a revised version of the Fear Survey Schedule for Children (FSS-FC) developed by Scherer and Nakamura in 1968. Items for the initial FSS-FC were compiled from adult fear survey schedules and from consultation with professionals familiar with childhood fears (Scherer & Nakamura, 1968). Items were selected to sample fears relevant to a variety of content areas, such as school, home, social, physical, animal, travel, classical phobias, and miscellaneous (Scherer & Nakamura, 1968). Each of the 80 items on the initial FSS-FC are rated on a 5-point scale describing how much the item is feared, from none to very much. The scale yields two scores: Total Number of Objects Feared and Total Degree of Fear. The scale has high internal consistency ($_2r_{xx}$ = .94, computed with the Spearman-

Brown prophecy formula) and is significantly correlated with the Children's Manifest Anxiety Scale (Castaneda, McCandless, & Palermo, 1956).

Although the initial work by Scherer and Nakamura (1968) suggested that the FSS-FC showed promise as a method to assess childhood fears, a number of factors limited the usefulness of the instrument (Ollendick, 1983). The use of a 5-point Likert-type scale was difficult for very young children and those with cognitive or developmental limitations. Further, there was limited information about the psychometric properties of the FSS-FC. Revision of the original scale was undertaken (a) to provide a response format (3-point scale) that could be used reliably by children with developmental or cognitive limitations and (b) to provide information about the psychometric properties of the revised version of the FSSC (Ollendick, 1983). The specific items were adopted directly from the FSS-FC because they appeared to sample the range of objects and events young children typically fear: going to the dentist, thunderstorms, being alone, and so forth.

The FSSC-R was developed by Thomas H. Ollendick, who is currently Professor of Psychology and Director of Clinical Training in the Department of Psychology at Virginia Polytechnic Institute & State University. Dr. Ollendick has conducted extensive research on childhood fear and anxiety. He has authored numerous research articles, chapters, and books in the area of child clinical psychology, including a book about childhood phobias (*Children's Phobias: A Behavioural Perspective;* King, Hamilton, & Ollendick, 1988). In addition, Dr. Ollendick is currently president of the Child Psychology section, Division of Clinical Psychology, of the American Psychological Association, and he serves as Representative-at-Large for the Association for Advancement of Behavior Therapy.

The FSSC-R, currently available from the test author, is a three-page questionnaire entitled "Self-Rating Questionnaire (FSSC-R)." The questionnaire includes directions that are easily understood by children 7 years of age and older. The instructions reassure the respondent that there are no right or wrong answers. Depending upon the child's age and reading level, the FSSC-R can be completed in fewer than 20 minutes. The scoring of the FSSC-R is straightforward. The Total Fear score can be derived in fewer than 5 minutes by simply adding up the appropriate numbers (1, 2, or 3) corresponding to the child's responses. Because there are currently no templates available, scoring the factors adds another 5 minutes. The questionnaire can be administered and scored by someone with little training, although interpretation requires knowledge of normal development of childhood fears.

The instrument is sensitive to gender differences. Boys consistently endorse less fear than girls (Ollendick, 1983; Ollendick, King, & Frary, 1989; Silverman & Nelles, 1987). It is unclear whether this reflects a reluctance on the part of boys to acknowledge fears, or actual differences in the amount of fear experienced by boys and girls (Ollendick, 1983). This finding is consistent with much of the research on fear in infancy (Jacklin, Maccoby, & Doering, 1983) and childhood (Lapouse & Monk, 1959). Overall scores on the FSSC-R do not differ consistently depending upon the age of the child, although some studies have reported greater fear scores among younger children (e.g., Ollendick et al., 1989). Studies that have not supported developmental differences in level of overall fear have noted developmental differences in the specific items children endorse (Ollendick, Matson, & Helsel, 1985a).

## Practical Applications/Uses

The FSSC-R may be useful in clinical, academic, and research settings, (a) to identify children who have specific fears or a high level of fear, (b) to identify specific sensitivities among highly anxious children, (c) to measure outcome in children undergoing treatment for excessive fears and anxiety, and (d) to gather normative information about children's fears. It is a relatively brief instrument that one can easily administer to children in group settings. Considerable support exists for using the FSSC-R with children from diverse backgrounds; the survey has been used in cross-cultural studies on populations from the United States (Ollendick, 1983; Ollendick et al., 1985a), Australia (Ollendick et al., 1989), and Britain (Ollendick & Yule, in press, Ollendick, Yule, & Ollier, in press), as well as in studies of normal children and those with psychopathology, physical handicaps (e.g., the blind), and developmental delays (Ollendick, 1983; Ollendick, Matson, & Helsel, 1985b).

According to the author, the FSSC-R is subject to the limitations inherent in self-report inventories administered to children (Ollendick, 1988). Children who are unwilling or unable to identify their fears accurately may deny them on the FSSC-R. As a partial solution to this difficulty, the instrument should be used in conjunction with other sources of information.

## Technical Aspects

In light of the relative newness of the FSSC-R, a considerable amount of information has been gathered about its psychometric properties. Initial information about internal consistency and test-retest reliability was gathered in a study (Ollendick, 1983) of two normal samples of children from different geographic locations ($N = 217$). The study included children 8–11 years of age, from either the Midwest or Southeast, who were in normal classrooms and had no prior history of mental health contacts or special education placements. The FSSC-R was administered in a group setting along with self-report inventories of anxiety, self-concept, and locus of control. Internal consistency of the FSSC-R for the two samples was high (.954 for the Virginia sample and .942 for the Indiana sample). The mean scores and standard deviations for the two samples were nearly identical (mean = 136, SD = 34.78 for the Virginia sample; mean = 134.61, SD = 37.34 for the Indiana sample). Test-retest reliability over a 1-week interval for Total Fear scores when the survey was administered to 50 children was .81 for boys, .82 for girls, and .82 overall. Test-retest reliability over a 3-month interval was .62 for boys, .58 for girls, and .55 overall. Overall Fear scores were significantly higher for girls than boys for both samples of normal children.

Ollendick (1983) further explored the instrument's convergent and divergent validity by examining the relationship between the FSSC-R and the other self-report measures. As predicted, the FSSC-R correlated positively with trait anxiety for boys and girls from both samples. Further, the FSSC-R was negatively correlated with self-concept and locus of control for girls and for boys and girls combined. The relationships were in the predicted direction, although not significantly, for boys alone.

Results of subjecting the FSSC-R to factor analysis (Ollendick, 1983) yielded a five-factor solution, similar to that reported by Scherer and Nakamura (1968). Factor 1 (Fear of Failure and Criticism) consists of items related to social-evaluative situations, such as "Giving an oral report" and "Looking foolish." The items that make up Factor 2 (Fear of the Unknown) relate to unknown events or uncertain outcomes, such as "Riding on the train" and "Meeting someone for the first time." Factor 3 (Fear of Injury and Small Animals) encompasses potentially harmful articles ("Sharp objects") and small animals ("Lizards"). Factor 4 (Fear of Danger and Death) incorporates items associated with extreme danger or death, such as "Bombing attacks--being invaded" and "Fire–getting burned." Factor 5 (Medical Fears) taps medically related issues, such as "Having to go to the hospital" and "Getting car sick."

Studies have supported the factor invariance of the FSSC-R. In the largest study to date, Ollendick et al. (1989) administered the FSSC-R to 1,185 children from 7 to 16 years old. The sample consisted of an equal number of children from Australia and the United States. Factor analysis of the results of the two populations revealed a high degree of congruity for four of the five factors. Differences in item loading were noted only on the Medical Fears factor. Interestingly, the two populations produced similar overall scores and identical mean number of fears (mean = 14) on the FSSC-R.

A subsequent study (Ollendick et al., in press) of fears among normal British children provides further support for the invariance of the factor structure of the FSSC-R. Estimates of the internal consistency of the factor scores were nearly identical to those found for samples of Australian and American children (Ollendick et al., 1989). Coefficient alpha was .94 for the total scale and above .80 for each of the factors except the Medical Fears scale.

To establish discriminant validity, Ollendick (1983) compared school-phobic children to matched controls on the FSSC-R. The school-phobic sample consisted of 25 subjects, ages 8–11, who were referred to a clinic for treatment. Twenty-five nonreferred children, matched to the clinical sample by age, sex, and grade in school, were recruited to serve as a comparison group. The FSSC-R Total Fear score for the school-phobic population was significantly higher than for the matched controls. Consistent with the results of the normal sample, Total Fear scores for girls were significantly higher than those for boys.

Strauss, Last, Hersen, and Kazdin (1988) provide further support for the discriminant validity of the FSSC-R in a study on the relationship between anxiety and depression among a sample of children referred to an outpatient anxiety disorders clinic. Three groups completed the FSSC-R along with other measures: (a) children who met DSM-III criteria for an anxiety disorder and major depression, (b) children who met the criteria for an anxiety disorder only, and (c) children who met criteria for disorders other than anxiety and depression. Subjects from the anxiety plus depression group scored significantly higher than the other two groups on the total score and on three FSSC-R subscales. Interestingly, however, neither the FSSC-R nor the Children's Manifest Anxiety Scale–Revised discriminated between children with anxiety and those in the psychopathology control group. Further, the mean score for the FSSC-R for these two groups was not higher than those reported elsewhere (Ollendick, 1983; Ollendick et al., 1989) for normal samples.

In a study of fear among a clinical population, Last, Francis, Hersen, Kazdin, and Strauss (1987) compared children with separation anxiety disorder ($n = 48$) and those with phobic disorder of school ($n = 19$) on the FSSC-R, the Children's Manifest Anxiety Scale–Revised, and the State-Trait Anxiety Inventory for Children. The two groups did not differ on any of these measures. Unfortunately, the means for the groups were not reported, so it is not clear whether both or neither obtained elevated scores. In light of the small number of children in each condition, the statistical power of the design may have been insufficient to detect actual differences.

In a subsequent study, Last, Francis, and Strauss (1989) administered the FSSC-R to 111 children who met criteria for one of three diagnostic groups: separation anxiety, overanxious disorder, or phobic disorder. Although the three groups did not differ on their overall FSSC-R scores, analysis of the most prevalent fears revealed significant differences across the groups. Comparison of the seven most common fears, excluding those commonly endorsed by normal children, for each of the groups revealed that the three groups differed on six of the items.

The utility of the FSSC-R has been supported by studies using the instrument to gather normative information about childhood fears (Ollendick et al., 1985a, 1985b; Silverman & Nelles, 1987), as an outcome measure in treatment programs (Williams & Jones, 1989), and as a screening instrument to identify fearful children (Jones, Ollendick, McLaughlin, & Williams, 1989). Most of the studies that have used the FSSC-R to gather normative data have provided information about age and gender differences in fear. In one such study, Ollendick et al. (1985a) reported significantly higher scores for girls than boys on the Total Fear score and on each of the five factors. No significant age effects were found for overall intensity of fear or for any of the factors, although individual item analysis revealed age differences on some of the items.

Silverman and Nelles (1987) explored whether peer perceptions of fears among girls and boys result in similar gender differences as do self-ratings on the FSSC-R. Sixty-two 9-year-old children were asked rate their own fears, the fears of their male peers, and the fears of their female peers. Results supported the notion that boys report fewer fears than girls. Further, both boys and girls rated girls as more fearful than they did the boys. This study lends some support to the notion that boys actually exhibit less fear toward objects and events in their environment than do girls because, presumably, ratings of peers reflect observations over time.

The FSSC-R has been used to examine differences in level of fear and patterns of fear between visually impaired and normally sighted children (Ollendick et al., 1985b). Results of the FSSC-R completed by 70 visually impaired and 106 normally sighted children showed that visually impaired respondents report significantly higher levels of fear overall and on one of the four factors (Danger/Death). Analysis of the 10 most commonly endorsed fears by the two groups revealed that the visually impaired children reported significantly greater fear on items reflecting potentially dangerous situations (such as getting a shock from electricity) than did their normally sighted peers. In contrast, the sighted children reported greater fears on items reflecting potentially psychologically harmful situations (such as being teased).

In a study comparing two programs designed to teach fire emergency skills,

Jones et al. (1989) used the FSSC-R as a screening measure to identify children with fears of fire. Children who reported "a lot" of fear on the item "Fire–getting burned" and scored poorly on a simulated behavioral assessment were assigned to receive behavioral rehearsal, elaborative rehearsal, or no training. Children in the elaborative and behavioral group evinced decreases on the fear of fire item (although the difference was significant only for the first group). The control group showed no reduction in fear to the item.

Williams and Jones (1989) administered the FSSC-R to 48 children prior to, at completion of, and 5 months following participation in a study of the impact of two training procedures on children's response to fire. Children assigned to a fear reduction condition, an instructional condition, and a waiting list control showed a nonsignificant decrease in fear at the end of the treatment compared to pretreatment levels. The gains made dissipated by the 5-month follow-up.

Turner, Beidel, and Costello (1987) used the FSSC-R along with other self-report inventories to measure fears among the offspring of adults with anxiety disorders. Differences on the FSSC-R among children whose parents had either anxiety disorder or dysthymia and two normal samples approached significance. Children of parents with anxiety disorders reported greater fears than normal schoolchildren and those with dysthymic parents. Surprisingly, a second group of normal children who were solicited via advertisement for participation in the study endorsed a similar level of fear as did the children of anxious parents. Elevations on a measure of trait anxiety suggest that the second group may have included children whose parents were concerned about possible behavioral difficulties (Turner et al., 1987).

## Critique

The Fear Survey Schedule for Children–Revised is a self-report inventory that appears to provide a measure of overall level of fear and to identify specific fears among children between 7 and 16 years of age. The instrument is easy to administer and score. It shows good test-retest reliability across a 1-week interval, though this stability falters over longer intervals. As childhood fears are known to be transient, changes on the FSSC-R over time may be attributable either to unreliability of the measure or to actual changes in children's fears.

A number of studies provide evidence that the instrument can discriminate children with clinical levels of fear from normal children. The factor structure of the instrument has been supported by studies of diverse groups of children from different nationalities. Support for the concurrent validity of the instrument has been provided by studies demonstrating positive correlations between the FSSC-R and measures of anxiety, along with studies demonstrating elevated scores on the FSSC-R among children with clinical levels of disruptive fears (e.g., school phobia). Further, the number of studies that have used the FSSC-R as a dependent variable attests to the utility of the instrument.

Because the FSSC-R is a fairly new revision of the FSS-FC, a number of questions about the instrument have yet to be answered. It is noteworthy that the test author has continued work on the instrument and has not yet promoted it as a clinical instrument. An immediate question focuses on content validity. The initial items on the FSS-FC were selected by experts, rationally rather than empirically. Thus, it is not yet established that the instrument measures the full range of objects and events feared by children.

A second question involves children's interpretation of the question being asked of them. The FSSC-R instructions ask children to describe their fear, but the concept may be interpreted differently across items and children. Depending on the item, children may respond according to how scared they imagine they would be if the event occurred (getting hit by a car), how much they avoid certain stimuli (spiders), or how much they worry about the event occurring (bombing attacks). It is interesting to note that many of the items children most commonly endorse as fear provoking are those on the danger and death factor, and include such events as "Being hit by a car" and "Not being able to breathe." Ollendick notes that the children may be actually visualizing the event and responding according to how scary it would be. The relationship between this notion and avoidance behavior needs to be explored. It could be clarified initially by making the items more consistent; some include implied pronoun/verb combinations (e.g., "[you] Getting punished") while others are simply nouns (e.g., "Lizards"). In addition, further specificity in the items would provide greater assurance that they are assessing similar constructs (e.g., change "Lizards" to "Being approached by a lizard").

Research on childhood fears lags considerably behind that on adults. Surprisingly little systematic research has explored the area. This may be due, in part, to difficulties quantifying childhood fears; though there are a number of well-validated instruments designed to assess fears in adults, no objective measure of childhood fear with established psychometric properties existed until the arrival of the FSSC-R. Although a relatively new instrument, the FSSC-R has accumulated an impressive amount of research to date. The instrument has been carefully developed and validated, promising to be an important vehicle for gathering information about children's fears.

### References

Castaneda, A., McCandless, B., & Palermo, D. (1956). The children's form of the Manifest Anxiety Scale. *Child Development, 27,* 317–326.

Jacklin, C.N., Maccoby, E., & Doering, C.H. (1983). Neonatal sex-steroid hormones and timidity in 6–18 month old boys and girls. *Developmental Psychology, 16,* 163–168.

Jones, R.T., Ollendick, T.H., McLaughlin, K.J., & Williams, C.E. (1989). Elaborative and behavioral rehearsal in the acquisition of fire emergency skills and the reduction of fear of fire. *Behavior Therapy, 20,* 93–101.

King, N.J., Hamilton, D.I., & Ollendick, T.H. (1988). *Children's phobias: A behavioural perspective.* Chichester, England: Wiley.

Lapouse, R., & Monk, M.A. (1959). Fears and worries in a representative sample of children. *American Journal of Orthopsychiatry, 29,* 803–818.

Last, C.G., Francis, G., Hersen, M., Kazdin, A.E., & Strauss, C.C. (1987). Separation anxiety and school phobia: A comparison using DSM-III criteria. *American Journal of Psychiatry, 144,* 653–657.

Last, C.G., Francis, G., & Strauss, C.C. (1989). Assessing fears in anxiety-disordered children with the revised Fear Survey Schedule for Children (FSSC-R). *Journal of Clinical Child Psychology, 18,* 137–141.

Ollendick, T.H. (1983). Reliability and validity of the revised Fear Survey Schedule for Children (FSSC-R). *Behaviour Research and Therapy, 21,* 685–692.

Ollendick, T.H. (1988). Fear Survey Schedule for Children–Revised. In M. Hersen & A.S. Bellack (Eds.), *Dictionary of behavioral assessment techniques.* New York: Pergamon.

Ollendick, T.H., & Francis, G. (1988). Behavioral assessment and treatment of childhood phobias. *Behavior Modification, 12,* 165–204.

Ollendick, T.H., King, N.J., & Frary, R.E. (1989). Fears in children and adolescents: Reliability and generalizability across gender, age, and adolescents: Normative data. *Behaviour Research and Therapy, 27,* 19–26.

Ollendick, T.H., Matson, J.L., & Helsel, W.J. (1985a). Fears in children and adolescents: Normative data. *Behaviour Research and Therapy, 23,* 465–467.

Ollendick, T.H., Matson, J.L., & Helsel, W.J. (1985b). Fears in visually-impaired and normally-sighted youths. *Behaviour Research and Therapy, 23,* 375–378.

Ollendick, T.H., & Yule, W. (in press). Depression in British and American children and its relationship to anxiety and fear.

Ollendick, T.H., Yule, W., & Ollier, K. (in press). Fears in British children and their relationship to manifest anxiety and depression.

Scherer, M.W., & Nakamura, C.Y. (1968). A fear survey schedule for children: A factor analytic comparison with manifest anxiety. *Behaviour Research and Therapy, 6,* 173–182.

Silverman, W.K., & Nelles, W.B (1987). The influence of gender on children's ratings of fear in self and same-aged peers. *The Journal of Genetic Psychology, 148,* 17–21.

Strauss, C.C., Last, C.G., Hersen, M., & Kazdin, A.E. (1988). Association between anxiety and depression in children and adolescents with anxiety disorders. *Journal of Abnormal Child Psychology, 16,* 57–68.

Turner, S.M., Beidel, D.C., & Costello, A. (1987). Psychopathology in the offspring of anxiety disorders patients. *Journal of Consulting and Clinical Psychology, 55,* 229–235.

Williams, C.E., & Jones, R.T. (1989). Impact of self-instruction on response maintenance and children's fear of fire. *Journal of Clinical Child Psychology, 18,* 84–89.

**Clifford M. DeCato, Ph.D.**
*Professor and Associate Director, Institute for Graduate Clinical Psychology, Widener University, Chester, Pennsylvania.*

# HAHNEMANN ELEMENTARY SCHOOL BEHAVIOR RATING SCALE

*George Spivack and Marshall Swift. Chester, Pennsylvania: George Spivack and Marshall Swift.*

## Introduction

The Hahnemann Elementary School Behavior Rating Scale (HESB) is an "instrument created to provide a standard system for identifying and measuring classroom behaviors of elementary school students in both regular and open classrooms" (Spivack & Swift, 1975, p. 1). The HESB, designed for children in Grades K–6, is a companion to the Hahnemann High School Behavior Rating Scale and the accompanying book *Alternative Teaching Strategies* (Swift & Spivack, 1976). The latter is a practical guide for teachers in the management of classroom behaviors relevant to classroom learning. The focus of the HESB is on those classroom behaviors that interfere with, facilitate, or reflect the student's level of ability to cope with academic expectations in both structured and "open" classroom settings.

The HESB was developed to provide a means of identifying and communicating observations about a wide range of positive and negative behaviors and to allow for one child's behavior to be compared with norms for others of his age and academic level (Spivack & Swift, 1975). The goal was to develop an instrument that would give teachers and mental health workers in school settings an effective means of communicating about student functioning in order to plan preventive and remedial action within the education setting. The manual describes the scale as follows:

> The *HESB* Scale form is comprised of a rating guide, 59 overt behavior items to be rated by the teacher and a profile sheet for graphic presentation of the pattern of student behavior based upon the ratings. Item 60 provides the teacher with an opportunity to make a global judgment about the child's progress in learning. This item is not used as an overt behavior item, but rather allows users of the Scale to relate actual judged achievement to the Scale factors for each child or group of children. (Spivack & Swift, 1975, p. 2)

George Spivack, Ph.D., ABPP, received his doctoral degree in psychology from the University of Pennsylvania in 1954. His career has focused primarily on research

The reviewer wishes to thank George Spivack and Marshall Swift for their support and advice for this review, in particular Dr. Spivack's generous efforts to supply research information and his insights on many aspects of the manuscript.

in educational and mental health settings and has included numerous positions of leadership and responsibility for programs. To note but a few, he has been director of research of the Devereaux Schools; director of research and evaluation services, John F. Kennedy Mental Health Center; and director of the Graduate Program in Evaluation and Applied Social Research, as well as the Preventive Intervention Research Center, both at Hahnemann University. Spivack is a certified school psychologist and a licensed psychologist in Pennsylvania and holds the Diplomate in clinical psychology from the American Psychological Association. He is currently a tenured professor at the Institute for Graduate Clinical Psychology at Widener University.

Marshall S. Swift, Ph.D., ABPP, took his doctorate from Syracuse University in 1966. He is a certified school psychologist and a licensed psychologist in Pennsylvania, holds the Diplomate in school psychology and is a Fellow of the American Psychological Association. His areas of expertise, research, and publication include prevention of behavioral and emotional problems, consultation in schools and clinics, and the translation of research into applied clinical and education programs. Swift's background includes experience in teaching in elementary school and junior high schools. Currently he is a tenured professor in Widener University's Institute for Graduate Clinical Psychology and serves as the principal investigator of a major foundation grant to develop curriculum to enhance the interpersonal competence of junior high school students.

The HESB was created over a period of 13 years by pooling the knowledge and experience of the authors and approximately 200 experienced teachers. The test was developed to fill a void: "Although the presumption of a relationship between student behavior and academic success has been generally accepted, little formal analysis of patterns of behavior in both regular and open elementary classrooms has been made" (Spivack & Swift, 1975, p. 1). A need existed for an instrument that would facilitate objective observation and communication of children's behavior among teaching and helping professionals, allow for comparison of individual children with norms, and provide a means of tracing the progress and development of a child in the formal classroom setting.

According to the authors, "factor analytic studies assessed the relationship of age, sex, background variables, psychiatric diagnosis, and subsequent behavioral adjustment and academic achievement in school" (Spivack & Swift, 1975, p. 5). They consulted with school staffs and administrators in a large number of school systems in many locations in the United States, Canada, England, and France. The final version of the HESB evolved out of a series of studies and included 294 urban and 192 suburban children from a major metropolitan area, 338 children in a midwestern Canadian city, 708 in a small eastern city, and 132 in a middle-sized city outside London, England, for a total of 1,664 children.

An additional normative sample is available in the literature based on a series of studies by Guidubaldi and others comparing a nationwide sample of 350 children from intact families with 336 children from divorced families (Guidubaldi, Cleminshaw, Perry, & McLoughlin, 1983; Guidubaldi, Cleminshaw, Perry, & Nastasi, 1984; Guidubaldi & Cleminshaw, 1985; and Guidubaldi, Cleminshaw, & Perry, 1985).

The final form of the HESB was published in 1975 and has not undergone any revisions, nor have other forms of the test been developed. A parallel form for use at junior and senior high school levels, the Hahnemann High School Behavior Rating Scale (HHSB), was published in 1973 and is still in use. The previously mentioned *Alternative Teaching Strategies* (1976) addresses the classroom interventions with youngsters whose patterns of maladjustive behavior have been identified using the HESB scale.

The HESB consists of a printed sheet of paper 11″ × 17″ that is folded in the center to provide four pages (8½″ × 11″). The first page bears the test title, four lines for recording demographic information and date, and eight specific steps spelling out how to use the rating guide. The next page provides the HESB Student Profile, where the student's status on the given behavior dimensions can be plotted and compared to the normative population. These first and second pages may be removed, producing a single 8½″ × 11″ sheet that becomes a convenient record for the student's file.

The third page of the HESB presents items 1–35, a 5-point rating scale, and the instruction "Compared with the average child, how often does this student . . . ." To the left of each behavioral item is a ¼″ box in which a rating from 1 to 5 is written. The authors suggest that the rating take place with the profile folded out of sight, to avoid the tendency to create behavioral patterns as the rating proceeds and to facilitate the independent rating of each item (Spivack & Swift, 1975, p. 11). The last page contains items 36–60 (e.g., "Friendly in his attitude toward the teacher?"), which are rated on a 7-point scale ranging from not at all (1) to extremely (7).

**Practical Applications/Uses**

The HESB is designed to allow elementary school teachers to record and describe individual children's academically relevant behaviors emerging in the classroom setting. The scale does not provide a measure of "personality" or of "character traits" (Spivack & Swift, 1975, p. 31). The authors' goal was to develop a scale that would be of practical use to the classroom teacher, school psychologist, and educational administrator, to aid in the observation and communication of behavior patterns important to a child's adjustment, achievement, and progress in school.

The manual describes each of the 14 behavioral dimensions derived from factor analyses and discusses their correlates with academic achievement. The factors are grouped together on the student profile to aid understanding and are arranged in order from 1 to 14 to indicate their relevance to regular and open classrooms.

> Factors 1–4 tap behavior dimensions that reflect a positive adaptation to the demands of the classroom environment and are positively related to academic achievement. Factors 5–13 tap behaviors that reflect varying aspects of inability to cope with classroom demands and relate negatively to achievement. Factor 14 reflects the appropriate balance in approach/avoidance in relating with the teacher (not too much or too little need to interact with the teacher). (Spivack & Swift, 1975, p. 14)

The four factors with the highest positive or negative correlations with actual classroom achievement are *independent learning, intellectual dependency* with peers, *originality,* and *unreflectiveness* (Spivack & Swift, 1975, p. 31).

This scale was developed to provide a means of tracking the behavioral progress of students in the classroom setting and detecting changes in behavior that could adversely impact on school achievement or signal improvement in school-related behaviors. This record permits communication among school staff and administrators and mental health workers and can be valuable to school counselors in working with the students. HESB results also may be used to assess the outcomes of special programs and preventive school interventions, as measures of academic progress that supplement the usual academic achievement measures, and as a means for teachers to communicate with parents about behaviors relevant to academic progress or problems.

In addition, although this reviewer found no reference to forensic psychology or parent counseling while perusing the literature, it seems reasonable that the HESB's record of behavioral observations could be a valuable source of information and understanding of the child for counseling parents, in custody cases and in a variety of other forensic proceedings where an objective record of the individual's classroom behavior before and after some event would be of importance (e.g., evaluating behavioral sequelae following neurological lesions).

The school classroom, regular or open, is the appropriate setting for making the observations on which the HESB ratings are based. The scale also may be used in special group classrooms for LD and ED children, if one wishes to define specific areas of behavior that interfere with learning as well as assist the teacher in working with the child. The profile also will allow the school administrator to compare a child being considered for special placement with the more usual child in the main stream.

The classroom teacher should do the ratings. On average, it takes about 1 month of classroom observation of a child to know the individual's behavior well enough to yield valid and reliable observations. In some situations it might be possible to train a teacher's aide to do the ratings, but the single most important factor is that the rater must have direct continual contact with the child in the classroom setting. The teacher must rate each child independently and should use only his or her own direct observations. Experience and research has shown that children may behave very differently with different teachers and classroom settings (Spivack & Swift, 1975).

The manual is a soft-covered, 48-page booklet containing double-spaced, highly readable print. Overall it is clear, concise, and supplies all the basic information needed to use the test. For anyone accustomed to the basics of psychological and educational tests, the HESB is easy to learn to use. Two suggestions to the authors that might enhance the manual's usefulness are (a) Add page numbers and (b) Add a table of contents and an index.

The authors report that most teachers appear to be willing to take the time to complete the HESB if they perceive there is a benefit to them in managing the child and tracking the child's progress. The manual notes in two ways the importance of the involvement of school administrators in preparing teachers to use the HESB: (a) teachers need reassurance that the behavior ratings will not be used as a measure of or reflection on their teaching performance, and (b) the time needed to complete the ratings must be provided as part of the teacher's regular work schedule.

The instructions are clear and reasonably easy to follow. The time required to learn to use the HESB will vary from one person to another, but somewhere between 1 and 3 hours would seem reasonable for both reading the materials and practicing with the scale. Once the scale is mastered, it is estimated that the process should take 10 to 15 minutes per student. The only forseeable difficulty might be a lack of opportunity to observe a particular type of behavior in a child. The authors have provided for an occasional omission with a simple prorating technique.

The score sheet provides clear instructions for using and scoring the HESB, and the manual gives further clarification (Spivack & Swift, 1975, pp. 11–13). Each of 59 items describe a discrete observable behavior, which then is rated on a scale described on the form. Items 1–35 are rated for frequency of occurrence of the behavior; items 36–60 are rated on a scale of degree. Item 60 provides the teacher with an opportunity to make a global rating of academic achievement rather than a behavioral observation. The individual items and each student are rated independently of each other. As mentioned previously, to avoid creating artificial or biased patterns, the examiner is instructed to fold the scoring sheet so that the profile is out of sight during the rating procedure.

There appear to be no inherent problems with scoring the instrument. The transposition of raw scores to the profile is a simple manual procedure (machine scoring is not available). Although even such simple clerical tasks sometimes produce errors, the sheet is well organized to keep such errors to a minimum. Transferring the raw score sums to the standard scale is clear and simple, all contained on the same page and clearly indicated for each separate factor so there is little opportunity for error.

The HESB profile is constructed from raw scores related to each of 14 behavioral dimensions or factors. The central point of the profile is 0, with a scale for each factor ranging from positive to negative in units of standard deviation. Raw scores for each factor item are recorded on the profile sheet to the left of the profile and added. Each total raw score is then marked along the scale line on the profile to the right. Joining these marks for the different factors yields a graphic profile picture of the particular child's pattern of behavior (Spivack & Swift, 1975, p. 12).

Interpretation is relatively simple and clear, and is based on objective scores yielding the 14 behavioral dimensions or factors. The profile presents a record or picture of the child's behavioral pattern as compared to children at the same grade level. Interpretation is based on relationships to academic performance as found in factor analytic studies. The manual describes each factor briefly and notes extra-test correlates of the behaviors in terms of the child's classroom and learning activities. The series of studies by Guidubaldi and others (1983, 1984, 1985) provides a nationwide normative sample that supports the norms set for the HESB profile as well as additional validity information showing the significant effects of divorce on many of the HESB ratings.

Some minimal appreciation of educational and psychological testing would appear necessary for interpreting the HESB, although not at a very sophisticated level. An appreciation of basic descriptive statistics would be needed in order to grasp the idea of the normal curve and deviations from central tendency. Although these ideas very likely comprise part of the training of elementary school teachers, they might not be part of the frame of reference for many teacher's aides.

**Technical Aspects**

Two series of studies were carried out to provide information on the reliability and validity of the HESB. The original series of studies conducted over a long period led to the final standardized published form of the scale. An additional series of studies by Guidubaldi et al. (1983, 1984, 1985) investigated the impact of divorce on children and used numerous measures, including the HESB.

The research by Spivack and Swift was conducted over a 13-year period, leading first to an experimental version. Factor analytic studies established the final form of the HESB, which is described along with the norms reported in the HESB manual. The studies by Guidubaldi et al. (1983, 1984, 1985) were part of a nationwide NASP study of the impact of divorce on children and served to provide information on HESB norms and validity based on a randomly selected sample of children. A wide array of data were gathered, including (but not limited to) teacher rating scales of classroom performance (one of which was the HESB), parent and child interviews, objective standardized measures (WISC-R and WRAT), and a follow-up sample that permitted inferences about predictions over time. The normative information produced by this nationwide sample were essentially similar to those produced by the original research (Spivack & Swift, 1975), thus confirming that the HESB norms have a high degree of generalizability within primarily urban U.S. populations.

Validity refers to the appropriateness of inferences drawn from test scores or other forms of assessment and requires empirical evidence. Spivack and Swift, using correlational techniques, established 14 factors or behavior dimensions relevant to coping with classroom demands and academic achievement. Factors 1–4 tap behaviors that are positively related to adaptation to the classroom environment and to academic achievement. Factors 5–13 reflect a variety of behaviors that relate negatively to classroom demands and to academic achievement.

Using ANOVAs (analysis of variance), analysis of covariance, and correlations, Guidubaldi et al. (1983, 1984, 1985) obtained significant results for most of the HESB factors. With IQ controlled, 15 of 16 teacher ratings of classroom behavior showed better performance of children from intact families (Guidubaldi et al., 1983); children from divorced families in general showed lower classroom adaptability and academic achievement. Measures of mental and physical health, family environment, and family support variables all revealed significant correlates to HESB teacher ratings of the childrens' classroom behavior. The Guidubaldi et al. studies yield a variety of information about relationships between classroom behavior, home environment, age, sex, parenting styles, and other extra-classroom behaviors all of which impact on a child's adaptation and achievement in the classroom. Following divorce, decreased mental and physical health, nightmares, fearfulness, parental emotional problems, and a variety of other factors too numerous to mention here predicted HESB teacher ratings of the children in the classroom.

Four additional studies have provided further evidence of the HESB's reliability and/or validity. Swift and Spivack (1968) studied 809 kindergarten through fifth-grade children. The sample was drawn by selecting a heterogeneous group of children from all the elementary schools in a small Pennsylvania town. Composition of the sample included a mixture of black (12%) and Caucasian, with the parents having an average education equivalent to high school. One week test-retest reliability analysis yielded a correlation of .85. Standard errors of measurement were also provided for each factor.

Information relevant to validity was generated by the relationships found between academic achievement as measured by grades and several factors of the HESB. Factors 2 and 5 were related to the age of entering kindergarten. Factors 2, 5, 3, and 13 were related to birth order. Factors 2, 3, 5, 6, 7, 9, 10, and 14 were related to parental education. Factors 2, 3, 5, 6, 7, 8, 9, and 10 were related to the number of siblings in the family, with the oldest sibling, especially if a girl, tending to perform best in school.

Spivack, Marcus, and Swift (1986) conducted a study on early classroom behaviors and predictions of later misconduct. A sample of 600 urban children from kindergarten through third grade were measured and followed up 10 years later using classroom and police records as criteria. Racial composition of the group included black (80%), Hispanic (10%), and white (10%) subjects drawn from a largely disadvantaged population. HESB factors 1, 2, 3, 9, and 13 were combined to yield a "core self-regulation" score. Teacher ratings on these factors were found to relate to classroom misconduct determined from school records and delinquent activities as reflected in police records 10 years after the initial measurement.

Spivack and Marcus (1987) studied the prediction of mental health from teacher ratings using several HESB factors. The subjects were the same 600 children as those in the earlier study (Spivack et al., 1986). Ten of the 14 factors that were rated while the children were in elementary school were divided into positive and negative behavioral groups. For the follow-up study, these two combined scores were correlated with a series of MMPI scores taken on the same subjects when they reached 20 years of age. Depending on the sex of the subject, early classroom behavior scores were related to one or more measures of mental health at age 20.

Spivack, Rapsher, Cohen, and Gross (1987) studied early signs of risk for delinquency using the same sample of 600 children previously cited (Spivack et al., 1986). A number of HESB factors were found to relate to such variables as placement in special classes, subsequent academic achievement using grades and standardized scores as criteria, and retention in a grade during the elementary school years.

By way of brief summary, the studies on reliability and validity present a variety of evidence that the behavioral dimensions measured have substantial stability over time and relate to a wide variety of important achievement factors, including but not limited to academic achievement, social adjustment, family stability (divorced or intact family), and mental and physical health. Certain factors have been found to relate to future behavior patterns, including but not limited to academic achievement, classroom placement, physical and mental health, and risk of delinquency.

## Critique

The HESB appears to be a succinct, objective instrument, clearly constructed, easy to use, and informative about a child's classroom behavior. It should provide useful information about the progress a child makes in adapting to the school environment while simultaneously helping to highlight emerging patterns that could spell trouble and could become the target areas for professional intervention, either of a remedial or preventive nature. The scale helps standardize observations in a way that should enhance communication among the professionals responsible for the child's school progress.

Although this scale was never intended to measure personality, character, or psychopathology, nor does it purport to, this reviewer cannot help but believe that interesting and useful relationships exist that could be teased out by research. The initial studies cited in this review provide at least beginning data toward understanding relationships between early behavior patterns and delinquency and certain MMPI variables. Certainly here is an area rife for future master's theses and doctoral dissertations. For example, is the whole greater than the part? That is, do different overall patterns of deviation on the profile signal different personality configurations or problems? Is there a significance to the size of the behavioral deviation or the specific type of behavioral deviation? In other words, could this empirically based behavioral instrument be approached in a manner similar to an MMPI and yield additional valuable information? Could it be used as a measure of therapeutic outcome or as a basis for recommending family or individual treatment for school age children?

These and similar validity questions remain largely unexplored, but the work of Guidubaldi et al. suggests a potential "gold mine" that has not yet been tapped for the HESB.

## References

Guidubaldi, J., & Cleminshaw, H. (1985). Divorce, family health, and child adjustment. *Family Relations, 34,* 35–41.

Guidubaldi, J., Cleminshaw, H., & Perry, J. (1985). The relationship of parental divorce to health status of parents and children. *Special Services in the Schools, 1,* 73–81.

Guidubaldi, J., Cleminshaw, H.K., Perry, J.D., & McLoughlin, C.S. (1983). The impact of parental divorce on children: Report of the nationwide NASP study. *School Psychology Review, 12,* 300–323.

Guidubaldi, J., Cleminshaw, H.K., Perry, J.D., & Nastasi, B.K. (1984). Impact of family support systems on children's academic and social functioning after divorce. In G. Rowe, J. Defrain, H. Lingren, R. MacDonald, N. Stinnett, S. VanZandt, & R. Williams (Eds.), *Family strengths* (pp. 190–207). Newton, MA: Education Development Center.

Guidubaldi, J., Cleminshaw, H.K., Perry, J.D., Nastasi, B.K., & Lightel, J. (1985). *The role of selected family environment factors in children's post-divorce adjustment.* (Available from John Guidubaldi, Director of Early Childhood School Psychology Program, Kent State University, Kent, OH 44242)

Spivack, G., & Marcus, J. (1987). Marks and classroom adjustment as early indicators of mental health at age 20. *American Journal of Community Psychology, 15,* 35–56.

Spivack, G., Marcus, J., & Swift, M. (1986). Early classroom behaviors and later misconduct. *Developmental Psychology, 22,* 124–131.

Spivack, G., Rapsher, L., Cohen, A., & Gross, R. (1987). *High risk, early signs for delinquency and related behavioral difficulties: Interim report I. National Institute of Juvenile Justice and Delinquency Prevention.* LEAA.

Spivack, G., & Swift, M. (1975). *Hahnemann Elementary School Behavior Rating Scale (HESB): Manual*. Chester, PA: Authors.

Swift, M., & Spivack, G. (1968). The assessment of achievement related classroom behavior. *The Journal of Special Education, 2,* 137–153.

Swift, M., & Spivack, G. (1976). *Alternative teaching strategies*. Champaign, IL: Research Press.

**Allan L. LaVoie, Ph.D.**
*Professor of Psychology, Davis & Elkins College, Elkins, West Virginia.*

# HEALTH PROBLEMS CHECKLIST

*John A. Schinka. Odessa, Florida: Psychological Assessment Resources, Inc.*

## Introduction

The Health Problems Checklist (HPC) was devised to provide a fairly comprehensive source of information on symptoms in 11 problem areas: skin, gastrointestinal, cardiopulmonary, and so on. There are no categories for emotional or mental symptoms except peripherally in the neurological section; there are two additional categories that ask about health habits (e.g., exercise, smoking, and drinking) and about history of major illness (e.g., stroke, diabetes). In addition, at the end of the four-page form the respondent is asked to list any other health problems, all medications currently being taken, and the names of all doctors and the illnesses they are treating. Once completed, the checklist is examined by the attending physician or psychologist but is not systematically scored. There is no final score, there are no risk assessments, no disease categorizations or diagnoses, and no standard scores. Clients do not provide information on this form about the illnesses of other family members, so one could not readily assess the likelihood of a genetic component for present symptoms (e.g., as in determining the likelihood of cardiac problems).

Related instruments are available, including the Hopkins Symptom Checklist (Derogatis, Lipman, Rickels, Uhlenhuth, & Covi, 1974) and a number that are available free from the professional literature. With the increasing attention psychologists are giving the health problems, a variety of other relevant assessment devices come to mind, such as the illness scale of Wyler, Masuda, and Holmes (1968, 1970) and Newcomb and Bentler's (1987) health status measure.

## Practical Applications/Uses

As the HPC is such an unusual measure when compared to standard psychological tests, it occupies an unusual niche as far as uses go. One obvious place is in a medical clinic, where completion would assure that the attending physician would have a complete symptom list. This instrument also could be used routinely in psychological practices, to provide a more detailed basis for medical referrals, to help rule out physical origins for psychological symptoms, and to ensure that the client's file was complete in the event of an audit or lawsuit.

A few published reports have appeared using the HPC. For example, Fordyce (1985, 1988) has used it in studies of happiness and finds that happy people have fewer physical symptoms. This may not be an efficient use of the HPC, for with 224 items (230 for women) it takes a fairly big commitment from the participant to complete it accurately. In fact, Fordyce cut the HPC down to a small subset in his studies.

It would be useful to have reports of the ability of the HPC to differentiate organic from psychological problems, to pick up all relevant medical history, or to see item analyses that describe the contribution each item makes in identifying problems in one of the content areas. In fact no such studies are available, and no manual is available describing the procedures used in developing the HPC. John Schinka, the author of the HPC, indicated (personal communication, February 18, 1991) that he developed the checklist for use in his private practice and for training graduate students, using expert panels of physicians to select the items from a large pool. It was never intended to be a formal test, it does not get scored, and he has not investigated its psychometric properties.

## Technical Aspects

No technical literature is available on the HPC's reliability or validity. In the absence of a manual and of research reports, no conclusion is possible about its suitability as a psychometric instrument. The HPC has ample face validity for its continuing informal use as an information-gathering tool. Comparisons with other instruments have not been undertaken, so one cannot evaluate relative efficiency. No published field trials are available to indicate which symptoms are actually most significant, which should most automatically trigger referrals, and which provide the most psychological information.

## Critique

In summary, the HPC is interesting and unusual. At present it costs about 40 cents for each administration, a small price to pay for a set of systematic information about medical symptoms. Its main use will be as a referral tool and to encourage psychologists to carefully review all possible symptoms before beginning treatment. This lengthy checklist also provides a record that a client's background information was collected, so in the event of a lawsuit or chart audit the psychologist will be able to document proper clinical practice.

## References

Derogatis, L.R., Lipman, R.S., Rickels, K., Uhlenhuth, E.H., & Covi, L. (1974). The Hopkins Symptom Checklist (HSCh): A self-report symptom inventory. *Behavioral Science, 19,* 1–15.

Fordyce, M.W. (1985). The Psychap Inventory: A multiscale test to measure happiness and its concomitants. *Social Indicators Research, 18,* 1–33.

Fordyce, M.W. (1988). A review of research on the Happiness Measures: A sixty second index of happiness and mental health. *Social Indicators Research, 20,* 355–381.

Newcomb, M.D., & Bentler, P.M. (1987). Self-report methods of assessing health status and health service utilization: A hierarchical confirmatory analysis. *Multivariate Behavioral Research, 22,* 415–436.

Wyler, A.R., Masuda, M., & Holmes, T.H. (1968). Seriousness of Illness Rating Scale. *Journal of Psychosomatic Research, 11,* 363–374.

Wyler, A.R., Masuda, M., & Holmes, T.H. (1970). The Seriousness of Illness Rating Scale: Reproducibility. *Journal of Psychosomatic Research, 14,* 59–64.

**María de la Luz Reyes, Ph.D.**
*Assistant Professor of Education, School of Education, University of Colorado, Boulder, Colorado.*

**Kenneth D. Hopkins, Ph.D.**
*Professor of Educational Psychology, School of Education, University of Colorado, Boulder, Colorado.*

---

# HENDERSON-MORIARTY ESL/LITERACY PLACEMENT TEST

*Cindy Henderson and Pia Moriarty. West Trenton, New Jersey: Alemany Press.*

### Introduction

The Henderson-Moriarty ESL/Literacy Placement Test (HELP) is designed for adult learners of English as a second language who have minimal or no oral English skills and who may fall into one of the following categories: (a) have no reading or writing skills in any language, (b) have minimal reading and writing skills in their native language (or an equivalent of less than 4 years of formal schooling), or (c) have reading and writing skills in a language that does not use the Roman alphabet. Specifically, HELP is an individually administered oral test designed to assess functional reading, writing, and oral proficiency in English.

The only background information on the authors of the HELP test (Cindy Henderson and Pia Moriarty) is that they have several years of experience teaching Southeast Asian refugees in San Francisco; no other specific credentials are reported. According to the manual, the test was developed to assist English as a second language (ESL) teachers in assessing Southeast Asians with little or no literacy skills in their native language. No information is provided regarding the history and development of the test in terms of content strata and item specifications.

Testing tools consist of materials provided in the HELP booklet and materials that must be furnished by the examiner. The test includes (a) a test booklet with pictures, (b) an intake form and answer sheet, (c) a multilingual sheet with a paragraph produced in Lao, Vietnamese, Khmer, and Cantonese, (d) writing paper (Circle the Word single sheet), (e) an identification form, (f) alphabet chips, and (g) appointment cards. The examiner must provide pencils with erasers, an ice cube tray to sort alphabet chips, a real telephone, real money in various denominations, a money box, and a large-print calendar.

There are three components to the HELP test: the intake information/first language assessment; the oral English assessment, including reading and manipulative skills; and the written English assessment, including reading skills. Intake information includes the examinee's background (country, languages spoken, first language literacy screening, and ESL background) and ideally should be gathered by someone who speaks both English and the examinee's first language.

The oral English assessment is the heart of the HELP test and is administered with the examiner facing the examinee across a table. All test items ($n = 30$) are read aloud by the examiner except for the Circle the Word and the Sight Word Recognition exercises ($n = 16$). The test booklet contains scripted questions that the examiner first should ask verbatim as they appear on the left-hand side of the page, but other variations of these questions (on the right-hand side of the page) may be substituted if needed for clarification. The items are very basic, asking the examinee what language he or she speaks, spelling first and last name with alphabet chips, showing competency in dialing a phone, telling time, reading an appointment date, identifying members of the family (father, mother, son, etc.), using real money for simulated purchases, and identifying signs in the environment (e.g., "Men," "Women," "No Smoking," etc.).

The last section of the HELP consists of a written English assessment that asks the examinee to fill out an identification sheet with name, address, telephone, sex, marital status, date of birth, signature, and date. The test is not timed.

Although it is primarily an entry-level placement test, the authors contend that HELP is a criterion-referenced test and hence that it can be used as a post-test "to measure learner achievement and evaluate program success." Further, they assert that certain items along with "test-taking behavior can also have diagnostic value" (Henderson & Moriarty, 1982, p. 3).

**Practical Applications/Uses**

The HELP test is designed to be used with examinees from Southeast Asia, but the basic level of functional English items in the test (except for the writing samples in Vietnamese, Lao, Khmer, and Cantonese) could also be used by bilingual and ESL teachers working with other limited-English-speaking groups from junior high school to adult to determine oral proficiency and functional literacy skills. Writing samples from other languages can be easily substituted.

The test takes approximately 20 minutes to administer, not including filling out the information form (where students are allowed as much time as needed). No special training for administering the test is required other than the examiner speak the examinee's native language for the intake information. After some familiarization with the test booklet, HELP could be easily administered by any adult. However, the pagination and the lack of clear labels for the various sections in the test (e.g., Circle the Word, identification form) make the process initially confusing.

Responses are evaluated on the basis of meaningful communication rather than grammatical correctness, putting the scoring on an all-or-nothing basis depending on whether the examiner understands a response or not. Except for the correct spelling of the examinee's name, other recognizable misspellings may be considered correct. The examiner fills out the score sheet by giving 1 point for each correct response. Scoring is simply a matter of counting correct responses. The answer sheet, however, presents some confusion. It has the numbers of 23 test items circled, suggesting some difference in those items, but no explanation is provided for either administering or scoring them. Two separate scores may be obtained: Oral (and reading) and Written (and reading). The booklet indicates cutoff points for Beginning Literacy (0–10 Oral score, 0–4 Written) and Intermediate Literacy (11–25 Oral score, 5–10 Written) levels. There is no mention of how the criteria for "beginning" and "intermediate" literacy were established.

The authors state that the scale and levels may vary, depending on the possible groupings of an ESL program. The range of item difficulty, however, is very small, suggesting that beyond separating readers from nonreaders, the literacy levels would not provide useful information or make fine distinctions in ability groupings. For this same reason, using HELP as a post-test would also be problematic. Identification of graphic signs in the environment (e.g., "Men" or "Women" on restroom doors) or names of family members (e.g., "son," "daughter") do not require repeated practice for mastery.

## Technical Aspects

No technical data are provided in the test materials.

## Critique

Of the 46 HELP items, 16 require an oral response, 3 require carrying out a command (i.e., dialing a phone), 3 require copying a word, 3 require word identification, 11 require fill-in-the-blank answers to personal information (e.g., name, address), and the remainder require oral comprehension. An analysis of these items suggests that the HELP test would be more useful for grouping students within an ESL class than grouping them for literacy instruction. Additionally, the entry-level nature of the test cannot provide much more than a mere screening of functional oral and writing skills; the quality of those skills cannot be detected. In fact, this test requires mostly word identification rather than reading connected text (except for the oral reading of the writing sample). With only two options in the Circle the Word section, for example, examinees have a 50% chance of accuracy. Writing is limited to filling blanks rather than constructing whole sentences or paragraphs. For this reason, the use of the label "literacy" in the title may be misleading.

In summary, the HELP test appears to have some practical utility for a quick screening measure at the most basic level of English literacy. It should not be viewed, however, as a carefully developed measure evidencing content validity and reliability. No data on items or any group of examinees are provided. Considerable work needs to be done and reported before the HELP test can be used with confidence.

## References

Henderson, C., & Moriarty, P. (1982). *The Henderson-Moriarty ESL/Literacy Placement Test (HELP).* Hayward, CA: Alemany Press.

**Dennis L. Calkins, Ph.D.**
*Postdoctoral Fellow in Pediatric Psychology, Department of Psychiatry and Behavioral Sciences, University of Oklahoma Health Sciences Center, Oklahoma City, Oklahoma.*

**C. Eugene Walker, Ph.D.**
*Professor of Pediatric Psychology, Department of Psychiatry and Behavioral Sciences, University of Oklahoma Health Sciences Center, Oklahoma City, Oklahoma.*

---

# HILSON ADOLESCENT PROFILE

*Robin E. Inwald. Kew Gardens, New York: Hilson Research, Inc.*

### Introduction

The Hilson Adolescent Profile (HAP) is a 310-item, behaviorally oriented, true-false questionnaire designed to assess the presence of pathological traits and problems in adolescents. The major objective of this instrument is to help professionals working with adolescents identify those at risk for behavioral and emotional problems. Scores are provided for the following scales: Guardedness (GR; 21 items), Alcohol (AL; 13 items), Drugs (DG; 15 items), Educational Adjustment Difficulties (ED; 19 items), Law/Society Violations (LV; 21 items), Frustration Tolerance (FT; 23 items), Antisocial/Risk-Taking Attitudes (AR; 19 items), Rigidity/Obsessiveness (RI; 21 items), Interpersonal/Assertiveness Difficulties (IA; 26 items), Homelife Conflicts (HL; 33 items), Social/Sexual Adjustment (SS; 22 items), Health Concerns (HC; 14 items), Anxiety/Phobic Avoidance (PP; 25 items), Depression/Suicide Potential (DP; 25 items), Suspicious Temperament (ST; 17 items), and Unusual Responses (UR; 10 items). Fourteen items contribute to more than one scale.

Dr. Robin E. Inwald is director of Hilson Research, Inc., a consulting firm specializing in computerized tests for psychological evaluation. She coauthored the HAP manual with Karen E. Brobst, M.A. and Richard F. Morrissey, Ph.D. Ms. Brobst was director of research at Hilson during the development of the HAP. Dr. Morrissey is a clinical psychologist at the Adolescent Pavilion of Hillside Hospital, Long Island Jewish Medical Center.

The authors of the HAP manual indicate that the adolescent assessment tools available prior to the development of the HAP in the 1980s failed to address current adolescent issues adequately (Inwald, Brobst, & Morrissey, 1987). Many were also noted to be nonbehavioral in content, while others were either downward extensions of instruments designed for the adult population or upward extensions of tests designed for young children. The HAP was developed consequently to provide a behaviorally based screening tool for the assessment of adolescent behavioral and emotional problems. To broaden the usefulness of this instrument, indicators of past behavior, current interpersonal skills, and social support systems were added to commonly assessed personality and clinical symptom variables.

The "rational-intuitive" approach was used to develop scales of relevance to the adolescent population and the items that would tap each dimension. Items addressed past and present behaviors as well as reactions to various situations. Inwald, Brobst, and Morrissey (1986) indicate that the HAP was initially derived from the Inwald Personality Inventory (IPI), which has been found useful in assessing young adults entering the law enforcement profession (Inwald, Knatz, & Shusman, 1983). However, it was more precisely the use of behaviorally oriented items that was borrowed from the IPI (R.E. Inwald, personal communication, December 6, 1990); only some items were taken from the IPI and rewritten to apply to the adolescent population. The more than 400 items generated were then checked for appropriateness to the teenage population. This resulted in deletions or rewording of some items and the creation of new ones to evaluate concerns that had not been addressed. The items were then assigned to scales.

Although the initial intention was for no HAP items to load on more than one scale, as noted previously the final form contains 14 items that contribute to more than one scale (Inwald et al., 1987). The number of items per scale ranges from 10 to 33, with an average of 20. The 16 scales are grouped into four clusters of related scales. The lone validity measure is the Guardedness scale. The acting out behavior measures include the Alcohol, Drugs, Educational Adjustment Difficulties, Law/Society Violations, Frustration Tolerance, Antisocial/Risk-Taking Attitudes, and Rigidity/Obsessiveness scales. The interpersonal adjustment measures encompass the Interpersonal/Assertiveness Difficulties, Homelife Conflicts, and Social/Sexual Adjustment scales. The internalized conflict measures include the Health Concerns, Anxiety/Phobic Avoidance, Depression/Suicide Potential, Suspicious Temperament, and Unusual Responses scales.

The basic normative data on 716 adolescents were collected by 92 professionals in 34 states between January 1985 and January 1987. This sample included 340 whites, 68 blacks, 72 Hispanics, and 236 adolescents from other or unknown racial backgrounds. Ages ranged from 10 to 19 years and averaged 15 years, 9 months. Included in the sample were 322 juvenile offenders, 148 hospitalized patients, 89 clinical outpatients, 78 high school dropouts, 47 beginning college students, 19 group home residents, 9 adolescents seen by a school counselor, and 4 for whom no information is available. Means, standard deviations, and critical scores are provided for every scale for each of the following variables: males, females, juvenile offenders, clinical in- and outpatients, troubled adolescents, beginning college students, race, and sex by age. Norms for the 10- to 12-year-olds were labeled "preliminary" due to small sample size. Norms are also provided by sex for another sample of 1,543 students in Grades 6 through 12 in Bedford County, Tennessee, and 78 high school dropouts from a special program in Arlington, Texas.

Comparison of juvenile offender and clinical in-/outpatient groups were made using *t*-tests. Juvenile offenders were found to have significantly higher scores on Alcohol, Drugs, Educational Adjustment Difficulties, Law/Society Violations, Antisocial/Risk-Taking Attitudes, and Social/Sexual Adjustment, while the clinical patients scored significantly higher on the Depression/Suicide Potential scale (Inwald et al., 1987). Some differences were noted between racial groups, but the number of subjects was small and the prediction within racial groups was equivalent (R.E. Inwald, personal communication, December 6, 1990).

The HAP materials consist of a manual, a test booklet, and individual answer sheets. Although the manual does not specify ages for administration and the answer sheet instructions provide the opportunity to indicate ages "10 or under" to age "19 or older," the means and standard deviations are only available for ages 10 to 19. A fifth-grade reading level is required; however, an audiotaped version is available for use with subjects who cannot comprehend written material at this level.

The HAP report is comprised of the following sections: a narrative report, a listing of critical items for follow-up evaluation, three personality profile graphs, and the item printout. The narrative report provides information on risk factors within each of the four clusters of scales. Items pertaining to suicidal ideation or attempts, eating disorders, and sexual problems that are answered in the pathological direction also result in specific statements in the printout. The critical items portion of the printout lists those items previously determined by a panel of clinical psychologists to be especially worthy of follow up (e.g., a response suggesting cocaine use) (Inwald et al., 1987). The HAP profile graphs provide information pertaining to a given subject's scores in relation to clinical patients, juvenile offenders, and adolescent students of the same sex. Scale scores have a mean of 50 and a standard deviation of 10. Scores of 60T may warrant exploration, while scores of 70T clearly fall outside the average range. If sufficient tests have been administered by a user, an additional graph is included in this section that reflects the norms for the user or his or her local area. (There is no indication in the manual, however, on how to request personal versus regional norms.) The HAP item printout is comprised of those items that were answered in the direction suggesting behavioral or emotional problems, printed out by scale.

The test publisher indicates that the narrative statements are somewhat general in nature to enable application to more than one person. It is also carefully stated that the report is not intended to take the place of the clinical interview, to serve as a final psychological report, or to be used as the only source in making treatment decisions.

**Practical Applications/Uses**

The HAP was designed for use by professionals working in or with school systems or juvenile justice departments, and/or who are providing mental health services to adolescents. Intended to be used as a screening instrument with those who may be at risk for behavioral and/or emotional problems, the HAP also could assist efforts to develop treatment programs. The HAP is easy to administer, having 310 true-false items, and usually takes about 45 minutes. No special procedures are necessary, and the measure can be given to one or more subjects simultaneously. Although the examiner is encouraged to read the instructions to respondents, this is not a requirement, as the instructions appear in each test booklet (Inwald, 1984). Subjects are asked to respond to items in the manner that best indicates how they "usually feel." Defining unknown words for subjects is permissible. The simplicity of administration would enable a nonprofessional to give the test.

Scoring keys are not available, as all scoring is accomplished by the test publisher. Users can either mail protocols to Hilson Research or use the Hilson Research Remote System Software and a modem to access the publisher's computer directly. The test publisher indicates that data received from every user are stored separately, and once at least 100 protocols have been received for each sex, norms are developed for the user and provided upon request. The test publisher also notes that ASCII data files containing case numbers, sex, race, HAP scale scores, and *t*-scores for each examinee can be provided to every user.

Users of the HAP should be thoroughly schooled in psychometrics, having a clear understanding of the limitations of test interpretation. The narrative portion of the HAP report may serve as a very useful hypothesis-generating tool in the hands of an experienced clinician. The interpretive statements are based upon comparisons of scale elevations to the normative sample and therefore represent statistically derived expectations. Although the sample reports included in the manual appear to integrate significantly elevated scales into coherent descriptions of the tested adolescents, a sample test report supplied separately from the manual does not contain much integration across the clusters of related scales and seems rather disjointed. Although this is not discussed in the manual, it will require the efforts of a skilled psychologist.

## Technical Aspects

The sample upon which the norms for the HAP were developed was not a stratified sample of the adolescent population of the United States. In a personal communication (February 6, 1991), the test author indicated that the profiles of juvenile offenders are very similar across the country and are readily discerned from those of clinical patients, thereby making a stratified sample helpful but not an absolute requirement, provided that test validation results and/or appropriate local norms are obtained. The basic normative sample included 716 subjects from 34 states, suggesting very small contributions from each state. Ninety-two professionals participated in the gathering of sample data, but further information about their precise role is unknown. Of the original sample, 236 "came from other racial groups or were those for whom no racial information was available" (Inwald et al., 1987). Only 14 subjects were in the 10- to 12-year-old age bracket. No details are provided on socioeconomic status (SES) or rural-urban breakdown. Data were also obtained on a sample of 1,543 school students in Bedford County, Tennessee; however, the manual provides no information about race (although Dr. Inwald reported that most of the sample was Caucasian), SES, or history of emotional and/or behavioral problems (R.E. Inwald, personal communication, February 6, 1991).

Internal consistency of the 16 HAP scales was evaluated on a sample of 569 adolescents from in-/outpatient clinical or juvenile populations by the Kuder-Richardson Formula 20 (KR-20) correlation coefficients, which were calculated by the *Statistical Package for the Social Sciences* (SPSS) reliability program. These coefficients range from .67 to .90 and average .77. Test-retest reliability was assessed on 33 adolescents who took the HAP after 2- to 4-week intervals. Pearson correlation coefficients for the HAP scales, which were calculated by the SPSS-PC+ Pearson correlation subprogram, range from .74 to .95 and average .85. Pearson correlations for a sample of 72 high school dropouts in Arlington, Texas, range from .60 to .86 and average .72, after 2- to 4-month intervals. A varimax rotated factor analysis of the HAP scales was also performed on the original sample of 716, using the factor analysis subprogram of the SPSS-PC+. The results suggested that the following three constructs are measured by the HAP: "internalized" problems; "externalized" or "acting out" behaviors; and "feelings of depression coupled with either health concerns or homelife conflicts, but without other clinical syndromes" (Inwald et al., 1987).

Pearson product moment correlations were also performed between the 16 HAP scales and 13 MMPI scales for the 254 adolescents on whom the data were available. Of the 208 correlations, 116 ranged from .23 to .64 and were found to be significant at the .001 level. The following correlations were ≥ .60: HAP Unusual Responses and MMPI F and Sc scales; HAP Depression/Suicide Potential and MMPI D and Sc scales; and HAP Interpersonal/Assertiveness Difficulties and the MMPI Si scale. Although these correlations do lend support to the construct validity of these three HAP scales, one cannot help noticing some other characteristics of the correlation coefficient matrix. For example, the correlation coefficients for 5 of the 16 HAP scales exceeded .22 with 10 or more of the 13 MMPI scales. Three of the HAP scales were similarly correlated with seven to nine of the MMPI scales. At the other extreme, one of the HAP scales, Alcohol, was not significantly correlated with any of the MMPI scales.

Criterion-related validity was evaluated by a step-wise discriminant function analysis, using SPSS-PC+, on each of the following criteria: suicide attempts, frequent drug use, alcohol abuse, running away history, sexual abuse history, and past conduct disorder diagnosis. Information on the presence of any of these behaviors in the normative sample was provided by the clinicians who administered the HAP. The percentages for correct predictions range from 66 to 90.5, with the average being 75.5. Another discriminant function analysis, using SPSS-PC+, correctly identified 86.5% of 126 juvenile offenders and 93.2% of 265 students (Inwald et al., 1987).

## Critique

The intention to develop a behaviorally oriented instrument for assessing behavioral and emotional problems in adolescents is sound. The creation of the HAP test items and their analysis was also done thoroughly and effectively. Although the test author contends that juvenile offenders and clinical patients present similarly across the country (R.E. Inwald, personal communication, December 6, 1990), the lack of a stratified sample of the national adolescent population on which to base norms is an unfortunate shortcoming.

The test norms are updated as additional data become available, which may prove significant in that the "norms" of adolescent behavior change over time. The possibility of some truly unique adolescent characteristic in a user's area makes the availability of local norms very appealing. The test authors will also provide free statistical analysis and follow-up research to any organization wishing to further validate the HAP on their own population(s). Although the manual does not indicate which items load on which scales, it is expected that the authors' willingness to work with every researcher will overcome this seeming limitation.

Some organizations may experience significant difficulties budgeting for the expense of an unknown number of test administrations 1 year in advance. However, the publisher will provide discounts on scoring services for government and nonprofit agencies (R.E. Inwald, personal communication, February 6, 1991).

### References

Inwald, R.E. (1984). *Hilson Adolescent Profile test book.* New York: Hilson Research.

Inwald, R.E., Brobst, K.E., & Morrissey, R.F. (1986). Identifying and predicting adolescent behavioral problems by using new profile. *Juvenile Justice Digest, 14*(13), 1, 4–9.

Inwald, R.E., Brobst, K.E., & Morrissey, R.F. (1987). *Hilson Adolescent Profile manual.* New York: Hilson Research.

Inwald, R., Knatz, H., & Shusman, E. (1983). *Inwald Personality Inventory manual.* New York: Hilson Research.

**Karen T. Carey, Ph.D., NCSP**
*Assistant Professor and Coordinator, School Psychology Program, California State University-Fresno, Fresno, California.*

# HOME ENVIRONMENT QUESTIONNAIRE

*Jacob O. Sines. Iowa City, Iowa: Psychological Assessment and Services, Inc.*

## Introduction

The home environment and other familial variables have long been thought to have an influence on children's behavior, achievement, and social interactions. Specifically, such factors as socioeconomic status, marital status (e.g., single, divorced), and the availability of educational materials in the home have been demonstrated to have a significant effect on children's development. The Home Environment Questionnaire (HEQ; Sines, 1983) was developed to objectively assess such environmental variables that can have an impact on a target child's behavior.

The theoretical foundations for the HEQ are based on Murray's (1938) concept of "alpha press." In contrast to beta press, which analyzes an individual's perception of his or her environment, alpha press refers to those environmental variables that can be assessed objectively. According to the HEQ's author, by evaluating alpha press variables, home environments that are not conducive to children's physical and mental health can be identified and modified as necessary.

Jacob O. Sines, author of the HEQ, obtained his Ph.D. in clinical psychology at Michigan State University in 1955. He was Professor of Psychology at the University of Missouri from 1961 to 1969 and served as professor and department chair in psychology at Case Western Reserve University from 1969 to 1970. Since 1970, Dr. Sines has been Professor of Psychology at the University of Iowa. He has published numerous articles examining rating scales and checklists for assessing children's behaviors and their environments.

This instrument is designed to assess environmental press variables for children from fourth to sixth grades. Two forms are available: the HEQ-2R and the HEQ-1R. The HEQ-2R was constructed to assess the environments of children living in two-parent families and consists of 123 true-false items; the HEQ-1R, for one-parent families, consists of 91 true-false items. The complete assessment kit includes the examiner manual, 18 transparent scoring templates (9 for HEQ-2R; 9 for HEQ-1R), 25 HEQ-2R questionnaire forms, and 25 HEQ-1R questionnaire forms. The questionnaire forms are color coded for easy identification (i.e., HEQ-2R—green form; HEQ-1R—yellow form). Both questionnaire forms are designed to be completed by the target child's mother. Ten dimensions of environmental press are assessed by the questionnaires: P(ress) Achievement, P Aggression–External, P Aggression–Home, P Aggression–Total, P Supervision, P Change, P Affiliation, P Separation, P Sociability, and P Socioeconomic Status.

The HEQ-2R was developed from an initial pool of 700 items encompassing life events and situations of children's environments identified from school and medical records of "several hundred children" (Sines, 1983, p. 2). Each item selected was then rated on a 10-point scale. A rating of "1" indicated the item described a specific child behavior, whereas a "10" indicated the item identified a specific facet of the child's environment (e.g., object, situation, or person), was descriptive of the environment (rather than inferred), and was written in simple, straightforward language (Laing & Sines, 1982). Those items with a median rating of 5.0 or higher were retained (*N* = 667).

Each item was also rated on a 10-point scale with respect to social desirability. A rating of "1" suggested that a response of "true" indicated highly undesirable environmental attributes; a rating of "10" suggested that a "true" response was evidence of strongly desired environmental attributes. All 667 items were retained following this procedure.

For Murray's 16 press variables, 10 to 12 items were selected for each variable (*N* = 174), and responses of "true" or "false" were identified as responding to each variable. A volunteer sample of 75 mothers completed the HEQ-2R at this stage of development. However, retention of items after this phase was based on Loevinger's (1957) general rational-statistical method. This method of item inclusion requires (a) an item-scale correlation of .30 or greater; (b) that the square of the correlation of each item with the variable to which the item is assigned be at least twice the square of the correlation of that item with any other variable; and (c) face validity of each item comprising a variable. Items for the questionnaire were then tested in a number of studies (Laing & Sines, 1982; Sines, Clarke, & Lauer, 1984) and were either attributed to a variable or dropped. According to the author, from the items available only 10 of the 16 press variables could be accurately measured by the items selected for final inclusion. The development of the HEQ-1R resulted from the exclusion of all items referring to two-parent families.

It should be noted that the number of items included for each variable on both questionnaires differ substantially. For example, the HEQ-2R contains 4 items on the P Sociability scale and 25 on the P Affiliation and P Socioeconomic Status scales. Factor analysis was not utilized during scale development.

**Practical Applications/Uses**

At present it appears the HEQ can be used only for research purposes. The author's overall goal is to develop methods for identifying children's behavior as attributed to environmental variables, specific individual personality variables, and interpersonal interactions. Further research with the instrument is needed to determine its usefulness.

The HEQ was normed on data collected from mothers of 620 fourth-, fifth-, and sixth-grade students (HEQ-2R = 544; HEQ-1R = 76) attending school in a Midwestern city with a population of 24,000. Approximately 95% of the mothers responding to the questionnaires were white, and the mean family income of the community was $18,000. Thus, the HEQ is not applicable for minority populations, children considered to be handicapped or at risk, or for families living at or below the poverty level.

The HEQ is designed to be completed by the target child's mother without examiner assistance. Instructions are provided on the face sheet of the questionnaire form, instructing the mother to provide written background information on the front of the form—child's name, age, sex, and grade, the respondent's name, and her relationship to the child. The mother is also instructed to answer each of the 123 items (or 91 if using HEQ-1R) "true" or "false" by making an × through the T or the F next to each item. The author recommends the mother be provided with a pencil in order to make erasures if necessary. The author also reports that mothers with "moderate reading ability" should be able to read and respond to the items (Laing & Sines, 1982).

HEQ administration procedures are relatively straightforward. However, it appears from an analysis of the items that a reading ability of at least the fifth- to sixth-grade level is necessary to complete the questionnaire. In addition, no information is provided relative to time required for administration or what should be done if the respondent answers items out of sequence.

Responses are scored using the appropriate nine transparent scoring templates for either the HEQ-2R or the HEQ-1R. The templates (which correspond to a particular variable) must carefully overlay the questions in the booklet to ensure the item numbers match those on the booklet. The templates have boxes to the left of the item numbers that identify those items contributing to the variable being scored. Each variable is scored based on the number of ×'s appearing in boxes on the templates. The user records raw scores in a blank space appropriate for each variable on the front of the questionnaire booklet. A raw score for the P Aggression–Total variable is obtained by adding the sum of the raw scores for P Aggression–External and P Aggression–Home variables. All raw scores are then converted to T scores using separate conversion tables for either the HEQ-2R or the HEQ-1R.

Information related to the interpretation of the HEQ is minimal and based on the author's own personal experience. Sines states that "clinical experience with the HEQ-2R suggests that a T score above 60 or below 40 on any scale should be considered significant and to warrant further exploration with the parents and the child" (1983, p. 7). No empirically based support for using the T scores in this manner is provided, however.

## Technical Aspects

Reliability data are not available for either form of the HEQ. Validity estimates are based primarily on predictive validity. However, the latter was assessed by correlating the raw score results of the HEQ with the Missouri Children's Behavioral Checklist—Parent Form (MCBC-P), another instrument developed by Jacob Sines. Through the utilization of the two scales (i.e., HEQ and MCBC-P), the manual states that the HEQ-2R can be used to estimate how much of a target child's behaviors can be expected from an "average child" exposed to similar environmental variables. Other statistical analyses have not been completed, although the manual outlines studies that should be undertaken in the future.

## Critique

The HEQ should not be used at the present time for professional decision making. Further experimental analyses and research are needed to determine the applicability of the HEQ, as numerous problems plague the instrument.

First, factor analysis was not used in scale development. Items were initially selected apparently on face validity for assignment to one of the 10 variables. Next, those items that met the general rational-statistical method were either included or deleted from the scale. Therefore, some items thought to be suitable for inclusion on a variable at the outset, based on the author's definitions of the variables, subsequently were deleted. Thus, it is difficult to determine whether items are actually measuring the specified variables to which they have been assigned.

Second, many items lack face validity for inclusion on specific variable scales. The items appear heavily loaded with respect to social desirability, and although the author provides information related to preliminary studies that address this issue, he concludes by stating "socially desirable characteristics of children's environments are, in fact, more frequent than socially undesirable ones" (Sines, 1983, p. 14). This conclusion is highly questionable and obviously dependent on the demographic characteristics of the norming population.

Third, though the HEQ was designed to assess environmental variables that can be assessed objectively, no such assessment is described. Naturalistic observations of the child's environment to evaluate the accuracy of the mother's reports are needed in order to determine the scale's internal reliability.

Fourth, although the rationale provided for the development of the HEQ and the underlying theoretical concepts are sound, the HEQ should *not* be used by practitioners at this time. Further validity and reliability studies are needed and are described in the manual. These must be undertaken before the HEQ will be applicable for day-to-day professional decision making.

## References

Laing, J.A., & Sines, J.O. (1982). The Home Environment Questionnaire: An instrument for assessing several behaviorally relevant dimensions of children's environments. *Journal of Pediatric Psychology, 7,* 425–449.

Loevinger, J. (1957). Objective tests as instruments of psychological theory. *Psychological Reports, 3,* 635–694.

Murray, H.A. (1938). *Explorations in personality.* New York: Oxford University Press.

Sines, J.O. (1983). *Home Environment Questionnaire.* Iowa City, IA: Psychological Assessment and Services.

Sines, J.O., Clarke, W.M., & Lauer, R.M. (1984). Home Environment Questionnaire. *Journal of Abnormal Child Psychology, 12,* 519–529.

**Charles W. Stansfield, Ph.D.**
*Director, ERIC Clearinghouse for Languages and Linguistics, and Director, Division of Foreign Language Education and Testing, Center for Applied Linguistics, Washington, D.C.*

# IDEA ORAL LANGUAGE PROFICIENCY TEST–II

*Enrique F. Dalton and Beverly A. Amori. Brea, California: Ballard & Tighe, Inc.*

## Introduction

Designed for students in Grades 7–12, the IDEA Oral Language Proficiency Test–II (IPT II) is an individually administered measure of speaking and listening proficiency in English as a second language (ESL). The test contains 91 items and requires between 5 and 25 minutes to administer, depending on the student's level of proficiency. The average administration time is 15 minutes. Raw scores are converted to one of seven proficiency level scores, which in turn classify the student as non-English-speaking (NES), limited English-speaking (LES), or fluent English-speaking (FES). The IPT II is a part of the IDEA Oral Language Proficiency Test series, which includes a Pre-IPT in English and Spanish for pre-kindergarten children, an IPT I English and Spanish for Grades K–6, and the IPT II in English and Spanish for Grades 7–12. This review focuses on the IPT II in English.

Because the IPT II is part of the IDEA Oral Language Proficiency Test series, its history is best described in the context of that series, which begins in the early 1970s. At that time, two public elementary school teachers, Wanda Ballard and Phyllis Tighe, were teaching in the Los Angeles area. During a 6-year period, these two teachers developed a set of oral language development materials for their students. The success of these materials, called Individualized Developmental English Activities (IDEA), led to their publication in 1976. The following year, a parallel set of materials (Ideas para el desarrollo del espanol por actividades) was developed in Spanish by Dr. Enrique F. Dalton. A natural consequence of the development of the oral language program was the development of a proficiency test that could be used to place students in the IDEA program or in others. This process began in 1978; Forms A and B of the IPT I in English were published in the fall of 1979. The validation studies for this test were directed by Dr. Dalton. He also played the lead role in the development of the IPT I in Spanish, which was published late in 1980, and he wrote the technical manuals for all the IPT tests. After these tests were completed, work began on the IPT II, which was published in September 1983. A description of the development of the IPT II follows.

In May 1982 a committee of language specialists that consisted of experienced teachers of ESL and bilingual education and specialists in oral language development in California was formed and met to advise the authors on the development of a comprehensive list of oral English language skills important at the secondary level. The authors, Enrique Dalton and Beveraly Amori, then began the process of developing such a list, which was refined in subsequent meetings of the committee. At least four items were written for each skill on the list, and these items were then ranked according to their suitability and quality by each committee member. The authors ultimately wrote over 300 items, some of which were based on the oral language skills contained in the eight levels of the IDEA program, and others of which came from research in second language development, including basic interpersonal communicative skills (BICS) and cognitive/academic language proficiency (CALP) (Cummins, 1984). Each item also was ranked according to the seven proficiency levels on the IPT scale.

Following deletion of items deemed inappropriate or repetitive, two parallel forms of a pilot test were developed and administered to a small group (number not indicated in the technical manual) of monolingual English-speaking students during December 1982. Using item difficulty and discrimination indices from this pilot testing, revisions were made on the items themselves and in their sequencing. Subsequently a field test of each form was conducted during the spring of 1983. This testing involved 306 monolingual native English-speaking students in Grades 7–12, as well as an additional 153 students in those grades who were classified as non-English-speaking (NES), limited English-speaking (LES), and fluent English-speaking (FES). A total of 120 of the 306 monolingual English-speaking students were retested in order to determine parallel form and interrater reliability. The data from these field tests form the basis of the reliability and validity information presented in the technical manual.

The IPT II materials set contains either 50 student test booklets or 50 diagnostic score cards (the component desired must be stipulated at the time the set is ordered). The set also contains a book of 15 stimulus pictures, an examiner's manual, a technical manual, 50 proficiency test level summaries (which describe the skills normally acquired by students at each level), and 10 group lists (which show students' test level scores and NES/LES/FES classifications).

Most IPT II items (93%) require an oral response. The remaining 7% test comprehension by requiring the student to make a physical response such as pointing to something in a stimulus picture. These five comprehension items focus on vocabulary while testing parts of the body, spatial relations, time, ordinal numbers, and superlatives.

Most of the oral production items test vocabulary either through a question/answer or a sentence completion format, with the response based on one of the stimulus pictures (e.g., "What is this?" or "We cook soup on the . . ."). The vocabulary tested relates to school, geometric shapes, pet animals, days of the week, and vegetables that make up a salad at the lower levels, and to coins, holidays, and a number of adjectives at the upper levels. Other oral production items test syntax, often through a question/answer format and also using the stimulus pictures (e.g., "Where's she going?" "To the movies"). In other cases, a descriptive prelude provides background information that is used to shape a desired response involving syntax (e.g., "Mr. Lee had a book about horses. His brother wanted to read it. What did Mr. Lee do with the book?"). Some items test syntax through a yes/no question format (e.g., "Do you know how to fly a helicopter?"); in the latter example, the student is told to answer in a complete sentence. Some items use questions and picture stimuli to test morphology (e.g.,

"Whose sweater is this?" "It's hers"). The critical feature being tested is the /s/ morpheme of third person singular feminine possessive pronoun. At the highest levels, the test also taps an organizational/expressive ability by asking the examinee to complete a story and to retell in his or her own words a story read by the examiner.

**Practical Applications/Uses**

The IPT II can be used to assess the oral language proficiency of students in Grades 7–12. Some confusion exists as to whether the IPT I and, by extension, the IPT II are tests of general proficiency or are achievement tests oriented to a specific set of instructional materials. The issue centers on the fact that the IPT I can be used to place students within the eight levels that make up the IDEA Oral Language Program, which is designed for use in Grades K through 8. Although this debate over the nature of the test may be logical for the IPT I, it is inappropriate to extend it to the IPT II. The IDEA Oral Language Program does not extend beyond Grade 8, and no claims are made in the IPT II examiner's or technical manuals that the test can be used for placement within another set of IDEA instructional materials.

Due to its length, the IPT is sensitive to gains in overall language proficiency. Therefore, the two forms of the test can be used as pre- and post-test measures to identify gains in language skills. The identification of such gains is often a desirable part of the evaluation of a special instructional program, such as an ESL program, migrant education, bilingual education, or compensatory education.

The IPT II can be used jointly with the IPT II in Spanish to determine language dominance; that is, the language in which the student is most proficient. To do this, first the IPT II–English level score is used to classify the student as NES, LES, or FES. Next, the level score in the child's native language is used to classify his or her proficiency in the home language in a similar manner. Thus, a child might be classified as non-Spanish-speaking (NSS), limited Spanish-speaking (LSS), or fluent Spanish-speaking (FSS). Finally, and if necessary, the two classifications can be compared to place the child in one of the five Lau language dominance categories (Office of Civil Rights, 1975).

The IPT II, like most tests, also can be used to diagnose a student's strengths and weaknesses. Diagnostic Score Cards (DSCs) link each item to a matrix of skills assessed by the test (vocabulary, morphology, syntax, and comprehension, as discussed at the end of the previous section). This matrix is similar to a test "blueprint," which is often used to demonstrate a content validity. When using the DSC, the examiner reads the questions from the test booklet, but records the response on the DSC. The DSC is then placed in the student's cumulative folder.

The IPT is administered to one student at a time. The authors recommend that the examiner be bilingual in English and the language of the student. Either English or the student's native language can be used to explain the test procedures prior to the start of the test. Following 4 sample items, the examiner begins with the first 14 items, which are associated with level score A. These items test very basic vocabulary. At the end of the section, the student's performance is scored. A student making four or more errors is given level score A and the test is discontinued. If three or fewer errors are made, the students is asked the 15 questions associated with level score B. A poor performance on this part (eight or more errors) will again place the student at level score A. If the student makes four to seven errors, he or she is given score level B and the test is discontinued. If a student makes three or fewer errors, the examiner proceeds to ask the 15 questions associated with level score C. The test continues in similar fashion through the last part, which contains the 16 questions associated with level score F. Thus, on any given part, the student may earn a score that either (a) places him or her at the previous level, (b) places him or her at the current level, or (c) advances him or her to the next level. Students who answer 75% of the items in level F correctly are assigned a level score of M, meaning mastery of the skills assessed on the test.

The examiner points to one of the IPT II test pictures on 31 of the 91 questions. Depending on the student's response, the examiner places a checkmark in the box labeled "Correct" or "Incorrect" in the student test booklet. To aid the examiner in scoring, the test booklet lists a critical feature of each response that must be present in order for the response to be marked correct. When there is more than one possible correct response, the alternatives are indicated with a slash mark (/). If the response calls for a complete sentence, the examiner cues the student to "answer in a sentence." Or, the examiner may say the first part of the sentence and wait for the student to continue the response and provide the critical feature. Because the IPT is scored in a relatively objective, straightforward manner, examiners can usually learn or be trained to administer and score it in half a day or less.

The time required to administer the IPT averages about 15 minutes and varies between 5 and 25 minutes according to the number of items presented to the student. This, in turn, may vary according to the student's proficiency. More proficient students are presented with more parts and more items. However, if an examiner has prior knowledge that a student has some ability in English, he or she may skip the items associated with the lower level scores and proceed directly to the middle level scores, thereby reducing the total administration time. In such cases, if the student misses more than one of the first six items on a given level, the examiner should descend to the previous level and begin again. At the end of the test, the examiner uses the level score attained by the student to assign an NES/LES/FES classification based on a chart on the back of the student's test booklet.

## Technical Aspects

Several studies were conducted to address the validity of the IPT II. However, the way they are reported in the technical manual is neither clear, organized, nor logical, and sometimes they used inappropriate subjects. As indicated previously, these studies were conducted in the spring of 1983.

The first studies involved 186 of the 306 monolingual English-speaking students who participated in the field testing. These students' English teachers were asked to predict the IPT II level scores of their students based on the list of oral language skills associated with each score level. (This list is printed on the IDEA Proficiency Test Summary, which is part of the test package.) The predicted score level of these students was then correlated with the attained score level. The correlations for both forms were low and not significant.

This should not be surprising for two reasons. First, as most English teachers do not emphasize instruction in oral language skills, they would not be prepared to make accurate judgments about their students' oral language skills. Indeed, they would probably base such judgments on their students' writing ability, which is what is emphasized in the secondary school English curricula. Second, as 93% of these native English speakers scored at levels F or M, there were few differences in their scores. Without differentiation in scores, there is no possibility of correlation, yet this latter is not mentioned in the technical manual. Finally, it seems inappropriate to correlate predicted with attained scores for a sample of native English speakers. The IPT II is a test for ESL learners, and such tests are, by definition, not designed for the native English-speaking population. Thus, in spite of the fact that this low correlation was needlessly included in the technical manual, its lack of significance should not be a source of concern.

Similar observations can be made regarding the efforts reported in the technical manual to correlate IPT II results with the CTBS scores, age, grade, writing proficiency, math proficiency, and so on of this sample of native English speakers. None of these correlations were significant, and it is not clear why these data were gathered or why they are presented in the technical manual.

One useful outcome of the above study on native English speakers was that it corroborated the designation of levels F and M as the Fluent English Speaking (FES) classification. Thus, nonnative English speakers who attain these levels can be said to score at the native English speaker level on the test.

Fortunately, a second study was conducted during the spring of 1983 involving 153 nonnative speakers of English. Seventy-eight of these students took Form A and 75 took Form B. Again, the technical manual reports the results of a correlation analysis with student age and grade for this sample. Not surprisingly, the IPT II was found not to correlate with age or grade. Of course, there is no reason why English proficiency should correlate with age or grade for a sample of nonnative English speakers. An 18-year-old immigrant who has just arrived in the United States usually will have far less proficiency than a 12-year-old who has been in the United States for 3 years. Thus, it would be more reasonable to expect English proficiency to correlate with the amount of time that each subject had been in the United States. This, in fact, is what the committee of language specialists recommended, with the result that additional data on time in country was gathered from student files. For a sample of 99 students, the correlation between IPT level score and time in country was found to be .62. Among this group, 49 took Form A while 50 took Form B, and the correlation for each group was almost identical. This provides some meaningful evidence of the validity of the IPT II.

The English teachers of the same group of 153 nonnative English-speaking students were asked to predict the IPT II level scores of their students based on the list of oral language skills associated with each score level. (This list is printed on the IDEA Proficiency Test Summary, which is part of the test package.) The predicted score level of these students was then correlated with the attained score level. The correlations for both forms (.66 and .43) was significant. This again provides some meaningful evidence of the IPT II's validity.

The technical manual reports that the IPT II scores of the same sample of 153 nonnatives were compared with the FES/LES/NES classifications previously determined by the school district. These classifications were obtained using three other tests approved for use in California by the California Department of Education: the Language Assessment Battery, the Language Assessment Scales, and the Bilingual Syntax Measure. The correlation with district classification was found to be .56 for Form A and .36 for Form B. Though both correlations were significant, it is not clear why Form B did not perform as well.

Finally, the IPT II scores of this sample were compared with the FES/LES/NES classifications made by teachers on the basis of their knowledge of the students' oral language ability, academic ability, and other unobtrusive measures. The significant correlations yielded were .68 for Form A and .59 for Form B.

An important validity issue is the method used to determine what constitutes an NES/LES/FES classification. In this case, the authors compared teacher and district classifications of 148 nonnative English-speaking students with their IPT II level scores. The results of this comparison were used to determine the IPT score levels that correspond to each classification. For the IPT II, score level A corresponds to a classification as non-English-speaking (NES). Score levels B through E correspond to classification as limited English-speaking (LES). And similarly, score levels F and M correspond to a classification as fluent English-speaking (FES). This latter correspondence agrees with the results of the first study of native English speakers reported earlier.

Two reliability studies are reported in the technical manual. In the spring of 1983, the 153 students mentioned earlier took one form of the IPT II; 78 took Form A and 75 took Form B. An analysis of internal consistency (Cronbach's alpha) produced a reliability coefficient of .98 for Forms A and B. This is exceptionally high reliability for any test, and especially for a productive skills test.

Test-retest reliability was determined in the following manner. A sample of 30 monolingual English-speaking students was administered Form A by different examiners at 1-week intervals. The correlation that emerged between the scores on the two different administrations was .43. This low correlation was due to the fact that little variance was found among the group on either administration; 22 of the 30 students attained level score M on both administrations, and 29 attained either E or M on both occasions. Again, this was due to the fact that an English-only sample was selected for this study. The study should have been conducted on nonnative rather than native speakers of English, as the test was designed to discriminate among nonnative speakers. A similar study involving 30 students who took Form B twice found a test-retest reliability of .73. Although this correlation is higher than that reported for Form A, it is probably well below the true test-retest reliability that would be attained with an appropriate sample of nonnative English speakers.

In another study, which attempted to assess parallel form reliability when different raters are used, 56 monolingual English-speaking students were administered both forms of the test, each by a different rater, within a 1-week interval. This approach takes into account error in measurement attributable to both different forms and different raters. The resulting correlation, .24, was not significant. Had the same rater been used, the parallel form reliability would probably have been slightly higher. However, the principal cause of this low correlation was the fact that an inappropriate sample was selected. Had the sample been composed of learners of English as a second language, undoubtedly the reliability coefficient would have been much higher. In theory, the parallel form reliability should approximate internal consistency reliability, which was found to be .98 for samples of nonnative English speakers.

## Critique

The IPT II was developed by practicing teachers with many years of classroom experience. The combination of their experience and the test's length have ensured that this measure has adequate content validity, which is outlined in a blueprint for each form in the technical manual. The IPT II is also easy to administer and score, and the 15-minute average administration is not excessive for an individually administered test, except perhaps for large districts with intake centers that need to assess thousands of students within a few days at the beginning of each school year. The system for converting level scores to language proficiency classifications appears sound.

Several validity studies show that this test correlates well with teacher ratings of language proficiency and with teacher classifications into an NES/LES/FES category for nonnative English-speaking students. There is also evidence that the IPT II relates to school achievement. Reliability is also high, perhaps due to the test's length, the similarity of its two forms, and the relative ease with which one can learn to score it accurately.

Only a couple of weaknesses can be identified in the IPT II. The major one seems to be the technical manual. The research reported there is not described clearly, and the text contains many tables but little narrative explanation. As a result, test user will find it difficult to put these tables together in order to arrive at a more complete understanding of the test's reliability and validity. Rivera and Zeller (1987) noted the same problem with the manual in their review of the IPT II. As use of the IPT II is increasing, especially in California and Texas, the publisher should consider producing a new manual that would present the development and validation of the test in a clear manner.

A second problem stems from using inappropriate samples, consisting of native English speakers, to present evidence of reliability and validity. The result of this is a failure to demonstrate adequate reliability or validity when such samples were involved. The test publisher should consider conducting further studies using samples of nonnative English speakers and then reporting the data in a revised technical manual. Correlations with other relevant data, such as scores on other ESL proficiency tests and on standardized achievement tests, could then be presented for nonnative English speakers, thereby providing a more comprehensive and meaningful analysis of the instrument. Given the large number of users of this test, it should not be difficult to collect such data.

Although it may be somewhat premature to say so given the dearth of relevant empirical research, this reviewer tends to agree with the publisher's claim that the test can be used as a test of overall oral language proficiency for students in Grades 7–12.

## References

Cummins, J. (1984). Wanted: A theoretical perspective for relating language proficiency to academic achievement among bilingual students. In C. Rivera (Ed.), *Language proficiency and academic achievement* (pp. 2–19). Clevedon, Avon, England: Multilingual Matters.

Dalton, E.F., & Amori, A.M. (1983). *IPT II technical manual English*. Brea, CA: Ballard & Tighe.

Office of Civil Rights. (1975). *Task force findings specifying remedies available for eliminating past educational practices ruled unlawful under Lau versus Nichols*. Washington, DC: U.S. Department of Health, Education, and Welfare.

Rivera, C., & Zeller, A.M. (1987). [Review of the Idea Proficiency Test II]. In J.C. Alderson, K.J. Krahnke, & C.W. Stansfield (Eds.), *Reviews of English language proficiency tests* (pp. 39–41). Washington, DC: Teachers of English to Speakers of Other Languages.

**Frank M. Bernt, Ph.D.**
*Assistant Professor of Health Administration, Department of Education and Health Services, St. Joseph's University, Philadelphia, Pennsylvania.*

---

# ILLNESS BEHAVIOUR QUESTIONNAIRE

*I. Pilowsky and N.D. Spence. Adelaide, Australia: I. Pilowsky, M.D.*

## Introduction

The Illness Behaviour Questionnaire (IBQ; Pilowsky & Spence, 1983) is a self-report instrument that provides information about various aspects of the respondent's illness behavior; that is, how one experiences and responds to his or her health status. The concept of illness behavior suggests that individuals respond to illness in a variety of ways that are more or less adaptive. Abnormal illness behavior consists of adopting a sick role that is considered inappropriate given the lack of any detected objective pathology (Pilowsky, 1978).

The IBQ represents an expansion of the Whiteley Index of Hypochondriasis (WIH), a short self-report measure designed to identify individuals with excessive hypochondriacal orientations (Pilowsky, 1967). Factor analyses of the 14 items on the WIH yielded three meaningful factors: bodily preoccupation, disease phobia/need for reassurance, and disease conviction/paranoia. In an effort to broaden the character of the instrument to include other dimensions of illness behavior, 38 additional items were generated. An exploratory factor analysis of the original 52-item version yielded seven meaningful factors. Ten additional items were generated and added to scales with less than five items to constitute the current 62-item version.

Descriptions of the seven IBQ scales follow:

1. *General Hypochondriasis* (9 items). Measures phobic concern about one's state of health and includes a secondary aspect of interpersonal alienation and some insight into inappropriateness of attitudes.

2. *Disease Conviction* (6 items). Measures the conviction that a physical disease exists (despite doctor's reassurance) and preoccupation with symptoms.

3. *Psychological vs. Somatic Perception of Illness* (5 items). Measures the extent to which the patient feels somehow responsible for illness and sees its cause as psychological rather than physical; a low score indicates a tendency to somatize concerns.

4. *Affective Inhibition* (5 items). Measures an individual's difficulty in expressing personal (especially negative) feelings to others.

5. *Affective Disturbance* (5 items). Measures an individual's feelings of anxiety and depression.

6. *Denial* (5 items). Measures one's tendency to deny life stresses and to attribute all one's problems to the effects of illness.

7. *Irritability* (5 items). Assesses the presence of anger and interpersonal friction.

Only 40 of the 62 items are included in the calculation of IBQ subscale scores; additional items are included to provide a score for the Whiteley Index of Hypochondriasis and "for research purposes."

The IBQ is currently available in at least 12 languages, including German, Spanish, Italian, Dutch, and Chinese.

**Practical Applications/Uses**

Though originally designed for clinical contexts, use of the IBQ has been expanded to include research as well. This is reflected in two slightly different forms of the IBQ: Form B differs from the original form (A) in that it rewords certain items that assume respondent illness in order to make it more appropriate for nonclinical settings.

The IBQ (simply entitled "Health Survey") consists of two pages of items. Individuals are instructed to respond "yes" or "no" for each item. The questionnaire generally can be completed in 15 minutes. Although it can be hand scored in less than 5 minutes, a computer-scoring program (in either BASIC or FORTRAN) also is available.

The questionnaire yields 11 scores: one for each of the seven subscales, one for the WIH, a discriminant function score (for classifying respondents as hypochondriacal), and two second-order scores representing Affective State (20 items) and Disease Affirmation (11 items). The report form for the IBQ presents raw scores and percentile scores for each of the above scales; percentile scores for each scale are also presented graphically. Norms for each of the subscales are listed in the technical manual for pain clinic, general practice, psychiatric, coronary artery bypass, and cardiac patient groups.

Space is provided at the bottom of the report form for clinical comments by the assessor. This reflects the authors' consistent position that the IBQ is not a substitute for, but only a supplement to, professional clinical judgment based on patient interview. In view of this insistence, recommended cut points suggested in the technical manual should be used very cautiously and tentatively. Readers intending to use the IBQ for clinical purposes may be interested in the interview-based Illness Behavior Assessment Schedule (Pilowsky, Bassett, Barrett, Petrovic, & Minniti, 1983).

**Technical Aspects**

Factor analytic studies of the 62-item version of the IBQ present an uneven picture. Four of the seven factors have been consistently replicated in three of the four studies reported by Pilowsky and Spence (1983): General Hypochondriasis (or Disease Phobia), Affective Inhibition, Affective Disturbance, and Denial. A later study (Main & Waddell, 1987) revealed that internal consistency estimates for these four scales ranged from .58 to .67 (mean $r$ = .58). Irritability, though replicated in only two of the four validation studies, possessed an internal consistency estimate of .71. Disease Conviction and Psychological vs. Somatic Perception of Illness scales were least replicable and received internal consistency estimates of

.48 and .36, respectively. Similarly low estimates were obtained recently using the German version of the IBQ (Wichmann, Nilges, Gerbershagen, Gamber, & Scheifling, 1990). Despite this unevenness, the scoring method described in the technical manual is still based on the original factor analysis of the 52-item version of the IBQ.

Zonderman, Heft, and Costa (1985), using the largest sample to date and applying an orthogonal rotation approach, obtained a six-factor solution that exactly replicated three of the seven original scales: Affective Inhibition, Denial, and Irritability. In addition, they obtained factors very closely resembling Affective Disturbance and General Hypochondriasis. As in earlier replication efforts, the Psychological vs. Somatic Perception of Illness scale was not represented at all, while the Disease Conviction scale was split between an "Illness Disruption" factor and the General Hypochondriasis factor. More recently, Main and Waddell (1987) factor analyzed a selected subset of IBQ items; though the appropriateness of some of their procedures and conclusions are questionable (Pilowsky & Spence, 1988), it is instructive to note that their three-factor solution confirmed the Affective Inhibition factor exactly. An "Affective and Hypochondriacal Disturbance" factor combined items from the General Hypochondriasis and Affective Disturbance scales, while a "Life Disruption" factor combined items from Denial and Disease Conviction scales.

Second-order factor analyses reported in the technical manual uncovered two higher order factors interpreted as Affective (General Hypochondriasis, Affective Disturbance, and Irritability) and Disease Affirmation (Disease Conviction and Psychological vs. Somatic Perception of Illness). Affective Inhibition fell outside either second-order factor. Zonderman et al.'s (1985) findings suggest a single general factor: intercorrelations among four of their six factors (excluding Affective Inhibition and Denial) ranged from .47 to .55.

Estimates of test-retest reliability using a Spearman correlation for each of the seven subscales and for the Whiteley Index range from .67 to .87 (mean $r = .82$); though this is convincing at first blush, it should be noted that the interval between initial test and retest varied from 1 to 12 weeks and that estimates are based on a sample of 42 (Pilowsky & Spence, 1983). Correlations between patients' scores and relatives' or friends' scores (or spouses'—the technical manual is unclear on this point) on each subtest (and the Whiteley Index) ranged from .50 to .78 (mean $r = .64$). In this case, friends or relatives were asked to complete the IBQ as they thought the patient would have responded. Again, the sample size was small (Pilowsky & Spence, 1983).

Studies examining the concurrent validity of the IBQ have yielded moderate correlations between the Affective Disturbance scale and a wide variety of depression and anxiety scales (Grassi, Rosti, Albierti, & Marangolo, 1989; Pilowsky & Spence, 1983). Affective Disturbance scores have also been found associated with Neuroticism scores on the Eysenck Personality Inventory (Harkins, Price, & Braith, 1989). Affective Inhibition was moderately negatively correlated with the Extraversion scale of the Eysenck Personality Inventory (Harkins et al., 1989; Zonderman et al., 1985). Perhaps more to the point, Zonderman et al. (1985) obtained moderate (though somewhat lower) correlations between all six of the IBQ scales derived from their study and three separate measures of neuroticism, suggesting that the IBQ is "saturated with neuroticism." Clayer, Bookless, and Ross (1984) confirmed this suggestion, finding that four of the seven IBQ scales (the same four that Zonderman et al. found moderately correlated with one another) discriminated neurotic from normal respondents.

Several studies appear to support the contention that the IBQ effectively discriminates individuals displaying abnormal illness behavior from those displaying normal illness behavior. Pilowsky, Murrell, and Gordon (1979) obtained discriminant score formulas that successfully identified 97% of pain clinic patients while incorrectly classifying 26% of general practice patients. Although the use of pain clinic patients in early studies may have weakened the credibility of the IBQ as a diagnostic tool for identifying hypochondriasis (in that pain clinic patients may probably, but not necessarily, be hypochondriacal), more recent studies comparing patients with nonorganic pain to those with organic pain have had similar success (Joyce, Bushnell, Walshe, & Morton, 1986; Pilowsky, Smith, & Katsikitis, 1987). Joyce et al. (1986) found that patients with nonorganic abdominal pain had significantly higher scores than their counterparts on General Hypochondriasis, Psychological vs. Somatic Perception of Illness, Affective Disturbance, and Denial subscales. Their findings partially replicate those of three separate discriminant analytic studies reported in the technical manual. Pilowsky and Spence (1983) refer to the resulting discriminant functions of these as "separate though similar"; although a recent analysis contests this similarity (Toshima & Kaplan, 1989), there does seem to be a notable overlap among studies.

Two important points deserve mention: First, there are differences in illness behaviors, which are probably best explained by the differences in the groups being discriminated or the pain subpopulations studied. It is instructive to note that while Pilowsky et al. (1987) found significant differences between patients with organic pain and those with nonorganic pain referred to a general practice, their efforts to apply the discriminant function formula based on the Adelaide pain clinic sample failed dismally. It would seem wise to avoid using such formulas without first conducting careful cross-validation studies. Secondly, it is interesting to note that the scales that are weighted strongly in the majority of studies discussed above include Psychological vs. Somatic Perception of Illness and Disease Conviction scales; both had weak internal consistency estimates, as indicated previously.

Different subsets of IBQ scales also have been found to discriminate effectively among various groups of patients; for example, pain patients from private practice patients (Chapman, Sola, & Bonica, 1979); intractable facial pain patients from dental pain patients (Speculand, Goss, Spence, & Pilowsky, 1981); poor sleepers from good sleepers (Pilowsky, Crettenden, & Townley, 1985); and patients with head/neck pain from patients with back pain and other pain site groups (Toomey, Gover, & Jones, 1984).

A number of moderating variables seem to influence how the IBQ performs. For example, Pilowsky and Spence (1976) found that disease conviction was associated with somatic symptomatology in gynecological patients with pain, but not in those without such pain. More recently, Pilowsky et al. (1987) found that correlations between certain IBQ scales and frequency of physician contacts were moderated by patient gender.

## Critique

Researchers and clinicians considering using the IBQ should carefully consider several points. First of all, the IBQ appears to behave differently for different populations; factor structures and estimates of concurrent validity seem unstable, so that relationships found in previous studies may not generalize beyond the specific groups studied. This is probably less a reflection of the IBQ's quality or stability than of the complex nature of illness behavior reactions to different types of pain experiences (Gordon & Hitchcock, 1983). The implication here is not that the IBQ is ill suited for such purposes, but that clinicians and students of illness behavior should be sensitive to the distinct characteristics of studied populations whenever using such measures.

Secondly, the original emphasis of the IBQ—to distinguish hypochondriacal from nonhypochondriacal patients—must be broadened in the face of its potential use in other areas. Analysts of the IBQ tend to agree that it is no less naive to use the IBQ to predict abnormal illness behavior than it is to use patient self-report to predict objective illness (Zonderman et al., 1985). Pilowsky and Spence probably would not dispute this point; however, the inclusion of discriminant function formulas and cut points in the technical manual provides occasion for users to stray from the important caution.

Third, it is this reviewer's opinion that the IBQ's real promise lies less in its use as a predictor or diagnostic measure of hypochondriasis (though there is evidence to support this use) than in its ability to articulate or identify those facets of the illness experience that are particularly prominent for different subpopulations of pain patients. Authors of the IBQ would do well to stress its wider application as a means of pinpointing maladaptive responses in "really sick" individuals. The question the IBQ is best suited to answer might not be "Is this patient really sick?" but rather "In what ways is this patient's reaction to his illness more or less adaptive?" Such use is clearly consistent with the purpose of the IBQ; several studies have taken steps in such a direction (Bassett & Pilowsky, 1985; Horgan, Davies, Hunt, Westlake, & Mullerworth, 1984; McFarlane & Brooks, 1988; Pilowsky & Barrow, 1990).

Finally, several weaknesses invite further research and revision. One such weakness concerns the considerable overlap among scales. Although this also may be more a function of the nature of illness perception than of the test itself, perhaps steps can be taken to minimize or at least to evaluate the strength of each scale in the face of such overlap. Critics have suggested that certain scales (notably, the Psychological vs. Somatic Perception of Illness and Disease Conviction scales) contain inappropriate items (Main & Waddell, 1987; Wichmann et al., 1990). Alternative multivariate analyses—for example, a theory-driven confirmatory factor analysis—could be used to evaluate the IBQ's factorial purity. It may be, as several studies have suggested, that illness behavior can be better represented by fewer than seven dimensions.

With regard to concurrent validity, a full-scale effort to determine the relationship between IBQ scales and other measures of illness behavior remains to be done. Other related scales include the Illness Attitude Scales (Kellner, 1983), the Hopkins Symptom Checklist (Derogatis, Lipman, Rickels, Uhlenhuth, & Covi,

1974), the General Health Questionnaire (Goldberg, 1979), and the Brief Symptoms Inventory (Derogatis, 1975). These instruments contain very similar types of scales; an assessment of concurrent validity and an evaluation of the comparative quality of these scales seems called for. One problem common to most of these measures seems to be their intent to measure as many different facets of illness behavior with as few items per scale as possible.

In summary, the IBQ's wide use as a measure of illness behavior seems justified, and it shows promise as a useful instrument. However, users should be cautious/ aware of the uneven quality of the scales used, and the authors should be encouraged to revise their scale in a manner that would (a) strengthen the internal consistency of the scales, (b) evaluate the factorial purity of the scales, and (c) emphasize uses other than the identification of hypochondriasis. Finally, although research to date generally points to the IBQ's promising quality, further studies addressing some of the fuzzy points mentioned above could strengthen it considerably.

## References

This list includes text citations and suggested additional reading.


Bassett, D.L., & Pilowsky, I. (1985). A study of brief psychotherapy for chronic pain. *Journal of Psychosomatic Research, 29,* 259–264.

Chapman, C.R., Sola, A.E., & Bonica, J.J. (1979). Illness behavior and depression compared in pain center and private practice patients. *Pain, 6,* 1–7.

Clayer, J.R., Bookless, C., & Ross, M.W. (1984). Neurosis and conscious symptom exaggeration: Its differentiation by the Illness Behaviour Questionaire. *Journal of Psychosomatic Research, 28,* 237–241.

Derogatis, L.R. (1975). *Brief Symptom Inventory.* Baltimore, MD: Psychometric Research.

Derogatis, L.R., Lipman, R.S., Rickels, K., Uhlenhuth, E.H., & Covi, L. (1974). The Hopkins Symptom Checklist (HSCL): A self-report symptom inventory. *Behavioral Science, 19,* 1–15.

Goldberg, D.P. (1979). *Manual of the General Health Questionnaire.* Windsor, England: NFER-Nelson.

Gordon, A., & Hitchcock, W.R. (1983). Illness behavior and personality in intractable facial pain syndromes. *Pain, 17,* 267–276.

Grassi, L., Rosti, G., Albierti, G., & Marangolo, M. (1989). Depression and abnormal illness behavior in cancer patients. *General Hospital Psychiatry, 11*(6), 404–411.

Harkins, S.W., Price, D.D., & Braith, J. (1989). Effects of extraversion and neuroticism on experimental pain, clinical pain, and illness behavior. *Pain, 36*(2), 209–218.

Horgan, D., Davies, B., Hunt, D., Westlake, G., & Mullerworth, M. (1984). Psychiatric aspects of coronary artery surgery: A prospective study. *Medical Journal of Australia, 141,* 587–590.

Joyce, P.R., Bushnell, J.A., Walshe, J.W., & Morton, J.B. (1986). Abnormal illness behaviour and anxiety in acute non-organic abdominal pain. *British Journal of Psychiatry, 149,* 57–62.

Kellner, R. (1983). *Abridged manual of the Illness Attitude Scales (IAS).* Albuquerque: University of New Mexico.

Main, C.J., & Waddell, G. (1987). Psychometric construction and validity of the Pilowsky Illness Behaviour Questionnaire in British patients with chronic low back pain. *Pain, 28*(1), 13–25.

McFarlane, A.C., & Brooks, P.M. (1988). Determinants of disability in rheumatoid arthritis. *British Journal of Rheumatology, 27,* 7–14.

McFarlane, A.C., Kalucy, R.S., & Brooks, P.M. (1987). Psychological predictors of disease course in rheumatoid arthritis. *Psychosomatic Research, 31,* 757–764.

Pilowsky, I. (1967). Dimensions of hypochondriasis. *British Journal of Psychiatry, 113,* 89–93.

Pilowsky, I. (1978). A general classification of abnormal illness behaviours. *British Journal of Medical Psychology, 51,* 131–137.

Pilowsky, I., & Barrow, C.G. (1990). A controlled study of psychotherapy and amitriptyline used individually and in combination in the treatment of chronic intractable, "psychogenic" pain. *Pain, 40,* 3–19.

Pilowsky, I., Bassett, D., Barrett, R., Petrovic, I., & Minniti, R. (1983). The Illness Behavior Assessment Schedule: Reliability and validity. *International Journal of Psychiatric Medicine, 13,* 11–28.

Pilowsky, I., Crettenden, I., & Townly, M. (1985). Sleep disturbance in pain clinic patients. *Pain, 23,* 27–33.

Pilowsky, I., Murrell, T.G.C., & Gordon, A. (1979). The development of a screening method for abnormal illness behaviour. *Journal of Psychosomatic Research, 23,* 203–207.

Pilowsky, I., Smith, Q.P., & Katsikitis, M. (1987). Illness behaviour and general practice utilisation: A prospective study. *Journal of Psychosomatic Resarch, 31*(2), 177–183.

Pilowsky, I., & Spence, N. (1976). Pain and illness behavior: A comparative study. *Journal of Psychosomatic Research, 20,* 131–134.

Pilowsky, I., & Spence, N. (1983). *Manual for the Illness Behaviour Questionnaire (IBQ)* (2nd ed.). Adelaide, Australia: University of Adelaide, Department of Psychiatry.

Pilowsky, I., & Spence, N. (1988). A critique of Main and Waddell (1987). *Pain, 32*(1), 127–130.

Pilowsky, I., Spence, N., Cob, J., & Katsikitis, M. (1984). The Illness Behaviour Questionnaire as an aid to clinical assessment. *General Hospital Psychiatry, 6*(2), 123–130.

Speculand, B., Goss, A.N., Spence, N.D., & Pilowsky, I. (1981). Intractable facial pain and illness behavior. *Pain, 11,* 213–219.

Toomey, T.C., Gover, V.F., & Jones, B.N. (1984). Site of pain: Relationship to measures of pain description, behavior and personality. *Pain, 19*(4), 389–397.

Toshima, M.T., & Kaplan, R.M. (1989). Review of the Illness Behaviour Questionnaire. In J.C. Conoley & J.J. Kramer (Eds.), *The tenth mental measurements yearbook* (pp. 365–367). Lincoln, NE: Buros Institute of Mental Measurements.

Waddell, G., Pilowsky, I., & Bond, M.R. (1989). Clinical assessment and interpretation of abnormal illness behaviour in low back pain. *Pain, 39,* 41–53.

Wichmann, E., Nilges, P., Gerbershagen, H.U., Gamber, J., & Scheifling, I. (1990). The Illness Behavior Questionnaire, psychometric properties and validity of a German version. *Pain, 5*(suppl.), 336.

Williams, R.C. (1988). Toward a set of reliable and valid measures for chronic pain assessment and outcome research. *Pain, 35,* 239–251.

Zonderman, A.B., Heft, M.W., & Costa, P.T., Jr. (1985). Does the Illness Behaviour Questionnaire measure abnormal illness behavior? *Health Psychology, 4*(5), 425–436.

**Robert J. Drummond, Ed.D.**
*Program Director, Counselor Education, University of North Florida, Jacksonville, Florida.*

# THE INSTRUCTIONAL ENVIRONMENT SCALE

*James E. Ysseldyke and Sandra L. Christenson. Austin, Texas: PRO-ED, Inc.*

## Introduction

The Instructional Environment Scale (TIES) is a systematic assessment system designed to gather information and make judgments about the effective instructional environment for an individual student. The system provides forms that help guide supervisors, peer teachers, consultants, researchers, or principals gather data through the observation of the student in a learning context, by interviewing both the teacher of the student and the student being observed. An Instructional Rating Form is completed by the observer or consultant after collecting these data, and a qualitative rating is made by the observer on 12 components of the instructional environment. The observer is then asked to identify intervention needs and actions based on the three data sources.

The major purpose of using the TIES is to describe the extent to which a learner's academic or behavior problems are a function of factors in the instructional environment. The system helps to facilitate the identification of appropriate instructional interventions for the learner.

The TIES authors, who have published consistently and extensively in the field of exceptional education, reviewed the literature on positive academic outcomes and the factors that contribute to these outcomes. The factors that were repeatedly mentioned in the literature as important for improving academic progress were thus identified, and the authors focused on aspects of the environment that could be easily observed. The factors selected also required empirical documentation and a basis in theory to be included in the list. Items were developed, tried out, and edited, and pilot studies conducted. The original pool of items was reduced from 200 to 40. The latter then were categorized into 12 components by identifying the ones that were most representative of the complex nature of the classroom.

Different formats of a rating scale were piloted, including 5- and 7-point Likert-type scales. A qualitative 4-point rating scale using "very much like," "somewhat like," "not much like," and "not at all like" was finally selected. Further revisions were made as a result of the pilot studies.

There are two forms used in the TIES, a Data Record Form and an Instructional Rating Form. The Data Record Form has three sections: Teacher Interview, Examiner Observation, and Student Interview. The first page, the Teacher Interview, consists of seven structured questions, with guidelines in some for probing for specific information. The Student Interview, the last page, is comprised of six general areas, with two to five questions under each. The middle two pages are provided for the examiner to write observations. There are 10 boxes for recording observations; 8 are square and 2 are rectangular and have a larger area than the others.

The second form, an Instructional Rating Form, calls for the observer to describe the instructional setting, the length of time of the observation, the instructional grouping used by the teacher, and the kind of tasks occurring in the classroom. The observer also is asked to describe any atypical circumstances that might have happened during the observation. The remaining three pages contain the rating scale of the 12 dimensions monitored by the observational schedule. Each item provides clarification of the construct being rated. The dimensions are rated on the 4-point scale previously described.

Descriptions of the 12 dimensions follow:

1. *Instructional Presentation,* which includes lesson development, clarity of directions, and checking for student understanding.

2. *Classroom Environment,* which includes classroom management, productive use of time, and class climate.

3. *Teacher Expectations,* which relates to the type of expectations the teacher has for the amount and accuracy of the work the student does.

4. *Cognitive Emphasis,* which focuses on the thinking skills used or required.

5. *Motivational Strategies,* which centers on what strategies the teacher used to heighten student interest and effort.

6. *Relevant Practice,* which includes the type of practice opportunities, task relevance, and instructional materials used.

7. *Academic Engage Time,* which covers student involvement and maintenance of student engagement.

8. *Informed Feedback,* which includes dimensions of feedback and the corrective procedures used.

9. *Adaptive Instruction,* which relates to the degree to which the teacher modifies the curriculum to meet student needs.

10. *Progress Evaluation,* which relates to how the teacher monitors the progress of the student and uses the information to plan future instruction.

11. *Instructional Planning,* which includes the dimensions of instructional diagnosis and instructional prescription used.

12. *Student Understanding,* which covers how the student demonstrates that he or she has an understanding of what is done in the classroom.

## Practical Applications/Uses

The test authors suggest that the TIES can be used for two major purposes. The first is to describe systematically the extent to which a learner's academic behavior problems are a function of factors in the instructional environment. The second is to help identify what might be the appropriate starting point for instructional interventions geared to the learner being observed (Ysseldyke & Christenson, 1987b, p. 3). The authors also suggest other uses, such as guiding program development for students referred to special education classes and for schools that have adopted the preferral intervention process. The scale could be used as a tool in the consultation process to help the consultant pinpoint specific areas in which the teacher needs help. This measure also could help in IEP development, teacher training, and research on teaching and the classroom environment.

The authors point out that the TIES should not be used as an instrument to evaluate teachers. It is a structured observation system that can be used with teachers who feel they would like some help in designing teaching strategies to help a problem learner. As the scale focuses on the individual learner and not on the class as a whole, the procedure would be appropriate for normal students with learning problems as well as for students with exceptionalities.

Anyone using the TIES needs to become familiar with the dimensions it covers by carefully reading the manual. The use of this scale requires six steps: conducting the classroom observation, interviewing the student, interviewing the student's teacher, deciding if additional data are needed, completing the instructional rating form and summary profile sheet, and providing feedback to the teacher and student.

It is suggested that the observer note both the lesson presentation and practice in one of the basic skill areas (e.g., mathematics, writing, language) and especially in the area in which the learner is having problems. The consultant needs to observe the teacher presenting, explaining, and demonstrating a lesson, as well as the student doing independent seatwork. More than one observation might be necessary. The recording form can be used to summarize the observations.

To get the best results in interviewing, the user must establish rapport with the teacher and student. The interviewer is cautioned to get enough information but not to lead the teacher into saying things that he or she feels the consultant wants to hear. In talking with students, the interviewer needs to consider the student's level of cognitive development and then modify or simplify the language of the questions accordingly.

The TIES is not an instrument that can be quickly completed; it demands observation time, interview time, analysis time, and feedback time. The process could take 3 to 4 hours at the minimum, and even longer when first used.

In scoring the scale, the observer has to integrate information from observations and interviews and qualitatively rate the 12 dimensions. The manual includes case materials to help users understand the rating process and how to complete the diagnostic profile. The criteria used in assigning the ratings are described in detail.

A sample case is presented to offer illustrative examples of how data are to be interpreted. The authors point out that interpreting this scale is not difficult, but the process demands sensitivity and good consultative skills on the part of the observer.

### Technical Aspects

The TIES is not a norm-referenced test but a structured observation and interview procedure. The scale has content validity, as its factors have both theoretical and research bases. Interrater reliability is provided for the 12 components, with coefficients ranging from a low of .83 on Cognitive Emphasis and Motivational Strategies to a high of .96 on Academic Engage Time, Informed Feedback, and Student Understanding. The median coefficient was .94.

The authors (Ysseldyke & Christenson, 1987a; Christenson & Ysseldyke, 1989) report on the need for looking at the instructional environment. They present an argument for the content validity of the scale and provide evidence from research and theory that the 12 components are important predictors of student achievement (Ysseldyke & Christenson, 1987b). In addition, a list of references is given for each component.

## Critique

The Instructional Environment Scale is a structured observation and interview schedule designed to be used to gather data on the nature of instruction for an individual student. The instrument is based on current theory and research on effective teaching. The manual provides a wealth of material to illustrate the use and interpretation of the instrument.

The authors should consider developing a videotape of sample observations and interviews, walking through the data recording, analysis, interpretation, and feedback stages. One of the main drawbacks here is the time it takes to complete the TIES process. In addition, the observer needs an extensive background in supervision, interpersonal, and consultative skills for the system to be effectively implemented. The clinical supervision models used by many trained supervisors probably would address the problems with less time and effort, focusing just on the problem area or areas rather than on all of the 12 components.

This reviewer is not certain that the instructional environment can be isolated from other components of the learning and teaching process. Diagnostic test information, past achievement, current achievement, scholastic aptitude, cognitive abilities, student learning style, and the like all need to be considered as well in the analysis and prescriptive process.

## References

Christenson, S.L., & Ysselydyke, J.E. (1989). Assessing student performance: An important change is needed. *Journal of School Psychology, 27*(4), 409–425.

Ysseldyke, J.E., & Christenson, S.L. (1987a). Evaluating students' instructional environments. *Remedial and Special Education, 8*(3), 17–24.

Ysseldyke, J.E., & Christenson, S.L. (1987b). *The Instructional Environment Scale.* Austin, TX: PRO-ED.

**Linda Leal, Ph.D.**
*Associate Professor of Psychology, Eastern Illinois University, Charleston, Illinois.*

# INVENTORY FOR CLIENT AND AGENCY PLANNING

*Robert H. Bruininks, Bradley K. Hill, Richard F. Weatherman, and Richard W. Woodcock. Allen, Texas: DLM Teaching Resources.*

## Introduction

The Inventory for Client and Agency Planning (ICAP; Bruininks, Hill, Weatherman, & Woodcock, 1986) is a self-administered instrument that was developed to systematically measure the current and potential levels of functioning of clients in a variety of educational, public, private, and human service settings. It covers the age range from infancy to adulthood (age 40 years and older) and can be used with handicapped as well as nonhandicapped populations. The ICAP identifies the diagnostic status and functional limitations of clients, measures both adaptive behavior skills and problem behaviors, and describes current status and anticipated needs for placement, support services, and activities. Administering and scoring the ICAP requires minimal training in test administration.

The authors of the ICAP have extensive backgrounds in both test development and statistics as well as a variety of experiences with special populations. Robert H. Bruininks has a Ph.D. in special education from George Peabody College of Vanderbilt University. He has served as a director or a consultant for numerous agencies and organizations that service the developmentally disabled. Bradley K. Hill has a doctorate from the University of Minnesota and also has experience working with the developmentally disabled. He has published articles on adaptive behavior and on residential services for retarded people. Richard F. Weatherman has an Ed.D. in special education from Michigan State University. He has been a special education teacher and consultant and was the principal investigator for the Minnesota Severely Handicapped Delivery Systems Project. Richard W. Woodcock received an Ed.D. in psychoeducation and statistics from the University of Oregon and was a postdoctoral fellow in neuropsychology at Tufts University School of Medicine. He has built a distinguished career in test construction and validation. Two of his publications include the Woodcock Reading Mastery Tests (Woodcock, 1973) and the Woodcock-Johnson Psycho-Educational Battery (Woodcock & Johnson, 1977). Additionally, all four authors of the ICAP also authored the Scales of Independent Behavior (SIB; Bruininks, Woodcock, Weatherman, & Hill, 1984).

The ICAP is statistically related to the SIB and to the Woodcock-Johnson Psycho-Educational Battery. Items measuring adaptive behavior on the ICAP were selected from the 14 subscales of the SIB based on their appropriateness and Rasch (Wright & Stone, 1979) difficulty values (*w* scores equivalent to derived Rasch scores). Through pilot testing and item analysis, a total of 77 items from the SIB were selected for inclusion in the four ICAP adaptive behavior domains. Items selected were separated from one another by approximately 8 *w*-scale points and were representative of the 14 SIB subscales. Items measuring problem behaviors on the ICAP are identical to those on the SIB.

The ICAP examiner's manual presents detailed information about the norming sample and norming procedures. The norming sample for both the adaptive behavior domains and problem behaviors sections of the ICAP are based on the same national sample as the SIB. ICAP scores were equated to SIB scores using regression procedures. ICAP norms, therefore, are directly comparable to the norms for the SIB. Normative data were collected from May 1982 to June 1983 from 1,764 subjects (ranging in age from 3 months to 44 years) in 40 communities throughout the United States. A stratified, representative sample based on 1980 U.S. Census data were selected based on sex, race, Hispanic origin, occupational status, occupational level, geographic region, and type of community using a three-stage sampling procedure. First communities were sampled; schools within the communities (for school-age subjects) were sampled next; and finally, subjects were randomly sampled from within the schools. Infants and preschool children in the standardization sample were contacted through newspaper birth announcements, social service agencies, day-care centers, and preschools. How adult subjects were procured is not directly addressed in the manual. A weighting procedure was used to correct for over- and underrepresentation in each cell of the sampling design. This was accomplished by assigning each subject a weight based on her or his required contribution to the database. Handicapped individuals were not included in the norming sample unless they were students in regular education programs. No information about how frequently this occurred is provided. The authors do report statistical results indicating that neither demographic factors nor sex influenced adaptive behavior scores for the sample as a whole.

The areas of the ICAP that yield descriptive information on clients' demographic and physical characteristics, diagnostic status, functional limitations, social support, and service needs were developed through a literature review on the functional assessments of clients and by consultation with relevant professionals. Items were selected based on their reliability, clarity, and usefulness as determined through field testing. Few specific details of this process, other than reliability and validity information, are provided in the manual.

The ICAP evaluates the functioning of clients ranging in age from infancy through adulthood with a 16-page self-administered response booklet. The respondent completing the response booklet should be someone who has known the client for at least 3 months and who sees the client daily. The cover page of the response booklet provides space for recording client and respondent identification information. The cover page also includes a profile for recording a summary of the client's adaptive behavior skills. Sections A through J of the response booklet collect information about the client's characteristics and abilities.

Sections A through C gather descriptive information about a client's status through a multiple-choice format. Section A, Descriptive Information, allows the respondent to record information about the client's sex, height, weight, race, Hispanic origin, primary language understood, primary means of expression, marital status, and legal status. Section B, Diagnostic Status, gathers information about the client's primary diagnosis as well as any additional diagnoses. Functional Limitations and Needed Assistance comprise Section C, which measures the client's level of mental retardation, visual and hearing abilities, frequency of seizures, health limitations, required care by nurse or physician, current medications, and mobility.

Section D measures adaptive behavior, divided into four broad domains: Motor Skills (18 tasks), Social and Communication Skills (19 tasks), Personal Living Skills (21 tasks), and Community Living Skills (19 tasks). Each task presented is scored on a 4-point rating scale (0 = never/rarely performs the task; 1 = does the task but not well; 2 = does the task fairly well; 3 = does the task very well without being asked).

Problem behaviors that limit personal and community adjustment are measured by Section E through eight broad categories: Hurtful to Self, Hurtful to Others, Destructive to Property, Disruptive Behavior, Unusual or Repetitive Habits, Socially Offensive Behavior, Withdrawal or Inattentive Behavior, and Uncooperative Behavior. Each category includes a definition as well as numerous examples of the behavior it measures. The respondent indicates whether or not the client displays this behavior by providing a description of the client's primary problem within this category. Both frequency and severity of this behavior is measured in a multiple-choice format. The respondent is also asked, in the same format, how people usually respond when the client exhibits problem behaviors.

Sections F through I provide descriptive information concerning placement and service use and needs through a checklist format. Section F, Residential Placement, solicits information on the client's current residence and any projected recommended changes that may be made within the next two years. Section G, Daytime Program, provides a format similar to Section F and assesses the client's current formal daytime activity as well as any recommended changes within the next two years. Support Services, Section H, measures those support services presently being used by the client as well as those not used currently but where an evaluation is needed. Section I, Social and Leisure Activities, allows the examiner to check the social and leisure activities the client has engaged in within the last month as well as factors that limit social activities.

Section J, General Information and Recommendations, provides space to record test scores from other sources and program decisions based on ICAP results, as well as additional, relevant information about the client. There is also space to record both program and service goals.

**Practical Applications/Uses**

The ICAP provides information about an individual client's abilities, particular problems, and present and future needs. It measures adaptive and problem behaviors and describes diagnostic status, functional limitations, and service needs. This information is obtained when an informant who is familiar with the client completes the ICAP self-administered response booklet. Professionals in educational and residential settings as well as other human service settings will find the information provided by the ICAP useful. Teachers, counselors, day program staff, social workers, psychologists, and family members will find the ICAP helpful in understanding a particular client's strengths and weaknesses. Although the ICAP is designed to facilitate the screening of clients in order to determine eligibility for specific services, it can also be used to plan programming. By periodically readministering the ICAP, the success of planned programming for an individual client can be determined. Gathering ICAP data from a group of clients allows the success of a specific program or programs to be evaluated, using pre- and post-program ICAP scores. The ICAP can be used in other research situations as well. It has applications for longitudinal research because of its wide age range (birth to adulthood), and ICAP information could also be used to match subjects in a research design.

The ICAP was developed to aid in evaluating, screening, and planning services for handicapped, disabled, and elderly individuals with a wide range of ability levels. Clients whose functioning ranges from profoundly retarded to nonhandicapped can be assessed. The ICAP is designed to help in determining the levels and types of services that these clients need. As the manual points out, however, whenever an in-depth assessment of certain abilities is needed, a more in-depth measure of those abilities may be necessary for planning purposes. For instance, a detailed measure of a particular client may be required in order to plan specific training activities in adaptive behavior. In this case, a more in-depth measure of adaptive behavior skills (i.e., the SIB) would be beneficial.

An extensive background in test administration is not needed to administer and score the ICAP, nor is any specific training. However, the respondent completing the booklet should read and study the instructions for administering and scoring the ICAP that are presented in the manual. The manual states that an experienced respondent will be able to complete the ICAP in 20 minutes.

Instructions for administering and scoring the ICAP are clearly presented in the manual. Chapter 2 offers step-by-step instructions for completing the response booklet in an easy-to-read fashion. The response booklet itself provides succinct directions for completing each section. Appendix D also outlines in five pages how to complete the ICAP response booklet.

The manual's chapter 3 provides the directions for scoring and interpreting ICAP responses. Most of this chapter is devoted to instructions for scoring Section D, Adaptive Behavior, and Section E, Problem Behavior. The manual provides clearly presented, detailed information about scoring these sections. The response booklet also provides prompts for scoring so that once scoring is learned, frequent references to the manual are unnecessary. A computer package for scoring the ICAP is also available from the publisher.

Chapter 3 begins by explaining how to calculate a client's chronological age, how to score individual items, and how to compute raw scores. After these computations have been made, the Training Implications Profile that is on the front cover of the response booklet can be completed for the four adaptive behavior domains. This presents a graphic representation of adaptive functioning when the client's raw scores are plotted on an age scale. The response booklet also provides a Summary of Scores worksheet for producing a number of derived scores for each of the four adaptive behavior domains as well as for calculating a score for the client's overall adaptive functioning (called Broad Independence). The examiner must refer to seven tables and carry out some mathematical calculations in order to determine a client's domain scores, standard error of measurement, age score, instructional range, average domain score, and confidence band. For all domains, a value of 500 represents a performance level approximately equal to that of a nonhandicapped child who is 10 years, 4 months old at the fifth-grade level. The range of domain scores extends from a low of about 270 to a high of 569 and is based on special *w*-score units.

Besides percentile ranks and standard scores, normal curve equivalents and relative performance indexes can also be determined for each adaptive behavior domain. Normal curve equivalent is a standard score with a mean of 50 and a standard deviation of 21.06 that has been used to evaluate performance in some federally financed programs. Relative performance indexes are used to indicate the percentage of independence predicted for a given client on a set of tasks that a reference group of individuals at the same chronological age level can perform with 90% independence. Relative performance indexes are based on the difference between a client's domain score and the average domain score for the reference group. For example, a relative performance index of 75/90 means that skills performed by individuals in a comparison group with 90% independence would probably be performed with 75% independence by the client.

The maladaptive behavior indexes can be calculated after the ratings (raw scores) for frequency and severity of problem behaviors are completed in Section E of the response booklet. Step-by-step instructions on the Maladaptive Behavior Worksheet in the response booklet are provided for calculating the maladaptive behavior indexes. The indexes have a mean of 0 for normal clients of the same age; index scores range from +5 to -70. Negative scores indicate problem behavior toward the maladaptive end of the scale. Nonhandicapped groups have a standard deviation of about 8; the typical standard deviation for various clinical samples is 10 points. After the maladaptive indexes are calculated on the Maladaptive Behavior Worksheet, the scores can be plotted graphically on the Maladaptive Behavior Indexes Profile on the back cover of the response booklet.

An ICAP Service Level score can be calculated after the adaptive behavior raw scores are summed and the maladaptive behavior indexes are computed. This Service Level score is a weighted combination of adaptive and maladaptive behavior. The total adaptive behavior raw score is weighted 70%, and the General Maladaptive Index score is weighted 30%. ICAP Service Level scores can range from 0 to 100; higher scores indicate increased independence and a decreased need for services. The back cover of the response booklet provides instructions for graphically calculating and representing the ICAP Service Level Profile.

Although several tables and numerous calculations must be undertaken to calculate a client's adaptive functioning and maladaptive behavior indexes, the manual presents clear instructions as well as numerous examples and practice profiles. The numerous calculations and tables to consult do, however, increase the likelihood of an error being made while scoring the ICAP. When scoring the ICAP by been made. Using the computer-scoring package would eliminate the need for recalculations.

hand, examiners should always check their work to be sure no errors have The manual provides several case study examples that include interpretations of ICAP results. As stated in the manual, the ICAP alone is not intended to replace the personal and professional judgments of family and interdisciplinary team members. The ICAP does provide a format for assessing client progress and for reporting and planning purposes. Even though formal training in test administration is not necessary for administering and scoring the ICAP, understanding and interpreting the scores require at least basic knowledge of standardized testing.

**Technical Aspects**

One of the most impressive aspects of the ICAP manual is the amount of reliability and validity information it presents. Chapter 5 is devoted to reliability. This chapter begins by defining standard error of measurement and *w* scores and explaining how both of these relate to reliability. Reasons why reliability coefficients may be low or high is also discussed. This is followed by reports of studies that investigated the internal consistency, test-retest, and interrater reliabilities of ICAP scores.

A total of 1,510 subjects from the technical research sample were included in a study of internal consistency. Internal consistency reliability statistics for all adaptive behavior domains were calculated using the split-half (odd and even) procedure and corrected by the Spearman-Brown formula. The median Broad Independence (total adaptive behavior) score reliability was .86 for three broad age groups (early childhood, childhood, and adolescent/adulthood). For the Motor Skills domain, the median internal consistency reliability was .58; for Social and Communication Skills, it was .70; Personal Living Skills was .76; and Community Living Skills was .69. Split-half reliabilities for handicapped samples also were computed and found to be considerably higher than those found with the nonhandicapped samples described above. Included in the handicapped sample were retarded children, adolescents, and adults; learning disabled children and adolescents; and behavior disordered adolescents. Split-half reliabilities corrected for length by the Spearman-Brown formula for the handicapped samples ranged from .68 to .98. The median coefficient for Broad Independence for all samples was .97.

Test-retest reliability data were collected from two elementary school samples of nonhandicapped subjects. The same respondent completed two ICAP booklets on the same child within a 4-week period. Test-retest reliabilities for the adaptive behavior domains and Broad Independence scores ranged from .52 to .96. Even though these data were gathered from a population with low rates of problem behaviors, test-retest correlations for the four maladaptive behavior indexes ranged overall from .75 to .86. The test-retest reliabilities for the ICAP Service Level score were in the high .80s and .90s.

Test-retest reliabilities from a sample of 30 mentally retarded adolescent and young adult subjects also were calculated after retesting within a 1- to 2-week period. The adaptive behavior domain and Broad Independence coefficients were all in the .90s. For the maladaptive behavior indexes these coefficients ranged from .73 to .90. The ICAP Service Level score test-retest correlation was .90 for this sample. Results from two other samples of mentally retarded subjects yielded similar findings. Test-retest reliabilities also were assessed for the four maladaptive behavior indexes with two samples of school-age subjects who had been placed in special education programs for conduct and behavior disorders. The two tests were administered 7 to 10 days apart. Reliability coefficients ranged from .74 to .88.

Although across all samples the test-retest reliability coefficients reported in the manual indicate fairly good stability for the adaptive behavior domains and maladaptive behavior indexes, two concerns should be kept in mind when interpreting these data. First, no test-retest reliability data are presented for a sample of nonhandicapped adults. The second concern questions what test-retest reliability measures over a short time interval. Is it measuring client stability or respondent memory? It is possible that over a 1- to 2-week period, respondents remembered how they responded to the first ICAP administration and these memories influenced their second set of responses.

The ICAP manual also presents data on interrater reliability. Two studies measured interrater reliability for two different samples of mentally retarded adults. In one study, direct-care personnel in licensed residential care facilities served as independent raters. Interrater reliability coefficients for the adaptive behavior domains ranged from .86 to .94, with a median coefficient of .92. In the second study, direct service personnel from two different environments (residential and day program) served as respondents for a sample of mentally retarded adults. Interrater reliabilities ranged from .72 to .83, with a median coefficient of .81. Another interrater reliability study was conducted with teachers and teachers' aides working with moderately and severely retarded students. The teachers and aides self-administered the Problem Behavior scale during the same week. Correlations between respondents ranged from .69 for the Asocial Maladaptive Index to .81 for the Internalized Maladaptive Index, with a median interrater reliability of .77 for the entire maladaptive behavior scale. The manual does not provide interrater reliability information for a nonhandicapped sample.

Reliability information for descriptive items (e.g., age, primary diagnosis, mobility) on the ICAP is also provided in chapter 5. One study measured agreement between two raters within a residential facility for mentally retarded clients. The percentage agreements ranged from 73% to 100%. Another study measured agreement between one staff member in a residential facility and another staff member in a daytime placement program that served the same clients. Response agreements were also high for this sample, ranging from 67% to 100%.

Chapter 6 of the ICAP manual presents validity information that documents the appropriateness of the ICAP for various uses and decision-making purposes. Construct, criterion-related, and content validity studies are described in detail. The validity of the ICAP Service Level score is also discussed with illustrative case vignettes.

Construct validity describes the extent to which test scores relate to some theoretical construct. The ICAP manual presents a series of studies that indicate that the ICAP has good construct validity. These studies investigated developmental, content, and handicapping constructs.

Because adaptive behavior skills increase with age, they have developmental characteristics. Pearson product-moment correlations between chronological age for three broad age groups (early childhood, childhood, and adolescent/adult) and

ICAP adaptive behavior scores for the technical sample ($N$ = 1,510) were curvilinear. A second-degree regression provided the best fit for the early childhood, childhood, and adolescent/adult ranges, and a fourth-degree regression provided the best fit for the sample as a whole. For the maladaptive behavior indexes, a third-degree regression provided the best fit. These results indicate that the ICAP adaptive behavior scores for a nonhandicapped sample are strong developmental measures. The low positive correlations reported for the maladaptive indexes suggest that these indexes are not developmental; they do, however, demonstrate a tendency for maladaptive behavior to decrease with age.

Intercorrelations among the four adaptive behavior domains revealed a moderate degree of overlap in their content. These correlations ranged from .40 to .80. Intercorrelations among the four maladaptive behavior indexes were also moderate. These results provide further evidence of the construct validity of the ICAP.

Several studies were conducted to compare the adaptive and problem behavior scores of handicapped subjects with normal peers to further assess construct validity. Subjects were matched whenever possible on age, sex, and community residence. The handicapped groups sampled included mildly to severely retarded children and adolescents/adults, learning disabled children and adolescents, hearing impaired children and adolescents, and behavior disordered children and adolescents. The findings indicate that ICAP adaptive behavior scores can differentiate among mildly and severely retarded people and their nonhandicapped peers. Fewer differences in adaptive behavior were found between the learning disabled and behavior disordered samples and their normal peers. Learning disabled and hearing-impaired samples scored within the normal range on the maladaptive behavior indexes. The moderately to severely retarded and behavior disordered samples evidenced significantly greater negative maladaptive behavior scores than did their nonhandicapped comparison groups.

Criterion-related validity is the extent to which scores on a test relate to scores on some criterion measure. Criterion-related validity for the ICAP was demonstrated, in part, by comparing it with scores on the SIB; the Adaptive Behavior Scale, School Edition (ABS-SE; Lambert, 1981); the Woodcock-Johnson Broad Cognitive Ability scores; and the Quay-Peterson Revised Problem Behavior Checklist (Quay & Peterson, 1983). Moderate to high correlations were found between the ICAP adaptive behavior domain scores and scores on these other tests.

Another measure of criterion-related validity presented in the manual was how well the ICAP discriminated school, residential, and day and vocational placements as well as handicapping status for handicapped and nonhandicapped subjects. Multiple discriminant analyses were conducted to accomplish this. Multiple discriminant analysis is a statistical technique used to distinguish between two or more groups by mathematically weighing and linearly combining a collection of discriminating variables in some fashion so that the groups are forced to be as statistically distinct as possible. Using adaptive behavior domain and maladaptive behavior scores as predictor variables, discriminant analysis findings provide evidence that the ICAP can predict classroom placement (regular versus special education), levels of residential placement (public institution, group home, semi-independent/independent settings), levels of day and vocational programs (day center, work center, sheltered workshop, supervised job placement, competitive employment), and ability groupings (moderately retarded, mildly retarded, and nonretarded). As the manual points out, however, these discriminations were not perfect. When using ICAP adaptive and maladaptive behavior scores for diagnoses and placement decisions, other measures and information as well as professional and family opinions should be considered as well.

Content validity refers to the degree to which the content of a test is representative of the domain it intends to cover. Content validity is usually evaluated with logic instead of statistical analyses. The content validity of the ICAP should be the degree to which it includes items that allow for the systematic evaluation of clients' current and potential levels of functioning in a variety of settings. In the manual, the authors present research findings, definitions, models, and theories to justify the content of the adaptive behavior domains and the items on the maladaptive behavior scale. They also note that the content of the ICAP is consistent with the reporting requirements for many state and federal laws (e.g., PL 94–142 and the Developmental Disabilities Act).

The ICAP Service Level score indicates the extent to which a client requires supervision and/or services by considering a weighted combination of the client's adaptive and maladaptive behaviors. Validity of the ICAP Service Level score was determined by examining the extent to which it could differentiate residential placement, level of retardation, and program staff ratings of independence for mentally retarded adults. Results indicate that the ICAP Service Level scores could differentiate among different levels of residential placement (institution, group home, semi-independent, independent) as well as level of retardation (mild, moderate, severe, profound). In general, ICAP Service Level scores increased with milder degrees of mental retardation and with less restrictive residential placements. Higher Service Level scores also correlated (range = .49 to .92) with higher ratings of independence by program staff.

The ICAP manual presents extensive evidence that documents both its reliability and validity. Terms and statistical analyses are described and defined. The use of many graphs and charts helps explain and reinforce the findings that are presented. A technical summary that overviews the development, norming, reliability, and validity of the ICAP is available from the publisher (Bruininks, Hill, Weatherman, & Woodcock, 1990). Anyone who is considering using the ICAP for planning and placement purposes should first review this technical summary.

## Critique

The ICAP provides a standardized format to gather information that can be used to screen and evaluate individuals needing special services. It provides information on client's strengths and weaknesses and as such can help with program planning decisions. The response booklet can be completed in a short amount of time because of its convenient checklist format, and no special training in test administration is required to self-administer the response booklet. The manual is comprehensive and provides sufficient information on the development and norming of the ICAP. Both the reliability and validity of the ICAP are documented. Directions for completing and scoring the response booklet are easy to follow and contain several examples and practice profiles. A computerized scoring package is also available. Overall, the ICAP is an exemplary test instrument.

Despite this favorable evaluation, several issues concerning the ICAP deserve attention. Even though no specialized training is needed to complete the response booklet, special competencies are required for interpreting scores and for decision-making purposes. For instance, standard error of measurement, standard scores, and especially normal curve equivalents and relative performance indexes are concepts that require some background in tests and measurements in order to understand and use the information they provide effectively. Even though the ICAP contains an adaptive and a maladaptive behavior scale, neither of these should be considered in-depth measures of behavior. Assessing an individual client's adaptive or maladaptive functioning should never be based on ICAP scores alone.

Finally, because the ICAP was published in 1986, it is a relatively new test instrument. During a recent library search, no articles relating to the ICAP could be found in refereed research journals. This will no doubt change in the near future. Until such time, however, no information (except from the publisher) is readily available about how successful the ICAP is in real-life planning, placement, and diagnostic situations.

## References

Bruininks, R.H., Hill, B.K., Weatherman, R.F., & Woodcock, R.W. (1986). *Inventory for Client and Agency Planning.* Allen, TX: DLM Teaching Resources.

Bruininks, R.H., Hill, B.K., Weatherman, R.F., & Woodcock, R.W. (1990). *Technical summary of the Inventory for Client and Agency Planning (ICAP).* Allen, TX: DLM Teaching Resources.

Bruininks, R.H., Woodcock, R.W., Weatherman, R.F., & Hill, B.K. (1984). *Scales of Independent Behavior.* Allen, TX: DLM Teaching Resources.

Lambert, N.M. (1981). *AAMD Adaptive Behavior Scale—School Edition.* Monterey, CA: Publishers Test Service.

Quay, H.C., & Peterson, D.R. (1983). *Revised Behavior Problem Checklist.* (Available from the authors, University of Miami, Box 248074, Coral Gables, FL 33124)

Woodcock, R.W. (1973). *Woodcock Reading Mastery Tests.* Circle Pines, MN: American Guidance Service.

Woodcock, R.W., & Johnson, M.B. (1977). *Woodcock-Johnson Psycho-Educational Battery.* Allen, TX: DLM Teaching Resources.

Wright, B.D., & Stone, M.H. (1979). *Best test design.* Chicago: MESA.

**Rick Myer, Ph.D.**
*Assistant Professor, Department of Educational Psychology, Counseling, and Special Education, Northern Illinois University, DeKalb, Illinois.*

**M. Cecil Smith, Ph.D.**
*Assistant Professor, Department of Educational Psychology, Counseling, and Special Education, Northern Illinois University, DeKalb, Illinois.*

# INVENTORY FOR COUNSELING AND DEVELOPMENT

*Norman S. Giddan, F. Reid Creech, and Victor R. Lovell. Minnetonka, Minnesota: National Computer Systems/PAS Division.*

## Introduction

The Inventory for Counseling and Development (ICD; Giddan, Creech, & Lovell, 1988) was developed over a 15-year period to measure characteristics useful in counseling, evaluating, and educating college students. These characteristics include both the intellectual and nonintellectual aspects of a student that help predict success in the college environment. The latter includes the student's academic, personal, and social functioning. The ICD is suitable for use with males and females who are currently attending a university or college.

Norman S. Giddan received a Ph.D. in psychology from Stanford University. He has worked in several university counseling centers and currently is employed at the Student Counseling Center, University of Toledo, Ohio. F. Reid Creech has a Ph.D. in social psychology from the University of North Carolina and a Psy.D. from the California School of Professional Psychology. At present he maintains a private practice in southern California. Victor R. Lovell has a Ph.D. in psychology from Stanford University, and he, too, is currently in independent practice in the southern California area.

As noted, the ICD has a 15-year history of development. The current form represents an analysis of scores from over 6,500 students in universities throughout the continental United States. Form F, the current form, was normed using 660 females and 520 males. The original form was conceived as a way to predict only academic performance. However, perceiving a lack of assessment instruments specifically designed for use with the college populations, the authors expanded the scope of the ICD over six revisions.

Each revision of the ICD used a convergent-discriminant method to refine the instrument. That is, items were tested during each refinement for face and content validity and correlation with its scale. All items in the current form met or exceeded the standards set by this method. The result is that each successive form has improved the power of the instrument to meet its stated objective.

A unique aspect of the ICD's development is that several theoretical perspectives were used as a philosophical base for the items. The theoretical perspectives include psychodynamic-clinical, cognitive-social learning, developmental paradigms, and trait, type, and factor theories. These various viewpoints were blended together to construct individual scales and to help the clinician in their interpretation.

Initially 541 items were generated for possible inclusion in the ICD. These items were developed using constructs thought to mediate academic performance. Examples of the constructs used are intellectual style, goals and values, motivation, and self-concept. Eventually 449 items were included in the ICD. Factor analysis grouped the items into 23 scales, which in turn fall into three categories: (a) Validity, (b) Substantive, and (c) Criterion. The Validity scales are sensitive to response sets such as random responding, faking good or bad, and other atypical patterns of responding. The Substantive scales assess aspects of personality and are divided into five categories, each embodying three scales. The Criterion scales also provide information about personality but add the dimension of the motivational components of an individual's academic behavior. The manual (Giddan et al., 1988, pp. 9–13) describes the scales as follows:

*Validity*

1. *Agreement*—the tendency to answer "true" when items are presented in a true/false format.
2. *Favorable Impression*—the tendency to answer questions in a socially desireable direction.
3. *Infrequent*—the tendency to respond in an atypical manner to test items.

*Substantive*

1. *Personal Discomfort*—personal consistency and individual variations in the areas of distress, discomfort, and perceived anxiety.
   a. *Insecurity*—the degree to which anxiety is present generally as well as in academic settings.
   b. *Alienation*—the degree of alienation and the presence of purposelessness.
   c. *Exam Tension*—the degree of anxiety about school performance in situations such as tests.
2. *External Motivation*—the degree to which external motivations (e.g., career goals, desire for recognition) affect performance.
   a. *Ambition*—the degree to which an individual emphasizes competition, productivity, and success.
   b. *Persistence*—the tendency to begin work and to persevere without interruption until completion.
   c. *Practicality*—the belief that academic performance is followed by extrinsic rewards.
3. *Internal and Social Motivation*—the degree to which learned motivations (internal and social) affect individual performance.
   a. *Sociability*—the importance an individual places on friendship and intimacy.
   b. *Teacher/Student Interaction*—the tendency or desire of an individual to communicate with teachers in or out of the classroom.

c. *Intellectuality*—the satisfaction an individual obtains from intellectual, scientific, or aesthetic pursuits.

4. *Creativity*—the affect of innovation and uniqueness on the potential for performance in academic or artistic endeavors.
   a. *Originality*—the tendency to seek or explore novel approaches to problems, activities, or experiences.
   b. *Adaptability*—the preference for a flexible, open-minded orientation toward both campus and community.
   c. *Orderliness*—the preference for planning and organization in academic and personal aspects of life.
5. *Ideology*—factors relating to an individual's developmental stage.
   a. *Liberal/Conservative*—the preference for a liberal or conservative political orientation.
   b. *Socio-Political Interest*—the interest in involvement with political issues and social change.
   c. *Sexual Beliefs*—the preference for permissive, liberal views on sexuality as opposed to more traditional or conservative views.

*Criterion*

1. *Sex Role Differences*—response tendency to personal, social, and interest items on which men and women differ most.
2. *Academic Performance*—personality and motivational tendencies associated with academic success; represents a summative assessment of Academic Excellence, Academic Capacity, and Academic Motivation scales.
3. *Academic Excellence*—personality and motivational tendencies associated with academic success while emphasizing the component of overachievement.
4. *Academic Capacity*—personality and motivational tendencies associated with academic success while emphasizing the component of ability or capacity.
5. *Academic Motivation*—personality and motivational tendencies associated with academic success, emphasizing motivation rather than ability.

**Practical Applications/Uses**

The ICD is a paper-and-pencil test using a test booklet and answer sheet that present 449 true/false items. Administration is similar to that of most tests of this nature. Examiners should take care to minimize factors that might distract the examinee (e.g., poor lighting, noise level, room temperature, etc.). As cheating is not an issue, no special seating arrangement is suggested except to assure adequate space for each examinee. The ICD can be administered to individuals or groups using the same instructions. Unless special instructions are required, the examiner should answer questions only regarding procedures. The manual states that examiners should not answer questions about the meaning, purpose, or content of any test item (Giddan et al., 1988). General instructions are included in the test booklet. There is no time limit for this test, yet most examinees can expect to complete the items in 50 to 60 minutes.

Users can score the ICD by computer or by hand; the manual contains clear instructions for doing so. Tables for converting raw scores to T-scores and percentile equivalents appear in the appendices of the manual. These tables are clearly labeled and generally easy to understand. Should hand scoring be used, the manual cautions examiners to confirm that they use the correct templates for each scale. Special care should be taken for scoring the criterion scales because there are male and female scoring templates. Caution should be exercised when converting raw scores as male and female norms are used for each scale. When using the computer-scoring services, a computer interpretation is included with the profile sheet that reports raw scores, T-scores, percentile equivalents, and the number of omitted and double-marked items. Having a variety of scoring templates that may result in errors is of concern. Computer scoring may be best and most convenient, although hand scoring is less costly. Work is currently being completed on the development of a computer-generated narrative to accompany computer-produced profiles (N. S. Giddan, personal communication, July 17, 1990).

The overall quality of the ICD manual is good. The writing style is concise and easily comprehended. However, at times readers should be aware that the authors describe the ICD in broad, general terms. For example, they claim that the ICD has "gained wider application because of need and opportunity" but neglect to be specific about whose needs and what opportunities are being served (Giddan et al., 1988, p. 44). The structure of the manual is very good. Divisions between chapters are distinct and provide examiners with the information required to use the ICD. A strength of the manual lies in its case studies, several of which have been included to help examiners understand how to interpret the ICD. These case studies appear to be from a variety of types of students representative of typical college populations. Several case studies are compared to demonstrate how similar problems might yield somewhat different profiles. However, the manual contains several editing problems. Figure 4.3 (p. 19) is labeled "Hand-Scored Answer Sheet" when it is clearly a profile sheet. Similarly, Figure 4.4 (p. 20) is labeled "Hand-Scored Profile Sheet" when it is clearly the answer sheet. The manual could also be improved by using the abbreviation "ICD" instead of writing out Inventory for Counseling and Development. Only twice does ICD appear in the manual, and readers are left to assume that these letters refer to the instrument.

The ICD uses two answer forms and profile sheets. One answer form and profile sheet is for computer scoring while the other set is to be used for hand scoring. All are easy to read and understand. The profile sheets use a multivariate rather than a nosological approach (Achenbach, 1984); that is, the profile enables examiners to develop a behavioral description of students as opposed to simply labeling them. One can easily see patterns useful in the interpretation of the ICD on the profile.

The ICD is intended to be used with both male and female college students. Research is currently being done to determine the measure's usefulness with entering college freshman (Giddan et al., 1988). College students of average and above-average ability should have no difficulty reading the test booklet or understanding the items (which are written in the first person using present tense verbs).

The uses of the ICD can be divided into two general categories, individual student evaluation and academic evaluation. Individual student evaluation entails selection of students for specific academic programs, facilitating the planning of students' academic and career experiences, providing assessment and evaluation as an adjunct to counseling and psychotherapy for students, and assisting students in identifying (behavioral) consistencies in motivation, cognitive style, or beliefs and attitudes that affect learning. Academic evaluation refers to evaluation at the college level to determine if objectives or outcomes related to students have been met, measurement of students' noncognitive changes, such as movement toward liberal thinking, changes in sexual beliefs, and alteration of social interaction patterns, and assessment of nontraditional students, minorities, women, and international students, to develop appropriate curricula, effective teaching methods, and culturally sensitive technology.

Doctoral and master's degree–level counselors in a university or college setting might use the ICD. A basic course in testing should prepare a counselor to use this instrument; however, counselors with just this training should use the ICD under the supervision of a person who has received more training, such as a psychologist.

A person charged with evaluating educational programs might also find the ICD useful in the appropriate situation; that is, one that would involve analyzing the educational process rather than educational outcomes. For example, the Teacher/Student Interaction scale could be used to determine if instructors are helping students increase their level of interaction in the classroom by conducting a repeated measures study. Another study might examine changes in political beliefs using the Liberal/Conservative and Socio-Political scales.

Interpretation of the ICD is similar to other tests of this nature. Examiners need to have a knowledge of T-scores and percentiles as well as understand that scales may form patterns. Examiners are warned to avoid "blind" interpretations of the ICD. The manual suggests that interpretation be made in conjunction with other data such as peer evaluations, ability and performance tests, and standard intake information (i.e., family history, presenting problem, etc.). The manual also cautions examiners to exercise care when making clinical interpretations because using the ICD in this manner is a recent development.

## Technical Aspects

Two studies assessing the reliability of the ICD are reported in the manual. These studies were conducted in 1985 and are based on a test-retest method. In the first study, 60 women and 6 men completed the ICD twice over a 3-week period. The second study involved 54 women and 7 men who completed the ICD over a 7-week period. Correlations ranged from .46 on the Agreement scale to .88 for Sexual Beliefs and Teacher/Student Interaction. The Substantive scales correlations emerged consistently in the .70s and .80s while the Criterion scales generally fell lower, with correlations in the .60s and .70s. The Validity scales produced the widest range of correlations from .46 to .87.

At this time, no estimates of internal consistency have been made for Form F. Analyses of data on other forms have shown high internal consistency. The manual states that data are being analyzed currently to estimate internal consistency.

Content validity of the ICD has been suggested through two methods. The first derives from the opinion of experts. During the development process, prospective items were screened by experts for their relativity to the purpose of the ICD. Items judged not relative were discarded. The second approach involved three separate research projects. The first two studies, qualitative in methodology, required participants to draw conclusions about item content and appropriate titling of the ICD from accumulated evidence. The third study involved factor analysis conducted during the instrument's development. The manual presents the results of a varimax-rotated principal factor analysis of Form C to lend credibility to the claim for content validity. These results suggest that the Substantive scales tap five distinct factors.

Construct validity of the ICD has been established through several lines of investigation. Care was taken to ensure as much as possible that results represented the population at large. In two studies, students' profiles were compared to their interest patterns. In the first, 80 students (43 men and 37 women) were given the ICD and the Strong-Campbell Interest Inventory (Campbell, 1977); in the second, 95 students (30 men and 65 women) completed the ICD along with the Career Assessment Inventory (Johansson, 1986). Bivariate correlations were calculated using the scales of the ICD and the other two inventories. Giddan et al. state that the results from these studies support the construct validity of the ICD.

Two other studies examined the relationships between students' scores on the ICD and measures of normal personality dimensions as assessed by two personality inventories. In one study, 168 students (47 men and 121 women) completed the ICD and the Self-Description Inventory (Johansson, 1983); in the other, 90 students completed the ICD and the Personality Description Inventory (National Computer Systems, 1986). Again, bivariate correlations were calculated and used to support the construct validity of the ICD.

Criterion-related validity is suggested by six studies using various forms of the ICD. These studies have examined criteria related to alienation, creativity, student activism, and academic performance. Concurrent validity is suggested by four of these studies, which examined alienation, teacher-student interaction, creativity, and political activism of students. Although mixed results were found, Giddan et al. conclude that the results support the ICD's concurrent validity.

In two studies examining the instrument's predictive validity, Giddan et al. tested the relationship between students' ICD scores and academic performance. The authors believe these results support an assertion of predictive validity.

## Critique

The authors of the ICD have developed an instrument that attempts a holistic assessment of students' lives in the college setting. Through the use of intellective and nonintellective factors, the authors have made an effort to predict college success. The result is an instrument that has interesting facets but may suffer from being overinclusive. That is, in the attempt to assess students in a holistic manner, what may emerge is an uninterpretable jumble. For example, how relevant is a student's sexual beliefs to his or her ambition, persistence, or practicality in approaching academic tasks?

A strength of the ICD is its usefulness in understanding academic difficulties.

The comprehensive nature of the instrument allows counselors to develop a picture of students' problems by seeing the interactions among the various scales. Viewing difficulties in this manner permits tailored intervention strategies. This individualized approach is needed as well as commendable, given the growing diversity among college students. Several other strengths of the ICD are noteworthy, including (a) the Teacher/Student Interaction scale, which seems particularly useful in helping students plan strategies that will maximize chances for success in college, (b) the number of subjects used to norm the ICD (several thousand students from universities throughout the continental United States), (c) the sample case studies presented in the manual, and (d) the ongoing research to refine the ICD (N. S. Giddan, personal communication, July 17, 1990).

A troubling aspect of the ICD arises in the various theoretical perspectives used to develop this instrument. Although the authors skillfully mixed these theories, it would seem that not all were needed. The use of developmental theories is commendable, as the impact of development on success in college seems logical, yet their relationships to academic performance is not made clear in the manual. Further discussion of the impact of development on academic performance would correct this oversight. Another concern is the use of trait, type, and factor theories in the development of this instrument. Although still debated in the literature, this approach to explaining behavior is somewhat anachronistic. The use of these theories does suggest to examiners how interpretations may be made.

Another concern involves the descriptions for some of the scales. Specifically, descriptions used for low scores on several scales seem to be value laden, particularly when no behavioral evidence is apparent. For example, on the Ambition scale, low scorers are described "as lacking initiative, as relatively indifferent to recognition or status, and as unmotivated" (Giddan et al., 1988, p. 11). A second example is found in the Orderliness scale, which describes high scorers as "organized, prompt, meticulous, and in control" and low scorers "careless, imprecise, unselfish, and unconcerned about rigid requirements" (Giddan et al., 1988, p. 12). Users of the ICD should be careful to avoid such value-laden terms when writing reports. For example, explanations other than lack of initiative, such as boredom or chronic depression, should be rejected before placing reports in students' files. The ICD would be improved by shifting away from scale descriptions that are conducive to placing value on behaviors during interpretation.

Four final criticisms concern the manual, the validation process, the length of the ICD, and the scoring method. With respect to the manual, several errors were made and some editorial "cleaning up" seems appropriate. For example, the manual often refers to research that has used the ICD, yet fails to cite these studies. This deserves the immediate attention of the authors and publisher. A question regarding the criterion-related validity seems logical because this contention is based on Form C of the ICD. Attention should be given to updating this information by conducting research using the current form, Form F. Another validity issue concerns the instrument's usefulness for clinical evaluations. The manual does advise discretion when using the ICD for clinical purposes, but a stronger caution probably would be more fitting. The ICD also seems overly long. It could be shortened by eliminating some of the less relevant scales (e.g., Sexual Beliefs) or items. Finally, the use of multiple-scoring templates is bothersome. Many users may elect to have the ICD computer scored.

In sum, the ICD seems to be useful in the assessment of academic difficulties. Yet, as a predictor of academic success, this measure may be limited. The best predictor of academic success is *always* current performance; perhaps, then, the ICD provides information that would help determine what factors might impede academic success. Beyond this application, the inventory's utility seems questionable. More research into its clinical usefulness must be conducted before application for this purpose can be supported.

### References

This list includes text citations and suggested additional reading.

Achenbach, T. M. (1984). Developmental psychopathology. In M. H. Bornstein & M. E. Lamb (Eds.), *Developmental psychology: An advanced textbook* (pp. 405–450). Hillsdale, NJ: Lawrence Erlbaum.

Andberg, J. (1987). *Correlations of GPAs and ICD Academic Performance scale scores for Edina High School students.* Unpublished raw data.

Bunnell, P. G. (1984). *A longitudinal study of the personality traits of college students identified by academic achievement and persistence.* Unpublished doctoral dissertation, University of Toledo, Ohio.

Campbell, D. P. (1977). *Manual for the SVIB–SCII.* Stanford, CA: Stanford University Press.

Giddan, N. S., Creech, F. R., & Lovell, V. R. (Eds.). (1985). *Working papers in the development of the Inventory for Counseling and Development.* (Available from National Computer Systems, 10901 Bren Road East, Minnetonka, MN 55343.)

Giddan, N. S., Creech, F. R., & Lovell, V. R. (1988). *Manual for the Inventory for Counseling and Development.* Minneapolis, MN: National Computer Systems.

Giddan, N. S., Lovell, V. R., Haimson, A. L., & Hatton, J. M. (1968). A scale to measure teacher-student interaction. *Journal of Experimental Education, 36,* 52–58.

Johansson, C. B. (1983). *Manual for the Self-Description Inventory.* Minneapolis, MN: National Computer Systems.

Johansson, C. B. (1986). *Manual for the enhanced version of the Career Assessment Inventory.* Minneapolis, MN: National Computer Systems.

National Computer Systems. (1986). *Personality Description Inventory* (unpublished version of the Self-Description Inventory). Minneapolis, MN: National Computer Systems.

**David A. Jepsen, Ph.D.**
*Professor, College of Education, Division of Counselor Education, The University of Iowa, Iowa City, Iowa.*

---

# JACKSON VOCATIONAL INTEREST SURVEY

*Douglas N. Jackson. Port Huron, Michigan: SIGMA Assessment Systems, Inc., Research Psychologists Press Division.*

## Introduction

The Jackson Vocational Interest Survey (JVIS) was constructed to measure vocational interests by scaling preferences between pairs of statements about work-related activities and work situations. It was designed principally to assist high school and college students and adults with their educational and vocational planning (Jackson, 1977). At the time it was released in 1977, the JVIS was acclaimed for several unique features among interest measures, including (a) a more theory-grounded approach than previous measures, based on a reconceptualization of occupational preferences in terms of both work roles *and* work styles; (b) elaborate, computer-based statistical strategies for scale development; (c) equal emphasis on application to males and females; and (d) an efficient, convenient scoring format open to user inspection.

The JVIS was developed by Professor Douglas N. Jackson, University of Western Ontario, who is widely recognized for his writing on issues in psychometric theory and especially the measurement of personality characteristics by structured inventories. The JVIS is, in many respects, the product of applying this expertise to interest measurement problems. Specifically, Jackson applied innovative multivariate statistical procedures in scale development to the interest domain. During his career, Dr. Jackson has also been active in the training of counseling psychologists, thus appreciating the problems of inventory interpretation with clients.

JVIS items are presented in a forced-choice format; test-takers are required to select the more interesting or preferred between pairs of "work-related activities." Instructions ask test-takers to consider only their preferences, regardless of the training or experience required for the activities. During scale development, however, each *activity* was considered as an item (a point to which the discussion will return in the "Critique" section of this review). Activity statements included in the survey were selected from among over 3,000 statements through extensive and rigorous procedures. The 13-page test booklet displays 289 activity-pair items in ample space for ease of reading. JVIS items are written at about the seventh-grade reading level according to the JVIS manual (Jackson, 1977), but some items contain terms that clearly require more advanced reading and conceptual background.

A unique feature of the JVIS is the broad range of scores it yields. The 34 Basic Interest (BI) scales are comprised of activity statement items showing the highest association with the total scale. The scales include separate activity items and are relatively independent from each other; therefore, each is considered to be interpretable in its own right. Eight BI scales reflect work style preferences and 26 BI scales are work role preferences.

The scales assessing work style preferences are an innovation in interest measurement and represent a more theory-based approach than earlier interest inventories. Jackson construed work preferences as pertaining to both activity and situation. Work style scales indicate "preferences for working in a certain kind of environment or working in a situation in which a certain mode of behavior is a norm" (Jackson, 1977, p. 2). The names of the work style scales (numbers indicate the order of appearance on interpretive materials) are 14. Dominant Leadership, 15. Job Security, 16. Stamina, 17. Accountability, 30. Academic Achievement, 32. Independence, 33. Planfulness, and 34. Interpersonal Confidence. Theoretical background for the work styles construct is not specified either in the manual or in Jackson's prior or subsequent writings. This is unfortunate because it handicaps both the interpreter of JVIS scores and the researcher interested in advancing this line of thinking. The manual is conspicuously silent on the source of these constructs and the corresponding items. Comparatively little information is presented about item selection for style scales as compared to role scales.

Work role scales reflect preferences for on-the-job activities associated with a certain group of occupations. The names of these scales are 1. Creative Arts, 2. Performing Arts, 3. Mathematics, 4. Physical Science, 5. Engineering, 6. Life Science, 7. Social Science, 8. Adventure, 9. Nature-Agriculture, 10. Skilled Trades, 11. Personal Service, 12. Family Activity, 14. Medical Service, 18. Teaching, 19. Social Service, 20. Elementary Education, 21. Finance, 22. Business, 23. Office Work, 24. Sales, 25. Supervision, 26. Human Relation Management, 27. Law, 28. Professional Advising, 29. Author Journalism, and 31. Technical Writing. The Basic Interest scales are arranged into areas on the interpretive materials on the basis of substantive similarity. For example, scales 1 and 2, Creative Arts and Performing Arts, are grouped under the rubric "The Arts," and scales 21–25 are called "Business, Administrative and Related Activities."

The General Occupational Themes (GOT) refer to broad patterns of interests rather than to interests in specific activities. Factor analytic studies with the JVIS revealed 10 distinct higher order dimensions named as follows: Expressive, Logical, Inquiring, Practical, Assertive, Socialized, Helping, Conventional, Enterprising, and Communicative. There is an obvious similarity to Holland's (1985) six personality types and the General Occupational Themes of the Strong interest inventories derived from Holland's work (Hansen & Campbell, 1985). The emergence of 10 dimensional themes rather than Holland's 6 seems to be a function of factor analyzing a large number (34) of comparatively homogeneous JVIS scales.

Six Administrative Indices aid the user in detecting cautions or reasons for confidence in profile interpretations. Five are simple response counts: number of "A" responses, "B" responses, omits, and double responses, and the percentage of scorable responses. An innovative profile Reliability (R) index provides "a measure of the consistency with which a person describes his or her interests" (Jackson, 1977, p. 26). It is simply an odd-even reliability computed on a single individual across all 34 BI scales. R scores below .50 should be interpreted with caution.

An Academic Orientation (AO) scale, the one nonoccupational scale on the

JVIS, estimates the degree of satisfaction in traditional academic settings. It was derived by contrasting scores of high school and university students on BI scales. The JVIS score interpreter is faced with a semantic challenge: a BI scale is labeled "Academic Achievement," and GOT scales are called "Inquiring" and "Logical."

Two sets of similarity scores compare the person's BI profile with the profiles of specified criterion groups: college students grouped in 13 academic majors and working adults grouped into 32 occupational clusters. The scores reflect the similarity between the individual's profile and those of people in the designated groups. Similarity scores range from +1.00 to –1.00, as a correlation coefficient would. The academic major similarity score is interpreted as "the probability of greater satisfaction in that particular course of study" (Jackson, 1977, p. 26). The occupational cluster similarity scores employ the same metric and roughly the same interpretation. The occupational cluster similarity scores were derived from an ingenious and complex method of cross-walking to the Strong interest inventory archival data.

The choice between the two answer forms depends on whether the test is scored manually or by computer. On the hand-scored format, the options A and B are placed on a diagonal for each numbered item. The sequence of items follows down a short, three- or four-row column and then goes to the top of the next column. The computer-scored answer grid has the two options placed side by side and the items appear in long columns.

Because item arrangement was critical for the hand-scored form, activity statements from the same scale appear in clusters of consecutive items. Furthermore, activities from half the scales are paired with activities from the other 16 scales. The second half includes activity pairs from only the second 17 scales. Therefore, the science-related activities, for example, appear only in the first half, and the business-related activities appear only in the second half. This item arrangement affects not only a test-taker's "set" but also score interpretation because of the ipsative item structure. There is an obvious pattern in the statements listed as A and those listed as B such that there is a strong possibility of a positional response set (Juni & Koenig, 1982).

Score report forms also differ depending on whether the profile was hand scored or machine scored. The hand-scored profile yields standard score scales (mean of 30 and standard deviation of 10) for the 34 Basic Interest scales. The scorer circles the appropriate raw score placed in order on the report form scale and estimates standard scores from the horizontal scale at the top of the form. The standard score scale is segmented into regions labeled "very low," "low," "average," "high," and "very high."

The computer-generated score report prints out the raw scores, standard scores, and percentiles by age group for 34 Basic Interest scales, the percentile ranks only for 10 General Occupational Themes, 7 Administrative Indices, similarity scores for 17 university major field clusters, and similarity scores for 32 occupational classifications. Extensive prose definitions of the scales and explanations of the scores are provided. Bar graph profiles are printed for BI and GOT scores. The lists of major fields and occupational groups are printed in rank order from most similar to least similar. In addition, several pages of descriptive information and sources of printed information about the three highest ranked occupational classifications are provided on the JVIS extended report to stimulate the user's career exploration.

**Practical Applications/Uses**

Purposes for using the JVIS are stated prominently, both in the manual (Jackson, 1977) and on the front cover of the inventory booklet. The JVIS is designed to help people discover their work-related interests and to assess their probable satisfaction in different occupational roles. The JVIS was designed for use by high school and college students and adults, especially those considering choices of educational programs or occupations. Counselors may use the JVIS in a broad range of settings including schools and colleges, university counseling centers, employment agencies, business and industry, and vocational rehabilitation and adult counseling centers. Undoubtedly, it is also appropriate for use by counselors in private practice and marital and family therapy. There are a few restrictions on the people for whom the JVIS is appropriate (such as the very young and those too disturbed or unstable emotionally to respond to the items). The relatively independent nature of the Basic Interest scales make the JVIS attractive for basic research on vocational interests and other aspects of personality and career development.

The JVIS is usually completed within 45–60 minutes, but there is no time limit. Group or individual administration follows clear and generally self-explanatory instructions that require no more than 10 minutes. The manual (Jackson, 1977, p. 5) provides a recommended guide for group administration when using computer-scored answer sheets. Appropriate precautions about accurate marking are mentioned throughout the administration. Adaptations for the hand-scored answer sheets are simple but will require calling attention to the item sequence on the answer sheet. Because administration of the JVIS does not require special knowledge, it can be administered by trained paraprofessionals as well as professionals. In some cases self-administration would seem reasonable, although a trained professional counselor should check the answer sheet prior to scoring.

Hand-scoring the JVIS is time-consuming, detailed work but imposes no great conceptual demands on the scorer. Nevertheless, the scoring system is not protected and allows both counselor and inventory taker to inspect the activities under each scale. This allows the user greater latitude in forming insights about the nature and origin of inventoried interests. Circled A and B responses are simply counted for a raw score total both across rows for the first 17 BI scales and then down columns for the other 17 scales. Accuracy is checked by totaling the row and column scores to see if the grand total is 289. The process requires at least 15 minutes and possibly much longer if errors are encountered. Machine (computer) scoring, although more expensive in time and money, is preferred for accuracy reasons but also because of the greater detail in the interpretive report.

The interpretive reports for the hand-scored answer sheets allow conversion of BI raw scores to standard scores derived from a norms group comprised of high school and college students. Line graphs on the profile allow approximate comparisons to separate sex groups. Means for the major and occupational similarity groups are available in the manual for inspectional comparisons.

The norms groups were derived from a combined group equally weighted from three samples: (a) students in U.S. and Canadian colleges and universities; (b) high school senior applicants to one large state university system; and (c) high school students in Ontario. Obviously, counselors who use the JVIS with adults and others who deviate significantly from this norms group (e.g., people from Latino populations, people with disabilities, people with limited education or economic means) will need to exercise caution in making generalizations from the norms group to their clientele. It is particularly puzzling to find both Spanish and French editions available but neither separate norms groups nor identification of these cultural groups within the norms population.

Because the eight work style BI scales are unique, their interpretation deserves elaboration. The manual suggests that the work style scale scores reveal insights into "more general dispositions toward work, other people, and self-attitudes" (Jackson, 1977, p. 18). The counselor or inventory user may have to distinguish these scales from the more familiar work roles and personality traits. Work style scales should be interpreted as interests in working in environments that reward and/or require the behavior implied by the scale name rather than as personality traits. The score report forms provide one- to three-sentence descriptions of the scales in exceptionally fine print. Most sentences contain the words "interested in" or synonyms such as "likes," "enjoys," or "prefers." Some work style scale descriptions deviate slightly and suggest traits. For example, the Planfulness description starts "Is organized . . ." and the Interpersonal Confidence scale includes "Reports not being afraid . . ." and "Believes in own ability . . . ." The manual singles out the latter scale and defines it as "confidence in interpersonal situations," using phrases like "are not bashful about speaking up" and "believe that they have skills in interpersonal activities." These phrases deviate unexplicably from the language employed elsewhere throughout the manual and interpretive folders and contrast with the admonition to avoid interpreting the scores as personality traits. Because the language implies something other than interests, clear interpretation is not facilitated. Work role BI scale interpretations seem straightforward because the language of scale descriptions and scale segments is likely to be grasped readily.

The manual suggests a three-level profile interpretation, (a) by considering individual high and low scales, (b) by considering the entire configuration of BI scale scores in relation to profiles for occupational clusters and individual occupations, and (c) by integrating the first two steps with other client information. The second step requires some elaboration because it involves unique statistical procedures for "bootstrapping" and clustering vocational interest profiles. The JVIS and the Strong Vocational Interest Blank (SVIB) Form T399 for men were both administered to 538 males entering Pennsylvania State University. Using multivariate, factor analytically based prediction procedures, JVIS BI profiles were predicted from SVIB Basic Interest scales. The JVIS profiles were created for each of 189 occupational groups in the Strong archival data. These profiles were factor analyzed to identify 26 clusters of occupations with similar JVIS interest profiles (Jackson & Williams, 1975). Through further application of the modal profile analysis, six more clusters were added. Thus, JVIS BI scale scores are used to predict scores on the 32 occupational clusters and the 189 male and 89 female occupational groups. Tables of mean predicted JVIS standard scores for these occupational groups and bar graphs for 52 occupational groups are available in the manual as interpretive aids.

The ipsative nature of the scales imposes limits on the interpretation of individual scores that are not addressed in the manual (e.g., the suggested interpretation of low scores as reflecting low interest in the activities). It would seem to be more accurate to say that the scale score is low *relative to* the scores from other scales *only in that half of the JVIS* from which the items were selected for the forced-choice format.

**Technical Aspects**

The JVIS is a product of Jackson's application of innovative multivariate statistical procedures to test development in the interest domain. He advocated for utilizing psychological theory and substantive item content in formulating a multifaceted item pool as well as for the importance of suppressing response biases (Jackson, 1971). The JVIS represents an exemplary approach to suppressing item response biases through applying two methods: (a) partialling out statistically and subtracting the component of activity statement scores attributable to a general like-dislike response bias factor, and (b) using the forced-choice format. It is important to note that "item response bias" and "item analysis" procedures are applied to the population of activity statements rather than the statement pairs that constitute the final forced-choice format.

Item analysis was based on the biserial correlation between activity statements and "purified" factor scores and those correlating highest with their "own" factor were retained. Low scale intercorrelations were ensured through applying an item efficiency index derived from Jackson's "minimum redundancy item analysis" (Neill & Jackson, 1976), thus increasing scale content saturation and minimizing scale redundancy. The surviving items were edited and arranged into pairs in the manner described earlier.

Scale homogeneity estimates reported for the BI scales are high and, as the author points out, approach the levels reported for academic achievement tests. The average item-factor biserial correlation for selected items was reported for all 34 BI scales; the median was .64 with a range from .46 for the Professional Advising scale to .99 for the Mathematics scale.

Average scale intercorrelations for a college entering class was .28 for males ($n$ = 779) and .24 for females ($n$ = 680). The aforementioned item arrangement—using activity statements from two sets of 17 scales each to form opposing items—contributed to a slightly higher correlation among each group. But the absence of a unipolar general factor and the relatively low intercorrelations suggests relatively independent interests are being tapped. The claim that these intercorrelations are "considerably lower than correlations reported for other vocational interest tests" (Jackson, 1977, p. 43) is subject to challenge. Subsequent factor analyses of BI scales on high school populations identified the 10 higher order factors named the General Occupational Themes, representing characteristic score patterns that aid in a more global interpretation of interests.

JVIS scale reliability was supported by test-retest and internal consistency estimates. The median 1-week test-retest reliability coefficient across 34 BI scales was

.84, with a range from .72 to .91 for 172 university students. Reliability coefficients for the 10 GOT scales over 1 week ranged from .82 to .92, with a median of .89 for 54 university students. Internal consistency was assessed by the theta statistic (Bentler, 1972), yielding a "dimension-free reliability coefficient." A median theta of .82 with range of .70 to .91 across BI scales was obtained for 1,573 high school students.

A distribution of the individual reliability index, the odd-even reliability coefficient computed for each student's BI profile, showed a majority of R scores over .70 and the median probably in the high .70s.

Basic Interest scale profile stability was assessed by intercorrelation of two profiles 2 weeks apart for each person. Three studies reported median correlations: the first was .87, with a range from .57 to .96 obtained for 54 students; the second was .88 for 172 students over 1 week; and the third was .84 for 102 successful medical school applicants over 6 months. The median correlation of GOT profiles for the first group was .94.

The validity claims for JVIS scales rest largely on evidence interpreted as supporting construct validity for the Basic Interest scales. The careful scale development already discussed could be construed as such. Further evidence that JVIS scales are distinct from abilities was based on generally low correlations with SAT scores for 2,154 entering Penn State students. Only a few correlations exceeded .20, as might be expected, with the highest a .37 between SAT Quantitative and JVIS Mathematics and a .21 between SAT Verbal and JVIS Author-Journalism.

Experimental evidence supporting BI scale construct validity was obtained from factor analyses of university student preferences for 51 different tasks when volunteering for psychological experiments and their JVIS BI scale scores. Twenty-five of the resulting 29 factors showed the highest factor loadings for the experimental task and the scale representing a similar interest. For example, the first factor contained preference for artistic drawings and the JVIS Creative Arts scale. The 29th factor contained preference for the task of writing a training manual and the JVIS Technical Writing scale.

The JVIS was administered to nine groups from six occupations ranging in size from 52 male elementary teachers to 286 male real estate agents. The five highest occupation cluster scores were displayed for five occupations and show obvious similarities to the subjects' current occupations. For example, the highest score for ministers was Occupations in Religion; for chemists, Occupations in Physical Sciences; and for elementary teachers, Occupations in Preschool and Elementary Teaching.

Concurrent validity evidence was obtained from correlations between scores on JVIS BI scales and SVIB Basic Interest scales for 159 college males and 153 college females. Generally scales sharing the same name were highly correlated: for example, SVIB Mathematics and JVIS Mathematics (.72 for males and .58 for females), SVIB Art and JVIS Creative Arts (.47 for males and .45 for females), and SVIB Social Services and JVIS Social Services (.53 for females).

Perhaps the most convincing concurrent predictions were for choice of one of eight academic colleges (e.g., Arts and Architecture, Business, Liberal Arts) among entering freshman at Penn State. Generalized distance measures (D2) between each pair of colleges were statistically significant for all male group comparisons and all but two female comparisons.

A subsequent study of academic majors by Jackson, Holden, Locklin, and Marks (1984) supported the construct validity of JVIS scales. Based on data from over 10,000 students, interest profiles for 17 academic major clusters were derived. Highest scores for students in each cluster were obtained on JVIS BI scales substantively related to the content area reflected in the cluster. For example, the Elementary Education and Teaching scales were the most highly associated with the education cluster.

Although no job satisfaction data are available, a study was reported of correlations between JVIS scales and real estate sales. High sales performance groups were differentiated from low performance groups on the Basic Interest scales.

## Critique

The JVIS is a complex instrument produced by applying sophisticated statistical methods that are probably not fully understood by a majority of test users. Even a careful study of the JVIS manual would not reveal all the information necessary to make a complete evaluation, and the JVIS manual is, arguably, no better or worse than most interest and personality test manuals. The sophisticated methods and incomplete information may have partly contributed to a delay of 14 years between publication and a review in *Test Critiques*. Minor difficulties with the JVIS today may be due, in part, to the fact it is still in its first edition and hence the inevitable "bugs" have not been corrected. The author and publishers are committed to starting a revision in 1991 (D.N. Jackson, personal communication, January 25, 1991).

The major limitations of the JVIS are (a) sparse theoretical background for the work style scales; (b) awkward items that create serious problems for test-takers and interpreters; (c) limited norm group descriptions and data; (d) lack of longitudinal predictive validity; and (e) the lengthy time required for taking and interpreting the test.

The case for JVIS Basic Interest scale validity rests heavily on arguments for construct validity. The work roles construct is familiar to psychologists and counselors and needs little elaboration beyond the brief definition in the manual. The work styles construct, on the other hand, is novel among interest inventories and has considerable promise both for theories of work behavior and for career counseling practice. It represents an effort to take seriously the idea of preferences based on work context, surroundings, or environment. Unfortunately, we are given only a brief conceptual definition in the manual, which may be forgivable in a field of assessment where so much work is empirical rather than conceptual but is surprising because the author has advocated strongly for theory-driven item pools (Jackson, 1971). At the least, the minimal definition of the work styles construct creates special problems for the test interpreter. How do we explain work style scale scores to the client?

A central issue in evaluating the JVIS from the perspective of test-takers is the nature of the forced-choice activity comparisons. Opinion varies about the quality of the JVIS items depending on what is construed as an item. Certainly, extraordinary attention was given to selecting the activity statements (called "items" in the manual) designated as the A and B options for each numbered item in the final test format. The sample of statements selected was "purified" by statistically eliminating response bias, ensuring substantive relations to defined interest dimensions, reducing statistical redundancy of items, and maximizing scale independence. All these elaborate steps were taken based on responses from about 2,000 people to single-stimulus, like-dislike items (i.e., the statements) and preceded the formation of the paired stimulus forced-choice items that constitute the final inventory form. These laudable item purifying steps notwithstanding, the test-taker is faced with a task of choosing between two carefully selected activities, and it is this *choice* that constitutes the test-taker's behavior and, in turn, determines scale scores and interest interpretations. When the choice is between two very different kinds of statements, no matter how carefully selected, the dimensions of judgment reflected by the choice are different than the judgments in rating individual activities.

The choice task is problematic for many of the 289 items, so much so that Juni and Koenig (1982) have observed seven different "anomalies" experienced by test-takers. The most serious of these are (a) choosing between a job and a trait (59 items), (b) choosing between a specific job and a general work style (20 items), and (c) choosing between a single event and an overall role (11 items). Although the general tone of their article may seem one-sided to those who appreciate the extraordinary care in selecting JVIS activity statements, nevertheless Juni and Koenig have identified a fundamental problem with using the JVIS scores to make generalizations about vocational interests. Whether forced-choice responses represent vocational interest may depend on more thorough empirical follow-up work.

The arrangement of activity statements in the forced-choice pairs to facilitate hand scoring has led to another serious problem inherent to JVIS item structure. Scale scores are based on frequency of selecting activities representing each scale. This ipsative scoring procedure means that one scale is given a point while the other scale is not given a point when there is an opportunity for adding to either score. But activities representing each scale are pitted against activities from only 16 of the 33 other scales. Thus, for example, the teaching activities are compared with business activities but not with science and mathematics activities. Precise interpretation of scale scores would emphasize that the score for a given scale (e.g., Teaching) is derived from some but not all choices between interest areas.

The norms are based on the group of 500 males and 500 females selected from about 5,000 cases of students in colleges and high schools. The manual supplies limited information about the nature of the norms groups, but there are apparent geographic biases and the potential for cultural biases as well. Furthermore, although the manual suggests applications to adult career changers, all the norm groups are college students or younger. Norm groups are not separated by age but appear as one heterogeneous group of students. The JVIS represents a clear improvement over other inventory norm groups assembled simply on the basis of gender and occupational membership, with little consideration to age or other important characteristics of typical users.

The JVIS is not unique either in claiming to assess probable satisfaction with occupations or in not providing supportive data for this claim. Nevertheless, this is a glaring limitation and should not be overlooked by inventory users. Is it accurate to say a high Basic Interest scale score indicates greater likelihood of satisfaction in the occupations associated with the scale? It isn't, of course, until the supportive data are forthcoming. The preferred validity data are those that show the predictive relationship between interest scores obtained from typical users (e.g., college students) and aspects of the person's later job experiences (e.g., satisfactions, commitments, etc.).

The JVIS manual hints at a modest claim to assess interests comprehensively, and, indeed, based on sheer number of activity statements and scales, this seems a reasonable claim. But such breadth is purchased at the cost of user time both in taking the inventory and in learning about the scale scores. Compared to other popular interest inventories, the JVIS is among the longest to take and interpret, which is a disadvantage to counselors and clients who feel they have tight schedules.

The special strengths of the JVIS, especially as compared to other interest inventories, are (a) the hand-scoring option and the ease of content interpretations of work role scales, using scale descriptions and their activity statement content as well as the normative tables; (b) the scale norming, which allows comparisons across occupations and majors; (c) the extraordinary attention to response bias and scale-activity correlations in scale construction; (d) the ingenious methods for relating JVIS scores to SVIB archival data; and (e) the breadth in coverage of vocational interest domain and the relatively homogeneous interest scales.

By contrast with interest inventories using secured scoring keys, the JVIS can be scored by hand whether or not the more desirable computer-scoring option is chosen. Hand scoring offers users the advantage of seeing the activities that define each scale and is likely to enhance their understanding of the scores and, probably, their interests. Interpretation of similarity of interests with occupational cluster groups and academic major groups is aided immensely by allowing direct comparisons among these groups (such as the ordering of occupational clusters most similar to the person's interests). This is possible because the interest scores are based on the same norms group rather than separate groups for each occupation or major.

This review has already described the elaborate "purifying" of activity statements, which is a distinctive JVIS strength, as much for demonstrating the feasibility of such methods in interest measurement as for the effect on JVIS scale construction. The JVIS also demonstrates that the construction of new interest inventories can utilize archival data from older inventories to enhance the generalization of scores. The success of the bootstrapping approach should encourage other test developers to attempt it.

The breadth of the vocational interest domain and the extensive list of homogeneous and independent scales makes the JVIS especially attractive for research as well as for counseling applications. Curiously, very few published studies have employed the JVIS, perhaps because it is so new (relative to, for example, the Strong or Kuder instruments) or because of the extra time it takes. The novel research studies reported in the manual should encourage more basic research on the nature and development of vocational interests.

In summary, the JVIS seems best suited for counseling with persons who have the motivation, skill, and time to acquire a comprehensive view of their vocational interests. The JVIS requires work: 289 choices must be made, occasionally between lengthy and complex activity statements. The reading level is sometimes sophisticated, and many activity descriptions involve multiple clauses. Interpretive materials require extensive explanation and time for clear and full discussion of the many scores. For those who extend these extra efforts, there is the possibility of achieving greater breadth and depth in understanding the nature of their interests than there is with other inventories. Because of the norm groups reported in the manual and the presence of college major scales, the JVIS would be most appropriate for college students, perhaps those early in their collegiate careers.

Promise of a planned JVIS revision is encouraging. Several of the JVIS problems are correctable with greater attention to detail in the revision (e.g., norm group descriptions). Some problems, such as the cumbersome item structure and the lack of predictive validity, will require considerable investment in order to make the JVIS outstanding compared with older vocational interest inventories.

### References

Bentler, P.M. (1972). A lower-bound method for the dimension-free measurement of internal consistency. *Social Science Research, 1,* 348–357.

Hansen, J.C., & Campbell, D.P. (1985). *Manual for the Strong Interest Inventory Form T325 of the Strong Vocational Interest Blanks, Fourth Edition.* Stanford, CA: Stanford University Press.

Holland, J.L. (1985). *Making vocational choices: A theory of vocational personalities and work environments.* Englewood Cliffs, NJ: Prentice-Hall.

Jackson, D.N. (1971). The dynamics of structured personality tests: 1971. *Psychological Review, 78,* 229–248.

Jackson, D.N. (1977). *Jackson Vocational Interest Survey manual.* Port Huron, MI: SIGMA Assessment Systems, Inc.

Jackson, D.N., Holden, R.R., Locklin, R.H., & Marks, E. (1984). Taxonomy of vocational interests of academic major areas. *Journal of Educational Measurement, 21,* 261–275.

Jackson, D.N., & Williams, D.R. (1975). Occupational classification in terms of interest patterns. *Journal of Vocational Behavior, 6,* 269–280.

Juni, S., & Koenig, E.J. (1982). Contingency validity as a requirement in forced-choice item construction: A critique of the *Jackson Vocational Interest Survey. Measurement and Evaluation in Guidance, 14,* 202–207.

Neill, J.A., & Jackson, D.N. (1976). Minimum redundancy item analysis. *Educational and Psychological Measurement, 36,* 123–124.

**Frederick T.L. Leong, Ph.D.**
*Assistant Professor of Psychology, The Ohio State University, Columbus, Ohio.*

**Alan Vaux, Ph.D.**
*Associate Professor of Psychology, Southern Illinois University at Carbondale, Carbondale, Illinois.*

---

# JOB DESCRIPTIVE INDEX

*Patricia C. Smith, Lorne M. Kendall, and Charles L. Hulin. Bowling Green, Ohio: Bowling Green State University.*

## Introduction

The Job Descriptive Index (JDI) is one of the most widely used measures of job satisfaction. It has been translated into many different languages and has been cited in over 400 publications dealing with job satisfaction (Smith et al., 1989). The original JDI, which consists of 72 items, is based on a multiple facet rather than global approach to job satisfaction. It was designed to assess an individual's satisfaction on the following dimensions of a job: (a) the work itself, (b) pay, (c) promotions, (d) supervision, and (e) co-workers. The original version of the JDI was published in 1969, and revisions were begun in the late 1970s that eventually added a global satisfaction scale entitled Job in General (18 items) to the five facets. Some of the items on the original five facets were also revised.

Research on the JDI began in a program of studies at Cornell University (Locke, Smith, & Hulin, 1965). However, it was Patricia Smith, Professor of Psychology at Bowling Green State University, who eventually completed the studies and launched the JDI in the now famous 1969 book, *The Measurement of Satisfaction in Work and Retirement: A Strategy for the Study of Attitudes.* The book was coauthored with Lorne Kendall (now deceased) and Charles Hulin. Hulin, a former student of Smith's, is now Professor of Psychology at the University of Illinois at Champaign-Urbana and, like Smith, has continued research on the JDI.

The JDI represented a 10-year effort to produce a reliable and valid measure of job satisfaction. Its development was based on a careful and comprehensive analysis of the major issues in the assessment of job satisfaction. Smith, Kendall, and Hulin (1969) argued that a good measure of job satisfaction would make significant contributions to practical issues as well as theoretical developments in our understanding of the sources of satisfaction and dissatisfaction at work. They pointed out that many of the problems of concern to management and unions, such as "supervisory training, organizational structure, job enrichment, automation, level and method of payment, retirement counseling, pension plans, and retirement-age policy, are based on the assumption that such factors affect the feelings and attitudes and, in turn, the behavior of the employees" (Smith et al., 1969, p. 2). That job satisfaction is a central variable in our understanding of worker motivation and preferences is beyond question. What Smith et al. (1969) had to address was more the question of whether another measure of job satisfaction was needed, given the ones already available (e.g., Brayfield & Rothe, 1951).

In an attempt to improve on existing measures, Smith et al. (1969) wanted to develop a measure of job satisfaction that would (a) be applicable to a wide range of situations and individuals, (b) be at low reading level so that almost any worker could be assessed, (c) be inexpensive to administer in terms of time and money, (d) have extensive norms for comparison, (e) be reliable and valid, and (f) measure different aspects of the job. Finally, they argued that the JDI, in using a job-referent rather than a self-referent descriptive format, has the advantage of requiring workers to describe their jobs rather than their internal states. The latter approach, which is more often used by other measures of job satisfaction, is presumed to be more difficult for workers to provide.

In identifying the dimensions or facets of job satisfaction to measure, Smith et al. (1969) relied on a study by Herzberg, Mausner, Peterson, and Capwell (1957), which found, through factor analytic studies, six relatively independent factors: general satisfaction and morale, attitudes toward the company and its policies, satisfaction with intrinsic aspects of the job, attitudes toward the immediate supervisor, attitudes toward satisfaction of aspirations, and satisfactions with conditions of present job. Based partially on this review, Smith et al. (1969) planned to investigate only four areas of satisfaction: work, pay and promotions (as a combined area), supervision, and co-workers. However, their preliminary analyses revealed that the pay-and-promotions factor could be broken down into two clearly discriminable factors. Therefore, the final scales of the JDI assessed the following five areas of job satisfaction: work, pay, promotions, supervision, and co-workers.

Having determined that the JDI would have the characteristics specified above, the focus shifted to the item content and the format of the index. Smith, Kendall, and Hulin chose a descriptive format, believing that it is easier for a worker to describe some specific aspects of a job than to describe internal states of feeling. Hence, the JDI items consisted of adjectives and short descriptive sentences (e.g., "Boring," "Gives sense to accomplishment" for the Work facet). Smith et al. (1969) developed the original item pool by selecting items from other job satisfaction inventories and from available lists of adjectives or short phrases that they felt could be applied to various aspects of a job. This resulted in 30 to 40 items for each of the scales.

To assess whether these items could elicit adequate responses from workers, the JDI was administered to several samples at Cornell University using a "triadic" procedure. Subjects were asked to describe their current job using the JDI, then to describe the best job and the worst job that they could imagine. For each of the original items, response frequencies were computed for descriptions of best and worst jobs. All items that failed to show significant differences in response frequency for best and worst jobs were discarded. Smith et al.'s (1969) rationale for this procedure was that "items which failed to differentiate between best jobs and worst jobs would not differentiate present jobs from either best or worst jobs and would, therefore, probably not be of great importance on a job" (p. 71).

The revised scales were then administered to other samples in order to determine if any other important items indicative of satisfaction or dissatisfaction had been omitted during the original item selection. Several new adjectives were added as a result of this assessment. Next, the JDI was administered to 192 male employees randomly selected from two plants of an electronics firm to assess its concurrent validity. The Faces Scale (i.e., faces ranging from unhappy to happy; Kunin, 1955), which had previously been shown to have convergent and discriminative validity, was also administered to this sample. The JDI was found to be significantly correlated with this measure of job satisfaction (Locke, Smith, Kendall, Hulin, & Miller, 1964). Smith et al. (1969) were also aware of the possible order effects among scales. Using a Latin-square design, they found no significant order effects. They also assessed the possible impact of acquiescence and other response sets by partialling out the response sets, and they found very little effect on the convergent validity coefficients of the JDI scales.

Revisions of the JDI began in late 1970 due to changes in the colloquial uses of language that called some items into question. In order to maintain the JDI's high scale reliability and validity, the JDI Research Group at Bowling Green, headed by Patricia Smith, began a 5-year effort to revise the JDI (Smith et al., 1989). Both standard psychometric and IRT criteria were used to select items from the original pool, as well as 41 new items, using a heterogeneous sample of 795. The original number and content of facets were retained, as were the number of items per facet. The new scales showed excellent internal consistency (.88 over six samples) and emerged in factor analyses. As a separate undertaking, a global satisfaction scale was added, called the Job in General scale (JIG; Ironson, Smith, Brannick, Gibson, & Paul, 1989). Although the JDI-Revised is now available, the focus of the present review will be on the original JDI as the revision has not yet accumulated much supporting information and because the original is likely to see continued use.

Roznowski (1989) has also reported on a modified version of the JDI. In addition to changes in language and job, she notes that the scales are asymmetrical and tend to provide more information on dissatisfaction than satisfaction. Items were selected in several stages through factor analysis and IRT analysis. The final scales yielded a near-perfect simple solution in factor analyses, which corresponded to the five proposed facet dimensions. The new scales also showed better internal consistency, lower interscale correlations, and greater scale information than the original scales. Finally, Roznowski provided a procedure for equating the new and old scale scores so that local norms might continue to be useful.

The JDI consists of five scales, each printed on a separate page: Work, Supervision, Pay, Promotions, and Co-workers. For each scale, there is a list of adjectives or short phrases, and the respondent is instructed to indicate whether each word or phrase applies with respect to the particular facet of his or her job (e.g., pay). If a word applies to pay, he or she is asked to write "Y" (for Yes) beside the word. If the word does not apply to pay, he or she is asked to write "N" (for No) beside the word. If he or she cannot decide, he or she is asked to enter a question mark (?).

## Practical Applications/Uses

The JDI was designed to be a multifaceted measure of job satisfaction that would be applicable to a wide range of workers. By measuring what the authors believe to be five major dimensions of job satisfaction, the JDI provides a more specific profile of workers' levels of job satisfaction on these dimensions. Smith et al. (1969) argue that a facet rather than a global approach to job satisfaction would be more likely to increase our substantive understanding of the antecedents and consequences of worker satisfactions and dissatisfactions with their jobs. Global measures of job satisfaction do not allow one to identify the most problematic areas of a person's job. On the other hand, a facet approach enables the design of interventions targeted at specific areas in need of improvement (e.g., one group of automobile workers may be dissatisfied with their pay while a similar group across town is most unhappy with their supervision).

The JDI has very broad uses within vocational and organizational psychology. It has been used extensively to research the correlates, antecedents, and consequences of job satisfaction among U.S. workers. O'Connor, Peters, and Gordon (1978) found that the JDI is the most often used measure of job satisfaction in the industrial psychology literature. Research has used the JDI to examine job satisfaction as both a predictor variable (e.g., high satisfaction predicting low turnover) and an outcome/criterion variable (e.g., congruence between person and work environment as a predictor of job satisfaction). Less well documented than research studies, the JDI has probably been used widely in organizations to assess employees' work attitudes for a variety of purposes. The extent of such practical uses is difficult to assess because they are usually not systematically documented. If and when such uses are documented, they usually appear in in-house publications with limited circulation.

According to Smith et al. (1969), the JDI would be appropriate for any worker with fourth-grade reading ability. It has been used with a very wide range of workers. As will be discussed in the "Technical Aspects" section of this review, the JDI is a very robust measure with wide-ranging applicability. However, there is doubt in some quarters as to whether it is appropriate for high level executives (e.g., CEOs) because the Supervision facet may not apply to them nor may some items of the Work scale (e.g., "Hot," "On your feet"). The JDI would certainly be appropriate for clinical and counseling uses, although such uses have not been well documented.

Administration of the JDI is very straightforward. The instructions are very simple, and respondents are required simply to write either a Y, N, or ? in reply to each of the items. The index can be administered individually or in groups and requires only a few minutes. No manual currently exists for the JDI, but copies of the book that serves this function may be purchased from Patricia Smith in the Department of Psychology at Bowling Green State University. A manual for the JDI/JIG is almost completed and soon will be available (Smith & Balzer, in press).

Scoring of the JDI is accomplished by aligning a template next to the items for each scale and assigning the appropriate weighted score to each item. The scores for all the items in each scale are then totaled to provide the scale score. Unlike the traditional scoring system for similar response options (i.e., yes, no, and undecided), Smith et al. (1969) recommend assigning a score of 0 to both Yes responses to negative items and No responses to positive items. (Traditional scoring normally assigns a 1 to such responses.) For ? responses to all items, Smith et al. (1969) recommend a score of 1 instead of the traditional 2. In both the traditional and the Smith et al. systems, Yes responses to positive items and No responses to negative responses both receive scores of 3. The items and their direction of scoring are provided in Smith et al. (1969). Machine or computer scoring is not available nor is it really necessary unless large samples of subjects are needed.

Interpretations of an individual's score on the various scales on the JDI can be accomplished by comparing that individual's score with those of a normative group. Extensive normative data are available in chapter 5 of Smith et al. (1969). The general norms for the five JDI scales are based on a sample of nearly 2,000 male and over 600 female workers representing 21 plants, 19 different companies, and 16 different standard metropolitan statistical areas. The normative samples were stratified according to five dimensions. Three of these stratification variables relate to personal characteristics: income, education, and job tenure. The two others concern situational characteristics: community prosperity and community decrepitude. Using an individual's raw score on a particular scale (e.g., Work), the individual's percentile rank may be obtained from the appropriate table in chapter 5. Tables are broken down by scale, gender, and stratification variables.

Smith et al. (1969) point out that the norm tables are designed only for use with individuals and that "any use of these tables for purposes of estimating the percentile standing of a MEAN score for a group of workers would result in serious errors of interpretation" (p. 93). They recommend using statistical tests of hypothesis for this purpose. Other information that may aid in the interpretation of JDI scores include the voluminous literature on the use of the JDI with various populations. Another alternative would be to accumulate local norms (e.g., an organization may collect JDI scores on all current employees and use those scores to interpret an individual's level of job satisfaction).

**Technical Aspects**

As noted previously, the Job Descriptive Index continues to be a very widely used measure of job satisfaction (Yeager, 1981). This popularity no doubt reflects the care taken in its initial development, its applicability across a wide range of employee types, its practical utility in monitoring facets of job satisfaction, and the quantity and quality of psychometric information available on the instrument. Indeed, apart from the standard efforts to establish reliability and validity, the JDI has been subjected to psychometric analyses involving a high degree of technical sophistication (e.g., Drasgow & Kanfer, 1985; Parsons, 1983; Parsons & Hulin, 1982).

*Reliability.* Often job satisfaction measures are used to monitor or evaluate the effects of organizational changes and interventions. However, as Schneider and Dachler (1978) have noted, measures used for these practical and research purposes must show stability under "normal" conditions. A number of studies have reported stability coefficients for JDI scales over substantial intervals, and, with some exceptions, these are quite good.

Schuler (1979) examined stability over a 7-month interval among public utility employees and reported test-retest correlations of .82 (Work), .77 (Supervision), and .79 (Co-workers). In contrast, Downey, Sheridan, and Slocum (1976) found that stability of the Work, Promotion, and Supervision scales over a 12-month interval was good for a sample of managers (.70, .73, and .70) but less so for machine operators (.64, .29, and .35). Such differences in stability across employee levels may reflect differential reliability or actual fluctuations in job conditions.

Schneider and Dachler (1978) addressed this issue directly. They examined stability over a 16-month period among managerial and nonmanagerial employees of a large utility company. These employees were drawn from all five departments in all five geographically dispersed divisions of the company. The stability coefficients were quite high, and the pattern was similar for the two employee groups: mean stability was .56 for managers and .58 for nonmanagement employees. For the Work, Pay, Promotion, Supervision, and Co-worker scales, respectively, the coefficients were .61, .61, .64, .46, and .47 for a management sample and .66, .62, .56, .45, and .58 for a nonmanagement sample. Further, test administration was examined as a method in a multitrait, multimethod procedure. This analysis indicated that for each trait (JDI facet), stability exceeded relevant interscale correlations both across and within administrations. Nor were any marked differences evident for the two samples.

Some fluctuation in job satisfaction should be expected over longer intervals; indeed, too much stability would imply insensitivity to change, detracting from the practical and evaluative utility of a job satisfaction measure. The moderate to high stability of JDI scales over substantial intervals supports the instrument's use in time-based studies.

The internal consistency of JDI subscales is quite good also. Smith et al. (1969) reported Spearman-Brown coefficients for a sample of 80 male employees as follows: .84 (Work), .80 (Pay), .86 (Promotion), .87 (Supervision), and .88 (Co-workers). In their review of the JDI, Cook, Hepworth, Wall, and Warr (1981) report Spearman-Brown and alpha statistics from another 16 studies published in the late 1970s. These studies involved a wide range of employees, including managers, technicians, salespeople, and blue-collar workers. The majority of coefficients were in the .80 to .90 range, quite comparable to those reported initially by Smith et al. (1969). Indeed, only 6 of 46 coefficients fell below .79, and there was no obvious indication of differential reliability by type or level of employee.

More recent studies have yielded comparable estimates of internal consistency. Roznowski (1989) examined data from employees in several organizations (hospital workers, secretaries, military personnel, and government workers). She reported alpha coefficients of .82 (Work), .76 (Pay), .81 (Promotion), .88 (Supervision), and .88 (Co-workers). In sum, the JDI facet scales show good internal consistency as well as stability. Nor is there any evidence that reliability has diminished over the two decades the instrument has been in use.

*Construct validity.* The JDI was designed to measure five distinct facets of job satisfaction: work, pay, promotion, supervision, and co-workers. A good deal of work has gone into examining how successfully it does so. Much of this work has concerned the internal structure of the instrument—its factor structure and the divergence of subscales. A complementary line of research, discussed later, has examined patterns of convergent and discriminant validity of JDI facet scales in relation to either related measures of job satisfaction or variables that are theoretical antecedents or consequences.

*Structure of the JDI.* Are the JDI facet scales distinct? The simplest form of that question involves examining the correlations among scales. Smith et al. (1969) reported median interscale correlations of .39 (range = .28–.42) and .32 (range = .16–.52), respectively, for their large samples of male and female employees. Cook et al. (1981) review comparable data from another 17 studies that yield median interscale correlations ranging between .22 and .43 (mean .31), with one notable exception: .79 for a predominantly female sample of company employees (Penley & Hawkins, 1980). In short, the facets of job satisfaction measured by the JDI appear to be moderately independent.

A more sophisticated form of the question about distinct facets involves factor analysis and related procedures. Smith et al. (1969) briefly reported the results of a factor analysis conducted by Maas on data from 80 male bank employees. Apparently the number of factors was set at five, and a quartimax rotation produced interpretable factors. Most, but by no means all, items showed their highest loadings on the appropriate scale. Making a case for the validity of the JDI as a measure of distinct facets, Smith et al. (1969) wrote that "subscales are discriminably different, have loaded on separate group factors with no general factor in repeated factor analysis studies, and do not intercorrelate highly despite their high reliabilities" (p. 25).

However, Smith, Smith, and Rollo (1974) conducted factor analyses of data from samples of white government employees, black government employees, and bank employees. Clear factors emerged for Pay, Promotion, and Co-worker, but Supervision items split into two factors with all three samples, and Work items did so for the white government employees. These findings suggest that the JDI might tap more than five facets of job satisfaction.

Yeager (1981) specifically addressed this possibility, predicting that with a larger sample both Supervision and Co-worker items would split into two factors reflecting interpersonal and performance aspects of these work relationships. Data from a large sample (over 2,000), representing the full range of employees from a large soft goods company, were subjected to factor analysis. A scree test suggested nine factors, which were then subjected to a varimax rotation. As predicted, both Supervision and Co-worker items loaded on parallel factors reflecting interpersonal and performance/ability dimensions. In addition, Work items loaded on three factors, which Yeager termed Challenging Work, Frustrating Work, and Fulfillment in Work. The Pay and Promotion items remained intact. New scales based on these factors had quite good internal consistency (median alpha = .80), except for Work Frustration (.52) and Fulfillment in Work (.45), both of which had few items. Further, interscale correlations were generally lower than for the original scales, except for the parallel Supervision (.50) and Co-worker (.56) scales. On the basis of these results, Yeager (1981) concluded that the JDI taps more than five facets of job satisfaction. In particular, he notes that the distinction between interpersonal and performance aspects of supervision and co-worker relationships may have theoretical and practical utility (cf. Blake & Mouton, 1964).

Jung, Dalessio, and Johnson (1986) pursued this matter further, reiterating the theoretical plausibility of the interpersonal-performance distinction and noting the indistinct convergence of relevant JDI scales with facet scales of related measures (e.g., Gillet & Schwab, 1975). They examined the generalizability of five-factor and nine-factor solutions using data from 11 samples (with an average *N*/

item ratio of 7:1). The five-factor solution was stable across samples, showing a very high degree of congruence (mean $C$ = .92 for the same factors, .31 for different factors). The congruence of the nine-factor solution was assessed relative to Yeager's (1981) matrix of factor loadings. The two Supervision factors emerged in 9 of 11 samples and showed a high degree of congruence with Yeager's factors. Two Co-worker factors emerged in eight samples, and these were congruent with Yeager's factors in five samples. Challenging Work emerged in all 11 samples and showed high congruence; Frustration with Work emerged in 10 samples and showed moderate congruence, while Fulfillment with Work emerged in only 1 sample. Jung et al. (1986) conclude that the traditional five-factor solution is not sample specific; rather, the JDI may be viewed as a measure of five facets of work satisfaction for a wide range of job situations. However, they note that the splitting of some items sets (Supervision, Work, and perhaps Co-worker) was consistent enough to warrant further study. Differentiated facet scales (possibly involving new items) may have theoretical or practical utility in some situations.

In a highly technical analysis, Parsons and Hulin (1982) employed item response theory (IRT) and hierarchical factor analysis to examine the structure of the JDI and, in particular, whether there was evidence of a general satisfaction dimension. JDI data (excluding Pay items and three Co-worker items) from 1,349 employees of 41 U.S. units of an international merchandising company were analyzed. Parsons and Hulin performed an oblique rotation of principal factors derived from a tetrachoric correlation matrix (one more appropriate for discrete variables). This factor pattern matrix was transformed to a hierarchical factor structure and compared to IRT results.

The authors conclude that the findings are consistent with the view that this modified JDI (the Pay scale was excluded) involves four facets of job satisfaction *and* a second-order general satisfaction dimension. It should be noted that many, but not all, items have high loadings on this general factor; that is, the results do not support summing scale scores to yield a general satisfaction score. Thus Parsons and Hulin (1982) suggest that the facet scales might be used when specific satisfactions are of interest, whereas the general factor might be of more use in studies involving "general acceptance or rejection of a work situation" (p. 833).

To summarize, a number of very sophisticated studies have examined the structure of the JDI. The traditional five-facet model is generalizable and congruent across a wide range of work situations (Jung et al., 1986). Further, both convergent and discriminant validity are stable over time (Jung et al., 1986). Yet there is also evidence that several facets may be further differentiated—a point to consider in further development of the instrument (Jung et al., 1986; Yeager, 1981). Finally, the JDI might also yield a measure of global job satisfaction (Parsons & Hulin, 1982).

*Convergent and discriminant validity.* The structural issues just discussed represent one approach to the validity of JDI subscales—an important but somewhat insular one. Do the JDI scales show appropriate patterns of convergence and divergence with related measures of job facet satisfaction?

Gillet and Schwab (1975) used the multitrait, multimethod procedure to compare the JDI to the Minnesota Satisfaction Questionnaire (MSQ), designed to measure 20 facets of job satisfaction. Data were derived from semiskilled production employees of a large consumer goods company. Convergence between corresponding JDI and MSQ scales was observed: Promotion with Advancement (.57), Pay with Compensation (.56), Co-worker with Co-worker (.49), and Supervision with Supervision Human Relations (.70). (Convergent validity of the Work scale was not discussed, though it correlated at .48 with the MSQ Working Conditions scale.) Further, the three criteria for discriminant validity were met. Convergent validities exceeded relevant heterotrait correlations involving either different or the same measures. The pattern of interscale correlations was concordant for the same and different measures. Finally, the Kavanagh, MacKinney, and Wolins (1971) analysis of variance procedure was employed and indicated good convergent and discriminant validity for the JDI scales. Gillet and Schwab (1975) also reanalyzed data reported by Evans (1969) comparing JDI scales to goal attainment measures for a sample of utility workers and nurses. These data, too, showed excellent convergent validity for the JDI though somewhat poorer discriminant validity.

Dunham, Smith, and Blackburn (1977) compared JDI facet scales to the MSQ, the Index of Organizational Reactions (IOR), and Faces scales, using data from a large sample of national retail employees, stratified by gender, job level, and territory. Although the results support the validity of the JDI, it appeared to have faired less well than the other measures. Thus all measures showed good convergence with corresponding scales (JDI scales had an average convergent validity coefficient of .47). All measures showed good discriminant validity by Campbell and Fiske's (1959) first criterion (larger associations for common traits than for different traits measured differently), but they did not all meet the second criterion (larger associations for common traits than for different traits measured similarly). Indeed, only 55% of relevant JDI tests met this criterion, compared to 77% for the IOR and 70% for the MSQ. Similarly, the concordance of trait associations across methods was acceptable for the JDI but better for all the other measures. The Dunham et al. (1977) study does need to be interpreted with some caution because the JDI may not have been scored correctly; namely, the Pay and Promotion scales were not doubled (P.C. Smith & W.K. Balzer, personal communication, May 15, 1990).

In an effort to develop an assessment device that might better predict important job-related behavior (e.g., departure), Hartman, Grigsby, Crino, and Chokar (1986) examined the relationship between JDI scales and corresponding "action tendencies." The action tendency measure (ATM) underwent considerable development, paralleling that of the JDI. A multitrait, multimethod procedure was used to compare versions of the ATM to JDI facets for two samples of employed students. The findings reflect on the validity of the established instrument (JDI) as well as the new one (ATM). In the first instance, all five facets showed quite good convergent validity and met two of the three criteria for discriminant validity. In the second analysis, ATM Pay and Promotion were combined, but again the data indicated adequate convergent and discriminant validity for the facet scales, with some minor exceptions that probably reflect sample characteristics.

Quite a few studies bear on the validity of *particular* JDI facet scales. For example, Keller and Szilagyi (1976) examined job satisfaction in relation to positive and punitive leader reward behaviors. The positive supervision style showed a particularly strong association with JDI Supervision ($r = .75$) relative to other facets. However, this pattern was not evident for the punitive style. Thus JDI Supervision may be more sensitive to variations in positive than punitive supervision. Dyer and Theriault (1976) found that salary level was associated with Pay satisfaction for a sample of managers. Alutto and Acito (1974) found that feeling deprived of decision-making power was associated particularly with JDI Promotion and Supervision satisfaction ($r = -.56$ and $-.44$, respectively), as might be predicted.

JDI facet scales have also been related to global job satisfaction measures in a number of studies, and the consistency of findings is instructive. Cook et al. (1981) review eight such studies involving diverse samples. In most cases, all the JDI scales showed small to moderate associations with various global job satisfaction measures. In every case, the Work facet scale showed the strongest association (mean $r = .66$, range = .53–.74).

Overall, comparisons to related measures support the convergent and discriminant validity of the JDI job facet satisfaction scales. That is not to say that the instrument's validity might not be further explored and improved. Studies involving comparisons with multiple measures of job satisfaction are particularly instructive because they suggest whether limits in convergent or discriminant validity reflect on the target instrument or comparison criteria. Were the Dunham et al. (1977) findings to be replicated with other samples and other comparison measures, efforts to improve the already good validity of the JDI might be warranted.

*Construct validity.* A great many studies have examined predicted relationships between JDI scales and a host of other variables.

One line of research concerns differences in job satisfaction by level of worker. There appears to be a relatively straightforward association between job status and Work satisfaction (Milutinovich, 1977; Ronen, 1978; Waters, Roach, & Waters, 1976), but satisfaction with other facets of the job may be curvilinear; that is, greatest among medium-level employees (Ronen, 1978). An important issue in such comparative studies is measurement equivalence: Differences among groups are only meaningful if the measure is assessing the same psychological characteristics. Drasgow and Kanfer (1985) examined this issue for the JDI using Joreskog's simultaneous factor analysis procedures. They analyzed data from both homogeneous and heterogeneous samples: employees of five hospitals and employees in three disparate industries (hospitals, retailing, and naval reserve). Both data sets yielded simultaneous factors consistent with the design of the JDI. The authors conclude that the JDI provides equivalent measurement across diverse groups and that mean differences in JDI scores reflect meaningful variations in job satisfaction.

A complementary line of research seeks to understand job satisfaction in relation to both personal and job characteristics. For example, Sterns, Alexander, Barret, and Dambrot (1983) found an inverse relationship between extraversion and job satisfaction, particularly with Work, Supervision, and Co-workers, but not Pay or Promotion. They explained this in terms of activation theory: extraversion was associated also with such work preferences as high cognitive task demands, high pace, a social task environment, and so on—job features that were not readily available to these nonmanagerial clerical employees.

A number of studies have related job involvement and commitment to satisfaction using the JDI. For example, in a study of insurance company employees, Newman (1975) found that job involvement showed modest correlations with facets of job satisfaction, but a stronger association with the Work satisfaction scale ($r$ = 57). Saal (1978) observed similar associations for a sample of nonsupervisory employees, particularly with JDI Work ($r$ = .52) and Supervision ($r$ = .47). Organizational commitment has shown similar associations with job satisfaction, especially with Work, Pay, and Co-workers among military aviation personnel (O'Reilly, Bretton, & Roberts, 1974) and with Work, Promotion, and Supervision among telephone company employees (Stone & Porter, 1975).

The JDI has been widely used in research on the relationship between job performance and satisfaction. These studies have not always yielded consistent findings. For example, Kesselman, Wood, and Hagen (1974) found moderate correlations between supervisor ratings of job performance and JDI satisfaction scores, especially Work and Pay, for a sample of draftswomen and telephone operators. However, Inkson (1978) found very modest correlations between supervisor ratings and satisfaction scores for New Zealand male manual employees. A good deal of research seeks to understand under what conditions the association holds. For example, Norris and Niebuhr (1984) found some evidence that organizational tenure operates as a moderator, job performance being related to global satisfaction and to satisfaction with Work and Supervision only for those with the company for less than 5 years.

The belief in an association between performance and satisfaction is longstanding, controversial, and the basis of several alternative models. It is also the focus of two recent meta-analyses (Iaffaldano & Muchinsky, 1985; Petty, McGee, & Cavender, 1984). Petty et al. (1984) restricted their review to studies using the JDI and/or measures of global satisfaction published between 1964 and 1983. Correcting for attenuation due to unreliability of measures, the average correlation between performance and global satisfaction was .41 for professional, managerial, supervisory samples and .20 for nonmanagerial samples. Most relevant for present purposes are the analyses involving facets of job satisfaction. The most consistent findings were for satisfaction with Promotion and Supervision and even these were modest (mean $r$ = .16 and .20).

Iaffaldano and Muchinsky (1985) reviewed 70 studies yielding 217 effect sizes for the association between satisfaction and performance. Their estimate of the relationship, corrected for sampling error and attenuation due to unreliability of measures, was .17, not substantially different from a review two decades earlier (Vroom, 1964). Analyses did not separate the JDI completely from, for example, the MSQ. Nevertheless, some findings are sobering. Larger effect sizes were *not* associated with a variety of study characteristics, including use of the JDI or MSQ overall score, use of an established measure (like JDI), use of JDI Work satisfaction, or examination of any particular facets of job satisfaction. These findings do not cast doubt on the validity of the JDI in particular. They do have implications for future efforts to evaluate its validity in relation to job performance. Indeed, Iaffaldano and Muchinsky (1985) conclude that the presumed association between job satisfaction and performance owes more to organizational program and policy assumptions than to empirical evidence.

Another major area of research involving the JDI concerns the relationship between job satisfaction and role conflict and ambiguity. Fisher and Gitelson (1983) conducted a meta-analysis of 43 studies from this literature. Again, studies employing the JDI were not treated separately, but these occur with sufficient frequency to throw some light on the validity of the measure. The mean effect sizes for overall satisfaction with role conflict and role ambiguity were moderate (−.35 and −.25). With respect to particular facets of job satisfaction, Supervision (−.37), Co-workers (−.31), and Pay (−.20) were most strongly related to role conflict, whereas Promotion (−.24) and Co-workers (−.22) were most strongly related to role ambiguity. Though modest, these population estimates are substantial, being greater than 2 standard deviations above 0 (Hunter, Schmidt, & Jackson, 1982). Efforts to examine variation in effects across job types proved unenlightening. There was some small but inconsistent indication of larger effects for professional relative to lower level and managerial employees. Again, these meta-analyses provide some support for the construct validity of the JDI along with other measures of job satisfaction. They also serve as a benchmark for more focused studies of validity.

## Critique

Overall the JDI is an excellent measure of job satisfaction. It is simple to administer, easily understood by workers with limited education, and is applicable to a wide range of job situations. Moreover, it appears to retain measurement equivalence over widely different occupations. A key feature of the measure is that it was carefully designed to assess five facets of job satisfaction. There is considerable evidence that it does so, certainly that the items reflect five relatively independent dimensions. The five scales show excellent internal consistency and stability. The dimensional structure of the measure is stable, robust, and congruent over a wide range of occupational types and levels. The five facets scales have consistently shown very good convergent and discriminant validity with related satisfaction measures and also predicted relationships with theoretically related variables. In sum, the widespread use of the JDI is justified by its simplicity and robust psychometric quality.

No measure is perfect, however. Even excellent measures can be improved, and they often need to be updated merely to retain their quality. Several minor problems with the JDI can be noted. First, though justified by the authors, scoring of responses (Yes, No, ?) is unusual and may lead to confusion. Several studies have examined Likert-type response formats for the JDI. Johnson, Smith, and Tucker (1982) compared the traditional and a 5-point agree/disagree format through a multitrait, multimethod procedure with data from college students. They found that facet scales with the new format showed good convergent validity with those in the traditional format (mean $r$ = .66). Scales from both versions also showed good discriminant validity. The Kavanagh et al. (1971) procedure indicated that the new format yielded greater discriminant validity, but also greater method bias, than the traditional format. Finally, several of the traditional format scales were skewed, though none of the new format scales were (see also Rassmussen, 1989; Watson, Watson, & Stowe, 1985). Johnson et al. (1982) conclude that the alternative method does not yield any substantial benefits.

Gregson (1987) analyzed a short form of the JDI, using the 30 best items from Smith et al. (1969), with Likert-type items. Data from a national sample of public accountants were factor analyzed. A clean interpretable factor solution emerged, consistent with the traditional five facets. Scales showed excellent internal consistency (mean alpha = .86, range = .84–.90) and moderate interdependence (mean $r$ = .41, range = .32–.53). In sum, Likert-type formats appear to have convergent and discriminant validity and a dimensional structure comparable to the traditional version.

The second problem concerns the variation in number of items per scale. Apparently not all researchers follow the recommended procedure of doubling scores for the short scales, leading to problems in comparing satisfaction levels across studies. The short scales might also underrepresent the content of those facets of satisfaction.

Third, the scales were developed prior to the rise of interest in intrinsic job satisfaction and underrepresent such facets (e.g., helping others, being challenged, learning, producing quality products, enjoying social aspects of work).

Fourth, Smith et al. (1969) discouraged use of the JDI as a measure of global job satisfaction, yet there appears to be a second-order factor reflecting general job satisfaction.

Fifth, evidence suggests that several facets (Supervision, Work, possibly Coworkers) might be further differentiated, possibly requiring development of new items. Heneman and Schwab (1985), for example, developed the Pay Satisfaction Questionnaire (PSQ), which taps four relatively independent aspects of compensation, and they found that both JDI and PSQ Pay scales only tap level of pay, not benefits, raises, structure, or administration.

Sixth and most important, the JDI still lacks a manual that provides a clear set of recommended procedures for use of the instrument along with a summary of reliability, validity, and normative data. However, Balzer and Smith (in press) have a manual in preparation and it will be available soon.

In summary, the JDI is a widely used measure and deservedly so. The new developments briefly discussed here should only improve this already excellent measure, which undoubtedly will see many more years of research and practical service.

## References

This list includes text citations and suggested additional reading.

Aldag, R.J., & Brief, A.P. (1978). Examination of alternative models of job satisfaction. *Human Relations, 31,* 91–98.

Alutto, J.A., & Acito, F. (1974). Decisional participation and sources of job satisfaction: A study of manufacturing personnel. *Academy of Management Journal, 20,* 334–341.

Balzer, W.K., & Smith, P.C. (in press). *User's manual for the Job Description Index (JDI) and the Job in General (JIG) scales.* Bowling Green, OH: Bowling Green State University.

Birnbaum, P.H., Farh, J.L., & Wong, G.Y.Y. (1986). The job characteristics model in Hong Kong. *Journal of Applied Psychology, 71,* 598–605.

Blake, R.R., & Mouton, J.S. (1964). *The managerial grid.* Houston, TX: Gulf Publishing.

Brayfield, A.H., & Rothe, H.F. (1951). An index of job satisfaction. *Journal of Applied Psychology, 35,* 307–311.

Campbell, D.T., & Fiske, D.W. (1959). Convergent and discriminant validation by the multitrait-multimethod matrix. *Psychological Bulletin, 56,* 81–105.

Candell, G.L., & Hulin, C.L. (1986). Cross-language and cross-cultural comparisons in scale translations: Independent sources of information about item nonequivalence. *Journal of Cross-Cultural Psychology, 17,* 417–440.

Cawsey, T.F., Reed, P.L., & Reddon, J.R. (1982). Human needs and job satisfaction: A multidimensional approach. *Human Relations, 35,* 703–715.

Cook, J.D., Hepworth, S.J., Wall, T.D., & Warr, P.B. (1981). *The experience of work: A compendium and review of 249 measures and their use.* New York: Academic Press.

Downey, H.K., Sheridan, J.E., & Slocum, J.W. (1976). The path-goal theory of leadership: A longitudinal analysis. *Organizational Behavior and Human Performance, 16,* 156–176.

Drasgow, F., & Kanfer, R. (1985). Equivalence of psychological measurement in heterogeneous populations. *Journal of Applied Psychology, 70,* 662–680.

Dunham, R.B., Smith, F.J., & Blackburn, R.S. (1977). Validation of the Index of Organizational Reactions with the JDI, the MSQ, and Faces scales. *Academy of Management Journal, 20,* 420–432.

Dyer, L., & Theriault, R.D. (1976). The determinants of pay satisfaction. *Journal of Applied Psychology, 61,* 596–604.

Evans, M.G. (1969). Conceptual and operational problems in the measurement of various aspects of job satisfaction. *Journal of Applied Psychology, 53,* 93–101.

Fisher, C.D., & Gitelson, R. (1983). A meta-analysis of the correlates of role conflict and ambiguity. *Journal of Applied Psychology, 68,* 320–333.

Gillet, B., & Schwab, D.P. (1975). Convergent and discriminant validities of corresponding Job Descriptive Index and Minnesota Satisfaction Questionnaire scales. *Journal of Applied Psychology, 60,* 313–317.

Gold, R.S., Webb, L.J., & Smith, J.K. (1982). Racial differences in job satisfaction among white and black mental health employees. *The Journal of Psychology, 111,* 255–261.

Gregson, T. (1987). Factor analysis of a multiple-choice format for job satisfaction. *Psychological Reports, 61,* 747–750.

Hanser, L.M., & Muchinsky, P.M. (1978). Work as an information environment. *Organizational Behavior and Human Performance, 21,* 47–60.

Hartman, S., Grigsby, D.W., Crino, M.D., & Chokar, J.S. (1986). The measurement of job satisfaction by action tendencies. *Educational and Psychological Measurement, 46,* 317–329.

Heneman, H.G., III, & Schwab, D.P. (1985). Pay satisfaction: Its multidimensional nature and measurement. *International Journal of Psychology, 20,* 129–141.

Herman, J.B., & Hulin, C.L. (1973). Managerial satisfactions and organizational roles: An investigation of Porter's need deficiency scales. *Journal of Applied Psychology, 57,* 118–124.

Herzberg, F., Mausner, B., Petersen, R.D., & Capwell, D.F. (1957). *Job attitudes: Review of research and opinion.* Pittsburgh, PA: Psychological Service of Pittsburgh.

Hulin, C.L. (1987). A psychometric theory of evaluations of item and scale translations: Fidelity across languages. *Journal of Cross-Cultural Psychology, 18,* 115–142.

Hunter, J.E., Schmidt, F.L., & Jackson, G.B. (1982). *Meta-analysis: Cumulating research findings across studies.* Beverly Hills, CA: Sage.

Iaffaldano, M.T., & Muchinsky, P.M. (1985). Job satisfaction and job performance: A meta-analysis. *Psychological Bulletin, 97,* 251–273.

Imparato, N. (1972). Relationship between Porter's Need Satisfaction Questionnaire and the Job Descriptive Index. *Journal of Applied Psychology, 56,* 397–405.

Inkson, J.H.K. (1978). Self-esteem as a moderator of the relationship between job performance and job satisfaction. *Journal of Applied Psychology, 63,* 243–247.

Ironson, G.H., Smith, P.C., Brannick, M.T., Gibson, W.M., & Paul, K.B. (1989). Construction of a job in general scale: A comparison of global, composite, and specific measures. *Journal of Applied Psychology, 74,* 193–200.

Johnson, S.M., Smith, P.C., & Tucker, S.M. (1982). Response format of the Job Descriptive

Index: Assessment of reliability and validity by the multitrait-multimethod matrix. *Journal of Applied Psychology, 67*, 500–505.

Joyce, W.F., & Slocum, J. (1982). Climate discrepancy: Refining the concepts of psychological and organizational climate. *Human Relations, 35*, 951–972.

Jung, K.G., Dalessio, A., & Johnson, S.M. (1986). Stability of the factor structure of the Job Descriptive Index. *Academy of Management Journal, 29*, 609–616.

Kavanagh, M.J., MacKinney, A.C., & Wolins, L. (1971). Issues in managerial performance: Multitrait-multimethod analysis of ratings. *Psychological Bulletin, 75*, 34–39.

Keller, R.T., & Szilagyi, A.D. (1976). Employee reactions to leader reward behavior. *Academy of Managerial Journal, 19*, 619–627.

Kesselman, G.A., Wood, M.T., & Hagen, E.L. (1974). Relationships between performance and satisfaction under contingent and non-contingent reward systems. *Journal of Applied Psychology, 59*, 374–376.

Kunin, T. (1955). The construction of a new type of attitude measure. *Personnel Psychology, 8*, 65–78.

Locke, E.A., Smith, P.C., & Hulin, C. (1965). *Cornell studies of satisfaction: V. Scale characteristics of the Job Descriptive Index.* Unpublished manuscript, Cornell University.

Locke, E.A., Smith, P.C., Kendall, L.M., Hulin, C.H., & Miller, A.M. (1964). Convergent and discriminant validity for areas and methods of rating job satisfaction. *Journal of Applied Psychology, 48*, 313–319.

Milutinovich, J.S. (1977). Black-white differences in job satisfaction, group cohesiveness, and leadership style. *Human Relations, 30*, 1079–1087.

Newman, J.E. (1975). Understanding the organizational structure–job attitude relationship through perceptions of the work environment. *Organizational Behavior and Human Performance, 14*, 371–397.

Norris, D.R., & Niebuhr, R.E. (1984). Organization tenure as a moderator of the job satisfaction–job performance relationship. *Journal of Vocational Behavior, 24*, 169–178.

O'Connor, E.J., Peters, L.H., & Gordon, S.M. (1978). The measurement of job satisfaction: Current practices and future considerations. *Journal of Management, 4*, 17–26.

O'Reilly, C.A., Bretton, G.E., & Roberts, K.H. (1974). Professional employees' preference for upward mobility: An extension. *Journal of Vocational Behavior, 5*, 139–145.

Parsons, C.K. (1983). The identification of people for whom Job Descriptive Index scores are inappropriate. *Organizational Behavior and Human Performance, 31*, 365–393.

Parsons, C.K., & Hulin, C.L. (1982). An empirical comparison of item response theory and hierarchical factor analysis in applications to the measurement of job satisfaction. *Journal of Applied Psychology, 67*, 826–834.

Penley, L.E., & Hawkins, B.L. (1980). Organizational communication, performance, and job satisfaction as a function of ethnicity and sex. *Journal of Vocational Behavior, 16*, 368–384.

Petty, M.M., McGee, G.W., & Cavender, J.W. (1984). A meta-analysis of the relationships between individual job satisfaction and individual performance. *Academy of Management Review, 9*, 712–721.

Pierce, J.L., McTavish, D.G., & Knudsen, K.R. (1986). The measurement of job characteristics: A content and contextual analytic look at scale validity. *Journal of Occupational Behavior, 7*, 299–313.

Rahim, A. (1982). Reliability and validity of Likert's profile of organizational characteristics. *The Journal of Psychology, 112*, 153–157.

Rasmussen, J.L. (1989). Score distributions of the Job Descriptive Index: An evaluation of the effects of transformation. *Educational and Psychological Measurement, 49*, 89–98.

Ronen, S. (1978). Personal values: A basis for work motivational set and work attitude. *Organizational Behavior and Human Performance, 21*, 80–107.

Rosse, J.G., & Hulin, C.L. (1985). Adaptation to work: An analysis of employee health, withdrawal, and change. *Organizational Behavior and Human Decision Processes, 36,* 324–347.

Roznowski, M. (1989). Examination of the measurement properties of the Job Descriptive Index with experimental items. *Journal of Applied Psychology, 74,* 805–814.

Saal, F.E. (1978). Job involvement: A multivariate approach. *Journal of Applied Psychology, 63,* 53–61.

Sawyer, J.E. (1988). Measuring attitudes across job levels: When are scale scores truly comparable? *Organizational Behavior and Human Decision Processes, 42,* 324–342.

Schneider, B., & Dachler, H.P. (1978). A note on the stability of the Job Descriptive Index. *Journal of Applied Psychology, 63,* 650–653.

Schneider, B., & Snyder, R.A. (1975). Some relationships between job satisfaction and organizational climate. *Journal of Applied Psychology, 60,* 318–328.

Schuler, R.S. (1979). A role perception transactional process model for organizational communication-outcome relationships. *Organizational Behavior and Human Performance, 23,* 268–291.

Smith, P.C., Balzer, W., Brannick, M.T., Chia, W., Eggleston, S., Gibson, W., Johnson, B., Josephson, H., Paul, K., Reilly, C., & Whalen, M. (1989). The revised JDI: A face lift for an old friend. *The Industrial-Organizational Psychologist, 24,* 31–33.

Smith, P.C., Kendall, L.M., & Hulin, C.L. (1969). *The measurement of satisfaction in work and retirement: A strategy for the study of attitudes.* Chicago: Rand McNally.

Smith, P.C., Smith, O.W., & Rollo, J. (1974). Factor structure for blacks and whites of the Job Descriptive Index and its discrimination of job satisfaction. *Journal of Applied Psychology, 59,* 99–100.

Sterns, L., Alexander, R.A., Barrett, G.V., & Dambrot, F.H. (1983). The relationship of extraversion and neuroticism with job preferences and job satisfaction for clerical employees. *Journal of Occupational Psychology, 56,* 145–153.

Stone, E.F., & Porter, L.W. (1975). Job characteristics and job attitudes: A multivariate study. *Journal of Applied Psychology, 60,* 57–64.

Vroom, V.H. (1964). *Work and motivation.* New York: Wiley.

Waters, L.K., Roach, D., & Waters, C.W. (1976). Estimates of future tenure, satisfaction, and biographical variables as predictors of termination. *Personnel Psychology, 29,* 57–60.

Watson, C.J., Watson, K.D., & Stowe, J.D. (1985). Univariate and multivariate distributions of the Job Descriptive Index's measures of job satisfaction. *Organizational Behavior and Human Decision Processes, 35,* 241–251.

Yeager, S.J. (1981). Dimensionality of the Job Descriptive Index. *Academy of Management Journal, 24,* 205–212.

**Susan M. Raza, Ph.D.**
*President, The People Planner, Tulsa, Oklahoma.*

# KEEGAN TYPE INDICATOR

*Warren J. Keegan. Rye, New York: Warren J. Keegan and Associates Press.*

## Introduction

The Keegan Type Indicator (KTI) is a self-administered and self-scored paper-and-pencil assessment of three aspects of the respondent's personality: way of perceiving reality (perception), way of making decisions (judgment), and attitude toward life (orientation). Each aspect is bipolar. People perceive by using either sensation or intuition, judge using thinking or feeling, and are oriented to the inner or outer world. The test is designed to expand adults' self-knowledge. Theoretically, through an understanding of type, the respondent can learn to be more effective in expressing talent and appreciating and using the talents and creativity of others. The author cautions against using the KTI to label and categorize individuals and suggests instead that test results be used as a framework for understanding perceiving, judging, and orientation. The test is based on C.G. Jung's theory of psychological types.

Dr. Warren J. Keegan took both his M.B.A. and D.B.A. from Harvard University and at present successfully pursues a career as a management consultant. He has been the president of Warren Keegan Associates for the past 20 years and the owner and operator of Warren J. Keegan and Associates Press for the past 10 years. He is the sole author and developer of the KTI, which he views a useful tool in his management consulting work.

Keegan developed the KTI as an aid to adults wishing to increase their self-understanding with regard to personality. He hoped that interested adults could apply this self-knowledge productively in their business, professional, and personal lives. Based on the conceptualizations of C.J. Jung, the test measures four functions of the mind organized into two bipolar pairs: perceptive functions (sensation/intuition) and judging functions (thinking/feeling). The members of the pairs are in opposition. One of the four functions will be superior or more conscious, dominant, and habitual than the others; its opposite is viewed as inferior or relatively unconscious, undeveloped, and repressed. The remaining two functions have intermediate strength. When one of the perceptive functions is superior, the individual theoretically prefers to live in a more flexible, spontaneous manner. In contrast, when one of the judging functions is superior, the individual prefers a more planned existence. Additionally, the test assesses a bipolar attitude or orientation to life. A person is either outer directed, object oriented, and extraverted, or inner directed, subject oriented, and introverted. The four functions of the mind and the two attitudes combine to form 16 personality types.

Type characteristics are believed to be inherited rather than learned and to go through three stages of development during a person's lifetime. In the first stage the dominant attitude of the child is clearly recognizable; in the second stage, early adulthood, one or more functions may be repressed in order to achieve success in the business or academic world. In the final stage, mid-life, people begin to give more attention to the repressed parts of their personality.

The KTI was originally copyrighted in 1979. The current KTI–Form B, a revision of the original, was copyrighted in 1982. Personal communication from the office of Warren Keegan Associates Incorporated (no published documentation is available) indicated that the original KTI took approximately 3 years to develop and the revision required an additional 3 years.

The KTI is a completely self-administered 44-item test. The two-page booklet includes a separate answer sheet designed to aid in the self-scoring process. Parts I and II of this three-part test have a forced-choice format. Part I consists of 27 items in which the respondent reads a sentence stem and chooses one of two endings; Part II presents nine adjective pairs and the respondent chooses the preferred member of the pair. Part III is a relative-ranking device. For each of the eight questions the respondent rank orders the four alternatives to reflect the degree to which the alternatives describe the respondent.

The directions for self-administration are very clear, although they may be difficult to follow in practice. The respondent is asked first to distinguish between "natural and innate preference," what he or she would like to be, and how he or she acts to meet the expectations of others, and then to respond based on natural and innate preference. Based on the Fog Index, the readability of the KTI is approximately 10th grade (Gunning, 1968). The response format is convenient and easy to use because the respondent circles and ranks the choices directly on the test form. The test can be self-scored by following directions enclosed with the test form. The examiner need only pass out and collect the surveys; however, because the scoring system is somewhat complex, he or she may wish to check the respondent's scoring or actually do the scoring for the respondent.

The KTI assesses four functions of the mind: sensation (perceiving reality through sight, hearing, taste, touch, and smell); intuition (perceiving reality via the sixth sense or holistic perception); thinking (determining the logical consequences of an action and deciding impersonally on the basis of cause and effect); and feeling (taking into account what matters to people and deciding on the basis of personal valuation). It also assesses two attitudes toward life: extraversion (outer directed and object oriented) and introversion (inner directed and subject oriented). When the scoring is complete, the respondent will obtain a three-letter code indicating which member of each the three bipolar scales is prominent. To interpret the results, the respondent or the examiner rank orders the four mental functions by determining whether perception or decision making is more prominent or superior. (The methods for doing this are discussed in the next section.)

**Practical Applications/Uses**

The KTI is intended to further self-awareness in adults and to promote understanding and appreciation of the personality of others. Armed with that understanding a person may be better able to use personality strengths, find ways to compensate for weaknesses, ensure that the working environment has all necessary types represented, and communicate more effectively with different types of people.

The author suggests a number of industrial organizational applications for the KTI. For example, a manager who is aware of personal strengths and weaknesses can play to the strengths and make certain that a person(s) of a complementary type is in a position to influence the manager. Also, by knowing the personality type, a manager can place a person in a type-appropriate position in which success is more likely.

To the extent that the KTI is a reliable and valid personality assessment instrument, it could be used by researchers wishing to investigate personality, by clinicians and counselors wishing to assess the personality characteristics of their clients as a treatment and planning aid, by vocational counselors advising clients as to personality-appropriate jobs, by industrial/organizational psychologists designing and validating selection batteries that include a personality measure, and by interested individuals wishing to gain a better understanding of self and others.

The user's manual (Keegan, 1982) does not specifically describe the type of subject for whom this test is appropriate, although it implies adults. The readability level of approximately 10th grade suggests individuals who are at least 16 years old and somewhat better than average readers. The manual also does not describe any details of test administration. However, because the test is self-administered and self-scored, it likely can be administered in both individual and group settings and would not require the presence of an examiner other than to pass out and collect the tests.

Upon completion of the test, the respondent is asked to transfer his or her responses first to an enclosed answer sheet and then to the scoring sheet located on the back of the test booklet. The test is scored by following the instructions detailed on the scoring sheet. The scoring system, requiring transferring answers from one place to another and multiplying scores by specific weights, is mildly complex. Instructions are given in step-by-step order, and, if they are precisely followed, a respondent who read the test with no difficulty would have little difficulty scoring it.

Interpreting the KTI results is much more challenging because it requires the interpreter to determine the individual's superior or most readily available function of the mind. In the user's manual, Dr. Keegan states that there are three methods for determining the superior function: (a) the function with the highest score in the pair with the greatest score difference, (b) the function with the highest score, and (c) the function that is opposite the weakest function, which is determined by reflecting on personal experience. If these three methods result in the same superior function, the latter is clear. However, if they do not result in the same superior function, Keegan recommends relying on personal experience and a rational estimation of the superior function. He states in the user's manual, "No instrument can substitute for self-reflection and self-knowledge" (Keegan, 1982, p. 2). A thorough interpretation of the wealth of information provided by personality types requires an in-depth understanding of C.G. Jung's theories and their application to individuals' daily lives.

**Technical Aspects**

The KTI has a good theoretical foundation. However, based on the limited technical information available (Mack, 1980), it is not psychometrically sound.

The above report prepared by Murray J. Mack and provided to this reviewer by the test author presents the results of an initial reliability study investigating the internal consistency of the KTI. As the report does not state whether Form B or some other form was investigated and does not specify the number or type of subjects who participated, it is difficult for the reader to evaluate the study. A personal communication from the office of Warren Keegan Associates Incorporated assured this reviewer that the technical report investigated Form B.

Assuming that an adequate number of subjects representing the population who would be using this tool participated in the reliability study, it is clear that the KTI needs a great deal of work before it can be seen as a reliable tool. The reliability study evaluated the results of Parts I and II separately from Part III due to the difference in response format. The study discussed three sets of results: scale intercorrelations, reliability estimates, and item intercorrelations. First, in all cases moderately high scale intercorrelations, ranging from –.16 to .27, suggest that the three bipolar dimensions are not independent. Second, measures of internal consistency (KR-20) were unacceptably low, ranging from .52 to .78, which suggests that the dimensions are not internally consistent. Rather, it is likely that they are measuring more than one construct. Finally, item intercorrelations revealed that, although items significantly correlated with the appropriate dimension, they also frequently significantly correlated with additional dimensions. This suggests the presence of an additional factor(s) or dimension(s) underlying the structure of the KTI.

As the KTI has an unacceptably low reliability, its validity becomes a moot point. No validity studies could be found.

**Critique**

The KTI has a fascinating and rich theoretical foundation as it is based on Carl Jung's conceptualizations of personality type. Unfortunately, the instrument is psychometrically unsound. It was designed to assess three independent bipolar aspects of personality, but a reliability study provided by the test author strongly suggests that the scales are not independent, that they are not internally consistent, and that there are additional factors or dimensions that underlie the instrument's structure. I echo the recommendations of the author of the reliability study (Mack, 1980), who suggested (a) a factor analysis of test items to determine what the test is actually measuring and (b) a test-retest reliability study to determine the stability of the measurement over time.

Keegan has done a fine job of discussing the theoretical aspects of personality type in the user's manual and has provided a wide variety of potential uses for the KTI, all focusing on self-awareness and using that knowledge to benefit self and others. The response format is easy to use and the test is short enough to hold the attention of even the most restless executive or manager. Reliability and validity studies and revisions of the KTI to create a sound instrument would add to our ability to assess personality and to communicate the assessments in a way that is immediately applicable to everyday life. Until that is done this reviewer cannot recommend the use of this instrument.

## References

Gunning, R. (1968). *The techniques of clear writing*. New York: McGraw-Hill.

Jung, C.G. (1976). *Psychological types: The collected works of C.G. Jung* (Vol. 6, Bollingen Series XX). Princeton, NJ: Princeton University Press. (Originally published in German as Psychologische Typen, Rascher Verlag, Zurich, 1921)

Keegan, W.J. (1982). *Keegan Type Indicator user's manual*. Washington, DC: Warren J. Keegan & Assoc.

Mack, M.J. (1980). *Psychometric evaluation of the Keegan Type Indicator.* Unpublished manuscript, George Washington University, Washington, DC.

**Zoa Rockenstein, Ph.D.**
*Assistant Professor of Applied Psychology, St. Cloud State University, St. Cloud, Minnesota.*

# KHATENA-TORRANCE CREATIVE PERCEPTION INVENTORY

*Joe Khatena and E. Paul Torrance. Bensenville, Illinois: Scholastic Testing Service, Inc.*

## Introduction

The Khatena-Torrance Creative Perception Inventory (KTCPI; Khatena & Torrance, 1976) consists of two separate autobiographical instruments designed to measure different dimensions of the creative personality. The two instruments, What Kind of Person Are You? (WKOPAY) and Something About Myself (SAM), may be administered separately or together. Both tests are appropriate for adolescents in Grades 7 through 12 and for adults. Each will be described separately in this review.

Torrance and Khatena are prolific writers in the area of creativity. Both have produced textbooks in this area as well as numerous journal articles and other publications. They also are authors of additional tests of creativity, the Torrance Tests of Creative Thinking being the most widely used of these.

*What Kind of Person Are You? (WKOPAY).* Biographical data have been found useful in identifying gifted and creative persons. Personality measures, such as the California Personality Inventory (Gough, 1957), the Omnibus Personality Inventory (Heist & Yonge, 1968), and the Myers-Briggs Type Indicator (Myers, 1962), have provided high or low creativity scores as a part of a personality profile. In using these measures in their own research, Khatena and Torrance felt a need for an instrument that would yield a single index of the "creative personality." The WKOPAY was developed with this purpose in mind.

Construction of the WKOPAY was based on theories concerning the relationship between self-concept and character development (Anderson, 1952). Rationale for the WKOPAY is based on the idea that the psychological self of the individual contains creative and noncreative ways of behaving. Test items were designed to provide verbal stimuli to the creative subselves so that response to the item would reveal creative aspects of the personality of the test subject.

Test items were selected from a survey of empirical studies on creative persons conducted by Torrance in 1962. Torrance chose 84 characteristics that had been found in over 50 studies to differentiate between creative and less creative individuals. The list was later reduced to 66 characteristics. The 66 characteristics were then rated by a panel of 10 research assistants knowledgeable in the area of the creative personality. Characteristics were ranked using the Q-sort technique (Torrance, 1965). The rankings resulted in 50 items arranged in a forced-choice format.

Normative data were derived from 4,362 subjects from various parts of the

United States. College students attending the University of Minnesota, University of North Dakota, Fresno State College, Emporia State Teachers College, University of Georgia, East Carolina University, Marshall University, Erskine College, Morgan State College, University of South Florida, and Indiana University contributed to the data, as did teachers from Macon, Georgia; Berkeley, California; St. Paul, Minnesota; and Daytona Beach, Florida. Adolescent norms were obtained in Georgia, Virginia, and West Virginia.

The WKOPAY is a self-report instrument containing 50 forced-choice items. The subject may be asked to choose between two socially desirable or two socially undesirable characteristics. In other items, the subject chooses between creative and relatively noncreative characteristics.

The *Khatena-Torrance Creative Perception Inventory Instruction Manual* (Khatena & Torrance, 1976) provides detailed information on test development, administration, and scoring. Tables summarizing a variety of studies on the KTCPI are included, as well as conversion tables for converting raw scores to standard scores.

The WKOPAY provides a wide range of information. In addition to the Creative Perception Index score, the test scores for five related factors described as follows (Khatena & Torrance, 1976, pp. 18–19):

1. *Acceptance of Authority:* obedient, courteous, conforming, and accepting the judgments of others.
2. *Self-Confidence:* socially well adjusted, self-confident, energetic, curious, and remembering well.
3. *Inquisitiveness:* always asking questions, being self-assertive, feeling strong emotions, being talkative and obedient.
4. *Awareness of Others:* courteous, socially well adjusted, popular or well liked, considerate of others, and preferring to work in a group.
5. *Disciplined Imagination:* energetic, persistent, thorough, industrious, imaginative, adventurous, never bored, attempting difficult assignments, and preferring complex tasks.

According to the factor analysis performed on these factors, Factor I (Acceptance of Authority) indicates a noncreative orientation whereas Factor V (Disciplined Imagination) indicates a creative orientation. The other three factors contain both creative and noncreative elements.

The profile for the WKOPAY shows the overall Creative Perception Index score plus scores for the five factor orientations. The scoring worksheet provides space for descriptive information on the subject along with columns for raw and standard scores. A graph at the bottom of the worksheet displays the five factors in relation to one another.

*Something About Myself (SAM).* Construction of the Something About Myself test followed as a result of Khatena's desire to provide an autobiographical screening device for creative people. The instrument is based on the work of Rhodes (1961), who suggested that creative people could be identified by their personality characteristics or "person," their thinking operations or "process," their results or "product," and their manner of coping with stress or "press." SAM is designed to provide information about the individual's creative personality characteristics, process, and products. The original 100 test items were based on a review of the literature. These were refined, through intercorrelation, to the 50 items that presently comprise the test.

SAM is a self-report checklist that can be administered to adolescents and adults, individually or in groups. In addition to the overall score, the SAM provides information about six factors described as follows (Khatena & Torrance, 1976, pp. 30–31):

1. *Environmental Sensitivity:* open to ideas of others, relating ideas to sensory experiences, interest in humor and beauty in experience, sensitivity to meaningful relationships.

2. *Initiative:* directing, producing, or playing leads in dramatic or musical performances, producing new formulas or new products, and acting as a change agent.

3. *Self-Strength:* self-confidence in talent competition, resourcefulness, versatility, risk taking, desire to excel, and organizational ability.

4. *Intellectuality:* intellectual curiosity, enjoyment of challenging tasks, imagination, preference for adventure over routine, delight in synthesizing ideas and things, dislike for routines.

5. *Individuality:* preference for working alone, self-starter, eccentric, critical of others' work, thinking for oneself, working tirelessly for long periods.

6. *Artistry:* production in the visual arts, musical composition, receiving awards or prizes, having exhibits, production of literary works.

## Practical Applications/Uses

*What Kind of Person Are You? (WKOPAY).* The WKOPAY was designed to provide an overall creativity index and to provide scores for the five personality factors: (a) Acceptance of Authority, (b) Self-Confidence, (c) Inquisitiveness, (d) Awareness of Others, and (e) Disciplined Imagination. The test was originally used to help graduate students in creativity classes understand their own creativity. In the process of taking and scoring the test, students gained some insight into the evaluation of creativity as a personality subself.

The WKOPAY serves other useful functions. It can be used by counselors in personality assessment and would be useful in personnel selection. It also could be used in early interview stages where creativity was a desirable characteristic of prospective employees. As a personnel tool, it might also assist managers and administrators in understanding the personality dynamics of creative employees. The WKOPAY is an excellent tool for researchers, especially those who are curious about the relationship of creativity to other dimensions of the personality.

Administration of the WKOPAY can be easily accomplished in either an individual or group setting. It requires no special qualifications of an examiner other than an ability to read the instructions, and it can be self-administered if desired. There is no time limit, and most subjects complete the test in 5 to 10 minutes.

A scoring key is provided in the manual. The test is scored rapidly by awarding 0 or 1 point to each item. The credit range for the Creative Perception Index is 0 to 50. This index is determined by adding the number of items for which 1 point was awarded. The five factors are also scored by awarding 0 to 1 point as indicated on the scoring key. The raw score for each factor is the total of points given for that factor.

Scoring instructions are clearly presented, and the instrument is easily scored by hand. The WKOPAY could be computer scored with the use of an appropriate answer sheet. Separate keys would be required for each factor. Interpretation of the scores is simplified by the separate scores on the five factors in addition to the total score (creative perception index). Scores are easily interpreted by trained or lay examiners.

*Something About Myself (SAM).* The SAM was designed to be used as a screening device for the identification of creative people, both adolescents and adults. It could be a useful tool in multiple-criteria evaluation, for selecting adolescents for gifted programs or for special schools for the performing arts. A high school guidance counselor also might find it useful. As it is product oriented, however, it would be a better indicator of manifested creativity than of creative potential. The SAM may have application in adult personnel selection where a productive creative person is sought, particularly if creative ability in the arts is a criterion.

The test can be quickly and easily administered by a lay examiner to individuals or groups. As with the WKOPAY, the SAM can be completed in 10–15 minutes and can be quickly and easily scored by the examiner. Instructions for administration and scoring are provided in the KTCPI test manual.

SAM can be machine or hand scored. Hand scoring might be preferable if certain types of creative achievements are more important to the examiner than others (e.g., if musical composition is valued over play production or scientific invention). Score interpretation may be highly objective or subjective, depending on the examiner's agenda. The overall score could be used as a screening element or in conjunction with the CPI score on the WKOPAY. Subjectively, responses to certain items on the test may have appeal for the examiner, depending on the nature of the evaluation.

**Technical Aspects**

*What Kind of Person Are You? (WKOPAY).* Test reliability was determined by attention to interscorer, test-retest, and internal consistency studies. The WKOPAY format and scoring procedure virtually ensure a high degree of interscorer reliability. Fifty randomly selected responses were independently scored by two student assistants. A Pearson product-moment correlation coefficient of .99 ($p < .01$) was found (Khatena & Torrance, 1976).

Test-retest reliability was measured by Joesting and Joesting (1973), Torrance and Khatena (1970a, 1970b), and Torrance and Wu (1966). The $r$'s obtained ranged from .71 to .97 and were significant ($p < .01$). These studies were conducted at three universities. Time between administrations of the test ranged from same day to 6 weeks.

The split-half method was used to determine the WKOPAY's internal consistency. Odd-even items from the same college students were correlated and corrected by the Spearman-Brown prophecy formula resulting in an $r$ of .98.

The determination of content validity was based on Torrance's attempt to derive an adequate and appropriate sample of test items that would reveal the relevant characteristics in the examinee. As summarized earlier, Torrance began with a list of 84 characteristics drawn from a survey of 50 studies on creative persons (Torrance, 1962). This list was reduced to 66 characteristics and then further refined to 50 characteristics by a group of 10 research assistants using the Q-sort technique. The question of the adequacy of this methodology depends, at least partly, on the content of the studies reviewed and the degree to which these 50 studies represent an adequate sampling of the universe of creative personality characteristics.

Construct validity was established in four studies exploring different aspects of the text. The first study (Torrance, 1971) compared the means of high, moderate, and low creative (as determined by the WKOPAY) with the scales of the Runner Studies of Attitude Patterns (Runner & Runner, 1965; Runner, 1973). Results supported the theoretical foundation of the WKOPAY. Next, Khatena (1970) addressed construct validity by preparing a frequency distribution of responses that rank ordered the characteristics according to creativity. In the third study, Phillips (1973) compared the WKOPAY to the Omnibus Personality Inventory (Heist & Yonge, 1968) and the Torrance Tests of Creative Thinking (Torrance, 1966). Evidence affirmed construct validity in both comparisons. Finally, a factor analysis was conducted by Bledsoe and Khatena (1973) to refine the differences between creative and noncreative aspects of the personality.

Criterion-related validity was determined by comparing the WKOPAY to the two verbal subtests in Thinking Creatively with Sounds and Words (Torrance, Khatena, & Cunnington, 1973). Validity indices ranged from $p < .05$ to $< .01$. The WKOPAY was also compared to a variety of other measures of creative thinking and personality, too numerous to review here. All results, however, supported the test's criterion-related validity.

*Something About Myself (SAM).* In determining content validity, the 50 SAM items were correlated with originality scores on both forms of Sounds and Images, and Onomatopoeia and Images (Torrance et al., 1973). The subject populations ranged from 87 to 135 adults and 110 to 176 adolescents. Seven of the items correlated significantly with verbal originality on Sounds and Images ($r$'s ranging from .20 to .39, $p < .05$). An additional 17 items correlated significantly with verbal originality as measured by Onomatopoeia and Images, with $r$'s ranging from .15 to .34 ($p < .05$). The test is weak in the area of content validity, and this issue requires further research.

An attempt to establish construct validity included three approaches, two looking at the relationship between the level of self-reported creativity and the tendency toward originality, and that between creative self-reports and various personality orientations, and the third a factor analysis. In the first approach, adult subjects identified as "high creatives" on the SAM had significantly higher originality scores on Sounds and Images and Onomatopoeia and Images than did "low creatives" (Khatena & Torrance, 1971). Construct validity was called into question, however, when the study was repeated with adolescents. Subjects were categorized as high, moderate, or low creatives, and the low group outscored the moderate group on originality (Khatena & Torrance, 1971).

In the second approach, Khatena claimed construct validity through comparing high, moderate, and low creatives on the SAM with the 12 personality scales on the Runner Studies of Attitude Patterns (Runner & Runner, 1965). High creatives significantly outscored low creatives on only 2 of the 12 scales. Even if high creatives outscored the moderate and low creatives on all 12 scales, however, the usefulness of these data in determining construct validity would be doubtful. The SAM purports to be a screening device for identifying creative people, while the Runner test makes no such claim.

A factor analysis of the items (Bledsoe & Khatena, 1973) accounted for 53% of the total variance, and the six SAM factors (environmental sensitivity, initiative, self-strength, intellectuality, individuality, and artistry) were designated in this study. The test was administered to 672 college men and women attending colleges in West Virginia, Florida, North Carolina, and Maryland.

Criterion-related validity was established through studies involving classroom experimentation (Khatena, 1973), correlation with a measure of personal-social motivation characteristics (Raina, 1975), and demonstrated ability to manipulate mental imagery (Khatena, 1975).

Reliability for the SAM was determined through studies involving interrater reliability, repeated administration, and internal consistency. The format of the test ensures interrater reliability ($p < .01$) as reported in the test manual (Khatena & Torrance, 1976). A random sample of 50 adults and 50 adolescents was drawn from the norm groups consisting of 1,358 subjects. Tests were scored independently by two student assistants.

The Spearman-Brown prophecy formula was used to measure split-half internal consistency. Responses of two subject groups (60 adults and 60 adolescents) were analyzed through odd-even correlation. *R*'s for the adolescents, adults, and the two groups combined were .92, .95, and .94, respectively (Khatena & Torrance, 1976).

Test-retest reliability coefficients were reported in a master's thesis (Raina, 1975). Responses of 35 adults were correlated after the test was readministered at 1- and 4-week intervals. *R*'s of .97 and .94 ($p < .01$) were recorded.

## Critique

In considering a critique of the Khatena-Torrance Creative Perception Inventory, several key questions come to mind. Is it a creativity test or a personality test? When should it be used? Should the two measures (WKOPAY and SAM) be administered separately or together? What benefits may be derived from the use of the inventory? What problems may arise?

The KTCPI attempts the complex and difficult task of measuring the interaction between creativity and personality. In this respect it is unique. It provides information that creativity tests and personality tests, used alone or in combination, probably would not provide.

When information on both creativity and personality is desired (for counseling, personal growth, or personnel purposes), the KTCPI could be usefully employed. This reviewer would recommend using it as a supplement to other instruments that measure creativity and personality factors separately and that have superior validity and reliability data.

If a measure of creative potential (as a subself of the personality) is desired, What Kind of Person Are You? could be administered alone. If a measure of past creative achievements would be helpful, Something About Myself would be the better instrument. Administered together, the results might identify creative underachievers or people with high creative potential who are in the early stages of their productivity.

When administering the KTCPI, examiners should be aware of possible disadvantages of its subtests. Although the authors have tried to cover the important validity and reliability issues to some extent, additional studies with larger subject populations are clearly called for. WKOPAY is a forced-choice measure. Many people dislike this type of test, as they often find that both or neither of the items is applicable. SAM is rather obvious in its approach. The more items the examinee checks, the more creative he or she is perceived to be. Many of the items are open to interpretation. In any case, examinee honesty is a clear issue.

Results from the Khatena-Torrance Creative Perception Inventory may benefit interviewers, counselors, examinees, and researchers; as creative thinkers become increasingly valued and valuable in our society, a market will exist for those instruments that identify them. Mental health professionals may lack training in the area of creative personality, and the KTCPI may help them understand the characteristics and needs of the creative person. Adults and adolescents taking the inventory, whether students in a creativity course, job applicants, or individuals seeking greater self-awareness, may gain new insights that could be helpful on the road to self-actualization. Much of the creative process remains a mystery, which makes it easier to take a creativity test apart than to build one. Researchers trying to understand more about the creative person and the creative process can make good use of existing instruments like the KTCPI.

Although we all acknowledge that creativity tests are far from perfect, the Khatena-Torrance Creative Perception Inventory offers useful information and insights concerning the creative personality.

## References

This list includes text citations and suggested additional reading.

Anderson, C.M. (1952). The self-image: A theory of the dynamics of behavior. *Mental Hygiene, 36*(2), 227–244.

Bledsoe, J.C., & Khatena, J. (1973). A factor analytic study of Something About Myself. *Psychological Reports, 32*, 1176–1178.

Clements, R.D., Dwinell, P.L., Torrance, E.P., & Kidd, J.T. (1982). Evaluation of some of the effects of a teen drama program on creativity. *The Journal of Creative Behavior, 16*, 272–276.

Gough, H.G. (1957). *California Psychological Inventory manual*. Palo Alto, CA: Consulting Psychologists Press.

Heist, P., & Yonge, G. (1968). *Omnibus Personality Inventory, Form F: Manual*. San Antonio, TX: Psychological Corporation.

Joesting, J., & Joesting, R. (1973). Some correlations of What Kind of Person Are You? A test of creativity. *Psychological Reports, 32*, 937–938.

Khatena, J. (1970). *Creative and non-creative sub-selves: A task for education*. Unpublished manuscript, Marshall University, Huntington, WV.

Khatena, J. (1973). Production of original verbal images by college adults to variable time intervals. *Perceptual and Motor Skills, 36*, 1285–1286.

Khatena, J. (1975). Relationship of autonomous imagery and creative self-perceptions. *Psychological Reports, 40,* 357–358.

Khatena, J., & Torrance, E.P. (1971). Attitude patterns and the production of original verbal images: A study in construct validity. *Gifted Child Quarterly, 15,* 117–122.

Khatena, G., & Torrance, E.P. (1976). *Khatena-Torrance Creative Perception Inventory—Instruction manual.* Chicago: Stoelting.

Myers, I.B. (1962). *Myers-Briggs Type Indicator.* Palo Alto, CA: Consulting Psychologists Press.

Phillips, V.K. (1973). Creativity: Performance, profiles, and perceptions. *Journal of Psychology, 83,* 25–30.

Raina, U. (1975). Creativity and teaching success. *Educational Trends, 10*(2), 153–157.

Raina, M.K., & Vats, A. (1979). Creativity, teaching style and pupil control. *Gifted Child Quarterly, 23,* 807–811.

Runner, K. (1973). *A theory of persons: Runner Studies of Attitude Patterns.* San Diego, CA: Runner Associates.

Runner, K., & Runner, H. (1965). *Manual of interpretation for the Interview Form III of the Runner Studies of Attitude Patterns.* Golden, CO: Runner Associates.

Tindall, J.H., Houtz, J.C., Hausler, R., & Heimowitz, S. (1982). Processes of creative problem solvers in groups. *Small Group Behavior, 13,* 109–116.

Torrance, E.P. (1962). *Guiding creative talent.* Englewood Cliffs, NJ: Prentice-Hall.

Torrance, E.P. (1963). *What Kind of Person Are You?* Unpublished manuscript, University of Minnesota, Minneapolis.

Torrance, E.P. (1965). *Rewarding creative behavior.* Englewood Cliffs, NJ: Prentice-Hall.

Torrance, E.P. (1966). *Torrance Tests of Creative Thinking: Norms-technical manual* (research ed.). Princeton, NJ: Personnel Press.

Torrance, E.P. (1971). Some validity studies of two brief screening devices for studying the creative personality. *Journal of Creative Behavior, 5,* 94–103.

Torrance, E.P., & Khatena, J. (1970a). *Technical-norms manual for What Kind of Person Are You?* Unpublished manuscript, University of Georgia, Athens.

Torrance, E.P., & Khatena, J. (1970b). What Kind of Person Are You?: A brief screening device for identifying creatively gifted adolescents and adults. *Gifted Child Quarterly, 14,* 71–75.

Torrance, E.P., & Wu, J.J. (1966). *Preliminary manual for the What Kind of Person Are You?* Unpublished manuscript, University of Minnesota, Minneapolis.

Torrance, E.P., Khatena, J., & Cunnington, B.F. (1973). *Thinking Creatively with Sounds and Words: Directions manual and scoring guide Forms 1A, 1B, 2B and 2B* (research ed.). Lexington, MA: Personnel Press.

**Thomas M. Dixon, Ph.D.**
*Postdoctoral Fellow in Medical Psychology, Rehabilitation Institute of Chicago, Chicago, Illinois.*

**Robert L. Heilbronner, Ph.D.**
*Coordinator, Brain Trauma Neuropsychology, Rehabilitation Institute of Chicago, Chicago, Illinois.*

---

# KNOX'S CUBE TEST

*Mark H. Stone and Benjamin D. Wright. Wood Dale, Illinois: Stoelting Company.*

## Introduction

Knox's Cube Test (KCT; Stone & Wright, 1980) is a nonverbal measure of attention span and short-term memory that requires its subjects to reproduce sequences of taps that the examiner presents on a row of four blocks. The sequences vary in length and complexity from two to eight taps, thereby providing a method for assessing the amount of information a subject can hold in immediate memory and repeat at one time.

The test manual (Stone & Wright, 1980, p. 2) furnishes a comprehensive review on the development of the KCT. Dr. Howard Knox, a physician with the U.S. Public Health Service, developed the test as part of a battery for evaluating the intellectual abilities of immigrants arriving at Ellis Island in the early 1900s. Subsequent versions of the KCT were incorporated into numerous intelligence test batteries for other populations, including Army candidates, deaf individuals, and preschool and school-age children. In addition, clinicians have used the KCT as a subtest of the Arthur Point Scale of Performance for children and adults (Arthur, 1943, 1947).

Stone and Wright (1980) revised the KCT in order to provide a version of the test based on contemporary psychometric techniques. They gathered items from eight existing versions of the KCT and graded the difficulty of these items via Rasch analysis (cf. Wright & Stone, 1979). This statistical procedure defines an underlying variable—in this case, attention and short-term memory—and calibrates individual items along an interval scale that reflects this variable.

Normative standards for the KCT are based on the performance of 440 subjects from 3 to 69 years of age. Stone and Wright (1980, p. 44) combined their data on these subjects with normative information from three other editions of the KCT. The demographic characteristics of the subjects in the various normative samples are poorly described in the test manual.

The current version of the KCT employs a form for test administration, a reporting form for presenting results, and four 1-inch black cubes fastened in a straight line 2 inches apart on a strip of plain wood. A fifth cube is used for tapping out the sequences. Although the block arrangement is not actually marked in any way, the examiner labels the blocks as 1, 2, 3, and 4 from the subject's left to right for the purpose of test administration. To administer an item, the examiner refers to a given numerical series on the test form (e.g., 1-2-4-3) and then taps the blocks in that order at the rate of one per second. The subject is then presented with the tapping cube and attempts to imitate the sequence. The verbal instructions are minimal; the examiner demonstrates the task and tells the subject, "Do what I did." Two practice trials are administered to illustrate the test procedure. One trial is given for each tapping series, and responses are scored either 1 or 0. The subject must reproduce a sequence exactly to receive credit, and testing is continued until five successive failures occur. Total administration time is approximately 2 to 5 minutes (Lezak, 1983, p. 454).

There are two forms of the KCT: the Junior Test Form (for children aged 2–8) contains 16 tapping sequences from two to six units in length. The Senior Test Form (for ages 9–adult) contains 22 sequences from three to eight units in length. Results are recorded on a reporting form that provides a raw score, a test age, and a "mastery" score based on an continuum derived from the Rasch analysis discussed above. In addition, the manual outlines a qualitative method of scoring responses.

Individual item scores from the test form are entered onto a reporting form. The raw score is the number of items correct. The reporting form includes scales to convert the raw scores into test ages (3–18 years) and "mastery units." The qualitative scoring system involves inspection of the subject's consistency of performance. For example, if a subject fails easy items and succeeds on more difficult ones, then this pattern is assumed to indicate fluctuating or inefficient attending behavior. The manual suggests drawing lines one and a half scores above and below an individual's score; any success or failure outside of these boundary lines constitutes a "surprising" or unexpected response.

## Practical Applications/Uses

Stone and Wright (1983) describe the benefits of using the KCT in educational settings, arguing that the ability to attend is a prerequisite for learning. The KCT also may be applied as a measure of attention in the neuropsychological evaluation of adults. Attentional impairment is a common consequence of many forms of brain injury, and an inability to attend may globally affect the efficiency of task performance. Mack (1986) points out that the poor memory skills observed in many brain-impaired individuals may occur as a function of poor attention when the material to be learned is presented initially. The KCT offers a method of quantifying the span of attention, analogous to the digit span measure traditionally used in mental status examinations and intelligence testing. Compared to digit span, the KCT may be particularly sensitive to attention deficits because reproducing nonverbal sequences is felt to be a more novel and less automatic task than repeating a series of numbers (Mack, 1986). On the other hand, Kaplan (cited in Lezak, 1983, p. 454) and DeRenzi (1968) have contended that some subjects may use a verbal strategy (i.e., numbering the blocks) to facilitate their performance.

Because of the simplicity, brevity, and nonverbal nature of the KCT, it can be administered to a variety of groups such as small children, deaf or aphasic patients, foreign language speakers, and elderly persons. The visually impaired or those unable to make a simple motor response likely would have greater difficulty completing the KCT. The task is nonthreatening, making it a suitable choice for inclusion in a comprehensive battery of tests administered by a psychologist or trained technician.

Although scoring the KCT is fairly straightforward, interpretation of the test results requires skill because the scoring system combines quantitative features (test ages, mastery unit scores) with a qualitative analysis of an individual's performance. One of the principal measures—the mastery unit—is never defined with respect to normative standards for subjects of different ages or diagnostic groups. D'Amato (1987) points out that interpreting the KCT with adults is problematic because test ages reach a ceiling at age 18.

## Technical Aspects

Stone and Wright (1980) do not provide any reliability information on their revision of the KCT. One study cited in their manual (Sterne, 1966), however, found a 1- to 4-day test-retest reliability of .64 for 56 adult males given Arthur's (1947) version of the KCT. In addition, the manual neglects any systematic account of the KCT's validity, although some investigations suggest that the test may be used to predict functional abilities (see Bornstein, 1983, for a review).

Bornstein (1983) studied the construct validity of the Arthur (1947) KCT by administering the test in combination with an extended neuropsychological examination including the Wechsler Adult Intelligence Scale, the Wechsler Memory Scale, the Halstead-Reitan Neuropsychological Test Battery, and the Wisconsin Card Sorting Test. In two separate samples of 150 patients referred for neuropsychological assessment, the KCT correlated most highly with Digit Span Backwards and the Trail Making Test. A factor analysis suggested that the KCT loaded primarily on a factor reflecting visual and auditory attention; a secondary loading was found on a factor reflecting visuospatial skills. Bornstein concluded that the KCT measures immediate visuospatial memory and sequencing abilities and felt that the test has some utility in clinical neuropsychological assessment. He recommended modification of the test format, however, including the administration of two trials for each tapping sequence and a delayed recall of the sequences. Bornstein's study seems to be the best one to date on the validity of the KCT in relation to established neuropsychological measures, although it is unclear whether his findings can be generalized to Stone and Wright's version of the test.

## Critique

The KCT appears potentially useful as a measure of visuospatial memory span. The task has a reasonable rationale, and it is rather easy to administer. The underlying skill measured by the KCT is important to clinicians, as immediate visuospatial memory is an ability required to perform other complex cognitive tasks such as learning and recalling geographic locations, navigating in the environment, and so forth. In fact, one of the new subtests of the Wechsler Memory Scale–Revised contains a visual memory span task similar to the KCT.

However, the use of the KCT in its present form cannot be highly recommended because of its inadequate reliability, validity, and normative data. It is unfortunate that the authors did not focus on establishing norms based on clearly described groups of subjects. The practice of combining normative data from various editions of the test seems questionable, even though the authors attempted to calibrate the different items with esoteric statistical methods. Equally disappointing is the lack of a sound measurement scale for the test; the manual's range of test ages is restricted, and the expression of scores in terms of "mastery units" does not seem especially helpful from a practical perspective. Further research would be necessary to determine how the mastery scores vary as a function of age, level of education, and clinical diagnosis.

**References**


Arthur, G. (1943). *A point scale of performance tests.* Chicago: Stoelting.

Arthur, G. (1947). *A point scale of performance tests* (revised form II). Chicago: Stoelting.

Bornstein, R.A. (1983). Construct validity of the Knox Cube Test as a neuropsychological measure. *Journal of Clinical Neuropsychology, 5,* 105–144.

D'Amato, R.C. (1987). Knox's Cube Test. In D.J. Keyser & R.C. Sweetland (Eds.), *Test critiques* (Vol. VI, pp. 292–296). Austin, TX: PRO-ED.

DeRenzi, E. (1968). Nonverbal memory and hemispheric side of lesion. *Neuropsychologia, 6,* 181–189.

Lezak, M.D. (1983). *Neuropsychological assessment* (2nd ed.). New York: Oxford University Press.

Mack, J.L. (1986). Clinical assessment of disorders of attention and memory. *Journal of Head Trauma Rehabilitation, 1,* 22–33.

Sterne, D.M. (1966). The Knox cubes as a test of memory and intelligence with male adults. *Journal of Clinical Psychology, 22,* 191–193.

Stone, M.H., & Wright, B.D. (1980). *Knox's Cube Test: Junior and Senior Version.* Chicago: Stoelting.

Stone, M.H., & Wright, B.D. (1983). Measuring attending behavior and short-term memory with Knox's Cube Test. *Educational and Psychological Measurement,* 43, 803–814.

Wright, B.D., & Stone, M.H. (1979). *Best test design.* Chicago: MESA.

**Keith S. Dobson, Ph.D.**
*Associate Professor of Psychology, University of Calgary, Calgary, Alberta, Canada.*

# LEVINE-PILOWSKY DEPRESSION QUESTIONNAIRE

*I. Pilowsky, S. Levine, and D. Boulton. Adelaide, Australia: I. Pilowsky, M.D.*

## Introduction

The Levine-Pilowsky Depression Questionnaire (LPD) was developed in order first to assess depressive symptoms and then to standardize decision rules based on responses in order to classify respondents as "endogenous" or "reactive" (Pilowsky, Levine, & Boulton, 1969). The need for this questionnaire arose from the general acceptance of the endogenous-reactive distinction in the depression literature at the time (cf. Mendels & Cochrane, 1968), as well as from the inability of other questionnaires to classify depressed patients along this dichotomy.

The items for the LPD were derived from standard psychiatric texts that dealt with the issue of endogenous and reactive depression. Based on the information available, 57 items were written, each having the form of an interrogative statement (e.g., "Is life worth living?") and a yes/no response. Subjects completing the LPD read each of the items and answer "yes" or "no" as appropriate. These responses are then subjected to a scoring procedure that ultimately classifies the subject into one of three categories:

1. *Class A.* Symptoms include loss of interest, suicidal ideas, housing and financial worries, irritability, overconcern about health, absence of sleep problems, guilt, self-depreciation, and potential paranoid ideation, representing (per Pilowsky et al., 1969) a neurotic or reactive profile of depression.
2. *Class B.* Symptoms include constant depression, retardation, loss of libido, loss of appetite, insomnia, dry mouth, and loss of interest, representing (according to the authors) endogenous depression.
3. *Class C.* Symptoms present a nondepressed profile.

The method used to derive the decision rules for scoring the LPD rests on a process referred to as "numerical taxonomy" (Pilowsky et al., 1969; Pilowsky & Boulton, 1970). Numerical taxonomy is essentially a cluster analysis procedure that uses a number of variables (in this case, scores on the depression inventory) and then tries to identify clusters of them that can maximally discriminate criterion groups (in this case, different subtypes of depression). In the original validation of the LPD, 200 psychiatric patients served as the criterion groups. This sample included patients with "endogenous depression" ($n$ = 38), "neurotic depression" ($n$ = 38), "other illnesses with depressive features" ($n$ = 30), "neurosis (non-depressive)" ($n$ = 75), and "psychosis (non-depressive)" ($n$ = 19). Phi coefficients

(McNemar, 1959) were computed between each variable and criterion group to determine those items that discriminated groups.

The scoring procedure for the LPD rests on the original validation sample, in that decision rules for categorizing subjects as belonging to Class A, B, or C come from the phi coefficients derived in the 1969 study. In order to score the LPD, the test user must obtain the scoring sheets from the author and then apply a weighting system that uses the critical items to decide if the test taker belongs to Class A or B, B or C, and A or C. In essence, the items that were identified in the original validation sample as discriminating subtypes of depression are reviewed vis-à-vis the test taker at hand.

**Practical Applications/Uses**

The original purpose of the LPD was "the identification and classification of depressed patients" (Pilowsky, 1979). In its most narrow usage, therefore, this is a self-report classification instrument. It is not surprising, therefore, that most of the research using the LPD has attempted to demonstrate its relationship to other assessment and classification instruments in the area of depression.

The major clinical utility of the LPD lies in its ability to identify depression in examinees, as well as to classify them provisionally into one of the three classes or depressive profiles. Use of the LPD as a screening instrument has been suggested (Boleloucky & Plevova, 1987; Pilowsky & Spence, 1978), and evidence suggests this is appropriate, as patients' LPD assessment profiles typically match clinical impressions.

The ability of the LPD to predict response to different treatments for depression has not yet been established. One early study (Pilowsky & McGrath, 1970) demonstrated a relationship between classification as a Class B (endogenous) patient and response to electroconvulsive therapy, but the test authors caution against using the LPD for the latter due to the presence of several poor responders who belonged to Class B in their study. Other research of this type does not appear to be available.

The LPD may have potential as an index of therapeutic change in depressed patients, because in addition to the classification procedure, its scores can be simply summed to derive a severity index of depression. Several studies (e.g., Levine, 1975; Levine, Deo, & Mahadevan, 1987) have used the LPD as an outcome measure in studies of depression.

A final major use of the LPD is to examine correlates of depression and the relationship of other variables to the three classes of depression the measure identifies. Some examples of such use include studies on pain (Chapman, Sola, & Bonica, 1979; Pelz & Merskey, 1982; Pilowsky & Bassett, 1982; Pilowsky, Chapman, & Bonica, 1977), hostility (Pilowsky & Spence, 1975), dependency (Pilowsky & Katsikitis, 1983), and suicidal tendencies (Goldney & Pilowsky, 1980; Goldney, Adam, O'Brien, & Termansen, 1983).

**Technical Aspects**

The major criterion for determining the adequacy of the LPD concerns the extent to which its classification scheme is consistent with diagnoses of "neurotic" and "endogenous" depression. In the original validation, for example, the items chosen for the LPD classification were selected by contrasting the two clinically identified depressive types (Pilowsky et al., 1969). Unfortunately, the method for deriving the clinical diagnoses in the validation study are not specified, and it is not clear that anything other than clinical impression formed the basis for diagnosis. Given that there were significant problems of diagnostic reliability and validity in the 1960s, due to the lack of standardized diagnostic systems (Beck, Ward, Mendelson, Mock, & Erbaugh, 1962; Spitzer & Fleiss, 1974), it is quite likely that the original validation sample itself may have included some invalid diagnoses.

To the authors' credit, validation studies on the LPD were undertaken early in the test's history (Pilowsky & Spalding, 1972). This research showed that the depression severity score related to treatment progress and was sensitive to clinical improvement, and that there were significant correlations between LPD depression severity scores and both a self- and observer rating of depression severity. A significant correlation ($r$ = .88) between the LPD depression severity score and the Zung Self-rating Depression Scale (Zung, 1965) also has been reported (Byrne, 1975).

Pilowsky reported another major validation study in 1979 in which 367 psychiatric patients received one of five diagnoses: depressive neurosis, endogenous depression, nondepressive neurosis, nondepressive psychosis, and other. Although the system for making clinical diagnoses apparently was not standardized, the relationship between clinical diagnosis and the LPD classification was significant. Of the 114 patients diagnosed as having depressive neurosis, the LPD correctly classified 38 as nonendogenous, but 42 as endogenous and 34 as having no depressive syndrome. Of the 99 endogenous depressives, 58 were correctly classified by the LPD as endogenous, while 9 were classified as nonendogenous and 32 as having no depression. Finally, of the 154 patients without depressive diagnoses, the LPD classified only 91 as having no depression; 28 were classified as having nonendogenous depression and 35 as having endogenous depression. It thus appears that the ability of the LPD to correspond with endogenous depression and a lack of depression (59% agreement in both above cases) is greater than for nonendogenous depression (33% agreement). It is also clear that a number of disagreements between the LPD and clinical diagnosis occurred.

Byrne (1975) provides other evidence of a relationship between LPD classes and clinical diagnoses. In that study, 7 out of 10 neurotic depressives were classified into Class A (the other 3 went into Class B), 8 out of 10 psychotic depressives were classified as Class B (the other 2 as Class A), while all 10 control subjects were classified as Class C (nondepressed). These data are stronger than Pilowsky's (1979) in supporting the classification utility of the LPD, although the correspondence of psychotic depression and Class B, as opposed to endogenous depression and Class B, is somewhat surprising.

Other evidence supporting the LPD as a severity instrument was obtained by Pilowsky (1979). He reported that the two depression classes (A and B) had higher severity scores than the nondepressed class (C). In addition, males had a lower overall severity score, which is consistent with the often-cited sex difference in depression (i.e., that females suffer more from this condition).

Aside from the preceding evidence related to concurrent validity, other psychometric data on the LPD are difficult to obtain. Apparently test-retest reliability has yet to be determined. One might suspect, in this regard, that the reliability would be low, as scores on the questionnaire should fluctuate with levels of clinical depression. The factor structure of the LPD appears not to have been assessed. Given the explicit three-factor model assumed by the LPD, validation of its factorial structure would seem an important step. Finally, predictive validity appears unexamined except in one preliminary uncontrolled study (Pilowsky & Boulton, 1970).

## Critique

Two aspects of the LPD deserve comment: its classification purpose and ability, and its assessment of depression severity. Turning to classification first, it does appear both that the LPD identifies discrete classes of examinees and that this classification relates to clinical diagnosis of endogenous or nonendogenous depression. At the time of its development, the availability of a questionnaire with such properties was of some value. Since that time, however, psychiatric diagnosis has advanced considerably. With the advent of DSM-III and DSM-IIIR (American Psychiatric Association, 1987), diagnoses have become much more reliable and standardized. The relationship between LPD classes and modern diagnostic systems is unclear.

Even more damaging for the original purposes of the LPD, however, is the fact that the reactive-endogenous distinction in clinical depression no longer features as part of the DSM nomenclature. Based on the preponderance of evidence that the reactive-endogenous distinction could not be maintained via diagnostic reliability or predictive validity, modern North American diagnosis has dropped this distinction. Although the ninth edition of the *International Classification of Diseases* (ICD; World Health Organization, 1980) incorporates endogenous depression, subsequent versions may not. As a consequence, the status of the basis for the LPD hangs in the balance. If both the DSM and ICD systems drop the reactive-endogenous distinction, then the utility of the LPD will be severely circumscribed.

The LPD's severity index, although inadequately validated to date, appears to have promise as a marker of improvement in clinical depression. It correlates with other measures of depression severity (although more evidence of this type would be beneficial), and it is sensitive to clinical change (Levine et al., 1987; Pilowsky & Spalding, 1972). What has yet to be established is whether the LPD provides a better measure of depression severity and change than instruments such as the Beck Depression Inventory (Beck, Ward, Mendelson, Mock, & Erbaugh, 1961), the Hamilton Rating Scale for Depression (Hamilton, 1967), or the Zung Self-rating Depression Scale (Zung, 1965). Concurrent validation studies of the LPD and other scales will be important to support its continued use.

In summary, although the need for the LPD was strong at the time of its development, its continued need given changes in diagnostic nomenclature and systems is unclear. Predictive validity studies of the classification scheme embedded in the LPD would go some distance to ensuring continued usage. Further, data related to the depression severity score are needed to determine the comparative utility of that score versus other depression inventories. Without such information, the future of the LPD as a depression questionnaire may be limited.

## References


American Psychiatric Association. (1987). *Diagnostic and statistical manual of mental disorders* (3rd ed. rev.). Washington, DC: Author.

Beck, A.T., Ward, C.H., Mendelson, M., Mock, J.E., & Erbaugh, J.K. (1961). An inventory for measuring depression. *Archives of General Psychiatry, 4,* 561–571.

Beck, A.T., Ward, C.H., Mendelson, M., Mock, J.E., & Erbaugh, J.K. (1962). Reliability and validity of psychiatric diagnoses II: A study of consistency of clinical judgments and ratings. *American Journal of Psychiatry, 119,* 351–357.

Boleloucky, Z., & Plevova, J. (1987). Self-assessed endogenous/neurotic-reactivity dichotomy in fully and partially hospitalized non-psychotic depressive patients. *Scripta Medica, 60,* 77–89.

Byrne, D.G. (1975). Some preliminary observations on a questionnaire technique for classifying depressive illness: Its relationship with clinical diagnosis and a biological technique for depressive classification. *Australia and New Zealand Journal of Psychiatry, 9,* 25–29.

Chapman, C.R., Sola, A.E., & Bonica, J.J. (1979). Illness behavior and depression compared in pain center and private practice patients. *Pain, 6,* 1–7.

Goldney, R., Adam, K., O'Brien, J., & Termansen, P. (1983). Depression in young women who have attempted suicide: An international replication study. In J.P. Soubrier & J. Vedrinne (Eds.), *Depression and suicide* (pp. 88–94). Paris: Pergamon.

Goldney, R., & Pilowsky, I. (1980). Depression in young women who have attempted suicide. *Australia and New Zealand Journal of Psychiatry, 14,* 203–211.

Hamilton, M. (1967). Development of a rating scale for primary depressive illness. *British Journal of Social and Clinical Psychology, 6,* 278–296.

Levine, S. (1975). A controlled comparison of maprotiline (Ludiomil) with imipramine avoiding observer bias. *Journal of International Medical Research, 3*(Supp. 2), 75–78.

Levine, S., Deo, R., & Mahadevan, K. (1987). A comparative trial of a new antidepressant, Fluoxetine. *British Journal of Psychiatry, 150,* 653–655.

McNemar, Q. (1959). *Psychological statistics.* New York: Wiley.

Mendels, J., & Cochrane, C. (1968). The nosology of depression: The endogenous-reactive concept. *American Journal of Psychiatry, 124,* 1–11.

Pelz, M., & Merskey, H. (1982). A description of the psychological effects of chronic painful lesions. *Pain, 14,* 293–301.

Pilowsky, I. (1979). Further validation of a questionnaire for classifying depressive illness. *Journal of Affective Disorders, 1,* 179–185.

Pilowsky, I., & Bassett, D.L. (1982). Pain and depression. *British Journal of Psychiatry, 141,* 30–36.

Pilowsky, I., & Boulton, D.M. (1970). Development of a questionnaire-based decision rule for classifying depressed patients. *British Journal of Psychiatry, 116,* 647–650.

Pilowsky, I., Chapman, C.R., & Bonica, J.J. (1977). Pain, depression and illness behaviour in a pain clinic population. *Pain, 4,* 183–192.

Pilowsky, I., & Katsikitis, M. (1983). Depressive illness and dependency. *Acta Psychiatrica Scandinavia, 68,* 11–14.

Pilowsky, I., Levine, S., & Boulton, D.M. (1969). The classification of depression by numerical taxonomy. *British Journal of Psychiatry, 115,* 937–945.

Pilowsky, I., & McGrath, M.D. (1970). Effect of ECT on responses to a depression questionnaire: Implications for taxonomy. *British Journal of Psychiatry, 117,* 685–688.

Pilowsky, I., & Spalding, D. (1972). A method for measuring depression: Validity studies on a depression questionnaire. *British Journal of Psychiatry, 121,* 411–416.

Pilowsky, I., & Spence, N.D. (1975). Hostility and depressive illness. *Archives of General Psychiatry, 32,* 1154–1159.

Pilowsky, I., & Spence, N.D. (1978). Depression inside and outside the hospital. *British Journal of Psychiatry, 138,* 265–268.

Spitzer, R.L., & Fleiss, J.L. (1974). A reanalysis of the reliability of psychiatric diagnosis. *British Journal of Psychiatry, 125,* 341–347.

World Health Organization. (1980). *International classification of diseases* (9th ed., clinical rev.). Geneva, Switzerland: Author.

Zung, W.W.K. (1965). A self-rating depression scale. *Archives of General Psychiatry, 12,* 63–70.

**Jon D. Swartz, Ph.D.**
*Chief of Psychological Services, Central Counties Center for MH-MR Services, and Professor of Psychology, Southwestern University, Georgetown, Texas.*

# MAKE A PICTURE STORY

*Edwin S. Shneidman. Los Angeles, California: Western Psychological Services.*

## Introduction

The Make A Picture Story test (MAPS)—originally called the MAPS method—is one of the many derivatives of the Thematic Apperception Test (TAT) of Morgan and Murray published over 55 years ago (Morgan & Murray, 1935). The MAPS consists of a set of 22 cardboard background pictures, 8½″ × 11″, each with a different setting, and 67 cut-out figures that the subject places in the various settings. Any figure(s) can be selected for any background without violating proportions.

The MAPS backgrounds are titled as follows: Living Room, Street, Medical, Bathroom, Dream, Bridge, Bedroom, Blank, Closet, Nursery, Stage, Schoolroom, Shanty, Doorway, Camp, Raft, Cave, Cemetery, Attic, Forest, Cellar, and Landscape. The backgrounds are depicted without people except for an ambiguous human head in the Dream background and a covered shape in the bed in the Bedroom background. The 67 figures include adult males and females, including minorities; children of both sexes; figures of indeterminate sex; fictitious figures (e.g., Santa Claus, Ghost, Witch); figures in silhouette or with blank faces; and animals. The figures are represented in various postures with a variety of facial expressions, and in different costumes and stages of dress (with completely nude figures of an adult male, an adult female, a boy, and a girl). Each figure is identified by a number and letter code as follows: 19, male adults (M); 11, female adults (F); 12, children (C); 10, minority group figures (N); 2, animal figures (A); 2, indeterminate sex (I); 6, legendary and fictitious characters (L); and 5, silhouettes and figures with blank faces (S).

The MAPS was published in 1949 by Edwin S. Shneidman, since 1975 a professor of thanatology at UCLA where he formerly was a professor of medical psychology. Shneidman received his Ph.D. from USC in 1948. When he published the MAPS he was a clinical psychologist with the VA Neuropsychiatric Hospital, Los Angeles. In 1976 he received the Bruno Klopfer Award for Distinguished Contribution from the Society for Personality Assessment. He is primarily known today for his work in the areas of suicide and thanatology.

In the administration of the MAPS, the subject is seated at a desk or table, with the examiner positioned behind the subject on either side. The Living Room background picture is placed directly in front of the subject while the examiner says, "What I am going to do is show you pictures like this, one at a time." The examiner places the figures on the table while stating that the task "is simply to take one or more of any of these figures and put them on the background picture as they might be in real life." The examiner then takes a couple of the figures and places them on the table so that the feet of the figures are toward the subject. The examiner then encourages the subject to arrange the remainder of the figures by saying, "You put the rest out." The examiner notes any peculiarities in the subject's arrangement of the figures. When the subject has arranged all the figures on the table, the examiner says

> Now I would like to go over the instructions in a little more detail. As I said before, all you have to do is take one or more of any of these figures, put them on the background as they might be in real life, and tell a story about the situation you have made. In telling your story, tell me who the characters are, what they are doing and thinking and feeling, and how the whole thing turns out. All right, go ahead.

The examiner records the subject's choice and placement of test figures onto the Figure Location Sheet, then offers feedback and subsequent instructions. He or she then selects the next background picture and puts it in front of the subject. The examiner records the subject's stories and, after the story for each new background is completed, introduces a new background picture with the phrase, "Try this one." For the Blank background *E* says, "In addition to selecting the figures and telling the story, in this case you also make up what the background might be. It can be anything. Tell me, sometime during your story, what background you have imagined."

Inquiry on the stories "may be done by the examiner in whatever fashion he does inquiry for TAT stories" (Shneidman, 1952, p. 8), but Shneidman recommends that only two questions be asked. The first is a general prompting question such as "Can you tell me more?" The second question, asked after each story, is for the title of the story: "What might you call this story?" or "If you were to give it a title, what would it be?" The examiner's recording tasks consist of obtaining accounts of the stories and completing the Figure Location Sheet (FLS).

The account of each story should be recorded verbatim and should include all verbal material (e.g., comments, mutterings, asides, questions, etc.). Reaction time is not taken because it was not found to be discriminating (Shneidman, 1948a). The purpose of the FLS is to record the identity and placement of the figures on each background so that the subject's performance can be repeated later. This recording is done by drawing an ellipse to represent each test figure used in the corresponding place on the picture of the background and by labeling it with the appropriate code. The FLS should be completed for each background, and the examiner should not be concerned with the code for each figure during administration of the test as identifications can be added to the FLS afterward.

**Practical Applications/Uses**

Shneidman (1952) saw all projective techniques as being used in two ways:

> In the *clinical* setting, the psychologist should use projective materials in such a manner so that he can administer, score, interpret, and report them as

> though he believed in their validity; and, as a separate function, in the *experimental* setting, he should investigate the techniques and their hypotheses as though they had no validity. (pp. 12–13)

He felt the MAPS added to the TAT by allowing the subject to construct his own stimulus situations, reasoning that by so doing the procedure would give a more complete picture of the subject's personal psychodynamics by revealing more facets of personality than are revealed in other story-telling techniques.

In his one-page 1988 addendum affixed to the inside front cover of the 1952 manual, Shneidman wrote that "chapters 1 through 5 can stand as they are, with some slight editing, to reflect the considerable social gains made since 1952." He felt, however, that a reprint of the manual would have to delete chapters 6 through 17 (the "MAPS Atlas," 50+ pages of generalizations about stories from various nosological groups) because it is now obvious "that one case cannot capture all the richness and nuances of large-scale categories, especially when the distinctiveness and veridicality of these categorizations are somewhat questionable in the first place."

Additional test materials include slotted wooden bases, by which the figures can be stood up, and a carrying case "theater" in which the backgrounds can be displayed in vertical positions. The theater is not ordinarily used, however (Shneidman, 1960). Usually not more than 10 of the background scenes are employed as the test can be very time-consuming, ranging from 45 to 90 minutes for each administration. A study in 1956 of the clinical use of the test revealed that a range of 2–12 scenes (mean = 8 scenes) were used in practice. In addition, the mean number of figures used per card was 3.9 (Spiegelman, 1956).

In an article on the MAPS test by its author as late as 1986 (in the 50th anniversary issue of the *Journal of Personality Assessment*), the most recent reference cited was Shneidman's 26-year-old chapter on the use of the MAPS with children (Shneidman, 1960).

## Technical Aspects

Shneidman (1952) reported that the MAPS was being published without knowledge of its validity and reliability, feeling that even the *concepts* of validity and reliability when applied to projective techniques were open to question. Since the publication of the MAPS, only a few studies have dealt with psychometric issues. The problems, as seen by Neuringer (1968) and by Zubin, Eron, and Schumer (1965), is that the flexibility found on the MAPS makes it difficult to validate the test. So many combinations of figures and backgrounds can occur that the number of possible themes is almost unlimited, making normative studies—the forerunner of most experimental treatments—difficult if not impossible to carry out.

The most comprehensive study of the MAPS's reliability and validity still is the one by Little and Shneidman (1959) carried out over 30 years ago. In this investigation experts' interjudge reliability correlations were in the .30s and .40s, and validity correlations ranged from .10 to .20. In addition, the assignment of diagnostic labels produced only chance results.

Jensen's (1965) comprehensive review of the MAPS in *The Sixth Mental Measure-*

*ments Yearbook* concluded that the reliability and validity coefficients reported were so low as to be "useless for individual assessment," and he found "no basis for recommending the MAPS for any practical use" (p. 470).

## Critique

The MAPS test was published at a time when scant attention was paid to questions of psychometric properties of assessment devices, especially in the development of projective techniques. The zeitgeist at that time held that if the TAT "worked," so would its derivatives, especially as used by trained clinicians in clinical settings. It was assumed that, in telling stories about characters in unstructured situations, subjects would be telling about themselves. All the examiner/therapist had to do was tease out this information.

The MAPS might not be accepted today if it were being published for the first time. Indeed, the same probably could be said of the TAT (Swartz, 1978). There have been no changes in the method since it was originally published by The Psychological Corporation in 1949. Shneidman originally saw his method as being more productive than the TAT because it separated figures and backgrounds in the stimuli, forcing the subject to select and place his own figures before telling his story and thereby respond to stimulus situations of his or her own making.

On the other hand, the clinical and research possibilities of the MAPS are many and never have been addressed, especially in any systematic fashion. Although old in years, the MAPS still remains new in possibilities. The basic premise that the MAPS is more productive than the TAT has never really been tested. Indeed, there is no firm evidence that the MAPS elicits more meaningful fantasy materials than the TAT (or other story-telling tests).

Morris (1951) concluded that the MAPS test "requires much work to be done in the areas of scoring, reliability, norms, and validity before it should be given general application" (p. 528). Unfortunately, this statement still holds 40 years later.

## References

This list includes text citations and suggested additional reading.

Hooker, E. (1957). The adjustment of the male overt homosexual. *Journal of Projective Techniques, 21,* 18–31.

Jensen, A.R. (1965). Make a Picture Story. In O.K. Buros (Ed.), *The sixth mental measurements yearbook* (pp. 468–470). Highland Park, NJ: Gryphon Press.

Little, K.B., & Shneidman, E.S. (1959). Congruencies among interpretations of psychological test and anamnestic data. *Psychological Monographs, 73*(6), 1–42.

Morgan, C.D., & Murray, H.A. (1935). A method for investigating fantasies: The Thematic Apperception Test. *Archives of Neurological Psychiatry, 34,* 289–306.

Morris, W.W. (1951). Other projective methods. In H.H. Anderson & G.G. Anderson (Eds.), *An introduction to projective techniques* (pp. 513–538). New York: Prentice-Hall.

Neuringer, C. (1968). A variety of thematic methods. In A.I. Rabin (Ed.), *Projective techniques in personality assessment* (pp. 222–261). New York: Springer.

Shneidman, E.S. (1948a). *A study of certain formal psychosocial aspects of the Make-A-Picture*

*Story (MAPS) test*. Unpublished doctoral dissertation, University of Southern California, Los Angeles.

Shneidman, E.S. (1948b). Schizophrenia and the MAPS test. *Genetic Psychology Monographs, 38,* 145–223.

Shneidman, E.S. (1949). *The Make A Picture Story Test.* New York: The Psychological Corporation.

Shneidman, E.S. (1952). Manual for the MAPS method. *Projective Techniques Monographs, 1*(No. 2).

Shneidman, E.S. (1960). The MAPS test with children. In A.I. Rabin & M.R. Haworth (Eds.), *Projective techniques with children* (pp. 130–148). New York: Grune & Stratton.

Shneidman, E.S. (1986). MAPS of the Harvard yard. *Journal of Personality Assessment, 50*(3), 436–447.

Shneidman, E.S., Joel, W., & Little, K.B. (1951). *Thematic test analysis.* New York: Grune & Stratton.

Spiegelman, M. (1956). A note on the use of Fine's scoring system with the MAPS tests of children. *Journal of Projective Techniques, 20,* 442–444.

Swartz, J.D. (1978). Thematic Apperception Test. In O.K. Buros (Ed.), *The eighth mental measurements yearbook* (pp. 1127–1130). Highland Park, NJ: Gryphon Press.

Zubin, J., Eron, L.D., & Schumer, F. (1965). *An experimental approach to projective techniques.* New York: Wiley.

**Rosemary Papalewis, Ed.D.**

*Professor of Educational Administration, California State University-Fresno, Fresno, California.*

# MANAGEMENT READINESS PROFILE

*London House. Park Ridge, Illinois: London House, Inc.*

## Introduction

The Management Readiness Profile (MRP) is designed to assess an individual's readiness for entry-level supervisory or management positions. It was developed for personnel selection and placement decisions, identification of training needs, and career development. The MRP was constructed by Jones, Orban, and Molcan (1988) to predict level of managerial status, ranging from non-managers (lowest level) to manager trainees/new supervisors (intermediate level) to experienced managers (highest level). The initial validation of this study was with a major Midwest grocery retail organization. The qualifications of the developers is not mentioned. Seven scale scores (Validity, Management Interest, Leadership, Energy Level, Practical Thinking, Management Responsibility, and Interpersonal Skills) and one overall score (Management Readiness Index) comprise the profile.

Theoretical underpinnings are mentioned in the Administrators' Guide for four of the seven MRP scales. Laws of control theory (Lefcourt, 1981; Rotter, 1966) formed the basis of the Management Responsibility scale. The Leadership, Energy Level, and Practical Thinking scales were patterned after various instruments. These three scales (Leadership, Energy Level, and Practical Thinking) have been reviewed by Thornton and Byham (1982).

The normative population as described in the MRP technical report initially entailed test scores from three groups of individuals: non-managers ($n$ = 63), manager trainees ($n$ = 13), and experienced managers ($n$ = 24). The purpose of this study was to determine if the MRP could differentiate between the three levels of management experience. Five of the six MRP subscales (Management Interest, Leadership, Energy Level, Practical Thinking, and Management Responsibility) significantly distinguished between the three management groups.

The MRP has been available since 1988 and has undergone some revision. For example, expansion of norm sets and revision of some decision rules that control behavioral feedback in the reporting system are reported to be under way.

The MRP test specimen is eight pages long, with clear directions at the top of the first page. Space is also provided for a signature of agreement by the examinee and for scoring and evaluation. Each of the 138 questions are followed by six squares, the first of which corresponds to the words "strongly agree" and the sixth to the words "strongly disagree." Questions 1 to 126 are typed in six question blocks separated by letters of the alphabet. The last such set of questions (letter V) comprises 127 to 130. On the eighth page of the questionnaire one finds 133 through 138. (Why questions 131 and 132 are missing from the test specimen is not known.) On the outside back cover appear the instructions for the MRP administrator.

Descriptions of the seven subscales and the overall readiness index follow:

1. *Management Interest*—designed to assess vocational interest in management and leadership positions.

2. *Leadership*—designed to assesses attitudes and behaviors that facilitate strong leadership performance.

3. *Energy Level*—designed as a measure of energy level, work pace, and endurance.

4. *Practical Thinking*—designed to identify people who enjoy new ideas and who think creatively.

5. *Management Responsibility*—designed as a measure of internal versus external locus of control in relation to management practices.

6. *Interpersonal Skills*—designed to assess interest in socializing with others.

7. *Validity*—designed to assess how candidly an examiner answers the MRP.

8. *Management Readiness Index (MRI)*—a composite score designed to reflect a person's overall orientation to a management position; based on the Management Interest, Leadership, Energy Level, Practical Thinking, and Management Responsibility subscales.

Supplemental information is provided by Favorable Management Indicators and Management Training Opportunities. The Favorable Management Indicators, as reported, reflect positive responses to MRP items and may be used to make a further evaluation of acceptable candidates. The Management Training Opportunities, as reported, reflect answers to questions that suggest the need for training and development.

**Practical Applications/Uses**

The MRP serves as an initial, preliminary screening instrument that identifies candidates who possess some of the basic psychological orientations that typically characterize successful managers. London House strongly states that the MRP scores should only be interpreted in conjunction with other sources of information, such as requirements of the job for which the candidate/incumbent is being assessed, work history, performance appraisals, assessment center ratings, mental abilities tests, reference checks, letters of recommendation, or job knowledge. Further, London House states that the MRP scores should only be interpreted by qualified psychologists or human resource professionals.

The MRP is administered individually. As noted in the instructions to the administrator, the testing area should be relatively free of noise or other distractions. The administrator is further instructed not to mention the name of the MRP to the candidate or to minimize the profile's importance. Directions for administering the MRP are easy to understand and follow. The MRP can be administered by clerical staff, management personnel, or a human resource specialist. Completion time is 20 minutes.

Procedures for scoring are presented in the manual. There are two phases: preliminary scoring, where the profile administrator transcribes the answers, and the ITAC Telephone Scoring System or the ITAC/PC Scoring System. With the telephone scoring system, after the numbers are read off, results are given immediately (while on the phone) for the standard scores of the seven subscales and the MRI. Written confirmation is mailed the next day. Operator-assisted scoring is available 60 hours a week (including Saturdays). Options for overseas customers are available via Telex. The ITAC/PC System, used with an IBM or compatible computer, can generate MRP results on-site within minutes. Also, completed test booklets can be mailed to London House for scoring, with a return to the client in a few days.

**Technical Aspects**

The reliability and validity of the MRP as a predictor of successful performance is presented in a series of technical reports. In MRP Technical Report #1, the internal consistency reliability for six subscales and the overall index is high (.8 and above). The intercorrelation of the six subscales is somewhat higher than desirable, indicating some degree of redundancy. The subscales' correlation with the total index is fairly high. For validity, the subscale and overall index correlations with management experience ($N = 100$) generally appear in the moderate (.4 to .5) range. No male/female or ethnic differences were found, although 90% of the sample was white.

MRP Technical Report #2, with a sample ($N = 24$) from an insurance company division, presents zero to moderate correlations of subscales with management experience, salary, supervisor ratings of performance, and promotion ratings. The total index correlated .3 to .7 with the same variables.

In MRP Technical Report #3, for 140 college students, five of the subscales were significantly differentiated, low from high interest in management.

MRP Technical Report #4 compares 36 managers rated as highly promotable to 393 college business students. Significant differences in favor of the highly promotable group were found on five subscales (not Interpersonal Skills) and the overall index.

In MRP Technical Report #5, assistant managers ($N = 65$) were rated for dimensions of management performance. An internal consistency reliability of .8+ was also reported. Correlations of five of the subscales (again, Interpersonal Skill subscale was not related) and total index were low (.21) to moderate (.46) with the four performance ratings.

MRP Technical Report #6 is an overview of all reports regarding the scale. It also presents a case study of a 24-year-old female, recommendations regarding the MRI profile, and literature regarding the management dimension in general. A long list of references is included.

MRP Technical Report #7 is a validation study that demonstrated the construct validity of the candidness scale using 25 females and 5 males. *MRP: A Reliability and Validity Summary* presents a summary of Technical Reports 1 through 5 with regard to each subscale.

The Adverse Impact Analyzer reports that blacks and Hispanics ($n = 117$ of over 2,668) were not adversely affected; for example, their score differences from whites were not significant. But less than 5% of all individuals identified were from non-white race/ethnic backgrounds.

## Critique

Overall, the MRP's internal consistency was generally high (.8 and above) in two separate samples. The validity for the overall index was moderate for a variety of areas, such as management experience, performance rating, and so forth. The technical adequacy, strong internal consistency, and moderate relation to criterion variables (e.g., performance, experience, etc.) supports London House's contention to supplement other information. As suggested by the case study, the MRP might be a source of confirmation or an initial screening device, but it should not be the only tool used for decision making.

The research basis for two subscales (Interpersonal Skills and Management Interest) should be more fully explained. Likewise, further research should address the age characteristic as well as gender and race/ethnicity issues (one assumes from the information provided that entry-level managers are in their twenties). Reentry workers as well as those that have changed jobs also should be considered in future studies (see Klein, 1985; Nkomo, Fottler, & McAfee, 1988). Finally, explanations regarding the validity of the subscale areas should be addressed for all of the subscales.

## References


Jones, J.W., Orban, J.A., & Molcan, J.R. (1988). *Psychological predictors of managerial status* (MRP Technical Report #1). Park Ridge, IL: London House.

Klein, S. (Ed). (1985). *Handbook for achieving sex equity through education.* Baltimore: Johns Hopkins University Press.

Lefcourt, H.M. (1981). *Research with the locus of control construct.* New York: Academic Press.

Nkomo, S.M., Fottler, M.D., & McAfee, R.B. (1988). *Applications in personnel/human resource management.* Boston: PWS-Kent.

Rotter, J.B. (1966). Generalized expectancies for internal versus external control of reinforcement. *Psychological Monographs, 80,* 288–294.

Thornton, G.C., & Byham, W.C. (1982). *Assessment centers and managerial performance,* New York: Academic Press.

**Mark Stone, Ed.D.**
*Professor of Psychology, Alfred Adler Institute, Chicago, Illinois.*

# MINI INVENTORY OF RIGHT BRAIN INJURY

*Patricia A. Pimental and Nancy A. Kingsbury. Austin, Texas: PRO-ED, Inc.*

## Introduction

The Mini Inventory of Right Brain Injury (MIRBI) is a screening instrument designed to evaluate the components of right-hemisphere syndromes. The MIRBI is an individually administered instrument for clinical assessment in the following applications: to determine the deficits associated with right-brain injury, to evaluate the relative severity of the injury, to locate the specific areas of right-hemisphere dysfunction, to determine the strengths and weaknesses of the client, to document patient progress during intervention, and to serve as a measurement tool in research studies on right-brain injury.

The MIRBI follows a four-dimensional model of right-hemisphere processing that covers 10 assessment areas: Visual Processing (Visual Scanning, Integrity of Gnosis, Integrity of Body Image, Visuoverbal Processing, Visuosymbolic Processing, Integrity of Praxis Associated with Visuomotor Skills; 13 items), Language Processing (Effective Language, Higher Level Receptive and Expressive Language; 10 items), Emotion and Affective Processing (Affect; 1 item), and General Behavior and Psychic Integrity (General Behavior; 3 items).

Item development for the MIRBI resulted from a survey of the literature on right-brain injury. Items were written to illustrate common deficit patterns and syndromes. A 63-item precursor test (also called MIRBI) was developed, and 50 patients from 18 pilot sites provided the data used for item analysis.

The revised MIRBI of 27 items was standardized on a sample of 30 patients with a diagnosis of right-brain injury and 13 patients with a diagnosis of left-brain injury. Subjects were evaluated by speech pathologists with at least a master's degree and current certification by the American Speech, Language and Hearing Association.

## Practical Applications/Uses

The MIRBI is intended to be used for patients between ages 20 and 80. The manual indicates that patients who are deaf, blind, or unable to speak "typical English" should not be administered the inventory. The manual also notes that test examiners should be professionals experienced in test administration who are thoroughly familiar with the test materials.

MIRBI materials include a 33-page manual and a 12-page record form. The latter provides the test administration directions, scoring criteria, and directions for recording responses. The materials are attractively printed and packaged.

The examination usually takes between 15 to 30 minutes and it must be administered individually. Specific directions for administration of each MIRBI item are provided in the test booklet. Scoring criteria are provided for each item. Persons administering the test must be completely familiar with the test materials and procedures given in the manual. The MIRBI is a screening instrument only and the results should be interpreted in that context. Further investigation of any clinical findings should be done by competent specialists.

## Technical Aspects

Coefficient alpha for 73 MIRBI protocols was reported to be .92. Interrater reliability was calculated between two raters on four subjects utilizing the Pearson product-moment correlation coefficient. These coefficients ranged from .65 to .87.

The standardization sample for right-brain injured persons included 21 males and 18 females. The average age of education was 11.7. Participants included 27 white, 2 black, and 1 "other," according to racial classifications. A left-brain standardization sample specified 8 males and 5 females, 12 whites and 1 black. Their average level of education was 13 years. The normal standardization sample contained 12 males and 18 females, all white. Average years of education for these participants was 13.6. The manual gives the average age of these three standardization samples as follows: right-brain injured = 63.9, left-brain injured = 60.07, and normal standardization sample = 59.06. These means suggest that a skewed distribution with a high total age mean constitutes the norm samples, although specific data are not provided.

Content validity for the MIRBI was based on "extensive and careful survey of the literature of right brain injury . . . [and] development and selection of items representative of right hemisphere syndrome components" (Pimental & Kingsbury, 1989, p. 29).

Predictive validity of the MIRBI "has yet to be explored," and the authors argue that the strongest evidence for construct validity is "diagnostic usefulness" (Pimental & Kingsbury, 1989, p. 29). Utility of the MIRBI was argued for by the authors but not demonstrated by data provided in the manual.

## Critique

It is the authors' contention that the MIRBI is the first and only standardized instrument for right-brain assessment. There is serious question as to whether the MIRBI is itself standardized, inasmuch as data expected in a typical standardization are not given in the manual. The age distribution of the normative sample is incomplete. From the table of standard errors, one can assume that the greater part of the sample distribution is between 40 and 60 years of age, with sparse data on subjects above and below this age range even though the MIRBI is described as appropriate from ages 20 to 80. Although we know the total number of persons in each subgroup and their average age, we do not know the standard deviation. For these three groups the reported sample sizes are too small to build norms. Distribution tables by all demographic criteria should be provided in the manual.

In a section called "Local Norms" (p. 10) the authors describe the steps for establishing such information. Unfortunately, they do not follow their own suggestions. They do not provide the normative data for their own sample groups that they recommend others collect, such as age levels, linguistic background, and socioeconomic factors. Furthermore, no standard or transformed score distributions are provided, although the authors recommend that such data be gathered.

More space is given in the manual to a narrative description as to what constitutes reliability and validity than is given to providing data demonstrating the reliability and validity of the MIRBI. The table of standard errors indicates that test scores can be as high as 5.5 raw score points on a total scale ranging from 0 to 43, which means that +1 standard error could reach as high as 25% of the total range of the instrument and consequently change the rating from one diagnostic category to another. This table also reports standard errors of 0.0, which can only indicate a sample of 1 at best or questionable data. Internal reliability appears to be high, with reported coefficients of .91 and above. However, Pimental's study of internal reliability produced much lower coefficients, as reported above. Rater reliability is a critical matter inasmuch as all scoring (and consequently diagnosis) is based on examiner judgment. It might further be pointed out that the product-moment coefficient is probably the least appropriate coefficient to calculate for interrater reliability; Cohen's (1960) kappa would be much more appropriate for the data reported.

Content validity of the MIRBI was considered to be demonstrated by "extensive and careful survey of the literature on right-brain injury" (Pimental & Kingsbury, 1989, p. 29). But how, in fact, this was accomplished is not explained in the manual. Criterion-related validity was evaluated by comparing the MIRBI to CT scans. A diagnostic accuracy of 99.9% was reported, but a problem commonly discussed in neuropsychology texts is that there is no one-to-one relationship between structure and function; that is, no two persons with the same brain structure dysfunction will necessarily show the same behavioral manifestations. If, as the authors argue, diagnostic usefulness is the strongest evidence of construct validity, then much more thorough information must be provided in order to demonstrate construct validity for the MIRBI.

In summary, it appears that the MIRBI can differentiate between normal and right-hemisphere dysfunction subjects. Data in the manual suggest less diagnostic utility in evaluating differences between right- and left-brain injured persons. Many of the deficiencies identified in the MIRBI no doubt result from the limited number of items per disorder area measured (i.e., four skill areas have only one item each to measure dysfunction). Only 5 of the 10 skill areas have three or more items.

The MIRBI manual provides questionable assurance that the instrument can support the level of accuracy required for such a subtle diagnosis as right-brain dysfunction without the accompanying expertise of a trained examiner. Until such time as more supportive data are provided, potential users of the MIRBI should understand that examiner skill is an indispensable prerequisite for use of the MIRBI.

### References

This list includes text citations and suggested additional reading.

Cohen, J. (1960). A coefficient of agreement for nominal scales. *Educational and Psychological Measurement, 20,* 37–46.

Pimental, P.A. (1985a). A *guide to right brain injury: Communication suggestions for patients with right hemisphere injury and the right hemisphere deficit checklist*. Chicago: Neurotest Associates.

Pimental, P.A. (1985b, November). *The aprosodias and right hemisphere syndromes*. Paper presented at the National Convention of the American Speech and Hearing Association, Washington, DC.

Pimental, P.A. (1987a, October). *Deficit patterns and lesion site in right brain injured subjects*. Paper presented at a meeting of the National Academy of Neuropsychology, Chicago.

Pimental, P.A. (1987b). *The Mini Inventory of Right Brain Injury (MIRBI): Development and standardization of a new screening instrument for assessment of right hemisphere brain injury*. Unpublished doctoral dissertation, The Chicago School of Professional Psychology.

Pimental, P.A. (1987c, October). *The MIRBI revisited: The first standardized right brain injury screening*. Paper presented at a meeting of the National Academy of Neuropsychology, Chicago.

Pimental, P.A., & Kingsbury, N.A. (1989). *Mini Inventory of Right Brain Injury*. Austin, TX: PRO-ED.

**Steven Arneson, Ph.D.**
*Project Manager, HRStrategies, Houston, Texas.*

# OCCUPATIONAL STRESS INDICATOR

*Cary L. Cooper, Stephen J. Sloan, and Stephen Williams. Windsor, Berkshire, England: NFER-Nelson Publishing Company Ltd.*

### Introduction

The Occupational Stress Indicator (OSI) is an integrated collection of seven questionnaires designed to identify human stress-related problems in organizations. The OSI questionnaires include an optional biographical questionnaire, measures of job satisfaction and current mental and physical health, an assessment of behavior patterns (specifically the Type A syndrome), a locus of control indicator, a review of sources of stress at work, and an assessment of coping skills. The OSI is self-administered and generally takes approximately 45 minutes to complete. In principle, the OSI is designed to help management focus attention on personal and organizational problems, while at the same time providing a structure for future decision making.

The OSI was developed by Cary L. Cooper, Stephen J. Sloan, and Stephen Williams in 1988. According to the authors, the OSI was developed because of a "frustration" with other measures of stress, which they maintain are "limited in practical application, offering the non-psychologist no better explanation than can be obtained by a simple observation" (Cooper, Sloan, & Williams, 1988, p. 9). Thus, their primary goal was to design an instrument that would solicit personal, accurate data that could be turned into a practical action plan for change and improvement.

Based on the extensive body of occupational stress research, the OSI is designed to identify and cross-reference four key elements: the sources of stress, personal characteristics, coping strategies, and the effects of stress, both individual and organizational. The authors intend the OSI to be a "working model" of stress, one that will be refined over time to reflect the changing nature of these key elements. For example, the early development of the OSI involved several modifications of the original assessment model. First, the OSI was circulated for comment to psychologists with experience in stress research. Based on their comments, a revised version was piloted to a group of middle managers selected at random from a variety of organizations. These managers were asked to make comments in addition to completing the survey. These comments and the collected data provided further questionnaire refinement, bringing the OSI to its current published form.

Normative data, including scale construction and factor analysis results, are based on a unspecified sample of British managers in a range of organizations. Although the exact *N* is not mentioned, the authors do cite some demographic information: Of the sample, 76% were male, 59% were married, and most (74%) were in the 20–40 age range. Normative data are presented for the total sample only and include raw scores, percentiles, means, and standard deviations for the subscales from each of the questionnaires (with the exception of the Biographical Questionnaire). Similar data are presented from an American follow-up study, collected from a group of female bank clerks ($N = 67$).

The OSI has not been revised since its development in 1988, although additional normative information is presented in a 1989 data supplement. In this supplement, scale means and standard deviations are presented from seven separate research studies, ranging in size from 14 to 225 respondents. The authors indicate that separate norms for males and females will be presented as more data become available. The Management Guide does not indicate whether non-English versions of the OSI are available.

The six assessment questionnaires are presented together in a nine-page booklet called the "Indicator" (the optional Biographical Questionnaire is printed separately). Each questionnaire has a 6-point rating scale, although scale anchors differ depending on the nature of the items in each questionnaire. Respondents mark their answers in the booklet; key-punch or scannable answer sheets are not provided. A brief description of each questionnaire follows, presented in order of its appearance in the Indicator.

The job satisfaction questionnaire consists of 22 items; respondents indicate their level of satisfaction with typical factors such as job security, communications, style of supervision, career development, and so forth. Next, respondents complete a questionnaire about their current state of health, both from a behavioral and physical perspective. Feelings and behaviors are assessed to provide a general, overall measure of mental health, while the physical health section examines the frequency of common ailments such as headaches, indigestion, decrease in appetite, and so on. This questionnaire includes 30 items, with scale points ranging from "very true" to "very untrue."

The third questionnaire presents 14 statements on general behavior; respondents indicate whether they agree or disagree with items that measure three different aspects of the Type A personality: attitude toward living (self-confidence, commitment, etc.), personal style of behavior (easygoing, impatient, etc.), and ambition. The fourth questionnaire is a locus of control indicator and assesses how individuals interpret the events around them. Respondents must rate 12 statements using a 6-point "agree-disagree" scale. The statements measure attitudes about such topics as organizational power, fairness, "luck versus ability," and responsibility.

The fifth questionnaire concerns sources of stress intrinsic to the job. A total of 61 different "pressure sources" are presented, including lack of power or influence, inadequate guidance, feelings of isolation, role ambiguity, and so forth. Respondents indicate the degree of pressure each source places on them. Finally, the sixth questionnaire assesses the individual's ability to cope with stressful job situations. Twenty-eight potential coping strategies are listed, and respondents indicate how often they use each to cope with job stress. Included are general tactics such as effective time management, support from family and friends, setting priorities, and so on.

The Indicator begins with an introduction to the sources and effects of occupational stress, followed by simple, easy-to-read directions for completing the questionnaires. The role played by the administrator is fairly passive, involving only a minimum of instruction and intervention. As with other assessment instruments, standard administration conditions apply (i.e., a quiet atmosphere, ample work space, no distractions, etc.).

**Practical Applications/Uses**

The Occupational Stress Indicator was designed to meet two specific objectives. The first was to develop an assessment tool that would operationally define a general model of stress research. The second was to design an instrument that would produce practical and useful information for managers. Specifically, the OSI should provide meaningful data about the hidden effects of occupational stress, which are difficult to identify at the group or organizational level.

Traditionally, companies have used indicators such as turnover, tardiness, or absenteeism to estimate the magnitude of stress in the organization. However, these indicators account for only a portion of the effects that stress-related behaviors have on production and, ultimately, profits. Behavioral outcomes such as increased accidents, missed deadlines, careless mistakes, increased difficulty in making decisions or in getting along with co-workers have a negative effect on performance and efficiency throughout the organization. As the authors note, these effects are "not easily pinned down or quantified by reference to 'normal' staff turnover or personnel-type data" (Cooper, Sloan, & Williams, 1988, p. 1). Thus, the OSI was designed to describe, analyze, and diagnose, in a practical manner, specific elements of stress in the organization.

As stated previously, the OSI measures four such elements of occupational stress: its sources, the characteristics of individuals who may experience it, coping strategies, and its individual and organizational effects. Together, these four variables allow managers, task-force groups, or other users to define problems and provide a structure for future decision making.

The OSI can be used in organizations of all sizes, although it is probably best applied in larger organizations where the symptoms of stress are more difficult to define. The Management Guide presents three case histories to illustrate how the OSI has been used to identify stressful working conditions, detail inadequate coping strategies, and recommend job redesign or small-scale system restructuring.

The OSI is designed to be administered to groups of employees, preferably away from the work setting; the authors recommend that groups be limited to about 15 employees at a time. Sessions can be conducted by a single administrator without the benefit of specialized training. The administrator opens the session with a formal introduction (which contains some explanation and instructions), monitors questionnaire completion, and closes with a brief statement read from the Administration Card. Individual questionnaire instructions are clear and descriptive, making it easy to adapt to the changes in rating scale anchors. As stated earlier, the Biographical Questionnaire is optional; if used, however, it should be administered before the Indicator questionnaires, which are to be taken in the order they appear in the booklet.

Once the OSI is completed, the user performs three analytic tasks: scoring the instrument, profiling the scores, and interpreting the results. Instructions for scoring the OSI are clearly presented in the Management Guide. The first task is to assess the responses to the Biographical Questionnaire, although this does not involve any quantitative analyses. Rather, the emphasis is on creating a qualitative, insightful impression of the group's responses. The scorer simply answers a series of questions about the biographical data and records any group characteristics or trends.

The Indicator questionnaires can be scored two ways: a detailed version produces results for 25 subscales, while a broader method generates scores on 17 subscales. Regardless of the method chosen, scoring involves the use of hand-scoring templates and a designated Score Sheet; computer or scan scoring procedures are not available. The first step is to label each respondent's Indicator so that it relates to a particular column on the Score Sheet. Then scoring templates are applied to the questionnaires; subscale scores are tabulated and transferred to the Score Sheet. When each Indicator has been scored, the next task is to produce a group profile for interpretation.

The process of profiling can involve as many as three steps. First, an examination of individual scores is made to assess the general distribution within the group. Second, the scores are compared with an external criterion, which is presented on the Score Sheet as a zone or band of scores. This band (derived from the pilot test results) represents the average level of scores one might expect to find in a random group of managers. Finally, a comparison of multiple groups is possible (i.e., various departments in an organization).

Having scored and profiled the Indicator, the final task is to interpret the results. Interpretation of the OSI is largely a subjective process. Although guidelines are presented that describe the process adequately, a certain amount of training, practice, and knowledge of occupational stress is required to reach a meaningful interpretation of the OSI results. The authors recommend that four fundamental questions be asked during the interpretive process. First, is there an effect (i.e., does one group experience more stress than another)? Second, can these effects be explained by underlying characteristics of the group? Third, what are the main sources of pressure for the group? Fourth, how does the group cope with the pressures it experiences? The Management Guide explains how each of these questions is interrelated and how each contributes to an overall understanding of OSI results. Case examples are presented to help demonstrate the procedure and possible outcomes of results interpretation.

## Technical Aspects

The Management Guide presents a brief statistical history of the Indicator questionnaires. Initially, the questionnaires were comprised of several items; factor analytic techniques were then applied, and an underlying factor structure was identified for each questionnaire. Items that did not fit the structure were deleted from subsequent versions of the OSI. Scale construction and factor analysis data taken from a pilot sample of 156 managers are presented for each questionnaire. In addition, questionnaire subscales are described along with their content and underlying meaning.

Data also are reported on the intercorrelation of subscales within each of the questionnaires. The intercorrelations seem somewhat moderate considering the "common ground" the individual questionnaires are designed to measure. The authors note, however, that the subscales were constructed to broadly define and assess the complex nature of occupational stress and therefore should not be expected to produce high intercorrelations.

The Management Guide presents reliability data in the form of subscale internal consistency results. Split-half coefficients are reported for each of the questionnaire subscales and range from .07 to .78. Although these correlations are all significant at the .01 level, 12 of the 28 reported correlations are less than .40. The authors note that some of the "scales" consist of only three items and therefore must be interpreted as not truly representing split-half reliability. A second form of reliability, test-retest, is "presently the subject of ongoing investigation" (Cooper, Sloan, & Williams, 1988, p. 57). The 1989 data supplement does not mention the results of this investigation.

Regarding the validity of the OSI, it must be noted that the Indicator is not a test and, as such, does not produce traditional criterion-related validity results. Rather, the pertinent validity evidence includes both content and construct validity. Regarding the former, a review of the occupational stress literature supports the view that the OSI is face valid and assesses the appropriate content. The authors took steps to ensure face validity during the pilot work, when preliminary versions of the OSI were reviewed by qualified stress researchers.

Construct validity evidence for the OSI is lacking. The research objective, of course, calls for an examination of the relationship between the OSI and other measures of occupational stress. The Management Guide states that construct validity is the subject of current background research, a statement that is essentially repeated (without support of data) in the 1989 data supplement. The data supplement notes that the authors are

> carrying out a number of construct and predictive validity studies. One is with managers and management consultants, one with factory workers and one with local authority managers and employees. A construct validity study on the OSI will be prepared for publication shortly. (Cooper, Sloan, & Williams, 1989, p. 1)

As of May 1990, no such reports had been forwarded for review.

## Critique

In general, the Occupational Stress Indicator appears to be a useful tool for identifying the sources of stress in the workplace. In fact, it is probably one of the better stress measurement devices available, largely because of the underlying model that grounds the OSI in the occupational stress literature. The authors have clearly done their research, and this state-of-the-art model of stress measurement is the best reason to recommend the OSI. Furthermore, the Indicator is short, easy to use, and appropriate for all levels of the organization. The Management Guide is clear and informative about nontechnical issues, especially in its treatment of the research on which the OSI is based. Another strength is the stated goal to make the OSI a "working model" instrument, one that will be open to feedback from users and the changing nature of future stress research. For all of its assets, however, the OSI also has a few technical shortcomings that need to be addressed in the future.

First, the Management Guide is lacking in its documentation of the normative database and other psychometric details. For example, it is unclear whether normative data were collected from the same sample that was used for scale construction and factor analysis work, or when exactly these data were collected. Also, important reliability and validity information is not reported. Though there is sufficient reason to consider the OSI a face-valid instrument, it remains to be seen how well the Indicator compares to other purported measures of occupational stress. Construct validity evidence is needed to really establish the OSI as a viable assessment tool in the field of stress research. Therefore, a high priority for the authors must be the ongoing collection and presentation of this validity evidence. Also, because it is difficult to establish meaningful criteria against which to measure the "success" of the OSI, this reviewer would like to see cost-accounting procedures or utility analyses used as criterion measures for the OSI. These measures would help quantify the impact the OSI is having in the organization.

Second, the Biographical Questionnaire data are not tabulated statistically, which may lead to errors or omissions in the analysis of trends within or across groups. Quantifying the data would not add much time or effort to the scoring process, yet would appear to make easier the task of describing group background characteristics.

Third, the OSI scoring and profiling systems follow this imprecise pattern of data collection when accounting for individual and group scores. Scores are recorded in blocks on the Score Sheet and are then transferred to "above," "average," and "below" categories on the Group Profile Sheet. Again, it would appear that meaningful differences between data points are lost with these scoring methods. Would not more significant conclusions be drawn on the basis of statistically derived results? In fairness to the authors, it should be noted that the typical user of the OSI is probably not sophisticated in the use of statistics; this must certainly have been a factor in developing the current scoring and profiling system. Nevertheless, it would be interesting to see if a more rigorous scoring method could be developed that would result in more precise interpretations.

Finally, because the OSI was developed in England, the language and grammar used throughout the instrument merit special attention. For the most part, users should have no difficulty with the English spelling of certain words (e.g., *organisation, programme* ). However, some phrases may be unfamiliar to U.S. users (e.g., the Biographical Questionnaire includes "O" and "A" educational levels among the choices for academic achievement). The Management Guide does not indicate if an American version of the OSI has been prepared; however, if the OSI is to be extensively used in the United States, certain revisions may be necessary.

In summary, the Occupational Stress Indicator is a welcome addition to the field of organizational stress research. Designed for managers, it appears useful in helping to identify the sources and consequences of work stress. With some minor technical adjustments, the OSI should become an even stronger measurement tool in the future, one that will warrant the attention of any organization interested in reducing organizational stress.

## References

Cooper, C.L., Sloan, S.J., & Williams, S. (1988). *Management guide for the Occupational Stress Indicator.* Windsor, England: NFER-Nelson.

Cooper, C.L., Sloan, S.J., & Williams, S. (1989). *Data supplement to the management guide for the Occupational Stress Indicator.* Windsor, England: NFER-Nelson.

**Terrence S. Luce, Ph.D.**
*Professor of Psychology, University of Tulsa, Tulsa, Oklahoma.*

# PARENTAL ACCEPTANCE-REJECTION QUESTIONNAIRE

*Ronald P. Rohner. Storrs, Connecticut: Center for the Study of Parental Acceptance and Rejection.*

## Introduction

Development of the Parental Acceptance-Rejection Questionnaire (PARQ) was begun by Dr. Ronald P. Rohner over two decades ago in his attempt to examine antecedents, consequences, and correlates of parental acceptance and rejection. The PARQ was originally published in 1980 and underwent revisions in 1984 and 1989. There are three versions of the PARQ: the Adult PARQ, the Mother PARQ, and the Child PARQ. This review will address all three versions.

Dr. Rohner is a professor of anthropology and human development at the University of Connecticut at Storrs and, since 1981, director of the University's Center for the Study of Parental Acceptance and Rejection. He holds a Ph.D. from Stanford University and is both an anthropologist and a psychologist. Rohner has authored numerous articles and books, including *The Warmth Dimension: Foundations of Parental Acceptance-Rejection Theory* (1986), *Handbook for the Study of Parental Acceptance and Rejection* (1990), and *They Love Me, They Love Me Not* (1975).

The fundamental theoretical framework guiding the development of the PARQ is the parental acceptance-rejection theory (PART), a theory of socialization that attempts to reveal the impact of parental acceptance and rejection on the behavioral, cognitive, and emotional development of children and on the personality formulation of adults throughout the world. The theory also attempts to discern why some children are able to withstand potentially damaging effects of parental rejection and emotional abuse and develop into basically healthy adults. Development of the instrument was guided by conceptual and methodological considerations that could eventuate in the establishment of cross-culturally valid principles concerning

> the world-wide antecedents, consequences, and correlates of parental acceptance and rejection—principles that can be shown empirically to hold true across social classes, racial groups and ethnic groups in both the United States and internationally, as well as across time as nations change. (Rohner, 1975, p. 13)

Once cross-culturally validated principles have been established, the possibility arises of formulating perhaps universally applicable policies and practices dealing with children and families.

In PART, parental warmth can be interpreted as a bipolar dimension, with rejection or the absence of parental warmth and affection standing at one pole and acceptance at the other. Given that nearly all persons have experienced during childhood some degree of warmth and affection from primary caregivers (usually parents), all people can be placed on this continuum. Accepting parents, as defined in PART, are those who show a constellation of behaviors toward their children consisting of love and affection, hugging, kissing, caressing, and other kinds of accepting gestures. Verbal affection also can be expressed, by means of praise and compliment. Such behaviors are likely to result in a child's feeling loved and accepted. The theory defines rejecting parents as those who dislike, resent, or disapprove of their children. Parental rejection generally manifests in the form of hostility and aggression on the one hand and indifference and neglect on the other. Although hostility refers to the subjective feelings of resentment or anger toward a child, verbal and physical aggression present observable manifestations of these feelings. Indifferent parents, by contrast, are more likely to be emotionally withdrawn and insensitive to their children's pleas for attention and comfort, and they usually are not attendant to the children's physical needs. Such parents are emotionally constricted toward their children and apt to spend little time with them. Either form of rejection, that revealed as hostility-aggression or that revealed as indifference-neglect, is likely to result in children who feel unacceptable or unloved.

Although PAR theory would predict that the impact of parental hostility and indifference on children would be devastating, it acknowledges evidence of parentally rejected children who seem minimally damaged by such parental behaviors. Here the theory introduces Piagetian concepts of cognitive capabilities and cognitive interpretations of social-situational factors that appear to distinguish "copers" from "non-copers." Copers are those who seem able to depersonalize apparently rejecting circumstances; that is, by being able to take another's perspective, the child can attribute what is ostensibly rejection to causes other than his or her unworthiness. Also, those children with a clearly differentiated sense of self seem less affected by rejecting parents than do those with less differentiated senses of self. Finally, those children who believe that what happens in their lives is controllable to some extent by themselves, who feel that their lives are self-determined, are relatively less affected by parental rejection or hostility.

In order to permit a comprehensive examination and thorough testing of PAR theory, Rohner also has developed the Personality Assessment Questionnaire (PAQ), a self-report instrument for the assessment of a person's perception of him- or herself, or his or her child, with respect to seven behavioral dispositions. In addition he has developed the Parental Acceptance-Rejection Interview Schedule (PARIS) for use with adult or child interviews. The PAQ and PARIS are both designed to complement the PARQ and are thoroughly discussed in Rohner's (1990) handbook, but these instruments lie beyond the scope of the current review.

All three versions of the PARQ provide a self-report format. The Adult PARQ asks an adult to respond to his or her perceptions of treatment by his or her mother from ages 7 through 12 years. The adult responds to these perceptions about the caregiver's treatment in terms of warmth-affection, hostility-aggression, indifference-neglect, and undifferentiated rejection, the four scales of the PARQ. The Mother PARQ asks the parent (usually, but not necessarily, a mother) to respond to her perceptions of her treatment of her child in terms of the same four scales. Finally, the Child PARQ asks child or adolescent examinees to respond to their perceptions of the manner in which their mother now treats them, also in terms of the four scales employed in the adult versions of the PARQ.

All questionnaires may be administered either individually or in group settings (such as classrooms) by persons without specific background in psychometrics or testing. On all three versions of the PARQ, the warmth-affection scale contains 20 items, the aggression-hostility and the neglect-indifference scales each contain 15 items, and the undifferentiated rejection scale contains 10 items, for a total of 60 items. The title page of each questionnaire presents associated instructions to read to respondents before they begin. However, for children or other respondents with reading difficulty, the item instructions also may be read aloud.

The accompanying handbook (Rohner, 1990) provides detailed information concerning all aspects of the PARQ. All versions of the questionnaire utilize an identical response format and scoring system, which permits comparability of scores across instruments. Respondents are instructed to ask themselves if each item is generally true or untrue about the way they were treated by their mothers, or about the way they (adult respondents) currently treat their own children. A response of "almost always true" is scored 4; "sometimes true," 3; "rarely true," 2; and "almost never true," 1. Seven items of the neglect-indifference scale must be reverse-scored; for these a 4 becomes 1, a 3 becomes 2, a 2 becomes 3, and a 1 becomes 4. Once derived, the total score depicts the composite level of acceptance-rejection as reported by the respondent. The handbook provides mean scores and standard deviations for each scale. These statistics were derived from 147 adult respondents and 220 children.

## Practical Applications/Uses

The PARQ, as stated earlier, has been developed from PAR theory for researching the antecedents and consequences of parental acceptance and rejection. The fundamental principle underlying the theory is that there are universal socialization principles that transcend race, social class, geography, and language. The instrument can be employed to further explore, discover, and refine cross-culturally validated socialization principles associated with parental acceptance and rejection practices. In the handbook, Rohner portrays the two guiding research questions of the PART as follows: 1. Do children everywhere throughout our species—regardless of differences in culture, language, race, or other limiting conditions—respond in the same way to the perception of parental rejection? and 2. To what extent do the effects of rejection in childhood extend into adulthood, and what personality dispositions are likely to be modified in the course of developing maturity?

To assure application cross-culturally, test items were screened and "decentered" from idiomatic English during a study of 101 societies. As a consequence of these translations, and consistent with the premise of PART that socialization practices can transcend culture and geography, potential research usage of

PARQ is vast. The following language versions were available at the time of this writing:

| | *Mother* | *Adult* | *Child* |
|---|---|---|---|
| Arabic | yes | yes | yes |
| Bengali | yes | yes | yes |
| Czech | yes | yes | yes |
| English | yes | yes | yes |
| French | no | no | yes |
| Greek | no | no | no |
| Hindi | yes | yes | yes |
| Korean | yes | yes | yes |
| Spanish (Mexican) | no | no | yes |
| Spanish (Puerto Rican) | no | no | yes |
| Swedish | no | yes | no |
| Telugu | yes | yes | yes |
| Tiv (Nigeria) | no | no | yes |
| Urdu | no | yes | no |

Although the user can interpret an individual respondent's scores by comparing them with the possible extremes of Rohner's reported scale scores, the instrument's primary application is for research with groups. Rohner claims (correctly) that social policies, programs, and practices are too often based on idiosyncratic beliefs rather than on established principles of human behavior. He buttresses this claim by citing Edwin Zigler, a renowned developmental psychologist, who charges that national policies in the United States dealing with family and children are "determined by waves of fashion substantially unrelated to empirical research—even when the results carry the risk of significant damage to whole generations and subclasses of the population . . ." (Zigler, 1978, p. 3). As theoretically driven and empirically based principles are discovered within the context of PAR theory, this universalist approach, which Rohner prefers to call "anthroponomy applications," can be further expanded to encompass such areas as the "cycles of violence" in child abuse and spouse abuse circumstances.

## Technical Aspects

Reliability and validity procedures on the PARQ were guided by the 1974 *Standards for Educational and Psychological Tests* (American Psychological Association). The primary measure of reliability used was Cronbach's coefficient alpha, a measure of the internal consistency of items within a scale. A high alpha score indicates that all items in a particular scale are, indeed, sampling the same content domain. Alpha coefficients for the Adult PARQ range from .86 to .95, with a median alpha of .91. Alpha coefficients for the child version range from .72 to .90, with a median reliability of .82. With such respectable reliability coefficients, users can feel confident that the PARQ has psychometric integrity with regard to reliability.

Convergent validity is determined by assessing the extent of agreement between different measures of a single trait, factor, or construct. Convergent validity is demonstrated when each of the PARQ scales correlates higher with its respective validation scales than it does with any other scale in the instrument. The convergent validity correlations for most of the scales demonstrate psychometric integrity. There are, however, two exceptions: perceived physical punishment and perceived neglect/indifference. Rohner (1990) explains that

> physical punishment was recognized in advance as being only an approximately satisfactory criterion for aggression/hostility. The physical punishment scale was used because no other validated scale measuring parental aggression/hostility could be located as a possible external criterion for determining concurrent validity.

Although the author provides a reasonable explanation for the relatively low correlations between these two PARQ scales and their respective validation scales, interpretations of these two scales must be made with caution.

The PARQ's construct validity was first assessed by means of a factor analysis. Items from the questionnaire were grouped into clusters of three to four items and subjected to a principal components factor analysis. Factor loadings, with associated percentages of variance accounted for, are presented in the handbook for all PARQ scales, both child and adult versions, and lend strong support to the conceptual interpretations (i.e., construct validity of the PAR theory). For example, in the adult version of the PARQ, the first three factors accounted for 75% of the variance.

Rohner (1990) produced further evidence for the construct validity of the PARQ scales by asking undergraduate students, who had studied the theoretical definition of each of the constructs measured by the four PARQ scales, to sort the items into four piles, each representing one of the four principal constructs. The warmth-affection items produced 100% accuracy, and both the aggression-hostility and the neglect-indifference items resulted in only 17% error. In contrast, the undifferentiated rejection scale resulted in considerable error rates (approximately 40%) for all three raters. It appears that the construct of undifferentiated rejection is conceptually ambiguous and, therefore, must be subjected to further theoretical refinement.

Other studies have attempted to assess the construct validity of the PARQ in a more global fashion. Potvin (1977) reported that the view of God held by rejected children is one of malevolence and punitiveness. In contrast, accepted and loved children tend to view God as benevolent and kind. However, the most compelling and comprehensive evidence of construct validity can be found Rohner's 1986 book, *The Warmth Dimension*. Here he reports the results of 15 studies regarding children's perception of parental acceptance and rejection in eight nations, including Canada, Czechoslovakia, India, Korea, and Nigeria. The general research method was to administer the PARQ and correlate those scores with Rohner's complementary instrument, the Personality Assessment Questionnaire (PAQ). In these studies of diverse societies, the "mental health" status of children in the samples, as inferred from the PAQ, was highly correlated with total PARQ scores. Still further confirmation emerges in a sample of 316 American schoolchildren whom Rohner studied to determine the relative contribution of various parenting styles to children's overall mental health. His findings demonstrate that the greatest emotional damage is produced by cold and rejecting parents (hostile-aggressive, indifferent-neglecting, and undifferentiated rejecting).

These studies provide considerable confirmation for the PAR theory's claim of the relationship between perceived acceptance-rejection and children's mental health status. Thus, Rohner's claim of the criticality of parental acceptance and rejection in children's socialization has been widely supported in numerous and varied sociocultural circumstances throughout the world.

## Critique

The PARQ, which was developed to test and refine parental acceptance-rejection theory, has been subjected to over two decades of rigorous cross-cultural research. Both the theory and the assessment instruments appear to have weathered these assaults well. The PARQ is an effective tool for examining parental practices cross-nationally and can be used over a wide age range. There are, however, some conceptual refinements/clarifications that must be addressed by the theory and reflected in the PARQ, such as the role of perceived physical punishment and that of perceived neglect/hostility.

A somewhat more serious concern stems from that part of the theory that predicts the likelihood of a rejected child becoming a dependent child. Though this has intuitive appeal (and jibes with Bowlby's [1969] attachment theory), PART appears also to explain the extreme "independence" found in some rejected children as follows: The child initiates a process of counter-rejection and postures with a "defensive independence" (Rohner's term). That is, the theory can comfortably explain either outcome of rejection—dependence or independence. A fundamental requirement of a theory is that it cannot be used to explain two contradictory outcomes. Although this concern does not assail the central postulates of parental acceptance-rejection theory, it is serious enough to be noted.

Professor Rohner has provided researchers with an immensely powerful tool for examining the impact of parental practices cross-culturally. Researchers and theoreticians in any of the behavioral or social sciences should feel confident in utilizing this instrument in virtually any sociocultural milieu. It has immense integrative potential for theory building, theory refinement, and theory testing in the social sciences. Rohner has begun a most ambitious task of integrating such separate bodies of theory as attachment theory, locus of control theory, and self theory. Such integrative efforts are both laudable and all too rare in social science disciplines, which too often dissect the complexity of human behavior in order to achieve methodological rigor. Rohner has scrupulously avoided this vapid approach while attempting to derive universal principles of human development and socialization, and he has already contributed greatly to our understanding of parental practices and associated consequences.

## References

American Psychological Association. (1974). *Standards for educational and psychological tests.* Washington, DC: Author.

Bowlby, J. (1969). *Attachment and loss: I. Attachment.* New York: Basic Books.

Potvin, R.H. (1977). Adolescent God images. *Religious Research, 19,* 43–53.

Rohner, R.P. (1975). *They love me, they love me not: A worldwide study of the effects of parental acceptance and rejection.* New Haven, CT: HRAF Press.

Rohner, R.P. (1986). *The warmth dimension: Foundations of parental acceptance-rejection theory.* Newbury Park, CA: Sage.

Rohner, R.P. (1989). *Handbook for the study of parental acceptance and rejection.* Storrs, CT: University of Connecticut, Center for the Study of Parental Acceptance and Rejection.

Zigler, E. (1978, December 4). Policy-making on a poor data base now the American rule. *Behavior Today,* pp. 3–5.

**Wyman E. Fischer, Ph.D.**
*Professor of Psychology and Chair, Department of Educational Psychology, Ball State University, Muncie, Indiana.*

# PEDIATRIC EXAMINATION OF EDUCATIONAL READINESS AT MIDDLE CHILDHOOD

*Melvin D. Levine. Cambridge, Massachusetts: Educators Publishing Service, Inc.*

### Introduction

The Pediatric Examination of Educational Readiness at Middle Childhood (PEERAMID) was developed to serve as a neurodevelopmental assessment of children ages 9 to 14. It is intended to measure those neurodevelopmental areas frequently associated with academic and/or behavioral difficulties. Though individual items of the examination receive a numerical value, the PEERAMID does not result in a composite score; instead, the examiner produces a narrative description based on test results and observations during the testing procedure (Levine, 1985).

Developed under the direction of Dr. Melvin D. Levine, the PEERAMID is the last in a chronologically arranged series of five batteries collectively identified as the Pediatric Assessment System for Learning Disorders. The others in the series are the Pediatric Extended Examination at Three (PEET), the Pediatric Examination of Educational Readiness (PEER) for ages 4 to 6, and the Pediatric Early Examination (PEEX) for ages 7 to 9. It is recommended that the PEERAMID, as well as the other batteries in the series, be complemented with data collected from additional sources such as medical examinations, detailed family histories, and cognitive tests of intelligence and achievement (Levine, 1985).

The Pediatric Assessment System for Learning Disorders was the product of many professionals associated with the Division of Ambulatory Pediatrics at the Children's Hospital in Boston. The examinations were the direct result of two major research programs, the Brookline Early Education Project and the Middle Childhood Project. Both projects were funded by the Robert Wood Johnson Foundation.

Dr. Melvin D. Levine, a licensed pediatrician and the primary author of the PEERAMID, is presently director of the Clinical Center for the Study of Development and Learning at the University of North Carolina at Chapel Hill and Professor of Pediatrics at the University of North Carolina School of Medicine. Prior to his present position, Dr. Levine was Associate Professor of Pediatrics at Harvard Medical School as well as chief of the Division of Ambulatory Pediatrics at the Children's Hospital in Boston. He and his collaborators spent approximately 5 years researching and developing the PEERAMID (Levine, 1985).

The PEERAMID set contains an examiner's manual, a stimulus booklet, a packet of response booklets, a packet of record forms, and a kit holding an eye-hand board and a cup and ball. The examiner's manual is attractively illustrated and includes instructions for administration, scoring, and interpretation of subtests grouped under the following six major sections: Minor Neurological Indicators, Fine Motor Function, Language, Gross Motor Function, Temporal-Sequential Organization, and Visual Processing. In addition, specific items scattered throughout the six major areas provide a measure of Selective Attention. The nature of each major section is described and its purpose for inclusion in a neurodevelopmental assessment battery is stated. The individual subtests (tasks) within each major section also are described and justified for inclusion. The interpretation section for each task identifies the specific disabilities or problems signaled by a poor score and, in a few cases, the remediation procedures that might be implemented.

As additional aids to the examiner, the manual contains a sample completed PEERAMID Record Form, a sample completed PEERAMID Response Booklet, a sample completed General Health Assessment, and a sample completed PEERAMID Task Analysis. As the same subject was used for each sample form, this presentation can clarify difficult administration, scoring, or interpretation problems during the initial stages of practice in learning to administer the battery (Levine, 1985).

The PEERAMID Record Form, if completed according to instructions, will contain a detailed quantitative and qualitative record of performance. Where deemed appropriate, the subject's performance on variables such as total correct, accuracy, and speed of performance is compared with normative age groups. Spaces are provided on the record form for computer coding of subtest responses to facilitate research efforts. As indicated earlier, the record form also includes a General Health Assessment (a form to be completed by a physician) and data summary forms titled "PEERAMID Clinical Summary" and "PEERAMID Task Analysis." The latter are intended to serve as aids in interpretation and treatment.

The PEERAMID Response Booklet provides a record of test items requiring a written or drawing response from the subject. After the testing session, the response booklet is to be placed with the record form in the subject's file. The PEERAMID Stimulus Booklet contains stimuli, both verbal and pictorial, for specific tasks related to language, temporal-sequential organization, and visual processing areas. As noted previously, the PEERAMID Kit contains a cup and ball plus an eye-hand board for visual-motor coordination tasks. In addition to these materials provided in the kit, the examiner is to have available sharp pencils, a paper tube for visual dominance testing, and a stopwatch for timed items. The total administration time for the PEERAMID should take approximately 40 minutes.

The 32 tasks grouped under the PEERAMID's six major neurodevelopmental sections are described as follows (Levine, 1985):

1. Minor Neurological Indicators
   a. *Lateral Preference*—a measure of hand and eye preference;
   b. *Left-Right Discrimination*—a measure of the ability to quickly and accurately identify left and right body parts;
   c. *Rapid Alternating Movement*—a measure of diadochokinesis of both the right and left hands;

d. *Sustained Motor Stance*—a measure of motor impersistence with possible concomitant spooning and/or choreiform twitches.

2. Fine Motor Function
   a. *Imitative Finger Movement*—a measure of finger agnosia;
   b. *Sequential Finger Opposition*—a complex task measuring motor speed, eye-hand coordination, motor sequential organization, and memory for simple motor patterns;
   c. *Alternating Fists*—a test of bimanual coordination involving two limbs simultaneously;
   d. *Complex Finger Opposition*—ability to master a novel fine-motor pattern or motor memory;
   e. *Eye-Hand Board*—a pure measure of eye-hand coordination and motor speed;
   f. *Graph Paper Copying*—a measure of motor planning and organizational ability and/or motor dyspraxia;
   g. *Pencil Speed*—a measure of fine-motor control similar in function to the eye-hand board;
   h. *Pencil Excursion*—a measure of propriokinesthetic feedback;
   i. *Cursive Alphabet*—a measure of long-term motor recall and pencil control;
   j. *Signature with Eyes Closed*—a measure of motor memory and propriokinesthetic feedback.
3. Language
   a. *Name Quickly Test*—a rapid retrieval of semantically encoded data;
   b. *Yes, No, Maybe Test*—a measure of verbal comprehension involving syntax;
   c. *Verbal Instructions*—a measure of auditory-motor integration;
   d. *Sentence Formulation ("Road Test")*—the ability to construct sentences involving cognitive flexibility and knowledge of grammar;
   e. *Category Naming*—a measure of verbal fluency, word finding, expressive vocabulary, and verbal cognition;
   f. *Picture Naming*—a measure of expressive vocabulary and/or dysnomia.
4. Gross Motor Function
   a. *Tandem Balance*—a measure of proprioceptive and kinesthetic feedback from muscles and joints;
   b. *Eye-Arm Coordination*—a measure of motor programming involving the eyes and upper body;
   c. *Sequential Hopping*—a measure of auditory–gross motor integration.
5. Temporal-Sequential Organization
   a. *Time Orientation Questions*—a measure of mastery of time concepts;
   b. *Digit Spans*—a measure of auditory sequential memory and/or auditory attention span;
   c. *Alphabet Arrangement*—a test of the interaction between short-term and long-term memory;
   d. *Geometric Form Tapping*—a measure of visual sequential organization;
   e. *Recall Complex Finger Opposition*—a measure of long-term motor memory and/or motor sequential organization.
6. Visual Processing
   a. *Visual Vigilance*—a measure of visual processing and/or impulse control;

b. *Visual Recognition*—a measure of visual memory and/or memory registration;
c. *Visual Retrieval*—a measure of revisualization or visual recall;
d. *Form Copying*—a measure of ability to integrate visual inputs with fine-motor drawing responses.

**Practical Applications/Uses**

The PEERAMID is described as a multipurpose instrument. As a clinical instrument, it serves as an aid in the diagnosis of neurodevelopmental problems often associated with specific learning and/or behavioral difficulties. As a teaching instrument, it can help students in training hone their diagnostic skills and increase their knowledge of neurodevelopment. As a research tool, it can establish or verify important links between neurodevelopmental impairments and learning/behavioral disorders (Levine, 1985).

Although specific levels of medical and/or psychological training are not specified, the PEERAMID is intended for use by "health care and other professionals" (Levine, 1985, p. 1). As mentioned previously, it is not intended to be used alone; rather, it should be part of a comprehensive evaluation including parent and teacher interviews, medical examinations, and cognitive tests of intelligence and achievement. Although the subtests of the PEERAMID are grouped into six major neurodevelopmental areas, purity of classification is not intended nor has it been demonstrated. Though a given task has a primary assessment purpose, it may in effect measure multiple functions. The test user is encouraged to complete both the PEERAMID Clinical Summary and the PEERAMID Task Analysis in addition to the PEERAMID Record Form for each subject evaluated. Such multiple analyses are intended to aid in arriving at a proper diagnosis and the formulation of an appropriate treatment plan.

**Technical Aspects**

Though the PEERAMID manual contains detailed instructions for test administration and scoring, it includes no reliability and only minimal validity data.

The author suggests that individuals in training who use the battery should undergo reliability testing by being observed by another professional familiar with the PEERAMID (Levine, 1985). However, there is no evidence in either the PEERAMID manual or in the test literature that any interrater reliability studies were ever conducted.

The author attempts to establish content validity by providing rationale statements for each of the tasks in the battery. For example, in relation to the Lateral Preference tasks, he states, "This item is included under Minor Neurological Indicators because poorly-established and mixed hand preference have been associated in the literature with various learning disorders (Orton, 1937)" (Levine, 1985, p. 5). Such documentations (a number of which have been discredited in more recent research) support some of the rationale statements. However, other rationale statements, written in support of a particular PEERAMID task, are not referenced even though they do not fall within the realm of common knowledge. For example, in reference to the tasks subsumed under Rapid Alternating Movement, the test author makes a very definitive statement without documentation. He says,

> when they try to execute rapid alternating movements, there is apt to be flailing and a lack of true rotary movements of the forearm. This imbalance between neuromuscular inhibition and facilitation can be taken as one indicator of a neuromaturational lag, as the finding is more common in younger children and becomes increasingly rare after age seven. (Levine, 1985, p. 7)

Other than referenced rationale statements in support of content validity, the manual of the PEERAMID contains no evidence of research-based criterion-related or construct validity.

Mention is made in the PEERAMID manual of normative data based on samples drawn from public school systems in New England blue- and white-collar communities. However, no tables are provided to describe the nature and size of these samples. Criterion values of acceptable performance on PEERAMID tasks for various age groupings are provided in the PEERAMID Record Form. However, because means and standard deviations from the normative samples are not available to the test user, it is difficult to determine what, if any, meaning the age-related criterion values have.

In general, instructions for scoring the PEERAMID should pose no serious problems for the examiner. However, in a few cases interrater reliability may suffer as a result of vagueness of scoring criteria. As noted by a previous reviewer of the PEERAMID (Hughes, 1989), an example of scoring vagueness is illustrated by the Category Naming task in which the examiner is instructed to score performance as 0 if performance is characterized by "considerable hesitancy, prolonged effort"; as 1 if performance involves "some hesitancy"; and as 2 if performance is characterized by "ease of production (quick response), no hesitancy" (Levine, 1985, p. 32).

## Critique

The PEERAMID is a neatly packaged and quality constructed test battery with a clearly defined purpose. Directions for administration are concise and except in a few cases, as alluded to in a previous section, scoring criteria are sufficiently definitive to ensure adequate interrater reliability among experienced examiners. The rationale and interpretation statements included in the PEERAMID manual, though not always adequately documented, provide meaningful context and establish relationships between the tasks of the battery and neurodevelopmental indicators believed responsible for a variety of academic and/or behavioral problems of 9- to 14-year-old subjects. The provisions for computer coding of subject responses are excellent and should facilitate research efforts with the instrument.

However, the PEERAMID is lacking in a number of key areas. No detailed description of normative data is provided in the manual. Levine, Rappaport, and Fenton (1988), in an article published after the PEERAMID was marketed, provide some additional normative data, but these are not readily available to test users. No statistical evidence of reliability, interrater or otherwise, is included in the manual. This should be of major concern to PEERAMID users because it seriously compromises meaningful use of the instrument. Except for evidence of content validity, the PEERAMID manual contains no other validity data. Users have no information as to how this battery compares with other instruments of similar purpose. Although Levine et al. (1988) did find that the PEERAMID discriminated statistically between children with school problems and those with normal academic performance, this in itself is not proof that the battery indeed measures neurodevelopment.

The author of the PEERAMID includes a disclaimer for the test when he says, "It should be stressed that there is no purity in this classification of test items into six areas of development" (Levine, 1985, p. 3). However, as the battery is divided into major sections and tasks with descriptive titles, the impression is created that differential diagnosis, based at least in part on the major sections, is possible. A factor analytic study is needed to determine if the six major sections of the PEERAMID are in effect unique and whether the individual tasks are placed appropriately within each section. Without such a study the usefulness of the instrument in providing data for differential diagnosis and treatment is questionable.

Although the test author provides considerable interpretative data (though of questionable value in light of the lack of statistical support), the manual provides little direction for treatment or remediation. This minimizes its value, particularly for those individuals not highly trained in behavioral neurology and/or psychoeducational intervention.

The PEERAMID is a well-developed instrument that has the potential to fulfill its intended purpose as a measure of neurodevelopment. However, until additional studies are conducted relative to reliability and validity, it should be considered a research instrument.

## References

Hughes, J.N. (1989). Pediatric Examination of Educational Readiness at Middle Childhood. In J.C. Conoley & J.J. Kramer (Eds.), *The tenth mental measurements yearbook* (pp. 608–609). Lincoln, NE: Buros Institute of Mental Measurements.

Levine, M.D. (1985). *Pediatric Examination of Educational Readiness at Middle Childhood.* Cambridge, MA: Educators Publishing Service.

Levine, M.D., Rappaport, L., & Fenton, T. (1988). Neurodevelopmental readiness for adolescence: Studies of an assessment instrument for 9 to 14 year old children. *Journal of Developmental and Behavioral Pediatrics, 4,* 181–188.

Orton, S.T. (1937). *Reading, writing and speech problems in children.* New York: Norton.

**Ric Brown, Ed.D.**
*Professor of Education, California State University-Fresno, Fresno, California.*

# PERFORMANCE LEVELS OF A SCHOOL PROGRAM SURVEY

*Frank E. Williams. East Aurora, New York: D.O.K. Publishers, Inc.*

### Introduction

The Performance Levels of a School Program Survey (PLSPS) was designed for easily assessing eight areas that the author suggests are guidelines for gifted and talented programs (Williams, 1979). The author, Frank Williams, suggests that all students possess these eight ability areas in some degree, with the implication that the PLSPS can be used at a school site for total program evaluation. The eight areas assessed are general intellectual abilities, specific academic abilities, leadership abilities, creative productive thinking abilities, psychomotor abilities, visual–performing arts abilities, affective abilities, and vocational career abilities.

The PLSPS was developed to reflect teachers' and administrators' perceptions of the degree to which their school was developing the ability areas. The results could then be used to identify areas of emphasis (or lack thereof) for future direction. For each of the eight areas, 10 items have been written covering the following 10 dimensions: measurement, enrichment, acceleration, individualization, recognition and reward, special activities, special personnel, staff development, student mentors, and out of school/class activities.

The test developer, Frank E. Williams, Ph.D., states that the survey was developed to determine need and direction of school programs to match students' unique learning styles. The survey attempts to diagnose a school's existing efforts and further analyze what is required to develop an optimum learning program for those whom the author refers to as "normal" students. He suggests that although the scale items have been derived from literature on how gifted and creative students learn, normal students differ only as to degree, not type, of abilities. He further states that the PLSPS can lead to the implementation of practices that can benefit approximately 80% of a school's student population. The survey is said to indicate the direction a program needs to take to develop the eight areas of human potential.

The test manual (16 pages, dated 1979) indicates that there have been three versions of the scale. A copy of the scale itself is dated 1988. The first form was field tested on 435 teachers and principals of K–12 schools in Alaska, Idaho, Washington, Oregon, Iowa, and California. The manual states that revision occurred after statistical analysis (not specified) and after the survey was given to other groups of teachers and administrators during in-service sessions in Oregon and California.

The scale itself is an eight-page, 8½" × 11" loose-leaf booklet. Ten questions appear on each page, yielding a total of 80. Each page covers one of the eight ability dimensions noted previously. The questions are in the form "Does your school . . ." or "Are students . . . ." To the right of each question, the respondent can check one of four answers: not being done, rarely being done, usually being done but need more, or adequately being done, leave as is. Some of the items have space for written comments that are solicited depending on the question, such as "If so, what? _____."

The instruction manual suggests that the test administrator (principal, department chair, etc.) be familiar with the entire survey. A statement is provided for reading aloud that attempts to encourage truthful answers are based on an individual's perception, not on what others are or should be doing. The statement also considers anonymity, suggesting that scores are evaluated by group, not individually. The survey is written to be answered by teachers and administrators at a school site, with a suggestion that the form be administered to two groups independently and then discussed after scoring is completed.

## Practical Applications/Uses

The PLSPS is intended to first report, in terms of staff perceptions, what a school program is doing and then to point out areas not usually considered by school sites. Although the manual contains no statements about appropriate timing for the survey, one can assume that a school site interested in information revealed by the PLSPS could give the scale when it was interested and/or ready to consider the data. As noted previously, the survey is to be completed by teachers and administrators at a school site. The survey has no time limit, but an estimate of 45 minutes to 1 hour is suggested for instructions and administration.

Directions and a format for scoring the scale are clearly presented, although exactly who is to do the scoring is not stated. A suggested time of 30 minutes for scoring (given in the manual) implies that respondents will score their own surveys or at least provide summary data. Space appears at the bottom of each of the eight pages of the test booklet with instructions to sum the checkmarks for each of the 10 questions in each of the response categories. For example, the scorer would sum the checks for the "not being done" category over the 10 questions and so on. After each page has been scored, the data are transferred to a summary sheet and then weighted, with a total score found. For example, on General Intellectual Abilities, if 2 items were checked as "not being done," 3 as "rarely being done," 4 as "usually being done but need more," and 1 as "adequately being done leave as is," the total score for that area would be calculated by weighing the checks on a 0 to 3 scale (2 × 0, 3 × 1, 4 × 2, 1 × 3) and then adding the results for a total of 14. After all areas have been scored in this manner, they are rank ordered in a space provided on the scoring key.

Users also may score the PLSPS for each of the 10 dimensions contained within each ability area. Basically, the same process as described previously would apply except that scoring would take place for all items numbered 1 (for dimension 1), all items numbered 2 (for dimension 2), and so on from each of the eight ability areas.

There is a scoring key for this analysis, and each of the 10 dimensions can be rank ordered for interpretation.

The manual suggests that the rank ordering of the ability areas be examined and discussed. Such discussion, it is suggested, could focus on the differences between teachers and administrators or on the ordering of the areas themselves. Once strengths and deficiencies are identified, the manual suggests bringing in competent professionals to help with program design.

### Technical Aspects

The PLSPS manual provides very little information regarding reliability and validity. For a sample of 51 teachers and administrators, a 6-month test-retest correlation coefficient of .61 is reported. The only validity noted was a review of the scale by six specialists in evaluation and measurement of gifted and talented programs. They indicated that although the PLSPS was self-report, they felt that school personnel would be frank.

### Critique

The development ideas for this scale began in the late 1970s, and it does not appear that the essential domains have been reconsidered in terms of reflecting the last 10 years of educational change. Without information provided by the author regarding the degree to which the PLSPS reflects contemporary thought, its value in 1990 is questionable. In fact, supporting references for the 1979 version are not given.

The eight ability areas covered by the PLSPS are generic to schools, and the 10 dimensions covered within each area encompass a variety of school aspects. However, the majority of questions ask about programs for above-average students. If a school and its staff do not endorse the author's viewpoint that provisions for bright students are essential for a strong, healthy school program, then the PLSPS will surely find the school deficient in all areas.

Current research and practice in gifted education (Feldhusen, 1989; Hershey, 1988), effective schools (Bancroft & Lezotte, 1985; Orlich, 1989), and educational reform (Conley & Bacharach, 1990; McDonald, 1988) may negate any information derived from the PLSPS unless they are considered in an update. In fact, use of any scales such as the PLSPS may be superfluous in the wave of state mandates regarding required programs and their evaluations (Timer & Kirp, 1989).

In terms of technical adequacy, very little is reported on the PLSPS. The manual states that the eight areas and 10 dimensions in each are developed from the literature, but they are not referenced. Even though the questions seem fairly literal and ask for what is actually happening at a school site, a test-retest correlation coefficient of .61 is very low. This could reflect a technical mistake by calculating an overall coefficient for a multidimensional scale or suggest that the questions are somewhat more ambiguous than they appear. More validity examination is necessary than by having six professionals do a content check. Though the reviewers indicated that honesty should not be a problem, the more serious concern of perception versus reality needs to be addressed.

As a tool to reflect Williams's perspective regarding the quality of a school, based on its provisions for bright students and in terms of 1979 standards, the PLSPS is probably as good as any survey of its type. However, in 1990, such a measure may be unnecessary not only in terms of mandated programs, but also in terms of more recent assessment methods that involve more than staff perceptions.

## References

Bancroft, B.A., & Lezotte, L.W. (1985). Growing use of effective schools model for school improvement. *Educational Leadership, 42,* 23–27.

Conley, S.C., & Bacharach, S.B. (1990). From school-site management to participatory school-site management. *Phi Delta Kappan, 71*(7), 539–544.

Feldhusen, J.F. (1989, March). Synthesis of research on gifted youth. *Educational Leadership,* pp. 6–11.

Hershey, M. (1988, February). Gifted child education. *The Clearing House,* pp. 280–282.

McDonald, J.P. (1988). The emergence of the teacher's voice: Implications for the new reform. *Teachers College Record, 89,* 471–486.

Orlich, D.C. (1989). Education reforms: Mistakes, misconceptions, miscues. *Phi Delta Kappan, 70*(7), 512–517.

Timer, T.B., & Kirp, D.L. (1989). Education reform in the 1980s: Lessons from the states. *Phi Delta Kappan, 70*(7), 509–510.

Williams, F.E. (1979). *Performance Levels of a School Program Survey.* East Aurora, NY: D.O.K. Publishers.

**Paul R. Hoffman, Ph.D.**
*Associate Professor of Communication Disorders, Louisiana State University, Baton Rouge, Louisiana.*

# PHONOLOGICAL PROCESS ANALYSIS

*Frederick F. Weiner. Austin, Texas: PRO-ED, Inc.*

## Introduction

The Phonological Process Analysis (PPA) was designed to assess the speech sound production of unintelligible children. Sixteen phonological process error patterns are each tested in 6 to 28 words. Delayed imitation of single words and recall of previously modeled sentences are used to elicit these words in utterances that are related to the actions of a cartoon character depicted in stimulus drawings.

PPA was developed by Frederick F. Weiner, currently an associate professor at Pennsylvania State University. Dr. Weiner received his M.A. and Ph.D. degrees in speech-language pathology from Wayne State University. He holds the Certificate of Clinical Competence in speech-language pathology from the American Speech-Language-Hearing Association. Dr. Weiner's research includes a number of studies directly related to the use of phonological processes in testing and remediation of children's delayed speech development, such as assessing the utility of phonological process analysis for describing normal and delayed speech development (Weiner & Wacker, 1982), describing a number of speech production errors that could not be accounted for using phonological processes (Weiner, 1981a), demonstrating that listener requests for clarification could affect children's speech sound production errors (Weiner & Ostrowski, 1979), and testing the utility of treating phonological process error patterns using requests for clarification directed at the contrast between minimal pairs of words (Weiner, 1981b).

The PPA was patterned after a component of Ingram's (1976) description of children's disordered speech sound development in which three major categories of phonological processes were defined: syllable structure processes, assimilation processes, and substitution processes. These have been incorporated into the PPA as syllable structure, harmony, and feature processes. The PPA was the first published testing instrument developed that specifically characterized children's speech production errors using phonological process notation. It adopted a variation of the picture articulation test format that had become the standard of traditional test administration through the 1970s.

The PPA is published as a spiral bound, $8^1/_2'' \times 11''$ book, with approximately 200 pages. It includes an introduction, description of phonological processes, instructions for administration and scoring procedures, suggestions regarding the clinical use of the test, a series of line drawings and prompts to be used in testing, scoring forms, and a summary analysis form. The back cover indicates that the scoring and summary analysis forms may be purchased separately in packages of 10. However, the publisher's 1990 catalog indicates that the forms supplied in the manual are reproducible.

Two line drawings of a cartoon character engaged in a variety of activities appear on the right page of the opened test book. The examiner's prompting statements and the targeted stimulus items appear on the left page. This orientation necessitates that the examiner and child sit side by side, with the child attending to the right page and the examiner attending to the left. A right-handed examiner will have some difficulty finding a place to hold scoring sheets while turning pages, pointing to drawings, and reading stimulus prompts that are all to his or her right in front of where the child is sitting.

The examiner is instructed to elicit each target word first via delayed imitation followed by sentence recall. In the delayed imitation procedure, the word being prompted occurs in the sentence preceding a sentence that the child is requested to finish. For example, the word *cat* might be elicited through the following prompting sequence: "Here is a cat. The man is feeding his ______." The examiner is instructed to use a rising intonation pattern to indicate that the child is to finish this utterance. Next, the examiner prompts sentence recall by saying "What is the man doing?" The use of two elicitations of each word is not specifically justified in the manual, but apparently is based on studies such as Dubois and Bernthal's (1978) showing that children produce more speech errors in phrase and sentence productions than in single-word naming tasks. More recent studies suggest that both picture naming and more contextual speech sampling methods result in identification of similar phonological process descriptions of children's speech (Andrews & Fey, 1986; Bankson & Bernthal, 1982).

Seventeen score sheets are used to record the child's responses. The scoring forms give the orthographic representation of each stimulus word, ample room for transcribing both the delayed imitation and recalled responses of the child, examples of transcriptions that would indicate that the phonological process of interest has occurred, and a check-off column for the occurrence of each process. The examiner is instructed to transcribe the child's production of each word and to record responses for later verification.

The summary sheet provides a listing of the 16 targeted processes, grouped by process type, with the number of possible occurrences. This format makes it relatively easy for the examiner to determine the percentage occurrence of each process. It also supplies a listing of consonants to be used in determining the speech sounds that are not present in the child's phonetic inventory. The lowest area of the form is supplied for notations regarding other error patterns that occur but are not accounted for by use of the targeted group of processes.

## Practical Applications/Uses

The PPA was designed to be used by speech-language pathologists who wish to describe the articulation errors of young children using phonological processes as the basic unit of analysis. It is intended for use with phonologically impaired children who are typically between the ages of 4 and 7 years. The manual suggests that 45 minutes is an appropriate administration time for this test. However, the young phonologically impaired child for whom the test is intended is likely to be language impaired to a degree that makes rapid recognition of the stimulus pictures or completion of the sentence tasks longer processes. Such children are also not likely to stay on task for a full 45 minutes to an hour. Newer test procedures make it possible to complete the test administration in a shorter time by targeting more than one process per word (Hodson, 1986). Assessment procedures that utilize spontaneous speech samples (Ingram, 1981; Shriberg & Kwiatkowski, 1980) are more complicated to analyze but offer the possibility that a single language sample would suffice for analysis of higher level language organization as well.

This test is designed to be administered individually in a quiet room where audio or video recording would be possible. The examiner must be trained in the use of phonetic transcription and knowledgeable about the nature of phonological processes. Any speech-language pathologist trained in the past 10 years should have such knowledge. For others, the manual provides a nicely written introduction to phonological processes that describes the processes targeted in this test.

The phonological processes identified by test administration are used to structure goals for treatment of the child's sound production. A number of treatment strategies have been developed for this purpose. Weiner (1981b) targeted phonological processes by teaching children to identify and produce minimal pairs of words that do not contrast in the child's speech because of a particular process (e.g., the words *bow* and *boat* would both be produced as *bo* by a child who deletes final consonants). Hodson and Paden (1983) suggest training perception and production of a small number of words affected by a phonological process without using the minimal pair words. Elbert and Geirut (1986) suggest training production of many words that are affected by an error pattern. Hoffman, Schuckers, and Daniloff (1989) provide feedback about misarticulated words within conversational interchanges.

A number of auxiliary analyses are suggested by the manual. These include (a) noting whether a phonological process pattern occurs only in restricted cases (e.g., *final consonant deletion* occurring only for fricatives but not stops), (b) noting interactions between feature processes such as stopping of fricatives and the absence of fricatives in the phonetic inventory, and (c) process blocking in which presence of one process precludes the occurrence of another. Such analyses are not specifically guided by the test format or forms, and would require considerable expertise on the part of the examiner.

**Technical Aspects**

Like all of the currently available phonological process analysis procedures and tests, there are no data supplied for comparing PPA results to a normative sample. In general, this type of procedure has been used with children who have already been diagnosed as phonologically impaired by some other means. Some data currently are being published regarding the percentage of children exhibiting phonological process errors at various ages (Haelsig & Madison, 1986) and the differences between error types produced by normal and phonologically impaired children (Hodson & Paden, 1981). Thus, the clinician seeking to compare an individual child to some standard of normal is forced to make comparisons to a literature in which speech sampling procedures and definition of phonological processes vary widely. Fortunately, the major phonological process patterns such as *consonant cluster reduction, final consonant deletion,* and *stopping* have relatively standard definitions in the literature. Furthermore, the decision that a child is exhibiting one of the major processes is relatively robust with respect to test procedure (Andrews & Fey, 1986; Bankson & Bernthal, 1982).

The validity of phonological processes as a construct is still much debated in the literature. The PPA's allusion to conditions of occurrence for processes and parallels between feature contrasts and the child's phonetic inventory are symptomatic of the issues involved. The PPA suggests that it is the process *stopping of fricatives* that causes a child's phonetic inventory to contain no fricatives. An alternative theoretical interpretation suggests that it is the absence of fricatives in the phonetic inventory that sometimes makes it appear that phonological processes occurred (Elbert & Geirut, 1986). Data from treatment studies indicate that a complex interaction among processing levels is the more probable possibility. For example, Weiner (1981b) trained children who deleted final consonants to produce a limited number of words containing final consonants. These children completely eliminated the process in untrained words, but the final consonants produced were appropriate to the words only 50% of the time. Possible explanations of this finding involve suggesting interactions between the appearance of phonological processes and the child's organization of interrelated feature, phoneme, syllable, and word level knowledge.

## Critique

The PPA may best be used as a form of verification of treatment results for children undergoing speech-language therapy. Such children will have probably been given a standardized test from which the clinician can identify possible phonological process error patterns. Selected subsections of the PPA then could be used to quantify percentage of usage of these processes. Both elicitation procedures could be utilized to effectively double the database for determining use of a process. Assuming that the clinician does not specifically target improved production of the particular words used as samples in the PPA, it should still provide a fair evaluation of the child's improvements with respect to these error patterns.

## References

Andrews, N., & Fey, M.E. (1986). Analysis of the speech of phonologically impaired children in two sampling conditions. *Language, Speech, and Hearing Services in Schools, 17,* 187–198.

Bankson, N.W., & Bernthal, J.E. (1982). A comparison of phonological processes identified through word and sentence imitation tasks of the PPA. *Language, Speech, and Hearing Services in Schools, 13,* 96–99.

Dubois, E.M., & Bernthal, J.E. (1978). A comparison of three methods for obtaining articulatory responses. *Journal of Speech and Hearing Disorders, 43,* 295–299.

Elbert, M., & Gierut, J. (1986). *Handbook of clinical phonology: Approaches to assessment and treatment.* London: Taylor & Francis.

Haelsig, P.C., & Madison, C.L. (1986). A study of phonological processes exhibited by 3-, 4-, and 5-year-old children. *Language, Speech, and Hearing Services in Schools, 17,* 107–114.

Hodson, B.W. (1986). *The assessment of phonological processes.* Austin, TX: PRO-ED.

Hodson, B.W., & Paden, E.P. (1981). Phonological processes which characterize unintelligible and intelligible speech in early childhood. *Journal of Speech and Hearing Disorders, 40,* 369–373.

Hodson, B.W., & Paden, E.P. (1983). *Targeting intelligible speech.* Austin, TX: PRO-ED.

Hoffman, P.R., Schuckers, G.H., & Daniloff, R.G. (1989). *Children's phonetic disorders: Theory and treatment.* Austin, TX: PRO-ED.

Ingram, D. (1976). *Phonological disability in children.* New York: American Elsevier.

Ingram, D. (1981). *Procedures for the phonological analysis of children's language.* Baltimore: University Park Press.

Shriberg, L.D., & Kwiatkowski, J. (1980). *Natural process analysis.* New York: Wiley.

Weiner, F.F. (1979). *Phonological Process Analysis.* Austin, TX: PRO-ED.

Weiner, F.F. (1981a). Systematic sound preference as a characteristic of phonological disability. *Journal of Speech and Hearing Disorders, 46,* 281–286.

Weiner, F.F. (1981b). Treatment of phonological disability using the method of meaningful minimal contrast: Two case studies. *Journal of Speech and Hearing Disorders, 46,* 97–103.

Weiner, F.F., & Ostrowski, A. (1979). Effects of listener uncertainty on articulatory inconsistency. *Journal of Speech and Hearing Disorders, 44,* 487–503.

Weiner, F.F., & Wacker, R. (1982). The development of phonology in unintelligible speakers. In N. Lass (Ed.), *Speech and language: Advances in basic research and practice* (Vol. 8, pp. 51–125). New York: Academic Press.

**Jerry B. Hutton, Ph.D.**
*Professor of Special Education, East Texas State University, Commerce, Texas.*

# PORTLAND PROBLEM BEHAVIOR CHECKLIST-REVISED

*Steven A. Waksman. Austin, Texas: PRO-ED, Inc.*

## Introduction

The Portland Problem Behavior Checklist-Revised (PPBC-R) is a 29-item norm-referenced behavior rating scale completed by teachers to rate the behaviors of students in kindergarten through 12th grades (Waksman, 1984a). Each of the items is rated by marking a 6-point scale (0 to 5) to indicate the degree of problem behavior observed, ranging from no problem (0) to severe (5). The ratings are added to form a total raw score, and the total is converted to a percentile by referring to separate tables for males and females in either Grades K-6 or 7-12. Separate, color-coded forms are used for rating the behavior of boys and girls. The PPBC-R is intended to be used to screen students for problem behaviors, to target behaviors for intervention, to supplement information to be used in comprehensive assessments, and to measure behavior change in response to various interventions.

Dr. Steven A. Waksman, author of the PPBC-R, received his Ph.D. from the University of Oregon in 1976. At present he is on the faculty of the counseling psychology department at Lewis and Clark College in Portland, Oregon. Dr. Waksman is also the author of the Waksman Social Skills Rating Scale (Waksman, 1984b).

The development of the original version of the PPBC-R (Waksman & Loveland, 1980) began in 1976 and was first published by the ASIEP Education Company in Portland. The initial step in the development of the behavior rating scale involved the collection of information from teachers who referred students to the Multnomah County School Mental Health Program. The teachers listed three behavior problems for each referred student, resulting in a total of 275 specific problems. The 29 items in the rating scale represent the 29 most frequently listed problems of the referred students. During the 1977-78 school year, 217 randomly selected students in Grades K through 8 were rated by their teachers on the original version of the PPBC-R. Another sample of students was randomly selected from 10 Portland schools and rated by their teachers in 1982-83. This sample consisted of 306 students from kindergarten through high school. The norms for the current version of the PPBC-R are based on the 1982-83 sample. The items in the original scale remain unchanged in the revision.

The PPBC-R manual is brief (17 pages including tables), well organized, and easy to read. The two forms, one for boys and one for girls, are used to rate individual students. The directions are clear and the format is simple. Scoring is easy, simply accomplished by adding the value (0 to 5) marked for each item and looking up the corresponding percentile rank in the manual according to the gender and level of the student.

The rating forms include a table for each level of student, either K–6 or 7–12. The teacher (or examiner) may add the values of the items grouped according to their factor or subscale groupings. The tables on the forms can be used to find the percentile ranks for each domain. The manual explains that the subscale percentiles can also be found in Tables 11 through 14, although these tables were not included in the manual provided for the current review.

The factor analysis of the PPBC-R was done separately for the four groupings of the 1982–83 sample of 306 students: (a) boys, Grades K–6, $n = 81$; (b) boys, Grades 7–12, $n = 79$; (c) girls, Grades K–6, $n = 81$; and (d) girls, Grades 7–12, $n = 65$. Although the factors are quite similar for each of the four groups, there are major differences. The factors and number of items in each for each group are as follows: (a) boys, Grades K–6, Conduct Problems (11), Academic Problems (7), Anxiety Problems (4), Peer Problems (4), and Other Problems (4); (b) boys, Grades 7–12, Academic Problems (8), Anxiety Problems (3), Conduct Problems (5), Peer Problems (3), Personal Problems (2), and Other Problems (8); (c) girls, Grades K–6, Conduct Problems (8), Peer Problems (2), Personal Problems (8), and Other Problems (11); and (d) girls, Grades 7–12, Academic Problems (9), Personal Problems (3), Conduct Problems (7), Anxiety Problems (3), and Other Problems (7).

## Practical Applications/Uses

Behavior rating scales provide an efficient and economic way to assess children's behavior, and teachers are in an excellent position to do so (Achenbach & Edelbrock, 1984). Although direct observation provides a valuable source of information in assessment, direct observation conducted by a classroom visitor is sometimes obtrusive and the behavior being observed is unduly influenced. Also, students may be sensitive to outside observers and tease the individual student who is targeted by the observation. Further, the reliability and validity of direct observation are dependent upon the number and length of observations, contributing to the expense of obtaining this type of information. Teachers who take data based on direct observation in their own classes may avoid these criticisms, but unless they are well trained in data collection, the activities may take the teacher away from instruction. As behavior rating scales may be used by teachers to systematically record their judgments based on direct observation, behavior rating scales may reduce some of the problems inherent in direct observation. Also, behavior rating scales may be used to evaluate behavior across different classes and/or teachers, contributing to an ecological view of assessment.

The PPBC-R is a behavior rating scale that may be used to collect information as part of a screening program, as part of a comprehensive assessment, or as an evaluation of student responses to intervention programs. Because it consists of only 29 items, teachers are likely to be cooperative in completing the checklist. Indeed, it is more practical and efficient to use brief checklists when rating behavior across several classes. When only one teacher rates the behavior of a student for one class period, the person using that information is limited to inferences concerning the behavior in only one setting.

Practitioners in private practice and/or clinical settings who evaluate children and adolescents are limited when information concerning school performance and adjustment is not available. Some information may be obtained from schools upon signed release and written request, and other information may be gained by interviews with the parents/guardians and student. It is usually not very practical for the practitioner to visit the school and interview the teacher(s) or perform classroom observations. The practitioner may greatly increase the information concerning the student's functioning at school by asking the student's teachers to complete behavior rating scales. When the practitioner needs to evaluate progress, the ratings can be repeated, thereby giving him or her more data on which to make treatment or intervention decisions. In addition, school counselors and teachers can improve their conferences with parents when they have information available concerning the student's behavior across various classroom settings.

As the items in the PPBC-R were taken from the 29 most frequently mentioned behaviors for students referred to a mental health clinic, mental health practitioners probably will find the items particularly appropriate for the school-age children and adolescents they assess. A teacher who uses the PPBC-R will need only about 5 to 10 minutes to rate a student's behavior. However, assessment or clinical personnel who request this information from teachers may need to deal with teacher resistance in some instances as teachers often have high paperwork demands. As a general rule, however, teachers who are concerned about or bothered by a student's behavior in their classes are likely to be quite willing to provide information.

The practitioner or assessment professional may facilitate the data collection by filling in the identifying information on the front of the rating scale form and writing on the form when the information is due and to whom it is to be sent. Although scoring is very easy when the manual is available, the assessment professional should do the scoring because teachers may not have access to a manual or have the time available to consult it. The interpretation of the scores is simple when percentile ranks are understood.

## Technical Aspects

The PPBC-R has two major technical problems. First, the sample on which the norms were developed consists of only 306 students for one specific geographic area. It should not be assumed that the sample is representative of students throughout the United States. As noted by Gable (1986), the pilot group used in the development of an "affective" instrument needs to be 6 to 10 times as large as the number of items in the instrument. In this respect, the PPBC-R was developed with an adequate number of students both in the original sample ($N$ = 217) and in the revised sample ($N$ = 306). The PPBC-R is now ready for the norming process. Simply stated, the PPBC-R cannot be assumed to be adequately normed on a sample size of 306. As noted by Hammill, Brown, and Bryant (1989), the minimal size for an adequate sample when norming an instrument is 1,000. Because age and gender differences on the PPBC-R require four different tables to determine percentile ranks, the PPBC-R minimal size may be 4,000. Of course, with a larger sample, age and gender differences may change. In addition, the sample needs to be taken so that the demographics are representative (geographic areas, residence, ethnicity/race, socioeconomic status, etc.) when compared to the U.S. census report.

The second major problem involves the factor analysis. The use of factor analysis is important in establishing the validity of an instrument. However, factor analysis requires 6 to 10 times as large a sample as the number of variables entering the procedure (Gable, 1986). The PPBC-R was factored on four groups: (a) boys, Grades K–6, $n = 81$; (b) boys, Grades 7–12, $n = 79$; (c) girls, Grades K–6, $n = 81$; and (d) girls, Grades 7–12, $n = 65$. Because the PPBC-R contains 29 items, each of the four groups require between 174 and 290 students if factor analysis is to be applied. Therefore, the conclusions drawn concerning the results of the factor analyses are suspect.

There is evidence in the manual that the author and his colleagues have done a lot of work on the PPBC-R to show its reliability and validity. The internal consistency (coefficient alpha) of the PPBC-R was strong (males, $n = 160$, .94; females, $n = 146$, .95; total sample, $N = 306$, .94). Test-retest reliabilities with a 1-month interval were mostly fair to adequate, ranging from .77 for seventh graders ($n = 36$) and .78 for middle-graders ($n = 100$) and females ($n = 122$) to .88 for high school students ($n = 22$). However, the test-retest reliability coefficient for sixth-graders was too low to be considered even fairly acceptable ($n = 28$, $r = .61$). The sample sizes were too small at some grade intervals, making the coefficients difficult to interpret (fifth, $n = 9$; kindergarten, $n = 14$; fourth, $n = 17$).

Evidence for the content validity of the PPBC-R rests on the identification of the 29 most frequently reported problem behaviors indicated by teachers referring students to a mental health facility. However, the item validities (correlations between each item and the total score) are not reported in the manual. As suggested by Anastasi (1988), minimum item validities should be .2 or .3 in order to retain items in a scale. Criterion validity studies reported in the manual suggest adequate validity. The PPBC and/or PPBC-R were correlated significantly with other instruments that measure similar constructs. For example, the PPBC and the Walker Problem Behavior Identification Checklist (Walker, 1970) were significantly correlated ($r = .66$), as were the PPBC and the Piers-Harris Children's Self Concept Scale (Piers & Harris, 1969; $r = .49$) and the Waksman Social Skills Rating Scale (Waksman, 1984b; $r = .65$). A comparison of PPBC scores for 24 emotionally disturbed children in a residential facility and 24 randomly selected middle school students was made. The ratings were significantly different ($t = 4.97$, $p < .001$), with the emotionally disturbed students receiving ratings suggesting greater behavior problems, lending support to the PPBC-R's discriminant validity.

## Critique

The PPBC-R has many positive aspects that may make it attractive to practitioners and assessment personnel in schools and clinics. It is brief, it may be used to assess behavior across classroom settings for an individual child or adolescent, it assesses behaviors that appear quite relevant to school adjustment and success, and it is easy to administer and interpret. There is some support for the reliability and validity of the PPBC-R when using the total score, but reliability and validity of the subscales have not been established to date. Two main shortcomings limit the use of the PPBC-R: a national standardization of the instrument has not yet been undertaken, and the factor analysis did not include enough subjects in the study. For these reasons the PPBC-R should be limited to experimental use until such major problems are overcome.

## References

Achenbach, T.M., & Edelbrock, C.S. (1984). Psychopathology of childhood. *Annual Review of Psychology, 35,* 227–256.

Anastasi, A. (1988). *Psychological testing* (6th ed.). New York: Macmillan.

Gable, R. (1986). *Instrument development in the affective domain.* Boston, MA: Kluwer-Nijhoff.

Hammill, D., Brown, L., & Bryant, B. (1989). *A consumer's guide to tests in print.* Austin, TX: PRO-ED.

Piers, E.V., & Harris, D.B. (1969). *The Piers-Harris Children's Self Concept Scale.* Nashville, TN: Counselor Recordings and Tests.

Waksman, S. (1984a). *The Portland Problem Behavior Checklist–Revised.* Austin, TX: PRO-ED.

Waksman, S. (1984b). *The Waksman Social Skills Rating Scale.* Austin, TX: PRO-ED.

Waksman, S., & Loveland, R.J. (1980). The Portland Problem Behavior Checklist. *Psychology in the Schools, 17,* 25–29.

Walker, H.M. (1970). *Walker Problem Behavior Identification Checklist.* Los Angeles, CA: Western Psychological Services.

**Brian Bolton, Ph.D.**
*Professor, Arkansas Research and Training Center in Vocational Rehabilitation, University of Arkansas, Fayetteville, Arkansas.*

# PRELIMINARY DIAGNOSTIC QUESTIONNAIRE

*Joseph B. Moriarty. Dunbar, West Virginia: West Virginia Rehabilitation Research and Training Center.*

## Introduction

The Preliminary Diagnostic Questionnaire (PDQ; Moriarty, 1981) was developed to assess the functional capacities of persons with disabilities in the context of employability. Implicit in this measure's development were the assumptions that (a) employability presupposes a certain amount of general knowledge, the ability to get around, general emotional wellness, and a desire to work; and (b) a preliminary assessment of these characteristics should be possible without special tools and equipment, and should take about an hour to administer. Initially designed for use by counselors in the state-federal vocational rehabilitation program, the application of this questionnaire has expanded to specialty disability facilities and programs, Worker's Compensation, Veterans Administration, and private practitioners working with persons who have disabilities.

The late author of the PDQ, Joseph B. Moriarty, was director of the West Virginia Rehabilitation Research and Training Center at West Virginia University from 1969 to 1991, where he held the title of Professor of Human Resources and Behavioral Medicine. An activist in rehabilitation for the past quarter century, Dr. Moriarty was president of the National Association of Research and Training Centers in 1980. Beginning with publication of his popular text on psychological tests (1971), Dr. Moriarty's research emphasized methodologies for functional assessment of persons with disabilities, program evaluation, and the application of information systems technologies to rehabilitation.

The PDQ was designed to assess four broad areas of functioning relevant to the employability of persons with disabilities: *Cognitive* (measured by the Work Information, Preliminary Estimate of Learning, Psychomotor Skills, and Reading Retention subtests); *Motivation*, or Disposition to Work (measured by the Work Importance and Internality subtests); *Physical* (measured by the Personal Independence subtest); and *Emotional* (measured by the Emotional Functioning subtest). In addition, a demographic table enables comparison of client characteristics and the probability of competitive employment based on historic occurrence with persons who have exited the vocational rehabilitation service system.

The nine subscales are described as follows:

1. *Work Information* measures the examinee's general knowledge about the world of work with 17 questions such as "What is a job reference?" and "What are fringe benefits?"

2. *Preliminary Estimate of Learning* measures the examinee's overall level of intel-

lectual functioning with 30 questions pertaining to general information, basic mathematics, and formal academic learning. If a recent IQ score is available it can be substituted for this subtest score using a conversion table provided in the manual (Moriarty, Minton, & Spann, 1989).

3. *Psychomotor Skills* measures the examinee's finger dexterity, hand-eye coordination, and visual-perceptual integrity using two tasks, paper folding/handling/writing and copying geometric figures.

4. *Reading Retention* measures the examinee's ability to read, retain, recall, and comprehend written material of general interest. The examinee reads a story aloud (or has it read) and responds to a series of 18 questions.

5. *Work Importance* measures the examinee's attitudes toward work, perceived support by family and friends, and optimism about obtaining employment with 10 statements like "People with disabilities like mine shouldn't be expected to work."

6. *Internality* measures the examinee's work motivation via 15 statements that reflect the internal versus external locus of control framework, such as "People are born to be good at certain jobs and not good at other jobs" and "I can get a good job if I just keep trying."

7. *Personal Independence* measures the examinee's limitations in three areas of functioning (self-care, mobility, and range of motion) using 20 questions about performance of daily living activities and 9 demonstrated movements.

8. *Emotional Functioning* measures the examinee's general psychological well-being in four areas (anxiety, depression, aggression, and withdrawal or bizarreness) with 20 statements like "I have trouble controlling my temper."

9. *Demographic Information* consists of patterns of psychosocial integration, employment/earnings history, perception of disability impact, and potential financial disincentives. In addition, six items (sex, marital status, work status, disability, education, and age) are translated into a probability of placement in competitive employment.

The PDQ is administered using a self-contained, consumable 12-page booklet. All examinee responses and examiner notes are recorded in the booklet. Item scoring is accomplished simultaneously by the experienced examiner, and the profile of standard scores can be calculated in just a few minutes. The normative sample consists of almost 3,000 vocational rehabilitation clients who are representative of the national population of clients. A computerized PDQ report is available on floppy disk, and a computer-based decision support system for rehabilitation counselors incorporates PDQ results as client database elements (West Virginia Rehabilitation Research and Training Center, 1988).

**Practical Applications/Uses**

The PDQ provides a comprehensive assessment of the employment potential of persons with handicaps who are candidates for vocational rehabilitation services. The instrument was designed to be administered, scored, and interpreted by counselors and other rehabilitation professionals, such as vocational evaluators. Specific uses of PDQ results are (a) establishing a basis for reaching decisions about an applicant's eligibility for vocational rehabilitation services, (b) identifying areas in need of more precise assessment, and (c) formulating a service plan that will restore the client to optimal functioning, including, whenever possible, placement in competitive employment.

Because the PDQ is administered in a structured interview format, the diagnostic interviewing skills of a professionally trained counselor are essential. The instrument can be administered in less than 1 hour in the counselor's office or the examinee's home. The manual (Moriarty et al., 1989) gives specific instructions on how to present each task, when to probe, and when to terminate questioning. The PDQ can be used appropriately with most adult applicants for vocational rehabilitation services. The single categorical exception to this statement would be persons with profound expressive or receptive language deficits.

Scoring the PDQ requires examiner judgment for the subtests that measure knowledge or skills with open-ended questions (e.g., Work Information and Preliminary Estimate of Learning) or that entail completion of tasks (e.g., Psychomotor Skills, Reading, and Personal Independence). In the cognitive scales, the scoring decision involves making the distinction between a correct response (1 point) and an incorrect answer (0 points). Scoring guidelines appear in the manual (Moriarty et al., 1989).

For each performance subtest, the raw scale score is the sum of the correct responses. For the subtests that measure attitudes (i.e., Work Importance, Internality, and Emotional Functioning), the raw score is the total of the self-ratings. The user then converts raw scores to stanine (*sta*ndard *nine* ) scores by locating the raw score interval on the PDQ profile report. After the scoring procedures are mastered, they probably require only a few minutes to complete.

Interpretation of PDQ results is based on both the objective test scores and the content of the examinee's responses to individual items. The manual (Moriarty et al., 1989) includes sections on profile interpretation, casework validity, interpretation of individual scales, and general interpretive principles. Proper use of the PDQ assumes graduate education in rehabilitation counseling, including courses in psychological and vocational testing, and completion of a PDQ training program.

The underlying assumption with this measure is that the individual with the disability is the expert with regard to his or her capacities and takes an active participatory role in the assessment and interpretation process. It is strongly recommended that a feedback interview follow the administrator's preliminary interpretation to clarify, expand, and explain findings as a first step toward plan development and service provision.

The PDQ's publisher, the West Virginia Rehabilitation Research and Training Center (WVRRTC), conducts training programs to prepare rehabilitation professionals to administer and interpret PDQ results. Training involves completion of a curriculum comprised of print and videotape materials. The modules include an introduction to functional assessment, administration and scoring, feedback and interpretation, diagnostic interviewing, and casework and management implications. A case study manual completes the training package (Spann, 1989). Certification requires completion of the training program and submission of five PDQ protocols for review by the WVRRTC training faculty. A self-instructional program is also available.

**Technical Aspects**

The normative sample that constitutes the basis for converting raw scores on the eight PDQ subtests to stanines consists of 2,972 vocational rehabilitation clients from 30 state agencies. The characteristics of the sample include 59% male, 77% white, mean age of 30, typical schooling of 11 years, and the following representation of disabilities: 53% physical/medical, 42% mental/emotional, and 5% sensory. Comparisons on demographic variables demonstrated that the PDQ normative sample was representative of the population of disabled persons who receive services through the state/federal vocational rehabilitation system (Moriarty, Walls, & McLaughlin, 1988).

Two types of reliability evidence are presented for the PDQ subscales: internal consistency, calculated for a sample of 986 clients with varying disabilities, and test-retest, conducted with a sample of 28 clients receiving services at a comprehensive rehabilitation center (the interval between PDQ administrations was 30 days). The internal consistency/test-retest reliability coefficients emerged as follows for the eight subtests: Work Information (.87/.78), Preliminary Estimate of Learning (.90/.97), Psychomotor Skills (.71/na), Reading (.84/.79), Work Importance (.69/.75), Internality (.77/.47), Personal Independence (.87/na), and Emotional Functioning (.86/.91). The two subtests for which retest data are not available (Psychomotor Skills and Personal Independence) have adequate internal consistency reliabilities, and the subscale with low retest reliability (Internality) also has adequate internal consistency reliability. The PDQ subtests do possess acceptable reliability characteristics.

Because the PDQ purports to assess the employment potential of persons with handicaps, evaluation of its validity should be based on the prediction of employment outcomes. Are the functional abilities measured by the PDQ significantly correlated with successful job placement? To answer this question, two dichotomous criteria of successful employment were formulated. The "earnings" criterion was defined as no earnings after case closure *versus* some earnings. The "minimum wage" criterion was defined as earnings below minimum wage after case closure *versus* earnings above minimum wage.

Employment information was ascertained for a sample of 219 former vocational rehabilitation clients who had completed the PDQ. Two subtests were statistically significant predictors of earnings after case closure (Psychomotor Skills and Work Importance), while three subscales were predictive of the minimum wage criterion (Work Information, Psychomotor Skills, and Work Importance). The magnitude of the typical relationship is indicated by these data: 51% of the minimum-wage earners scored in the top third on Work Importance and only 10% scored in the lowest third (Moriarty, Walls, & McLaughlin, 1987).

Although only some of the relationships were statistically significant, all eight PDQ subscales correlated positively with the two employment criteria. In order to include all assessment components in the validity study, a discriminant analysis on 33 PDQ variables was carried out for the purpose of developing a global feasibility index. Ninety-five percent of minimum-wage earners in the validity sample scored in the top third on the feasibility index, providing further support for the PDQ as a predictor of employability (Moriarty et al., 1988).

Additional evidence of the PDQ's validity includes the careful scale construction procedures and the correlations with standard aptitude, intelligence, and achievement tests. For example, to identify item content for the Emotional Functioning subtest, case folders of former vocational rehabilitation clients who experienced job failure due to emotional difficulties were analyzed. In developing the Personal Independence subscale, a continuum of "essentiality" was established, ranging from eating and drinking, through self-care activities, to agility and balance.

Illustrating the variety of convergent and divergent relationships with well-known standardized tests, PDQ Psychomotor Skills correlated higher with General Aptitude Test Battery (GATB) Spatial Aptitude and Form Perception than with Verbal Aptitude, and higher with Wechsler Adult Intelligence Scale (WAIS) Performance IQ than with Verbal IQ. In general, GATB aptitudes and WAIS IQ scores correlated more highly with PDQ cognitive subtests than with the motivation, physical, and emotional subtests.

The validity of the Demographic Information probability figure derives from its empirical mode of construction. The probability estimates were calculated by determining the proportion of clients in the national vocational rehabilitation population with each combination of demographic characteristics who became competitively employed.

## Critique

Although there are many excellent instruments for assessing the employment potential of persons with handicaps (see Bolton, 1988), the PDQ represents a truly innovative approach to the psychosocial evaluation of applicants for vocational rehabilitation services. Several features of the PDQ are noteworthy:

1. It was designed to facilitate the counselor's eligibility decision-making and case service–planning responsibilities.

2. It may be administered, scored, and interpreted by trained counselors rather than consulting psychological examiners.

3. It measures comprehensively the functional capacities that are considered essential in preparation for competitive employment.

4. It is administered in a structured interview format and therefore provides both clinical and psychometric information of value to the counselor.

5. It can be administered and scored in less than 1 hour in the counselor's office or the examinee's home.

6. It has been demonstrated to be adequately reliable and valid for the purpose of assessing the employment potential of rehabilitation clients (more technical studies are desirable, of course).

7. The manual for administering, scoring, interpreting, and using the results in case planning is well organized, detailed, and user friendly.

8. A training and certification program is available for vocational rehabilitation professionals who wish to become qualified to use the instrument. (See Publisher's Index in this volume for contact information.)

### References

Bolton, B. (1988). *Special education and rehabilitation testing: Current practices and test reviews.* Austin, TX: PRO-ED.

Moriarty, J.B. (1971). *How to select, administer and interpret psychological tests: A guide for the rehabilitation counselor.* Dunbar, WV: West Virginia Rehabilitation Research and Training Center.

Moriarty, J.B. (1981). *Preliminary Diagnostic Questionnaire.* Dunbar, WV: West Virginia Rehabilitation Research and Training Center.

Moriarty, J.B., Minton, E.B., & Spann, V. (1989). *Manual for the PDQ* (2nd ed.). Dunbar, WV: West Virginia Rehabilitation Research and Training Center.

Moriarty, J.B., Walls, R.T., & McLaughlin, D.E. (1987). The Preliminary Diagnostic Questionnaire (PDQ): Functional assessment of employability. *Rehabilitation Psychology, 32,* 5–15.

Moriarty, J.B., Walls, R.T., & McLaughlin, D.E. (1988). Employability of clients served in state vocational rehabilitation agencies: A national census. *Rehabilitation Counseling Bulletin, 32,* 108–121.

Spann, V. (Ed.) (1989). *Preliminary Diagnostic Questionnaire (PDQ). Case study manual: A guide to interpretation.* Dunbar, WV: West Virginia Rehabilitation Research and Training Center.

West Virginia Rehabilitation Research and Training Center. (1988). *Excellence through information management: A decision support system.* Dunbar, WV: Author.

**Daryl Sander, Ph.D.**
*Professor Emeritus, School of Education, University of Colorado, Boulder Colorado.*

# PROGRAM FOR ASSESSING YOUTH EMPLOYMENT SKILLS

*Educational Testing Service. Princeton, New Jersey: Educational Testing Service.*

## Introduction

The Program for Assessing Youth Employment Skills (PAYES) is a career counseling tool that was designed for use with adolescents and young adults who are relatively deficient in verbal skills. It provides for administering seven untimed measures orally in order to compensate for negative attitudes toward traditional multiple-choice, paper-and-pencil tests, which might be difficult to read or comprehend. The program covers attitudinal measures (Job-Holding Skills, Attitude Toward Supervision, Self-Confidence), cognitive measures (Job Knowledge, Job-Seeking Skills, Practical Reasoning), and a vocational interest inventory.

PAYES was developed in the early 1970s by the Educational Testing Service (ETS) with assistance from a general advisory committee, which dealt with matters such as sex bias and general design considerations, and a standards setting committee, which assisted in establishing scoring standards. The project grew out of the need for more appropriate assessment tools for persons served by federally funded manpower training programs. This pool of trainees included in many cases persons with low verbal skills and impoverished educational backgrounds. An initial battery of 13 measures was constructed to correspond with specific areas of trainee behavior, and this battery was administered on a trial basis to several groups of Neighborhood Youth Corp trainees to obtain initial validation data. Subsequent refinements and longitudinal studies led to the present seven-scale format. The rationale for PAYES and the history of the early developmental work on it is described in detail in the technical manual. The PAYES packet also includes the user's guide, the PAYES Individual Profile, and three booklets that contain the inventory items.

## Practical Applications/Uses

PAYES was designed specifically for young adults and adolescents who are deficient in verbal skills, and many of the items include illustrations depicting the content of that item. For example, several questions in Booklet II that deal with knowledge about a carpenter's work are positioned alongside a cartoon-like picture of a person nailing boards onto an upright structure with a hammer. The corresponding questions inquire about where this work would be done, when it would likely be done, and the kinds of tools used by the worker. Care has been taken to select items that would minimize cross-cultural bias, thus ensuring applicability to ethnic minorities.

Because the directions require that questions be read aloud by the administrator, lack of reading skill is expected to have minimum effect on test scores. Further, all tests are untimed, and test administrators are cautioned to gear the pace of reading the items to the particular ability level of those being tested. Provision is made for administrators to repeat questions that may not have been clearly understood the first time. Thus an atmosphere of low-key informality is likely, in contrast to traditional test administration.

The publisher acknowledges and justifies the obvious cultural bias of the three attitudinal measures in the following manner:

> Most employers and supervisors are influenced by a strong middle-class work ethic. PAYES incorporates these values because they determine the attitudes and behavior that are currently associated with successful adaptation to work. (ETS, 1979, p. 4)

Scoring standards were established by a panel of educational experts who made judgments about "the probability of a minimally competent student choosing each option" (ETS, 1979, p. 11). Scoring weights were then developed for each possible response to each item. Scoring procedures are relatively simple, and it is intended that counselors who use PAYES will hand score the tests locally. Profile sheets are provided on which to plot seven scores for the interest inventory and three each for the attitudinal and the cognitive measures.

Career counselors' interpretation of PAYES scores is intended to focus on the occupational clusters with the highest scores. The user's guide offers suggestions for counselors to consider in their interpretations as well as cautions regarding patterns of low scores and the problems that may be contributing to them.

**Technical Aspects**

Several aspects of construct validity are offered in the PAYES technical manual (Freeberg & Vitella, 1979); these are based largely on data derived on the original 13 measures that were administered to Neighborhood Youth Corps trainees. The technical manual provides criterion-related validity coefficients based on a wide variety of job-training criteria, including counselor ratings, instructor ratings, and work supervisor ratings. Other validity criteria are factor scores derived from clusters of outcome variables obtained through factor analysis as well as scores obtained on other independent measures of cognitive performance (e.g., vocabulary and arithmetic tests). Only validity coefficients significant at .05 or beyond are shown. Validity for the vocational interest inventory is discussed briefly, but data on predicting job performance following placement or differentiation among various occupations do not appear.

Standard errors of measurement and reliabilities for the seven scales are provided in the technical manual as well as the user's guide. Alpha coefficients, which describe the tests' degree of internal consistency, are used as reliability coefficients. They range from .59 on Job-Holding Skills to .85 on Practical Reasoning, with a median *r* value of .70. Test-retest reliabilities are not given. The inter-test correlations shown among the three attitudinal measures and also among the three cognitive measures suggest the existence of the two separate clusters, one cognitive and the other attitudinal.

## Critique

PAYES appears to be a potentially valuable tool for its intended purpose. It fills a need that has been apparent for some years and for which there have been too few assessment resources available. Thus, it represents a unique option for vocational testing and counseling. The inclusion of substantial proportions of inner-city ethnic minority youth in the groups from which the validity data were derived is especially commendable. PAYES can provide valuable data to be combined with observational and other appraisal information to assist counselors in their work with these youth.

Some additional validity data demonstrating long-term predictability of success in jobs following training would be useful. Likewise, most counselors would prefer to see test-retest reliabilities to get an idea of the stability of scores over time. Nonetheless, the PAYES's publishers have provided excellent reliability and validity data and have suggested directions for further research. PAYES is a valuable counseling tool, and with some further research, it will become a major part of any program of vocational assistance to those with verbal deficiencies.

## References

This list includes text citations and suggested additional reading.

Educational Testing Service. (1979). *User's guide.* New York: Cambridge Book Co.

Freeberg, N.E. (1970). Assessment of disadvantaged adolescents: A different approach to research and evaluation measures. *Journal of Educational Psychology, 61,* 229–240.

Freeberg, N.E., & Vitella, P.E. (1979). *PAYES technical manual.* New York: Cambridge Book Co.

**Pattey L. Fong, Ph.D.**
*Assistant Professor of Psychology, California State University-Fresno, Fresno, California.*

# QUESTIONNAIRE ON RESOURCES AND STRESS FOR FAMILIES WITH CHRONICALLY ILL OR HANDICAPPED MEMBERS

*Jean Holroyd. Brandon, Vermont: Clinical Psychology Publishing Company, Inc.*

## Introduction

The Questionnaire on Resources and Stress (QRS) for Families with Chronically Ill or Handicapped Members was developed for the quantitative assessment of families' coping and adaptational responses to a disabled family member. The QRS consists of 285 self-administered, true-false items that form 15 rationally derived scales. These scales are grouped into three general response categories: Personal Problems (seven scales), Family Problems (three scales), and Problems of Index Case (five scales). The QRS is intended to measure sources of stress and variables that attenuate stress as well as family members' responses to stress. A 66-item short form (QRS-SF) can be used for screening purposes; however, the full 285-item long version is recommended for use in clinical assessment (e.g., to determine family needs for social services) and clinical research.

The developer of the QRS is Jean Holroyd, a clinical psychologist and director of Clinical Psychology Internship Training in the Department of Psychiatry at the University of California, Los Angeles. Since she first reported on the instrument's development in 1974, the QRS has had a significant impact on the study and measurement of stress in families with a disabled family member. Unfortunately, since the publication of the QRS by the Clinical Psychology Publishing Company in 1987, Dr. Holroyd has discontinued her work on family stress and now conducts research in the unrelated area of hypnotherapy. However, the number of studies reporting the use of the QRS and examining its psychometric properties continues to grow from year to year, and researchers in other laboratories will undoubtedly continue this examination.

The QRS in its present (1987) form remains essentially identical to the original 1974 report. The current manual (Holroyd, 1987) reports that the 285 QRS items were culled from a pool of 556 items generated by a psychologist, psychiatrist, social worker, two teachers, and a parent. These items were then reduced to 251 items by 12 raters (psychologists, social workers, and public health nurses) who examined the items for appropriateness, content, clarity, and redundancy. An additional 29 items were added for their theoretical and/or empirical importance, and 15 items that exaggerated the stress of caring for a handicapped family member were added to form a validity scale. (The author[s] of these additional items is not reported in the manual. Furthermore, at least one of these figures must be in error because the numbers total 295, rather than 285 as stated in the manual on p. 31.) Items were rewritten so that half would be answered "true" and half would be answered "false" when answered in the well-adjusted direction.

The QRS scales were rationally derived by deductively grouping items; this process originally resulted in 18 scales. An inductive procedure that involved regrouping all 285 items based on significant interitem correlations from the scores of 43 unmatched parents resulted in 15 shorter, more homogeneous scales using 206 nonoverlapping items. Use of the remaining 79 items is not explained in the manual. The 285-item, 15-scale QRS has not been validated through factor analysis. However, a factor analysis of the 285-item QRS completed by 526 respondents yielded 11 factors, rather than 15. Fifty-three items on these 11 factors were not among the original 206 items that formed the basis of the 15 QRS scales. The 11 factors were used to develop the short form of the QRS (QRS-SF), which consists of 11 scales with six items retained on each. Various alternatives were attempted (best five items per scale, variable number of items per scale, etc.), resulting in a decision to include six items on each scale as this solution resulted in high correlations between the short scales and the 11 factors.

Normative data for the QRS are based on parents of 107 normal children from Holroyd's laboratory in California and other research groups in Georgia and New Zealand. The samples included families nominated by parents with disabled children who were completing the QRS at the UCLA clinic (California sample); families on preschool rolls, waiting lists, or public health records (New Zealand sample); and low SES volunteers (Georgia sample). These data were used to establish T-score conversions and percentile scores for both the 15-scale QRS and 11-scale QRS-SF. Separate norms were established for preschool and school-age children because some scales showed significant correlations with age. However, the preschool norms are based on a slightly shortened version of the 285-item QRS. The New Zealand researcher (Wilton, unpublished raw data, see QRS manual) eliminated certain items from the QRS that parents without a disabled child were unlikely to answer in the scored direction. Adult norms (i.e., for families with an adult disabled member) have not been established.

Norms for special populations of families with members with different handicapping conditions have been established for four major classifications: developmental disabilities, psychiatric problems, chronic medical illness, and neuromuscular disease. These norms are based on 329 cases, including 145 developmentally disabled children, 98 children with psychiatric problems, 49 children with medical illnesses (renal disease, leukemia, cystic fibrosis), and 37 children with neuromuscular diseases (Duchenne's dystrophy, cerebral palsy).

Different factor analyzed short-form versions of the QRS have been developed by other researchers (e.g., Friedrich, Greenberg, & Crnic, 1983; Salisbury, 1986). These versions were developed to produce psychometrically stronger versions of the QRS.

The 285 QRS items are listed in randomized order in an eight-page booklet, and all items are written at a sixth-grade reading level. Instructions for completing the questionnaire appear on the front page of the test booklet, including those for respondents who do not have a disabled family member. Respondents mark their answers ("T" or "F" for each item) on a separate answer sheet. Because the test is self-administered and the instructions for completing it are clear, an examiner need not be present when the respondent completes the questionnaire. The QRS kit includes scoring templates, or the test can be computer scored (the manual includes programming instructions for the latter).

The resulting profile is plotted on a separate profile sheet that includes T-score distributions for preschool and school-age children. The appearance of the plotted profile is very similar to an MMPI profile. Inexplicably, the profile sheets use the terms "Your name," "Your date of birth," and so forth for listing identifying data. As respondents are not likely to score their own questionnaires or plot their own profiles, it is unclear why this terminology appears on the profile sheets. An appendix in the manual lists percentile norms for special populations; however, profile plotting charts are not provided for special populations or for adults.

The 15 scales on the full-length QRS are grouped and identified as follows: Personal Problems scales—Poor Health/Mood, Excess Time Demands, Negative Attitude toward Index Case, Overprotection/Dependency, Lack of Social Support, Overcommitment/Martyrdom, and Pessimism; Family Problems scales—Lack of Family Integration, Limits on Family Opportunity, and Financial Problems; and Problems of Index Case scales—Physical Incapacitation, Lack of Activities for Index Case, Occupational Limitations for Index Case, Social Obtrusiveness, and Difficult Personality Characteristics.

The 11 scales on the 66-item short form (QRS-SF) cover Dependency and Management, Cognitive Impairment, Limits on Family Opportunities, Life Span Care, Family Disharmony, Lack of Personal Reward, Terminal Illness Stress, Physical Limitations, Financial Stress, Preference for Institutional Care, and Personal Burden for Respondent. The test kit does not contain any materials for administering or scoring the QRS-SF.

## Practical Applications/Uses

The QRS is intended for the assessment of family responses to a family member with chronic physical illness or a mental, emotional, or developmental handicap. This measure covers a broad range of variables, including stressors related to the disabled family member (e.g., difficult personality characteristics, physical incapacitation), individual and family resources (e.g., social support, financial problems), and individual and family responses to the disabled family member (e.g., pessimism, degree of family integration).

Given the comprehensive nature of the information the QRS provides, clinicians can use this instrument to determine which families need help the most and which specific family problems to address first. In short, "the QRS was developed to assist clinicians in deciding which families need social assistance more in a time of shrinking resources" (Holroyd, 1987, p. 2). The QRS also has been used in clinical research to examine the differential impact of certain handicaps on families as well as of various child, parent, and family characteristics on family stress responses (for a review, see Holroyd, 1988). The QRS has potential for a wide range of settings—day treatment centers, special education settings, and respite care services, to name just a few. Professions that may find this test of interest include psychology, social work, and special education.

Any member of the family other than the identified patient may complete the questionnaire. The test is appropriate for use in families wherein a member has any type of chronic physical illness or other handicap. Although the QRS has been used most often with the families of young children or adolescents, the QRS is appropriate for families with adult disabled children and those caring for other adults (e.g., a parent with Alzheimer's disease) as well. However, the manual does not provide norms for adult populations, so any such clinical use must be restricted to an examination of items endorsed by the respondent, as the QRS raw scores would be uninterpretable.

The manual describes administration of the QRS in a setting in which the examiner is available to answer any questions. However, other studies have described administration by mail and over the telephone, and the QRS manual does not caution against doing so. The manual also makes no mention of examiner qualifications.

The QRS instructions are easy to understand, so respondents should not have much difficulty answering questions, even without an examiner present. However, families with a less severely handicapped family member might have some difficulty answering items such as "If I knew when ____ would die I wouldn't worry so much" or "It is difficult for me to stand back and watch ____'s condition get worse," which assume the presence a severely handicapped or terminally ill family member. Completion of the full-length QRS takes about 1 hour, whereas the short form requires about 20 minutes.

Special skills or training are not necessary for scoring the QRS. The kit contains five templates, each of which is used to score three scales (openings of differents shapes—square, circle, triangle—are used for each scale). Templates are placed over the answer sheet, and each marked item that appears through the template for a particular scale is scored "1." The scale score is the number of items that appear through the template. The manual also includes instructions for computer scoring.

Interpretation of the QRS scale scores for preschool and school-age children is based on objective scores. T-scores above 70 are considered clinically significant, while tentative interpretations should be made for those between 60 and 70. T-scores under 60 are considered to fall within the normal range. The manual describes each scale in a fair amount of detail; however, interpretation of the QRS profile is not straightforward.

The manual describes a sample profile in which 10 of the 15 scales are elevated (i.e., six scales with T-scores of 70 or more and four scales with T-scores between 60–70). A naive user might assume this pattern represented a family under a great deal of stress, but instead this profile is said to represent a group that is fairly stable emotionally and financially, with the mother assuming the burden of care; thus, the main recommendation is to make this family more aware of community resources that they can well afford.

Clearly Holroyd intends the QRS scale scores to be interpreted in relation to each other; that is, the *pattern* of scale elevations appears to be most important, rather than the simple *number* or *magnitude* of scale elevations. However, the manual unfortunately does not elaborate on interpretation of different profile patterns, nor does it describe appropriate training for individuals who plan to use and interpret QRS scores.

As stated earlier, norms for adult patients are not provided; thus, interpretation is limited to examination of individual QRS items endorsed by the family. Percentile scores (but not T-scores) are provided for four general groups—developmental disabilities, psychiatric problems, chronic medical illness, and neuromuscular diseases—which also limits interpretation.

**Technical Aspects**

Little in the way of reliability and validity has been examined for the QRS, and the reports that do exist are not entirely encouraging. Reliability reported in the manual is limited to Kuder-Richardson 20 estimates for internal consistency. The KR-20 reliability correlation was .96 for the full-length QRS and .79 to .85 for the 66-item short form (QRS-SF). Scale coefficients ranged from as low as .24 to .88 on the QRS, and from .31 to .82 on the QRS-SF. In general, scales with fewer items produced lower internal consistency coefficients. In a sample of 189 parents examined by Salisbury (1985), KR-20 correlations ranging from .314 to .843 were obtained for scales on the QRS-SF. Item-total correlations ranged from .02 to .74. Item-total correlations from 289 QRS respondents reported by another laboratory (Friedrich et al., 1983) revealed that only 96 items had item-total correlations of .40 or more. Test-retest reliability coefficients for the QRS are not available.

Reliability between the QRS and QRS-SF is questionable. When the 285 QRS items were factor analyzed in the Holroyd laboratory, 11 factors emerged that did not necessarily "fit" with the original 15 factors. (The procedures used in the factor analysis are not described in the manual.) In fact, 53 items on these 11 factors do not overlap with the 206 items on the 15 scales of the full-length QRS. The best correlations with the 11 factor analyzed factors and the original 15 scales ranged from .37 to .81. From these 11 factors, the six items correlating most highly with the factor were selected to comprise the short-form QRS. These correlations ranged from .64 to .90.

The lack of congruity between the QRS and QRS-SF became quite apparent when Holroyd and Guthrie (1986) found that the QRS and QRS-SF provided different results for various groups of families with medically ill children. For example, when a group of parents with children with neuromuscular disease was compared with a normal control group of parents, statistically significant group differences were found on Limits on Family Opportunity on the QRS-SF but not on the QRS. In the same study, when a group of parents with children with cystic fibrosis were compared to a normal control group, 3 of the 15 scales on the QRS were statistically different (Lack of Social Support, Physical Incapacitation, and Social Obtrusiveness), while 4 of the 11 QRS-SF scales were significantly different (Cognitive Impairment, Life Span Care, Terminal Illness Stress, and Financial Stress). The QRS-SF is recommended for use as a screening device, yet these data suggest that significant findings on the QRS-SF may not be replicated when the full-length QRS is examined.

The manual reports that QRS content validity was established "by having 12 experts select the most relevant items from a large pool during initial questionnaire development" (Holroyd, 1987, p. 45). The manual summarizes the results of numerous studies in which QRS scales significantly differentiate various groups of respondents (e.g., parents of handicapped vs. nonhandicapped children, or younger vs. older autistic children) as evidence of criterion validity. The manual does not describe studies of criterion validity in which QRS scores are compared to those of other established measures of stress or family resources. However, other researchers (e.g., Friedrich, 1979; Friedrich et al., 1983; Salisbury, 1989) have compared the QRS and adapted versions of it with established measures such as the Beck Depression Inventory, Locke-Wallace Marital Adjustment Inventory, and Marlowe-Crowne Social Desirability Scale and have found significant correlations.

The construct validity of the QRS has not been addressed systematically. The QRS was not developed with an explicit theory of family stress in mind; furthermore, the different methods (rational vs. factor analytic) used to develop the short and full-length forms of the QRS have resulted in conceptually different scales.

## Critique

The development of the QRS in the mid-1970s occurred during a time of growing interest in parental and family responses to a handicapped child, particularly in terms of family stress and resources. Prior to the initial report on the QRS in 1974, the assessment of family responses to a young handicapped member consisted primarily of interview data and measurements (e.g., MMPI) that did not focus directly on the child's impact on family functioning. Thus, the QRS provided a sorely needed comprehensive, quantitative measure of family stress and resources at a time of dwindling funds for such families.

Unfortunately, the QRS has many weaknesses that preclude meaningful use of scores derived from either its full-length or short forms. First, the theoretical basis for the QRS is not clear. Exactly what does it measure? Does the QRS measure the degree of the child's disability or the parent's *perception* of the degree of the child's disability? Does the QRS measure stressors faced by the family or the family's response to these stressors? The instrument is purported to measure all of these things as well as subtle interactions among these variables. If either scores on different scales or certain patterns of scale scores could convey this type of information, the QRS would be a very useful measure.

Even research coming out of Holroyd's laboratory has failed to produce consistent, clearly interpretable results. For example, to explain a finding in which parents of children with neuromuscular disease did not report more problems in the area of Dependency and Management than control parents, Holroyd and Guthrie (1986) state that "it is possible that this factor reflects a patient's demanding personality rather than the amount of care actually required and that in this instance the parents do not feel that the child is demanding more attention than is appropriate" (p. 558). In another example, Holroyd, Brown, Wikler, and Simmons (1975) found that stress levels based on interview ratings that differentiated mothers of older versus younger autistic children were not supported by the mothers' QRS responses. The study's authors suggest that "the difference might be attributable to greater sensitivity to family problems on the part of the raters, or possibly rater bias" (Holroyd et al., 1975, p. 31). The absence of a theoretical foundation for the QRS has resulted in different interpretations of QRS scores from study to study as researchers attempt to explain both significant and nonsignificant data.

The incongruence between the full-length QRS and its short form (QRS-SF) presents another problem. Holroyd recommends using the QRS for clinical decision making and research, and the QRS-SF for screening purposes. However, the rationally derived scales on the QRS were not supported by the factor analytic process used in the development of the QRS-SF. Short forms of the QRS with stronger psychometric properties have been developed by Friedrich et al. (1983) and Salisbury (1986), and the psychometric properties of these short forms have been examined in subsequent studies (e.g., Salisbury, 1989; Scott, Sexton, Thompson, & Wood, 1989).

In addition, this reviewer found the test kit materials less than ideal for regular use. The respondent answer sheets and scoring templates are oddly sized (about 10½" × 13½"), which makes storage of the test cumbersome. The templates are rigid and cannot be folded for storage. Furthermore, pages from the manual fell out during this reviewer's first reading; unless I received an odd defective copy, the manual clearly may not hold up to regular use. Finally, the manual was not written or organized in a "clinician friendly" manner. As stated earlier in this review, appropriate clinical interpretation of QRS profiles is not clearly explained.

In summary, this reviewer would not recommend employing the QRS for the primary purpose stated in the manual—that is, to help clinicians make decisions about which families and which problems to address first in circumstances of limited resources. Furthermore, researchers should not assume that the QRS is a reliable or valid instrument for measuring family stress and resources. Numerous studies (see Holroyd, 1988, for a review) have demonstrated the QRS's ability to differentiate various groups of parents (e.g., handicapped vs. nonhandicapped, institutionalized vs. noninstitutionalized). However, the ultimate test of the QRS will be whether it can detect intragroup variation; that is, can the QRS detect which parents within a diagnostic category are experiencing greater levels of stress?

When the research literature is considered as a whole, the QRS does not appear to measure family stress and resources with an acceptable degree of consistency or certainty. The short forms developed by Friedrich et al. (1983) and Salisbury (1986) are better measures in terms of their psychometric properties, although the questions concerning exactly what these questionnaires measure remain. Nonetheless, the QRS presents an important assessment measure to examine further, given its comprehensive content and the need for such an instrument for both research and clinical purposes. If researchers continue to publish reports on the properties of the QRS and its adapted forms, an instrument with more robust psychometric properties and clinical validity will likely emerge.

## References

Friedrich, W.N. (1979). Predictors of coping behaviors of mothers of handicapped children. *Journal of Consulting and Clinical Psychology, 47,* 1140–1141.

Friedrich, W.N., Greenberg, M.T., & Crnic, K.A. (1983). A short form of the Questionnaire on Resources and Stress. *American Journal of Mental Deficiency, 88,* 41–48.

Holroyd, J. (1974). The Questionnaire on Resources and Stress: An instrument to measure family response to a handicapped family member. *Journal of Community Psychology, 2,* 92–94.

Holroyd, J. (1987). *Questionnaire on Resources and Stress for Families with Chronically Ill or Handicapped Members.* Brandon, VT: Clinical Psychology Publishing.

Holroyd, J. (1988). A review of criterion validation research on the Questionnaire on Resources and Stress for Families with Chronically Ill or Handicapped Members. *Journal of Clinical Psychology, 44,* 335–354.

Holroyd, J., Brown, N., Wikler, L., & Simmons, J.Q. (1975). Stress in families of institutionalized and noninstitutionalized autistic children. *Journal of Community Psychology, 3,* 26–31.

Holroyd, J., & Guthrie, D. (1986). Family stress with chronic childhood illness: Cystic fibrosis, neuromuscular disease, and renal disease. *Journal of Clinical Psychology, 42,* 552–561.

Salisbury, C.L. (1985). Internal consistency of the short form of the Questionnaire on Resources and Stress. *American Journal of Mental Deficiency, 89,* 610–616.

Salisbury, C.L. (1986). Adaptation of the Questionnaire on Resources and Stress–Short Form. *American Journal of Mental Deficiency, 90,* 456–459.

Salisbury, C.L. (1989). Construct validity of the adapted Questionnaire on Resources and Stress–Short Form. *American Journal on Mental Retardation, 94,* 74–79.

Scott, R.L., Sexton, D., Thompson, B., & Wood, T.A. (1989). Measurement characteristics of a short form of the Questionnaire on Resources and Stress. *American Journal on Mental Retardation, 94,* 331–339.

**M. Cecil Smith, Ph.D.**
*Assistant Professor, Department of Educational Psychology, Counseling, and Special Education, Northern Illinois University, DeKalb, Illinois.*

---

# RETIREMENT DESCRIPTIVE INDEX

*Patricia C. Smith, Lorne M. Kendall, and Charles L. Hulin. Bowling Green, Ohio: Bowling Green State University.*

### Introduction

The Retirement Descriptive Index or RDI (Smith, Kendall, & Hulin, 1969) was developed to measure the satisfaction of retirees with their retirement status. The development of this instrument followed from that of a measure of job satisfaction, the Job Descriptive Index (Smith et al., 1969; see review in this volume). The authors define satisfaction as the "feelings or affective responses to facets of the situation" (Smith et al., 1969, p. 6). In the case of the RDI, the situation is, of course, retirement, and the assessment considers individuals' satisfaction across four dimensions: retirement activities, financial status, health, and people (associates). This measure is suitable for both male and female retirees, at all educational and occupational levels.

Patricia C. Smith (the senior author of the RDI) is Professor Emerita of Psychology at Bowling Green State University in Ohio, best known for her work in the field of industrial psychology. Work on the RDI grew out of research referred to as the Cornell Study of Satisfactions, in which Smith and her coauthors (Lorne M. Kendall and Charles L. Hulin) were involved. This research, in turn, comprised part of the Cornell University Studies of Retirement Policies and Practices funded by the Ford Foundation in the late 1950s.

The RDI is a self-report paper-and-pencil instrument that presents 63 items across four subscales. The Activities, Financial, and People subscales consist of 18 items each, and the Health subscale has 9 items. The scales resemble an adjective checklist. Representative items for each subscale are "tiresome," "exciting" (Activities); "satisfactory," "worry about it," "self-supporting" (Finances); "hard to meet," "intelligent," "active" (People); and "excellent," "failing" (Health). Respondents simply place a Y ("yes"), an N ("no"), or a ? ("can't decide") beside every item to indicate whether the item does or does not describe their retirement situation. Items are considered to be positive ("exciting") or negative ("same thing every day").

As noted, the RDI evolved from research on a measure of job satisfaction entitled the Job Descriptive Index (JDI). Smith et al.'s 1969 book, *The Measurement of Satisfaction in Work and Retirement,* describes in detail the theoretical basis for the JDI, extensive validation studies, scale characteristics, and norms for both instruments. The 1969 text is now out of print, but a photocopied text (copyright 1975) was available from Dr. Smith at BGSU for $18.00 plus postage and handling at the time of this writing.

Smith et al. believe that a scientific understanding of the sources of satisfaction/dissatisfaction is worthwhile with regard to promoting mental health, developing appropriate industrial management and retirement counseling programs, and retirement policies. Further, the study of satisfaction in general can "contribute to the general psychology of motivation, preferences, and attitudes" (Smith et al., 1969, p. 3). Instruments such as the RDI and JDI provide a means toward this end.

Because the RDI was an offshoot of research that examined job satisfaction, Smith et al. devote much of their attention to describing the lengthy series of studies that concerned the validation, scaling, and norming of the JDI. Unfortunately, the authors do not devote as much attention to explaining the rationale for and development of the RDI as for the JDI; therefore, the rationale for developing the RDI can only be understood in the context of the development of the JDI. Three of the four RDI subscales (Activities, Finances, and People) correspond closely to JDI subscales (Work, Pay, and Co-Workers, respectively).

**Practical Applications/Uses**

The purpose of the RDI is to assess the retiree's satisfaction with his or her retirement situation. This measure also can be employed to examine workers' expectations about retirement and so may be useful for preretirement planning and counseling. The RDI has applications in both research and clinical (nondiagnostic) practice.

The RDI was normed on heterogeneous samples of workers and retirees and is suitable for use with all occupational and educational levels. It can be administered orally to illiterate workers and retirees or those whose vision impairs their reading of printed materials. For example, the researcher/examiner may find it convenient to prepare an audiotape to facilitate administration of the RDI to those with poor reading skills or to visually impaired respondents. The RDI can be administered in a group or individually.

The directions and response format of the RDI are very simple and easy to understand. Each of the four subscales is presented on a separate page. The instructions for each scale ask the subject to put a "Y" beside an item if the item describes the particular aspect of his or her retirement situation, an "N" if the item does not describe that aspect, and a "?" is he or she is uncertain. A respondent can complete the RDI in a matter of 5–15 minutes.

Scoring is relatively simple. A weight of 3 is given for a "yes" response to each positive item (e.g., "fascinating") and a "no" response to each negative item (e.g., "same thing every day"). A weight of 1 is given to every ? given for any item. A scoring key appears in Smith et al. (1969). Scores can range from 0 to 56 on the Activities, Finances, and People subscales and 0 to 27 on the Health subscale. A high score indicates that an individual is very satisfied with the particular aspect of his or her retirement situation and a low score indicates dissatisfaction.

**Technical Aspects**

The majority of effort in the development of the JDI, and correspondingly the RDI, was concerned with establishing validity. Validity issues were of two types:

establishing the construct validity of the instrument by determining its agreement with other measures assumed to measure the same concepts (convergent validity), and what Smith et al. refer to as "intrinsic" validity or understandability. Specifically, Smith et al. desire that the instrument assess the effects of changes in situations; that is, changes in the individual's retirement situation. So, the RDI should have a certain "dynamic" quality to it.

Smith et al. attempted to establish the RDI's validity via a factor analytic study of its scale scores in association with 57 other measures of biographical, situational, and attitudinal information. A sample of 631 male retirees in various occupations was given the four RDI subscales. These measures were intercorrelated and factored by the centroid method. Based on the results of this analysis, Smith et al. claim the RDI is a reasonable measure of retirement satisfaction.

Other research has shown that the RDI correlates significantly with life satisfaction ratings of retirees (Hooker & Ventis, 1984) and self-actualization measures (Keahey & Seaman, 1974). Thus, several sources of evidence demonstrate that the RDI assesses retirees' perceptions of and satisfaction with retirement.

Smith et al. admit that little is known about the RDI's scale characteristics (e.g., test-retest reliability, item order effects, response set), and this problem has no doubt limited the use of the RDI in studies of retirement satisfaction. The subscale statistics for the RDI, based on a sample of 601 male retirees, emerged as follows: Activities, $M = 36.43$ ($SD = 12.49$); Finances, $M = 30.96$ ($SD = 11.06$); People, $M = 42.25$ ($SD = 10.90$); and Health, $M = 33.13$ ($SD = 13.40$). Correlations among the subscales range from $r = .43$ (Health and Activities) to $r = .19$ (People and Finances).

The authors were unable to employ the large scale sampling research used for the JDI in the development of the RDI, and so initial development of the RDI was based on a sample of 600 male and 240 female retirees ages 51 and older. All of the subjects had retired (or were nearing retirement) from work in both white- and blue-collar occupations at 19 different companies in 16 communities across 12 states. No other demographic data are reported. Tables of norms appear in Smith et al. (1969). These norms are based on the sample described above and are stratified by age, sex, and income. Although it would be of great interest to have normative data by occupation, no such data are provided.

## Critique

The Retirement Descriptive Index is a simple instrument to employ in retirement satisfaction research and, possibly, retirement counseling. The measure evolved from careful, extensive research regarding workers' attitudes. The format is easy to understand, the directions are straightforward, and subjects can respond orally or in writing. The RDI can be used with a wide variety of retirees and persons anticipating retirement. These are its virtues.

Because of the attention devoted to the development of the JDI, an explicit rationale for the RDI's development is lacking. Further, additional information is needed regarding the steps taken in the RDI's development. An up-to-date report concerning recent use and a manual with contemporary norms is needed. Apparently few studies exist in the literature that have employed the RDI to assess retirement satisfaction.

Although the directions to respondents for completion of the RDI are relatively simple, directions for how to appropriately administer the instrument are lacking. Is the instrument sensitive to different instructions and settings? How explicit should the directions for completing the RDI be? This information is not in Smith et al.'s report.

The RDI suffers from a lack of established reliability, although with sufficient data, this problem could be remedied readily. Dr. Smith has requested that researchers who employ the RDI submit data to her to assist in determining the instrument's reliability, and she does anticipate updating the norms. Although the RDI has been shown to correlate strongly with measures of life satisfaction, because no reliability data are available it may be best for researchers simply to use life satisfaction measures to assess, in a more general manner, a retiree's satisfaction with his or her retirement condition.

## References

Hooker, K., & Ventis, D.G. (1984). Worth ethic, daily activities, and retirement satisfaction. *Journal of Gerontology, 39,* 478–484.

Keahey, S.P., & Seaman, D.F. (1974). Self-actualization and adjustment in retirement: Implications for program development. *Adult Education, 24,* 220–226.

Smith, P.C., Kendall, L.M., & Hulin, C.L. (1969). *The measurement of satisfaction in work and retirement: A strategy for the study of attitudes.* Chicago: Rand McNally.

**Michael D. Franzen, Ph.D.**
*Associate Professor of Behavioral Medicine and Psychiatry and Director of Neuropsychology, West Virginia University Medical Center, Morgantown, West Virginia.*

# RIVERMEAD PERCEPTUAL ASSESSMENT BATTERY

*S. Whiting, N.B. Lincoln, G. Bhavnani, and J. Cockburn. Windsor, Berkshire, England: NFER-Nelson Publishing Company Ltd.*

### Introduction

The Rivermead Perceptual Assessment Battery (RPAB) was designed to evaluate visual-perceptual deficits, attendant upon stroke or closed head injury, that might interfere with an individual's ability to perform common activities. The RPAB consists of 16 subtests that evaluate a subject's ability to match two pictures of the same objects, to match two of the same objects, to match colors, to perceive size constancy, to sequence cards either in order of increasing size or in order of probable narrative, to pair different halves of animals, to identify missing objects in a picture, to identify objects in overlapping line drawings, to identify body parts from wooden two-dimensional representations and from the subject's actual body, to copy shapes, words, and three dimensional designs, to copy two-dimensional designs using cubes, and to scan and cancel letters. The manual (Whiting, Lincoln, Bhavnani, & Cockburn, 1985) further states that the RPAB is sensitive to the level of severity of the deficits as well as to changes in the level over time.

The RPAB was originally designed to allow occupational therapists to evaluate the visual-perceptual deficits of their patients when access to a neuropsychologist was limited. Therefore, the battery does not allow the fine-grained analysis one would expect from a neuropsychological instrument. Despite this limitation, the RPAB may be useful to general clinical psychologists who need to evaluate these aspects of these patients, and further development may increase the battery's utility for clinical neuropsychologists.

The development of the RPAB started in 1979. The battery was originally designed by occupational therapists who wished to standardize their assessment of visual-perceptual functions. There were several suggested assessment strategies but little agreement regarding the relative utility of each. Additionally, the individual strategies did not have standardized administration, scoring, or interpretation, severely limiting their applicability. The authors of the RPAB surveyed the techniques used by occupational therapists in Great Britain and compiled those tasks into a battery. The interest in perceptual aspects of disability is a relatively new concern for occupational therapists treating stroke patients; traditional concerns had lain in the areas of motor activity. The RPAB tasks were designed so that they could be administered by occupational therapists without specialized training in test administration or interpretation. The scoring system was designed to be objective. Originally there were 27 tasks in the battery. Initial studies indicated that some of the tasks had poor test-retest reliability, poor inter-rater reliability, or low correlations with other measures of visual perception. Following the removal of those deficient tasks, 16 tasks remained.

The RPAB was standardized on a normative group of 69 subjects with no history of brain damage or epilepsy. The subjects were stratified into three age groups: 16–32 years, 33–49 years, and 50–69 years. Each of the age groups was further stratified into three levels of intellectual functioning as assessed by the synonyms test of the Mill Hill Vocabulary Scale. The three levels are described in the manual as above average, average, and below average. The manual does not give the decision criteria used to classify the subjects into the intellectual functioning groups, although later it does provide criteria for determining the subject's pre-morbid intelligence based upon Mill Hill Vocabulary Test scores, and it is possible that these criteria were used. The subjects were distributed approximately 2:1, male to female. The normative group was administered the entire 27 tests of the original battery. All of the normative subjects were obtained either from the hospital staff or from the surrounding community. In the normative sample only the Body Image and Cancellation subtest scores correlated significantly with age. On the other hand, 11 of the subtest scores were significantly correlated with the score from the Mill Hill Vocabulary Test.

Following the original collection of normative data, reliability studies indicated that administration and scoring instructions needed to be changed for five of the subtests. The manual does not describe the changes in the subtests, however. Normative data then were collected on these five subtests from a sample of 20 subjects. Because these five subtests (Missing Articles, Figure Ground Discrimination, Body Image, 3D Copying, and Body Image–Self Identification) were normed on a different sample from the other subtests, the scores from these subtests should not be compared to the scores from the other subtests until such time as the entire set has been normed on the same sample.

The RPAB arrives in a large briefcase that contains all the materials needed to administer the tests. There is a cloth layout guide on which the test stimuli are to be arranged. The Picture Matching subtest uses 10 pictures (five pairs of objects). The Object Matching subtest uses five pairs of objects: toothbrushes, toy cars, matchboxes, combs, and cups. The Color Matching subtest uses a paper sheet of colors and colored wooden blocks. The Size Recognition subtest uses 10 pictures of variously sized objects. The Series subtest uses cards with pictures that represent some form of series. The Animal Halves subtest uses incomplete pictures of objects that, when matched, form a complete object. The Figure Ground Discrimination subtest uses a card with overlapping line drawings of objects and smaller cards with line drawings of individual objects, some of which are also on the larger card. The task is for the subject to separate the smaller cards into two piles: objects that are on the larger card and objects that are not on the larger card. The Sequencing Pictures subtest uses two sets of cards that the subject arranges into a sequence that reflects an implicit narrative. The Body Image subtest uses small wooden representations of body parts that the subject is to arrange into a model of a body. The Right/Left Copying Test for Shapes and the Right/Left Copying Test for Words use stimulus cards and a copy sheet. The 3D Copying Test uses wooden models of abstract constructions that the subject is to copy with loose wooden components. The Cube Copying Test uses two-dimensional representations of designs that the subject is to copy with three-dimensional cubes. The Cancellation Test uses sheets of repeated letters. The Body Image–Self Identification requires only the body of the subject.

### Practical Applications/Uses

The examiner is seated opposite the subject during the RPAB, administering the instructions and records responses. The record form used is a four-page protocol that includes places to record demographic information as well as the scores obtained from the administration of the procedures. There is also space to record behavioral observations and comments. The obtained scores are then separately compared to cutoff scores by estimate of intelligence for each subtest. The cutoff scores for the subjects of average intelligence correspond to scores that are 2 standard deviations below that of the normative group; the derivation of cut-off scores for the below-average and above-average intelligence groups is not described in the manual. The final page of the response protocol is a profile sheet on which the examiner can graph obtained scores in order to show areas of relative strength and weakness.

There is a 3-minute time limit for each subtest except for the two Right/Left Copying tests (5 minutes) and the Body Image–Self Identification test (no limit). There are general guidelines for scoring as well as specific guidelines for individual tests. Scoring is generally objective exception for the Body Image test, where accuracy of placement of the face parts is of necessity somewhat subjective, and the Copying-Shapes test, where some subjective judgments also are required.

The user interprets the RPAB on the basis of the number of tests for which the obtained score falls below the cutoff, as well as on the basis of the extent of deviation from the cutoff. The manual states that subjects who produce more than three test scores above the cutoff should be diagnosed as having a perceptual deficit. Unfortunately, there is no information given related to the accuracy of using such a diagnostic system, and there are no guides for interpreting the size of deviation from the cutoff, but future research should address this issue. Interpretation of the RPAB takes place at a basic enough level that it could be accomplished by most psychologists with experience in testing. However, to use the RPAB for other purposes (e.g., to delineate differential profiles of strengths and weaknesses, to diagnose specific brain impairments, or to identify specific psychological skills deficits in order to suggest treatment approaches) would require expertise in clinical neuropsychology.

### Technical Aspects

RPAB test-retest reliability was evaluated using a sample of 19 patients who had left hemiplegia following right-hemisphere stroke and whose strokes had occurred more than 1 year previously. All of the patients were rated as stable by their occupational therapists. The subjects were evaluated twice by the same examiner over a 4-week test-retest interval. Spearman rank-order correlation coefficients were computed for all of the tests except Picture Matching and Size Recognition, which did not show any variability in scores. The Object Matching, Series, and Figure Ground Discrimination tests did not show adequate reliability, and their reliabilities were then checked in a separate sample of 20 subjects. Even with the revisions, the reliability for the Series test was insignificant. The reliabilities for the other tests ranged from 1.00 for Animal Halves to 0.59 for Right/Left Copying Words (Bhavnani, Cockburn, Whiting, & Lincoln, 1983).

Interrater reliability was evaluated by videotaping administration of the RPAB to six subjects. The videotapes were then scored independently by three occupational therapists. The Left/Right Copying tests and the Cancellation test were scored from patient protocols. The reliability of the 3D Copying test was evaluated by presenting five arrangements of the blocks to three raters and then checking agreement. Kendall coefficients of concordance were calculated, with the result that Object Matching, Missing Articles, and Cancellation showed perfect agreement and the remaining tests showed agreement ranging from 0.72 to 0.98.

In order to evaluate the validity of the RPAB, its scores were correlated with scores from tests thought to evaluate similar skills (WAIS Block Design and Object Assembly, Cube Counting, Rey-Osterreith Complex Figure, Gollin Incomplete Figures, Warrington Non-Verbal Retention, and the Benton Visual Retention Test) and with scores from tests not thought to evaluate the same skills (WAIS Vocabulary, Token Test, Logical Memory section of the Wechsler Memory Scale, and Object Naming). Spearman rank-order correlation coefficients were calculated, with the result that most of the correlations with tests of perception were larger than correlations with other tests. The exceptions were related to the Right/Left Copying Words test and the Body Image–Self Identification test, which correlated significantly with tests of verbal skills and naming skills. The subjects used were 41 stroke patients and 16 head-injury patients.

These same 57 subjects were then compared to the 69 subjects used in the normative study in order to see if the RPAB could discriminate between brain injured and normal subjects. Individual *t* tests were computed, and all except the Series test were found to be sensitive to brain impairment. The comparisons computed involved multiple *t* tests, but no effort was made to control for experiment-wide error. Comparing the right-hemisphere stroke patients from this group (20 subjects) with the normal subjects indicated significant differences on all of the tests except Picture Matching. Comparison of the right-hemisphere stroke patients with the left-hemisphere patients (18 subjects) indicated that only the Object Matching, Size Recognition, Series, Animal Halves, and Cube Copying tests showed significant differences, and these differences might not be significant if the number of comparisons were taken into account.

As yet another check on the validity of the RPAB, scores were compared to scores obtained on the Rivermead Activities of Daily Living Assessment by the 57 patients mentioned in the original validity study. Activities of Daily Living (ADL) scores were available on only 54 of these patients. Increasing scores on the RPAB appeared to be associated with increasing numbers of activities of daily living that a patient could do, although for the Picture Matching and Missing

Article tests, the patients with medium-level ADL scores gave better performance on the RPAB than did the patients with high-level ADL scores.

## Critique

The RPAB was originally designed for use by occupational therapists; however, with increases in the amount of information regarding its properties, it could become very useful for psychologists. Although the manual describes the type of psychological skill thought to be tapped by each test in the RPAB, there has not been any formal, empirical test evaluations of these suppositions. A better understanding of the constructs underlying each procedure would be helpful in applying the test to perceptually disordered patients.

Some confusion exists because the test scores appear to be sensitive to brain impairment in general, regardless of hemispheric location of injury. Additionally, some of the tests correlate with tests of psychological skills other than perception. Of greatest significance perhaps is the fact that the tests correlated significantly with the Mill Hill Vocabulary Test in the normative sample. Therefore, we cannot be sure that the tests are actually measuring the level of perceptual integrity. The RPAB tests appear to have good face validity and are taken from the tradition of clinical lore; thus empirical verification is now needed to confirm the hypotheses.

## References

Bhavnani, G., Cockburn, J., Whiting, S., & Lincoln, N. (1983). The reliability of the Rivermead Perceptual Assessment. *British Journal of Occupational Therapy, 45,* 67–68.

Whiting, S., Lincoln, N., Bhavnani, G., & Cockburn, J. (1985). *Rivermead Perceptual Assessment Battery manual.* Windsor, England: NFER-Nelson.

**Ron D. Cambias, Jr., Psy.D.**
*Psychology Staff, Children's Hospital, New Orleans, Louisiana.*

**Grant Aram Killian, Ph.D.**
*Associate Professor of Psychology, Nova University, Ft. Lauderdale, Florida.*

**Jan Faust, Ph.D.**
*Assistant Professor of Psychology, Nova University, Ft. Lauderdale, Florida.*

# ROBERTS APPERCEPTION TEST FOR CHILDREN: SUPPLEMENTARY TEST PICTURES FOR BLACK CHILDREN

*Glen E. Roberts. Los Angeles, California: Western Psychological Services.*

### Introduction

The Roberts Apperception Test for Children (RATC; McArthur & Roberts, 1982) is a thematic apperceptive technique designed to elicit hidden drives, conflicts, and feelings from children ages 6 to 15 (for an excellent review, see Friedrich, 1984). The RATC follows in a long line of apperception tests, most notably the Thematic Apperception Test (TAT; Murray, 1971) and the Children's Apperception Test (CAT; Bellak & Bellak, 1980). In response to the lack of stimulus pictures for black children, Roberts (1986) published the Supplementary Test Pictures for Black Children as an addition to the original RATC.

Central to apperception tests, as well as projective tests in general, is the concept of apperceptive distortion, which refers to the individual's subjective interpretation of a stimulus. Beginning in the latter part of the 19th century and the early part of 20th, professionals began to recognize that clients' unconscious drives and conflicts could be manifested through verbalizations made in response to an otherwise ambiguous stimulus. Through the ambiguity of the stimulus, the client "projects" his or her personality traits, drives, defenses, and unconscious conflicts. Thus, the subject's unique history of accumulated past experiences results in a distortion of current perceptions. In other words, an individual subjectively perceives more than what is objectively extant in the stimulus (Bellak, 1975). The individual's personality colors how he or she perceives the world. As a result, projective techniques like the Roberts Supplementary Test Pictures for Black Children allow access to an individual's internal world.

A review of the apperception test literature reveals a paucity of tests for use with minority groups. Perhaps the first thematic apperception test devoted to use with a minority population was the Thompson Modification of the TAT (T-TAT;

Thompson, 1949). The T-TAT was developed for use with blacks to provide a culturally relevant alternative to existing thematic apperceptive techniques, particularly the TAT. However, interest in the Thompson TAT dwindled, due in part to a lack of receptivity to minority issues in psychological testing during the 1950s (Costantino, Malgady, & Rogler, 1988). The only other reference to a thematic apperception test for black populations is the Themes Concerning Blacks test (TCB; Williams, 1972), which apparently never attained any degree of popular use, perhaps due to a lack of adequate research on its psychometric properties and applications (Daum, 1985).

The Roberts test manual states that "preliminary findings suggest that the RATC may be a valid and appropriate instrument for assessing children from diverse ethnic and socioeconomic backgrounds, not just middle-class white children" (McArthur & Roberts, 1982, p. 6). Unfortunately, no reference to specific studies supports this claim. Recent studies have presented conflicting findings regarding the RATC's use with different ethnic populations. One study indicates that the RATC is culturally sensitive to groups of children from diverse cultural backgrounds (Cadavid-Hannon, 1988). However, another suggests that the RATC may measure different constructs in Anglos and Hispanics (Burns, 1986). Despite questions regarding the validity of the RATC in cross-cultural testing, it behooves test developers to construct tests in general, and apperception tests in particular, that contain stimulus pictures that are culturally relevant. Lubin and Wilson's (1956) study demonstrating the relationship between increased identification and similarity of test subject to picture hero figures is germane to this point.

The supplementary stimulus pictures consist of black-and-white charcoal drawings paralleling the original RATC stimulus situations. There are 27 stimulus pictures (all $8^{1}/_{2}'' \times 11''$), 11 for use with boys, 11 for use with girls, and 5 for both sexes (for a total of 16 cards to use with each subject). The pictures all represent common interpersonal situations of childhood and pull for such themes as aggression, sibling rivalry, parental support, and relationship to maternal figures. For example, Card 11, depicting a girl with hands raised in front of her while shrinking back, pulls for a reaction to a fearful situation. This particular picture seeks to evoke the subject's ability to cope with a fear-provoking situation; that is, to see whether the subject tells a story in which the main figure handles the situation alone or seeks the help of others.

The original RATC scoring system comprises several areas. Profile Scales include the Adaptive Scales, which are designed to measure the types of solutions to problems; the Clinical Scales, which are designed to measure the types of clinical reactions to a problem; and the Critical Indicators, which are designed to signify the presence of significant deviations from typical responses to cards. In addition, there are three Supplementary Measures, which provide further clinical information but were intended primarily as research measures in the continuing validation of the RATC. Also, the Interpersonal Matrix is designed to elucidate the relationship between the interaction of story characters with the various scales and indicators.

The eight Adaptive Scales are described as follows:

1. *Reliance on Others:* use of others' help in the resolution of a problem (e.g., a character asks mother for a drink of water).

2. *Support-Other:* offer of support to other people (e.g., a young boy helps an old lady walk across the street).

3. *Support-Child:* self-sufficiency, assertiveness, or experience of positive feelings (e.g., a character creates a picture for his parents; a character feels good about himself).

4. *Limit Setting:* appropriate restriction of behavior by any authority figure (e.g., a girl is punished for breaking a dish).

5. *Problem Identification:* ability to identify and articulate a problem (e.g., a character wants to please her parents but also wants to do what her friends want her to do).

6. *Resolution 1:* easy, unrealistic resolution of a problem (e.g., a boy wishes for a bike and then magically receives one).

7. *Resolution 2:* constructive resolution of a problem without accompanying explanation or insight (e.g., a character finds out who stole his bike but does not explain how he found out who it was).

8. *Resolution 3:* constructive resolution of a problem with explanation and/or insight (e.g., a girl finds her doll and fully explains the steps in retrieving it).

The five Clinical Scales are described as follows:

1. *Anxiety:* anxiety, guilt, remorse, apprehension, or stressful situations (e.g., a character feels anxious over a test, guilty for hurting a friend, apprehensive about going home, or relates a story about the death of a parent).

2. *Aggression:* expression of anger or aggression (e.g., a boy gets into a fight at school).

3. *Depression:* sadness, despair, or physical symptoms of depression (e.g., a character feels tired and sad over losing her dog).

4. *Rejection:* any type of separation from others or jealousy (e.g., a girl's classmates make fun of her and she feels left out of the group; a girl is jealous of another girl's clothes).

5. *Unresolved:* a problem in the story is not resolved (e.g., a character fights with his sister, but no solution is attempted).

Finally, the three Critical Indicators are described as follows:

1. *Atypical Response:* extreme deviation from the normal themes or primary process thinking (e.g., a boy sees a witch on one of the stimulus cards).

2. *Maladaptive Outcome:* action makes solutions to problems more difficult, inappropriate behavior occurs in the resolution of a problem, or a main character dies at the end of a story (e.g., a character runs away from school; a character threatens another person to get her way; a character is killed for not doing what her mother wanted her to do).

3. *Refusal:* subject refuses to give a response to the stimulus card.

In addition, there are three Supplementary Measures:

1. *Ego Functioning Index:* measures the type of perception present within the projective material along a continuum from psychotic to stereotyped to creative.

2. *Aggression Index:* measures the quality of aggression present within aggressive responses along a continuum from physically destructive aggression (e.g., death of a character) to creative, constructive resolution of aggression (e.g., a boy is angry, but talks to a friend who helps calm him down).

3. *Levels of Projection Scale:* measures the degree of story complexity along a

continuum from simple description of people and objects to a complete story with discussion of feelings, thoughts, or motivations.

Finally, the Interpersonal Matrix allows the examiner to visualize the relationship between the various scales and indicators and the story figures. This system is based on the assumption that children will project conflicts regarding specific figures from their lives in the stories told to stimulus cards. The Interpersonal Matrix is used as an aid to clinical interpretation by offering a way of visualizing potentially significant interactions between scales and indicators and story characters. For example, it may become evident that there is a clustering of Depression scores in the row for Mother story figures. This information may prove useful in gaining further insight into the nature of individual scale/indicator scores.

**Practical Applications/Uses**

At the time of this writing, no information had been published regarding these supplementary test pictures. When and if the psychometric properties are adequately established, this set of cards presumably will be appropriate for use with any child or adolescent black population. The RATC manual states the following purpose for the original instrument: "Its primary purpose is to assess children's perceptions of common interpersonal situations as an aid to general personality description and clinical decision making" (McArthur & Roberts, 1982, p. 1). Undoubtedly the supplementary test pictures will be used for the same purpose. In addition, on the condition that the supplementary pictures eventually demonstrate adequate psychometric integrity, this reviewer would recommend these pictures for use in research regarding racial attitudes.

No normative, reliability, or validity data currently exist for the RATC Supplementary Test Pictures for Black Children. However, it is assumed that once these studies are completed, the test user will administer, score, and interpret the supplementary pictures in the same manner as the original RATC stimuli. In the meantime, only a subjective analysis of the responses can be conducted at present. Such use, though, leaves the examiner open to the criticism that he or she may be projecting as much as the subject.

Each of the 16 stimulus cards is administered in order to the test subject. The directions are similar to those given with the TAT, asking the subject to tell a story: what is happening now, what led up to the present, and how the story ends. In addition, the subject is asked to tell what the people in the story are saying and feeling. Responses are recorded verbatim. Additional inquiry, restricted to the use of five basic questions (i.e., What is happening? What happened before? What is he or she feeling? What is he or she talking about? How does the story end?), may be used during the first two cards if aspects of the story are omitted. However, further inquiry after this point, other than clarifying the identity of a character or the meaning of a word or phrase, is not permitted. Administration requires approximately 20 to 30 minutes.

Scoring involves the profile scales, indicators, and completion of the Interpersonal Matrix. The three supplementary measures, although primarily used for research purposes, may also be utilized during the interpretive process. Following the administration, all responses are examined, with the appropriate scales and indicators marked on the Summary Score Sheet. For example, a story in which the main character is punished for killing his brother would result in checking the following items: Limit Setting (an Adaptive Scale), Aggression (a Clinical Scale), and Atypical Response (one of the Critical Indicators).

Raw scores for the scales and indicators are determined by summing the checkmarks for each. Scores for the Adaptive and Clinical Scales are then transformed into T-scores, with a mean of 50 and a standard deviation of 10, by plotting raw scores on the RATC Profile Form appropriate for the subject's age (profiles are provided for ages 6–7, 8–9, 10–12, and 13–15). The conversion of raw scores into T-scores allows the examiner to compare the subject to others of his or her age. The totals for each of the three indicators are checked against critical cutoff scores. Anything equal to or above the cutoff scores is considered clinically significant.

Next the Interpersonal Matrix is completed. The matrix is composed of rows/columns of boxes corresponding to the various possible characters represented (located by row) and the various scales and indicators (located by column). The examiner looks at each story and marks the stimulus card number in the box associated with a particular figure (by row) and profile scale and/or indicator (by column). The marking of each story by character and scale/indicator allows the examiner to visualize the relationship between the various scales and indicators and the story figures. Finally, each of the stories may be rated on a number of categories specific to each of the three Supplementary Measures. For example, for the Ego Functioning Index, each story is scored along an 8-point continuum from distorted to creative. The frequency of scores for each of the various categories can then be tallied to provide a visual display of clusters of scores. Scoring an average RATC protocol takes approximately 20 to 30 minutes.

Interpretation consists of both quantitative and qualitative analysis. Quantitative analysis, referring to the examination of the RATC profile scores, involves the following steps: "(1) sequential analysis of the individual profile scales and indicators; (2) comparison of mean scale scores for the adaptive and clinical scales; (3) examination of interscale variability (i.e., 'scatter'); and (4) use of the Interpersonal Matrix" (McArthur & Roberts, 1982, p. 23). Qualitative analysis refers to a more subjective approach to interpretation and entails consideration of behavioral data, structural components (e.g., ability to comply with tests instructions), and thematic content (e.g., areas of conflict). The examiner then integrates information gleaned from both quantitative and qualitative analyses in order to construct an accurate psychological "picture" of the subject. The manual reports an average time of 10 to 15 minutes for interpretation.

## Technical Aspects

As noted in the previous section, when this review was written there was no published information regarding the reliability, validity, or standardization of the Roberts supplemental test pictures. However, the developer does state that this information is forthcoming (G.E. Roberts, personal communication, July 1989). When and if such data are published, there will be a need either for a manual to accompany these pictures or else for a revision of the current RATC manual (McArthur & Roberts, 1982), per the *Standards for Educational and Psychological*

*Testing* (American Educational Research Association, American Psychological Association, & National Council on Measurement in Education, 1985).

## Critique

The original Roberts Apperception Test for Children was one of the first apperception tests to provide an objective scoring system based on normative data. The addition of a set of stimulus pictures targeting black populations is part of a growing movement to develop apperception tests that show sensitivity to ethnic differences while addressing the need for psychometric rigor (e.g., the Children's Apperceptive Story-Telling Test [CAST; Schneider, 1989] and the Tell-Me-A-Story test [TEMAS; Costantino et al., 1988]). However, with the current lack of normative, reliability and validity data, test users would be unwise to use this additional set for anything other than research purposes.

When and if psychometric rigor is attained, the Supplementary Test Pictures for Black Children will take its place among the more sound apperception tests developed in recent years, of which the original RATC was a significant forerunner.

## References

This list includes text citations and suggested additional reading.

American Educational Research Association, American Psychological Association, & National Council on Measurement in Education. (1985). *Standards for educational and psychological testing*. Washington, DC: American Psychological Association.

Anastasi, A. (1982). *Psychological testing* (5th ed.). New York: Macmillan.

Bailey, B.E., & Green, J., III. (1977). Black Thematic Apperception Test stimulus material. *Journal of Personality Assessment, 41*(1), 25–30.

Baty, M.A., & Dreger, R.M. (1975). A comparison of three methods to record TAT protocols. *Journal of Clinical Psychology, 31*(2), 348.

Bellak, L. (1975). *The T.A.T., C.A.T., and S.A.T. in clinical use* (3rd ed.). New York: Grune & Stratton.

Bellak, L., & Bellak, S. (1980). *A manual for the Children's Apperception Test* (7th ed.). Larchmont, NY: C.P.S.

Burns, C.W. (1986). The validity of the Roberts Apperception Test for Children across ethnic groups and between sexes. *Dissertation Abstracts International, 47,* 1773B. (University Microfilms No. 8614934)

Butkus, M. (1984). Comparison of the predictive/descriptive accuracy and improvements to the incremental validity of a projective and two objective personality tests for children and adolescents. *Dissertation Abstracts International, 45,* 3930B. (University Microfilms No. 8502508)

Cadavid-Hannon, E.B. (1988). A study of children's adaptive adjustment across multi-cultural groups using the Roberts Apperception Test for Children. *Dissertation Abstracts International, 49,* 5062B. (University Microfilms No. 8822710)

Cambias, R.D., Jr., Killian, G.A., & Faust, J. (1992a). Children's Apperceptive Story-Telling Test (CAST). In D.J. Keyser & R.C. Sweetland (Eds.), *Test critiques* (Vol. IX, pp. 66–79). Austin, TX: PRO-ED.

Cambias, R.D., Jr., Killian, G.A., & Faust, J. (1992b). Tell-Me-A-Story Test. In D.J. Keyser & R.C. Sweetland (Eds.), *Test critiques* (Vol. IX, pp. 545–560). Austin, TX: PRO-ED.

Costantino, G., Malgady, R., & Rogler, L.H. (1988). *TEMAS (Tell-Me-A-Story) manual.* Los Angeles: Western Psychological Services.

Daum, J.M. (1985). Themes Concerning Blacks. In J.V. Mitchell, Jr. (Ed.), *The ninth mental measurements yearbook* (pp. 1617–1619). Lincoln, NE: Buros Institute of Mental Measurements.

Friedrich, W.N. (1984). Roberts Apperception Test for Children. In D.J. Keyser & R.C. Sweetland (Eds.), *Test critiques* (Vol. I, pp. 543–548). Austin, TX: PRO-ED.

Henry, W.E. (1956). *The analysis of fantasy.* New York: Wiley.

Killian, G.A. (1984). House-Tree-Person Technique. In D.J. Keyser & R.C. Sweetland (Eds.), *Test critiques* (Vol. I, pp. 338–353). Austin, TX: PRO-ED.

Kline, P. (1986). *A handbook of test construction: Introduction to psychometric design.* New York: Methuen.

Korchin, S., Mitchell, H., & Meltzoff, J.A. (1950). A critical evaluation of the Thompson Thematic Apperception Test. *Journal of Projective Techniques, 13,* 445–452.

Light, B.H. (1955). A further test of the Thompson TAT rationale. *Journal of Abnormal Social Psychology, 51,* 148–150.

Lubin, N.M., & Wilson, M.O. (1956). Picture test identification as a function of "reality" (color) and similarity of picture to subject. *Journal of General Psychology, 54,* 31–38.

McArthur, D.S., & Roberts, G.E. (1982). *Roberts Apperception Test for Children manual.* Los Angeles: Western Psychological Services.

Mercer, J.R. (1978–79). Test "validity," "bias," and "fairness": An analysis from the perspective of the sociology of knowledge. *Interchange, 9*(1), 1–16.

Murray, H.A. (1971). *Thematic Apperception Test manual.* Cambridge: Harvard University Press.

Obrzut, J.E., & Cummings, J.A. (1983). The projective approach to personality assessment: An analysis of thematic picture techniques. *School Psychology Review, 12*(4), 414–420.

Roberts, G.E. (1986). *Roberts Apperception Test for Children: Supplementary Test Pictures for Black Children.* Los Angeles: Western Psychological Services.

Schneider, M.F. (1989). *CAST: Children's Apperceptive Story-Telling Test manual.* Austin, TX: PRO-ED.

Schwartz, E., Reiss, B., & Cottingham, A. (1951). A further critical evaluation of the Negro revision of the TAT. *Journal of Projective Techniques, 15,* 394–400.

Sines, J.O. (1985). Roberts Apperception Test for Children. In J.V. Mitchell, Jr. (Ed.), *The ninth mental measurements yearbook* (pp. 1289–1291). Lincoln, NE: Buros Institute of Mental Measurements.

Stevens, H. (1984). A comparative study of the Roberts Apperception Test for Children between well-adjusted, average and guidance clinic adolescents. *Dissertation Abstracts International, 45,* 1926B. (University Microfilms No. 8419105)

Thompson, C.E. (1949). The Thompson modification of the Thematic Apperception Test. *Journal of Projective Techniques, 17,* 469–478.

Williams, R.L. (1972). *Themes Concerning Blacks.* St. Louis, MO: Robert L. Williams & Associates.

**Virginia Brabender, Ph.D.**
*Assistant Professor and Director of Internship Training, Institute for Graduate Clinical Psychology, Widener University, Chester, Pennsylvania.*

# RUST INVENTORY OF SCHIZOTYPAL COGNITIONS

*John Rust. Windsor, Berkshire, England: NFER-Nelson Publishing Company Ltd.*

## Introduction

The Rust Inventory of Schizotypal Cognitions (RISC) is an instrument designed to measure the presence of those aberrant thought patterns associated with schizotypal and schizophrenic disorders. It distinguishes itself from other similar instruments in two respects. First, this test is geared to measure the positive rather than negative symptomatology of the aforementioned disorders. Second, the psychometric method by which it was developed allowed for the selection of subtle items and thereby enabled its use with a normal population. This test is based on the assumption that schizotypal cognitions occur not only in certain diagnostic groups but in the nonpatient population at large. The RISC is intended to identify those nonpatients who by virtue of their high scores show themselves to be at greater risk for schizophrenia and schizotypal disorders than others in the population.

This test was developed by John Rust, Senior Lecturer in Psychometrics at the University of London Institute of Education, using a three-stage psychometric process. In Stage I, a pool of 450 items was created by a group of psychologists and psychiatrists. The items reflected the DSM-III (American Psychiatric Association, 1980) characterization of the thought patterns associated with schizophrenic (Category A) and schizotypal disorders (Categories 1, 2, 4, and 7). The initial pool was then reduced to a pilot scale of 300 items. A preliminary study done on this scale involved the testing of 183 students (primarily part-time) at London University. The subjects were presented the 300 items in a forced-choice, agree/disagree format. The analysis of their responses ultimately led to Stage II, in which the item pool was reduced to 120. From a factor analysis of the 300 responses emerged 10 factors that appeared to describe the data. A first set of three factors related to paranoid symptoms: paranoia, delusions of grandeur, and secretiveness. A second set pertained to more general schizophrenic symptoms: hallucinations, derealization and depersonalization, and thought direction. A third set concerned defensive operations: maintenance of personal identity, avoidance of uncomfortable thoughts, and avoidance of uncomfortable situations. A final factor related to rituals.

On the basis of the 10 factors, 10 subscales, each with 12 items, were constructed, guided by the application of four criteria: (a) the mean of the sample of the population must approximately correspond to the midpoint of the subscale; (b) a normal distribution must characterize scores on the subscale; (c) the number of positive items must equal the number of negative items; and (d) the subscale must withstand a validity test with extreme items (i.e., items answered in a consistent direction by 9 out of 10 individuals in the population). Although the test author eliminated the extreme items to reduce the influence of various test-taking sets, a strong relationship with such items was required of the total of the subscale items.

In Stage II, the resultant scale with 120 items, randomly combined, was subjected to further analysis. In contrast to the binary forced-choice format in Stage I, the options were increased to four alternatives in Stage II: strongly disagree, disagree, agree, and strongly agree. The items of the 10 subscales were administered to 27 students at the University of London Institute of Education on two occasions separated on average by 8 weeks but at least for 3 weeks. Test-retest reliabilities ranged from .68 to .89 with a mean and median of $r$ = .80. A further analysis was performed on the test protocols of 117 faculty and students from the same institution to determine if the pilot subscales met criterion "a" described above (i.e., that the midpoint of the subscales of 18 approximately coincide with the population means). The means of the subscales ranged from 16.07 to 19.37.

The subscales were subjected to factor analysis, which yielded a best fit solution of three factors. Each of the three factors concerned paranoid, schizoid, and experiential ideation, respectively. The test author dropped the last factor. After the factor analysis of the first two factors, a rotation was performed, yielding a schizotypal dimension that appeared to be congruent with the intended purpose of the test.

The third stage in the development of this test involved the reduction in the number of items to create a single schizotypal scale. The author obtained three samples of subjects to ensure that any subject's score on this scale would be unbiased in terms of sex, language, culture, and religion. The first sample consisted of 140 persons (70 men and 70 women) who were affiliated in some way with London University. Their mean age was 33.43 years. The second group included 315 Asian Hong Kong students (161 males and 154 females) from English-medium colleges. These subjects had a mean age of 18.3 years. The third group consisted of 608 Spanish-speaking subjects (104 men and 504 women) at the University of Venezuela in Caracas. The test was administered to them in Spanish.

A factor analysis was performed for each of the groups and a projection scale constructed using items from the first two factors. Items were selected for the final scale on the basis of item correlations and adjusted item correlations with the projected scales. Items were chosen (a) on the basis of their good discriminability and (b) their lack of gender and culture bias. An equal number of positively biased versus negatively biased items was sought. The final scale involved the selection of 26 items. An analysis of variance test of nonadditivity was nonsignificant.

## Practical Applications/Uses

The primary purpose of this scale is to identify individuals within the nonpatient population who are at risk for the development of the symptoms associated with schizophrenic and schizotypal disorders. A primary application of this instrument is for clinical research (J. Rust, personal communication, July 30, 1990). Use of the RISC enables the creation of groups of subjects who produce considerable bizarre ideation. On the individual clinical level, however, this test should be used for descriptive rather than prognostic purposes.

This instrument might be used to identify a possible thought disorder underlying a person's obvious difficulty in adjusting to his or her environment. For example, if a student was referred to a psychologist because of difficulties in concentration in school, the psychologist might use this test as one avenue of pursuit to determine if the kinds of ideas to which the test is sensitive are distracting the student from more reality-oriented concerns. Also, this test, particularly because of its brevity, might be used as a screening device in a clinical situation to alert the clinician to the possible presence of ideational patterns that may warrant intervention. A high RISC score could trigger a referral for a full battery of psychological tests in which the subject's thinking could be explored more fully. However, for reasons to be discussed subsequently in this review, the absence of a high score should not be interpreted to rule out the presence of a thought component to the patient's symptomatology.

This test is suitable for use with late adolescents and adults. It may also be useful with younger adolescents (below 16), although no data are, as of yet, available on this population. Rust indicates that the items of the test "all have been shown to be understandable by people from a wide variety of backgrounds and levels of literacy" (1989, p. 3). Although the author does not specify the reading grade level required by the test, it appears to necessitate approximately the same level of reading ability as the MMPI (i.e., sixth grade). There is an English and Spanish form of this test. Items may be read to visually impaired subjects.

The 26 items of this test typically can be administered in 4 to 8 minutes. The author indicates that the subject should be told that the test examines variability in the normal personality. The examiner should avoid revealing the test's capacity to detect psychopathology, and if schizotypal cognitions are discussed at all, their creative aspect should be given emphasis. It seems to this reviewer that these instructions are not truly neutral (especially in the instance in which the subject is led to believe that creativity is being measured). Although the emphasis on normality or creativity may diminish the subject's apprehension about the test, it may also lead him or her to endorse eccentric or bizarre thoughts on the notion that the examiner may regard such endorsements positively.

The test manual does not specify what skill level is necessary for the examiner. However, it would seem that a testing technician who is skilled at handling patient resistances to test taking and to the specific content of this test would be adequately qualified for this role.

Scoring for the RISC is extremely simple and convenient. Responses are completed by the subject on a carbonized scoring sheet. For hand scoring, all that is required of the examiner is to sum the values that are circled by the subject (the subject only sees letters, not numbers, on the attached overlay sheet). Scores range from 0 to 78, with 78 representing the highest level of schizotypal thinking.

RISC scores are interpreted through use of a key provided on the carbonized scoring sheet. Intervals of RISC scores are listed with corresponding interpretive labels such as "average," "above average," and "extremely high," with each representing the extent of schizotypal cognitions. Also offered in the key is the percentage of individuals in the population scoring in each interval as well as the transformation of the RISC to stanine norms.

In his item selection, Rust made a prodigious cross-cultural effort to minimize the influence of subject variables. Indeed, the data he presents suggest that the effects of the variables of culture, language, and gender have been minimized sufficiently to obviate the need for separate norms for different cultural and gender groups. Nonetheless, there is evidence to suggest that there are other subject variables that one must consider in the interpretation of the data. The subject variable that appears most determining of RISC scores is age. Unfortunately, it is not possible for the test author to disentangle the effects of age from other variables because in the reported studies, age covaries with other subject variables. For example, Rust tested a group of part-time British students (average age = 33.23 years) who obtained a stanine mean of 4.81. A group of Hong Kong students with an average age of 18.27 obtained a stanine mean of 5.56. As the author himself admits, this difference could be attributed to age, culture, or their interaction. Although the comparison of any two groups that Rust tested does not lead to an unambiguous interpretation, a comparison of subjects across all groups and within each group provides support for a negative relationship between age and RISC scores.

The average correlation between age and RISC scores in the control groups was -.18. This consistent but rather weak correlation appears to be due to a tendency of scores to drop sharply between 17 and 21 years. That Rust obtained this finding is not unusual in view of similar findings on the relationship between age and measures of cognitive slippage on other psychological tests such as the Rorschach (e.g., see Exner, 1986). Rust also found that after 21 years, there is a slight downward trend increasing with age with a somewhat inexplicable elevation at 28 years and a further decline thereafter. The age-specificity of RISC scores may be sufficiently great to warrant norms for different age groups or at least adolescent versus adult norms. For the present, the test interpreter must recognize that subjects of approximately 16 years are likely to obtain a score that places them a full interval higher than adult subjects.

Another subject variable that may be relevant to the interpretation of an individual's RISC score is his or her religious affiliation. Rust collected data on two religious sects and seven occult groups. On comparing their scores with those of a control group, Rust found that some groups had scores significantly below the mean of the controls while others had scores significantly above the mean. Rust was not able to identify a factor among the nine that accounted for the direction of the deviation. At the present time, these results can only alert the examiner to a possible association between the two variables. Given, however, that individuals with thought pathology may be attracted to participation in certain ideological groups, the existence of a relationship between religious affiliation and RISC scores does not necessarily require that the examiner modify his or her interpretation of a subject's RISC score given knowledge of the subject's religious affiliation.

Although more empirical work needs to be done on the relationship between subject variables and RISC scores, this necessity is not unusual given that the test was new at the time of this writing. A more serious problem in interpreting RISC scores is the lack of clarity concerning the meaning of the RISC score in relation to the purpose of the test (i.e., to identify individuals who may be at risk for the eventual manifestation of schizophrenic-like symptoms). For example, if a subject obtains a score of 43, which is labeled "high," what is the probability that he or she will manifest schizophrenic-like symptoms at some later point? Rust does not provide data to answer this question. Moreover, the interpreter receives little aid in the interpretation of low scores. Although Rust suggests that extremely low scores may be associated with a high level of defensiveness, he provides no empirical evidence to support this hypothesis.

## Technical Aspects

The test author reports split-half reliabilities based on 1,866 subjects of $r = .71$. Test-retest reliabilities on 108 subjects, part-time students and their associates in inner London, were obtained after a mean interval of 1 month (range = 2 weeks to 3 months). The average $r$ was 0.87, and the group means for the two testings were not significantly different.

Currently, several concurrent validity studies exist to suggest that RISC scores do indeed reflect the extent of schizotypal cognitions within the thinking of an individual. Rust has done a small series of studies on schizophrenic subjects. As bizarre, magical, and eccentric cognitions are known to typify the mental life of schizophrenics, the demonstration that such subjects achieve relatively high RISC scores constitutes one line of support for the validity of the scale. Rust reports a study in which acute schizophrenics, outpatients and inpatients, were compared with the British control group described in the discussion of his Stage II of test development. Rust found that the difference between the two groups was significant at the .001 level. The acute schizophrenics achieved a mean RISC score of 35.67 ($SD = 7.67$). This study provides only weak support for the RISC as a measure of schizotypal cognitions because items reflecting any kind of pathology are likely to discriminate between these two extreme groups.

A second stronger study involved the administration of the RISC to 36 chronic schizophrenic patients. In addition, each patient's psychiatrist was asked to give, without knowledge of the RISC score, the degree of schizotypal symptomatology the subject exhibited on a 7-point scale. Rust found that the subjects in the sample obtained a mean RISC score of 33.0, which actually appears to be lower than that of several of the control groups (although Rust does not report a statistical comparison between these groups). A correlation between the RISC scores and the psychiatric ratings yielded a moderate $r$ of .52 ($p > .001$). Rust then compared the RISC scores of his acute and chronic schizophrenic samples and obtained a significant difference ($p > .001$), with the acute schizophrenics obtaining higher scores.

A second set of studies involved correlating RISC scores with scores on other tests that purport to measure similar phenomena. RISC scores were correlated with scores on the Eysenck Personality Questionnaire (EPQ), another scale measuring psychoticism. The subjects tested were those in the Venezuelan pilot group described earlier. The RISC scores correlated significantly but minimally ($r = .12$, $p > .001$) with the Psychoticism scale and somewhat more highly with the Neuroticism scale ($p > .001$). The $r$ of –0.04 with the Extraversion scale was not significant. The author sees this low correlation between the Psychoticism scale and the RISC scores as being due to a design problem in the Psychoticism scale.

In another study, the relationship between RISC scores and the Minnesota Counselling Inventory (MCI), a test derived from the Minnesota Multiphasic Personality Inventory, was examined (Rust & Chiu, 1988). Both tests were given to the Hong Kong control sample described earlier. Because the 120-item pilot version of the RISC was used, the 26 items needed to be extracted from the larger body. The investigators found that the RISC correlated significantly with all four subscales of the MCI. A positive correlation between the RISC and nonconformity ($r = .40$, $p > .001$), poor social relations ($r = .26$, $p > .001$), negative mood ($r = .27$, $p > .001$), and emotional instability ($r = .45$, $p > .001$) was obtained. These results indicate that labile adolescents with negative social relations are likely to obtain relatively high scores on the RISC. Although the author interprets that finding as suggesting a relationship between negative and positive symptoms of schizophrenia, another possibility is that the negativism of the unconventionally, emotionally excitable adolescents would lead them to endorse items in a deviant direction.

The test author also reports an effort to correlate RISC scores with measures of creativity from the Comprehensive Ability Battery (Hakstain & Cattell, 1976). Subjects were individuals affiliated with City University. Low but significant correlations were obtained between RISC scores and spontaneous flexibility ($r = .19$, $p > .05$), ideational fluency ($r = .22$, $p > .05$), and originality ($r = .28$, $p > .05$), supporting Rust's view that schizotypal thinking can at times have a creative aspect.

## Critique

In introducing his test, Rust (1989) points out that a fundamental premise underlying its construction is not only schizotypals or schizophrenic individuals produce schizotypal cognitions. Rather, this symptom, like the other symptoms of schizophrenia, exists on a continuum from mild to severe. Individuals within the nonpatient population can be placed at all points along this continuum. This continuum model has received considerable empirical support over the years (e.g., Strauss, 1969; Quinlan, Harrow, Tucker, & Carlson, 1972). Although this important aspect of the test rests on a sound foundation, what might be brought into question is Rust's assumption about the most sensitive way in which to detect schizotypal cognitions and how to interpret their presence when they are so detected in an individual.

The test author distinguishes his test from those of others in the field in that he focuses on the positive rather than the negative symptoms of schizophrenia. For example, rather than examining cognitive deficits, Rust focuses on the content of the cognition, looking for common schizotypal and schizophrenic themes. In this reviewer's opinion, there are three limitations to a technique designed to uncover positive symptoms only. First, a test of positive symptoms is inefficient in that it duplicates information that could be obtained from a good clinical interview. In fact, sensitive interviewers have the advantage of gearing the tone, timing, and phrasing of their interview questions to their immediate impressions of the subject.

Second, it is dubious whether positive symptoms have the same discriminating value as negative symptoms. Consider, for example, the negative symptom of the inability to think logically. Except for persons with central nervous damage, the inability to think logically is characteristic of schizophrenics only (Whitaker, 1992). On the other hand, the positive symptoms of delusions and hallucinations are typical of various diagnostic groups such as persons with affective disorder with a psychotic component.

Third, a focus on positive symptomatology may be unsuited to serve a major purpose of this test, which is the early detection of schizotypal cognition. Generally, the more subtle negative symptoms are observed to occur before the more florid positive symptoms manifest themselves. The negative symptoms are what have commonly been described as characterizing the prodromal period. Moreover, this observation of the early onset of negative symptoms is compatible with a developmental model of regression in which the more developmentally advanced processes are the first to show deterioration. Subtle difficulties in thinking logically that involve sophisticated cognitive processes are likely to be challenged sooner than those perceptual processes whose subversion at least in part underlies hallucinatory experiences.

Optimally sensitive or not, this test undoubtedly will identify some persons who, relative to the general population, exhibit a high number of schizotypal cognitions. How might the elevated scores of a subject be interpreted? As implied in an earlier section, Rust provides the user with little direction. Presumably, the interest in early detection is in the possibilities it creates for early intervention. If an individual is exhibiting adaptive difficulties, a high RISC score may have some explanatory (albeit not necessarily predictive) power and may provide a direction for interventions. However, in the absence of any clear adaptive difficulties on the part of a subject, the clinical value of that subject's high RISC score is not evident. To claim that a high score is highly predictive of later schizophrenic symptoms is to ignore the role of other factors such as the particular stressors a person is facing, how these stressors interact with the person's psychodynamics, and the family context of the person.

What has become increasingly clear over the years is that the course of schizophrenia and its related disorders is not inexorable as Kraepelin once thought but highly variable (Harding, 1988; Marengo & Harrow, 1987). In fact, the RISC might be one useful research tool in the continuing quest to learn more about how these factors interact as well as how positive and negative symptoms covary. However, at present, it would seem premature to use this test predictively. In this reviewer's opinion, the RISC currently has its greatest utility in its descriptiveness of an aspect of the subject's present cognitive functioning.

In addition to the conceptual points that have been made about this approach to the assessment of schizophrenic-like thought patterns, several technical points might be offered about the RISC's psychometric properties. Although Rust provides a good demonstration of test-retest reliabilities over brief intervals, it would be helpful to the user to know about long-term reliability so as to make correct inferences about the stability of the psychological property this test is measuring.

The RISC is seen as in need of further validation work, an unsurprising conclusion given the recent publication of the test. Perhaps the most convincing study to date of this test's validity is that showing a relationship between RISC scores and psychiatrist's ratings of schizotypal thinking. However, three future lines of investigation would be important in providing a more substantial validational base for this test and giving stronger indication of the uses for which it is appropriate. First, the test should be correlated with other tests that purport to measure the same or similar phenomena. Examples of these are the Schizotypal scale of the MCMI-II (Millon, 1987), the Whitaker Index of Schizophrenic Thinking (Whitaker, 1980), the Harris and Lingoes (1968) subscales Sc2A (Lack of Ego Mastery, Cognitive) and Sc3 (Bizarre Sensory Experiences) of the MMPI, and the special scores of the Rorschach (Exner, 1986).

Second, the capacity of this test to distinguish between persons with ego deficits at equal levels of severity who do and do not carry diagnoses involving positive thought pathology must be demonstrated because the test is designed to reflect a type of disorder. Moreover, the potential ability of the test to discriminate between various diagnostic categories of persons exhibiting positive thought pathology should be explored. For example, do persons with schizotypal personality disorder obtain lower scores on this scale than acute schizophrenics? How do the scores of persons with an affective disorder with psychotic features compare to those of schizophrenic persons?

Third, as the test author sees this test as an estimator of risk for schizophrenia or schizotypal disorders, then longitudinal predictive validity studies would be essential. Individuals at various score levels should be followed to determine the percentage of persons within each RISC category that ultimately develops the appropriate cluster of symptoms to qualify for a schizophrenic or schizotypal diagnosis.

From a more practical standpoint, the handbook for this test is in great need of expansion. The proper administration of the RISC should be described in greater detail. A more concrete discussion of the uses of the test with illustrations should be provided. Finally, an exposition of the limitations of the test as well as a description of its potential misapplications (e.g., how the author would regard the use of the test to screen out persons for psychologically demanding work positions) would encourage the most responsible use of this instrument.

## References

This list includes text citations and suggested additional reading.

American Psychiatric Association. (1980). *Diagnostic and statistical manual of mental disorders* (3rd ed.). Washington DC: Author.

Exner, J.E. (1986). *The Rorschach: A comprehensive system* (Vol. 1, 2nd ed.). New York: Wiley.

Hakstain, A.R., & Cattell, R.B. (1976). *The Comprehensive Ability Battery.* Champaign, IL: Institute for Personality and Ability Testing.

Harding, C.M. (1988). Course types in schizophrenia: An analysis of European and American studies. *Schizophrenia Bulletin, 14*(4), 633–643.

Harris, R., & Lingoes, J. (1968). *Subscales for the Minnesota Multiphasic Personality Inventory.* Mimeographed materials, The Langley Porter Clinic.

Marengo, J.T., & Harrow, M. (1987). Schizophrenic thought disorder at follow-up: A persistent or episodic course? *Archives of General Psychiatry, 44*, 651–659.

Millon, T. (1987). *Millon Clinical Multiaxial Inventory-II* (2nd ed.). Minneapolis, MN: National Computer Systems.

Quinlan, D.M., Harrow, M., Tucker, G., & Carlson, K. (1972). Varieties of "disordered" thinking on the Rorschach: Findings in schizophrenic and non-schizophrenic patients. *Journal of Abnormal Psychology, 79*(1), 47–53.

Rust, J. (1987). The Rust Inventory of Schizoid Cognitions (RISC): A psychometric measure of psychoticism in the normal population. *British Journal of Clinical Psychology, 26*, 151–152.

Rust, J. (1988). The Rust Inventory of Schizotypal Cognitions (RISC). *Schizophrenia Bulletin, 14*(2), 317–322.

Rust, J. (1989). *The Rust Inventory of Schizotypal Cognitions.* San Antonio, TX: Psychological Corporation.

Rust, J., & Chiu, H. (1988). Schizotypal estimators in adolescence: The concurrent validation of the RISC. *Social Behavior and Personality, 16*(1), 25–31.

Rust, J., Moncada, A., & Lepage, B. (1988). Personality dimensions through schizophrenia borderline. *British Journal of Medical Psychology, 61*, 163–166.

Strauss, J.S. (1969). Hallucinations and delusions as points on continua function: Rating scale evidence. *Archives of General Psychiatry, 21*, 581–586.

Whitaker, L.C. (1980). *Objective measurement of schizophrenic thinking: A practical and theoretical guide to the Whitaker Index of Schizophrenic Thinking.* Los Angeles: Western Psychological Services.

Whitaker, L.C. (1992). *Diagnosis of schizophrenia: Sense and nonsense.* New York: Plenum.

**Ellis D. Evans, Ed.D.**
*Professor and Chair of Educational Psychology, University of Washington, Seattle, Washington.*

# SCALE: SCALES OF CREATIVITY AND LEARNING ENVIRONMENT

*Steven W. Slosson. East Aurora, New York: Slosson Educational Publications, Inc.*

## Introduction

SCALE: Scales of Creativity and Learning Environment (Slosson, 1986) consists of a pair of descriptive rating scales formulated to sensitize educators to the characteristics and needs of gifted individuals, and to assist school personnel in recognizing salient attributes of creative, divergent thinkers. Age ranges or grade levels of the target population of gifted thinkers for which SCALE is intended are unspecified, as are the developmental history of the instrument and identifying information about the author.

The SCALE is packaged in kit form, containing a manual and two separate, but similar, rating scales—the Scale of Gifted Students and the Scale of Divergent/Convergent Thinking. The 20-page manual contains brief instructions for administering each separate scale by an evaluator who is positioned to observe student behavior over an extended period of time. This manual includes directions for scoring each scale and converting raw scores to "ordinal range scores" from 1 to 100, a brief section about differences between divergent and convergent thinking and stimulating a creative environment, a collection of techniques or projects for teachers interested in cultivating a creative learning environment, and a bibliography. Commentary about the features of the manual is reserved for later sections in this review.

Although the Scale of Gifted Students and the Scale of Divergent/Convergent Thinking are similar in format and scoring, their content differences warrant separate introductions. First, the Scale of Gifted Students is formatted on both sides of a two-page, 8½" × 11", folder-type document for use in guiding a rater's evaluations of an individual student. Page 1 (face sheet) provides space for student identifying information (name, address, school, sex, grade, and age), rater's name and date of rating, scoring results (including a profile of scale ratings), and a chart for converting raw scores into ordinal range scores from 1 to 100. When completed by an examiner, page 1 provides a detailed summary of ratings for the individual student concerned. Pages 2, 3, and 4 of the Scale of Gifted Students provide the scoring key and directions for 105 items distributed unequally across seven titled subscales: Cognitive area (19 items), Comprehension (15 items), Language (11 items), Affective Area (14 items), Behavioral Area (13 items), Problem Solving (21 items), and Hobbies and Play (12 items). All items are scaled for rating in a 5-point, Likert-type format, with a range from superior (5) and above average (4), through neutral (3), to below average (2) and critical impediment (1). This scaling is intended to guide the rater's judgment about how a specific characteristic influences the student's creativity. Items for each of the seven subscales are arranged in vertical order on the rating protocol pages, with the 5-point scaling guide reproduced horizontally for each subscale (item cluster) across pages 2, 3, and 4 of the protocol. Each specific item rating from each subscale is accomplished by circling the chosen number placed along the aforementioned 5-point scale.

The format for the Scale of Divergent/Convergent Thinking is identical to its partner scale in every way except for item content and meanings for the 5-point rating scale values. As for content, this second scale has 65 items grouped into six subscales or item clusters: Knowledge (9 items), Ability (9 items), Creativity (11 items), Divergence (15 items), Synthesis (12 items), and Evaluation (9 items). Scaling is ordered to guide a rater's judgment of the degree of influence of each item (personal attribute) on the student's *divergence* (Strong = 5, Mild = 4), through *neutral* (3), to the student's *convergence* (2 = Mild, 1 = Strong). Consequently, divergent thought is assigned higher scale values.

To summarize, both components of the SCALE share common properties in terms of layout, scaling and scoring, and provision for charting their respective subscale scores to portray a profile of scale results for the individual student. This measure is designed for easy administration by capable teachers or other evaluators, preferably in the context of a rapport established between rater and student over a sufficient period of time to enable confident rating. Slosson recommends that a minimum of 30 days of observation should precede administration but states a preference for the end of a school term or school year, by which time teachers will have come to know their students well enough for a valid evaluation.

**Practical Applications/Uses**

The SCALE was constructed to facilitate recognition or identification of attributes of gifted or exceptionally talented individuals, and to distinguish attributes of the divergent (or convergent) thinker in educational settings. No further uses are stated explicitly in the SCALE manual. It follows that beyond this general information-gathering function, any specific applications would be discretionary and exploratory. Potential SCALE users might be advised to envision such exploratory uses—including screening for program placements, research on learning environments, and educating for creativity—with a most critical eye.

Whether one considers using SCALE components simultaneously or separately and independently, any use will be encumbered by conspicuous shortcomings in the manual. For example, measurement validity and reliability are not addressed, and explicit decision guidelines for selecting target populations for rating are absent. Without such basic information, a potential SCALE user might assume (with risk) that the instrument is equally well suited for use with children and youths from preschool through college age who give indication of creative potential in any kind of educational setting. User cautions are accentuated by the fact that SCALE items are generally highly inferential by nature and are phrased cryptically to capture a wide range of the personal characteristics, attributes, or behavioral tendencies of individual students. No conditions of rater training are advised by Slosson beyond the aforementioned recommendation that a rater should be sufficiently familiar with the student of interest.

In contrast, SCALE scoring directions and procedures are provided in ample detail to guide a potential user toward summative profile ratings of a person. These directions and procedures are identical for both the Scale of Gifted Students and the Scale of Divergent/Convergent Thinking. For each component, scoring is hand-done in a prescribed sequence. First, each item within each subscale is scored by circling a number, from 5 to 1, that corresponds to the rater's judgment about the degree to which a student shows an attribute, as compared to other students of the same age. This comparative scoring feature presumes a sufficient wealth of rater experience with students of a given age to establish a reliable normative frame of reference. Again, it is important to emphasize that scores for each item are evaluated serially on the common 5-point, Likert-type scale in terms of the extent of influence an attribute might have on an individual's giftedness or divergent/convergent thought, depending on which of the two SCALE components are being used.

The second step in SCALE scoring requires the examiner to tally the number of entries in each column of circled scores, from 5 to 1, for each subscale on either the Scale of Gifted Students or the Scale of Divergent/Convergent Thought. The resulting sum for each column is weighted by multiplying that sum by the column number designation. This result is a weight score for each column numbered 5 to 1. In turn, the five weighted scores are summed to provide a *total raw score* for each of the subscales that define the two SCALE components. Thus, a fully rated individual will receive seven raw scores for the Scale of Gifted Students and/or six raw scores for the Scale of Divergent/Convergent Thinking. Each raw score is then recorded in a small box created for that purpose, which is printed adjacent to its applicable subscale on the rating protocol.

It is important here to emphasize that Slosson's rating and scoring procedure compensates for unobserved or unknown attributes. Any such items so judged are not factored into the raw scores. Slosson warns that an "overabundance of unknown/unobserved characteristics will invalidate screening score statistics" (1986, p. 4). Because the term *overabundance* is not operationally defined, a potential user will need somehow to adjudicate this matter.

The third and final major step in scoring involves converting raw scores to ordinal range scores. This procedure calls for each raw score to be recorded in a horizontal row at the bottom of page 1 of the rating protocol. This row cuts across the bottom of the subscale score columns in which raw score values are also marked. These columns are formed as individual graphs that encompass nearly the full range of possible raw scores, presented in descending order. A scorer is guided to mark individual subscale raw score values on each column (graph) for the purpose of deriving an overall profile of a student's ratings. This is accomplished by using a reference scale of "ordinal range scores" printed in vertical form on both sides of the graphed column (i.e., the right and left margins of page 1). For both SCALE components, the scorer uses a ruler to line up the raw score entry in each subscale graph with its corresponding ordinal range score on the same horizontal line. Once each ordinal range score is located, it is recorded in a small, segmented, rectangular box above the individual raw score columns (subscale graphs) designed to accommodate these subscale results. When completed, the box of ordinal range scores constitutes an individual student's profile of scale results.

It should be noted that this score conversion process differs slightly for each SCALE component in terms of the ordinal range score gauge. For the Scale of Gifted Students, the reference gauge accommodates the score range of 0 to 100. Once the seven ordinal scores for this SCALE component are determined by using the ruler alignment procedure just described, these scores are summed and then divided by 7 to determine the average ordinal score. This mean score is then recorded in a space for this purpose in the upper right corner of page 1 of the score sheet, an act that completes the scoring.

In contrast, the ordinal range score reference gauge for the Scale of Divergent/Convergent Thinking differs in that it embraces a "range of divergence" in descending range of order from 100 to 0 (neutral point) and a "range of convergence" from 0 to 100 in ascending order on the same vertical gauge. Use of this gauge, again by way of ruler alignment of column raw scores to locate ordinal range scores, provides a profile description of the individual student. This profile is defined in terms of divergence *or* convergence scores for each of the six subscales. Those scores are recorded separately in small rectangular boxes reserved for this purpose in a space below the identifying information section on the protocol face sheet. Because the ordinal range scores derive from a divergence-convergence continuum rather than a standard linear scale, no average score is calculated.

Time estimates for administering and scoring either SCALE component are not provided in the SCALE manual. Moreover, score interpretation guidelines for these components are undifferentiated. Score interpretation directives are limited to three main points. One point is a disclaimer about the usefulness of general norms for the SCALE on the grounds that norms will "fluctuate" according to the rater's use of the provision for unknown or unobserved item ratings. A second point for score interpretation is the argument that average SCALE scores will "vary considerably" according to context variables such as institution type and locale and a rater's level of experience and training. The third point for interpretation appears as a recommendation for teachers to develop their own local norms. In the absence of such norms, a potential SCALE user is left to infer that mean ordinal range scores for the Scale of Gifted Students and range of divergence/convergence scores for the Scale of Divergent/Convergent Thinking serve a function similar to percentile norms. Yet, these ordinal range scores clearly are not grounded in a norming population. To compound this score interpretation ambiguity, no explanation is provided in the manual about how the ordinal range score distributions (gauges) were derived or formulated in relation to SCALE raw score distributions. Short of efforts to establish local norms, a potential SCALE user must proceed with score interpretations on the perilous assumption that raw-score, ordinal-range score interpretations are equivalent across different age, grade, ability, and socioeconomic group configurations.

**Technical Aspects**

The Slosson SCALE manual provides no information about measurement reliability or validity. Potential users who are concerned about these fundamental technical qualities are therefore challenged by a leap of faith. Otherwise, users must be both willing and able to seek their own technical evidence. Standard reliability issues, including the qualities of internal consistency, stability, and interrater congruence, applicable to rating scales in general are no less applicable to the SCALE. Relatively speaking, however, these reliability issues seem less serious for local utilization than are issues of validity. That is, resourceful users can achieve their own reliability estimates if they determine that the SCALE offers advantages over competing measures for their particular research or evaluation purposes.

Validity issues are more serious for several reasons. Aside from measurement theory concerned with the interrelationships of validity and reliability, construct validity for the SCALE is the foremost issue: How confident can a user be about the degree to which SCALE scores permit inferences about the underlying traits of giftedness and divergent thinking ability? This question cannot be answered directly from the SCALE manual, nor can those about the discriminant or concurrent validity of SCALE components and their subscales. Finally, there are no indications that factor or cluster analytic work underlies the subscale construction or that any field-test research has taken place to explore predictive validity.

Considering these shortcomings, a potential SCALE user must rely mainly on two remote cues from the manual that could pertain to validity. The first cue appears early in the manual where Slosson cites Gallager (1979), Guilford (1967), and Torrance (1969) for agreement that the "creative child is generally a divergent thinker" (Slosson, 1986, p. 1), and follows with a claim that both SCALE components "rely on Bloom's theories of taxonomy and his realization that learning takes place at varying levels of cognitive thinking" (p. 1). The second cue to validity appears two pages later where Slosson writes that the Scale of Divergent/Convergent Thinking "consists of a list compiled from various sources" (p. 3). These sources remain unidentified, although it seems reasonable to assume that they reside among those listed in the manual bibliography. This bibliography reveals 42 references dated from 1925 to 1984, approximately 15% of which are reports of original research from juried journals. Of the two SCALE components, the Scale of Divergent/Convergent Thinking seems somewhat more clearly linked to established work on creativity, divergent thinking, and hypothetical structures of intelligence (Guilford, 1967), as an inspection of item content suggests. If so, some degree of face validity for this SCALE component might be acknowledged. Origins of subscales and their items for the Scale of Gifted Students are comparatively more obscure. These origins reside in a liberal interpretation of the *Taxonomy of Educational Objectives: Cognitive Domain* (Bloom, Englehart, Furst, Hill, & Krathwohl, 1956) and are augmented by hypotheses about children's language, affect, problem solving, and hobbies and play—the bases for which are not made explicit.

## Critique

From information presented in the SCALE manual, it is apparent that its two components, the Scale of Gifted Students and the Scale of Divergent/Convergent Thinking, are untested, unvalidated measures of unknown reliability. Taken together, these two components are predicated upon the value premise that educators should be more sensitive to characteristics of gifted and divergent thinkers and take steps to nurture these characteristics. Regarding measurement, the fundamental assumption for the SCALE is that the presence of some degree and combination of attributes shown by students and capably rated by teachers indicates at least a potential for giftedness and creative achievement. As implied in the preceding section on technical aspects, considerable mystery enshrouds SCALE, a mystery defined by four major questions: (a) What are the author's qualifications for developing this measure? (b) What is the utility of this measure apart from alerting educators to the human characteristics represented by SCALE items? (c) Why were technical qualities of reliability and validity unexplored prior to SCALE publication for commercial distribution or, if they were explored, why were the results of this exploration excluded from the manual? (d) How and why does material of this genre reach publication short of meeting acceptable standards of scholarship?

The first three questions, unanswerable from the SCALE manual, address limitations that are highlighted in previous sections of the present review. The fourth question, concerning the SCALE's publication, requires justification, in fairness to the author, and, ultimately, speculation about commercial test markets and the nature of consumer psychology beyond the scope of this review. The remainder of this critique is therefore limited to the justification aspect of this fourth question and is based on this reviewer's claim that the SCALE fails to meet minimum professional standards for educational and psychological measurement (American Educational Research Association, American Psychological Association, & National Council on Measurement in Education, 1985).

First, Slosson provides no clarification of who or by what means SCALE items were created in the initial sense. Perhaps it can be assumed that items were created by Slosson himself, exercising his selective judgment about information from a potpourri of books, articles, and companion measures listed in the SCALE manual. Particularly puzzling are subscale identities for each of the two SCALE components. Recall that both components embrace subscales showing no evidence of factorial independence or subscale intercorrelation and weak evidence (at best) of grounding in conceptual domains. These inadequacies prompt an inference that SCALE subscales are the result of unilateral and largely arbitrary work from sources about creativity and taxonomies of educational objectives that are themselves vulnerable to legitimate criticism about validity (Travers, 1980; Weisberg, 1986).

Second, validity concerns aside, documentation or substantiation of content is weak throughout the entire SCALE manual. This weakness occurs at two levels. One level is the pervasive absence of linkage from specific points in the SCALE text to sources listed in the bibliography. In fact, the only direct citations in the entire manual are in an introductory paragraph (p. 1) and a footnote (p. 7). This is not to demean the bibliographic references themselves, for many involve work by recognized authorities in the field of giftedness (e.g., Khatena, 1982; Renzulli, 1973; Torrance, 1969). If a SCALE revision is forthcoming, however, it would behoove the author to articulate his source material more directly, without which this measure provides only a façade of legitimacy. It would also be important to include references to independent work about SCALE use in the school environment.

The second level of weakness in SCALE content documentation concerns the supplemental material that Slosson proffers to classroom teachers. Well over one half of the SCALE manual concerns advice, suggestions, and projects for teachers interested in arranging an open learning environment, creating divergent test questions, and seeking information via self-assessment and student feedback about accommodating students' learning styles, enhancing their self-image, and generally facilitating their creative expression. By implication, these themes underscore an educational philosophy consistent with the humanistic tradition in psychology and education (Hamachek, 1987). Although the classroom projects recommended may be exemplary, no evidence is presented in the manual as to their efficacy. A conservative view would consider each project as only a hypothesis for experiment-minded teachers to test for outcomes in relation to project objectives.

A final point of criticism concerns an unusual number of distracting misspellings, punctuation errors, and syntax problems in the SCALE manual text, which apparently escaped the proofreading eyes of those responsible for the SCALE's preparation. To illustrate, consider one particularly puzzling sentence that is intended to explain the brainstorming process: "This process is central to gifted education to transcending the normal boundries [*sic*] of what is currently thought by modern man" (Slosson, 1986, p. 5).

To date, the SCALE story clearly is incomplete. This measure may survive to contribute to educational research and practice in useful ways, but potential users are advised to proceed cautiously and at their own risk. SCALE seems to be in need of serious pilot research before any degree of confidence can be expressed in this measure. Such pilot research would begin with standard questions about reliability and validity and could be followed by any number of studies about individual differences and classroom practice. In the absence of such work, the SCALE is best considered on its own merits as a rating procedure focused on student attributes or characteristics that are frequently mentioned in discourse about giftedness and creativity. Accordingly, the SCALE may show some utility as a supplement to teacher evaluations concerned with how students compare with one another on the target characteristics.

## References

American Educational Research Association, American Psychological Association, & National Council on Measurement in Education. (1985). *Standards for educational and psychological testing*. Washington, DC: American Psychological Association.

Bloom, B.S., Englehart, M.D., Furst, E.J., Hill, W.H., & Krathwohl, D.R. (1956). *Taxonomy of educational objectives: Handbook I. Cognitive domain*. New York: David McKay.

Gallagher, J.J. (1979). *Teaching the gifted child* (2nd ed.). Boston: Allyn & Bacon.

Guilford, J.P. (1967). *The nature of human intelligence*. New York: McGraw-Hill.

Hamachek, D.E. (1987). Humanistic psychology: Theory, postulates, implications for educational processes. In J.A. Glover & R.R. Ronning (Eds.), *Historical foundations of educational psychology* (pp. 159–182) New York: Plenum.

Khatena, J. (1982). *Educational psychology of the gifted*. New York: Wiley.

Renzulli, J.S. (1973). *New directions in creativity*. New York: Harper & Row.

Slosson, S.W. (1986). *SCALE: Scales of Creativity and Learning Environment*. East Aurora, NY: Slosson Educational Publications.

Torrance, E.P. (1969). *Creativity.* Belmont, CA: Dimensions.

Travers, R.M.W. (1980). Taxonomies of educational objectives and theories of classification. *Educational Evaluation and Policy Analysis,* 2(2), 5–23.

Weisberg, R.W. (1986). *Creativity: Genius and other myths.* New York: Freeman.

**Nancy A. Busch-Rossnagel, Ph.D.**
*Associate Professor of Psychology, Fordham University, Bronx, New York.*

# THE SCHEDULE OF GROWING SKILLS

*Martin Bellman and John Cash. Windsor, Berkshire, England: NFER-Nelson Publishing Company Ltd.*

## Introduction

The Schedule of Growing Skills is a developmental screening procedure designed to check that children ages 0 to 5 years are developing normally for their age, as measured against prescribed criteria. The Schedule was developed in Britain as part of a health surveillance project and was derived, in part, from the STYCAR sequences (Sheridan, 1976). The Schedule consists of 180 items hierarchically organized within 23 skill sets. The skill sets cover nine skill areas: passive posture (ages 0 to 6 months), active posture (ages 0 to 12 months), locomotor (ages 9 to 60 months), manipulative, visual, hearing and language, speech and language, interactive social, and self-care social (6 to 60 months).

The background of the test authors lies in community health: Dr. Martin Bellman is Consultant Community Pediatrician, Bloomsbury Health Authority, and Honorary Clinical Senior Lecturer at the Department of Pediatrics, University College London. Dr. John Cash is Senior Lecturer in Community Pediatrics and Child Health at the Institute of Child Health, University of Birmingham.

The Schedule was originally a research tool for the National Child Encephalopathy Study (NCES), a research project investigating the incidence and severity of the alleged neurological reactions to immunization against whooping cough. The design of the NCES required a developmental assessment of children 0 to 3 years that met the following requirements: broad clinical scope, proven validity, reproducibility, simplicity, brevity, minimum equipment, quantification, and standardization on British children. Two tests, the Griffiths Mental Development Scales (Griffiths, 1967) and the Sheridan Developmental Sequences (published as the STYCAR sequences, Sheridan, 1976), were standardized on British children and had sufficient scope to be considered for this assessment. The Griffiths, however, was too lengthy, required special equipment, and needed specially trained personnel for its administration. Thus, the NCES researchers looked at the STYCAR sequences. However, if all the items from the STYCAR sequences were administered, it would be as lengthy as the Griffiths. Therefore, it was decided to abstract cardinal items from the STYCAR sequences (to retain the validity) for the NCES.

Using the "age of performance" specified by Sheridan, developmental ages for each of the nine skill areas were obtained to allow for quantification of performance. The NCES schedule thus produced (Bellman et al., 1985) was used over 3-year period in the 1970s to assess approximately 500 children. A modification of the NCES schedule was used for a developmental surveillance program in a district health authority, which resulted in some minor modifications. To make the schedule applicable to more health districts, items to cover the 3- to 5-year level were added to the NCES schedule. The 3- to 5-year-old items were selected primarily from the STYCAR sequences. After the addition of the 3- to 5-year-old items, the authors felt that the NCES research tool had become a clinical instrument, and this modification was renamed the Schedule of Growing Skills.

The Schedule consists of the 180 items arranged in developmental sequence on the Child Record, the Profile (a visual summary of the child's performance), the set of materials (e.g., pegs, a brush, a doll, a picture book), and the User's Handbook, all of which are contained in a lightweight carrying case. The *Schedule of Growing Skills in Practice* (Bellman & Cash, 1987a) is available separately and provides test development history, psychometric information, training information, and more details about the Schedule. Users without extensive knowledge of the STYCAR scales will want to consult this book when first mastering administration of the Schedule.

### Practical Applications/Uses

The goal of the authors of the Schedule is to provide a standard for developmental screening for various professional groups and for different health authorities within Great Britain. It is designed to be used, along with growth records, hearing and vision screening, immunization, continuing care of the disabled, prompt treatment of illness, advice to parents, and health education as part of a child health surveillance program. Furthermore, developmental screening is seen as the first stage in the process of child health care and must be followed by assessment (full diagnostic assessment by specialists) and management (the provision of appropriate treatment or support) for the system to be effective. The Schedule also may be used to document results of interventions.

The Schedule was designed for use by a wide range of professionals (e.g., general practitioners, clinical medical officers, and health visitors). Regardless of professional background, the authors suggest that a 1-week course in health surveillance training be given to users of the Schedule. This course should cover not only the administration and interpretation of the developmental screening schedule but also allow updates on immunizations, health education, sensory testing, emotional problems, relationships with other service agencies, and so forth.

The authors designed the Schedule to allow for rapid testing (about 15 minutes) in the home, and the kit is very portable. The information about the items in the Child Record form is very limited; further elaboration on a few items is provided in the User's Handbook. However, all the materials presuppose knowledge of the STYCAR sequences or introduction in a training course. The examiner goes through each skill area appropriate to the child's age (e.g., active postural skills is only for ages 0 to 12 months). Testing involves identifying the most advanced item that the child can perform within each skill set, and it can begin at any level (e.g., the child's expected level of performance) to minimize testing time. The order of administration of the skill sets is likewise flexible.

Scoring of individual items is accomplished through a simple check for those items passed; a "Q" is entered for items the child passes but with questionable performance. A total score for each skill area is the sum of the scores of the highest items achieved within each skill set. These raw scores are transferred to the Profile for conversion into developmental ages. The Profile consists of a chart with the nine skill areas heading the columns and the age intervals covered by the Schedule as the rows. The age intervals on the Profile are 0, 1, 3, 6, 7, 9, 12, 15, 18, 24, 30, 36, 48, and 60 months. The child's chronological age is indicated by a dark horizontal line at the appropriate age level. The examiner darkens the block that corresponds to the child's raw score for each skill area, and the developmental age is obtained by simply reading across to the row label.

For interpretation, a significant delay is one where the developmental age obtained falls more than 1 age interval below the child's chronological age. However, the authors do not provide cutoffs for referral, preferring instead to allow for clinical judgment. They do suggest that a significant delay (developmental age more that 1 age interval below CA) is a reason to consider referral. The case example provided by the authors also suggests that moderate delays (within 1 age interval) in several areas is also reason to consider referral.

**Technical Aspects**

Bellman and Cash (1987b) used a sample of 20 to establish interobserver reliability for the 0 to 3 age group. The correlations between the two observers were above .90 for each of the four general areas covered by the Schedule (posture and large movement, vision and fine movements, hearing and speech, and social behavior and play). In a sample of 20 3- to 5-year-olds, the correlations between the two observers' scores for four areas (manipulation, vision, hearing, and speech) were high (above .85), but the areas of gross movements ($r$ = .58), interactive ($r$ = .79), and self-care social ($r$ = .47) were lower.

The validity of the Schedule rests in great part on the validity of the STYCAR sequences, and these in the form of the NCES tool were compared with the Griffiths scales. On a theoretical comparison, the STYCAR ages at which items were expected to be performed by "normal" children were higher than the Griffiths. This may represent cohort effects from differing standardization times or the wide range of performance regarded as normal. However, 60% of the items compared were within 1 month in developmental age.

In a clinical comparison of the NCES schedule and the Griffiths scales, 25 children received both assessments. The posture and large movements section of the Schedule were compared with the Griffiths's locomotor scale, the vision and fine movements with eye-hand coordination, hearing and speech with hearing and speech, and social behavior and play with personal-social and performance. The correlations between the two scores were high (above .90). Forty-five children ages 3 to 5 were administered the Schedule of Growing Skills and the Griffiths scales to check the validity of this portion of the test. These correlations are lower for three of the four comparisons: vision and fine movements (Schedule) and eye-hand coordination and performance (Griffiths), $r$ = .52; hearing and speech ($r$ = .81); and interactive and self-care social behavior (Schedule) and personal-social (Griffiths), $r$ = .68.

The content validity of the Schedule continues to be analyzed. Since the studies reported above, certain tests that experienced users of the STYCAR sequences felt had the least association with the developmental level at a particular age have been omitted from the Schedule. The authors request further feedback on the use of the Schedule, indicating that modifications are appropriate given the dynamic nature of developmental screening.

## Critique

In designing the Schedule of Growing Skills, Bellman and Cash have certainly met their goal of providing a practical and portable method of developmental screening. Certain features of the Schedule are designed to fit easily into a health care system. For example, the Profile has three (carbonless) copies and the top sheet can be used as a referral or report, a wonderful time-saver. However, for the U.S. user, the Schedule is not up to the basic standards set out for psychological testing. For example, details about the samples of the validity and reliability studies are not provided. Likewise, the Schedule relies on developmental ages for scoring, a practice discouraged here (Salvia & Ysseldyke, 1988). From their discussion of developmental screening, it is clear that Bellman and Cash developed the test from a medical model, and they probably would not consider it a psychological test. However, for U.S. users, tests standardized on U.S. children with more detailed psychometric information are available (e.g., the Early Screening Inventory; Meisels & Wiske, 1988), and their use is recommended here.

## References

Bellman, M.H., & Cash, J. (1987a). *The Schedule of Growing Skills in practice.* Windsor, England: NFER-Nelson.

Bellman, M.H., & Cash, J. (1987b). *The Schedule of Growing Skills: User's handbook.* Windsor, England: NFER-Nelson.

Bellman, M.H., Rawson, N.S.B., Wadsworth, J., Ross, E.M., Camerson, S., & Miller, D.L. (1985). A developmental test based on the STYCAR sequences used in the National Childhood Encephalopathy Study. *Child: Care, Health and Development, 11,* 309–323.

Griffiths, R. (1967). *Griffiths Mental Development Scales for testing babies and young children from birth to eight years of age.* High Wycombe, England: Test Agency.

Meisels, S.J., & Wiske, M.S. (1988). *Early Screening Inventory.* New York: Teachers College Press.

Salvia, J., & Ysseldyke, J.E. (1988). *Assessment in special and remedial education* (4th ed.). Boston: Houghton Mifflin.

Sheridan, M.D. (1976). *Children's developmental progress from birth to five years: The STYCAR sequences* (4th ed.). Windsor, England: NFER-Nelson.

**Selma Hughes, Ph.D.**
*Professor of Psychology and Special Education, East Texas State University, Commerce, Texas.*

# SCREENING CHILDREN FOR RELATED EARLY EDUCATIONAL NEEDS

*Wayne P. Hresko, D. Kim Reid, Donald D. Hammill, Herbert P. Ginsburg, and Arthur J. Baroody. Austin, Texas: PRO-ED, Inc.*

## Introduction

Screening Children for Related Early Educational Needs (SCREEN) is an individually administered test of educational achievement designed to assess early academic ability in children ages 3 through 7 years. It should not be confused with SCREEN (the Senf-Comrey Ratings of Extra Educational Needs), which is a group-administered, machine-scored test of general readiness for school instruction also published in 1988.

The SCREEN was developed in 1988 from four existing tests: the Test of Early Language Development (TELD; Hresko, Reid, & Hammill, 1981); the Test of Early Written Language (TEWL; Hresko, 1988); Test of Early Reading Ability (TERA; Reid, Hresko, & Hammill, 1981) and the Test of Early Mathematics Ability (TEMA; Ginsburg & Baroody, 1983). The examiner's manual points out that the most discriminating items from each of these tests were selected for inclusion in the SCREEN, which was developed to identify children whose achievement in beginning reading, writing, and arithmetic is significantly below that of their peers. (See *Test Critiques: Vol. V* for reviews of the TELD and the TERA.)

The authors of this test are active researchers in the field of learning disabilities, concerned with the early recognition of children with learning problems and skilled in test construction. The senior author, Wayne P. Hresko, is currently at the University of North Texas and well known as coauthor of a standard text embodying a cognitive approach to learning disabilities with the second author D. Kim Reid. Dr. Reid was for many years at the University of Texas at Dallas and has specialized in the study of young children with problems in language development. Donald Hammill, the third author, is president of PRO-ED, Inc. in Austin and distinguished author of many widely used textbooks and tests in language and learning. Herbert Ginsburg and Arthur Baroody have published in the area of mathematics learning and are associated with the University of Rochester.

The SCREEN kit consists of the Examiner's Manual, Picture Book, Student Workbook and Profile/Record Form contained in a small practical cardboard box. The objects needed for the test are not included in the kit, but each test item clearly indicates the materials needed and the examiner is reminded to have all items assembled before starting testing. A comprehensive set of basic testing procedures outlined in the manual would be helpful even for experienced test practitioners.

The Examiner's Manual contains the administration and scoring procedures, an overview of early academic screening, technical data on the construction of the test, and interpretive information. The instructions to be read to the student are given in uppercase letters so that they are easy to read (prompts are provided when needed). The student response is noted on the Profile/Record Form. When a response other than an oral one is required, the response is made in the Student Workbook.

Oral language is assessed by 18 items that measure knowledge of use of syntax, understanding of semantics, and ability to use language. The items are written in a format that is appealing to young children, (e.g., "Billy was tired. He hadn't taken a nap. What do you think he said to his mother?"). The language items are interspersed with the reading, writing, and mathematics items so that the nature of the task varies. This makes the testing more motivating in this reviewer's opinion. There is a naturalness about the items that is often lacking in many tests. The ordering of the items was based on a preliminary item analysis.

The reading component consists of 18 items that assess concepts about print, such as "Here is a story. Show me where it starts." Knowledge of the alphabet is assessed by items such as "What letter is this? Tell me its name." There are also a number of excellent questions on construction of meaning involving retelling a story and completing cloze items.

Sixteen items assess the mechanics of writing and the ideational aspects of written expression. Constructs of transcription are assessed by tasks such as copying from a model. Convention items include questions such as "What does a question mark tell you?" Knowledge of letter sequences and spelling is assessed, as is knowledge of creative expression. The writing test items are not as imaginatively worded as the reading and oral language items (e.g., "Write a sentence for each of these words"). The criteria for scoring do not require correct spelling or correct punctuation, so that a more appealing task would be, for example, "Will you write a little story for me and use all of these words as well as any words you want to use?"

Early mathematics achievement is tested with 18 items. These require understanding of quantitative concepts (e.g., "Point to the side that has more dots"; "Count out loud for me"). The mathematics items assess both informal concepts, which the child acquires without formal teaching, and formal concepts, which depend on having been taught. Rote counting, use of the numbers line, and mental calculations are considered examples of informal aspects of mathematics. Number conventions, basic number facts, place value, and written calculations are considered formal aspects of mathematics ability. It is questionable that children are aware of the use of a number line without being formally taught. Many of the items require more rote learning than conceptual knowledge, even among the formal items. There is little assessment of the spatial and topological relationships on which mathematical understanding depends.

The items in the test overall are scored as either "correct" or "incorrect," making scoring relatively simple. An entry point is given for each age, 3 through 7 (e.g., an age 5 entry point is item 30), which shortens the testing time. Testing is continued until six consecutive items are missed, which establishes a ceiling. The basal consists of six consecutive correct items and full credit is given for items not attempted below the basal.

The SCREEN yields three types of score: raw scores, percentile ranks, and standard scores. The standard scores have a mean of 100 and standard deviation of 15 (which facilitates comparison with the widely used individual test of intelligence [potential], the Wechsler Preschool and Primary Scales of Intelligence). The standard scores are shown in the form of a quotient for each of the four areas assessed (e.g., Language Quotient [LQ], Reading Quotient [RQ]) and a SCREEN Early Achievement Quotient (SEAQ), which is a composite of the four component quotients.

The Profile/Record Form provides space for background data, other test results, child characteristics, examiner observations, interpretations, and recommendations. The form is very usable yet at the same time quite comprehensive. A chart for showing test results in graphic format is also provided, which is helpful when explaining the results to parents, for example.

An optional scoring system known as the SCREEN PRO-SCORE System is described by Hresko and Schlieve (1988). PRO-SCORE is a computerized program available for Apple and IBM computers that generates a four-page report from the raw scores and background information fed into the computer. The program converts the raw scores to standardized scores and percentile ranks, and it provides an interpretive analysis of the four quotients and overall composite.

**Practical Applications/Uses**

There is considerable interest at the present time in the identification of high-risk children, both those at environmental risk (e.g., disadvantaged children) and those at established risk with specific disabilities (e.g., Down's syndrome). The most substantial body of efficacy literature is that on the effects of early intervention with children at environmental risk (Hanson & Lynch, 1989). Several major reviews have concluded that early intervention is effective for this group of children (e.g., Lazar & Darlington, 1982).

The SCREEN is of practical use in identifying students at high risk for failure by screening out those who fall significantly below their peers in the academic areas of language, reading, writing, and arithmetic. The SCREEN also may be used to identify specific strengths and weaknesses in students as a preliminary to providing intervention. This measure may be helpful to program planners in evaluating the effectiveness of intervention, as it may be used to document progress in specific areas as a consequence of early intervention.

The manual also points out that the test is useful in research studies where there has been a lack of academically related tests. Readiness may be viewed from a process orientation or a skill orientation (Salvia & Ysseldyke, 1989). In the former, readiness is seen as the underlying processes believed to be necessary for the acquisition of skills and knowledge. In the latter, readiness is viewed as the specific skills and knowledge necessary for beginning instruction. The SCREEN embodies a skill orientation to readiness and, as such, should be a better predictor of academic achievement than more generalized or global measures.

The performances of preschoolers are so variable that relatively little long-term prediction is possible from short, quickly administered readiness tests unless the test has good content mastery (Salvia & Ysseldyke, 1989). It would seem that the

SCREEN does embody much of the newer research on the importance of oral language and knowledge of concepts about print to beginning reading. The skills assessed are directly related to reading. The closer the predictor measure (readiness test) is to the criterion or predicted measure, the greater the accuracy of the prediction. It would appear that the SCREEN is an accurate predictor of achievement.

The test may be given by anyone who has had some formal training in test administration. As extensive experience is not required for this measure, the SCREEN could be used by classroom teachers, diagnosticians, psychologists, counselors, and any professional with experience in achievement testing. The Examiner's Manual makes reference to the use of the test by regular education teachers, paraprofessionals, aides, and so forth, and points out that in these cases specific instruction and training should be given and the person administering the test should be under direct supervision by someone with the necessary expertise.

The SCREEN can be administered in 15 to 40 minutes (according to the manual), depending on the age and ability of the child. With younger children it is suggested that no more than 10 minutes of testing transpire and then a break is taken. Scoring would take about 10 minutes, which makes this a very efficient test.

The interpretation of SCREEN scores centers on the standard scores and in particular on the SCREEN Early Achievement Quotient (SEAQ). The SEAQ is interpreted similarly to intelligence quotients; for example, the "Average" range is represented as 90–110, 80–89 is "Below Average," and 70–79 is "Poor." Thus a score has to be more than 2 standard deviations below the average to be rated as "Very Poor."

The limitations in interpreting the test are pointed out, and the examiner is urged to rely on clinical judgment and observation. Diagnosis should not be based on test results alone, according to the authors. Nevertheless, the four quotients do provide a basis for making judgments about the child's aptitude in the areas assessed by the test. In addition, qualitative data derived from the testing situation may be included in the write-up. The manual makes specific reference to "testing the limits," which the examiner may choose to do while testing. Examples of probes are provided in the manual (e.g., "How did you decide on this item? Why were the other pictures incorrect?"), which would aid in testing the limits.

**Technical Aspects**

The SCREEN was standardized on a sample of 1,355 children residing in 20 states. The percentages in the sample of sex, residence, race, ethnicity, and geographic region was similar to these percentages nationwide. The data present clear evidence of the sample's representativeness.

According to the manual, reliability for the SCREEN was established by examining error variance associated with content sampling and time sampling. To assess the amount of test error due to content, the internal consistency of the items was investigated using Cronbach's coefficient alpha. Coefficient alphas were computed by age on the whole sample of 1,355 children, for the four components of SCREEN and for the overall quotient. The coefficients ranged from .71 to

.98, with 94% exceeding the .80 level for acceptable reliability established by Anastasi (1976). The small size of the standard error of measurement also supports the test's internal reliability.

To assess the amount of error due to time, the stability of the test was measured using a test-retest model. The size of the group to which the test was administered twice is not stated, but the participants were two groups of older children who varied in age from 6.0 to 7.3. The resulting coefficients for the subtest and composite scores exceed .80, indicating that the SCREEN is stable over time for children of that age group. No doubt the reliability would be much lower if the younger children had been included.

Three types of validity are reported for the SCREEN: content, criterion related, and construct. Content validity was demonstrated through an item analysis to identify the most discriminating items from the four tests that constituted the item pool—TELD, TERA, TEWL, and TEMA. The final items were tested on a sample of 220 children, and the appropriateness of the retained items was substantiated in a second item analysis that was made with all the children in the sample. Validity coefficients of discrimination (which were reported for the TELD and the TERA) were not reported for SCREEN, but median discrimination indexes ranging from 45 to 62 were said to indicate acceptable levels of discrimination and difficulty at all age levels.

The criterion-related validity of the SCREEN was established by correlating the component score of each of the items with the test from which it was derived. The manual reports that all the correlations exceeded .90, which indicates a high level of validity.

Construct validity refers to the psychological constructs inherent in the test. The authors of the SCREEN describe at length the premises on which the test is based and the hypotheses to which the constructs give rise. They tested these hypotheses by logical or empirical means. For example, to support the hypothesis that the SCREEN measures abilities that are affected by cognitive processes, SCREEN scores were correlated with scores obtained on major tests of intelligence such as the Weschler Intelligence Scale for Children–Revised, the Wechsler Preschool and Primary Scales of Intelligence, and so forth. Another measure of construct validity was to ascertain whether the SCREEN scores increased with age and school experience; correlations significant at the .01 level are reported. A final measure of construct validity was provided by showing that the test does differentiate between children who are learning and children who are not.

In summary, the SCREEN manual provides good evidence of validity as discussed by Hammill, Brown, and Bryant (1989).

### Critique

The SCREEN is a relatively new test about which little has been written at present. It is a soundly constructed, individually administered test that should have strong appeal for teachers and clinicians. Though relatively simple to administer, score, and interpret, much thought has been put into the design of the tasks and the wording of the items. The SCREEN is therefore more interesting and may be more motivating to younger students than the usual "readiness" tests.

The SCREEN is more a test of early academic achievement than a measure of global readiness. The test does appear to meet admirably the purpose for which it was designed, namely, the early detection of potential academic problems. It embodies a sound philosophy in relation to early academic screening, and its authors have developed an excellent instrument that researchers could use to investigate the problems and parameters of early learning difficulties.

### References

Anastasi, A. (1976). *Psychological testing* (4th ed.). New York: Macmillan.

Ginsburg, H.P., & Baroody, A.J. (1983). *The Test of Early Mathematics Ability.* Austin, TX: PRO-ED.

Hammill, D., Brown, L., & Bryant, B. (1989). *A consumer's guide to tests in print.* Austin, TX: PRO-ED.

Hanson, M.J., & Lynch, E. (1989). *Early intervention.* Austin, TX: PRO-ED.

Hresko, W.P. (1988). *The Test of Early Written Language.* Austin, TX: PRO-ED.

Hresko, W.P., Reid, D.K., & Hammill, D.D. (1981). *The Test of Early Language Development.* Austin, TX: PRO-ED.

Hresko, W.P., & Schlieve, P.L. (1988). *PRO-SCORE system for the SCREEN* (Apple and IBM versions). Austin, TX: PRO-ED.

Lazar, I., & Darlington, R. (1982). Lasting effects of early intervention: A report from the Consortium for Longitudinal Studies. *Monographs of the Society for Research in Child Development,* 47(Serial No. 195).

Reid, D.K., Hresko, W.P., & Hammill, D.D. (1981). *The Test of Early Reading Ability.* Austin, TX: PRO-ED.

Salvia, J., & Ysseldyke, J. (1989). *Assessment in special and remedial education,* Boston: Houghton Mifflin.

Senf, G., & Comrey, A. (1988). *Senf-Comrey Ratings of Extra Educational Needs.* Novato, CA: Academic Therapy Publications.

Widerstrom, A. (1986a). Test of Early Language Development. In D.J. Keyser & R.C. Sweetland (Eds.), *Test critiques* (Vol. V, pp. 464–469). Austin, TX: PRO-ED.

Widerstrom, A. (1986b). Test of Early Reading Ability. In D.J. Keyser, & R.C. Sweetland (Eds.), *Test critiques* (Vol. V, pp. 470–474). Austin, TX: PRO-ED.

**Mary Ann Rafoth, Ph.D.**
*Associate Professor of Educational Psychology, Indiana University of Pennsylvania, Indiana, Pennsylvania.*

# SCREENING TEST FOR EDUCATIONAL PREREQUISITE SKILLS

*Frances Smith. Los Angeles, California: Western Psychological Services.*

## Introduction

The Screening Test for Educational Prerequisite Skills (STEPS) is designed to provide a quick, psychometrically accurate, and theoretically based screening test for children entering kindergarten. The test includes sections addressing some traditional readiness skills (letter naming and writing, color identification, counting), basic speech and language skills (articulation errors, prepositions, following directions), fine- and gross-motor skills (copying shapes, balancing on one foot), and cognitive development (ability to make classifications, short-term memory for digits).

In addition, the child's attitude toward school is assessed through a series of forced choices in a self-report scale. The examiner also completes brief observational questions covering sensory problems, activity level, and test attitude. A short Home Questionnaire given to parents is optional. These features are similar to most screening tests available. The STEPS, however, regroups these typical items into groups of tasks that are said to be representative of Robert Gagné's theory of learning capabilities or outcomes (Gagné & Driscoll, 1988).

The test author, Frances Smith, Ph.D., apparently began work on the STEPS as a doctoral dissertation and completed the first standardization study at that time. The national standardization study was completed under the direction of Western Psychological Services. Little information is provided in the manual to describe item selection or test development except to note that items relate to school curricula and are linked to Gagné's theory of instruction.

The STEPS is designed to be used as a means of identification of children at risk for difficulties in kindergarten and/or in need of additional psychoeducational evaluation. The test might be given in the spring prior to school entrance, at the time a child registers for school in the fall, or during the first few weeks of kindergarten. Examinees typically will be age 4 or 5, although others planning to enter kindergarten might also be tested. Use of the test in preschool settings for 4-year-old children is not generally recommended.

The STEPS may be administered and scored by a trained paraprofessional or volunteer under the supervision of either a teacher trained in educational assessment or a school psychologist. Because the recording of results is done on a top sheet that automatically transfers the information to a scoring sheet that in turn automatically transfers the information to a teacher and parent report form, test interpretation is fairly automatic and very general. A trained paraprofessional could administer the STEPS, score it, and complete the two report forms within 15 minutes. Testing time should be between 8 to 10 minutes. Although there is no time limit, assessments taking over 12 minutes are judged to indicate lack of examiner familiarity with materials.

The STEPS is indeed brief and scores easily. When examiner judgment is necessary, criteria are described specifically and in behavioral terms. The test author argues that test items measure behaviors that correspond with successful classroom performance. The STEPS tasks are representative of the readiness skills found to be predictive of early school success. However, the STEPS also purports to identify specific *skill* deficits (rather than *knowledge* deficits) that can be remediated through classroom instruction. Given the brevity of the instrument and the generally poor success of prescriptive-diagnostic approaches (see Arter & Jenkins, 1978), this claim merits further investigation.

**Practical Applications/Uses**

Although volunteers and teacher aides may administer the STEPS under supervision, persons not familiar with standardized testing may find the score sheet initially confusing. In addition, because the child's cooperation is vital to the interpretation of the instrument, examiners must be skilled in working with young children while keeping within appropriate test limits. A few task refusals will invalidate the use of several of the key interpretive areas (e.g., intellectual skills and verbal information). Likewise, the presence of a permanent or temporary physical impairment will affect the test's usefulness to such a degree that it has questionable utility with such children.

The STEPS manual and promotional material frequently note the inclusion of a Home Questionnaire as an important asset, as it allows for parental inclusion in the assessment process. The parent questionnaire is, however, optional only and so not an integral part of the assessment. The Home Questionnaire is short (23 descriptive statements), requires simple responses (parent circles "yes" or "no"), and is automatically scored and interpreted (the results are easily included on the teacher and parent report forms). The parent also supplies some demographic and health information. The child's main caregiver should complete the form; no provisions are made for both parents to complete a form or to discriminate between one parent completing the form or both parents completing the form in concert. Response-set problems are somewhat controlled by variation in the direction of positive versus negative responses, although a parent could easily discern how to answer questions in such a way as to present his or her child in a good or bad light. In addition, because parents have to make an all-or-nothing choice on items that would be better answered on a gradient for most children (e.g., "My child is difficult to manage," "My child does not listen well"), there is a tendency to receive a skewed picture. In general, the superficiality and optional nature of the Home Questionnaire makes its utility as part of the STEPS questionable.

The STEPS itself has 14 separate tasks:

1. Gross motor (stand on each foot for 15 seconds);

2. Fine motor (pencil grasp; rated as adequate or poor);
3. Write name (rated on a continuum from 1 "tried but could not copy" to 6 "first and last names with no errors");
4. Copy lowercase word (copies the word *beds*; points deducted for capitalization and reversals);
5. Copy shapes (circle, cross, square, and triangle);
6. Classification (able to classify by color without help, with encouragement, with direct instruction, or unable to);
7. Name classification concept (labels the concept demonstrated in task 5);
8. Color naming (red, yellow, blue, green);
9. Counting (receives points for correctly counting up to 8);
10. Prepositions ("in front," "over," "under," "behind," and "in");
11. Story/articulation errors (child tells a story about a real or imagined pet and examiner rates articulation errors on a scale of 1 to 4; descriptive anchors provided);
12. Following directions (three-step physical directions; child receives up to 5 points for listening, performing each task, and for performance in the correct order);
13. Memory for digits (two trials for sequences of two to five digits); and
14. Self-report pictures (child looks at six sets of pictures and chooses one that is most like him or her; intended to address attitude toward working with others and school entry, and feelings about persistence, self-competency, and self-esteem).

In addition, the examiner makes three observations concerning the presence of any notable sensory problems in the child, the child's activity level, and the child's test attitude.

The test materials are efficient but do not seem durable (an important consideration, as this test might be given to a large number of children over the course of 1 or 2 days). The paperback manual is relatively brief and easy to understand. The test protocols are "autoscore" carbon sheets that are a little awkward to separate easily. They are convenient but expensive. The last sheet on the STEPS protocol rips off so that the examiner can use it for tasks 3, 4, and 5. Along with places for identifying information, there is a place for the child to write his or her name, copy the lowercase word, and copy the shapes. This sheet is flimsy, cluttered, and inappropriate for use with young children. Their performance will likely be impaired by space limitations. Errors made in articulation are to be noted on the back of this sheet. A preschool pencil is provided with the test kit. When screening a large number of children, a box of such sharpened pencils would be advised. Many of the tasks use a set of small "counting bears." These eight bears come in sets of two (blue, yellow, red, and green) and are in a very small drawstring pouch. The bears are indestructible but easily lost because of their size. My pouch ripped after only one administration of the test. The self-report cards come in a cardboard easel that can be reversed to show cards of the correct sex. The easel is also flimsy but turns easily. The pictures are black-and-white line drawings that depict children from different racial groups. The materials fit into a slim cardboard box.

The STEPS protocol contains the actual instructions for administering the test; it is not necessary to refer to the manual after becoming familiar with the instrument. Although the manual is very explicit regarding administration, the use of bold type or italics to indicate actual examiner directions would make quick reference to the manual during administration easier. The general instructions are written in such a way as to be easily understood by novice examiners. Scoring the protocol is automatic, but the examiner must press firmly on the top sheets and erasure is difficult. Understanding the score sheet will take several readings, particularly for paraprofessionals. The appendix contains good examples of pass/fail items for scoring reference.

Once the test is scored, two reports in letter format addressed to the parent and receiving teacher are created automatically. (When scoring categories are circled on the score sheet, the circles show up on the report forms around interpretive descriptions). The teacher report provides a record in terms of pass/fail for the child's performance on tasks involving copying symbols (said to be examples of Gagné's intellectual skills), ability to tell information (said to be examples of Gagné's verbal information skills), and ability to take in and use information (said to be examples of Gagné's cognitive strategies skills). In addition, a summary recommendation is circled, indicating whether a child has adequate skills to succeed, may need monitoring in two of the areas noted above (intellectual skills and verbal information), or should be referred for additional assessment. Results of performance in the cognitive strategies section are reported as adequate to good or possibly weak; in the fine and gross motor tasks as pass, fail, or refusal to do (+, -, or R); and in attitude toward learning as a single plus or minus from the child's report and the examiner's rating. A place also exists to either circle the parents' overall rating of their concerns as "generally pleased" or "have some concerns," or to indicate that they did not complete the Home Questionnaire. A similar report is also automatically produced for the parents. Instead of explaining the tasks in reference to Gagné's models as does the Teacher Report, the Parent Report gives some examples of the tasks performed by the child.

The STEPS is similar to a criterion-referenced test and is not interpreted on a normative basis. Cutoff points are established in terms of relationship to success in kindergarten and to curricular goals. Although the items were chosen on the basis of amenability to instruction, missed items are not intended to be taught as would normally occur as a result of criterion-referenced testing. The STEPS attempts to relate screening to specific educational goals and to identify skill levels that are associated with the learning process, not with specific products. Thus, the STEPS recommendations "point toward specific kinds of monitoring or assessment that may be necessary to help children succeed in school" (Smith, 1990, p. 26). The manual explains each of Gagné's learning capabilities/outcomes and their importance to learning. What teachers should do to "monitor or assess" progress in these areas is not clear, however.

**Technical Aspects**

As noted previously, the STEPS has elements of a criterion-referenced instrument. Judgments about a child's potential for success in school are made on the basis of his or her ability to perform certain tasks selected because of their applicability to early school success. Because the test is intended only for screening purposes, missed items are not meant to suggest a specific course of instruction but rather to act as warning flags to teachers and parents. Nevertheless, the STEPS cutoff scores are based on the performance of a large group of children on the test, and it is a standardized instrument.

The STEPS standardization sample consisted of 1,527 children aged 4–0 to 5–11, tested either in the late spring or early fall prior to or at the beginning of kindergarten. Private and public settings were used, including Head Starts, private day-care centers, and public and private kindergartens. Sample demographic characteristics adequately match U.S. normative characteristics and exceed those often found in readiness and screening tests. The proportion of children tested who were from high-risk groups was somewhat exaggerated to ensure a representative enough sample to produce stable estimates of performance. Statistical procedures to correct for the overrepresentation of high-risk groups were used in the analysis.

As might be expected, children with specific demographic characteristics were found to score lower on the STEPS. Children from minority ethnic groups, lower socioeconomic levels, and boys were more likely to be judged in need of monitoring or further referral.

Test-retest reliability was assessed by administering the STEPS twice to 80 children with a 1-week time lag. All but four of the items showed adequate test-retest reliability. Items receiving no reliability coefficients were those that all children in the sample passed both times (a not unusual occurrence in a screening test designed to assess minimal competency). In general, test-retest reliability was not strong enough for any conclusions to be drawn from a child's performance on any single item. Instructional decisions should not be made from this test. Item factor analysis revealed strong support for a factor comprised of the tasks for copying and symbolic capability and adequate support for the other three capabilities.

Overall reliability was assessed by comparing the recommended rates of referral for either monitoring or additional evaluation with the rates obtained from the second administration. The valid positive rate (children identified at risk both the first and second times) was 92%, and the overall hit rate was 89%. When only those children recommended for additional testing were compared, the valid positive rate dropped to 80%, indicating that one out of five children was inaccurately identified as significantly at risk. The two most reliable categories (copying/symbolic and language) are the only two used to make decisions regarding the summary recommendation.

Test validity was assessed in a manner appropriate for the goals of a screening test, in terms of false positives and negatives and accuracy of hit rate. Content validity was argued for on the basis of the relevance of the skills tested to classroom instruction. Although each item's connection to one of Gagné's learning outcomes is discussed in the manual, no information is presented to show either a research base for the inclusion of these tasks or their validity as representative samples of each learning outcome. Construct validity is not addressed in the manual but is threatened by the small number of items chosen to represent each domain. Intellectual skill deficits, for example, are identified by only three very similar tasks—name writing, letter copying, and shape copying. There is also potential for contamination from one domain to the next. Poor fine-motor skills might inhibit performance on the copying tasks mentioned previously and cause the child to appear to have an intellectual deficit. Classification by color (used to sample verbal information on the test) could also be viewed as a process of discrimination, concept development, and rule application more appropriate to an intellectual skill (see Gagné & Driscoll, 1988).

Concurrent validity was established by comparing the results of the STEPS with several other assessment measures used in kindergarten. None of the instruments used cutting scores to identify risk as does the STEPS. In order to compare hit rates accurately, therefore, cutting scores were identified artificially on the basis of equivalent percentages of children who would be identified as at risk. Given the differences between the stated purposes of the STEPS and the other measures and difficulties in this procedure, the comparable hit rates are strong enough to establish adequate concurrent validity between the STEPS and other measures used in kindergarten. The outcome prediction rate between the STEPS and the Goodenough-Harris Drawing Test (a developmental draw-a-person test) was about twice what might be expected by chance. Similarly, the outcome prediction rate between the STEPS and the School Behavior Checklist (a teacher judgment rating scale) was four to five times as good as chance would predict. The Test of Behavioral Experience (a norm-referenced objective test) had a prediction rate about 20% better than chance would predict, and the Brigance K & 1 Screen (a criterion-referenced objective test) had an outcome prediction rate about five times greater than a chance prediction.

Predictive validity is extremely important in instruments designed for screening if they are to be valid for their stated purpose. Smith did attempt to establish predictive validity with this new test by predicting the results of the Metropolitan Readiness Test (MRT), administered in the spring to 186 children who had been screened with the STEPS the previous fall. The MRT is a widely used readiness test with adequate reliability and validity. When both at-risk categories on the STEPS ("monitor progress" and "refer for additional evaluation") were combined, hit rates ranged from 84% to 88%, and outcome prediction rates were four to five times above a chance prediction.

These results indicate that the STEPS was able to accurately identify most children who would later score poorly on the MRT, a measure of basic readiness skills for first grade. These results do not indicate that the STEPS predicts which children would function poorly *in the classroom* at the end of kindergarten, which children would be placed in special programs (special education, Chapter I, speech and language services), or which children would be recommended for retention or transitional class placement. Nor does this assess the validity of any interventions suggested by the identification procedure of the STEPS in preventing the development of school problems. These are important questions that should be addressed before the real utility of the STEPS can be determined.

## Critique

The STEPS was designed to serve the needs of school systems to speedily, but accurately, identify children at risk for learning problems at the beginning of their school careers. It is not meant to test academic readiness specifically or to provide teachers with information on which to base instructional decisions. Concurrent and predictive validity and reliability data provided in the manual indicate that the STEPS can adequately identify most children who may be at risk. The test is certainly brief, is easy to administer, scores almost completely automatically, and can be interpreted almost as automatically. In large school screenings it is often difficult to offer teachers and parents immediate feedback, but the parent and teacher reports generated from the STEPS score sheets provide almost immediate feedback.

However, the STEPS is limited by its very advantages. Its brevity means that few questions are used to represent important skill areas. The test's ties to Gagné's theory of learning capabilities are weakened by threats to construct validity and inadequate domain sampling. The very general and sweeping information provided to teachers could be easily overinterpreted. For example, a child might receive a recommendation for monitoring due to suspected weakness in the area of intellectual skills. The brief explanation at the top of the teacher report may not be enough to protect against overinterpretation of this as a suspected cognitive deficit, particularly as no trained person makes a specific interpretation. Finally, the lack of specific implications for intervention with those children identified as having suspected weakness in one of the learning capabilities seriously affects the ability of the STEPS to serve as a significant aid to early prevention of learning problems.

### References

Arter, J., & Jenkins, J.R. (1978, January). *Differential diagnosis–prescriptive teaching: A critical appraisal* (Technical Report No. 80). Urbana, IL: University of Illinois at Urbana-Champaign, Center for the Study of Reading.

Gagné, R.M., & Driscoll, M.P. (1988). *Essentials of learning for instruction.* Englewood Cliffs, NJ: Prentice-Hall.

Smith, F. (1990). *Test manual for the Screening Test for Educational Prerequisite Skills.* Los Angeles: Western Psychological Services.

**Alice G. Friedman, Ph.D.**
*Assistant Professor of Psychology, State University of New York at Binghamton, Binghamton, New York.*

# SELF-PERCEPTION PROFILE FOR CHILDREN

*Susan Harter. Denver, Colorado: University of Denver.*

## Introduction

The Self-Perception Profile for Children (SPPC; Harter, 1985b) is a self-report measure designed to assess children's perceptions of their competence and self-adequacy across a number of specific domains, including scholastic competence, social acceptance, athletic competence, physical appearance, and behavioral conduct, as well as global self-worth. The instrument is intended for children ages 8 to 13 and can be administered in groups or individually. There are currently a number of versions of the instrument available for use with other populations: younger children (the Pictorial Scale of Perceived Competence and Social Acceptance for Young Children; Harter & Pike, 1983), adolescents (the Self-Perception Profile for Adolescents; Harter, 1988c), college students (the Self-Perception Profile for College Students; Neemann & Harter, 1986), adults (the Self-Perception Profile for Adults; Messer & Harter, 1985), and learning disabled students (the Self-Perception Profile for Learning Disabled Students; Renick & Harter, 1989). This review focuses exclusively on the Self-Perception Profile for Children.

The SPPC was developed by Susan Harter, who is currently a professor at the University of Denver. Dr. Harter has published extensively in the area of self-concept and understanding of emotions in children. The SPPC differs from other well-known measures of self-concept (e.g., the Piers-Harris Children's Self-Concept Scale, Piers; Piers & Harris, 1964) or self-esteem (e.g., Coopersmith Self-Esteem Inventories; Coopersmith, 1967), which conceptualize global self-worth as a unidimensional construct, an aggregate of the child's responses to specific areas of competency. According to Harter (1981), instruments that yield a single self-esteem score may be masking important distinctions that children make about their abilities across different domains of functioning. The SPPC considers the multidimensional nature of the self-concept by including domain-specific judgments as well as those about global self-worth (Harter, 1985a). To that end, children's perceptions of self-growth are not simply summations of their perceptions of abilities in different areas of functioning.

This instrument requires children to make judgments about their abilities in specific realms represented by six subscales. The Scholastic Competence (SC) subscale was designed to measure a child's perception of his or her ability in academic areas and includes items related to whether the child views him- or

---

Preparation of this review was supported by the Institute for Research and Training in Clinical Psychology, State University of New York at Binghamton, Binghamton, New York.

herself as being smart, good at school, able to remember things, and so forth. The Social Acceptance (SA) subscale is included to reflect the extent to which a child perceives him- or herself to be accepted by peers and asks about ease of making friends, popularity, and whether most children like him or her. The Athletic Competence (AC) subscale attempts to reflect the extent to which the child feels competent in sports and includes items related to doing well in sports and playing rather than watching. The Physical Appearance (PA) subscale was designed to reflect a child's satisfaction with his or her physical appearance and asks the examinee to evaluate aspects of how he or she looks, including overall appearance, body, face, and height/weight. The Behavioral Conduct (BC) subscale is intended to reflect a child's perceptions of the acceptability of his or her behavior and includes statements related to whether he or she gets into trouble and acts kindly toward others. Lastly, the Global Self-Worth (GSW) subscale is included to reflect a child's judgments about his or her worthiness as a person through questions about how happy the child is with him- or herself. Each subscale consists of six items, which do not overlap across subscales.

Materials for the SPPC include two questionnaires, labeled "What I Am Like" and "How Important Are These Things to How You Feel About Yourself as a Person?", plus a teacher rating scale. The questionnaire labeled "What I Am Like" (SPPC) is the primary instrument (and focus of this review), with the other two providing supplementary information. The SPPC consists of 36 items presented in a structured alternative format (Harter, 1985b). Each item contains two statements referring to an identical skill: one presents a positive description (e.g., some kids do very well at their classwork), the other presents a negative one (e.g., other kids don't do well at their classwork). The child is asked first to determine which of the two kinds of kids he or she is most like, then to decide whether the statement is "really true for me" or "sort of true for me." Consequently, each item has four possible responses. The format was designed to reduce the tendency for children to respond in a socially desirable manner. The wording of the statements is counterbalanced across scales such that half of the items are worded in a positive direction first and the remaining items are worded in a negative direction first. Scoring is accomplished by assigning a number from 1 to 4 to each item depending on the child's response, with higher numbers reflecting greater self-perceived competency. Subscale scores are the sum of the numbers assigned to the six items of the subscale.

The manual for the Self-Perception Profile for Children includes information about its administration, scoring, and psychometric properties, a teacher rating scale, and forms to enable scoring and plotting the SPPC profile. Means and standard deviations for each of the six subscales are available for boys and girls in Grades 3 through 8. The Teacher Rating Scale was designed for completion by teachers or others familiar with the child. Respondents are asked to rate their perceptions of the child's behavior in five of the SPPC domains (excluding global self-worth). The items in this rating scale are similar to those administered to the children. The questionnaire labeled "How Important Are These Things to How You Feel About Yourself as a Person?" is provided to enable a comparison of the child's perception of importance of a skill to her or his judgments of competency in the area. Presumably, the impact of a child's judgment about his or her competency in a given area on the child's overall self-esteem is mediated by how important he or she considers the area. A discrepancy score can be calculated to determine the relationship between the child's perceptions of competency and judgments of importance of each of the five domains. Mean discrepancy scores for a normative sample are included for determining if a child's scores "fit the normative pattern" (Harter, 1985b, p. 25).

The Self-Perception Profile for Children (SPPC) is a recent revision of the Perceived Competence Scale for Children (PCSC; Harter, 1982). The original scale included subscales reflecting three competence areas (cognitive, social, and athletic competence) and global self-esteem. The revision added two subscales (Behavioral Conduct and Physical Appearance), changed the names of some of the subscales to better represent item content, and expanded the name of the instrument, both to reflect a broadening of its focus to include forms of self-adequacy that do not necessarily refer to competency in a particular skill area and to suggest that scales be compared to each other (Harter, 1985b). Additionally, several items in the original scale were revised (Harter, 1985b).

**Practical Applications/Uses**

The Self-Perception Profile for Children was designed to assess children's perceptions of their competency and adequacies across a range of domains as well as to provide a measure of global self-worth. According to the author, a decision to use this instrument as opposed to others measuring self-esteem ought to be guided by a consideration of the specific dimensions of interest. The author stresses the need to consider the specific assessment question being asked prior to choosing an instrument to ensure that the instrument is sensitive to the dimensions of interest (Harter, 1988b).

The SPPC was developed for use with third- through sixth-grade children, although the author notes that it may be administered to older children. The instrument may be administered individually or in group settings. Harter warns against use of the instrument with special groups of children, such as those with learning disabilities or mental retardation, because the factor structure and interpretation of the subscales may be quite different. This warning probably could be extended to include all populations that differ from the standardization sample, which consisted of predominantly Caucasian children from lower middle class to upper middle class families in Colorado. This reviewer could find no information about the impact of factors such as race, socioeconomic status, or physical and emotional disabilities on responses to the SPPC. In the standardization sample, boys obtained significantly higher scores on Athletic Competence, Physical Appearance, and Global Self-Worth subscales, while girls scored higher on Behavioral Conduct.

Each questionnaire contains space for the child to record his or her name, age, and date of birth. The author suggests that children in Grades 5 and above can read the items themselves, but that children in the third and fourth grades should have items read aloud to them. The instructions, which may be read verbatim from the manual, stress the notion that the questionnaire is a survey, not a test, and that there are no right or wrong answers. The format of the SPPC is quite different from questionnaires the children may have completed in the past. Care must be made to ensure that examinees endorse only one response per question. As part of the instructions to be read aloud, the author provides a sample question and specific directions for making decisions. Harter notes that "invariably there will be one or two children who check both sides initially" (1988b, p. 11). Thus it is particularly important that the examiner checks the child's response to the first few items to ensure that he or she has understood the directions.

**Technical Aspects**

Test construction of the SPPC was accomplished in a systematic manner that is described only minimally in the manual. More thorough information can be obtained through articles written by the author and available in peer-reviewed journals. This instrument is one of the only (if not *the* only) measures of self-concept for which the developer used factor analytic methods to select items for specific domains and global self-esteem (Wylie, 1989), a fact not emphasized in the manual. Harter's model of self-concept has guided the development of the instrument, and new information about perceived self-competency in children has influenced its scope.

The SPPC has undergone a number of revisions. The original version (the Perceived Competence Scale for Children; PCSC) was developed to tap content areas in four domains considered significant to children's self-concept: cognitive, social, physical, and general (Harter, 1982). The initial items for each domain derived from information gathered during interviews with children. An early version of the PCSC, consisting of 40 items selected on the basis of face validity, was administered to a sample of 215 children in Grades 3 through 6. Results were subjected to factor analysis, yielding a four-factor solution. Items were eliminated from each subscale because they did not meet the following stringent criteria for inclusion: acceptable loadings on one factor, high loading on only one factor, mean value near the midpoint, acceptable variability, and contribution to the internal consistency of the subscale. Three or four items on each subscale did not meet these criteria and were replaced by new ones. A revised version of the scale was administered to a sample of 133 children, with all items reaching the inclusion criteria (Harter, 1982).

The new measure was subjected to considerable analysis to establish its psychometric properties. The instrument was administered to a total of 2,271 children representing populations from different geographic locations. Factor analysis using both orthogonal and oblique solutions resulted in the same factor structure, which was found to be stable across grade levels. Internal consistency (coefficient alpha) for the subscales ranged from .73 to .86. Test-retest reliability coefficients for each of the subscales for a subsample of children retested after 3 months ranged from .70 to .87. Test-retest reliability coefficients for each of the subscales for a subsample of children retested after 9 months ranged from .69 to .80. Subscale means were fairly stable across grades and samples. The four subscales are moderately and significantly correlated (Harter, 1982).

A number of studies provided support for the convergent validity of the original measure. Harter (1982) examined the relationship between teachers' ratings and the children's own ratings. Across samples of children in Grades 3 through 9, correlations between child and teacher ratings were in the .40s and reflected a clear developmental pattern of increasing correlations with age of the children. Mean correlation between children's ratings of physical competence and that of gym teachers well acquainted with the child was .62.

The construct validity of the original instrument has been supported by a number of studies examining the relationship of the PCSC and behaviors assumed to be related to perceived competency. According to Harter (1981), perceived competence is positively related to intrinsic motivational orientation. Children who prefer to be challenged and engage in mastery activities should obtain higher scores on perceived cognitive competence. This hypothesis was supported in a study demonstrating positive correlations between scores on perceived cognitive competence and preference for challenge, independent mastery, and curiosity. Further support for the construct validity of the instrument is provided by a study (Harter, 1982) demonstrating that, given a choice of anagrams varying from easy to difficult, children who obtained high scores on perceived cognitive competence chose significantly more difficult anagrams than those who scored low on perceived competence.

Support for the discriminative validity of the SPPC subscales is provided by a study (Baarstad, cited in Harter, 1982) demonstrating that children with learning disabilities rate their cognitive competence significantly lower than children without learning disabilities. Scores on the other subscales of the SPPC were not significantly lower for the learning disabled children compared to children without learning disabilities. Harter (1982) showed that children selected for sports teams scored higher on perceived physical and social competence than their peers.

The original measure was expanded by adding two new subscales (Physical Appearance and Behavioral Conduct) and then renamed the Self-Perception Profile for Children. The revised instrument was administered to four samples of children ($N$ = 1,543) in Grades 3 through 8 from lower middle class to upper middle class Colorado households. Internal consistency reliabilities for the six subscales are primarily in the .80s but range from a low of .71 to .86. Alpha coefficients for Behavioral Conduct, though lower than those for the other subscales, are in the .70s. Three items (one each in Behavioral Conduct, Social Acceptance, and Global Self-Worth) consistently lowered the reliability of their respective subscales and were subsequently modified. The resulting instrument constitutes the current SPPC.

The manual presents means for each of the six subscales for the four normative populations. The means are typically close to 3.0; all but one falls above the midpoint of 2.5 for each scale, suggesting that the distribution is negatively skewed (Wylie, 1989). There is considerable variation in responding across children. Standard deviations range from .43 to .94, depending on subscale and population.

The revised scale was subjected to factor analysis to determine whether the new subscales actually constituted separate factors. Only five of the six subscales were included in the analysis because, according to the author, items that load on Global Self-Worth vary from child to child and should not emerge as a distinct factor (Harter, 1985b). Factor analysis, using oblique rotation, yielded five specific subscales for three samples of children in Grades 5 through 8, with no cross-loading greater than .18. A four-factor solution was obtained for third- and fourth-graders in two of the samples. The author concluded that the addition of the two new subscales "provides a more differentiated and meaningful profile of self-perceptions for children" (Harter, 1985b, p. 18). Intercorrelations among subscales are higher among younger children than older ones. Scholastic Competence and Behavioral Conduct are moderately correlated (*r*'s ranging from .29 to .58), as are Social Acceptance, Athletic Competence, and Physical Appearance. Social Acceptance is related to Scholastic Competence for younger but not older children. Physical Appearance is consistently related to self-worth (*r*'s ranging from .62 to .73). The other subscales are moderately related to Global Self-Worth, particularly for younger children (Harter, 1985b).

The appropriateness of considering the importance of test-retest reliability as a criterion for test evaluation depends on the expected stability of the to-be-measured trait or behavior (Harter, 1988b). If the latter is considered a stable construct, the instrument's test-retest reliability ought to be high. However, if the behavior is subject to change over time, test-retest reliability should be low if the instrument reliably measures what it purports to measure. As the stability of children's self-judgments appears to vary depending on environmental and developmental factors, low reliability coefficients do not necessarily indicate poor psychometric properties (Harter, 1988a). On the original instrument, test-retest reliability over a relatively short period of time (3 and 9 months) within the same school year was high. However, stability across school years may be expected to be considerably lower, reflecting actual changes in the children's perceptions of themselves relative to their peers (Harter, Whitesell, & Kowalski, n.d.). In fact, Harter et al. (n.d.) reported test-retest reliability coefficients in the .60s for children tested 7 months apart but in different school years. These correlations are lower than those reported for children tested 9 months apart during the same school year.

Establishing the validity of the SPPC poses interesting psychometric challenges. As noted by Harter (1988b), the instrument is not designed to measure actual performance in different spheres; rather, it is an assessment of children's perceptions of their competency. Therefore, although comparing SPPC scores to an external criterion may be an appropriate test of a child's accuracy in appraising his or her abilities, it does not produce evidence of the instrument's validity (Harter, 1988b). Validity evidence must come either from comparison with other well-validated instruments purporting to measure similar constructs or from empirical results confirming a priori hypotheses based on previous research findings. In fact, a number of studies focusing on the relationship between SPPC scores and children's responses to other measures, and the SPPC and other behaviors hypothesized to be related to perceived self-competency, have provided support for the scale's construct validity. Harter (1986) examined self-worth among children judged by their teachers to manifest affective and motivational symptoms of depression. As expected, their overall self-worth scores were low compared to norms. These children rated success in their lowest perceived competency domains as being as important to them as success in their highest domains. In an unpublished study of the impact of education transitions on perceived scholastic competence and classroom motivational orientation, Harter et al. (n.d.) demonstrated that children who showed increased perceived competence across grades also showed increased intrinsic motivation. Conversely, those who showed decreased perceived competence across grades showed decreased intrinsic motivation. Renick and Harter (1989) reported that children with learning disabilities who compared themselves with children with normal scholastic achievement perceived themselves as less academically competent than did those who compared themselves to other children with learning disabilities.

## Critique

The Self-Perception Profile for Children is a new instrument that has undergone careful, systematic construction. The use of subscales assessing specific domains, verified through factor analytic techniques to be distinct, as well as global self-worth makes the SPPC unique among instruments purporting to measure self-esteem in children. According to Wylie (1989), a well-respected expert on self-concept, a number of threats to validity common to other measures of self-concept were avoided, including "item ambiguity, forced-choice format, ipsative scoring, dichotomous scoring, and overlap between scales" (p. 114). The SPPC appears to be a significant improvement over other instruments purporting to measure self-worth.

The SPPC is closely tied to the author's theoretical model of self-concept. It was developed to facilitate study of the impact of domain-specific judgment on global self-worth in children, and it has been used to generate considerable information on the determinants of self-worth in children. However, those who intend to use the instrument in clinical settings should carefully consider how they interpret the results of the SPPC in light of other information they have about a child. A finding that a child perceives him- or herself as highly competent in all areas is not necessarily a desirable outcome. For example, although one may expect that higher scores on self-worth would correlate with other indices of adjustment, this has not been demonstrated empirically. Further, the meaning of high scores in specific areas is even less clear. High scores on the subscales in the absence of actual competency may indicate more of a problem than low scores on the subscales in areas in which the child is actually quite competent. Therefore, while the SPPC may facilitate the generation of hypotheses regarding a particular child, it provides little information if not used in conjunction with other data about the child. This is not a criticism of the instrument, as any assessment of a child should include information from multiple measures and sources.

Although very new, the SPPC has already proven useful for generating information about children's self-perceptions and their correlates. Few instruments for children have undergone such careful and systematic development, and this one seems to provide more information about how children view themselves than do the more well-established measures of self-concept in children.

## References

Coopersmith, S. (1967). *The antecedents of self-esteem.* San Francisco: W.H. Freeman.

Harter, S. (1981). A new self-report scale of intrinsic versus extrinsic orientation in the classroom: Motivational and informational components. *Developmental Psychology, 17,* 300–312.

Harter, S. (1982). The Perceived Competence Scale for Children. *Child Development, 53,* 87–97.

Harter, S. (1985a). Competence as a dimension of self-evaluation: Towards a comprehensive model of self-worth. In R. Leahy (Ed.), *The development of the self* (pp. 55–122). New York: Academic Press.

Harter, S. (1985b). *Manual for the Self-Perception Profile for Children.* Denver, CO: University of Denver.

Harter, S. (1986). Processes underlying the construction, maintenance, and enhancement of the self-concept in children. In J. Suls & A.G. Greenwald (Eds.), *Psychological perspectives on the self* (pp. 136–182). Hillsdale, NJ: Lawrence Erlbaum.

Harter, S. (1988a). Developmental changes in self-concept and emotional understanding: Implications for psychotherapy. In S. Shirk (Ed.), *Cognitive development and child psychotherapy.* New York: Plenum.

Harter, S. (1988b). Issues in the assessment of self-concept of children and adolescents. In A. LaGreca (Ed.), *Through the eyes of the child.* Boston: Allyn & Bacon.

Harter, S. (1988c). *The Self-Perception Profile for Adolescents.* Denver, CO: University of Colorado.

Harter, S., & Pike, R. (1983). The Pictorial Scale of Perceived Competence and Social Acceptance for Young Children. *Child Development, 55,* 1969–1982.

Harter, S., Whitesell, N., & Kowalski, P. (n.d.). *The effects of educational transitions on young adolescents' perceptions of competence and motivational orientation.* Unpublished manuscript.

Messer, B., & Harter, S. (1985). *The Self-Perception Scale for Adults.* Unpublished manuscript, University of Denver.

Neemann, J., & Harter, S. (1986). *The Self-Perception Profile for College Students, manual.* Denver, CO: University of Denver.

Piers, E., & Harris, D. (1964). *The Piers-Harris Children's Self-Concept Scale.* Nashville, TN: Counselor Recordings and Tests.

Renick, M.J., & Harter, S. (1989). Impact of social comparisons on the developing self-perceptions of learning disabled students. *Journal of Educational Psychology, 81,* 631–638.

Wylie, R. (1989). *Measures of self-concept.* Lincoln, NE: University of Nebraska Press.

**Selma Hughes, Ph.D.**
*Professor of Psychology and Special Education, East Texas State University, Commerce, Texas.*

---

# SENF-COMREY RATINGS OF EXTRA EDUCATIONAL NEEDS

*Gerald M. Senf and Andrew L. Comrey. Novato, California: Academic Therapy Publications.*

## Introduction

The Senf-Comrey Ratings of Extra Educational Needs (SCREEN; Senf & Comrey, 1988) is a group-administered, norm-referenced test for screening children in kindergarten through third grade for potential learning difficulties. The subscales are designed to measure both social- and academic-related skills necessary for learning and can provide an efficient way of identifying high-risk children before they become underachievers. The test may also be used as a means of identifying from a large population of children a smaller group whose learning difficulties are such that further diagnostic testing on an individual basis is suggested.

The test was developed in 1975 from an earlier 1974 edition. The extensive studies noted in the technical manual were carried out on the 1975 edition of the test, which represented a substantial reduction in length from the 1974 edition. No content changes were made in the 1988 edition except for the elimination of the Figure Copying test.

The 1975 test formed part of the state of Illinois's publicly funded Project SCREEN, which was developed to identify high-risk children before failure further lowered their academic and adjustment potential. The senior author of the test, Gerald Senf, was the principal investigator with Computer Psychometric Affiliates Inc., which carried out the screening. (For a full description of Project SCREEN, see Senf & Comrey, 1975; Senf & Sushinsky, 1975; and Senf, Luick, & Larsen, 1976.) Dr. Senf has a background in the study of learning problems, having been editor for many years of the *Journal of Learning Disabilities.*

The second author, Andrew Comrey, is Professor of Psychology at the University of California at Los Angeles. He has a background in the psychometric investigation of personality inventories, particularly those developed in the early '50s and '60s. He also is the author of the Comrey Personality Scales (see *Test Critiques: Vol. IV* for a review).

According to the authors, the SCREEN was developed to avoid or at least minimize the problems associated with procedures that then existed. The procedures involved labeling children as learning disabled in order to determine their eligibility for special services. Phinney (1988) points out that labels often libel a child as inadequate and fail to provide information about the processes of learning in that child. The SCREEN attempts to remedy this by providing teachers information about the child's learning strengths and a broader basis for making educational decisions.

The SCREEN consists of an administrator's manual, a student booklet, and a technical manual. The 24-page student booklet has full-color illustrations, which are appealing and may be more meaningful to the student than the black-and-white line illustrations found in some readiness tests. The same booklet is used for kindergarten through third grade, though the results are interpreted differently.

The student booklet contains five subtests that are completed by the student, a 40-item checklist completed by the teacher, and a pupil information sheet that is also completed by the teacher. The five subtests are Self Concept and School Adjustment, Visual Skills, Auditory Skills, Basic Knowledge, and General Readiness. The SCREEN is administered in four sessions. Each session is color coded, and the tests within each session are arranged in order of administration.

The Self Concept and School Adjustment test consists of 36 items, which are answered "yes" or "no" by making a "happy" face or a "sad" face. There is a training session of six questions (requiring a "yes" or "no" answer) that the examiner checks for accuracy after demonstrating with a large model of the two faces. Twenty-four questions elicit information about how the child does in school, how he or she feels about school, and the attitude that he or she holds about school. Some of the questions relate to self-concept (e.g., "Are you good looking?"). The majority of the statements are worded negatively, requiring a negative answer to indicate a positive attitude. It is difficult to know the significance of some questions (e.g., "Do you like your clothes?"), the choice of which would not seem to be under the control of a child of the age for which the test is designed.

Visual skills are assessed by three types of tasks. The first is a measure of visual memory for the animals who "asked the questions" in the Self Concept and School Adjustment scale. It is given in the first testing session, while the other two tasks are administered in a later session. The second task assesses letter and number knowledge (e.g., "Mark the letter [or number] that comes after ____"). The test directions themselves require recognition of numbers (e.g., "Go to the next page with the large number 3 on top"). The third visual task asks the child to identify which of four pictures represents what a cut-up picture would look like if it were put back together again.

Three kinds of items assess auditory skills: auditory discrimination, listening comprehension, and digit memory. In the test of auditory discrimination, the child indicates whether three words are the same or different. Some of the discriminations are easier than others (e.g., "cry, try, try" is easier than "think, think, thing"). In the listening comprehension measure, the child answers factual questions about a brief story (110 words at the third-grade level). The story is only read once (although the questions may be repeated), making the test a measure of auditory memory as much as a test of listening comprehension. In the opinion of this reviewer, the use of colored animal to ask the questions is confusing in this test (e.g., "The yellow bird asks, Did Tom tell the dog that his mother would not let him have a dog?"). In the test of digit memory, the child identifies which of four number sequences matches the one read by the teacher.

The Basic Knowledge scale assesses "a variety of cognitively oriented items" (Senf & Comrey, 1975, p. 7). It relies heavily on the child's ability to interpret directions given orally and on his or her knowledge of language. The child must mark one of the four pictures that best illustrates the qualitative concept presented by the teacher. The items include simple concepts (e.g., "widest," "on top"). Another task requires marking the one picture out of four that does not belong. This task forms part of the Matrices subscale and resembles the Absurdities subscale where the child has to mark one frame out of four that has something wrong with it (e.g., cat in a nest).

Test booklets must be returned to the publisher for machine scoring, the rationale for which will be discussed in the next section. The publisher prepares a three-page individualized report on each child, which synthesizes the data provided by the teacher and interprets the test results.

A typical profile includes identifying information (name, age, grade, placement, etc.) and a summary of the child's past history of medical, sensory, and educational testing as far as the school knows (e.g., "Harry has had a hearing test and was not found to have a hearing problem"). A chart summarizes the test performance in each of the four areas with a Performance Index (x 50 SD 10) and percentile scores. A fifth General Readiness Score is derived from the four subtests. The teacher ratings are combined into four areas: Cognitive Perceptual, Behavioral Adjustment, Social Adjustment, and Maturity, again with a Performance Index (x 50 SD 10) and percentile ranks. In addition, an interpretation is provided for each score. The interpretation is based on the normal curve where scores of $\pm 1$ SD of the mean are "average or above," scores 2 SD below the mean are "possible problems," scores 3 SD below the mean are "moderate problems," and scores 4 SD below the mean are "severe problems." No designations are established for students scoring more than 1 SD above the mean because the test focuses on children who may have learning difficulties (N.A. Martin, personal communication, March 12, 1990).

The SCREEN individualized report provides, in addition, a narrative interpretation of each of the subtests pointing out significant areas of weakness (e.g., "Harry missed 5 out of 11 items on the Letters and Numbers subtest. He did not know the letter *c*, the letter *k*, the letter that comes after *s*, etc."). The four Performance Indexes of pupil behavior are also interpreted with statements such as "Harry frequently or usually tries to get attention by misbehaving" (Behavioral Adjustment) or "Harry always or almost always hangs on to the teacher instead of relating to other children" (Social Adjustment).

## Practical Applications/Uses

The SCREEN was developed as a practical, group-administered screening device that would both assist teachers in the early identification of children with extra educational needs and provide them with a better basis for referral recommendations (Senf & Comrey, 1975).

The technical manual describes the philosophical orientation of the test. The SCREEN was designed to identify children at "high risk" for school problems before they fail. The test identifies children who need extra educational assistance and thereby enables more to realize their potential.

The test was designed to remedy some of the deficits in present screening techniques that the manual outlines. These include the cost of screening, the diagnostic orientation of many of the tests with intent to label the child, and the identification of the whole range of functioning rather than focusing on high-risk pupils. The SCREEN remedies many of these by providing a relatively short, easy test that incorporates both formal testing and teacher referral. The test is practical in that it attempts to collect, integrate, and return useful information to the teacher with a minimum of child and teacher time, without compromising psychometric standards (Senf & Comrey, 1975).

The rationale underlying the computer scoring of the test is that this technology increases scorer accuracy and reduces scorer bias. The scoring and analysis of SCREEN data are objective, and the SCREEN Individualized Report is free from subjective interpretations that might influence how results are interpreted.

The SCREEN provided a cost-effective assessment of children in kindergarten through third grade. An entire class can be screened by the classroom teacher in four sessions of 15 minutes or less, and the teacher requires no special training. The test would not be of use to private practitioners or clinicians in a mental health service agency; it is strictly designed for use in school settings.

The SCREEN is different from other readiness tests (e.g., Metropolitan Readiness Tests) in that it is a global index of readiness for academic work in general and is not geared to specific academic areas. The overall item difficulty is low so that the subscales are easy for students without significant deficits. The test looks at readiness as a relationship between the adequacy of the child's capacity in relation to the demands of the beginning primary curriculum.

**Technical Aspects**

In May and June of 1975, the 1975 version of the SCREEN was administered to approximately 10,000 Illinois elementary schoolchildren. The technical data are derived from samples of varying sizes that were taken from the survey. The technical manual reports that 1,275 males and 1,226 females were used at the kindergarten level; 1,192 males and 1,098 females at the first-grade level; 789 males and 693 females at the second-grade level; and 770 males and 730 females at the third-grade level.

Extensive studies are described with regard to the validity of the test. Validity refers to the extent to which the results of an evaluation procedure serve the particular uses for which they are intended (Hammill, Brown, & Bryant, 1989). The SCREEN is designed to predict students at risk of failure, and several kinds of validity studies are described: content, concurrent, reverse longitudinal, and predictive.

Content or curriculum validity is supported by nonempirical evidence that shows the test to be an adequate sampling of skills over several domains. Factor analysis is reported of items included in the subtests, and detailed descriptions are given on the choice of items included in the various scales.

Concurrent validity was demonstrated by studying the scores obtained on the SCREEN and on standardized measures of achievement. SCREEN multiple *r* correlations with seven achievement tests (e.g., Metropolitan Achievement Test, Stanford Early School Achievement Test) are shown separately for kindergarten, first- and second-grade students. The average multiple correlation is shown separately by grade level and ranges from .71 for kindergarten to .73 for third grade, with the average of the tests (total Score correlation) being slightly higher.

Reverse longitudinal studies are reported from data collected during kindergarten compared with SCREEN performance in first and second grades. Concurrent validity was demonstrated, and it was shown that the SCREEN tests predict widely accepted achievement indices while in no way measuring what the other tests measure.

Predictive validity studies carried out in 1974 are described, and a lengthy discussion of the issues is provided in the technical manual. The authors report that the SCREEN does better in predicting group achievement test performance than individually administered achievement test performance, which one would expect.

The manual's section on reliability, which is the extent to which a test is stable and consistent, reports reliabilities by grade for each of the 10 major SCREEN scales based on split-half, Kuder-Richardson 20, and test-retest methods. Because of the way in which the SCREEN was constructed with a deliberate positive skew, the restriction in range at the upper end of the scale has tended to reduce the split-half reliabilities of SCREEN scores. The technical manual points out that the reliabilities reported can be considered conservative estimates of the actual internal consistency of the SCREEN scores.

The split-half reliabilities are computed separately for each grade for each of the nine SCREEN scores, and the average coefficient is about .80. Kuder-Richardson 20 reliabilities also are reported and are slightly higher. The test-retest reliability coefficients quoted tend to be somewhat lower than those derived by either the split-half or KR-20 methods, with the exception of the teacher rating scales. The test-retest reliability study was carried out on children in an inner-city school, with a higher error rate among the children tested. The technical manual points out that other test-retest reliability studies carried out on different sample subjects may obtain higher reliabilities.

Considerable demographic information is provided for each of the studies from which the technical data derive, and graphic data are provided on the test results at each level in 21 figures (charts). Although the technical data are impressive, the user must remember that the information relates only to children in Illinois and is more than 15 years old.

## Critique

The SCREEN does indeed meet the need for a cost-effective assessment of children in kindergarten through third grade. It is a group-administered measure by means of which an entire class can be screened for potential learning disabilities by the classroom teacher. No special personnel or specialized training is needed to administer the test.

The profiles provided by the test are comprehensive and give valuable information about the status of students. The SCREEN clearly identifies students who are high risk for failing. At the present time, with so much emphasis on early recognition of high-risk students, the SCREEN should appeal to school districts that desire a proven method of screening based on a process orientation toward readiness (i.e., underlying skills and processes; Salvia & Ysseldyke, 1989).

In addition, the test profiles provide useful data on individual differences that would be helpful in planning intervention programs. The SCREEN may not be of use in clinical practice and would not be of use to school systems that wished to hand-score the data, as scoring criteria are not available.

## References

Hammill, D., Brown, L., & Bryant, B. (1989). *A consumer's guide to tests in print.* Austin, TX: PRO-ED.

Phinney, M.Y. (1988). *Reading with the troubled reader.* Portsmouth, NH: Heinemann.

Salvia, J., & Ysseldyke, J. (1989). *Assessment in special and remedial education.* Boston: Houghton Mifflin.

Senf, G., & Comrey, A. (1975). State initiative in learning disabilities: Illinois' Project SCREEN. *Journal of Learning Disabilities, 8,* 451–457.

Senf, G., & Comrey, A. (1988). *Senf-Comrey Ratings of Extra Educational Needs.* Novato, CA: Academic Therapy Publications.

Senf, G., Luick, A.H., & Larsen, R.P. (1976). Consistent SCREEN performance profiles isolated among first graders with school problems using cluster analysis. In *Proceedings of the Association for Children with Learning Disabilities International Conference,* Seattle.

Senf, G., & Sushinsky, L.W. (1975). State initiative in learning disabilities: Illinois' Project SCREEN, report II. Definition and Illinois practice. *Journal of Learning Disabilities, 8,* 524–533.

**Zoli Zlotogorski, Ph.D.**
*Professor of Psychology, The Hebrew University of Jerusalem, Mount Scopus, Israel.*

# SENSE OF COHERENCE QUESTIONNAIRE

*Aaron Antonovsky. Beersheba, Israel: Aaron Antonovsky, Ph.D.*

## Introduction

The Sense of Coherence Questionnaire is an easily administered 29-item self-rating instrument that assesses a subject's orientation to life. The questionnaire was developed by Antonovsky (1983) as part of a wider conceptual and theoretical effort whose focus was a salutogenic orientation. This orientation focuses on the origins of health and poses a radically different question than that of the pathogenic orientation that dominates physical medicine. The salutogenic question asks, "Why are people located toward the positive end of a health ease/disease continuum?" In other words, most people successfully cope with difficult circumstances, and some even seem to mature in the face of overwhelming hardships.

The model proposed by Antonovsky suggests that the impact of a high stressor load will be pathological, neutral, or health-improving, depending on the generalized resistance resources or resistance deficits available to an individual. The culling rule introduced by Antonovsky (1979) is the sense of coherence concept. By the sense of coherence he meant the global orientation in which one has a pervasive and enduring, though dynamic, feeling of confidence that one's internal and external environments are predictable and that there is a high probability that things will work out as can be reasonably expected. The operationalization of the sense of coherence concept theoretically necessitated a global or dispositional orientation. The questionnaire was constructed to refer to a wide variety of stimuli and situations while reflecting the three core elements of coherence: comprehensibility, manageability, and meaningfulness.

Comprehensibility is defined as the extent to which one perceives the stimuli that confront one as making sense, as information that is ordered, consistent, structured, and clear. Manageability is seen as the extent to which one perceives that one's resources are at one's disposal and are adequate to meet the demands posed by the stimuli that bombard one. Finally, meaningfulness is the extent to which one feels that life makes sense emotionally, and it includes a sense of commitment, engagement, and a robust investment of energy in the demands posed by living.

The development of the questionnaire was based on the notion of Cartesian space and facet design as developed by Guttman (Shye, 1978). Facet design requires the researcher to propose a mapping sentence (Fig. 1) by specifying the essential facets of what is to be measured and then to list the important elements in each facet. Thus any given item in a questionnaire represents a structure or particular combination of one element in each facet. In the mapping sentence proposed by

Antonovsky (1987), he defined five essential facets: sense of coherence, modality of stimulus, source of stimulus, nature of demand, and time reference. The 29-item questionnaire is then a sample of the possible 243-item pool as defined by the mapping sentence. The final questionnaire includes 11 comprehensibility items, 10 manageability items, and 8 meaningfulness items.

**Fig. 1.** Sense of Coherence mapping sentence

**A. Modality**
{1. instrumental}
Respondent X responds to a(n) {2. cognitive} stimulus which has
{3. affective}

**B. Source**
{1. the internal}
originated from {2. the external} environment(s) and
{3. both}

**C. Demand**
{1. concrete}
which poses a(n) {2. diffuse} demand, the stimulus being in
{3. abstract}

| | |
|---|---|
| **D. Time** | **E. Sense of Coherence** |
| {1. past} | {1. comprehensibility} |
| the {2. present} in response dimension | {2. manageability} |
| {3. future} | {3. meaningfulness} |

{1. high}
which is {2. medium} in terms of Facet E (Sense of Coherence).
{3. low}

The questionnaire was field tested in a number of different studies both in its Hebrew and English versions. An Israeli national sample ($n$ = 297), three separate studies of Israeli army officer trainees ($n$ = 117, $n$ = 338, $n$ = 228), and a study of Israeli health workers ($n$ = 33) provided the normative data for the Hebrew version. The English version was employed in three studies of U.S. undergraduates ($n$ = 336, $n$ = 59, $n$ = 308), a study of New York State production workers ($n$ = 111), Edmonton health workers ($n$ = 108), and Nordic occupational health workers ($n$ = 30). It is important to note that the questionnaire was used cross-culturally and with both homogeneous and heterogeneous groups. Antonovsky (1987) reports coefficients of variation ranging from .10 to .20, which indicates heterogeneity of responses even in the most homogeneous populations.

## Practical Applications/Uses

The 29 sense of coherence items are brief questions relating to various aspects of the respondent's life. A subject responds by circling a number from 1 to 7. These extreme answers are clearly explained in the instructions and are highlighted with clear wording of both extremes. The questionnaire contains 13 items that are reversed and 13 items that are recommended for use as a short form.

The Sense of Coherence Questionnaire is primarily a research instrument, although the author suggests that the clinical uses of the instrument remain unexplored. In an early empirical study, Margalit (1985) investigated the perceptions of parents' behavior, familial satisfaction, and sense of coherence in hyperactive children. In this study, a sample of 32 teacher-identified hyperactive children had a significantly lower sense of coherence than a control group. Their environment was reported to be less ordered and predictable, less manageable, and to a large extent meaningless. In another study, Dana and his colleagues (1985) investigated relations among the components of the coherence concept. Correlations between each component and its construct equivalent were significant. However, they note that the construct measures did not distinguish among the subscales. In other words, these component scores were empirically not separable. This finding, Antonovsky (1987) correctly points out, is an inherent feature of facet design.

## Technical Aspects

The reliability of the questionnaire was studied by computing Cronbach's alpha in each of the normative studies. The scores ranged from .84 to .93, which represents a reasonable degree of internal consistency and reliability of the instrument.

A number of studies have attempted to establish the validity of the questionnaire. Rumbaut (1983) and his colleagues developed a separate instrument designed to measure the same concept of coherence. They administered a 22-item sense of coherence scale and the Sense of Coherence Questionnaire to a sample of 336 undergraduates. The alphas of the two scales were .903 and .881, and the correlation between the two was .639, indicating a degree of concurrent validity. In addition to the Rumbaut study, Antonovsky cites the normative data as providing further evidence of validity. Employing the known-groups technique, he argues that a valid scale should provide differences on mean scores among samples that would be expected to differ. An inspection of the normative sample means indicates that the rank order of the means reflects a priori expectations, while the psychometric properties of the data on the homogeneous samples are nearly identical. Validity data were also presented by Dana (1985), who administered the questionnaire and a battery of other health measures to 179 subjects. Dana's findings indicate that the Sense of Coherence Questionnaire was related in a significant and positive direction to all health measures and in a significant but negative direction to all illness measures.

## Critique

The Sense of Coherence Questionnaire appears to be a reliable instrument for the assessment of a subject's orientation to living. However, at this point there is insufficient evidence regarding its validity. As the author of the measure suggests, judgment of the questionnaire should be held in abeyance until further research is published with regard to its psychometric properties. Yet despite this note of caution, there appears to be sufficient evidence that the scale is an adequate representation of the sense of coherence construct.

It is important to note that the questionnaire represents a serious attempt to operationalize a salutogenic orientation. Although behavioral medicine and health psychology have made significant strides in the past few decades, questions concerning the maintenance of health are as yet unanswered. How are we to understand the brain as a health care system? Or, how do enduring coping styles and personality factors interact with stressors? As we all know, the loss of one's job may lead to debilitating stress, subsequent depression, and even immunosuppression and illness. But under what conditions may the same stressor lead to a reevaluation of career objectives, subsequent increased self-esteem, even immunoenhancement and improved health? It is to this latter question that the Sense of Coherence Questionnaire addresses itself. Despite the methodological limitations discussed earlier, the Sense of Coherence Questionnaire represents a significant step toward the eventual exploration of the salutogenic question.

## References

Antonovsky, A. (1979). *Health, stress, and coping: New perspectives on mental and physical well-being.* San Francisco: Jossey-Bass.

Antonovsky, A. (1983). The sense of coherence: Development of a research instrument. *W. S. Schwartz Research Center for Behavioral Medicine, Tel Aviv University, Newsletter and Research Reports, 1,* 1–11.

Antonovsky, A. (1987). *Unravelling the mysteries of health: How people manage stress and stay well.* San Francisco: Jossey-Bass.

Dana, R.H. (1985, April). *Sense of coherence: Examination of the construct.* Paper presented at the Southwestern Psychological Association, Austin, TX.

Margalit, M. (1985). Perceptions of parents' behavior, familial satisfaction, and sense of coherence in hyperactive children. *Journal of School Psychology, 23,* 355–364.

Rumbaut, R.G. (1983). Stress, health, and the sense of coherence. In M.J. Magenheim (Ed.), *Geriatric medicine and the social sciences.* Philadelphia: Saunders.

Shye, S. (1978). *Theory construction and data analysis in the behavioral sciences.* San Francisco: Jossey-Bass.

**Kirk R. John, Ed.D.**
*Associate Professor of Psychology, California University of Pennsylvania, California, Pennsylvania.*
**Gurmal Rattan, Ph.D.**
*Professor of Educational Psychology, Indiana University of Pennsylvania, Indiana, Pennsylvania.*

# SHIPLEY INSTITUTE OF LIVING SCALE–REVISED

*Robert A. Zachary. Los Angeles, California: Western Psychological Services.*

## Introduction

The Shipley Institute of Living Scale (SILS) is a self-administered test of intellectual ability and, in some cases, cognitive impairment. The SILS is comprised of a 40-item vocabulary subtest and a 20-item abstract reasoning subtest. Administration time is brief (20 minutes or less) and the scale can be administered to examinees ranging in age from 14 years through adulthood. Group or individual assessment is possible, and administration can be completed via a paper-and-pencil or computerized format.

When the SILS was first introduced, it was intended as a measure of cognitive impairment by its developer, Walter Shipley. Building on earlier research findings that indicated certain cognitive abilities deteriorate at different rates, Shipley (1940) hoped to diagnosis mental impairment by comparing the relative status of two cognitive processing skills. Specifically, Shipley decided to compare vocabulary knowledge, which was reported to be resistant to deterioration because of its overlearned nature, to abstract thinking, which had been found to deteriorate at a more rapid pace. However, as several threats to the validity of the SILS to predict cognitive impairment have been identified, use of the scale for this purpose has been questioned (Johnson, 1986; Zachary, 1986). Today, the SILS is probably most used as a screening measure for overall intellectual ability (Zachary, 1986). The SILS Total Score has a high correlation with two measures of complex intellectual functioning: the Wechsler Adult Intelligence Scale (WAIS; Wechsler, 1955) and the Wechsler Adult Intelligence Scale–Revised (WAIS-R; Wechsler, 1981).

In 1986 the SILS was revised by Robert A. Zachary. Substantial changes were made, including age-adjusted norms for computing IQ scores, the use of standard scores to enhance interpretation, a new impairment index accounting for the examinee's age and educational level, and an updated standardization sample (Zachary, 1986). Most notable among these changes is the inclusion of the age-adjusted norms for computing T-scores and IQ scores. As exemplified by Morgan and Hatsukami's (1986) research, without consideration for the normal decline in abstract thinking that accompanies advancing age, the SILS consistently overidentifies adults over the age of 45 as having cognitive impairment. Likewise, without age correction, prediction of IQ scores may be very imprecise at times (Zachary, 1986).

The design of the SILS is simplistic, as the entire test is reproduced on a single administration form. The Vocabulary subtest, including instructions and an example, is printed on the front side of the administration form. The Vocabulary subtest consists of 40 multiple-choice items, which the examinee answers by circling the best synonym from four choices provided. In the Vocabulary sample item, for example, the word *big* is circled as the correct choice for the stimulus word *large* from the alternatives of *red, big, silent,* and *wet.* The examinee is encouraged to complete all items and to guess if necessary.

The Abstract Thinking subtest appears on the reverse side of the administration form. This 20-item subtest assesses abstract thinking through a pattern analysis format; that is, the examinee is required to complete a logical sequence by placing a missing number(s), letter(s), or word(s) in a predetermined blank(s). As an illustration, the sample item for this subtest demonstrates that the letter *E* completes the sequence *A B C D.* As with the Vocabulary subtest, written instructions and the example are provided at the beginning of the test.

## Practical Applications/Uses

Although the SILS has been purported to provide an index of cognitive impairment, it is most widely used as a measure of intellectual ability (Zachary, 1986). Ease of administration, brevity, and group administration are appealing features of this measure. In this regard, the SILS would be very suitable for screening purposes in psychiatric settings, in personnel selection, and in vocational guidance. As well, the SILS has also been frequently used in research.

Zachary (1986) recommends that the SILS be used with persons 14 to 55 years of age. Use of the test with individuals below 14 is not advised because of a lack of age-appropriate norms. Likewise, for individuals older than 55 (even though norm tables are provided in the manual for this age group), use of the SILS is tenuous due to age effects and the limited number of subjects in the norm group in this age range.

Administration of the Shipley is quick and uncomplicated. In fact, paraprofessionals can be used to administer the test as special training is not required. However, Zachary (1986) cautions in the test manual that interpretation should always be completed by a trained professional (i.e., a holder of a master's degree in psychology or its equivalent). Ten minutes is allotted for completion of each subtest.

The SILS can be hand or computer scored. In either case, six summary scores can be calculated, which include a Vocabulary score, an Abstraction score, a Total test score (i.e., Vocabulary plus Abstraction score), a Conceptual Quotient (i.e., the ratio of the Abstraction score to the Vocabulary score), an Abstraction Quotient (i.e., the Conceptual Quotient adjusted for age and education level), and an estimated IQ score. To compute these scores by hand, a scoring key is available that is quick and easy to use. Guide marks are incorporated on the test form to ensure correct alignment of the scoring key.

On the Vocabulary test, the raw score is computed by adding the total number of correct responses to a correction factor. The correction factor (i.e., the total number of responses left blank divided by 4) is computed to correct for guessing by the examinee on this multiple-choice test. All items with two or more responses circled are scored as incorrect. Fractional scores are rounded to the nearest whole number.

The Abstraction test is scored in a like fashion with the scoring key. However, for responses to be marked as correct, there must be an exact match to the predesignated pattern in content and form. For example, if the answer calls for an arabic numeral, the written form of the numeral would be considered incorrect. However, writing style and capitalization are not considered in scoring decisions.

Once correct responses have been tabulated on the Abstraction subtest, they are multiplied by 2 to arrive at the Abstraction raw score. The Total raw score for the test is then arrived at by summing the Vocabulary and Abstraction raw scores. Tables are provided to convert raw scores for each area (Vocabulary, Abstraction, Total score) into standard scores (T-scores), percentile ranks, and mental ages. Tables are also provided to calculate a Conceptual Quotient (CQ), an Abstraction Quotient (AQ), and an estimated IQ score.

The CQ is a comparison of performance on the Abstraction test to performance on the Vocabulary test. This comparison is intended to provide a measure of cognitive impairment based on the assumption that Abstraction scores are more susceptible to mental deterioration than are Vocabulary scores. However, as age and/or educational level can also differentially affect performance on the Abstraction and Vocabulary subtests, an AQ can be computed. The AQ, as developed by Mason and Ganzler (1964), is simply the CQ adjusted for age and educational level.

Tables are also provided to convert the Shipley Total score into an estimated IQ score (WAIS or WAIS-R). These tables were constructed with statistical procedures to correct for the effects of age on scores (Zachary, Crumpton, & Spiegel, 1985; Zachary, Paulson, & Gorsuch, 1985). Recent studies (Jacobsen & Tamkin, 1988; Schear & Harrison, 1988) have supported the use of age-adjusted scores in estimating IQ scores with the SILS. Schear and Harrison (1988) reported that Zachary, Paulson, and Gorsuch's prediction formula was robust and especially effective with middle-aged to older age groups. Likewise, Jacobsen and Tamkin (1988) found Zachary, Paulson, and Gorsuch's formula to be among the best methods available for predicting IQs of older subjects.

As noted, computer scoring for the test is also available. A diskette for microcomputer use can be acquired through a limited licensing agreement. The computer program generates a four- to six-page report of the test results. The report provides a profile of quantitative scores, an estimated IQ score, interpretative hypotheses, and possible caveats in interpreting results.

Although the determination of Shipley raw scores is straightforward and objective, interpretation of SILS scores requires considerable caution. To his credit, Zachary provides a thorough discussion of the major confounding variables to be aware of during test interpretation. To begin with, the SILS should only be administered to individuals within the low average to high average range of intellectual ability. The SILS will tend to underestimate the ability of individuals who possess subnormal or superior intellectual skills because of floor and ceiling effects, respectively. Furthermore, as the SILS measures verbal knowledge, the test is inappropriate for persons with low verbal ability, language handicaps (including bilingual individuals), and those persons with limited formal educational experiences. All of these factors will tend to underestimate the true ability of the examinee. Another confounding variable is the individual's motivation level. Poor motivation may differentially affect performance and result in a higher Vocabulary score relative to the Abstraction score, given that the former requires less mental effort. To familiarize users of the SILS with such diagnostic pitfalls, Zachary has provided several case studies in the manual to illustrate appropriate interpretive techniques.

After a careful review of the examinee's background for the aforementioned factors and other pertinent data, various score comparisons can be made. The Vocabulary, Abstraction, and Total scores can be compared to the mean performance of the standardization group for an estimate of relative standing. The Total raw score can also be converted to an IQ score to be more easily understood by the nonprofessional. In addition, patterns of scores can be compared, according to Shipley's initial plan, to assess cognitive impairment. This is done by computing the CQ and/or AQ scores, which utilize the ratio of Abstraction scores to Vocabulary scores. A CQ or AQ of more than 1 standard deviation below the mean (indicating an Abstraction score significantly lower than the Vocabulary score) suggests the need for a more extensive evaluation.

**Technical Aspects**

The SILS was originally standardized by Shipley on a sample of 1,046 students (Shipley, 1940). The majority of the students ($n$ = 572) were reported to have come from Grades 4 through 8. The remaining students in the sample were either high school ($n$ = 257) or college ($n$ = 217) students. Because of the restricted age range of the sample and the use of the mental age concept in deriving scores, the SILS has been restandardized. Using a group of 290 psychiatric patients examined by Paulson and Lin (1970), new norms for the SILS were developed using a continuous norming procedure to adjust for the effects of age on test scores (Zachary, 1986). Equivalent numbers of males and females were selected from all socioeconomic levels. However, the sample was not systematically selected, and only a small portion of the subjects were older than 54 years of age (Johnson, 1986). In view of the restricted standardization sample, generalization of the results may be questionable.

A comprehensive review of reliability and validity of the SILS is provided in the manual (Zachary, 1986). Looking first at internal consistency, a study completed by Shipley (1940) is representative of the ratings obtained on the SILS. Shipley's investigation resulted in internal consistency coefficients of .87 for Vocabulary, .89 for Abstraction, and .92 for the Total test score. However, test-retest coefficients have been found to be considerably lower. For example, Zachary (1986) reported median test-retest coefficients of .60 for Vocabulary, .66 for the Abstraction test, and .78 for the Total score. The median time interval between the test administrations was reported to be 12 weeks. To summarize, results from the split-half reliability studies suggest satisfactory internal consistency for the SILS; however, its stability over time as noted by the magnitude of the test-retest coefficients does not appear to be very high.

Validity studies on the SILS have concentrated on its efficacy as a predictor of IQ. Seventeen criterion-related studies were reviewed by Zachary (1986), comparing the SILS with various Wechsler scales. Correlations range from .68 to .90 with Wechsler Full Scale IQs and the SILS Total score. Median coefficients for the various Wechsler scales are .77 for the Wechsler-Bellevue, .79 for the WAIS, and .79 for the WAIS-R. These coefficients support the concurrent validity of the SILS.

However, studies examining the validity of the CQ have been mixed. Criticisms of the CQ consist of its susceptibility to the influences of normal aging, educational level, and socioeconomic status (Johnson, 1986; Zachary, 1986). Although the AQ does correct for age and educational level, it only accounts for 38% of the variance in Abstraction scores, suggesting that other unexplained factors may be affecting performance on this measure. In conclusion, the overall psychometric characteristics of the SILS have been well documented by the author. Moreover, Zachary has provided a very forthright and honest appraisal of the SILS's strengths and limitations.

## Critique

The SILS is a brief, easy to administer test that yields a reasonably accurate estimate of verbal intelligence for individuals of low to high average ability. Its major advantage is its ability to be used as a group assessment instrument. However, as Zachary (1986) points out in the SILS manual, the scale should be used only as a screening device. The user should also be cognizant of variables that may affect the validity of SILS test scores, such as low socioeconomic status, poor language skills, limited educational background, advanced chronological age, and low motivation to perform. Additionally, the lack of a representative sample in the standardization may preclude generalization of results to various clinical groups (Fowles & Tunick, 1986). Notwithstanding the above, to provide a quick estimate of cognitive ability, the SILS is recommended as a useful screening measure.

## References

Fowles, G.P., & Tunick, R.H. (1986). WAIS-R and Shipley estimated IQ correlations. *Journal of Clinical Psychology, 42*, 647–649.

Jacobsen, R.H., & Tamkin, A.S. (1988). Converting Shipley Institute of Living Scale scores to IQ: A comparison of methods. *Journal of Clinical Psychology, 44*, 72–75.

Johnson, R.G. (1986). Shipley Institute of Living Scale. In D.J. Keyser & R.C. Sweetland (Eds.), *Test Critiques* (Vol. V, pp. 425–443). Austin, TX: PRO-ED.

Mason, M.F., & Ganzler, H. (1964). Adult norms for the Shipley Institute of Living Scale and Hooper Visual Organization Test based on age and education. *Journal of Gerontology, 19*, 419–424.

Morgan, S.F., & Hatsukami, D.K. (1986). Use of the Shipley Institute of Living Scale for neuropsychological screening of the elderly: Is it an appropriate measure for this population? *Journal of Clinical Psychology, 42*, 796–798.

Paulson, M.J., & Lin, T. (1970). Predicting WAIS IQ from Shipley-Hartford scores. *Journal of Clinical Psychology, 26*, 453–461.

Schear, J.M., & Harrison, W.R. (1988). Estimating WAIS IQ from the Shipley Institute of Living Scale: A replication. *Journal of Clinical Psychology, 44*, 68–71.

Shipley, W.C. (1940). A self-administering scale for measuring intellectual impairment and deterioration. *Journal of Psychology, 9*, 371–377.

Wechsler, D. (1955). *Manual for the Wechsler Adult Intelligence Scale.* San Antonio, TX: Psychological Corporation.

Wechsler, D. (1981). *Manual for the Wechsler Adult Intelligence Scale–Revised.* San Antonio, TX: Psychological Corporation.

Zachary, R.A. (1986). *Shipley Institute of Living Scale: Revised manual.* Los Angeles: Western Psychological Services.

Zachary, R.A., Crumpton, E., & Spiegel, D.E. (1985). Estimating WAIS-R IQ from the Shipley Institute of Living Scale. *Journal of Clinical Psychology, 41*, 532–540.

Zachary, R.A., Paulson, M.J., & Gorsuch, R.L. (1985). Estimating WAIS IQ from the Shipley Institute of Living Scale. *Journal of Clinical Psychology, 41*, 820–831.

**Janet F. Carlson, Ph.D.**
*Assistant Professor, Graduate School of Education and Allied Professions, Fairfield University, Fairfield, Connecticut.*

# SIMILES TEST

*Charles E. Schaefer. Teaneck, New Jersey: Fairleigh Dickinson University, Division of Psychological Services.*

## Introduction

The Similes Test (Schaefer, 1969) was developed to measure creativity through the assessment of poetic expression and thus identify literary talent in children and young adults. Creativity is tested by measuring the individual's prowess in forming original similes when provided the simile stems. The test relies on the notion that creativity and divergent thinking are strongly related.

Charles Schaefer received his Ph.D. from Fordham University while he was a research psychologist. Early in his career, he began working at the Children's Village in Dobbs Ferry, New York, as a supervising psychologist and later became director of psychological services. Since 1986, he has been at Fairleigh Dickinson University, serving as director of training.

The elusive nature of creativity has given rise to a variety of measures designed to quantify this quality. Many of the metrics employed rest on the premise that originality, or divergent thinking, is a mainstay of the construct, as advanced in Guilford's structure-of-intellect model (e.g., Guilford, 1967; Stumberg, 1928; Torrance, 1966). Even before tests of creativity were contrived, the ability to extract similarity between seemingly dissimilar objects was regarded as the standard by which genius was judged.

The Similes Test, too, makes use of this widely accepted proposition, by presenting the test taker with a series of 10 simile stems (e.g., "The young girl was as playful as _____"; Schaefer, 1975, p. 144). Following each stem, there is space for three responses. Two equivalent forms (I and II) of the test are available, and each version contains open-ended simile stems similar in structure to the sample cited but covering a range of senses and feeling states. The test was designed for group administration, although individual administration is clearly an option. The age range for which the test is appropriate is not specified, but normative data are provided for males and females from fourth grade through college.

## Practical Applications/Uses

The Similes Test was designed for use in situations where one needs to, or would like to, evaluate creativity or the potential for creative, literary achievement. Educational settings, such as those serving gifted and talented students, might find the instrument helpful, as might vocational counselors who are attempting to match abilities with prospective career opportunities. The test may prove useful in discriminating between the creative individual who uses an unusual approach and the purely oppositional person who also follows an unusual path but does so for a different reason.

The Similes Test is easily administered to a classroom-size group of test takers. The examiner need not have any specialized training, primarily due to the limited role in which the examiner serves. The instructions on the front cover of the test are read aloud by the examiner. Fifteen minutes are allowed for completion of the test, and test takers are told when half of the allotted time has elapsed. The test is readily modified for administration to smaller groups or individuals. It would also be possible to administer the test orally on a one-to-one basis if the test taker were unable to write his or her responses (e.g., due to blindness or other physical handicap); however, in any of these cases norms and validity would differ from those provided by the test author.

Scoring guides are contained in the appendices of the test manual. Each response is scored for originality using a 6-point scale, with higher values denoting greater originality. Scores were "designed to reflect both the uniqueness and aptness of the responses" (Schaefer, 1969, pp. 3–4). Thus, merely providing unusual responses does not necessarily warrant a high score for originality. Unless the responses are also appropriate endings for the simile stems provided, the test taker will receive low scores. Scores for the 30 responses (three responses for each of 10 stems) are summed for a total score. Although scoring must be done by hand, tests can be scored in about 10 or 15 minutes each once the procedure is mastered.

The difficulties in scoring and interpreting the Similes Test primarily relate to the open-ended format of the instrument itself and the subjectivity of the rating procedure required to score the responses. Although the test manual contains numerous examples for each simile stem at each score level, the general principles on which such fine discriminations are to be made are not clearly provided in the test manual. Interpretation of test results should be conducted only by a professional trained and skilled in measurement principles.

Normative data are provided for rather irregularly spaced grade levels. Hence, the test user must be cautious when attempting to interpret results from individuals or groups not specifically included in the normative sample. Ten groups, ranging in size from 33 to 130 (total $N = 720$), were included in the normative sample for Similes I. Five of these groups also took Similes II. Nearly half of the sample ($n = 322$) were fifth-grade students, stratified by socioeconomic status. Other grade levels in the total sample included 4th ($n = 80$), 6th ($n = 129$), 9th ($n = 54$), 10th ($n = 46$), college males ($n = 56$), and college females ($n = 33$). Means and standard deviations for each of the 10 groups are presented in the manual, together with percentile ranks for four groups, one at each of the 5th-, 6th-, 9th-, and 10th-grade levels. The total score for a given test taker may be compared to the performance of the group that he or she most closely matches. It is not clear why means for males and females at the college level are presented separately rather than collapsed, as were the values for the younger grade levels.

## Technical Aspects

Two interscorer reliability studies were conducted by the test author at the time the Similes Test was normed. In each study, 30 Similes I and 30 Similes II response sheets were selected at random from a much larger pool. Two trained scorers scored the responses independently, and correlation coefficients were computed, presumably between the set of total scores obtained by each rater. Reliability coefficients ranged from .93 to .98. Split-half reliabilities, using an odd-even split and adjusting for length by the Spearman-Brown formula, yielded coefficients of .84 for Similes I and .89 for Similes II for a group of 5th-grade students, .87 for Similes I for 9th-graders, and .82 for Similes I for 10th-graders. All item–total score correlation coefficients were significant at the .01 level for both Similes I and II, with median values of .50 and .56, respectively. Delayed alternate-forms reliability was assessed over a 2-week interval, using a sample of 65 fifth-grade students. The reliability coefficient of .60 was significant at the .01 level.

Concurrent validation of the Similes Test was assessed in four studies. The first used a sample of 47 fifth-grade students from one of the 10 groups in the normative sample who had completed Similes II. These students also completed the Similes Preference Inventory (Pearson & Maddi, 1966) and five subtests of the Torrance Tests of Creative Thinking (Torrance, 1966): Incomplete Figures, Repeated Figures, Ask Questions, Unusual Uses, and Just Suppose. Significant correlation coefficients were obtained between performance on Similes II and three of the Torrance measures: Ask Questions ($r$ = .41), Unusual Uses ($r$ = .32), and Just Suppose ($r$ = .58). In the second study (Anastasi & Schaefer, 1969), 52 female college students completed Similes I and a biographical inventory that measured creative achievement in the literary field. The correlation coefficient indicating the relationship between the two instruments was .31, significant at the .05 level.

The third and fourth studies relating to concurrent validation used nominations. In the third study, four fifth-grade teachers were asked to identify two groups of students from one of the norm groups: (a) those who had demonstrated creative work in the classroom and (b) those who had produced no such creative work but were comparable in terms of academic achievement. Ten students were identified as creative by more than one teacher, and 10 were considered controls (i.e., not creative). The mean scores of the two groups, using the total score on Similes I as the dependent measure, indicated that the creative group scored significantly higher than the control group ($p < .05$). In the fourth study, a similar procedure was used to identify 40 creative and 111 control students from the fourth and fifth grades at three public schools in The Bronx, New York. On Similes I, the creative group performed significantly better than the control group ($p < .01$).

## Critique

At the time the Similes Test was constructed, it was popular to attempt to quantify creativity, with the hope of identifying creative geniuses or at least those with that potential in a variety of fields. A number of these instruments have perished in the face of changing views of creativity (especially regarding its complexity and the variety of forms in which it may be expressed) and the value placed on tests intended to measure the elusive construct. Indeed, Thurstone (1951) commented, albeit indirectly, on the validity of such efforts when he noted that creative solutions to problems were most likely to occur when an individual was relaxed and attention was diffuse, rather than focused or concentrated on the specific problem at hand. Thus, even open-ended, loosely structured techniques, such as those employed in the Similes Test and other similar measures, may thwart the expression of the construct they are intended to measure: creativity. It is not unlike the frequently noted paradoxical directive to be spontaneous.

The Similes Test is an aged measure in need of updating. With revision, many of the technical inadequacies born some 25 years ago would undoubtedly be rectified. It, like several other such tests produced in its time, has not enjoyed particularly wide circulation. At present, it is probably best thought of as a research instrument rather than one with clinical utility. In fact, Mehrens suggested in 1982 that the few creativity tests available at that time should all be considered no more than research instruments, and little else has appeared in the literature since then that argues otherwise.

**References**


Anastasi, A., & Schaefer, C.E. (1969). Biographical correlates of artistic and literary creativity in adolescent girls. *Journal of Applied Psychology, 53*, 267–273.

Guilford, J.P. (1967). *The nature of human intelligence*. New York: McGraw-Hill.

Mehrens, W.A. (1982). Aptitude measurement. In H.E. Mitzel, J.H. Best, & W. Rabinowitz (Eds.), *Encyclopedia of educational research* (5th ed., pp. 137–145). New York: Free Press.

Pearson, P.H., & Maddi, S.R. (1966). The Similes Preference Inventory: Development of a structured measure of the tendency toward variety. *Journal of Consulting Psychology, 30*, 301–308.

Schaefer, C.E. (1969). *Similes manual*. Teaneck, NJ: Author.

Schaefer, C.E. (1975). The importance of measuring metaphorical thinking in children. *Gifted Child Quarterly, 19*, 140–148.

Stumberg, D. (1928). A study of poetic talent. *Journal of Experimental Psychology, 11*, 219–234.

Thurstone, L.L. (1951). Creative talent. In *Proceedings of the 1950 Invitational Conference on Testing Problems* (pp. 55–69). Princeton, NJ: Educational Testing Service.

Torrance, E.P. (1966). *Torrance Tests of Creative Thinking: Norms–technical manual*. Bensenville, IL: Scholastic Testing Service.

**Robert C. Reinehr, Ph.D.**
*Associate Professor of Psychology, Southwestern University, Georgetown, Texas.*

# SOCIAL RETICENCE SCALE

*Warren H. Jones. Palo Alto, California: Consulting Psychologists Press, Inc.*

## Introduction

The Social Reticence Scale (SRS) is a 20-item self-report inventory intended to measure shyness in adolescents and adults (Jones, 1986). Although originally developed for the conduct of basic personality research, it is now available commercially for use in applied as well as scientific settings.

The present SRS is an outgrowth of an earlier version (Jones & Russell, 1982) that contained 21 items, 3 for each of seven components of shyness. All the items on the original version were worded such that positive endorsement of an item indicated greater shyness. Although the reliability was adequate and validity findings were promising, there was concern that having all the items worded in the same direction might cause an acquiescence response set to confound results. There was also a small but significant correlation with an independent measure of social desirability. The current version consists of 10 of the original items, slightly rewritten, and 10 new items.

## Practical Applications/Uses

The SRS is self-administered, with each of the 20 items on the scale endorsed on a 5-point Likert-type scale ranging from not at all characteristic of the examinee to extremely characteristic. Ten of the items are worded such that a positive endorsement of item indicates greater shyness; for the other 10 items a negative endorsement indicates greater shyness.

The manual suggests that individual administration is preferable and that reliability and validity will be improved if verbal assurances are given of the confidentiality of respondent's answers. Means and standard deviations are provided for several populations, including a large sample of college students and smaller samples of high school students, general adults, convicted felons, hospital workers, and parents of adolescents in counseling. Separate means and standard deviations are provided for males and females within each standardization sample.

Although slim, the manual is well organized, well written, and follows quite closely the guidelines suggested in the *Standards for Educational and Psychological Testing* (American Educational Research Association, American Psychological Association, & National Council on Measurement in Education, 1985). Suggestions are made for the use of the scale in applied settings, but they are very conservative, and it is plainly stated that the scale should not be used for individual clinical diagnosis. In all, the manual is a model of scientific restraint, confining itself to presenting a description of the development of the scale and to a summary of the reliability and validity information available at the time of publication.

## Technical Aspects

The SRS manual reports a test-retest reliability coefficient of .87 for a sample of 101 college students, with 8 weeks between administrations. Estimates of internal reliability for this and other samples were above .90. Factor analysis suggests that there are two principal, and highly correlated, factors involved in the scale: one set of items that assesses feelings of isolation from others, and another set that focuses on ease of communication with others.

Several types of validity information are provided. The scale scores correlate .67 with shyness self-labeling, although none of the SRS items contain the word *shyness*. SRS scores also correlate significantly with scores on the UCLA Loneliness Scale (Russell, Peplau, & Cutrona, 1980) and the Differential Loneliness Scale (Schmidt & Sermat, 1983). Jones and Carpenter (1986) report an inverse correlation between scores on the SRS and the number of friends or number of persons in the support network of college students. SRS scores also correlate highly and in the expected direction with the two subscales of the 16PF (Cattell, 1967) that appear to be most directly related to shyness. It should be noted, however, that the subscales of the 16PF are themselves suspect from a psychometric point of view, and that substantial correlations were also found between the SRS and several 16PF factors that are less obviously related to shyness.

In addition to these relationships with other paper-and-pencil measures, SRS scores have been found to correlate substantially with judges' ratings of college students' shyness (Cherulnik, Way, Ames, & Hutto, 1981) and to descriptions of college students by their friends and family members.

## Critique

The shortcomings of the SRS are those associated with all self-report trait measures: insufficient information concerning situational determinants, substantial correlations with traits that bear little theoretical relation to the trait in question, and the possibility that a social desirability response bias may account for some of the reported findings. It should be noted, however, that the developers of the SRS have recognized most of these problems and have made an attempt to address them. In addition to the validity information provided, the manual suggests seven general areas where further research is needed and outlines the previous findings in each of these areas briefly.

The SRS is essentially a tool for personality research rather than for use in applied settings. Although possible clinical applications are discussed in the manual, no unsupported claims are made for the scale. Development has been sound to this point and the suggestions made for possible directions of future research are thoughtful and informative. This is an excellent tool for personality research and holds at least some promise of value in clinical settings.

## References

American Educational Research Association, American Psychological Association, & National Council on Measurement in Education. (1985). *Standards for educational and psychological testing*. Washington, DC: American Psychological Association.

Cattell, R.B. (1967). *The Sixteen Personality Factor Questionnaire*. Champaign, IL: Institute for Personality & Ability Testing.

Cherulnik, P., Way, J., Ames, S., & Hutto, D. (1981). Impressions of high and low Machiavellian men. *Journal of Personality, 49*, 388–400.

Jones, W.H. (1986). *Manual for the Social Reticence Scale*. Palo Alto, CA: Consulting Psychologists Press.

Jones, W.H., & Carpenter, B.N. (1986). Shyness, social behavior and relationships. In W.H. Jones, J.M. Cheek, & S.R. Briggs (Eds.), *Shyness: Perspectives on research and treatment* (pp. 227–238). New York: Plenum.

Jones, W.H., & Russell, D. (1982). The Social Reticence Scale: An objective instrument to measure shyness. *Journal of Personality Assessment, 46*, 629–631.

Russell, D., Peplau, L.A., & Cutrona, C. (1980). The Revised UCLA Loneliness Scale: Concurrent and discriminant validity evidence. *Journal of Personality and Social Psychology, 39*, 472–480.

Schmidt, N., & Sermat, V. (1983). Measuring loneliness in different relationships. *Journal of Personality and Social Psychology, 44*, 1038–1047.

**Jan Hankins, Ph.D.**
*Senior Research Associate, University of Tennessee, Knoxville, Tennessee.*

# SPECIFIC APTITUDE TEST BATTERY

*U.S. Employment Service. Washington, D.C.: U.S. Department of Labor.*

## Introduction

A Specific Aptitude Test Battery (SATB) measures an untrained or inexperienced individual's potential to acquire the skills involved in a specific occupation. The SATBs combine two, three, or four aptitudes as measured by subtests derived from the U.S. Employment Service's General Aptitude Test Battery (GATB). Each SATB has a cutoff score that purportedly relates to successful performance in a given occupation. To date, more than 450 SATBs have been developed through studies on specific occupations (U.S. Department of Labor, 1977).

To understand the SATB, an overview of the "parent" battery is necessary. The General Aptitude Test Battery (GATB) measures an individual's vocational aptitudes and is used to help him or her in choosing an occupation. First published in 1947, the GATB consists of 12 tests (Name Comparison, Computation, Three Dimensional Space, Vocabulary, Tool Matching, Arithmetic Reason, Form Matching, Mark Making, Place, Turn, Assemble, and Disassemble) that measure nine vocational aptitudes. Descriptions of these aptitudes follow:

1. *General Learning Ability (G):* ability to understand instructions and underlying principles and the ability to reason and make judgments (measured by Three Dimensional Space, Vocabulary, and Arithmetic Reason).
2. *Verbal Aptitude (V):* covers several abilities—understanding word meanings and ideas associated with them, using words effectively, understanding language and the relationships between words, understanding entire sentences and paragraphs, and presenting information or ideas clearly (measured by Vocabulary).
3. *Numerical Aptitude (N):* ability to perform arithmetic operations quickly and accurately (measured by Computation and Arithmetic Reason).
4. *Spatial Aptitude (S):* ability to understand forms in space and the relationships of planes and solid objects (measured by Three Dimensional Space).
5. *Form Perception (P):* ability to perceive pertinent details in objects or pictorial or graphic material, and to make visual comparisons and discriminations in slight differences in shapes and shadings as well as widths and lengths (measured by Tool Matching and Form Matching).
6. *Clerical Perception (Q):* ability to perceive pertinent detail in verbal or tabular material, to see differences in copy, to proofread words and numbers, and to avoid perceptual errors in arithmetic computation (measured by Name Comparison).
7. *Motor Coordination (K):* ability to coordinate eyes, hands, and fingers rapidly

and accurately while making precise movements with speed, and to make a movement response quickly and accurately (measured by Mark Making).

8. *Finger Dexterity (F):* ability to move the fingers and manipulate small objects with the fingers quickly and accurately (measured by Assemble and Disassemble).

9. *Manual Dexterity (M):* ability to move the hands easily and with skill, and to work with the hands in placing and turning motions (measured by Place and Turn).

Finger Dexterity and Manual Dexterity (GATB tests Place, Turn, Assemble, and Disassemble) are measured with the use of apparatus tests; paper-and-pencil tests tap the remaining aptitudes.

A Spanish edition of the GATB (Bateria de Examenes de Aptitud General) became available in 1977. It is designed for use with Spanish-speaking employment service applicants, including those in Puerto Rico. There are also GATB administration methods suitable for deaf examinees. Separate norms are available on the Manual Dexterity tests when administered to persons who must remain seated (U.S. Department of Labor, 1982).

A great deal of research has been done on the GATB. In addition, several reviews have appeared (see Humphreys, 1959; Keesling, 1985; Kirnan & Geisinger, 1986; and Weiss, 1972). The remainder of this review will pertain only to the specific SATBs developed from the GATB. Readers interested in the total battery are referred to the U.S. Employment Service and the earlier reviews.

**Practical Applications/Uses**

The Specific Aptitude Test Batteries (SATBs) comprise from two to four of the GATB aptitudes that, in combination, are used to predict an individual's chance of success in a given occupation. In addition to a cutoff score for specific occupations, each SATB also has a system of Occupational Aptitude Patterns (OAPs). The OAPs consist of combinations of aptitudes, with associated cutoff scores for groups or families of occupations. The OAPs indicate the aptitude requirements for groups of occupations. The current 66 OAPs cover 97% of all nonsupervisory occupations (U.S. Department of Labor, 1982).

An individual's score on the specific tests composing the SATB are compared with the aptitude cutoff scores for the OAP, and a letter grade of H, M, or L is assigned for that OAP. If the examinee obtained scores that meet or exceed the cutoff scores in a given OAP, an H is assigned. If the examinee's score plus 1 standard error of measurement meets or exceeds the OAP's cutoff scores, an M is assigned. If the individual's score plus 1 standard error of measurement does not meet all the cutoff scores for the OAP, the individual receives an L. For those receiving an H, their scores exceed current workers judged to be satisfactory in the occupation; there is a good probability that those individuals will do well on the job. Examinees who receive an M score are close to workers judged to be satisfactory in the occupation, but their probability of doing well on the job will be lower than for those assigned an H. An individual who receives an L scores similarly to or lower than current workers found to be unsatisfactory in the occupation. The probability that such examinees will succeed on the job is low (Kirnan & Geisinger, 1986).

The process by which tests are chosen for a SATB becomes a little confusing. First, a job analysis is performed to determine which aptitudes appear important to that particular job. Second, the entire GATB battery is administered to applicants or current employees. If administered to applicants, they are hired without regard to test scores. Third, supervisory ratings are obtained for each employee. The ratings are dichotomized into a high and a low group by placing a certain percentage, usually 34–36%, of the workers into the low group to correspond with the percentage of workers considered unsatisfactory or marginal. Next, an analysis of the GATB tests is performed. The mean, standard deviation, and correlation with supervisory ratings is obtained for each aptitude. The aptitudes with the highest means, highest correlations with supervisory ratings, and that appear important to the occupation based on the job analysis are chosen for further consideration. Last, two to four aptitudes are chosen that yield the optimum differentiation between the high and low groups. Cutoff scores are set at approximately 1 standard deviation below the mean scores. A phi coefficient is used to determine to which OAP, if any, the occupation can be assigned.

**Technical Aspects**

Research to develop SATBs for specific occupations has been a continuing effort since the GATB was published in 1947. Until 1967, most of the studies were done at a single location, and samples usually consisted of workers who happened to be available at the time of the study. Minority group membership was not one of the considerations in sample selection, and no information on group membership was obtained. Subsequent studies have indicated that blacks, Native Americans, and Mexican-Americans tend to score lower than whites on the GATB aptitudes, especially those involving General Learning Ability, Verbal Aptitude, and Numerical Aptitude. In studies since 1967, the emphasis in SATB research has been placed on obtaining samples containing minority groups. In 1972, an effort was begun to revalidate the SATBs separately on samples of minority and nonminority persons; as of 1982, 36 SATBs had been revalidated. The samples used contained sufficient numbers of one minority group to allow separate analysis of minority and nonminority groups, and were shown to be fair and valid for minority groups (U.S. Department of Labor, 1977, 1982).

The correlation coefficients reported as validities for the SATBs in the technical information this reviewer received ranged from .17 to .68. Only two were above .60, while the rest ranged from .17 to .31. Unfortunately, there is no rule of thumb regarding exactly how high a validity coefficient should be (Cronbach, 1971). However, a validity coefficient of .31 or lower is surely less than desirable.

Validity was established using a phi coefficient in some reports, while a tetrachoric correlation coefficient is used in others. The technical reports received, however, did not indicate exactly what variables were correlated. One is left to assume that the scores on the aptitudes are somehow combined from the tests to achieve one global score that is then correlated with supervisory ratings, as this is the only criterion described anywhere. How such a global score was obtained is not described.

Because each SATB contains a unique set of aptitudes, reliability must be established for each one. No information provided to this reviewer by the U.S. Employment Service addressed the reliability of the specific SATBs or how such reliability was established.

## Critique

There are a number of sources of confusion and concern regarding how aptitudes are chosen for specific SATBs. First, when dichotomizing employees into high and low groups, no evidence is provided to document the claim that 34% to 36% of the workers can be considered unsatisfactory or marginal in their performance. Second, when selecting aptitudes that provide optimum differentiation between the high and low groups, there is scant information provided on how such maximum differentiation is determined. Last, the statistical analysis is performed in terms of the *aptitudes* measured by the GATB rather than on the specific GATB *tests*. This reviewer could find no information on how scores on the aptitudes are determined. For example, many of the aptitudes are measured by more than one test. Are the test scores combined in some fashion? If so, how?

A major criticism of the SATB program is that a number of different aptitudes are equally effective in predicting job success. This affects the OAPs, which rely heavily on the validity information of the SATB for their development (Kirnan & Geisinger, 1986).

Nunnally (1978) states that "at least two types of reliability coefficients should be computed and reported for any test that is employed widely" (p. 236), which is also implied in Standard 2.6 of the *Standards for Educational and Psychological Testing* (American Educational Research Association, American Psychological Association, & National Council on Measurement in Education, 1985). Further, Standard 2.1 states:

> For each total score, subscore, or combination of scores that is reported, estimates of relevant reliabilities and standard errors of measurement should be provided in adequate detail to enable the test user to judge whether scores are sufficiently accurate for the intended use of the test. (p. 20)

Standard 2.10 goes on to say that

> Standard errors of measurement should be reported at critical score levels. Where cut scores are specified for selection or classification, the standard errors of measurement should be reported for score levels at or near the cut score. (p. 22)

Feldt and Brennan (1989) indicate that the standard error is more stable from group to group than is the reliability coefficient. However, no reliabilities or standard errors of measurement were reported in any of the information received by this reviewer.

The *Standards for Educational and Psychological Testing* state that validity is the most important consideration in test evaluation (p. 9). Mehrens and Lehmann (1984) agree. The *Standards* go on to indicate that an ideal validation includes several types of evidence. This reviewer found evidence for only one type of validity and only one source of that validity evidence. The technical reports this reviewer received on specific SATBs were weak in reported validity.

Standard 1.14 in the *Standards* indicates that when rater judgments are used as criteria in concurrent validity studies, the training and experience of the raters should be described if possible. There is no indication that raters were trained. Further, Mehrens and Lehmann (1984) indicate that supervisor ratings have many inadequacies as a criterion. For example, if the test score does not correlate highly with the ratings, it is not possible to determine if the test did not predict job success or whether the supervisor could not rate the individual accurately, or both. In addition, the reliability of the criterion measure will affect validity (Thorndike, 1982). An unreliable criterion measure will produce a low validity coefficient.

The only validity data provided were dichotomized for scores on the aptitudes as well as supervisory ratings. Aptitude scores were dichotomized into those above the cutoff score and those below, while supervisory ratings were dichotomized into a high and low group. Technically speaking, as both of these may be thought of as continuous variables that have been dichotomized, a tetrachoric correlation is the correct correlation to use (Welkowitz, Ewen, & Cohen, 1976). Thus, a technically incorrect coefficient was used when the phi coefficient was applied. Another concern arises from the fact that this reviewer was unable to replicate reported phi coefficients using the procedure described by Nunnally (1978) for computing phi using tabular data. Apparently the developers made use of the fact that the phi coefficient is equal to the square root of chi square divided by the total sample size (Nunnally, 1978). However, they apparently used Yates's correction (Walpole, 1968) for computing chi square because there is only one degree of freedom. Thus, the Yates correction has affected the computed phi coefficient.

Guion (1965) indicates that a chi square can be used appropriately to establish evidence of validity, as was done for tests 5-A and 6-A. Guion contends, however, that one should not stop with the use of the chi square because it does not indicate the strength of the relationship. He suggests using expectancy tables. Thorndike (1982) suggests the use of *taxonomic validity,* which indicates whether persons in different occupations have different means on the test. He suggests use of analysis of variance procedures and a point-biserial correlation to differentiate the two groups. This will provide evidence of the strength of the relationship. The reports contain a chi square analysis to determine if there is a significant relationship between job performance criteria (supervisory ratings, presumably) and the SATB. In all reports received, the significant relationship did exist. Although use of Yates's correction for the chi square is appropriate in these cases, the developers failed to mention use of the correction in some of the reports. This can create confusion.

Mehrens and Lehmann (1984) indicate that face validity is important from an acceptance viewpoint. If the test appears relevant, the examinees may take it more seriously. None of the GATB tests appear to have any type of face validity whatsoever.

Guion (1965) contends that predictive validity is the most relevant of the types of validity to personnel practice. The common practice of using concurrent validity is an inadequate substitute. Only one report received by this reviewer involved predictive validity. All others reported concurrent validity studies.

In general, this reviewer found it difficult to obtain accurate and timely information from the publishers for this review, and the review is, therefore, based on scant information. For example, despite several requests to see a copy of the administration manual, it was never provided and a copy could not be obtained locally. Thus, no information could be provided here on the administration of the test(s), scoring, and so forth. Previous reviews of the GATB discuss these briefly, but how administration and scoring differs for the SATB is not known.

## References


American Educational Research Association, American Psychological Association, & National Council on Measurement in Education. (1985). *Standards for educational and psychological testing*. Washington, DC: American Psychological Association.

Cronbach, L.J. (1971). Test validation. In R.L. Thorndike (Ed.), *Educational measurement* (2nd ed., pp. 443–507). Washington, DC: American Council on Education.

Feldt, L.S., & Brennan, R.L. (1989). Reliability. In R.L. Linn (Ed.), *Educational measurement* (3rd ed., pp. 105–146). New York: American Council on Education.

Guion, R.M. (1965). *Personnel testing*. New York: McGraw-Hill.

Humphreys, L.G. (1959). General Aptitude Test Battery. In O.K. Buros (Ed.), *The fifth mental measurements yearbook* (pp. 698–700). Highland Park, NJ: Gryphon Press.

Keesling, J.W. (1985). General Aptitude Test Battery. In J.V. Mitchell, Jr. (Ed.), *The ninth mental measurements yearbook* (pp. 1645–1647). Lincoln, NE: Buros Institute of Mental Measurements.

Kirnan, J.P., & Geisinger, K.F. (1986). General Aptitude Test Battery. In D.J. Keyser & R.C. Sweetland (Eds.), *Test critiques* (Vol. V, pp. 150–167). Austin, TX: PRO-ED.

Mehrens, W.A., & Lehmann, I.J. (1984). *Measurement and evaluation in education and psychology* (3rd ed). New York: Holt, Rinehart, & Winston.

Nunnally, J.C. (1978). *Psychometric theory*. New York: McGraw-Hill.

Thorndike, R.L. (1982). *Applied psychometrics*. Boston: Houghton Mifflin.

U.S. Department of Labor. (1956). *Technical report on standardization of the General Aptitude Test Battery for scrapper (paper goods)*. Washington, DC: Government Printing Office.

U.S. Department of Labor. (1970). *Development of USES Aptitude Battery for selected aircraft assembly occupations* (Technical Report S-76R). Washington DC: Government Printing Office.

U.S. Department of Labor. (1972). *Development of USES Aptitude Battery for yarn texturing-machine operator* (Technical Report No. 168). Washington, DC: Government Printing Office.

U.S. Department of Labor. (1973). *Development of USES Specific Aptitude Test Battery for operating engineer II (construction)* (Technical Report S-343 R). Washington, DC: Government Printing Office.

U.S. Department of Labor. (1975). *Technical report on development of USES Specific Aptitude Test Battery for production mechanic, tin cans (tinware), preventive maintenance mechanic, cup forming (paper goods), line mechanic, cup forming (paper goods)*. Washington, DC: Government Printing Office.

U.S. Department of Labor. (1977). *USES Test research report no. 31*. Washington, DC: Government Printing Office.

U.S. Department of Labor. (1978). *Development of USES Specific Aptitude Battery S-470: Weaver (basketry)* (Technical Report S-470). Washington, DC: Government Printing Office.

U.S. Department of Labor. (1982). *USES Test research report no. 32*. Washington, DC: Government Printing Office.

Walpole, R.E. (1968). *Introduction to statistics.* London: Macmillan.

Weiss, D.J. (1972). General Aptitude Test Battery. In O.K. Buros (Ed.), *The seventh mental measurements yearbook* (pp. 1058–1061). Highland Park, NJ: Gryphon Press.

Welkowitz, J., Ewen, R.B., & Cohen, J. (1976). *Introductory statistics for the behavioral sciences.* New York: Academic Press.

**James A. Moses, Jr., Ph.D.**
*Clinical Associate Professor of Psychiatry and Behavioral Sciences, Stanford University School of Medicine, and Coordinator, Psychological Assessment Unit, Veterans Administration Medical Center, Palo Alto, California.*

---

# STATE-TRAIT ANGER EXPRESSION INVENTORY, RESEARCH EDITION

*Charles D. Spielberger. Odessa, Florida: Psychological Assessment Resources, Inc.*

## Introduction

The State-Trait Anger Expression Inventory (STAXI) is a 44-item, self-report, objectively scored questionnaire. The STAXI was designed to measure the experience, control, and mode of expression or suppression of anger as a situational response and as a general stress response predilection. It consists of six scales, one of which (Trait Anger) has two component subscales. Descriptions of the STAXI scale dimensions follow (Spielberger, 1988, p. 1):

1. *State Anger (S-Anger):* a 10-item scale for measuring the intensity of angry feelings at a particular time.
2. *Trait Anger (T-Anger):* a 10-item scale for measuring individual differences in the disposition to experience anger. The two subscales of the T-Anger scale are
   a. *Angry Temperament (T-Anger/T),* a 4-item measure of a general propensity to experience and express anger without specific provocation; and
   b. *Angry Reaction (T-Anger/R),* a 4-item measure of individual differences in the disposition to experience anger when criticized or treated unfairly by other individuals.
3. *Anger-in (AX/In):* an 8-item scale for measuring the frequency with which angry feelings are held in or suppressed.
4. *Anger-out (AX/Out):* an 8-item scale for measuring how often an individual expresses anger toward other people or objects in the environment.
5. *Anger Control (AX/Con):* an 8-item scale for measuring the frequency with which an individual attempts to control the expression of anger.
6. *Anger Expression (AX/EX):* a research scale based on the responses to the 24 items of the AX/In, AX/Out, and AX/Con scales that provides a general index of the frequency that anger is expressed, regardless of the direction of expression.

The STAXI was developed to objectively assess specific components of the experience, expression, and control of anger as an emotional response tendency in a variety of normal and clinical groups. Spielberger and his colleagues have been concerned with application of these dimensions to the study of normal and abnormal personality processes as well as a variety of stress-related medical conditions. They have reviewed and contributed to an extensive and rapidly growing literature that supports the relevance of anger and other stress-related affective states to the development and progression of hypertension, coronary heart disease, and some forms of cancer. Assessment of specific psychosomatic elements that are modifiable has potentially important implications for the diagnosis, treatment, and prevention of stress-related disorders.

The author of the STAXI, Charles D. Spielberger, Ph.D., received his Ph.D. from the University of Iowa in 1954. Currently he is Distinguished University Professor of Psychology and Director, Center for Research in Behavioral Medicine and Health Psychology at the University of South Florida, Tampa, where he has been a faculty member since 1972. He has held tenured faculty positions at Duke University (1955–62), Vanderbilt University (1963–66), and Florida State University (1967–72), where he served as director of the Clinical Psychology Training Program. He also has served as a training specialist in psychology at the National Institute of Mental Health (1965–67) and was twice as a research fellow at the Netherlands Institute for Advanced Study (1979–1980 and 1985–1986). His extensive bibliography includes authorship, coauthorship, or editorship of more than 280 professional publications through October 1989.

Spielberger currently serves as the treasurer of the American Psychological Association and as president of its Division of Clinical Psychology. In 1991 he will become the 99th president of the Association. He is a past president of numerous learned societies, including The Society for Personality Assessment, the International Council of Psychologists, and Psi Chi, the National Honor Society in Psychology, and he is a Fellow of Sigma Xi, AAAS, the Society for Behavioral Medicine, and 10 American Psychological Association divisions. He is a Diplomate in Clinical Psychology of the American Board of Professional Psychology and a Distinguished Practitioner of the National Academies of Practice. He founded the *American Journal of Community Psychology,* served as editor for 7 years, and is currently an associate editor of four other learned journals, as well as an editorial board member of 10 additional professional periodicals.

The STAXI represents an advance over previous instruments for evaluation of anger and hostility due to its theoretically based and empirically confirmed multivariate specification of anger components, and to the relevance of these dimensions to the behavioral analysis of the etiology of a wide variety of stress-related or stress-influenced medical disorders. Prior to the development of the STAXI there was considerable ambiguity in the operational definition of anger and the related but distinct constructs of hostility and aggression.

Spielberger and his colleagues have been concerned with parametric analysis of *anger,* which they define as "an emotional state that comprises feelings that vary in intensity from mild annoyance or aggravation to fury and rage, and that are accompanied by arousal of the autonomic nervous system" (Spielberger, 1988, p. 6). Hostility is distinguished from anger by the presence of complex attitudes that motivate an individual to behave in verbally or physically aggressive and vengeful ways. Aggression typically refers to physical or verbal behavior that results in destructive or punitive action, which is often motivated by hostility but may also be instrumental to achieving the goals (for example, the bombardier who impassively devastates an enemy city and may actually feel guilt about the death of civilians rather than anger toward them). The characterization of anger that emerges from the analyses of Spielberger and his colleagues is multidimensionally complex and shows that the experience and expression of anger can form many individualized patterns that may have different implications for health, emotional status, illness vulnerability, and illness resistance.

**Practical Applications/Uses**

Spielberger notes that the phenomenology of anger is conceptually difficult to define and that this unique and important aspect of anger has been overlooked in much of the research literature prior to the development of the STAXI. It has central relevance to many contemporary theories of personality and health status, however, and must be systematically studied. In particular the distinction between situational or state, and predispositional personality or trait, characteristics has not been previously addressed in the literature on anger and hostility measurement. State anger is defined by Spielberger (1988, p. 6) as "an emotional state or condition that consists of subjective feelings of tension, annoyance, irritation, fury and rage, with concomitant activation or arousal of the autonomic nervous system." The level of state anger is thought to vary with the perception and interpretation of the situational stressor experienced by the individual. Trait anger involves individual differences in a general predisposition to experience state anger with greater or lesser frequency over time in response to situational stress.

The STAXI also assesses the mode of anger expression in the individual. Recent research findings suggest that the mode of anger expression as well as the degree and type of anger experienced along state or trait dimensions are important factors that influence cardiovascular health status and possibly vulnerability to some types of cancer (for reviews see Spielberger, 1988; Spielberger, Krasner, & Solomon, 1988; McMillian, 1984). These phasic and tonic behavioral and affective dimensions must be evaluated separately. The manner of expression of anger is categorized as suppressive or self-directed ("anger in") or openly expressive and other directed ("anger out") toward the frustrating, anger-provoking person, situation, or object, or a symbolic equivalent of it. The "anger out" expressive alternative typically involves an increase in state anger and verbal or physical aggression toward the object.

Literature reviewed in the test manual by Spielberger (1988, pp. 9–10) shows a consistent relationship between higher scores on the "anger in" coping style and phasic blood pressure elevation and tonic hypertension. Although this general relationship supports the relevance of the suppressive anger expression dimension to these cardiovascular risk factors, most studies in the area are exploratory and as yet have not employed the refined dimensional anger experience and expression dimensions that are available with use of the STAXI. Spielberger's review of the literature in the manual also notes that investigators have begun to evaluate a variety of demographic and health variables such as race, sex, socioeconomic status, and hypertension risk in examining the relationship of anger variables to health status. It appears likely that investigations relating variations on each of these demographic variables and STAXI dimensions to each other in graded factorial or multivariate experimental designs will be necessary to work out the relevance of the behavioral variables to health risk.

The STAXI is designed for administration to persons aged 13 years through adulthood. A fifth-grade reading ability is required to complete the STAXI, which is the level of reading comprehension necessary to read most newspapers and popular magazines. Separate norms are provided by sex in three age groups: adolescent, college student, and adult. Separate norms by sex also are provided for "special populations" of general medical and surgical patients, prison inmates, and military recruits. Spielberger refers to this release of the STAXI as a "research edition" because there are gaps in the normative database for STAXI scales for men and women in some age ranges. Specifically, normative data remain to be reported for the AX/Con and AX/EX scales for women. Norms for adolescents were available at the time of this review. The normative database for this test is very extensive and consists of more than 9,000 subjects through the time that the manual appeared in 1988. Although some fine-tuning of the scaling remains to be completed for some groups, available norms can be used with confidence.

The STAXI can be administered in hand-scored (Form HS) or machine-scored (Form G) formats. Form G (group) is for large-scale applications of the test, particularly in research and evaluation work. The Form G respondent must answer with a No. 2 pencil on a special answer sheet provided by the publisher, who offers an automated machine scoring service for this form in which the answer sheet is scanned by an OCR device. The mail-in scoring service provides raw scores and their percentile and standardized linear T-score equivalent values. Form G has a single answer sheet with directions for marking answers and spaces for demographic data reporting. Essential information that must be provided by the subject to allow for machine scoring is an identification number (typically the social security number), age, date of completion, sex, and highest educational grade completed. Optional codes for demographic research information gathering include categories for marital status, ethnic group, and "special codes" that are not otherwise defined in the manual. The test can be machine scored without these optional codes.

The STAXI Form HS test materials consist of a single-use item booklet and a single-use, two-page answer or rating sheet. Routine demographic information collected on the answer sheet consists of the subject's name (or code number), sex, age, date of testing, educational level, occupation, and marital status. Age, sex, and educational level are necessary to choose the appropriate set of STAXI norms. The answer sheet is divided into three parts, which are presented in separate block formats. Items are numbered within blocks with four numbered circles to the right of each item number. The subject blackens in a circle to indicate his or her response for that item. Respondents rate items for Part 1 (State Anger) on a 4-point scale according to "How I Feel Right Now." Items for Part 2 (T-Anger, T-Anger/T, T-Anger/R) are rated according to "How I Generally Feel." Items for Part 3 (AX/Con, AX/In, AX/Out, AX/EX) involve ratings of the frequency of behavioral reactions listed "When Angry or Furious."

There are two pages to the STAXI rating sheet. Page 1 is for the respondent's use, and page 2 is a pressure-sensitive answer sheet that has a listing of the scale on which each item is scored next to the item. When the subject marks an answer on page 1, page 2 is marked simultaneously. Page 2 alone is used by the scorer to tally the subject's raw scores on each scale. Formulas for scoring each of the STAXI summary scores are provided at the bottom of the scorer's carbon-copy answer sheet.

Raw scores are transferred from the scoring sheet to the tabular scoring grid on the last page of the STAXI item booklet. The appropriate normative group is selected for the subject, and raw scores are translated to percentiles and T-scores for plotting on the STAXI Profile Chart (which also is on the final page of the item booklet). Spielberger advises in the manual (p. 17) that percentile ranks are most appropriate for comparison of the score of an individual on a STAXI measure with the appropriate normative group. Normalized linear T-scores are provided to make STAXI scores equivalent across scales and subscales to allow for statistical analysis that requires comparable metric values across measures for parametric analyses.

STAXI administration does not require specialized training in psychology or education, although an examiner with professional experience is preferred. With careful attention to administration and scoring procedures that are presented in the manual, administration of the STAXI need not be more than a clerical task. Few administration difficulties are foreseeable if the subject has the required reading proficiency, but Spielberger advises that confusion, distractibility, or hesitancy in responding on the part of an examinee should be cues for assistance on the part of the examiner. Respondents who have questions about the nature of the test, which is referred to as a "self-rating questionnaire" on the question booklet and answer sheet, should generally be advised that the test "inquires about feelings, attitudes, and behavior" (Spielberger, 1988, p. 2).

The STAXI is not timed, but the manual advises that the majority of adolescent and adult examinees can complete the inventory in 10 to 15 minutes. The clerical scoring and profiling of the test results averages less than 5 minutes for an experienced examiner. Interpretation of STAXI results, however, requires professional training in psychology, psychiatry, or a related mental health field. Specialized technical knowledge of the research literature that relates the anger constructs as measured by the STAXI scales to both normal personality functioning as well as stress-influenced psychosomatic disorders and medical illnesses is necessary for valid interpretation in the clinical or research setting. A knowledge of psychometrics also is essential to appreciate the strengths and limitations of the test. The utility and validity of the STAXI scores as indices of a patient's clinical status can only be endorsed if the interpreter is professionally qualified by training and experience to make such evaluations.

Spielberger recommends normative interpretation of the STAXI scores, which typically involves percentile referencing. Scores between the 25th and 75th percentiles are considered within normal limits. Higher scores within this normal range suggest greater likelihood that the individual will become angry, express anger outwardly, or suppress angry affect. Such scores do not reflect sufficient anger levels to predispose respondents to increased risk for development of stress-related physical or psychological syndromes. Scores that exceed the 75th percentile for the appropriate reference group do suggest sufficient anger experience or expression to be maladaptive, in that such respondents are at increased risk for development of stress-related physical or psychological disorders. The combination of high AX/In and low AX/Out with a high anxiety level has been related to elevated blood pressure and hypertension. Scores above the 90th percentile on AX/In and AX/Out are related to increased risk of coronary artery disease and myocardial infarction (Spielberger, 1988, p. 4).

The manual presents interpretive statements for high scores on each of the STAXI scales (p. 5, Table 4). Although an abstract of these trends is presented here to suggest differences among the indices as anger experience, expression, and control parameters, more detail is available in the manual's descriptions:

*High S-Anger scores:* suggest the intensity of anger experienced at the present time according to the associated percentile value.

*High T-Anger scores:* suggest frustration as a result of perceived unfair treatment.

*High T-Anger/T scores:* suggest ready expression of anger with minimal provocation, tenuous anger control, and impulsiveness in anger expression.

*High T-Anger/R scores:* suggest high sensitivity to criticism, perceived affronts, and negative evaluation by others.

*High AX/In* scores: suggests frequent experience of anger that is suppressed rather than voiced or acted out physically.

*High AX/Out scores:* suggests frequent experience of anger that is openly expressed toward people or objects in the environment by verbal or physical means.

*High AX/Con scores:* suggests much effort is invested in "monitoring and preventing the experience and expression of anger."

*High AX/EX scores:* suggests experience of intense anger that may be suppressed or expressed verbally or physically, or both suppressed and expressed alternately.

AX/In and AX/Out scores are the primary indicators of the mode of anger expression. If both AX/In and AX/Out are elevated, there is likely to be a generalized expression of anger in behavior. Persons with this pattern typically have great difficulty relating to others interpersonally and are at increased risk for medical disorders, particularly cardiovascular syndromes.

Low-scoring individuals on the STAXI scales are not finely differentiated, as these scales were not designed for this purpose. Generally low scores across measures may reflect denial or repression of angry affect. When there is no apparent stress-related disorder or psychopathology, these individuals may be defending against anger as a personality style (Spielberger, 1988, p. 5).

### Technical Aspects

Development of the S-Anger and T-Anger scales has proceeded rationally and empirically. The operational definitions of each construct presented previously in this review were used to develop initial item pools of 20 S-Anger and 22 T-Anger items. The initial pool of T-Anger items was administered to 146 college students as a preliminary item validation group. Each respondent was asked to rate themselves on each item as to "how you generally feel" on a 4-point frequency scale: 1 = almost never, 2 = sometimes, 3 = often, or 4 = almost always. The T-Anger items were administered with measures of trait anxiety and trait curiosity that had been developed independently by Spielberger and his colleagues (Spielberger, Gorsuch, & Lushene, 1970; Spielberger, Peters, & Frain, 1981).

The initial pool of 22 T-Anger items was reduced to 15 items, based in part on their relatively lower correlations with the trait anxiety and trait curiosity scale scores. The 15 remaining items also had the highest correlational values with the corrected total scale score (item-remainder score). In these analyses the T-Anger item to be correlated with the total T-Anger scaled score was omitted from the total scaled score for that analysis. This provides the remainder score for the scale (scale total – item score). The item is then correlated with this remainder score to produce the item-remainder score correlation. This procedure prevents correlational inflation, which is particularly important when the number of items is relatively small and the influence of a single item is correspondingly increased.

The Cronbach coefficient alpha statistic, a measure of internal consistency or item homogeneity, also was computed for this 15-item T-Anger scale. Coefficient alpha values of .80 or greater minimize error variance for practical purposes (Nunnally, 1978) and may be considered to be highly consistent measures of a unitary construct. The mean coefficient alpha value of .86 for a scale as brief as 15 items is exceptionally high and shows very accurate measurement of a unitary construct. These results were comparable across samples that were divided by sex (coefficient alpha = .87 for men and .84 for women; Spielberger, 1988, p. 8, Table 6). Similar results (.87 for both sexes) for the T-Anger scale were reported by Spielberger et al. (1981; cited in Spielberger, 1988, p. 7).

The S-Anger scale was constructed rationally from the previously mentioned working definition of state anger. Multiple thesauruses and dictionaries were consulted to produce a list of synonyms for key components of the state anger construct as it had been defined. An initial pool of 20 S-Anger items was composed based on these sources. These items and the 15 T-Anger items were administered to a sample of 270 naval recruits. The respondents were instructed to answer the S-Anger items according to their feelings "right now" by noting themselves on the following 4-point scale: 1 = not at all, 2 = somewhat, 3 = moderately so, and 4 = very much so. The same item analysis procedures were followed for the S-Anger items that had been used to select and finalize the T-Anger items.

The initial pool of 20 S-Anger items was reduced to 15 S-Anger items through retention of items with the highest intrascale item-remainder correlations. The items selected also were required to have relatively low correlations with simultaneously administered measures of state anxiety and state curiosity so that the measures were specific for the state anger construct. The median item-remainder correlations for the S-Anger items were consistently high across sexes (median values of .64 for men, .67 for women, and .68 for total sample). The 15 best discriminating S-Anger items with the highest item-remainder correlation coefficients had a coefficient alpha value of .93 for each sex analyzed separately (Spielberger, 1988, p. 7, Table 5).

Principal components factor analysis of the S-Anger and T-Anger scales was carried out with varimax orthogonal rotation of the factor matrix to simple structure. Salient items (i.e., those that contributed adequate explanatory variance to be included as exemplars of constructs or dimensions underlying each scale) were defined as having factor loadings of .30 or greater. Multiple criteria were used to determine the number of factors (for details see Spielberger, 1988, p. 8). These same criteria were used in all subsequent factor analytic investigations of the

STAXI. Data for each sex were analyzed separately and produced comparable factorial solution results across samples.

The S-Anger scale items were found to measure a unitary emotional state dimension. The T-Anger items, in contrast, were found to have two correlated but factorially independent dimensions, which were labeled "Angry Temperament" (T-Anger/T) and "Angry Reaction" (T-Anger/R). These composed the two subscales of the STAXI T-Anger scale. The item-remainder correlation and coefficient alpha item analyses were carried out for each of the two T-Anger subscales and were computed independently for the two sexes within the college and naval recruit samples. The median item-remainder correlational value for the T-Anger/T subscale was .73, and the alpha coefficients for this subscale varied from .84 to .89. The median item-remainder correlational value for the T-Anger/R subscale was .50, and the alpha coefficients for this subscale varied from .70 to .75. Given that each of these subscales consisted of only four items, the results are exceptionally good. Values for the item-remainder correlations optimally should be .25 or higher (Nunnally, 1978) but should not be exceptionally high because that would suggest item redundancy. Thus, values for the T-Anger subscales are in an optimal range.

Development of the Anger Expression scales proceeded independently and subsequently to the S-Anger and T-Anger scales. Initially Spielberger and his colleagues intended to develop a unitary, bipolar measure that might range from strong inhibition or suppression of anger to strong, overt expression of this emotion, as in aggressive behavior toward other people or things in the environment. Rather than a general rating of anger expression, the STAXI Anger Expression scales required subjects to respond according to the *frequency* with which they respond to angry feelings in a particular way. Subjects were instructed to rate the frequency of their responses when they felt "angry or furious" according to the following scale: 1 = almost never, 2 = sometimes, 3 = often, or 4 = almost always. The Anger Expression items involved a variety of modes of concealing or expressing angry affect. The preliminary Anger Expression scale item pool, consisting of 33 items, was administered to 1,114 high school students as part of a dissertation study carried out by Johnson (1984). Three of the initial 33 items were eliminated after preliminary item analyses due to "poor psychometric properties" (presumably low item-remainder correlations) or because they proved to be unclear (i.e., numerous questions from examinees arose about their meaning during the validational study).

The remaining 30 items of the initial Anger Expression scale were factor analyzed by the method of principal components with orthogonal varimax rotation of the factor matrix to simple structure. Multiple criteria for determination of the number of factors to be retained for the final solution were used as in the previous study with the S-Anger and T-Anger scales. Contrary to the test authors' theoretical expectations, two distinct factors emerged from these analyses, and there was high correspondence of the bimodal factorial solution for both sexes. Each of these factors had quite robust psychometric characteristics that best met all of the statistical criteria. The analysis of item content suggested interpretation of the factors as indices of anger concealment or suppression (Anger-In; AX/In) and anger expression (Anger-Out; AX/Out). Based on the robustness of these preliminary findings with the initial 30-item Anger Expression item pool, separate scales for measuring "anger-in" and "anger-out" were developed. The number of Anger Expression scale items was further reduced to 22 items through elimination of items with factor loadings less than .35 on both the AX/In and AX/Out scales. This procedure eliminated items that were less robust exemplars of the underlying constructs. Two additional items were eliminated because they had relatively low item-remainder values for the sample of women.

The 20-item combined Anger Expression scale items (AX/In and AX/Out) were then refactored. The results again were statistically optimal for the two-factor simple structure solution and were comparable across analyses by sex. Factor structure was improved with analysis of the 20-item scales that proved to be more homogeneous. The final AX/In scale consisted of eight items with high loadings on the AX/In dimension and minimal loadings on the AX/Out dimension. The median item factor loading on the AX/In factor was .67, and the alpha values for the AX/In items were .84 and .81 for men and women, respectively. Item-remainder correlations for AX/In for men ranged from .49 to .63, while for women the range was from .47 to .60. The median item loading on the AX/Out factor was .59. The coefficient alpha internal consistency reliability values for the AX/Out Scale were .73 for men and .75 for women. Again these values are quite robust for a relatively brief scale. Item-remainder correlations on AX/Out for men range from .32 to .49 and for women, from .37 to .57.

For the Anger Expression total scale scores (AX/In plus AX/Out), the item remainder correlations ranged from .15 to .56 for men and from .14 to .53 for women. Coefficient alpha values for the total Anger Expression scale were .80 for men and .77 for women. Although the total Anger Expression scale is internally consistent with or without division into subscales, clearly there is more homogeneity of the items with the scale construct as a whole when the items are divided into a subscale. This increased specificity and accuracy contributes to the further differentiation and explication of the anger expression construct. Given the brevity of the subscales, the statistical indices of item-scale homogeneity are quite robust and they show excellent scale accuracy and specificity. It is important to note that the AX/In and AX/Out dimensions are orthogonal factors that vary independently of each other and thus comprise two independent components of a more general anger expression dimension or construct.

The final subset of STAXI items consists of the Anger Control (AX/Con) subscale items. The precursor of this scale emerged in the factor analysis of the 20-item Anger Expression scale and was comprised of three of the four items that were not scored on the AX/In or AX/Out subscales. Additional items subsequently were added. Content sampling methods were based on dictionary definitions of synonyms for the word *control*. The initial 20-item AX/Con scale was developed from anger control statements based on these synonyms and idioms, plus the three anger control items in the original Anger Expression scale. The preliminary AX/Con scale was administered to 409 undergraduates enrolled in introductory psychology classes. The results were factor analyzed by the method of principal components for each sex separately. One robust primary factor and several incidental (chance-influenced/based) factors that explained little additional variance were found in analyses for both males and females. The AX/In, AX/Out, and AX/Con items were jointly factored to determine whether the three scale dimensions were orthogonal (i.e., independent of each other). The AX/In, AX/Out, and AX/Con items consistently loaded most highly on their three respective orthogonal dimensions for each of the three scales.

Using a somewhat more conservative factor loading criterion of .40 to minimize chance sampling, one notes that items that describe temper control or temper loss loaded on both AX/Out and AX/Con across sexes. A few multiply loading items of this kind are probably consistent with sampling bias or chance capitalization alone. This interpretation is supported by the findings that AX/In and AX/Out are orthogonal to each other and to AX/Con. Zero-order correlations of AX/In with AX/Out and AX/Con are near to 0, which confirms their univariate independence as well. Correlations between AX/Con and Ax/Out scaled scores for men and women were –.59 and –.58, respectively, indicating that persons with high AX/Con scores frequently are involved in contributing the overt expression of anger.

An overall Anger Expression Index (AX/EX) also has been developed for the STAXI. In earlier work with the scale, this index was based only on AX/In and AX/Out scores. Subsequent work with AX/Con showed the need to include it as a construct with the other two measures as a correction factor in the calculation of the AX/EX index. The AX/EX metric is computed according to the following formula: AX/EX = AX/In + AX/Out – AX/Con + 16. The final constant term is added to exclude negative values for the index. The psychometric characteristics of this measure are under investigation, and currently it is available only as a research measure.

Several studies have been carried out by Spielberger and his colleagues to establish the concurrent validity of the STAXI state and trait anger scales against established measures of anger-related constructs. One such study compared T-Anger scale scores with the Buss-Durkee Hostility Inventory (BDHI) and the Hostility and Overt Hostility scales of the Minnesota Multiphasic Personality Inventory (MMPI). Samples studied were 270 naval recruits and 280 college undergraduates. The range of correlations for T-Anger was from .66 through .73 with the BDHI, from .43 to .59 with the MMPI Hostility scale, and from .27 to .32 with the MMPI Overt Hostility scale. Correlational values were comparable across samples and sex of subject. All correlations were significant at the .001 level with the exception of the correlation of T-Anger with MMPI Overt Hostility, which was significant at the .01 level.

The correlations of the STAXI T-Anger and S-Anger scales with the Eysenck Personality Questionnaire (EPQ) subscales and the Trait and State Anxiety and Curiosity scales of the State-Trait Personality Inventory (STPI) were computed for a large sample of 879 college students (545 women, 334 men). The correlations between the EPQ Neuroticism scale and S-Anger were moderate (.43 for men, .27 for women). Correlations between T-Anger and the EPQ Neuroticism scale also were moderate on the average (.50 for men, .49 for women). These correlations, which were all significant at the .001 level, were interpreted by Spielberger as supportive of the validity of the STAXI measures because neurotic individuals frequently experience unexpressed angry feelings.

Correlations of the T-Anger scale with the EPQ Extraversion scale and the STPI State Curiosity and Trait Curiosity scales by sex were consistently low (–.08 to –.15 for S-Curiosity; –.07 to –.08 for T-Curiosity; –.06 to –.07 for EPQ Extraversion).

Because these values were uniformly low, Spielberger concluded that the T-Anger scale showed no significant or consistent relationship to these measures. Demonstration of discriminant validity, in which the measure of interest is related to expected dimensions (convergent validity) and is unrelated to irrelevant dimensions (divergent validity), is an important source of evidence that the STAXI T-Anger scale has concurrent validity. A comparison of the STAXI measures with the Marlowe-Crowne Social Desirability Scale also should be performed to rule out social desirability as a self-report response bias on the STAXI measures.

Correlations of the S-Anger scale with Trait Anxiety (.30 for women, .35 for men), EPQ Neuroticism (.27 for women, .43 for men), and EPQ Psychoticism (.26 for men, .27 for women) are in the low-to-moderate range, but all of these values were significant at the .001 level due to the large sample size. Spielberger (1988, p. 12) concluded that persons with a variety of psychopathological syndromes and tendencies are more likely to experience state or situational anger than are people without such conflicts. However, on the whole these correlations are relatively weak, and this inference should be considered tentative at best for the time being. There was a moderate correlation of State Anxiety with State Anger (.63 for both sexes, $p < .001$), but whether this reflects social learning history characteristics as Spielberger suggests or a more general neurotic dimension to which both anger and anxiety contribute remains to be clarified.

Spielberger noted the moderate concurrent validity of the S-Anger and T-Anger scales with the BDHI and the MMPI measures of Hostility and Overt Hostility. Although his review of the literature suggested that it was important to distinguish between anger, hostility, and aggression, these measures showed convergent validity at a variety of levels. He performed a factor analysis of the *items* from the T-Anger scale, the Trait-Anxiety scale, and the Trait-Curiosity scale, with the T-Anger total score, the BDHI total and subscale scores, the MMPI Hostility and Overt Hostility Scales scores, and the Trait Anxiety and Trait Curiosity scale scores as marked variables. Principal components extraction with orthogonal varimax rotation of the factor matrix to simple structure was employed with multiple criteria as previously described to determine the final number of factors to be interpreted.

Three- and four-factor solutions were invariant across sex of subject and meaningfully interpretable. The three-factor solution differed from the four-factor solution in that its first factor was interpreted as a mixed construct of Anger-Hostility, whereas in the four-factor solution these two constructs could be distinguished as the first (Anger) and fourth (Hostility) factors. The Anger factor was defined by high loadings on the T-Anger scale and the majority of the T-Anger scale items. The Hostility factor was marked by high loadings on all of the BDHI measures except Guilt and by the MMPI Hostility scale. The second factor was termed Anxiety, which showed higher secondary loadings on a number of BDHI subscales (Irritability, Suspicion, and Resentment) and the MMPI Hostility Scale than the first (Anger) factor.

Spielberger did not report the factor matrix for this analysis in the manual when the results above were described (Spielberger, 1988, pp. 12–13), and he does not report the characteristics of the second and third factors in that source. His primary aim in the study was to clarify the differences between Anger and Hostility constructs across measures, and the results presented provide impressive evidence for the construct and concurrent validity, as well as for the specificity of the T-Anger scale as the measure of a construct that is differentiable from hostility. Unfortunately the original reference cited as the source of the factor analytic study in which the results are presented and discussed in more detail is an unpublished master's thesis (Westberry, 1980) that is not publicly available.

Validation of the Anger Expression scale is summarized by Spielberger et al. (1985). Students were classified dichotomously as "anger-in" or "anger-out" on the basis of their responses to experimental vignettes that were designed to measure type of anger response (Harburg, Blakelock, & Roeper, 1979). Moderate biserial correlations were found between the STAXI Anger Expression scales (AX/In, AX/Out, and AX/EX) and the experimentally classified anger expression subject subtypes. The correlations with AX/EX were somewhat higher on the average than the correlations with either AX/In or AX/Out, suggesting that these components of anger expression both contributed to the relationship of the STAXI scales to the experimental measure responses. Correlations of AX/In with AX/Out and AX/Con were essentially 0.

Johnson (1984; cited in Spielberger, 1988, pp. 13–14) administered the original 20-item form of the Anger Expression scale to 1,114 high school students as part of a larger study of the relationship of anger expression to systolic (SBP) and diastolic (DBP) blood pressure levels. Correlations between AX/EX and SBP were negative and moderate (–.45 for men, –.30 for women), and more robust than the AX/EX relationship to DBP across sexes (–.27 for men, –.16 for women). All of these correlational values were highly significant, at the .001 level, due to exceptionally large sample size. AX/In showed moderate positive correlations with SBP across sex of subject groups (.47 for men, .27 for women) and lesser but significant values for the relationship to DBP (.29 for men, .16 for women). Again all of these values were significant at the .001 level. Across sexes AX/Out showed correlations with SBP (–.13 for men and women) and DBP (.09 for men, .05 for women). The AX/EX and AX/In correlational values with the blood pressure measures were of approximately the same magnitude but oppositely signed.

Overall, the findings suggest that elevated blood pressure may be related to anger suppression and that the total effect of expressed anger (AX/EX) is attributable to anger suppression alone (AX/In). Additional analyses of a number of demographic and medical history variables showed that blood pressure has a wide variety of significant cofactors beyond anger expression type. These variables were analyzed in partial and multiple correlational analyses with the STAXI anger expression measures. Johnson reported that AX/In remained as a significant predictor of systolic and diastolic blood pressure even after the other variables had been statistically controlled. More impressive is the finding that AX/In scores were the best predictors of blood pressure in stepwise multiple regression analyses that were done to predict elevated systolic and diastolic blood pressure level.

## Critique

The STAXI has been painstakingly developed and validated. It meets strict psychometric criteria for validity and reliability in investigations reported to date.

Its psychometric investigation continues and should be completed before the test is used extensively in clinical practice. Spielberger notes that the test-retest reliability of the STAXI measures has been investigated by Jacobs, Latham, and Brown (in press), but these results were not cited in the manual. Such results must be reviewed and replicated at acceptable levels in large, independent samples. Intertest interval should be approximately 2 weeks in a medically stable sample and in a control group. Different samples should be run with these reliability analyses, particularly the age groups and special population groups for which normative data are provided in the manual. It would be desirable to have retest data for comparison in common medical groups of interest, such as patients with hypertension, cancer (varied by malignancy level and not subject to medication side effects), heart disease, and so forth.

Although the STAXI scores are highly reliable on internal consistency indices, this does not assure that scores are temporally stable. One sort of reliability does not substitute for another, as they estimate different aspects of error variance and true score variance. Interrater reliability is not at issue as this test is scored objectively by actuarial means and errorless scoring can be assured with automation. If the STAXI scores are temporally stable at acceptable levels, then changes in scores over time can be reliably related to true changes in state or trait construct levels that reflect treatment or experimental effects rather than measurement error.

The high levels of demonstrated divergent and convergent validity of the STAXI measures and their exceptionally high internal consistency values suggest that they have much promise as measures of psychosomatic risk factors for cardiovascular disease, particularly disorders that are related to blood pressure elevation. One would hope that STAXI investigators would continue to work closely with physicians and experimental physiologists with applied interests to investigate specific parameters of stress so that the STAXI measures may be further refined and related to biological variables. In this manner we may begin to understand key features of the ways in which stress emotions, particularly anger and anxiety, affect normal and abnormal physiological reactions in health and disease. One exploratory study cited in the manual attempted to relate the STAXI measures to adjustment of patients undergoing treatment for Hodgkin's disease or lung cancer (McMillian, 1984), but the results are not presented in the manual. This work is an unpublished master's thesis and not publicly available for review. In future work of this kind it would be advisable to study stages of the disease process in a single disease or related disease group and to obtain behavioral health and adaptive coping ratings, STAXI measures, and biological parameters in order to determine adaptive and maladaptive components of the syndrome.

Spielberger and his colleagues have shown the relevance of anger experience, expression, and control to blood pressure elevation in particular. Use of specific physiological marker variables to validate STAXI indices is desirable, as suggested above. We probably will learn more about the specific biological correlates of the STAXI indices in health and disease states through the study of specific STAXI measures in specific syndromes, particularly with specific physiological indices, symptoms, and signs instead of complex, multiply determined, symptomatically variable disease states. Spielberger (1988, p. 14), for example, cites a variety of studies that have addressed STAXI correlates of Type A behavior as risk factors for cardiovascular disease.

The role of the STAXI measures in normal individuals without evidence of physical disease or psychological disorder also should be investigated to learn how healthy persons adaptively cope with stress and anger. Adaptive coping is more than the absence of stress and emotional disturbance, and the correlates of healthy adjustment as they relate to the STAXI scales remain to be specified in detail. Some initial work along these lines has been reported by Johnson-Saylor (1984) and by Schlosser and Sheeley (1985a, 1985b), both of which are cited by Spielberger (1988). Unfortunately, these references are unpublished and their specific results are not summarized in the manual. As more work on the STAXI accumulates it is hoped that more authors will publish their work.

The role of anger dimensions in normal personality functioning remains exploratory with the STAXI to date (Johnson, 1984) and also should be of interest to personality theorists. The role of the STAXI variables, along with Spielberger's other measures of trait and state anxiety and curiosity as well as related indices of hostility and adaptive coping, should be explored as logical extensions of the validation process to place affective management of anger and other emotions into context.

Systematic studies of sex differences in anger experience, expression, and control under experimental conditions rather than in naturalistic clinical groups or in college or military samples would be valuable contributing to the study of relationships of the STAXI variables to physiologic and personological variables. The relationship of anger to anxiety variables is just beginning to be explored. More systematic investigation is needed to determine if a relationship to the Type A or other maladaptive personality type is reflected in these relationships. Geriatric studies also are needed to study change in STAXI measures as a function of age and health status. Studies of clinical groups with stress-related or stress-influenced disease, particularly chronic pain syndromes, who do well or poorly in response to standard, controlled medical treatments would be of interest. Issues that relate STAXI variables to treatment type, response, acceptance, outcome, and efficiency are needed. Modifiability of STAXI indices by standard cognitive-behavioral methods and the relationship of such controlled treatment to the modifications of physiological variables such as blood pressure and clinical status (to be operationally defined) remain to be explored. Affective response in patients with unilateral hemispheric lesions, particularly stroke, is known to vary and could be studied effectively with the STAXI measures. The list of applications is quite varied; these suggestions are only illustrative.

Demographic predictors of physiological marker variables also need to be consistently blocked (varied by level) rather than "controlled" by partial correlational methods, in order to evaluate possible interactions of these variables with the STAXI dimensions in future work. Each level of key demographic variables should be included in a series of factorially designed experiments to ask more specific, limited-scope questions now that the general effectiveness of the STAXI has been established. Specification and control should extend to demographic variables, STAXI patterns, disease (if any) subtype, and adaptive level. Just as the STAXI was developed as a very specific, well-operationalized measure, so its applications to problems of normal and dysfunctional personality assessment must proceed parametrically and operationally if we are to build a model of psychosomatic disease risk and prevention that will have high predictive and therapeutic value.

Considerably more validation of the STAXI measures themselves is needed, and the way to approach this work has been shown in the excellent work done to date. Spielberger provides evidence that the STAXI measures can explain approximately 10–20% of the variance in multiply determined, complex physiological indices such as blood pressure (Johnson, 1984), at least in normal youthful populations. These findings are more robust in men than in women and stronger for systolic than for diastolic blood pressure. Extension of these findings to other age groups of men and women who are normal, at risk for cardiac disease due to demographic variables alone, hypertensive but asymptomatic, or who manifest specific types and stages of cardiac disease would be useful. Relationships of STAXI variables to Type A behavior in particular should continue to be studied extensively and meticulously. This work has begun (cf. Booth-Keyley & Friedman, 1987; Goffaux, Walston, Heim, & Shields, 1987; Herschberger, 1985; Janisse, Edguer, & Dyck, 1986; Krasner, 1986; Spielberger et al., 1988), but much of it as yet remains to be published. These references are cited in the manual by Spielberger (1988).

In conclusion, the STAXI is a specific, sensitive, psychometric instrument that can become invaluable in the assessment of some aspects of stress-related symptomatology in health and disease states as well as in the investigation of normal personality processes. Its promise is most likely to be fulfilled when it is used in conjunction with other specific behavioral and physiological indices to study specific adjustment patterns. If future applications of the STAXI are as experimentally rigorous as the development of this measure, there is great potential for its use to significantly further our understanding of important stress-based and stress-influenced syndromes and to help in identifying effective means by which such disorders may be reversed and prevented.

## References

Booth-Keyley, S., & Friedman, H.S. (1987). Psychological predictors of heart disease: A quantitative review. *Psychological Bulletin, 101,* 343–362.

Goffaux, J., Wallston, B.S., Heim, C.R., & Shields, S.L. (1987, March). *Type A behaviors, hostility, anger and exercise adherence.* Paper presented at the Eighth Annual Session of the Society of Behavioral Medicine, Washington, DC.

Harburg, E., Blakelock, E.H., & Roeper, P.J. (1979). Resentful and reflective coping with arbitrary authority and blood pressure: Detroit. *Psychosomatic Medicine, 3,* 189–202.

Herschberger, P. (1985). *Type A behavior in non-intensive and intensive care nurses.* Unpublished master's thesis, University of South Florida, Tampa.

Jacobs, G.A., Latham, L.E., & Brown, M. (in press). Test-retest reliabilities of the State-Trait Personality Inventory and the Anger Expression scale. *Journal of Personality Assessment.*

Janisse, M.P., Edguer, N., & Dyck, D.G. (1986). Type A behavior, anger expression, and reactions to anger imagery. *Motivation and Emotion, 10,* 371–385.

Johnson, E.H. (1984). *Anger and anxiety as determinants of elevated blood pressure in adolescents: The Tampa study.* Unpublished doctoral dissertation, University of South Florida, Tampa.

Johnson-Saylor, M.T. (1984). *Relationships among anger expression, hostility, hardiness, social support, and health risk.* Unpublished doctoral dissertation, University of Michigan, Ann Arbor.

Krasner, S.S. (1986). *Anger, anger control, and the coronary prone behavior pattern.* Unpublished master's thesis, University of South Florida, Tampa.

McMillian, S.C. (1984). *A comparison of levels of anxiety and anger experienced by 2 groups of cancer patients during therapy for Hodgkin's disease and small cell lung cancer.* Unpublished master's thesis, University of South Florida, Tampa.

Nunnally, J.C. (1978). *Psychometric theory* (2nd ed.). New York: McGraw-Hill.

Schlosser, M.B., & Sheeley, L.A. (1985a, August). *The hardy personality: Females coping with stress.* Paper presented at the 93rd Annual Convention of the American Psychological Association, Los Angeles.

Schlosser, M.B., & Sheeley, L.A. (1985b, August). *Subjective well-being and the stress process.* Paper presented at the 93rd Annual Convention of the American Psychological Association, Los Angeles.

Spielberger, C.D. (1988). *State-Trait Anger Expression Inventory, Research Edition: Professional manual.* Odessa, FL: Psychological Assessment Resources.

Spielberger, C.D., Gorsuch, R.L., & Lushene, R. (1970). *Manual for the State-Trait Anxiety Inventory: STAI ("Self-Evaluation Questionnaire").* Palo Alto, CA: Consulting Psychologists Press.

Spielberger, C.D., Johnson, E.H., Russell, S.F., Crane, R.S., Jacobs, G.A., & Worden, T.J. (1985). The experience and expression of anger: Construction and validation of an anger expression scale. In M.A. Chesney & R.H. Rosenman (Eds.), *Anger and hostility in cardiovascular and behavioral disorders* (pp. 5–30). New York: Hemisphere McGraw-Hill.

Spielberger, C.D., Krasner, S.S., & Solomon, E.P. (1988). The experience, expression and control of anger. In M.P. Janisse (Ed.), *Health psychology: Individual differences and stress.* New York: Springer-Verlag.

Spielberger, C.D., Peters, R.A., & Frain, F. (1981). Neugier und angst (Curiosity and anxiety). In H.G. Voss & H. Keller (Eds.), *Neugierforschung: Grundlagen-theorien-andwendungen* (pp. 197–225). Weinheim, Federal Republic of Germany: Beltz.

Westberry, L.G. (1980). *Concurrent validation of the Trait-Anger scale and its correlation with other personality measures.* Unpublished master's thesis, University of South Florida, Tampa.

**Lizanne DeStefano, Ph.D.**
*Assistant Professor of Educational Psychology, University of Illinois at Urbana-Champaign, Champaign, Illinois.*

# STREET SURVIVAL SKILLS QUESTIONNAIRE

*Dan Linkenhoker and Lawrence McCarron. Dallas, Texas: McCarron-Dial Systems.*

## Introduction

The Street Survival Skills Questionnaire (SSSQ) was designed as a measure of adaptive behavior for use with persons with developmental disabilities ages 9½ years to adult. For this test, adaptive behavior is defined as fundamental community living and prevocational skills. The test consists of nine subtests, each relating to a specific area of adaptive behavior: Basic Concepts; Functional Signs; Tool Identification and Use; Domestic Management; Health, First Aid, and Safety; Public Services; Time; Money; and Measurement. The SSSQ may be used as a stand-alone measure of adaptive behavior or in conjunction with the McCarron-Dial System as a component of the Integration-Coping factor.

At present the SSSQ is packaged in nine separate volumes; however, in the current reprinting the nine volumes will be integrated into one three-ring binder. Each subtest consists of 24 questions presented in a multiple-choice pictorial format, administered directly to the individual being evaluated. Test administration is untimed but usually takes about 1 hour. Two types of scores are available. For each subtest, a scaled score (mean = 10, standard deviation = 3) may be obtained. In addition, raw scores across all subtests can be summed and converted to a standard score (mean = 100, standard deviation = 15) known as the Survival Skills Quotient. An SSSQ profile can also be drawn to identify strengths and weaknesses as an aid to individual planning. A curriculum guide and master planning charts accompany the test. A computer-scoring package also is available.

The SSSQ is designed to serve as a baseline measure of adaptive behavior from which an individual training program may be formulated. It may also be used to monitor an individual's progress over time or as a result of an intervention. The authors cite the test's usefulness in predicting an individual's probable success in adapting to community living conditions and vocational placements. The SSSQ is targeted for use in secondary education, vocational, and rehabilitation programs working with persons with developmental disabilities. When considered in conjunction with additional measures of sensorimotor skills, emotional adjustment, cognitive ability, academic skills, vocational skills, and social skills, the SSSQ is intended to provide guidelines for the placement of individuals into the community.

The first step in the construction of the test was format selection. Six design principles guided this process: objectivity, individual administration, simple administration, short administration time, minimal reading requirements, and emphasis on power rather than speed. Five separate content selection procedures were used. First, analysis of several major adaptive behavior scales provided a description of those behavior domains that were most frequently assessed. Second, a review was conducted of the research findings concerning the validity of various domains for describing and predicting social adaptation. Third, the number of dimensions to be included in a measure of adaptive behavior was considered and set at nine. Fourth, in order to determine content areas relevant to training, informal interviews were completed with staff persons responsible for rehabilitation efforts with mentally retarded persons. After the appropriate content areas had been identified, the final criterion applied was that items were amenable to objective and quantifiable assessment. This requirement eliminated content areas that could not be administered in a multiple-choice format, such as maladaptive behavior.

Following the selection of content areas and the choice of format, a large pool of 216 items was generated. The manual states that items were written to require recall, recognition, and/or inferential ability. The first draft of these items was reviewed, and ambiguous items were rewritten. The entire series of items was administered, item analyzed, and revised as necessary. Field testing and statistical analysis resulted in four complete revisions of the SSSQ. Information on the subsequent revisions was not included in the examiner's manual or located by this reviewer.

The SSSQ kit contains the test itself, an examiner's manual, answer booklets, and a curriculum guide, all packaged in a brown vinyl attaché. The test consists of nine separate subtests, each related to a specific area of adaptive behavior:

1. *Basic Concepts*—color recognition, color matching, and knowledge of spatial and quantitative concepts.
2. *Functional Signs*—recognition of basic signs and symbols used in workshops, schools, public facilities, and other public services.
3. *Tool Identification and Use*—knowledge of various tools commonly used in sheltered workshops or for minor repairs around the home.
4. *Domestic Management*—familiarity with the requirements for successfully managing an apartment; ability to use utensils or appliances for food preparation and clothing maintenance.
5. *Health, First Aid, and Safety*—understanding of personal health care, hygiene, first aid, and safety skills needed in daily living.
6. *Public Services*—knowledge of a wide range of public services utilized in community living.
7. *Time*—ability to tell time and understand time-related concepts.
8. *Money*—recognition and handling of money, such as identifying coins and currency, recognizing money equivalence, and making change.
9. *Measurement*—ability to use common measurements, including temperature measures, liquid measures, and linear measures.

The SSSQ examiner's manual includes sections on purpose and development, reliability and validity, administration, scoring, norms tables, interpretation guidelines, and curriculum materials. The four-page answer booklet provides room for the examiner to score each item as pass/fail on the nine subtests. The face page of this booklet contains summary charts for plotting the adaptive behavior profile and for recording raw scores, scaled scores, and the Survival Skills Quotient.

A 269-page text, *Curriculum Guides for the SSSQ*, provides objectives, material, suggested performance criteria, teacher strategies, and specific student activities for each of the 24 items on each of nine subtests. In addition, a booklet containing instructions for administering the SSSQ to persons with hearing impairments using American Sign Language is also available from the publisher.

**Practical Applications/Uses**

The Street Survival Skills Questionnaire (SSSQ) has been constructed to assess community-relevant adaptive skills in a comprehensive fashion. As stated by the authors, the instrument was designed to serve the following functions (Linkenhoker & McCarron, 1983):

1. The SSSQ provides an objective measure of specific aspects of adaptive behavior. The instrument's coverage excludes the affective, motoric, and motivational aspects of adaptive behavior and focuses instead on the functional skills that facilitate living and working in the community. Consequently, the SSSQ may serve as an objective supplement to direct situational assessments of adaptive behaviors.

2. The SSSQ provides a baseline behavioral measure to gauge the effects of training on individual clients. This initial assessment of the individual's basic resources can serve as a reference point for comparing the impact of various training or intervention strategies.

3. The evaluation data obtained from the SSSQ can be used to design an individualized educational or rehabilitation plan.

4. The SSSQ may be used as a research and evaluation tool to measure the effectiveness of educational and rehabilitation programs. The relevance of specific adaptive behavior skills to successful placement in the community might also be identified with this instrument.

Given these proposed uses, it is likely that the SSSQ would be used by vocational evaluators, psychologists, and direct service personnel in schools, adult service agencies, and other educational and rehabilitation facilities as one part of a comprehensive assessment.

The present version of the SSSQ has been constructed to assess adolescents and adults who are characterized by lower intellectual functioning, psychiatric disorders, social disadvantagement, or a history of prolonged institutional living. The authors refer to this group as developmentally disabled or neuropsychologically disabled. Normative data for the revised test items were obtained from developmentally disabled subjects ($N$ = 400, ages 15–55) in five sheltered workshops and community employment programs in Illinois, Indiana, New York, Ohio, and Texas. A group of mentally retarded residents from state institutions was also included in this sample. The subjects were randomly selected from a list of daily participants in various rehabilitation and educational settings. The average IQ of the group as measured by the Wechsler scales ranged from 23 to 77 across groups defined by participation in day care, work activities, extended/sheltered work, and community programs. The average IQ using the Peabody Picture Vocabulary Test (PPVT; Dunn, 1965) was 58, with a range of 28 to 80.

In addition, data from two secondary school prevocational programs located in

Indiana and Texas were obtained. The normal adolescent group had an average age of 17 years, with a range from 14 to 18 years. There were 100 males and 100 females included in this sample. The mean IQ score for this group was 97, with a range of 80 to 121.

The manual states that norms are available for neuropsychologically disabled adults (based on a norm group of 500, ages 15–55); normal adolescents and adults (based on a norm group of 200, ages 16–40); and normal children (based on a norm group of 271, ages 9–15). It is not clear how these three groups relate to the samples described above. Furthermore, norms tables are provided for the first two groups alone. It is unclear how the test is to be scored for subjects under 15. In all samples, distribution of subjects by age is not provided. Given the small sample sizes and the large age ranges, it is likely that the norms are based on very few subjects at each age level.

The administration of the SSSQ requires approximately 30 to 50 minutes in a formal individual testing situation. All items in each subtest must be administered to obtain a subtest score. The presentation is similar to that of the PPVT in that the evaluator sits opposite the individual, who faces the page of plates. The examiner orally presents the question according to the script presented on his or her side of the examination booklet. The examinee responds by pointing to one of the four pictures presented on a page (or verbally responding "A," "B," "C," or "D"). The small black-and-white drawings may be problematic for persons with visual and motor deficits, but the authors state that the test can be used with individuals with visual acuity of 20/200 or better in either eye. Fundamental reading skills are only required for specific items that involve the use of a telephone book and the identification of signs, products, and currency.

Directions for administration are provided in the examiner's manual. The usual administration begins with the first subtest and proceeds in sequence through nine, but the sequence of administration may be varied if desired. The examiner need only read the script on his or her side of the booklet to introduce each item, prompt as necessary, provide special materials (ruler, phone card) when appropriate, and record correct/incorrect responses. Other than familiarity with test content and format, no specialized training is necessary.

Scoring the SSSQ is quick and easy. The front of the SSSQ Score Form provides space for demographic data, conversion of raw scores to standardized scores, and profiling the individual's performance on each of the subtests. The raw score for each subtest is obtained by summing the correct responses within that section. The results of each of the nine subtests can be converted into scaled scores enabling a comparison with a specific norm group (neuropsychologically disabled adults, 15–55 years of age, and average adults, 16–40 years of age). In addition, the scores can be plotted on the SSSQ Score Form Profile to indicate how the individual's performance in one area compares to performance in the other areas. The profile indicates relative strengths and needs, which facilitates the writing of an Individualized Education Plan (IEP) or any other individualized program. Conversion tables to convert raw scores into scaled scores or a Survival Skills Quotient (SSQ) are included in the manual. These tables are poorly labeled, and no instructions are provided for their use. Norms are not provided for smaller age groupings within the 15 to 55 or 16 to 40 age range.

A computer-generated report for the SSSQ is also available from McCarron-Dial Systems. In addition to the automatic scoring and plotting of scores according to age-appropriate norms, the SSSQ computer report provides narrative interpretations of the examinee's performance in the nine content areas of functioning. Each of these areas is then broken down into content subareas, which are analyzed with respect to the individual's own average level of performance. A list of relative strengths and needs is given as well as specific page references to the Curriculum Guides for the SSSQ.

Interpretation of the SSSQ is based on the examinee's performance on individual items and on the subtest profile. The Master Planning Chart provides a means of describing an individual's level of achievement in each of the nine content areas. Each of the 24 items that comprise a content area is identified on the chart by a word corresponding to the content of the item. Construction of this chart provides a rapid overview of deficit areas and an efficient method for structuring individual program goals. Each item deficit can be associated with an objective in the Curriculum Guides. These objectives can be used in writing individualized program plans.

Scaled scores on the SSSQ have a mean of 10 and a standard deviation of 3. The range of scaled scores from 7 to 13 indicates typical performance, 4 to 77 indicates moderate deficits, and scaled scores from 0 to 4 indicate severe deficits in adaptive behavior.

The authors state that comparisons may be made between IQ and SSSQ score when both are converted to standard scores. A table based on a sample of normal adults is provided to convert total SSSQ raw scores into Survival Skills Quotients (SSQ), with a mean of 100 and a standard deviation of 15. Cautions are provided concerning the appropriateness of this practice, given that the distribution of adaptive behavior scores are negatively skewed rather than normally distributed.

## Technical Aspects

Content, construct, concurrent, and predictive validity studies are presented in detail in the SSSQ manual, as is item analysis information. Content validation of the test was addressed during the content selection process through analysis of existing tests, literature review, and interviews with rehabilitation staff. The authors report that pilot studies in prevocational and work adjustment programs in secondary schools and sheltered workshops indicated that the SSSQ had broad enough content area coverage to provide information for program planning.

The procedures and results of item analyses involving item difficulty, item-total correlation, item discrimination, and distractor analysis are reported in detail in the examiner's manual. Empirical and rational procedures were used in the selection, rejection, and rewriting of items. Empirical criteria were determined; that is, items with difficulty level less than .30 or greater than .70, discrimination level less than .20, and corrected item-total correlation less than .20 were considered for rewrite or exclusion. These criteria were tempered by rational considerations (i.e., if the item appeared to be face valid and to be of fundamental importance in activities of daily living). The dual criteria resulted in the retention of some items with low or negative item-total correlations or high difficulty levels.

The construct validity of the SSSQ was investigated by (a) an analysis of the intercorrelations among SSSQ subtests, (b) factor analysis, and (c) an analysis of the correlation of the SSSQ with measures of intelligence and reading skills.

Intercorrelations among SSSQ subtests ranged from .32 to .78, with an average correlation of .55. These correlations demonstrate a moderate amount of shared variance (approximately 30%) and indicate that specific content accounts for the largest proportion of variance. Factor analysis produced a single, unitary factor, capable of explaining the greatest variance in the test and supporting the interpretation of the SSSQ score as a general measure of adaptive behavior.

SSSQ subtest and total scores were highly correlated with PPVT scores (range = .61 to .76). This is not surprising, given the similarity of the two tests in terms of format and response demand. The authors report this finding as evidence of the test's relationship with intelligence. More correctly, the PPVT is a measure of receptive language, and the high correlations are probably more supportive of the test's use as a measure of verbal rather than daily living skills. It is not clear why the authors chose the PPVT and not its later revision or more traditional measures of intelligence such as the Wechsler scales or the Stanford-Binet as correlates. Another correlations study done using the Wide Range Achievement Test (WRAT; Jastak & Jastak, 1965) reading scores, IQ scores, and SSSQ scores concluded that knowledge of specific adaptive behaviors has limited relationship to intelligence. Limited information about the sample (juvenile delinquents) and the IQ measures used restricts the utility of the findings.

Concurrent validity studies examined the relationship between SSSQ scores and the San Francisco Vocational Competency Scale (SFVCS; Levine & Elzey, 1968) as a measure of vocational competency and the Progress Assessment Chart (PAC; Gunzberg, 1963) as a measure of adaptive behavior. Analyses suggest that SSSQ scores bear a relationship to both vocational competence and adaptive behavior as measured by these instruments. The characteristics of the samples used in these validity studies were not clearly described in the manual, nor was the rationale for choosing these tests as correlates rather than more recently developed and more popular measures of adaptive behavior and vocational competence.

A predictive validity study reported that the SSSQ in conjunction with the Dial Behavioral Rating Scale (BRS; Dial, 1976) had a high predictive relationship with work competency ($r = .91$) as measured by the SFVCS. When the SSSQ was used alone, $r = .65$. It should be noted that work competency was not measured by the ability to perform actual work or to maintain a job but by another standardized measure. Therefore, the relationship of SSSQ scores to actual daily living is still unknown.

The characteristics of the sample used in reliability studies were not clearly reported, but general reliability appears high. Test-retest reliability was examined over a 1-month interval. Reliability coefficients ranged from .87 to .95 over the nine subtests. Test-retest reliability for the total score was high at .99.

Internal consistency was measured using the Kuder-Richardson Formula 20 (Guilford & Fruchter, 1973). KR-20 coefficients ranged from .68 to .96 across subtests. Internal consistency for the entire test was .97. Interrater reliability was not reported.

The standard error of estimate for the test was found to be 3.0, meaning that there is a 66% probability that the individual's true score is within 3 points of the obtained raw score. This error estimate should be considered when interpreting the degree of dependability of particular test scores or when interpreting changes in scores over time or as a result of intervention.

## Critique

The SSSQ differs from other popular methods of adaptive behavior, such as the Vineland Adaptive Behavior Scales (Sparrow, Balla, & Cicchetti, 1984) or the Scales of Independent Behavior (Bruininks, Woodcock, Weatherman, & Hill, 1984), in that it attempts to assess adaptive behavior directly, through pictorial cues and a multiple-choice format, rather than using a third-party informant to report on an individual's day-to-day functioning. Direct assessment is often considered more objective than third-party interviewing; further, it allows the examiner first-hand knowledge of the individual being assessed and, in some cases, is easier to schedule and conduct than meetings with parents or direct-care staff. However, given the target population of this test and the applied nature of the construct it purports to measure, it is questionable that many individuals in this group could respond reliably to the abstract format of the test, and, more importantly, it is unclear that their responses to the multiple-choice items bear any relationship to how they might behave in a real-life situation. For example, on item 1 in the Public Services subtest, the examinee is shown four stylized black-and-white drawings of a city bus, a small truck, a big truck, and a van and asked to "point to the bus." Success or failure on this item is difficult to interpret in terms of its application to real life. If the examinee failed to recognize the stylized drawing of the bus, do we infer that he would not recognize the large, loud, moving, full-color bus as it pulled up to the stop to take him to work? That would be risky, because we know that persons with mental retardation and developmental disabilities have difficulty with abstraction and generalization, yet that is what this test requires them to do.

Validity studies fail to illustrate the relationship of test scores to real-life performance in independent living and employment. This shortcoming becomes particularly troublesome when one considers the heavy emphasis the test authors place on the use of the test for classification and placement decisions. The examiner's manual goes so far as to associate SSSQ raw score and standard score ranges with vocational and residential program placements through the use of tables and a regression formula in the examiner's manual. The danger with this use is that persons may be placed into inappropriate vocational and residential programs based on test results that bear little relationship to daily performance in real-life situations. With supported employment initiatives demonstrating that persons who were thought previously to be "incapable" of work can work in integrated settings, the idea of restricting opportunity on the basis of a test score is inappropriate and unethical.

The SSSQ is probably most viable as an aid to program planning when used in conjunction with direct observation, situational assessment, and other standardized measures of adaptive behavior. The Curriculum Guides offer suggestions for activities to address areas of need, some of which are community based and quite appropriate for inclusion in an individualized program.

### References

This list includes text citations and suggested additional reading.


Blackwell, S., Dial, J., Chan, F., & McCollum, P. (1985). Discriminating functional levels of independent living: A neuropsychological evaluation of mentally retarded adults. *Rehabilitation Counseling Bulletin, 29*(1), 1–3.

Bruininks, R.H., Woodcock, R.W., Weatherman, R.F., & Hill, B.H. (1984) *Scales of Independent Behavior.* Allen, TX: DLM Teaching Resources.

Dial, J. (1976). *Behavior Rating Scale.* Dallas, TX: Common Market Press.

Dial, J., Chan, F., Parker, H., Carter, S., & Pomeroy, V. (1985). SSSQ predictors of independent living skills: A criterion validity study. *Vocational Evaluation and Work Adjustment Bulletin, 18*(4), 141–145.

Dunn, L.M. (1965). *Peabody Picture Vocabulary Test manual.* Circle Pines, MN: American Guidance Services.

Giller, V., Dial, J., & Chan, F. (1986). The Street Survival Skills Questionnaire: A correlational study. *American Journal of Mental Deficiency, 91*(1), 67–71.

Guilford, J.P., & Fruchter, B. (1973). *Fundamental statistics in psychology and education* (5th ed.). New York: McGraw-Hill.

Gunzberg, H. (1963). *Progress Assessment Chart of Social and Personal Development manual.* Bristol, IN: Aux Chandelles.

Jastak, J., & Jastak, S. (1965). *The Wide Range Achievement Test manual.* Wilmington, DE: Jastak Associates.

Levine, S., & Elzey, F. (1968). *San Francisco Vocational Competency Scale manual.* San Antonio, TX: Psychological Corporation.

Linkenhoker, D., & McCarron, L. (1983). *Street Survival Skills Questionnaire.* Dallas, TX: McCarron-Dial Systems.

Sparrow, S., Balla, D., & Cicchetti, D. (1984). *Vineland Adaptive Behavior Scales.* Circle Pines, MN: American Guidance Service.

**Ann H. Stoddard, Ed.D.**
*Professor of Education, University of North Florida, Jacksonville, Florida.*

# TEACHER STRESS INVENTORY

*Michael J. Fimian. Brandon, Vermont: Clinical Psychology Publishing Company, Inc.*

## Introduction

The Teacher Stress Inventory (TSI; Fimian, 1988) is designed to assess the degree of occupational stress experienced by teachers in public schools. The TSI consists of 49 items divided into 10 factors that comprise some elements of teacher stress. Five of these factors are considered stress sources (Time Management, Work Related Stress, Professional Distress, Discipline and Motivation, and Professional Investment) and five represent stress manifestations (Emotional, Fatigue, Cardiovascular, Gastronomic, and Behavioral). The TSI scores serve three functions: assessment of individual stress levels, assessment of stress levels in a workshop and school setting, and assessment of stress on a school, district, or statewide level.

The test developer, Dr. Michael J. Fimian, is an associate professor in the Department of Language, Reading, and Exceptionalities at Appalachian State University, Boone, North Carolina, and has published extensively in the area of teacher stress. He initially began item development for the TSI in 1979.

This inventory has undergone two modifications. The initial form of the test, with 63 items and a 7-point Likert-type scale, was administered to 365 special education teachers in a northeastern state. The 41-item second version, now called the Teacher Stress Inventory, was distributed to both regular and special education teachers. In 1982 eight time management items were added. For 5 years thereafter the instrument was used in workshops, research projects, and dissertations. The resulting data were combined to form an aggregate sample of 3,401 regular and special education teachers, representing seven states. The population description includes regular elementary, middle, and high school teachers, as well as special education teachers across an identical spectrum.

The TSI is contained within a three-page consumable booklet that asks for demographic and stress-related data. The demographic information covers the respondent's sex, age, type of students taught (regular or handicapped), number of years taught, number of students taught each day, level of students taught, degree held, and support of and from peers and/or supervisors. The inventory itself is divided into two major sections that gather information on sources of stress and stress manifestations.

The stress sources covered on the TSI except for time management are job specific and related directly to the classroom. However, the fact that the directions ask respondents to identify factors that are specifically job related poses a difficulty in the area of time management. These items are practically impossible to separate from other aspects of the respondent's life-style. What occurs in time management outside the job situation tends to affect one's performance and attitude toward the job. Items that ask about overcommitment, impatience, and use of time cannot be distinctly divided into everyday living and job orientation. After stress sources are examined, the remaining five subscales address physical and behavioral manifestations of teacher stress.

To avoid sensitizing teachers to their beliefs and attitudes about stress, the title on the inventory booklet reads "Teacher Concerns Inventory." It is recommended that the TSI be completed on the job site and that the term *work-related problems* be used in lieu of *stress*. Only after the inventory has been completed should one allow the topic of "stress" to emerge and be discussed.

The profile for the TSI is a graphic representation of the separate subscales, each having an average mean score. An individual's score is interpreted according to cutoff points set at -1 and +1 standard deviations from the mean. Scores at or above the 84th percentile indicate strong stress levels, while weak stress levels are indicated by scores at or below the 16th percentile. Those scores falling between -1 and +1 standard deviations represent moderate stress levels and are considered average. Cutoff points are different for each of the following categories: type of teacher, gender of teacher, and grade level of teacher. The manual does not describe how to accommodate the three reference groups. For example, a female special education teacher in an elementary school will have three reference comparisons. At any rate, an individual high score on any of the subscales should cause concern and draw attention to that category for consideration toward reduction.

**Practical Applications/Uses**

The TSI can be very useful in identifying teachers who are potential candidates for stress reduction training and counseling. As noted, two sets of variables are measured: five *sources* of stress and five of its *manifestations*. Without proposing to measure all aspects of these factors, the instrument tries to measure selected areas of each. To have a maximal effect on identifying stress, the TSI score should be used in conjunction with other scales or inventories that assess personality, anxiety, and stress. Although Fimian (1988) claims to present a different model for identifying stress-related problems than those currently in use, the inventory includes items that could be classified under the Maslach Burnout Inventory (MBI; Maslach & Jackson, 1986) subscales. The TSI also uses the MBI to confirm its relationship to stress indicators.

The TSI can be applied in several educational situations. Teachers can use its results to help make realistic decisions about occupational stress reduction and to recognize stress areas that need attention to deter or circumvent burnout. Educational administrators could use the TSI results to recommend a change in principal management style and leadership and to look more closely at sources of teacher job stress and role conflict for the purpose of both stress reduction and burnout prevention. The TSI results also can help identify and enhance levels of job satisfaction and administrative support. With group scores, TSI results can reveal teacher stress–related problems in schools, systems, or statewide surveys. In any case, attention should be given to devising plans of action to decrease the sources of stress and to alter situations that induce stress.

Directions for administering and scoring the TSI are clearly written and easily carried out. The inventory is self-administered, taking approximately 15 minutes to complete. According to the author, no "special qualifications, techniques, or procedures are required of the examiner administering the TSI" (Fimian, 1988, p. 12). The respondent circles the appropriate response on a 1 to 5 rating scale. To minimize response bias and ensure confidentiality and privacy, an examiner who is not a member of the educational power structure should administer the inventory. The selected examiner should also be able to provide an environment in which the examinee feels comfortable in providing honest responses, without feelings of guilt, intimidation, and so forth.

Scoring the TSI is extremely simple and can be done by the respondent or a clerk. Uncompleted items are rated as 1 (no strength; not noticeable). Each subscale should be scored separately, then the total for each divided by the number of items in the subscale. The total TSI score is derived by totaling all the subscale scores and dividing the sum by 10.

The TSI can be computer scored if respondents use OpScan sheets. If computer scoring is used, the computer program should employ a "blanks equal" component that is coded to compute 1 for each missing item. Respondents are encouraged to answer all items relevant to their role on the job site.

General interpretation of the TSI scores can be made using the graphic representation as the profile. More specific interpretations are possible with reference group comparisons, gender comparisons, and grade level comparisons. Reference group comparisons include regular and special education teachers, and grade level comparisons include elementary, middle, and secondary schools. Interpretation is straightforward: The higher the TSI score, the stronger the stress-related trait is manifested by the respondent; a low TSI score indicates either an absence or an insignificant presence of the trait. Teachers producing high ranges on any of the subscales should seek intervention measures. For example, a high range in Discipline and Motivation should prompt the teacher to consider improvement in class management skills and to examine additional procedures and activities that may stimulate students toward classroom success.

## Technical Aspects

Several types of validity were reported for the TSI. Face validity, used for item selection, was addressed by summarizing the literature on teacher stress and developing 79 items that then were distributed to 2 college faculty members, 14 graduate students, and 16 public school teachers. Raters were asked to sort the items into two categories, one for items most related to teacher stress and the other for those least related. District teachers provided written feedback about the appropriateness of the items. The 79 items were ranked based on frequency of selection. Sixty-three items were considered usable for the pilot scale.

Factor analysis was used to establish construct validity. As items were added to the pilot test, a second analysis was conducted. All items exceeded the .35 loading criteria with only three items falling between .35 and .40. A total score for the stress strength dimension was developed, using the mean data. Each subscale score fell within the 1- to 5-point strength range, from 1.4 to 3.7.

Content validity was provided by five samples of 226 experts from three categories: authors of books or articles on stress, researchers in the area of stress, and persons conducting stress management workshops. These experts used 4-point Likert-type scale, ranging from 1 = not relevant to 4 = quite relevant, to determine the degree to which each item was related to her or his concept of teacher stress. Finn's $r$ was then used to explain the interrater reliability correlation, the estimates being larger for stress source than stress manifestation. The $r$'s ranged from .42 to .72 for the subscales, with .82 achieved for the total TSI.

Convergent validity was manifested in three ways. First, 47 teachers' TSI scores were correlated with independent ratings by significant others (in this case, other teachers who knew the 47 subjects well). These ratings were found to be significantly related in each of the subscales ($r = .46$ to $.69$; $p = .001$) and in the total scale score ($r = .65$; $p = .001$). Second, teachers' total TSI scores were correlated with personal and professional variables. Personal variables were sex, age, experience, and professional development, none of which showed a high significant relationship to teacher stress levels. The professional variables examined were student number and grade level; class size was related to teacher stress to a very limited degree, whereas grade level showed no relationship to teacher stress.

The third type of convergent validity was established by correlating TSI total scores with various psychological and organizational measures reported to be related to teacher stress, namely burnout, role problems, counseling, training adequacy, central life interest, supervisory/peer support, job satisfaction, job stress, substance abuse, anxiety, physiological symptoms, social readjustment, tedium, principal management style, principal leadership, and stress inoculation programs. When TSI scores were correlated with the Maslach Burnout Inventory, data showed that teachers who (a) experienced job ambiguity, (b) received inadequate teacher training, (c) were not enrolled in a counseling program, (d) were primarily interested in their personal lives, (e) did not receive peer support, (f) rated their job as very stressful, (g) reported being very anxious, and (h) experienced stressful life events tended to report the strongest stressful experiences associated with teaching. Tedium, principal management style, and principal leadership were significantly related to teacher stress. In addition, teachers who were stressful tended to experience more frequent psychosomatic disorders and to use drugs to reduce stress to more manageable levels. It was also determined that stress inoculation training tended to reduce stress.

Four types of reliability were investigated. Based on Cronbach's coefficient alpha, whole scale alpha estimates of .93, .92, and .93 for three separate groups of teachers indicated a high degree of overall internal consistency. All TSI subscales ranged from .67 to .88. Test-retest reliability estimates ranged from .42 to .99 for the subscales and .67 to .99 for the entire scale. Although a split-half reliability study and an alternate forms reliability study were conducted, the data were not reported in the manual.

## Critique

The TSI is a tool designed to access occupational stress in both regular and special education teachers at both elementary and secondary levels. It appears to do so adequately, meeting a need for stress identification and awareness in educational settings. TSI results seem to support other research and clinical findings showing that teachers who score at or above the 84th percentile are experiencing strong stress levels and should consider the use of intervention techniques, counseling, or stress inoculation training programs.

The TSI can be considered to be an instrument with potential but in need of further study to determine how effective it is in designating levels of teacher stress. There are at least two reasons why additional research is needed. First, with all of the analysis reported on validity and reliability, it is reasonable to expect the TSI to perform well. The inventory's careful construction establishes a strong case for both content validity and convergent validity. However, the failure to provide split-half and alternate forms reliability indicates, perhaps, moderate or insignificant *r*'s that would affect generalizability (as the author has referred to these *r*'s in other papers, such as Fimian & Gastenau, 1987). The omitted information would further substantiate the measure's reliability and provide a stronger case for the TSI, especially if the coefficients were adequate. In addition, Fimian should report a standard error of measurement.

Second, some of the relationships between the TSI and certain specific variables are based on a sample size that was somewhat limited. Sometimes the *N* was an aggregated 2,247 and 3,401, while other times the number fell to 39, 14, and 9. Samples came from two settings, a survey format and workshop format, with no indication of what setting provided what data what part of the time.

Fimian (1988) merits some recognition for his efforts to achieve acceptable levels of validity and reliability. The results of this study are exceedingly well presented in the manual. He also is to be commended for recognizing the need for further research in the area of sample size with regard to concurrent validity and reliability and the TSI's relationship to specific variables, which would help clarify the "larger picture" of teacher stress. He reports on the treatment of and further need for longitudinal studies from levels of teacher training through the verification of teaching careers, as well as the exploration of the validity of stress reduction through workshops and other intervention measures.

All in all, despite these limitations the TSI appears to be a strong measure for identifying stress factors and their origins, with great potential as a research tool. It promises to help illuminate specific areas of concern so that stress intervention can be more specific, particularly if used in conjunction with other assessments for stress and anxiety or with other organizational variables. The TSI presents a careful study in the preparation of a self-report for stress indicators and their sources.

**References**

Fimian, M.J. (1988). *Teacher Stress Inventory.* Brandon, VT: Clinical Psychology Publishing.
Fimian, M.J., & Gastenau, P.S. (1987). *The factorial validity, content validity and alpha reliability of the Teacher Stress Inventory: A re-analysis of aggregate data.* Manuscript submitted for publication.
Maslach, C., & Jackson, S.E. (1986). *Maslach Burnout Inventory.* Palo Alto, CA: Consulting Psychologists Press.

**Jerome Siegel, Ph.D.**
*Professor of Psychology, The City College of New York, New York, New York.*

# TEAM EFFECTIVENESS SURVEY

*Jay Hall. The Woodlands, Texas: Teleometrics International.*

## Introduction

The Team Effectiveness Survey (TES) was developed in 1968 to assess the process issues that characterize the internal workings of a team. The instrument emphasizes issues of interpersonal style, expressiveness, and team member communication patterns, which are all important in achieving team effectiveness.

The emphasis of the TES relies on assessments of each team member by all members as well as a self-assessment. The resulting data provide information for each team member on how he or she impacts the performance of the team as perceived and evaluated by the rest of the team members. In addition, the self-evaluations can be compared with team members' assessments and total team data and performance. These assessments can be shared by team members and then discussed and evaluated as part of a team-building exercise.

The TES consists of an attractive, self-contained, 10-page booklet, which explains the test and provides instructions for taking, scoring, and interpreting the results. A rating scale is provided that lists 20 behaviors that individuals may use in team exercises or projects. These are stated as descriptions of members' behaviors using bipolar dimensions. For example, a behavior may be described as, "This person is empathetic of other team members (as opposed to being indifferent and lacking understanding)." The task for each team member is to rate him- or herself and every other team member on each of the behaviors, using a 10-point scale in which 1 denotes a minimum use of the behavior and 10 is the maximum use of the behavior described. All of the 10 scale values are described in the booklet on the same page as the 20 behavioral statements. A chart next to the 20 behaviors provides space for team members' names, a rating on each behavior for each team member, and a self-rating.

The TES is a self-scoring instrument. After all of the team members complete their ratings, envelopes are passed around the group with one member's name on each. The perforated scoring sheet is torn so that team members will get their ratings for each of teammate in their envelope. Their data forms the basis of a scoring system that involves tallying the ratings of each team member on a tally page and then being able to sum and average scores, depending on what information is to be interpreted or discussed.

The TES is based on a model of interpersonal relationships, the Johari window, developed by Drs. Joseph Luft and Harry Ingram (1970). This model is used in scoring and interpreting individual performances within the group. By plotting scores in the 2×2 window, team members obtain information about their own interpersonal styles and how they are used in developing relationships with other team members. Their styles are categorized based on how open they are in their relationships and how they obtain information from others about their feelings and knowledge. This typology of interpersonal style is then compared with descriptive normative interpretations of each type and examined to see whether it results in defensive or supportive behavior by other members in the group. Each individual can then profile his or her results and how that compares with a defensive or supportive climate created by the behavior of the other members of the team.

The TES is self-administered and self-scored. Interpretations are also made by individual team members, and the results are usually discussed by all team members in terms of individual team members and average team scores. There is no time limit for the TES because the amount of time for the completion will be a function of what team members do with the results.

## Practical Applications/Uses

The author's main claim for the TES is that it "yields data which may prove helpful in assessing each individual's impact and it affords an index of general team climate and procedural effectiveness, as these are perceived by the total membership" (Hall, 1986, p. 1). The emphasis of TES is on issues of interpersonal style, expressiveness, trust, and openness within the communication process. It deals with listening skills, understanding feelings, degree of support, feedback processes, personality dynamics, and other issues of team-oriented behavior. It does not deal with technical skills and knowledge required, on the assumption that this may vary from team-to-team. The author states the following in the instruction guide:

> it is what team members do with the data they get from the TES that will really determine its utility for achieving team effectiveness; therefore, be prepared to deal with the questionnaire and the ensuing team analysis as objectively and candidly as possible. (Hall, 1986, p. 1)

According to these instructions and objectives stated by the author, the TES can be used to generate data for almost any type of a team-building exercise. Although it was probably designed for use in the work situation for small project-oriented groups, it most likely can be used, as can many other team-building exercises, with groups in a variety of institutional settings, including hospitals, universities, government agencies, and even voluntary work groups and those in therapeutic communities. The task of rating 20 behavioral statements is specific, but the objectives, interpretation, and uses of the data are very general within the framework of the theory used to interpret the results.

The administration and scoring of the instrument is clear, simply presented, and results in a set of data for every team member and for the team as a unit. It is based on a summation of all evaluations by each team member on the 1- to 10-point scale for each of the 20 behavioral statements. The scores are added for two separate behaviors labeled *exposure* (the tendency to engage in open expressions of one's own feelings and knowledge) and *feedback* (the tendency to solicit information from others about their feelings and knowledge). Therefore, scores on each of these factors can range from 10 to 100. These scores are added, averaged,

**Fig. 1** The Johan window model of interpersonal relationships

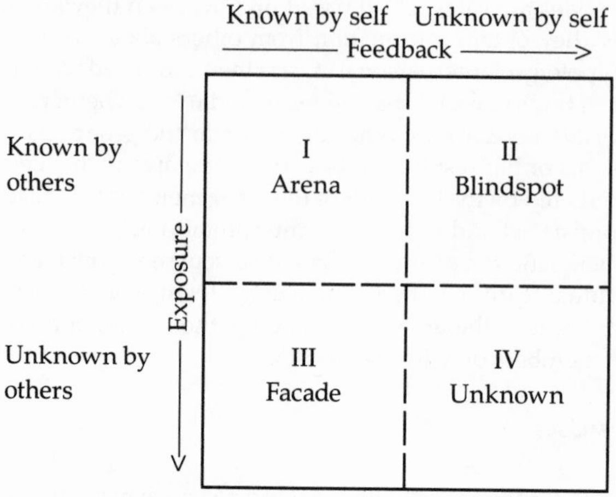


and then plotted in Johari windows for each team member and for the total team (see Fig. 1).

This model allows each member to measure their tendency to facilitate or hinder the flow of interpersonal information in their relationships with other team members. Interpersonal styles will vary, resulting in changes in the size of each quadrant for different team members. Those with large arena scores (+) make best use of exposure and feedback and have trust, openness, and sensitivity with other group members; those with a large unknown (IV) area have great difficulty since they make minimal use of feedback and exposure to facilitate the group process. This data and model are then also used to interpret the team climate.

## Technical Aspects

There is very little information available regarding the psychometric properties of TES. This may be, in part, because of the type of instrument it is and the unstructured format for the use of the data. The publishers provide no information regarding the 20 behavioral statements and how they were selected. Unless there are specific item analysis procedures utilized in this process, there could have easily been other behavioral statements more relevant to the group process. No evidence of team member reliability is given, which would be important if the quantitative data are used to evaluate individual member or total team effectiveness. Scorer reliability would also be a useful piece of information in evaluating the effectiveness of TES. Through personal communication with the publisher (S.M. Donnell, February 1990), they report interjudge reliability coefficients of .41 for exposure and .46 for feedback, which is reported as significant at the .01 level. However, the nature and size of the sample is not given, and the reported reliability coefficients are considerably below what would normally be acceptable levels of test score consistency.

There are no reported validity data in any of the published material. In fact, there is no evidence to suggest whether this instrument has been useful in any of its intended applications. Therefore, the user really has no empirical data to suggest what this instrument is really measuring. Some construct validation procedures would certainly be appropriate.

## Critique

The TES is a well packaged and attractively designed instrument that is simple to administer and score. The interpretation is based on a theoretical model of interpersonal relations that can provide some insight for team members regarding how others perceive his (her) behavior as contributing to team effectiveness. It is, however, like many other team-building exercises in that it provides a vehicle for discussion and self-analysis of team member and team effectiveness. Some of the behavioral items seem arbitrary, as does the scoring, but the end product can produce an effective process as a team-building instrument. Unfortunately, the author does not provide any guidelines or recommendations regarding its utility as a team-building exercise. Suggestions regarding how a group leader can use the instrument, or how teams or groups can best discuss the data generated by the TES, are not available. Readers are referred to Francis and Young (1979) for other examples of team-building tools and exercises that provide explicit instructions to leaders and team members regarding practical suggestions for team building.

The TES was reviewed by Mollenkopf in *The English Mental Measurements Yearbook* (1978). His major criticism, shared by this review, was the total omission of technical skills and knowledge from the TES. The publishers' rationale is that "this may vary from team to team." Mollenkopf, in his review, states: "weaknesses in the various skills required to play a full part in a work team can have a great impact on the effectiveness of the team and the quality of the relationships among members of the team" (1978, p. 1682). It is well documented that individual differences in skills, knowledge, and abilities will influence decision making, problem solving, and who plays which roles in the performance of a group. Power and influence often are based on individual levels of expertise, which will have a marked influence on the characteristics being evaluated with the TES.

Other limitations of the TES are the lack of appropriate psychometric properties of reliability, specification of appropriate normative samples, and of validity evidence pertaining to what constructs the test is really measuring. It would also be helpful to know something about its past applications and the level of success achieved as a diagnostic/evaluative instrument.

In short, this reviewer perceives the TES as another instrument to initiate a team-building process. Its positive characteristics are simplicity and ease of administration and scoring, its interpretation being tied to a specific model of interpersonal effectiveness. The limitations center around an absence of appropriate psychometric data, and insufficient guidelines regarding applicability as a team-building tool. In the hands of a skilled facilitator, the TES has the potential of being a useful instrument.

## References

Francis, D., & Young, D. (1979). *Improving work groups: A practical manual for team building.* San Diego: University Associates.

Hall, J. (1986). *Team Effectiveness Survey.* The Woodlands, TX: Telemetrics International.

Luft, J. (1970). *Group processes: An introduction to group dynamics* (2nd ed.). Palo Alto, CA: Mayfield.

Mollenkopf, W.G. (1978). Team Effectiveness Survey. In J.V. Mitchell, Jr. (Ed.), *The eighth mental measurements yearbook* (pp. 1054–1055). Lincoln, NE: Buros Institute of Mental Measurements.

**Ron D. Cambias, Jr., Psy.D.**
*Psychology Staff, Children's Hospital, New Orleans, Louisiana.*

**Grant Aram Killian, Ph.D.**
*Associate Professor of Psychology, Nova University, Ft. Lauderdale, Florida.*

**Jan Faust, Ph.D.**
*Assistant Professor of Psychology, Nova University, Ft. Lauderdale, Florida.*

---

# TEMAS (TELL-ME-A-STORY)

*Giuseppe Costantino, Robert G. Malgady, and Lloyd H. Rogler. Los Angeles, California: Western Psychological Services.*

## Introduction

The Tell-Me-A-Story test (TEMAS; Costantino, Malgady, & Rogler, 1988) is a thematic apperceptive technique designed for children and adolescents that follows in the tradition of the Thematic Apperception Test (TAT; Murray, 1971) and the Children's Apperception Test (CAT; Bellak & Bellak, 1980). The TEMAS (meaning "themes" in Spanish) differentiates itself from other apperception tests through its suitability for both minority (i.e., Hispanic, black) and nonminority populations, while respecting psychometric demands (e.g., reliability, validity, and standardization).

The first author, Giuseppe Costantino, Ph.D., has been clinical director at the Sunset Park Mental Health Center of the Lutheran Medical Center in Brooklyn, New York, since 1985, and Research Associate at the Hispanic Research Center of Fordham University in The Bronx since 1978. The second author, Robert G. Malgady, Ph.D., has been a Research Associate at the Hispanic Research Center since 1981 as well as a professor in the department of mathematics, science, and statistics at New York University. The third author, Lloyd H. Rogler, Ph.D., director of the Hispanic Research Center since 1977, has received many prestigious honors as well as city and national government appointments.

The TEMAS developed out of the first author's experiences while working in Harlem during the early 1970s. During that time, he became aware of the lack of responsiveness of both Hispanic and black children to traditional projective instruments. This lack of responsiveness and the unavailability of apperception tests with adequate psychometric properties led him to begin work in 1977, with the help of artist Phil Jacobs, on the TEMAS cards. Dr. Costantino brought the TEMAS with him to the Hispanic Research Center, where he and the other two authors have worked on its development. The nonminority version of the test was developed in 1980, at the advice of David Lachar, Ph.D., of Western Psychological Services. The TEMAS stimulus cards eventually were published by Western Psychological Services in 1986, with the manual following in 1988.

The TEMAS is based on a dynamic-cognitive model, encompassing aspects of ego psychology, interpersonal psychology, social-cognitive learning theory, and cognitive psychology. The core of the TEMAS is its nine personality functions, which were developed greatly from the contributions of ego psychology (Bellak, Hurvich, & Gediman, 1973). These personality functions are related to the contributions of ego psychology by redefining ego functions as personality constructs. Ego psychologists, specifically Bellak and his associates (1973), defined a number of ego functions that assist the individual in meeting the demands of the environment (e.g., reality testing, thought processes, etc.). These ego functions are seen by ego psychologists as internal modulators of behavior. From the perspective of interpersonal psychology, Sullivan (1953) posited that the various ego or personality functions resulted from the child's interactions with significant others. Thus, both the ego's internal and interpersonal aspects are defined through the theories of ego and interpersonal psychology.

Bandura (1977), from the viewpoint of social-cognitive psychology, developed a modeling theory consisting of four basic processes: attention, retention, motoric reproduction, and reinforcement. These processes are further complemented by three effects of modeling that facilitate learning: (a) imitation, (b) disinhibition, and (c) elicitation. The influence of social-cognitive theory on the TEMAS is reflected through the use of familiar, colored stimulus situations to enhance the child's attention and to elicit responses through disinhibition. The purpose of these features is to facilitate projection of intra- and interpersonal material.

Finally, the cognitive theories of Piaget and Inhelder (1969, 1971) also are reflected in the dynamic-cognitive framework of the TEMAS. With the rise of symbolic thinking, the child is able to symbolize experiences through imagery and words. Costantino, Malgady, and Rogler (1988), extrapolating from the research of Piaget and Inhelder, point out that "the memory image elicited by a pictorial representation of the TEMAS becomes a symbol which integrates the percept, the emotional state, and the elicited past learning experience of the subject" (p. 12).

The stimulus cards were developed out of research regarding stimulus ambiguity, the use of color, and the contrasting nature (or bipolarity) of personality functions. Although the traditional assumption has been that an ambiguous stimulus facilitates greater projection than a structured one (Murray, 1943), the TEMAS was constructed with unambiguous stimuli. This decision to use unambiguous stimuli was based on research that unambiguous stimuli activate specific drives and provide more easily interpreted responses, due to the elicitation of responses from a stimulus of known significance (Epstein, 1966). Thus, the historically poor reliability of projective instruments is likely related to the greater difficulty in quantifying results derived from ambiguous stimuli. The use of color was based on findings that colored stimuli increase verbal fluency and encourage expression of emotions (Brackbill, 1951; Thompson & Bachrach, 1951).

Each stimulus situation consists of bipolar personality functions requiring the resolution of psychological conflicts, similar to Kohlberg's moral dilemma situations (Kohlberg, 1976). For example, if the personality function of delay of gratification is depicted in a scene, then so is its opposite, the inability to delay gratification. The stimulus situations require the resolution of psychological conflicts, which are judged according to their adaptiveness or maladaptiveness. For example, Card

10G depicts a girl holding a coin over her piggy bank as she considers either buying an ice cream or saving her money to buy a bicycle. This card pulls for delay of gratification. The resolution of this conflict will fall on a continuum, from highly adaptive to highly maladaptive. An example of an adaptive response would be the girl's saving her money to buy the bicycle; a maladaptive response would entail stealing money to buy the ice cream and bicycle.

The development of the TEMAS began in September of 1977 with the creation of the first stimulus pictures (Costantino, 1978). Originally, 100 stimulus cards were constructed to portray (a) scenes with which children could identify, (b) scenes that were interesting to children, and (c) scenes that were in color to enhance realism. A pilot study was conducted in which a group of eight children, ages 6 to 12, were asked to tell a story about each picture and answer four questions concerning the action, characters, relationships, and setting portrayed in the pictures (Costantino, 1978; Costantino, Malgady, & Rogler, 1988). Those pictures on which the children reached a .80 level of interrater agreement for all four questions were retained, while the rest were either discarded or redrawn. Fifty-three pictures were selected in this manner. Through clinical research, some pictures were found to be clinically insignificant and were discarded. By 1980, 47 cards were developed. Further studies (not specified in the manual) on the psychometric properties of this set resulted in the final set of 23 pictures, which was ready by early 1983.

The TEMAS was standardized on a sample of 642 children who ranged in age from 5 to 13 years. The standardization group included 281 males and 361 females selected from New York City area public schools. However, the TEMAS manual (Costantino, Malgady, & Rogler, 1988) does not describe the criteria for selection. Subjects, generally from lower and lower middle income families, represented four different ethnic/racial groups: whites, blacks, Puerto Ricans, and Other Hispanics. Due to significant correlations between age and many of the TEMAS scores, the standardization sample was broken down into three age levels: 5–7, 8–10, and 11–13.

Tables for converting raw scores into T-scores allow the examiner to compare each subject to the standardization group by age and ethnic/racial group. Seven ethnic/racial groups are broken down into three age levels: whites, blacks, Puerto Rican, Other Hispanic, Combined Hispanic, Minority, and Total Sample. These numerous choices allow the examiner to choose the group that best reflects the ethnic/racial identification of the subject while providing larger, more statistically stable comparison groups. For example, the Other Hispanic, 5- to 7-year-old sample contains only 19 subjects (8 females and 11 males), far too small to provide for statistically reliable results. A minimum for such subgroups would be around 300 subjects (Kline, 1986). However, the test authors attempt to minimize this problem by combining the Puerto Rican and Other Hispanic subgroups into a Combined Hispanic group, thus yielding a larger subgroup of 67 subjects (35 females and 32 males).

In addition to the small subgroups, another problem with the normative sample is the failure to employ a stratified sampling procedure during the standardization of the TEMAS. Because of the unstratified nature of the standardization sample, the test authors warn that the TEMAS normative data should be regarded as preliminary estimates and should be used with caution.

The TEMAS Short Form (comprising 9 cards) was standardized by extracting scores from the Long Form protocols of the general standardization sample. Because they were extracted from Long Form protocols, these norms should also be used with caution. Whether or not subjects might have responded differently to a shorter administration of TEMAS cards remains uncertain.

The TEMAS kit consists of the manual, stimulus cards (individual sets of minority and nonminority versions), administration instruction card, and packages of 25 record booklets. The manual covers the test's theoretical framework, administration and scoring, interpretation of results, three case studies, development and standardization information, and a consideration of the test's psychometric properties (i.e., reliability and validity data).

Both minority and nonminority versions consist of thirty-six 8½" × 11" full color stimulus picture cards. The minority version presents Hispanic and black characters in an urban setting. The nonminority version consists of nonminority characters in an urban setting. Most stimulus pictures portray unambiguous scenes from urban life and fantasy scenes that require the resolution of a conflictual situation. For example, Card 1B portrays a scene in which a boy is outside with a group of peers, one of whom is holding a basketball. A man and a woman are looking at the boy through an open window, with the woman holding a piece of paper in her hand. This particular picture is designed to elicit themes concerning interpersonal relationships and delay of gratification. The dilemma inherent in this picture is between the boy's playing basketball with his friends or obeying the command of his parents. The Long Form encompasses 23 cards for use with each subject (12 cards are used with both sexes, 11 are used with either males or females). The Short Form encompasses 9 cards for use with each subject (4 cards for both sexes, 5 that are sex-specific).

The administration instruction card is intended to assist the examiner with the test instructions in order to ensure standardized administration procedures. The first page of the TEMAS Record Booklet consists of sections for recording demographic information (e.g., the subject's name, age, dominant language, language used during administration, ethnic/racial background, and form administered—long or short, etc.), behavioral observations, and normative group employed (e.g., white, black, Puerto Rican, etc.). The second and third pages are devoted to scoring the Quantitative Scales and the Qualitative Indicators, respectively. Finally, the last page is devoted to profiling the Quantitative Scales.

The TEMAS addresses 18 Cognitive Functions, 9 Personality Functions, and 7 Affective Functions. The 18 Cognitive Functions are described as follows:

1. *Reaction Time:* the time elapsed from moment of presentation of stimulus card to verbalization of response by examinee.

2. *Total Time:* the total amount of time required for the examinee's response to the card, including responses to all inquiries.

3. *Fluency:* the total word count for each response.

4. *Total Omissions:* the total number of characters, events, and settings that are present in the stimulus situations but not mentioned in the subject's response.

5. *Main Character Omissions:* omissions of main characters from the stimulus situations in the subject's response.

6. *Secondary Character Omissions:* omissions of characters, other than main characters, from the subject's response.

7. *Event Omissions:* refers to the examinee's failure to identify what is happening in the picture.

8. *Setting Omissions:* refers to the examinee's failure to identify where the story is taking place.

9. *Total Transformations:* the total number of perceptual distortions of characters, events, and settings in the subject's response.

10. *Main Character Transformations:* incorrectly identified main characters in the subject's response.

11. *Secondary Character Transformations:* incorrectly identified characters, other than main characters, in the subject's response.

12. *Event Transformations:* incorrectly identified events in the examinee's response.

13. *Setting Transformations:* incorrectly identified locations in the examinee's response.

14. *Conflict:* recognition of the conflict portrayed by the individual stimulus card (e.g., the conflict of delay of gratification with Card 14, in which the main character may choose to dance or study).

15. *Sequencing:* refers to the ability of the subject to relate the events in the response to past, present, and future.

16. *Imagination:* refers to material that goes beyond mere description of the stimulus and reflects the personality of the subject (e.g., projection of personal material).

17. *Relationships:* refers to identification of characters and how they relate to each other.

18. *Inquiries:* refers to questions asked regarding the clarification of material or omitted information.

The nine Personality Functions are described as follows:

1. *Interpersonal Relations:* the degree and quality of the relationships expressed in the subject's responses.

2. *Aggression:* either the verbal or physical expression of harm to self, others, or property.

3. *Anxiety/Depression:* irrational fears, worries, or unhappiness (these two are combined due to their oftentimes combined presence in children, and they are scored as a Personality Function due to their nature as defense mechanisms and coping styles).

4. *Achievement Motivation:* the desire to achieve a goal or excel on some task.

5. *Delay of Gratification:* the ability to relinquish immediate pleasure in order to acquire a greater future reward.

6. *Self-Concept:* the realistic perception of one's abilities and mastery over one's environment.

7. *Sexual Identity:* the realistic perception of one's sex roles.

8. *Moral Judgment:* the ability to distinguish between right and wrong, to act responsibly, and to experience appropriate guilt for wrongdoing.

9. *Reality Testing:* the ability to distinguish between fantasy and reality and to anticipate consequences of one's behavior.

Finally, the seven Affective Functions are described as follows:

1. *Happy:* contentment over the resolution of conflict.
2. *Sad:* discontentment over the resolution of conflict.
3. *Angry:* strong displeasure over the resolution of conflict.
4. *Fearful:* feeling of impending danger over the resolution of conflict.
5. *Neutral:* emotional indifference to the resolution of conflict.
6. *Ambivalent:* emotional indecision over the resolution of conflict.
7. *Inappropriate Affect:* incongruence between the feelings and behaviors of the main character(s) in the story over the resolution of conflict.

The first four Cognitive Functions (Reaction Time, Total Time, Fluency, and Total Omissions), the entire set of nine Personality Functions, and the first four Affective Functions (Happy, Sad, Angry, and Fearful) compose the Quantitative Scales. These scales consist of raw scores that are converted into normalized T-scores, thereby allowing a comparison of a subject's scores with children from the standardization sample. The rest of the Cognitive and Affective Functions, a total of 17 functions, compose the Qualitative Indicators. These functions did not have the same psychometric properties as the other scales due to the more limited variability of scores for each during the standardization of the TEMAS. Instead of converting raw scores to T-scores, critical cutoff points were calculated to indicate which scores were at or above the 90th percentile for the normative sample.

**Practical Applications/Uses**

The TEMAS is most appropriate for school and clinical psychologists in the evaluation of both minority and nonminority children and young adolescents regarding emotional/adjustment problems. The TEMAS manual states that the three major uses for the test are to "(a) gain better understanding of both strengths and deficits in cognitive, affective, and intrapersonal and interpersonal functioning of the individual; (b) give problem-specific information in order to develop a more accurate treatment plan; and (c) assess therapeutic progress and outcome" (Costantino, Malgady, & Rogler, 1988, p. 2). For example, a clinical psychologist might use the TEMAS in evaluating an urban boy referred by his school for depression. The results would help the clinician assess strengths and weaknesses and develop a treatment plan, and then the test could be employed again 1 year later, following psychotherapeutic intervention, to measure treatment progress.

The test authors state that the TEMAS is intended to be used in conjunction with other evaluation measures to corroborate information as part of a personality assessment. However, if used as part of a test battery for the purpose of diagnostic assessment, it is important to note that thematic apperception tests have been shown to reduce the diagnostic validity of more psychometrically robust measures, like the MMPI or the Personality Inventory for Children (Wildman & Wildman, 1975; Butkus, 1984). Although the TEMAS may prove to complement the other personality tests of an assessment arsenal, the point is questionable until established by research.

The manual states that the TEMAS is suitable for use with black, Hispanic, and white children and adolescents, ages 5 to 18. However, at present no normative data are available for ages 14 to 18. Despite the fact that the manual clearly states that the TEMAS may not be used normatively with these adolescents, even a subjective analysis may lead to inaccurate interpretation of test data: In this way, the chances increase of the examiner projecting onto test material as much as the test subject (Killian, 1984). Further, due to the makeup of the normative sample, the TEMAS is only appropriate for use with urban populations. Neither suburban nor rural children were included in the standardization sample. Finally, the test requires that subjects have basic comprehension and verbal skills to understand directions and communicate a story, motivation to cooperate with the instructions of the test, and no acute sensory and intellectual deficits.

Prior to administration of the TEMAS, the examiner first decides whether to administer the minority or nonminority version, according to which best reflects the ethnic/racial identification of the test subject. Due to findings that suggest a lack of verbal fluency on projective tests calls their validity into question (Anderson & Anderson, 1955), it was important for the TEMAS to encourage the verbal fluency of minority subjects by presenting culturally relevant stimuli. Research has demonstrated the increased verbal fluency of black and Hispanic subjects when using the minority version of the TEMAS compared to their performance on the TAT (Costantino, Malgady, & Vazquez, 1981; Costantino & Malgady, 1983). Also, the examiner decides whether to administer the Long Form (23 cards, 2 hours) or the Short Form (9 cards, 45 minutes to 1 hour).

The examiner must be thoroughly familiar with the administration and content of the TEMAS. Although it is preferable that the examiner be of the subject's ethnic or racial background, the test authors suggest that this is not necessary provided the examiner is familiar with the subject's cultural background (Malgady, Rogler, & Costantino, 1987). However, if the examinee is bilingual or lacks proficiency in English, the test must be administered by a bilingual examiner and allow the examinee to respond in his or her preferred language. Costantino et al. (1981) discovered that Hispanic children were more likely to respond in Spanish to the TEMAS than to the TAT. Ideally, it would seem necessary for the examiner to have training in projective testing on at least a master's degree level.

The TEMAS is administered individually in any quiet, well-lit room free from distractions. The manual states that responses should be recorded verbatim by hand. Though such a method undoubtedly saves time, recording by hand may interfere with the flow of responses and building of rapport should the examiner need to interrupt the examinee in order to clarify or repeat what the subject had said. Furthermore, this method is less efficient than audiotaping and may result in loss of information, as demonstrated by TAT research comparing machine recording with recording by hand (Baty & Dreger, 1975).

The examiner begins administration with a set of instructions similar to those given with the TAT. The test subject is handed each picture (apparently in any order) and asked to look at it and relate a story about it that has a beginning and an end. The examiner instructs the child to tell a complete story for each picture that answers the following three questions: What is happening in the picture now? What happened before? What will happen in the future? These instructions may be repeated, if necessary, for each picture—especially when testing young children or those with short attention spans. In addition, certain prescribed inquiries are conducted at the end of each response if clarification is needed. These questions are aimed at clarifying the relationship of characters, the setting, the sequence of action (present, past and future), and the thoughts and feelings of the main character. The examinee is encouraged to talk about each story for at least 2 minutes, with a maximum time limit of 5 minutes for each response.

Scoring the TEMAS involves the Quantitative Scales and the Qualitative Indicators. Cognitive Functions are each scored as to their presence or absence for each response. In the case of Fluency, the number of words for each response is totaled; Reaction Time and Total Time are converted into two-digit numbers and proportions of an hour (e.g., 6″ = 06; 4′15″ = 4.25). The raw scores are totaled and either checked against a critical cutoff score (90th percentile or above) for the Qualitative Indicators or converted into normalized T-scores for the Quantitative Scales. The decision to use each type of scoring system was based not on relative clinical value but on the psychometric properties for each type of score.

The Personality Functions are scored using a 4-point, Likert-type scale, with 1 indicating the greatest maladaptive functioning and 4 indicating the greatest adaptive functioning. For example, Card 9 depicts a scene in which a child is standing at the edge of a woods with one road diverging in two directions (adapted from Robert Frost's poem, "The Road Not Taken"). The child may either take the road to the right, where peers can be seen persuading the child to follow them, or take an empty road to the left. This picture pulls for themes concerning the Personality Functions of Achievement Motivation and Anxiety/Depression. An example of a 1-point response to this picture for Achievement Motivation, indicating highly maladaptive functioning, would be deciding to take the road to the right in order to steal the other children's money. A 2-point response for Achievement Motivation, indicating moderately maladaptive functioning, would be taking the road to the right in order to avoid doing homework. A 3-point response for Achievement Motivation, indicating partially adaptive functioning, would be avoiding work by going down the road to the left but then returning to the other road to finish a school project with classmates. Finally, a 4-point response for Achievement Motivation, indicating the highest adaptive functioning, would be taking the road to the left in order to run an errand for one's parents, though preferring to have joined friends to play. Responses that fail to relate themes intended to be elicited by a particular stimulus card are marked "N," for "Personality Function Not Pulled."

The scores for each function are summed and then divided by the number of responses containing like themes to derive a mean score. This mean score is then converted into a normalized T-score by referring to the norm tables in the back of the manual. Norm tables are listed by age range (5–7, 8–10 and 11–13 years of age) and by ethnic/racial group (e.g., black, Hispanic, etc.). The "N" responses are totaled and checked against cutoff scores, marking performance at the 85th percentile. Such responses were rare in the standardization sample and are indicative of maladaptive "selective attention" (Hallahan & Reeve, 1980), reflecting deficits in the self-awareness necessary for proper personality growth.

Finally, the Affective Functions are scored for their presence (Happy, Sad, Angry, Fearful, Neutral, or Ambivalent) and congruence to story content (Inappropriate Affect). More than one affect may be marked at one time. As with the Cognitive Functions, the scores are summed into raw scores, which are either compared to critical cutoff points (for the Qualitative Indicators) or converted to normalized T-scores (for the Quantitative Scales).

Overall, the TEMAS scoring system is straightforward and comprehensive. The use of such an objective scoring system facilitates comparison of scores within a subject's protocol as well as between subjects from the normative sample. The uniform 4-point, Likert-type scoring system for the Personality Functions and simple marking of discrete scores for the other functions simplifies and reduces the subjectivity of scoring. Although there may be some subjective judgment involved in scoring the Personality Functions (e.g., deciding whether to score a response as 2 points or 3 points), the manual's numerous, clear examples enhance the examiner's ability to learn accurate response scoring.

The major part of interpreting the TEMAS involves an examination of the Quantitative Scales and the Qualitative Indicators. Examination of the TEMAS Profile scores, consisting of the Quantitative Scales, entails looking for significant high and low scores. The TEMAS Profile scores are based on a T-distribution, a method for expressing a subject's relative position within a group, with a mean T-score of 50 and a standard deviation of 10. Therefore, significant scale scores are those that fall 1 standard deviation above or below the mean (outside the T-score range of 40 to 60). Each function is inspected as to the magnitude of its deviation from the mean. Examination of the Qualitative Indicators entails examining scores that exceed the cutoff points marking performance at the 90th percentile for each score. Each function is inspected to see which ones exceed the cutoff score.

The Cognitive Functions should be interpreted together, regardless of whether they are Quantitative or Qualitative Scales. For example, Total Omissions of the Quantitative Scales should be interpreted together with Omissions of Main Character, Secondary Character, Events, and Settings of the Qualitative Indicators. Likewise, the Affective Functions should also be interpreted together, regardless of whether they are Quantitative or Qualitative Scales. For example, Happy, Sad, Angry, and Fearful of the Quantitative Scales should be interpreted together with Neutral, Ambivalent, and Inappropriate of the Qualitative Indicators. Both Cognitive and Affective Functions are interpreted according to their deviation from the mean, for the Quantitative Scales, or exceeding cutoff points, for the Qualitative Indicators.

The Personality Functions are examined for the magnitude and direction of the T-scores. These functions are interpreted in groups and with other Cognitive and Affective Functions, as relevant. Sums of "N" scores for Personality Functions that were not pulled should be compared to critical cutoff points, marking that point at which 15% or fewer of the standardization subjects scored. Significant "N" scores should be interpreted in conjunction with omissions of Cognitive Functions due to their similar nature as indicators of selective attention.

The interpretation of the TEMAS should include an attempt to integrate the various functions together to enhance understanding of the test subject's overall functioning. For example, a significant high T-score on Aggression, together with significantly elevated scores on Conflict (a Qualitative Indicator signifying failure to verbalize the depicted conflict in the stimulus situations) and Happy (an Affective Function of the Quantitative Scales) likely signify denial and/or repression over aggressive impulses. Other unscored Qualitative Indicators (i.e., test behavior, rejection of cards, and content analysis of stories) are also examined for their contribution to a comprehensive understanding of test results. In addition, the test authors intend to develop a Popularity Index to indicate which response themes are most popular (Costantino, Malgady, & Rogler, 1988); this index would be similar to the Popular Response on the Rorschach (Exner, 1986).

Interpretation of the TEMAS is moderately complex and requires an examiner skilled in the interpretation of psychological tests. A background in child development and psychopathology is required to interpret results adequately. The test examiner must also be cognizant of the limits of projective testing. For example, test results should not be overinterpreted but should be compared with data from other sources, such as clinical interviews and behavior rating scales.

**Technical Aspects**

As noted before, the TEMAS is one of the few apperception tests developed with any amount of psychometric rigor. The psychometric properties of any psychological test refer to its validity and reliability. The types of validity addressed with respect to the TEMAS are content (Costantino, Malgady, & Rogler, 1988), construct (Costantino, Malgady, Rogler, & Tsui, 1988; Costantino, Malgady, Bailey, & Colon-Malgady, 1989; Costantino, Colon, Malgady, & Perez, 1989), and criterion-related (Malgady, Costantino, & Rogler, 1984). The types of reliability addressed are internal consistency (coefficient alpha) (Costantino, Malgady, & Rogler, 1988; Costantino, Malgady, Casullo, & Castillo, 1989), test-retest (Costantino, Malgady, & Rogler, 1988; Costantino, Malgady, Rogler, & Tsui, 1987), and interrater (scorer) (Costantino, Malgady, & Rogler, 1988; Costantino, Malgady, Casullo, & Castillo, 1989).

Content validity was established by a study (Costantino, Malgady, & Rogler, 1988) in which 14 psychologists rated the stimulus cards according to personality function "pulled for." Examiners were presented the TEMAS cards in random order and asked which of the nine Personality Functions, if any, were exhibited in the picture. Results indicated high agreement (71–100%) among raters as to the thematic content of the TEMAS cards, thus lending support for content validity.

Evidence for construct validity is supported by recent studies demonstrating the utility of the TEMAS in distinguishing between clinical and nonclinical groups (Costantino, Malgady, Rogler, & Tsui, 1988; Costantino, Malgady, Bailey, & Colon-Malgady, 1989; Costantino, Colon, Malgady, & Perez, 1989). In the first study, Costantino, Malgady, Rogler, and Tsui (1988) administered the TEMAS to two groups of Hispanics and blacks, comprising 100 outpatients from psychiatric centers and 373 public school students (outpatients: 67 Hispanics, 33 blacks; students: 167 Hispanics, 206 blacks). A discriminant analysis yielded a classification rate of 89%, thus lending support for the TEMAS's ability to differentiate clinical from nonclinical test subjects. However, the authors of the study point out that it would be premature to use the TEMAS to distinguish between specific diagnostic categories of patients and normals. Also, the authors caution against overgeneralizing results from this and earlier studies to other subgroups of blacks and Hispanics, as mostly lower SES and Puerto Rican subjects from New York City have been employed in these studies. The generalizability of the TEMAS could be furthered by studies that include higher SES black and Hispanic groups and other Hispanic subgroups (e.g., Cubans, Mexicans, etc.).

In the second study, Costantino, Malgady, Bailey, and Colon-Malgady (1989) attempted to further the findings of the previous discriminant analysis study (Costantino, Malgady, Rogler, & Tsui, 1988) by adding a subgroup of clinical and nonclinical white children. They administered the TEMAS to Hispanic, black, and white outpatients and public school students (outpatients: 67 Hispanics, 33 blacks, 36 whites; students: 71 Puerto Ricans, 40 blacks, 49 whites). Discriminant analyses yielded classification rates of 89% for Hispanics, 91% for blacks, and 86% for whites, thus demonstrating the test's utility in classifying clinical and nonclinical groups according to racial/ethnic background. Again, the authors warn that profiling specific diagnostic categories is premature.

Finally, in the third study, Costantino, Colon, Malgady, and Perez (1989) administered the TEMAS to 95 outpatients from mental health centers and 163 public school students, consisting of Hispanics, blacks, and whites (outpatients: 35 Hispanics, 25 blacks, 35 whites; students: 71 Hispanics, 40 blacks, 52 whites). The outpatients comprised a group of children/adolescents meeting the diagnosis for Attention-Deficit Hyperactivity Disorder (ADHD; American Psychiatric Association, 1987). It was hypothesized that ADHD children would be more likely to omit perceptual details of pictorial stimuli than would normal-functioning children. Two-tailed *t* tests between group means indicated that all three ADHD groups (Hispanic, black, and white) were more likely to omit details regarding characters, settings, and events than the public school students. These results suggest the possible use of thematic apperceptive techniques for distinguishing ADHD children from normals.

Criterion-related validity encompasses both concurrent and predictive validity. The concurrent validity of the TEMAS was examined by correlating eight different measures with results from TEMAS protocols using a sample of 210 Puerto Rican children. These children were chosen to participate in a study of behavioral problem children from New York City public schools (Malgady et al., 1984). The eight measures were measures of ego development (the Sentence Completion Test of Ego Development, Loevinger & Wessler, 1970; or its Spanish version, Brenes-Jette, 1987), trait anxiety (the Trait Anxiety scale of the State-Trait Anxiety Inventory for Children, Spielberger, Edwards, Lushene, Montuori, & Platzek, 1973; or its Spanish version, Villamil, 1973), teacher behavior rating (the Teacher Behavior Rating Scale, Costantino, 1980), mother behavior rating (Mother Behavior Rating Scale, Costantino, 1980), delay of gratification, self-concept, disruptiveness, and aggression (the last four assessed via observer ratings of role-playing situations). Regression analyses resulted in significant correlations for all of these measures with TEMAS profiles, except for trait anxiety. The significant correlations ranged from .32 to .51. Thus, this study demonstrated the ability of the TEMAS to predict criterion-related measures.

Predictive validity was assessed using 123 subjects from the same sample used in the concurrent validity study (Malgady et al., 1984). This time, subjects underwent a period of treatment before being retested. A hierarchical multiple regression analysis was performed, using the same eight criterion measures in the study above. Pretherapy TEMAS profiles significantly predicted all posttherapy measures, except for self-concept of competence, ranging from 6% to 22% variance increments.

Coefficient alpha was computed by ethnic group for the TEMAS Long Form on a group of 73 Hispanic and 42 black children selected by their teachers for absence of behavior problems (Costantino, Malgady, & Rogler, 1988). Alpha coefficients for the Long Form yielded a range of .41 to .98 (with a median value of .73) for the Hispanic sample and a range of .31 to .97 (with a median value of .62) for the black sample. Internal consistency was generally lower for the Personality Functions, perhaps in part due to the few cards pulling for each function. However, the sample size in this study falls short of the recommended minimum number of 200 subjects to ensure statistically reliable results in such studies (Kline, 1986).

Reliability coefficients were computed for the Short Form on a group of 210 Puerto Rican children chosen to participate in a study of behavioral problem children from New York City public schools (Costantino, Malgady, & Rogler, 1988). Alpha coefficients for the Short Form yielded a range of .30 to .92 (with a median value of .74). Internal consistency could not be calculated for the Personality Functions due to the few cards pulling for each function.

In a more recent study, the TEMAS Long Form was administered to 140 public school students, 140 private school students, and 50 clinical subjects from San Juan, Puerto Rico (Costantino, Malgady, Casullo, & Castillo, 1989). Alpha reliability coefficients ranged from .13 to .96 (with a mean of .72) for the public school group, .18 to .95 (with a mean of .62) for the private school group, and .27 to .96 (with a mean of .74) for the clinical group. Internal consistency was generally higher for the more objective indices, moderate to high for the Affective Functions, and somewhat lower for the Personality Functions (again, perhaps due to the few pictures pulling for each function).

Two studies examined test-retest reliability (Costantino, Malgady, & Rogler, 1988; Costantino et al., 1987). In the first (Costantino, Malgady, & Rogler, 1988), 51 subjects randomly selected from the group of 210 Puerto Ricans in the behavioral problem study were tested twice with the TEMAS Short Form with an 18-week interval. Only 8 of the 34 functions measured by the TEMAS resulted in significant correlation coefficients. Correlations were generally in the low to moderate range (ranging from −.01 to .53).

In the second study (Costantino et al., 1987), two random subsamples of 70 public school and 70 private school students from San Juan, Puerto Rico, were administered the TEMAS Long Form twice at a 2-month interval. Correlation coefficients were computed for the nine Personality Functions. Results, again, were generally disappointing: coefficients ranged from .09 to .59. However, these studies were confounded by numerous variables. For example, different raters were used at pre- and posttesting, large samples were not used, and variables, such as age, sex, and SES, were poorly controlled. In addition, the authors posed the problem, inherent with all projective instruments (see Obrzut & Cummings, 1983), of the instability of constructs when measuring young children to explain the poor results.

Interrater reliability of the TEMAS was assessed by two separate studies (Costantino, Malgady, & Rogler, 1988; Costantino, Malgady, Casullo, & Castillo, 1989). In the first (Costantino, Malgady, & Rogler, 1988), 27 Hispanic and 26 black children were randomly selected from a group of 73 Hispanics and 42 blacks participating in a previous study. Two raters independently scored each of these protocols, and the results were then correlated. Results indicated correlations ranging from .31 to 1.00. In the second study (Costantino, Malgady, Casullo, & Castillo, 1989), two raters independently scored 20 Argentinian protocols as part of a study validating the TEMAS with various Hispanic subcultures. Results were generally higher than the previous study, with correlations ranging from .75 to .95 (with a mean of .81). The authors point out that the higher interrater reliabilities for the second study may have reflected refinements to the scoring system in the interim between the first study (conducted in 1983) and the second (conducted in 1987).

## Critique

The *Standards for Educational and Psychological Testing* (American Educational Research Association, American Psychological Association, & National Council on Measurement in Education, 1985) is a seldom-used but critical reference for how well a test meets technical standards of construction and application. Although the TEMAS would seem to be one of the few apperception tests that approximates these standards, there are a couple of standards with which the test does not yet comply.

One primary standard concerning criterion-related validity studies states that (a) the amount of time that elapses between administering the test and collecting criterion data should be reported, and that (b) validation reports should be dated clearly and specify the time interval in which data were collected. Although this information is presented in the study establishing the TEMAS's predictive validity (Malgady et al., 1984), unfortunately it does not appear in the manual.

The *Standards* also warn that when translating a test into another language, the reliability and validity of that version need to be established. As the TEMAS was standardized utilizing bilingual examiners who tested Hispanic subjects in their predominant language, no assumption can be made as to the equality of these two forms of administration. Separate reliability and validity studies should have been conducted for the Hispanic sample because some of these subjects were administered the test in Spanish and some were administered in English. There is no evidence demonstrating the comparability of both forms of administration.

However, the TEMAS represents a serious attempt to address the lack of psychometric rigor so characteristic of other apperceptive techniques. Indeed, the numerous studies undertaken by the test's authors to validate their instrument are quite impressive. At the time of this writing, further studies were in progress, especially those aimed at cross-cultural validation (G. Costantino, personal communication, July 1989). Future normative studies should be composed of larger, stratified samples to ensure accurate representation of target populations. In addition, it is recommended that further test-retest reliability studies be conducted, as this form of reliability has not yet been adequately established for the TEMAS (Costantino, Malgady, & Rogler, 1988; Costantino et al., 1987). Although the generally disappointing results may reflect true developmental changes in children, other confounding variables must first be ruled out in order to have confidence in what the TEMAS is measuring. Finally, a study on the relative effectiveness of the TEMAS and other apperception tests in discriminating clinical from nonclinical samples is recommended. Such a study would demonstrate the relative effectiveness of the TEMAS with regard to other available instruments.

The TEMAS stands with the Michigan Picture Test—Revised (MPT-R; Hutt, 1980), the Roberts Apperception Test for Children (RATC; McArthur & Roberts, 1982), and the Children's Apperceptive Story-Telling Test (CAST; Schneider, 1989) as one of the few thematic apperceptive techniques currently available that address the need for psychometric rigor and approximate the standards of psychological testing.

## References

This list includes text citations and suggested additional reading.

American Educational Research Association, American Psychological Association, & National Council on Measurement in Education. (1985). *Standards for educational and psychological testing*. Washington, DC: American Psychological Association.

American Psychiatric Association. (1987). *Diagnostic and statistical manual of mental disorders* (3rd ed. rev.). Washington, DC: Author.

Anderson, H., & Anderson, G. (1955). *An introduction to projective techniques*. New York: Prentice-Hall.

Bandura, A. (1977). *Social learning theory*. Englewood Cliffs, NJ: Prentice-Hall.

Baty, M.A., & Dreger, R.M. (1975). A comparison of three methods to record TAT protocols. *Journal of Clinical Psychology, 31*(2), 348.

Bellak, L. (1975). *The T.A.T., C.A.T., and S.A.T. in clinical use* (3rd ed.). New York: Grune & Stratton.

Bellak, L., & Bellak, S. (1980). *A manual for the Children's Apperception Test* (7th ed.). Larchmont, NY: C.P.S.

Bellak, L., Hurvich, M., & Gediman, H.K. (1973). *Ego functions in schizophrenics, neurotics, and normals*. New York: Wiley.

Brackbill, G.A. (1951). Some effects of color on thematic fantasy. *Journal of Consulting Psychology, 15*, 412–418.

Brenes-Jette, C. (1987). *Mother's contribution to an early intervention program for Hispanic children*. Unpublished doctoral dissertation, New York University, New York.

Butkus, M. (1984). Comparison of the predictive/descriptive accuracy and improvements to the incremental validity of a projective and two objective personality tests for children and adolescents. *Dissertation Abstracts International, 45*, 3930B. (University Microfilms No. 8502508)

Costantino, G. (1978, November). *Preliminary report on TEMAS: A new thematic apperception test to assess ego functions in ethnic minority children*. Paper presented at the Second American Conference on Fantasy and the Imaging Process, Chicago.

Costantino, G. (1980). *The use of folktales as a new therapy modality to effect change in Hispanic children and their families* (National Institute of Mental Health Grant No. 1-R01-MH33711-01). Rockville, MD: National Institute of Mental Health.

Costantino, G., Colon, G., Malgady, R., & Perez, A. (1989, August). *Assessment of attention deficit disorder using a thematic apperception technique*. Paper presented at the 97th Annual Convention of the American Psychological Association, New Orleans.

Costantino, G., & Malgady, R. (1983). Verbal fluency of Hispanic, black and white children on TAT and TEMAS, a new thematic apperception test. *Hispanic Journal of Behavioral Sciences, 5*(2), 199–206.

Costantino, G., & Malgady, R.G. (1989, August). Multicultural standardization and validation of TEMAS, a thematic apperception test. In M.F. Schneider (Chair), *Utilizing personality assessment within the school context: Assessment to intervention.* Symposium conducted at the 97th Annual Convention of the American Psychological Association, New Orleans.

Costantino, G., Malgady, R.G., Bailey, J., & Colon-Malgady, G. (1989, April). *Clinical utility of TEMAS: A projective test for children.* Paper presented at the 50th Anniversary Midwinter Meeting of the Society for Personality Assessment, New York.

Costantino, G., Malgady, R.G., Casullo, M.M., & Castillo, A. (1989, June). *Cross-cultural standardization of TEMAS in three Hispanic subcultures.* Paper presented at the XXII Congreso Interamericano de Psicologia, Buenos Aires, Argentina.

Costantino, G., Malgady, R.G., & Rogler, L.H. (1985). *Cross-cultural validation of TEMAS, a minority projective test.* Rockville, MD: National Institute of Mental Health, Center for Minority Group Mental Health Program. (ERIC Document Reproduction Service No. ED 265 174)

Costantino, G., Malgady, R., & Rogler, L. (1986). *Standardization and validation of TEMAS, a pluralistic thematic apperception test.* New York: Fordham University, Hispanic Research Center.

Costantino, G., Malgady, R., & Rogler, L.H. (1988). *TEMAS (Tell-Me-A-Story) manual.* Los Angeles: Western Psychological Services.

Costantino, G., Malgady, R., Rogler, L.H., Casullo, M.M., & Castillo, A. (1988, August). *Cross-cultural validation of TEMAS (minority and nonminority versions).* Paper presented at the 96th Annual Convention of the American Psychological Association, Atlanta.

Costantino, G., Malgady, R.G., Rogler, L.H., & Tsui, E.C. (1987). *Cross-cultural validation of TEMAS (minority version), a pluralistic projective test.* Rockville, MD: National Institute of Mental Health, Center for Minority Group Mental Health Program. (ERIC Document Reproduction Service No. ED 294 879)

Costantino, G., Malgady, R.G., Rogler, L.H., & Tsui, E.C. (1988). Discriminant analysis of clinical outpatients and public school children by TEMAS: A thematic apperception test for Hispanics and blacks. *Journal of Personality Assessment, 52*(4), 670–678.

Costantino, G., Malgady, R., & Vazquez, C. (1981). A comparison of the Murray-TAT and a new thematic apperception test for urban Hispanic children. *Hispanic Journal of Behavioral Sciences, 3*(3), 291–300.

Epstein, S. (1966). Some considerations on the nature of ambiguity and the use of stimulus dimensions in projective techniques. *Journal of Consulting Psychology, 30,* 183–192.

Exner, J.E. (1986). *The Rorschach: A comprehensive system: Vol. 1. Basic foundations* (2nd ed.). New York: Wiley.

Hallahan, D.P., & Reeve, R.E. (1980). Selective attention and distractibility. In B.K. Keogh (Ed.), *Advances in special education* (Vol. 1). Greenwich, CT: JAI Press.

Hutt, M.L. (1980). *The Michigan Picture Test–Revised.* New York: Grune & Stratton.

Killian, G.A. (1984). House-Tree-Person Technique. In D.J. Keyser & R.C. Sweetland (Eds.), *Test critiques* (Vol. I, pp. 338–353). Austin, TX: PRO-ED.

Kline, P. (1986). *A handbook of test construction: Introduction to psychometric design.* New York: Methuen.

Kohlberg, L. (1976). Moral stages and moralization. In T. Lickona (Ed.), *Moral development and behavior: Theory, research and social issues* (pp. 31–53). New York: Holt, Rinehart & Winston.

Loevinger, J., & Wessler, R. (1970). *Measuring ego development 1. Construction and use of a sentence completion test.* San Francisco: Jossey-Bass.

Lubin, N.M., & Wilson, M.O. (1956). Picture test identification as a function of "reality" (color) and similarity of picture to subject. *Journal of General Psychology, 54,* 31–38.

Malgady, R., Rogler, L., & Costantino, G. (1987). Ethnocultural and linguistic bias in mental health evaluation of Hispanics. *American Psychologist, 42,* 228–234.

Malgady, R.G., Costantino, G., & Rogler, L.H. (1984). Development of a thematic apperception test for urban Hispanic children. *Journal of Consulting and Clinical Psychology, 52*(6), 986–996.

McArthur, D.S., & Roberts, G.E. (1982). *Roberts Apperception Test for Children manual.* Los Angeles: Western Psychological Services.

Mercer, J.R. (1978–79). Test "validity," "bias," and "fairness": An analysis from the perspective of the sociology of knowledge. *Interchange, 9*(1), 1–16.

Murray, H.A. (1943/1971). *Thematic Apperception Test manual.* Cambridge: Harvard University Press.

Obrzut, J.E., & Cummings, J.A. (1983). The projective approach to personality assessment: An analysis of thematic picture techniques. *School Psychology Review, 12*(4), 414–420.

Piaget, J., & Inhelder, B. (1969). *The psychology of the child.* New York: Basic Books.

Piaget, J., & Inhelder, B. (1971). *Mental imagery in the child.* New York: Basic Books.

Schneider, M.F. (1989). *CAST: Children's Apperceptive Story-Telling Test manual.* Austin, TX: PRO-ED.

Spielberger, C.D., Edwards, C.D., Lushene, R.E., Montuori, J., & Platzek, D. (1973). *Preliminary test manual for the State-Trait Anxiety Inventory for Children.* Palo Alto, CA: Consulting Psychologists Press.

Sullivan, H.S. (1953). *The interpersonal theory of psychiatry.* New York: Norton.

Thompson, C.E., & Bachrach, J. (1951). The use of color in the Thematic Apperception Test. *Journal of Projective Techniques, 15,* 173–184.

Villamil, B. (1973). *Desarrollo del Inventorio de Ansiedad Estado Y Rasgo para ninos* [Development of the State-Trait Anxiety Inventory for Children]. Unpublished master's thesis, University of Puerto Rico.

Wildman, R.W., & Wildman, R.W., II. (1975). An investigation into the comparative validity of several diagnostic tests and test batteries. *Journal of Clinical Psychology, 31,* 455–458.

**Jerry Johns, Ph.D.**
*Professor of Reading, Northern Illinois University, DeKalb, Illinois.*
**Peggy VanLeirsburg, Ed.D.**
*Teacher, Elgin Public Schools, Elgin, Illinois.*

# TEST BEHAVIOR CHECKLIST

*Glen P. Aylward and Robert W. MacGruder. Brandon, Vermont: Clinical Psychology Publishing Company, Inc.*

## Introduction

The Test Behavior Checklist (TBC) was developed to provide a descriptive, easily scored, systematic means of describing test behaviors. Test examiners and psychologists can record observed test behaviors of children and adolescents on a four-page booklet of descriptive rating scales. The TBC is organized into three main sections (Aylward & MacGruder, 1986a), and items are rated on a 5-point, Likert-type scale.

The first section, General Information, permits the rater to record demographic data and physical appearance, followed by checklists of descriptive behaviors appropriate to motor skill development, articulation/language, activity level, and test-taking anxiety. The second section, Test-Taking Approach and Behavioral Characteristics, consists of the following behavioral indices: Attention Span, Ability to Follow Directions, Goal Directedness and Frustration Tolerance, Response Latencies, Response Variability, Capacity to Change Mental Set, Approach to Problem Solving, Motivation and Need for Encouragement, and Fear of Failure. The final item in this section permits the examiner to estimate the validity and reliability of the test results. The third section, Personality and Social Characteristics, provides for recorded observations of the student's social-emotional style, cooperativeness, and social skills. Space for additional comments is included in each of the three sections.

The 5-point rating scale is simple to apply, taking only 5 to 10 minutes per student. For example, under Test-Taking Approach and Behavioral Characteristics is "Ability to Follow Directions." The rating options range from "grasped directions very quickly; no elaboration of standardized instructions needed" to "constantly needed elaboration and repetition of directions; became confused often." Another example is "Social-Emotional Style," an index within the Personality and Social Characteristics section. The five options here range from "emotionally withdrawn; resisted examiner's efforts to establish working rapport" to "socially intrusive; solicitous of attention from outset of testing session; may be manipulative."

## Practical Applications/Uses

The Test Behavior Checklist is designed for use in any standardized test situation, particularly in "intellectual evaluations, achievement testing, or assessment of possible learning disabilities" for children in the 4-year through adolescent age range (Aylward & MacGruder, 1986b, p. 3). It provides written evidence of behaviors on one or several tests, facilitating consistency in writing behavioral observations that may accompany some test reports, such as psychologicals. The examiner records behaviors occurring over the course of an examination immediately following the testing session. Completion of the TBC usually takes less than 10 minutes. There are no scores to be added and no interpretation is necessary. This checklist is a method of recalling the particular behaviors of a testing situation.

The TBC authors state that "the behavioral observations section is the portion of the psychological report that is typically underemphasized, least standardized, and utilized least effectively" (Aylward & MacGruder, 1986b, p. 1). An attractive feature of the TBC is that the examiner can "subsequently dictate directly from the TBC forms, thereby saving considerable time and increasing efficiency" (Aylward & MacGruder, 1986b, p. 3). The dictation would include both behavioral descriptions from the TBC, as well as additional examiner comments, providing an overall profile of relevant behaviors of the child.

The manual is clearly written and includes three examples of completed TBC results plus the resulting paragraphs developed for inclusion in the sample child's psychological report. These examples illustrate the ease of scoring and reporting the behavioral information gained by the use of this checklist.

## Technical Aspects

The Test Behavior Checklist is a simple measurement tool. No norm groups are reported for standardization purposes. Validity is not indicated; reliability coefficients are not reported. Although the authors apparently did not set out to develop a sophisticated psychometric tool, such lack of an interrater reliability coefficient or analysis of content validity is inappropriate (Phelps, 1989).

As measurement tools, checklists are subject to error variance in that data are collected by observational techniques. Interrater reliability can evaluate such error variance. The authors report data on a pilot sample of 30 children ages 3½ through 9 years old. Standardized testing instruments included the Stanford-Binet Intelligence Scale, the Wechsler Intelligence Scale for Children–Revised, the Bender Visual Motor Gestalt Test, and the Wide Range Achievement Test–Revised. Agreement existed only if both raters chose the same response descriptor on the TBC. Interrater agreement for a specific test session ranged from 88% to 96% during this field testing. A coefficient of reliability, however, was not calculated.

Content validity depends on the choice of the behavioral descriptors chosen in the TBC. The manual offers no discussion of how the descriptors were chosen or, further, of how the descriptors represent the "language, depth, and scope of the behavioral indices" (Phelps, 1989, p. 822) as components of the checklist.

## Critique

The Test Behavior Checklist, a descriptive instrument, is an organized and simplified means of recording student's test behaviors. It may be useful in individual psychological examination situations to consistently view like behaviors across students and to dictate observations directly from the TBC forms. The ease of recording behaviors on a checklist with a simple format that is quickly completed is an attractive feature. The simplicity of the format may stimulate its use in programs or courses designed to train professionals in psychological testing. Such uses may help guide observations in the various areas contained in the checklist.

The lack of data regarding the basis on which the TBC was developed, including its validity and reliability, severely limits the confidence users can place in it. Coefficients regarding interrater reliability are necessary. Validity, both content and concurrent, should be examined and reported. Phelps (1989) suggests content and concurrent validity coefficients be measured against other available checklists such as Sattler's (1982) 28-item Behavior and Attitude Checklist. Without such sound statistical evidence, the Test Behavior Checklist cannot be recommended for sophisticated psychometric purposes.

## References

Aylward, G.P., & MacGruder, R.W. (1986a). *Test Behavior Checklist*. Brandon, VT: Clinical Psychology Publishing.

Aylward, G.P., & MacGruder, R.W. (1986b). *Test Behavior Checklist manual*. Brandon, VT: Clinical Psychology Publishing.

Phelps, L. (1989). Test Behavior Checklist. In J.C. Conoley & J.J. Kramer (Eds.), *The tenth mental measurements yearbook* (pp. 821–822). Lincoln, NE: Buros Institute of Mental Measurements.

Sattler, J.M. (1982). Behavior and Attitude Checklist. In J.M. Sattler (Ed.), *Assessment of children's intelligence and special abilities* (2nd ed., p. 497). Boston: Allyn & Bacon.

**Patrick Groff, Ed.D.**
*Professor of Education, San Diego State University, San Diego, California.*

# TEST OF AUDITORY DISCRIMINATION

*Victoria Risko. San Rafael, California: Academic Therapy Publications.*

## Introduction

The Test of Auditory Discrimination (TAD; Risko, 1975a) is designed as a means of determining how well someone learning to read can (a) decide whether pairs or trios of monosyllabic words spoken to him or her begin or end with the same consonant speech sound or whether they have the same middle vowel sound, and (b) listen to words whose parts are pronounced in isolation (e.g., /f/-/ăt/) and infer and produce their correct pronunciations. The TAD is a measure of learners' previously developed abilities to identify (segment) speech sounds (phonemes) in spoken words and to judge whether a target phoneme in one word is the same as one in another word, as well as to "blend" word parts spoken in isolation into pronounceable words.

The TAD was developed by Victoria Risko, Ed.D., in 1975. At that time she was a professor of education at State University College, Fredonia, New York. No other information as to her qualifications as a test constructor, or over what period of time the TAD was developed, was available to this reviewer. Risko gives no citation to any publication in her name in the reference section of her book, *The Testing-Teaching Module of Auditory Discrimination* (Risko, 1975b), the first part of which acts as a manual for administrators of the TAD. According to the *Educational Index*, she has written no articles on subjects relating to the TAD since 1975. As there were no age or grade-level norms developed for the TAD, no history of the test in terms of normative populations, the criteria used for selecting such populations, and so forth are given by its author (Risko, 1975b).

There also is no indication from the TAD's author that the published version of the test was developed through a series of revisions of prior-developed forms. Neither does she provide any indication that special editions of the TAD have been developed for diverse groups such as foreign-language speakers, those who use a nonstandard dialect, or for people who are hearing impaired.

The TAD is presented in an eight-page, 8½" × 11" booklet. On the first page of the test booklet, space is provided to record information about the subject taking the test. The remaining seven pages contain the test itself. The TAD's format is uncluttered, which makes the test easy to read. It is user friendly in this respect.

The TAD is divided into six sections. In each successive section subjects are directed to judge if pairs or trios of closed-syllable monosyllabic words (e.g., *bad*) spoken to them (a) begin with the same single consonant phoneme, (b) begin with the same cluster of consonant phonemes, (c) end with the same single consonant phoneme, (d) end with the same cluster of consonant phonemes, or (c) have the same middle vowel sound. Section VI directs subjects to infer the correct pronunciation of monosyllabic and multisyllabic words after having heard their parts pronounced in isolation (e.g., /d/-/ish/, /pub/-/li/-/ca/-tion/).

The content of the TAD consists of 125 items divided among the six sections. Fifty-five additional items are designated as "optional." Each of Sections I through IV consists of two subsections, A and B, each of which contains 10 items. Section V has four subsections, A through C of which present 5 items each. Subsection D presents 10 items. In Sections I through IV, subjects identify consonant phonemes. In Section V they identify vowels. Section VI presents 20 items that require subjects to listen to the parts of a word pronounced in isolation and then infer and produce its correct pronunciation.

In addition, Sections I through V offers "optional" items. In these items subjects are directed to listen to pairs of words and then to say, in isolation, their beginning or ending consonant phoneme or their middle vowel. There are 10 optional items for Sections I–IV, and 15 for Section V.

The TAD is designed to be administered on a one-to-one basis. The examiner holds the TAD booklet as he or she reads directions for the subjects to follow in answering the requirements of the test. For example, the directions for subsection A of Section I are, "I shall say two words. Tell me if they begin with the same sound or with a different sound. Listen carefully to the beginning sounds" (Risko, 1975a, p. 2). Some readiness for performing upcoming items also is addressed: "First, let's try a few examples. (Read each pair [of words] one time. Pause about three seconds between the words)" (Risko, 1975a, p. 2).

One can infer that the author of the TAD intended it to be used with primary-grade pupils. The research that she conducted to determine the relationship between scores on the TAD and those from a standardized reading test was conducted with children in Grades 1–3 (Risko, 1975b). There seems to be no legitimate reason why the TAD could not be administered, however, to determine the abilities of subjects of any age who cannot read or are functionally illiterate.

Whether subjects could understand the requirements posed by the TAD would depend to a great extent on how well they were able to comprehend the directions given for the test. Whether the TAD is appropriate for a given subject depends on whether he or she has gained a conscious awareness of clauses, words, and syllables. All this knowledge develops earlier and more easily than does the conscious awareness of phonemes. On the other hand, it appears that the TAD presents a simpler challenge than counting the number of phonemes in a spoken word–which about 30% of children at the end of Grade 1 cannot do successfully (Adams, 1990).

Although the instructions for taking the TAD were clear to this reviewer, there may be primary-grade children who will not understand the concepts and vocabulary involved in this direction-giving. For example, young children may not know what the administrator means when he or she says, "Tell me if they begin with the same sound," or "Listen carefully to the beginning sounds," or "Tell me the beginning (ending, middle) sound," or "Listen to the sounds and tell me the word." This problem is complicated by directions given in the TAD that would even be confusing to skilled readers. For example, subjects are directed to believe that *clam/crop* and *bland/bred/brig* "do not begin with the same sounds" (Risko, 1975a, p. 3). It is known that if directions are cleverly phrased, young children likely will have a much greater chance of understanding them. The author of the TAD has not taken this advice seriously enough.

**Practical Applications/Uses**

As noted, the TAD was constructed to provide information about subjects' previously developed conscious awareness of phonemes and about their ability to infer the correct pronunciations of words after hearing approximate pronunciations of them. The TAD was not designed to present age- or grade-level norms of these two accomplishments, however. The goal of the TAD, instead, is to provide specific examples of subjects' weaknesses in the above capabilities. Teachers who administer the TAD and discover such deficiencies in their pupils are advised by the author to remediate these failings. For this purpose she provides a 160-page book, *The Testing-Teaching Module of Auditory Discrimination* (Risko, 1975b), which as noted also acts as the examiner's manual for the TAD. This book presents activities the teacher can conduct with pupils that will provide practice to overcome the phoneme segmentation or phoneme blending inadequacies that they have demonstrated on the TAD.

As the TAD is a relatively uncomplicated test, it should be easy for almost anyone to administer (at least to subjects who can understand its directions). The scoring procedure is simple as well. The examiner indicates in a space provided alongside each item whether a subject has or has not performed the given task satisfactorily. It is not difficult to determine what is a correct answer, which probably accounts for the fact the TAD does not include a correct-answer key.

The uncomplicated nature of the TAD suggests that "nonprofessional" people (i.e., parents, teachers' aides, and literacy organization volunteers) could successfully administer the test. There thus would be many settings outside of the school in which an administration would be appropriate and feasible. In fact, as the TAD is designed as an individual rather than a group test, its application might be more practical in out-of-classroom settings than in school surroundings. Today's busy teacher might not be able to find the time to test his or her pupils individually with the TAD. If one calculated the time needed to do this, based on the author's directions to "pause about three seconds" between the words read aloud, the administration of the test would take at least 20 minutes.

Sections I through V of the TAD could be administered as a group test, however, and scored by the subjects themselves. All that would be required for this group testing would be for subjects to listen to the words being read aloud and then to indicate on numbered scoring sheets whether they believed the target phonemes they heard were the same or different.

The scores on the TAD also might be used for insights into the needs of students who have had difficulty in learning to spell. Research has revealed the close relationship of phoneme awareness and spelling development (Adams, 1990). Once it was discovered which of the TAD items proved difficult for children who spell poorly, this information could be converted into direct, systematic, and intensive practice in the development of phonics information.

Risko does not present any data to verify whether the order in which TAD items are assembled is a valid one. She does not reveal, for example, whether she based the order of item presentation on the relative ease with which various groups of subjects could respond correctly to them. Because people learning to read tend to make fewer mistakes in the beginnings than at the ends or middles of words, it seems logically defensible to sequence phoneme recognition tasks in this order, as the TAD does.

Risko relates that words used in various items were "grouped according to their phonetic categories of articulation . . . plosives, fricatives, affricatives, nasals, and glides" (1975b, p. 11). She has followed through carefully in this regard in Sections I through V, which improves the chance that responding to one test item is not more inherently difficult, from a linguistic standpoint, than is responding to any other item.

**Technical Aspects**

The validity of the TAD as a useful test of reading readiness is suggested by the findings of a study its author conducted to determine the coefficients of correlation (*r*'s) between TAD scores and those obtained on a standardized reading test (Metropolitan Achievement Test) by 81 pupils in Grades 1–3. These *r*'s for pupils in Grades 1, 2, and 3 were .91, .97, and .88, respectively. In addition, Risko found that first-graders' scores on Section III, subsection A, and on Section VI of the TAD "predicted [their] reading achievement, accounting for 61 percent of the variance at the .01 level" (Risko, 1975b, p. 15). For Grade 2 subjects, Section IV, subsection B scores accounted for 63%. For Grade 3 subjects, Section IV, subsection A and the subjects' abilities to identify and say in isolation targeted clusters of consonant phonemes (an "optional" task of Section IV) accounted for 48%.

**Critique**

The TAD fulfills an essential need in reading instruction. The experimental research indicates consistently that reading programs "explicitly designed to develop sounding and blending skills produce better word readers than do those that do not" (Adams, 1990, p. 293). It is vital in reading instruction, therefore, that phonemes "be dug out of their normal subattentional status" (Adams, 1990, p. 294). The leading predictor of beginning reading achievement is the ability to discriminate between phonemes. The ability to "blend" phonemes likewise is important. Therefore, to the extent that children who do not learn to identify individual phonemes are not consciously aware of them, they will experience difficulty in learning letter-phoneme correspondences (i.e., phonics information). And without knowledge of phonics information, the research findings emphasize, students will be handicapped in learning to recognize written words in an automatic fashion. Risko's discovery that TAD scores relate closely to reading success thus is not at all surprising.

Nonetheless, despite the importance of a working knowledge of phonemes in order to learn how to speak a language, and notwithstanding the fact that young children have overlearned the phonemes of English, they "are not naturally set up to be consciously aware of them" (Adams, 1990, p. 66). Hence the need for means by which to discover the extent of children's awareness of phonemes and to employ systematic, direct, and intensive instruction to develop this awareness if it is lacking. The TAD thus can serve a critical function in assisting the course of reading development for anyone in want of that skill by supplying notice of what phonics information should be taught.

This is not to say that the TAD is free from shortcomings or errors. Foremost among its several flaws is its apparent assumption that subjects who are given the test will understand the directions provided for its administration. The TAD would be strengthened, therefore, if its manual warned about this potential problem and gave instructions as to how to make sure, before the test is applied, that all subjects fully understand what is demanded of them.

In this respect, the TAD generally presents its subjects with trial items before the main body of the test is begun. Unfortunately, this is not always the case. In addition, subjects at times are told to listen to the ending or beginning sound of a word, when in fact they are required to listen to clusters of consonant sounds. In one part of the TAD, subjects hear the administrator of the test say, "*Pen* and *yen* have the *e* sound." In the very next section, they hear, "These words [*leach-speak*] have the *e* sound" (Risko, 1975a, pp. 7–8).

It is also readily noticeable that the "optional" sections of the TAD should have been included as a regular part of the test. The author unintentionally concedes that this is so when she reports that an optional section of the test proved to be more predictive of children's general reading ability than did some regular sections (Risko, 1975b). It is highly recommended, therefore, that users of the TAD administer the optional sections. This action would run the item count of the TAD from 125 to 180 items, therefore significantly lengthening the time taken to administer it.

Other defects in the TAD also are observable. For example, in its Section VI, the administrator is directed to mispronounce 5 of the 20 words presented in that part. There is no justifiable reason in this section for mispronouncing the separate parts of *immediate*, for instance, as /ĭm/-/mē/-/dĭ/-ăt/. This mispronunciation will not help children learn to blend parts of words into pronounceable wholes as much as would /ĭm/-/ēd/-/ĭ/-/ăt/.

The criterion for successful performance for each item in the TAD is 100%. The TAD thus implies that teachers using the scores on the test as a basis for remedial instruction purposes also should demand 100% performance by pupils in this teaching before criterion performance is attained. This seems an extraordinarily high standard, which users of the TAD may want to modify.

Although there are certain obvious mistakes in the TAD, it is important to stress that these faults are not structural in nature. That is, TAD users can remove or remediate them without negatively affecting the worthwhile functions of the test. In fact, this reviewer recommends that before anyone applies the TAD he or she revise the test, taking into account the shortcomings cited in this review. This revision of the TAD will improve its validity as a test of phonics knowledge.

## References

This list includes text citations and suggested additional reading.

Adams, M.J. (1990). *Beginning to read: Thinking about learning about print.* Cambridge, MA: MIT Press.

Coleman, E.B. (1970). Collecting a data base for a reading technology. *Journal of Educational Psychology Monographs, 61,* 1–23.

Feitelson, D. (1988). *Facts and fads in beginning reading.* Norwood, NJ: Ablex.

Groff, P., & Seymour, D.Z. (1987). *Word recognition: The why and the how.* Springfield, IL: C.C. Thomas.

Henderson, L. (1982). *Orthography and word recognition in reading.* New York: Academic Press.

Pearson, P.D. (Ed.). (1984). *Handbook of reading research.* New York: Longman.

Perfetti, C.A. (1985). *Reading ability.* New York: Oxford University Press.

Resnick, L.B., & Weaver, P.A. (Eds.). (1979). *Theory and practice of early reading.* Hillsdale, NJ: Lawrence Erlbaum.

Risko, V. (1975a). *Test of Auditory Discrimination.* San Rafael, CA: Academic Therapy Publications.

Risko, V. (1975b). *The testing-teaching module of auditory discrimination.* San Rafael, CA: Academic Therapy Publications.

**Douglas L. Weeks, Ph.D.**
*Assistant Professor of Exercise Science, Motor Behavior Laboratory, Ball State University, Muncie, Indiana.*

# TEST OF GROSS MOTOR DEVELOPMENT

*Dale A. Ulrich. Austin, Texas: PRO-ED, Inc.*

## Introduction

The Test of Gross Motor Development (TGMD) is an individually administered, standardized assessment instrument designed to evaluate gross motor skill performance in children between 3 and 10 years of age. The test assesses level of mastery in 12 different fundamental gross motor skills commonly included as content in preschool and elementary motor skill instructional programs. The battery of 12 skill items is divided into two subtests that assess different aspects of gross motor functioning: a locomotor skills subtest and an object control skills subtest. The Locomotor Skills subtest, designed to provide a composite score indicating ability to dynamically change body position, consists of seven specific items (run, gallop, hop, skip, horizontal jump, leap, and slide tests). The Object Control Skills subtest, designed to provide a composite score indicating propulsion and reception skill ability, consists of five specific items (two-handed striking, a stationary [ball] bounce, [ball] catch, [ball] kick, and overhand throw tests). Each subtest yields raw scores from which standard score norms and percentile-rank equivalents have been developed at each age in years. Subtest standard scores can be summed and converted to a final standard score based on the examinee's age, which is said to be representative of overall gross-motor skill functioning and termed the Gross Motor Development Quotient (GMDQ).

Dale A. Ulrich, Ph.D., an adapted physical education specialist, released the current version of the TGMD in 1985. Motivation for developing the test was based in part on Ulrich's observation that existing tests of gross motor functioning, such as the gross motor development subtest of the Bruininks-Oseretsky Test of Motor Proficiency (Bruininks, 1978), tended to focus on the outcome or product of motor performance rather than assessing the processes or movement patterns employed in performing a skill. A need for assessment of movement process, which could provide a more in-depth analysis of performance problems, had also been noted by Thomas (1984). The TGMD was designed to fill this void by focusing assessment on the form or technique employed in fundamental skill performance. The test requires examiners to make subjective judgments as to whether specific performance criteria for each skill item are present in a child's performance. Performance criteria for each of the 12 skills were developed by observing commonalities in the form of individuals judged as having mature movement patterns. The test can, therefore, be used to identify deficiencies in skill mastery based on an observed absence of specific performance criteria in an individual's performance. Thus, the intent of the TGMD was "qualitative" assessment of movement patterns for a variety of skills as opposed to "quantitative" assessment of movement outcome.

Ulrich was further motivated to develop a test that would provide nationally representative norms while maintaining the ability to be used for individual instructional decisions. Thus, an individual's test scores can be used in a norm-referenced capacity by comparing test scores to standards established for age-group peers or used in a criterion-referenced capacity to assess individual progress in attaining skill mastery.

The initial phase of test development involved a literature review and consultation with three motor development content experts in order to establish three to four performance criteria readily observable in a mature movement pattern for 50 different fundamental motor skills. Data for each of the 50 skills was collected on 279 children ranging in age from 3 to 12 years (the test manual does not provide information about how the 279 were selected). Indices of discrimination from a subsequent item analysis were used to make decisions to narrow the 50 skills to the 12 currently comprising the test. A second item analysis was performed on the 12 skills utilizing data collected from a sample of 909 children ranging in age from 3 to 10 years from eight states. The resulting item analysis yielded biserial discrimination coefficients indicating that scores for each of the 12 items were effective in discriminating between high and low achievers within the sample. Biserial coefficients obtained at each age for skills within the locomotor subtest ranged from .12 to .76, while coefficients for skills within the object control subtest ranged from .32 to .84.

Once the discrimination ability was viewed as adequately established, data from the same sample were utilized to develop age-representative norms. A sampling plan had been employed to select the 909 children to ensure that characteristics of the normative sample would approximate those of the U.S. population based on the 1980 census on such demographic variables as gender, race, community size and socioeconomic status, and geographic region. A cluster sampling procedure was used to select preschools and elementary schools within designated geographic regions and community types from which subjects would be drawn. With schools selected, a stratified random sampling technique was employed to construct the normative sample using gender and race as stratification variables. Sample size at each age ranged from 103 to 153. Separate norms for males and females were not constructed because inferential tests of the normative sample data indicated no significant differences in male and female subtest scores at the .01 level of significance. Although the test manual was not clear as to percentage of individuals with handicapping conditions included in the normative sample, it was reported that individuals with severe handicaps were excluded from the normative sample.

Following the development of norms, test materials were released in 1985. Test materials include a 38-page test manual and a four-page student record book for each individual tested. The testing manual consists of four chapters encompassing an overview of the TGMD, test administration and scoring procedures, results interpretation, and test development information. The test administration and scoring chapter provides a written description of the equipment utilized, testing area layout, directions, and performance criteria for each of the 12 skills tested. In addition, the manual includes illustrations representing the preparatory, propulsive, and follow-through phases of mature performance for the skills. Equipment necessary to administer the TGMD, such as playground balls, sponge balls, tennis balls, and plastic bats, is commonly available in elementary schools.

The individual student report form is designed to allow recording of scores for two separate administrations of the test, with additional space included for examiner's comments and data pertaining to the student and the examiner. The report form lists the same performance criteria for each of the 12 skills as is listed in the test manual. Each performance criterion is scored separately, with scores based on a dichotomous measurement scale. A score of 1 is entered on the student report form if the criterion is exhibited on at least two of the three sequential performances of a skill. A score of 0 is entered if a given criterion is exhibited only once across three trials or not at all. It should be noted that lack of achieving any particular criteria at a particular age does not necessarily represent a skill performance deficiency because younger individuals are not expected to exhibit fully mature movement patterns indicated by mastery of each performance criterion within a skill. For each subtest, performance criteria raw scores are summed across items, with the resulting subtest raw scores converted to a standard score listed in the test manual for each age. Standard score norms, with a mean of 10 and a standard deviation of 3, were derived for each subtest from a cumulative frequency distribution of raw scores at each age in the normative sample. Use of this scale renders the TGMD scores not immediately comparable to other standardized test scores of gross motor performance; however, the test manual does provide tables transforming subtest standard scores to *z*, *T*, and stanine scores to expedite the process across test comparisons. The subtest standard scores can be summed, with the resulting score transformed to the GMDQ, which is based on a standard score scale with a mean of 100 and a standard deviation of 15. Thus, the GMDQ is intentionally similar in scale to the Wechsler Intelligence Scale for Children–Revised.

When interpreting subtest standard scores and the GMDQ, it must be kept in mind that these are composite scores of the total number of performance criteria exhibited across skills. It is, therefore, not possible to draw conclusions about any single gross motor skill from these composite scores. Likewise, a direct comparison of raw scores between the 12 specific skills cannot be made as scales have not been equated for differences in skill difficulty or standardized for individual skills. Within any single skill test, though, comparison of raw scores across multiple administrations can be useful in interpreting progress a child has made in mastering the performance criteria.

Accuracy in scoring performance criteria is integrally related to the examiner's ability to reliably judge presence or absence of exhibited performance criteria in a child's movement pattern. For this reason, the test manual encourages the examiner to create a "mental picture" of mature performance by reading the performance criteria, studying the illustrations in the testing manual, and practicing administering the test. Although this may be sufficient for some examiners, future revisions of the TGMD might benefit from employing more concrete means to enhance formation of this cognitive representation of mature performance by using, perhaps, videotaped examples of mature/immature movement patterns. Ten of the 12 skill tests involve passive viewing of student performance by the examiner; however, the two-handed striking test and the catching test require the examiner to toss a ball to the subject just prior to observing subject performance. Thus, for these two tests, subject performance will be dependent to some degree on examiner consistency in ball tossing.

**Practical Applications/Uses**

This test is designed to be of utility to a wide variety of professionals familiar with children's motor skill functioning who are concerned with assessing mastery of the processes or movement patterns involved in psychomotor performance. Preschool and elementary educators may find the TGMD useful for measuring current state of functioning to assist in instructional programming at both the individual level and class level. An examinee's level of mastery for each of the 12 motor skills assessed will be dependent to a large degree on the amount and type of previous instruction and practice the individual has experienced. Thus, the TGMD is potentially useful to educators as a criterion-referenced tool to identify skills in need of enhanced instruction. Use of the test in a norm-referenced capacity to assess a child's relative standing among age-group peers, for such concerns as adapted physical education placement decisions, is possible at the subtest level. However, relative standing on any single skill is not determinable due to unavailability of norms on a skill-by-skill basis.

Clinicians such as physical therapists may find the test useful as one tool in a battery of instruments to assess progress in performance during a period of rehabilitation. The test may also be used in a clinical setting for making norm-referenced decisions as long as measurement fidelity needs are no greater than at the entire subtest level.

Researchers concerned with measuring children's gross motor skill performance may also find the test of utility. In fact, the ability to record performance criteria scores for two occasions on a single student report form will expedite data recording in a pretest-posttest research paradigm. Because TGMD test scores have been shown to improve following specific instruction involving the tested skills (Ulrich & Ulrich, 1984), researchers will find the test a useful indicator of the efficacy of specific gross motor skill instructional methods.

The utility of the test is further enhanced by the minimal amount of training time required to be able to administer the test. Training consists of familiarizing oneself with the performance criteria and illustrations provided for each skill and briefly studying the student report form to become comfortable with the scoring procedures. Recommended procedures for test administration are straightforward, involving a demonstration by the examiner of the skill to be assessed, followed by the subject performing three trials of each skill as the examiner observes and records scores. The testing manual reports an average testing time of 15 minutes per subject, which may be prohibitive if a large number of students must be tested in a classroom setting.

**Technical Aspects**

An important psychometric consideration with respect to the validity of this test is content validity. Two primary content validity concerns must be fulfilled to judge the test as content valid. First, the 12 skills assessed must represent an adequate sampling of the gross motor skills children ages 3 to 10 possess in their motor skill repertoire. With respect to this concern, care was taken in the test development phase to gain a consensus from content experts that the skills assessed were representative of the domain of behaviors children within this age range would experience in an instructional setting. This condition, therefore, seems sufficiently fulfilled. A second content validity concern is whether the performance criteria established for each skill are generally representative of mature form. Again, construction of the lists of qualitative performance criteria were done under the guidance of content experts (cf. Gallahue, 1982; Thomas, 1984). Attention to each of these aspects of content validity has resulted in the TGMD being judged as sound with regard to traditional standards for content validity.

However, contrary evidence as to the test's soundness with respect to content validity has been provided by Cole (1989) and Cole, Wood, and Dunn (1990) by analyzing TGMD scores in the framework of item response theory (IRT). Within these analyses, each performance criterion was treated as a separate item on the test. Analysis of individual performance criteria scores indicated that many of the criteria did not fit a two-parameter model effectively. Poor model-data fit can be an indicator of a need for content revision at the individual test item level (in this case, performance criterion level). However, further investigation of model-data fit with other models (for example, three-parameter models) seems necessary to make a more robust judgment that content revisions are warranted.

Another psychometric consideration is the reliability of observed scores obtained from the TGMD. Judgments of reliability are based on both interrater reliability and test score or intrasubject reliability. Interrater reliability depends on the consistency of performance criteria scores obtained from different examiners rating the same performances. The consistency of various examiner's scores will be contingent in part on the cognitive representation or mental reference for mature performance each examiner possesses, as well as on each examiner's ability to detect when a performance criterion has been exhibited. A generalizability study by Ulrich and Wise (1984) examined interrater generalizability across 2, 10, and 20 raters obtained from an undergraduate adapted physical education course. Raters received a 45-minute training session prior to observing a videotape of 10 students performing the 12 skills. Generalizability coefficients reported in the test manual for the rater facet were of adequate magnitude for each of the 12 skills, with the lowest generalizability coefficient obtained equal to .77 for two raters on the run skill test. The study indicated that the TGMD delivered consistent scores across the particular raters included in the study, with generally good agreement obtained with a minimum of two raters. However, it is not clear how generalizable these results are because the specially trained undergraduates who served as raters in the study may not be representative of the typical professional who would use the TGMD. In addition, generalizability coefficients were not reported for each age group to determine scoring consistency at each age.

Ulrich and Wise (1984) also included a facet to determine a type of intrasubject reliability defined as the stability of scores assigned to the examinees' performances by the raters across two rating occasions. This was accomplished by having raters view the videotape to rate performances a second time 1 week following the first viewing. The obtained generalizability coefficients should not be viewed as similar to test-retest reliability coefficients, as subjects did not perform the test twice following an appropriate time interval. Instead, coefficients represented stability of scores from the same performance viewed on different occasions. The lowest generalizability coefficient reported in the test manual was .84, again for the run skill test. A mean generalizability coefficient for skills within the locomotor subtest was .96, and a mean generalizability coefficient for skills within the object control subtest was .97. These results indicated that each subtest rendered stable ratings of identical performances.

Another measure of test reliability, the internal consistency of scores across the various skills within a subtest, was reported in the test manual by employing split-half reliability coefficients adjusted with the Spearman-Brown prophecy formula. Coefficients obtained from data for 25 children drawn from each age level in the normative sample (no information given about sampling method employed) revealed generally good internal consistency with the lowest $r = .71$ for the object control subtest for 8-year-olds. It was not made clear why data for the entire normative sample of 909 children were not used to render coefficients. Further, calculation of Cronbach's alpha would have been a small additional improvement.

No estimates have been reported for the intrasubject reliability of the TGMD for handicapped versus nonhandicapped populations, although generation of coefficients for these populations could have been handled expeditiously by including handicapped/nonhandicapped as a facet within the Ulrich and Wise (1984) study. However, the IRT studies of Cole (1989) and Cole et al. (1990) have provided some evidence as to the accuracy of the test across various ability levels. Use of IRT methods liberates derived test and item statistics from dependency on the ability levels of the specific individuals tested. Thus, estimates of the accuracy of test scores can be generated for ability levels other than those from which the data were derived. The IRT statistic of interest for determining the effectiveness of the TGMD to deliver accurate scores across a broad range of psychomotor abilities is the test information function. The classical test theory analog to the test information function is the reliability coefficient. However, the reliability coefficient is a single measure of effectiveness of test accuracy applied across an entire range of examinee ability levels. The distinct advantage of the test information function over estimates of reliability lie in its ability to deliver estimates of test accuracy at each different ability level encountered within a group of subjects from possibly low functioning handicapped individuals to high functioning individuals exhibiting mature movement patterns.

Typical IRT test information functions are bell shaped, indicating that at high and low ability levels less accuracy is obtained in measuring the underlying trait, while at middle levels of ability test information increases. Thus, scores will more accurately represent the underlying trait at middle levels of ability. A function of this sort is acceptable for most tests because greatest measurement precision will be obtained for middle ability levels at which the majority of examinees function. Using the same data from which TGMD norms were derived, Cole (1989) determined that both TGMD subtests displayed typical bell-shaped test information functions, with peak information lying at ability levels just below average. Plots of the information functions indicated that subtest scores were most accurate within 1 standard deviation either side of peak information, with test information asymptotic at low and high ability levels. Based on these findings, it was evident that test precision decreased progressively for low and high ability individuals. Thus, a need may exist to more closely investigate the test's ability to assess motor functioning for those at the extremes of the ability continuum.

In all, evidence from classical test theory studies, generalizability studies, and item response theory studies indicate that the TGMD provides reasonably reliable scores for at least middle ability subjects. As this is likely to be where the majority of individuals tested will function, one can be reasonably confident of consistency in scores across raters and within individuals.

A final psychometric consideration pertains to the degree to which TGMD scores correspond to the underlying theoretical construct purportedly measured, gross motor development. Two common methods used to assess this correspondence are construct validity, as indicated by correlation coefficients, and factor analytic techniques of individual skill test scores. Ideally, factor analysis would reveal a simple structure in which each subtest was extracted as a separate factor and skills within a subtest were highly related to their respective factors as indicated by significant factor loadings. A factor analysis of normative data reported in the test manual extracted three factors accounting for 75% of the common variance. Nine of the 12 skills loaded significantly on the first factor, which accounted for 62% of the total common variance. Ulrich determined that this first factor represented a general gross motor development factor, indicating that most of the separate skill tests were measuring a similar construct and thus providing some support for internal construct validity. However, Langendorfer (1986) is at odds with the notion that this first factor indicates that the TGMD measures development. Instead, Langendorfer suggests that the TGMD assesses current level of motor control and not development or change in motor function. Thus, Langendorfer contends that this first factor would be more representative of a gross motor control factor. Because the use of the term *development* in the test title is not a trivial matter, further consideration of Langendorfer's claim that change (i.e., development) is not assessed seems warranted.

A second factor accounting for 8% of the common variance was extracted, with significant loadings for each of the skills assessed in the locomotor subtest except the run skill test, which was extracted alone as a final factor accounting for 5% of the common variance. The second factor indicated that skills within this subtest were highly related, supporting internal construct validity for this particular subtest. However, failure of the run test to load significantly on either of the first two factors and its extraction alone as a third factor indicated that this test was not highly related to the others. This could be a function of the run test representing a separate locomotor skill dimension substantially different from the other 11 skills measured, or a function of this particular test being the least reliably scored of the 12.

Unfortunately, correlation coefficients between the TGMD and other standardized tests of gross motor development have not been reported to assess external construct validity. Thus, statistical confirmation that the test measures similar constructs as other established gross motor development tests is lacking. This is due, perhaps, to the lack of other standardized tests that assess process mastery (an exception being the Motor Skills Inventory; Werder & Bruininks, 1988). However, correlations of TGMD scores with those of outcome-oriented gross motor skill tests would be instructive. Indeed, if low correlation coefficients were obtained, the value of the TGMD would be enhanced as this would be indicative of the different tests measuring separate constructs related to either process or outcome.

## Critique

The TGMD is designed to assess children's level of mastery in a number of fundamental gross motor skill movement patterns that are precursors to more complex motor skills utilized in sport and leisure settings. Studies of the test's reliability and validity seem to indicate that it generally delivers accurate scores for age-related norm-referenced decisions about general motor functioning and for criterion-referenced decisions about skill mastery/nonmastery (Ulrich, 1984). Though it is generally accepted that children progress through various stages of skill development due to both biological and experiential factors, TGMD scores should be viewed as primarily representing mastery based on experiential factors. That is, TGMD performance will be heavily influenced by prior instructional experiences. Thus, educators may find the TGMD beneficial as a tool for making instructional planning decisions for individuals and groups or as an indicator of progress in motor skill learning. The TGMD will also be especially useful to researchers needing an assessment instrument to indicate changes in fundamental motor skill learning.

It is hoped that future versions of the test consider use of an interval scale of measurement, with performance criteria scores based on a 0–3 scale rather than the currently used dichotomous scale. This would alleviate the loss of information encountered when transforming observations from the three performances per skill to an "all-or-none" scale, hopefully increasing test precision. In addition, consideration might be given to more refinement in age group norms by using age in years and months, rather than just in years, as the basis for calculation of standard scores. This feature hopefully would provide greater measurement fidelity during a period of life in which gross motor functioning is changing rapidly.

Based on minimal examiner training time, low cost to administer, relative ease in scoring, and adequate indicators of reliability and validity, the Test of Gross Motor Development seems a useful measure of children's gross motor skill proficiency. The test's focus on process rather than outcome makes it ideal for assisting professionals in planning appropriate instructional experiences leading to skill mastery.

## References


Bruininks, R.H. (1978). *Bruininks-Oseretsky Test of Motor Proficiency examiner's manual.* Circle Pines, MN: American Guidance Service.

Cole, E.L. (1989). *An application of item response theory to the Test of Gross Motor Development.* Unpublished master's thesis, Oregon State University, Corvallis, OR.

Cole, E.L., Wood, T.M., & Dunn, J.M. (1990, April). *An application of item response theory to the Test of Gross Motor Development*. Paper presented at the annual conference of the American Alliance for Health, Physical Education, Recreation, and Dance, New Orleans.

Gallahue, D.L. (1982). *Understanding motor development in children*. New York: Wiley.

Langendorfer, S. (1986). Test of Gross Motor Development. *Adapted Physical Activity Quarterly, 3*, 186–190.

Thomas, J.R. (1984). *Motor development during childhood and adolescence*. Minneapolis: Burgess.

Ulrich, D. (1984). The reliability of classification decisions made with the objectives-based motor skill assessment instrument. *Adapted Physical Activity Quarterly, 1*, 52–60.

Ulrich, D.A., & Ulrich, B.D. (1984). The objectives-based motor skill assessment instrument: Validation of instructional sensitivity. *Perceptual and Motor Skills, 59*, 175–179.

Ulrich, D.A., & Wise S.L. (1984). The reliability of scores obtained with the objectives-based motor skill assessment instrument. *Adapted Physical Activity Quarterly, 1*, 230–239.

Wechsler, D. (1974). *Wechsler Intelligence Scale for Children–Revised*. San Antonio, TX: Psychological Corporation.

Werder, J.K., & Bruininks, R.H. (1988). *Body Skills: A developmental curriculum for children*. Circle Pines, MN: American Guidance Service.

**Priscilla A. Drum, Ph.D.**

*Professor of Educational Psychology, Graduate School of Education, University of California-Santa Barbara, Santa Barbara, California.*

**Carol N. Dixon, Ph.D.**

*Senior Lecturer and Director, Education Reading Clinic, Graduate School of Education, University of California-Santa Barbara, Santa Barbara, California.*

# TEST OF INFERENCE ABILITY IN READING COMPREHENSION

*Linda M. Phillips and Cynthia C. Patterson. St. John's, Newfoundland: Institute For Educational Research and Development, Memorial University of Newfoundland.*

### Introduction

The Test of Inference Ability in Reading Comprehension (TIA; Phillips & Patterson, 1989) is intended to assess the ability of students in Grades 6–8 to draw appropriate inferences from material they have read, to provide diagnostic information on the level of sophistication of students' inference-making ability, and to provide information that will be useful in planning instruction for those students. The authors view reading as "meaning construction" and define inferring as "a constructive thinking process because a reader expands knowledge by proposing and evaluating hypotheses about the meaning of text" (Phillips, 1989b, p. 4). The TIA is a 36-item scaled-answer test, available in either a multiple-choice or constructed-response format. It may be administered as either an individual or group test.

The manual provides no biographical information on either of the test authors and little historical information regarding the timeframe or steps undertaken during test development. However, the manual does indicate that there were six phases in test development, and that a complete description of test development and design is available in a separate technical report (Phillips, 1989a). The manual contains a brief review of relevant literature as the rationale for development of this test.

The manual states that the norming population for the TIA was four groups of sixth- through eighth-graders ($N$ = 888) from schools across Canada. The norming groups represented a demographic range from small rural settings to large urban districts and low to middle class economic levels. The manual does not indicate that any other forms of the test have been developed to meet the needs of special populations (e.g., ESL students).

---

The reviewers would like to acknowledge and thank Janet H. Brown for her assistance in preparing this review.

"The Test of Inference Ability in Reading Comprehension consists of three full-length stories representative of the three kinds of discourse found at the middle grade levels: narration, exposition, and description" (Phillips, 1989b, p. 7). The stories are four or five paragraphs long. Each paragraph consists of approximately 100 to 150 words and is followed by 2 to 4 questions, for a total of 12 questions for each story. In the multiple-choice format, the questions consist of a statement followed by four possible answers. The present reviewers have attempted to simulate one of these items as an example. Although our simulation may not be considered appropriate by Phillips and Patterson (1989), we felt such a device was necessary in order to indicate the nature of items in this somewhat unusual test:

*Example.* Weather may be a factor in UFO sightings because
(A) Weather conditions may distort what people think they see.
(B) Weather conditions are checked out by scientists.
(C) Weather interferes with people's view of UFOs.
(D) Weather may cause UFOs to work improperly or actually damage them.

In the constructed-response format, an incomplete statement such as "Weather may be a factor in UFO sightings because" is followed by a five-line space in which the student writes an answer. Students are instructed to use both the information from the passage and their background knowledge to answer the questions.

The TIA is intended to be administered by a classroom teacher, without special training. The manual provides a script for examiners to use during administration as well as clear directions for procedures. No time limit is set (as this is a "power" test), although it is suggested that testing time will average 40–45 minutes, including test distribution and completion of one sample item.

Both formats of the TIA are scored against scaled answers. The four choices provided in the multiple-choice format were derived from student responses during test development and range in value from 0 to 3 for the answer deemed both most consistent and complete. Answers to the constructed-response version also are scored on a scale of 0 to 3, using criteria provided in the manual. The manual states that format choice does not make a difference in student performance, although no alternate-forms comparison data are provided. It is possible that students with poor writing skills would do less well on the constructed-response format or that different scorers would award different point values for responses. The authors caution that students must be competent with the difficulty level of the text before one can make appropriate judgments about their inferencing ability.

## Practical Applications/Uses

The TIA was designed to help educators, particularly teachers and researchers, appraise the inferential ability of middle grade students and, in research applications, study the nature of inference-making. It can be used as a measurement instrument or a teaching tool, in classrooms or with individual students, but not as a sole criterion for making placement decisions (Phillips, 1989b, p. 11). The authors suggest that this test is constructed in a way that allows the teacher or researcher to closely examine the thinking processes of students confronted with questions requiring inferential thinking. In the multiple-choice format, each detractor has been designed to identify a particular kind of error. Some students use circular reasoning, thereby giving incomplete answers; others may use only factual information, again missing the more complete answer. Because the multiple-choice test gives partial credit for these incomplete answers, the test examiner can see more clearly the way a student reads, comprehends, and infers about a given passage.

As described in the previous section, two formats are available for this test: multiple choice and constructed response. The multiple-choice format can be scored in one of two ways: dichotomously, that is, 1 point for right, 0 for wrong, or on a partial credit scale, from 0 to 3 points, where each answer gets either 0, 1, 2, or 3 points (with 108 points possible). Scores for each story are added separately. In addition, examiners can gain information by looking at types of error patterns made across the three types of passages, narrative, expositive, and descriptive.

The constructed-response format is scored on a subjective basis, giving each answer 0 to 3 points. Model answers are available, and guidelines established; however, scoring these answers is difficult at first. The authors recommend that graders "be open-minded and flexible to recognize and to assign appropriate values to interpretations different from the model answers provided in the Constructed-response Key" (Phillips, 1989b, p. 19). In other words, scoring these tests requires examiner judgment but also allows great insight into the student's thinking process. The multiple-choice format is an objective test and the constructed-response format a subjective one. Therefore, the latter requires a scorer who is knowledgeable about inference-making.

The Test of Inference Ability in Reading Comprehension is a norm-referenced test. The raw scores become meaningful when they are compared with the distribution of scores of the norming groups—888 sixth- through eighth-grade Canadian students. The manual provides tables showing raw scores, means, and standard deviations for the four norming groups used, by age and sex, as well as a table showing percentiles.

**Technical Aspects**

The technical aspects of the Test of Inference Ability in Reading Comprehension are explained most clearly in the technical report (Phillips, 1989a) rather than in the manual that accompanies the test; therefore, this discussion will be based on that report. The five pilot studies conducted to develop the test are described and results and revisions explained. These data will be used to explore the TIA's validity. Because of the subjective nature of the "constructed-response format," the reliability and validity descriptions generally will be limited to the multiple-choice format.

The internal consistency of the total test (36 items with an upper limit of 3 points per item for a possible perfect score of 108) was .79 as determined by the Kuder-Richardson 20 procedures on the normative sample. This coefficient is somewhat lower than those found for typical achievement tests, where the values for coefficients are estimated as high at .98 and at the median at .92 (Borg & Gall, 1989, p. 258). However, as noted by Phillips in the manual, the reliability of .79 is comparable to those obtained for the Cornell Critical Thinking Test at .72 and the Watson-

Glaser Critical Thinking Appraisal at .80. The quality of inferences, from poor to excellent, is a difficult decision process and is not well defined in the literature (van Dijk & Kintsch, 1983).

The need for background knowledge in constructing appropriate inferences is acknowledged (Ennis, 1973; Markhan, 1981; Govier, 1985), yet such knowledge varies from individual to individual depending on life experiences. This variation is corroborated by the KR-20 coefficients for 12 items or 36 points available for the three passages: .60 for UFO's, .49 for Money, and .77 for Newspapers. The latter passage is a narrative about home delivery of newspapers, considered an easier genre (Bereiter & Scardamalia, 1982) and with a higher level of background knowledge in Phase 2 of test development (90% as compared with 80% for UFOs and 75% for money). The standard deviations for the other two passages were smaller than for the newspapers passage, indicating that some of these sixth- through eighth-grade students knew a great deal about newspaper deliveries and others very little, while they were quite homogeneous in their knowledge on the other topics. In any case the means are quite low at 67% correct for all three passages, with the distribution of scores at the 99th percentile with 70 correct out of a possible 108.

The steps taken to validate the TIA were thorough. The materials present a clear summary of the research that led to the definition of reading inference used for test development. A good inference is defined as follows:

> Inferences in reading comprehension tend to be good to the extent that a reader integrates relevant text information and relevant background knowledge to construct interpretations that more completely and more consistently explain the meaning of the text than alternative interpretations. (Phillips, 1989a, p. 5)

Passages were selected through six stages using graduate students, teachers, and pupils representing Grades 5 to 9. Five pilot studies were run to develop both the constructed-response and the multiple-choice formats. Results of a construct validation of oral and written thinking protocols and test item responses were high, showing an average correlation of .55. No cross-validations with other reading scores outside the test itself are provided. It would be difficult to establish predictive validity given the recency of test construction. However, the fact that the mean scores increased by grade, significant at $<.01$, indicates a reasonable pattern of growth for this instrument. Thus, the steps taken to validate the TIA seem reasonable.

**Critique**

Inferencing is an ability that pervades all human endeavors, whether realized through oral or written language or through actions. When the present reviewers administered this test in order to critique it, six of our subjects answered the questions without the passages and two with the passages, following Tuinman's (1973–74) example. The six subjects without the passages produced higher total scores than those with the passages. Our small *N* makes this finding questionable, but a study should be designed to test this condition. Most of the items do require inferential reasoning in our judgment, but again most of them do not require passage information to select the best answer. The information in the concatenated items for a topic in both the stems and the choices provide sufficient information to select the best choice if the examinee is knowledgeable.

The weighting of the answer choices from 0 to 3 represents an advance over most standardized tests. An appropriate design in these choices could lead to tests that provide some diagnostic information. However, a scoring format is needed so that the selection pattern for individual subjects and for classes is apparent. Teachers could use this information to teach inferencing skills where needed.

Inference tests similar to this one could be developed for content area classes in order to estimate the prior knowledge of a class for instruction and grouping purposes. Passages would not be needed, just topics, although it is likely that the tendency to seek face validity would require passage inclusion. In its current form this test purports to be a general test of inference ability. It is our contention that inferencing is a skill that depends mainly on prior knowledge, and that no generalized *g* score for this ability has meaning.

## References

Bereiter, C., & Scardamalia, M. (1982). From conversation to composition: The role of instruction in a developmental process. In R. Glaser (Ed.), *Advances in instructional psychology* (Vol. 2, pp. 1–64). Hillsdale, N.J.: Lawrence Erlbaum.

Borg, W.R., & Gall, M.D. (1989). *Educational research: An introduction* (5th ed.). New York: Longman.

Ennis, R.H. (1973). Inference. In H.S. Broudy, R.H. Ennis, & L.I. Krimerman (Eds.), *Philosophy of educational research*. New York: Wiley.

Govier, T. (1985). *A practical study of argument*. Belmont, CA: Wadsworth.

Markhan, E. (1981). Comprehension monitoring. In P. Dickson (Ed.), *Children's oral communication skills* (pp. 61–82). New York: Academic Press.

Phillips, L.M. (1989a). *Developing and validating assessments of inference ability in reading comprehension* (Technical Report No. 452). Urbana, IL: University of Illinois, Center for the Study of Reading.

Phillips, L.M. (1989b). *Manual for Test of Inference Ability in Reading Comprehension*. St. John's, Newfoundland: Institute for Educational Research and Development, Memorial University of Newfoundland.

Phillips, L.M., & Patterson, C.C. (1989). *Phillips-Patterson Test of Inference Ability in Reading Comprehension*. St. John's, Newfoundland: Institute for Educational Research and Development, Memorial University of Newfoundland.

Tuinman, J.J. (1973–74). Determining the passage dependency of comprehension questions in five major tests. *Reading Research Quarterly, 9*, 206–223.

van Dijk, T., & Kintsch, W. (1983). *Strategies of discourse comprehension*. New York: Academic Press.

**Diane J. Tedick, Ph.D.**
*Assistant Professor of Second Languages and Cultures Education, Department of Curriculum and Instruction, University of Minnesota, Minneapolis, Minnesota.*

# TEST OF WRITTEN ENGLISH

*Velma R. Andersen and Sheryl K. Thompson. Novato, California: Academic Therapy Publications.*

### Introduction

The Test of Written English (TWE; Andersen & Thompson, 1979) is an informal instrument designed to assess students' writing performance in Grades 1 through 6. A paper-and-pencil test, the TWE screens for mastery in four major areas: capitalization, punctuation, written expression, and paragraph writing. The test, primarily designed for individual administration, requires approximately 10 to 20 minutes to complete. According to the test authors, it can also be administered to a small group of students, provided that each is able to read at the second-grade level or higher (Andersen & Thompson, 1979).

The TWE was developed by Velma R. Andersen and Sheryl K. Thompson in response to "an apparent lack of instruments on the market that were designed to measure a student's performance" in writing (Andersen & Thompson, 1979, p. 5). According to the test authors, previous teaching experience and a number of sources, such as curriculum guides, language books, and readings, were used to develop the items and grade level descriptors for the various skill areas. The authors do not, however, list the actual sources or describe the nature of the teaching experience to which they referred. Furthermore, specific information regarding the development of the test and the qualifications of the test authors is not provided.

The TWE is packaged in a sturdy plastic folder that holds the TWE manual and 50 individual test forms. The first page of each test form provides space for recording the date; the student's name, grade, birthdate, age, school, and teacher; the examiner's name; notes; and scores. The remaining three pages contain the test items, organized into sections that encompass the four major areas tested. Items in the first three sections are grouped according to degree of difficulty (least difficult to most difficult) for Grades 1 through 6.

The test authors emphasize that because the TWE is an informal device, the written directions and test items can be read aloud to students unable to read these elements themselves. The examiner, who may or may not be the student's teacher, administers the test to individual students or a small group of students by covering each section of the test in order. Students respond on the individual test forms provided.

In the Capitalization section, the student is asked to circle the words that need to be capitalized in nine sentences. The first five sentences are brief and contain from one to three errors that require capitalization of the first words of the sentences, the pronoun *I*, and proper nouns specifying names of persons. The remaining four sentences are longer and contain from three to eight errors that require capitalization of proper nouns specifying names of persons and places, days of the week, and months. The Punctuation section is composed of 13 sentences that the student must correct by inserting the appropriate punctuation marks. Each sentence contains from one to three errors requiring correct insertion of periods, question marks, exclamation points, commas, apostrophes, and quotation marks. In the third section, Written Expression, the student is to demonstrate correct usage by (a) creating two sentences using the words *boy* and *what,* (b) writing words to finish a sentence, (c) inserting appropriate words in blanks within two sentences, (d) correcting two run-on sentences, (e) combining two pairs of sentences, and (f) selecting and underlining the correct pronoun or verb form from two choices in eight sentences. In the final section, Paragraph Writing, which is meant only for students in the second grade or higher, the student is expected either to use at least four sentences to complete a story from a two-sentence story starter provided or to write a paragraph of his or her own choosing. The test authors suggest that older students be instructed to include "descriptive words and/or words in a series" in their paragraphs (Andersen & Thompson, 1979, p. 6).

The TWE manual is composed of 95 pages. The first seven pages contain recommendations for administering and scoring the test. The next four list resources from 21 different publishers. The rest of the manual is devoted to exercises, materials, and instructional strategies for teaching 17 different skills areas, ranging from capitalization and punctuation to subject-verb agreement to paragraph writing. It appears that these are provided for the teacher-examiner so that he or she can examine a student's performance on the test, determine which skills need remediation, and then choose appropriate strategies and exercises for use in instruction.

**Practical Applications/Uses**

According to the test authors, the primary purpose of the TWE is to measure a student's performance in writing. Presumably, the TWE can be used by classroom teachers or resource teachers at any time during the school year to determine a student's approximate grade level in writing skills. Although primarily designed for students in Grades 1 through 6, the TWE also can be administered to students beyond Grade 6 who are experiencing difficulty in school. In addition, the test authors claim that the TWE is appropriate for learning disabled students because the examiner may read the test items and directions aloud (Andersen & Thompson, 1979).

The TWE is administered individually or to a small group of students in a 10- to 20-minute period. As specified in the manual, the examiner should begin with the first item in each section. In the Capitalization and Punctuation sections, the examiner is to continue testing until items are missed in two consecutive sentences. In the Written Expression section, the examiner is to discontinue testing after two consecutive items are missed. Andersen and Thompson (1979) emphasize that *"credit should be given for any correct items within these sentences or written expression items"* (p. 5, emphasis original). They also offer to examiners the option of administering all of the items to students who are in or above the fifth grade. Given these stipulations, it is difficult to see how the test could be administered accurately and efficiently to a small group composed of students below the fifth grade.

Quoted directions for administering the TWE are provided in the manual, but they are presented "as a source of information for the examiner only" (Andersen & Thompson, 1979, p. 6). Apparently the examiner is free to reword the intent of instructions using words deemed as appropriate for the particular student being tested. As pointed out in an earlier review of the TWE (Poteet, 1985), some of the instructions provided are not precise. In the Written Expression section, for example, it is not clear whether the student is to write in just the necessary change to correct run-on sentences or to combine sentences, or whether he or she is to rewrite the sentences in a corrected form (Poteet, 1985).

The scoring guidelines are straightforward for the first three sections of the test. In the answer key provided in the manual, each item for the first three sections of the test is written in its corrected form, with the original errors in the Capitalization and Punctuation sections marked clearly. The examiner scores each test by hand, awarding students 1 point for each correct response. For example, if the student is able to correct two of a total of three errors in one sentence, he or she receives 2 points. In the Capitalization section, 1 point is also awarded to the student if he or she capitalizes his or her own name, yet it is not specified in the instructions that the student is to write his or her own name.

In order to determine the grade level for each student on the first three sections of the test, the examiner is instructed to refer to the "Scoring Breakdown" section of the manual once the total number of points has been determined for each section. In the scoring breakdown, the number of points the student received on the first three sections corresponds to a grade-level placement ranging from first grade, second semester to sixth grade, second semester. For example, a student who scores between 14 and 17 points out of a total of 30 in the Capitalization section is said to be at the level of third grade, first semester. Similarly, a student who scores 11 points out of the 21 possible in the Written Expression section is assigned a level of fourth grade, second semester.

> The scoring for each of the sections was based upon the approximate following percentage cutoffs for the second semester of each grade: first grade—75 percent; second grade—80 percent; third grade—85 percent; fourth grade—90 percent; fifth grade—95 percent and sixth grade—better than 95 percent. (Andersen & Thompson, 1979, p. 5)

The test authors claim that an overall performance level can be determined by calculating an average of the grade level scores for the first three sections of the test.

Interpretation of the results of the test is vague at best. The test authors provide four lists to assist the examiner in scoring and interpreting the test: (a) Guidelines for Written Language, a list of skills for the six grade levels that correspond to the Capitalization, Punctuation, and Written Expression sections of the test; (b) Grade Level Determinations, a list of items from the first three sections of the test that correspond to the six grade levels; (c) Interpretation of Scores, a list of suggested observations that should be made by the examiner during the administration and interpretation of the instrument; and (d) Scoring Breakdown (described earlier). Because the test authors fail to provide the list of sources they consulted to develop these sections, it is difficult at best to know whether they are appropriate for all elementary contexts.

The final section of the test, Paragraph Writing, is not scored, even though it is the *only* section that asks the students to engage in an actual composing task. No guidelines for scoring the paragraph or interpreting a student's performance are provided. The test authors simply suggest that a student's performance on this section be compared with his or her performance on the Capitalization, Punctuation, and Written Expression sections. They state that "the purpose for writing the paragraph is to see whether the student can apply the skills that he knows as measured by the preceding sections of this test" (Andersen & Thompson, 1979, p. 6). They also claim that "an approximate grade level can be established for the paragraph writing section by using the Guidelines for Written Language—Written Expression section for each grade level" (p. 7). These guidelines summarize skills that the authors propose "should be mastered by the *end* of that school year" (Andersen & Thompson, 1979, p. 7, emphasis original).

These guidelines, however, are neither descriptive nor complete enough for an examiner to provide an accurate assessment of a student's ability to write a paragraph. For example, as stated in the Guidelines for Written Language—Written Expression section, a fourth-grade student should be able to demonstrate "correction of run-on sentences" (p. 8). Clearly, this descriptor is not at all appropriate for assessing the Paragraph Writing section of the test; this descriptor, and many others listed in this set of guidelines, are only appropriate for the Written Expression section of the test. It is as though the test authors suggested the use of these guidelines for assessing the Paragraph Writing section as an afterthought.

## Technical Aspects

The test authors provide neither norms for the test nor data regarding attempts to establish validity or to determine reliability. They claim that "some initial comparisons were made between the students' performance on this test and on other instruments," including the Wechsler Intelligence Scale for Children-Revised Verbal IQ score and the Reading and Spelling subtest scores on the Wide Range Achievement Test, but they make no mention of what these comparisons revealed (Andersen & Thompson, 1979, p. 5). There is no excuse for the test authors' failure to report at least minimal information regarding validity and reliability indices (Poteet, 1985).

## Critique

Research has indicated that children begin to develop as writers at very young ages when they are free to experiment with writing, when they are encouraged to take risks, and when composing processes are emphasized and nurtured (e.g., Bissex, 1980; Calkins, 1983; Clay, 1975; Graves, 1983; Harste, Woodward, & Burke, 1984; Smith, 1982; Temple, Nathan, & Burris, 1982). In addition, research has shown that "young children demonstrate their knowledge of written language best when tasks are highly contextualized, similar to their uses in daily life" (Shanklin, 1989, p. 631). Given these indications, it is clear that the TWE lacks a sound theoretical framework.

The authors of the TWE claim that it "was based upon the concept that written language is the ability to express oneself clearly on paper" (Andersen & Thompson, 1979, p. 5), yet the one section of the test that requires students to express themselves on paper, Paragraph Writing, is the only section that is *not* scored. The TWE is clearly biased toward the measurement of writing conventions, as indicated by the emphasis the authors put on the Capitalization, Punctuation, and Written Expression sections. Perhaps these sections are emphasized because they are easier to measure than are writing processes or written products. It is important to remember, however, that ease of measurement should not guide test construction. Shafer (1985), in an earlier review of the TWE, puts it simply: "The underlying message of this test seems to be that conventions of writing are more important than writing itself" (p. 1599). The danger of a test such as this one is precisely the communication of this message to students, teachers, parents, and administrators.

Paragraph Writing is also the only section that excludes first-grade students. Shafer (1985) cites the work of Graves (1975) to support the notion that many first-grade students are quite capable of writing paragraphs as well as longer pieces of text. Indeed, many researchers have shown that these young children are able to create rich paragraphs and stories, though they are often just beginning to understand and use writing conventions (Bissex, 1980; Clay, 1975; Harste et al., 1984; Temple et al., 1982). The writing abilities of children such as these could not be measured accurately by the TWE because of its bias toward writing conventions (Shafer, 1985).

As mentioned earlier, the test authors emphasize that the TWE can be used with young children and/or learning disabled children who cannot read because the examiner can read the directions and items to those students. What remains unclear is precisely how a student is supposed to be able, for example, to circle the correct word that needs to be capitalized if he or she cannot read that word or the context in which it is placed. Children learn the conventions of writing by *reading* and *writing,* not by being taught rules (e.g., Smith, 1982).

The test authors stress that the TWE is an informal device, yet it seems more like a standardized measure. Teachers who already emphasize the importance of meaningful writing in the classroom are capable of informally assessing their students' writing strengths, weaknesses, and progress by observing them and recording brief comments to be placed in a cumulative folder; they do not need a test such as the TWE to obtain this information (Newkirk & Atwell, 1982; Samway, 1987; Strickland & Morrow, 1989). The TWE and other instruments like it "ignore the multifaceted nature of writing when it evolves in a human environment" (Samway, 1987, p. 297).

In sum, the problems associated with the TWE as just described, coupled with the test authors' failure to provide even minimal indices of validity and reliability, lead to the conclusion that the TWE is not acceptable as an informal instrument for measuring the writing abilities of children. Classroom teachers would be wise to refer to the literature regarding informal strategies for assessing writing (see, for example, Barrs, 1990; Clay, 1990; Newkirk & Atwell, 1982; Samway, 1987; and Stires, 1991) in order to develop systematic, comprehensive guidelines for informally assessing students' writing that correspond to the characteristics of their individual writing programs.

## References

This list contains text citations and suggested additional reading.

Andersen, V.R., & Thompson, S.K. (1979). *Test of Written English (TWE).* Novato, CA: Academic Therapy Publications.

Barone, D., & Lovell, J. (1987). Bryan the brave: A second grader's growth as reader and writer. *Language Arts, 64,* 505–515.

Barrs, M. (1990). The Primary Language Record: Reflection of issues in evaluation. *Language Arts, 67,* 244–253.

Bissex, G.L. (1980). *Gnys at wrk: A child learns to read and write.* Cambridge, MA: Harvard University Press.

Calkins, L.M. (1983). *Lessons from a child.* Portsmouth, NH: Heinemann Educational Books.

Calkins, L.M. (1986). *The art of teaching writing.* Portsmouth, NH: Heinemann Educational Books.

Clay, M.M. (1975). *What did I write?* Portsmouth, NH: Heinemann Educational Books.

Clay, M.M. (1990). Research currents: What is and what might be in evaluation? *Language Arts, 67,* 288–298.

Cramer, R.L. (1982). Informal approaches to evaluating children's writing. In J.J. Pikulski & T. Shanahan (Eds.), *Approaches to the informal evaluation of reading* (pp. 80–93). Newark, DE: International Reading Association.

Dyson, A.H. (1989). *Collaboration through writing and reading: Exploring possibilities.* Urbana, IL: National Council of Teachers of English.

Farr, M., & Daniels, H. (1986). *Language diversity and writing instruction.* Urbana, IL: National Council of Teachers of English.

Graves, D.H. (1975). An examination of the writing processes of seven year old children. *Research in the Teaching of English, 14,* 227–241.

Graves, D.H. (1983). *Writing: Teachers and children at work.* Portsmouth, NH: Heinemann Educational Books.

Gregg, L.W., & Steinberg, E.R. (Eds.). (1980). *Cognitive processes in writing.* Hillsdale, NJ: Lawrence Erlbaum.

Harste, J.C., Woodward, V.A., & Burke, C.L. (1984). *Language stories and literacy lessons.* Portsmouth, NH: Heinemann Educational Books.

Heinemann Educational Books. (1989). *The Primary Language Record Handbook.* Portsmouth, NH: Author.

King, M.L., & Rentel, V. (1979). Toward a theory of early writing development. *Research in the Teaching of English, 13,* 243–253.

Morrow, L.M. (1989). *Literacy development in the early years.* Englewood Cliffs, NJ: Prentice-Hall.

Newkirk, T., & Atwell, N. (Eds.). (1982). *Understanding writing: Ways of observing, learning, & teaching.* Chelmsford, MA: Northeast Regional Exchange.

Poteet, J.A. (1985). Test of Written English. In J.V. Mitchell, Jr. (Ed.), *The ninth mental measurements yearbook* (pp. 1598–1599). Lincoln, NE: Buros Institute of Mental Measurements.

Power, B.M., & Hubbard, R. (Eds.). (1991). *Literacy in process.* Portsmouth, NH: Heinemann Educational Books.

Samway, K. (1987). Formal evaluation of children's writing: An incomplete story. *Language Arts, 64*, 289–298.

Shafer, R.E. (1985). Test of Written English. In J.V. Mitchell, Jr. (Ed.), *The ninth mental measurements yearbook* (pp. 1599–1600). Lincoln, NE: Buros Institute of Mental Measurements.

Shanklin, N.L. (1989). Test of Early Written Language (TEWL). *The Reading Teacher, 42*, 630–631.

Smith, F. (1982). *Writing and the writer.* New York: Holt, Rinehart & Winston.

Stires, S. (1991). Thinking throughout the process: Self-evaluation in writing. In B.M. Power & R. Hubbard (Eds.), *Literacy in process* (pp. 295–310). Portsmouth, NH: Heinemann Educational Books.

Strickland, D.S., & Morrow, L.M. (1989). Assessment and early literacy. *The Reading Teacher, 42*, 624–635.

Teale, W., Hiebert, E., & Chittenden, E. (1987). Assessing young children's literacy development. *The Reading Teacher, 40*, 772–777.

Temple, C.A., Nathan, R.G., & Burris, N.A. (1982). *The beginnings of writing.* Boston, MA: Allyn & Bacon.

**Robert H. Bauernfeind, Ph.D.**
*Professor of Education, Northern Illinois University, DeKalb, Illinois.*

# TESTS OF ADULT BASIC EDUCATION—FORMS 5 AND 6

*SRA Staff. Monterey, California: CTB/Macmillan/McGraw-Hill.*

## Introduction

The Tests of Adult Basic Education (TABE) are designed to measure adult proficiency in reading, mathematics, and language. This reviewer earlier had issued a fairly negative critique of TABE Forms 3 and 4 (Bauernfeind, 1986); however, in 1987 the publisher issued two new forms—5 and 6—that are rather different from Forms 3 and 4. The 1987 forms provide an objective (multiple-choice) measure of the reading, mathematics, and language/editing skills that are needed by adults for two reasons: to pass the GED high school graduation equivalency test and to concentrate on "basic skills that are required to function in society" (TABE Examiner's Manual, 1987, p. 1).

The 1987 TABE program consists of eight test booklets, two each (Form 5 and Form 6) at four levels of difficulty. *Level E (Easy)* is color coded dark violet. Its type size is large (about 14 point), with spacious vertical leading and excellent page layouts. Level E provides grade equivalent scores ranging from 0.3 or 1.6 (for a raw score of 0) to 8.9 (for raw scores at the top of the test). *Level M (Medium)* is color coded dark blue. It is also set in large type (about 12 point) with spacious vertical leading and excellent page layouts. Level M provides grade equivalent scores ranging from 0.8 or 2.2 (for a raw score of 0) to 10.9 (for raw scores at the top of the test). *Level D (Difficult)* is color coded dark brown. Its type size and leading are the same as Level M, and again the page layouts are excellent. Level D provides grade equivalent scores ranging from 0.9 or 3.3 (for a raw score of 0) to 12.9 (for raw scores at the top of the test). *Level A (Advanced)* is color coded teal. Set in about 11-point type with reasonable leading, again the page layouts are excellent. Level A provides grade equivalent scores ranging from 1.4 or 4.5 (for a raw score of 0) to 12.9 (for raw scores at the top of the test). The raw scores of 0 yielding respectable grade equivalents are unnerving. These obviously are editorial mistakes, but the same thing happened in TABE Forms 3 and 4.

All eight booklets cover the same curriculum areas, with the same numbers of items and the same time limits. Thus, there is only one Examiner's Manual for all eight booklets (an achievement that should be a model for all publishers of graduated [growth] test booklets).

Examinees begin by taking a "practice test" for marking answers and a "locator test" to identify the test level that would be most appropriate for diagnostic purposes and to establish a baseline for growth studies. The Locator Test is composed of 25 Vocabulary items and 25 Mathematics items. The examinees' raw scores on this test are used to suggest the most appropriate level for the baseline test.

If the Locator Test scores indicate a significant difference in an examinee's verbal and number skills, "e.g., more than two TABE levels apart, it may be appropriate to assign the examinee one TABE level test book for Reading, Language, and Spelling and a different level test book for Mathematics" (TABE Examiner's Manual, 1987, page 21). However, the only combination "more than two levels apart" would be E and A. With positive correlations between these two skill areas, such discrepancies should be extremely rare.

The TABE comprises the following curriculum areas, numbers of items, and time limits: Reading Vocabulary—30 items, 17 minutes; Reading Comprehension—40 items, 37 minutes; Math Computation—48 items 43 minutes; Math Concepts, Applications—40 items, 37 minutes; Language Mechanics—30 items, 15 minutes; Language Expression—45 items, 41 minutes; and Spelling—30 items, 13 minutes. The practice items plus Locator Test and the preliminary fill-ins add an additional 80 minutes. Thus, the 1987 TABE provides 263 multiple-choice items that yield seven scores. Given in four sessions, with breaks, TABE requires approximately 5½ hours' administration time. There is also a shorter "survey" battery at each level, with about half as many items, requiring about half as much time, but not providing the Spelling score or the kinds of curriculum part scores that one obtains from the full-length versions.

The TABE answer sheets are well designed, and the Examiner's Manual is an excellent model for those who test unsophisticated clients. The authors recommend that examiners and proctors take the test themselves before attempting to give it to a group. The authors also recommend that there be one proctor for every 15 examinees (TABE Examiner's Manual, 1987, p. 8).

Although the testing materials have been carefully designed to provide a smooth testing program, the publisher's catalog presents a great variety of choices for examinees' answers and data processing. One cannot begin to present all choice combinations in a meaningful way but suffice it to say that

- There is one large-print edition for clients who are visually impaired.
- There are two standard-print answer sheets for hand scoring.
- There are four different answer sheets for electronic scoring.
- Software systems are available for the IBM/PC, XT, AT, or 100% compatibles, and for the Apple IIe or II+.

Whichever scoring system is used, students are given some or all of the following score interpretations:

1. *An IRT standard score growth scale.* The TABE scale runs from 1 to 999, presumably with equal units of measurement (like inches on a yardstick). Its effective zone of measurement runs from around 500 to around 850—scores that avoid random chance markings at the bottom and ceiling effects at the top.

2. *Grade equivalent (GE) scores.* These data were developed by equating TABE standard scores to GE scores on the current California Achievement Tests, Form E.

3. *Estimated GED scores.* These data were developed by equating TABE standard scores to the five curriculum scores and an overall average score on the current Tests of General Educational Development (GED).

4. *Percentile-rank or stanine scores.* These scores are determined within four different norms groups—students in (a) basic education programs, (b) adult offender

programs, (c) juvenile offender programs, and (d) vocational/technical training programs.

**Practical Applications/Uses**

The TABE Individual Diagnostic Profile provides a record for use in improving each examinee's skills. The profile lists the objectives covered in the TABE, provides spaces for indicating mastery or nonmastery of each skill area, and allows a graphic picture of student performance on each subtest.

Where low skill areas are noted, the TABE can be used to plot student growth via subsequent retests. Both the standard score scale and the grade equivalent scale can be used to show student growth. The TABE also can be used to show students how close they are to scoring a 45 on the GED scale (which is the most usual benchmark for saying that a student has achieved high school graduation equivalency and that he or she should be reasonably competent in these skill areas in real life).

Finally, TABE scores can be used as dependent (outcome) variables in all sorts of studies involving different treatments for ABE (adult basic education) students.

**Technical Aspects**

Technical data on the 1987 TABE are presented in two publications—the *TABE Technical Report* (1987) and the *TABE Norms Book* (1987). Neither publication is included in the Multi-Level Test Review Kit (Specimen Set), which is irritating, and neither is very useful, which is discouraging. At their best, these publications provide detailed raw-score-to-scale data for the four score interpretations cited previously, and they provide extensive reports of Kuder-Richardson Formula 20 reliabilities. Data from 224 studies (four groups, four levels, two forms per level, and seven scores per form = 224) showed KR-20 reliabilities ranging from .71 to .94, with a median of .89 and a mode of .90. Reliabilities for the Reading Comprehension scores tended to run highest, and those for the English Mechanics (capitalization and punctuation) scores tended to run lowest. However, there are significant omissions of data: there are no reports of test-retest reliability coefficients, and there are no reports of correlations among the seven TABE scores (though dozens of such studies could have been generated from data already available).

Further, the technical report's sections on "validity" do not provide the kinds of studies usually associated with the concept. The chapter on validity includes passages on test development, procedures for reducing bias, tryout and item selection, distractor information, choosing items for tests, item card printouts, computer interactive displays and computer printouts, item parameters, and establishment of Locator Test cutpoints. One would expect to find such material in a chapter on "development" rather than one on "validity."

There are no studies showing that those who score high on the TABE tend to function more effectively in American society than those who score low. The 1987 technical report cites one study ($N$ = 678) showing correlations between TABE scale scores and scale scores on the Tests of General Educational Development

(GED). This study shows a top correlation of .70 between the total scores of the two batteries; correlations between corresponding part scores run in the .50s and .60s.

When we use tests to predict similar tests, we should be able to obtain correlation coefficients of .80 or higher. One study relating TABE Forms 3 and 4 to the GED yielded a correlation of only .56 between the total scores of the two batteries (TABE Technical Report, 1978, p. 18). If one assumes that those two studies can be compared, the data would suggest that the 1987 TABE is more harmonious with (i.e., shares more common variance with) the GED. Still, it seems that the two testing programs continue to be rather remote from each other. Differing content/curriculum emphases are probably the cause of these less-than-encouraging correlations.

The authors seem to focus unduly not on validity, but on the TABE three-parameter IRT standard score scale and on the concept of "standard error of measurement." The standard error of measurement comes up again and again, even inappropriately at times, as in the norms booklet (pp. 14–17 and 66–69). Moreover, a full 14 pages in the 57-page technical report are devoted to showing SEm data in graphic form, with SEm lines running high at the extremes of each scale and low in the middle ranges of each scale. In those middle ranges, the SEm averages around 15 units on the standard score scale, which is what most users are probably most interested in.

The GE norms conversion tables are extremely difficult to read. In a two-score area, such as Reading Vocabulary and Reading Comprehension, GE scores for Vocabulary are given in a vertical column, GE scores for Comprehension are given in a horizontal row, and GE scores for Vocabulary-plus-Comprehension are given at the intersection of the Vocabulary raw score and the Comprehension raw score. Don't these two-score totals give redundant GE conversions? No. For example, in the table for Reading, Form 6, Level D, raw scores of 8 + 20 yield a GE score of 4.5, while raw scores of 20 + 8 yield a GE score of 5.1. Such minor discrepancies are undoubtedly a function of unequal variances between the two tests, but are such discrepancies worth pursuing in such a complicated table? Might we not settle for 8 + 20 = 20 + 8 = GE 4.8?

## Critique

The 1987 TABE can be given three grades. First, it gets an A+ for its design. Its booklet format, answer sheets, and single Examiner's Manual for all eight booklets mark it as one of the best engineered testing programs this reviewer has ever seen. It is like a magnificent music hall, waiting for a concert by a magnificent symphony orchestra.

Second, it gets a B for test content. The item writing is first rate, but too much of the TABE material is oblique to real life for American adults:

> The idea of having adults—whose primary concern often is to improve their employment situation—read poetry and passages about Greek gods and animals is not readily justifiable. More of the passages should be related to adult topics, needs, and interests, and they should address the idea of functioning in the real world more directly. (Flynt, 1990, p. 102)

This reviewer would extend Flynt's criticism to include many of the TABE's choices of spelling words (e.g., *canteen, rehearsal, bristles, forfeit, exceed, edible, coarse, val-*

*iant, pall, rhapsody, sentinel, crescent* ) and exercises with fractions (e.g., $^7/_8 \times {}^3/_4 \times {}^1/_3 =$ ____; $^2/_3 \div {}^4/_7 =$ ____), for example.

Third, the norms book and the technical report get, for reasons cited previously, a D.

There is one more major problem with the 1987 TABE: This program desperately needs a benchmark for score interpretations. The standard score scale provides no benchmarks for score interpretations, nor do the grade equivalent scores, and nor do the four groups for which norms scores are provided. As one purpose of the TABE is to predict standard scores on the high school equivalency GED tests, one could use the GED Average Score (specifically, an average of 45) as a benchmark for "effective adult behavior." A majority of states, territories, and Canadian provinces use 45 as such a benchmark score (ACE, 1987, p. 107). Although that score of 45 could be raised or lowered, let us accept it for the moment. TABE scores then could be interpreted in this way:

| *TABE SS* | *Grade equivalent* | *GED Total SS* | *Interpretation* |
|---|---|---|---|
| 500 | 1.1 | 9 | |
| 525 | 1.4 | 13 | |
| 550 | 1.7 | 17 | Low |
| 575 | 2.0 | 21 | functioning |
| 600 | 2.3 | 24 | for |
| 625 | 2.7 | 28 | real life |
| 650 | 3.1 | 32 | |
| 675 | 3.8 | 36 | |
| 700 | 4.9 | 40 | Marginal |
| 725 | 6.3 | 44 | functioning |
| 750 | 8.4 | 48 | for real life |
| 775 | 12.6 | 52 | |
| 800 | 12.9+ | 56 | High |
| 825 | 12.9+ | 60 | functioning |
| 850 | 12.9+ | 63 | for real life |

All data in this illustration have been culled from the norms book (1987) and, of course, all are approximate. But, here is the point: This table provides a useful benchmark (TABE SS 725) that can be used to chart student growth, estimate students' GED prospects, and show students their prospects for effective adult functioning in these cognitive areas. This is what is missing from the present potpourri of scales and norms in the TABE program. A useful fourth column in such a table would include ITED/ACT standard scores; thus students who had grown rapidly in the TABE program could begin to consider college possibilities.

In summary, the 1987 TABE program is not yet a magnificent symphony orchestra that will do justice to a magnificent music hall—but it is close. This reviewer agrees with Flynt, who called this newest edition a marked improvement over earlier versions. Pending the arrival of TABE Forms 7 and 8, one can recommend TABE Forms 5 and 6 for adult programs aimed at diagnosing weak skills and measuring cognitive growth.

## References

American Council on Education. (1987). *GED teacher's manual for the official practice tests* (2nd ed.). Englewood Cliffs, NJ: Prentice-Hall Regents.

Bauernfeind, R.H. (1986). Tests of Adult Basic Education. In D.J. Keyser & R.C. Sweetland, *Test critiques* (Vol. V, pp. 494–498). Austin, TX: PRO-ED.

Flynt, E.S. (1990). Tests of Adult Basic Education, Forms 5 and 6. In R.B. Cooter (Ed.), *The teacher's guide to reading tests* (pp. 98–107). Scottsdale, AZ: Gorsuch Scarisbrick.

*TABE examiner's manual.* (1987). Monterey, CA: CTB/McGraw-Hill.

*TABE norms book.* (1987). Monterey, CA: CTB/MCGraw-Hill.

*TABE technical report.* (1978). Monterey, CA: CTB/MCGraw-Hill.

*TABE technical report.* (1987). Monterey, CA: CTB/McGraw-Hill.

**Jan Hankins, Ph.D.**
*Senior Research Associate, University of Tennessee, Knoxville, Tennessee.*

# TESTS OF GENERAL EDUCATIONAL DEVELOPMENT

*GED Testing Service Staff and Consultants. Washington, D.C.: American Council on Education.*

## Introduction

The Tests of General Educational Development (GED) are designed to measure the major and lasting outcomes generally associated with 4 years of high school education. The primary purpose of the GED is to provide individuals with the opportunity to earn a high school equivalency diploma. The tests are designed to measure an individual's knowledge of broad concepts and his or her ability to use information to solve problems. Specific facts, details, and definitions are not measured. The focus of the test is on the *use* of knowledge and information rather than on recitation of facts. Items require critical thinking and problem solving.

All states, the District of Columbia, most U.S. territories, and Canadian provinces, as well as employers and college and university admissions policies accept the GED credential or GED test report in lieu of a high school diploma or transcript. About 95% of 2,236 postsecondary institutions accept the GED. Fewer Canadian universities accept it, however (Spille, 1982).

About 700,000 to 800,000 people take the GED tests every year. Cervero (1983) concluded that nearly 15% of the high school diplomas awarded in the United States are based on GED tests. Since its beginning, over 10 million adults have earned their high school equivalency through the GED. There are over 3,000 official GED testing centers. Testing is also provided for military personnel stationed overseas, persons in federal and state correctional and health institutions, and American civilians and foreign nationals overseas.

The GED is administered through the American Council on Education (ACE). The first editions of the GED were developed in 1942 by the U.S. Armed Forces Institute (USAFI) to aid active duty military personnel who had not received a traditional high school diploma in future educational endeavors and employment once they were no longer in the armed forces. The Veterans Testing Service (VTS) was charged with administration of the GED test battery. During the 1950s, many states requested and received permission to administer the GED tests to civilian adults who had not received a high school diploma. The GED testing program changed from one serving only military personnel to one serving both military personnel and civilians. By 1959, civilians represented the majority of test takers. In recognition of this, the VTS was renamed the General Educational Development Testing Service (GEDTS) in 1963.

During the 40-year history of the GED testing program, the nature and purpose of the test battery has remained essentially the same. However, the GED tests are periodically updated. There have been three generations of GED tests since its original inception. The original five tests, used from 1947 to 1978, were titled Correctness and Effectiveness of Expression, Interpretation of Reading Materials in the Social Sciences, Interpretation of Reading Materials in the Natural Sciences, Interpretation of Literary Materials, and General Mathematical Ability. In the early 1970s, the original test specifications were changed. New specifications that were more consistent with secondary school curriculum and that included a larger variety of source materials relevant to the lives of adults were written. This led to the introduction of a new battery of tests in 1978: Writing Skills, Social Studies, Science, Reading Skills, and Mathematics.

The third generation of GED tests was introduced in 1988. In the mid-1980s, a committee of secondary school and adult education specialists defined another set of specifications to which the GED items were matched. These specifications were constructed from a representative sample of high school curriculum and skills. The committee charged with creating the new specifications consisted of many teachers, curriculum specialists, and content experts. The committee's report focused on the following themes: (a) the tests should demand higher level thinking and problem-solving skills; (b) the tests should emphasize the relationship of the skills measured to the workplace; (c) the tests should acknowledge the impact of computer technology. (This includes the way in which computers affect the lives of examinees rather than the skills required to operate and/or program a computer. The panel rejected testing knowledge of programming languages, hardware operations, or specific programs. Thus, the GED tests do not measure computer proficiency or literacy.) (d) The tests should address consumer skills; (e) the tests should use settings adult examinees would recognize; and (f) calculators should not be used. There were two *major* changes in the tests introduced in 1988: the Writing Skills test was expanded to include an essay, and there was a greater emphasis placed on higher level thinking skills in the multiple-choice items.

Testing times have been reduced significantly from the original GED tests. The original battery could be completed in about 10 hours of testing time. The second-generation battery could be completed in about 6 hours. With the inclusion of the essay, the newest version of the GED battery can be completed in about 7 hours. These time limits are sufficient to allow 85% or more of examinees to complete the tests while working at a comfortable pace. Thus, the GED tests are not considered speeded. Once examinees finish a test, they may proceed to the next one if administrative circumstances permit.

English-language GED tests are available in U.S. and Canadian editions. The Canadian edition was developed to separate specifications (e.g., the Social Studies test focuses on Canadian social studies, and all five Canadian tests use the metric measurement system). There are also Spanish and French editions of the tests available. Although the specifications to which these tests were developed are similar to the English editions, they are unique tests, not just translations. Emphasis within a content area may be altered to reflect language differences. The Spanish version includes a sixth 2-hour test of English for states that require it.

There are also audiocassette versions of the GED test battery for both English- and Spanish-language editions. Braille and large-print editions are available for individuals who are physically handicapped or who have a diagnosed educational disability. These editions, unlike the French and Spanish editions, are identical to the regular English language GED tests.

There are five separately timed GED tests. With the exception of Part II of the Writing Skills test, all items are 5-option multiple choice. The five components of GED tests break down as follows:

1. Writing Skills:
   - Part I—55 items, 75 minutes
     - 35% Sentence Structure
     - 35% Usage
     - 30% Spelling, Punctuation, and Capitalization
   - Part II—Essay, 45 minutes
2. Social Studies (64 items, 85 minutes):
   - 25% History
   - 20% Economics
   - 20% Political Science
   - 15% Geography (20% in Canada)
   - 20% Behavioral Science (15% in Canada)
3. Science (66 items, 95 minutes):
   - 50% Life Science (Biology)
   - 50% Physical Science (Earth Science, Physics, and Chemistry)
4. Interpreting Literature and the Arts (45 items, 65 minutes):
   - 50% Popular Literature
   - 25% Classical Literature
   - 25% Commentary on Literature and the Arts
5. Mathematics (56 items, 90 minutes):
   - 50% Arithmetic
     - 30% Measurement
     - 10% Number Relationships
     - 10% Data Analysis
   - 30% Algebra
   - 20% Geometry

In the multiple-choice Writing Skills test, examinees are required to perform a variety of tasks. Sentence correction requires the examinee to identify what is wrong with a sentence and how it should be corrected. Sentence revision requires an examinee to determine how to correct an underlined section of a sentence. Construction shift measures the ability to rewrite existing items using a different structure while maintaining the overall relationship between ideas. The essay presents an issue or situation familiar to examinees. It requires no specialized knowledge, but asks examinees to present a point of view or explain a situation. The essay is restricted to expository writing to help control for topic variability. All topics for the essay are of approximately equal length, reading level, and format.

For the writing test, the multiple-choice items and essay are combined and reported as one composite standard score. The multiple-choice section of the Writing Skills test comprises 60% to 65% of the composite score, while the essay comprises 35% to 40%. The differences in weights are due to differences in difficulty in the essay and multiple-choice items. The essay is weighted as heavily as possible without diminishing the estimated test-retest reliability below a level acceptable to the GEDTS. The reliability of the weighted composite score cannot be less than the test-retest reliability for the old multiple-choice Writing Skills test taken alone. This is usually .90 for high school seniors and .85 for GED examinees.

The Social Studies test measures the individual's ability to use knowledge and information about social studies concepts. Recall of facts is not tested. The Behavioral Science section includes items on anthropology, psychology, and sociology. All Social Studies and Science items are based on either a written or graphic stimulus. About two thirds have a written stimulus and about one third (20–40%) have a graphic stimulus. A written stimulus may be up to 50 words. More than one item may be based on a stimulus, and these are called "item sets." Item sets may consist of up to 250 words or a graphic followed by four to six items. About two thirds of the items present in item sets, while about one third stand alone. Abstract reasoning and problem solving are very important aspects of the Science test.

The reading selections used as stimuli in Interpreting Literature and the Arts range from 200 to 400 words and are written at a level of difficulty appropriate for an average high school student. All items are based entirely on reading selections, and no prior knowledge of literature or familiarity with the vocabulary of literary analysis or criticism is required. All selections are preceded by a purpose question, which highlights the focus of the reading.

In the Mathematics test, 30–40% of the items may be solved using ratio and proportion techniques. Approximately 15% involve identifying a correct formula from among a list of formulas and solving. About two thirds of the Mathematics items have a written stimulus, and about one third have a graphic stimulus.

More detailed information on the test content and test description may be found in *The Official Teacher's Guide to the Tests of General Educational Development* (GED Testing Service, 1987a).

The GED uses a cognitive skills hierarchy to describe the skills measured by the items. This hierarchy is a modification of Bloom's (1956) taxonomy and contains five levels:

1. *Comprehension*—measures the ability to restate information, summarize ideas, and identify implications.
2. *Application*—measures the ability to use ideas in a new or different context.
3. *Analysis*—measures the ability to distinguish between facts and hypotheses or opinions, recognize assumptions, distinguish conclusions from supporting statements, or identify cause-effect relationships.
4. *Synthesis*—measures the ability to produce hypotheses, theories, and so forth. Only the essay exam is classified as synthesis.
5. *Evaluation*—measures the adequacy or appropriateness of data to support hypotheses or conclusions, recognize the role of values in beliefs and decision making, assess the accuracy of facts determined by documentation, and indicate logical fallacies.

The percentages of items at each cognitive area are equal in the Social Studies and Science tests (i.e., Evaluation, 20%; Analysis, 30%; Application, 30%; Comprehension, 30%). In Interpreting Literature and the Arts, 60% of the items are Comprehension. Two types of Comprehension items are used: literal, which measures an individual's ability to restate information or ideas or to summarize ideas, and inferential, which measures the ability to identify implications, understand consequences, and draw conclusions. Of the remaining items, 15% are Application and 25% are Analysis.

The ability to read and understand written material is a basic skill required for all subject test areas. Many items are based on written or graphic stimulus materials, requiring the student to use the information provided in the stimulus in some fashion to answer the items. Selections used as stimulus materials in the GED tests are not screened using readability formulas because these formulas do not take into account the level of abstraction contained in the material. Instead, stimulus materials are chosen through a process of review by teachers and content experts. All stimulus materials are field tested and may be removed based on reviewer advice or student data.

The GED tests are normative. That is, they compare the performance of GED examinees with the performance of graduating high school seniors. Graduating high school seniors were chosen as a norm group because of the GED test's purpose to measure the lasting outcomes of 4 years of high school education. The developers of the GED felt that examinees who receive a GED credential should perform similarly to graduating high school seniors.

Although training courses are available for individuals who wish to prepare for the GED, candidates are not required to complete a course in order to take the test. Libraries and bookstores often carry GED study materials, and there is also a television series carried by cable and most public television stations that guides students in preparation. There are practice versions of the GED available in English (U.S. and Canadian) and Spanish editions. The purpose of the practice tests is to help examinees determine if they are ready to take the regular GED. The practice tests provide practice in test-taking skills and in using the answer sheets. The same specifications were used to develop the practice tests as were used to develop the regular tests. Practice tests are about half as long as the regular tests and scores are reported on the same standard score scale. The practice tests have acceptable reliability for their purpose. Predictive validity has not been established yet for the 1987 administration of the practice tests, however.

**Practical Applications/Uses**

As mentioned previously, the GED tests are designed to measure the lasting outcomes associated with a 4-year high school education. These tests may be used for the purpose of awarding a high school equivalency diploma or as an early exit examination in some states. Testing high school graduates or graduates of other adult education programs is prohibited. Although some employers and postsecondary education institutions have required high school graduates to take the GED to verify their level of educational achievement, this violates the purpose for which the GED tests were intended. The tests may not be used in such a fashion except when they comprise part of a research study conducted by or authorized by the GEDTS.

Retesting of persons who have already received a GED credential may be done if, and only if, a higher score is required for admission to a postsecondary educational institution or an employer requires scores to exceed current requirements of the jurisdiction.

The official GED practice tests are not designed to serve as diagnostic tests; there are too few items in each category to produce reliably precise indications of deficiencies. The practice tests may, however, be used in a pretest-posttest methodology as *one* measure of training program effectiveness. They are not to be used as a graduation or completion requirement at the end of an adult education course.

The *Teacher's Manual for the Official Practice Tests* (GED Testing Service, 1987b) provides information on the current use of the practice tests. The practice tests may be used to (a) determine a student's readiness to take the full-length GED, (b) help students identify areas in which they may need additional study, and (c) provide experience in taking tests under standardized conditions. The manual also describes inappropriate uses of the practice tests, which include (a) administration to examinees known to be deficient in preparation, (b) administration as a graduation or completion requirement at the end of an adult education course or program, (c) administration to examinees who have not been informed about the limitations of the test and appropriate use of test scores, (d) administration to the same individual repeatedly (more than twice), (e) use of item clusters within the tests as the sole source of information for diagnosing need for remediation, and (f) use to evaluate the effectiveness of teachers.

Not all individuals are eligible to take the regular GED tests. Individuals are eligible to take the GED only if they are not currently enrolled in high school, have not graduated from high school, or meet requirements set by the state, territory, or province in which they reside. These requirements specify minimum age, length of time since leaving school, and residence requirements. The nearest GED Testing Center or the Department of Education in the state, territory, or province may provide interested individuals with information on local requirements.

Administration of the GED tests takes place at an official GED testing center. Each testing center has a chief examiner, responsible for testing at the entire center. There must be one examiner or proctor to 20 or fewer candidates. Candidates taking the GED for the first time must be given the opportunity to complete all five tests before retesting on any one test. It is recommended that the initial testing be completed in two testing sessions within a maximum period of 6 weeks.

Retesting is permitted. Some jurisdictions may require a waiting period before retesting, however. An individual may retest over an entire battery or individual test(s). The criteria for retesting are established by the Department of Education in each jurisdiction. There is no limit on the total number of times an individual may be retested, although availability of alternate forms may limit the number of possible retestings in a 12-month period to two (the initial exam and two retestings). If an examinee is retested, a different form of the English edition must be administered. No form is designed exclusively for retesting. A different form of the Spanish, French, audiocassette, large-print, and braille editions is required if available.

Special administrations may be arranged at the candidate's request and with the approval of the chief examiner and the state GED administrator. The examiner's manual (GED Testing Service, 1989) contains in-depth information on the problems that warrant special administration, the adaptation allowed, and documentation required.

The examiner's manual is quite complete and easy to follow. Instructions are specific and clear, with examples provided when needed. The manual is divided into sections, which makes administration easier, as one simply turns to the test administration section rather than having to search through the entire manual to find specific directions for administration.

Each jurisdiction determines the minimum passing score, age, or other qualifications for the GED tests. It is recommended that these all be consistent for the French, Spanish, and English versions. Although each jurisdiction sets its own passing score, jurisdictions must require at least one of the following conditions: examinees obtain a standard score of 40 or more on each of the five tests, or examinees get an average standard score of 45 or above on all five tests. The jurisdictions may require higher, but not lower, standards. This lowest minimum score means that to qualify for a GED credential, individuals must demonstrate a level of proficiency higher than that of about 30% of the norm group.

Scoring of the multiple-choice items may be done either using templates or by sending answer sheets to a centralized location that may have mechanical scoring. There is no penalty for guessing.

For the essay, two trained raters score the essay independently using holistic (or general impression) scoring. Holistic scoring is basically a process of rank-ordering papers. A scoring guide helps to control for drifting of standards (i.e., what score you receive depends on who you are compared with). Holistic scoring was chosen because it is quick, relatively simple, and efficient for a large number of essays, and because it offers the most accessible method of obtaining a high degree of correlation between the essay and multiple-choice components of the Writing Skills test. Handwriting is not considered. The score the individual receives on the essay is the average of the two ratings. Raters may differ by 1 point. If more than 1 point separates the two ratings, a third rater reads the essay. The total score is equal to twice the average of the sum of the three scores. A detailed scoring guide exists for readers to use in assigning scores to the essay. This guide is detailed, yet generic enough so that it may be used for all topics and readings. This guide helps to provide scale stability across topics, readers, and scoring sessions. Length is not specified in the scoring guide. The directions to the students suggest "about 200 words," but this is for the benefit of the examinee, not the reader. Readers must assign a whole number score to the essay.

Essays are scored at a decentralized scoring site. Rigorous procedures are in place for controlling and monitoring essay scoring. There are several scoring options available for the essay. First, the GED has an essay scoring service. There are three scoring sites in Iowa, which are coordinated by the Iowa GED Administrator. Each jurisdiction may have its own scoring site(s), and commercial scoring services may be used. For those jurisdictions that elect to have their own scoring site, there is usually only one site for the entire jurisdiction. Each scoring site has a chief reader and alternate chief reader who are trained at one central site with one set of materials. The chief reader is then responsible for training and certifying site readers. Once readers have been certified, a site must be certified. Patience and Auchter (1989) provide detailed information on the selection and training of readers, site certification, and monitoring of sites.

For the subtests, scale scores may range from 20 to 80 for each test. This score scale is a T-score, with a mean of 50 and standard deviation of 10, and a normal distribution. The essay score ranges from 1 to 6 for each rater (2 to 12 for both). This 1-to-6 scale has no midpoint and forces raters away from the tendency to drift toward the middle. The score of the essay is then combined with the multiple-choice section and the composite raw score placed on the common score scale.

**Technical Aspects**

As mentioned previously, the GED tests are normative. Candidate performance is evaluated relative to the demonstrated achievement of a representative sample of graduating high school seniors. High school seniors were chosen as the norm group because the achievement represented by a high school diploma and the GED diploma should be equivalent. Thus, a national sample of graduating high school seniors was used in establishing the standard score scales for the GED. Norming studies, conducted periodically to establish new sets of norms, have taken place in 1943, 1955, 1967, 1977, 1980, and 1987.

In 1987, over 20,000 high school seniors in more than 1,000 high schools took pairs of the five GED tests. Approximately 1,000 subjects took all five tests. The school population chosen for the norming study included all public and nonpublic schools that had students enrolled in Grade 12 except those that did not graduate a senior class, did not enroll their own students but received students enrolled in other schools, or were exclusively schools for handicapped or special education students. Eligible schools were stratified according to geographic region and nature (public or nonpublic). For the public schools, districts were stratified according to socioeconomic status information. Each of five geographic regions contained approximately 20% of the 12th-grade enrollment. A sample of schools was chosen by randomly selecting schools in each stratum in proportion to their estimated Grade 12 enrollment. Testing was done in April and May. Within each school, a list of eligible students was prepared by school officials. All senior students were eligible except those who would not receive a high school diploma prior to September 1987 or those who were handicapped to the extent that a special administration would have been required.

The norm group for the Canadian edition of the GED was drawn from graduating Grade 12 students in Canada. Norm groups for the Spanish-language edition were drawn from graduating seniors in Puerto Rico. The French edition was standardized using the results of high school seniors in New Brunswick and Quebec, Canada.

The average of the five standard scores on the 1988 GED tests were about the same as in 1980. Scores on the Science and Social Studies were higher in 1988 than in 1980; scores in Interpreting Literature and the Arts were about the same as the 1980 Reading Skills test. Scores were lower on the Mathematics and Writing Skills test in 1988 than in 1980. Preliminary results indicate that pass rates for the 1988 GED are slightly lower than the 1980 pass rates. Pass rates are expected to increase as preparation for the new test increases.

For the 1987 English-language standardization administration of the regular GED, KR-20 reliabilities ranged from .90 to .94. The standard errors of measurement ranged from 2.63 to 3.18. For the 1988 standardization administration, KR-20 reliabilities ranged from .90 to .95, with standard errors of measurement ranging from 2.34 to 3.28. These reliabilities and standard errors of measurement are for high school seniors and may be slightly different for GED examinees. (See GED Testing Service, 1987c, for additional information.)

Whitney, Malizio, and Patience (1985) discuss the internal consistency and parallel forms reliability of GED tests administered in 1980. The slightly lower KR-20 reliabilities observed for the GED examinees may be attributed to several sources. First, the distribution of GED examinees tends to be slightly positively skewed, rather than normal. Second, the distribution of GED examinees tends to be more homogeneous and less variable (W. Patience, personal communication, December 1989).

Studies are currently under way to further assess the reliabilities of the 1988 multiple-choice GED tests. The most recent results indicate that reliabilities for the 1988 GED tests are slightly higher than the 1980 administration, with reliabilities ranging from .91 to .93 for GED candidates. This increase in reliability may be attributed to greater variance among the candidates and higher item discrimination indices (W. Patience, personal communication, December 1989).

The GED tests are evaluated for content validity, concurrent validity, and predictive validity. Although much research has been done on the previous editions of the GED, little has appeared in the way of formal studies on the validity of the 1988 GED multiple-choice tests because not enough time has elapsed since its introduction. Initial studies of concurrent validity and predictive validity are promising, however, showing validities similar to or higher than those found for the 1980 GED tests (W. Patience, personal communication, December 1989).

Whitney et al. (1985) make a strong case for the content and concurrent validity of the 1980 GED tests. The magnitude of these reported intercorrelations suggest that the GED tests are strongly related but also measure somewhat distinct skills and knowledge. If the tests measured the same skills, one would expect the correlations to be slightly higher than those observed. Similarly, if the tests measured completely different skills, one would expect the correlations to be slightly lower than those observed.

A number of studies have focused on the predictive validity of the GED tests. Several studies have suggested that a GED credential is helpful in obtaining employment and that the GED credential can increase an individual's opportunity for promotions and pay raises (Carson, 1986; Cervero, 1983; Valentine & Darkenwald, 1986). In addition, studies have shown that many employers accept a GED credential as equivalent to a high school diploma when making decisions about hiring, salary levels, and promotions (Carson, 1986). GED credential holders are most often employed in craft and repair trades (Ladner, 1986). Another study has shown that although persons holding a GED credential are more likely to be employed and earn a higher wage than individuals who have neither a GED credential nor a high school diploma, individuals with a high school diploma are more likely to be employed and earn a higher wage than those with the GED credential (Passmore, 1987).

Some studies have attempted to establish the predictive validity of the GED tests by looking at the relationship of the GED tests and college or community college grades. These studies have generally found that there is little difference between individuals with a GED credential and those with a regular high school diploma with regard to academic success in a community college (Wilson, Davis, & Davis, 1981; Wolf, 1980), program completion and employment placement (Wilson et al., 1981), and academic success in first-year studies at a small Canadian university (Colert, 1983). One study did find, however, that those individuals with a regular high school diploma were more likely to be attending a postsecondary institution than those with a GED credential (Ladner, 1986). All these studies, though focusing on slightly different outcome variables, all suggest the predictive validity of the GED tests.

There are three reliability concerns in essay tests. The first is scale stability, or the degree to which raters uniformly apply a defined score scale in scoring essays both within readings and across readings. The second reliability concern is reading reliability, the consistency with which raters in a given reading award the same scores to a particular set of essays. The third concern is score reliability, or the consistency with which an individual receives the same score on two similar, equally demanding essays.

Score scale drift, or the tendency of raters to change the way in which they apply standards of behavior over time, may impact the accuracy of score scale stability without affecting interrater reliability. The GEDTS uses systematic and random monitoring techniques to eliminate score scale drift. For the systematic monitoring process, scoring sites are mailed four sets of 10 essays to be included in the next scoring session. All four sets of essays are read by each reader. The scores assigned by the readers are then compared against the scores assigned by the writing committee. For the random monitoring process, a random sample of 40 essays is selected from each site. The scores given to the essays by the site readers are masked, and the writing committee members read each essay and assign a score independently. Scores are discussed and recorded for each essay, then compared. Random monitoring differs from systematic monitoring in two important ways. First, readers are not aware that they are being evaluated; and second, the essays and topics vary across sites. (See Patience & Auchter [1989] for complete results of these monitoring processes.) Results suggest that it is possible to maintain score scale stability across multiple scoring sites even when the distributions of scores across the sites varies.

To help assure a high degree of reading reliability and maintain score stability, the GEDTS trains and certifies all readers, certifies scoring sites to ensure that the scoring site performs well enough to score essays, and monitors scoring sites to evaluate whether the site's performance warrants continued certification to score essays. The GEDTS uses three additional methods to assess reading reliability. The first is the percentage of readers giving the same scores, contiguous scores (scores differing by 1 point), and discrepant scores (scores differing by 2 or more points). Second, correlations of first and second ratings are obtained. Third, means between the first and second ratings are compared. To assess score stability (the consistency of an essay score given on the same essay on two separate readings), the correlations of scores and comparison of mean scores for reading are obtained.

All potential essay topics are reviewed by the GED Writing Committee. To ensure that the topics use the same skills and are of comparable difficulty, all potential topics are field tested with GED examinees and high school seniors.

Essays are scored to determine if the examinees have sufficient information to respond in the rhetorical form intended. Scores are analyzed to ensure that examinees perform as well as they did on previous actual essays. Topics are retained or rejected based on the judgment of the writing committee and statistical analysis. The statistical analysis includes the Kruskal-Wallis test of homogeneity of score distributions and a test of the equality of correlations between the multiple choice and essay scores. Only topics that yield nonsignificant results on both tests are retained.

The validity of indirect measures of writing have been frequently challenged (e.g., Bamberg, 1982, Charney, 1984; Godshalk, Swineford, & Coffman, 1966). This, in part, led to the addition of the essay examination for measuring writing skills. The addition of the essay has improved the test's content validity. To assess concurrent validity, GEDTS computed the correlation between scores earned on the 1980 multiple-choice GED Writing Skills test and scores earned on the essay component. For high school seniors, the correlations between essay scores and scores on the Writing Skills test ranged from .55 to .69, depending on the essay topic (Swartz & Whitney, 1985). The magnitude of these correlations suggest that the two tests are measuring related but somewhat different sets of skills. The overall validity of the test was improved by combining reliable scores from an indirect measure of writing with a more valid (though less reliable) direct measure of writing. This is consistent with previous research findings (Godshalk et al., 1966; White, 1985).

## Critique

The GED is both well researched and well documented. A bibliography of the GED this reviewer obtained contained well over 300 listings. The *GED Research Briefs*, published periodically by the GEDTS, contain summaries of completed research relating to the development, use, and interpretation of the GED tests. The studies I read on the GED were conducted in a manner consistent with well-accepted research practices.

One aspect of the GED that does seem problematic concerns a study conducted to set the time limits for each subtest. This study did not use a representative sample of examinees, a serious methodological limitation. Only examinees in New Jersey, New York, and Pennsylvania were used to establish the time limits, with examinees in Wisconsin serving as a cross-validation sample. One is left to wonder if different time limits would be established if some examinees from poorer states or states in a different geographic region were included in the sample. In addition, the study made no reference to whether examinees serving as the subjects were mainly from urban or rural areas. If they were mainly from urban areas, one is left to wonder how including rural-dwelling examinees would affect the time limits. Despite the limitations of this study, use of these time limits in the testing situation has suggested that they are sufficient to allow 85% or more of the examinees to finish the test while working at a comfortable pace.

This reviewer was unable to find any reference to whether bias studies have been carried out on the GED, and if so, which methodology or methodologies have been used. If no such studies have been performed to date, they would make a valuable addition to current GED research.

Research to date on the GED has used classical measurement analyses and equapercentile equating (W. Patience, personal communication, December 1989). Classical measurement analyses have a number of problems, some of which have been delineated by Hambleton and van der Linden (1982) and by Hambleton and Swaminathan (1985). First, the values of the item statistics (e.g., the difficulty and discrimination indices) are dependent on the particular sample of examinees upon which they are based; thus the average ability level and range of ability scores influence, perhaps substantially, the value of the classical item statistics. Second, the assessment of classical test reliability is related to the variability of the examinees' scores; the greater the variability, the greater the reliability (this phenomenon has already been noted for the GED).

Third, test reliability relies heavily on the concept of parallel forms, which are often difficult if not impossible to achieve in practice. Hambleton and van der Linden (1982) have noted that test administrators must be content with either lower bound estimates of reliability or estimates of reliability with unknown biases. Fourth, classical measurement provides no basis for determining how an examinee might perform on any given item; this ability could be extremely useful when choosing new items to include on the test.

Fifth, classical measurement assumes that the standard error of measurement is the same for all examinees, which is not a valid assumption. It can be demonstrated that some examinees perform more consistently than others and that the standard error of measurement varies with test score (Feldt, Steffen, & Gupta, 1985; Mollenkopf, 1949). The consistency of performance may covary with ability. Sixth, classical methods of assessing bias are not usually successful because they cannot take into account true differences in ability among the groups of interest. Last, equating using classical methodologies can also be problematic (Hambleton & Swaminathan, 1985).

Given the large number of individuals taking the GED, it would seem highly desirable that some sort of item response theory (IRT) analysis of the GED be done and that different GED forms be equated using IRT methodologies. IRT analysis holds a number of advantages over classical measurement. IRT estimates of examinees' ability are independent of the sample of items administered. Second, the item characteristics (statistics) are independent of the sample of examinees used to calibrate the items. Third, an Information Index, which indicates the precision with which an examinee's ability is estimated, is provided. Another advantage of IRT is that its assumptions may be tested, while those of classical test theory cannot. With its emphasis on item-free and person-free measurement and the use of information rather than reliability, IRT would seem to serve the GED well. If the scale on which the typical IRT analysis is done is of concern, any linear transformation would suffice to remove negative values from score reports.

While research on equating has not yet provided any clearly definitive answers as to which type of equating is best in any given situation, three-parameter IRT equating has consistently shown positive results, while results for equapercentile equating have been mixed. Thus, although equapercentile equating may be adequate for the GED, three-parameter IRT equating would serve just as well and would be part and parcel of the regular IRT analysis so no special equating would need to be carried out. In their review of equating studies, Skaggs and Lissitz (1986) suggest that it is advisable for any testing program to have the ability to use several equating methodologies and compare their effectiveness for the specific application to which the test is being put. They also suggest establishing a sample on which to cross-validate results. These suggestions would certainly serve the GED well, given the importance of the use of GED test scores.

### References

Bamberg, B. (1982). Multiple-choice and holistic essay scores: What are they measuring? *College Composition and Communication, 33,* 404–406.

Bloom, B.S. (1956). *Taxonomy of educational objectives handbook I: Cognitive domain.* New York: David McKay.

Breland, H.M. (1986, April). *Study objectives and outcomes of reliability and predictive validity analyses.* Paper presented at the annual meeting of the American Educational Research Association, San Francisco, CA.

Carson, B.W. (1986, August). *Acceptance of General Educational Development (GED) in hiring policies of Denver area employers* (GED Research Brief No. 11). Washington, DC: American Council on Education.

Cervero, R.M. (1983, April). *A national survey of GED test candidates: Preparation, performance, and 18 month outcomes.* Paper presented at the annual meeting of the American Educational Research Association, Montreal, Quebec.

Charney, D. (1984). The validity of using holistic scoring to evaluate writing: A critical review. *Research in the Teaching of English, 18,* 69–71.

Colert, S. (1983, December). *High school equivalency and high school diploma students at Brandon University: A comparison of academic success* (GED Research Brief No. 15). Washington, DC: American Council on Education.

Feldt, L., Steffen, M., & Gupta, N. (1985). A comparison of five methods for estimating the standard error of measurement at specific score levels. *Applied Psychological Measurement, 9,* 351–361.

GED Testing Service. (1987a). *The official teacher's guide to the Tests of General Educational Development.* Chicago: Contemporary Books.

GED Testing Service. (1987b). *Teacher's manual for the Official Practice Tests* (2nd ed.). Englewood Cliffs, NJ: Cambridge Adult Education.

GED Testing Service. (1987c). *Tests of General Educational Development reliabilities and standard errors of measurement: 1987 standardization administration.* Washington, DC: American Council on Education.

GED Testing Service. (1989). *1989 examiner's manual for the Tests of General Educational Development.* Washington, DC: American Council on Education.

Godshalk, F. Swineford, E., & Coffman, W. (1966). *The measurement of writing ability.* New York: College Entrance Examination Board.

Hambleton, R.K., & Swaminathan, H. (1985). *Item response theory: Principles and applications.* Boston: Kluwer-Nijhoff.

Hambleton, R.K., & van der Linden, W.J. (1982). Advances in item response theory and applications: An introduction. *Applied Psychological Measurement, 6,* 373–378.

Ladner, R.A. (1986). *Educational and occupational activities of GED and conventional high school graduates in Florida* (GED Research Brief No. 8). Washington, DC: American Council on Education.

Mollenkopf, W. (1949). Variation of the standard error of measurement. *Psychometrika, 14,* 189–229.

Passmore, D.L. (1987, September). *Employment of young GED recipients* (GED Research Brief No. 14). Washington, DC: American Council on Education.

Patience, W., & Auchter, J. (1989, April). *Monitoring score scale stability and reading reliability in decentralized large-scale essay scoring programs.* Paper presented at the annual meeting of the National Testing Network in Writing, Montreal, Quebec, Canada.

Skaggs, G., & Lissitz, R.W. (1986). Test equating: Relevant issues and a review of recent research. *Review of Educational Research, 56,* 495–529.

Spille, H.A. (1982, March). *Interpreting the GED scores of college applicants who have earned a high school equivalency credential* (GEDTS Memo #23). Washington, DC: American Council on Education.

Swartz, R., & Whitney, D.R. (1985, June). *The relationship between scores on the GED Writing Skills Test and on direct measures of writing* (GED Testing Service, Research Studies, No. 6). Washington, DC: American Council on Education.

Valentine, T., & Darkenwald, G.G. (1986). The benefits of GED graduation and a typology of graduates. *Adult Education Quarterly, 87,* 23–37.

White, E.M. (1985). *Teaching and assessing writing.* San Francisco: Jossey-Bass.

Whitney, D.R., Malizio, A.G., & Patience, W.M. (1985, May). *The reliability and validity of the GED Tests* (GED Research Brief No. 6). Washington, DC: American Council on Education.

Wilson, R.C., Davis, P.D., & Davis, J.C., Sr. (1981, April). *The success of high school diploma and GED equivalency students in vocational programs at Lake City Community College, Florida* (GED Research Brief No. 4). Washington, DC: American Council on Education.

Wolf, J.C. (1980, March). *Predictive validity of the GED Tests for two-year college study South Plains College, Texas* (GED Research Brief No. 1). Washington, DC: American Council on Education.

**Dan Zakay, Ph.D.**

*Senior Lecturer, Department of Psychology, Tel Aviv University, Ramat Aviv, Israel.*

# TIME USE ANALYZER

*Albert A. Canfield. Los Angeles, California: Western Psychological Services.*

## Introduction

The Time Use Analyzer (TUA) was developed as a tool for providing "a yardstick against which individuals can compare their relative feelings about how their time is being utilized" (Canfield, 1990, p. 1). There is no doubt that time management is an important factor influencing everyone's life. Mackenzie (1977) calls time the "critical resource," and Saifullah and Kleiner (1988) claim that "how you arrange your time is how you arrange your life" (p. 60). Hence, a tool for helping people in analyzing the way they use time is needed.

The TUA is an intuitive instrument based on practical experience gained in time management workshops and seminars. It is not a theory-based instrument, neither is it supported by any empirical study.

The TUA materials consist of a manual accompanied by response sheets and a scoring sheet (the last two are bound together). Scores transfer from the response sheet to the scoring sheet via carbon paper. Respondents are asked to examine the time they spend engaged in the following eight areas of life activities:

1. *Work*—time spent at work, on the job, at home, on trips, and so forth.
2. *Sleep*—regular sleep, naps, sleeping in, and so forth.
3. *Personal Hygiene*—bathing, dressing, hair care, and so forth.
4. *Personal/Family Business*—shopping, banking, check writing, home and yard maintenance, cleaning, and so forth.
5. *Community/Church*—time spent at church, in church events, club activities, and political activities.
6. *Family/Home*—time with spouse, children, and other relatives in family activities (movies, sports events, etc.), watching TV, casual reading, conversation, and so forth.
7. *Education/Development*—job or career-related study, training sessions, seminars, professional reading, professional meetings, and so forth.
8. *Recreation/Hobbies*—golfing, boating, woodworking, collecting antiques, hunting, bicycling, fishing, and so forth.

Regarding each one of these life activities areas, respondents are asked to think how much time they would like to spend relative to the amount of time they actually spend. One response out of five is to be selected and marked in an appropriate column for each area. The response categories are "a lot less time," "a little less time," "no more or no less time," "a little more time," and "a lot more time."

Next, respondents are asked to choose three areas that are most important to them and to rate each by placing one of the following importance weights in the corresponding box in the appropriate column: 4 (most important), 3 (second most important), or 2 (third most important). All other areas are actually assigned an importance weight of 1, although this is not specified in the manual on the response or scoring sheets.

Scoring and interpreting the TUA is simple, and the procedure is well explained in the manual. Scoring is done on the scoring sheet provided. When one starts to score, one response out of five is already marked on the response sheet. Two numbers are preassigned to each possible response and are preprinted on the scoring sheet. One number reflects the level of dissatisfaction (D) with time use. These D factors are identical for each response category across all eight life activities areas. The D factors are 0 for "no more or no less time," 1 for "a little more time" and for "a little less time," and 3 for "a lot more time" as well as for "a lot less time." The higher the D factor, the higher the level of dissatisfaction. The second factor reflects the level of typicalness (T) of each response. The factors differ for various response categories in various areas, reflecting the percentages of respondents in a normative group that chose each specific response category in each area. The T values range from 0 to 5.

Two total scores can be calculated: the Total Dissatisfaction score and the Total Typicalness score. The Typicalness score shows how typical one's responses are compared to the normative group. The Dissatisfaction score reflects how satisfied one is with the way his or her time is spent. The total Typicalness score is obtained by summing up the eight T scores attached to the eight response categories selected across eight life activities areas. The total Dissatisfaction score is obtained by first multiplying each D score attached to each chosen response in each area by the importance weight assigned to that area, then summing up all eight products.

Interpretation of the total scores is done by comparing the obtained scores with a profile table on the back of the scoring sheet. This comparison enables each respondent to locate the percentage of normative group respondents who gained a specific score. For instance, a Dissatisfaction score of 13 is equivalent to the 50th percentile, meaning that 50% of the respondents in the norm group obtained higher scores and 50% obtained 13 or less. Canfield states in the TUA manual that

> a high score or a high percentile indicates more typicalness or more dissatisfaction with time utilization. A high score does not mean that the respondent has more time problems, it only means that the individual expresses relatively more concern about time problems than the people in the normative group. (1990, p. 3)

The TUA can be utilized individually, but the author recommends using it in small group settings such as time management seminars. No special training is needed to administer the TUA, but respondents are asked to read the instructions carefully and are urged to be as honest and objective about their feelings as possible. Completing the TUA is indeed very simple, and typically takes no more than 5 to 10 minutes.

## Practical Applications/Uses

The Time Use Analyzer should be judged as an instrument for enhancing awareness and stimulating thinking about patterns of time use. As such, it should not be judged according to scientific criteria. Topics like psychometric structure, reliability, and validity do not seem to be relevant here; no serious research probably would be done using the TUA, neither would one draw any serious conclusions on the basis of this instrument. It seems that no harm can be caused by using the TUA, as long as no claim is made that the results reflect any personality traits and so forth. Nevertheless, there are some problems with the TUA, even as a nonpretentious instrument:

1. The rationale for choosing the eight areas of time use is not clear. Claiming that these are the only areas of importance in misleading. Factors like the type of managerial position one holds influence patterns of time use (Webber, 1972).
2. The engineering of the scoring sheet can be improved. One problem is that importance weights are not copied via the carbon paper from the response to the scoring sheet.
3. Scoring could become easier if the manual mentioned clearly that the five areas that are not chosen as most important should be assigned importance weights of 1.
4. It is not clear what one should do in case of two or more areas that are identical in importance.
5. The major flow of the TUA has to do with the normative group on which the interpretation of scoring is based. The normative group consisted of 283 managers and educators. This sample was more than 90% male, mostly between the ages of 30 and 45 (Canfield, 1990, p. 4). This is a very restricted sample in regard to important dimensions such as sex, age, jobs, and culture. Hence, interpretation based on such a nonrepresentative sample might be misleading in many cases.

## Technical Aspects

Because of the nature of the TUA, technical information is not presented.

## Critique

Canfield (1990) states that the Time Use Analyzer provides both a yardstick against which individuals can compare their relative feelings about how their time is being utilized as well as a considerable amount of information on how one feels about his or her time use. These statements seem exaggerated. The TUA is a simple tool that can evoke some awareness. It should be treated as a stimulus for discussion and thinking, and no more than that. In this reviewer's opinion, users should ignore the Typicalness score because it is based on a nonrepresentative normative group. The Dissatisfaction score should be utilized as a nominal score, without referring to the normative group profile. The best application of the TUA would be in time management seminars, in which participants would be encouraged to compare scores and discuss their subjective meanings.

**References**

Canfield, A.A. (1990). *Time Use Analyzer manual*. Los Angeles: Western Psychological Services.
Mackenzie, R.A. (1977). *The time trap.* New York: McGraw-Hill.
Saifullah, E.D., & Kleiner, B.H. (1988). Effective time management. *Management Decision*, *26*(5), 60–64.
Webber, R.A. (1972). *Time and management*. New York: Van Nostrand Reinhold.

**Zoli Zlotogorski, Ph.D.**
*Professor of Psychology, The Hebrew University of Jerusalem, Mount Scopus, Israel.*
**Edythe A. Wiggs, Ph.D.**
*Consulting Psychologist, National Institutes of Mental Health, Rockville, Maryland.*

---

# TINKER TOY TEST

*Muriel Lezak. New York, New York: Oxford University Press.*

## Introduction

The Tinker Toy Test (Lezak, 1982, 1983) is a standardized measure of executive functions developed to give patients an opportunity to demonstrate their capacity to initiate, plan, and organize an activity. The test attempts to replicate the minimal structure inherent in many activities of daily living.

Muriel Lezak, author of the test, is Associate Professor of Neurology and Psychiatry at the Oregon Health Sciences University and a clinical neuropsychologist at the Portland Veterans Administration Medical Center. As a neuropsychologist, Lezak utilizes a flexible approach to assessment with a focus on patient care. Her 1983 text, *Neuropsychological Assessment*, is a standard in the field. Throughout her work she has emphasized the whole person, including family, work, and leisure activities.

Traditionally, psychological tests are highly structured and rigid in their administration. Lezak recognized that the very nature of the neuropsychological evaluation precluded gathering data on the patient's ability to carry on an activity independently. The Tinker Toy Test was devised to meet the need for observing how a patient would proceed when given minimal structure, directions, or feedback.

Lezak's (1982) initial evaluation of the effectiveness of the Tinker Toy Test was made on a total of 35 patients. One group ($n = 18$) was seen as dependent and required supervision in their activities of daily living, while the second group ($n = 17$) was considered independent. The latter managed their own daily routines, were responsible for their transportation needs, and included five gainfully employed individuals. The control group consisted of 10 hospital employees who were both younger and better educated than the patient groups. Later investigators (Bayless, Varney, & Roberts, 1989; Cicerone & DeLuca, 1990; Tupper, Wiggs, & Cicerone, 1989) have provided additional normative data on the test with larger samples of both patients and nonpatients.

The Tinker Toy Test utilizes 50 pieces from a standard set of children's Tinker Toys. The newer versions of this toy differ slightly in their composition from the original set used by Lezak (1983). The pieces that Lezak specified include 24 wooden dowels, 14 wooden rounds, and 12 plastic pieces. Representative samples of the work of both patients and controls are photographed and presented in her 1983 text article on the test (Lezak, 1983, pp. 513–519). The complete scoring system used for evaluating the constructions is also included in this article.

The test is simple to administer. The pieces are placed on the table in front of the patient and he or she is told, "Make something with these. You may make anything you wish. You have at least 5 minutes or as much time as you need" (Lezak, 1983, p. 514). Further direction is avoided in order to elicit as much independent activity as possible from the patient.

Although the materials are widely recognized as children's toys, few patients (or normal controls) object. Lezak (1983) as well as other investigators have found that most people are interested or amused by the test. The difficulty level depends on the ability of the patient to initiate and carry out purposeful behavior. To the extent that patients experience difficulty with these executive functions, they will have problems with the test. Severely impaired patients may touch the pieces and move them around but will be unable to make anything. Because the pieces are small, patients who do not have use of both hands will be unable to take the test.

## Practical Applications/Uses

The Tinker Toy Test is of practical value to neuropsychologists and psychologists in their assessment of patients for rehabilitation treatment planning. The executive functions, defined by Lezak (1983) as "goal formulation, planning, carrying out goal-directed behaviors and effective performance" are essential to "appropriate, socially responsible and effectively self-serving adult conduct" (p. 507). The minimal structure provided by the test renders it a suitable instrument for the elicitation of these behaviors or, conversely, a diminished capacity for these behaviors. Therefore, the test has its greatest utility in cases where the ability to act independently is in question. Injuries to the brain, particularly to the frontal lobes, may compromise an individual's ability for planning and executing an unstructured task.

Bayless et al. (1989) administered the Tinker Toy Test to 50 closed-head injured patients and 25 controls. The patients were divided into a currently employed group ($n$ = 25) and a vocationally disabled group ($n$ = 25). Both patient groups were at least 2 years post-injury. The findings of this study indicate significant differences among the three groups. None of the controls and only one of the currently employed group evidenced impaired scores on the Tinker Toy Test, while 13 of the vocationally disabled group showed impaired functioning. The authors point out that the extent of the head injuries sustained by all of the patients was relatively mild, and all 50 had been cleared for return to work.

Tupper et al. (1989), in a study of 41 head-injured patients, found significant differences between the Complexity scores generated from the constructions of head-injured patients and a control group. In addition, in the patient sample, the Complexity score obtained from the Tinker Toy Test was significantly correlated with measures of fluid intelligence: Performance IQ on the Wechsler Adult Intelligence Scale-Revised, Trails B, and the Reasoning cluster from the Woodcock-Johnson Psycho-Educational Battery. There was a significant correlation between postdischarge employment status and the Complexity score on the Tinker Toy Test.

Mendez, Ashla-Mendez, and Martin (1990) administered the Tinker Toy Test as part of a more comprehensive neuropsychological battery to three groups of elderly individuals: 18 patients with a diagnosis of multi-infarct dementia, 18 patients with a diagnosis of Alzheimer's disease, and 18 normal elderly controls. The patients with multi-infarct dementia obtained significantly lower Complexity scores on the Tinker Toy Test than either the Alzheimer's patients or the controls. The multi-infarct dementia patients also generated fewer words per minute and fewer words per phrase in a free-speech task from the Boston Diagnostic Aphasia Battery. The authors interpreted these results as indicative of frontal system impairment in multi-infarct patients.

Despite the simplicity of administration and the ease with which the materials can be procured, caution must be exercised in the interpretation of the results of this test. As with all psychological tests, extratest behavior is as important to the interpretation of the results as the test behavior itself. Although most patients find no objection to the materials, it is incumbent on the psychologist to observe and to critically evaluate the individual's investment in the task. It is essential that adequate rapport be established prior to the administration of this test. Furthermore, no single test is sufficient for any diagnosis. This test must be administered as part of a comprehensive battery of tests designed to evaluate the whole person.

Research directly addressing the issues of objections to the test materials and clarity of instructions was carried out by way of a questionnaire. One hundred twenty-one individuals ages 15 to 44 took the Tinker Toy Test as part of a larger battery of neuropsychological tests (Wiggs, 1988). All of these subjects were either employed or enrolled in school at the time of the assessment, although 20 reported a previous history of trauma or other condition that might affect cognition. Interest in the task was measured on a 5-point scale from 1 = very interesting to 5 = not at all interesting. The mean score was 2.1+1.1. Furthermore, the subjects were asked if the instructions were clear. Using the same scale, the mean score was 1.3+.6. These results clearly suggest that the Tinker Toy Test is not aversive to most people. In addition, the instructions, although minimal and nondirective, are clear to the average person.

Scoring is based on the construction that the patient indicates is complete. There are no time limits, although the instructions are meant to encourage the patient to continue to work on the test for at least 5 minutes. In instances where the subject has not spontaneously given a name to the constructions, an appropriate query is made after the subject indicates completion of the task. The construction is then scored on two primary dimensions: number of pieces used to complete the object and complexity.

The first score is self-explanatory. The Complexity score is comprised of points awarded for each of the following categories: attempt to complete the task; the construction is free-standing; the construction is three-dimensional; the construction is given an appropriate name; the construction has wheels that move; and the construction has moving parts. In addition, up to 4 additional points are awarded for the number of pieces used, and a point is subtracted for errors (e.g., dropping pieces and failing to pick them up). In Lezak's scoring a total of 12 points is possible for "complexity." Scoring takes only a few minutes and can be completed before the structure is broken down.

Some scoring problems have been recognized. Lezak (1983) cautioned that her scoring system was preliminary, and other investigators (Bayless et al., 1990) have modified the Complexity score somewhat. These authors increased the value of the score for the name of the object to reflect a continuum that ranged from appropriate to vague to unnamed. Another problem exists when attempting to score constructions that are composed of more than one "thing." At times, severely impaired patients will construct multiple sets of two or three pieces, each of which they are unable to identify. Clearly, these constructions present difficulties in terms of the scoring system and pose a problem in research applications of the test. However, it should be noted that the clinical information provided by such constructions is valuable (M. Lezak, personal communication, August 31, 1987).

**Technical Aspects**

Few studies have directly addressed the reliability of the Tinker Toy Test. An alpha coefficient to determine internal consistency of the test was generated by Wiggs (1988) in a sample of 121 individuals (alpha = .57). In another study (Tupper et al., 1989), interrater reliability was acceptable, although a numerical value was not reported. Test-retest reliability studies have not been reported.

Validity studies typically have focused on the ability of the test to predict employment status after rehabilitation. Researchers have reported that the test shows good promise as a predictor of postdischarge employment status (Cicerone & DeLuca, 1990; Tupper et al., 1989; Bayless et al., 1989). Cicerone and DeLuca (1990) administered a battery of neuropsychological tests to 87 head-injured adults. The Tinker Toy Test Complexity score and Trails B correlated .40 with postdischarge employment status. The authors interpreted the results as evidence that executive functioning tests (i.e., Tinker Toy Test, Trails B), may reflect the ability to benefit from rehabilitation.

In another outcome study, Tupper, Fenster, and Atcachunas (1985) presented a case study of a 19-year-old head trauma victim with repeated test results during his 4-month rehabilitation course. The Tinker Toy Test, along with Mazes and the Means-End Problem Solving Test, predicted the patient's eventual improvement in therapists' ratings of self-control and extratest problem-solving behaviors. It is interesting to note that test results showed improved scores several months before they appeared in staff ratings. Test gains were maintained post-rehabilitation, while staff ratings of self-control and problem-solving strategies declined to pretreatment levels. The authors suggest that the results are indicative of the necessity for environmental structure even after formal rehabilitation has ended. An alternate parsimonious explanation for these findings is the practice effect. Thus, judgment as to the utility of the Tinker Toy Test in situations that require multiple test administrations should be held in abeyance until the test-retest reliability is known.

In a study of the Tinker Toy Test among young adult nonpatients, Wiggs (1988) found very low correlations between the scores on this test and scores on other standard tests of neuropsychological functioning, such as Mazes, Picture Arrangement, and Controlled Oral Word Fluency. Tinker Toy Test Complexity scores did not correlate with measures of crystallized ability such as reading, mathematics, and vocabulary. If these results can be replicated, they indicate that the Tinker Toy Test may be independent of previously learned skills. This supports the contention of Lezak (1983) that the executive functions are independent of performance on traditional structured tests of neuropsychological functioning.

## Critique

Although there is some promise shown by the Tinker Toy Test, particularly in rehabilitation settings, further research is necessary before the results can be considered reliable and valid predictors of extratest behaviors. The test has numerous advantages, however, which should encourage research. It is inexpensive, easy to administer and score, and provides a method of observation that is unique to the testing situation. In addition, the test appears to measure something independent of previous learning and experience. However, much work needs to be done before the Tinker Toy Test can be considered anything but experimental.

## References

Bayless, J.D., Varney, N.R., & Roberts, R.J. (1989). Tinker Toy Test performance and vocational outcome in patients with closed-head injuries. *Journal of Clinical and Experimental Neuropsychology, 11*(6), 913–917.

Cicerone, K.D., & DeLuca, J. (1990, February). *Neuropsychological predictors of head injury rehabilitation outcome.* Paper presented at the 18th Annual International Neuropsychological Society Meeting, Kissimmee, FL.

Lezak, M.D. (1982). The problem of assessing executive functions. *International Journal of Psychology, 17,* 281–297.

Lezak, M.D. (1983). *Neuropsychological assessment* (2nd ed.). New York: Oxford University Press.

Mendez, M.F., Ashla-Mendez, M.E., & Martin, R. (1990, February). *Differences between multi-infarct dementia and Alzheimer's disease on unstructured neuropsychological tasks.* Paper presented at the 18th Annual International Neuropsychological Society Meeting, Kissimmee, FL.

Tupper, D.E., Fenster, J., & Atcachunas, L.J. (1985, October). *Remediation of problem-solving and initiation deficits following bilateral frontal lobe trauma: A case study emphasizing transfer.* Poster presented at the Fifth Annual Meeting of the National Academy of Neuropsychologists, Philadelphia.

Tupper, D.E., Wiggs, E.A., & Cicerone, K.D. (1989, October). *Executive functions in the head-injured: Some observations on Lezak's Tinker Toy Test.* Poster presented at the Ninth Annual Meeting of the National Academy of Neuropsychologists, Washington, DC.

Wiggs, E.A. (1988). *Neuropsychological assessment of executive functions in healthy young people.* Unpublished doctoral dissertation, University of Maryland, College Park.

**Ann H. Stoddard, Ed.D.**
*Professor of Education, University of North Florida, Jacksonville, Florida.*

# TLC-LEARNING PREFERENCE INVENTORY

*Harvey F. Silver and J. Robert Hanson. Moorestown, New Jersey: Hanson, Silver, Strong and Associates, Inc.*

## Introduction

The TLC-Learning Preference Inventory (LPI) is designed to identify individual students' learning styles. It consists of 144 items that indicate individual preferences for perception and judgment and provides insight into orientation toward ideas and things in the individual's world. Basically the inventory provides teachers with information about how students learn best.

The LPI was constructed by Harvey F. Silver and J. Robert Hanson. Silver holds a doctorate from Teachers College, Columbia University, and presently serves on the graduate faculty of Pace University. In the past he served as director of several educational programs and consulted throughout the United States. Silver has written extensively and co-authored another instrument with Hanson entitled Teacher Self Assessment: Dealing with Diversity. Dr. Hanson holds degrees from Yale and the University of the South. Prior to joining Silver, he was president of Educational Management and Evaluation Consultants, and at present he serves on the graduate faculty of Kean College of New Jersey. As a management consultant, he works closely with departments of education in the northeast and mid-Atlantic states. Hanson is also responsible for a series of diagnostic instruments that measure cognitive preferences among children and adults.

According to the authors, the LPI is based on the Jungian thesis that (a) all behaviors result from two sets of functions, perceiving (which includes sensing and intuition) and making judgments (which includes thinking and feeling), and (b) learning behavior is directly influenced by the choice of functions for perception, judgment, and attitude. The attitudinal dimensions fall into two categories: introversion (I) and extraversion (E). In other words, the interaction of these combinations produces a different style of learning for each individual. Four styles of learning emerge, mediated by attitude: sensing-feeling (S-F), sensing-thinking (S-T), intuitive-feeling (N-F), and intuitive-thinking, (N-T). The LPI profile provides a student's dominant attitude, using Jung's definitions of these dimensions; that is, two different ways of perceiving one's world rather than the popular misinterpretation of these two dimensions, a shy wallflower (introvert) versus an articulate aggressive type (extravert).

The LPI is a two-page booklet, with the first page designed to collect demographic data, introduce the LPI, and direct the user in how to respond. The next page and a half contain 36 open-ended statements plus four responses to be rank ordered. Each response is numbered consecutively from 1 to 144. The statements are written on an elementary-school level but are not suitable for primary students K through Grade 2. (There is no indication that students at this level were included in the sample population.)

It appears that the teacher of the class being evaluated makes the best administrator. The three steps for collecting student data require that, first, a checklist of preferred student behaviors be used to garner the teacher's perception about the students' learning styles. Second, students need to be prepared for the administration of the LPI through warm-up exercises that develop the concept of "preference" (e.g., writing down four favorite desserts and then, while pretending that all four are on the table at the same time, choosing which they would eat first, second, third, and last). The third step emphasizes establishing set for responding to the LPI.

The one-page scoring sheet uses both sides of the page. On the front side, students' first preferences are recorded in columns headed SF, ST, NT, NF, I, and E. Each column then is added and multiplied by a weighted sum. The products next are added to provide a preference score for each of the four styles and each of the two attitudes. The other side of the score sheet describes directions for scoring and computing the scores and describes the student profile. The profile indicates the dominant learning style, the auxiliary style, the supportive style, and the least used of the four styles. The profile also specifies the student's dominant attitude.

**Practical Applications/Uses**

Although the LPI was designed specifically to identify an individual's learning style, the authors state that the inventory also may furnish teachers with information for making daily decisions about optimal student learning. Best use occurs in an educational setting with upper elementary, secondary, college, and adult learners. In addition to information gleaned from the LPI about student learning preferences, the authors encourage teachers to use a variety of other sources, such as observations, tests, interviews, and parent conferences.

The LPI user's manual devotes 60 pages to suggestions on how to best apply the LPI results. The topics discussed center around how to motivate students, create varied and effective learning environments, plan and develop curriculum, teach for maximum learning, develop abilities to function across all four learning styles, diversify class activities, create a climate of sharing and trust, and work more effectively with teachers and students (Silver & Hanson, 1980). Materials are provided for creating environments that facilitate the suggestions just listed.

The user's manual additionally provides an extensive characterization of each of the four learning styles, including descriptions, combination of functions, approach to learning and problem solving, assets and liabilities, and how one learns best. Two pages also are devoted to an overview of teaching behaviors that support each learning style. These categories emphasize the themes of curriculum objectives, learning environments, instructional strategies, teaching strategies, and evaluation procedures.

The LPI may be individually or group administered. The manual suggests that students need to be prepared prior to administration. They must understand clearly the concept of "preference." As described previously, younger students should complete some exercises in rank ordering their preferences as warm-up training. Examinees should be reminded that there are no right or wrong answers, that they may ask for assistance to help understand a word or phrase, that the LPI is not a speed test, that all questions must be answered, and that their answers should reflect how they prefer to behave, not how someone expects them to.

For nonreaders who can understand the task, the LPI can be administered orally. Even though the LPI user's manual does not refer to non-English-speaking students, "nonreader" could be stretched to include this group if the oral administration is in the examinee's native language. Likewise, physically handicapped students may be included in this group, especially those who are visually impaired. When oral examination is necessary, the manual suggests that students make a single most preferred response rather than rank ordering the four responses. A single response, however, tends to reduce the reliability of the test results because of the fewer response options.

The person who administers the LPI needs no special skills for the task. The manual suggests that the classroom atmosphere should be conducive to self-learning and self-appreciation. This condition helps avoid the pitfalls of using a self-assessment and attitudinal measure. One might conclude, then, that the classroom teacher is the appropriate administrator of the LPI.

The LPI is easily scored in any one of three ways: by the administrator, by computer, or by older students scoring their own inventories. Each response has a preference value of 1 to 4. The response ranked first is transferred to the appropriate column on the scoring sheet. Total sums are found for each column then multiplied by the weighted value found directly below each column total. The four weighted scores are added next, and this sum represents the student's preference score for that particular learning style. The preference scores are placed in descending order, beginning with the largest number. The beginning score is indicative of the examinee's dominant learning style. Every third score measures an attitudinal preference, which is determined in the same way as the learning style. Question 36 is considered a dummy item and is not included in the scoring procedure. Further, when single responses are collected, no weighted values are used. The selected responses are added and the sums are regarded as learning preferences.

To analyze the scores, maximum points are presented for both style and attitude. Very high preference for style and attitude is 100–125 and 65–80, respectively. Other classifications are high preference, moderate preference, some preference, and little or no preference. The user can plot a learning style profile in the form of a histogram or a line graph. There are four variations of interpretation: (a) the graduated profile, where the student receives a different score for each learning style; (b) the double dominant profile, where the student has selected two different styles with equal preference; (c) the balanced profile, where the student chooses across three learning styles with little difference of choice among them; and (d) the clear dominant learning preference with identical auxiliary and supporting styles.

The authors also suggest another way to interpret LPI scores. The dominant and auxiliary choices can be scrutinized in terms of either the judgment or perception functions. For example, if the student's dominant style is S-F and the auxiliary style is N-F, then in both instances the student prefers *feeling* as the "judgment" mode; *thinking* is least preferred or is limited to the least preferred or least used learning preference. Similarly, if the student scores S-F and S-T, one may conclude that the "perception" function is dominant, and the intuitive function is third or last choice.

Class profiles can be developed by transferring the scores to a two-way chart entitled Class Style Profile. Scores are separated by gender and placed in a column for extraverts or introverts and in a row that stipulates the preferred learning style.

**Technical Aspects**

Prior to a psychological test being considered appropriate for effective use, it must furnish evidence of technical adequacy in its manual or some other research publication that provides data to support claims for its use. Unfortunately neither the LPI user's manual nor Research Monograph #4 (Hanson & Silver, n.d.) report any validity or reliability coefficients. The only reference to reliability is found in the user's manual, where the authors report that a single most preferred response reduces reliability because the response options are fewer (Hanson & Silver, 1980, p. 23). For an inventory such as the LPI to be usable and generalizable, both criterion-related and construct validity, as well as internal consistency reliability, need to be demonstrated.

The user finds a description of the subject pool in Research Monograph #4. Two separate populations were used: 600 third-, fourth-, fifth-, and sixth-graders in an urban school district, and 250 third-, fourth-, fifth-, and sixth-graders from a school district represented by a mix of urban, suburban, and rural students.

The research monograph discusses the use of Jungian-based psychological type classification to assess school-age learners' learning styles. A factor analysis of the LPI items was conducted, and items representing each factor were retained if they loaded at .40 or higher on that factor. Thirteen items were deleted on the basis of the principal components analysis and nonmatch of hypothesized styles. The conclusion drawn from the research findings was that the LPI corresponded to learner types defined by Jung (1921) and by the Myers-Briggs Type Indicator (Myers, 1962, 1976).

**Critique**

The idea of having another inventory to assess learning preferences is a very good one. These data can be exceedingly useful both to teachers and parents. The LPI has a substantial theoretical background but little documentation of its research. The lack of reported validity and reliability coefficients should make users cautious about categorizing learners into various learning styles.

The LPI user's manual contains excellent information that is very worthwhile for teachers and other educational personnel. The importance of knowing what learning abilities are developed and need to be developed is a worthy goal for instruction, especially in the early school years. However, no rationale is offered for the weighted scores, and no test norms are provided. Because the class profile is separated by gender, it would be helpful to compare norms in this area. Norms by school type would also be advantageous when comparing elementary, secondary, and college students.

Areas for needed research on the LPI include (a) interrater reliability for the items, (b) validity, particularly criterion-related and construct, and reliability for the three different school populations, (c) validation through teacher ratings of the test's efficacy and utility, and (d) significantly relating the measure to Jung's theory and to the Myers-Briggs Type Indicator and/or Gregorc's (1979) student learning style model/instrument.

There is clearly a need for an instrument that will identify students' learning preferences early on in their formal schooling. Such a tool would assist teachers not only in modifying their teaching behavior but in teaching students other learning styles. Although the LPI seems to have strong potential as an assessment of learning styles, given the lack of specific technical information it is difficult to determine its present effectiveness. Until such data are ascertained, it would be better to use the LPI as a possible indicator of learning preferences. Motivating students and helping them develop the requisite abilities for academic success is a significant element in the teaching/learning process.

## References

Gregorc, A.F. (1979). Learning/teaching styles: Their nature and effects. In J.W. Keefe (Ed.), *Student learning styles: Diagnosing and prescribing programs.* Reston, VA: National Association of Secondary School Principals.

Hanson, J.R., & Silver, H.F. (1980). *Learning Preference Inventory user's manual.* Moorestown, NJ: Hanson, Silver, Strong and Associates.

Hanson, J.R., & Silver, H.F. (n.d.). *A factor analytic study of the Learning Preference Inventory based on C.G. Jung's psychological types theory.* Moorestown, NJ: Hanson, Silver, Strong and Associates.

Jung, C.G. (1921). *Psychological types: The collected works* (Bollingen Series XX). Princeton, NJ: Princeton University Press.

Lawrence, G. (1979). *People types and tiger stripes: A practical guide to learning styles.* Gainesville, FL: Center for the Application of Psychological Types.

Myers, I.B. (1962). *Manual: The Myers-Briggs Type Indicator.* Palo Alto, CA: Consulting Psychologists Press.

Myers, I.B. (1976). *Introduction to type.* Gainesville, FL: Center for the Application of Psychological Types.

**James A. Moses, Jr., Ph.D.**
*Clinical Associate Professor of Psychiatry and Behavioral Sciences, Stanford University School of Medicine, and Coordinator, Psychological Assessment Unit, Veterans Administration Medical Center, Palo Alto, California.*

# UNIVERSITY RESIDENCE ENVIRONMENT SCALE

*Rudolf H. Moos. Palo Alto, California: Consulting Psychologists Press, Inc.*

## Introduction

The University Residence Environment Scale (URES; Moos, 1974; Moos, 1988; Moos & Gerst, 1974) is designed to provide multidimensional descriptive information about the social environmental characteristics of a wide variety of university-based housing facilities from the individuals and groups who live in them. The URES is a self-report questionnaire that consists of 100 brief declarative statements to which the subject responds "true" or "false."

Three forms of the URES are available for comparison of real, ideal, and expected social environmental characteristics of university residential settings. Items of the *real* form (Form R) are phrased in the present tense and are used by residents who are familiar with the housing setting and the other current residents of the setting. The other forms of the URES are modifications of Form R. They differ in verb tense but not in item content. The *expected* form (Form E) items have the same content as those of Form R but are phrased in the future tense. This form is applicable to persons who are entering a new university residential housing environment or to those who are about to experience some significant change in the residential environment. The *ideal* form of the URES also has the same item content as Form R but phrases the items conditionally, and describes what an ideal university residential setting might be like.

A short form (Form S) of the URES also is available for use in settings where time for data collection is limited and where only a brief impressionistic overview of the social climate of the setting is desired as a screening procedure. Empirical findings support the use of Form S in the evaluation of residential settings but not individuals, as Form S has too few items to reliably evaluate individual differences. Form S results are very similar overall to those of Form R for group evaluation (Moos, 1988).

The URES has not been revised since its initial appearance (Moos, 1974), but the original administrative and interpretive manual (Moos & Gerst, 1974) has been revised (Moos, 1988). In the revised manual Moos has expanded the scope of recommendations for clinical, consultative, evaluative, and research applications of the URES to social ecological evaluation of university residence programs. He also has provided a detailed overview of the literature on the URES and has updated several previously published literature reviews on the scale. Users of the URES are advised by the author to use only the revised manual in current work with the URES.

The author of the URES, Rudolf H. Moos, received the B.A. with honors (1956) and the Ph.D. (1960) degrees from the University of California, Berkeley. Thereafter he was a postdoctoral fellow at the University of California, San Francisco for 2 years. He is a diplomate in Clinical Psychology of the American Board of Professional Psychology (1965), a recipient of the Hofheimer Award for Research of the American Psychiatric Association (1975), a Veterans Administration Career Scientist (since 1981), and a fellow of numerous learned societies. Moos has been a faculty member of the Department of Psychiatry and Behavioral Sciences at Stanford University since 1962 (Professor since 1972), and he serves as the director of the Postdoctoral Research Training Program at that institution. At the Veterans Administration Medical Center, Palo Alto, California, he serves as the director of the Social Ecology Laboratory, as the chief of psychiatric research, and as the director of the Far West Health Services Research and Development Service Field Program. He had published 12 books and 270 book chapters, manuals, literature reviews, and professional research articles through January 1988. Dr. Moos is best known for his pioneering work in the development and implementation of the social ecological approach to classification, description, evaluation, and consultation.

Development of the initial URES item pool began with several convergent procedures. The social climate model posed by Moos and his colleagues was followed in the development of the URES as was the case with their nine other social climate scales. Application of the model to university residence settings led the test developers to seek descriptive items that would reflect "emphasis on interpersonal relationships (such as involvement), on goals in personal growth (such as academic achievement) or on living group structure and change (such as order and organization or innovation)" (Moos, 1988, p. 14). Items were developed from observation of student living settings and from information gained from unstructured interviews with both students living in university-based residential housing and staff in university-based residences and housing offices.

The initial URES item pool consisted of 238 items. This form of the scale was administered to students who were living in 13 dormitories. The initial item pool was reduced through item analysis to 140 items. Items were selected that discriminated at statistically significant levels between the residential settings by eliminating (a) those that described only extreme or atypical living groups and (b) those that correlated significantly with the Crowne-Marlowe Social Desirability Scale. The test developers also included a "a halo scale from 10 items that did not discriminate among houses and that were endorsed in the keyed direction by fewer than 10 percent of the respondents" (Moos, 1988, p. 14).

The 140-item experimental form of the URES then was administered to students living in 74 different residence halls that represented a wide range of demographic, social, and architectural settings. Test statistics used for final item selection were item intercorrelations, URES subscale intercorrelations, and item-to-subscale correlations for three successive samples. The test statistics were recomputed and the experimental form of the test was restructured to reflect each of these successive evaluations to regroup useful items and to eliminate others that were poorly discriminative. Items that were selected for the final 100-item URES scale met three key criteria. They showed high item-to-subscale correlations. This criterion ensured that the items selected for a subscale were related to each other and measured a common, well-defined theoretical construct. Low-to-moderate correlations among subscales also were necessary to ensure that the subscales of the URES were not redundant with each other. Each of them was required to measure a separate behavioral dimension. Finally each item selected for the final form of the URES was required to show maximal item discrimination among residential units that were prototypically different in kind. For detailed reviews of the URES item development, see Gerst and Moos (1972) and Moos (1979).

Instructions to the respondent for Form R are relatively simple and require one to mark the answer sheet "true" if the statement is definitely or mostly true or "false" if the item is definitely or mostly false as it applies to the respondent's current view of the residential setting. For Form E the resident is asked to answer "true" or "false" to the same item content statements, which here are phrased in the future tense. In this case one is asked to describe what one imagines a new residential setting about to be entered "will be like." For Form I the resident is asked to describe what he or she thinks an ideal living unit "would be like." The URES is recommended for self-report group administration, with assurances of anonymity to encourage candor in descriptions of the living setting rather than socially desirable or defensive response tendencies in those who may fear censure if they are critical of the setting or the administrative staff.

The URES test form consists of a four-page reuseable question pamphlet. The subject records on the answer sheet the form of the URES that is being completed, the date, and basic identifying information: name (or code number), age, sex, living group, corridor/floor, room number, student or staff status, title (if a staff member), year in college, preferential ordinal choice of this living unit among others on campus (first, second, etc.), all quarters or semesters respondent has lived in setting rated (4 maximal for current year, previous year), a 5-point Likert scale of desirability of living in same setting next year, date test completed, and other (brief) demographic information.

A worked example is given for true and false responses. Numbered boxes that correspond to each question are horizontally divided in half. True is indicated by marking an X in the top half of the box; false is indicated by marking an X in the bottom half of the box. The profile sheet can be used with any of the 10 social climate scales. The residential setting rated is indicated in addition to the social climate scale used, the scale form, the normative group used to convert raw scores to standardized scores, and the date. The legend of the profile has boxes to indicate the scaled score and the subscale title acronym for the appropriate social climate scale.

Separate URES norms are provided in the test manual for translating living group mean raw scores and individual respondent raw scores to standard scores based on the full 100-item form of the test. In addition, there is a conversion table for translating Form S raw scores to standard scores for living groups only.

*Form R normative sample.* The norms for Form R of the URES are based on 168 residential units with widely different demographic characteristics. The units are sampled from 16 American colleges and universities. Moos provides the following descriptive characteristics of these units:

> The 16 schools include 2 state colleges, 5 state universities, 2 private women's colleges, 5 private coeducational colleges and universities, a medical school, and a college of fine arts. Units in the normative sample include 32 women's houses, 23 men's houses, and 37 coed houses—all integrated by class; 6 upperclass women's houses, 4 freshman women's houses, 2 freshman coed houses; 16 fraternities; and several houses with graduates and undergraduates living together. The size of these units ranges from fewer than 20 to more than 300 students. (Moos, 1988, p. 8)

Descriptive statistics that measure central tendency and variability for Form R are presented separately for a mean of the 168 living groups just described and for 505 individuals drawn from them. These subjects are said to be "representative" of the larger group, but their demographic characteristics and method of selection are not reported in the test manual. Apparently they were selected from the larger sample to reflect group trends and the range of variability in the sample as a whole, as well as to eliminate the biasing influence of outliers on the various social climate dimensions. The size of the overall sample from which they were chosen is not reported in the test manual, so the selection ratio is unclear.

Norms are provided based on student samples only. If the URES is administered to a group of staff members in the residential setting as well as students (as indicated on the answer sheet as an alternative), it is unclear how the staff responses would be normed. The examples in the manual are for analysis of perceptions of students and student groups only, so the application of the URES method to staff members at present appears to be exploratory or experimental only. For an application of the URES to the analysis of student and staff perceptions of university residential settings, see Ford (1975).

*Form S normative sample.* Descriptive statistics for the short form of the URES are provided in the test manual for the 168 living groups described above for the Form R normative sample. Form S statistics are available for group description only, as short form statistics of this test are not sufficiently reliable to describe individual differences.

*Form I normative sample.* Form I descriptive statistics are presented in the manual for a sample of 948 students who were sampled from three universities. These academic institutions were of average enrollment size and included two private universities and one state-supported public college. Standard score conversions are not currently available for Form I but could be calculated from the raw score values in the test manual.

*Form E normative samples.* Form E descriptive statistics are presented in the test manual for a sample of 1,424 entering freshmen prior to matriculation at an average-size public college and a comparably sized private university. Standard score conversions are not currently available for Form E but could be calculated from the raw score values in the test manual.

Typically two or more of the forms of the URES are used in conjunction. Form R may be compared with Form E, for example, to judge expected change from a known baseline in a program about to undergo planned change. Administration before and after the programmatic alteration would be particularly useful for comparison of expected and experienced change. Alternatively Form R and Form I could be compared to evaluate program satisfaction and areas of dissatisfaction between actual and optimal social environments.

**Practical Applications/Uses**

The URES scale development is modeled on a three-category social ecological model that has been developed and extensively validated in a variety of social living and institutional settings by Moos and his colleagues. Their work is derived theoretically from the formulations of Henry Murray (1938), who was the first social personality theorist to recognize the complementary roles of individual needs and environmental press as codeterminants of complex social perception and behavior. The model on which the URES was developed postulates three categories of relationship, personal growth or goal orientation, and system maintenance and change dimensions. Moos (1984) has shown that the three-domain orientation to analysis of various social living groups has a wide range of applications across a variety of social settings. On the URES these three domains are measured with 10 subscales that tap a wide variety of perceived social environmental characteristics of university residential settings. Moos (1988, p. 2) describes the URES subscales in the revised manual as follows:

1. Relationship dimensions:

*Involvement*—degree of commitment to the house and residents; amount of interaction and feeling of friendship in the house.

*Emotional Support*—amount of concern for others in the house; effort to aid one another with academic and personal problems; emphasis on open and honest communication.

2. Personal Growth or Goal Orientation dimensions:

*Independence*—diversity of residents' activities allowed without sanctions versus socially proper and conformist behavior.

*Traditional Social Orientation*—emphasis on dating, going to parties, and other traditional heterosexual activities.

*Competition*—degree to which social and academic activities are cast into a competitive framework.

*Academic Achievement*—prominence of academic accomplishments and concerns.

*Intellectuality*—emphasis on cultural, artistic, and other scholarly intellectual activities as distinguished from strictly academic achievements.

3. System Maintenance and Change dimensions:

*Order and Organization*—amount of formal structure or organization in the house.

*Student Influence*—extent to which student residents (not staff or administration) control the house, formulate and enforce the rules, and make decisions about the use of money, selection of staff, roommates, and so on.

*Innovation*—spontaneity of behaviors and ideas; number and variety of new activities.

The URES Relationship dimensions (Involvement, Emotional Support) are designed to assess the degree to which residents feel involved as members of the living group, their experience of group congeniality and mutual support, and the degree of perceived staff support of residents in the group. The Personal Growth or Goal Orientation dimensions evaluate personal and social skill development (Independence, Traditional Social Orientation) as well as orientation toward professional preparation and academic maturity (Competition, Academic Achievement, Intellectuality). The System Maintenance and Change dimensions assess the efficiency and orderly organization of social relationships in the living residence (Order and Organization), the degree of democratic orientation of the house that reflects student concerns and desires (Student Influence), and the perceived level of flexibility and receptiveness to novelty and change (Innovation).

The URES has been validated in a wide variety of applications (Moos, 1979). The scale has found its primary applications in descriptive evaluation and comparison of student residential groups, in program evaluation and consultation, and in student counseling. URES findings may be used to define objectively and compare perceptions of the living environment between students and staff within and among settings that are similar or dissimilar in systematic ways. It may be used to evaluate characteristics of the living setting that contribute to student and staff productivity and achievement of various goals, such as personal and social growth and academic orientation. It can be of value to plan assignments of various groups of students to residential settings of different types and to evaluate what characteristics of students are likely to lead them to choose those living settings. Those results can be obtained before and after the residential assignment and compared with objective indicators of achievement to determine predictors of educational success, which may be variably defined.

The URES is particularly useful for comparing the perceptions of residents, resident house manager assistants, and housing administrators. Moos (1988) also notes that the URES has proven useful when it is completed by nonresident visitors, such as parents of current and prospective residents and prospective student residents. Empirical evidence summarized by Moos (1979) shows that the URES information is descriptively accurate and can be used to provide feedback to staff that positively motivates them to become more involved in residential program planning that is responsive to student needs, desires, and satisfaction with the living setting. These variables have been shown to impact on academic performance as well (Moos, 1988).

In the revised manual, Moos (1988, pp. 21–28) provides multiple worked examples in which data from the URES have been used to evaluate and recommend modification of student living settings. For details the interested reader is referred to the original sources; key trends are summarized in the discussions that follow. Typical applications of the URES are illustrated in the manual. These examples include comparison of systematically different coeducational residential settings on a single campus with URES Form R, comparison of real (Form R) and ideal (Form I) descriptions of a single freshman coeducational dormitory, and comparison of initial entering expectations (Form E) with real perceptions of the residential setting obtained during fall and spring sessions. These examples reflect the usefulness of the URES for comparison of specific differences between similar settings, the systematic multidimensional contrast of dissimilar living settings, and multiple baseline comparisons of initial and subsequent real environmental perceptions with an expected preentry ideal. These various applications of the URES are modally illustrative.

Innovative applications of the URES have included design and evaluation of living-learning residential programs in which there is a common academic major topic of interest among the residents. In such settings there is an academically oriented, supportive environment in which academic achievement pursuits are fostered. Senior members of the unit commonly serve as social and professional role models and as peer counselors for the junior students in the setting. Evaluation of such a program by Schroeder and Griffin (1976) showed that for engineering students enrolled in the living-learning program, there were systematic differences in academic performance relative to that shown by comparable students who lived in traditional residential settings. The living-learning center group showed a higher grade point average, a considerably greater likelihood of continuing with this difficult major subject into upper division levels, and continuing affiliation with their residential setting relative to a comparison group of engineering majors who were living in traditional settings. For other examples of similar programs that showed similar results that were analyzed with the URES, see Schroeder and Belmonte (1979) and Richman (1977).

Use of the URES to assist student groups to analyze, modify, optimize, and evaluate change in a university residential program was investigated by Daher, Corazzini, and McKinnon (1977). Use of the URES in organizational development with university housing staff was reported by Schroeder (1979). Those results were based on integrated use of the Myers-Briggs Type Indicator as an index of personality variables with the Group Environment Scale (Moos, 1986) and the URES as joint indices of social and environmental variables. Matching of personality types to social living situations optimally could enhance adjustment through use of feedback to residents and housing office staff at each stage of program development and implementation.

Brandt and Chapman (1980) used the URES to show that students who were allowed to adaptively modify their dormitory environment developed a multidimensionally specific, enhanced positive outlook toward their living setting relative to residents who were denied such environmental control. Similar findings were reported and extended by Werring, Winston, and McCaffrey (1981), who found that residential participants who took an active role in improving and modifying their social environments also showed an enhanced multidimensional appreciation of the perceived positive aspects of their residential setting and their role in it. Other residents of the same programs who did not participate in the environmental improvement did not share these enhanced perceptions to a like degree.

Another approach was employed by Crouse (1982), who made use of family network therapy technique with one randomly assigned group of students in a dormitory setting who were matched with a comparison group from the same setting. As assessed by the URES, the students who participated in a series of group sessions of the kind noted showed enhanced positive perception of their social environment relative to the nonparticipants.

Moos (1988, p. 28) has concluded that direct student participation in residential program planning, evaluation, and modification is associated with their enhanced positive perception of the social living environment. Residential programs that provide for direct student involvement in program evaluation, change, and modification appear to be more effective and to lead to less dissatisfaction than programs that teach resident assistants to conduct didactic skill-learning workshops for their residential peers (Dalton, 1981; Wilson, 1980).

From these examples it is clear that the URES is useful for comparing different types of living groups and intervention methodologies. Moos, Van Dort, Smail, and DeYoung (1975) performed a cluster analysis of URES findings from different living groups and identified six prototypical student residential-living group types: relationship oriented, traditionally socially oriented, competition oriented, supportive achievement oriented, independence oriented, and intellectually oriented (for a detailed review of URES profile characteristics for each of these living group types, see Moos, 1988, pp. 35–39). In the URES manual there are graphic representations of dimensional contrasts between the relationship oriented and traditionally socially oriented, the competition oriented and supportive achievement oriented, and the independence oriented and intellectually oriented living group profiles. The six types of living groups are systematically different as they are described on the URES profile categorical and subscale dimensions.

Systematic differences between the six prototypical living group types were found as a function of sex of resident. Competition oriented settings were predominantly male. Independence and intellectually oriented residences were predominantly coeducational. Traditional socially oriented units were almost exclusively female. Supportive achievement oriented and relationship oriented residential settings also were predominantly female or coeducational. For further details of these analyses, the reader is referred to Moos (1979) and to Moos et al. (1975).

Professional qualifications for program consultants who use the URES are not explicitly stated in the manual, but one would expect a qualified consultant to have graduate level training in a mental health specialty and at least a journeyman's-level working knowledge of psychometric theory and statistics. University administrators who make use of the URES results would do well to seek the assistance of such a professional consultant when URES profile results are interpreted for their programs. A professional psychologist would be the preferred consultant for URES interpretation in programmatic description and evaluation.

The URES is suitable for administration in a wide variety of collegiate and university settings. The target audience consists of undergraduate and graduate university students who are living in communal housing settings. The target audience would thus involve people aged 18–22 in the modal undergraduate population as well as adults of various ages who are pursuing postbaccalaureate degrees.

The URES typically is self-administered as a self-report measure. Moos recommends anonymity for individual resident and staff respondents. Comparison of anonymous and identified respondents typically shows more conservative response trends when respondents identified themselves on the answer sheets (Cox, 1977). A quiet, well-lighted, well-ventilated room with sufficient working space for each respondent should be provided for completion of the URES. The role of an examination proctor in administration of the URES seems to be mostly limited to assurance that the respondents remain task oriented and that they do not share responses while answering the test items. Foreign students may need assistance with translation or reinterpretation of some words or phrases they may not fully understand. Simple restatements of individual word meanings are allowable, but the proctor must not influence the responses of the students or staff.

The proctor should read the directions aloud to the respondents while they read them silently and follow the response examples. Lead pencils with erasers should be provided so that respondents do not use pens. Individuals who have difficulty answering questions as true or false should be advised to answer questions true if in their opinion the statement is "true most of the time." Persons who still are unable to answer decisively should be encouraged to guess as an alternative to non-response. Particularly on Form S, respondents should be encouraged to answer every item. Incomplete protocols endanger reliability of measurement and hence test validity. Answer sheets should be checked for completeness of demographic information and responses to test questions as the forms are collected.

In most situations administration of the URES is straightforward and should pose no difficulty for the proctor or for the respondents. The questions are written at a sixth-grade reading level. For residents who may have physical disabilities, Moos (1987, p. 23) recommends the use of tape-recorded or computerized instructions. In such cases, however, the proctor may simply wish to read the questions aloud to the respondents, as the audiovisual devices suggested are not typically available in university residential settings. Each form of the URES usually requires 15 to 20 minutes to complete.

Forms I and E of the test may be obtained from the publisher in a master form suitable for reproduction. The publisher normally will authorize reproduction of these copyrighted materials after review of a written request that describes their intended use (Moos, 1988, p. 7). If more than one form of the URES is to be administered to the same person, the test author recommends administration of the two forms at separate sittings to keep the descriptions independent.

Scoring of the URES is a clerical task. The items of the 10 URES subscales are arranged in columns on the answer sheet. One places the clear plastic scoring template over the answer sheet and counts the number of answer marks (X's) that show through the circular marks on the scoring template. These subscale raw scores are entered in boxes below the response portion of the sheet. The raw scores are translated to scaled scores using tables provided in Appendix A of the manual (Moos, 1988, pp. 60–63).

Normative standards are provided for raw-to-standard score conversions of mean data for *living groups* on Form R and Form S of the URES and for *data from individuals* on Form R only. Normative values for Form E and Form I of the URES are not yet available; as a result, these forms of the test should be considered experimental. Manual scoring and profiling of the URES results for a single individual would require only about 10 minutes for an experienced user. No mention is made in the manual about automated scoring, but an automated URES administration and scoring program would be relatively easy to develop. One should be careful to make use of the appropriate normative database in such applications.

Interpretation of the URES is typically normative. Differences in profile elevations between groups or individuals or between forms for the same group are interpreted as clinically relevant when the difference between scores on a dimension approaches 1 standard deviation. As noted in a previous review of a related social climate scale (Moses, 1991), it would be useful to report standard error of measurement and standard error of difference statistics for the URES in the test manual. From these data one could construct reference tables that would display objective statistical criteria for significant score differences (elevations or depressions) relative to the mean of the profile at various levels of probability. This information also could be incorporated into an automated computer program for the URES and would help to objectify standards for rigorous performance level interpretation.

Currently one must attempt to infer from the examples given in the manual nonchance significance levels through impressionistic comparison of the mean profile differences for one's individual patient or residential program modal descriptive profile. Whether these are normal variations consistent with chance alone or truly significant differences is difficult to judge, particularly when difference or change scores are relatively small. It is also worth noting that the interpretable differences change considerably with the form of the test and the type of comparison. For description of *individuals* on Form R, the standard deviation across URES scales is on the order of 3 to 4 raw score points. For description of *living group mean data,* the standard deviation is the order of 1 to 2 points for the URES scales. This lesser variability result is statistically logical but may not be apparent to the average interpreter of the URES who is concerned with clinical application.

Relatively small differences in living group mean data, either between different living groups at the same time or in the same group over time, thus should be meaningfully interpretable. This is so because individual variation is averaged in calculation of the group mean, and the results show consistent trends in the data over individuals. For the case of Form S, the trend is most pronounced. There is a standard deviation value range of approximately one half to one full raw score point across living group mean raw scores for Form S. One would wish to be particularly sensitive to the relative deviations required for interpretive significance on each form of the URES and with each normative sample. As yet standards for profile elevation and variation for Forms E and I of the URES are unknown.

These points could be made more explicit in the discussion in the manual. Operational definition of statistically significant differences for each scale also could alert less experienced interpreters of the URES to relatively small but consistent mean differences that are of value in description of subtle programmatic variation.

The interpretive strategy modeled by Moos (1988) in the test manual suggests prototypical applications of the URES to residential program development, modification, and evaluation, as discussed earlier in this review. Directed practice with implementation of this methodology is essential. Initially one would probably wish to study the worked examples of Moos and his colleagues in the literature and in the test manual. Thereafter, it would be useful to describe familiar residential programs with the URES and to correlate the test findings with the known program characteristics in order to improve one's understanding of the psychometric indices and their behavioral correlates. Practice of this kind with individual and group mean analysis would be advisable before clinical or consulting application of the URES is attempted. It is important to emphasize that while the URES is a brief instrument that is easy to administer and score, its interpretation is not simple. New users of the URES are cautioned against simplistic performance level interpretation of the measure.

Mechanisms for provision of feedback based on the URES results should be coordinated with the housing authorities and the house manager and discussed with the residents before data are collected. It would be advisable to make explicit the reasons for the data collection and the intended use of the results. Respondents may have a quite different response task orientation toward the inventory if they view it as personally relevant and a potential referent for adaptive programmatic change rather than a means of administrative evaluation only.

### Technical Aspects

Reliability is an important psychometric property of all tests because it serves as an objective index of the accuracy of measurement of those dimensions the test is designed to measure. Three types of reliability are commonly distinguished. In tests where there is a formal rating or scoring system that is not actuarial, one must establish interrater reliability. This is unnecessary for the URES because the test is actuarially scored, and perfectly consistent scoring can be assured through automation or cross-checking results when hand scoring is done. Of these two options, machine scoring is preferable because it is cost effective and errorless. There is no ambiguity in the URES procedures that would lead to variance in careful clerical scoring.

A second kind of reliability is internal consistency. The items of a test must relate to each other if they are to describe a common dimension or theoretical construct that underlies a specific behavior pattern. The degree to which test items are interrelated in this manner can be measured by means of a variety of correlational statistics. Moos calculated the internal consistencies of the URES scales by means of the Kuder-Richardson Formula 20 (see Guilford, 1954, pp. 380–383, for technical details), a standard procedure used for this purpose. Most authorities in psychometric theory agree that an internal consistency value of approximately .80 minimizes error variance for practical purposes (for discussion, see Nunnally, 1978). The URES Form R very closely approximates this ideal standard across its 10 scales. The internal consistency values were calculated for a sample of 13 living groups. The URES Form R scalewise internal consistency statistics range from .77 (Independence, Competition, and Innovation subscales) to .88 (Involvement subscale). All of the URES Form R subscales thus measure their behavioral characteristics very accurately.

Cross-validation of these results in a sample of at least 300 subjects using the alternative internal consistency analytic procedure of Cronbach's coefficient alpha would be desirable. The same psychometric standard for internal consistency (.80 reliability) would apply to these analyses. Results based on a sample of 300 subjects drawn at random from the population should generalize to a very large sample. An advantage of coefficient alpha is that it is the mean of all possible split-half values for a test, and as such it is the overall best estimate of internal consistency (Nunnally, 1967, 1978).

The third aspect of reliability is test-retest reliability, which measures the temporal stability or reproduceability of the test results. Establishment of this sort of reliability is necessary to show that the test can accurately measure enduring and consistent patterns. The test-retest reliability of the URES Form R was evaluated by twice retesting students in one men's and one women's dormitory in a public university over periods of 1 and 4 weeks after the initial date of testing. After 1 week the test-retest reliability correlations ranged from .66 (Student Influence subscale) to .77 (Emotional Support subscale). Four weeks after the initial testing, the retest reliability values ranged from .59 (Independence subscale) to .74 (Traditional Social Orientation and Academic Achievement subscales). These values are within acceptable limits for the time periods.

A supplementary analysis evaluated the stability of the URES Form R profile as a whole across retest sessions relative to the baseline evaluation. The intraclass correlation coefficients were .96 over 1 week and .86 over 1 month in the men's residences for the URES profile reliability. Even more consistent findings were found for the women respondents, who showed .96 retest reliability on the URES Form R after 1 week and .98 retest reliability after 1 month on the intraclass correlational measure. Although there was some individual variability on some of the scales, the profile as a whole remained a stable indicator of key social climate variables in the residential living situations of respondents of both sexes.

The URES Form R subscale intercorrelations range from negligible (-.01, Emotional Support with Traditional Social Orientation) to moderate (.62, Involvement with Emotional Support). The mean URES subscale intercorrelation is approximately .20. These results are desirable in that they show relative independence of the URES Form R subscales from each other. This indicates that the subscales measure related but distinct and nonredundant behavioral features.

A complementary analysis of the URES Form R subscales investigated the correlation of each item on each subscale with the remainder of items on the subscale. This analysis provides an itemized index of internal consistency. Items should show a moderate univariate correlation with the scales to which they have been assigned. A low correlation would suggest that the item was unrelated or irrelevant to the subscale dimension; too high a correlation of many items with the subscale total would suggest redundancy of the item content in that subscale. A moderate correlational value of the scale items with the scale total score is consistent with a complementary relationship among the items that suggests there is a unique contribution of each of them to the common construct. This inference is supported when the internal consistency values also are high, as in the case of the URES Form R. The URES Form R mean item-to-subscale correlations are consistently at the optimal moderate level (range of .44 for Innovation to .62 for Involvement). The grand mean of the URES Form R item-to-subscale correlations is .52; on the average each item shares approximately 25% of its variance with its subscale total score. These values are based on a sample of 505 student respondents (Moos, 1988, p. 16).

Validity of a psychological test also is measured in various ways. Face validity refers to the apparent relevance of the item content to the dimension that the item is intended to measure. Content validity refers to the more important consensus agreement among expert raters that the item indeed is an accurate measure of a theoretically relevant aspect of the dimension that it is intended to measure. Face validity of an item may be plausible to a layman or nonspecialist in the assessment area under question and yet it may not be judged content valid by experts. Conversely some items that are content valid may not appear to be face valid.

Moos and his colleagues worked to build both face and content validity into the

URES items through definition of *specific* content dimensions for each subtest of the scale, by obtaining consensual agreement among independent raters that the dimensions were accurate and relevant and by writing items to define specific aspects of those dimensions. In addition, items that were selected for the final URES form had to meet the stringent multiple reliability criteria previously outlined. Scale independence and specificity was enhanced by assignment of each URES item to a unique scale.

Another aspect of validity that was built into the development of the URES is concurrent or criterion-related validity. According to this standard, a test must demonstrate agreement with some independent standard that has been established as a criterion. The criterion can be a variety of measures and typically involves objective behavior ratings or other tests that have been well studied and validated in previous research.

Moos and his colleagues obtained information for their concurrent validation of the URES from a series of semistructured interviews and feedback questionnaires from students and staff in eight university-based student residences. Students typically agreed that the URES results provided an accurate description of salient behavioral dimensions that were typical of their settings. Goebel (1977) reported that URES profiles agreed with descriptions of the residences provided by the program directors and with brochure descriptions of the residences that were available through promotional literature for prospective residents.

An important series of criterion-related validation studies of the URES showed that the scale can discriminate among different styles of living groups on the same campus and on different campuses (Goebel, 1977). For additional examples, see McHugo (1979) and Moos (1979). Detailed review of the rather extensive literature on the URES, though beyond the scope of this overview, is provided in the test manual (Moos, 1988, pp. 24–54). Some trends in that literature, however, will be noted.

The URES has been used successfully to measure student off-campus residential living situations and to contrast them with university-based residential programs. This work has also been extended to cross-cultural comparison of student subcultures in America and Taiwan (Tsai, 1985). Kerce and Royle (1984) modified the URES to study the social climate of Marine Corps barracks and adaptation to it among women with traditional and nontraditional career and family goals.

The URES has been used to investigate the influence of residential architecture features such as single versus shared room units, group study areas, recreational facilities, and amenities such as a snack bar on the social climate of the residence. Interestingly no influence on social climate was found as a function of the age of the residence hall or the presence of a group dining room in the facility. Small living units (suites) were found to promote social cohesion, perceived peer support, innovation, and sense of student independence more than large dormitory settings (Null, 1980; Gerst & Sweetwood, 1973). Freshman students in high-rise dormitories reported less social involvement, cohesion, social support, and organization than students in low-rise structures, but the high-rise dwellers reported greater emphasis on independence (Wilcox & Holahan, 1976; Holahan & Wilcox, 1979). Central campus dormitories tend to emphasize competition and social heterosexual activities more strongly, while more peripherally located campus residential living groups favor "achievement, independence, and intellectuality" (Moos, 1988, p. 43; see also Moos, 1979, chapter 4). The URES also has been used to investigate the effect on social climate of program size, major field choice, personality type, student satisfaction with the collegiate experience, personal growth in the freshman year, and comparison of coeducational versus unisex living settings (for an overview, see Moos, 1988, pp. 44–50).

Health status and psychopathology also have been linked to the URES dimensions. Moos and Van Dort (1979) developed a 12-item URES Symptom Risk subscale to identify risk factors that were related to development of physical symptoms during the academic year. These symptoms appear to be stress related, as they typically develop in highly competitive, socially unsupportive living settings and are significantly reduced in student living settings that are achievement oriented but socially peer supportive.

Patterns of alcohol consumption also have been related to social climate. Different patterns of URES item endorsement were found in single-sex as compared with coeducational residence halls. Items related to increased drinking in single-sex residential facilities were drawn from the Traditional Social Orientation, Order and Organization, Student Influence, and Innovation subscales. In coeducational residential programs, items related to alcohol consumption were drawn from the Support, Independence, Academic Achievement, Innovation, and Intellectuality subscales. Clearly there may be quite different reasons for student residents to drink to excess in different social settings, and the URES appears to be sensitive to many of them. Items for each of these special alcohol consumption scales are provided in Appendix B of the URES manual (Moos, 1988, p. 64).

## Critique

The URES is an accurate, valid, generally adaptable measure for multidimensional description, evaluation, and planned modification of actual, idealized, and expected collegiate social living settings. It is well validated as an index of the nuances of social living across a wide variety of settings.

There has been some preliminary and successful use of the scale for describing student living settings cross-culturally. Extension of this work could be quite useful to broaden the use of the URES and to objectively clarify cultural differences in coping and adaptation patterns among university students. For example, cross-cultural application of the URES cluster analytic typology of living groups could be of particular interest to educators at universities with large groups of overseas students. The URES could be used productively to match living settings for specific groups of foreign students to their cultural background experiences. Whether foreign students socially adapt and educationally achieve better in same-language, same-culture or mixed linguistic and cultural groups would be useful to investigate.

Another application might involve cross-cultural studies of university settings for foreign students in their native culture and in American university settings. Such questions could be of interest to cultural anthropologists, housing administrators, and educators alike. Cooperative work among different academic specialty groups to optimize adaptation of foreign students to American university settings and to learn adaptive coping skills from overseas groups that would aid in the adaptation of American students to their own universities and overseas academic settings would be useful to investigate with the help of the URES. Because many American students also study overseas during their collegiate or graduate careers, investigation of major overseas educational centers to aid students to learn academic and cultural expectations and mores in the overseas cultures could enhance American student adaptation and achievement in those overseas collegiate living settings.

The investigation of psychopathology among university students, particularly problem drinking, is just beginning. The alcohol consumption scales for single-sex and coeducational living programs should be cross-validated and widely applied in prospective prevention programs to lessen the prevalence and severity of alcohol abuse among student groups. The presence of different social ecological patterns in different living groups as a function of sex highlights the potential complexity and specificity of the problem. Students may drink for various reasons, and one would want to build on current findings so as not to oversimplify the question. In essence, one would not want to search for *one* reason that students become prone to substance abuse any more than one would seek a unitary cause for the experience of stress. Abuse of illicit substances other than ethanol among university groups also would be useful to investigate as a function of the URES dimensions.

The usefulness of stress inoculation and other behavioral programs to encourage students to resist abuse of illicit drugs and alcohol is an important one in high stress university settings. Investigation of the URES in combination with measures of psychopathology also remains to be investigated. Anxiety and depression are the most probable diagnostic categories of interest in most university settings. The URES might also identify groups of students at risk for substance abuse and serve as a means of monitoring life-style change that is associated with objective behavioral measures of adaptive coping and achievement.

Specialists in behavioral medicine could make productive use of the URES to study stress symptomatology and coping strategies among student groups at undergraduate and graduate levels. It would be useful to study those students who are successful in these areas, to clarify the coping difficulties of the distressed students, and to develop and evaluate systematic programs that could reduce the coping difficulty of the university environment among students who cope less adaptively. Relationship of the URES dimensions to standardized measures of health behavior, anxiety, and stress could be studied productively to see which variables singly and in combination predict coping success. Change in life-style on URES dimensions after psychotherapy or programmatic consultation would also be useful.

Study of living setting characteristics that are conducive to social growth and enjoyment for physically disabled students also remains to be explored with the URES. There has been a greatly increased advocacy for and by disabled student groups in recent years, but optimization of their living setting through use of the URES analytic methodology has not yet been reported. The special needs of this heterogeneous group would require careful evaluation to ensure that meaningful groups of students are compared. They might be compared on their type of physical disability and environmental adaptive needs, but it would also be important to be sensitive to personality type, major field of interest, social interests, career goals, and so forth.

Each of the areas in which the URES has been investigated has been essentially *exploratory,* and many lines of research investigation have been shown by the work that has been accomplished to date. Consultation with housing administrators, model student groups who would like to have their particular achievements and skills documented and publicized, and dysfunctional student living groups that would benefit from consultative advice for programmatic change suggest immediate applications for the URES. Study of groups of students who share similar common fields of study (mathematics/physical science, biological science, humanities, fine arts, etc.) would be useful to characterize the types of collegiate residences that are relevant to topically mixed versus topically similar living settings.

Retrospective study of undergraduate living settings of students who go on to become highly successful as graduate students in various fields also could offer ideas to develop pilot data for predictive studies of the relationship of URES dimensions to later success in various career fields. Application of the URES typology of living types to average and superior students in different fields might give insights into the aspects of the living situation that are conducive to achievement in those specialties. Relationship of the URES dimensions to completion of the collegiate career, to grade point average, to pursuit of graduate status, to career achievement 5 years after graduation, and to other outcome variables would also appear to be useful to investigate.

A combination of the URES with other social climate scales, such as the Community Oriented Programs Environment Scale (COPES) and the Military Environment Inventory (MEI), could be useful. Initial work with use of the MEI in the analysis of Marine Corps barracks was productive and should be expanded greatly with a variety of military groups. Studies to compare living groups of cadets at the American and foreign service academies with the URES would be particularly interesting. Studies of military living groups and work groups at various levels of the command hierarchy also could be related to measures of stress, job performance, job satisfaction, and reenlistment.

As with other social climate scales, one would recommend that the test author provide ipsative statistics to provide an objective standard for profile subscale deviation from the mean as a standard for clinical interpretation of nonchance profile elevations on the various URES scale measures. Provision of commercially available automated scoring for the URES is encouraged, particularly as most applications of the URES are likely to involve relatively large samples of subjects.

The URES is a brief, elegant, cost-, and time-efficient measure of important perceived behavioral dimensions in university residential living settings that are significantly related to important outcome variables. In preliminary clinical and research applications, it has been shown to have broad scope areas of usefulness and detailed descriptive specificity. It is relevant to program evaluation and modification as well. It predicts important elements of psychopathology and has been shown to enhance student adaptation to the collegiate environment. With appropriate modifications, the URES can have cross-cultural applicability as well.

The URES methodology has just begun to be applied systematically. Continued careful, hypothesis-driven applications of the methodology doubtless will continue to enhance the quality of the collegiate living and learning experience for university students and should increase our growing knowledge of the relevance of social ecological variables to student adaptation and performance in a variety of university residential settings.

## References


Brandt, J., & Chapman, N. (1980). Student alterations of dormitory rooms: Social climate and satisfaction. In R. Strough & A. Wandersman (Eds.), *Optimizing environments: Research, practice, and policy.* New York: Environmental Design Research Association.

Cox, G. (1977). *Environmental study of the Memphis Correctional Center.* Memphis, TN: State Technical Institute, Correctional Research and Evaluation Center.

Crouse, R.H. (1982). Peer network therapy: An intervention with the social climate of students in residence halls. *Journal of College Student Personnel, 23,* 105–108.

Daher, D., Corazzini, J., & McKinnon, R. (1977). An environmental redesign program for residence halls. *Journal of College Student Personnel, 18,* 11–15.

Dalton, J. (1981). An initial assessment of the radiating effects of an adaptive skills training program in university dormitories (Doctoral dissertation, University of Connecticut, Storrs, 1980). *Dissertation Abstracts International, 41,* 3173B.

Ford, M. (1975). The social ecology of University of Northern Colorado residence halls (Doctoral dissertation, University of Northern Colorado, Greeley). *Dissertation Abstracts International, 36,* 7233A.

Gerst, M., & Moos, R. (1972). Social ecology of university student residences. *Journal of Educational Psychology, 63,* 513–525.

Gerst, M., & Sweetwood, H. (1973). Correlates of dormitory social climate. *Environment and Behavior, 5,* 440–464.

Goebel, J. (1977). Alienation in dormitory life (Doctoral dissertation, Texas Christian University, Ft. Worth, 1976). *Dissertation Abstracts International, 38,* 415B.

Guilford, J.P. (1954). *Psychometric methods.* New York: McGraw-Hill.

Holahan, C.J., & Wilcox, B. (1979). Environmental satisfaction in high and low rise residential settings: A Lewinian perspective. In J. Aiello & A. Baum (Eds.), *Residential crowding and design* (pp. 127–140). New York: Plenum.

Kerce, E., & Royle, M. (1984). *First term enlisted Marine Corps women: Their backgrounds and experiences* (Report No. TR 84-57). San Diego, CA: Navy Personnel Research and Development Center.

McHugo, G. (1979). A multivariate analysis of self-selection and change due to college experience (Doctoral dissertation, Darmouth College, Hanover, NH). *Dissertation Abstracts International, 40,* 1867B.

Moos, R.H. (1974). *University Residence Environment Scale Form R test booklet.* Palo Alto, CA: Consulting Psychologists Press.

Moos, R.H. (1979). *Evaluating educational environments: Procedures, methods, findings and policy implications.* San Francisco, CA: Jossey-Bass.

Moos, R.H. (1984). Context and coping: Toward a unifying conceptual framework. *American Journal of Community Psychology, 12,* 5–25.

Moos, R.H. (1986). *Military Environment Inventory manual* (2nd ed.). Palo Alto, CA: Consulting Psychologists Press.

Moos, R.H. (1987). *The social climate scales: A user's guide.* Palo Alto, CA: Consulting Psychologists Press.

Moos, R.H. (1988). *University Residence Environment Scale manual* (2nd ed.). Palo Alto, CA: Consulting Psychologists Press.

Moos, R.H., & Gerst, M. (1974). *University Residence Environment Scale manual.* Palo Alto, CA: Consulting Psychologists Press.

Moos, R.H., & Van Dort, B. (1979). Student physical symptoms and the social climate of college living groups. *American Journal of Community Psychology, 7,* 31–43.

Moos, R.H., Van Dort, B., Smail, P., & DeYoung, A. (1975). A typology of university student living groups. *Journal of Educational Psychology, 67,* 359–367.

Moses, J.A., Jr. (1991). Correctional Institutions Environment Scale. In D.J. Keyser & R.C. Sweetland (Eds.), *Test critiques* (Vol. VIII, pp. 118–131). Austin, TX: PRO-ED.

Murray, H.A. (1938). *Explorations in personality.* New York: Oxford University Press.

Null, R. (1980). University residence hall suites: A progression of approaches to evaluation research. *Housing and Society, 7,* 67–76.

Nunnally, J.C. (1967). *Psychometric theory.* New York: McGraw-Hill.

Nunnally, J.C. (1978). *Psychometric theory* (2nd ed.). New York: McGraw-Hill.

Richman, J. (1977). The effects of homogeneous housing assignments upon the adjustment of transfer students (Doctoral dissertation, Florida State University, Tallahassee). *Dissertation Abstracts International, 38,* 3296A.

Schroeder, C. (1979). Designing ideal staff environments through milieu management. *Journal of College Student Personnel, 20,* 129–135.

Schroeder, C., & Belmonte, A. (1979). The influence of residential environment on prepharmacy student achievement and satisfaction. *American Journal of Pharmaceutical Education, 43,* 16–19.

Schroeder, C., & Griffin, C. (1976). A novel living-learning environment for freshmen engineering students. *Engineering Education, 67,* 159–161.

Tsai, B. (1985). *The relationship between the university environment and creative attitudes among Chinese graduate students in Taiwan and in the United States.* Unpublished doctoral dissertation, Stanford University, Palo Alto, CA.

Werring, C.J., Winston, R.B., & McCaffrey, R.J. (1981). How paint projects affect residents' perceptions of their living environment. *Journal of College and University Student Housing, 11,* 3–7.

Wilcox, B., & Holahan, C. (1976). Social ecology of the megadorm in university student housing. *Journal of Educational Psychology, 68,* 453–458.

Wilson, J. (1980). An action research project to facilitate person-environment congruence (Doctoral dissertation, University of Massachusetts, Amherst, 1979). *Dissertation Abstracts International, 40,* 4506A.

**Robert J. Drummond, Ed.D.**
*Program Director, Counselor Education, University of North Florida, Jacksonville, Florida.*

# THE VALUES SCALE: RESEARCH EDITION

*Donald E. Super and Dorothy D. Nevill. Palo Alto, California: Consulting Psychologists Press, Inc.*

## Introduction

The Values Scale (VS; Super & Nevill, 1986) is a paper-and-pencil inventory designed to measure 21 intrinsic and extrinsic life-career values (Ability Utilization, Achievement, Advancement, Aesthetics, Altruism, Authority, Autonomy, Creativity, Economic Rewards, Lifestyle, Personal Development, Physical Activity, Prestige, Risk, Social Interaction, Social Relations, Variety, Working Conditions, Cultural Identity, Physical Prowess, and Economic Security) via 106 items, five items per scale (item 106 is not scored). The authors define values as the objectives sought in behavior. Intrinsic values are those inherent in an activity, such as Ability Utilization and Creativity. Extrinsic values, such as Economic Rewards and Prestige, are concomitants or outcomes in an activity. The VS can be used by career counselors and researchers interested in assessing the life-career values of clients or groups.

This scale was one of the instruments developed by Donald E. Super and associates for the Work Importance Study (WIS). The WIS, an international study, was designed to identify the values that persons seek or hope to find in their different life roles and to study the importance of the work role as a means of value realization in the context of other life roles (Nevill & Super, 1989, p. 1). Many countries participated in the study: Australia, Belgium, Canada, France, Israel, Italy, Japan, Poland, Portugal, the Republic of South Africa, the United States, and Yugoslavia. The U.S. version of the scale was authored by Donald E. Super and Dorothy Nevill.

Specialists from the countries represented in the WIS helped to define the variables to be studied and to write items for the project. The VS was developed, piloted, and then refined through the efforts of numerous researchers and professors. Items were empirically checked through interitem correlations and factor analysis. Certain scales were dropped and others added in the process. The five best items for each scale were kept. The 1980 version of the VS contained 10 items for each of the 23 original scales developed. The current VS was published as a research scale in 1986 and the manual revised in 1989. This revised manual (Nevill & Super, 1989) contains normative information for high school students, university students, and adults, and reports additional validity and reliability information.

Donald E. Super, Professor Emeritus of Psychology and Education at Teachers College, Columbia University, is a major career development theorist and has published extensively in this field. His numerous research studies on career development and career decision making have led to the formation of his developmental model. He and his associates have constructed several major assessment instruments used by career counselors and counseling psychologists, such as the Career Development Inventory, the Salience Inventory, and the Adult Career Concerns Inventory.

Dorothy Nevill is Professor of Psychology at the University of Florida and was an associate of Dr. Super's in the WIS. She also co-authored the Salience Inventory in addition to numerous articles in the area of career development.

The VS test booklet consists of four pages: the cover sheet, which describes the purpose of the test; two pages for the directions and the 106 test items; and a final page that asks test takers to identify the occupational group to which they belong. The matrix is an adaptation of a section of the Career Planning Questionnaire from the Differential Aptitude Test.

The separate answer sheet can be machine or hand scored. The front side presents 10 demographic items to be bubbled in: name, age, educational level, marital status, occupational status, how examinees feel about themselves as a student, citizen, leisurite, and worker, what type of work they do, the level of work they do, and the kind of work they do. The second side of the answer sheet contains five columns of item response spaces.

The VS profile sheet contains high school, college, and adult norms on one side and a graph on which individuals can record raw scores and draw their profile on the other.

Examinees are asked to respond to each item on a 4-point scale, where 1 means "of little or no importance" and 4 means "very important." The same stem is considered for evaluating each item, asking the examinee where the activity is now or will be in the future on the scale of importance. An example of activity similar to those on the test would be "to have my job for life."

The VS can be self-administered or given by an examiner. No special competencies are needed to administer the test. The VS is designed for use with high school, college, and adult groups or individuals, although the authors suggest (Nevill & Super, 1989) that it could be used as early as middle school. This test, which requires eighth-grade reading ability, is said to be appropriate for adult members of semiskilled, skilled, clerical, sales, professional, and managerial occupations.

## Practical Applications/Uses

The VS is designed to measure or assess the importance of intrinsic and extrinsic work values to the individual and can be used as a tool in career and personal counseling. The authors suggest that the scale can enhance individual counseling, group assessment, career development, needs surveys, and research with variables such as interests, career maturity, sex, and socioeconomic status. The VS can be used in research on dimensions of vocational behavior and measurement of values. Counseling psychologists, as well as career, employment, and personal counselors, could find this scale a valuable assessment tool.

Many career guidance assessment systems, both pencil and paper and computer assisted, require clients to assess their values. However, the type of constructs measured by the VS might help clients better gain an understanding of their value structure than do other systems of organizing values. Apropos of these differences, the VS also can be used in teaching to illustrate Super's theory.

Other language versions of the test used in the WIS have been published, but not by Consulting Psychologists Press. In addition, no special forms are available for hearing- or sight-impaired persons.

An examiner with experience administering group tests would have no difficulty with the VS, and, as noted previously, it also can be self-administered. Directions are printed on the front cover of the test booklet, and administrative procedures are described in chapter 2 of the manual. Administration is easy and could be performed by a proctor or secretary. Most individuals can complete the VS in 30 to 45 minutes, and (in this reviewer's experience with college students and adults) even 10 to 15 minutes is possible.

The completed scale can be sent to Consulting Psychologists Press for scoring or one can score it by hand. With the latter in mind, the VS answer sheet is designed to be scored quickly either by the test taker or the examiner. Each row represents one of the values. For example, items 1, 22, 43, 64, and 85 appear in the first row of each column and represent Ability utilization. The responses across each row are added to yield a score for each subscale. The score is the summation of the weights (degree of importance) the test taker has given to each of the five items. A test can be hand scored in 2 to 3 minutes. The computer scoring service provides users with results on a floppy disk, including means and standard deviations as well as individual profiles.

VS scores can be interpreted either normatively or ipsatively. Norms are presented for high school, college, and adult groups on the profile sheet. The individual's raw or standard scores can be compared across the 21 subscales to identify the highs and lows in his or her profile. The authors present a sample case of a 25-year-old male to illustrate VS interpretation.

**Technical Aspects**

The manual presents evidence of internal consistency using Cronbach's alpha and of stability using the test-retest method. Although the coefficients of both the 1980 and 1986 versions are presented, this review will focus on the current version. The manual reports alpha coefficients based on 2,816 high school students, 2,140 college students, and 323 adults. For the high school group, alpha coefficients ranged from a low of .60 on Lifestyle to a high of .80 on both Creativity and Risk, with a median of .71. Eight of the coefficients here fell in the .60 to .69 range. For the college group, the coefficients ranged from a low of .62 on Variety to a high of .85 on Risk, with a median of .75. Six of the coefficients for this group ranged from .60 to .69. For the adult sample, alpha coefficients ranged from a high of .87 on Economic Security to a low of .67 on Cultural Identity, with a median of .77. Two of the coefficients fell between .60 and .69. Nevill and Super (1989) point out that at the high school level, values are still forming and more variability in responding is expected (p. 21).

Test-retest data come from two samples of university students. One sample ($n$ = 83) produced coefficients ranging from a low of .52 on Ability Utilization to a high of .82 on Physical Activity, with a median coefficient of .71. In the second sample reported ($n$ = 140), coefficients ranged from a low of .59 on Physical Prowess to a high of .82 on Economic Security (median = .70). Ten scales yielded coefficients lower than .69. Ability Utilization, Lifestyle, and Personal Development had consistently low reliabilities across sample by both methods; Physical Prowess had low test-retest coefficients.

The authors make an argument for content validity through the rational methods in which the values were determined, defined, and developed. Nevill and Super state that the most important types of validity data are those showing that the instrument actually measures what the theory claims it should measure (1989, p. 24). The authors present means and standard deviations by gender and indicate that sex differences are to be expected with certain values.

Factor analyses of the VS items were computed for each group. Similarities in the factor structure were found across groups and are reported in the manual's Appendix F. On only three of the scales do the items occur as pure factors: Authority, Creativity, and Prestige. The authors report that the same combination of items make up three additional factors. The Economic Rewards, Economic Security, and Advancement items have high loading on one factor and are labeled the Material factor. The items from Ability Utilization, Achievement, and Personal Development have high loadings on another factor and are labeled Ability Utilization. Social Interaction and Social Relations have high loadings on another factor and are labeled Sociability. There are some differences in the factor structure of the remaining items across groups. A few studies appear in the literature comparing the VS with other measures (e.g., Macnab & Fitzsimmons, 1987; Drummond & Stoddard, 1990).

## Critique

The assessment of values can be an important part of the career counseling process, for knowledge of one's values can provide important information for career development. The VS presents one assessment possibility for counselors, but there are some problems that prospective users need to recognize.

1. Although there was an effort to identify important work values through rational and empirical methods, many of the VS subscales are not independent and are highly correlated with one another. The factor analyses of the items also demonstrates the lack of independence of some of the items belonging to the same scale. (As noted previously, only three scales occur as pure factors: Authority, Creativity, and Prestige.)

2. Some of the scales have questionable reliability, as evidenced by both the internal consistency and test-retest methods. In general, the standard error of measurement for some of the subscales would be fairly large and needs to be taken into consideration when interpreting individual profiles.

3. Very few studies have compared the VS with other values inventories, including the Work Values Inventory (WVI; Super, 1970). Actually, there is little evidence presented of this scale's criterion-related validity.

4. Three of the scales are not presented in alphabetical order on the VS profile sheet. Further, with regard to the profile, the WIS has been concluded and proba-

bly very few individuals would be interested in the comparisons across the different cultures represented (especially as the test would have to rescored). Also, why not drop item 106, as it is not used in scoring? If the VS is to be utilized, it needs to have its own identity and not just be a research tool that was used in the WIS.

5. The subscales are defined by only one item in the manual, and the authors should consider providing more complete definitions. (This should be relatively easy, as the judges of the definitions apparently achieved consensus.) The pattern that Nevill and Super might consider is the way that Edwards defines the 15 needs measured by the Edwards Personal Preference Scale (EPPS).

The revised manual is an improvement over the 1986 version but still has a way to go to meet the criteria of a good manual. The item pool and the values included on the VS need to be reviewed. The internal consistency data would indicate considerable variability in how some of the items fit the scales.

The present reviewer has used the VS in counseling, research, and teaching contexts. In general, clients rate it somewhat redundant and tedious to take (they like the WVI better). They do not see the importance of certain values to their work situation. The VS is influenced by response set and has to be cautiously interpreted. Some clients rate all items a "4," while others tend to rate all items "1" or "2." As respondents could fake on this instrument without much effort, they need to see the importance of taking the VS and the relevance of the instrument to their life situation.

The test does have sufficient reliability to use in research contexts, and it presents an excellent teaching tool for stimulating discussion on values and Super's theory and for illustrating differences in values by Holland's personality type.

This reviewer is not certain that there was that much gain in either the validity or reliability of the VS over the WVI. Counselors following Super's developmental assessment model will find the VS a useful tool, but others will prefer direct questions on values or some other quicker technique to get at a client's value structure. In general I conclude, as I did in a previous review (Drummond, 1988), that the VS is a potentially useful instrument in career and developmental counseling, even in the face of some technical problems.

### References

Drummond, R.J. (1988). Test review: The Values Scale. *Journal of Employment Counseling, 25,* 136–138.

Drummond, R.J., & Stoddard, A. (1990, April). *Values inventories: Issues of validity and reliability.* Paper presented at the annual meeting of the American Educational Research Association, Boston.

Macnab, D., & Fitzsimmons, G.W. (1987). A multitrait-multimethod study of work-related needs, values, and preferences. *Journal of Vocational Behavior, 30,* 1–15.

Nevill, D.D., & Super, D.E. (1989). *Manual to The Values Scale.* Palo Alto, CA: Consulting Psychologists Press.

Super, D.E. (1970). *Work Values Inventory.* Chicago: Riverside.

Super, D.E., & Nevill, D.D. (1986). *The Values Scale.* Palo Alto, CA: Consulting Psychologists Press.

**Bonnie C. Konopak, Ph.D.**
*Associate Professor and Assistant Chair, Department of Curriculum and Instruction, Louisiana State University, Baton Rouge, Louisiana.*

# VOCABULARY COMPREHENSION SCALE

*Tina E. Bangs. Allen, Texas: DLM Teaching Resources.*

## Introduction

The Vocabulary Comprehension Scale (VCS; Bangs, 1975) was developed to assess language/learning handicapped children's comprehension of pronouns and words of position, quality, quantity, and size. In contrast to more traditional tests (e.g., Peabody Picture Vocabulary Test, Dunn, 1959; PPVT-Revised, Dunn & Dunn, 1981) that measure size of vocabulary, the present instrument is a criterion-referenced tool that evaluates knowledge of specific types of words important for children to know when entering school. From the baseline information obtained, an educator is able to construct curricular activities to assist a child in developing vocabulary appropriate for kindergarten or first grade. The scale is suitable for use with both females and males, ranging in age from preschool (2.0 years) to first grade (6.0 years).

Tina E. Bangs received her Ph.D. from Stanford University in 1958, with a specialization in speech pathology and audiology. Upon moving to Houston, Texas, she co-directed the Speech and Hearing Center in the Texas Medical Center. Throughout her lengthy academic career, her interests have focused on clinical research and instruction/learning experiences in the area of language/learning disabilities. She has written numerous articles and books on young children's developmental learning and is particularly known for her text, *Language and Learning Disorders of the Preacademic Child* (1st ed., 1968; 2nd ed., 1982). She retired in 1984 and is now Professor Emerita at the Speech and Hearing Institute, University of Texas Health Science Center at Houston.

Research on the Vocabulary Comprehension Scale was begun in order to provide more diagnostic information than was normally obtained from previous tests (e.g., Dunn, 1959; Wechsler, 1974). Two important considerations were addressed: (a) the kinds of words children have in their lexicon, and (b) the age level at which these words are acquired. First, research on types of words was grounded in Clarke's (1973) semantic feature hypothesis; new vocabulary words added to a child's lexicon may be used appropriately (extension) or inappropriately (overextension). In particular, overextended words may be one of two types: (a) pronoun generalizations (e.g., using the pronoun *he* with all children) and (b) misuse of paired opposites (e.g., using *big* to cover small to large sizes). Second, research on children's language development (e.g., Palermo, 1974) indicated that different types of words are acquired at different age levels. For example, children under 4 years have difficulty demonstrating their comprehension of *more* and *less*, with *more* being acquired before its opposite *less.*

In the VCS, children are asked to manipulate objects in order to exhibit their knowledge of target words. Eighty-five words were originally selected from first- through third-grade readers in the categories of pronouns and words of position, quality, quantity, and size. Of the 85 words, 24 were deleted from the final scale due to (a) not meeting criteria by 6.0 years of age and (b) eliciting erratic responses from the normative group. The subjects included 80 children of mixed ethnic backgrounds from low middle to high middle income families; they were all enrolled in preschool programs in Houston. Children were selected based on average or above ability and a score no greater than 6 months below age level on the Peabody Picture Vocabulary Test. Ten children in each 6-month age level between 2.0 years and 6.0 years were tested (e.g., 2.0–2.6 years; 2.6–3.0 years). Analysis of the data revealed distinct cutoff points between 80–100% correct. The age level selected for comprehension was at the point where 80% or more of the subjects responded correctly. An exception included three words (*less, their,* and *different*) that met criteria for a 12-month span but slipped to 70% at a higher level. The author chose to use the lower age level, with a caution to educators regarding the stability of these words. The VCS has recently undergone changes and will be published in a second edition as the Receptive Vocabulary Checklist (Bangs, in press).

The Vocabulary Comprehension Scale consists of a set of manipulatives, individual scoring forms, and a manual containing test administration, scoring procedures, and suggestions for instructional activities. The manipulatives include (a) a tea set, with female and male dolls, cups, plates, knives, forks, spoons, and napkins; (b) a garage set, with a garage, ladder, fence with short and tall trees, dog, big cars, and little cars; and (c) miscellaneous items, including buttons of different sizes (large/small), cubes of different densities (soft/hard) and weights (light/heavy), and sticks of different lengths (short/long).

The individual scoring forms list different activities for each set of manipulatives, based on different types of words. The tea party activity focuses on pronouns and includes such tasks as "Give *me* a cup," "*She* wants a plate," and "*He* wants a napkin." The garage activity focuses on words of position and size; sample tasks include "Put the car *in/behind/beside* the garage" (position) and "Show me a *big/little* car" (size). The button activity focuses on positions, "Put the button *under* the car"; quality, "Show me the one that is the *same/different* as this one"; and quantity, "Show me a *full/empty* box." The blocks and sticks activities focus on quality, such as in "Show me the *thin/fat* one, *hard/soft* one." The last page is a summary sheet on which the examiner scores each task (+/pass, –/fail, and blank/not administered). Each task is designated by the age criterion level; all tasks are listed developmentally from the lowest (2.0–2.6) to the highest age level (5.6–6.0).

The manual includes directions for administration, using the manipulatives, and completing the scoring forms. Prior to administration, the examiner asks the child to identify each item used in the various activities to ensure that an inappropriate response is not due to his or her lack of object knowledge/vocabulary. When beginning the test, the examiner sets up the manipulatives into a tea party scene and a garage scene, each with appropriate objects; the miscellaneous items are grouped according to type. The examiner then proceeds to read each task from the scoring form, to elicit the child's response, and to record a pass, fail, or not administered score. The test is concluded when all 61 items are completed or when the examiner feels the test should be terminated (e.g., the child fails to meet criteria on succeeding tasks). The scores are then transcribed to the summary section of the scoring form, and each word type (e.g., pronouns) is totaled.

**Practical Applications/Uses**

In developing the Vocabulary Comprehension Scale, Bangs had a two-fold purpose: (a) to determine the developmental sequence of selected target word acquisition, and (b) to construct a criterion-referenced measure that would indicate a child's knowledge of these words. The test was designed for use in clinical and educational settings, wherein an examiner works one-on-one with a young child to obtain diagnostic information. It functions as a pretest, as an educator can determine which words are known or need to be known and then construct instructional activities for learning. It also functions as a posttest, as an educator can subsequently determine the extent of acquisition.

The VCS originally was intended for young children ages 2.0–6.0 who may prove to be language/learning handicapped. By obtaining information on a normative group of average and above ability learners, the vocabulary knowledge of this handicapped group could be evaluated. In particular, objects rather than pictures were utilized in order to increase the reliability of these young subjects' responses. Because the target words included pronouns and words of position, quality, quantity, and size, pictures were felt to be appropriate for correct identification. The test has been used successfully with a range of language handicaps (e.g., hearing impaired, language different; Bangs, 1982); consequently, it could potentially serve as a screening tool for language development of all preacademic children.

The directions for administration are briefly described in the test manual and on the scoring form itself. The most appropriate setting for administration is an individual session with an examiner, within a clinic or classroom context. Because of the simplicity of the test and its administration, the examiner may be a clinician, an educational specialist, or a classroom teacher. The directions are not detailed, leaving concerns regarding time, order of items, and alternative responses unanswered. However, because it is a criterion-referenced measure, some adjustments could probably be made according to individual children and their abilities.

Scoring the results is not difficult. Of the 61 items listed, 17 test pronouns, 26 test words of position, 6 test words of quality, 6 test words of quantity, and 6 test words of size. On the instrument itself, the words are ordered by activity (i.e., garage scene, buttons, tea party, and miscellaneous); when transcribing the results to the summary sheet, the words are ordered by developmental age within word type. By tallying the results of each word type, an educator can obtain a quantitative measure across words; by examining those words judged to be known/unknown, he or she can address specific words at specific age levels.

Actual interpretation of the data appears to be limited to a numerical gain from pretest to posttest on number of words as well as on age level for each word type. In addition, Bangs suggests that particular unknown words be selected for instructional activities. Because of its criterion-referenced nature, an examiner would need little training in order to adequately and properly interpret this test.

Finally, in addition to the administration/scoring instructions in the test manual,

Bangs provides detailed follow-up instructional activities for teachers, support personnel, and parents. In an introduction, she explains the need for (a) pretesting and posttesting in order to obtain the child's level of functioning, and (b) the development of objectives and lesson plans. Following this, she provides specific lesson plans for language handicapped students, including objectives, classroom activities/materials, support teaching from educational specialists/clinicians, and family involvement. Within these activities, selected target vocabulary words are addressed, as well as other language development areas (e.g., increasing sentence length).

**Technical Aspects**

The manual contains little information on validity and reliability; further, citations on the use of the instrument (Bangs, 1982) indicate that it has been used successfully but no critical detail is provided. In examining the standardization procedure, it appears to have been thoughtfully undertaken. However, information regarding who the examiners were, where the testing took place, under what conditions the test was administered, and so forth is not provided. In addition, while the total number of subjects was 80, they were stratified by 6-month intervals, with 10 subjects per level between the ages of 2.0 to 6.0 years. It is difficult to determine the generalizability of these results.

However, Bangs does provide a table of the percentage of students meeting criterion for each word at the 6-month age intervals. The 61 words are listed by word type; within each type, words are ordered from most to least known by age level. For example, the pronoun *I* met criterion across all age intervals; the position word *behind* did not meet criterion until the 5.0–5.5 age level. Such data are informative, as they delineate word acquisition developmentally as well as note any inconsistency in meeting criterion across levels (e.g., *less*).

**Critique**

Because vocabulary is a critical indicator of success in school (Bangs, 1975; Graves, 1987), it is important to evaluate a preacademic child's knowledge of words. Prior to the development of the Vocabulary Comprehension Scale in 1975, researchers (Dunn, 1959; Terman & Merrill, 1960; Wechsler, 1974) were primarily interested in the size of children's lexicons, particularly with local/national norming groups. Further, their tests (Peabody Picture Vocabulary Test, Stanford-Binet Intelligence Scale, Wechsler Intelligence Scale for Children) and similar later tests (e.g., the National Tests of Basic Skills; American Testronics, 1985) consist of paper-and-pencil instruments wherein children are asked to respond to a target word by selecting an appropriate drawing/picture.

Bangs' scale, in contrast, addresses (a) the content of a child's lexicon as well as (b) the child's use of manipulatives within particular contexts. Although more recent criterion-referenced tests (e.g., Assessment of Children's Language Comprehension; Giddan & Stark, 1983) also focus on specific word knowledge, they generally still include written materials. It is these two factors—focus on content and use of physical objects—that recommend the VCS as an appropriate screening tool for young children.

However, limitations to the use of this scale exist, primarily due to the standardization process in test development and the brevity of detail in the test manual. As discussed earlier, the group of subjects used to develop the instrument were limited in number, particularly when stratified by age intervals; the conditions for testing were not explained; and, most importantly, no information is given in terms of test validity and reliability. In addition, important information concerning test administration and interpretation is lacking; indeed, more detail is provided for the instructional plans suggested as follow-up activities. Given that the revised VCS will be published soon, it should be more comprehensive regarding these critical points.

## References

American Testronics. (1985). *National Tests of Basic Skills.* Iowa City, IA: Author.

Bangs, T.E. (1968). *Language and learning disorders of the preacademic child.* New York: Prentice-Hall.

Bangs, T.E. (1975). *Vocabulary Comprehension Scale.* Allen, TX: DLM Teaching Resources.

Bangs, T.E. (1982). *Language and learning disorders of the preacademic child* (2nd ed.). New York: Prentice-Hall.

Bangs, T.E. (in press). *Receptive Vocabulary Checklist.* Tucson, AZ: Communication Skill Builders.

Clarke, E.V. (1973). What's in a word? On the child's acquisition of semantics in his first language. In T.E. Moore (Ed.), *Cognitive development and the acquisition of language* (pp. 65–110). New York: Academic Press.

Dunn, L.M. (1959). *Peabody Picture Vocabulary Test.* Circle Pines, MN: American Guidance Service.

Dunn, L.M., & Dunn, L.E. (1981). *Peabody Picture Vocabulary Test–Revised.* Circle Pines, MN: American Guidance Service.

Giddan, J., & Stark, J. (1983). *Assessment of Children's Language Comprehension.* Palo Alto, CA: Consulting Psychologists Press.

Graves, M. (1987). The roles of instruction in fostering vocabulary development. In M. McKeown & M. Curtis (Eds.), *The nature of vocabulary acquisition* (pp. 165–184). Hillsdale, NJ: Lawrence Erlbaum.

Palermo, D.S. (1974). Still more about the comprehension of "less." *Developmental Psychology, 10,* 827–829.

Terman, L., & Merrill, M. (1960). *Stanford Binet Intelligence Scale.* Boston: Houghton Mifflin.

Wechsler, D. (1974). *Wechsler Intelligence Scale for Children* -Revised. San Antonio, TX: Psychological Corporation.

**Michael D. Franzen, Ph.D.**
*Associate Professor of Behavioral Medicine and Psychiatry and Director of Neuropsychology, West Virginia University Medical Center, Morgantown, West Virginia.*

---

# WIDE RANGE ASSESSMENT OF MEMORY AND LEARNING

*David Sheslow and Wayne Adams. Wilmington, Delaware: Jastak Associates, Inc.*

## Introduction

The Wide Range Assessment of Memory and Learning (WRAML) represents an attempt to provide a means of evaluating the memory of children aged 5 years, 0 months to 17 years, 11 months. Because modern developments in memory theory analyze memory in terms of its various aspects (e.g., visual and verbal, semantic and episodic, short term and long term, etc.), the WRAML contains procedures that are designed to assess those aspects separately. Additionally, the WRAML contains some procedures in which the information to be memorized is presented across multiple trials, thereby allowing an evaluation of the subject's learning efficiency. Finally, both recall and multiple-choice recognition procedures are included so that both encoding and retrieval can be assessed.

There are nine subtests in the WRAML. Additionally, there are delayed recall procedures for the Verbal Learning, Visual Learning, Sound Symbol, and Story Memory subtests, and recognition procedures for the Story Memory subtest. If all of the subtests are administered, the average amount of time required for each subject is about 1 hour. The first four subtests can be given as a screening procedure, in which case the amount of time required decreases to about 15 minutes. The WRAML provides scores for Verbal and Visual Memory Indices as well as for a Learning Index. These indices combined result in a General Memory Index. The differences between the immediate recall scores and the delayed recall scores for the Verbal Learning, Story Memory, Sound Symbol, and Visual Learning subtests provide indices of decay and savings.

There is no single theory underlying the WRAML. Instead, various theories were reviewed and the clinically most relevant aspects were incorporated into the design of the battery. There are separate norms for the age groups, and for some of the subtests, younger children are started at a different level than are older children. The learning tasks (Verbal Learning, Visual Learning, and Sound Symbol Learning) have smaller sets of stimuli for younger children than for older ones. These considerations are good ideas, but all of the tasks are the same for older and younger children, differing only in level of difficulty. There does not seem to be a consideration of the developmental aspects of memory, such as the idea that children do not systematically use active encoding strategies until about age 8 or 9 years and that children older than 10 gradually refine their use of strategies, making them both more effective and more flexible (Kail & Hagen, 1982). Furthermore, the test authors do not directly discuss the concept that children will vary in the degree to which they benefit from multiple trials as a function of developmental status (Boyd, 1988). The use of multiple trial procedures with age norms will help account for differences that might occur across the ages, but a more directly articulated method would have been preferable.

David Sheslow and Wayne Adams are psychologists who practice at the A.I. duPont Institute, which is a hospital for children with chronic illnesses, mainly related to injuries of the brain or spinal cord. In the manual, the test authors describe their frustration in not having a sound memory assessment instrument available to evaluate children. Out of this frustration, the plan for the WRAML was designed and executed over the course of a 2½-year period.

The original battery included 14 subtests rather than the current 9. Each of the subtests also had a larger number of items than is presently the case. All of these items were administered to 200 subjects at three age levels across the difference between first grade and high school. Item analyses (not described in the manual) suggested that certain of the items and subtests be dropped. The remaining items were ordered into graduated scales of item difficulty.

This collection of items was then administered to a stratified normative sample of 2,363 children in 21 different age groups. There was one age group for each 6 months between 5 years, 0 months and 13 years, 11 months, one age group for the 14-year-olds, and one age group for the 15-year-olds. A final age group included subjects between the ages of 16 years, 0 months and 17 years, 11 months. The size of the age groups ranged from 110 to 119. Population figures from the 1980 U.S. Census and the 1988 Rand McNally commercial atlas and marketing guide were used to stratify the sample in terms of sex, race, and region of the country. Additionally, the proportion of urban versus rural residences reflected the Rand McNally values. Socioeconomic variables were evaluated by randomly sampling 10% of the normative group and recording the higher occupational level of the parents. There were no differences between the distribution in the 1980 census and the distribution in this group of 263 individuals. The children were sampled from regular school classrooms, and children with special educational needs were included in the same proportions in which they occurred in the larger sample. Children with disabilities that precluded administration of the entire WRAML were not included in the normative sample.

The WRAML is contained in a box approximately the size of a briefcase. The assessment of each child requires a test protocol and a response booklet. The word lists and stories are included on the recording protocols; the subject uses the response booklet to respond to the Picture Memory subtest items and those of the Design Memory subtest. The first, Picture Memory, uses a set of four pictures that vary in complexity. The child is shown each picture for 10 seconds and then is given an approximate replica of the picture in the response booklet. He or she is told to draw a line through each part of the picture that differs from the original. The second subtest, Design Memory, involves showing the child a set of four cards that have abstract designs drawn in various quadrants. He or she is then asked to reproduce the designs in blank quadrants on the response booklet.

The third subtest, Verbal Learning, involves administering a list of words (13 for children 8 years and younger, 16 for older children). Every child receives all four trials, and a delayed recall trial is administered following the next subtest (Story Memory). The relevant scores are the total number of words recalled over the four trials and the difference between recall on the fourth trial and recall on the delayed trial. The Story Memory subtest uses two stories for younger children, one of which is one of the two stories used for older children. For each of the stories, some points must be remembered verbatim to receive credit and some can be remembered as gist. The scoring instructions include examples of acceptable gist replies. However, the same amount of credit is given for the exact responses as for the gist responses.

The fifth subtest is called Finger Windows. This procedure uses a card with nine cut-out circles or "windows," which the examiner touches in a prespecified order. The subject is asked to reproduce the series of touches in the same order, and the test is discontinued after three consecutive failures. The sixth subtest, Sound Symbol, has two different forms, one for younger children and one for older children. The form for older children has the same items as the one for younger children plus four additional items. The procedure involves showing the subject an abstract line drawing from a small easel booklet and giving him or her a single-syllable sound to associate with the symbol. Some of the associations are easy, such as the symbol for the sound "wah," which looks like stylized water waves, and the symbol for "tabe," which resembles a stylized table. However, there are no scoring distinctions between easy and difficult, and the manual does not address this point. If the child gives the incorrect answer or is unable to answer within 5 seconds, the sound is again given. This procedure continues for four trials. A final, delayed trial is given at the end of the immediate recall procedures, and the two relevant scores are the sum across Trials 1 to 4 and the difference between Trial 4 and the delayed trial.

The fifth subtest is Sentence Memory. All responses are scored verbatim. Perfect performance is given 2 points, one error receives 1 point, and two or more errors receive 0 points. There are 20 sentences arranged in increasing length and difficulty, but the subtest is discontinued after three consecutive 0-point responses. The next subtest, Visual Learning, has two separate forms, depending on the age of the subject. This subtest requires a stimulus board divided into a 4 × 4 matrix with a different color design in each cell. The designs are covered by yellow soft plastic covers. One by one the different designs are uncovered. The child is then shown the designs from a spiral-bound booklet and asked to point out the location of that design on the stimulus board. If the child points to an incorrect location, the examiner removes the correct cover and provides verbal feedback. If the child is correct, the examiner uncovers the design. There are four trials, and the relevant scores are the total correct over Trials 1 to 4 and the difference between the number correct on the fourth trial and the number correct on a delayed trial.

The ninth subtest is called Letter/Number Memory. The examiner reads a series of letters and numbers intermixed and asks the subject to repeat the series. The subtest is discontinued after three consecutive failures. After the Letter/Number Memory subtest, the delayed trials of the Sound Symbol, Visual Learning, and Story Memory subtests are given. Additionally, a delayed recognition test of the Story Memory subtest is administered in a multiple-choice format.

The examiner form has space to plot scale scores for each subtest, where 10 is the average score and 3 is the standard deviation. Assignment of scaled scores differs by age group. The scale scores are then summed into four indices: Verbal Memory, Visual Memory, Learning Scale, and General Memory. The four indices use two different transformations, one for children 8 years and younger and one for those 9 years and older. The delayed recall subtest scores and delayed recognition scores are translated into a five-level scale of Atypical, Borderline, Low Average, Average, and Bright Average. One of the complications in using this scheme is that if a child receives a 0 score at the initial administration and a 0 score at the delayed recall, the difference is 0, placing the subject in the Bright Average range, the same as would be the case if the child had a perfect performance at the initial trial and a perfect performance at the delayed recall. Therefore, these difference scores should always be interpreted with respect to the absolute level of score. The manual does not indicate how these rankings were derived. Finally, there are instructions for prorating a General Memory Index when only eight of the nine subtests have been given.

## Practical Applications/Uses

The manual states that qualified users of the WRAML include trained clinicians with experience in the administration of psychometric instruments. Administration and scoring may also be conducted by a teacher or technician under the supervision of a psychologist. The authors also recommend the test for speech-language pathologists, learning disability specialists, and educational diagnosticians. There is some behavioral skill required of the person administering the test, especially for the Picture Memory subtest, and practice is recommended.

The WRAML requires that the subject have intact visual integrative and visual scanning skills. Additionally, he or she should have intact verbal receptive language skills, especially for phonemic discrimination. These prerequisites must be determined by separate evaluation, and there is no administration flexibility to allow for the assessment of perceptually disabled children. All of the subtests must be administered in the order specified in the manual.

Because of the wide range of ages in the normative group, the WRAML would be appropriate for testing schoolchildren from kindergarten until high school. Other appropriate subjects would include children with psychiatric and neurological disorders in which memory impairment is a complaint. The materials are easily portable, and this test would also be useful in a hospital setting. The optimal setting for administration of the WRAML is a quiet, distraction-free room where the examiner can sit opposite the subject. This is the first well-normed such instrument for the evaluation of children (although others are planned), and as such the WRAML possesses great potential for contributing to the neuropsychological assessment of children.

Scoring is described clearly in the manual. For the most part, the process is objective, and where the subject's response is ambiguous, the examiner is allowed to probe for clarification. There are subjective aspects to scoring Story Memory and Design Memory, and the manual contains extra instructions and examples for these two subtests. If the examiner has recorded the responses clearly, scoring should not take more than 15 minutes.

The manual also contains a few clinical case examples. The results of the WRAML are best conceptualized as providing clinical hypotheses to be evaluated against other clinical information. Further research will allow greater certitude in the independent interpretation of WRAML.

### Technical Aspects

The WRAML was evaluated using both classical test theory methods and item response theory methods (Rasch modeling). The manual provides tables with item separation statistics (range = 1.00–0.99) and person separation statistics (range = 0.79–0.94) for each of the subtests. The values for coefficient alpha range from 0.78 to 0.90 for the subtests, and from 0.90 to 0.96 for the memory indices. Test-retest reliability was evaluated over an average of 108 days with a range of 61 to 267 days. This study used 87 individuals from the normative sample. General Memory had a stability coefficient of 0.84. For Verbal Memory the coefficient was 0.82, for Visual Memory, 0.61, and for Learning Memory, 0.81. Mean differences between the two occasions are not presented in the manual, so it is difficult to determine why the stability coefficient for Visual Memory was relatively lower than the others. In any event, test-retest reliability is difficult to evaluate in tests of memory and learning. The manual presents standard errors of measurement (SEM) calculated on both the coefficient alpha values and on the person separation indices.

Interscorer reliability was evaluated by having two individuals independently score 82 sets of Design Memory protocols randomly chosen from the normative sample. The interscorer reliability coefficient for the total subtest score was 0.99 with no significant difference between mean scores. The manual states that item bias was investigated for both gender and race, but that the information will be published in a separate monograph.

The WRAML is designed to measure memory functions in children. The different subtests have complex constructs and may not be well articulated as single unitary behaviors. This is not necessarily a fault in the instrument, as many neuropsychological skills are complex interplays of overlapping skills. However, the presence of complex constructs will make it difficult to validate the subtests individually in terms of their behavioral referents.

Validity was evaluated by correlating the WRAML with the memory section of the McCarthy Scales of Children's Ability for 41 subjects aged 6 and 7 years. The WRAML General Memory Index correlated 0.72 with the McCarthy Memory Index, but the WRAML Learning Index correlated only 0.10 with the McCarthy. The WRAML was correlated with the Memory Scale of the Stanford-Binet, Fourth Edition in a sample of 50 children aged 10 and 11 years. Coefficients ranged from 0.62 for WRAML Visual Memory and Stanford-Binet Memory to 0.80 for WRAML General Memory and Stanford-Binet Memory. Finally, the WRAML was correlated with the Wechsler Memory Scale–Revised (WMS-R) in a sample of 71 subjects aged 16 and 17 years. The respective Verbal Memory indices correlated 0.44, the respective Visual Memory indices correlated 0.47, and the respective General

Memory indices correlated 0.61. Although the participants were randomly selected from a group of supposedly nonimpaired subjects, the mean WMS-R Verbal Memory was 88.0 and the mean Visual Memory was 109.0, indicating that there may have been some anomalous results clouding the interpretation of the study.

As a check on the factorial validity, two principal components analyses with varimax rotation were conducted on the normative sample, one for the children 8 years and younger and one for those 9 years and older. For the most part, the various subtests loaded on the factors or indices to which they had been assigned. The exception was in Visual Learning, which loaded more highly on the Visual Memory factor than on the Learning factor.

The WRAML was also correlated with the WISC-R in a sample of 40 children aged 6 years to 8 years, 11 months. The results indicate small to moderate correlations between these two sets of variables. The WRAML was correlated with the WRAT-R in a sample of 40 children aged 6 years to 8 years, 11 months and in a sample of 40 children aged 16 to 17 years. Here again there were small correlations. This information is preliminary, and interpretation should be limited.

## Critique

The WRAML is the first standardized and well-normed, broad-based instrument devised to assess memory in children. The authors have taken great pains to ensure that adequate standardization and normative information has been provided. However, there are a few problems that will limit the utility of this instrument.

The first problem is that the WRAML was designed with current memory theory serving as only a broad guide. In that sense, it is mainly an atheoretical instrument. The WRAML shares this limitation with the WMS-R and most other memory instruments. It also does not contain a developmental perspective or allow evaluation of the manner in which memory changes qualitatively as a function of age. The WRAML is incompletely validated, largely because of its recent publication. The initial comparison with the McCarthy, Stanford-Binet, and WMS-R indicate intriguing possibilities, but further research to articulate those results as well as to determine whether the WRAML is sensitive to brain impairment or demonstrated memory dysfunction is needed. As noted previously, the difference scores for delayed recall of Learning subtest materials can be misleading, and greater information regarding interpretation is indicated. The subtests are combined into the indices by simple addition without any consideration of whether weighted scores may have been preferable. Some empirical evaluation of this point may help determine whether the indices could have increased utility.

Even with these problems, the WRAML is the best children's memory instrument available, and additional empirical evaluations may establish it as the standard instrument.

## References

Boyd, T.A. (1988). Clinical assessment of memory in children: A developmental framework for practice. In M.G. Tramontana & S.R. Hooper (Eds.), *Assessment issues in child neuropsychology* (pp. 177–204). New York: Plenum.

Kail, R., & Hagen, J.W. (1982). Memory in childhood. In B. Wolman, G. Stricker, S. Ellman, P. Keith-Siegel, & D. Palermo (Eds.), *Handbook of developmental psychology* (pp. 350–366). Englewood Cliffs, NJ: Prentice-Hall.

Sheslow, D., & Adams, W. (1990). *Wide Range Assessment of Memory and Learning administration manual.* Wilmington, DE: Jastak Assessment Systems.

**James E. Jirsa, Ph.D.**
*School Psychologist, Madison Metropolitan School District, Madison, Wisconsin.*

---

# WISC-R SPLIT-HALF SHORT FORM, SECOND EDITION

*Kenneth L. Hobby. Los Angeles, California: Western Psychological Services.*

## Introduction

The WISC-R Split-Half Short Form, Second Edition (S-H; Hobby, 1989) uses a selected-item approach to reduce, by approximately 50%, the administration/scoring time for the Wechsler Intelligence Scale for Children–Revised. The average time required for the S-H is reported to be 30 to 40 minutes, compared to 60 to 75 minutes for the standard form. The S-H uses only odd-numbered items on all subtests except Coding, Digit Span, and Mazes, where the entire subtest is administered, and on Block Design, where both odd- and even-numbered items constituting 6 of the 11 designs are used.

The S-H was developed by Kenneth L. Hobby and initially published in 1980. A second edition, published in 1989, was prompted by the availability of data associated with referrals of students for entrance consideration into programs for the intellectually gifted.

Kenneth Lester Hobby is currently Associate Professor of Psychology at Harding University in Searcy, Arkansas. His previous positions have included testing supervisor/chief psychologist at an Oklahoma mental health center, adjunct psychology faculty instructor, mental health clinic director, and school psychologist in private practice and in public school settings. Professor Hobby received his Ph.D. in applied behavioral studies/educational psychology from Oklahoma State University at Stillwater in 1981. He has published a number of supplemental forms for use in psychological assessments and has written and presented extensively on a variety of psychology-related topics. Hobby is a licensed and certified psychologist, a member of the American Psychological Association, and an active member of other professional organizations.

The S-H WISC-R uses the same materials for the same age range as the standard administration, and the standardized subtest directions are not altered. A record form is used to compute scores and IQs with a separate version provided for the gifted referral. An available scoring booklet is an adaptation of the more familiar WISC-R profile form, in this case a six-page folded form that can be used for response recording during the test administration process and also as a scoring guide. Although the scoring booklet cannot be used for the gifted referral, its availability for all of the remaining assessments should prove highly beneficial. The S-H process is sufficiently complicated to benefit from the assistance and guidance provided by the scoring booklet.

## Practical Applications/Uses

Hobby emphasizes that the S-H is to be used only by experienced examiners who are thoroughly familiar with, and completely understand, the S-H rationale, procedures, special instructions, and statistical properties. He suggests that the administration of 100 WISC-Rs would probably be sufficient for ensuring the development of the skills and competencies required to use S-H procedures.

When evaluating an individual referred for assessment related to providing opportunities for the gifted, the same starting point, basal, ceiling, items, and scoring method are used. However, at certain ages, specific subtests are not shortened (e.g., Information at ages $13\frac{1}{2}$ and $16\frac{1}{2}$; Picture Arrangement at age $9\frac{1}{2}$) because this would have resulted in lowered internal consistency at the higher scaled score levels commonly reached with this population. The standardization sample for the gifted referral process consisted of 1,155 students ages 6–0 to 16–11 from more than 100 Oklahoma school districts.

## Technical Aspects

The standardization sample of the S-H consisted of 1,100 students ages 6–0 to 16–11 from approximately 50 school districts. According to the manual, all of these students had been referred by schools or parents for individual testing and represented a continuum from the gifted to the trainable mentally retarded. The summary IQ scores derived from this group were approximately 1 standard deviation below the normal population, reflecting a referral population, according to the test author, that is typical of that with which the psychologist in a school setting is involved.

In order to look at concurrent validity, S-H raw scores were extracted from the standard WISC-R protocols of the 1,100 individuals comprising the standardization sample. This procedure would permit the randomizing of all variables with the exception of those influencing the internal consistency of the instrument. Following the raw score extraction, scaled score equivalents from the WISC-R manual were obtained and corrections were applied. Corrected S-H scale scores were then used to compute the Verbal, Performance, and Full Scale IQs. Corrections subsequently were applied to the IQ scores so that only corrected scaled scores and IQs were used in computing the Pearson correlation coefficients. The resulting correlations ranged from a low of .78 (accounting for 60% of the variance) on Object Assembly at age $12\frac{1}{2}$ to a high of .98 (accounting for 96% of the variance) on a number of subtests at various ages throughout the range. The S-H manual also provides data regarding the differences between variances, between means, and an analysis of individual score differences. The data reported support the conclusion that variability of S-H scores from the standard form is within acceptable and reasonable limits.

With regard to stability, S-H scores were extracted from the protocols of 50 students who had been reassessed with the WISC-R. Therefore, the scores from both the standard and S-H WISC-Rs were obtained at the same time at each of the two test administrations. For the purpose of determining relative stability, the standard form WISC-R stability was defined as optimal, and any deviation was considered "error variance."

This procedure allows four test-retest permutations: comparisons of (a) standard form at the first and second administrations, (b) S-H at the first and second administrations, (c) standard form at the first administration and S-H at the second administration, and (d) S-H at the first administration and standard form at the second administration.

Correlation data for the standard form repeated measure were .86, .82, and .88 for the Verbal, Performance, and Full Scale IQs. Repeated measure S-H correlations were .88, .75, and .82, respectively. The manual also provides variance differences, the differences between means, and individual score differences. Overall, the stability data indicate no significant differences in IQ scale stability between the standard and S-H WISC-R forms. IQ score increases are to be expected in standard form and S-H reassessments; the largest difference is to be expected when the initial assessment used the standard form and the reassessment used the S-H.

## Critique

Short forms of the Wechsler scales generally have received highly critical reviews. In the present case, Gutkin (1985) and Mealor (1985) represent this point of view, especially with respect to technical issues related to norms and sampling issues regarding the standardization populations. However, as the test author points out in regard to not establishing S-H norms, "the whole purpose of the research was to determine whether the internal consistency of the WISC-R was such that the S-H could be extracted from it and be equivalent" (K.L. Hobby, personal communication, March 8, 1990).

The extent to which the S-H parallels the standard WISC-R scoring patterns in a typical school-based referral population appears to be essentially the same. The primary reason for the S-H is to reduce the time required to obtain meaningful diagnostic information. Hobby argues, convincingly, that the S-H is capable of providing those data in an acceptable manner. In addition, he indicates that information regarding personality dimensions tied to subtest responses is not lost because of the reduced item load. Behaviors including boredom and frustration, for example, probably would not be as common when using the S-H, but they could still be observed and appropriately noted.

In summary, Hobby has devoted a great deal of careful attention to developing the rationale, procedures, and technical properties of the S-H. He seems thoroughly familiar with the relevant research literature, and he is willing to identify various limitations and methods to minimize procedural or interpretive concerns. By reducing the evaluation time required, the S-H is more likely to reduce student frustration and discouragement and consequently provide a more accurate appraisal of optimal potential functioning. When used in its intended role, as an instrument for evaluating intellectual performance in assessment/reassessment procedures associated with exceptional education decision making, the S-H should prove a worthwhile and valuable tool for psychologists and students.

## References

This list includes text citations and suggested additional reading.


Bersoff, D.N. (1971). Short forms of individual intelligence tests for children: Review and critique. *Journal of School Psychology, 9,* 310–320.

Carleton, F.O., & Stacey, C.L. (1954). Evaluation of selected short forms of the Wechsler Intelligence Scale for Children (WISC). *Journal of Clinical Psychology, 10,* 158–261.

Erikson, R.V. (1967). Abbreviated form of the WISC: A re-evaluation. *Journal of Consulting Psychology, 31,* 635–636.

Finch, A.J., Jr., Childress, W.B., & Ollendick, T.H. (1973). Comparison of separately administered and abstracted WISC short forms with the full scale WISC. *American Journal of Mental Deficiency, 77,* 755–756.

Flann, C. (1975). An abbreviated WISC compared against the fully administered WISC. *Association of Educational Psychologists Journal, 3,* 8–22.

Gayton, W.F., Wilson, W.T., & Berstein, S. (1970). An evaluation of an abbreviated form of the WISC. *Journal of Clinical Psychology, 26,* 466–468.

Gurvitz, M.S. (1945). An alternate short form of the Wechsler-Bellevue Test. *American Journal of Orthopsychiatry, 15,* 727–732.

Gutkin, T.B. (1985). WISC-R Split-Half Short Form. In J.V. Mitchell, Jr. (Ed.), *The ninth mental measurements yearbook* (pp. 1742–1743). Lincoln, NE: Buros Institute of Mental Measurements.

Hobby, K.L. (1989). *WISC-R Split-Half Short Form manual* (2nd ed.). Los Angeles: Western Psychological Services.

Levy, P. (1968). Short-form tests: A methodological review. *Psychological Bulletin, 69,* 410–416.

Mealor, D.J. (1985). WISC-R Split-Half Short Form. In J.V. Mitchell, Jr. (Ed.), *The ninth mental measurements yearbook* (pp. 1743–1744). Lincoln, NE: Buros Institute of Mental Measurements.

Mumpower, D.L. (1964). The fallacy of the short form. *Journal of Clinical Psychology, 20,* 111–113.

Silverstein, A.B. (1975). Validity of WISC-R short forms. *Journal of Clinical Psychology, 31,* 696–697.

**Alan Vaux, Ph.D.**
*Associate Professor of Psychology, Southern Illinois University at Carbondale, Carbondale, Illinois.*

# WORK ENVIRONMENT SCALE

*Rudolph H. Moos. Palo Alto, California: Consulting Psychologists Press, Inc.*

## Introduction

The Work Environment Scale (WES) is a multidimensional measure of the social climate of work settings. Social climate may be viewed as the style or atmosphere of a setting, its characteristic mode of functioning. Settings, like people, vary in how friendly, goal oriented, open, and organized they are. Social climate is a characteristic of settings, though it is assessed through the global impressions of participants. The WES examines 10 dimensions of work settings organized around three major themes: relationships, personal growth, and system maintenance or change.

*Relationship dimensions* address the nature of social relationships in the workplace through three subscales: Involvement—the extent of employee commitment to their work; Peer Cohesion—the degree to which employees are friendly and supportive; and Supervisor Support—the degree to which supervisors are supportive and encourage a supportive atmosphere. *Personal growth dimensions* have to do with the way in which the setting promotes growth and functioning within the setting. Three subscales reflect this theme: Autonomy—the degree to which employees are encouraged to make their own decisions; Task Orientation—the degree of emphasis on efficiency and productivity; and Work Pressure—the degree of press to work and of time urgency. *System maintenance dimensions* concern how the setting maintains order and manages change. This theme is examined through four subscales: Clarity—the clarity and explicitness of expectations and policies; Control—the extent to which employees are constrained by rules and regulations; Innovation—the degree of openness to change and emphasis on variety; and Physical Comfort—the degree to which the work setting is pleasing and comfortable.

The WES is one of 10 social climate measures developed by Rudolph Moos at the Social Ecology Laboratory, Stanford University. Comparable instruments were developed to assess the social climates of families, classrooms, and various treatment settings. This work constitutes a major contribution to the assessment of human environments. Up until the late 1960s, theoretical and empirical attention to the context of human functioning was severely limited in psychology. Even the assessment of such critical environments as the workplace and family was quite restricted. With the growing recognition of the role that social context played in

The reviewer wiskes to thank Joseph Watkins for his assistance in processing the large literature on the WES.

well-being and adjustment, there came a need for instruments to assess the main features of settings. The social climate scales were part of the response to that need.

The work of Moos and his colleagues has spanned two decades (Moos, 1974). This research and that of many others using the instruments has generated a substantial body of knowledge on the nature and impact of social climate. Findings have linked the social climate of work, family, learning, and treatment settings to participant well-being, health, treatment success and relapse, and functioning generally (Moos, 1985a, 1985b). All the instruments reflect the three themes of how settings shape participant relationships and goals and how they maintain order and manage change. This common framework provides an integrative theoretical system for research on disparate settings and with diverse foci. The WES is intended to provide a fairly comprehensive assessment of the workplace. The goal was to capture the main features of the work setting through a multidimensional measure. The broad social ecological framework within which the WES was developed make it a versatile tool for those examining the workplace and its impact.

The WES was developed through both rational and empirical strategies. The specification of dimensions and selection of items was guided throughout by the theoretical assumption that relationships, personal growth, and system maintenance are important themes in all settings. An initial pool of 200 items was generated from findings of structured interviews with employees and by adapting items from other social climate scales. Pretesting led to a 138-item form that was subjected to extensive psychometric analysis using data from 624 employees and managers in 44 highly disparate work groups (Moos, 1981). Several psychometric criteria provided a basis for the final form of the instrument. Items were selected that had nonextreme endorsements and that were shown to discriminate between work settings and to have a higher correlation with their designated scale than any other. Subscales were constructed to balance the direction of items (to avoid acquiescence), to have an equal number of items, to discriminate among work settings, and to show low to moderate intercorrelation. This procedure led to the current 90-item, 10-subscale Form R of the WES.

Normative data are available for several large, diverse, and, in some cases, random samples. WES data were obtained from 1,442 employees from representative work groups and 1,607 employees from health-care settings. The test development sample of 624 from 44 groups was included. Also included were 400 persons randomly selected from census tracts in the San Francisco area. Data from the random and nonrandom samples showed similar WES means and standard deviations, so the data appear to be representative of general work settings. The manual includes descriptive data and standard score conversion tables for both general and health-care work settings (Moos, 1986b). Further, in light of the large body of published research with the WES, researchers using all but the most idiosyncratic samples should be able to find some useful data on comparable samples. Researchers or practitioners using the WES certainly should seek such published data, especially from random samples, to complement the published norms. Also, the WES is short enough to be administered routinely, particularly in large corporations, allowing the development of local norms. These would be particularly useful in evaluating organizational change, whether planned or imposed.

The WES has not been subject to any major revisions since the initial development of Form R. Arguably, the careful development of the instrument, as well as subsequent findings supporting its reliability and validity, have obviated any need for substantial changes. The theoretical underpinnings of the instrument also have worn well. The instrument has proved adaptable, and researchers creative, so that new research foci have been accommodated quite easily by combining subscales: for example, to measure work stress or work support.

The active research teams working with Moos have generated several alternative forms of the social climate scales including the WES. An Ideal version (Form I) was developed through rewording items and instructions, designed to assess participants' ideal work setting. The goal here was not to aid in the design of some utopian workplace but rather to help identify setting problem areas, directions for change, discrepancies between subgroup ideals, and shifts in values. An Expected version (Form E) also was developed through rewording items and instructions, in order to assess participants' expectations prior to entering a work setting. This can be useful in employee counseling to identify a mismatch between expected and actual climate, which might suggest pre-entry preparation or a recommendation to seek a more congruent setting. Subscale internal consistencies and intercorrelations for Forms I and E are comparable to those for Form R, reviewed below. Preliminary normative data are available for small samples of 348 (Form I) and 81 (Form E) (Moos, 1986b).

The WES has been adapted for use in several countries and has been translated into Dutch, French, German, Hebrew, Japanese, Portuguese, Spanish, and Vietnamese (Moos, 1986b). Available psychometric data from these studies, though somewhat limited as yet, are encouraging.

The WES is a 90-item self-report instrument presented in a small reusable booklet. The instructions and items are straightforward and quite simple. A true/false response format is used and research participants simply mark "T" or "F" for each item on a separate answer sheet. Administration of the test is straightforward, requiring only a quiet room with space for respondents to write. Group administration is quite feasible. Under most circumstances, the administrator's role is supervisory, maintaining quiet, limiting interaction, ensuring that each participant is completing the form correctly, and encouraging indecisive respondents to consider whether an item is true or false "most of the time." As the instrument is short and not very demanding, most employees should be able to complete it without difficulty.

Scoring is simple. A template is laid over the answer sheet, which is organized so that each column of responses relates to a scale. A quick count of visible marks yields raw scores for the 10 subscales. Individual scales or work group means can be easily converted to standard scores. Individual or group profiles can be plotted easily on supplied profile forms. All this work, prior to interpretation, can be done by conscientious nonprofessional staff.

**Practical Applications/Uses**

The WES is sufficiently versatile that it should be considered by anyone with an interest in assessing or changing the psychosocial aspects of work settings.

Whether a consultant trying to diagnose problems in an organization or evaluate an organizational intervention, or a researcher trying to understand the impact of workplace on well-being or the effect of structure on productivity, the WES almost certainly would shed light on the problem. A relatively brief instrument, given what it delivers, it always should be considered as an addition to an assessment package. In many cases, it should be one of the first instruments included.

The WES manual (Moos, 1986b) provides an excellent discussion of some likely applications both in consulting and research contexts. Other useful sources include the User's Guide to the social climate scales (Moos, 1987) and various review articles by Moos and his colleagues (e.g., Finney & Moos, 1984; Moos, 1979, 1984, 1985a, 1985b, 1986a). Some of these will be noted here. First, a point implicit through the discussion so far should be clarified. The WES is a measure of a setting's social climate through the impressions of participants. Thus, applications may focus on the setting (assessed through mean group scores for a sample of workers) or on individual setting participants or subgroups of participants. This feature is a major source of the measure's versatility.

*Characterizing work settings.* What is this work setting like? How do these settings differ? What are the major types of work settings from the perspective of participants? These are some of the questions that the WES can help answer. Simply assessing and profiling a work setting may be instructive to supervisors, workers, and consultants. Notable features should be evident from the profile and allow an interpretation of potential strengths and weaknesses. Thus the profile serves as a valuable basis for discussion, facilitates an enriched understanding of setting features, and may suggest future difficulties that need to be anticipated. The WES has been used quite extensively to describe and compare work settings. For example, Hoiberg (1978) contrasted five Navy training schools using the WES. Fawzy, Wellisch, Pasnau, and Leibowitz (1983) used the WES to describe and compare the work environments of nurses in five clinical hospital services (e.g., oncology, surgery, etc.).

Settings sometimes differ in actuality or phenomenology for different subgroups of participants—an issue that may be extremely important in the context of workplace justice. The WES can be extremely useful in examining this process. For example, Booth and Lantz (1977) used the WES to examine gender issues in the social climate of Navy health-care settings. A general psychosocial typology of work settings may not be possible, but such typologies might be developed within more limited spheres such as sectors of work or particular corporations. Work with the Family Environment Scale has yielded a typology of families (Moos & Moos, 1986). Similar typologies of work settings might prove useful for a variety of purposes.

*Planning, monitoring, and evaluating change.* What is wrong with this work setting? Why is morale low among this group of workers? How can we improve the functioning of the work setting? Is this intervention working? These, too, are questions that the WES can help answer. Comparisons of actual social climate to norms or to participant ideals can be very helpful in diagnosing problems and suggesting directions for change. For example, an assessment might reveal that workers experience an unusually low level of clarity or very high levels of control, or that they would prefer considerably more autonomy or clarity than currently exists—problems that might be resolved easily or suggest changes implemented on a trial basis. Waters (1978) examined real-ideal discrepancies in the social climate of a law enforcement agency and suggested how the WES might be used to diagnose and resolve difficulties. A common problem, an organization might have to decide whether high work demands are worth the cost in burnout and turnover, or whether the effects of such demands might be moderated by improving relationship dimensions or by modifying system maintenance dimensions. For example, Koran, Moos, Moos, and Zasslow (1983) used the WES to identify work stressors among the staff of a burn unit and used real-ideal discrepancies to guide various organizational changes. Both social climate theory and a growing body of research provide a framework to guide intervention goals.

The WES can also be used as an aid in planning change by assessing social-climate discrepancies (current or ideal) across different work groups or across workers and management. This may be helpful in resolving obstacles to team-building or in working out conflicts in objectives. The WES can also be extremely useful in both process and outcome evaluation of organizational interventions (cf. Finney & Moos, 1984). For example, it has been used to evaluate interventions designed to reduce burnout among mental health workers (Hunnicutt & MacMillan, 1983). The WES can also be useful in monitoring the effects of imposed changes due to new technology or organizational restructuring. Sinclair and Frankel (1982) used it to assess the impact of quality assurance programs introduced in outpatient treatment programs. Given the complexity of social ecologies, the effects of planned or imposed change are often dependent on contextual factors. Here, too, the WES may prove valuable—for example, Roberts (1985, cited in Moos, 1986b) found that acceptance of office automation was influenced by social climate factors.

The social ecology of work settings is complex. In diagnosing problems, planning interventions, or monitoring change, it is important to take a multidimensional perspective, as contingent or contextual effects probably are the rule rather than the exception. This is what makes the WES so valuable. The measure facilitates examination of the interplay of climate dimensions and social climate theory provides a valuable guide for doing so.

*Examining setting effects on functioning.* What characteristics of a work setting promote high productivity? What features influence worker morale and satisfaction? What aspects engender health problems? The WES is a valuable tool in addressing these questions. Research has generated principles that seem to have applicability across a range of work settings. For example, heavy work demands appear to promote low morale, dissatisfaction, and burnout—an effect that can be countered to some degree by clarity, autonomy, and positive relationships at work (e.g., Brady, Kinnaird, & Friedrich, 1980; Rosenthal, Teague, Retish, West, & Vassell, 1983). By looking at several dimensions of work settings, researchers can better understand when work pressure and task orientation will lead to demoralization and when to a sense of accomplishment, or when positive setting relationships will lead to a low-productivity, complacent work force and when to high-powered, flexible teamwork.

An important research application of the WES involves the examination of stressors and resources in the workplace as they affect the well-being of workers.

Reflecting the recent interest in social support, Holahan and Moos (1983) developed the Work Relationships Index (WRI) composed of the WES Involvement, Peer Cohesion, and Supervisor Support scales. Although questions have been raised about the general utility of this index as a measure of support, it has proved useful in the work context and provides an added benefit of using the WES (Vaux, 1988). The WES also is an adaptable measure of work stressors—Work Pressure often will play a key role, exacerbated in different work contexts by low Clarity, high Control, low Autonomy, and high Task Orientation (Billings & Moos, 1982).

Moos (1986b) reports a number of other research foci involving the WES, suggesting its versatility. Studies of social climate and somatic complaints indicate the potential negative consequences of high work demands and low autonomy. Studies of role socialization suggest that, at least in some settings, an emphasis on support and autonomy may help new employees learn their new occupational roles. Social climate in work and other settings appear to be interrelated. Thus, the work climate of teachers is reflected in the classroom social climate experienced by students, and the work climate of staff has implications for the treatment group climate in residential treatment facilities. Also the joint effects of climates in different settings, such as work and family, can be investigated using the WES with other social climate measures. These research applications—looking at indirect or joint setting effects—provide a much-needed strategy for examining what Bronfenbrenner (1979) terms *exo-* and *meso-system effects* on human development. The relationships tend to be complex, but such findings can shed light on the complex effects of interventions, as well as help us understand why some settings work better than others.

*Vocational counseling and personnel applications.* What work setting might best suit this person? Might this employee function better in a different department? What setting might best serve this employee, rehabilitating after an illness or a psychological problem? The WES can be helpful in answering these practical questions. A central notion in the guidance, placement, and retention of employees is fit or congruence (Holland, 1985). The WES can provide additional information on the match between an employee and a work setting. Moos (1986b, Appendix B) reports social climate characteristics for five of Holland's occupational categories. Comparing a person's ideal climate to these descriptions should aid placement recommendations. More specifically, an individual's ideal or expected climate might be compared to that of a prospective work setting. Discrepancies would suggest an alternative recommendation or perhaps pre-entry preparation. Campbell (1973, cited in Moos, 1986b) found such discrepancies to be related to attrition among new staff nurses and suggested the need for pre-entry orientation.

All these uses of the WES might be especially helpful in dealing with employees undergoing rehabilitation. For example, in a series of studies Moos and his colleagues found links between the functioning of alcoholics and social climate at work (Bromet & Moos, 1977; Finney & Moos, 1981). Similar research with depressed psychiatric patients (e.g., Billings & Moos, 1985) also has practical implications for vocational guidance.

In sum, the WES has a multitude of practical and research applications, some of which have been outlined above. It is suitable for a broad range of employees and work settings and is easily administered. In many applications, merely profiling standardized data or comparing data to local norms will be highly instructive. More sophisticated interpretations depend on familiarity with social climate theory and research and experience in using the WES in the particular context, though a great deal can be learned from the test manual alone and several bibliographies aid the newcomer in mastering relevant literature.

### Technical Aspects

*Reliability.* Moos (1986b) reports internal consistency coefficients for data from 1,045 general and health-care employees. These range from .69 (Peer Cohesion) to .86 (Innovation), with eight subscales at or above .76. WES subscales also show good stability (Moos, 1986b). A sample of 75 employees from four work groups retook the WES after a 1-month interval, yielding stability coefficients that ranged from .71 (Cohesion) to .83 (Involvement). Stability coefficients for a larger sample ($N$ = 254) for a 12-month interval ranged from .51 (Supervisor Support) to .63 (Work Pressure). Finally, the stability of WES profiles over 12 months was assessed for 90 individuals. The individual profiles were highly stable, .50 or above for 75 of the 90 persons (mean = .61) (Moos, 1986b).

*Structural validity.* The WES subscales were not designed to be independent. Using data from the same large sample noted above, Moos (1986b) reports intercorrelations that range from .54 to almost 0. The three relationship dimensions tend to correlate around .50 and, indeed, most correlations above .30 involve these dimensions (e.g., Involvement with Autonomy, Task Orientation, and Innovation; Supervisor Support with Autonomy, Clarity, and Innovation). In general, the higher correlations make sense—subscale independence would not be an expected or desirable feature in a social climate instrument, given the underlying theoretical rationale.

Several studies have involved factor analysis of WES data. For example, Booth, Norton, Webster, and Berry (1976) analyzed WES data (both Forms R and E) obtained from 580 Navy enlisted personnel. Five of the original WES subscales were represented by factors emerging from this analysis. Clarity items merged with Supervisor Support items, Involvement items merged with Task Orientation items, and Autonomy did not emerge. Factor analyses of WES items is to be encouraged, if driven by some theoretical rationale or psychometric concern: for example, a belief that the three relationship dimensions are better represented as two dimensions, or that a particular subscale can be usefully split and requires additional items. The use of scales other than the designated WES scales may be justified but has the disadvantage of obscuring the link to an established theory and body of research.

*Convergent and discriminant validity.* The WES is somewhat unique. To this reviewer's knowledge, no comparable multidimensional measure of work setting social climate exists. Consequently, explicit tests of convergent and discriminant validity involving most or all of the subscales have not been conducted. An exception is the finding that work and family social climate scores are independent, and that spouses provide independent scores for the work setting (not shared) but correlated scores for the shared family setting (Holahan & Moos, 1983).

*Intervention-related change.* WES scores are quite stable for employees who do not change jobs (see above). However, they are also responsive to changes in the workplace. McCormack and DeVore (1986) used the WES in a process consultation with staff of a VA psychology service. Following the intervention, increases in Supervisor Support, Autonomy, Task Orientation, and Clarity were observed. Williamson and Sanderson (1986) studied the effects of changing the rate of shift rotation of controllers of an emergency service in an effort to diminish the negative consequences of shiftwork. Significant reductions in work pressure were observed. Not all efforts to improve work climate are successful, however, as observed by Darou (1985) in his research with staff of a street-work program.

*Differences among groups.* As noted earlier, the WES shows differences across different work settings. For example, virtually every subscale has shown some significant variation across Holland's occupational categories: higher Involvement for investigative than realistic jobs, higher Innovation in enterprising than conventional jobs, and so forth (Moos, 1986b). A number of studies have observed theoretically meaningful differences in WES scores across groups of participants within the same or related settings. Booth and Lantz (1977) found that expected social climate differed for men and women entering naval health-care jobs: men had higher expectations in terms of Physical Comfort, Control, Task Involvement, and Communication. Following experience with the setting, no gender differences in social climate were evident except in Control, suggesting a possible difference in supervision of men and women in this setting. Booth and Lantz (1977) also found that the social climate of the job setting was rated as significantly more favorable than that of the training setting on most dimensions.

Lusk, Diserens, Cormier, Geranmayeh, and Neves (1983) found significant differences between preclinical and clinical dental students on several dimensions (the latter experienced more Support, less Task Orientation, less Work Pressure, and less Control) and between students in a traditional and experimental training program, with the latter reporting a more favorable climate on all dimensions. Mohl, Denny, Mote, and Coldwater (1982) found significant differences in the social climate reports of nurses on general medical and intensive care units. Drude and Lourie (1984) found significant differences in work climate among three admission units in a psychiatric hospital. These apparently reflected patient/staff ratios, which were significantly related to greater Work Pressure and to a less favorable Relationship climate as well as less Autonomy and Physical Comfort. Turnipseed (1988) found the work climate reports of teachers in more and less effective school districts, although matched on a variety of variables, differed significantly in terms of Involvement, Cohesion, Work Pressure, Clarity, Control, Innovation, and Physical Comfort.

*Construct validity.* A great many studies bear on the construct validity of the WES; that is, yield findings that to a greater or lesser degree conform to theoretical predictions. One important area has to do with social climate and psychological well-being, especially depression. Because most of this work focuses on social support, using the Work Relationship Index, only a few illustrative studies will be noted. More attention will be given to another important area, related to social climate and morale.

Holahan and Moos (1981) conducted a longitudinal study of work and family support in relation to psychological distress among almost 500 randomly selected participants. Findings were generally consistent with the view that decreases in support within the work or family setting during a year were associated with increases in psychological distress. In a related study, Holahan and Moos (1982) found that support from the work environment adds to life stressors and quantitative support measures in predicting somatic complaints and depression, but only for men, while a supportive family environment is beneficial to both men and women. Wetzel and Redmond (1980) also examined depression in relation to work and family climate. They found that a controlling and unsupportive work environment as well as an unsupportive family environment discriminated depressed from nondepressed men and women.

In a study of depressed patients during treatment, Billings and Moos (1985) found that the supportiveness of the workplace added significantly to other social resources in the prediction of depression even when initial functioning was controlled. Consistent with the view that the WES measures climate and not solely features of the reporting participant, work support remained quite stable during treatment, whereas improvements in several other social resources variables were observed. Finally, in a study of almost 300 families, Billings and Moos (1982) found that psychological distress (depression, anxiety, somatic complaints, and low self-confidence) tended to be positively associated with stressful aspects of work climate (high Work Pressure and Control, low Autonomy and Clarity) and negatively associated with supportive aspects of the workplace. Work stressors appeared to have a greater impact on men, although such impact also was attenuated more by support than was the case for women.

Turning to studies of work morale, Brady et al. (1980) found that mental health staff who were high in job satisfaction reported social climates with significantly more Involvement, Peer Cohesion, Staff Support, Autonomy, and Innovation than did their less satisfied peers. Savicki and Cooley (1987) found that burnout among mental health workers was related to many work climate dimensions, particularly Relationship dimensions. In regression analyses, each of the components of burnout were related to different climate indices (e.g., emotional exhaustion with Work Pressure, depersonalization with low Control, personal accomplishment with Peer Cohesion). Rosenthal et al. (1983) examined the relationship between burnout and social climate among park and recreation employees. In canonical correlation analyses, emotional exhaustion and, to a lesser extent, depersonalization were associated with work climate reports of high Work Pressure and low Involvement, Staff Support, and Clarity.

In another study of burnout, Golembiewski and Roundtree (1986) tested an eight-phase model of progressive burnout using data from a large sample ($N$ = 2,123) of employees of a retirement community chain. The phases of burnout proceed from the point where depersonalization, lack of personal accomplishment, and emotional exhaustion are all low to where all are high, through various combinations. Significant differences across phases were observed for all work climate dimensions, with increases in Work Pressure and Control and decreases in all other dimensions.

## Critique

Overall the Work Environment Scale is an excellent measure of the social climate of work settings. Factors contributing to its strength include the following: (a) it rests on a provocative theoretical base, (b) it belongs to a family of measures that address a wide range of settings in a similar fashion, (c) a substantial body of research has built up around it, (d) it was developed with due concern for psychometrics, (e) its multidimensional nature allows a more sophisticated examination of settings, and (f) an excellent, quite recently updated, manual exists.

The WES is a versatile instrument with a wide range of practical and research applications. The former include the description and comparison of work settings, an aid in diagnosing organizational problems and planning change, a tool for process and outcome evaluation, a means for monitoring developmental or imposed change, and an aid in vocational guidance and human resource management.

The WES is a complex instrument. To establish its validity as a measure of 10 dimensions of work climate within an evolving theory is an enormous challenge. A considerable body of findings relevant to validity have accumulated, and generally these are encouraging. Yet the quality of this research is variable. Two issues are especially salient. First, many studies take statistical advantage of the 10 WES subscales either by performing multiple tests without predicting which scales should show effects or adjusting alpha levels, or by using unreplicated stepwise multivariate procedures. Future research should be more precise both in terms of specific predictions and the correct use of multivariate analyses. Second, much of the work involving the WES examines person-level data. There is a great need for more work looking at social climate as a setting variable, measured through group means or through the reports of fellow workers.

In sum, the WES is a strong multidimensional measure of the social climate of work settings. The psychometric properties of the instrument are good. Existing validity data are encouraging, and the measure has a broad range of practical applications for those interested in the workplace. It is strongly recommended for the consideration of vocational, human resource, and I/O practitioners as well as researchers of vocational, management, or organizational issues.

## References

This list includes text citations and suggested additional reading.

Billings, A.G., & Moos, R.H. (1982). Work stress and the stress-buffering roles of work and family resources. *Journal of Occupational Behavior, 3,* 215–232.

Billings, A.G., & Moos, R.H. (1985). Life stressors and social resources affect posttreatment outcomes among depressed patients. *Journal of Abnormal Psychology, 94,* 140–153.

Booth, R., & Lantz, K. (1977). Sex differences in psychosocial perceptions toward naval work environments. *Perceptual and Motor Skills, 44,* 1155–1161.

Booth, R., Norton, R., Webster, E., & Berry, N. (1976). Assessing the psychosocial characteristics of occupational training environments. *Journal of Occupational Psychology, 49,* 85–92.

Brady, C., Kinnaird, K., & Friedrich, W. (1980). Job satisfaction and perception of social climate in a mental health facility. *Perceptual and Motor Skills, 51,* 559–564.

Bromet, E., & Moos, R. (1977). Environmental resources and the posttreatment functioning of alcoholic patients. *Journal of Health and Social Behavior, 18,* 326–335.

Bronfenbrenner, U. (1979). *The ecology of human development.* Cambridge, MA: Harvard University Press.

Campbell, F.C. (1973). *Mutual expectations for the neophyte staff nurse: A cooperative effort of nursing education and service* (Report of Phase II: Role adaptation). Los Angeles, CA: Children's Hospital.

Cangelosi, V.E., & Lemonine, L.F. (1988). Effects of open versus closed physical environment on employee perception and attitude. *Social Behavior and Personality, 16*, 71–77.

Darou, W.G. (1985). Improving the work environment of youth workers. *Canadian Counsellor, 19*, 183–185.

Drude, K.P., & Lourie, I. (1984). Staff perceptions of work environment in a state psychiatric hospital. *Psychological Reports, 54*, 263–268.

Fawzy, F., Wellisch, D., Pasnau, R., & Leibowitz, B. (1983). Preventing nursing burnout: A challenge for liaison psychiatry. *General Hospital Psychiatry, 5*, 141–149.

Finney, J., & Moos, R. (1981). Characteristics and prognoses of alcoholics who became moderate drinkers and abstainers after treatment. *Journal of Studies on Alcohol, 42*, 94–105.

Finney, J., & Moos, R. (1984). Environmental assessment and evaluation research: Examples from mental health and substance abuse programs. *Evaluation and Program Planning, 7*, 151–167.

Golembiewski, R.T., & Roundtree, B.J. (1986). Phases of burn-out and properties of work environments: Replicating and extending a pattern of covariants. *Organization Development Journal, 4*, 25–30.

Hoiberg, A. (1978). Women in the Navy: Morale and attrition. *Armed Forces and Society, 4*, 659–671.

Holahan, C.J., & Moos, R. (1981). Social support and psychological distress: A longitudinal analysis. *Journal of Abnormal Psychology, 90*, 365–370.

Holahan, C.J., & Moos, R. (1982). Social support and adjustment: Predictive benefits of social climate indices. *American Journal of Community Psychology, 10*, 403–415.

Holahan, C.J., & Moos, R. (1983). The quality of social support: Measures of family and work relationships. *British Journal of Clinical Psychology, 22*, 157–162.

Holland, J. (1985). *Making vocational choices: A theory of careers.* Englewood Cliffs, NJ: Prentice-Hall.

Hunnicutt, A.W., & MacMillan, T.F. (1983). Beating burn-out: Findings from a three-year study. *Association of Mental Health Administrators Journal, 10*, 7–9.

Koran, L., Moos, R., Moos, B., & Zasslow, M. (1983). Changing hospital work environments: An example of a burn unit. *General Hospital Psychiatry, 5*, 7–13.

Lusk, E., Diserens, D., Cormier, P., Geranmayeh, A., & Neves, J. (1983). The Work Environment Scale: Baseline data for dental schools. *Psychological Reports, 53*, 1160–1162.

McCormack, J.C., & DeVore, J.R. (1986). Survey-guided process consultation in a Veterans Administration medical center psychology service. *Professional Psychology: Research and Practice, 17*, 51–57.

Mohl, P.C., Denny, N.R., Mote, T.A., & Coldwater, C. (1982). Hospital unit stressors that affect nurses: Primary task vs. social factors. *Psychosomatics, 23*, 366–374.

Moos, R. (1974). *The social climate scales: An overview.* Palo Alto, CA: Consulting Psychologists Press.

Moos, R. (1979). Improving social settings by social climate measurement and feedback. In R. Munoz, L. Snowden, & J. Kelly (Eds.), *Social and psychological research in community settings* (pp. 145–182). San Francisco, CA: Jossey-Bass.

Moos, R. (1981). *Work Environment Scale manual.* Palo Alto, CA: Consulting Psychologists Press.

Moos, R. (1984). Context and coping: Toward a unifying conceptual framework. *American Journal of Community Psychology, 12*, 5–25.

Moos, R. (1985a). Creating healthy human contexts: Environmental and individual strategies. In J.C. Rosen & L.J. Solomon (Eds.), *Prevention in health psychology* (pp. 366–389). Hanover, NH: University Press of New England.

Moos, R. (1985b). Evaluating social resources in community and health care contexts. In P. Karoly (Ed.), *Measurement strategies in health psychology* (pp. 433–459). New York: Wiley.

Moos, R. (1986a). Work as a human context. In M.S. Pallack & R.O. Perloff (Eds.), *Psychology and work: Productivity, change, and employment* (Master Lecture Series, Vol. 5). Washington, DC: American Psychological Association.

Moos, R. (1986b). *The Work Environment Scale manual* (2nd ed.). Palo Alto, CA: Consulting Psychologists Press.

Moos, R. (1987). *The social climate scales.* Palo Alto, CA: Consulting Psychologists Press.

Moos, R., & Fuhr, R. (1982). The clinical use of social-ecological concepts: The case of an adolescent girl. *American Journal of Orthopsychiatry, 52,* 111–122.

Moos, R., & Moos, B. (1986). *Family Environment Scale manual* (2nd ed.). Palo Alto, CA: Consulting Psychologists Press.

Roberts, V. (1985). Personality characteristics and work environments: Their impact on receptivity toward office automation technology (Doctoral dissertation, University of Missouri, Columbia, 1984). *Dissertation Abstracts International, 45,* 3406A.

Rosenthal, D., Teague, M., Retish, P., West, J., & Vessell, R. (1983). The relationship between work environment attributes and burnout. *Journal of Leisure Research,* 125–135.

Savicki, V., & Cooley, E. (1987). The relationship and client contact to burnout in mental health professions. *Journal of Counseling and Development, 65,* 249–252.

Shannon, R. (1983). An examination of relationships between work structure and perceptions of family and work environments reported by teachers (Doctoral dissertation, University of Nebraska, Lincoln, 1982). *Dissertation Abstracts International, 45,* 1661A.

Sinclair, C., & Frankel, M. (1982). The effect of quality assurance activities on the quality of mental health services. *Quality Review Bulletin, 8,* 7–15.

Turnipseed, D.L. (1988). An integrated, interactive model of organizational climate, culture and effectiveness. *Leadership and Organizational Development Journal, 9,* 17–21.

Vaux, A. (1988). *Social support: Theory, research and intervention.* New York: Praeger.

Waters, J. (1978). Evaluating organizational environments in law enforcement agencies: A social climate perspective. *Criminal Justice Review, 3,* 1–6.

Wetzel, J., & Redmond, F. (1980). A person-environment study of depression. *Social Service Review, 54,* 363–375.

Williamson, A.M., & Sanderson, J.W. (1986). Changing the speed of shift rotation: A field study. *Ergonomics, 29,* 1085–1095.

**Janet A. Norris, Ph.D.**
*Associate Professor of Communication Disorders, Louisiana State University, Baton Rouge, Louisiana.*

# WRITTEN LANGUAGE ASSESSMENT

*J. Jeffrey Grill and Margaret M. Kirwin. Novato, California: Academic Therapy Publications.*

## Introduction

The Written Language Assessment (WLA; Grill & Kirwin, 1989) is designed to measure writing ability in children from ages 8 to 18 and above. Meaningful composition, rather than isolated subskills of writing, are evaluated to provide both derived scores for normative comparisons and informal analyses of content, function, and form. Three different kinds of written discourse are assessed to test the ability to write for different purposes. The results of the WLA are intended to provide a basis for making formal instructional and placement decisions about students in regular and special education settings, and for planning instruction in writing.

The authors, J. Jeffrey Grill, Ed.D., and Margaret M. Kirwin, Ed.D., teach in the areas of special education and elementary and early childhood education, respectively, at the College of Saint Rose in Albany, New York. Collectively they have previous teaching experience with learning disabled, emotionally disturbed, high school English and journalism, and elementary students. Both authors adhere to the belief that the most authentic way to assess an expressive skill such as writing is to evaluate something that is actually expressed, rather than individual subskills.

The WLA was developed in order to provide teachers and other professionals with a standardized test of writing ability that reflects all of the composition decisions that authentic writing requires, including the selection of form, audience, purpose, text, and style. Instructional methods and goals tend to correspond with the behaviors assessed on tests, and so this instrument is designed to influence the teaching of writing by providing a method of evaluating whole, purposeful writing. Three different writing samples are elicited in order to comprehensively assess writing. The three samples evaluate different modes of written discourse based on Britton's (1975) categorization of writing functions.

The first task corresponds to Britton's expressive mode, characterized by relatively unstructured and self-revealing writing. Knowledge, feelings, and reactions are expressed in this mode. The instructive, or transactional, mode of writing is elicited in the second task. This mode requires specific instructions to be given in order to persuade, inform, explain, report, and/or express similar goal-oriented intents. The third mode, creative or poetic, requires knowledge of the literate forms of writing found in narration, poems, plays, songs, and so on.

Efforts were made to develop tasks that are culturally and geographically unbiased as well as appropriate to students across a wide age range. For example, a photograph of an adult holding hands with a child shows only the hands and not the people, their location, or additional activity. The subject is instructed to write about hands and is free to generate ideas from personal experience or reaction. The pictures used in two of the tasks were selected because they appropriately limited the range of potential topics, were sufficiently open-ended to permit a range of interpretations, and provided students with a motivation to write. The instructions for the third task were selected because the concept of giving information to someone younger than the writer had credibility and was relevant to the experience of most students.

Two different versions of each task were developed for field testing. For example, two photographs of hands were used in the field test to elicit expressive writing. The photograph depicting an adult and a child holding hands was selected from the field test results because it elicited a wide range of responses, while the photograph of cupped hands elicited stereotypic compositions. Similarly, two different versions of instructions were field tested for the instructive and creative modes of writing, and those that elicited the greatest amount and quality of writing were included on the final version of the WLA.

However, the picture used to elicit the narrative composition for the creative writing task may be biased in favor of older students. The picture shows the painting "You," a depiction of a woman lying down with a cat nestled in the blanket. The picture is not action based, does not suggest any problem or goal, does not indicate that a conclusion must be drawn, does not show relationships between events occurring in one situation that may have a cause or effect on another character or situation, nor does it suggest any other elements of story structure. To derive a story from this picture, the writer must be able to make high level inferences and activate elaborate background information. The task may fail to measure narrative abilities that young children possess and that this task purports to measure because the picture selected is not conducive to storytelling. In the field testing, the effectiveness of this picture relative to others in eliciting stories was not compared, but only the instructions used to elicit the writing sample. No rationale for selecting this picture is given.

Field testing was conducted on 86 students in Grades 1 through 7 (7 to 13 years of age) who were attending an after-school tutorial program at the College of Saint Rose. Participants included high and average achievers who attended for enrichment activities and low achievers who attended for corrective instruction. Students were recruited from public, private, and parochial schools. One version of each writing task was randomly assigned to each of the subjects on each of three separate testing days. Sixty complete sets of three writing samples and 26 sets of fewer than three samples were collected. These 200+ writing samples were used to select the tasks to be used in the final version and to develop scoring categories and criteria.

The scoring categories and criteria used in field testing were designed to focus on the qualitative aspects of writing rather than on the mechanistic, or subskill, components. First, the level of difficulty of the text produced by the student was judged using the Fry (1977) readability formula. This formula uses the average number of sentences and syllables found in a passage to provide an estimate of grade-level difficulty. The field testing found that the readability grade level for compositions produced by students tends to lag behind (by one or more grade levels) the readability of text that can be read, so that a passage written by a good third-grade writer may have a readability level of second grade. Therefore, the authors developed normed scaled scores based on the distribution of readability levels produced by subjects at each grade level for the final version of the test. The scaled scores, and not grade level, are to be used as the basis for making judgments on readability adequacy.

Secondly, rating scales were selected to assess the quality of writing. Originally, the rating categories included the task, vocabulary, rhetoric, legibility, ideas, and overall quality. Checklists of characteristics and differing criteria across each task were part of the initial scoring procedures. Field testing revealed that many of the determinations were too complex to apply easily and/or not sufficiently reliable, and so several of the categories were eliminated, leaving Rhetoric, Legibility, and Overall Quality. Finally, the mechanics of writing were focused on by analyzing spelling, punctuation, grammar, and usage. Field testing eliminated all of these categories. Scoring grammar and usage separately proved redundant, punctuation scores revealed little variation between students at any age or grade level, and the scoring of spelling was unreliable and produced a range of scores in each age group too narrow for the development of norms. Although unsuitable for deriving norms, these behaviors were considered important to the process of writing, and so guidelines for informally analyzing them are included in the manual.

In place of some of the original scoring strategies, two additional scoring categories were investigated. The Productivity score corresponds to the number of words written and has been shown in research to be a reliable indicator of the quality of writing produced. Word Complexity represents the difference between the total number of syllables written minus the total number of words produced and provides a general measurement of vocabulary level because it indicates use of multisyllabic words and affixes. Both of these scoring categories proved to be easy to calculate, reliable, and discriminating in the development of norms, and thus they were included in the final version of the WLA.

The final four WLA scoring categories cover General Writing Ability (a composite of the Rhetoric, Legibility, and Overall Quality ratings), Readability, Productivity, and Word Complexity.

The WLA in its final form was normed on 1,025 students in Grades 3 through 12 (ages 8 through 18–19 years). The geographic representation is poor, with all subjects residing in upstate New York. Attempts were made to obtain a representative sample of other significant demographic variables. Compared to the *Statistical Abstract of the United States* (U.S. Bureau of the Census, 1985), the WLA included an appropriate distribution of a nearly equal number of males versus females but a higher than representative proportion of white subjects (94% compared to 86% nationally) and a low representation of urban residence (54% compared to 74% nationally). Various types of schools (public, private, parochial) were represented. Intelligence test scores and socioeconomic status data were not available to the test developers. Students who were receiving instruction in special education classes for any handicapping condition were not included in the normative sample.

The practice of eliminating students with any handicapping conditions from the normative population negates one primary intent of the test: to provide a basis for making formal placement decisions about students in regular and special education settings (Grill & Kirwin, 1989, pp. 9, 33, 36). The norms do not represent a normal range of abilities found in the general school population but rather only a narrow range of writing variability. Therefore, as no students who fall within the low ranges of school performance are included in the WLA norms, the derived scores that are supposed to represent "seriously deficient performances" (i.e., 2 or more standard deviations below the mean) are in actuality within the average range of students' writing abilities. The results of this nonrepresentative sample are serious. Students in the regular classroom will be inappropriately identified as being poor writers, even eligible for special education services. Children with handicapping conditions, such as a learning disability or language disorder, are at risk for appearing to fall in the severely to profoundly handicapped range. Rather than serving to make decisions about handicapped children, the norms are invalid and should not be applied at all to this population.

Another problem with the standardization exists in the number of subjects in the norm sample for some age levels, particularly at the two extreme age ranges. One hundred subjects are the minimum number for which a full range of percentiles can be computed and for which standard scores between ±2.3 standard deviations can be computed without extrapolation (Salvia & Ysseldyke, 1978). Only 30 subjects in the 8–0 to 8–11 age range were included, 85 in the 9–0 to 9–11, and 56 in the 18 to 19 category. Four other age groups had 90–97 subjects. Thus, the norms for the lowest and highest age ranges lack stability and are not dependable, as another group consisting of the same number of subjects might yield very different results.

The materials for the WLA consist of three different test sheets to correspond with the three writing tasks, an individual scoring sheet, and the Examiner's Manual (Grill & Kirwin, 1989). Two of the test sheets contain black-and-white pictures, the Expressive task showing a photograph of an adult and a child holding hands and the Creative task showing a picture of a woman lying down with a cat. The third task presents the written instructions to "Write how you would tell a little kid about the danger of fire." The remainder of the test sheet consists of lined space for writing the composition. Additional paper may be provided if needed.

The front page of the score sheet provides a summary of raw scores for the three writing tasks, equations for calculating totals, and areas to record the derived scaled scores, percentile ranks, and the total Written Language Quotient. A profile chart comparing total performance across scoring categories also is provided. Additional pages are designed to score each writing task, including forms to rate each composition for Rhetoric, Legibility, and Overall Quality (e.g., General Writing Ability), formulas for calculating Readability, Productivity, and Word Complexity, and space for making notations regarding Informal Assessments.

The scaled scores for General Writing Ability, Productivity, Word Complexity, and Readability each have a mean of 10 and a standard deviation of 3. Tables for converting raw scores to scaled scores for students at each age level from 8 to 18+ years are found in the appendix. According to the manual, performances below 1 standard deviation from the mean are considered below average, and those 2 or more standard deviations are substantially below average. The authors recommend that individual scaled scores be reserved for intraindividual comparisons of a student's strengths and weaknesses in writing skills. They provide too little information, when used alone, for making decisions about educational placement.

The authors state that the composite Written Language Quotient (WLQ), derived from the sum of the scaled scores, is appropriate for use in making educational placement decisions because it is a global index of writing skills. The WLQ has a mean of 100 and a standard deviation of 10, making comparisons between performance on the WLA to other intelligence or achievement tests possible. However, the authors caution that the WLA measures only writing ability, and the content of the test is not directly comparable to the content of other tests. Further, the norm samples used for various other tests are not identical to each other or the WLA sample, and thus the practice of comparing quotients across tests must take differences in norming populations into consideration. The manual states that quotients below 70 (i.e., 2 standard deviations below the mean) indicate marked inadequacy in writing skills.

**Practical Applications/Uses**

The WLA is designed to be scored and interpreted by trained professionals, including classroom teachers, reading or speech and language specialists, school psychologists or psychometrists, school administrators, and others familiar with standardized tests. It can be administered by any responsible practicing paraprofessional or professional in either an individual or group setting. The test can be used in making placement and instructional decisions, although it is recommended that test results be used in combination with other assessment data.

Administration in regular classrooms or other "normal" working environments is recommended. Familiar settings and familiar adults administering the test may serve to elicit more suitable writing samples from students. Students must work unassisted, and unrevised first drafts of compositions must be scored, but students do not have to be spatially isolated while writing. The three writing tasks must be presented in sequence, beginning with the expressive task, then the instructive task, and finally the creative task, to correspond with the normative procedures and the typical sequence of development of children's writing.

Administration instructions are standard but not rigid. Students are directed to complete spaces for their name, date, school, and grade, and to read along as the directions for the writing task are read aloud. Students are to be prompted to write if necessary with neutral statements that encourage the child to make independent decisions about what or how much to write.

Each task on the average requires approximately 15 minutes to complete (45–60 minutes in total), although the WLA is not a timed test. Students with special needs or disabilities may require more time and encouragement. The three writing tasks ideally should be administered one per day over a period of 3 to 5 days, but they may be given over as few as 2 days or as long as 2 weeks. Under no circumstances should all three writing tasks be given in one session because of diminishing interest in writing when too much is required. This requirement places restrictions on the use of the test for purposes of diagnostics. Often students are evaluated by appraisal teams in school or clinical settings and are seen only once, precluding the use of this test in these situations.

The direct product, or composition, is scored. An experienced WLA scorer requires approximately 15 minutes to complete the ratings, calculate the raw scores, and convert them to derived scores. Three of the scoring procedures, Productivity (word counts), Word Complexity (word and syllable counts), and Readability (word, syllable, and sentence counts), are relatively objective and easy to calculate. Adequate justification for including these counts and the different types of information that they provide is described in the manual with reference to supporting research. Additional informal qualitative analyses of the writing samples, including spelling, punctuation, thematic content, and organization, are encouraged.

Scoring for General Writing Ability is more subjective, and while the scoring procedures attempt to provide reliable and valid methods for standardizing these scores, they are problematic in many respects. Each of the General Writing Ability components (e.g., Rhetoric, Legibility, Overall Quality) is scored by assigning a rating of 0 to 4. Ratings are assigned from a single standard and are applied without regard to the writer's age or grade. For example, the standard for a rating of 4 (superb rhetoric) is a composition that has well-developed style, fluency, appropriate wording, figures of speech, and humor at an adult level of writing. The authors state that this rating is reserved for only the best and will be earned by few writers (Grill & Kirwin, 1989, p. 26). This criterion essentially eliminates a rating of 4 as one choice for the majority of the age levels tested, rendering this rating level meaningless. One would assume the same adult standard is held for the ratings of 3 (excellent) and 2 (good). Thus, even though a child may write better than his or her age-mates, the rating is to be judged in comparison to the standard (Grill & Kirwin, 1989, p. 25). As most young children will not write as well as a good or excellent adult writer, the range of potential ratings for most age levels tested is really not a 5-point scale but rather a 2- to 3-point scale (from 0 to 2).

The choice of labels attached to each of the rating categories then becomes problematic. A rating of 0 is referred to as "illiterate" and a rating of 1 is "poor." The passages produced by most children in the lower age ranges will rate an "illiterate" or "poor" when in fact they may be developmentally appropriate or even good for an 8-year-old. The negative connotations associated with these terms may make judges reluctant to use them, especially when rating compositions that are developmentally appropriate. Interestingly, the scale for the Legibility component is not similarly biased against young writers. A rating of 4 is assigned when the handwriting of every word is clear and easily read, regardless of the style or sophistication of the writing. Many compositions at all age levels are likely to be awarded this rating.

The rating criteria for the points on the scale are fairly well defined for Legibility (i.e., 3 = handwriting is clear but mildly distracting to the eye and slows reading a bit; 1 = handwriting requires many stops to decipher words and is only minimally legible), but the same is not true for Rhetoric and Overall Quality. For these categories, the ratings are defined only by terms, with 4 = superb, 3 = excellent, and so forth. No characteristics are given to guide the evaluator in making an objective judgment. Five examples of scored compositions are provided in an appendix;

these are helpful but not sufficient to represent the range of compositions that the examiner must judge.

The format for presenting these examples also could be improved. The present appendix profiles each example of a child's test performance as a complete test (six pages of writing samples and scored protocol forms). This requires the examiner who is attempting to judge, for example, the Rhetoric of the Expressive writing passage to flip back and forth through 34 pages of the manual in order to locate and compare the five examples of Rhetoric scoring to the composition being judged. A more useful strategy would be to present a series of examples of compositions (two or three that were rated 0, two or three rated 1, etc.) for each scoring category and writing task. A short description of the common characteristics that resulted in that rating would also improve the ease and reliability of scoring immensely.

**Technical Aspects**

Test-retest reliability is not reported in the manual. This type of reliability is important to a test such as the WLA where the response requirements are open-ended and have potential for varying greatly across administrations. An examiner using the test to make placement and/or instructional decisions about a child would need to know the level of confidence at which the same test results are likely to be obtained if the test was readministered.

Internal consistency reliability was established for the WLA by comparing the raw scores for each writing task to each of the other writing tasks. Thus, for each of the four scores—General Writing Ability (GWA), Productivity (P), Word Complexity (WC), and Readability (R)—the scores on the Expressive task were compared to the scores of the Informative task, the Informative to the Creative, and the Expressive to the Creative. The Pearson product-moment correlation coefficient for each pair of writing samples was calculated, resulting in three correlational coefficients for each score at each age level. The average of the three correlational coefficients at each age level were then found, and the average reliability coefficients were corrected for statistically. The resulting coefficients for scores at various age levels were only moderate, ranging from .42 through .91. The median coefficients across age levels for the four scoring categories were GWA = .86, P = .81, WC = .81, and R = .61. These are all below the minimum level of reliability recommended for tests used for diagnostic or placement decisions (Salvia & Ysseldyke, 1988). The authors do recommend that the individual scaled scores not be used for making decisions about educational placement.

Although the reliabilities for the individual scores are only moderate, the reliability of the composite Written Language Quotient (WLQ) is adequate at most age levels. The median coefficient across age levels for this composite is .90. The authors recommend that only the WLQ be used for making placement decisions about individual students.

Interrater reliability, or the extent to which independent examiners agree on the performances of test-takers, was assessed through three separate studies. For each study, completed sets of WLA writing samples from the normative group were randomly selected and rescored by new raters. The percentages of agreement among raters were then calculated. Including each rating category for each of the three writing tasks, there were a total of 200 possible agreements between pairs of raters. Overall, the levels of exact agreements between examiners was low, ranging from .44 to .65 agreement. Close agreement, or a rating with no more than 1 point difference between the two ratings, was also calculated, resulting in high agreements ranging from .92 to .98. These raters were all trained by the authors and were experienced at the time of the studies. It is probable that raters who must make judgments based only on information provided in the manual would attain lower percentages of agreement.

Criterion-related validity was established by comparing performance on the WLA to the Picture Story Language Test (PSLT; Myklebust, 1965). Correlations between the four WLA and three PSLT scores ranged from .05 to .77. A syntax score on the PSLT had no correlation with the scores on the WLA, but the other two score types reached correlations significant beyond the .01 level of confidence, yielding support for criterion-related validity.

The validity of two assumptions underlying the test construction were examined. The intercorrelations among the four raw scores at each age level were calculated for all 1,025 subjects in the norm sample. Appropriately moderate scores were obtained except for the relationship between Productivity and Word Complexity scores, which were high. The authors state that these correlations support the assumption that the four scores measure different aspects of writing. The relationship between increasing age and test performance was also tested. Results indicated only a moderate relationship (correlation coefficient = .54) between WLA scores and age. Although the authors claim that both of these measures support construct validity, neither is an assessment of construct validity. They neither suggest what constructs account for test performance, derive hypotheses from the theory involving the construct, nor test the hypotheses empirically (Cronbach, 1970).

The "diagnostic validity," or the ability of the WLA to differentiate between students with normal abilities and those with learning disorders, was tested by comparing scores of students placed in special education resource rooms with a matched sample of regular class students. Eighteen students from each population were tested, and group means were subjected to an analysis of variance. A significant main effect for groups was found in favor of the regular class students. No data are provided regarding individual performances, including the number of students who were correctly identified by group or differences in performance between matched pairs.

## Critique

The WLA is a theoretically appealing test instrument that unfortunately has serious flaws in test construction, normative data, and scoring procedures. The test evaluates authentic writing and uses measures that attempt to sample the quality of written expression rather than isolated subskills. The whole, meaningful compositions can be evaluated informally to obtain information in addition to that provided by the norms, such as stage of narrative development exhibited or abstractness of ideas expressed. Comparisons can be made between the three different functions of writing represented by the three samples, providing a means of evaluating strengths and weaknesses exhibited by the writer. These are all extremely desirable features of the test.

The WLA norms cannot be used with confidence. Because test-retest reliability was not established, it remains questionable whether the same quality of composition will be produced across different administrations. The reliability of the scoring is also unstable. Both intrarater and interrater coefficients were only moderate when experienced scorers trained by the authors were used. The rating scales themselves are not equivalent. For some scoring categories the full rating scale from 0 to 4 can be applied for all age groups, but for other categories the higher ratings in practice do not apply to younger age groups. Even if the administration and scoring were highly reliable, the norms are not representative of the school-age population. The test cannot be used to make placement and instructional decisions regarding special education when no students participating in special education were included in the norm sample.

The WLA represents a theoretically important shift in assessment practices for language skills, in this case writing. The difficulty in developing quantitative scoring procedures to evaluate qualitative aspects of writing is well appreciated. Unfortunately, the WLA has not overcome the problems inherent in this endeavor.

## References

Cronbach, L. (1970). *Essentials of psychological testing* (3rd ed.). New York: Harper & Row.

Fry, E.B. (1977). Fry's readability graph: Clarifications, validity and extension to level 17. *Journal of Reading, 21*, 242-243.

Grill, J.J., & Kirwin, M.M. (1989). *Written Language Assessment—Manual*. Novato, CA: Academic Therapy Publications.

Myklebust, H.R. (1965). *Development and discourse of written language: I. Picture Story Language Test*. New York: Grune & Stratton.

Salvia, J., & Ysseldyke, J.E. (1988). *Assessment in special and remedial education*. Boston: Houghton Mifflin.

U.S. Bureau of the Census. (1985). *Statistical abstract of the United States*. Washington, DC: GPO.

# INDEX OF TEST TITLES

# INDEX OF TEST PUBLISHERS


Academic Therapy Publications, 20 Commercial Boulevard, Novato, California 94949; (415) 883-3314—[II:621; IV:172, 213, 278, 627; V:237, 244, 396; VI:447, 635; VII:346; VIII:70, 637; IX:480, 564, 584, 676]

Alemany Press (Janus Book Publishers, Inc.), P.O. Box 7604, West Trenton, New Jersey 08628; (609)394-9679—[IX:258]

American Association of Teachers of Spanish and Portuguese, National Spanish Examinations, University of Delaware, Academy Street 413, Newark, Delaware 19716; (302) 451- 6961—[VII:27]

American College Testing Program, The, 2201 North Dodge Street, P.O. Box 168, Iowa City, Iowa 52243; (319)337-1051—[I:11; VII:398]

American Council on Education, GED Testing Service, One Dupont Circle, NW, Washington, D.C. 20036; (202)939-4490—[IX:597]

American Foundation for the Blind, 15 West 16th Street, New York, New York 10011; (212)620-2000—[IV:390]

American Guidance Service, Publisher's Building, Circle Pines, Minnesota 55014; (800) 328-2560, in Minnesota (612)786- 4343—[I:322, 393, 712, 715; III:99, 304, 480, 488; IV:327, 368, 704; V:172; VI:153; VIII:492, 557]

American Orthopsychiatric Association, Inc., The, 19 West 44th Street, Suite 1616, New York, New York 10036; (212)354- 5770—[I:90]

American Psychiatric Association, *American Journal of Psychiatry,* 1400 K Street N.W., Washington, D.C. 20005; (202)682-6000—[III:439]

American Psychological Association, *Journal of Consulting and Clinical Psychology,* 1200 17th Street N.W., Washington, D.C. 20036; (202)955-7600—[V:198, 412]

American Society of Clinical Hypnosis, *The American Journal of Clinical Hypnosis,* 2250 East Devon, Suite 336, Des Plaines, Illinois 60018; (312)297-3317—[V:447]

American Testronics, 8600 West Bryn Mawr, Chicago, Illinois 60631; (800)553-0030—[III:164]

Ann Arbor Publishers, Inc.—[VI:26 *See* Academic Therapy Publications]

Antonovsky, Aaron, Ph.D., Ben-Gurion University of the Negev, Beersheba, Israel; no business phone—[IX:486]

ASIEP Education Company—[I:75; II:441; V:86; VII:456 *See* PRO-ED, Inc.]

Assessment Systems Corporation, 2233 University Avenue, Suite 440, St. Paul, Minnesota 55114; (612)647-9220—[VIII:470]

Associated Services for the Blind (ASB), 919 Walnut Street, Philadelphia, Pennsylvania 19107; (215)627-0600—[II:12; VII:371]

Aurora Publishing Company, 1709 Bragaw Street, Suite B, Anchorage, Alaska 99504; (907) 279-5251—[V:444]

Australian Council for Educational Research Limited, The, P.O. Box 210, Hawthorn, Victoria 3122 Australia; (03)819-1400—[IV:560; VII:82]

Ballard & Tighe, Inc., 480 Atlas Street, Brea, California 92621; (714)990-4332—[VIII:264; IX:271]

Barber Center Press, The, 136 East Avenue, Erie, Pennsylvania 16507; (814)453-7661—[VI:127]

Behar, Lenore, 1821 Woodburn Road, Durham, North Carolina 27705; (919)489-1888—[V:341]

Behavior Science Systems, Inc., P.O. Box 1108, Minneapolis, Minnesota 55458; (612) 929-6220—[II:472; V:252, 348; IX:201]

Bloom, Philip, 140 Cadman Plaza West, #3F, Brooklyn, New York 11201; (718)855-9784—[VI:48]

Book-Lab, 500 74th Street, North Bergen, New Jersey 07047; (201)861-6763 or (201) 868-1305—[V:209; VI:421; VIII:570]

Bowling Green State University, Department of Psychology, Bowling Green, Ohio 43402; no business phone—[VIII:679; IX:319, 422]

Brink, T.L., 1103 Church Street, Redlands, California 92374; (415)592-3570—[V:1688 VII:250, 536]

Bruce, Martin M., Ph.D., P.O. Box 248, Larchmont, New York 10539; (914)834-1555—[I:70; IV:496; V:529]

Cacioppo, John T., Department of Psychology, University of Iowa, Iowa City, Iowa 52242; no business phone—[III:466]

Callier Center for Communication Disorders, The University of Texas at Dallas, 1966 Inwood Road, Dallas, Texas 75235; (214)905- 3106—[IV:119]

Carney, Weedman and Associates, 4368 42nd Street, #6, San Diego, California 92105; (619)582-2005—[VII:173]

Carousel House, 450 Mission at First Street, Suite 504, San Francisco, California 94105; (415)777-2334—[IX:114]

Center for Child Development and Education. *See* Center for Research on Teaching and Learning

Center for Cognitive Therapy, 133 South 36th Street, Room 602, Philadelphia, Pennsylvania 19104; (215)898-4100—[II:83]

Center for Educational Assessment, College of Education, University of Missouri, 403 South 6th Street, Columbia, Missouri 65211; (314)882-4694—[VII:342]

Center for Epidemiologic Studies. *See* Epidemiology and Psychology, Research Branch, Division of Clinical Research, NIMH

Center for Faculty Evaluation and Development, Kansas State University, 1623 Anderson Avenue, Manhattan, Kansas 66502- 4098; (913)532-5970—[VIII:271]

Center for Psychological Service, 1511 K Street N.W., Suite 430, Washington, D.C. 20005; (202)347-4069—[VI:512]

Center for Research on Teaching and Learning, College of Education, University of Arkansas at Little Rock, 33rd and University, Little Rock, Arkansas 72204; (501)569-3422—[II:337]

Center for the Study of Adolescence, Michael Reese Hospital, 31st and Lakeshore Drive, Chicago, Illinois 60616; (312)791- 4199—[V:297; VI:387]

Center for the Study of Parental Acceptance and Rejection, University of Connecticut, P.O. Box U-158, Storrs, Connecticut 06268; (203)486-4513—[IX:378]

Chandler, Louis A., Ph.D., The Psycho-educational Clinic, University of Pittsburgh, 606 Illini Drive, Monroeville, Pennsylvania 15156; (412)327-6164—[VI:570]

Chapman, Brook & Kent, P.O. Box 3030, Blue Jay, California 92317; (805)962-0055—[IV:183]

CHECpoint Systems, Inc., 1520 North Waterman Avenue, San Bernardino, California 92404; (714)888-3296—[IX:24]

Childcraft Education Corporation, 20 Kilmer Road, Edison, New Jersey 08818; (800)631-5652—[IV:220]

Chronicle Guidance Publications, Inc., Aurora Street Extension, P.O. Box 1190, Moravia, New York 13118; (315)497- 0330—[IX:48]

Clinical Psychology Publishing Company, Inc., 4 Conant Square, Brandon, Vermont 05733; (802)247-6871—[III:461; VIII:692; IX:414, 534, 561]

Clinical Psychometric Research, P.O. Box 619, Riderwood, Maryland 21139; (301)321-6165—[II:32; III:583]

Coddington, R. Dean, P.O. Box 307, St. Clairsville, Ohio 43950; (614)695-4805—[III:383, 388]

College Board Publications, The, 45 Columbus Avenue, New York, New York 10023; (212) 713-8000—[VI:120, 609; VII:10]

College-Hill Press, Inc., 34 Beacon Street, Boston, Massachusetts 02108; (617)859-5504—[III:293]

Communication Research Associates, Inc., P.O. Box 11012, Salt Lake City, Utah 84147; (801)295-8046; III:669; VII:290]

Communication Skill Builders, Inc., 3830 East Bellevue, P.O. Box 42050, Tucson, Arizona 85733; (602)323-7500—[II:191, 562; V:118; VII:202; VIII:34]

Consulting Psychologists Press, Inc., 577 College Avenue, P.O. Box 60070, Palo Alto, California 94306; (415)857-1444—[I:34, 41, 146, 226, 259, 284, 380, 482, 623, 626, 663, 673; II:23, 56, 113, 263, 293, 509, 594, 697, 729; III:35, 51, 125, 133, 349, 392, 419; IV:42, 58, 132, 162, 570; V:141, 189, 226, 303, 556; VI:29, 87, 97; VII:20, 55, 59, 66, 87, 446; VIII:111, 115, 118, 241, 251, 384, 436, 516, 563, 574, 630, 734; IX:132, 500, 625, 643, 664]

C.P.S., Inc., P.O. Box 83, Larchmont, New York 10538; (914)833- 1633—[I:185; III:604; IX:210]

Creative Learning Press, Inc., P.O. Box 320, Mansfield Center, Connecticut 06250; (203) 423-8120—[II:402; VII:110]

Croft, Inc., 2936 Remington Avenue, Baltimore, Maryland 21211-2891; (301)235-1700—[III:198]

CTB/McGraw-Hill. *See* CTB/Macmillan/McGraw-Hill

CTB/Macmillan/McGraw-Hill, Del Monte Research Park, 2500 Garden Road, Monterey, California 93940; (800)538-9547, in California (800)682-9222 or (408)649-8400—[I:3, 164, 578; II:517, 584, 780; III:186; IV:79, 238; V:406, 494; VI:149, 615; VII:102, 144, 189; VIII:521, 652; IX:591]

Curriculum Associates, Inc., 5 Esquire Road, North Billerica, Massachusetts 01862-2589; (800)225-0248, in Massachusetts (617)667-8000—[III:79]

Dean, Raymond S., Ph.D., Ball State University, TC 521, Muncie, Indiana 47306; (317) 285-8500—[VI:297]

Delis, Dean, Ph.D., 3753 Canyon Way, Martinez, California 94553—[I:158]

Denver Developmental Materials, Inc., P.O. Box 6919, Denver, Colorado 80206-0919; (303) 355-4729—[VII:234]

Devereux Foundation Press, The, 19 South Waterloo Road, P.O. Box 400, Devon, Pennsylvania 19333; (215)296-6905—[II:231; III:221; V:104]

Diagnostic Specialists, Inc., 1170 North 660 West, Orem, Utah 84057; (801)224-8492—[II:95]

DLM Teaching Resources, One DLM Park, Allen, Texas 75002; (800)527- 4747, in Texas (800) 442-4711—[II:72; III:68, 521, 551, 726; IV:376, 493, 683; V:310; VI:80, 586; VII:49; VIII:77, 319; IX:290, 648]

DMI Associates, 615 Clark Avenue, Owosso, Michigan 48867; (517)723- 3523—[VI:115]

D.O.K. Publishers, Inc., P.O. Box 605, East Aurora, New York 14052; (800)458-7900—[II:211; VI:303, 582; VIII:708; IX:391]

Eagleville Hospital, 100 Eagleville Road, Eagleville, Pennsylvania 19408; (215)539-6000—[VII:561]

Economy Company, The, P.O. Box 25308, 1901 North Walnut Street, Oklahoma City, Oklahoma 73125; (405)528- 8444—[IV:458]

Educaional Activities, Inc., 1937 Grand Avenue, Baldwin, New York 11520; (800)645-2796, in Alaska, Hawaii, and ew York (516)223-4666—[V:290; VI: 249]

Educational and Industrial Testing Service (EdITS), P.O. Box 7234, San Diego, California 92107; (619)222-1666—[I:279, 522, 555; II:3, 104, 258; III:3, 215; IV:199, 387, 449; V:76]

Educational Assessment Service, Inc., 6050 Apple Road, Watertown, Wisconsin 53094; (414)261-1118—[II:332, VI:415; VIII:235]

Educational Development Corporation, P.O. Box 470663, Tulsa, Oklahoma 74147; (800) 331-4418, in Oklahoma (800)722- 9113—[III:367;VI:244]

Educational Evaluation Enterprises, Awre, Newnham, Gloucestershire GL14 1ET England; (0594)510503—[VIII:308]

Educational Performance Associates, 600 Broad Avenue, Ridgefield, New Jersey 07657; (201)941-1425—[VIII:713]

Educational Studies and Development, 1428 Norton, Muskegon, Michigan 49441; (616)780-2053 or 755-1041—[IX:3]

Educational Testing Service (ETS), Rosedale Road, Princeton, New Jersey 08541; (609) 921-9000—[III:655; VI:404; VIII:44, 717; IX:411]

Educators/Employers' Tests & Services Associates (ETSA), 341 Garfield Street, Chambersburg, Pennsylvania 17201; (717)264- 9509—[IX:219]

Educators Publishing Service, Inc., 75 Moulton Street, Cambridge, Massachusetts 02238-9101; (800)225-5750, in Massachusetts (800)792-5166—[IV:195, 611; VI:188, 392; VIII:22; IX:385]

El Paso Rehabilitation Center, 1101 E. Schuster Avenue, El Paso, Texas 79902; (915)566-2956—[III:171, 628]

Elbern Publications, P.O. Box 09497, Columbus, Ohio 43209; (614)235-2643—[II:627]

Elsevier Science Publishing Company, Inc., 52 Vanderbilt Avenue, New York, New York 10017; (212)867-9040—[III:358]

English Language Institute, Test Publications, University of Michigan, 3004 North University Building, Ann Arbor, Michigan 48109-1057; (313)747-0456 or 747-0476—[IX:214]

Epidemiology and Psychology, Research Branch, Division of Clinical Research, NIMH, 5600 Fishers Lane, Room 10C-05, Rockville, Maryland 20857; (301)443-4513—[II:144]

Essay Press, P.O. Box 2323, La Jolla, California 92307;(619)565- 6603—[II:646; IV:553]

Evaluation Research Associates. *See* FAAX Corporation

FAAX Corporation, 770 James Street, Suite 216, Syracuse, New York 13203; (315)422-0064—[II:551; III:158]

Fairleigh Dickinson University, Division of Psychological Services, Teaneck, New Jersey 07666; no business phone—[IX:496]

Family Social Science, University of Minnesota, 290 McNeal Hall, St. Paul, Minnesota 55108; (612)625-5289—[VII:209, 417]

Family Stress, Coping and Health Project, School of Family Resources and Consumer Sciences, University of Wisconsin, 1300 Linden Drive, Madison, Wisconsin 53706; (608) 262- 5712—[VI:10, 16]

Foreworks, P.O. Box 9747, North Hollywood, California 91609; (818)982-0467—[III:647]

Foundation for Knowledge in Development, The—[I:443 *See* Psychological Corporation, The]

G.I.A. Publications, 7404 South Mason Avenue, Chicago, Illinois 60638; (312)496-3800—[V:216, 351]

Grune & Stratton, Inc.—[I:189; II:819; III:447, 526; IV:523; V:537; VI:52, 431 *See* Psychological Corporation, The]

Guidance Centre, Faculty of Education, University of Toronto, 10 Alcorn Avenue, Toronto, Ontario M4V 2Z8, Canada; (416)978- 3211/3210—[III:271]

Halgren Tests, 873 Persimmon Avenue, Sunnyvale, California 94087; (408)738-1342—[I:549]

Hanson, Silver, Strong and Associates, Inc., 10 West Main Street, Moorestown, New Jersey 08057; (609)234-2610—[VII:589; IX:620]

Harding Tests, P.O. Box 5271, Rockhampton Mail Centre, Queensland 4702, Australia; no business phone—[IV:334]

Harvard University Press, 79 Garden Street, Cambridge, Massachusetts 02138; (617)495-2600—[II:799]

Hilson Research Inc., 82-28 Abingdon Road, P.O. Box 239, Kew Gardens, New York 11415; (718)805-0063—[VI:265; IX:261]

Hiskey, Marshall S., 5640 Baldwin, Lincoln, Nebraska 68507; (402)466-6145—[III:331]

Hodder & Stoughton Educational, A Division of Hodder & Stoughton Ltd., P.O. Box 702, Mill Road, Dunton Green, Sevenoaks, Kent TN13 2YD England; (0732)450111—[IV:256; VII:646; VIII:544, 647, 749; IX:204]

Hodges, Kay, Ph.D., 801 Duluth Street, Durham, North Carolina 27710; (919)684-6691—[VI:91]

Humanics Limited, 1389 Peachtree Street, P.O. Box 7447, Atlanta, Georgia 30309; (404) 874-2176—[II:161, 426]

Humanics Media—[V:522, 524; VI:76 *See* Western Psychological Services]

Industrial Psychology Incorporated (IPI), 111 North Market Street, Champaign, Illinois 61820; (800)747-1119—[II:363]

Institute for Child Behavior Research, 4182 Adams Avenue, San Diego, California 92116; (619)281-7165—[VII:185]

Institute for Educational Research and Development, Memorial University of Newfoundland, St. John's, Newfoundland A1B 3X8, Canada; (709)737-8625—[IX:579]

Institute for Personality and Ability Testing, Inc. (IPAT), P.O. Box 188, 1602 Coronado Drive, Champaign, Illinois 61824-0188; (217)352-4739—[I:195, 202, 214, 233, 377; II:357; III:139, 246, 251, 319, 567; IV:595; V:283; VI:21, 359, 560; VII:374; VIII:190, 278, 289, 294]

Institute for Psycho-Imagination Therapy, 179 South Burrington Place, Los Angeles, California 90049; (213)652- 2922—[I:593]

Institute for Psychosomatic & Psychiatric Research & Training/Daniel Offer. *See* Center for the Study of Adolescence

Institute for the Advancement of Philosophy for Children, Montclair State College, Upper Montclair, New Jersey 07043; (201)893- 4277—[VII:365]

Institute of Psychological Research, Inc., 34 Fleury Street West, Montreal, Quebec H3L 1S9, Canada; (514)382-3000—[II:530; VI:601]

Instructional Materials & Equipment Distributors (IMED), 1520 Cotner Avenue, Los Angeles, California 90025; (213)879- 0377—[V:109]

International Association for the Study of Pain, 909 N.E. 43rd Street, Room 306, Seattle, Washington 98105-6020; (206)547- 6409—[VIII:402]

International Universities Press, Inc., 315 Fifth Avenue, New York, New York 10016; (212) 684-7900—[III:736]

INTREX Interpersonal Institute, P.O. Box 55218, Madison, Wisconsin 53705; (801)363-6236—[VII:541]

Jamestown Publishers, P.O. Box 9168, 544 Douglass Avenue, Providence, Rhode Island 02940; (800)USA-READ or (401)351- 1915—[V:212]

Jastak Associates, Inc., P.O. Box 4460, Wilmington, Delaware 19807; (800)221-9278—[I:758, 762; IV:673; VI:135; IX:653]

Johnson, Suzanne Bennett, Ph.D., Childrens's Mental Health Unit, Box J-234, J. Hillis Miller Health Sciences Center, University of Florida, Gainesville, Florida 32610—[VI:594]

Jossey-Bass, Inc., Publishers, 433 California Street, San Francisco, California 94104; (415) 433-1740—[III:395]

Keegan, Warren, and Associates Press, 210 Stuyvescent Avenue, Rye, New York 10580; (914)967-9421—[IX:335]

Kent Developmental Metrics, 1325 South Water Street, P.O. Box 845, Kent, Ohio 44240-3178; (216)678-3589—[III:380]

Khavari, Khalil A., Ph.D., Midwest Institute on Drug Use, University of Wisconsin-Milwaukee, Vogel Hall, Milwaukee, Wisconsin 53201; (414)963-4747—[VII:193]

Kovacs, Maria, Ph.D., 3811 O'Hara Street, Pittsburgh, Pennsylvania 15213-2593; (412)624-2043—[V:65]

Krieger, Robert E., Publishing Company, Inc., P.O. Box 9542, Melbourne, Florida 32901; (305)724-9542—[III:30]

Ladoca Publishing Foundation—[I:239 *See* Denver Developmental Materials, Inc.]

Lafayette Instrument Company, Inc., P.O. Box 5729, Lafayette, Indiana 47903; (317)423-1505—[V:534; VIII:337]

Lake, David S., Publishers, 19 Davis Drive, Belmont, California 94002; (415)592-7810—[II:241]

Lea and Febiger, 600 Washington Square, Philadelphia, Pennsylvania 19106; (215)922-1330—[I:117]

Learning House, distributed exclusively by Guidance Centre, Faculty of Education, University of Toronto, 10 Alcorn Avenue, Ontario, Canada M4V 2Z8—[VI:66, 70, 73]

Lefkowitz, Monroe M., Ph.D., P.O. Box 1685, Lenox, Massachusetts 01240; (413)637-2113—[VII:432]

Lewis, H.K., & Co. Ltd., 136 Gower Street, London WC1E 6BS, England; (01)387-4282—[I:47, 206, 595; IV:408]

Libraries Unlimited, P.O. Box 3988, Englewood, Colorado 80155-3988; (303)770-1220—[VII:505]

LinguiSystems, Inc., 716 17th Street, Moline, Illinois 61265; (800)ALL-TIME, in Illinois (309)762-5112—[II:831; V:221; VII:282, 600]

London House Press, 1550 North Northwest Highway, Park Ridge, Illinois 60068; (800) 323-5923, in Illinois (312)298- 7311—[III:510; IV:463; V:565; VI:529; VII:570; VIII:173; IX:18, 363]

Macmillan Education Ltd., Houndmills, Basingstoke, Hampshire RG21 2XS, England; (0256)29242—[VII:40; VIII:163, 374]

Marathon Consulting and Press, P.O. Box 09189, Columbus, Ohio 43209-0189; (614)235-5509—[II:138, 535; VI:640; VII:159]

Martinus Nijhoff—[III:288 *See* SWETS and Zeitlinger, B.V.]

McCarron-Dial Systems, P.O. Box 45628, Dallas, Texas 75245; (214)247-5945—[IX:526]

Medical Research Council—[V:314 *See* Elithorn & Levander]

Merrill, Charles E., Publishing Company, 1300 Alum Creek Drive, P.O. Box 508, Columbus, Ohio 43216; (614)258-8441 or (800)848- 6205—[I:125; II:35; IV:3, 176, 590; VII:34. *Editors' note:* Most C. E. Merrill tests now published by The Psychological Corporation.]

MetriTech, Inc., 111 North Market Street, Champaign, Illinois 61820; (217)398-4868—[VIII:315]

Midwest Publications Critical Thinking Press, P.O. Box 448, Pacific Grove, California 93950; (408)375-2455—[IX:123]

Modern Curriculum Press, Inc.—[IV:229; V:37; VI:143 *See* PRO-ED, Inc.]

Monitor, P.O. Box 2337, Hollywood, California 90028; no business phone—[V:21, 113; VI:3]

National Business Education Association, 1914 Association Drive, Reston, Virginia 22091; (703)860-8300—[VI:373]

National Computer Systems/PAS Division, 10901 Bren Road East, Minnetonka, Minnesota 55343; (612)939-5118—[I:455, 466, 660; II:128; III:454; IV:425; VI:216, 252; VIII:457, 485; IX:36, 300]

National Institute on Mental Retardation, Kinsmen NIMR Building, York University Campus, 4700 Keele Street, Downsview, Ontario M3J 1P3, Canada; (416)661-9611—[VI:622]

National Study of School Evaluation, 5201 Leesburg Pike, Falls Church, Virginia 22041; (703)820-2728—[VII:423, 557, 586]

NCS Professional Assessment Services. *See* National Computer Systems/PAS Division]

Neimeyer, Robert A., Ph.D., Department of Psychology, Memphis State University, Memphis, Tennessee 38152; (901)454- 4680—[VII:566]

Nelson Canada, 1120 Birchmount Road, Scarborough, Ontario M1K 5G4, Canada; (416) 752-9100—[II:350; IV:127; V:48]

Neuropsychiatric Institute, 760 Westwood Plaza, Los Angeles, California 90024; (213)825-0458—[IX:29]

Neuropsychology Laboratory, University of Wisconsin, University Hospitals, Madison, Wisconsin 53711; no business phone—[I:478]

New York University, Department of Educational Psychology, New York, New York 10003; no business phone—[IX:184]

NFER-Nelson Publishing Company Ltd., Darville House, 2 Oxford Road East, Windsor, Berkshire SL4 1DF, England; (0753)858961—[I:51, 130; II:88, 169, 388, 642; III:546, 608; IV:7, 281, 469, 656; VI:192, 197, 369; VII:76, 307, 473; VIII:18, 200, 229, 423; IX:371, 426, 438, 455]

Office of Public and Professional Services, College of Education, Western Michigan University, Kalamazoo, Michigan 49008; (616)383-1690—[VII:582]

Ollendick, Thomas H., Ph.D., Department of Psychology, Virginia Polytechnic Institute & State University, Blacksburg, Virginia 24061; no business phone—[IX:239]

Organizational Tests (Canada) Ltd., P.O. Box 324, Fredericton, New Brunswick E3B 4Y9, Canada; (506)452-7194—[III:209; VII:386; VIII:95, 617]

Oxford University Press, 200 Madison Avenue, New York, New York 10016; (212)679-7300—[V:475; IX:615]

Pacific Psychological, 710 George Washington Way, Suite G, Richland, Washington 99352; (800)523-4915—[V:3]

P.A.R., Inc., 290 Westminster Street, Providence, Rhode Island 02930-3416; no business phone—[VIII:3]

Peacock, F. E., Publishers, Inc., Test Division, 115 North Prospect Road, Itasca, Illinois 60143; (312)773-1590—[IV:516]

Pediatric Psychology Press, 320 Terrell Road West, Charlottesville, Virginia 22901; (804)296-8211—[I:504]

Perceptual Learning Systems, P.O. Box 864, Dearborn, Michigan 48121; (313)277-6480—[III:276; V:137]

Personal Life Skills Center, 1201 Second Street, Corpus Christi, Texas 78404; (512)883-6442—[V:318]

Personality Research Services Ltd., 2000 Fairlawn Parkway, Schenectady, New York 12309; (518)370-0955—[IV:48]

Personnel Decisions, Inc., 2000 Plaza Seven Tower, 45 South Seventh Street, Minneapolis, Minnesota 55402; (612)339- 0927—[VIII:548]

Pilowsky, I., M.D., Department of Psychiatry, University of Adelaide, Adelaide 5000, Australia; (08)2230-230, Ext. 5141—[IX:279, 352]

Plenum Press, *Cognitive Therapy and Research*, 233 Spring Street, New York, New York 10013; (212)620-8000—[IV:20]

Precision People, Inc., 3452 North Ride Circle South, Jacksonville, Florida 32217; (904)262-1096—[VI:208]

Price Systems, Inc., P.O. Box 1818, Lawrence, Kansas 66044; (913)843-7892—[VI:308]

Priority Innovations, Inc., 128 Washington Street, Glenview, Illinois 60025; (312)729-1434—[VI:481]

PRO-ED, Inc., 8700 Shoal Creek Boulevard Austin, Texas 78758; (512)451-3246—[I:688; II:223, 235, 787; IV:68, 76, 87, 92, 189, 659; V:43, 94, 100, 179, 358, 464, 485; VI:232, 287, 453; VII:3, 131, 177, 196, 496, 516, 628; VIII:26, 144, 443, 598, 607, 623, 656, 688, 703; IX:66, 80, 286, 367, 395, 400, 459, 570]

Programs for Education, Inc., P.O. Box 167, Rosemont, New Jersey 08556; (609)397-2214—[II:310, 314, 681]

Psychodiagnostic Test Company, Box 859, East Lansing, Michigan 48823; (517)372-4460—[IV:484]

Psychodynamic Instruments, P.O. Box 1172, Ann Arbor, Michigan 48106; (805)962-6524—[I:99]

Psychological Assessment and Services, Inc., P.O. Box 1031, Iowa City, Iowa 52240; (319) 338-9316—[I:473; IX:267]

Psychological Assessment Resources, Inc., P.O. Box 998, Odessa, Florida 33556; (813)977-3395—[I:113, 491; II:288; III:175, 542; IV:677; V:6, 278, 388, 419, 545; VI:103, 177, 463; VII:119, 245, 485; VIII:61, 106, 195, 527, 663; IX:58, 256, 510]

Psychological Corporation, The, A Subsidiary of Harcourt Brace Jovanovich, Inc., 555 Academic Court, San Antonio, Texas 78204; (800)228-0752—[I:47, 106, 117, 206, 252, 295, 328, 494, 499, 595, 608, 614, 648, 720, 728, 740, 750; II:16, 63, 175, 182, 319, 326, 436, 446, 463, 495, 579, 653; III:13, 58, 226, 296, 427, 434, 633, 682, 698, 711; IV:149, 320, 394, 414, 478; V:271, 287; VI:38, 56, 158, 226, 322, 336, 341, 476, 536; VII:44, 264, 338, 350, 389, 438, 523, 633, 639; VIII:54, 158, 641; IX:167]

Psychological Publications, Inc., 5300 Hollywood Boulevard, Los Angeles, California 90027; (213)465-4163—[I:654; IV:294]

Psychological Services, Inc., Test Publication Division, 100 West Broadway, Suite 1100, Glendale, California 91210; (818)244- 0033—[I:266; VIII:583, 589]

Psychological Test Specialists, P.O. Box 9229, Missoula, Montana 59807; no business phone—[I:530; II:299, 376, 451, 603; III:375; V:128]

Psychologistics, Inc., P.O. Box 033896, Indiatlantic, Florida 32903; (305)259-7811—[VIII:7]

Psychologists and Educators, Inc., P.O. Box 513, St. Louis, Missouri 63006; (314)576-9127—[I:568; III:206; V:323, 483; VI:412; VII:381; VIII:347, 394]

Psychometric Affiliates, P.O. Box 807, Murfreesboro, Tennessee 37133; (615)890-6296 or 898-2565—[IV:519; V:367; VI:437, 486]

Psychonomic Society, Inc., *Psychonomic Science*, 2904 Guadalupe, Austin, Texas 78705; (512)476-9687—[V:513]

Psytec, Inc., P.O. Box 300, Webster, North Carolina 28788; (704)227-7361—[V:55]

Pumroy, Donald K., Ph.D., CAPS, College of Education, University of Maryland, College Park, Maryland 20742; (301)454- 2026—[VII:328]

Purdue University Bookstore, Division of Sponsored Programs, Patents and Copyright Office, Room 328, Building ENAD, West Lafayette, Indiana 47907; (317)494-2610—[V:326]

University of Wisconsin–Stout, Stout Vocational Rehabilitation Institute, Materials Development Center, Menomonie, Wisconsin 54751; no business phone—[VIII:209]

Valett, Robert E., Department of Advanced Studies, California State University at Fresno, Fresno, California 93740; no business phone—[II:68]

Variety Pre-Schooler's Workshop, 47 Humphrey Drive, Syosset, New York 11791; (516)921-7171—[III:261]

Vocational Psychology Research, University of Minnesota, N620 Elliott Hall, 75 East River Road, Minneapolis, Minnesota 55455-0344; (612)625-1367—[II:481; IV:434; V:255; VI:350]

Vocational Research Institute, 2100 Arch Street, 6th Floor, Philadelphia, Pennsylvania 19103; (215)496-9674—[VII:623]

Walker Educational Book Corporation, 720 Fifth Avenue, New York, New York 10019; (212)265-3632—[II:689]

West Virginia Rehabilitation Research and Training Center, #1 Dunbar Plaza, Suite E, Dunbar, West Virginia 25064; (304)766- 7138—[VIII:301; IX:405]

Western Psychological Services, A Division of Manson Western Corporation, 12031 Wilshire Boulevard, Los Angeles, California 90025; (213)478-2061—[I:315, 338, 511, 543, 663; II:108, 430, 570, 607, 723, 826; III:145, 255, 282, 340, 402, 415, 615, 714, 717; IV:15, 33, 39, 259, 274, 300, 351, 382, 440, 501, 565, 606, 649; V:9, 73, 83, 378, 382, 425, 458, 549; VI:60, 260, 505, 519, 576, 629; VII:277, 301, 313, 404, 463, 480; VIII:358, 668; IX:10, 51, 99, 358, 431, 465, 490, 545, 611, 660]

Westwood Press, Inc., 251 Park Avenue South, 14th Floor, New York, New York 10010; (212)420-8008—[VII:466]

Wilmington Press, The, 13315 Wilmington Drive, Dallas, Texas 75234; (214)620-8531—[VI:383; IX:145]

Wolfe Personnel Testing and Training Systems, Inc., P.O. Box 319, Oradell, New Jersey 07649; (201)265-5393—[VIII:741]

Wonderlic, E.F., & Associates, Inc., Frontage Road, Northfield, Illinois 60093; (312)446-8900—[I:769]

World of Work, Inc., 2923 North 67th Place, Scottsdale, Arizona 85251; (602)946-1884—[VI:644]

Wyeth Laboratories, P.O. Box 8616, Philadelphia, Pennsylvania 19101; (215)688-4400—[V:499]

York Press, Inc., 2712 Mount Carmel Road, Parkton, Maryland 21120; (301)343-1417—[VII:163]

Zung, William W.K., M.D., Veterans Administration Medical Center, 508 Fulton Street, Durham, North Carolina 27705; (919)286- 0411—[III:595]

# INDEX OF TEST AUTHORS/REVIEWERS

# SUBJECT INDEX

## PSYCHOLOGY

### Child and Child Development



### Intelligence and Related

**Marriage and Family: Family**

**Marriage and Family: Premarital and Marital Relations**



**Neuropsychology and Related**

**Personality: Adolescent and Adult**

**Personality: Child**

**Personality: Multilevel**

**Academic Subjects: Mathematics: Basic Math Skills**



**Academic Subjects: Mathematics: Upper Math Skills**



**Academic Achievement and Aptitude**

**Education Development and School Readiness**

**Reading: High School and Above**



**Reading: Multilevel**



**Sensorimotor Skills**



**Special Education: Gifted**

**Special Education: Learning Disabled**



**Special Education: Mentally Handicapped**

**Special Education: Physically Handicapped**



**Special Education: Special Education**



**Speech, Hearing, and Visual: Auditory**



**Speech, Hearing, and Visual: Speech and Language**

**Student Evaluation and Counseling: Study Skills Attitudes**



**Student Evaluation and Counseling: Vocational Guidance**



**Teacher Evaluation**

## BUSINESS AND INDUSTRY

### Aptitude and Skills Screening



### Clerical



### Computer



### Intelligence and Related



### Interests

**Interpersonal Skills and Attitudes**



**Management and Supervision**

# ABOUT THE EDITORS

**Daniel J. Keyser, Ph.D.** Since completing postgraduate work at the University of Kansas in 1974, Dr. Keyser has worked in drug and alcohol rehabilitation and psychiatric settings. In addition, he has taught undergraduate psychology at Rockhurst College for over 15 years. Dr. Keyser specializes in behavioral medicine—biofeedback, pain control, stress management, terminal care support, habit management, and wellness maintenance—and maintains a private clinical practice in the Kansas City area. Dr. Keyser has co-edited each edition of *Tests: A Comprehensive Reference for Assessments in Psychology, Education, and Business* and has made significant contributions to computerized psychological testing. More recently, he was involved in the development of the *Applied Testing Series.*

**Richard C. Sweetland, Ph.D.** After completing his doctorate at Utah State University in 1968, Dr. Sweetland completed postdoctoral training in psychoanalytically oriented clinical psychology at the Topeka State Hospital in conjunction with the training program of the Menninger Foundation. Following appointments in child psychology in the University of Kansas Medical Center and in neuropsychology at the Kansas City Veterans Administration Hospital, he entered the practice of psychotherapy in Kansas City. In addition to his clinical work in neuropsychology and psychoanalytic psychotherapy, Dr. Sweetland has been involved extensively in the development of computerized psychological testing. Dr. Sweetland has co-edited each edition of *Tests: A Comprehensive Reference for Assessments in Psychology, Education, and Business* and was involved in the development of the *Applied Testing Series.*